BEST PRACTICES
IN SCHOOL PSYCHOLOGY

SYSTEMS-LEVEL SERVICES

BEST PRACTICES
IN SCHOOL PSYCHOLOGY

SYSTEMS-LEVEL SERVICES

EDITED BY
PATTI L. HARRISON & ALEX THOMAS

From the NASP Publications Board Operations Manual

The content of this document reflects the ideas and positions of the authors. The responsibility lies solely with the authors and editors and does not necessarily reflect the position or ideas of the National Association of School Psychologists.

Published by the National Association of School Psychologists

Copies may be ordered from:
NASP Publications
4340 East West Highway, Suite 402
Bethesda, MD 20814
301-657-0270
301-657-3127, fax
866-331-NASP, Toll Free
e-mail: *publications@naspweb.org*
www.nasponline.org/publications

Best Practices in School Psychology: Systems-Level Services
ISBN: 978 0932955-55-5 (print);

Best Practices in School Psychology (4-book series)
ISBN: 978-0-932955-52-4 (print), ISBN: 978-0-932955-51-7 (electronic)

Printed in the United States of America

19 10 9 8 7 6 5

Table of Contents

School-Wide Practices to Promote Learning

Preventive and Responsive Services

Family–School Collaboration Services

Introduction

BEST PRACTICES IN SCHOOL PSYCHOLOGY: OVERVIEW OF THE SERIES

Best Practices in School Psychology is the sixth iteration of an intraprofessional collaborative effort to provide a single source for contemporary knowledge about many valued topics within school psychology. It has been more than 30 years since the first edition of *Best Practices in School Psychology* was published. In those 30 years and six editions, there have been substantial changes in the quantity of chapters, range of topics, and intended outcomes of school psychology services. However, the purpose of all editions of *Best Practices in School Psychology*, including the current edition, has remained constant over the years: to provide the current, relevant, and valued information necessary for competent delivery of school psychological services. Thus, chapters across editions have focused on *practices* by school psychology practitioners. Although chapters are not intended to be detailed reviews of research, research documentation is included in the chapters to provide an evidence-based foundation for recommended best practices.

This edition of *Best Practices in School Psychology* is designed to be a comprehensive resource, allowing readers to refer to chapters in the process of gaining information about specific, important professional practice topics and updating readers about contemporary techniques and methods. The primary target audience is school psychology practitioners who provide services in school settings, as was the case for previous editions. Similarly, the chapters may provide useful resources for other school-based professionals, as well as those who provide services to children in other settings. *Best Practices* also may serve as a helpful supplement for graduate courses when used in conjunction with primary course textbooks. As a compilation of best practices on major topics, *Best Practices in School Psychology* will assist school psychology practitioners, graduate students, interns, faculty, and others by providing readings on many specific areas of interest.

The content in this edition of *Best Practices in School Psychology* is expanded from earlier editions to include a broader range of topics, with considerable attention to multitiered, problem-solving, and evidence-based approaches for the delivery of effective school psychology services. The school psychology services outlined in this edition focus on improving student outcomes through data-based and collaborative activities in schools. Chapters emphasize prevention and intervention efforts for both student-level and systems-level services that recognize the importance of culture and individual differences across students, families, schools, and communities.

This edition of *Best Practices* was developed over 5 years, with multiple focus groups consisting of practitioner school psychologists, as well as graduate students and faculty, assisting the editors with organization and new topics for chapters to represent current and future needs. In addition, chapter authors and reviewers identified additional chapter topics.

The result is that this edition is organized a bit differently than previous editions. This edition is a four book series, with each book corresponding to one of the four interrelated components of the broad framework of the 2010 National Association of School Psychologists (NASP) *Model for Comprehensive and Integrated School Psychological Services* (i.e., the NASP Practice Model; see http://www.nasponline.org/standards/2010standards/2_PracticeModel.pdf): (a) *practices that permeate all aspects of service delivery*, including data-based and collaborative decision making; (b) *student-level services*, including instructional and academic supports and social and mental health services; (c) *systems-level services*, including school-wide learning practices, preventive and response services, and family–school collaboration; and (d) *foundations* of school psychological services, including diversity, research and program evaluation, and legal/ethical/professional practices.

About half of the chapters in this edition are updates of chapters included in earlier editions, and the other half focus on new and topical issues of importance in contemporary school psychology. Although it is impossible to include chapters for *all* areas of relevance to school psychology, it is hoped that the resulting 150 chapters provide a good representation of major services and issues in the field.

Organizational Framework of the Series

Each of the four books in the series has two or three separate sections corresponding to the specific domains of school psychology established in the 2010 NASP Practice Model. The titles of the four books and of the sections within each are outlined below:

1. *Best Practices in School Psychology: Data-Based and Collaborative Decision Making*

   Introduction and Framework
   Data-Based Decision Making and Accountability
   Consultation and Collaboration

2. *Best Practices in School Psychology: Student-Level Services*

   Interventions and Instructional Support to Develop Academic Skills
   Interventions and Mental Health Services to Develop Social and Life Skills

3. *Best Practices in School Psychology: Systems-Level Services*

   School-Wide Practices to Promote Learning
   Preventive and Responsive Services
   Family–School Collaboration Services

4. *Best Practices in School Psychology: Foundations*

   Diversity in Development and Learning
   Research and Program Evaluation
   Legal, Ethical, and Professional Practice

Chapter Structure

Typically, chapters include the following components, which provide readers with a predictable chapter structure:

Overview. Includes a definition and history of the topic and may provide situations for which a practicing school psychologist may wish to consult the chapter. This section orients the reader to the major issues, characteristics, and needs related to a chapter topic. It is introductory and establishes the context for the information presented.

Basic Considerations. Provides background information, research, training, experience, equipment, and other basics that school psychologists should know to effectively deal with the topic.

Best Practices. The heart and most extensive part of a chapter. Authors were asked to provide best practices and to include options and perspectives so that school psychologists can mesh their professional orientation with other successful possibilities.

Summary. A synopsis of the topic, which includes a brief review and discussion of the best practices.

References. Publications and resources that support the chapter authors' information. Authors were asked to not make exhaustive lists, because chapters are intended to focus on evidence-based practices and not simply present a compilation of research.

Unlike previous editions of *Best Practices*, the current edition does not include Annotated Bibliographies at the end of each chapter. Instead, readers have online access to each chapter's Annotated Bibliography on the NASP website (http://www.nasponline.org/publications). Annotated Bibliographies include articles, books, Web-based information, and other resources suggested by authors of each chapter for follow-up reading to gain a more detailed view of best practices for the topic discussed in a chapter.

It is our hope that this edition of *Best Practices in School Psychology* will support current and future school psychologists in their ongoing quest for improved procedures and practices and the acquisition of professional skills needed to enhance students' success in their schools, homes, and communities.

INTRODUCTION TO THE BOOK: BEST PRACTICES IN SCHOOL PSYCHOLOGY: SYSTEMS-LEVEL SERVICES

This book includes three sections of chapters about school psychology practices related to systems-level services, including school-wide learning practices, preventive and responsive services, and family–school collaboration.

School-Wide Practices to Promote Learning

Chapters in this section focus on the School-Wide Practices to Promote Learning domain of the 2010 NASP *Model for Comprehensive and Integrated School Psychological Services*. The domain represents practices for systems-level services (see http://www.nasponline.org/standards/2010standards/2_PracticeModel.pdf, p. 6):

School psychologists have knowledge of school and systems structure, organization, and theory; general and special education; technology resources; and evidence-based school practices that promote learning and mental health. School psychologists, in collaboration with others, demonstrate skills to develop and implement practices and strategies to create and maintain effective and supportive learning environments for children and others. Professional practices associated with school-wide promotion of learning include the following:

- School psychologists, in collaboration with others, incorporate evidence-based strategies in the design, implementation, and evaluation of effective policies and practices in areas such as discipline, instructional support, staff training, school and other agency improvement activities, program evaluation, student transitions at all levels of schooling, grading, home– school partnerships, and more.
- School psychologists use their knowledge of organizational development and systems theory to assist in promoting a respectful and supportive atmosphere for decision making and collaboration, and a commitment to quality instruction and services.
- School psychologists are actively involved in the development of school improvement plans that impact the programs and services available to children, youth, and families, and the manner in which school psychologists deliver their services.
- School psychologists incorporate evidence-based strategies when developing and delivering intervention programs to facilitate successful transitions of students from one environment to another environment (e.g., program to program, school to school, age-level changes, and school to work transitions).
- School psychologists promote the development and maintenance of learning environments that support resilience and academic growth, promote high rates of academic engaged time, and reduce negative influences on learning and behavior.

- School psychologists participate in designing and implementing universal screening programs to identify students in need of additional instructional or behavioral support services, as well as progress monitoring systems to ensure successful learning and school adjustment.
- School psychologists work collaboratively with other school personnel to create and maintain a multitiered continuum of services to support all students' attainment of academic, social, emotional, and behavioral goals.
- School psychologists apply the problem-solving process to broader research and systems-level problems that result in the identification of factors that influence learning and behavior, the evaluation of the outcomes of classroom, building, and system initiatives and the implementation of decision-making practices designed to meet general public accountability responsibilities.

Preventive and Responsive Services

Chapters in this section focus on the Preventive and Responsive Services domain of the 2010 NASP *Model for Comprehensive and Integrated School Psychological Services*. The domain represents practices for systems-level services (see http://www.nasponline.org/standards/2010standards/2_PracticeModel.pdf, pp. 6–7):

School psychologists have knowledge of principles and research related to resilience and risk factors in learning and mental health, services in schools and communities to support multitiered prevention, and evidence-based strategies for effective crisis response. School psychologists, in collaboration with others, demonstrate skills to promote services that enhance learning, mental health, safety, and physical well-being through protective and adaptive factors and to implement effective crisis preparation, response, and recovery. Examples of effective practices associated with preventive and responsive services include the following:

- School psychologists promote recognition of risk and protective factors that are vital to understanding and addressing systemic problems such as school failure, truancy, dropout, bullying, youth suicide, or school violence.
- School psychologists participate in school crisis teams and use data-based decision making methods, problem-solving strategies, consultation, collaboration, and direct services in the context of crisis prevention, preparation, response, and recovery.
- School psychologists provide direct counseling, behavioral coaching, and indirect interventions through consultation for students who experience mental health problems that impair learning and/or socialization.
- School psychologists develop, implement, and evaluate prevention and intervention programs based on risk and protective factors that are precursors to severe learning and behavioral problems.
- School psychologists collaborate with school personnel, parents, students, and community resources to provide competent mental health support during and after crisis situations.
- School psychologists promote wellness and resilience by (a) collaborating with other healthcare professionals to provide a basic knowledge of behaviors that lead to good health for children; (b) facilitating environmental changes conducive to good health and adjustment of children; and (c) accessing resources to address a wide variety of behavioral, learning, mental, and physical needs.
- School psychologists participate in the implementation and evaluation of programs that promote safe and violence-free schools and communities.

Family–School Collaboration Services

Chapters in this section focus on the Family–School Collaboration Services domain of the 2010 NASP *Model for Comprehensive and Integrated School Psychological Services*. The domain represents practices for systems-level services (see http://www.nasponline.org/standards/2010standards/2_PracticeModel.pdf, p. 7):

School psychologists have knowledge of principles and research related to family systems, strengths, needs, and culture; evidence-based strategies to support family influences on children's learning and mental health; and strategies to develop collaboration between families and schools. School psychologists, in collaboration with others, demonstrate skills to design, implement, and evaluate services that respond to culture and context and facilitate family and school partnerships and interactions with community agencies for enhancement of academic and social–behavioral outcomes for children. Examples of professional practices associated with family–school collaboration include the following:

- School psychologists use evidence-based strategies to design, implement, and evaluate effective policies and practices that promote family, school, and community partnerships to enhance learning and mental health outcomes for students.
- School psychologists identify diverse cultural issues, contexts, and other factors that have an impact on family–school partnerships and interactions with community providers, and address these factors when developing and providing services for families.
- School psychologists promote strategies for safe, nurturing, and dependable parenting and home interventions to facilitate children's healthy development.
- School psychologists advocate for families and support parents in their involvement in school activities, for both addressing individual students' needs and participating in classroom and school events.
- School psychologists educate the school community regarding the influence of family involvement on school achievement and advocate for parent involvement in school governance and policy development whenever feasible.
- School psychologists help create linkages between schools, families, and community providers, and help coordinate services when programming for children involves multiple agencies.

ACKNOWLEDGMENTS

It is fascinating to compare the assembling and publication of this sixth edition of *Best Practices in School Psychology* with the circumstances surrounding the first edition. The comparison highlights the growth and diversity of the profession, the organizational vitality and commitment of NASP, and the increasing influence and importance of school psychologists during the intervening 30+ years.

In 1982, when work began on the first edition, NASP had 7,500 members (2014 membership exceeds 25,000), and training, field placement, practice, and credentialing standards for school psychology were at a much earlier stage of development. For the first edition of *Best Practices,* the acknowledgments section thanked six individuals who assisted in reviewing the 39 chapters and in typesetting—yes, literally setting type of the text. Selection of font style and size, space between lines, paper stock, cover art, selection of the printer, obtaining copyright, design of shipping cartons, method of shipping, cost, and the like were made by the coeditors, and communications with authors and reviewers were primarily by U.S. mail along with occasional phone calls. Three thousand copies of the first edition of *Best Practices* were printed and then trucked to, stored at, and eventually distributed from a school psychologist's garage in Connecticut. The introductory price to members, including shipping, was $22. Times change.

For this sixth edition of *Best Practices,* there are hundreds of people to thank and acknowledge. First, the approximately 300 authors of our 150 chapters spread across four books deserve our gratitude. We appreciate the dedication, enthusiasm, and efforts of this highly talented group.

In addition to our editorial review, an earnest effort was made to have each chapter peer-reviewed by at least three school psychologists (two current practitioners and a university- or other non-school-based school psychologist). We must heartily thank the reviewers who read first drafts, provided important feedback to authors, and shared their suggestions for improvement of the chapters. Once these reviews were received, the reviewed chapters were forwarded to the author along with copies of comprehensive reviewer notations and editor comments. It was a time-consuming process for the reviewers, and our authors' final manuscripts substantially benefited from these extensive reviewer efforts. Reviewers who contributed to this edition, and who receive our appreciation, are:

Melinda Adkins
Elsa Arroyos
Barry Barbarasch
Brian J. Bartels
John Biltz
Alan Brue
Elliot J. Davis
Bill Donelson
Amy N. Esler
René Fetchkan
Beth Glew
Bryn Harris
Denise Hildebrand
Daniel Hyson
Jessica (Dempsey) Johnston
Cathy Kennedy-Paine
Laurie McGarry Klose
Brian Leung
Jane Lineman-Coffman
Courtney L. McLaughlin
Dawn Miller
Karin Mussman
Karen O'Brien
Rivka I. Olley

Ronald S. Palomares
Anna M. Peña
Madi Phillips
Pamela M. Radford
Alecia Rahn-Blakeslee
Tracy Schatzberg
Nicole Skaar
Marlene Sotelo-Dynega
Vicki Stumme
Jackie Ternus
Lori Unruh
Ellie L. Young
Ashley Arnold
Michelle S. Athanasiou
Susan Bartels
Jill Berger
Brandee Boothe
Kelly R. Swanson Dalrymple
Emma Dickinson
Katie Eklund
Pam Fenning
Marika Ginsburg-Block
Julie Hanson
Jasolyn Henderson

Candis Hogan
Susan Jarmuz-Smith
Rita Lynne Jones
Regina K. Kimbrel
Misty Lay
Mary Levinsohn-Klyap
Monica McKevitt
Katherine Mezher
Sara Moses
Mary Alice Myers
Ed O'Connor
Leslie Z. Paige
Shamim S. Patwa
Debbie Phares
E. Jeanne Pound
Stephanie Rahill
Nancy Peña Razo
Margaret Sedor
Carole A. Sorrenti
Patricia Steinert-Otto
James M. Stumme
Lynne Ostroff Thies
Nate von der Embse

This sixth edition of *Best Practices* is the first edition that does not include Jeff Grimes as coeditor. Jeff worked with Alex Thomas as coeditor of all previous editions and made many contributions to the framework and content of *Best Practices* editions over the years. Further, Jeff has been a long-time leader in school psychology, and our field has benefitted greatly from his commitment, wisdom, and vision. We thank Jeff for all he has done for *Best Practices* and school psychology.

The efforts of Mike Schwartz have proved invaluable to the completion of this edition. Mike Schwartz has been the copyeditor for every chapter in this and in the last two editions of *Best Practices*. He read and reread each of the chapters and contributed substantive comments and perspectives in addition to making sure that references were properly cited, tenses agreed, tables aligned, verbs and nouns were compatible, and ideas remained focused. We thank him for his talent and good humor.

The look and feel of this edition, and the consistency and ease of reference, is due to the metadiligent efforts of Linda Morgan, NASP Director of Production. She actively participated in the myriad details associated with this work and took the lead in the design and presentation. Additionally, she fact checked and triple fact checked every reference and citation. NASP is fortunate to have her talents, and this edition of *Best Practices* is richer due to her involvement.

There are other people at the NASP national office who quietly and competently worked to enhance this edition of *Best Practices*. We thank Brieann Kinsey, Manager of Editorial Production, for her time fact checking, proofreading, and ensuring that what was printed was accurate and consistent with the overall "feel" of the publication. We also thank Denise Ferrenz, Director of Publications, for dealing with the multitude of planning, publication, and marketing considerations associated with a project of this magnitude.

Alex Thomas
Patti Harrison

EDITOR NOTE

Authors were invited to write chapters for this edition of *Best Practices* because of their expertise and experience in a specific topic. In a number of cases, these authors have written other publications or developed resources on the same topic and reference these materials in their *Best Practices* chapters. Therefore, authors were instructed to include a disclosure statement at the end of their *Best Practices* chapters, in line with the 2010 NASP *Principles for Professional Ethics*, Standard III.V.6 (see http://www.nasponline.org/standards/2010standards/1_%20Ethical%20Principles.pdf), which requires school psychologists to disclose financial interests in resources or services they discuss in presentations or writings.

Disclosure. Alex Thomas and Patti Harrison have financial interests in publications they coauthored or coedited and that are referenced by authors of several chapters in this edition of *Best Practices in School Psychology*. These include, for Alex Thomas, previous editions of *Best Practices in School Psychology* and, for Patti Harrison, *Contemporary Intellectual Assessment: Theories, Tests, and Issues; Adaptive Behavior Assessment System;* and *ABAS-II: Clinical Use and Interpretation.*

Section 1
School-Wide Practices to Promote Learning

1 Best Practices in Systems-Level Change

Jose M. Castillo
Michael J. Curtis
University of South Florida

OVERVIEW

Recent policy developments have radically changed the educational landscape in which school psychologists practice. The No Child Left Behind Act (NCLB) of 2002 and the 2004 reauthorization of the Individuals with Disabilities Education Act (IDEA) established clear expectations for implementation of scientifically based practices and data-based evaluation of student outcomes. Implementation of the instructional, intervention, and assessment practices mandated in federal legislation has forced educators to grapple with massive cultural, structural, and practical changes in the way that the nation educates its children. Moreover, the introduction of new school reform efforts has seemed to accelerate over the past few years, increasing the external demands placed on educators to change their practices. Recent reform efforts initiated in many states include adopting the Common Core State Standards, mandating more rigorous teacher evaluation systems, creating more sophisticated data systems to evaluate student progress, revising rules that determine processes and procedures for eligibility for special education services, and developing accountability processes for improving student outcomes. Any one of these changes represents a significant undertaking that has an impact on the services delivered by educators. Together, these policy developments represent a systematic effort to revolutionize American education.

Although recent reform efforts are not without controversy, the challenges inherent in implementing these innovations provide school psychologists with long sought after opportunities to expand their roles. Special-education-related activities continue to dominate the professional lives of many school psychologists (Castillo, Curtis, & Gelley, 2012) despite calls for major changes in the field. One outcome of the 2002 Multisite Conference on the Future of School Psychology was a proposed paradigm shift in the foundational philosophy of school psychology away from a special-education-focused medical model to a public health model in which health promotion and problem prevention are dominant themes (Dawson et al., 2004). The 2012 Multisite Conference on the Future of School Psychology continued this theme with multiple presentations, including an emphasis on school psychologists promoting and delivering services consistent with a public health framework (see http://www.indiana.edu/~futures/).

Data from schools and districts across the nation suggest that opportunities for school psychologists to answer these calls are becoming increasingly available. The vast majority of districts responding to a nationwide survey regarding response to intervention (RTI), a multitiered system of supports (MTSS) for matching instruction/intervention to student need, indicated that they are at some stage of implementation of the model (Spectrum K–12, 2011). Importantly, most districts report implementing RTI for the purpose of individualizing instruction for all students (62%) and providing early intervening services and supports to students identified as at risk (88%). These data reflect an emphasis on prevention and intervention services in addition to special education eligibility determination requirements introduced by the reauthorization of IDEA.

Whether supporting implementation of MTSS (e.g., RTI) or other school reform efforts, the National Association of School Psychologists (NASP) *Model for*

Comprehensive and Integrated School Psychological Services (NASP, 2010a) emphasizes practices that place school psychologists in a position to be leaders in improving the outcomes of students. This chapter, then, focuses on knowledge, skills, and practices that are reflected in the model's Consultation and Collaboration domain. Specifically, the application of consultation skills at a systems level is discussed. Furthermore, the role of systematic problem solving when engaging in systems-level consultation is detailed throughout. Critically, school psychologists who engage in collaborative problem solving during systems-level consultation can indirectly facilitate the improved student outcomes that are the focus of educational stakeholders.

However, one major obstacle to sustained improvements in student outcomes is a persistent disconnect between our knowledge about what research tells us about effective innovative practices and our knowledge about what research tells us about principles for systems change (Fixsen, Naoom, Blase, Friedman, & Wallace, 2005). In other words, the problem school psychologists face in responding to accountability demands does not lie with the availability of effective practices; rather, it lies with the failure to implement those practices effectively in a specific school setting. However, in almost every case (e.g., positive behavior support at the school level and mental health programs), implementation of the proposed program or practice would represent a significant school-wide change initiative, the success of which would depend on knowledge and skills in systems-level change. The reality is that knowledge and skills relating to both the innovative practice and systems change are essential if we are to be successful in bringing about meaningful change in our schools. It is apparent that there is an overriding need to engage in organizational change through the carefully planned application of systems change principles if school reform is to be successful.

Unfortunately, the preparation of most school psychologists has not included knowledge and skills relating to systems change. In fact, the 2010 standards for training programs adopted by NASP (see NASP, 2010b) and guidelines for the provision of school psychological services (see NASP, 2010a) include a focus on systems change for the first time. Nevertheless, the inclusion of systems change in these documents attests to the growing recognition of the importance of this area. In addition, *School Psychology: A Blueprint for Training and Practice III* (Ysseldyke et al., 2006) places special emphasis on knowledge and skills in understanding and changing systems.

As a result of the recent emphasis on systems change, this professional function has not been emphasized by many school psychologists. According to Castillo et al. (2012), the average school psychologist reports spending less than 6% of his or her time engaged in systems-focused consultation. Nevertheless, it is an area to which many school psychologists could contribute valuable knowledge and expertise.

The central foundation of psychology is the understanding of human behavior. A special strength of school psychology is understanding human behavior within the context of schools and educational institutions as they function in relationships with families and the larger community. In other words, school psychologists understand human behavior within the ecology of the school as part of a larger system. This understanding and expertise can allow school psychologists to emerge as leaders in the implementation of changes that are important to educational stakeholders.

The purpose of this chapter is to increase school psychologists' understanding of the knowledge, skills, and practices that facilitate systems change. It is hoped that after reading this chapter, school psychologists will understand schools as complex social systems, understand the role of consultation skills in facilitating systems change, and understand critical systems change principles and their application in school settings.

BASIC CONSIDERATIONS

There are some circumstances in which a school psychologist might function in the role of a systems-level change agent from outside the organization (e.g., the school psychologist would be hired for the specific purpose of facilitating systems change). However, in most cases, the school psychologist will be an employee of the school district, typically assigned to serve one or more schools, and facilitating systems change will represent only one of a variety of direct and indirect professional service functions. In order to effectively facilitate systems-level change, school psychologists need to call upon three areas of expertise:

- An understanding of human behavior from a social systems perspective
- An ability to use collaborative planning and problem-solving procedures
- A familiarity with principles for organizational change

Social Systems Perspective

Although schools usually can be identified by their physical appearance, without students and the personnel who work there, schools are very much like any other building. Bricks, mortar, steel beams, and glass do not tell much about the character of a school. Regardless of physical structure, it is the people within who give it life. Because of its people, a school is a social system. Furthermore, no two schools are functionally alike because of the uniqueness of the individuals who inhabit and affect each of the schools. It is for this fundamental reason that, despite efforts to affect district policies and operational procedures, the school building most often is the focus of systems-level change efforts. This is not to suggest that district and state administrators do not play an important role in facilitating change. In fact, establishing and communicating expectations, allocating resources (e.g., professional development opportunities, matching funding to identified needs) to meet school staff needs, and facilitating shared accountability for student performance are among the critical roles that these leaders play (e.g., Leithwood, 2010; Sharratt & Fullan, 2009). However, delivery of the services that will have an impact on student outcomes ultimately occurs at the school level, necessitating a focus on changing the practices of teachers, principals, instructional support personnel, and other school-level stakeholders.

Understanding of Schools as Systems

A system is an orderly combination of parts that interact to produce a desired outcome or product. An automobile engine is an example of a system. It consists of a number of specific parts that interact to produce power and motion. However, in contrast to a living system, an automobile engine is an example of an inert system (i.e., as long as the parts continue to function in the same way, the engine should continue to produce power in essentially the same way). Because it is people who give schools their real meaning, schools are living systems. A critical difference between a living system and an inert system is the ability of the living system to learn from its experiences and to adapt to its environment.

For the purposes of this chapter, a system is the orderly combination of two or more individuals whose interaction is intended to produce a desired outcome. A school is a system because it consists of component parts (e.g., students, teachers, cafeteria workers, parents, principal) that are organized and interact for the purpose of producing a definable outcome (e.g., academic achievement by all students). As is true of all

systems, the school building also is part of a larger system; that is, the school district. Individual classrooms, grade-level teams of teachers, local school improvement committees, and problem-solving teams are examples of systems within the school. Each consists of component parts that interact for the purpose of attaining desired outcomes, and each exists within a larger system.

Reciprocal Influence

In order for a living system to interact with and to react to its environment, both internally and externally, it must be an open system. Each of the parts of a system influences all of the other parts, as well as the performance of the system as a whole. A change in one part of the system will cause changes in other parts of the system. For example, if the current building principal is replaced by a new principal, that change is likely to affect, for example, classrooms, students, teachers, the school psychologist, and cafeteria workers. Although changes in one particular component of the system may tend to have more impact than would change in others because of the role played by that particular part (a principal versus one student), each part, regardless of role or size, influences the system as a whole to some degree. Also, circumstances may significantly alter the system more than normally would be expected (e.g., a tragedy involving one student that affects everyone in the school). Similarly, changes in the larger surrounding environment influence the school building as a system, as well as the components within the building. For example, a district decision to implement a specific behavioral intervention program in every building would influence not only the individual school but its teachers, students, and other personnel as well.

Gutkin (2009) advocates for viewing the individual child within a systems or ecological framework. From this perspective, the child is one element in a larger interactive environment. The child influences and is influenced by various forces in the system of which he or she is a part. Thus, improving student outcomes will sometimes require interventions that address systemic barriers to academic, behavioral, and social–emotional learning.

Capacity of the System to Solve Problems

One of the ways in which systems differ is the extent of their openness to environmental influences, both internal and external. Healthy systems—based on their identified goals—screen environmental information, accepting that which is important, rejecting that which is not, and responding in a manner that is appropriate for the information received. In other words, healthy systems demonstrate the capacity to analyze problems and to solve them in a manner that facilitates the attainment of their goals.

Of course, some systems lack the capacity to solve problems effectively. In some cases, systems are not sufficiently open to accept important information or systems may have been open at an earlier time, but because they did not have the ability to solve problems confronting them, they became closed, somewhat like the ostrich with its head in the sand. The inability to interact with influential forces, internally as well as externally, creates tremendous tension in closed systems. If the tension reaches a high enough level, a crisis occurs that causes some type of change in the system.

On the other end of the continuum, some systems are too open and are unable to screen environmental forces. They essentially accept all input and try to respond to everything, often with the same level of intensity. They are overwhelmed and operate in a constant state of crisis. As a result, the school is in a constant state of change. In such systems, because there is a lack of stability and continuity, it is exceedingly difficult to set goals, make plans to attain them, and monitor progress. In addition, the energy invested and the attention required to constantly respond to all forces, regardless of importance, is not available to address issues that should be a priority.

The primary goal of facilitating systems-level change is to increase the problem-solving capacity of the system so that it can deal with all problems more effectively. In this way, facilitating systems-level change is exactly like one-to-one consultation. While the immediate objective in one-to-one consultation is to help the person requesting assistance solve the problem, the primary objectives are to help that person become more effective in solving similar problems in the future and to become a more effective problem solver in general. In facilitating systems-level change, the system serves as the consultee. While the immediate goal is to help the system solve a specific problem, the primary goal is to facilitate the development of the system as an effective problem solver.

Collaborative Planning and Problem-Solving Skills

Collaboration serves as the foundation for facilitating systems-level change. For our purposes, whether one-to-one or systems level, collaboration means two or more people working together, using systematic planning and problem-solving procedures, to achieve desired outcomes. The principles of collaborative planning and problem solving that apply to individual consultation are directly relevant when facilitating systems-level change as well. In fact, collaborative one-to-one consultation and the facilitation of systems-level change are directly parallel in almost every respect. Although we will not discuss one-to-one consultation skills in depth here, it would be helpful to note very briefly some of the fundamental characteristics of effective consultation that should be present in the facilitation of systems-level change, specifically those relating to interpersonal relationships and planning and problem-solving skills.

Interpersonal Relationships
Effective consultation is based on mutual respect, trust, and coordinate power status among the participants. In facilitating systems change, the intent is to support the efforts of the group to achieve the goals that the group has decided upon in a manner that the group chooses. Effective communication skills are essential whether we are functioning as a consultant or as a member of a problem-solving/planning team. The ability to listen, ask open-ended questions, paraphrase, and summarize and synthesize information, all within a nonjudgmental climate, are especially important. These skills take on added significance when attempting to facilitate change from within the system. Group members are often not very tolerant of a member whose behaviors tend to alter the coordinate power status among members (e.g., by giving unsolicited feedback to the group).

Planning and Problem-Solving Skills
It is essential to remember that consultation is a problem-solving process and that attention to both interpersonal skills and problem-solving procedures are critical in determining success. Whether functioning as a consultant or as a member of the team, effectiveness in each area is necessary but insufficient by itself.

Fundamental planning and problem-solving procedures are very similar, with the major difference being one of direction. Whereas planning is intended to achieve a desirable goal, problem solving is intended to alleviate an undesirable condition. Many planning and/or problem-solving models exist; however, most models reflect the inclusion of four major stages:

- Problem identification and definition of the desired outcome(s)
- Problem analysis and identification of resources and barriers

- Strategy development and implementation
- Program evaluation

Regardless of the specific model chosen, effective problem solving must include all four of these stages. However, although such models typically describe a specific sequence of stages, actual problem solving often does not proceed in such a mechanical, lockstep manner. Rather, movement back and forth among the stages is common. Nevertheless, the general sequence of stages typically should occur as described and all stages must be included. For a comprehensive review of consultation processes, including interpersonal relationships, as well as problem solving, see Gutkin and Curtis (2009).

BEST PRACTICES IN SYSTEMS-LEVEL CHANGE

A growing body of literature exists that is focused on school change (e.g., Fullan, 2010; Hall & Hord, 2011; Sharratt & Fullan, 2009). Although conceptual frameworks for approaching systems change may differ in terms of the number of principles to attend to and terminology used, the critical concepts are similar. From our review of the literature on systems change and our experiences working with schools, districts, states, community agencies, and professional organizations, we have organized the important components of change into seven principles.

Principles for Organizational Change

The application of the concepts and strategies represented in these principles has been identified as critical to schools and districts that have been successful in improving student outcomes (e.g., Fielding, Kerr, & Rosier, 2007; Fullan, 2010; Sharratt & Fullan, 2009). Each of the seven principles is described below. Important concepts and strategies school psychologists can use to facilitate change and examples of how these principles have been applied in the context of educational settings are provided.

Change Principle 1: Leadership

Perhaps no change principle is more important than leadership. Formal and informal leaders play a critical role in creating the conditions necessary for change to occur. It is essential to identify all persons who function as gatekeepers before any aspect of the change process is initiated. The role of a gatekeeper is characterized by

decision-making power, ability to distribute resources, and authority within the system. Gatekeepers must not only give sanction for the change process but, it is hoped, provide support and fully participate with all other members of the system as well. Sometimes, just the nonparticipation of the gatekeeper can be a negative factor. The role of gatekeeper is most commonly held by personnel who serve in designated leadership positions, such as building principals and superintendents. However, staff in less obviously powerful positions, such as a school secretary or specific teachers who are highly respected, can be very influential in determining the success or failure of change efforts.

Success of a change effort often hinges on whether leadership is demonstrated by those responsible for facilitating the change. Effective leaders articulate a clear vision for where the organization needs to go, establish a sense of urgency, and maintain focus on implementing change over time. Effective leaders understand that meaningful change happens when those responsible for serving students (teachers) alter their practices. They cultivate an environment for such changes to occur by creating relationships with stakeholders (e.g., teachers, parents) based upon mutual respect and responsibility, engage in problem solving to remove barriers to student success, and invest in staff professional development (Crawford & Torgesen, 2007; Leithwood, 2010).

Although principals and district administrators play a critical role in facilitating change, the idea of mutual respect and shared responsibility is evident in school and district leadership teams being responsible for facilitating change in many settings. The composition of a team will vary according to the unique context of a school or district; however, it is critical that such teams include representation from the major stakeholders of the organization. In the context of schools, key stakeholders who should be involved typically include administrators (i.e., principals), general and special education teachers, support personnel (e.g., school psychologists, content specialists, interventionists), parents, and community members. The roles and responsibilities of leadership teams are not just to set expectations for change, but also to plan for and support the change. This often requires team members to work with the educators responsible for implementing the change through existing structures in order for stakeholders to analyze and improve their practices (see Nellis, 2012, for more information on teaming). However, when administrators support a change effort, they are often willing to be creative to ensure that the new practices are implemented.

In one elementary school in which the first author served as a school psychologist, the school principal scheduled three full-day sessions for kindergarten teachers to discuss their perspectives on MTSS, analyze data on the performance of their students, and engage in data-based problem solving to improve Tier 1 instruction. What is noteworthy about this example is that the principal was initially skeptical about embracing MTSS. However, after participating in district-provided professional development and engaging in consensus-building discussions with the school's leadership team, the principal not only decided to set the expectation that MTSS would be implemented, but also provided substitute teachers for each of the full-day sessions to ensure adequate time for problem solving and instructional planning to occur. Although the sessions were facilitated by the school psychologist and literacy coach, the principal was an active participant in the meetings, demonstrating the importance of this initiative to the teachers.

Returns on the significant time investment made by the principal were evident at the end of the school year when 71% of kindergarten students met the school district's standards for proficiency. Although additional work was clearly needed, 71% of students meeting district expectations represented a substantial increase over recent years when 59%, 62%, and 55% of students met expectations during the three previous school years. This increase occurred despite the fact that the school's student population remained largely the same across the years (the majority of students were eligible for free or reduced lunch and the school received Title 1 supports).

Calls have been emanating from the field for school psychologists to play a leadership role in schools. In fact, the 2012 Multisite Conference on the Future of School Psychology dedicated an entire strand to the topic (see http://www.indiana.edu/~futures/ for more information). Some school psychologists serve in a formal leadership role (e.g., supervisor of psychological services); however, most school psychologists will play more informal roles in leading change efforts. School psychologists are ideal candidates to serve on school leadership teams, facilitate planning and problem-solving meetings, and support educators in implementing effective practices. In the above example, the school psychologist not only facilitated problem solving but also served as a member of the school leadership team. These roles allowed the school psychologist to provide input regarding implementing MTSS and be directly involved with key stakeholders responsible for implementing the assessment, curricular, and instructional practices.

Change Principle 2: Involvement of Key Stakeholders

All stakeholders in the system must participate in every stage of the change process. Stakeholders are all the members of the system who will be affected by the change. Decisions about systems-level change in schools are often made at the administrative level. Failure to involve important stakeholders, such as classroom teachers, will negatively affect the organizational change effort.

Many efforts to implement intervention-focused services have violated this critical principle. Typically, the discussion, planning, and even implementation of changes have involved seemingly everyone but classroom teachers. Principals, special education personnel, school psychologists, and other related services professionals then inform teachers about the new procedures. Confusion and frustration result among these well-intentioned change agents when teachers are not included early in the process. Common sense suggests that classroom teachers are the primary stakeholders among the professional staff in a school who will be affected by the implementation of changes.

Parents represent another critical group of stakeholders. Parents are often glaringly absent from systems-level change efforts in schools. IDEA mandates that parents are to be meaningfully involved in the education of children with disabilities. However, the involvement of parents in all school-change initiatives would seem self-evident from the perspective of the organizational change literature. It also should be apparent that, where possible and appropriate, students should be involved in systems change. The literature is very clear: All stakeholders should be meaningfully involved in every aspect of systems-level change efforts, beginning with initial discussions regarding potential change and continuing through implementation and evaluation of the change effort.

Two specific organizational change concepts discussed by Hall and Hord (2011) have been found to be particularly helpful in guiding efforts to meaningfully involve key stakeholders. People within a system vary in their level of willingness and ability to adopt specific innovations. Moreover, innovation spreads through a system as increasing numbers of stakeholders begin using it. Therefore, it is important to focus change efforts on those members who are interested or willing to consider change rather than on those who are resistant. Those who remain resistant to the systems change efforts may represent personnel issues that must be addressed by formal leadership (e.g., the building principal).

It also is important to understand how individuals' levels of concern toward an innovation can affect their level of commitment to the procedures necessary to implement that innovation. The stages of concern that individuals pass through begin with concern about how the innovation will affect them personally, then concern about how to implement the innovation, and finally concern about how the innovation will have an impact on the system. How quickly individuals pass through levels of concern often will vary as a function of their willingness and ability to adopt innovations. Therefore, understanding individuals' stages of concern will help in deciding what type of information to provide and how much effort to invest in those individuals. (See Hall and Hord, 2011, for additional information as well as tools to help identify educators' willingness and readiness to adopt an innovation.)

Involving teachers, parents, and other key stakeholders (e.g., community members) can be challenging in an increasingly stressed educational system. In our experience, time is the number one barrier cited by educators when discussions about, planning for, or implementation of new practices occur. School psychologists engaged in change efforts can help key stakeholders address this barrier by working with school leaders (typically administrators) to use existing structures and/or create new ones to facilitate involvement of stakeholders. Faculty meetings, professional learning communities, grade-level meetings, parent–teacher organization/association meetings, school advisory committee meetings, and open houses are some examples of already existing communication structures that can be used to share information with key stakeholders as well as gather input from them. When these structures are not available or sufficient, leaders must be creative regarding how to facilitate the involvement of stakeholders who cannot be left out of the change process. In addition, school psychologists should not underestimate the value of informal conversations with key stakeholders. When educators, parents, and other stakeholders trust those facilitating change, they become a rich source of information about how the change process is progressing. Exchanging ideas in the hallway, having conversations during lunch in the teachers' lounge, and engaging in discussions before and after school are just a few examples of using opportune moments to gather information.

Because an organizational change effort must be planned and sustained over time, it is important that key personnel and other stakeholders have a realistic understanding of what may be involved. Otherwise,

the absence of immediate change (an unrealistic goal to begin with) could lead to the loss of commitment and investment in the process. Therefore, it may be helpful to demonstrate change methods so the group can gain familiarity with such procedures, as well as experience success in addressing real concerns. For example, the second author taught an entire school staff group problem-solving techniques as a means for demonstrating organizational change methods and for securing their commitment to the change process. After having the participants identify real concerns and establish related goals for change, group problem-solving skills were taught and used to develop strategies to achieve the identified goals. Using this strategy served to teach the problem-solving skills necessary for planned change while addressing real concerns that were considered important by the participants (see Curtis & Metz, 1986, for additional information).

Change Principle 3: Shared Vision, Mission, Beliefs, and Values

Involvement of key stakeholders in a change effort presumes a common understanding of the organization as well as a shared belief in its direction. In the accountability era, schools and districts are under increasing pressure to improve student outcomes. Although we agree that ambitious expectations for student performance and accountability structures are important elements of school reform, relying too heavily on a mandate-driven approach to change ignores the culture and climate of schools. Fullan (2010) discusses the importance of establishing what he calls a moral imperative for changing practices. When educators are provided the opportunity to discuss and reflect upon how changes in their practices fit into the bigger picture of improving student functioning, they are much more likely to embrace new practices.

Although schools and districts typically have vision and mission statements intended to create a shared moral imperative among stakeholders, they are often developed by a small group and posted on a website or a wall in an office. Little opportunity for input and discussion is provided for teachers and other stakeholders (e.g., parents) whose contribution is necessary to achieve the vision and mission. School psychologists can change this dynamic by working with school leaders to facilitate staff and parental discussions regarding what they believe and value. Issues should be discussed, such as the purpose of schooling; how students best learn; staff, family, and community roles in contributing to the learning of all students; and what should be done when a student is not meeting expectations. The goal of these types of discussions is to develop consensus among staff and other stakeholders regarding how a school educates its students. This information can be used by leadership to develop vision, mission, beliefs, and value statements that truly reflect stakeholders' shared perspectives. These statements should be publicly stated and reaffirmed regularly to remind people why they are engaging in the change effort.

As an example, in her assignment to a new building, the principal of an elementary school solicited the assistance of the second author in developing vision, mission, and beliefs and value statements for her school. An all-day session was held at the beginning of the school year before the return of students. All stakeholders for the building participated, including the principal and assistant principal, classroom teachers, special subject teachers (e.g., physical education), support services personnel (e.g., school psychologist), cafeteria and custodial staff, and the leadership of the parent–teacher organization. Initial activities were intended to build personal and professional familiarity among all of those present. Ground rules were established to guide the rest of the day (e.g., everyone would participate, all ideas and perspectives were welcome). The group was presented with the scenario that the facilitator's son would be starting in their school the following week, and, as a parent, the facilitator wanted to know what could be expected for his child (What were the beliefs and values that would determine his son's experiences in that school?). When all ideas were exhausted following a brainstorming process, the ideas generated were discussed and used to formulate several values and belief statements that everyone could live with. Those statements then served to guide all subsequent discussions and the development of both a vision statement for what education should be like for all students and a mission statement for that school's goals in pursuing that vision. The resulting statements were publicly posted, were distributed to all parents, and were used to guide decision making throughout the year.

Change Principle 4: Having a Systems Perspective

The same intervention would not be employed to address different concerns relating to different students. The intervention would have to fit the specific problem in each situation. Yet, in facilitating systems change there sometimes seems to be a tendency to use the same change strategies, regardless of the specific characteristics and needs of different systems. To be successful in facilitating systemic change, change agents must possess an understanding of the uniqueness of the system and how each of its parts interrelate. Because schools are social systems in which educators from various disciplines bring different backgrounds, experiences, and roles and responsibilities to the table, it is important to build a common understanding of what the organization does and how an individual, unit, department, or other entity contributes to the overall vision and mission of the organization. Having this type of shared systems perspective allows stakeholders to better determine who should be involved and what changes may need to be made in the system when engaging in planning and problem solving.

Facilitating a common understanding of the big picture regarding how the parts of a school or district work together is necessary but not sufficient for change to occur. Successful collaboration among stakeholders across a system requires a shared way of working. Importantly, a shared way of working is not just a program or procedures but a way of educating students and solving problems that becomes how staff does business. For example, using data-based problem solving to identify supports students and schools need within a multitiered framework is the way of working within schools and districts implementing MTSS.

School psychologists are ideal candidates to help build the capacity of other stakeholders to engage in problem solving as a way of working. School psychologists' ecological perspectives regarding student learning and development provide a foundation for understanding how different levels of a system relate to student outcomes. Furthermore, school psychologists collaborate with multiple stakeholders in the educational system (e.g., teachers, parents, school administrators, guidance counselors, school social workers, district personnel) who can provide unique insights into how the personnel that constitute a school system could contribute to improving student outcomes in MTSS. Communicating with key stakeholders about the vision for how the system can better organize itself and use problem-solving practices to produce improved outcomes is critical for staff to gain an understanding of what this way of working entails. Awareness presentations, systematic professional development, and ongoing dialogue with key stakeholders are common examples of strategies for facilitating a systems perspective.

Change Principle 5: Data-Based Decision Making

Systems change is built upon careful analysis of the organization and the resulting plan that is designed to address the unique needs and characteristics of a particular system. Using data to inform decisions increases the probability that the actions taken will succeed. Importantly, data-based decision-making concepts that apply to ways of addressing the needs of students apply to systems change. The specific data sources may be different or may be applied at larger units of analysis than the individual student (e.g., grade level, school level, district level); however, the concept of multimethod, multi-informant assessment is the same. Importantly, multimethod, multi-informant assessment should occur throughout the process of diagnostic, input, and program evaluation.

Diagnostic evaluation (i.e., needs assessment) is helpful for identifying the needs of the system. Formal techniques such as surveys and questionnaires may be combined with informal measures such as interviews and observations to provide a complete understanding of the organization. Needs assessments are particularly useful not only for gathering information about the organization but also for involving all members of the system in the change process. Once the needs of the system have been clearly identified, the resources available that may be relevant to addressing those needs are examined through input evaluation (i.e., resource mapping). The skills and resources of the staff, support of parents and district personnel, and financial resources are examples of factors to be considered. When focusing on problems it is sometimes easy to overlook the importance of acknowledging and building upon the existing strengths, resources, and successes of the system. Attitudinal factors may be just as important as tangible resources. A thorough understanding of all relevant factors, both negative and positive, must be developed before moving forward.

Once diagnostic and input evaluations have been conducted and the process of change begins, ongoing program evaluation efforts are critical to increasing the likelihood of success. As with individual consultation or a student-focused intervention effort, it is essential that progress in systems-level change efforts is also monitored and evaluated on an ongoing basis through the collection and analysis of data. Measuring progress is necessary at multiple levels, beginning with the lowest levels of the structured problem-solving process and progressing through the major goals of the organization. Evaluation at each level enables us to determine the extent to which the problem-solving strategy has been successful. When necessary, the strategy can be modified or replaced by a new action plan. When successful, a new barrier can be targeted or a new problem or goal

identified. Importantly, data on the fidelity of implementation of the plan as well as data measuring progress on the identified goal or outcome are critical to making informed decisions regarding next steps in the change process. School psychologists' skills in assessment, research, and program evaluation suggest that they can and should take an active role in the data collection, analysis, and interpretation tasks required for school and district personnel to make reliable and valid data-based decisions.

Change Principle 6: Capacity Building

Organizational change leaders ensure that the capacity for change is continuously addressed. Too often, mandates for change have been placed upon educators without ensuring the availability of the appropriate professional development and systems supports necessary for implementation to occur. Common elements of capacity building include addressing the beliefs, attitudes, knowledge, and skills of educators through professional development; using resources (time, personnel, materials, funding) to support implementation of an initiative; and ensuring that policies and procedures are developed and communicated that support implementation. Although professional development and resource allocation are common processes in education, the manner in which they traditionally have been carried out is a contributing factor in the history of the reform failures noted above. Fullan (2010) argues for approaching professional development and resource allocation in a way that results in the collective capacity of educators to implement practices that improve student outcomes.

Alignment and integration of systems and resources are important concepts when focusing on collective capacity building. Although several factors influence what professional development should be provided, the organization's priorities (goals) and the needs of staff identified through data need to inform the scope and sequence of content delivered. When the scope of what schools and districts are responsible for doing is considered, the sheer volume of knowledge and skills educators need to possess can become overwhelming. Knowing what the building is focusing on accomplishing during a given year, and collecting data to determine what staff will need in order to accomplish those goals, can help focus professional development targets. In the absence of these elements, leaders run the risk of covering content that results in little meaningful professional learning. (See Learning Forward, 2011, for more information on effective professional development practices.)

The concept of collective capacity also involves aligning and integrating resources in a way that maximizes their contribution to the system. Traditionally, resources have been thought of as unitary entities that operate separately to support the system. For example, school and district leaders have often bought additional personnel and programs to meet a need without consideration for how they should be integrated into the larger system. However, Fullan (2010) argues that collective capacity is achieved when resources are compounded in such a way that they support each other. Purchasing a Tier 2 program to address the phonemic awareness and phonics needs of students identified by data is an example of acquiring a material resource. To maximize the usefulness of this new resource, leaders need to determine who needs to be trained on the new program and what knowledge and skills should be the focus of ongoing professional development (including how the program relates to Tier 1 instruction in the building). Furthermore, schedules must be altered to ensure time for professional development, delivery of the intervention program, and meetings to discuss student progress. Progress monitoring systems that incorporate technology must be put in place to facilitate efficient collection, analysis, and interpretation of the data needed to inform decisions about student performance. Thus, the intervention program in this example has the potential to become an effective resource because of thoughtful consideration of how it, along with other available resources, improves the capacity of the human resources in the building to deliver effective instruction.

We have seen the role school psychologists can play in capacity building firsthand on a number of occasions. The above scenario regarding purchasing a Tier 2 intervention program is based on a school in which both authors worked with the school's principal, reading specialist, and kindergarten teachers to implement the evidence-based Tier 2 intervention program. Importantly, these stakeholders were involved in every aspect of making decisions about the identification, implementation, and evaluation of the program. In fact, evidence of increased rates of learning for the majority of students receiving the Tier 2 intervention program was one of the major factors that contributed to school personnel sustaining the practices in subsequent years. Moreover, the primary role of many of the school psychologists in the school district in which the first author worked was to provide training and technical assistance to school and district personnel implementing MTSS. Importantly, the psychologists did not focus solely on the delivery of professional development, but also on collaborating with members of the school and district leadership teams to support the scheduling, funding, and other decisions that needed to be coordinated to build staff capacity to implement MTSS.

Change Principle 7: Planning and Problem-Solving Skills

Application of the preceding six principles is necessary but not sufficient for ensuring that sustainable change will occur. Systems-level change must be planned and pursued in a systematic manner over time. It does not just happen. Furthermore, it is not an event or activity but an ongoing process that should never end. Having skills in and using planning and problem-solving procedures is the mechanism for facilitating a sustainable effort to implement change. A few considerations when applying planning and problem-solving concepts to systems-level issues follow.

Goal identification. Specific desirable outcomes based on needs and resource evaluations should be identified. It is critical that these goals reflect information derived from the data. The goals will determine the types of systems-level intervention to be considered and specifically those chosen for implementation. It is at this stage that groups often discover that they have identified several different, although related, goals. Refinement of goals and the selection of one goal at a time to pursue through specific change strategies will enhance the likelihood that the group will be successful in its efforts.

It is also important to establish realistic, concrete, systems-level goals, especially during the early stages of an organizational change effort. When seeking organizational change, it is easy to get lost in an all-or-nothing view of the system. The school psychologist can assist the group in breaking larger goals into more reasonable steps according to which change can be measured. Even a small initial change has the potential to create a ripple effect that leads to more significant change later.

Strategy development and implementation. Facilitating systems-level change involves ongoing activities to address long-term goals. Intervention is not conceptualized as a single event. Therefore, it is helpful to identify a staff member who will serve as the on-site facilitator of the change process. Although school psychologists may be well suited for this role, the itinerant nature of some school psychology assignments may make involvement in the ongoing monitoring of change difficult. In systems change efforts, it is easy for individuals to get lost in the details of their daily routines. It is essential that someone monitor systems-level initiatives and, when necessary, refocus the group on the change process. Although formal leaders such as the principal are ideal for this role, others may serve in this role provided that administrators are supportive of the effort. The overall plan for change may involve intervention methods that target the cognitive, affective, and/or structural components of the organization. Interventions that address cognitive aspects include the activities that are instructional such as training staff in new knowledge or skills. Affective interventions are those that address interpersonal relationships among the staff. Examples include training in communication and effective listening skills. Structural interventions focus on the way the organization is put together and its relationship to its various component parts, as well as the larger system of which it is a part. Because these components are somewhat interrelated, systems-level intervention plans that address all three are usually most effective. The intervention activities should be carefully selected to achieve aspects of the overall goals of the system.

Evaluation of progress. It is important for school psychologists and other educators facilitating change to remember the importance of evaluating the extent to which strategies selected and implemented achieved the desired goals. Similar to student-focused interventions, the selection and implementation of strategies does not guarantee success. The plan may not be implemented as intended, it may not be the right match for the problem or not be implemented intensively enough to be effective, or the dynamics of the situation may change, necessitating a different set of strategies to be successful. In our experience, educators who engage in systems-level problem solving often develop action plans but do not develop plans to evaluate progress toward a goal. Several barriers exist to engaging in program evaluation (e.g., lack of time, lack of perceived importance, skill deficits); however, the foundational knowledge and skills that school psychologists possess in research and program evaluation (NASP, 2010a) place them in a prime position to support evaluation efforts.

Teaching of planning and problem-solving procedures. As noted above, the development of problem-solving skills by the system is the primary goal in facilitating systems-level change. The most effective method for achieving this goal is through direct instruction, practice, and follow-up. One-time didactic presentations that do not provide opportunities for practice, feedback, and rehearsal of desired skills are ineffective (Joyce & Showers, 2002). The school psychologist could be a valuable resource in providing training to as many of the major stakeholders in the system as possible. It may be necessary to begin by training only a few members; however, providing all members with training in problem-solving skills should still be maintained as an eventual goal. For example, in working at the building level, it very often is necessary to begin by training a specific group such as the school leadership team. Once the group has been trained and has had an opportunity to practice using collaborative planning and problem-solving procedures and then refined their use of such methods through feedback, discussion, and perhaps further training, members of the group can become a vehicle for planning training for the remainder of the staff. However, improving the problem-solving skills of any members of the system represents progress, even if training the entire staff is not possible. Any improvement should be recognized as a positive outcome of systems change efforts.

Model for Systematic and Structured Planning and Problem Solving

Although many different approaches to problem solving might be used, the model described below has been used by the authors to train a wide range of individuals and groups in a variety of settings, including schools, districts, state departments of education, and professional organizations. Each of the steps is explained briefly. The effectiveness of this model depends on strict adherence to the following steps in the sequential order described and on thoroughly completing one step before moving on to the next. For ease of presentation, each step is explained in terms of problem-solving procedures. However, the same steps would be used to achieve goals identified for planning purposes.

Step 1

Describe the problem to be addressed as concretely and in as much detail as possible. Once the problem has been defined, identify the desired outcome of the problem-solving efforts, again using concrete, descriptive terms. Often, what initially is thought to be a single problem is recognized to be several distinct, although perhaps related, problems. Record all problems identified. Although all of the problems may not be dealt with during one session, those not dealt with can be addressed during subsequent sessions. Identify the specific problem that will be addressed first. Then, describe the desired outcome that would result from resolution of that one specific problem. It is essential that all members of the problem-solving team have the same understanding of both the problem to be addressed and the desired outcome.

Step 2

Analyze the specific issue chosen in terms of factors that might help in reducing or eliminating the problem (resources), as well as factors that might serve as barriers to its resolution. All members of the team should participate in a brainstorming process to generate a list of potential resources and barriers. The use of only concise statements should be encouraged. It is essential that ideas not be discussed, evaluated, or even clarified at this point. The intent is to produce as much information as possible by involving all members of the group in a free flow of ideas. Record only enough about each idea to allow clarification by its originator after brainstorming is completed. The intent is to develop a thorough understanding of the problem and its context (i.e., problem analysis).

Step 3

Select one barrier identified in Step 2 that is preventing resolution of the problem defined in Step 1. The barrier selected should be viewed as only the first barrier to be addressed, not the only one. Avoid trying to identify the most important barrier; this will help diminish issues relating to ownership associated with who generated which ideas. However, the barrier selected should be one for which there is shared interest across the group. If the team is inexperienced in using systematic and structured problem-solving procedures, it also would be desirable to initially choose a barrier for which there is a reasonable chance of generating strategies for reducing or eliminating it. Experiencing success is important in developing team skills and confidence. Other important barriers can be identified for attention during subsequent efforts.

Step 4

Focusing only on the one obstacle selected in Step 3 and brainstorm strategies that might be used to reduce or eliminate that specific barrier. The list of resources identified in Step 2 serves only as a stimulus for the generation of ideas. Again, because a brainstorming process is being used, the intent is to generate and record as many ideas as possible. Specific ideas can be clarified after brainstorming is complete. Remind team members that this is only an idea stage. They should not

filter out potential strategies because they are unsure of how the strategies would be implemented. At this stage, no decisions have been made regarding strategies to be implemented.

Step 5

Design multiple action plans to guide the implementation of the systems intervention for the purpose of reducing or eliminating only the barrier identified in Step 3. If possible, several action plans for interventions should be developed to address the same barrier. That way, if one plan is not carried out as intended or does not attain the desired results, the identified barrier still may be reduced or eliminated through other action plans. Each plan should clearly identify who (by name or position) is responsible for carrying out what specific activity (include as much detail as possible) and by when (the deadline for completion) to promote accountability. The greater the detail provided in a plan, the greater the likelihood that it will be carried out as intended and on time. Sometimes it is desirable to try out an action plan on a limited scale before proceeding with full implementation. If the person identified as being responsible for the action plan is not a member of the group developing the plan, an action plan should be created that identifies a group member who will contact that individual about his or her willingness to take responsibility for the plan (what) and the date by which contact is to occur (when).

Step 6

Develop a plan for following up with each action plan or intervention that explains how implementation will be monitored as well as how support will be provided to the person responsible, if needed. Intervention integrity is as important in dealing with systems-level issues as it is in addressing student-specific issues. Failing to implement an action plan or not implementing the plan as intended undermines the effectiveness of the change effort. A range of factors can represent potential barriers to the implementation of action plans. People typically have busy schedules and many other responsibilities under the best of circumstances. Follow-up procedures serve as a prompt for the team to attend to the action plan in spite of other pressures. In addition, when unanticipated events crop up that require the time, energy, and attention of the individual responsible for a given action plan, follow-up procedures may provide a mechanism for securing additional resources or the services of other members of the team in pursuing the action plan.

Step 7

Develop a detailed plan that explains how data will be collected to evaluate progress at two different levels: (a) reduction or elimination of the barrier identified in Step 3 and (b) progress toward attainment of the desired outcome of the problem-solving effort identified in Step 1. For each level, the team should decide on the nature of the data that will be used to measure progress and who will collect the data and on what schedule. In addition, the team should decide before implementation of any action plan what would be considered an acceptable level of progress for each level. With regard to the desired outcome identified in Step 1 in particular, multiple types and sources of data should be collected whenever possible.

Step 8

Describe the process and time line for using data collected through Step 7 to decide if satisfactory progress is being made toward reduction or elimination of the barrier and attainment of the desired outcome of problem solving as well as next steps in the problem-solving process. Depending on the level of progress being made toward reduction or elimination of a barrier, the team should decide whether the intervention should be continued as implemented, intensified, modified, or terminated. If the team does not believe that adjusting the intervention will attain the desired level of results, a new intervention should be developed. If it is decided that satisfactory progress is being made in addressing a specific barrier, depending on the availability of time and resources, the team may return to an earlier stage in the problem-solving process to address a new barrier.

Illustrations of the Use of Principles for Change and the Planning and Problem-Solving Model

The key principles discussed earlier and the specific model described above could be used to facilitate systems change at what would be considered macro level (e.g., the design and implementation of a specific plan at a school building, district, state, or even national level). They also could be used to pursue systems change at a micro level (e.g., addressing a particular aspect of student behavior in the cafeteria, on buses, or in a specific classroom). Application at both the macro and micro levels typically is necessary to facilitate attainment of an organization's goals.

Implementation of MTSS that includes systematic problem solving represents a major change effort for most schools and districts. Given the importance of such a change but the challenges that it represents, implementation of MTSS will be used to illustrate the use of the principles for change and the planning and problem-solving model presented above to address macro- and micro-level systems change. The information provided is based on the authors' experiences. Both cases are based on real examples of school psychologists' contributions to systems change efforts.

Example of Macro-Level Systems Change

Being located within a district in which the department of education is supporting MTSS, and based on district-wide data that suggest that its students would benefit from such a change, school psychologists located within Typical School District have decided to solve the problem of how to facilitate implementation of MTSS, beginning with elementary schools. The supervisor of psychologists in the district, Howard, has been working with district-level leadership to gather support for implementing the model but recognizes that many schools are not ready for the change. He asked Sheldon, a school psychologist who is very familiar with the model and has good collaborative problem-solving skills, to facilitate a planning and problem-solving session to help the school psychologists get started with the process. The goal of the change effort was defined as gaining consensus among all of the district's elementary schools to implement MTSS. See Table 1.1 for a description of each of the problem-solving steps that occurred to help the staff achieve this goal.

Example of Micro-Level System Change

Third-grade teachers in an elementary school have brought to the principal's attention that they are having difficulty finding the time to implement Tier 2 interventions. The expectation for teachers in the school is to provide 30 minutes of Tier 2 interventions to students identified as needing additional support. At the beginning of the school year, teachers were told that they had the flexibility to determine when to deliver the interventions within their schedule. However, disagreements existed in terms of whether it could be done, whether they could sufficiently differentiate instruction to meet the various needs evidenced by student data, and whether the students' assigned teacher should be responsible or whether students could be shared during the intervention time. Given that one of the primary emphases of the schools was to improve the reading proficiency of students, the principal scheduled a half-day problem-solving session and asked all of the

Table 1.1. Description of the Steps Used to Plan for Implementation of a Multitiered System of Supports by School Psychologists in a Typical School District

Planning/Problem-Solving Step	Outcome of the Step
Step 1: State the problem/goal and desired outcome	The goal of the change effort was defined as gaining consensus among all of the district's elementary schools to implement MTSS. The psych services unit defined consensus as belief in the model and active participation in the process of implementation. Stakeholders to involve in the development of consensus include administrators, members of the schools' leadership teams, teachers, support staff, and parents.
Step 2: Analyze the organizational situation and identify resources and barriers to achievement of the desired outcome	*Resources* • District vision for the change to MTSS exists • Teachers believe kids need to learn • Participation of administration in MTSS discussions is occurring • The law requires MTSS to be implemented • Teachers are analyzing data in the district • Collaboration of district office administration is expected • Selection of team members facilitating MTSS implementation is done well in some places *Barriers* • Changing leadership team member beliefs contrary to MTSS is difficult • Active participation of administrators is a challenge in some places • Selection of members on team implementing MTSS is not done well in some places • Schools are focusing on Tier 3 implementation rather than Tier 1 • Turf issues make it a challenge to collaborate
Step 3: Select one barrier to achievement of the desired goal	The psych services unit identified "changing the beliefs of leadership teams" to be consistent with the tenets of the MTSS model.
Step 4: Brainstorm ideas to reduce or eliminate the barrier identified	• Better define beliefs we need to possess about issues such as NCLB, MTSS, core instruction, etc. • Use available presentations done by staff members • Access knowledge base from university settings that have been addressing MTSS implementation • Access data/research from pilot schools in the district and state • Use MTSS coaches and/or district office personnel to address beliefs • Capitalize on the fact that many teachers, staff, and administrators are ready to change
Step 5: Design multiple action plans	• *Action plan 1*: Each school psychologist will dialogue with administrators about their beliefs and support for implementation of the MTSS model between the statewide assessment and the end of the school year; the goal is to develop a plan with administrators that includes the Beliefs Survey and needs assessment data collected from staff as well as presentations to the leadership team in the fall (show data from pilot schools, show our school's data, present philosophy behind MTSS) • *Action plan 2:* Howard will ask Raj (director of student services) to ask for time during the district leadership team's April meeting to address implementation of MTSS by 3/15 • *Action plan 3:* Howard will schedule time during each month's scheduled psychologist staff meeting to revisit the plan 1 week prior to each meeting
Step 6: Establish procedures for follow-up and support	• *Action plan 1:* Sheldon will e-mail all school psychologists reminders to try to chat with principals about the change by the beginning of April, May, and June (i.e., monthly reminders) • *Action plan 2:* Leonard (a school psychologist) will e-mail about materials and supports he needs by 3/7 • *Action plan 3:* Sheldon will discuss time and materials needed to revisit the plan during that week's Friday office day

Continued

Table 1.1. Continued

Planning/Problem-Solving Step	Outcome of the Step
Step 7: Develop evaluation plan	*Selected barrier: Changing beliefs of school leadership teams* • *Step 1:* Sheldon will send copies of the Beliefs Survey used to measure beliefs of educators regarding multitiered system of supports to all school psychologists today • *Step 2:* All school psychologists will show a copy of the survey to principals as part of the discussion outlined above regarding implementing MTSS • *Step 3:* All school psychologists will have informal conversations with leadership team members and e-mail themes to Sheldon 1 week before each staff meeting *Desired outcome: Build consensus for MTSS implementation in elementary schools* • *Step 1:* All school psychologists will record salient themes of school leadership team discussions regarding MTSS and send to Sheldon 1 week before each staff meeting • *Step 2:* Sheldon will summarize information and prepare the data for presentation at the monthly psychologist meeting 2 days before each meeting so materials can be copied
Step 8: Describe the process and time line for making decisions regarding how to proceed	All psychologists will report on their progress talking with principals during each team meeting. The information summarized by Sheldon will be shared and discussed in terms of implications for continued planning.

third-grade teachers, the school's literacy specialist, intervention teachers responsible for providing additional support to students, and the school psychologist to attend. The school psychologist was asked to facilitate the meeting with active support from the principal. Following some discussion of the general issues, during which all key stakeholders were given a chance to voice their perspectives and concerns, the team identified "teachers not having sufficient time to implement 30 minutes of Tier 2 intervention a day" as the priority to address (i.e., the problem). All members agreed that the desired long-range outcome is to "provide 30 minutes of Tier 2 intervention to all students with fidelity." See Table 1.2 for a summary of the problem-solving steps that followed.

Multicultural Competence and Systems Change

Change agents often become frustrated when key stakeholders do not have the same perspective regarding the importance of a change effort. Furthermore, although federal policy (e.g., NCLB, IDEA) requires that student outcomes are disaggregated by demographic subgroups, consensus among educators regarding whether schools should be held accountable for the outcomes of diverse children is lacking. Such differences in perspectives among key stakeholders can lead to frustration when well-intentioned attempts to facilitate change are met with resistance.

School psychologists should question, however, the extent to which perceived resistance is actually resistance versus varying perspectives based on cultural differences. School psychologists not only must work to understand the perspectives of others who have backgrounds and experiences different from their own, but also need to develop an awareness of their own biases and worldview. In addition, school psychologists should work to develop an understanding of the institutional (e.g., inequitable distribution of resources) and societal (e.g., educators' beliefs about the capability of diverse students to be successful in school) factors that contribute to disenfranchisement of diverse students and their families. Through the use of consultation skills, school psychologists can collaborate with key stakeholders to further their understanding of these issues as well as meaningfully involve diverse stakeholders in all aspects of the change effort.

Evaluation of School Psychologists' Efforts in Facilitating Change

The role of program evaluation in planning and problem solving was addressed earlier in this chapter. However, in the age of accountability, school psychologists should pay particular attention to evaluating the outcomes of change efforts in which they are involved. Ultimately, the success of any initiative will be judged by whether it improves student outcomes. However, determining whether an initiative contributed to improved student outcomes requires a systems perspective. Factors such as the extent to which essential practices were implemented with fidelity, educators'

Table 1.2. Description of the Steps Used to Solve the Difficulty Teachers in an Elementary School Were Having Implementing Tier 2 Interventions With Fidelity

Planning/Problem-Solving Step	Outcome of the Step
Step 1: State the problem/goal and desired outcome	The team identified "teachers not having sufficient time to implement 30 minutes of Tier 2 intervention a day" as the priority to address (i.e., problem). All members agree that the desired long-range outcome is to "provide 30 minutes of Tier 2 intervention to all students with fidelity." Importantly, all students were included in the goal (rather than just those students identified as at risk) because a major barrier to the teachers embracing the 30 minutes of Tier 2 intervention concept was ensuring that students meeting standards were provided with opportunities for enrichment.
Step 2: Analyze the organizational situation and identify resources and barriers to achievement of the desired outcome	*Resources* • Principal is willing to provide supports • School psychologist can support using data to identify common needs • Literacy coach has expertise in reading • Teachers want to provide additional support • Intervention teachers are available • Tier 2 intervention programs are available in district-adopted curriculum series • Parent volunteers are available *Barriers* • Time in schedule is difficult to find • Teachers do not want to give up other subjects • Students are already overloaded with task demands • Teachers are not experts in all of the interventions • It is difficult for some teachers to share students • Differentiation of interventions with diverse needs within one classroom is very difficult
Step 3: Select one barrier to achievement of the desired goal	The team selected the barrier "differentiating interventions with diverse needs occurring within a classroom is difficult."
Step 4: Brainstorm ideas to reduce or eliminate the barrier identified	• Create a common intervention time • Reassign intervention teachers supporting other grade levels to third grade • Use paraprofessionals to deliver interventions • Assign students to Tier 2 stations based on identified needs; teachers could be responsible for particular knowledge/skill interventions
Step 5: Design multiple action plans	• *Action plan 1*: Penny (principal) and Amy (literacy coach) will identify which staff will be responsible for delivering which interventions (identified based on student need) by 3/15 • *Action plan 2:* Amy will schedule and meet with each teacher implementing Tier 2 interventions to plan for the intervention block (first meeting will occur by 3/27; second meeting will occur by 4/30) • *Action plan 3:* Identified teachers will begin implementing the Tier 2 intervention plan for identified students every day from 12:35 to 1:05 starting 4/1 • *Action plan 4:* All participants from today's meeting (3/8) will meet to evaluate whether action plans 1–3 were successful in providing time for Tier 2 interventions by 5/31
Step 6: Establish procedures for follow-up and support	• *Action plan 1:* Sheldon (psychologist) will contact Penny and Amy by 3/10 to see what support is needed • *Action plan 2:* Penny will contact Amy by 3/25 to see what additional support may be needed • *Action plan 3:* Penny and Amy will follow up during third grades' regular planning meetings to address barriers and provide support • *Action plan 4:* Penny will schedule another half day meeting and send an e-mail to all team members by 4/1

Continued

Table 1.2. Continued

Planning/Problem-Solving Step	Outcome of the Step
Step 7: Develop evaluation plan	*Selected barrier: Differentiating interventions with diverse needs occurring within a classroom is difficult* • *Step 1:* Amy will collect copies of the intervention plans for each teacher and give them to Sheldon (by 4/1 for meeting 1 and 5/1 for meeting 2) • *Step 2:* Sheldon will review intervention plans and count (a) the number of different knowledge and skill sets being focused on and (b) the number of students in each group (will send to Penny and Amy prior to team meeting to occur before 5/31) • *Step 3:* Sheldon will gather input from third-grade teachers regarding whether the intervention block structure is meeting the needs of students with different needs (will summarize perspectives of teachers and send to Penny and Amy prior to team meeting occurring before 5/31) *Desired outcome: Provide 30 minutes of Tier 2 intervention to all students with fidelity* • *Step 1:* Teachers will complete Intervention Documentation Worksheet each day to record which students were present, the focus of the intervention, and how many minutes they received (teachers agreed to place the worksheet on a clipboard near their reading tables to facilitate completion) • *Step 2:* Amy will collect worksheets from teachers each Friday and give to Sheldon beginning the week of 4/1 • *Step 3:* Sheldon will calculate the number of days that 30 minutes of Tier 2 intervention was provided for each identified need as well as the percentage of days each student received the intervention (will send to Penny and Amy prior to team meeting to occur before 5/31)
Step 8: Describe the process and time line for making decisions regarding how to proceed	All team members will review the data and information described above to determine whether the barrier was reduced and goal was eliminated during the team meeting to be scheduled before 5/31

knowledge and skills, and level of buy-in regarding implementing the practices also should be evaluated. Many models for developing and implementing evaluation plans exist. Regardless of the model chosen, the data must be used by key stakeholders regularly to facilitate decisions about the effectiveness of strategies and to help determine the next steps in the change process. The use of data also can serve to keep educational stakeholders focused on the change effort when other issues (e.g., mandates, funding concerns, other initiatives) compete for attention.

SUMMARY

Major forces affecting education in general, services for students with disabilities, and school psychological services have created a tremendous need for professionals with knowledge and skills in the facilitation of systems-level and organizational change. Many opportunities exist for school psychologists to respond to that need by expanding their roles to include this area of professional expertise. By building on current competencies, school psychologists can increase participation in systems-level change efforts by viewing behavior from a systems perspective, using collaborative planning and

problem-solving procedures, and pursuing strategies that are based in principles for organizational change. Any planned change effort, no matter how small, can be an important step toward improved services for students. Critically, school psychologists can, should, and must play a leadership role in helping our schools to improve student outcomes.

REFERENCES

Castillo, J. M., Curtis, M. J., & Gelley, C. D. (2012). School psychology 2010: Part 2: School psychologists' professional practices and implications for the field. *Communiqué, 40*(8), 4–6.

Crawford, E., & Torgesen, J. (2007). *Teaching all students to read: Practices from Reading First schools with strong intervention outcomes.* Tallahassee, FL: Florida Center for Reading Research. Retrieved from http://www.justreadflorida.com/reading_first.asp

Curtis, M. J., & Metz, L. W. (1986). Systems-level intervention in a school for handicapped children. *School Psychology Review, 15,* 510–518.

Dawson, M., Cummings, J. A., Harrison, P. L., Short, R. J., Gorin, S., & Palomares, R. (2004). The 2002 Multisite Conference on the Future of School Psychology: Next steps. *School Psychology Review, 33,* 115–125.

Fielding, L., Kerr, N., & Rosier, P. (2007). *Annual growth for all students, catch-up growth for those who are behind.* Kennewick, WA: New Foundation Press.

Fixsen, D. L., Naoom, S. F., Blase, K. A., Friedman, R. M., & Wallace, F. (2005). *Implementation research: A synthesis of the literature* (FMHI Publication 231). Tampa, FL: University of South Florida, Louis de la Parte Florida Mental Health Institute.

Fullan, M. (2010). *All systems go: The change imperative for whole system reform*. Thousand Oaks, CA: Corwin Press.

Gutkin, T. B. (2009). Ecological school psychology: A personal opinion and a plea for change. In T. B. Gutkin & C. R. Reynolds (Eds.), *The handbook of school psychology* (pp. 463–496). Hoboken, NJ: Wiley.

Gutkin, T. B., & Curtis, M. J. (2009). School-based consultation: The science and practice of indirect service delivery. In T. B. Gutkin & C. R. Reynolds (Eds.), *The handbook of school psychology* (pp. 591–635). Hoboken, NJ: Wiley.

Hall, G. E., & Hord, S. M. (2011). *Implementing change: Patterns, principles and potholes* (3rd ed.). Boston, MA: Allyn & Bacon.

Joyce, B., & Showers, B. (2002). *Student achievement through staff development* (3rd ed). Alexandria, VA: Association for Staff and Curriculum Development.

Learning Forward. (2011). *Standards for professional learning*. Oxford, OH: Author.

Leithwood, K. (2010). *Turning around underperforming school systems: Guidelines for district leaders*. Edmonton, AB, Canada: College of Alberta School Superintendents. Retrieved from http://o.b5z.net/i/u/10063916/h/Pre-Conference/CASS_Research_Paper_3_Leithwood_Turning_Around_School_Systems.pdf

National Association of School Psychologists. (2010a). *Model for comprehensive and integrated school psychological services*. Bethesda, MD: Author. Retrieved from http://www.nasponline.org/standards/2010standards/2_PracticeModel.pdf

National Association of School Psychologists. (2010b). *Standards for graduate preparation of school psychologists*. Bethesda, MD: Author. Retrieved from http://www.nasponline.org/standards/2010standards/1_Graduate_Preparation.pdf

Nellis, L. M. (2012). Maximizing the effectiveness of building teams in response to intervention implementation. *Psychology in the Schools, 49*, 245–256.

Sharratt, L., & Fullan, M. (2009). *Realization: The change imperative for deepening district-wide reform*. Thousand Oaks, CA: Corwin Press.

Spectrum K–12 School Solutions. (2011). *Response to intervention adoption survey 2011*. Towson, MD: Author. Retrieved from: http://www.spectrumk12.com/rti/the_rti_corner/rti_adoption_report

Ysseldyke, J., Burns, M., Dawson, P., Kelley, B., Morrison, D., Ortiz, S., … Telzrow, C. (2006). *School psychology: A blueprint for training and practice III*. Bethesda, MD: National Association of School Psychologists. Retrieved from http://www.naspcenter.org/blueprint/FinalBlueprintInteriors.pdf

Best Practices in Strategic Planning, Organizational Development, and School Effectiveness

2

Howard M. Knoff

Arkansas Department of Education–Special Education; Project ACHIEVE Incorporated

OVERVIEW

The ultimate educational goal is to maximize the academic and social, emotional, and behavioral progress and proficiency of all students, from preschool through high school, so that they are college or career ready. Since the 1980s virtually every state and school district in the country has been required—often by state law or statute—to coordinate its planning, resources, and activities at the school, staff, and student levels to annually reach this goal. All of this involves strategic planning and organizational development processes that focus on school effectiveness. While many practicing school psychologists may not be formally trained in these processes, their typical professional activities (e.g., assessment, consultation, intervention) are a direct result of their districts' strategic planning processes. Given this, school psychologists are encouraged to become students of strategic planning and become more active at the systems levels so that they can (a) have a more direct impact on their roles and activities and (b) share their knowledge of psychology as applied to education to assist administrators and educators alike in planning and executing the best services, supports, strategies, and programs for all students.

Strategic planning and organizational development is an ongoing process that has specific stages distributed across the school year. Often tied to districts' annual budget cycles, strategic planning focuses on the staff and skills, materials and resources, instruction and intervention, and formative and summative evaluations needed to educate a diverse and often complex student body.

Moreover, as guided by federal education laws (e.g., the Elementary and Secondary Education Act and Individuals with Disabilities Education Act) and complemented by state education laws and regulations and other local initiatives, most districts and schools now embed school improvement into their strategic planning processes, setting goals in the following areas: (a) organizational development, including resource mapping and development, capacity building and sustainability, and systems-level support to schools, staff, and students; (b) effective school and schooling, including the use of science- or research-based practices at the administrative, curriculum and instruction, progress monitoring and evaluation, and multitiered (i.e., prevention, strategic intervention, and intensive need) service and support levels; (c) positive behavioral support systems, including attention to school safety, school and classroom climate, effective classroom management, and student health, mental health, and wellness; (d) professional development, supervision and mentoring, and teacher and educator effectiveness, accountability, and evaluation; and (e) parent and community outreach and involvement. All of this planning focuses on student, staff, school, and district goals, objectives, activities, and outcomes. Once again, however, the ultimate goal relates to student outcomes.

As noted, it is essential that school psychologists understand and, it is hoped, be actively involved at the organizational and strategic planning levels in identifying and facilitating the services, supports, strategies, and programs that most strongly predict and result in students' academic and social, emotional, and behavioral learning and success. Indeed, when school psychologists, in collaboration with other district and school leaders and colleagues, help plan and implement these practices at the prevention levels, fewer students will need to be individually assessed or to receive more multitiered strategic or intensive services or supports (Louis, Leithwood, Wahlstrom, & Anderson, 2010; Perlman & Redding, 2009). Clearly, this organizational, systems-level focus is consistent with the National Association of School Psychologists (NASP) *Model for Comprehensive and Integrated School Psychological Services* (NASP, 2010) domain of School-Wide Practices to Promote School Learning.

To this end, this chapter will describe a number of strategic planning, organizational development, and effective school and schooling practices that help schools and districts plan for staff and student success while supporting a multitiered system and the problem-solving process needed when students are not successful and require strategic or intensive supports and interventions. It is important to note that strategic planning has an extensive history and scientific foundation, and this science is simply being applied here to education as represented by a district or school.

BASIC CONSIDERATIONS

In order to coordinate and facilitate school-based organizational change and strategic planning processes, it is important for school psychologists to recognize four prerequisite areas: (a) the evidence-based components and processes underlying effective school and schooling practices at the school, staff, and student levels; (b) data-driven leadership and decision-making processes, integrating these into a school's strategic planning and organizational development cycles; (c) shared leadership structures and approaches, coordinated through a building-level School Leadership Team (or the equivalent) and other school-level committees; and (d) the creation and implementation of comprehensive, school-level professional development programs that build school capacity and staff skills through training, supervision, mentoring, evaluation, and accountability.

For some, these are not traditional school psychology role and function areas. And yet, these areas already exist in most schools, and their effectiveness often is enhanced when school psychologists add the psychological, developmental, behavioral, and cognitive/learning perspectives of children and adolescents. On a more pragmatic level, involvement in these areas may (a) increase the probability of expanding the role of the school psychologist in a district and (b) increase the

potential to have a positive impact on the largest number of students while, once again, decreasing the number of students who need more strategic or intensive services (because effective school and schooling practices are simply missing or not effectively implemented in the schools). While the sole school psychologist working in a district clearly can assume this strategic planning role (among his or her many other roles), it may be more realistic to have one or more school psychologists assume these roles in districts where multiple school psychologists are working together.

Effective School and Schooling

While guided independently by a number of experts (e.g., Marzano, Daggett, Sizer, Lezotte, Comer), the research-based components that result in effective schools have been clearly identified since the 1980s (Louis et al., 2010; Perlman & Redding, 2009). These components should be the foundation of any strategic plan and process, and they share key constructs that are implicit to any school's continuous improvement efforts. These constructs involve a school-wide commitment to the following:

- A culture of high and realistic expectations for all students that is supported by a shared mission, vision, values, and goals
- Data-driven decision making that focuses on continuous improvement
- Validation, verification, evaluation, and accountability
- Articulated and differentiated academic and social, emotional, and behavioral (or health, mental health, and wellness) curricula
- Rigorous and relevant instruction delivered through a multitiered system of prevention, strategic intervention, and intensive services, supports, strategies, and programs
- Personalized learning, resulting in students who are college and career ready
- Professional learning communities where cross-disciplinary teaming focuses on effective instruction that results in student learning, mastery, proficiency, and the ability to solve real-world problems
- Partnerships that reach out to and actively engage families and community partners
- Positive and safe school climates that engage and connect students in sustained, meaningful relationships
- A formal and informal system of shared, multilevel leadership

Beyond these key constructs, the common core of effective school components include the following: (a) strategic planning and organizational analysis and development; (b) problem-solving, teaming, and consultation processes; (c) effective school, schooling, and professional development; (d) academic instruction linked to academic assessment, intervention, and achievement; (e) behavioral instruction linked to behavioral assessment, intervention, and self-management; (f) parent and community training, support, and outreach; and (g) data management, evaluation, and accountability.

Data-Driven Leadership and Decision-Making Processes

Just as school psychologists use data-based problem-solving processes when assessing students, problem solving should similarly be used to make data-based decision at a systems level and during strategic planning. While there may be more variables and circumstances to consider, and the analyses may be more complex, effective strategic planning is dependent on sound problem identification, problem analysis, intervention planning and implementation, and formative and summative evaluation.

Beyond this, the science and practice of decision making must be used wisely. Different decisions may require different approaches. For example, some decisions are made by collaboration and consensus, others through a vote (where specific percentages are required for a motion or recommendation to pass). Some decisions are made administratively by the superintendent, but with the advice and counsel of his or her strategic planning team. Finally, some decisions are unilateral or command decisions, where the superintendent makes a decision without involving others. Critically, the key to decision making during strategic planning is that those involved know beforehand which decision-making approach will be used to make a particular decision. In this way, missteps in the decision-making process that sometimes cause dissension can be avoided, allowing participants to focus on the quality and potential impact of the decisions that are made.

Shared Leadership Structures and Approaches

In order to maximize the impact of strategic planning and continuous school improvement processes, effective schools use shared leadership structures and approaches. This involves identifying, nurturing, and using formal and informal school leaders who (a) take responsibility for different school improvement goals and activities, (b) have the permission to independently guide or make certain decisions, and (c) accomplish their tasks by collaborating with other colleagues, often with minimal supervision or oversight. In shared leadership schools, administrators delegate more responsibilities to their staff, and staff and administrators make more collaborative decisions through discussion, debate, consultation, and consensus. As a result, more people are committed to and are enthusiastic about the decisions made, more initiatives are implemented in timely and high-quality ways, and more goals are accomplished relative to students' academic and social, emotional, and behavioral success.

Recognizing that most schools are like large, multidimensional businesses, the presence and interactions of effective school-level committees are a core element of successful shared leadership schools. Indeed, from a strategic planning perspective, school-level committees help to identify on an annual basis, and are responsible for implementing during the school year, many of the activities written into a school's strategic or school improvement plan. Moreover, in effective schools, the committee structure parallels the components that drive effective school and schooling practices. Thus, a blueprint for a school's building-level committees might include the following (Knoff, 2011a): School Leadership Team, Curriculum and Instruction; School Discipline/School Climate, Professional Development/Teacher Support and Mentoring, and Parent Involvement/Community Outreach committees; and the Student Assistance, Building Intervention, or Response-to-Intervention (RTI)/Child Study team (or the equivalent). While this blueprint should be adapted to the size and complexity of the school and its strategic needs, organizational realities, and desired outcomes, the components and activities that make schools successful still must be embedded in whatever committee structure the school uses.

Beyond the existence of a practical school committee structure, committees still need to use effective collaborative practices that result in sound decisions and actions. And yet few school psychologists have ever been formally trained in these practices and processes. Below is a brief summary of some of the characteristics or processes that help committees to run smoothly and effectively (Branigan & Jones, 2006; Conzemius & O'Neill, 2002). All committees (a) have representatives from every grade level or instructional team (except for the RTI/child study team), as well as from all relevant school-level and other support staff; (b) are organized so that most staff members have staggered 3-year terms of office; (c) have a designated chair (or cochairs) and a recorder who takes the minutes of all meetings; (d) have a written mission, role, and function statement or document that is consistent with the school's mission statement; (e) have annual written goals and objectives that have been included in the annual school improvement plan; (f) meet at a fixed (whenever possible) predesignated time each month; (g) have a set agenda that is consistent from month to month and a fluid agenda that may change according to the committee's goals or activities from month to month; (h) have meetings that are consistently attended by at least 80% of its members; (i) have agreed-upon meeting expectations and processes for making decisions; and (j) publicly post minutes or summaries of all meetings that are available to all school staff within 2–3 days following each meeting.

Professional Development That Builds School Capacity

Effective professional development consists of informa-tion and knowledge that is demonstrated through effective skills and practice and that results in profes-sional confidence and competence. Professional devel-opment may involve research and self-study, workshop or inservice instruction, clinical supervision and collegial consultation, and case study practice and application occurring in, for example, a mentoring or professional learning community. From a strategic planning per-spective, there are always new initiatives, programs, curricula, and resources planned and introduced during every school year. Without effective professional devel-opment, these new elements may not be embraced, implemented, or implemented with integrity. This may undermine the new elements' desired outcomes, thereby creating a resistance to future planned innovations. Given this, strategic planning needs to address not just what needs to be added and accomplished but how the additions should be introduced, taught, applied, and institutionalized.

BEST PRACTICES IN STRATEGIC PLANNING, ORGANIZATIONAL DEVELOPMENT, AND SCHOOL EFFECTIVENESS

As previously noted, strategic planning focuses predom-inantly on students' previous, current, and future academic and social, emotional, and behavioral progress and proficiency. To get there, however, strategic

planning must also look at how effectively classroom teachers provide differentiated instruction and facilitate positive classroom climates and interactions through effective classroom management. From a school-wide multitiered service delivery perspective, strategic plan-ning also must ensure that school psychologists and other related services professionals have the numbers and resources needed to address the academic and behavioral needs of at-risk, underachieving, unrespon-sive, and unsuccessful students. Finally, at a systemic level, strategic planning needs to reinforce and sustain productive organizational climates, supportive policies and procedures, effective administrative leadership, sound staff decision making, and positive interprofes-sional and interpersonal interactions. The ultimate product of strategic planning is an annual strategic or school improvement plan that helps schools build capacity and autonomy; identify, develop, and deploy resources; facilitate communication, collaboration, com-mitment, and innovation; and sustain student, staff, and system success.

In the context of continuous school improvement (or any other planned change process), it is important to note that organizational change and strategic planning are natural, necessary, and ongoing characteristics of healthy, evolving, and effective schools. Indeed, as schools focus on students' academic, social, emotional, and behavioral learning, mastery, application, and proficiency, schools must attend to the organizational, planning, and interactional processes that build the resources and capacity of the school and facilitate the implementation—by staff and students—of the services and supports that maximize success. While compre-hensive problem-solving approaches are implicit to this process, the more explicit elements include (a) an understanding of the possible activities within the strategic planning process, (b) what resources might be available to facilitate the implementation of the plan, (c) the components of a school improvement plan, (d) how to identify consultants and their areas of expertise from existing staff, and (e) the specific activities that facilitate the organizational and motivational readiness of school staff and partners. The first four areas are discussed below, while the fifth area is addressed across the entire discussion.

Strategic Planning

Strategic planning is a continuous, systematic process that helps schools and districts identify, plan, prepare for, execute, and evaluate their short- (i.e., annual) and long-term (i.e., 3–5 year) goals, activities, and explicit outcomes. Designed to attain these short- and long-term outcomes, strategic planning also results in actions that are (a) consistent with the school's vision, mission, and needs of its students and staff; (b) reflective of the school's (and community's) strengths and assets, weaknesses and limitations, opportunities and resources, and threats and barriers; (c) focused on strengthening the school's organizational capacity and resources while increasing effective and efficient staff collaboration and leadership; (d) committed to fiscal and technological integrity; and (e) unapologetic in emphasizing data-based decision making, the use of science- or research-based approaches and practices, and staff accountability and consistency. While virtually every school and district is now mandated to use a strategic planning process that results in an annual school or district improvement plan, many have not been trained, or trained effectively, in the science and practice of strategic planning.

In the context of organizational change and continuous improvement, strategic planning can be organized in five phases at the school level (Cook, 1990; Knoff, 2012; Knoff & Dyer, 2013; Knoff, Finch, & Carlyon, 2004; see Table 2.1):

- *Phase 1:* Determining the organizational and motivational readiness of school staff for change; conducting needs assessments, resource and status audits, and gap analyses
- *Phase 2:* Addressing the school's needs; writing and resourcing the school improvement plan
- *Phase 3:* Establishing the infrastructure needed to implement the plan
- *Phase 4:* Implementing, monitoring, and evaluating the plan
- *Phase 5:* Reviewing, retooling, and renewing the plan

Phase 1

During Phase 1, the following primary activities need to occur.

The School Leadership Team is established (or reconfirmed), and it organizes the strategic planning process. While the School Leadership Team's mission, role, and function will be discussed below, the School Leadership Team is chaired by the principal and is made up of the chairs or co-chairs of all the other school-level committees and selected others, all to ensure that the team consists of a representative sample of teachers, related service professionals, other support staff, and administrators. As needed, the School Leadership Team receives training and support (perhaps from a district administrator or outside consultant) on how to implement an effective strategic planning process, and it documents its mission, role, function, processes, and annual activities and time lines.

Typically, a school's strategic planning process is chronologically aligned with the district's budgeting cycle. Working backward, most districts begin their fiscal year on July 1, and the school board often passes the budget by the end of May (at the latest). Thus, schools in the district must submit their strategic plans and budgets to the superintendent by the end of February so that all requests can be analyzed, approved, and then integrated into the district's improvement plan by April. This means that schools must begin their strategic planning processes by early January. Moreover, once the school board passes the budget, each school then needs to revisit its school improvement plan, adjusting and finalizing all goals and activities based on the now-approved district and school priorities and the funds and other resources provided.

The School Leadership Team identifies and reaches out to community stakeholders, gatekeepers, and other constituent groups, involving them in the strategic planning process. Here, the School Leadership Team and other school staff identify different governmental and public safety, social service agency and business, and community and neighborhood groups that have a stake in the activities and success of the school. Along with the school's parents and students, these stakeholders are briefed on the strategic planning process and its importance, invited to participate in its formal and informal activities, informed of the timelines and intended outcomes, and told that they will be involved, as relevant, both in the needs assessments and other information-collection activities and in the later plan implementation and evaluation process.

The School Leadership Team completes an external environmental scan and analysis. This scan occurs as (a) national, state, regional, and local economic, demographic, social, political, and education trends are analyzed and predicted; (b) the impact of these trends and predictions on the district's (and its schools') educational policies, practices, and procedures are determined; and (c) the district its schools identify the resources and responses needed to address both

Table 2.1. An Overview of the Strategic Planning Process

Phase 1. Assessing Organizational Readiness/Needs Assessments and Audits	Phase 2. Writing the School Improvement Plan	Phase 3. Establishing the Infrastructure to Implement the School Improvement Plan	Phase 4. Implementing, Monitoring, and Evaluating the School Improvement Plan	Phase 5. Reviewing, Retooling, and Renewing the School Improvement Plan
The School Leadership Team is established; it organizes the strategic planning process.	The school improvement plan is written based on the Phase 1 results.	The school builds (or continues to build) its resources and capacity in preparation for the school improvement plan implementation (beginning at least by May or June).	The school improvement plan is implemented at the beginning of the new school year (or during the planning days immediately before the beginning of school).	A summative evaluation of all areas of the school improvement plan is completed (typically in April).
Community stakeholders and other important constituent groups are involved.	The school improvement plan is checked for its consistency with the school's vision and mission statements.	The school completes a year-end Consultation Referral Audit.	Individual teacher professional development plans are written and approved, and they are evaluated biannually.	The evaluation and review process eventually leads back to the relevant activities in Phases 2 and 3.
An external environment scan and analysis are completed.	The school improvement plan is submitted to the superintendent and is integrated into the district's budgeting and strategic planning process (typically by the end of February).	The school completes a year-end Get-Go process.	Progress in the different areas of the school improvement plan are evaluated at the school, committee, staff, grade, classroom, and student levels.	
An internal organizational scan and analysis are completed.		The school and its committees complete other end-of-year articulation activities to prepare for the transition to the next school year.	The school improvement plan is formally evaluated at the end of the first 6 weeks of the school year, and then on a quarterly basis (typically the end of October and during January).	
The organizational readiness of the school for strategic planning and implementation is evaluated.			The January evaluation reinitiates the strategic planning process relative to the relevant activities needed in Phases 1 and 2.	
The motivational readiness of the school for strategic planning and implementation is evaluated.				

existing conditions as well as the most likely future situations. This scan also includes analyses at the state, regional, and local levels of some of the same governmental and public safety, social service agency and business, and community and neighborhood groups noted immediately above to identify and prepare for how their policies, practices, and procedures are having or may have an impact on the district or its schools.

The School Leadership Team completes an internal organizational scan and analysis. Here, the strengths and assets, weaknesses and limitations, opportunities and resources, and threats and barriers within the school are identified (often through what is called a SWOT analysis) by using the effective school components as an organizing structure. As part of this process, a number of audits are conducted, and the results of these audits are contrasted with the current status and outcomes of the students, staff, and school, along with its effective school and schooling characteristics. In this way, effective practices that need to be maintained are identified, and critical weaknesses or gaps that need to be addressed are isolated.

At the school level, for example, the School Leadership Team needs to audit (a) the student, staff, and school outcomes written into the last three school improvement plans; (b) the academic curricula currently in use, and their alignment with the Common Core (or equivalent) State Standards and other state or district academic standards documents; (c) the school's computer and other technology-based systems and supports; and (d) its professional development, supervision, and staff evaluation program, procedures, and outcomes.

At the staff level, the School Leadership Team needs to audit (a) the presence of high-quality and consistently effective classroom instruction and classroom management (e.g., using its state or district teacher evaluation system); (b) staff understanding of the standards, benchmarks, and criteria for student mastery relative to the academic and social, emotional, and behavioral curricula being taught; (c) staff use of effective progress-monitoring approaches and formative and summative assessments in evaluating student learning and mastery; and (d) staff understanding and participation in grade- and school-level multitiered problem solving, consultation, and instructional and intervention services, supports, strategies, and programs particularly for struggling or challenging students.

Finally, the School Leadership Team needs to audit every grade level of students relative to (a) their academic and behavioral skill acquisition and mastery,

their ability to transfer skills to real-world applications, and their academic progress over time; (b) their need for strategic or intensive academic or behavioral services, supports, strategies, or specialized programs; and (c) their proficiency on high-stakes state and national tests, including the predominant reasons why specific students or groups of students have been unsuccessful on those tests.

Relative to resources, a comprehensive audit would scan, survey, and identify staff, school, district, and community resources in the following areas: money and finances; facilities and physical plant; materials (e.g., books, videos, equipment) and activities; time, scheduling, deployment, and logistics; people and professional development; technology; and creativity and hard work. Specific examples in each of these areas are listed in Table 2.2 (Knoff, 2011b, 2012).

The School Leadership Team determines the organizational readiness of the school. Based on the needs assessments, external environmental and internal organizational scans, audits and gap analyses, and investigations of existing resources, the School Leadership Team can determine the organizational readiness of the school relative to the school improvement plan goals, objectives, and activities needed to bring it to the next level of excellence. Clearly, as school, staff, student, curricular, technological, professional development, and other resource gaps are identified and analyzed, specific goals and objectives will be prioritized in the plan, along with the funds and resources needed to eliminate those gaps.

The School Leadership Team determines the motivational readiness of the school. Based on the conversations and collaborations of staff within their grade or instructional teams, on school-level committees, and during the needs assessment process above, the School Leadership Team can evaluate how cohesive the staff is and the staff's motivational readiness to participate in the school improvement plan's new or next initiatives and activities. Functionally, motivational readiness can be determined by evaluating how the staff communicates, collaborates, and celebrates; demonstrates caring, commitment, and collegial consultation; and how consistent the staff is across these different interactions. When staff motivation is an issue, the underlying reasons need to be determined through a problem-solving process, and strategic interventions linked to the staff assessment results need to be implemented and evaluated.

Table 2.2. A District or School Resource Analysis: Areas and Examples

Money/Finances
Possible areas to investigate:
- Federal, state, and district funding
- Discretionary money controlled by the school due to site-based management
- Grant or foundation money
- Business or other local donations

Facilities and Physical Plant
Possible areas to investigate:
- Areas of the school available before and after school, during evenings, and during weekends
- Rooms where space is underutilized due to low student enrollments or that could be better utilized with more efficient student and staff scheduling
- Empty or unused rooms
- Effective use of computer, media, physical education, and cafeteria
- Effective use of hallways for more effective traffic and transition patterns

Materials and Activities
Possible areas to investigate:
- Effective use of art, physical education, computer, media, and textbook materials
- Effective use of audiovisual and other technological equipment
- Sharing, from teacher to teacher, of curriculum-specific or instructional activities to support classroom learning
- Sharing, from parents, businesses in the community, or other community resources, of relevant activities to support classroom learning
- Accessing donations of support materials (e.g., software, books, equipment) for school or classroom use

Time/Scheduling/Deployment/Logistics
Possible areas to investigate:
- Block and other more effective approaches to scheduling
- Efficient student and staff transitions when moving from outside to inside a classroom and when moving from one subject area to other subject areas within the same classroom
- Efficient use of grade level, committee, and whole staff meeting times
- Amount of out-of-class interruptions of classroom instruction (e.g., due to announcements, students going to pull-out groups) that decrease academic engagement
- Amount of in-class interruptions of classroom instruction (e.g., due to discipline problems, off-task behavior, lack of preparation) that decrease academic engagement
- Amount of staff absenteeism requiring the use of substitute teachers
- Degree and level of student tardiness

People/Professional Development
Possible areas to investigate:
- Knowledge and use of existing student, staff, and parent skills and talents for those within or currently interacting with the school
- Knowledge and use of existing district-level staff who could become available to the school
- Knowledge and use of community-based resource people who could become available to the school
- Knowledge and use of resource people, accessed through the Internet or other technological means, who could become available to the school

Technology
Possible areas to investigate:
- Hardware and software programs or other advances
- Web-based and cloud computing advances
- Audiovisual, instructional, and telecommunication advances
- Distance learning and assistive support advances

Creativity and Hard Work
Possible areas to investigate:
- Levels of and approaches to facilitate staff communication, cooperation, motivation, and innovation
- Survey for and completion of a staff Consultant Resource Directory
- Available rewards and incentives to staff and students to motivate them toward exceptional accomplishments
- Opportunities to celebrate exceptional accomplishments for staff and students

Phase 2

During Phase 2 the school improvement plan is written by integrating everything accomplished during Phase 1 into a specific, outcomes-oriented document organized by goals, objectives, activities, time lines, resources, criteria of success, and formative and summative evaluation tools and procedures. The school improvement plan focuses on what the school, staff, and students need to achieve in order to maximize students' academic and social, emotional, and behavioral progress, development, mastery, and proficiency.

At times, the district may require additional school improvement plan goals and objectives that are part of its district-wide improvement plans. At other times, these additional goals are designed to ensure that the district and its schools are in compliance with or responding to new national or state statutes, regulations, or initiatives (e.g., the Common Core State Standards), or to take advantage of new evidence-based strategies, programs, or innovations. Ultimately, these district-set goals may require or encourage all of the elementary and secondary schools to cross-collaborate horizontally or vertically on sections of their school improvement plans so that activities, time lines, and funds are effectively and efficiently aligned.

Consistent with the school's vision and mission statements, the school improvement plan should have prominent sections focusing on each component of school effectiveness: (a) strategic planning and organizational development processes; (b) early intervention, problem-solving, teaming, consultation, and RTI processes; (c) effective school, schooling, and professional development processes; (d) student-focused academic achievement and curriculum and instruction processes; (e) student-focused behavioral outcomes and positive behavioral support processes; and (f) parent and community training, support, and outreach processes. In addition, embedded in each relevant section should be services, supports, strategies, and programs that address the needs of all students, that is, from those who are gifted, talented, and excelling to those who are at risk, struggling, and challenging. Finally, in each goal area, the school improvement plan should explicitly describe how and when implementation integrity will be measured, how staff and student accountability will be tracked, and when quarterly (or more frequent) formative and summative evaluations will occur and under whose auspices.

As noted earlier, when schools submit their school improvement plans to the superintendent by the end of February, their goals, objectives, and activities then are integrated into the district's planning processes and its district improvement plan. Eventually, everything is submitted to the school board for its approval and funding.

Phase 3

In Phase 3 the school builds (or continues to build) onto its existing resources in preparation for the implementation of the school improvement plan. At the very latest this occurs in May or June, immediately after the superintendent approves and the school board funds the school improvement plan. This is an ongoing process. Indeed, when schools are committed to continuous progress and the systematic improvement of academic and social, emotional, and behavioral systems and approaches, schools expand their capacity each year by building onto the strengths of the previous year. This process is guided by the goals and activities in each year's new school improvement plan, and it is facilitated by the funds that allow the school to hire new staff; purchase new equipment, curricula, and software; and provide needed professional development and other technical assistance services.

At a more functional level, schools need to operate with the mantra, "The beginning of the school year starts in April." This suggests that schools need to systematically tag-team or articulate their successes and lessons learned—at the school, staff, and student levels—from the current year to the next school year. To do this, schools need to catalog the academic, social, emotional, and behavioral progress of all students at the individual, classroom, grade, and whole-school levels, while reevaluating the organizational accomplishments of the school, guided by the most-recent SWOT analyses of their strengths, weaknesses, opportunities, and threats, and by the audits discussed earlier in Phase 1. School staff then need to determine how best to prepare for the first day of the new school year by building on the school's strengths and accomplishments and the instructional processes, procedures, interactions, and practices that had the greatest success. All of this is done in April and May as a continuation of the strategic planning process and then in June when the school year has ended and the school improvement plan and new funds and resources have been approved.

Relative to committee functioning, every school-level committee needs to prepare in April and May for the immediate implementation in August and September of the school improvement plan goals, objectives, and activities that relate directly to them. Assuming that most of these committees significantly contributed to their section of the school improvement plan, this should occur logically, naturally, and fluidly. Critically, when committees complete these preparations before the summer break, they do not need the first few meetings of the new school year to gear up, and this readiness translates into an effective and efficient start to the school year with no confusion, no need for initial start-up meetings, and no implementation downtime.

Relative to student functioning, two important articulation activities are recommended, especially for struggling and challenging students: the year-end Consultation Referral Audit and the Get-Go process. The results of these two activities help (a) determine the success of specific school improvement plan goals and activities from the current year and (b) identify specific gaps or next steps that need to be included, through the strategic planning process, in the next school improvement plan.

Conducting a year-end Consultation Referral Audit.
In order to assess and provide early, strategic, or intensive instruction or intervention services and supports to academically struggling or behaviorally challenging students, all schools should have a student assistance, building intervention, or RTI/child study team (or the equivalent). Working throughout the year to help teachers address the needs of at-risk, under-achieving, unresponsive, and unsuccessful students, this team also should conduct at least one annual Consultation Referral Audit. Typically done in April or May, this audit involves summarizing all of the referrals for the current year across the following dimensions: (a) student age and grade, (b) time of year when referred, (c) specific presenting problems (e.g., reading fluency, mathematical applications, ability to sustain academic attention and engagement), (d) assessments conducted and their results, and (e) specific instructional or intervention approaches linked to the assessments and implemented with success.

With this information, the RTI team can identify referral trends and patterns and early warning indicators so that younger students, who may eventually experience similar problems, can receive early preventive instructional or intervention services. The team also identifies specific professional development needs based on the consultation referral audit analysis so that teachers can be trained to provide (a) preventive early intervening services at their grade levels as well as (b) other more strategic interventions for the student problems that are likely to be needed by their respective struggling or challenging students.

This analysis becomes part of each year's strategic planning process, and its outcomes are codified in relevant sections of the school improvement plan. All of this facilitates the data-based problem-solving, consultation, and instruction or intervention processes needed by the students who are typically referred for more strategic or intensive attention during the school year. This analysis also increases the probability that more students will receive these strategic instructional or intervention services and supports more quickly and successfully from general education teachers who, over time, may have less need for additional school psychological or RTI team services or consultations.

Identifying Get-Go students for the new year.
Too often, after spending a lot of time completing functional analyses of students with academic or behavioral challenges and implementing successful strategic or intensive interventions, teachers and RTI team members do not systematically transfer these lessons learned to the next year's teaching teams. For the students involved, this often results in a service delivery gap (if services are delayed) or loss (if redesigned services are less effective than the previous services). For the new staff, it may mean a loss of time and success as the staff reinvents the wheel from both assessment and intervention perspectives.

In order to strategically transfer successful student interventions from one school year to the next, it is recommended that RTI teams, with relevant classroom teachers, complete a review of every student who received early intervention or RTI services at any level of intensity during the school year, as well as all students on individual education; Section 504; state-required academic intervention; or social, emotional, or behavioral intervention plans. We call this the get-go process (Knoff, 2011c) and, as with all other articulation activities that factor into strategic planning, it occurs in April or May.

During the Get-Go process, three groups of students are identified: (a) get-go students, who need (or may need) immediate academic or behavioral interventions on the first day of the new school year; (b) at-risk students, who have such notable instructional or intervention needs that their new teacher must be briefed by their current teachers (and relevant others) before the next school year begins; and (c) check-in students, who need someone (e.g., from the RTI team, the mental health team, or the curriculum and instruction committee) to check in with them, their parents, or their teacher at some point during the first day, week, month, or quarter of the new academic year. In addition to students with academic or behavioral needs, medically fragile students with attendance problems and students with unique home or life circumstances also are considered during the Get-Go review process.

The Get-Go process increases the effective transfer of functional assessment, consultation, instructional, and intervention information from one school year to the next. This is especially important for students who are transferring not just from one grade level to another in the same school but from one school building to another (e.g., from a fifth-grade elementary to sixth-grade middle school, from an eighth-grade middle to ninth-grade high school) or in the same district. At the elementary level especially, this process also may help determine how students are grouped into homerooms or skill-based instructional groups for the next year, and it may influence the process whereby specific students are matched with the teachers who have the best expertise to meet their needs. Finally, the Get-Go process ensures that teachers or instructional teams receive the instructional or intervention training and support before the new school year begins so that they are fully prepared to deliver required (e.g., 504 or Individualized Education Program based) or needed services and supports to struggling or challenging students on the first day of school.

Phase 4

In Phase 4 the school improvement plan is implemented at the classroom, grade, committee, and school levels, and it is formatively evaluated by the School Leadership Team and other school-level committees on a regular basis. Thus, after reviewing the school improvement plan at the beginning of the new school year (e.g., in August), it is formatively evaluated (a) at the end of the first 6 weeks of school (i.e., mid-September) to ensure that all of its activities have been successfully initiated and then (b) on a quarterly basis (i.e., at the end of October and during January). The January formative evaluation coincides with the reinitiation of the strategic planning process for the next year, and thus the renewal of Phases 1 and 2.

While the school improvement plan guides all school, staff, and student activities, it often is supplemented by a professional development plan, or the equivalent, for every staff person in a school. The professional development plan documents each staff member's professional goals, objectives, and responsibilities for the school year, and it identifies the outcomes and procedures needed to evaluate every staff member's year-long performance and accomplishments. Significantly, professional development plans are based on the activities outlined in the school improvement plan, and those plans help the school and district accomplish specific planned goals and outcomes while holding staff accountable to them. Thus, school improvement and professional development plans are interdependent and critical to the success of the entire strategic planning and service delivery process.

Phase 5

During Phase 5 (typically in April), the school improvement plan is summatively evaluated relative to the progress and accomplishments of the current year. This also initiates the articulation process that prepares the school for the next year, and it leads eventually back to the relevant activities needed in Phases 2 and 3.

Ultimately, the school improvement plan is a public document of accountability, and it synthesizes all of the planning and implementation processes needed in a school and district. The essential question for a school, however, is: Is the school improvement plan a piece of paper written annually by one or two individuals to meet a state mandate, or is it a functional, comprehensive document that is developed by staff, with feedback from other stakeholders, and that guides the monthly, weekly, and daily operation of the entire staff in the school? The answer to this question often discriminates the effective school from the ineffective school.

Components of a School Improvement Plan

While there are many ways to organize a school improvement plan, typically there are two layers. The first layer, as suggested earlier, identifies critical components of the effective school and schooling process. Thus, there may be sections devoted to (a) students' academic achievement supported by curriculum and instruction; (b) students' social, emotional, and behavioral development supported by classroom management and school-wide positive behavioral support systems; (c) multitiered academic and behavioral services, supports, strategies, and programs for at-risk, underachieving, unresponsive, and unsuccessful students; (d) school-wide professional development, staff supervision, and staff evaluation; (e) school and administrative initiatives and supports, along with committee activities; and (f) parent and community training, support, and outreach.

The second layer reflects a planning and execution template that is used for all of the first-layer areas. This template includes (a) specific goals or targets; (b) evidence-based methods or approaches that will be used; (c) the sequence of activities needed to fully implement the service, support, strategy, or program area from start to finish; (d) the personnel needed to directly or indirectly help implement or support the initiative; (e) the funding, materials, professional development or training, and technological resources needed (and their respective sources); (f) how implementation or treatment integrity will be formatively and summatively evaluated; (g) what short-term success will look like and how it will be formatively evaluated; and (h) what long-term success, related to a specific goal or outcome, will look like and how it will be summatively evaluated. Once the plan has been written and approved, and the resources needed to implement it have been acquired, it is ready to be executed.

Identifying Consultation Expertise From Existing Staff

A critical part of the strategic planning process is the identification of resources. While the first source of resources are the professionals in or available to a school, many schools or districts do not systematically survey their staff to identify and share these professionals' areas of expertise. To this end, the development of a school (or district) Consultant Resource Directory is recommended.

Developed after a school's entire staff has completed a brief questionnaire, this directory identifies staff members' degrees and areas of certification or specialization; areas of inservice training and professional development; academic or behavioral areas of expertise; and special skills, talents, or hobbies. Staff specifically describe consultation skills in the following areas: (a) curriculum and academic instruction; (b) student behavior and classroom management; (c) technology or special instructional techniques; (d) student assessment and progress monitoring; and (e) strategic or intensive academic and social, emotional, or behavioral instruction or intervention techniques. School psychologists, along with their counseling, social work, special education, and instructional specialist colleagues, might develop their own related services directory, identifying the assessment and intervention skills that they provide to school staff for academically struggling and behaviorally challenging students.

The goal of this activity is to identify and publicize the skills and resources that already exist in a school, making everyone aware of the different people who are available to consult with others in specific areas. From a strategic planning perspective, the directory can be used to assign the right people to different school improvement activities or initiatives so that they have the highest probability of success. In the end, this resource can be posted on the shared drive of a school's computer system. The front section of the directory can be organized by instructional staff, support staff, and administrators, while the back section can be organized across specific skill areas.

SUMMARY

Today's children continue to come to the schoolhouse door significantly at risk for both educational and social failure. Schools and districts must use systematic and strategic planning and implementation processes in order to build the infrastructures—at the staff, school, system, and community levels—that help coordinate resources, build capacity, support school-wide programs, and maximize the academic and social, emotional, and behavioral success of all students. To do this, strategic planning must guide a multitiered process that focuses on providing prevention, as well as needed strategic or intensive services, supports, strategies, and programs, to struggling learners and challenging students. Strategic planning success facilitates student, staff, and school success as current and future generations of students learn, master, and apply the important skills that they need, not just in school but in their homes, when they enter the workforce, and as they become leaders in their communities.

AUTHOR NOTE

Disclosure. Howard M. Knoff has a financial interest in Project ACHIEVE Incorporated and Project ACHIEVE Press and in books he authored or co-authored referenced in this chapter.

REFERENCES

Branigan, H. M., & Jones, R. D. (2006). *Leadership for rigor, relevance, and relationships*. Rexford, NY: International Center for Leadership in Education.

Conzemius, A., & O'Neill, J. (2002). *The handbook for SMART school teams*. Bloomington, IN: National Education Service.

Cook, W. J. (1990). *The planning discipline*. Cambridge, MA: The Cambridge Management Group.

Knoff, H. M. (2011a). *A Project ACHIEVE blueprint toward an effective and integrated school-level committee structure: Process, preparation, and implementation.* Little Rock, AR: Project ACHIEVE Press. Retrieved from http://www.projectachieve.info/assets/files/pdfs/Proj_ACH_Schl_Committee_TA_Final_111.pdf

Knoff, H. M. (2011b). *Analyzing a school's readiness for positive behavioral support system implementation and conducting the initial SWOT and resource analysis: Process, preparation, and forms.* Little Rock, AR: Project ACHIEVE Press.

Knoff, H. M. (2011c). *The "Get-Go" process: Identifying students' services and needs for the beginning of the school year.* Little Rock, AR: Project ACHIEVE Press.

Knoff, H. M. (2012). *School discipline, classroom management, and student self-management: A positive behavioral support implementation guide.* Thousand Oaks, CA: Corwin.

Knoff, H. M., & Dyer, C. (2013). *Effective multi-tiered RTI approaches for academically and behaviorally struggling students.* Rexford, NY: International Center for Leadership in Education.

Knoff, H. M., Finch, C., & Carlyon, W. (2004). Inside Project ACHIEVE: A comprehensive, research-proven whole school improvement process focused on student academic and behavioral outcomes. In K. Robinson (Ed.), *Advances in school-based mental health: Best practices and program models* (pp. 19-1–19-28). Kingston, NJ: Civic Research Institute.

Louis, K. S., Leithwood, K., Wahlstrom, K. L., & Anderson, S. E. (2010). *Investigating the links to improved student learning: Final report of research findings.* Minneapolis, MN: University of Minnesota. Retrieved from http://www.wallacefoundation.org/knowledge-center/school-leadership/key-research/Documents/Investigating-the-Links-to-Improved-Student-Learning.pdf

National Association of School Psychologists. (2010). *Model for comprehensive and integrated school psychological services.* Bethesda, MD: Author. Retrieved from http://nasponline.org/standards/2010standards/2_PracticeModel.pdf

Perlman, C. L., & Redding, S. (Eds.). (2009). *Handbook on effective implementation of school improvement grants.* Lincoln, IL: Center on Innovation and Improvement.

3

Best Practices in Implementing Evidence-Based School Interventions

Susan G. Forman
Audrey R. Lubin
Alison L. Tripptree
Rutgers, The State University of New Jersey

OVERVIEW

Implementation can be thought of broadly as the process of supporting an individual or group to do something new, or the process of putting a new program or practice into place in an organization such as a school. Implementation has also been defined more specifically as the use of strategies to adopt and integrate evidence-based interventions in practice settings. When thinking about interventions, school psychologists usually focus on considering which interventions are likely to have positive outcomes for students and learning about the content of such interventions. Implementation focuses on the actions that need to be taken in the school and related systems to ensure that the selected intervention is delivered to students completely and appropriately.

Over the past few decades many interventions have been developed that have a research base supporting their potential to prevent and/or reduce emotional, behavioral, social, and academic problems of children and adolescents in schools (Kazdin & Weisz, 2010). These include interventions that target anxiety, depression, anger, aggression, disruptive behavior, substance use, and low reading and math achievement. Unfortunately the frequency of use of these interventions is low, indicating a gap between research and practice (Ennet et al., 2003). Efficacious interventions will not produce positive outcomes for students unless they are used, and used appropriately. Implementation addresses how to put these interventions into practice in

schools and what school psychologists can do to ensure that their efforts to deliver evidence-based interventions to students are successful.

Brief History

Implementation draws from multiple disciplines, including anthropology, sociology, public health, agriculture, medicine, business, and communication, as well as psychology and education. Early work in this area targeted the use of new practices by farmers, the use of new medical procedures by physicians, the spread of news, and adoption of new products. More recent work in this area has focused on health promotion, evidence-based medicine, innovation in organizations, and use of teaching and learning innovations. Everett Rogers' book, *Diffusion of Innovations*, originally published in 1962, was the first effort to bring the work of these separate disciplines together, and is now in its fifth edition (Rogers, 2003).

Fixsen, Blase, Duda, Naoom, and Van Dyke (2010) have described the various approaches to implementation that have been used in attempts to support implementation of evidence-based programs. Early attempts focused on diffusion, with researchers publishing their findings and hoping that practitioners would find and use the information contained in their publications. Later, the focus was on dissemination, with researchers providing their findings directly to practitioners through manuals, toolkits, and training sessions. Implementation refers to an active approach to providing the supports and conditions necessary for those using new practices and programs. This historical continuum of approaches to translating research to practice has been referred to as "letting it happen" versus "helping it happen" versus "making it happen" (Fixsen et al., 2010, p. 437).

Relevance to School Psychology Practice

Implementation is relevant to the school psychologist in several roles and to the three-tier model of service delivery. It is relevant for school psychologists working in the area of prevention programming and school- and district-wide efforts to enhance mental health and learning (Tier 1 services). It is also relevant for the delivery of mental health and/or academic interventions for students at risk (Tier 2 services) or with identified problems (Tier 3 services). Consideration of issues related to implementation is important when the school psychologist is the provider of direct services to students or is in the role of consultant recommending that teachers or other school staff use evidence-based interventions with students.

For example, Alphabet Middle School is in a state that recently mandated implementation of suicide screening at all middle and high schools. The school psychologist has been asked to chair a school-district-wide task force on carrying out this state mandate. Understanding the implementation process will help the school psychologist plan for successful implementation of the screening program selected for his district.

The school psychologist in Jersey Strong Elementary School has received teacher reports and observed that a few students in each of the classes in the school appear to have anxiety symptoms, and the school psychologist would like to provide anxiety management groups at the school. Knowledge of the implementation process will help the school psychologist understand what type of support will be needed from the principal and from other school staff and parents in order for anxiety management group implementation to be successful. Implementation process skills will help the school psychologist develop and maintain that support.

The principal of Pleasantville Elementary School asks the school psychologist to work with three teachers who have high incidences of severe disruptive behavior in their classrooms. The school psychologist intends to begin a series of consultation sessions with the teachers with the goal of assisting the teachers in implementing applied behavior analysis procedures in their classrooms. Understanding the implementation process can help the school psychologist plan the best ways to support these teachers in initiating and maintaining these procedures that are new to their classrooms.

Relationship to NASP Practice Model Domains and the General Problem-Solving Method

For the school psychologist, the implementation process consists of a variety of activities and considerations that relate to several domains of the National Association of School Psychologists (NASP) *Model for Comprehensive and Integrated School Psychological Services* (NASP, 2010). The implementation process involves Data-Based Decision Making and Accountability, and Consultation and Collaboration, and will assist school psychologists in delivery of academic and mental health interventions to individual students, classroom groups, and school-wide populations. The implementation process has special relevance to the domain of School-Wide Practices to Promote Learning. This domain focuses on promoting the use of "evidence-based school practices that promote learning and mental health" through program development and implementation skills (NASP, 2010). The implementation process focuses on putting evidence-based interventions in place in schools so that the school can improve the emotional, social, and academic development of students. It is a complex process that requires knowledge of systems and organizational theory, approaches to adult and organizational behavior change, and the science of establishing the effectiveness of interventions. It requires skill in collaboration with others, provision of school staff training and technical assistance, and program evaluation.

Consideration of the implementation process also relates to the general problem-solving method used in school psychology. Consideration of what the problem is, why it is happening, what can be done about the problem, and whether a potential solution to the problem worked can be used to gain an understanding of why efforts to implement an evidence-based intervention may not be working as well as expected, to develop strategies that can improve implementation, and to evaluate the success of those strategies.

This chapter provides an introduction to the process of effective implementation of evidence-based school interventions. It focuses on how to put interventions into place in school settings and how to enhance the quality of program delivery by working with school staff, school administrators, and others who influence school functioning and implementation success. Readers of this chapter will acquire a basic understanding of the definition of implementation, its foundations, and major elements. Readers will also learn about steps in planning for successful implementation including (a) considering intervention characteristics in intervention selection, (b) developing implementer and stakeholder support, (c) providing effective training and technical assistance, (d) developing organizational and systems-level support for an intervention, (e) adapting interventions for diverse populations, (f) evaluating implementation, and (g) planning for sustainability.

BASIC CONSIDERATIONS

Consideration of the difference between intervention activity and implementation activity is important in understanding how to implement evidence-based interventions successfully. Most school psychologists typically focus on intervention activity and intervention outcomes when planning to implement evidence-based interventions.

Intervention Activity Versus Implementation Activity

Intervention activity is the provision of an evidence-based intervention to students, while implementation activity consists of the actions that need to be taken to develop the conditions necessary at the school so that the intervention can be delivered as intended to students.

For example, intervention activity related to an evidence-based intervention for anxiety might include providing training in understanding the physical and cognitive components of anxiety, identifying the antecedents of anxiety, and using cognitive coping techniques and relaxation strategies. This training might be provided to a group of students who have reported anxiety problems and be led by school psychologist and guidance counselor group leaders using didactic instruction, modeling, behavior rehearsal, role-playing, and feedback. Implementation activity related to this intervention might include building support for the program by presenting information about it at parent organization meetings and school staff meetings so that parents will be willing to give permission for their children to attend and so that teachers will be willing to make accommodations for their students who attend the group and miss a class or lesson. Implementation activity might also include procuring resources needed for the group, such as appropriate space for group meetings, manuals for the group leader and students,

and any instructional technology equipment needed, such as audio and video equipment. In addition, implementation activity might include designing a screening program and referral process for the group, developing a means of tracking group participant outcomes, and providing information about these outcomes to relevant stakeholders. Obtaining training and technical assistance for the group leaders might also be a necessary implementation activity, as well as making adaptations to the program so that it is culturally appropriate for the student participants. A final important implementation activity might be developing a means of tracking whether this group intervention is delivered completely and appropriately to students.

Theoretical Roots

Implementation science and practice is rooted in systems theory, social learning theory, and behaviorism. A basic understanding of these areas is necessary for effective professional functioning in this area. Such theoretical understanding will assist in understanding an implementation context and developing effective implementation strategies in various professional practice situations.

Systems theory was initially developed in the biological and physical sciences but has also been used to describe school and student functioning (Forman & Selman, 2009). A social system, such as a school, consists of two or more individuals interacting to produce a desired outcome. Systems theory assumes that everything is interrelated and interdependent, and views the social and organizational world as systems within systems. For example, a classroom can be viewed as a system because it consists of students and one or more teachers, and sometimes support staff, interacting to increase student knowledge and skill.

The classroom is related to and dependent on its suprasystems; that is, the school, the school district, the community, the state department of education, and the U.S. Department of Education. Suprasystems are the larger system contexts within which a social system functions. When planning for implementation in the context of a particular social system, it is important to recognize that the suprasystems within which the implementing system exists will have an influence on how that implementing system functions and reacts to new practices and programs (Glisson, 2002).

Social systems have norms (established ways for behaving), and individuals in social systems have roles (patterns of behavior) and values (general justifications for roles and norms; Glisson & Green, 2006). Those who lead implementation efforts need to be aware of the norms, roles, and values of the system in which they are working in order to develop and maintain the support of stakeholders and potential implementers. In the process of putting new programs into place, it is important to understand whether the work patterns and attitudes of individuals in the system will be compatible with the new intervention. If not, strategies can be developed to change those behavior patterns and attitudes to provide a supportive implementation context.

Social learning theory (Bandura, 1977) has also provided an important theoretical anchor for implementation science and practice. Social learning theory explains that behavior change, such as implementing a new practice or program, is influenced by social factors, such as observing another person's behavior. It supports viewing the implementation process as one in which social interaction is important in determining implementation success and one in which the attitudes and behaviors of potential implementers' peers will influence willingness to implement a new intervention. For example, a teacher who is asked to implement a token economy in the classroom is likely to ask other teachers what they think about this procedure before deciding whether to commit to implementing it.

Behaviorism's (Skinner, 1969) focus on the influence of the environment and contingencies of reinforcement in behavior change emphasizes the importance of linking organizational rewards to the implementation of new programs if those programs are to be successfully initiated and maintained. For example, in the interest of successfully initiating the use of social–emotional learning programs in all classrooms within a school, it will be important for the teachers who implement those programs to receive recognition and reward. This could be accomplished by citing the use of social–emotional learning programs in teacher performance reviews, giving public recognition at meetings, and/or providing access to any other rewards used in the school, such as extra teaching supplies/materials/equipment, appointment to school committees that are perceived to be of high status, or any financial rewards available such as salary bonuses.

Components of Implementation

Understanding the basic elements or components of implementation provides a basis for beginning efforts in this area. Implementation typically includes (a) an innovation; (b) a change agent; (c) a communication process; (d) implementers, both primary and secondary;

(e) stakeholders; and (f) a social system (Fixsen, Naoom, Blase, Friedman, & Wallace, 2005; Rogers, 2003).

An *innovation* is an intervention that is perceived as new, such as a depression screening measure or school-wide bullying prevention program that has not been used in a particular school before. The *change agent* is the individual, such as the school psychologist, who is actively working to bring the innovation to a school setting. The *communication process* is the process through which information and opinions about the innovation are communicated between the change agent and others in the school setting. For example, this might consist of workshops, presentations at faculty meetings and parent organization meetings, newsletters, and/or informal discussions. *Implementers* are the individuals who will carry out the innovation. Primary implementers are those who have a direct role in carrying out the innovation, while secondary implementers are those who play a supporting role in the program. For example, the school psychologist may be the primary implementer for a new anger management group, and the teacher may be a secondary implementer because the teacher is asked to cue group members to use newly learned anger management skills while in the classroom. Other *stakeholders* are any individuals who have an interest in the innovation, such as parents or school administrators. The social system is the school context and its larger community within which implementation occurs, and social systems considerations may include state and federal regulations and policies such as those pertaining to the No Child Left Behind Act (NCLB) or the Individuals with Disabilities Education Act (IDEA).

Stages of Implementation

The implementation process consists of stages. Understanding the stages of implementation is important because the various stages require different actions on the part of the change agent and implementers to support successful implementation. Authors writing about implementation have differed in the way they conceptualize the stages of implementation; however, there are common themes that cut across the different conceptualizations. The stages typically include a *dissemination stage*, in which information about the new practice or program is dispersed; an *adoption stage*, in which a decision is made to try the innovation; an *initial implementation stage*, in which the innovation is first tried; and a *sustainability stage*, in which the innovation is maintained over time after the first complete trial (Durlak & Dupre, 2008).

Hall and Hord (2001) have explored the stages of implementation in school settings. Their research indicates that in the early stages of implementation, provision of information about the new intervention is of primary importance and that potential implementers need to become aware of the intervention and understand what it does, how to use it, and how it will affect them personally. During early use of an innovation, success is more likely if implementers have training and support related to how the intervention works and how to fit it into their daily work tasks. Later in the implementation process, feedback about the outcomes of implementation and information about how to adapt the innovation for specific local contexts and clients become important.

Among the authors who have advanced-stage models of implementation, there appears to be consensus about the importance of information provision as well as of matching of intervention resources and requirements to organizational resources in the beginning stages. Rogers (2003) emphasizes that in addition to information about the intervention, potential implementers look to opinions of peers in making a decision about whether or not they will implement, and thus the decision to implement is a social process, heavily influenced by the opinions of those in the implementer's social system. Adaptation of the intervention to the needs of the implementing organization is seen as particularly important in the later stages. Therefore, implementers will need to understand how they can make appropriate adaptations to evidence-based interventions without eroding effectiveness.

BEST PRACTICES IN IMPLEMENTING EVIDENCE-BASED SCHOOL INTERVENTIONS

The first step in planning for successful implementation is choosing an appropriate intervention to implement. This involves two major issues for consideration.

Making a Good Match: Considering Intervention Characteristics

What is the evidence base for the intervention under consideration? Is this intervention a good fit for the school context in which it will be implemented?

Evidence-based interventions are those that have research support indicating that these interventions are likely to yield positive outcomes with clients. Various professional organizations and federal agencies have more specifically defined the meaning of the term

evidence based. Although these definitions vary somewhat, in general, evidence-based interventions are those that have two or more research studies in which there has been specification of the target population; random assignment of participants to conditions; use of intervention manuals that specifically describe the intervention procedures; use of multiple outcome measures, including measurement of the target problem; statistically significant differences between the intervention group and a comparison group after treatment; and replication of outcomes, ideally by an additional investigator (Kazdin & Weisz, 2010).

The U.S. Department of Education (2003) indicates that interventions that have strong evidence of effectiveness are ones that have been tested in well-designed randomized controlled trials in which individuals have been randomly assigned to an intervention group or a control group in order to measure the effects of the intervention. For school interventions, randomized controlled trials should show effectiveness in two or more typical school settings, including a setting similar to the practice setting for which the intervention is being considered. In an additional category, interventions that have possible evidence of effectiveness (U.S. Department of Education, 2003) are defined as interventions that have been tested in studies that fall short of the criteria for strong evidence. This may occur when experimental and control groups are not randomized, there is only one well-designed study, the studies are not done in schools, the study participants have different characteristics from the practice setting target population, or there are high attrition rates among the study participants.

An intervention that is evidence based is greatly preferred to one that is not. However, evidence-based interventions are not available to deal with all problems and needs that may arise in schools. When evidence-based interventions do exist, it is essential to choose those interventions over other programs that may be available. In the absence of strong or possible evidence of effectiveness, it may be necessary to use empirical evidence related to the determinants or causes of a problem or need as a means of choosing an appropriate intervention. Several federal agencies and national and international organizations have vetted the research on interventions to identify evidence-based interventions for a variety of school problems, such as the Collaborative for Academic, Social, and Emotional Learning (http://www.casel.org), the U.S. Department of Education What Works Clearinghouse (http://ies.ed.gov/ncee/wwc), the Center for the Study and Prevention of Violence (http://www.colorado.edu/

cspv/blueprints/index.html), and the National Institute on Drug Abuse (http://www.drugabuse.gov). The school psychologist can use these websites alone or in conjunction with their own reading of intervention studies and literature reviews to identify appropriate interventions for a specific target problem and population. As the individual who is frequently the most knowledgeable among school staff members about research-related issues, the school psychologist can play a lead role in identifying interventions with appropriate research support and in communicating this information to other school staff.

Once an intervention's evidence base is evaluated, other intervention characteristics should be considered that are likely to affect adoption and implementation success in a specific school context (Rogers, 2003). When implementing a new intervention, those that are perceived by potential implementers and other stakeholders as being better than what is currently being used (relative advantage) are more likely to be successfully implemented. In addition, the compatibility of the intervention with the needs, values, norms, and past positive programs of the school is important. Interventions that are perceived as more compatible are more likely to be adopted and implemented. Interventions that are more likely to be implemented successfully are those perceived as being easy to understand and use (less complex), those that can be tried out on a limited basis before full implementation (trialability), and those for which the results of the intervention can be observed (observability). In addition, interventions that are perceived as risky are less likely to be adopted and implemented, and those that are seen as having the potential to improve the implementer's work performance (task relevance) are more likely (Greenhalgh, Robert, Macfarlane, Bate, & Kyriakidou, 2004). Finally, interventions that are viewed as adaptable (flexible) and able to be modified to better fit the specific school context are more likely to be successfully implemented (Durlak & Dupre, 2008). The school psychologist should assess interventions in relation to these characteristics, the characteristics of their school, and attitudes of school staff in order to select an intervention that is likely to be an appropriate fit for the school context in which it will be implemented.

Developing Implementer and Stakeholder Support

Although some of the evidence-based interventions that address emotional, social, behavioral, and academic problems of children and adolescents are designed to be implemented by a school psychologist, many are designed to be implemented by teachers or other support services personnel in schools. For example, the school psychologist may recommend that the intervention Bringing Words to Life (Beck, McKeown, & Kucan, 2002) be implemented in a classroom in order to increase reading comprehension through vocabulary development. The school psychologist may be in the role of consultant, but the teacher is the primary implementer of the procedures that constitute this intervention.

Even for those interventions designed to be implemented by the school psychologist, support from others in the school setting and from parents is frequently helpful, if not necessary. For example, if the school psychologist is conducting an anger management group with students and is teaching students about how to use cognitive coping skills, it is helpful if the classroom teacher and the parents proactively cue their student or child to use these coping skills in situations that may potentially trigger an anger response. Further, the school psychologist may need the permission of parents to include their children in the group, may need support or permission from the principal to conduct the group, and may need permission from teachers to allow students in their classes to attend the group.

Thus, support from potential implementers and other stakeholders is essential for successful implementation in situations where the school psychologist is the primary implementer of the intervention and in situations where other school staff are the primary implementers. In working to develop implementer and stakeholder support, it is important to develop an understanding of the pattern of relationships and communication within a school or a school district. An individual's decision to implement or support implementation of an intervention is based in part on their perceptions of how significant others in their social system think about the intervention (Rogers, 2003). In this respect, it is important to identify with whom the potential implementers and stakeholders communicate regularly, because it is likely that those individuals may influence implementers' and stakeholders' attitudes and behaviors.

Opinion leaders are individuals in an organization who are able to influence many other individuals' attitudes and behaviors (Rogers, 2003). Opinion leadership is not necessarily a function of an individual's formal position in an organization. Thus, an opinion leader in a school is not necessarily the principal or other administrator, but may be someone others perceive to be socially accessible, technically competent, and/or an exemplar of system norms. Opinion leaders can be identified through observation of and informal conversation about relationships among school staff. For example, in order to identify a school opinion leader, it will be important to determine to whom many school staff go for advice and who might take over ceremonial duties on important occasions.

An important goal for the school psychologist planning for successful implementation of an intervention is to develop school opinion leaders into champions for the intervention. A champion is an individual who puts his or her support behind a new program or practice. If the champion is an opinion leader, then that support can overcome indifference or resistance and play an important role in contributing to the success of the new intervention. Discussing the intervention with school opinion leaders in terms of the intervention characteristics that support implementation, described above, can help in efforts to turn opinion leaders into champions who will work to develop widespread support for the intervention.

In general, teacher support is crucial for the success of most school interventions (Forman, Olin, Hoagwood, Crow, & Saka, 2009). If teachers do not support an intervention, they may resist it or only half-heartedly implement it, and half-hearted implementation frequently leads to poor outcomes for students. Teacher buy-in can be increased if the teacher can witness the effectiveness of the intervention through observing either a demonstration or a small-scale trial in another classroom or school. In addition, involving teachers in the selection of an intervention is important, as is including teachers, when appropriate, in planning activities that are part of the intervention and in developing materials.

Administrator support, especially principal support, has also been viewed as essential for implementation success (Forman et al., 2009). In this respect, as indicated above, the permission of the principal is sometimes needed to implement interventions. In addition, the principal can be instrumental in getting school staff to support an intervention by providing professional development opportunities and material resources needed for the intervention, linking the reward structure of the school to implementation, and providing encouragement and opportunities to reflect on progress. For the school psychologist, it is important to develop a positive relationship with the principal through formal and informal discussions, prior to implementation attempts, to set the stage for later effective implementa-

tion. The school psychologist's skills and special areas of expertise should be discussed with the principal as part of this process. It will also be important for the school psychologist to develop an understanding of the goals of the principal and the school, allowing the proposed intervention to be linked to those goals.

Providing Training and Technical Assistance

A prerequisite of successful implementation is competence and skill in conducting the intervention. Thus, provision of high-quality training and technical assistance for implementers is key. Professional development in a workshop format can be used to provide background information about the intervention, to introduce the components of the intervention, and to provide opportunity to practice new skills and receive feedback. The content of initial training for interventions should focus on the rationale and principles of the intervention, including the theory and research bases, the content and process of the intervention, and acceptable forms of flexibility and adaptation. Literature on the process of good professional development tells us that training should be multisession; should include written materials; should include goal-setting, modeling, practice, feedback; and should include follow-up booster sessions, and/or technical assistance, after the initial session (Joyce & Showers, 2002). These characteristics of effective training should be used in the development of workshops and presentations that the school psychologist may use to train other school staff in the content and process of evidence-based interventions.

Technical assistance or ongoing implementation support can help implementers turn knowledge of a new intervention into skillful practice. This is sometimes referred to as coaching. Coaching can serve several functions, including modeling the use of the intervention in a real professional practice situation, assessing and providing performance feedback about implementation attempts, and providing encouragement and emotional support to deal with setbacks and the general difficulty of doing something new. Performance feedback for implementers has been found to be particularly effective in assisting those learning new skills to maintain a high level of accuracy. Such feedback can be given in the form of oral comments, written notes, and graphs (Noell et al., 2005).

Provision of performance feedback for school staff implementers fits well within the consultation role of school psychologists. Within a consultative relationship of this type, the school psychologist consultant would observe the implementers' delivery of an intervention and students' responses to intervention delivery. The school psychologist consultant would also provide feedback on those implementation efforts, discuss problems, and collaboratively develop solutions; model new strategies; discuss student response to the intervention; and emphasize connections between the use of the intervention and student functioning (Han & Weiss, 2005).

Developing Organizational Support Within Existing Systems

When viewed in the context of systems theory, an effort to implement an intervention in a school setting occurs within a school organization, which in turn is influenced by external systems such as the school district, the local community, the state department of education, and the U.S. Department of Education. The potential impact of all of these systems should be considered in planning for implementation of an evidence-based intervention.

The impact of the organization in which implementation occurs has been studied most frequently. In a major review of studies related to factors that influence implementation success, Durlak and Dupre (2008) found organizational capacity to be of significant importance. Aspects of organizational functioning that were found to have an impact on the success of implementation efforts included positive work climate, organizational openness to change and incorporation of new programming, shared organizational vision, shared decision making, effective communication mechanisms, effective procedures and structures to accomplish work tasks, coordination with other local agencies that may be able to contribute resources to the implementation effort, effective leadership and administrative support, and existence of a program champion.

Other reviews of the implementation literature indicate that a monitoring and feedback system is important (Fixsen et al., 2005; Greenhalgh et al., 2004), as is ensuring that the organizational reward system recognizes implementation of the intervention (Fixsen et al., 2005; Klein & Sorra, 1996).

What does this mean for the school psychology practitioner attempting to implement an evidence-based intervention? Some of these factors are beyond the control of the school psychologist, but they provide an indication of whether a specific school will offer a supportive context for implementation of evidence-based interventions. However, these factors do point to a number of actions that the school psychologist can take to make successful implementation more likely.

First, development of a positive relationship with the principal, prior to implementation attempts, is essential. If that is established, then it will be possible to work with the principal to ensure that structures such as new committees or workgroups and procedures such as referral systems are developed to support the intervention when appropriate. In addition, the principal can ensure that implementers are recognized through the reward system of the school and that the implementation effort is recognized using school communication vehicles such as faculty meetings, newsletters, and parent association meetings.

Second, the school psychologist can work to develop an implementation champion among school staff and administration, with recognition of the place the potential champions hold in the social network of the school. Again, it is best to work to understand the social network of the school and to identify and develop positive relationships with school opinion leaders before specific efforts to implement evidence-based interventions are initiated.

Third, development of a monitoring and feedback system related to the intervention is within the competency of school psychologists and the generally accepted importance of data-based decision making in school psychology practice. In this regard, the school psychologist can work to develop the methods and measures that will be used to monitor whether the intervention is implemented completely and appropriately (see below for a more extended discussion of this) and whether the intervention is resulting in positive student outcomes. The information gained from continuous monitoring can be used to make rapid changes to the implementation process in order to improve implementation. It can also be used to inform implementers and other stakeholders about the positive outcomes of the intervention in order to maintain enthusiasm for its use.

Systems external to the school may also have an impact on implementation. There may be laws or regulations at the state or federal level that support the use of evidence-based interventions, and in some cases there may be grant funding that can be used to provide financial support for these interventions. For example, IDEA and NCLB contain language, guidelines, and regulations aimed at meeting the mental health needs of students and use of evidence-based interventions (Dahl, Hoff, Peacock, & Ervin, 2009). State and federal laws and regulations can be used to bolster the stated need and rationale for use of evidence-based interventions to prevent and address student problems. The school psychologist should also consider joining advocacy efforts aimed at development of laws and regulations that support use of evidence-based interventions in schools.

Adapting Interventions for Diverse Populations

The students school psychologists work with are diverse on many dimensions, including race, ethnicity, national origin and immigrant status, language, level of acculturation, socioeconomic status, family structure, and sexual orientation. Participants in the studies that have established the efficacy of many interventions do not represent the diversity of youth in the public schools. Knowledge about the effectiveness of many evidence-based interventions with diverse students and families is limited.

Most of the research that has examined the use of evidence-based interventions with diverse populations has focused on African American and Hispanic/Latino ethnic minority youth. Huey and Polo (2008) have reviewed published randomized trials of efficacious treatments for outcomes with ethnic minority youth. They found 13 treatments to be "probably efficacious" (one placebo-controlled trial or two trials comparing treatment and no treatment) and 17 to be "possibly efficacious" (one study showing that a treatment is more efficacious than control) for several problems, including attention deficit disorder, conduct problems, trauma, depression, substance use, anxiety, suicidal behavior, and mixed/comorbid problems. Ethnic minority youth in these studies were found to benefit as much as non-ethnic-minority youth. The treatments were mostly group or family based and most used cognitive–behavioral procedures. Thus, several evidence-based interventions have been found to work well for African American and Hispanic/Latino youth; however, other ethnic minority groups and recent immigrant groups are absent from this literature, as are students who have other diverse characteristics.

When implementing interventions with culturally diverse students, it is important for school psychologists to understand their own culture and how it has an impact on their professional functioning, including their attitudes toward and reactions to student behavior. It is also important for school psychologists to develop an understanding of the attitudes and beliefs of school staff concerning culturally and linguistically diverse students (Sheridan, 2000), as these attitudes and beliefs may have an impact on their willingness to implement or support implementation of evidence-based interventions with diverse populations. In addition, cultural differences may mean that families may have different expectations and goals than school personnel for their culturally diverse students, and culturally diverse families may differ in their attitudes toward commonly accepted interventions. In general, intervention fidelity and success can be supported by selecting interventions collaboratively with families in a culturally sensitive manner.

Following from the principles described above related to selecting interventions that have a strong evidence base, some evidence is better than no evidence when selecting interventions. In attempting to use evidence-based interventions with diverse student populations for which they may not have been tested, practitioners are advised to proceed cautiously using the following guidelines: (a) maintain essential ingredients or core components of the intervention, (b) adapt the intervention with respect to language or the situational examples provided to increase relevancy, and (c) continuously monitor student outcomes to gauge effectiveness.

Evaluating Implementation

Evaluating implementation or monitoring the success of implementation efforts is essential for successful implementation (Werner, 2004). Implementation evaluation can serve several purposes. It can provide the practitioner with knowledge about what is happening in attempts to carry out an intervention and about whether what is occurring is desired. It can also provide information about why implementation is proceeding as it is. Implementation evaluation can provide rapid feedback so that implementation strategies can be adjusted to increase success. It provides a means of monitoring delivery and fidelity of the intervention ensures that the intended students are being served.

Implementation evaluation typically addresses two questions: Are the intervention and its supports consistent with the way in which the intervention was designed? Is the intervention reaching the appropriate students?

In addressing the first question, the focus is on whether the resources needed to operate the intervention are in place. If they are not, what is missing and why? Specific issues include adequacy of funding, availability of needed staff and staff skills, availability of materials or resources, existence of appropriate administrative and organizational structures, availability of information systems that may be required for the intervention, and stakeholder support for the program. An additional issue of interest is whether the intervention processes are proceeding as planned. Sometimes interventions may have adequate resources and seem to have all components in place, yet may still not operate as planned because implementers are not implementing correctly. In addressing the second question (Is the intervention reaching the appropriate students?), the focus is on whether the intended population is receiving the intervention at the appropriate rate, dosage, and quality.

The degree to which an intervention is implemented as planned has been referred to in the literature as *intervention fidelity* or *integrity* (Sanetti & Kratochwill, 2009). High intervention fidelity has been associated with positive outcomes for clients (Durlak & Dupre, 2008). The relationship of intervention fidelity to positive student outcomes emphasizes the importance of assessing and evaluating implementation.

Multiple measurement methods are used in implementation evaluation. The methods chosen are determined by the specific evaluation questions, the nature of the implementation context, and the nature of the intervention. A large portion of the data used in implementation evaluation focuses on knowledge, perceptions, and attitudes of implementers and stakeholders, including affect toward the intervention, perceived usefulness, satisfaction, ease of use, and commitment to implementing the intervention in the future. Data collection methods include interviews, focus groups, and surveys. Documentation of intervention operations can be conducted through the use of administrative data typically collected by the school (e.g., referrals for service, disciplinary incidents) and examination of intervention documents such as manuals, forms, and brochures. Observation of intervention processes can be conducted using direct observation or implementer self-report of the occurrence of essential intervention components and the quality of delivery of those components (e.g., timing, affect, responsiveness to clients).

For example, a school psychologist is working with several third- and fourth-grade teachers to implement the Good Behavior Game (Embry, 2002) and is using several strategies to evaluate implementation. The school psychologist checks to see how many of the third- and fourth-grade teachers are using the game and how many of the components of the game they are using. The school psychologist also asks the third- and fourth-grade teachers to complete a brief, anonymous survey asking them to rate their level of satisfaction with

the game, how useful they think it is in reducing classroom behavior problems, how easy it is to use, and whether they intend to use it in the future. In addition, the school psychologist conducts a focus group with the teachers in which the topics for discussion are their perceptions of the usefulness of the game, the barriers and difficulties they encountered when using it, and suggestions for making use of the game more effective.

Evaluating Sustainability

Sustainability is the degree to which an intervention continues to be used after its initial implementation is complete. Sometimes this is also referred to as institutionalization. Han and Weiss (2005) conducted a review of the literature on implementation and sustainability of teacher-implemented classroom mental health programs and developed a four-factor model of the essential ingredients of sustainable programs. Their model indicates that a sustainable program must be (a) acceptable to school and teachers, (b) effective, (c) feasible, and (d) flexible and adaptable.

Acceptability is influenced by teacher judgments of intervention characteristics (as described above), as well as the perceived support of the school and school district for the intervention. Han and Weiss (2005) indicated that teachers must perceive the intervention as meeting the needs of their students and as being compatible with their teaching style. Effectiveness can be achieved by selecting interventions with empirical support and by teacher observation of change in their students' behavior, as well as attribution of this change to the intervention. This can be facilitated by providing ongoing feedback to implementers to emphasize the link between intervention implementation and positive student outcomes. Feasibility involves having sufficient resources for ongoing implementation. Thus, interventions that required minimal resources are more likely to be sustained in the face of limited school funds. Flexibility refers to the degree to which the intervention can be adapted to changing student and classroom circumstances. Another important component of flexibility is the degree to which implementer understanding of the intervention allows for appropriate adaptation. This occurs when the implementers understand the core principles and core components of the program so that they can make changes in the intervention without eroding intervention effectiveness.

Han and Weiss (2005) presented a model in which sustainability can be enhanced through teacher implementer training and performance feedback from a consultant. In this model, when teachers implement an efficacious intervention correctly, positive changes in student behavior will result that will generate teachers' experience of success. Resulting efficacy beliefs and attribution of student functioning to the intervention will lead to increased motivation and skill in implementing the intervention, as implementers learn what is effective and what does not work in their classroom. Thus, a self-sustaining feedback loop occurs.

This model emphasizes the importance of providing intensive training for implementers, as well as performance feedback from a consultant, both roles that are within the skill set of school psychologists. Intensive initial training should address the theoretical and empirical rationale for the program, program principles, processes and strategies, the importance of maintaining fidelity, and acceptable forms of flexibility and adaptation. Within this model, consultation has two functions. The first focuses on improving implementation skills and involves observing implementation efforts and student responses to the intervention, providing performance feedback to the implementer and collaboratively resolving implementation problems, and modeling intervention techniques. The second focuses on increasing motivation to continue the intervention and involves focusing the implementer's attention on improvements in student behavior, interpreting the short-term effects of the intervention on students, and making accurate attributions connecting improved student functioning to the intervention.

Financial resources are also an issue when planning for sustainability. When initiating new interventions, it is important to develop a long-term plan for supporting the program financially. This has been especially problematic for interventions or programs that are started with grant funds. Eventually, after grant funds run out, a continuous stream of funding must be identified, and this typically means local school district officials must be convinced that the program should become part of the regular school budget. Thus, designing a means of informing school- and district-level administrators about the intervention and its resulting successes is important.

Finally, staff turnover in schools has been a concern for those working to sustain programs. Schools experience frequent turnover in teaching and administrative staff, and this can have an impact on the availability of trained, competent implementers as well as supportive stakeholders. This requires planning for continuing communication and training related to the intervention focused on bringing new staff and administrators on board and maintaining the organizational capacity to deliver the intervention in the face of personnel changes.

SUMMARY

Implementation is the process of putting a new program or practice into place in an organization such as a school. It also refers to the use of strategies to adopt and integrate evidence-based interventions in practice settings. Implementation activities include actions that need to be taken in the practice setting to develop the conditions necessary so that an intervention can be delivered as intended to students.

Basic components or elements of implementation include (a) innovation or intervention that is new to the users; (b) a change agent, such as the school psychologist, who is working to bring the innovation to the school; (c) a communication process between the change agent and others in the school setting; (d) implementers who will carry out the intervention; (e) other stakeholders who have an interest in the intervention; and (f) the social system (school and larger community context for implementation). The implementation process proceeds in stages that require different actions on the part of the change agent and implementers. Stages include dissemination, adoption, initial implementation, and sustainability.

The Appendix provides an implementation planning worksheet based on the practices described above. Best practices in implementation require the following:

- Choosing an appropriate intervention that fits the needs of students and the organizational context of the school, with consideration of the evidence base for the intervention and intervention characteristics
- Developing implementer and stakeholder support, including a champion for the intervention, and support from teachers and administrators
- Providing good training and ongoing technical assistance, which includes goal setting, modeling, practice, and feedback
- Developing organizational and systemic support and ensuring that use of the intervention is rewarded and supported
- Adapting the intervention for use with diverse populations when appropriate and maintaining core components of the intervention
- Evaluating the implementation process to ensure that the intervention is being implemented with fidelity and that intended students are being served, and using the information gained to adjust implementation strategies when necessary

- Planning for sustainability so that the intervention continues to be used after its first implementation

Planning and action in these areas will provide the conditions for successful implementation and increased use of interventions that have the potential to enhance the development of students in schools.

REFERENCES

Bandura, A. (1977). *Social learning theory*. Englewood Cliffs, NJ: Prentice Hall.

Beck, I. L., McKeown, M. G., & Kucan, L. (2002). *Bringing words to life: Robust vocabulary instruction*. New York, NY: Guilford Press.

Dahl, A., Hoff, K. E., Peacock, G. G., & Ervin, R. A. (2009). The influence of legislation on the practice of school psychology. In M. A. Bray & T. J. Kehle (Eds.), *The Oxford handbook of school psychology* (pp. 628–646). New York, NY: Oxford University Press.

Durlak, J. A., & Dupre, E. P. (2008). Implementation matters: A review of research on the influence of implementation on program outcomes and the factors affecting implementation. *American Journal of Community Psychology, 41*, 327–350. doi:1007/s10464-008-9165-0

Embry, D. D. (2002). The Good Behavior Game: A best practice candidate as a universal behavioral vaccine. *Clinical Child and Family Psychology Review, 5*, 273–297.

Ennet, S. T., Ringwalt, C. L., Thorne, J., Rohrback, L. A., Vincus, A., Simons-Rudolph, A., & Jones, S. (2003). A comparison of current practice in school-based substance use prevention programs with meta-analysis findings. *Prevention Science, 4*, 1–14.

Fixsen, D. L., Blase, K. A., Duda, M. A., Naoom, S. F., & Van Dyke, M. (2010). Implementation of evidence-based treatments for children and adolescents: Research findings and their implications for the future. In A. E. Kazdin & J. R. Weisz (Eds.), *Evidence-based psychotherapies for children and adolescents* (pp. 3–9). New York, NY: Guilford Press.

Fixsen, D. L., Naoom, S. F., Blase, K. A., Friedman, R. M., & Wallace, F. (2005). *Implementation research: A synthesis of the literature*. Tampa, FL: University of South Florida.

Forman, S. G., Olin, S., Hoagwood, K., Crowe, M., & Saka, N. (2009). Evidence-based intervention in schools: Developers' views of implementation barriers and facilitators. *School Mental Health, 1*, 26–36. doi:10.1007/s12310-010-9038-1

Forman, S. G., & Selman, J. S. (2009). Systems-based service delivery in school psychology. In M. A. Bray & T. J. Kehle (Eds.), *The Oxford handbook of school psychology* (pp. 628–646). New York, NY: Oxford University Press.

Glisson, C. (2002). The organizational context of children's mental health services. *Clinical Child and Family Psychology Review, 5*, 233–253.

Glisson, C., & Green, P. (2006). The effects of organizational culture and climate on the access to mental healthcare in child welfare and juvenile justice systems. *Administration and Policy in Mental Health and Mental Health Services Research, 33*, 433–448.

Greenhalgh, T., Robert, G., Macfarlane, F., Bate, P., & Kyriakidou, O. (2004). Diffusion of innovations in service organizations: Systematic review and recommendations. *The Milbank Quarterly, 82*, 581–629.

Hall, G. E., & Hord, S. M. (2001). *Implementing change: Patterns, principles, and potholes*. Boston, MA: Allyn & Bacon.

Han, S. S., & Weiss, B. (2005). Sustainability of teacher implementation of school-based mental health programs. *Journal of Abnormal Child Psychology, 33*, 665–679.

Huey, S. J., Jr., & Polo, A. J. (2008). Evidence-based psychosocial treatments for ethnic minority youth. *Journal of Clinical Child & Adolescent Psychology, 37*, 262–301. doi:10.1080/15374410701820174

Joyce, B., & Showers, B. (2002). *Student achievement through staff development* (3rd ed). Alexandria, VA: Association for Supervision and Curriculum Development.

Kazdin, A. E., & Weisz, J. R. (2010). Introduction: Context, background, and goals. In A. E. Kazdin & J. R. Weisz (Eds.), *Evidence-based psychotherapies for children and adolescents* (pp. 3–9). New York, NY: Guilford Press.

Klein, K. J., & Sorra, J. S. (1996). The challenge of innovation implementation. *Academy of Management Review, 21*, 1055–1080.

National Association of School Psychologists. (2010). *Model for comprehensive and integrated school psychological services*. Bethesda, MD: Author. Retrieved from http://www.nasponline.org/standards/2010standards/2_PracticeModel.pdf

Noell, G. H., Witt, J. C., Slider, N. J., Connell, J. E., Gatti, S. L., Williams, K. L., & Duhon, G. J. (2005). Treatment implementation following behavioral consultation in schools: A comparison of three follow-up strategies. *School Psychology Review, 34*, 87–106.

Rogers, E. M. (2003). *Diffusion of innovations*. New York, NY: The Free Press.

Sanetti, L. M. H., & Kratochwill, T. R. (2009). Toward developing a science of treatment integrity: Introduction to the special series. *School Psychology Review, 38*, 445–459.

Sheridan, S. M. (2000). Considerations of multiculturalism and diversity in behavioral consultation with parents and teachers. *School Psychology Review, 29*, 389–400.

Skinner, B. F. (1969). *Contingencies of reinforcement: A theoretical analysis*. New York, NY: Appleton-Century-Crofts.

U.S. Department of Education. (2003). *Identifying and implementing educational practices supported by rigorous evidence: A user friendly guide*. Washington, DC: Author.

Werner, A. (2004). *A guide to implementation research*. Washington, DC: Urban Institute Press.

APPENDIX. IMPLEMENTATION PLANNING WORKSHEET

1. What is the evidence base for use of the intervention with the target problem and population?

2. What are the intervention's characteristics and resource requirements? How do these fit with my school context?

3. Which teachers and other school staff support use of the intervention? How will I develop additional support of school staff, especially opinion leaders?

4. Which administrators support use of the intervention? Does the principal support its use? How will I develop additional administrative support?

5. Who will be a champion for the intervention?
6. How will training on intervention use (e.g., goal setting, modeling, practice, and feedback) be provided for implementers?
7. How will continuing technical assistance and coaching for implementers be provided?
8. Are needed organizational supports for the intervention (e.g., committees, work groups, referral systems, data collection, data management systems) in place? If not, how will they be developed?
9. Have I considered how state and federal law or policy may have an impact on implementation of this intervention? How will I use this information to support implementation?

10. Do I need to adapt the intervention for use with diverse populations? If so, how will I do this while maintaining core components?
11. What is my plan to monitor the success of implementation efforts, using multiple measurement methods?
12. What is my plan for sustainability, including use of ongoing feedback to implementers and stakeholders about the outcomes of the intervention?
13. How will staff turnover be addressed? How will new staff members be incorporated in use of the intervention?
14. How will needs for continuing financial support for the intervention be addressed?

4

Best Practices in Curriculum Alignment

Bradley C. Niebling
Iowa Department of Education
Alexander Kurz
Arizona State University

OVERVIEW

Curriculum alignment—the extent to which and how well curricular categories and the elements within them (e.g., content standards, instructional content, and assessment practices) work together to guide instruction and, ultimately, facilitate and enhance student learning (e.g., Webb, 1997)—is an underexamined aspect of the educational process and is often taken for granted. Curriculum alignment is important for students because of the role of standards-based reform, multitiered systems of supports (MTSS; also referred to as response to intervention), and the complementary role they play in ensuring that all students receive equity in their opportunity to learn a rigorous set of knowledge and skills in school. Although school psychologists are not typically involved in curriculum alignment efforts in their schools and districts, they are typically involved in standards-based reform and MTSS efforts. Given the importance of curriculum alignment to the success of standards-based reform and MTSS, and the role of school psychologists in supporting these two complementary efforts, it is important that school psychologists develop knowledge and skills in the area of curriculum alignment. These skills apply to several domains of the National Association of School Psychologists (NASP) *Model for Comprehensive and Integrated School Psychological Services* (NASP, 2010), but can be most closely associated with the domain of School-Wide Practices to Promote Learning.

Historical Context

At the heart of standards-based reform is the idea that all students can learn if they are held to a common or universal set of high academic standards (Porter & Smithson, 2001). Several social and political forces prompted the movement to include this aspiration in educational policies. For example, the National Commission on Excellence in Education (1983) claimed that educational goals for all students needed to be identified because students from the United States were performing poorly on standardized tests when compared to students in other countries. In addition, the Second International Mathematics Study and Third International Mathematics and Science Study revealed national differences in the content, depth, and breadth of instruction and the relationship of this instruction to student achievement (e.g., McKnight et al., 1987). This mile wide, inch deep curriculum was blamed for the poor academic performance of students in the United States when compared to students in other countries. These studies also highlighted the lack of clearly defined standards in the United States when compared to other developed countries.

Important Policies

These studies provided the impetus for federal legislation mandating the creation of content and performance standards at the state level. The cornerstone policy for standards-based reform is known as the 1965 Elementary and Secondary Education Act (ESEA). ESEA was reauthorized in 2001 as the No Child Left Behind Act (NCLB). NCLB places an increased emphasis on the results of tests used in accountability systems. An aspect of this policy that often goes unnoticed is that states are not considered to be "in compliance" with NCLB unless they have ensured a sufficient degree of alignment between content standards and large-scale accountability measures.

The spirit and intent of NCLB was reinforced for students with disabilities in the reauthorizations of the Individuals with Disabilities Education Act both in 1997 before NCLB reauthorization in 2001 and in 2004. One means of demonstrating the connections to the general education curriculum is through a standards-based Individualized Education Program. Students with disabilities are required to participate in accountability assessments, and schools and districts are held accountable to making sure increasing proportions of them are proficient.

Current Context of Alignment

In a series of studies summarized by Porter (2002), (a) content standards typically were no better aligned with accountability measures designed for that state than tests designed for other states, (b) the content of teachers' instruction typically was no better aligned with accountability measures within their own state than it was to measures designed for other states, and (c) the content of teachers' instruction aligned much better with what was taught by other teachers (both within and across states) than it did with their own state accountability measures. In other words, there is little compelling evidence that teachers are using content standards as the primary source to make decisions about instructional content, particularly if the content of what they teach aligns more tightly with the practices of teachers in other states than with the content standards or accountability measures found in their own state.

Findings such as these are even more troubling for students with disabilities. For example, Kurz, Elliott, Lemons, et al. (2014) examined the extent to which opportunities to learn were similar or different for students with and without disabilities in school settings using a full inclusion model of special education delivery. They found that students with disabilities experienced less time on standards, more noninstructional time, and less content coverage compared to students without disabilities in their class. Although students with disabilities may need at least as much opportunity to learn, if not more, than students without disabilities, these findings suggest that the exact opposite is occurring.

The Common Core State Standards for K–12 define what students are to know and be able to do in English/language arts and mathematics. The Common Core is designed to ensure that, if implemented as intended, all students would be prepared to graduate from high school ready to enter either higher education or the workforce. The standards were developed as a state-led initiative by the National Governor's Association and the Council of Chief State School Officers. Although the development of the standards was not a federal initiative per se, it can be viewed as the latest effort in the national standards-based reform movement. To date, most states and U.S. territories have adopted the Common Core.

Evaluating and facilitating curriculum alignment, grounded in the Common Core, are essential to implement Tier 1, a critical component of an MTSS. Poorly aligned Tier 1 instruction can have a ripple effect across all three tiers of the system. For example, if only 50% of students are judged to be proficient on accountability measures, and one of the identified problems with Tier 1 instruction is a lack of sufficient curriculum alignment, then the system has created a large number of "instructional casualties" (Vaughn, Linan-Thompson, & Hickman, 2003) because the students were not given the chance to learn the content. This, in turn, can place a burden on the system to provide additional supports and services (i.e., Tiers 2 and 3) to these students who may not have otherwise needed it. Given the research on the importance of opportunity to learn and curricular access, and corresponding evidence that some schools and classrooms have done an insufficient job providing students with an opportunity to learn the core curriculum (e.g., Gamoran, Porter, Smithson, & White, 1997), evaluating curriculum alignment is a useful place to start when trying to improve the schools.

Role of Alignment in Student Outcomes

In a series of independent studies, Cohen (1987) found that students of varying academic ability demonstrated greater growth when assessments were more tightly aligned with instructional content. Effect sizes from these studies ranged from 1.0 to 3.0, indicating that alignment between instructional content and assessments can have an extremely large impact on student achievement.

The studies examined by Cohen focused on narrowly defined learning objectives with individual and small groups of students. However, there is evidence that the importance of opportunity to learn for student outcomes holds true at the group level as well. For example, in a broad review of research on the alignment between what was taught and tested, Marzano (2000) found an effect size of 0.88, indicating a large effect. Gamoran et al. (1997) found that higher degrees of alignment between the content of mathematics curriculum and a standardized test of mathematics was predictive of student gains in achievement on that standardized test for low-achieving, low-income high school students. Students in remedial courses, which consisted of primarily low-achieving, low-income students, had smaller gains in achievement scores on average when compared to their peers in transition or college preparatory courses. Data indicated that the degree of alignment between instructional content and the assessments used was higher in the transition and college preparatory courses than it was in the remedial courses. Collectively, there is strong research support for a relatively basic idea: Students perform better on assessments when they have had the opportunity to learn the content.

BASIC CONSIDERATIONS

Before engaging in high-quality curriculum alignment work, it is essential to have clear definitions of the key concepts and terms associated with the work. The framework and definitions presented here are intended to detail one potential approach to defining curriculum alignment.

Defining Key Concepts: Curriculum

We use Porter's (2006) curriculum framework as the foundation for the key curriculum concepts and terms used in this chapter. He breaks curriculum down into four

components: intended, enacted, assessed, and learned. As seen in Figure 4.1, defining these terms is critical because there are many potential aspects to examine both within and between curricular components.

Intended Curriculum

Intended curriculum is the set of knowledge and skills that all students should know and be able to do (Porter, 2006), and it should be based on content standards, currently the Common Core. Within districts, the intended curriculum is often an unpacking or further detailing of the content standards, a scope and sequence document, and/or instructional units. Districts and buildings can then acquire or develop support materials like assessments, textbooks, workbooks, and other instructional resources that can help facilitate the implementation of the content standards. Kurz (2011) has further elaborated this model to include the planned curriculum, which is a teacher's cumulative set of plans developed to teach the intended curriculum defined by content standards, elaborated in local curriculum documents, and supported by assessments and instructional materials.

Enacted Curriculum

The enacted curriculum is the set of knowledge and skills actually delivered during instruction (instructional content) in the classroom and other learning settings, and how it is taught (instructional practices; Porter, 2006). The distinction between instructional practices and content is typically made in alignment analyses to

Figure 4.1. Visual Depiction of the Learning-Centered Curriculum Framework

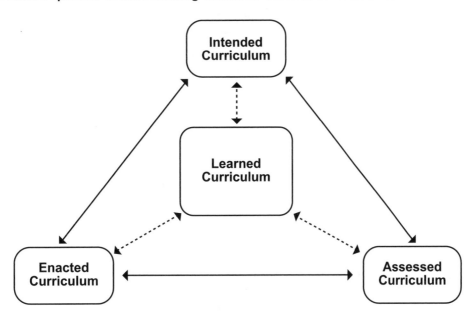

help clarify what needs to be examined. When conducting curriculum alignment analyses, it is best to focus specifically on what teachers deliver in their classrooms and not how they deliver it.

Assessed Curriculum

The assessed curriculum is the knowledge and skills that are assessed to determine student achievement (Porter, 2006). The focus of curriculum alignment analyses here is the degree to which there is agreement between the assessed curriculum and other curricular components.

Learned Curriculum

The learned curriculum is the set of knowledge and skills students actually acquire (Porter, 2006), as demonstrated via the assessed curriculum. It is strongly influenced not only by the enacted curriculum, but by the curriculum the students actually engage in as well (Kurz, 2011). In order to understand the degree to which the learned curriculum is aligned with the intended, enacted, and/or assessed curricula, the results should be displayed in those contexts (i.e., standards referenced).

Defining Key Concepts: Alignment

Alignment is the extent to which and how well curricular components work together to guide instruction and, ultimately, facilitate and enhance student learning (e.g., Webb, 1997). The three characteristics of alignment are directionality, dimensions, and level of analysis (Figure 4.2). It is important to purposefully consider each of these characteristics whenever engaging in alignment work, as each of these characteristics is in action, even if they are not being explicitly addressed. Furthermore, each of these characteristics will be dependent on the purpose of the alignment analyses and stakes attached to the decisions made with the data collected.

Directionality

Directionality is the direction within the system in which the alignment work is being done. For the purpose of this chapter, vertical alignment is defined as the degree of match or agreement within one component (i.e., intended, enacted, assessed, or learned) across multiple levels (e.g., different grades, leveled assessments, or textbooks). For example, an examination of vertical alignment could be to measure the degree of match between a state's third- and fourth-grade mathematics content standards.

Horizontal alignment examines the degree of match or agreement, typically across two components (e.g., enacted and assessed) within a single level (e.g., same-grade comparisons, multiple forms of an assessment at the same difficulty level). For example, an examination of horizontal alignment could be measuring the degree of match between the content of math instruction in a fifth-grade classroom and a district fifth-grade math

Figure 4.2. Visual Depiction of the Three Characteristics of Alignment

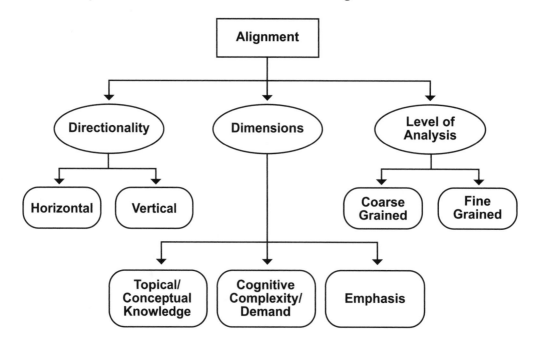

benchmark assessment. Sometimes, horizontal alignment work can occur within a single curricular component. For example, third-grade teachers collaboratively developing a common summative assessment in English/language arts is an example of horizontal alignment within the intended curriculum.

Dimensions

Dimensions represents the substance of what is either aligned or misaligned. It is the characteristic of alignment educators typically think about when they hear the term alignment. There are typically three alignment dimensions: topical/conceptual knowledge, cognitive complexity/demand, and emphasis.

Topical/conceptual knowledge.

Topical/conceptual knowledge are the "things" students are supposed to know and be able to do as a result of engaging in school. This may be described as the subjects, information, and ideas students are supposed to learn. For example, in English/language arts, topical/conceptual knowledge can be as broad as phonemic awareness or comprehension, or as specific as spelling–sound correspondences or main purpose of a text.

Cognitive complexity/demand.

Cognitive complexity/demand can be defined as what students are expected to be able to do with topical/conceptual knowledge. The cognitive complexity approach that most educators are familiar with is Bloom's Revised Cognitive Taxonomy (Krathwohl, 2002). Another approach to understanding cognitive complexity/demand was developed by the creators of the Surveys of Enacted Curriculum, which are called performance expectations (Porter & Smithson, 2002). A third approach is Webb's Depth of Knowledge (Webb, 2005). Although topical/conceptual knowledge and cognitive complexity/demand can be and often are examined separately within alignment analyses, it is helpful to consider them together (i.e., topic-by-cognitive demand combinations).

Emphasis.

Emphasis is defined as how extensively each topic-by-cognitive demand combination is addressed by the curricular component. Emphasis is often considered in terms of amount of time or points allocated to a topic-by-cognitive demand combination. For example, if a first-grade teacher spends more instructional time on Common Core mathematics standards related to understanding place value than on measuring lengths indirectly and by iterating length

units, in most cases the teacher should make sure that student learning on place value is assessed more frequently, and/or allocate more "points" to place value than to measuring lengths.

Level of Analysis

The level of analysis can be very general (i.e., coarse grained) or it can be very specific (i.e., fine grained; Porter & Smithson, 2002). Coarse-grained analyses tend to be more categorical in nature and often result in higher estimates of alignment. For example, when examining the degree of alignment between content standards and accountability measures in the area of mathematics, a coarse-grained level of analysis may be used to examine the documents for terms and skills like algebra or geometry.

Fine-grained analyses tend to be more subskill and performance oriented in nature, and may result in lower estimates of alignment. Using the same example of comparing content standards to accountability measures, a fine-grained level of analysis may be used to examine the documents for terms like multistep equations and inequalities.

BEST PRACTICES IN CURRICULUM ALIGNMENT

First, curriculum alignment work needs to be linked to clearly defined purposes or drivers. Second, several quality factors need to be considered. Third, curriculum alignment data are needed for decision making. Fourth, the curriculum alignment work should be grounded in the problem-solving process. Note that the best practices can be applied to any of the identified purposes in this chapter, but student achievement problems are likely to be the most frequently encountered purpose by school psychologists.

Determining the Purpose of the Work

School psychologists, with their knowledge of policy requirements, organizational theory, and systems-level services, should be part of any district or school collaborative team working to determine the purpose of proposed curriculum alignment work. School psychologists should work to proactively facilitate discussions about why their district or school should engage in curriculum alignment work based on one or more thoughtfully determined purposes. There are multiple potential purposes, or drivers, for engaging in curriculum alignment work. Furthermore, for any driver there are additional factors to consider. Together, these help frame the alignment work.

Identification of Drivers

Drivers are policies or strategies used to direct or move improvement efforts (Fullan, 2011). Within curriculum alignment, drivers could include policy requirements, student achievement, curriculum cycles, and research and evaluation. Policy requirement driver examples are NCLB requirements or, in Common Core adoption states, requirements for teachers to align their enacted curriculum to the intended curriculum of the standards. Examples of student achievement drivers include reteaching concepts and Common Core-based training for teachers in formative assessment practices based on low student achievement. Examples of curriculum cycle drivers are adoption of universal-level instructional materials that are tightly aligned with the Common Core, and development of common benchmark assessments that are tightly aligned with the Common Core. Finally, examples of research and evaluation drivers are examining changes in enacted-to-intended alignment after implementation of professional development with teachers, and examining the extent to which increased enacted-to-assessed alignment has an impact on student achievement.

A single alignment activity could be used for multiple drivers. For example, the adoption of Tier 1 instructional materials tightly aligned with the Common Core (curriculum cycle driver) could be at least partially based on low student achievement (student achievement driver). If the decision has already been made by the district or school to engage in curriculum alignment work without thoughtful consideration of the driver, best practices for school psychologists include sharing the drivers with the collaborative decision-making team, facilitating a conversation to help the group determine if the proposed curriculum alignment work fulfills at least one of the drivers, and determining if any modifications need to be made to the proposed curriculum alignment work based on the identified driver.

Consideration of Additional Factors

School psychologists should also review the proposed curriculum alignment work to determine the scope, relationship, and characteristics that are most appropriate, given the proposed driver for the work. The scope of the curriculum alignment work deals with the range of students and educators considered. It could involve individual students, groups of students, a single building, multiple buildings within a district, a whole district, multiple districts, an entire state, or the entire country.

Examples for school psychologists include the extent to which a student who has been referred for an evaluation has had an opportunity to learn the Common Core and the extent to which two same-grade teachers are aligned with each other and with the Common Core.

A curriculum alignment relationship describes the curricular components (intended, enacted, assessed, learned) involved in the curriculum alignment work, known as between-component curriculum alignment relationships. For example, an examination of what a teacher teaches compared to the Common Core is an example of an enacted-to-intended curriculum alignment relationship. There are also additional within-component curriculum alignment relationships, such as the Common Core and the teacher's planned curriculum within the intended curriculum.

Recall that there are three general alignment characteristics: directionality (horizontal, vertical), dimensions (topical/conceptual knowledge, cognitive complexity/demand, emphasis), and level of analysis (coarse grained, fine grained). For each of these the characteristics are involved in all curriculum alignment work, whether they are included intentionally or not. For example, examining a curriculum alignment relationship of a fourth-grade teacher's enacted curriculum to the intended curriculum of the fourth-grade Common Core standards in English/language arts standards would be considered a horizontal comparison. Examining how much time is spent on reading compared to writing strands is an example of examining emphasis alignment. Finally, looking at alignment at the strand level, instead of the standard level, would be a relatively coarse-grained examination.

Considering Quality Indicators

Once the driver of the curriculum alignment work has been determined, the next step is to ensure that the approach to the work results in a high degree of educators' confidence in the data. It is best practice for school psychologists to review the quality indicators with the collaborative decision-making team once the driver of the alignment work has been determined. In addition to linking the curriculum alignment work to the driver, quality indictors include (a) content area expertise, (b) curricular component expertise, (c) number of people involved, (d) independent versus consensus approach, (e) sufficiency criteria, and (f) data display (see Table 4.1). Reviewing the quality indicators is important for planning the action necessary to successfully execute the curriculum alignment work.

Table 4.1. Indicators of High Quality Curriculum Alignment Work

Quality Indicator	Description
Linkage to driver	The driver of the curriculum alignment activities should inform all subsequent decisions.
Content area expertise	The person facilitating the curriculum alignment work does not need content area expertise. Those involved need content area expertise.
Curricular component expertise	The curricular components of focus in the curriculum alignment work (i.e., intended, enacted, assessed, learned) should inform the type of curriculum component expertise needed to successfully engage in the work (e.g., educators with assessment background involved if assessed curriculum is part of the work).
Number of people involved	When the enacted curriculum is involved, only one or two educators are needed. If the intended or assessed curriculum is involved, five or more educators are typically needed (Porter, Polikoff, Zeidner, & Smithson, 2008).
Independent versus consensus approach	Curriculum alignment work may be done independently or collaboratively. The results should be derived via consensus and/or average (or other measure of central tendency) across multiple educators.
Sufficiency criteria	Curriculum alignment is considered "good enough" if it meets the criteria set forth in a policy requirement or if the results are predictive of student outcomes.
Data display	Curriculum alignment results should be reported as a matter of degree, as opposed to "aligned" versus "not aligned." Quantitative alignment data should be displayed either graphically or in tables. Qualitative alignment data are better suited for tabular or textual display.

Since curriculum alignment is primarily about the strength of the relationship between curricular components, the extents to which those relationships are both consistently determined and accurate are of central importance. Estimates of reliability and validity are relatively straightforward to determine and understand when measuring the degree of alignment to determine data quality. School psychologists, with their skills in research and program evaluation, are the ideal educators to ensure that the necessary reliability and validity estimates are derived from the data collected during the curriculum alignment process.

Collecting Curriculum Alignment Data

Before the school psychologist can help lead the problem-solving process in the area of curriculum alignment, quantitative curriculum alignment data are needed. Examples include examining the degree of alignment between instructional units, common benchmark assessments, and enacted curriculum and the intended curriculum of the Common Core. Many school systems do not have an existing process for collecting quantitative curriculum alignment data. Therefore, school psychologists should not take for granted that quantitative curriculum alignment data will be readily available. Best practice for school psychologists is to start by determining if there is a process to

collect quantitative curriculum alignment data. The most likely method for making this determination in most school systems is to ask the curriculum director or director of assessment for the district or school.

If no quantitative curriculum alignment data exist in the system, then it is important to understand why that is the case. Simply picking and using a method to collect the data may not address the underlying issues that led to no data existing in the first place. Potential hypotheses could be that the leaders in the system thought they already had sufficient information about curriculum alignment, or that they did not know how to quantify curriculum alignment. Methods for school psychologists to collect information to test these or other hypotheses could be reviewing a record of meeting notes or asking the system leaders questions about their knowledge of measuring curriculum alignment. Best practice for school psychologists is to begin collecting quantitative curriculum alignment data as quickly as possible.

Once the school psychologist determines why there are no quantitative curriculum alignment data available, an action plan should be developed focused on collecting the alignment data, paying attention to mediating factors why the data are not present. For example, if no quantitative curriculum alignment data are available because system leaders did not know curriculum alignment could be quantified, then the plan should likely include professional learning for system leaders to learn about why and how curriculum alignment data can be quantified, as well as the methods by which processes and tools are selected and used to collect the curriculum alignment data. In general, a plan should include the following five steps:

- Step 1: Determine the alignment relationships to examine.
- Step 2: Select the processes and tools to use for collecting the curriculum alignment data. There are a wide range of possibilities for collecting curriculum alignment data (see Martone & Sireci, 2009; Roach, Niebling, & Kurz, 2008). The tools with the strongest evidence base are the My Instructional Learning Objectives Guidance System (MyiLOGS), the Surveys of Enacted Curriculum, and Webb methods. (All of these will be discussed below.)
- Step 3: Determine the resources needed to complete the alignment work. Important resource considerations for doing the work include time and scheduling, finances, required technical assistance, and technology and tool requirements.
- Step 4: Identify any potential obstacles to successfully implementing the plan to collect curriculum alignment data, as well proposed solutions to those obstacles. For example, an obstacle could be a lack of sufficient time in the professional development schedule to teach teachers how to use the alignment tools. A potential solution may be to determine the importance of the alignment work compared to the other professional learning opportunities. If curriculum alignment is a higher priority, system leaders may need to reschedule existing professional learning activities not related to the curriculum alignment work.
- Step 5: Assign roles and responsibilities for each part of the plan.

Once the plan is developed, it must be implemented with fidelity. It is important for the school psychologist to help ensure that the educators in their system have patience with this process. Several trainings conducted by vendors or consultants may be needed to ensure that the educators in the school system have the knowledge and skills they need to engage in the data collection process. If the enacted curriculum is involved, it can take a full school year to collect these data. School psychologists should work with the collaborative decision-making team to make sure that the appropriate amount of time is planned for, clearly communicated, and taken to reliably and validly collect the curriculum alignment data.

MyiLOGS

MyiLOGS is an online teacher log that provides teachers with data-based feedback on their instructional planning and documentation efforts along key indices of opportunity to learn that extend beyond just curriculum alignment. Kurz (2011) and Kurz and Elliott (2012) designed this online teacher log to assess opportunity to learn indices related to three enacted curriculum dimensions: time (e.g., instructional time), content (e.g., coverage of standards), and quality (e.g., cognitive process expectation, instructional practice, grouping formats). MyiLOGS provides several percentage-based opportunities to learn scores and more than a dozen charts that illustrate aspects of a teacher's instruction, such as time emphases across applicable Common Core standards or differences in instructional practices for students in the same class. Evidence for usability, score reliability, and validity support a majority of intended score inferences (Kurz, Elliott, Kettler, & Yel, in press), and initial findings on opportunity to learn for students with disabilities have been reported (Kurz, Elliott, Lemons, et al., 2014). The intended behavior change based on self-monitoring and self-reflection through ongoing logging and reviewing of instructional feedback reports is further supported through targeted professional development activities.

The instructional feedback reports provided by MyiLOGS can be used in the context of an Instructional Growth Plan. The Instructional Growth Plan engages teachers in their own instructional data by establishing growth targets and monitoring progress via goal attainment scaling. Teachers can use the various MyiLOGS scores or other forms of evidence to support their progress toward self-established goals. MyiLOGS is free for individual teachers but requires the successful completion of a performance-based, online professional development course. More information and examples of the MyiLOGS report and the MyiLOGS Instructional Growth Plan can be found at http://www.myilogs.com.

Surveys of Enacted Curriculum

The Surveys of Enacted Curriculum are a set of tools developed by Porter (2002) and Porter and Smithson (2001) that include a teacher-completed survey, as well as a set of procedures that can be used to conduct content analyses and subsequent data analyses, of different sets of educational materials (e.g., assessments, standards, textbooks). The primary features of the Surveys of Enacted Curriculum methodology include a common language framework for examining the content of the intended, enacted, and assessed curriculum; a single alignment statistic (i.e., a scale ranging from 0.0 to 1.0); and graphical output of intended, enacted, and assessed curriculum content. The common language framework results in an array of topic-by-cognitive demand intersections that describe the component being examined and allows for direct cell-by-cell comparisons across components that permit the single-statistic calculations.

Information collected when using Surveys of Enacted Curriculum tools can also be used to inform various professional development activities (e.g., new findings from research regarding critical math skills, how to incorporate this content into daily lessons) and in research and program evaluation. These tools are also capable of providing a wide range of alignment analyses and can be used to measure vertical alignment, teacher-to-teacher alignment, building-to-building alignment, district-to-district alignment, state-to-state alignment, and additional comparisons. The Surveys of Enacted Curriculum framework is capable of generating coarse- and fine-grained data. More information on the Surveys of Enacted Curriculum can be found at http://www.seconline.org.

Webb's Alignment Model

Webb's alignment model provides a series of statistics that indicate the match or correspondence between content standards and the content covered in assessments. The information provided by alignment analyses using Webb's method is typically used for modifying assessments and revising content standards. It is also useful in examining the degree of alignment for state alternate assessments for students with disabilities and English language learners (e.g., Cook, 2006; Roach, Elliott, & Webb, 2005).

In Webb's model, alignment is examined along the following dimensions: (a) categorical concurrence (same categories covered in both documents), (b) balance of representation (degree to which one curriculum objective or benchmark is given more emphasis on the assessment than another), (c) range-of-knowledge correspondence (similarity in the span of knowledge expected of students by a standard what students need in order to correctly answer corresponding assessment items/activities), and (d) depth-of-knowledge consistency (similarity in the level of complexity required to respond to the curricular objectives and assessment items). Webb's model also includes recommended criteria for the degree of expected alignment along each dimension. Although Webb's methods have not histori-cally been used to collect information about the

enacted curriculum, recent efforts have taken place to explore this possibility (Niebling, 2012). More informa-tion on the Webb model can be found at http://facstaff. wcer.wisc.edu/normw/.

Engaging in Problem Solving

At this stage of the process, the school psychologist should have already worked with the collaborative decision-making team in their school system to link the proposed curriculum alignment work to one or more clearly defined drivers, considered the seven quality indicators (Table 4.1), and developed a plan to collect quantitative curriculum alignment data to use for decision making. Next, there needs to be a transition from measuring curriculum alignment to improving curriculum align-ment. Improving curriculum alignment involves actively working to align different curricular components. Examples include school psychologists developing instructional units or common benchmark assessments that are tightly aligned to the Common Core, and teachers enacting instructional content that is tightly aligned to the Common Core. While the school psychologists' strengths in research and evaluation are needed to help facilitate the collection of curriculum alignment data, it is their strengths in the areas of school-wide practices to promote learning, data-based decision making and accountability, and problem solving that they can contribute to taking those data and turning them into action to improve curriculum alignment.

Case Example

A hypothetical curriculum alignment scenario can help illustrate how the problem-solving process can be used to engage in curriculum alignment work. The scenario takes place at North County Elementary School. The principal at North County Elementary is concerned because the school did not make adequate yearly progress and has been identified as a school in need of improvement under the state's NCLB accountability plan for the last 3 school years. Previous efforts to implement MTSS focused on interventions have not led to significant improvements to overall student learning. Universal screening data have historically been used only to identify which students need supports and services at Tiers 2 and 3, not to examine the overall health of Tier 1. However, the state department of education is recommending that North County Elementary examine Tier 1 practices, including working to determine if teachers are teaching the Common Core to all students.

At the August building-level collaborative decision-making team meeting, the team decides that collecting curriculum alignment data focused on the enacted-to-intended curriculum (directionality = horizontal) can help them fulfill the recommendation. The school psychologist has provided an overview of the four potential drivers for curriculum alignment work (i.e., policy requirements, student achievement, curriculum cycles, and research and evaluation), and the team decides that the driver for the work is student achievement. After reviewing several processes and tools, the team decides to use the MyiLOGS. Results at the end of the school year from the MyiLOGS data indicate that, on average, teachers are addressing only 70% of the Common Core (dimension = topical/conceptual knowledge), with wide variations between teachers in the amount of instructional time spent on each of the standards (dimension = emphasis; level of analysis = fine grained).

Definition of the problem or need. In an MTSS system, schools collect universal screening data to determine which students are likely to be proficient on a meaningful outcome measure (e.g., statewide accountability assessment) and to determine the sufficiency of Tier 1 services and supports. A typical goal is that at least 80% of students be proficient as determined by a universal screening assessment while only receiving Tier 1 services and supports. At North County Elementary, the collaborative decision-making team discovered that only 60% of students were proficient on the universal screening assessment while receiving only Tier 1 services and supports. In this scenario, the 20% gap defines the problem or need.

The school psychologist can play an integral role in the curriculum alignment work using his or her skills in data-based decision making and accountability throughout the problem definition process. Educators will likely need assistance collecting both universal screening and curriculum alignment data. Educators will also likely need support to interpret and use those data to define the problem, yet another skill school psychologists typically can use to support schools. In this example, a lack of sufficient curriculum alignment is a viable hypothesis for why the achievement discrepancy exists.

Problem analysis. In the given example, North County Elementary has misalignments with both topical/conceptual alignment to the Common Core, as well as the amount of time spent on the Common Core across teachers. Problem analysis should focus on why these misalignments exist. There are a wide range of potential hypotheses to test, which can quickly become overwhelming. Best practice for school psychologists is to help the school organize potential hypotheses into helpful categories, such as (a) systems/policy issues (e.g., instructional materials do not align tightly with the Common Core), (b) professional learning issues (e.g., lack of teacher content knowledge, lack of sufficient training to implement instructional materials with fidelity), and (c) instructional need issues (e.g., students' lack of sufficient opportunity to learn in previous grades or courses, disparately low achievement across multiple sections of the same grade level). School psychologists should also take the lead in developing methods to collect information to test these hypotheses. In this scenario, strategies could include interviewing staff at North County Elementary, engaging in more detailed review of universal screening results, and examining curriculum alignment data from the MyiLOGS for grade- and/or teacher-specific misalignment patterns.

Plan development. Plan development should focus on addressing the causes of the curriculum misalignment. In the case of North County Elementary, those causes would come from an examination of the information collected via educator interviews, reviews of universal screening data, and alignment data from the MyiLOGS. The goal of this plan should be to increase the degree of alignment, which should in turn help increase student achievement. The curriculum alignment data collected serve as a baseline against which the impact of plan implementation can later be evaluated. In general, a plan should include the following five steps. Best practices for school psychologists include working with educators in the system to ensure that the plan is regularly monitored for implementation fidelity and each of these planning steps is followed:

- Determine how the curriculum alignment data will be shared and how staff will be trained to interpret and use the data. Although most quantitative curriculum alignment data are relatively easy to interpret, additional training is likely needed to help educators use the data to answer specific questions such as: "To what extent is my enacted curriculum aligned with the Common Core? To what extent is my enacted curriculum aligned with other same-grade teachers in my building?"
- Identify the action steps necessary to address the causes of the curriculum misalignments. For example, if one of the validated hypotheses was that instructional materials are not tightly aligned with the

Common Core, a curriculum adoption or development process may be one of the primary activities a system engages in to address curriculum misalignments. Action steps could include a systematic analysis of alignment between several evidence-based instructional programs and the Common Core.

- Identify any potential obstacles to successfully implementing the plan to address the causes of curriculum misalignments, as well proposed solutions to those obstacles. For example, an obstacle could be that the district's curriculum materials adoption cycle for English/language arts has not come around when the school or district wants to address curriculum misalignments in English/language arts due to a lack of tight alignment between existing curriculum materials and the Common Core. Some potential solutions may be to seek school board permission to modify the adoption/development cycle, or to seek additional external funding to support new materials adoption sooner than originally scheduled.
- Determine the resources needed to complete the action steps. Important resource considerations for doing the work include time and scheduling, finances, required technical assistance, and technology and tool requirements.
- Assign roles and responsibilities for each part of the plan.

Plan implementation. There are several considerations for the school psychologist to support plan implementation. In the case of North County Elementary, the school psychologist should support the principal to address these considerations. Support could come in the form of regularly scheduled meetings to review plan implementation with the principal, or to directly ensure that the considerations are addressed during plan implementation.

First, the details of the plan should be documented. Second, someone should have the role of monitoring the fidelity of plan implementation. Third, implementation fidelity data should be collected at regularly scheduled intervals. Fourth, frequent check-ins by team members who developed and are implementing the plan should occur to help facilitate monitoring and adjusting the plan if needed, as well as to troubleshoot any issues that may arise. Since North County Elementary selected the MyiLOGS, formative curriculum alignment data would be available to incorporate into both troubleshooting and providing ongoing coaching and support to teachers as the plan is implemented over the course of the school year.

Evaluation. During the evaluation stage of the problem-solving process, the same processes and tools used to collect baseline curriculum alignment data should be used again. In the case of North County Elementary, the tool would be the MyiLOGS. The frequency with which evaluation occurs should be defined in the implementation plan. It may occur annually or less frequently (e.g., every 2–3 years). Changes in practice can take multiple years, as can the impact on student achievement. Regardless of the frequency, student achievement data should also be examined with the curriculum alignment data. In the case of North County Elementary, this should at least include universal screening data. Given the school's status as a school in need of improvement, reviewing student achievement on the statewide accountability assessment would also be warranted. Changes in curriculum alignment can help schools to understand the extent to which those changes may have an impact on student achievement. School psychologists' skills in data-based decision making and accountability, as well as research and evaluation, are particularly important during the evaluation stage.

Identifying the Role of the School Psychologist

Since curriculum alignment is a relatively new concept for most school psychologists, it can be difficult to know what roles a school psychologist could play to support a school or district that wants or needs to engage in curriculum alignment activities. There are no particular differences in practice for children of different ages in curriculum alignment. Neither are there any multicultural competencies needed by school psychologists for curriculum alignment as defined in this chapter. However, school psychologists can evaluate their own effectiveness when providing curriculum alignment-related services, either in terms of the outcomes defined in the problem-solving process and/or their role in it.

For example, a consumer of curriculum alignment information may read or attend workshops about curriculum alignment issues and practices to better understand how these issues have an impact on system functioning. Consuming research and other information on curriculum alignment can help a school psychologist be a more knowledgeable and skilled member of a team that is working on curriculum alignment issues. It is likely that most school psychologists working in districts and schools would fall into the category of consumer.

As a distributor of curriculum alignment information, a school psychologist might provide an inservice for teachers on curriculum alignment issues or processes. A school psychologist might also consult with a teacher to help the teacher know whether or not an assessment the teacher is developing for students is aligned with the Common Core. Engaging in these types of practices would require a wider and deeper understanding of curriculum alignment than a consumer and yet would not require the school psychologist to have primary responsibility for being the expert.

In the role of conductor, a school psychologist would have the knowledge, skills, and expectations to take a leadership role collecting curriculum alignment data and engaging in processes to increase the degree of curriculum alignment in a school or district. For example, a school psychologist may coordinate the logistics of using an enacted curriculum data collection tool like MyiLOGS or Surveys of Enacted Curriculum. Although a small proportion of school psychologists may become conductors of curriculum alignment work, those who have an interest or need to be a conductor could engage in advanced study and training in specific alignment strategies.

MyiLOGS, Surveys of Enacted Curriculum, and Webb methods have numerous potential applications for school psychologists in all three roles just described, particularly for conductors. For example, the MyiLOGS or Surveys of Enacted Curriculum could be used to help troubleshoot problems with Tier 1, as was discussed in the example of North County Elementary School. Current MTSS models assume the existence of an effective Tier 1 system that will allow the majority of students to be successful with limited or no additional support. As with North County Elementary, school psychologists may encounter situations where the quality of Tier 1 is resulting in inadequate progress for enough students. In these situations, the MyiLOGS or Surveys of Enacted Curriculum could provide a method for identifying areas of strength and weakness in current classroom practice. After setting up MyiLOGS or Surveys of Enacted Curriculum accounts for the teachers, the school psychologist can (a) coordinate training by a MyiLOGS or Surveys of Enacted Curriculum trainer, (b) provide ongoing coaching and support to teachers around data collection throughout the school year (MyiLOGS) or at the end of the school year (Surveys of Enacted Curriculum), and (c) help facilitate data interpretation sessions. Once enacted curriculum gaps are identified, school psychologists can provide instructional consultation to help improve teachers' ability to facilitate student learning.

School psychologists could also use the Webb alignment model in their assessment support of teachers,

such as leading the development of district benchmark assessments aligned to the Common Core. This would require (a) downloading and reading the training manual (Webb, 2005), (b) assembling a team of teachers to develop assessment items/tasks, (c) entering the item information into the online Webb Alignment Tool, and (d) using the Webb Alignment Tool reports to modify the assessment items/task to improve alignment as desired.

Although school psychologists may be new to some of these skills and tools, they have a deep set of skills to draw upon to learn how about curriculum alignment can improve system functioning, skills that many other educators in systems do not typically have (e.g., measurement and assessment, system functioning). As school psychologists provide the services and supports they typically offer, curriculum alignment can and should be a new area of practice that can have a significant impact on student achievement.

SUMMARY

This chapter has outlined a number of important components of quality universal instruction in Tier 1 of an MTSS. Tier 1 can be enhanced by examining and improving the degree of alignment between the intended, enacted, and assessed curriculum. Research on curriculum alignment indicates that, as students' opportunity to learn the content on which they are assessed increases, so does their achievement. Not only can insufficient Tier 1 instruction result in a low percentage of students meeting proficiency without additional support, it also can put additional stress on the resources and effectiveness of Tier 2 and Tier 3 services. Since Tier 2 and Tier 3 are the levels in which school psychologists typically work (e.g., students at risk for academic failure, students receiving special education services), poor curriculum alignment in Tier 1 may have a drastic effect on the caseloads of school psychologists.

Because the provision of high-quality universal instruction is essential to the success of policies such as high-stakes accountability and MTSS, it is essential that school psychologists be familiar with and use research-based tools and strategies for examining and improving curriculum alignment. Examples of these tools and strategies include MyiLOGS, Surveys of Enacted Curriculum, and Webb's alignment model. Each of these tools examines the degree of curriculum alignment across the three alignment characteristics for engaging in deep, meaningful alignment work:

directionality (horizontal and vertical), dimensions (topical/conceptual knowledge, cognitive complexity/demand, and emphasis), and level of analysis (coarse grained and fine grained).

It is important for educators to identify the drivers of the curriculum alignment work. Identifying the drivers influences which tools are chosen, necessary resources needed to do the work, and what the next steps will be once the curriculum alignment analyses have been completed.

It is also important to use a problem-solving approach. Curriculum alignment is a critical aspect of building effective universal instruction. School psychologists, with their extensive background and training in assessment, research, evaluation, and problem solving, have the opportunity to provide both leadership and support in completing meaningful curriculum alignment work that can have a positive impact for all students.

AUTHOR NOTE

Disclosure. Alexander Kurz has a financial interest in books he authored or coauthored referenced in this chapter. He also has a financial interest in the My Instructional Learning Opportunities Guidance System (MyiLOGS), which is also referenced in this chapter.

REFERENCES

Cohen, S. A. (1987). Instructional alignment: Searching for a magic bullet. *Educational Researcher, 16*, 16–20.

Cook, H. G. (2006). *Aligning English language proficiency tests to English language learning standards.* Washington, DC: Council of Chief State School Officers.

Fullan, M. (2011). *Choosing the wrong drivers for whole system reform* (Seminar Series 204). East Melbourne, Victoria, Australia: Centre for Strategic Education. Retrieved from http://www.edsource.org/today/wp-content/uploads/Fullan-Wrong-Drivers1.pdf

Gamoran, A., Porter, A. C., Smithson, J. L., & White, P. A. (1997). Upgrading high school mathematics instruction: Improving learning opportunities for low-achieving, low-income youth. *Educational Evaluation and Policy Analysis, 19*, 325–338.

Krathwohl, D. R. (2002). A revision of Bloom's taxonomy: An overview. *Theory Into Practice, 41*, 212–218.

Kurz, A. (2011). Access to what should be taught and will be tested: Students' opportunity to learn the intended curriculum. In S. N. Elliott, R. J. Kettler, P. A. Beddow, & A. Kurz (Eds.), *Handbook of accessible achievement tests for all students: Bridging the gaps between research, practice, and policy* (pp. 99–129). New York, NY: Springer.

Kurz, A., & Elliott, S. N. (2012). MyiLOGS: My Instructional Learning Opportunities Guidance System (version 2). Tempe, AZ: Arizona State University.

Kurz, A., Elliott, S. N., Kettler, R. J., & Yel, N. (in press). Assessing students' opportunity to learn the intended curriculum using an online teacher log: Initial validity evidence. *Educational Assessment.*

Kurz, A., Elliott, S. N., Lemons, C. J., Zigmond, N., Kloo, A., & Kettler, R. J. (2014). Assessing opportunity-to-learn for students with disabilities in general and special education classes. *Assessment for Effective Intervention.* Advance online publication. doi:10.1177/1534508414522685

Martone, A., & Sireci, S. G. (2009). Evaluating alignment between curriculum, assessment, and instruction. *Review of Educational Research, 79*, 1332–1361.

Marzano, R. J. (2000). *A new era of school reform: Going where the research takes us* (REL No. RJ96006101). Aurora, CO: Mid-Continent Research for Education and Learning.

McKnight, C. C., Crosswhite, F. J., Dossey, J. A., Kifer, E., Swafford, J. O., Travers, K. J., & Cooney, T. J. (1987). *The underachieving curriculum: Assessing U.S. school mathematics from an international perspective.* Champaign, IL: Stipes.

National Association of School Psychologists. (2010). *Model for comprehensive and integrated school psychological services.* Bethesda, MD: Author. Retrieved from http://www.nasponline.org/standards/2010standards/2_PracticeModel.pdf

National Commission on Excellence in Education. (1983). *A nation at risk.* Retrieved from http://www2.ed.gov/pubs/NatAtRisk/risk.html

Niebling, B. C. (2012). *Using Webb's alignment model to measure intended-enacted curriculum alignment: A brief treatment.* Sun Prairie, WI: Midwest Instructional Leadership Council. Retrieved from http://milcleaders.org/media/cms/files/Content/Pages/Using%20Webb%20DOK%20for%20Intended-Enacted%20Curriculum%20Alignment%20AnalysesD2(1).pdf

Porter, A. C. (2002). Measuring the content of instruction: Uses in research and practice. *Educational Researcher, 31*, 3–14.

Porter, A. C. (2006). Curriculum assessment. In J. L. Green, G. Camilli, & P. B. Elmore (Eds.), *Complementary methods for research in education* (3rd ed.). Washington, DC: American Educational Research Association.

Porter, A. C., Polikoff, M. S., Zeidner, T., & Smithson, J. (2008). The quality of content analyses of state student achievement tests and content standards. *Educational Measurement: Issues and Practice, 27*(4), 2–14.

Porter, A. C., & Smithson, J. L. (2001). *Are content standards being implemented in the classroom? A methodology and some tentative answers.* In S. Fuhrman (Ed.), *From the capitol to the classroom: Standards-based reform in the states.* Chicago, IL: University of Chicago Press.

Porter, A. C., & Smithson, J. L. (2002, April). *Alignment of assessments, standards, and instruction using curriculum indicator data.* Paper presented at the annual meeting of the American Educational Research Association, New Orleans, LA.

Roach, A. T., Elliott, S. N., & Webb, N. L. (2005). Alignment of an alternate assessment with state academic standards: Evidence content validity of the Wisconsin Alternate Assessment. *Journal of Special Education, 38*, 218–231.

Roach, A. T., Niebling, B. C., & Kurz, A. (2008). Evaluating the alignment among curriculum, instruction, and assessments: Implications and applications for research and practice. *Psychology in the Schools, 45*, 158–176.

Vaughn, S., Linan-Thompson, S., & Hickman, P. (2003). Response to instruction as a means of identifying students with reading/learning disabilities. *Exceptional Children, 69*, 391–409.

Webb, N. L. (1997). *Criteria for alignment of expectations and assessments in mathematics and science education* (Research Monograph No. 8). Madison, WI: National Institute for Science Education, University of Wisconsin–Madison.

Webb, N. L. (2005). *Web Alignment Tool (WAT) training manual: Draft version 1.1.* Madison, WI: Wisconsin Center for Education Research, University of Wisconsin–Madison. Retrieved from http://wat.wceruw.org/index.aspx

5

Best Practices in Facilitating Professional Development of School Personnel in Delivering Multitiered Services

Melissa Nantais
Kimberly A. St. Martin
Aaron C. Barnes
Michigan's Integrated Behavior and Learning Supports Initiative

OVERVIEW

Over the past decade the educational landscape began changing and affecting the focus of professional development as well as the role of the school psychologist. These changes began with the increased focus on effective instruction, strong intervention, and prevention efforts emphasized in the federal No Child Left Behind Act of 2001 and the 2004 reauthorization of the Individuals with Disabilities Education Act. As part of these changes, response to intervention (RTI) was viewed as a means for increasing student achievement through effective instruction, prevention, and provision of increasingly intensive layers of intervention. Inherent in RTI is the development of multitiered systems of supports (MTSS) as a framework for providing a comprehensive system of differentiated supports that includes evidence-based interventions matched to student needs and educational decision making using student outcome data.

Over the past few years, educational policies have continued to emphasize the critical components of MTSS through the LEARN ACT, Learning Forward, and the Common Core State Standards. The critical role of professional development in facilitating the delivery of multitiered services to support the continuum of learners cannot be underestimated. Learning Forward defines professional learning as "a comprehensive, sustained, and intensive approach to improving teachers' and principals' effectiveness in raising student achievement" (Learning Forward, 2011, p. 2). Similarly, the introduction of Common Core State Standards in 2010, and its subsequent adoption by 45 states and three territories, has contributed to a new backdrop for education in the 21st century. This backdrop focuses on linking educator evaluation to the achievement and outcomes of students, thus highlighting the need for learning new skills and maintaining those already acquired. Taken together, these factors create an unprecedented opportunity for school psychologists to engage in systems change by promoting and directly providing professional development opportunities for school staff. These opportunities are aimed at building competency in using evidence-based programs and practices within an MTSS framework as well as supporting these programs and practices within school settings. While seemingly broad, the systems-level model of MTSS remains focused on promoting positive outcomes for students by, as VanDerHeyden and Tilly (2010) summarized, "using student performance data to allocate instructional resources to improve learning for the greatest number of students who are particularly vulnerable to failure, and to do these things in the most efficient way" (p. 3).

In light of school psychologists' critical role in promoting and facilitating professional development, it is important that they are aware of the skills necessary to support and sustain these systems. It is particularly important for school psychologists to understand the key features of MTSS-focused professional development so they are well equipped to provide necessary supports. Barnes and Harlacher (2008) describe several key features of MTSS-focused professional development. Considerations should include (a) ongoing professional development as opposed to a single workshop or train and hope approach, (b) addressing of beliefs and attitudes in education, including the rationale for why the model is being implemented, (c) both knowledge and skills needed for implementation, and (d) involvement across the various levels of educators, including administrators and school psychologists.

The role of school psychologists in the context of current educational policies and systems is both broad and varied. Opportunities may exist to serve as change agents, leaders, coaches, and resources for the other educators around them. By facilitating the success of other educators, school psychologists can further promote positive outcomes for students. This chapter's focus is well aligned with the domain of School-Wide Practices to Promote Learning within the National Association of School Psychologists (NASP) *Model for Comprehensive and Integrated School Psychological Services* (NASP, 2010). As providers and facilitators of necessary professional development and technical assistance for promoting successful implementation of an MTSS model, school psychologists will be actively engaged in consultation and collaboration as well as promoting many direct and indirect services for children, families, and schools. They will also be actively engaged in data-based decision making and accountability.

This chapter outlines and promotes a framework for school psychologists to facilitate professional development in support of an integrated academic and behavioral MTSS model of service delivery. The framework will outline basic considerations for increasing the likelihood that staff will use what it has learned in training for the purpose of improving student outcomes. It will also discuss how school-level practices can be improved through frequent problem solving of a district-level team. Relevant practices for school psychologists to advocate for and support this type of multilayered district and school level of implementation will also be presented.

BASIC CONSIDERATIONS

As more schools and districts begin implementing an MTSS framework, the likelihood that a school

psychologist will be in a position to facilitate the professional development of school personnel increases. To prepare for planning, delivery, and growth of professional development, school psychologists must take several considerations into account. Time invested in these considerations will increase the likelihood that implementation efforts will result in improved student outcomes.

School psychologists must understand that implementation of an MTSS framework will occur in stages, that the stages are recursive, and that in the current stage implementation should directly have an impact on the content of the professional development. For example, a school or district that is in a very early stage of MTSS implementation would benefit most from professional development content that is primarily focused on describing MTSS and how a school might benefit from implementation, whereas a school that has advanced in MTSS implementation would need professional development focused more on establishing the necessary systems, data, and practices. In order to differentiate the content for professional development, a school psychologist should account for a school's stage of implementation as defined by Fixsen, Blase, Horner, and Sugai (2009). Table 5.1 provides a summary of the stages along with suggestions for framing professional development content related to MTSS.

Understanding that professional development extends beyond the actual training event is another important consideration. School psychologists seeking to promote the transition of learning into practice will advocate for both formal training and coaching efforts as part of MTSS professional development. (Joyce & Showers, 2002). These types of coaching supports can occur at the systems and the classroom levels. In many cases a school psychologist's training in consultation, collaborative problem solving, and data-based decision making may position them favorably as a system-level coach. For example, a key component of MTSS is the use of universal screening data to inform academic instruction and intervention. A school psychologist can provide coaching to a building-level leadership team based on the skills presented during a training to support the interpretation of the data and the application of data-based decisions related to the types and levels of support provided to students.

Similarly, school psychologists can advocate that in the planning of any MTSS professional development opportunities, careful consideration be given to the system as a whole. This should include determining whether or not the necessary supports (e.g., resources,

Table 5.1. Considerations for Content Based on Stages of Implementation

Stage of Implementation	Focus	Professional Development Content Considerations
Exploration/adoption	Should we do it	• Information defining MTSS • Data that identify the need for change to the MTSS framework • Information identifying what the change involves
Installation	Work to do it right	• Identify resources needed to support implementation with fidelity • Create necessary materials to support implementation • Establish necessary data systems to evaluate student outcomes and program quality/fidelity • Action plans based on setting up the infrastructure needed to support implementation • Multiple examples provided as models
Initial implementation and full implementation	Work to do it right	• Clearly defined steps for implementation • Modeling and practicing with feedback • Use of data to inform implementation efforts (both program quality/fidelity data and student outcomes) • Data review and action planning
Elaboration	Work to do it better	• Expand training and implementation beyond initial efforts based on learning from initial and full implementation • Data review and action planning
Continuous regeneration	Work to do it better	• Data review and action planning • Identify strategies to make the work easier and more efficient • Review and revise policies and practices to embed MTSS work

personnel) are in place for the actual implementation efforts to take hold and whether or not the system actually has the capacity for implementation with fidelity. A valuable tool in this effort would be the Assessing Evidence-Based Programs and Practices tool (also known as the Hexagon Tool) developed by the National Implementation Research Network (Blase, Kiser, & Van Dyke, 2013; http://implementation.fpg. unc.edu/resources/hexagon-tool-exploring-context). This tool is set up to walk through the early stages of exploration and planning and can help make important decisions related to the professional development efforts a system is set up to best support. This type of planning and problem solving occurs best in collaboration with a district-level team leading implementation of MTSS.

School psychologists are in a position where they are likely to be asked to facilitate the professional development of school personnel related to MTSS implementation. When faced with this opportunity, school psychologists will increase the positive impact of the professional development when considerations are given to the school's current stage of implementation, the provision of related follow-up coaching, and the adequacy of the system to support implementation.

BEST PRACTICES IN FACILITATING PROFESSIONAL DEVELOPMENT OF SCHOOL PERSONNEL IN DELIVERING MULTITIERED SYSTEMS

Successful district-wide implementation of an integrated MTSS model requires continuous professional development, data analysis, and technical assistance at multiple levels of the educational system (e.g., intermediate school district, district, school building, grade level, and individual student level). School psychologists can play a critical role in the implementation process at each of these levels by facilitating professional development as well as being able to offer technical assistance in data analysis, systems development, and implementation of evidence-based practices.

It is imperative that school psychologists work collaboratively with other school psychologists, teachers, administrators, and ancillary staff to support implementation efforts to provide continuity of supports across all school buildings within a district. It is not uncommon for school psychologists to have a broader implementation lens beyond the school level when they may provide services to multiple school buildings within a district.

Thus, this chapter will focus primarily on school psychologists with the assumption that they are working collaboratively with district staff with the goal of improving student outcomes. The following sections outline the best practices in professional development necessary to successfully implement an integrated MTSS model of academic and behavior support. The practices include (a) focus on school and district implementation of evidence-based practices with fidelity within an MTSS framework supported by an infrastructure that promotes continuous improvement and sustainability and (b) emphasis on developing local implementation capacity by accessing a comprehensive professional development model that increases the likelihood of translating what is taught into action. These practices are supported by research (Fixsen et al., 2009; McIntosh, Filter, Bennett, Ryan, & Sugai, 2009) along with the authors' experiences in implementing a professional development and technical assistance model for district-wide MTSS implementation.

Levels of Implementation Support

Successful implementation of any school reform initiative requires direct and indirect support to each level of the cascading system (Figure 5.1) to ensure practices are developed and have meaningful impact on student outcomes that endure over time. Professional development, data analysis, and technical assistance are necessary supports at each level. The recipients and providers of the supports will vary depending on the level of the cascading system.

School psychologists provide a critical leadership role in supporting each level of the cascading system, from the individual teacher/staff level to the district implementation team level and perhaps even at a regional implementation team level through providing professional development and/or coaching supports. However, the lens required to support each level is slightly different. A part of a school psychologist's leadership role includes determining professional development needs within the

Figure 5.1. Cascading Model of Support

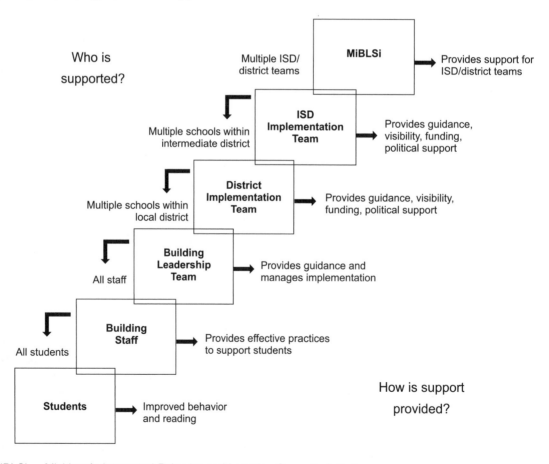

Note. MiBLSi = Michigan's Integrated Behavior and Learning Supports Initiative

school/district as well as thoughtfully planning how best to support implementers. It is also common for school psychologists to manage multiple requests from building administrators to facilitate professional development in a particular topic area. Before responding to requests or contemplating whether to facilitate professional development, school psychologists should consider the following: (a) whether or not the practice and/or system will meet an identified need; (b) how the practice and/or system fits with existing priorities within the school and district; (c) if there are sufficient resources (people, time, materials) to adequately implement with good effect; and (d) whether or not the practice is research validated and, when implemented well, will improve student outcomes. Intentionally thinking through each of these four factors during the exploration phase of implementation will increase the likelihood of efficient and effective action.

Once the exploration process is complete, the focus should shift to planning how best to facilitate and evaluate efforts of professional development for school personnel. It is important for school psychologists to define ideal implementation of the practice and/or system that will be trained. This allows for a clear lens of what leadership, district capacity, and implementation supports are needed at each level of a cascading system. After considering whether adequate supports exist and/or how to create adequate supports if they do not already exist, school psychologists will identify possible ways for evaluating the impact of professional development: (a) determining if staff behavior changes as directed by the training and (b) determining if student outcomes are improved. After thoughtful planning occurs, school psychologists should meet with their building administrator and district supervisor to share their plans for facilitating professional development of the particular practice thus far and to determine how best to proceed.

While meeting with leaders, it will be important for school psychologists to provide some description around the differences in implementation supports across the cascading system to ensure there is common understanding. Teacher-level supports tend to be more practice specific, with data analysis focused on classroom level and individual student data. Those supports differ from the supports provided to school building leadership teams, which focus primarily on systems development within the school building to support the implementation of classroom-level practices. District-level supports will focus more broadly on implementation across school buildings to ensure each building has the resources necessary for successfully implementing the systems and practices necessary.

School psychologists should monitor and evaluate outcomes of staff professional development and overall implementation. Implementation needs to be evaluated at each level of the cascading system. An analysis of program quality data (data that indicate the degree to which the practices are being implemented with fidelity) and student outcome data will occur on a regular basis and will help to determine the successes and the implementation barriers. The data provide a feedback loop to the teachers, school building leadership teams, and to the district implementation team so that quick and efficient problem solving occurs without stifling momentum. School psychologists are integral to the data analysis and problem-solving process since their role tends to support multiple layers of the system.

Infrastructures to Promote Continuous Improvement

We have found district implementation supports are essential to supporting practices being implemented at the building level. A district model provides advantages not available with a building-based implementation approach. Owing to efficiencies of scale, schools may access professional development and technical assistance from the district that would not be possible at the building level. There is increased motivation for implementing well at a district level, with central administration as a priority for accountability and allocation of appropriate implementation resources.

Since school psychologists tend to interact with building-level leaders and staff across the district, broaching a conversation around the necessity of district-level supports prior to facilitating professional development might be challenging. We continue to recommend that school psychologists schedule an initial meeting with their building administrator and their district supervisor to develop a plan for how best to support implementation. During this time it is possible to discuss the purpose of district-level infrastructures in supporting the sustainable implementation of the practices and systems within an integrated MTSS model. School psychologists should not be surprised if the concept is unheard of for the integrated function of the district executive leadership team and implementation planning team. Given this fact, it will be important to be prepared to fully explain the concept.

When beginning to describe the infrastructures, school psychologists should begin by explaining there

Figure 5.2. District Infrastructure

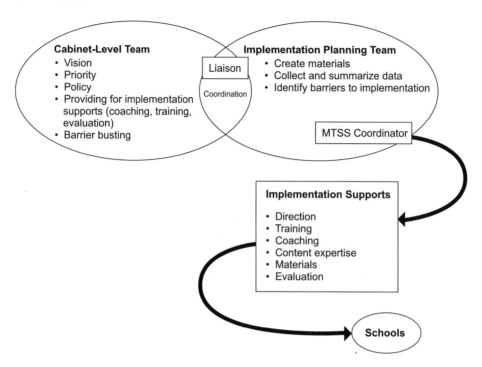

are two distinct yet equally important functions for supporting district implementation (Figure 5.2). The first is the executive leadership function (cabinet-level team) that is composed of individuals who are responsible for identifying district priorities and allocating resources to support the implementation of the priorities. This cabinet-level team must hold the vision for how successful student outcomes will be achieved across the district. Alignment of the priorities and allocated resources of the vision is critical. This group addresses barriers impeding the attainment of the vision in an efficient manner so as not to hinder forward progress. The executive leadership function already exists within a district; however, the composition of the team may vary depending on the size and circumstance of the district.

One example that may be helpful in conceptualizing the role of the cabinet team for removing barriers involves aligning job descriptions with assigned responsibilities. Since the school psychologist's role is broad and critical in supporting the implementation of an MTSS service model, adequate time needs to be devoted to fully engage in the duties that are assigned. These duties span the continuum of facilitating staff learning of MTSS data and systems and practices to determining student eligibility for services. Too often, new responsibilities are layered on the existing responsibilities, resulting in frustration and limited time for

school psychologists to fully meet expectations. Prioritizing what school psychologists need to do to support an MTSS model and then creating adequate space for those responsibilities has implications for work assignments. Typically, only individuals on the cabinet team can adequately address issues concerning redistribution of responsibilities, thus requiring an established feedback loop to the cabinet. The absence of quick and efficient feedback to this team will slow or even halt implementation efforts.

The second function is implementation and planning. Ideally, the implementation planning team would be composed of five to seven members, and they should be knowledgeable about the practices and fluent in applying the problem-solving process. The implementation planning team closely monitors the impact of implementation efforts by collecting, summarizing, and evaluating data across the district. The data analysis coupled with systematically applying the problem-solving model results in identification of areas of strength, need, and barriers that are impeding implementation efforts. Based on an analysis of the data, the team will provide direction for how to address the needs and by doing so will develop a district plan for cabinet-level approval that will act as a blueprint for district-wide MTSS implementation. If such a team does not currently exist, school psychologists can advocate that a team be formed to serve these functions.

One of the components the plan will address is developing staff competency in implementing the practices encompassed in an MTSS model. School psychologists have a leadership role in facilitating professional development and providing coaching supports following the professional development. Given this fact, it is essential to approach the meeting with the building administrator and the district supervisor with a clear understanding of what ideal implementation of the practice or system in which school staff will be trained looks like. Without a clear description of the critical components of the practice and the continuum of implementation variations ranging from what is ideal to what would be harmful for improving student outcomes, the district plan will be lacking in detail and will have a negative impact on successful implementation.

The school psychologist should next discuss why his or her membership on that team will add value to furthering the district's implementation process. There are many reasons for why a school psychologist's participation on the district team could be beneficial. First, school psychologists typically have a broader implementation lens that extends across the buildings within the district to identify patterns of implementation successes, needs, and barriers that exist across the district. Second, school psychologists are knowledgeable about the practices being implemented and also fluent in applying the problem-solving process using both program quality data and student outcome data.

Additionally, the skill set of school psychologists could serve a dual function both by being an active contributor to supporting implementation efforts and by developing competency among implementation team members. This is accomplished by modeling the problem-solving process, combining both program quality and student outcome data, and by deepening knowledge about the systems and practices necessary to implement a sustainable, integrated MTSS model.

Developing Local Implementation Capacity

A sustainable approach to moving a school system toward implementing an integrated MTSS model requires developing local capacity to successfully train and coach educators in how to implement the data, systems, and practices within an MTSS framework. The critical concepts require accessing a comprehensive professional development model. The professional learning provided in any such model must include the following best practices: (a) utilize a combination of theory, demonstration, and practice; (b) provide opportunities for

coaching the implementation of the practices in the classroom (Barnes & Harlacher, 2008); and (c) address key findings from the implementation research.

When planning to facilitate professional development, school psychologists must try to guard against traditional spray and pray methods of delivering professional development. That is, they should try to avoid being put in a position to conduct a 1-day training for school staff that does not encompass best practices of professional development and does not adequately address developing competency at multiple levels. It is critical for school psychologists to discuss with leaders during the planning stage about how competency will be developed for others who are expected to lead staff through the implementation process and for the district implementation team. School psychologists may find it helpful to ask the leaders to reflect on a recent implementation of an initiative, practice, or program to identify challenges that occurred during the process. The school psychologist can then suggest that the challenges described are common implementation pitfalls and can be prevented if competency can be developed at levels beyond the practitioner level and if the findings from the research on implementation can be consistently addressed.

The comprehensive school psychological services promoted by the 2010 NASP Practice Model, particularly those encompassed in the Consultation and Collaboration domain, place school psychologists in a prime position to fulfill a coaching function before, during, and after professional development. School psychologists will always want to ask themselves if they are building capacity across team members or dependency on the support being provided. If an overreliance on the coach occurs, then an honest conversation with the building principal about how to alter the trajectory will need to occur immediately. There will also need to be a plan for how to delegate responsibilities to other team members in a way that does not make the school psychologist appear as though he or she is no longer willing to fulfill the responsibilities being delegated. The process of weaning team members from the coach could cause some discontent between the team and the coach if it is not handled tactfully and right away.

School psychologists can be intimately involved in supporting the cascading model of support described earlier in this chapter. They should deepen the knowledge of cabinet-level leaders, the district implementation team, administrative team, and individual principals and serve as building-level coaches who participate in the school building leadership team trainings and follow-up meetings. To accomplish all of the work, there will need to be a significant investment of school psychologist's time to fulfill the roles in facilitating professional development and supporting staff through coaching the implementation of the systems and practices. The reality is school psychologists may or may not have time within their schedules. For this reason, the exploratory conversations with the building administrator and district supervisor are critical. If implementation of the data, systems, and practices within an MTSS model are a priority, then adequate resources must be allotted to support the work. The cabinet-level team will need to tackle this potential barrier to reconceptualize the role of school psychologists in supporting student achievement across the district. This will undoubtedly mean a traditional school psychologist role focused primarily on testing and placing students will be a thing of the past.

School psychologists should be mindful of the unintended consequences of coaching supports. At times, teachers may not be receptive to individuals entering into their classrooms in order to model, co-teach, observe, and provide feedback around how they are implementing a particular practice. This uneasiness, coupled with the use of an observation tool aligned with the practice, can cause a great deal of angst on the part of the coach and the people receiving coaching supports. We are not equating an observation tool with the staff evaluation process. Coaching and staff evaluation should be separate because it should be standard practice for any teacher regardless of his or her effectiveness to have access to coaching supports when working to implement new things. Districts should not inadvertently place school psychologists (or any other staff member who is expected to provide coaching supports) in a position where their coaching support is viewed as evaluative or forced or the intent will be lost. If a school psychologist is feeling as if the line between coaching and evaluation is becoming blurred, then it will be important to speak to the building administrator and district supervisor.

When school psychologists are asked to facilitate professional development for staff implementing MTSS, they should also be responsible for developing a participant evaluation, which generally occurs at the end of the professional development event and asks participants to respond to a series of statements using a Likert-type scale. Ongoing evaluation of the impact of professional development must also occur following the training session. As staff works to implement MTSS in the classroom, further retraining and implementation

support occurs in the form of coaching supports. The evaluation of learning now occurs through observation of school staff implementing the critical features of the practice and their application of feedback received from the coach for enhancing implementation. Too often, observation tools specific to the practices are not readily available. Consequently, school psychologists will want to work to develop a tool that can be used when coaching staff. Once the tool is developed, it will be important to present it to the district implementation team so it can incorporate its use into the MTSS implementation plan. As data are being collected, the school psychologist will want to organize the data in such a way that areas of strength and need are easily identified. The data will need to be presented to the district implementation team during predetermined intervals so the team can act on any data indicating retraining or any data suggesting more resources are required to support efforts.

Michigan's Integrated Behavior and Learning Supports Initiative

Michigan's Integrated Behavior and Learning Supports Initiative (MiBLSi) provides an example of a comprehensive professional development model. Since 2003, the Michigan Department of Education has made significant investment into an integrated model of school-wide behavior and reading support. MiBLSi utilizes a multitiered system of support in an integrated behavior and academic model (Bohanon, Goodman, & McIntosh, 2009). This model emphasizes developing competency at multiple levels (Figure 5.3), starting at the central administrative level down to the school team level. Since the beginning of this statewide initiative, school psychologists have played integral roles in the facilitation of professional development for staff implementing MTSS, and we use MiBLSi as an example to describe the implementation of the previously identified best practices.

MiBLSi's comprehensive professional development model begins with an initial meeting with the cabinet-level team to ensure there is an understanding of the scope of the MTSS work that will be taking place within the district. It will also provide an opportunity to clarify resource allocations necessary to support implementation efforts, to answer questions, and to address concerns. During this initial meeting, teaching and learning are occurring even though it would not necessarily look like a formal professional development opportunity. Foundational knowledge is provided to

Figure 5.3. Professional Development at Multiple Levels

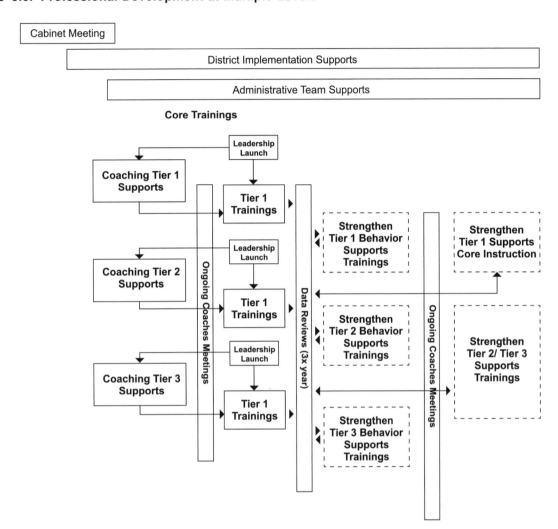

Note. Each box represents multiple days of training. Program quality/fidelity and student outcome data will be used to determine entrance/exit out of a particular tier as well as when reading and/or behavior will be the focus of professional learning. Customized implementation supports may not always be necessary if data do not support the need.

district leaders that apply to the scope of their role in effectively leading and supporting MTSS implementation efforts, basic knowledge about the practice is that requires implementation support and the need to support implementation at multiple levels.

The next level of professional development occurs with the implementation planning team. The training topics will emphasize fostering effective team functioning, aggregating school-level data for frequent analysis and problem solving, and differentiating school building supports based on the building's stage of implementation. During early implementation efforts there should be regularly scheduled sessions (e.g., monthly) with the team. Each session builds upon each other session for continuity and aligns with the key features of MTSS-focused

professional development described by Barnes and Harlacher (2008).

The administrative team addresses the role the district leaders have in leading the implementation of an integrated MTSS model. Monthly professional learning opportunities are provided with the administrative team that includes K–12 administrators who attend the sessions together with their district supervisor. The emphasis throughout is on building continuity across the district. School psychologists should clearly articulate the benefits of working with the administrative team, including emphasizing research-validated leadership practices that have a positive impact on student outcomes (Hattie, 2009); effectively managing the resistance some staff might have to changing the practice (Fullan, 2010); understanding what implementation of the practice should look like when principals are entering classrooms to observe student learning; and knowing how to analyze the program quality data and student outcome data in advance of initial implementation.

Access to the administrative team and agreement that this time will be time well spent given the administrators' already busy schedules could be challenging. For this reason, emphasizing the benefits and the short duration of the monthly sessions will be critical. It will also be important to ask that the professional learning opportunities for the administrative team be incorporated into an existing meeting schedule. Most districts have a reoccurring schedule for the administrators to meet with central office leaders, so leveraging a small portion of that meeting time might cause leaders to be more supportive.

Within this model there is a coaching relationship between school psychologists and building administrators throughout the implementation process to further facilitate professional learning. Because of the importance of building-level leaders holding staff accountable for high-quality implementation of MTSS practices, building administrators will need to have accurate information about what ideal implementation of the practice looks like as well as the variations of implementation. Leaders are faced with the difficult task of sifting through research and information provided by staff, albeit sometimes conflicting, in order to make decisions that undoubtedly have an impact on expectations for implementation. School psychologists leverage their consultation and collaboration skills by serving as confidants to leaders and helping leaders sift through the information provided by staff, and in other venues, such as professional development sessions

that communicate clear expectations to staff around implementation. Consultation can be provided during a regularly scheduled meeting with the building administrator to discuss what the principal should be seeing in the classroom and how best to continue to move staff toward ideal implementation. High-quality professional development and coaching support to staff can help to increase the likelihood that ideal implementation is attainable.

School-level professional development is undoubtedly more complex than the other layers presented in Figure 5.3 because the learning is different depending on the intended audience. There are two main categories of professional development provided: (a) core trainings that focus on building foundational knowledge of universal, targeted, and intensive reading and behavior supports included in an integrated MTSS model and (b) implementation supports that are accessed only after core training for the specific tier has occurred and sufficient time for implementation of what was trained has been provided. Data analysis is essential regardless of which category of professional development schools are accessing, and it determines entrance into and exit out of a particular tier of support.

Audiences for the core MTSS training content include principals, individuals identified as providing coaching supports to the buildings, and three to five additional members of the leadership team who are representative of the school staff. An example of the training sequence for the principal, coaches, and school building leadership teams outlined in Table 5.2 represents what training would look like in the first year when an implementation planning team has identified in its 5-year MTSS implementation plan that leadership teams will begin training in positive behavior interventions and supports. School psychologists are often

Table 5.2. Example Year 1 Training

Session Title	Audience	Assessment Measure
Leadership launch (3 days)	Principals and coaches	• PBIS self-assessment survey • Student risk screening scale • School-wide information system
Coaching supports for Tier 1 behavior (3 days)	Coaches	• Student risk screening scale • School-wide information system • Benchmarks of quality
School-wide PBIS (3 days)	School-based leadership team	• Student risk screening scale • School-wide information system • Benchmarks of quality

Note. PBIS = positive behavior interventions and supports.

identified as building-level coaches. This has the potential to be a challenge for some school psychologists if they are also expected to facilitate the professional development session. In these situations, it is important to have a cofacilitator who can manage questions from the teams and carefully monitor activity completion across teams. Trying to fulfill both roles, as a lead facilitator and coach, will dilute focus across both functions.

Within the MiBLSi model, it is the responsibility of the implementation planning team to frequently review implementation data and determine when to layer on additional focus areas and tiers of support. The time line for implementing practices with fidelity is at a minimum a 3- to 5-year process (Fixsen, Naoom, Blase, Friedman, & Wallace, 2005). This duration requires the implementation planning team to maintain focus, continually align priorities, and actively work to avoid distractions that might compete for staff time, resulting in a dip in implementation fidelity. Communication processes across all layers of the cascading model of support (Figure 5.1) are essential to providing feedback along the stages of implementation so issues impeding efforts can quickly and efficiently be addressed by the implementation planning team or cabinet-level team. Developing local capacity for understanding the data, systems, and practices within an integrated MTSS model is necessary for managing the complexities of large-scale school reform.

Evaluating the impact of professional development is important at every layer of support. However, failing to evaluate professional development at the school level could have disastrous consequences. Remember that it is the interactions between teachers and students that will yield the greatest amount of student growth. For that reason, ensuring that school staff have both the competency necessary to effectively implement MTSS and opportunities for continuous coaching supports is an important aspect of the MiBLSi model. Participant evaluations following a professional development session use a procedure referred to as a *retrospective self-assessment* (D'Eon, Sadownik, Harrison, & Nation, 2008).

Retrospective self-assessment asks participants to rate their level of knowledge for each of the outcomes from the professional development session at the end of the day compared to their knowledge at the beginning of the day across four different categories: (a) mastery, (b) competence, (c) developing competence, and (d) need more training/practice. Although the retrospective self-assessment requires participants to assess their knowledge at the beginning of the day as well as the end of the day, reflecting on beginning-of-the-day knowledge still

occurs at the end of the day. This is because participants often do not know at the beginning of the day what they should know by the end of the day. It is only after participating in the learning throughout the day that participants can more accurately assess their level of knowledge before the session began.

The data from the retrospective self-assessments are summarized and examined to inform future iterations of the professional development content as well as to inform areas in need of additional support. These data are presented to the district implementation team as part of the overall evaluation of MTSS efforts within the district and are used to inform future planning as well as to support the development and refinement of the skills of local trainers.

SUMMARY

Professional development related to an integrated MTSS model of academic and behavior supports should be systematically designed and implemented so as to focus on the use of evidence-based practices with fidelity, an infrastructure that promotes continuous improvement and sustainability, and on the development of local capacity for coaching, training, and evaluation. Leveraging the knowledge from implementation science, particularly the application of the implementation drivers and understanding of the stages of implementation, increases the likelihood that this type of professional development will translate research on evidence-based practices and programs into practice within a district, school, and classroom. School psychologists have an unprecedented opportunity to apply their skills in collaboration and consultation to assist in the delivery and/or coaching of this type of professional development. Adequate preservice training and continuous professional learning of school staff are essential to addressing the changing educational landscape, for meeting student needs, and for improving outcomes.

REFERENCES

Barnes, A. C., & Harlacher, J. E. (2008). Clearing the confusion: Response to intervention as a set of principles. *Education and Treatment of Children, 31*, 417–431.

Blase, K., Kiser, L., & Van Dyke, M. (2013). The hexagon tool: Exploring context. Chapel Hill, NC: National Implementation Research Network, FPG Child Development Institute, University of North Carolina at Chapel Hill.

Bohanon, H., Goodman, S., & McIntosh, K. (2009). *Integrating academic and behavior supports within an RTI framework, Part I: General overview*. Washington, DC: RTI Action Network. Retrieved from http://www.rtinetwork.org/learn/behavior-supports/integrating-behavior-and-academic-supports-general-overview

D'Eon, M., Sadownik, L., Harrison, A., & Nation, J. (2008). Using self-assessments to detect workshop success: Do they work? *American Journal of Evaluation, 29*, 92–98. doi:10.1177/1098214007312630

Fixsen, D. L., Blase, K. A., Horner, R., & Sugai, G. (2009). *Readiness for change: Scaling up brief #3*. Chapel Hill, NC: University of North Carolina, FPG, SISEP.

Fixsen, D. L., Naoom, S. F., Blase, K. A., Friedman, R. M., & Wallace, F. (2005). *Implementation research: A synthesis of the literature.* (FMHI Publication 231). Tampa, FL: University of South Florida, Louis de la Parte Florida Mental Health Institute, National Implementation Research Network.

Fullan, M. (2010). *Motion leadership: The skinny on becoming change savvy.* Thousand Oaks, CA: Corwin.

Hattie, J. A. C. (2009). *Visible learning: A synthesis of meta-analyses relating to achievement.* New York, NY: Routledge.

Joyce, B., & Showers, B. (2002). *Student achievement through staff development: Fundamentals of school renewal.* (3rd ed.). Alexandria, VA: Association for Supervision and Curriculum Development.

Learning Forward. (2011). *Evidence of effectiveness: A report from Learning Forward.* Oxford, OH: Author.

McIntosh, K., Filter, K. J., Bennett, J. L., Ryan, C., & Sugai, G. (2009). Principles of sustainable prevention: Designing scale-up of school-wide positive behavior support to promote durable systems. *Psychology in the Schools, 47*, 5–21. doi:10.1002/pits

National Association of School Psychologists. (2010). *Model for comprehensive and integrated school psychological services.* Bethesda, MD: Author. Retrieved from http://www.nasponline.org/standards/2010standards/2_PracticeModel.pdf

VanDerHeyden, A. M., & Tilly, W. D., III. (2010). *Keeping RTI on track: How to identify, repair and prevent mistakes that derail implementation.* Horsham, PA: LRP Publishing.

6 Best Practices in Decreasing Dropout and Increasing High School Completion

Shane R. Jimerson
University of California, Santa Barbara
Amy L. Reschly
University of Georgia
Robyn S. Hess
University of Northern Colorado

OVERVIEW

Contemporary data from the U.S. Department of Education reveal that each year more than 1 million youth drop out of school. This is equivalent to more than 7,000 youth dropping out each day of the school year (*Education Week*, 2010). The social, economic, and moral case for addressing the dropout problem in the United States was detailed in a report titled *Left Behind in America: The Nation's Dropout Crisis* (Center for Labor Market Studies, 2009). The report highlights that students who drop out represent a serious socioeconomic problem, given that most are undereducated and ill-equipped to fulfill the rapidly advancing technological needs of society's workforce. Moreover, societal costs include an enormous loss of taxable income because of unemployment and increased participation of dropouts in social welfare programs. Costs due to unemployment, welfare, and crime related to dropouts have been estimated at billions of dollars per year (Center for Labor Market Studies, 2009).

Clearly, the problem of students leaving school before completion is an important topic among education professionals (Rumberger, 2011). The purpose of this chapter is to provide school psychologists with background information essential to understanding high school dropout and interventions and provide a tiered framework for interventions intended to increase school completion among youth. A focus on enhancing school completion is aligned with the National Association of School Psychologists (NASP) *Model for Comprehensive and Integrated School Psychological Services* (NASP Practice Model; 2010) in that the chapter encompasses prevention-oriented services, the provision of universal as well as individualized support, and, depending on students' needs, both support and interventions in academic and social–emotional domains. Thus, the chapter emphasizes the NASP Practice Model domain of School-Wide Practices to Promote Learning.

Defining and Measuring School Dropout

Although there is general consensus that leaving school before graduation represents an important concern for our society, there is rarely agreement on how best to measure the number of students who do not finish their education. In general, a school dropout is defined as an individual who quits school before graduation and has not enrolled in or completed an educational equivalency program. As simple as this definition seems, we do not know exactly how many students drop out of school because most states have difficulty following individual students over time, and historically, schools have determined who is a dropout. The most recent No Child Left Behind regulations provide more guidance on how to count dropouts, stating that only those who earn a traditional high school degree at the end of their fourth year (or the following summer) should be considered a graduate (National Research Council & National Academy of Education, 2011).

The federal government has traditionally reported three types of dropout statistics: event (number of students who have dropped out within an academic year), cohort (follows the same group of students over time), and status (percentage of dropouts in a particular age range). Each of these methods can be used to answer different types of questions regarding school dropout. For example, cohort data are useful measures because they help schools to determine their promotion power, or the degree to which secondary students advance from grade to grade as expected within a given school or district. Unfortunately, cohort dropout rates can overestimate the total number of dropouts because they do not account for individuals who transfer in and out of the district and those who are expelled or incarcerated, or who are deceased (National Research Council & National Academy of Education, 2011). The status dropout rate, which represents the percentage of an age group in the civilian, noninstitutionalized population who were not enrolled in a high school program and had not received a high school diploma or obtained an equivalency certificate, avoids some of the aforementioned complications in reporting. For example, dropout rates of young people ages 16–24 have gradually declined between 1972 and 2010, from 15% to a low of 7.5% in 2004 (U.S. Department of Education, 2012). The status dropout rate remained relatively stable during the 1990s. However, millions of youth continue to not complete high school each year (*Education Week*, 2011). This statistic is helpful in providing a broad snapshot of how the United States is performing as a nation, but it does not help individual schools or districts to evaluate their effectiveness in facilitating school completion.

In more recent years, states have been encouraged to use aggregated cohort rates that are designed to account for individuals who transfer in and out of a cohort as well as those who are at the greatest risk of dropping out. The U.S. Department of Education (Seastrom et al., 2006) uses a metric called the *averaged freshman graduation* rate, a measure of the percentage of an incoming freshman class who graduate 4 years later. The averaged freshman graduation rate is the number of graduates with a regular diploma divided by the estimated count of incoming freshmen 4 years earlier, as reported through the National Center for Education Statistics Common Core of Data. The survey system is based on state education departments' annual administrative records. The following method is used to compute this estimate:

the sum of (a) the number of eighth graders 5 years earlier, (b) the number of ninth graders 4 years earlier, and (c) the number of 10th graders 3 years earlier is calculated, and then the total is divided by 3. Graduates include only those who earned regular diplomas or diplomas for advanced academic achievement (e.g., honors diploma), as defined by the state or jurisdiction. More information on measures of student progress and persistence can be found in the summary prepared by the Intercultural Development Research Association (2012). The U.S. Department of Education (2013) provides the averaged freshman graduation rate for public high school students for each of the states. Providing such information at the state, county, and local school levels enhances transparency and also provides further comparative data to inform policy and prevention efforts in schools across the country.

This demonstration of three different methods for counting dropouts illustrates the wide degree of variation that exists across studies and reports. Furthermore, the lack of consistency or agreement about how to estimate school completion rates has led to difficulties in comparing rates across states or districts, determining whether schools are meeting accountability standards, and evaluating the relative effectiveness of prevention and intervention programs. It is important that school psychologists understand each of these calculation methods to inform their efforts to provide systems-level assistance to schools and districts regarding the impact of school policies and dropout prevention efforts.

Demographic Characteristics

Despite the different methods used to measure school dropout, it is clear that in the United States some groups of students are at higher risk for dropping out, particularly students who come from backgrounds of low socioeconomic status (i.e., those who are Hispanic, African American, or Native American) and students with disabilities. Dropout rates among Hispanic youth remain much higher than other ethnic groups, although the rate has declined in last few years from 30% in 1998 to 24% in 2004 to 15% in 2010 (U.S. Department of Education, 2012). Higher dropout rates among recent Hispanic immigrants partially account for the elevated rates. For example, 44% of Hispanic 16- to 24-year-olds who were born outside the United States were not enrolled in school and had not earned a certificate of high school completion, a rate more than double the rates for first- or second-generation Hispanic youth born in this country and approximately six times the rate for non-Hispanic immigrant populations (7.4%; National Center for Education Statistics, 2002). These data reflecting the dropout rates among immigrant and minority youth further reveal the importance of multicultural competence among school psychologists working to promote graduation among all groups of students.

Historical and Contemporary Approaches in School Dropout Scholarship

Extensive reviews of the dropout literature have identified numerous variables associated with the likelihood of dropout and completion (Rumberger, 2011). Several categorizations of variables related to dropout and completion have been offered (see Table 6.1). Variables may be classified according to amenability to intervention, proximity to students, and so forth.

Recently, attention has turned to addressing questions of "why" or "how" by attempting to articulate multidimensional models to explain the process influencing students' decisions to drop out instead of descriptions of correlates. These models also suggest developmental pathways to dropout that involve family expectations and involvement, early school difficulties, poor peer relations, lack of school engagement, drug use, and cumulative family stress (e.g., Evans & DiBenedetto, 1990; Finn, 1989). Moreover, only some of the risk factors for dropping out of high school are characteristics of the students while many others are characteristics of the schools these students attend or their family's origin (see Table 6.1). Dropping out of school is at least partially a product of school practices that are ineffective in promoting the success of all students and of community pressures that fall disproportionately on underprivileged families. Early childhood experiences have been related to school adjustment and dropout or completion years later (e.g., Jimerson, Egeland, Sroufe, & Carlson, 2000). The confluence of empirical evidence illustrates that school dropout is best conceptualized as a process that occurs over many years.

BASIC CONSIDERATIONS

Understanding why students drop out of school may hold important clues to developing effective prevention and intervention approaches. However, identifying the causes of school dropout is very difficult because it is

Table 6.1. Categorizations of Variables Predictive of High School Dropout and Completion

Nonschool Correlates[a]		Status Variables[b]
Socioeconomic status	*Family process*	*Dropout*
Minority group status	Those with parental involvement	Low socioeconomic status
Gender	and monitoring less likely to drop	Reside in Southeastern and Western regions
Males slightly more likely to drop out	out	Students with disabilities
Community characteristics	*Student involvement with education*	English language learners
Dropout more likely in urban areas,	Dropouts have lower aspirations	From Native American, Hispanic, or African
Southeastern and Western	and achievement, less	American racial/ethnic backgrounds
regions, poorer communities,	participation, etc.	
single-parent families, non-	*Social conformity versus autonomy*	
Caucasian communities,	Dropouts have a higher need for	
communities with high rates of	autonomy, less conformity, less	
foreign-born individuals	accepting of authority, lower	
Household stress	church involvement, etc.	
Several stress variables related to	*Social deviance*	
dropout (e.g., single parenting,	Dropouts more likely to be	
substance abuse, mobility,	deviant (e.g., substance abuse,	
neighborhood violence)	conduct disorder, runaway)	
Taking adult roles	*Personality*	
Teen pregnancy, employment,	Dropouts have lower self-	
other adult responsibilities	esteem and confidence, more	
Social support for staying in school	impulsive, difficulty	
Valuing education by parents and	communicating, etc.	
peers reduces likelihood of dropout		
(e.g., parental expectations and		
achievement)		

Continued

Table 6.1. Continued

Alterable Variables[b] By context	Protective	Risk
Student	• Completes homework • Comes to class prepared • High locus of control • Good self-concept • Expectations for school completion	• High rates of absences • Behavior problems • Poor academic performance • Grade retention • Working
Family	• Academic support (e.g., help with homework) and motivational support (e.g., high expectations, talk to children about school) for learning • Parental monitoring	• Low educational expectations • Mobility • Permissive parenting styles
School	• Orderly school environments • Committed, caring teachers • Fair discipline policies	• Weak adult authority • Large school size (>1,000 students) • High pupil–teacher ratios • Few caring relationships between staff and students • Poor or uninteresting curricula • Low expectations and high rates of truancy

Push	Pull[c]	Proximal	Distal[d]
Conditions or events in the school environment that push kids out (e.g., disciplinary policies, grade retention)	Events or conditions outside of school that pull kids away (e.g., caring for a family member, having to get a job)	School attendance and behavior	Family background, early school experiences
	Demographic risk variables Socioeconomic status, disability or English learner status, race/ethnicity, etc.	*Functional risk[e]* Attendance, behavior, academic performance, credits earned, low levels of participation, etc.	

Note. From "Jingle, Jangle and Conceptual Haziness: Evolution and Future Directions of the Engagement Construct" (pp. 3–19), by A. L. Reschly and S. L. Christenson, 2012, in S. L. Christenson, A. L. Reschly, and C. Wylie (Eds.), *Handbook of Research on Student Engagement*, New York, NY: Springer. Copyright 2012 by Springer. Adapted with permission. [a]Rosenthal (1998). [b]Reschly and Christenson (2006b). [c]Jordan, McPartland, and Lara (1999). [d]Rumberger (1995). [e]Christenson (2008).

influenced by an array of factors related to both the individual student and the family, school, and community settings. Several conceptual models of processes and pathways to dropout have been proposed based on theory and research. Two of these models are described to illustrate the varied and complex processes that underlie dropout to aid school psychologists in their efforts to understand and address the dropout problem.

Finn's (1989) participation–identification model emphasizes that the students' active participation in school and in classroom activities and their feeling of identification with the school affected school completion. Identification with school referred to an internalized conception of belonging and valuing school success. From this perspective, lack of school engagement was central to the process of dropout. Engagement is composed of the student's behavior (involvement with classroom and school activities) and identification with school. The participation–identification model explains dropout in terms of a behavioral antecedent (lack of participation) and a psychological condition (lack of identification). It portrays dropping out as a process of disengagement over time rather than as a phenomenon that occurs in a single day or even a single school year. Participating in the school environment includes attending school, being prepared to work, and responding to the teacher's directions and questions. Other levels of participation include students' initiative to be involved in the classroom and school, participation in social and extracurricular activities, and involvement in decision making. This model has a developmental emphasis in that it reflects how participation in the school environment changes as students progress through school with greater opportunities to become involved in the nonacademic aspects of the school environment.

Evans and DiBenedetto (1990) provide four possible pathways that focus on the interaction of the individual and school factors that lead to early school withdrawal: (a) unexpected events, (b) long-term underlying problems, (c) early skill deficits, and (d) entry problems. Consistent with Finn (1989), these authors suggest that dropouts can be better identified by examining behaviors rather than searching for predetermined characteristics of students. Furthermore, they propose that dropping out may be characterized by a snowballing effect, wherein events that occurred earlier have an impact on subsequent events.

The first pathway emphasizes unexpected events such as a pregnancy or the death of a loved one occurring that subsequently influences school enrollment. Such unforeseen events may be more likely to appear in certain contexts and thus these events are not completely unexpected. Moreover, adaptation and coping following these unexpected events will also be influenced by the context and support available to the student. In regard to dropout prevention, the emphasis in this pathway is on immediate and appropriate interventions to assist students who experience such unexpected events.

The second pathway focuses on long-term underlying problems. Students on this pathway may not display any psychological difficulties, but over time as the student engages in deviant behaviors, the student perhaps begins to associate with maladjusted peers or possibly begins using drugs, which ultimately influences school enrollment. Clearly this pathway takes time as the student follows a deviant pathway that may ultimately lead to school dropout. Intervention strategies to avoid this pathway place a premium on the family context, including family monitoring, disciplinary strategies, and communication.

In the third pathway, a student may possess cognitive and/or social deficits that interact over time and influence school enrollment. For example a child who experiences early reading difficulties may subsequently lack the motivation to continue to struggle with reading. It is possible that the student may also be shy or may be actively neglected by peers because of the student's academic performance, and over time both dimensions may interact and result in early withdrawal. The emphasis for intervention is on identifying and remediating early cognitive and social deficits such that they are not exacerbated over the years and result in dropping out.

The fourth pathway recognizes that some children begin school with emotional and/or behavior problems. For instance, if a student is immature and overactive, this is likely to lead to problems with classroom behavior and possibly struggles with teachers, and over time the student may dislike school and may ultimately choose to withdraw. Again the emphasis is on this process occurring across time, and early intervention with students displaying emotional or behavioral problems would be essential in avoiding subsequent deleterious outcomes.

As illustrated in the above models, there are numerous pathways that potentially lead to school dropout, and thus it is particularly important to consider the multiple influences that may facilitate school completion. The models illustrate the combined impact of diverse influences across the individual's development (including social, behavioral, and academic considerations). A recent comprehensive synthesis (Rumberger, 2011) of the numerous influences on developmental trajectories resulting in high school dropout emphasizes two types of factors: (a) individual factors associated with students themselves, such as their attitudes, behaviors, school performance, and experiences, and (b) contextual factors found in students' families, schools, and communities. Because school policies and practices are the most amenable to change, a consideration of the school variables that contribute to school dropout is warranted.

According to Rumberger (2011), four types of school characteristics influence student performance, including the propensity to drop out or to graduate: (a) social composition, such as the characteristics of students attending the schools, particularly the socioeconomic composition of the student body; (b) structural characteristics, such as size, location, and school control (public traditional, public charter, private); (c) school resources, such as funding, teacher quality, and the student and teacher; and (d) policies and practices, such as the academic and social climate. For example, large school size is positively correlated with decreased attendance, lower grade point averages and standardized test scores, higher dropout rates, and higher crime compared with smaller schools serving similar children (Rumberger, 2011). Other school-related factors, such as high concentrations of low-achieving students and less qualified teachers, are also associated with higher dropout rates (National Research Council & National Academy of Education, 2011). School practices, such as tracking, grade retention, and high rates of suspension, have a negative correlation with school completion rates independent of the student's ability level (Jimerson, Anderson, & Whipple, 2002; Lee, Cornell, Gregory, & Fan, 2011).

Considering the multiple pathways that may lead to school dropout, there is an array of potential intervention strategies to facilitate the academic success of students who may be at risk of dropping out. It is important that school psychologists and other educational professionals are knowledgeable about the individual strengths and needs of youth and are prepared to provide appropriate prevention and interventions to promote their success. So, too, educational professionals must understand how school policies and practices may act as barriers to school completion. The warning signs for students at risk of dropping out are often apparent in elementary school, and thus there is an opportunity to provide early intervention that will promote school completion.

BEST PRACTICES IN PROMOTING SCHOOL COMPLETION

Contemporary science provides much information regarding the characteristics of students who drop out. However, there is a relative paucity of information regarding effective interventions to prevent school dropout and promote school completion. Recent efforts to evaluate dropout prevention programs through the Institute of Education Science What Works Clearinghouse (http://ies.ed.gov/NCEE/wwc/) underscore the paucity of rigorous evaluation of programs and practices, even those that are widespread. Reviews of the dropout prevention literature (Dynarski & Gleason, 2002; Lehr, Hansen, Sinclair, & Christenson, 2003) may guide school psychologists and other educators in their efforts to link current knowledge to school-based prevention and intervention practices. What follows provides a brief summary of important considerations emerging from these reviews:

- There are many dropout prevention programs and practices in use across the United States. However,

evaluations of these programs are either not conducted or are of poor methodological quality. Few replications have been published.
- Dropout is best conceptualized as a long-term process, not an instantaneous event. However, most interventions are administered at a middle or high school level after problems are severe.
- Students with disabilities drop out at an alarming rate. However, few interventions in the literature have targeted, or even included, these students.
- Programs to prevent school dropout often focus solely on changes within students. However, these programs do not address other important influences (e.g., peer groups, schools, families, or communities).
- Programs are often implemented as an add-on to existing services. However, isolated supplemental programs have a negligible impact on reducing dropout.
- School-wide restructuring programs designed to improve rates of school completion may be intuitively appealing. However, such system reform efforts are challenging and are often met with resistance, or they lack fundamental elements of successful systems change (e.g., leadership, consensus).
- Restructuring efforts that appear promising are those that focus on changing what happens within classrooms, specifically on improving curriculum and instruction. However, programs typically welcomed by districts are those that accommodate the district and/or school.

Given these limitations and caveats, dropout prevention strategies described in this chapter and elsewhere must be viewed as suggestions or tentative recommendations. Furthermore, given the lack of empirical data supporting these strategies, the need for ongoing program evaluation is paramount. On the basis of their extensive work, Christenson and Thurlow (2004) have outlined three fundamental guidelines for implementing school completion programs: understanding dropout as a process and not an event, attending to the role of context, and adopting a positive orientation toward school completion.

Understanding dropout as a process, not an event: As described previously, there are numerous pathways that may lead to the outcome of dropping out of school. School dropout is best understood as a gradual process of disengagement from school and learning. Prevention strategies should be designed to address dropout as a process, beginning early and continuing over time.

Attending to context: Implicit in this classic intervention research question is the realization that context does matter: what works, for whom, and under what conditions? A strategy or program that is effective with one group of students may not work with another. As noted by Dynarski and Gleason (2002), it is difficult to match programs to students; or in other words, any one program or strategy is limited in its capacity to address the needs of diverse groups of students. One size does not fit all.

Adopting a positive orientation toward school completion: Preventing dropout and promoting school completion appear to be similar goals. However, a positive orientation, one in which the goal is to promote skills, behaviors, and attitudes needed to be successful in school and life, is a categorically different orientation from that of preventing a negative outcome (i.e., dropout). Programs and strategies will benefit from a positive, competence-enhancement orientation rather than a deficit or dropout prevention viewpoint.

With these caveats in mind, there is emerging evidence that comprehensive, individualized, long-term interventions positively affect school completion among youth (Christenson & Thurlow, 2004). Other promising practices may include early reading interventions, tutoring, counseling, mentoring, caring environments and relationships, block scheduling (Lehr et al., 2003), and alternative middle school environments for younger students (e.g., smaller classes, greater personalization and support) and GED programs for older students (Dynarski & Gleason, 2002). Strategies and programs must be chosen based on student needs and context. Across interventions, however, a key component to promoting school completion is the systematic monitoring of all students for signs of disengagement, such as attendance and behavior problems, failing of courses, off track in terms of credits earned toward graduation, or problematic or few close relationships with peers and/or teachers, and then following up with those who are at risk (Reschly & Lovelace, 2010).

Tiered Framework of Intervention to Increase School Completion

Given the long-term developmental process that accompanies a student's decision to discontinue school, a multitiered model is a valuable heuristic in conceptualizing matching student needs with essential supports. Within this framework, a variety of interventions and resources can be applied to increase a student's engagement in school by addressing academic achievement, positive peer relationships, and motivation for learning. Conceptualizing the three-tiered model as levels of support facilitates decisions about adjusting services based on student need and intensity of assistance. As illustrated in the NASP Practice Model (NASP, 2010), use of the three-tiered model emphasizes developing the capacity of the system to meet the needs of all students. Comprehensive strategies at multiple levels are important in facilitating student success and school completion. The What Works Clearinghouse provides recommendations based on the extant empirical literature, including diagnostic, targeted, and school-wide interventions (see Table 6.2).

Tier 1

At Tier 1, the universal level of intervention, school psychologists can work with the leadership teams within their schools to ensure that all children experience the core components that promote school completion. Although some of these interventions might be delivered in a more intensive format at Tiers 2 and 3, these interventions provide a basic foundation for helping all children experience success in school. Drawing on the work of Reschly and Lovelace (2010) and the National Dropout Center (Schargel & Smink, 2001), among others, these components include high-quality early educational experiences, good instruction and opportunities for academic success, schools that provide a climate of caring and support and provide opportunities for student participation, and school policies that promote best practices.

Early Educational Experiences

The importance of early family and educational experiences as related to later outcomes for students, including school completion, cannot be overstated. There are enormous disparities in the educative value of home learning environments and access to high-quality preschool learning experiences for students before school entry and, not surprisingly, in students' own skills and behaviors at entry to primary school. The goal of early childhood intervention and preschool programs is to ensure that students have the requisite skills, attitudes, and behaviors necessary to succeed in school and, by extension, in life. Although early parent–child or child-focused interventions and high-quality preschool experiences are not a panacea for reducing risk of poor outcomes such as school dropout, there is evidence to support the use of early childhood programs and high-quality preschool experiences for improving

Table 6.2. Institute of Education Sciences Report: Recommended Strategies and Corresponding Levels of Empirical Support

Topic	Recommendation	Level of Evidence
Diagnostic	• *Utilize data systems that support a realistic diagnosis of the number of students who drop out and that help identify individual students at high risk of dropping out:* States, districts, and schools should develop comprehensive, longitudinal, student-level databases with unique IDs that, at a minimum, include data on student absences, grade retention, and low academic achievement. Data should be reviewed regularly, with a particular emphasis before the transitions to middle school and high school.	Low
Targeted interventions	• *Assign adult advocates to students at risk of dropping out:* Adult advocates should have an appropriate background and low caseloads, and be purposefully matched with students. Adequate training and support should be provided for advocates.	Moderate
	• *Provide academic support and enrichment to improve academic performance:* Help students to improve academic performance and reengage in school. This should be implemented in conjunction with other recommendations.	Moderate
	• *Implement programs to improve students' classroom behavior and social skills:* Students should establish attainable academic and behavioral goals and be recognized when they accomplish them. Schools can teach strategies to strengthen problem-solving and decision-making skills, and partner with community-based agencies to provide students with supports to address external factors affecting social and behavioral interactions.	Low
School-wide interventions	• *Personalize the learning environment and instructional process:* A personalized learning environment creates a sense of belonging and fosters a school climate where students and teachers get to know one another and can provide academic, social, and behavioral encouragement.	Moderate
	• *Provide rigorous and relevant instruction to better engage students in learning and provide the skills needed to graduate and to serve them after they leave school:* Engagement can be increased by providing students with the necessary skills to complete high school and by introducing students to postsecondary options.	Moderate

Note. From *Dropout Prevention: A Practice Guide* (NCEE 2008–4025), by M. Dynarski, L. Clarke, B. Cobb, J. Finn, R. Rumberger, and J. Smink, 2008, Washington, DC: National Center for Education Evaluation and Regional Assistance. Copyright 2008 by the National Center for Education Evaluation and Regional Assistance. Adapted with permission.

school and life outcomes of students who are at risk. Long-term studies of intensive early childhood intervention programs such as the Perry Preschool Program, the Abcedarian Project, and the Child–Parent Center preschool program have consistently demonstrated that participants attain more years of education and have higher rates of school completion than comparison groups (Ou & Reynolds, 2006). These programs focus on increasing school readiness by involving parents in their children's education, focusing on early literacy skills, and providing comprehensive services such as nutritional programs and healthcare. School psychologists who work within preschool programs can assist in developing structured ways for families to be involved (e.g., volunteering in the classroom), helping to implement high-quality early literacy programming, and supporting preschool teachers in meeting the needs of young children from high-risk settings through consultation and inservice training.

Opportunities for Academic Success and Individual Assistance

The academic expectations of schooling can be very challenging for some students, particularly those with learning disabilities or behavior problems, or who speak English as their second language. An important component in promoting school completion is ensuring that students have many opportunities to experience academic success. Although not specific to school completion, school psychologists can help ensure that best practices for academic success are being used in their own settings. For example, effective literacy programs incorporate screening of students at the beginning and middle of each school year to determine which students would benefit from additional support and in what areas (Gersten et al., 2009). School psychologists can assist teachers in the interpretation of their data and problem solve around strategies for addressing student needs. Often, teachers will incorporate differentiated instruction through the use of multiple academic centers. These types of settings require effective classroom management skills, and school psychologists can assist by consulting with teachers on how best to implement smooth transitions between centers.

At the secondary level, students who struggle academically are often discouraged, frustrated, and disengaged. Through intensive academic supports such as tutoring, homework assistance, and other enrichment programs (e.g., summer school, credit recovery options), these academic skill gaps can be addressed and students may become reengaged (Dynarski et al., 2008). School psychologists can assist with these efforts by developing partnerships with local businesses and service agencies that may be able to provide volunteers to serve as tutors and additional resources such as incentives, computer equipment, or financial support that can help offset the cost of implementing additional programming.

Climate of Caring and Support

Although students who drop out of school often have difficulty with academics, surveys and interviews conducted with dropouts reflect the consequence of the social and interpersonal aspects of schooling. These former students reported difficulty getting along with teachers and peers, believed they were treated unfairly, and felt that they did not belong at school (Reschly & Christenson, 2006a). More generally, positive relationships between students and teachers have been associated with engagement behaviors, attitudes, feelings of belonging, motivation, and achievement. At a systems level, opportunities for this type of personalized interaction can be enhanced by extended class periods, advisory periods, and smaller class sizes (Dynarski et al., 2008).

Similar results are found for peer relationships (Christenson & Anderson, 2002). A focus on creating climates that are experienced by students as caring and supportive is a common component of school completion strategies and programs.

Opportunities for Participation

As schools and communities have grown larger and our population more mobile, extracurricular activities and involvement in prosocial organizations have become more competitive and/or less accessible to all youth. Yet

these activities can play an important role in keeping students connected to other students and adults, schools, and their community. These activities also positively affect how students use their time, reducing opportunities for youth to engage in risky behaviors and opportunities for increased competence. In the positive youth development literature, constructive use of time and engagement in organized activities are associated with fewer risk behaviors, greater school engagement, and lower rates of school dropout (Barber, Abbott, Blomfield, & Eccles, 2009). There are numerous ways students can be engaged in activities, ranging from band and sports participation, special interest clubs, governance at schools, volunteer work, service learning, and cross-age tutoring programs. School psychologists can help build connections between schools and community organizations (e.g., Boys & Girls Club) to ensure that these programs are available and that students have access to them (e.g., resources, transportation).

Policies and Systems Change

Systems change is challenging, but it is a worthy undertaking. Within any given school there are a number of variables related to school dropout and completion, even after accounting for the characteristics of students who attend that school. School-level variables related to dropout include teacher quality, student–teacher ratios, teacher salaries, and school-wide attendance (Rumberger, 2011). When class sizes are too large and teachers are not adequately prepared, instruction and student–teacher relationships suffer. Furthermore, rigid policies related to suspension and expulsion are associated with lower academic achievement and higher rates of student disengagement and school dropout (American Psychological Association Zero Tolerance Task Force, 2008). School psychologists and educators may work together to incorporate professional development opportunities for teachers and to review policies that may disadvantage certain youth. Efforts to address school completion and the factors that create risk for school dropout across systems must include working together with families, schools, and the community.

Tier 2

At Tier 2, interventions are directed toward students who are at higher risk of dropping out because of academic failure and/or problematic behavior. As a result, ensuring that schools have methods for providing early academic and behavioral interventions can help prevent more intense challenges in the future. When students struggle in school, one of the beginning signs of disengagement is school truancy. It is important that schools develop strong policies and programs that focus on regular school attendance and support families in their efforts to prevent chronic truancy. Focused interventions can also be implemented at vulnerable points (e.g., transitions from one school to another) for students who are struggling.

Timely Academic and Behavioral Interventions

Early identification and intervention for both academic and behavioral problems are more effective than later identification and intervention (Donovan & Cross, 2002). The logic and evidence to support this statement are clear. However, day-to-day practice in many schools is not oriented to prevention or early intervention for academic or behavioral issues. Systemic use of problem-solving consultation (e.g., Kratochwill, 2008) is one method of service delivery oriented toward screening, early intervention, and evaluation that may be particularly useful for addressing academic and behavioral concerns in a timely manner. Early identification and intervention are of principal importance for increasing school completion because students who are at risk for dropping out often experience difficulties with academic coursework and/or behavior at school very early in their educational careers. These academic and behavioral difficulties affect motivation, effort, and learning of new material, which, in turn, further exacerbate academic and/or behavioral problems. School psychologists can work with problem-solving teams to prevent or remediate these difficulties before they become severe to increase the likelihood that students will successfully complete school. Additional targeted strategies for increasing school completion include pairing youth who are at risk for school dropout with peer mentors.

Adult Advocate Programs

Strategies that focus on pairing at-risk students with adult mentors are common elements in many dropout prevention programs (e.g., Check & Connect; Christenson, Stout, & Pohl, 2012). As described earlier, positive relationships with teachers and peers are associated with effort, belonging, and a host of other important outcomes (Christenson & Anderson, 2002). Check & Connect has been recognized in the What Works Clearinghouse as an intervention program that effectively promotes student engagement in school

and with learning. Student engagement in school is continuously assessed through regular tracking of tardies, truancies, and behavioral referrals. Through ongoing consultation with their monitors, at-risk students are given information and feedback about their educational progress, reminded frequently of the importance of staying in school, and helped to solve some of the problems that placed them at risk for dropping out. If a student's engagement in school falters, the program provides more services, including convening the family and school to problem solve barriers to school attendance, providing intensive academic instruction, and promoting extracurricular activities for the student.

This program has been replicated and expanded for use with elementary students at risk for dropout, implemented as a truancy intervention, and used as a service delivery model in combination with interventions to address aggressive behavior and literacy skill deficiencies. Furthermore, when students have difficulty with academics and few close relationships at school, holding power is greatly reduced. If, on the other hand, there are close relationships (e.g., someone knows the student is there, cares about the student and the student's future), even if a student struggles with academic work, the climate and those relationships help keep students connected and progressing in school. School psychologists can help develop and promote this type of programming to help increase the school engagement of youth who are at risk for school dropout.

Promoting Regular School Attendance

As might be expected, students who are engaged in school are more likely to attend regularly than those who are not. Unfortunately, when students do not see the value in school or do not perceive school as a safe and welcoming place, then they are more likely to be absent. Attendance, even in the very early grades, is a robust predictor of dropout and completion (Alexander, Entwisle, & Kabbani, 2001). If students are not present at school, they miss not only the academic instruction necessary for subsequent work but also the opportunity to interact with peers and teachers. In addition to promoting student engagement, the Check & Connect program is also effective as a truancy prevention program (Christenson et al., 2012). However, because there are many different reasons for why students are truant, it is important for schools to have multiple strategies to address this problem. Key elements to many truancy prevention programs include parent involvement, incentives for school attendance, consequences for truancy, community involvement, and ongoing comprehensive supports within the school environment that address multiple risk factors. Effective truancy prevention programs are available on the Office of Juvenile Justice and Delinquency Prevention website (http://www.ojjdp. gov/mpg/programTypesDescriptions.aspx). School psychologists can work with principals and district leaders to develop and implement these types of comprehensive programs across different grade levels to promote regular school attendance.

Facilitating Successful School Transitions

Many students struggle with transitions between school levels (e.g., middle to high school). Transitions often disrupt social and interpersonal relationships between students and teachers and students and peers, but they also tend to involve moving to larger, more impersonal school environments (Barber & Olsen, 2004). These transitions require additional attention and care to ensure students do not get lost or begin to disengage from school following a transition. School psychologists can help develop and facilitate transition programs that help students successfully navigate these school changes. Specifically, programming that helps students connect with their teachers and peers in these new settings are helpful in reducing the academic and behavioral problems that are sometimes seen after one of these major transitions.

Tier 3

At the most intensive programming level, Tier 3, interventions will focus on providing a broad range of services to students who are at the highest risk of school dropout. These types of services would likely be delivered in collaboration with community resources to ensure the broadest level of support, such as those seen in a wraparound model for students who are struggling because of emotional and/or behavioral problems. For some students, alternative programming may be the best option because the smaller, more flexible format may be better suited to the students' needs.

Availability of Help for Students' Personal Problems

There are a variety of reasons why students prematurely leave school. A number of these students have significant personal or family problems that interfere with their school performance and commitment. Many prevention programs offer counseling services for students who are at risk of dropping out of traditional schools and as part

of alternative schools and recovery programs. School psychologists should be cautious about implementing counseling services as stand-alone interventions. If there is an underlying mental health issue, such as social anxiety, that is interfering with a student's ability to attend and complete school, then providing an evidence-based intervention may prove helpful in reducing symptoms and allowing a student to return to school. However, counseling services only for the purpose of increasing school completion have not been shown to be successful. Often these services are supplemental or add-on services that are available as part of a comprehensive intervention strategy.

Alternative School Programming

Alternative schools have attempted to increase opportunities for success in a number of ways, sometimes using the traditional curriculum in smaller classes, offering acceleration and/or creating more challenging curricula, and sometimes allowing students to be self-directed and progress at their own pace (Dynarski & Gleason, 2002). For many students, key components of these alternative programs include opportunities for students to accrue credits through online programming, after-school programs, summer school, or some other format. When students are significantly behind in credits, they often become discouraged and consider dropping out as their only reasonable option. Through these credit recovery options they are able to accelerate their time to high school completion.

Postdropout Services

Educators, school psychologists, and policy makers must work together to provide postdropout follow-up services (e.g., keeping track of students who have left school, encouraging students to return to school). Diverse strategies are needed to address the different needs of these students, such as child care, vocational programming, or evening classes. In addition to flexible high school curricular options, there should be access and support for students to attend alternative schools or GED programs.

Incorporating Multiple Strategies

There are a number of ways to integrate these components in working with individual students and within classrooms and schools. Strategies within classrooms (e.g., peer tutoring) and at the school level (e.g., discipline policies), such as promoting relationships between teachers and students, ending the practices of tracking and grade retention, and enhancing school climate (e.g., effective management, clear leadership, discipline, no tolerance for bullying/victimization) are each important considerations when attempting to promote school completion. School psychologists can serve as the catalysts for system reform and engage other education professionals, because effective collaboration is essential to actualize systems-level changes within a school or district. School administrators, curriculum coordinators, guidance counselors, school psychologists, and others need to collaborate to support the implementation of programs that will promote school completion.

Many services to support student success would benefit from collaborative efforts with other community professionals. School psychologists can provide leadership in engaging and working with other community professionals to promote student success. For example, community mental health professionals, social workers with the welfare department, vocational and career professionals, and community college representatives are all potential partners and should be considered as resources that may contribute to supporting a student's school success. Likewise, school psychologists should facilitate communications with parents and actively engage them in promoting their child's success. Collaboration with all caring adults and talented professionals is important in addressing the needs of children and facilitating school completion.

SUMMARY

Students who drop out are likely to face numerous deleterious life outcomes. Dropout is a process that begins early and is influenced over time by individual and contextual factors. School psychologists can serve as catalysts for system reform, expand services to meet the needs of students at risk for dropout, and facilitate successful student outcomes. Furthermore, school psychologists can provide important leadership in engaging other professionals in the community (e.g., community mental health professionals, vocational professionals, community college representatives) to support all students' school success. Comprehensive strategies at multiple levels across the multitiered systems of support are important in promoting students' success and school completion.

The change in focus from preventing dropout to promoting school completion reflects a shift in thinking, allowing school psychologists to address this issue through a range of services, from targeted interventions to broad systemic reforms. From a systemic perspective, ensuring that schools have safe learning environments, promote policies that are consistent with school success,

and develop close collaborative ties with community resources and families can help to create a network that supports the needs of many students. Targeted interventions to increase school attendance, raise achievement, reduce challenging behaviors, and support positive peer relationships can be provided to those students who are most at risk for dropout. In addition, it is important to ensure that there are systematic efforts to engage in dropout recovery by providing practical alternatives such as flexible hours and individualized curricula in a smaller, supportive setting. Finally, we cannot overlook the aspects of the school environment that may contribute or serve as a barrier to academic success for students who are at risk for school failure. Thus, we must continue to research practices and policies within schools that promote the highest level of positive outcomes for all students.

AUTHOR NOTE

Disclosure. Amy Reschly has a financial interest in books she authored or coauthored that are referenced in this chapter.

REFERENCES

Alexander, K. L., Entwisle, D. R., & Kabbani, N. S. (2001). The dropout process in life course perspective: Early risk factors at home and school. *Teachers College Record, 103,* 760–822.

American Psychological Association Zero Tolerance Task Force. (2008). Are zero-tolerance polices effective in schools? An evidentiary review and recommendations. *American Psychologist, 63,* 852–862. doi:10.1037/0003-066X.63.9.852

Barber, B. K., & Olsen, J. A. (2004). Assessing the transitions to middle and high school. *Journal of Adolescent Research, 19,* 3–30. doi: 10.1177/0743558403258113

Barber, B. L., Abbott, B. D., Blomfield, C. J., & Eccles, J. S. (2009). Secrets of their success: Activity participation and positive youth development. In R. Gilman, E. S. Huebner, & M. J. Furlong (Eds.), *Handbook of positive psychology in schools* (pp. 273–289). New York, NY: Routledge.

Center for Labor Market Studies. (2009). *Left behind in America: The nation's dropout crisis.* Boston, MA: Author. Retrieved from http://hdl.handle.net/2047/d20000598

Christenson, S. L. (2008, January 22) *Engaging students with school: The essential dimension of dropout prevention programs* [Webinar]. Clemson, SC: National Dropout Prevention Center for Students with Disabilities.

Christenson, S. L., & Anderson, A. R. (2002). Commentary: The centrality of the learning context for students' academic enabler skills. *School Psychology Review, 31,* 378–393.

Christenson, S. L., Stout, K. E., & Pohl, A. (2012). *Check & Connect: A comprehensive student engagement intervention: Implementing with fidelity.* Minneapolis, MN: University of Minnesota, Institute on Community Integration.

Christenson, S. L., & Thurlow, M. L. (2004). School dropouts: Prevention, considerations, interventions, and challenges. *Current Directions in Psychological Science, 13,* 36–39.

Donovan, M. S., & Cross, C. T. (Eds.). (2002). *Minority students in special and gifted education.* Washington, DC: National Academies Press.

Dynarski, M., Clarke, L., Cobb, B., Finn, J., Rumberger, R., & Smink, J. (2008). *Dropout prevention: A practice guide* (NCEE 2008–4025). Washington, DC: National Center for Education Evaluation and Regional Assistance. Retrieved from http://ies.ed.gov/ncee/wwc

Dynarski, M., & Gleason, P. (2002). How can we help? What we have learned from recent federal dropout prevention evaluations. *Journal of Education for Students Placed at Risk, 7,* 43–69.

Education Week. (2010, June 10). "Diplomas count 2010: Graduation by the numbers: Putting data to work for student success." Retrieved from http://www.edweek.org/ew/toc/2010/06/10/index.html

Evans, I., & DiBenedetto, A. (1990). Pathways to school dropout: A conceptual model for early prevention. *Special Services in School, 6,* 63–80.

Finn, J. (1989). Withdrawing from school. *Review of Educational Research, 59,* 117–142.

Gersten, R., Compton, D., Connor, C. M., Dimino, J., Santoro, L., Linan-Thompson, S., & Tilly, W. D., III. (2009). *Assisting students struggling with reading: Response to intervention and multitier intervention for reading in the primary grades: A practice guide* (NCEE 2009-4045). Washington, DC: National Center for Education Evaluation and Regional Assistance. Retrieved from http://ies.ed.gov/ncee/wwc/publications/practiceguides/

Intercultural Development Research Association. (2012). *Types of dropout data defined.* San Antonio, TX: Author. Retrieved from http://www.idra.org/Attrition/Study/Types_of_Dropout_Data_Defined/

Jimerson, S. R., Anderson, G., & Whipple, A. (2002). Winning the battle and losing the war: Examining the relation between grade retention and dropping out of high school. *Psychology in the Schools, 39,* 441–457.

Jimerson, S. R., Egeland, B., Sroufe, L. A., & Carlson, E. (2000). A prospective longitudinal study of high school dropouts: Examining multiple predictors across development. *Journal of School Psychology, 38,* 525–549.

Jordan, W. J., McPartland, J. M., & Lara, J. (1999). Rethinking the causes of high school dropout. *The Prevention Researcher, 6,* 1–4.

Kratochwill, T. R. (2008). Best practices in school-based problem-solving consultation: Applications in prevention and intervention systems. In A. Thomas & J. Grimes (Eds.), *Best practices in school psychology V* (pp. 1673–1688). Bethesda, MD: National Association of School Psychologists.

Lee, T., Cornell, D., Gregory, A., & Fan, X. (2011). High suspension schools and dropout rates for Black and White students. *Education and Treatment of Children, 34,* 167–192.

Lehr, C. A., Hansen, A., Sinclair, M. F., & Christenson, S. L. (2003). An integrative review of data-based interventions: Moving beyond dropout toward school completion. *School Psychology Review, 32,* 342–364.

National Association of School Psychologists. (2010). *Model for comprehensive and integrated school psychological services.* Bethesda, MD: Author. Retrieved from http://www.nasponline.org/standards/2010standards/2_PracticeModel.pdf

National Center for Educational Statistics. (2002). *Dropout rates in the United States: 2000.* Washington, DC: U.S. Department of Education.

National Research Council & National Academy of Education. (2011). *High school dropout, graduation, and completion rates: Better data, better measures, better decisions.* Washington, DC: National Academies Press.

Ou, S-R., & Reynolds, A. J. (2006). Early childhood intervention and educational attainment: Age 22 findings from the Chicago Longitudinal Study. *Journal of Education for Students Placed at Risk, 11,* 175–198. doi:10.1207/s15327671espr1102_4

Reschly, A. L., & Christenson, S. L. (2006a). Prediction of dropout among students with mild disabilities: A case for the inclusion of student engagement variables. *Remedial and Special Education, 17,* 276–292.

Reschly, A., & Christenson, S. L. (2006b). Promoting school completion. In G. G. Bear & K. M. Minke (Eds.), *Children's needs III: Understanding and addressing the developmental needs of children.* Bethesda, MD: National Association of School Psychologists.

Reschly, A. L., & Christenson, S. L. (2012). Jingle, jangle, and conceptual haziness: Evolution and future directions of the engagement construct. In S. L. Christenson, A. L. Reschly, & C. Wylie (Eds.), *Handbook of research on student engagement.* New York, NY: Springer.

Reschly, A. L., & Lovelace, M. (2010). Promoting student engagement to enhance school completion: Information and strategies for educators. In A. S. Canter, L. Z. Paige, & S. Shaw (Eds.), *Helping children at home and at school III* (S2H23-1–S2H23-4). Bethesda, MD: National Association of School Psychologists.

Rosenthal, B. S. (1998). Non-school correlates of dropout: An integrative revire of the literature. *Children and Youth Services Review, 20,* 413–433.

Rumberger, R. W. (1995). Dropout of middle school: Amultilevel analysis of students and schools. *American Educational Research Journal, 32,* 583–625.

Rumberger, R. (2011). *Dropping out: Why students drop out of high school and what can be done about it.* Cambridge, MA: Harvard University Press.

Schargel, F. P., & Smink, J. (2001). *Strategies to help solve our school dropout problem.* Larchmont, NY: Eye on Education.

Seastrom, M., Chapman, C., Stillwell, R., McGrath, D., Peltola, P., Dinkes, R., & Xu, Z. (2006). *User's guide to computing high school graduation rates: Vol. 1. Review of current and proposed graduation indicators* (NCES 2006-604). Washington, DC: National Center for Education Statistics.

U.S. Department of Education. (2012). *NCES Common Core of Data: State dropout and completion data file, school year 2007–08; 2008–09.* Washington, DC: Author. Retrieved from http://nces.ed.gov/ccd/drpcompstatelvl.asp

U.S. Department of Education. (2013). *Public school graduates and dropouts from the Common Core of Data.* Washington, DC: Author. Retrieved from http://nces.ed.gov/pubs2013/2013309rev.pdf

7

Best Practices in Focused Monitoring of Special Education Results

W. Alan Coulter

Louisiana State University Health Science Center

OVERVIEW

Fulfilling the promise of special education is the intention of every school psychologist, advocate, and educator as they design and deliver services to children with disabilities and the children's families. When a decision is made that a child has a disability and needs special education, the intention of federal and state law is that special education confer an educational benefit (Goldschmidt, 2011). Monitoring the implementation and results of special education services is the most important aspect of determining compliance with federal and state law and a key aspect of child advocacy. In instances of noncompliance, federal and state agencies are required to compel correction and, in some instances, levy sanctions on local programs. The purpose of this chapter is to describe the concepts and processes by which the U.S. Office of Special Education Programs (OSEP) and states monitor their special education accountability system in a focused manner and to describe best practices for school psychologists.

Consistent with the domain of School-Wide Practices to Promote Learning in the National Association of School Psychologists (NASP) *Model for Comprehensive and Integrated School Psychological Services* (NASP, 2010), school psychologists must gain knowledge of how federal and state agencies monitor compliance with federal and state law and regulations in order to support and implement school-wide practices that promote learning. Maintenance of levels of service consistent with regulations requires that school psychologists use their knowledge of organizational development and systems theory in working with other educators. Further, maintaining compliance with state and federal law is an

ethical requirement for school psychologists, and advocacy for children and families begins with a thorough understanding of legal requirements. School psychologists should consult this chapter when evaluating or consulting on their school system's special education accountability design, when preparing for monitoring by the state or independent evaluator, and/or when participating in their state's accountability monitoring process. Compliance with federal and state regulations by the school administration of the setting in which a school psychologist works represents a minimum level of effective working conditions for providing ethical school psychological services.

OSEP and State Accountability

OSEP designs and implements monitoring processes to determine if states are accountable for compliance with federal law. OSEP determines the foci of federal monitoring (e.g., graduation, access to least restrictive environment) and promulgates guidance to states. OSEP requires each state to design an accountability system to examine implementation of special education, termed *general supervision*, compliant with federal and state law and monitor those implementation and monitoring processes to determine compliance. General supervision in the 2004 Individuals with Disabilities Education Act (IDEA) is synonymous with accountability. General supervision is defined by Congress as "including child find, effective monitoring, the use of resolution sessions, mediation, voluntary binding arbitration, and a system of transition services" Section (616(a)(3)(B)). States design a system of special education services and an accountability system to supervise implementation and results of those services. A state monitors local school systems using its particular system of general supervision to determine that implementation complies with federal law and regulations as well as state law. States modify their monitoring processes to mirror what OSEP determines as foci for monitoring. Local school systems often develop self-monitoring processes, in which school psychologists often play a key role, based on their state's monitoring process. In this manner, OSEP's process and foci for monitoring cascade to local levels as a generally consistent means of determining accountability and compliance with federal and state law.

OSEP Requirements: Accountability and Monitoring

According to the Merriam-Webster website (http://www.merriam-webster.com), *accountability* is defined as "the state of being accountable; liability to be called on to render an account; the obligation to bear the consequences for failure to perform as expected; accountableness." Monitoring is a process defined as "the systematic process of collecting, analyzing and using information to track a programme's progress toward reaching its objectives and to guide management decisions" (UNITE, 2013). Accountability and monitoring have been central to the general supervision of special education and a potential means for producing improvement since its inception at the national level in 1977 (Wolf, 2003). Yet, until recently, the processes by which federal and state monitoring occur have changed very little in 35 years.

Prior to the reauthorization of IDEA, traditional monitoring of more than 755 specific special education requirements was criticized as ineffective in ensuring full implementation of law (i.e., compliance; President's Commission on Excellence in Special Education, 2002). To address the criticism and provide for improvements in general supervision and accountability, Congress, in 2004, modified federal law to shift the emphasis in monitoring to a focused approach.

> The primary focus of Federal and State monitoring activities described in paragraph (1) shall be on (A) improving educational results and functional outcomes for all children with disabilities; and (B) ensuring that States meet the program requirements under this part, with a particular emphasis on those requirements that are most closely related to improving educational results for children with disabilities." (IDEA, Section 616)

Focused monitoring is a process that purposefully selects priority areas to examine for compliance and results while not specifically examining other areas for compliance to maximize limited resources, emphasize important requirements, and increase the probability of improved results (National Center for Special Education Accountability Monitoring, 2005). The emphasis on results by Congress was driven by its assertion, "the implementation of this title has been impeded by low expectations, and an insufficient focus on applying replicable research on proven methods of teaching and learning for children with disabilities" (IDEA, Section 601(c)(4)). This assertion was based, in part, on an analysis of national data of graduation rates for students with disabilities over time.

The U.S. Department of Education (2011) reported a gap of more than 19 percentage points in graduation rates between students with disabilities and students without disabilities. From 1991 to 2011 OSEP has reported annual diploma rates hovering at 50% (OSEP, 2011). Congress viewed monitoring for compliance with federal special education law as a method for improving results and ensuring compliance. However, Congress also intended that the focus of such monitoring be on those indicators most closely related to results (i.e., access to less restrictive environments, lower complaints, better achievement, and graduation).

The goal of an accountability model using focused monitoring is to orient a state's system of general supervision toward those requirements, indicators, and activities that continuously improve results for children with disabilities and their families while maintaining compliance with federal law. Focused monitoring uses data analyses of selected indicators related to a small number of carefully chosen priorities to significantly shape the accountability process. The focused monitoring of accountability for general supervision generates written reports of findings and includes intervention to correct noncompliance and support improved results.

OSEP monitors states' compliance in two ways: (a) status determination of state performance plans and annual performance reports and (b) on-site visits to state education agencies designed to be intensive monitoring. To sharpen the focus for states on special education results, IDEA requires states to develop a state performance plan organized around 20 indicators for school-age children with disabilities (U.S. Department of Education, 2013; see Table 7.1) and to file to OSEP and the public. OSEP annually monitors each state's annual performance report to determine compliance with IDEA and issues a report of findings and a determination of

Table 7.1. Required OSEP Indicators for School-Age Programs in State Performance Plans: Part B Measurement Indicators

B-1. Graduation (diploma)	B-11. Timely Evaluations
B-2. Dropout	B-12. Transition From C to B
B-3. Achievement (participation and performance)	B-13. Transition Preparation
B-4. Suspension/Expulsion	B-14. Postschool Outcomes
B-5. Educational Environment	B-15. Corrected Noncompliance
B-6. Preschool Environment	B-16. Resolved Complaints
B-7. Preschool Outcomes	B-17. Due Process
B-8. Parent Involvement	B-18. Resolutions
B-9. Disproportionality	B-19. Mediations
B-10. Specific Disproportionality	B-20. Timely Data

Note. Based on information from OSEP (2013a).

status as required by IDEA. Each state is determined by OSEP to be in one of four categories: "meets requirements," "needs assistance," "needs intervention," or "needs significant intervention." Similarly, states are required to determine the status of each local special education program.

OSEP also intensively monitors states on a cyclical basis with an on-site visit. During this visit, OSEP follows a protocol designed to examine the state accountability system and the state's capacity to detect and correct noncompliance in local programs. Whenever a state special education program is monitored, OSEP posts its written report of findings on its website. The most recent date of an OSEP report for a state reflects the last time that state received a formal on-site monitoring visit. School psychologists can review the most recent federal monitoring report for their state at the following website: http://www.ed.gov/policy/speced/guid/idea/monitor/osep-monitoring-reports.html.

In 2012, OSEP announced a significant refinement in its approach to focused monitoring. Results Driven Accountability draws significantly more attention to student performance measures, especially student achievement (see http://www2.ed.gov/about/offices/list/osers/osep/rda/index.html of the Office of Special Education Program's Results Driven Accountability home page). Results Driven Accountability continues a shift by OSEP away from hundreds of specific requirements toward compliance indicators that measure through aggregated data the effectiveness of special education programs by how well students with disabilities perform in academic curricula. While all states will be monitored via their submissions of annual performance reports, OSEP has constructed a methodology for selecting a limited number of low-performing states for more intensive on-site monitoring (National Center on Educational Outcomes, 2012).

OSEP Accountability and School Psychologists

School psychologists should be concerned about how OSEP monitors a state's accountability for implementing federal and state law because this federal agency holds the principal responsibility for ensuring implementation of IDEA. School psychologists, as advocates for students with disabilities and their families, should be informed about both the state's status as determined by OSEP and any concerns or citations that OSEP has reported. Any citation by OSEP requires corrective action, and the specific actions can affect local policies and practices. Corrective actions may be imposed on local programs and frequently require the active participation of school psychologists to achieve a satisfactory result. Further, because OSEP's methods of monitoring are frequently mirrored in state monitoring practices, familiarity with OSEP's findings informs the practicing school psychologist about the priorities or focus that his or her state will adopt. The principle agent for change and improvement in special education is a state's accountability system and its monitoring processes. In order to improve their own practice and the services that are delivered, school psychologists should be well informed about how compliance is determined, their state's plans for improvement, how corrective actions are implemented, and when sanctions on local programs have become necessary.

BASIC CONSIDERATIONS

School psychologists interested in monitoring compliance with special education requirements and how it affects their practice should be familiar with basic principles of focused monitoring, which include systems perspective, limited scope of intensive investigation, and extensive use of data. Given that consideration of compliance has shifted away from many indicators and variables to those assumed most likely to affect results (i.e., Results Driven Accountability), school psychologists should be attuned to how compliance monitoring supports greater implementation of evidence-based practices keyed to student performance. A state's monitoring process and its public reports offer an important perspective on the functioning of local systems.

Student Advocacy Versus Systems-Level Monitoring

In considering principles of focused monitoring, it is important to note a key difference between advocacy for an individual student and monitoring at a systems level. Typically, school psychologists, parents, and others advocate for services to meet the unique needs of an individual student. Disputes or conflicts regarding the scope or adequacy of services for an individual student are managed through dispute resolution and due process and may result in child-specific corrections. However, in federal and state monitoring, it is the local system's response to large numbers of students with disabilities and their performance that is at the heart of the examination of compliance and improved results. The level of analysis is typically directed at summative numbers about students and their performance, comparing students with disabilities to students without disabilities, and to comparable local systems or state averages. Hence, school psychologists should adopt a systems-level perspective when considering monitoring processes.

Emphasis on Limited Priority Indicators

A second basic principle of focused monitoring is a limited scope of investigation of a priority area as measured by a few selected indicators. Time and other resources are always limited, so focus on a priority or key priorities is essential in order to ensure that an in-depth investigation of compliance and performance is efficiently accomplished. Rather than examine all the more than 755 requirements of IDEA, as was typical in traditional monitoring, focused monitoring devotes intensive attention to only those requirements closely related to the selected priority area. Traditional variables used in compliance monitoring have been criticized as having little effect on improving student performance indicators (Luster & Coulter, 2012). Results Driven Accountability, as described by OSEP, narrows the monitoring focus to student performance

indicators. Each priority area is investigated by following a protocol that specifies both methods (data analyses, document examination, interviews, observations) and explicit compliance standards. States typically post the monitoring protocols that they use so that local programs can use these in self-monitoring. For example, in 2011–2012, Illinois selected school systems based on the magnitude of the gap in reading achievement between students with and without disabilities. Monitoring was principally focused on the design and delivery of special education instruction in reading.

Emphasis on Data and Student Outcomes

Focused monitoring places a heavy emphasis on the use of data in making decisions about what to monitor and which local systems in the state should receive the most attention for monitoring. As previously noted, Congress was concerned about the poor results of special education when it reauthorized IDEA. OSEP determined that poor results should be defined as student performance on achievement, graduation, and post-school outcomes (OSEP, 2012a). Arguably, other measures could have been chosen but OSEP, following a basic principle of focused monitoring, used data to select what to monitor (i.e., student performance).

Given limited resources, focused monitoring uses data to select which states (OSEP's national process) or local school systems (state level) will be monitored most intensively. For example, while national graduation data for 2011 show a gap of 19 percentage points between typical students and students with disabilities, data disaggregated by state show a wide range of differences across states (TIERS Group, 2013). Graduation is considered one of the most important indicators of school success (OSEP, 2012a). (See Figure 7.1.)

Using the graduation data by state in focused monitoring would lead OSEP to select states where the graduation gap was greatest or where a matrix similar to that proposed for student performance (National Center on Special Education Outcomes, 2012) indicated greatest potential noncompliance. Similarly, states could disaggregate graduation data by school district to select those with the poorest performance.

BEST PRACTICES IN MONITORING SPECIAL EDUCATION RESULTS

Focused monitoring of general supervision, whether of a state or local system, examines compliance with what is required by IDEA and what is reasonably assumed to

Figure 7.1. 2010–2011 Top 10 and Bottom 10 States' Gap in Special Education Graduation Rate

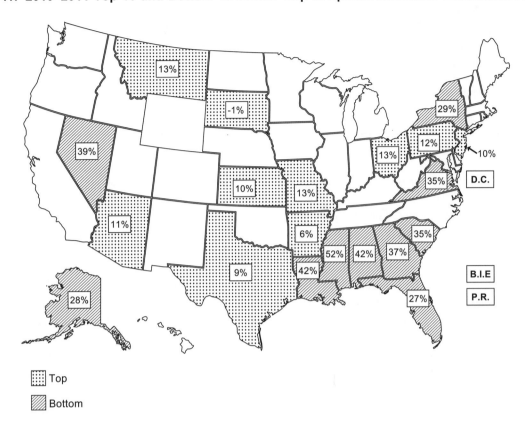

Note. From *Did You Know?*, by TIERS Group, 2013, Baton Rouge, LA: Human Development Center. Copyright 2013 by Human Development Center. Reproduced with permission.

produce improvements. Seven components, at a minimum, frame a system of general supervision for special education: (a) a state performance plan with goals and rigorous targets; (b) policies, procedures, and effective implementation; (c) data on processes and results; (d) targeted technical assistance and professional development; (e) effective dispute resolution; (f) integrated on-site and off-site compliance monitoring activities; and (g) improvement and corrective action, including sanctions and incentives (National Center for Special Education Accountability Monitoring, 2007). When school psychologists are familiar with all seven components, they are able to identify opportunities at a local level where best practices can be applied.

Component 1: State Performance Plan With Goals and Rigorous Targets

IDEA requires each state to develop a state performance plan using a uniform format for articulating goals and measurable and rigorous annual targets for improvement of special education services and results (OSEP, 2012a, 2012b). The state performance plan requires a

description of how the state will monitor implementation of IDEA and a minimum of 20 indicators for school-age children with disabilities (ages 3–21; see Table 7.1) and 14 indicators for infants and toddlers with disabilities (birth through age 2; see Table 7.2). Each indicator must report baseline for 2005 and set measurable and rigorous annual targets through 2013–2014. While Congress conceived in 2004 that a state performance plan would be for 5 years, OSEP in 2012 extended the current state performance plan process for 9 years because reauthorization has not occurred.

Congress required that state performance plans be developed with stakeholder input, reviewed and approved by the U.S. Department of Education, disseminated to the public, and posted on each state's website. Stakeholders are an important aspect in the operation of general supervision and, specifically, in the development and review of the state performance plan. A state's stakeholder group provides a purposive sample of all stakeholders with communities of interest in the effective implementation of IDEA. Given that stakeholders have had input into the measurable targets of the state performance plan, their other critical role is in

Table 7.2. Required OSEP Indicators for Infant/Toddler Programs in State Performance Plans: Part C Measurement Indicators

C-1. Infants/Toddlers Receiving Services	C-8. Exit Part C With Transition
C-2. Infants/Toddlers With Services in Natural Environments	C-9. Corrected Noncompliance
C-3. Infants/Toddlers With Improved Outcomes	C-10. Written Complaints
C-4. Families Report Services Have Helped	C-11. Due Process in Time Lines
C-5. Birth to 1 Identified Compared	C-12. Resolutions
C-6. Birth Through 2 Compared	C-13. Mediations
C-7. Timely Evaluations	C-14. Timely Data

Note. Based on information from OSEP (2013b).

the designation of priority areas to focus the monitoring process. The work of stakeholders helps refine the priorities for focused monitoring. For example, stakeholders in Louisiana, given a very low diploma rate for students with disabilities (40.6%), determined that local systems with a poor record of graduating students with disabilities (Indicator B-1) be selected for focused monitoring. Similarly, Georgia used student performance (Indicator B-3) to select local systems. Most states use no more than two or three priorities (indicators) for focused monitoring while monitoring all other OSEP indicators in a cursory manner.

States are required to monitor the performance of all local programs each year, report annually each program's performance compared to the state's annual target, and designate the status of each local program. Parallel to OSEP's designation of states, local program status must be designated by a state each year as "(a) meets requirements, (b) needs assistance, (c) needs intervention, or (d) needs substantial intervention" (OSEP, 2012a, p. 1). Each state must develop criteria by which the status designations are made and develop plans to provide assistance. The state's annual performance report must document the performance of the state and each local program on each of the OSEP indicators using data and the results of its focused monitoring activities (see Component 6).

Best practices for school psychology: School psychologists should be critical observers, if not participants, in a state's stakeholder process. School psychologists should examine the following in evaluating a state's use of a stakeholder group: (a) Does the stakeholder group include parents, advocates, service providers, administrators, advocates, policy makers, and individuals with disabilities? (b) Does the stakeholder group meet at least annually? (c) Does the stakeholder group participate in setting rigorous targets? (d) Does the stakeholder group annually review the results of focused monitoring? (e) Does the school psychology association directly play a role in the state stakeholder group?

School psychologists should be familiar with the baseline and targets for each state performance plan indicator, especially those directly related to student performance. Following the publication of the annual performance report, school psychologists should analyze the state's performance to determine where relatively poor performance has occurred. School psychologists should note the number of local school systems that their state determines as "needs intervention" or "needs substantial intervention." Local school systems with these designations likely are challenged in adequately meeting the needs of students with disabilities and their families. Such systems are in need of a variety of services and the expertise of school psychologists who bring a broad knowledge base in students with special needs, curricula, instruction, and behavior management.

Component 2: Policies, Procedures, and Effective Implementation

State agencies are required to establish policies and procedures at the state level to ensure effective implementation of IDEA. This is a fundamental organizational requirement that provides structures for implementation of special education law (Wright & Wright, 2005). State activities following these policies and procedures include approving local applications or grants for the expenditure of federal funds; requiring signed assurances; and approving local policies, procedures, and forms. State law, regulations, and policies have been used as a tool for traditional compliance monitoring of federal regulations since the passage of federal special education legislation in 1975 (Levinson, 2012; Wright & Wright, 2005). However, in recent years, state policies and procedures have been modified to require specific practices, such as research-based instruction in reading, lending support to implementation of best practices.

Best practices for school psychology: Knowledge of state policies and procedures is the fundamental basis for advocacy for students with disabilities and their families. School psychologists should be familiar with the particular process by which state and local policies and procedures are developed and approved. School psychologists and state school psychology associations can play a significant role in shaping policies and procedures in support of best practices, including implementation of multitiered systems of support.

Component 3: Data on Processes and Results

Data are critical to accountability and monitoring and raise the potential that limited resources for monitoring can have an effect on compliance and on improving results by selecting programs most in need of intensive monitoring. Since the initiation of a federal role in special education, some data have been required, reported, and used to determine needs and effectiveness of programs (IDEA, Section 618). These data, typically referred to as 618 data, have formed the basis for the *Annual Report to Congress on the Implementation of the Individuals with Disabilities Education Act*. Since 1975, requirements for the type and extensiveness of data have increased with each reauthorization of the special education law as Congress has recognized the value of data in determining how the Act is being implemented. The most recent annual report to Congress presents more than 400 pages of data on special education (U.S. Department of Education, 2011).

Essential to the focused monitoring of results are data that can be disaggregated by a local program or school. Many aspects of special education services, including the prevalence of disabilities, settings where students receive services, and results of services (diploma, dropout), are depicted in 618 data. However, these data are especially useful when comparisons are made to show relative performance of states or local programs. Almost all states now publicly report education data, including special education data, by local program (Data Quality Campaign, 2012a). Standard profiles (e.g., formats for reporting data) facilitate comparison of programs and can be rank ordered to detect low system performance. Using data to depict variance in performance is one of the critical concepts in focusing a state or local program's monitoring. By selecting programs that are performing least well on the indicator, focused monitoring can closely examine the degree of compliance and need for correction and improvement.

With the increasing importance of data as a basis for determining compliance with federal law (i.e., No Child Left Behind, IDEA), procedures for data verification are integral to monitoring accountability. States and local programs have developed audit routines and software that identify key entry errors to increase the accuracy of submitted data. The importance of accurate and timely data is further emphasized in state performance plans with a specific OSEP indicator (B-20 or C-14) that reports on the accuracy and timeliness of reporting required data.

Best practices for school psychology: School psychologists are accustomed to collecting and using data in evaluating individual student performance. School psychologists are also familiar with measurement error and inaccuracy in reporting. School psychologists can take a lead role in training and supporting local programs and schools in using data to identify specific areas to improve student performance (Allison & Besser, 2010; McNulty & Besser, 2011). School psychologists can measure implementation integrity of data action teams and provide coaching to improve functioning (Telfer, 2011).

School psychologists should increase their knowledge and expertise with federally required data on local program performance because these are used in states' focused monitoring processes. When evaluating a state's use of data in focused monitoring processes, school psychologists should consider: (a) Is the state's database an individual student record system (i.e., can data be disaggregated at the individual child level)? (b) Is the data system capable of analyzing trends in data over time? (c) Are data on local programs compared to the state's rigorous targets? (d) Are data analyzed to determine progress of students with disabilities? (e) Are data verified as a routine procedure within the state's focused monitoring process?

School psychologists can assist state and local programs in routines to verify data accuracy. Best practices exist for data depiction (Cairo, 2013; Few, 2004). Depicting data so that results and implications are easily understood by educators and the public (e.g., use of maps, line graphs) promotes educator and public awareness of data about local program performance.

Component 4: Targeted Technical Assistance and Professional Development

Given that states adopt a restricted focus toward rigorous targets, limited resources for technical assistance and professional development can be directed toward specific needs indicators in local programs with the greatest need. A state's annual performance report identifies the outcomes of targeted professional development and technical assistance and links these to system performance (i.e., approaching or meeting rigorous targets) on state performance plan indicators. When local programs evidence a need for improvement in knowledge and skills, OSEP requires the state to identify sources for technical assistance and professional development.

Comprehensive System of Personnel Development plans describe strategies for how the state will address the identified needs related to professional development and preservice preparation to ensure that all personnel who work with children with disabilities have the skills and knowledge necessary to meet the needs. Strategies include (a) working with institutions of higher education and other entities that prepare personnel to ensure that those institutions develop the capacity to support quality professional development programs that meet state and local needs as well as (b) those enhancing the ability of current personnel to use scientifically research-based approaches to meet the needs of children. Recently, states have integrated plans to improve special education personnel with plans for other personnel as part of waiver applications to the U.S. Department of Education.

Best practices for school psychology: School psychologists should carefully monitor the provision of technical assistance and professional development. OSEP supports the State Personnel Development Network School (http://www.signetwork.org) that lists all funded projects and provides resources useful in developing technical assistance for local programs. School psychologists can increase expertise in professional development by gaining familiarity with current national standards (Learning Forward, 2011) and with contemporary methods of delivery that emphasize improvement based on measurable indications of program improvement (e.g., state performance plan indicators).

Component 5: Effective Dispute Resolution

With the assistance of legal counsel, states will institute an effective dispute resolution system that includes a number of components (Zirkel & McGuire, 2010). These procedures ensure that parental concerns be resolved in a timely manner and provide a safety net for families in protecting individual rights. State agencies are required to encourage mediation and preappeal processes, allowing for resolution of parental concerns through less invasive procedures and to reduce the number of requests for impartial due process hearings.

Data are collected and analyzed to identify issues and areas of dispute emerging from all phases of the dispute resolution process. The Center for Appropriate Dispute Resolution in Special Education routinely analyzes data by state and reports on trends (http://www.directionservice.org/cadre/). State performance plans include four OSEP indicators related to dispute resolution (B-16, B-17, B-18, and B-19). These data inform all areas of general supervision including the identification of priority areas, on-site investigations, and needed training and dissemination of promising practices.

Best practices for school psychology: School psychologists may serve as mediators in a state's dispute resolution process. Advocacy for individual students is based on a thorough understanding of mediation, due process, and alternative methods of resolution. School psychologists can access data about their state's dispute resolution system and analyses of issues and trends from the state's website. These data may indicate significant gaps and a need for professional advocacy. State school psychology associations may want to consult with advocacy groups and other professional associations to address issues raised by trends in dispute resolution data.

Component 6: Integrated On-Site and Off-Site Compliance Monitoring Activities

Compliance monitoring has changed significantly since the reauthorization of IDEA. Prior to 2004, it was not uncommon to erroneously assume that an on-site monitoring visit of local programs composed the entirety of a state's system of general supervision. However, the system of general supervision is intended to ensure appropriate implementation of IDEA and protection of the rights of children with disabilities and their families (de facto noncompliance). Hence, multiple methods of focused monitoring within a system of general supervision are critical in ensuring effective implementation of federal law.

As described in this chapter, monitoring is incorporated in all aspects of general supervision. The intensity of monitoring is determined, in part, on the local program's performance on the state performance plan and indicators of the focus priority. The least intensive monitoring, applied to all local programs, is an off-site inquiry about the accuracy of reported data. States have developed multiple inquiry methods that do not require an on-site visit, including surveys, submission of documents, and telephone interviews. The most intensive degree of monitoring is an on-site focused monitoring visit investigating compliance and current practices in the priority area selected by the state. On-site visits are limited to instances where the method to collect needed monitoring data is an on-site visit. Using multiple monitoring methods varying in intensity preserves limited resources for when on-site focused monitoring is needed.

Off-Site Focused Monitoring

Focused monitoring may be limited to analysis of data within a priority area followed by inquiry before a decision is reached to conduct on-site focused monitoring because more information is needed. Analysis of the data might suggest inaccuracy of the data, noncompliance, and/or a need for program improvement. Reference to the monitoring protocol for the priority area helps frame the inquiry. If the questions are answered in ways that do not suggest noncompliance (meet compliance standards) or a need for improvement, then the focused monitoring is completed. When answers to the multiple inquiry method suggest either noncompliance and/or a need for improvement, an on-site visit may be conducted.

Many states implement a self-review process whereby local agencies/programs are required to complete a comprehensive self-review on a cyclical basis to ensure the state has adequate data and information regarding local agencies' provision of appropriate services and supervision and monitoring of their programs and services. Local agencies are provided with clear procedures and guidelines to act in accordance with the self-review requirements including (a) conducting a review of their policies, procedures, and practices with an emphasis on the extent to which results are being achieved as measured on state performance plan indicators; (b) determining areas of noncompliance and/or need for improvement; (c) developing corrective actions addressing all areas of noncompliance and areas needing improvement; and (d) reporting the results of implementation of these plans to the state agency.

An array of methods is used by state agencies to validate local self-review processes, results, and progress on corrective actions. Validation methods range from designing contacts specifically designed to collect data about the most recent self-review to incorporating self-review validation activities into other existing on-site activities conducted by the state (e.g., school or program improvement visits). A state's use of a self-review can be an important monitoring process within its accountability system, ensure compliance with all requirements of law, and serve as an important means of obtaining data and information about local performance when using a focused monitoring process.

On-Site Focused Monitoring

School psychologists may have been involved in general supervision by serving as a member or leader of an on-site monitoring team. On-site focused monitoring typically includes three phases: previsit, on-site visit, and postvisit/reporting. States routinely disseminate monitoring protocols used in the on-site visit to assist local programs in complying with accountability requirements. On-site focused monitoring is planned and initiated when the state hypothesizes, based on data analyses and other information obtained off-site, that noncompliance exists within a priority area or areas. The decision to conduct on-site focused monitoring is primarily based on the need to collect additional data and information where the program is geographically located in order to prove or disprove a hypothesis of noncompliance.

Monitoring Teams

Members and leaders of on-site focused monitoring teams, including school psychologists, typically receive training in the state's monitoring processes as frequently as needed, but at least once a year. Often team members and leaders benefit from on-site or off-site technical assistance or coaching as well.

Previsit Phase

Planning for the on-site visit includes the analysis of disaggregated data (selected state performance plan indicators and other data) leading to the development of hypotheses of noncompliance or poor performance and a preliminary plan for on-site investigation. Given the installation of longitudinal data systems in every state, trend data are becoming increasingly available (Data Quality Campaign, 2012b). Other information that should be examined include other available statewide data; parent survey data; complaints filed against the district; results of due process hearings; previous state and/or federal monitoring findings; local policies, procedures, and applications for funds; and self-assessment or self-review documents.

The team examining these data should carefully analyze or disaggregate the data to determine what may be affecting performance. For example, the on-site team might determine if specific disability groups, schools, age groupings, and/or regions of the district appear to account for any negative differences between the local data regarding students with disabilities and state data, performance targets, and/or local data regarding nondisabled students.

Based upon this analysis, and augmented by the analysis of any other available information, specific hypotheses of noncompliance and factors affecting performance are developed. A number of hypotheses can flow from this consideration (e.g., time to write reports, difficulty in scheduling team for Individual Family Service Plan meeting). Noncompliance, when determined from the on-site investigation, may fully or partly account for poor student results in the priority area.

After hypotheses of noncompliance are developed, the team develops a preliminary plan to investigate and thereby validate or disprove the hypotheses. Specific sites within a program (school buildings or service locations) to be visited are determined, as are the techniques to be used. Techniques used by the team are typically indicated by the monitoring protocol and may include review of documents in child records, interviews, classroom and building observations, and focus groups or public meetings. Selection of sites, records, determination of staff, parents and students to interview, and observations of students and classrooms may be randomly or purposefully selected as part of the preliminary plan for the on-site visit.

On-Site Visit

Given the preliminary plan for the visit, the monitoring team typically meets with the administrator of the program and explains the purpose and working agenda for the visit. On-site focused monitoring teams meet nightly to review preliminary results, refine the hypotheses if necessary, and decide on the most promising activities for the next day. Further, it is sometimes necessary for teams to add a hypothesis of noncompliance during the visit in response to information uncovered through monitoring activities. On-site activities can also result in eliminating a hypothesis during the course of the visit if preliminary results indicate that the hypothesis is not promising to detect noncompliance.

Postvisit and Reporting Phase

Typically, a postvisit staffing is conducted to draw final conclusions by reviewing the evidence supporting or negating noncompliance with statutory and regulatory requirements and by identifying areas for program improvement, leading to better results for children with disabilities. A monitoring report should be issued by the state agency or program within its prescribed time lines.

Best practices for school psychology: Two roles can be played by school psychologists. They should actively solicit opportunities to participate in on-site monitoring activities. These events often provide a school psychologist with the occasion to inform educators about the contributions school psychology can make to accountability and advocacy for students. Focused monitoring is a dynamic construct subject to changes in governmental policies and legal intervention. School psychologists should remain vigilant to changes at federal and state levels. Just as Results Driven Accountability has sharply narrowed OSEP's focus in examining compliance with IDEA, future policy changes could significantly alter what is monitored by OSEP and states.

School psychologists can assist a local program in developing a self-monitoring process or preparing for on-site monitoring. There are a number of critical considerations: (a) As state monitoring protocols increasingly focus on student performance measures as indicators, are current practices of schools aligned with what could be monitored? (b) Does the local program have efficient methods to monitor compliance in priority areas and detect problems? (c) Does the local program have established methods to engage training and technical assistance to make corrections before state monitoring occurs?

For many school psychologists the only experience with accountability they may have is an on-site monitoring visit by a state or federal team. Clearly, focused monitoring of a system of general supervision is much more than the on-site visit. When examining a state's implementation of monitoring in order to support a local program it is important to ask: (a) Is the ranking of local programs providing special education services used in evaluating the state's implementation of IDEA? (b) How are local programs not selected for on-site monitoring accountable in some manner for the requirements of IDEA? (c) How are local programs selected for on-site monitoring? (d) Do written standards exist to determine compliance for requirements related to each requirement to be monitored? (e) Are all members of the on-site monitoring team well trained to implement their responsibilities? (f) What methods does the on-site monitoring team use to collect information and data about possible noncompliance? (g) Is the written report of monitoring findings made available to the public?

School psychologists should be members of on-site monitoring teams. Their knowledge, skills, and advocacy make them effective on-site team members. In considering whether or not to be a member of an on-site monitoring team, the school psychologist should consider: (a) Is training provided to all members so that all are prepared to function in their roles? (b) Are there methods used to establish the reliability of team members to collect data? (c) What evaluation data have been collected about the on-site monitoring process? (d) Have recommended or needed improvements been made to the on-site monitoring process?

Component 7: Improvement and Corrective Action Planning

An effective accountability system for the implementation of IDEA must ensure that any noncompliance is identified and corrected in a timely manner. There is a logical, systematic relationship between focused monitoring and corrective actions; that is, evidence-based solutions are linked to identified problems based on data-based investigations. Corrective actions ensure a change in behavior that fully corrects the noncompliance, improves child and student performance, and is evidenced by improvement in data. OSEP requires states to correct all identified noncompliance within 1 year. This time requirement typically requires the state to frame noncompliance in a very specific manner amenable to correction within 1 year.

States must ensure that high-quality professional development and technical assistance (as described in Component 4) are available to assist in the development and implementation of corrective action plans, if necessary. The implementation of the activities in corrective action plans is typically tracked by the state and local agencies/programs in terms of effort expended within time lines. States are mandated to intervene quickly and effectively if tracking indicates a lack of progress in implementation.

State-level intervention may take a variety of forms. Examples include provision of information by state or regional technical assistance centers or other dissemination entities, provision of assistance to low-performing programs by high-performing programs (e.g. through mentoring programs), publication of successful and effective practices, and provision of new funding for initiatives such as improvement grants from state discretionary funds.

After the corrective action planning has been fully implemented, the state conducts a follow-up monitoring to ascertain whether the areas of noncompliance have been corrected. Successful completion of a corrective action plan means that the state or local program/ agency has corrected the noncompliance or made significant progress toward reaching the required target in a priority area. This is verified through data analysis,

documentation of evidence of change, and other methods selected by the state.

Sanctions

When correction of noncompliance does not occur, the state agency must implement sanctions. There should be a range of sanctions available to states that provide an effective means of ensuring compliance and efficient improvement of results. Sanctions will typically be imposed in two instances: (a) when noncompliance has been identified and has not been remedied through successful implementation of the corrective action planning and (b) for local programs, when performance targets are not met by the identified deadline in the corrective action or improvement plan. Sanctions will be different for failure to implement corrective actions than for failure to meet the targets of a state performance plan.

The decision about what sanction is most likely to be effective is made by the state after an analysis of the corrective action plan or improvement plan, previous monitoring reports, determination of any unique characteristics of the state program, and assessment of the local agency's willingness to fix the identified problem. Sanctions should be selected based on likelihood of effectiveness and are a part of a state's focused monitoring procedures.

Incentives

Seemingly logical, but infrequently used, incentives are provided by states to encourage improvement in local program results. While federal and state funds are routinely provided to support special education services, rarely are funds provided as incentives for documented needs or improved performance. States can provide supports, including effective building of infrastructure in poorly functioning local programs/districts (without defeating the monitoring/enforcement process). It is advisable that incentives be provided to states or local programs when they meet or exceed the targets in the performance plan. In providing the incentive, the state agency would specify which target the state or local program has met. The state will need to validate the data on which the judgment of good performance is based. Incentives may include, but are not limited to, (a) provision of money to the state or local agency for mentoring other agencies and telling the story of how they achieved success; (b) a letter, publicly disseminated, to the governor of the state or local superintendent or governing board, praising the accomplishments of the agency; (c) a plaque or other recognition provided to high-performing states; and (d) national or local press releases or other publicity.

Best practices for school psychology: School psychologists know that focused monitoring of accountability for general supervision has little value without effective correction of noncompliance. Certainly, if the intent of Congress to fully implement the law is to be achieved, then any noncompliance detected by focused monitoring must be corrected. When examining the corrective actions and sanctions within a state, the school psychologist might ask: (a) Do corrective action plans identify the evidence of correction that must be demonstrated by the local program? (b) Does the corrective action plan specify activities that will lead to evidence of improvement on the selection indicator, that is, the data that initially indicated problems in implementation of IDEA? (c) Does the state monitor the implementation of the corrective actions plan? (d) Are the results of implementation of the corrective action plan verified by an on-site visit? (e) Does a range of sanctions exist for violations or failure to implement the corrective action plan?

School psychologists have long recognized the value of rewards or incentives in improving human performance and the cautions in their use guided by the professional literature. In examining a state's use of incentives, school psychologists should ask: (a) Are programs reported to be performing at or above the state's targets recognized or provided some form of incentive? (b) Does a range of incentives exist to support good program performance? (c) Has the effectiveness of incentives been evaluated?

SUMMARY

School psychologists can implement their advocacy for children and families by becoming informed and involved in monitoring. Accountability for effective and meaningful implementation of IDEA is fundamental to achieving the intent of Congress in providing "that all children with disabilities have available to them a free appropriate public education that emphasizes special education and related services designed to meet their unique needs and prepare them for further education, employment, and independent living" (IDEA, Section 601 14 (D)(1)(a)). Focused monitoring, a system of accountability for general supervision, encouraging continuous improvement in results, and ensuring that implementation of law is enforced are responsibilities of the U.S. Department of Education, states, and local programs, with the ongoing advice and oversight of monitoring stakeholders. Focused monitoring is a coherent set of principles and components that school psychologists can utilize to advocate for better results for children with disabilities and their families.

REFERENCES

Allison, E., & Besser, L. (2010). *Data teams: The big picture.* Englewood, CO: Lead + Learn Press.

Cairo, A. (2013). *The functional art: An introduction to information graphics and visualization.* Berkeley, CA: New Riders.

Center for Appropriate Dispute Resolution in Special Education. (2012). *Trends in dispute resolution under the Individuals with Disabilities Education Act (IDEA).* Eugene, OR: Author. Retrieved from http://www.directionservice.org/cadre/pdf/FINAL_TrendsInDRUnderIDEA_5Oct12.pdf

Data Quality Campaign. (2012a). *10 essential elements of a state longitudinal data system.* Washington, DC: Author. Retrieved from http://www.dataqualitycampaign.org/build/elements/

Data Quality Campaign. (2012b). *10 state actions to ensure data use.* Washington, DC: Author. Retrieved from http://www.dataqualitycampaign.org/build/actions/

Few, S. (2004). *Show me the numbers: Designing tables and graphs to enlighten.* Oakland, CA: Analytics Press.

Goldschmidt, S. (2011). A new idea for special education law: Resolving the "appropriate" educational benefit circuit split and ensuring a meaningful education for students with disabilities. *Catholic University Law Review, 60,* 749, 1–34.

Learning Forward. (2011). *Standards for professional learning.* Oxford, OH: Author. Retrieved from http://www.nsdc.org/standards/index.cfm

Levinson, N. (2012). *Boosting the quality and efficiency of special education.* Washington, DC: Fordham Institute.

Luster, J. N., & Coulter, W. A. (2012, November). *The story of IDEA compliance and results.* Paper presented at the annual meeting of Mid-South Educational Research Association. Lexington, KY. Retrieved from http://www.hdc.lsuhsc.edu/tiers/publications/TheStoryofIDEAComplianceandResults.pdf

McNulty, B., & Besser, L. (2011). *Leaders make it happen: An administrator's guide to data teams.* Englewood, CO: Lead + Learn Press.

National Association of School Psychologists. (2010). *Model for comprehensive and integrated school psychological services.* Bethesda, MD: Author. Retrieved from http://www.nasponline.org/standards/2010standards/2_PracticeModel.pdf

National Center for Special Education Accountability Monitoring. (2005). *Accountability and advocacy: Concepts of focused monitoring.* Unpublished working paper. New Orleans, LA: Author. Retrieved from http://www.accountabilitydata.org/

National Center for Special Education Accountability Monitoring. (2007). *Developing and implementing an effective system of general supervision: Part B.* New Orleans, LA: Author. Retrieved from http://www.accountabilitydata.org/General%20Supervision/1%20EffectiveGeneralSupervisionfinal%201-16-07.pdf

National Center on Educational Outcomes. (2012). *Sample approaches for using assessment data as part of a results driven accountability system.* Minneapolis, MN: Author. Retrieved from http://www2.ed.gov/about/offices/list/osers/osep/rda/sample-approaches.pdf

Office of Special Education Programs. (2011). *Thirtieth annual report to Congress on the implementation of the Individuals with Disabilities Education Act, Parts B and C, 2008*. Washington, DC: Author. Retrieved from http://www2.ed.gov/about/reports/annual/osep/index.html

Office of Special Education Programs. (2012a). *Part B state performance report and annual performance report* (OMB Number 1820-0624). Washington, DC: Author. Retrieved from http://www2.ed.gov/fund/data/report/idea/partbspap/allyears.html?exp=2

Office of Special Education Programs. (2012b). *Part C state performance report and annual performance report* (OMB Number 1820-0578). Washington, DC: Author. Retrieved from http://www2.ed.gov/fund/data/report/idea/partcspap/allyears.html

Office of Special Education Programs. (2013a). *Part B indicators*. Washington, DC: Author. Retrieved from http://nichcy.org/laws/idea/partb/indicators-partb

Office of Special Education Programs. (2013b). *Part C indicators*. Washington, DC: Author. Retrieved from http://www2.ed.gov/policy/speced/guid/idea/capr/crelreqdoc.doc

President's Commission on Excellence in Special Education. (2002). *A new era: Revitalizing special education for children and their families*. Washington, DC: U.S. Government Printing Office. Retrieved from http://education.ucf.edu/mirc/Research/President's%20Commission%20on%20Excellence%20in%20Special%20Education.pdf

Telfer, D. M. (2011). *Moving your numbers: Five districts share how they used assessment and accountability to increase performance for students with disabilities as part of district-wide improvement*. Minneapolis, MN: University of Minnesota, National Center on Educational Outcomes.

TIERS Group. (2013). *Did you know?* Baton Rouge, LA: Human Development Center. Retrieved from http://www.hdc.lsuhsc.edu/tiers/Did.php

UNITE. (2013). *What is monitoring and evaluation?* New York, NY: Author.

U.S. Department of Education. (2011). *Provisional data file: SY2010–11 four-year regulatory adjusted cohort graduation rates*. Washington, DC: Author. Retrieved from http://www2.ed.gov/documents/press-releases/state-2010-11-graduation-rate-data.pdf

U.S. Department of Education. (2013). *Part B state performance plans (SPP) letters and annual performance report (APR) letters*. Washington, DC: Author. Retrieved from http://www2.ed.gov/fund/data/report/idea/partbspap/allyears.html

Wolf, P. J. (2003). Sisyphean tasks. *Education Next, 3*, 24–31.

Wright, P., & Wright, P. (2005). *Wrightslaw: Special education law* (2nd ed.). Hartfield, VA: Harbor House Law Press.

Zirkel, P., & McGuire, B. (2010). A roadmap to legal dispute resolution for students with disabilities. *Journal of Special Education Leadership, 23*, 100–112. Retrieved from http://www.directionservice.org/cadre/pdf/Roadmap%20to%20Legal%20Dispute%20Resolution%20for%20Students%20with%20Disabilities.pdf

8 Best Practices in Supporting the Education of Students With Severe and Low Incidence Disabilities

Franci Crepeau-Hobson
University of Colorado Denver

OVERVIEW

Low-incidence disabilities (LID) are defined in the 2004 Individuals with Disabilities Education Act (IDEA) as "a visual or hearing impairment, or simultaneous visual and hearing impairments; a significant cognitive impairment; or any impairment for which a small number of personnel with highly specialized skills and knowledge are needed in order for children with that impairment to receive early intervention services or a free appropriate public education" (20 U.S.C. 1400 § 673(a)(3)). Students with severe incidence disabilities and LID clearly comprise a small, heterogeneous population and school personnel charged with meeting their academic and social–emotional needs in the school setting are confronted with a daunting task.

Because these disabilities are by definition relatively rare—fewer than 2% of students enrolled in public schools in 2009–2010 (Office of Special Education and Rehabilitative Services, 2012)—they present unique challenges to schools, particularly in relation to the amount and intensity of services required to support them in general education settings. Under the No Child Left Behind (NCLB) legislation, all students, including those with LID, are required to be educated in a milieu of high standards (Campbell, Reilly, & Henley, 2008; Jackson, 2005), and, consequently, school psychologists are confronted with the difficult responsibilities of identifying and assessing these students, as well as participating in the planning and implementation of school programs and services within this context (Cole & Shapiro, 2005). Access, participation, and progress in

the general education curriculum depend on the development and implementation of high quality Individualized Educational Programs (IEPs) that blend specialized curriculum within that of the general education setting (Jackson, 2005). School psychologists and other IEP team members must maintain high expectations of students with LID for achievement of state- and district-level standards (Wehmeyer, Sands, Knowlton, & Kozleski, 2002) and approach the IEP development process as such.

Although students with disabilities are classified by individual categories under IDEA, in many instances common curriculum and instructional practices can be applied. Students with severe complex healthcare issues, multiple disabilities, and significant developmental delays require critical and highly specialized assessment as well as approaches that offer greater intensities of supports to enable school and community inclusion (Jackson, 2005: Rude et al., 2005). In addition to a greater degree of support, students who have physical or sensory impairments (blind, deaf, deaf-blind, or cerebral palsy) may also need curriculum or teaching approaches that are highly specialized as well (Jackson, 2005). Further, these students generally need supports or services from specialized service providers (e.g., audiologists for youth who are deaf; orientation and mobility specialists for students who are blind; Jackson, 2005) and, in some situations, assistive technology activities and materials (Rude et al., 2005) or specialized environments (Jackson, 2005). All of these must be routinely available as part the student's educational service plan (Rude et al., 2005).

Consistent with the National Association of School Psychologists (NASP) *Model for Comprehensive and Integrated School Psychological Services* (NASP 2010), supporting students with LID is most effectively done within the context of a multitiered system of supports. This approach is intended to provide greater access to the general education curriculum for all students, including those with disabilities, by addressing the needs of students who present with a range of academic, social, emotional, physical, and behavioral difficulties (Sailor, 2008–2009). Students with LID will often need more intensive interventions than only those available at the universal level. Thus, inclusion of these students in the general education environment with integrated Tier 2 and Tier 3 supports and interventions is recommended. This way, all services, including academic, social, and emotional learning and positive behavior supports, and related services, are integrated into the general education environment so that school psychologists and other related service professionals can have the greatest impact on as many students as possible (Freeman et al., 2006; Sailor, 2008–2009). In this model, not only do students with LID have greater access to the general curriculum, but they are also included in the regular classroom more fully and in more meaningful ways so that they have opportunities for interactions and friendships with classmates with and without disabilities (Sailor, 2008–2009).

The purpose of this chapter is twofold. First, the broad area of psychoeducational assessment of students with LID is addressed, including assessment of cognitive ability, as well as assessment for the purposes of transition planning. Second, educational planning for students with LID is detailed with the concept of data-based decision making in mind. While this chapter is aligned specifically with the NASP Practice Model domain School-Wide Practices to Promote Learning (NASP, 2010), virtually all aspects of the NASP Practice Model inform support of and service delivery to students with LID as outlined below.

BASIC CONSIDERATIONS

The severity of the impairments that result from LID requires the use of alternative forms of assessment, intervention, and inclusion that are not necessarily specific to the type of disability. It is the common thread of disability severity that drives nontraditional school psychological practice with these individuals (Cole & Shapiro, 2005). Customary approaches used with students with high incidence disabilities, such as specific learning disabilities and speech/language impairments, are insufficient and often ineffective with students with LID. Consequently, school psychology practitioners must be willing to maintain flexibility and think outside of the box when working with these students and, at times, also seek specialized knowledge and skills, especially in the area of assessment (Cole & Shapiro, 2005).

Effectively supporting students with LID requires closer collaboration with common adults such as parents, classroom teachers, special educators, and paraprofessionals, as well as other related services personnel (Giangreco, 2000). Although all school psychologists are trained to work with students with high incidence disabilities such as learning disabilities, most school psychology training programs do not offer any specialized training in working with students with LID (Cole & Shapiro, 2005). Thus, it is also critical that school psychologists work closely with those special educational professionals who specialize in working with children with LID to help plan the student's curriculum and pedagogies. It is this collaboration, as well as a shared commitment among general and special education personnel on IEP teams, that is key to developing and implementing a plan that will ensure access, participation, and progress in the general education curriculum (Nolet & McLaughlin, 2005).

Often, students with LID require an educational team that is up to double in size what is typical (Giangreco, 2000). For example, in addition to the typical multidisciplinary team members of classroom teacher, special education teacher, and school psychologist, a student with LID may also have an orientation and mobility specialist, audiologist, vision specialist, occupational therapist, deaf educator, and adaptive physical education teacher participating in educational planning. Although all these invested participants can bring fresh ideas, important knowledge, relevant skills, and valuable resources to the table, it can make for a challenging proposition when it comes to educational planning and programming for the student and coordinating the contributions of different team members. In this context, it is the school psychologists who must be prepared to facilitate the integration of data from these various team members and facilitate data-driven discussions to ensure the development of an educational program that is student centered and can be implemented efficiently and effectively.

Given that various team members working with LID often have roles and functions that overlap, Giangreco (2000) suggests a number of considerations for IEP teams, such as determining the specific disciplines and related service providers that are necessary for the student to receive an appropriate education; establishing what each team member should be doing; deciding how and when team members will collaborate; and identifying how services from multiple service providers will be coordinated. Making these decisions during the planning process can help prevent problems for students and families such as gaps in services, unnecessary overlaps in services, or contradictory service recommendations offered by professionals from various disciplines. Because the student with LID generally has a larger IEP team than students with high incidence disabilities, delineating which team member has primary responsibility for each of the student's IEP goals in writing is a helpful first step (Janney & Snell, 2011). Once clear roles and responsibilities have been determined, the team should decide how decisions about instruction and supports will be made and communicated, as well as who will assume team leadership roles, and how this sizeable team will function as a unit (Janney & Snell, 2011). Highly trained in consultation and collaboration, school psychologists can take the lead in facilitating these processes.

BEST PRACTICES IN LOW-INCIDENCE DISABILITIES

Supporting students with LID begins with a valid and strategic assessment of needs. However, assessing students with severe physical, communicative, or sensory impairments is not an easy proposition. There are limited numbers of standardized tests that are valid for use with children with LID, particularly measures of cognitive ability. In addition, school psychologists often have limited experience with both assessment and provision of direct interventions to these students (Bowen & Ferrell, 2003; Cole & Shapiro, 2005).

Assessment

School psychologists must keep in mind that formal assessment practices are often impractical or not useful for specific program-planning purposes and of questionable validity for students with LID (Bowen & Ferrell, 2003). For example, many psychoeducatonal tests used by school psychologists require functional sensory and motor systems. Moreover, standardized tests are generally not sensitive to small changes in functional behavior that is characteristic of individuals with LID. Further, because an individual's disability label may

mask his or her actual ability, it is important that assessment information be comprehensive and accurate to identify strengths as well as needs (Cole & Shapiro, 2005). Given the numerous shortcomings of standardized tests with this population, school psychologists must adapt their assessment practices when working with students with LID and generally not rely on the use of traditional methods of evaluation.

Because of the aforementioned limitations of many formal assessment tools, reliance on other measures such as interviews and rating scales is considered a valuable and necessary supplement for gathering relevant data about a student with LID (Cole & Shapiro, 2005). Often, third-party informants serve as the primary informational sources for individuals with LID, especially those with severe communication/language impairments, when developing educational and/or rehabilitation programs. Third-party measures can provide a wealth of information related to the strengths and needs with students with LID. However, despite the usefulness of third-party informant data, too much reliance on such sources may be risky in that the information provided may not necessarily yield valid and reliable results (Lohrmann-O'Rourke & Browder, 1998). For example, third-party respondents may base their responses about the student's capabilities on their experiences with the student in contexts in which their presence actually influences the student's behavior. The ways in which the student behaves in such situations may actually be considerably better or worse than in similar situations with other individuals who are familiar with the student.

In order to get an accurate estimate of the child's current level of functioning, assessment must include a variety of instruments and informants across settings. School psychologists and other team members should utilize a combined approach that is composed of direct observation and both professional expertise and parental knowledge of the student. These data should be obtained through formal and informal assessment strategies (Campbell et al., 2008). Best practice methods include observation, interviewing, functional behavioral assessment, and rating scales (Cole & Shapiro, 2005) and assess both the functional and educational implications of cognitive, sensory, and motor impairments. Areas that should be assessed include daily living skills, functional skills/academics, social skills, and recreational skills, as these are essential components of the educational programs of students with LID (Browder, 2001). In some situations, assessment of cognitive ability may also be appropriate. The best assessment method accounts for differences in experiences of children with LID, seeks to obtain the best possible performance, and recognizes the limitations of traditional, formal assessment practices that have primarily been developed with samples of children who do not have severe impairments.

Transition Assessment

Transition assessment is a dynamic process intended to identify strengths, interests, and needs in relation to educational, vocational, and postschool environments. Transition assessment for secondary students with LID should include informal transitional assessment procedures, including direct observations of the individual in a variety of real-world situations and environmental analyses (Test & Mazotti, 2011), as well as formal assessment tools. Formal assessments can provide information about a range of skills in a number of areas that may include adaptive behavior, intelligence, aptitude, achievement, personality, interests, and preferences (Test & Mazotti, 2011). Conversely, systematic informal assessments in the community contexts where daily choices are made can be extremely helpful as they may yield more reliable information than formal transition assessment practices or third-party informants. In addition, these tools often provide the most useful information for program planning purposes for these students (Lohrmann-O'Rourke & Browder, 1998). For example, ecological assessment is an informal assessment method that involves referencing behaviors against what is required for independent functioning in authentic contexts and yields practical and functional instructional targets (Jackson, 2005).

Vocational assessments should also be completed with secondary students with LID, as vocational rehabilitation counselors are increasingly using data from these assessments to determine needed services for individuals with developmental and other LID (Lohrmann-O'Rourke & Browder, 1998). Vocational assessments should provide information about the strengths, career interests, and training needs of the student with LID. Vocational assessment should include assessment of the individual with LID and both current and future environments. Individual vocational assessment tools include ecological assessment, standardized and informal checklists and questionnaires, behavior observation, performance or work samples, interviews, and situational assessments (Neubert, 2012). As with other assessments, some adaptations may be necessary when using particular vocational assessment tools with students with LID in order to obtain meaningful data for

vocational planning. For many students with LID, work samples and situational assessments will likely yield the most meaningful information. Secondary course analyses, task and job analyses, and community assessments that examine adult services, community resources, and transportation options are all helpful tools for assessing the environmental domain (Neubert, 2012). Data from the various transition assessment tools can then be used to identify the best match between the individual student with LID and various environments.

Although many school psychologists lack training in the area of vocational assessment and most are not significantly involved in transition-related services, as data and assessment experts, school psychologists should participate in this process as members of the multidisciplinary team. At the very least, school psychologists should be knowledgeable about effective ways to assess vocational-related areas and they should be able to interpret assessment data through a vocational lens (Fives, 2008). For example, school psychologists can consider how a student's executive functioning, cognitive, sensory, or motor deficits might have an impact on the student's ability to complete certain types of tasks or to function in various occupational environments. School psychologists must also be able to incorporate vocationally relevant information into psychological reports and also learn about available resources that can be considered in vocational planning and will facilitate progress toward vocational goals (Fives, 2008). Further, as noted, many individuals with LID will need services from vocational rehabilitation or developmental disabilities systems after exiting the school system. For these students, it is important to ensure that required assessments for those resources are updated to determine eligibility for adult services. Often, it is the school psychologist who will assume responsibility for determining what and how assessment data will be collected as well as ensuring that this information is used for transition planning in IEP meetings.

Assessment of Cognitive Ability

In those situations where assessment of cognitive ability is deemed appropriate for a student with LID, the school psychologist is presented with a number of challenges. For example, school psychologists may have access only to published norm-referenced tests that provide little in the way of meaningful information that can be used for educational and treatment planning and programming (President's Commission on Excellence in Special Education, 2002). Children with significant motor, visual, hearing, or linguistic limitations are often unable to be comprehensively and accurately assessed utilizing most widely used cognitive assessments. The result is that a significant number of children with severe physical, communicative, or sensory impairments are currently assessed in ways that may underestimate their abilities, and their sensory deficits may be confused with cognitive deficits (Sattler, 2008). Thus, while these assessments can produce a comprehensive picture of intellectual functioning for most typically developing children, it is much more difficult to obtain a valid picture of overall cognitive functioning and to delineate relative strengths and weaknesses for children with LID. Consequently, assessment of cognitive ability in students with LID may require adjustments to standardized administration and/or the use of measurement tools developed specifically for use with individuals with that particular disability (Crepeau-Hobson & Vujeva, 2012).

Most standardized measures of cognitive functioning assess a range of visual, linguistic, and motor skills in order to generate a comprehensive representation of the child's intellectual functioning. Consequently, these assessments require that the examinee have adequate vision, hearing, language functioning, and visual–motor skills (Sattler, 2008). If a child lacks any of these essential skills, calculations of the Index Scores and Full Scale IQ could exclude relevant subtests that rely heavily on a particular modality or modifications such as nodding or pointing could be utilized to make the subtests accessible (Sattler, 2008). Suggested accommodations are listed in Table 8.1. However, school psychologists should interpret results with caution when standardized administration procedures have not been adhered to as little research has been conducted on the reliability and validity of these test scores. These results must be interpreted in the context of a broad body of evidence, including observational measures, interview data, and educational and developmental history, in order to best understand a child's level of functioning and in order to make appropriate placement and intervention decisions (Sattler, 2008).

There are some assessment tools that have been developed specifically for individuals with certain LID (e.g., blindness) that can provide a valid estimate of cognitive ability. Examples include the Intelligence Test for Visually Impaired Children (Dekker, 1993) and the Cognitive Test for the Blind (Dial et al., 1990). In addition, there are some cognitive ability tests that are minimally loaded in those modalities most affected by certain LID. For example, tests such as the Leiter International Performance Scale-Third Edition (Leiter-3), the Universal Nonverbal Intelligence Test, and the

Table 8.1. Adaptations to Standardized Tests and Test Administration for LID

Blind/Visually Impaired	Deaf/Hard of Hearing	Severe Language Disabilities	Physical Disabilities/Severe Motor Disabilities	Disabilities With Severe Language and Motor Impairment[a]
Administration of verbal subtests only; use of verbally mediated measures of visual–spatial skills; use of a sheet magnifier with visual items	Administration of nonverbal subtests only; translation of verbal items via sign language; use of FM system during test administration	Administration of nonverbal subtests only; allow pointing, nodding, and/or pantomime in lieu of verbal responses	Administration of verbal subtests only; use of verbally mediated measures of visual–spatial skills (e.g., Stanford-Binet Intelligence Scales-Fifth Edition)	Administration of nonverbal subtests only; allow pointing and/or nodding, in lieu of verbal responses

Note. [a]Cerebral palsy is an example of a disability with severe language and motor impairment.

Comprehensive Test of Nonverbal Intelligence-Second Edition (CTONI-2) are not heavily verbally loaded and may be useful in assessing students who are deaf or have severe language impairments, including those with autism. The Leiter-3 and CTONI-2 can also be used with individuals who have physical disabilities and severe motor impairments as these tests do not include a timed component and do not require manipulation of objects. For those students with severe intellectual disabilities, cognitive assessments that include lower limits of measurement such as the Stanford-Binet Intelligence Scales-Fifth Edition and the Differential Ability Scales-Second Edition are good choices for obtaining the most accurate estimate of ability.

Case example: Jennifer is a fifth-grade student who has cerebral palsy. She is unable to walk and uses an electric wheel chair. Jennifer is able to speak in very short sentences (two to three words) and her speech is about 25% intelligible. Her fine motor skills are an area of significant weakness and she has virtually no pencil control. For her triennial reevaluation, the school psychologist utilized a variety of methods and sources to obtain information that would provide a comprehensive picture of Jennifer's functioning. Interviews were conducted with both Jennifer's mother and teacher and both of them also completed measures of adaptive behavior and behavior checklists that assess social–emotional functioning. The school psychologist observed Jennifer several times in her classroom during different activities and at different times of the day. To assess cognitive ability, including memory, reasoning, and spatial skills, the school psychologist administered the Leiter-3, since it requires little motoric skill and no expressive language, and it has no speeded/timed components. On this test, Jennifer is able to point to the answers and/or indicate responses with one-word responses. Receptive language and vocabulary are assessed with a picture vocabulary test. Although oral reading fluency cannot be evaluated, Jennifer's reading skills are assessed by having her silently read passages and respond to comprehension questions by pointing or orally responding to multiple choice questions by indicating A, B, C, or D. Mathematics is also assessed this way. Together, these assessment data provide a clear picture of Jennifer's strengths and needs in all areas that will be considered in developing her individual education plan.

Assessment of Preferences

One final area that should be examined is the preferences of the student with LID as this area is often less obvious and more difficult to communicate than for students who have high incidence disabilities. Investment in the educational plan and opportunities for self-determination are enhanced when students' preferences are considered (Spooner, Browder, & Uphold, 2011). In this context, choice allows for the expression of a preference and an opportunity to feel in control. Because it may be difficult for some students with LID to express their preferences due to atypical means of communication, school psychologists and other IEP team members may need to rely on the observation of those things that the student chooses consistently in order to infer preference (Lohrmann-O'Rourke & Browder, 1998). Accordingly, opportunities for choice making must be provided so that student preferences can be communicated and assessed. For example, students can be allowed to choose which writing utensil to use or specific items from a restaurant menu. Teaching skills that promote self-determination such as setting goals, solving problems, and self-regulating the learning process can support student involvement and access to the general curriculum (Wehmeyer et al., 2002).

Accommodations and Modifications

Both IDEA and Section 504 of the Rehabilitation Act mandate the provision of appropriate accommodations and modifications to students with disabilities, including LID, to allow them to receive instruction in the general educational environment and to be included in school, district, and state required assessments. When access and involvement in the general curriculum are hindered by the student's disability, specialized accommodations and/or modifications must be utilized to address these issues (Jackson, 2005; Nolet & McLaughlin, 2005). These adaptations should be made systematically and should facilitate both social and instructional participation in the classroom (Janney & Snell, 2011). School psychologists must be knowledgeable about the different types of adaptations and those that are most appropriate for the individual student with LID.

Accommodations

An accommodation is an adaptation that helps a student overcome or work around the disability (Bowen & Ferrell, 2003). Testing accommodations are alterations to tests' standard administration procedures that are made to overcome individuals' functional impairments in order to increase the validity of inferences that can be made from the resulting scores. Classroom accommodations are intended to give the student with LID an equal opportunity to participate in and benefit from instruction by removing or minimizing the impact of disability on performance (Jackson, 2005). These support structures accommodate a student's disability without altering standards and provide access to the curriculum so students with disabilities may complete a test and/or tasks without barriers related to test format, administration, or responding (Bowen & Ferrell, 2003). Accommodations that enable students with LID to participate in the general curriculum should also be applied during assessments so that they are assessed fairly against state standards of proficiency (Jackson, 2005).

Nolet and McLaughlin (2005) describe three general categories of accommodations: alternative acquisition modes, content enhancers, and alternative response modes. Alternative acquisition modes are alternative ways for students with disabilities to access the same materials used by their nondisabled peers and vary depending on the specific disability being addressed. These accommodations are intended to augment, bypass, or compensate for a motor, sensory, or information-processing deficit (Nolet & McLaughlin, 2005) and are often the most important accommodations for students with LID. Examples of alternative acquisition modes include braille materials for blind students and sign language interpreters for deaf students. Content enhancements help students recognize, organize, interpret, and remember information (Nolet & McLaughlin, 2005). Some examples are graphic organizers, concept diagrams, and semantic maps. These may also include study guides and mnemonic memory devices. Alternative response modes are intended to support the student in overcoming barriers to instruction created by sensory or motor deficits. These accommodations allow students to express what they know and what they can do by unconventional means of responding such as skits, role-play, pantomimes, and simulations (Nolet & McLaughlin, 2005). For students whose disability has a significant impact on communication modes, such as those who are deaf or have cerebral palsy, alternative response modes may be the only way of demonstrating learning.

Finding the right balance of appropriate accommodations for students with LID can be challenging. Because there clearly is risk when students with LID are under accommodated, there may be a tendency to over accommodate these students. The problem here is that over accommodating may limit the opportunities of students with LID to develop independent skills. For example, providing a blind student with a scribe to record written responses might interfere with the development of literacy skills, whereas allowing that student to use voice-to-text software or a braille typewriter would more appropriately accommodate the student's disability. Accommodations should be provided on the basis of demonstrated need only.

Modifications

Nolet and McLaughlin (2005) define a modification as an alteration in what is being taught to or expected from the student. Curricular modifications include teaching less content, teaching different content, or having individualized curricular goals. Reductions in content may make sense for those students who cannot learn at the same pace as their peers, including those with intellectual disabilities. Teaching a different content indicates that the student needs to learn something not offered in the general curriculum, such as functional or life skills. This is typically the case for most students with LID whose instructional needs often fall outside of the general curriculum. For some students with LID, highly individualized curricular goals may be appropriate (Nolet & McLaughlin, 2005). For example, although goals related to communication and social awareness may be linked to the general education content standards, these would clearly be unique to the individual student with LID.

Students with LID typically have numerous accommodations and modifications written into their IEP to support their learning, and, consequently, an organized and collaborative approach to identifying and implementing appropriate accommodations and modifications is recommended (Snell & Brown, 2011). This process can begin with detailed descriptions of class activities and the student's degree of participation in them. Janney and Snell (2011) suggest using an ecological assessment of classroom activities for this purpose. This assessment involves a detailed observation of the student's performance on various aspects of classroom activities and lessons to identify those activities that need to be adapted and the adaptations that will increase participation. Once those things have been identified, an individualized adaptations plan can be developed (Janney & Snell, 2011) that includes general applications or those that apply to predictable aspects of classroom routines such as restroom use and specific adaptations for particular lessons or activities. As experts in observational and behavioral assessment techniques, school psychologists are in a perfect position to conduct ecological assessments in this context and to facilitate data-based discussions related to the planning of appropriate adaptations for students with LID.

Educational Planning and Programming

The role of the school psychologist in supporting the education of students with LID is typically done within the context of related service provider. While school psychologists may provide direct services to some students with LID who have social–emotional or behavior needs, school psychologists will almost always provide consultation services to parents and teachers of students with LID, as well as participate in IEP development for these students. School psychologists must have a solid knowledge base related to effective educational and instructional practices that can maximize the learning and development of students with significant disabilities. The development of an understanding of concepts such as inclusive practices, universal design for learning, and person-centered practices is key for school psychologists to participate in meaningful ways in supporting students with LID in the educational setting.

Inclusive Practices

Though there is not a one-size-fits-all inclusive practice, some empirical studies have shown that inclusive educational programs may produce important educational and social outcomes for students with severe and LID such as increased academic engagement; gains in communication, social, and adaptive behavior skills; and increased social interactions and friendships with typical peers (see Downing & Peckham-Hardin, 2007, for a review). Students without disabilities may also benefit from inclusive programs by developing increased sensitivity to and an awareness of the needs of people who are different from themselves, improving their own self-concept and self-identity, and establishing sustained social relationships with peers who have disabilities.

Inclusive educational planning should be interdisciplinary and focus on the student's strengths and capabilities (Jackson, 2005). The general education curriculum and routines should be examined so as to determine when and how the learning needs of a student can be addressed within that context (Jackson, 2005). In addition, students with LID often experience healthcare needs that present challenges for both instruction and assessment and these issues should be taken into consideration as appropriate when planning the student's educational program, including in the context of inclusive educational settings (Jackson, 2005).

There is great variability in how and when inclusive practices are implemented. This issue should be considered within the context of effectively meeting the student's needs in the least restrictive environment as well as in consideration of available resources. Not all students with LID should have a full-inclusion placement. For some students with LID, the team may determine that an alternative or separate setting is the most appropriate and, consequently, the least restrictive placement available for meeting the student's individual needs and providing access to the general curriculum (Jackson, 2005). Regardless, IEP teams should be open to the provision of inclusive settings as they enter into the educational planning process with each individual student and school psychologists should advocate for the inclusion of students with LID in general classroom environments as appropriate.

Universal Design

According to Jackson (2005) and Spooner, Browder, and Mims (2011), universal design can greatly enhance access to the curriculum for students with LID. Universal design for learning concepts can provide a solid foundation for curriculum reform (Jackson, 2005) as these approaches are developed to meet the needs of all students within the general education environment (Nolet & McLaughlin, 2005). Curricula that align with universal design include "multiple means of representation (to allow various ways of acquiring information and knowledge), multiple means of expression (to allow alternatives for demonstrating knowledge), and multiple means of engagement (to challenge appropriately, to motivate, and to allow learners to express and participate in their interests)" (Jackson, 2005, p. 1). Universal design involves designing materials and curricula to increase access to subject matter and instruction by both students with disabilities and their typical peers with fewer teacher modifications and prompts (Snell & Brown, 2011). Flexibility should be built into the design to help reduce barriers to learning (Nolet & McLaughlin, 2005). Universal strategies can be successfully applied in the general educational setting with students with disabilities as well as their peers without disabilities. These strategies create a positive learning environment and utilize appropriate instructional materials, supports, and methods that are suitable to the student's level of learning and preferences as well as to the target skill (Snell & Brown, 2011). For students with LID, these are especially critical considerations in meeting their needs.

Meeting Both Functional and Academic Needs

Historically, many students with LID had IEPs that focus almost exclusively on functional life skills rather than academic skills. Functional skills are those that can be used in everyday life in natural domestic, vocational, and community environments and support inclusion and independent functioning (Jackson, 2005). However, as noted above, with the passage of NCLB, all students are required to demonstrate progress on general education core content. Consequently, there is a need for a balance between functional skill and academic skill goals in order to best meet the needs of students with LID (Snell & Brown, 2011). Such a balanced approach requires a combination of curriculum focused on meeting unique, disability-specific needs and curriculum that allows for the development of those skills needed for optimal functioning (Jackson, 2005). Access to the general curriculum by students with LID is determined through assessment, planning, and evaluation conducted by the IEP team, including the school psychologist. The team must consider the content taught to typical peers and determine appropriate entry points to the curriculum, as well as determine if any individualized instructional strategies are required to address disability-related needs (Jackson, 2005). These data then drive the development of an IEP that includes a range of services and supports that allow for access to the general education curriculum (Nolet & McLaughlin, 2005). Instruction for students with LID should occur within meaningful activities and provide systematic prompting and feedback and should include opportunities to learn general education content and allow the student to demonstrate progress on state standards. Grade-level content can also be adapted and implemented in a self-contained setting if needed (Browder, 2001).

According to Jackson (2005), there should be a connection between educational goals and desirable adult outcomes such as living independently and obtaining employment so that traditional special education goals are nested in or aligned with general curriculum goals. In this way, students with LID are able to both access the general curriculum and demonstrate progress in that context as well as develop the skills needed for more positive adult outcomes.

Consideration should be given to the appropriateness of various instructional practices that have been used effectively with students with a variety of LID including peer tutoring, cooperative learning groups, and observational learning opportunities. In addition, the majority of students with LID will need some instruction related to functional academic and daily and independent living skills as well as some training in communication and social skills. Specific curricular approaches for specific LID should also be considered (Jackson, 2005). Students who are blind or deaf-blind will also require instruction-related to orientation and mobility and perhaps visual efficiency training. Education in deaf culture is an important area of curricular content for deaf students, as is auditory skill building. For deaf-blind students, experiential and tactile learning activities are key components of their education, while those with significant physical or multiple disabilities require special instruction in functional mobility and communication. Consistent with requirements outlined in IDEA (Sec 614 (d)(l)(A)(i)), students with LID also need opportunities to be involved in recreational, leisure, and extracurricular activities as these are key in developing friendships and ultimately increase the likelihood of community integration, postschool success, and the overall quality of life (Heward, 2006). Many extracurricular activities such as using computers, working on school newsletters and yearbooks, and participating in science programs provide opportunities for students with LID to practice and extend their academic skills. Issues related to transportation, teacher support, and parental involvement are critical considerations when planning for inclusion of students with LID in such extracurricular and community activities. The educational plan for students for LID should also address the need for community-based instruction to teach functional skills (Spooner, Browder, & Mims, 2011).

Instructional Scheduling

Educational planning and programming for students with LID also requires consideration of the schedule for instruction. Snell and Brown (2011) emphasize the importance of having planned and predictable schedules from the very beginning. They recommend constructing a matrix of IEP objectives and general education activities for instructional planning that considers when, where, and how often instruction will take place. For example, *yes* would be marked on the matrix in places where certain IEP objectives can be taught during regular class time and *no* would be listed when those objectives do not fit in within class routines.

Consideration must also be given to the time and pace of instruction (Jackson, 2005). Through assessment, school psychologists can obtain critically important data related to the student's ability to sustain attention, process and remember various types of information, and persist on tasks of varying levels of difficulty. These data can then be used for planning in the context of instructional speed and timing. Students with LID generally need increased time for all aspects of learning from skill acquisition to maintenance and generalization, and the educational plan should reflect this need as appropriate (Spooner, Browder, & Mims, 2011). Schedules consistent with systematic instruction can be considered in this context. Systematic instruction is based on principles of behavior analysis and includes several different teaching trial schedules in which the student is prompted and reinforced for a particular response (Spooner, Browder, & Mims, 2011). Massed trial instructional schedules provide for multiple opportunities for the student to respond in rapid succession. Spaced trial instruction provides breaks between responses and distributed trials require responses across a lesson or the school day. As experts in the areas of behavior analysis and reinforcement schedules, school psychologists have a key role to play here: It is the school psychologist who has the skills required to collect and analyze the data needed for this aspect of educational planning.

Programming to Meet Social–Emotional Needs

Finally, the educational program of the student with LID must include consideration of behavior and social–emotional functioning. Addressing problem behaviors is critical to supporting students with LID in accessing the curriculum as this issue often results in alternative placements (Freeman et al., 2006). Implementing positive behavior interventions and supports (PBIS) is an effective means of tackling problem behaviors. PBIS is a positive and proactive means of supporting the student to reduce problem behaviors while teaching alternative skills and increasing desirable behaviors (Simonson, Sugai, & Negron, 2008). Ideally, PBIS should be implemented on a school-wide basis and include supports at the universal, secondary, and tertiary levels (Freeman et al., 2006). The intent of this multilevel approach is the provision of a continuum of supports that address the needs of all students including those with the most significant learning and/or behavioral challenges by matching the intensity of educational practice and intervention to each student's unique needs (Simonson et al., 2008). It is important to keep in mind that students with LID who need support at the tertiary level often have communication, social, learning, or health/physiological difficulties that require more in-depth functional behavioral assessment (Freeman et al., 2006). Tertiary-level prevention plans, especially those for students with LID, should generally include interventions across multiple settings (i.e., home,

school, community) that address a variety of life domains. Wraparound or person-centered planning can facilitate success at the tertiary prevention level as these strategies address support needs of the family, general quality of life, and any needed technical assistance for teachers and school staff to help support effective implementation of tertiary-level interventions (Freeman et al., 2006).

In addition to addressing problem behaviors of student with LID, educational programming should attend to any socially related needs of the student. Because the opportunities of students with LID to develop social relationships are often limited, Spooner, Browder, and Knight (2011) suggest that both environmental arrangements to provide opportunities for social interaction and to foster social relationships as well as social skill intervention/instruction to address deficits in social and communication skill be considered.

Planning for these opportunities should occur in the context of where the student receives instruction, where and with whom the student eats lunch, how and with whom the student travels to and from school, etc. Consideration of the most appropriate opportunities for providing the student with direct or embedded instruction in social-communication skills will maximize potential classroom-based instructional learning activities for this purpose (Janney & Snell, 2011). Using an IEP planning matrix such as the one described above and recommended by Snell and Brown (2011) can be very helpful in this regard. However, just ensuring that the student with LID has opportunities to mix with peers is often insufficient in promoting the development of social skills and relationships. Some students with LID will require additional environmental supports such as building disability awareness in the peer group or having peers who agree to spend time with the student or invite the student to join their established group of friends (Spooner, Browder, & Knight, 2011).

For some students with LID, their social skills deficits require direct instruction to facilitate development in this area. There are a number of research-based strategies and programs that promote social skills that school psychologists can provide to students with LID (see Spooner, Browder, & Knight, 2011, for a review). These practices are often aimed at improving social-perception and strategy-generation skills as students with LID often need assistance with focusing simultaneously on multiple social cues and in selecting appropriate social strategies. Specific intervention techniques include modeling, coaching, joint attention interventions, peer training strategies, and story-based interventions.

Case example: Robert is a ninth grader who has a significant visual impairment. He uses a cane to help him navigate around the school and in the community. Assessment results indicate that Robert is very bright in terms of verbal comprehension and reasoning but he has significant weaknesses in working memory and processing speed. Robert also struggles with frustration tolerance and explosive outbursts, and his social skills are relatively weak. Robert's education plan includes support from the orientation and mobility specialist to foster independent movement. The school psychologist consults with the orientation and mobility specialist, as well as Robert's classroom teachers, to help them understand how Robert's memory deficits have an impact on his ability to follow directions and learn new material and how his slow processing speed relates to response time and academic fluency. Robert is in the general education setting for all of his classes and repetition of material as well as additional time for assignments, tests, and oral responses are explicitly indicated in Robert's IEP as instructional strategies and accommodations. He is provided with a scribe, voice-to-text software, books in braille and audiobooks, and he is getting instruction in keyboarding so that he can write his own essays and short answers. In addition, the school psychologist provides direct services to Robert to help Robert improve his social skills and peer interactions and his ability to manage his anger. The school psychologist works with Robert one-on-one to help Robert develop anger management strategies and on picking up on auditory nonverbals, such as sighs and the speed, tone, and volume of voices, and he works with Robert in a group to improve initiating and sustaining conversations with peers. The school psychologist also collaborates with the school guidance counselor regarding development of postsecondary goals and exploration of career options within the context of Robert's strengths and interests.

Developmental Considerations

Supporting the education of students with LID at various ages and grade levels does not generally require a great deal of adaptation. Students with LID of all ages will need to have adjustments made to many standardized assessments in order to obtain valid and meaningful data to drive educational planning. All students with LID should have access to inclusive learning environments and to the general curriculum as appropriate. The one area that does require some additional consideration relates to transition planning as

it is a requirement for secondary students with LID. For these older students, school psychologists will need to consider psychoeducational assessment data through a transition and vocational lens (Fives, 2008) and they may need to utilize additional measures relevant to career interests and environmental design.

Multicultural Competencies

Students from minority backgrounds are disproportionately represented in several categories of LID, including intellectual disabilities and multiple disabilities (Office of Special Education and Rehabilitative Services, 2012). Consequently, application of culturally responsive practices for students with significant support needs from diverse backgrounds is critical. Most importantly, school psychology practitioners must be sensitive to the family's perspectives, values, and unique concerns in the context of having a child with a significant disability. This is key to encouraging family–school collaboration and developing an educational plan and providing services that are congruent with the family's views (Lynch & Hanson, 2004). This understanding is best developed through open conversations with caregivers of students with LID who come from diverse backgrounds.

Evaluation of Effectiveness

Owing to the rare occurrence of LID, opportunities to provide school psychological services to these students arise relatively infrequently. Consequently, it is imperative that school psychologists utilize all available data to evaluate effectiveness. For example, surveys of students and their families, as well as other IEP team members regarding the value of their contributions to the interventions and educational plans of the student with LID, can be quite valuable in informing the school psychological practices. These types of data are likely to be much more meaningful in this context than are data such as progress monitoring and preintervention and postintervention measures as gains made by students with LID are often much smaller and take more time than those of students with high incidence disabilities.

SUMMARY

The daunting task of supporting students with severe and LID is one that is both immensely challenging and rewarding. First and foremost, collaboration is key to success. School psychologists must work closely with parents and other professionals to effectively support access, participation, and progress in both the general and special curricula. It is essential that the student's entire IEP team collectively examines curriculum, instructional context, and available instructional resources in order to effectively plan for each student's access and participation.

School psychologists working with this population must be mindful of the various interconnected aspects of educational planning and programming for these students that allow for a seamless continuum of supports: assessment, accommodations and modifications, instructional and curricular considerations, and behavioral and social–emotional supports. Best practices emphasize approaches such as observation, formal assessment, functional behavioral assessment, rating scales, and community-based assessment techniques. These assessment methods provide data that are directly applicable to a student's current functioning and future academic planning, including the identification of the least restrictive environment for individual students and the implementation of positive behavioral supports. Appropriate accommodations and modifications that mediate the negative effects of the student's disability and increase access to the general curriculum must be mindfully developed and implemented. Instruction pertaining to both functional and academic skills must be carefully planned for and provided, keeping in mind that the educational and quality-of-life outcomes for students with LID are improved when supports for academic and social behavior development are integrated in all education settings. Finally, consideration must be given to addressing problem behaviors and to facilitating the development and maintenance of social relationships of students with LID.

REFERENCES

Bowen, S. K., & Ferrell, K. A. (2003). Assessment in low-incidence disabilities: The day-to-day realities. *Rural Special Education Quarterly, 22*(4), 10–19.

Browder, D. M. (2001). *Curriculum and assessment of individuals with moderate and severe disabilities.* New York, NY: Guilford Press.

Campbell, D. J., Reilly, A., & Henley, J. (2008). Comparison of assessment results of children with low incidence disabilities. *Education and Training in Developmental Disabilities, 43,* 217–225.

Cole, C. L., & Shapiro, E. S. (2005). Perceptions of trainers and practitioners regarding assessment and intervention for students with low incidence disabilities. *Psychology in the Schools, 42,* 677–689. doi:10.1002/pits.20118

Crepeau-Hobson, F., & Vujeva, H. (2012). Assessment of cognitive ability of students with severe and low-incidence disabilities: Part 1. *Communiqué, 41*(2), 12–13.

Dekker, R. (1993). Visually impaired children and haptic intelligence test scores: Intelligence Test for Visually Impaired Children (ITVIC). *Developmental Medicine & Child Neurology, 35,* 478–489.

Dial, J., Mezger, C., Gray, S., Massey, T., Chan, F., & Hull, J. (1990). *Manual: Comprehensive Vocational Evaluation System.* Dallas, TX: McCarron-Dial Systems.

Downing, J. E., & Peckham-Hardin, K. D. (2007). Inclusive education: What makes it a good education for students with moderate to severe disabilities? *Research and Practice for Persons With Severe Disabilities, 32,* 16–30.

Fives, C. J. (2008). Vocational assessment of secondary students with disabilities and the school psychologist. *Psychology in the Schools, 45,* 508–522. doi:10.1002/pits.20320

Freeman, R., Eber, L., Anderson, C., Irvin, L., Horner, R., Bounds, M., & Dunlap, G. (2006). Building inclusive school cultures using school-wide positive behavior support: Designing effective individual support systems for students with significant disabilities. *Research and Practice for Persons With Severe Disabilities, 31,* 4–17. doi: 10.2511/rpsd.31.1.4

Giangreco, M. F. (2000). Related services research for students with low-incidence disabilities: Implications for speech-language pathologists in inclusive classrooms. *Language, Speech, and Hearing Services in Schools, 31,* 230–240.

Heward, W. L. (2006). *Exceptional children: An introduction to special education* (8th ed.). Columbus, OH: Merrill/Prentice-Hall.

Jackson, R. (2005). *Curriculum access for students with low-incidence disabilities: The promise of universal design for learning.* Wakefield, MA: National Center on Accessing the General Curriculum. Retrieved from http://aim.cast.org/learn/historyarchive/backgroundpapers/promise_of_udl

Janney, R. E., & Snell, M. E. (2011). Designing and implementing instruction for inclusive classes. In M. E. Snell & F. Brown (Eds.), *Instruction of students with severe disabilities* (7th ed., pp. 224–256). Upper Saddle River, NJ: Pearson.

Lohrmann-O'Rourke, S., & Browder, D. M. (1998). Empirically based methods to assess the preferences of individuals with severe disabilities. *American Journal of Mental Retardation, 103,* 146–161.

Lynch, E. W., & Hanson, M. J. (2004). *Developing cross-cultural competence: A guide for working with young children and their families.* Baltimore, MD: Brookes.

National Association of School Psychologists. (2010). *Model for comprehensive and integrated school psychological services.* Bethesda, MD: Author. Retrieved from http://www.nasponline.org/standards/2010standards/2_PracticeModel.pdf

Neubert, D. A. (2012). Transition assessment for adolescents. In M. L. Wehmeyer & K. W. Webb (Eds.), *Handbook of adolescent transition education for youth with disabilities* (pp. 73–90). New York, NY: Routledge.

Nolet, V., & McLaughlin, M. J. (2005). *Accessing the general curriculum: Including students with disabilities in standards-based reform* (2nd ed.). Thousand Oaks, CA: Corwin Press.

Office of Special Education and Rehabilitative Services. (2012). *31st annual report to Congress on the implementation of the Individuals with Disabilities Education Act 2009.* Washington, DC: U.S. Department of Education. Retrieved from http://www2.ed.gov/about/reports/annual/osep/2009/parts-b-c/31st-idea-arc.pdf

President's Commission on excellence in Special Education. (2002). *A new era: Revitalizing special education for children and their families.* Washington, DC: Author. Retrieved from http://www.ed.gov/inits/commissionsboards/whspecialeducation

Rude, H., Jackson, L., Correa, S., Luckner, J., Muir, S., & Ferrell, K. (2005). Perceived needs of students with low-incidence disabilities in rural areas. *Rural Special Education Quarterly, 24*(3), 3–14.

Sailor, W. (2008–2009). Access to the general curriculum: Systems change or tinker some more? *Research and Practice for Persons With Severe Disabilities, 33–34*(4-1), 249–257.

Sattler, J. M. (2008). *Assessment of children: Cognitive foundations* (5th ed.). San Diego, CA: Jerome M. Sattler.

Simonson, B., Sugai, G., & Negron, M. (2008). School-wide positive behavior supports: Primary systems and practices. *Teaching Exceptional Children, 40*(6), 32–40. doi:10.1300/J019v24n01_03

Snell, M. E., & Brown, F. (2011). *Instruction of students with severe disabilities* (7th ed.). Upper Saddle River, NJ: Pearson.

Spooner, F., Browder, D. M., & Knight, V. F. (2011). Social skills and positive behavioural supports. In D. M. Browder & F. Spooner (Eds.), *Teaching students with moderate and severe disabilities* (pp. 283–307). New York, NY: Guilford Press.

Spooner, F., Browder, D. M., & Mims, P. J. (2011). Evidence-based practices. In D. M. Browder & F. Spooner (Eds.), *Teaching students with moderate and severe disabilities* (pp. 92–124). New York, NY: Guilford Press.

Spooner, F., Browder, D. M., & Uphold, N. (2011). Transition to adult living. In D. M. Browder & F. Spooner (Eds.), *Teaching students with moderate and severe disabilities* (pp. 364–382). New York, NY: Guilford Press.

Test, D. W., & Mazotti, V. L. (2011). Transitioning from school to employment. In M. E. Snell & F. Brown (Eds.), *Instruction of students with severe disabilities* (7th ed., pp. 569–611). Upper Saddle River, NJ: Pearson.

Wehmeyer, M. L., Sands, D. J., Knowlton, H. E., & Kozleski, E. B. (2002). *Providing access to the general curriculum: Teaching students with mental retardation.* Baltimore, MD: Brookes.

9

Best Practices for Working in and for Charter Schools

Caven S. Mcloughlin
Kent State University (OH)

OVERVIEW

Charter schools were first developed to provide diversity in educational opportunity. They offer an option for parents seeking an alternative to traditional local education authority (LEA) neighborhood schools for their children. Thus, they may be viewed as a bellwether indicator of parental dissatisfaction with local, traditional educational options suggesting that some parents believe charter schools provide superior opportunities (Bushaw & Lopez, 2012). Charter schools also afford an employment alternative for school psychologists.

The first charter schools were created in Minnesota in 1992. About 1.4 million children attend more than 6,700 public charter schools in 40 states and the District of Columbia (about 4% of America's children; National Alliance for Public Charter Schools, 2012). Fundamental to the rapid increase in numbers and acceptability of public charter schooling is strong public support for school choice. In the nine "Highlights" from the 2013 PDK/Gallup poll is this statement: "Charter schools probably offer a better education than traditional public schools" (Phi Delta Kappan, 2013). Charter schools are becoming established in all U.S. states and territories. One of the agendas for those engaged in attempting reform in public education is to achieve more academically at a lower cost. For this reason, charter schools are popular with some policy makers, legislators, and business leaders, because they promise cost-effective scalable alternatives for delivering high-quality elementary and secondary education.

Few issues exercise the ire of LEA school professionals more than charter schools. Historically, the working relationship between LEAs and charters has been nonexistent at best and antagonistic at worst. When most of the concerns about charters are stripped away, they generally focus on the dual guild issues of protecting employment terms for educators and the fiscal imperative of securing a consistent funding stream for LEAs. Advocates contend that strong bipartisan community-based support is the real strength of charter schools, and that charter schools' competition helps traditional public schools improve. Critics contend that charter schools' siphoning of funds from public school systems weakens education. As charter schools become more common these tensions are abating.

An important purpose for this chapter is to provide a balanced, evidence-based appraisal of the possibilities and perils today experienced within the charter movement with particular focus on the admittedly relatively small part played by school psychologists in the daily life of a typical charter school. This chapter addresses the origin and development for the charter education movement, the opportunities and the restrictions experienced by charter schools, their implications for neighborhood LEA schools, workplace considerations for school psychologists serving charters, and typical service delivery in charters for students with special education needs. Additionally, it addresses the barriers that practitioners experience both in systemically changing and in supplementing services to charter schools. Data interpretation is provided to assist readers in determining whether there has been adequate delivery on the promise that charter schools can provide high quality education to all students, at lower cost, within sound fiscal parameters.

However, evidence-based recommendations regarding the delivery of best practices by psychologists to charter schools has received scant concern in the school psychology professional literature ever since charter education became an option. A literature search of the primary journals in school psychology, and the extensive resources and publications of the National Association of School Psychologists (NASP), discloses no empirical studies comparing school psychologists' practice models in traditional and charter schools, no evidence-sourced recommendations have emerged, and this field's researchers have yet to become engaged in this research line, even tangentially. Speculation abounds. Commentary is frequently partisan and based on localized fragmentary experience flavored by self-interest related to guild concerns. One presumption is virtually always made that if only the model currently in place in traditional LEAs could be imported into charter schools then all would be well for children, families, and school psychology professionals. While it is possible that this is the case, there is no extant evidence to address this contention.

As this chapter will outline, there are multiple pragmatic limitations to the wholesale importation of the traditional LEA model into charter schools that relate to fiscal and organizational imperatives. The information in this chapter is organized to assist school psychologists in understanding their employment options and obligations so that they may make decisions that compare their professional aspirations to the typical mission and priorities of the charter education movement.

In its *Model for Comprehensive and Integrated School Psychological Services* (NASP, 2010), NASP describes an array of options for the delivery of high quality, comprehensive services incorporating multitiered service delivery and problem solving that is unrestricted solely to children eligible for special education. This chapter reflects upon professional activities related to the domain of School-Wide Practices to Promote Learning. This best practice model has yet to be influential in typical charter school service delivery by school psychologists. Rather, school psychology services are typically limited to the initial identification of exceptional children (for direct service by others in the school), are absent intervention foci, and only exceptionally rarely are mental health services contemplated for all children.

Charter schools are not alone in not incorporating NASP's contemporary mandates of evidence-based best practices. However, it is the exception rather than the rule for school psychologists serving charter schools to provide direct services (such as intervention and instruction to provide support for academics or the provision of mental health services to develop social and

life skills) or to engage in systems-level change (including preventive services and meaningful engagement in supporting family–school collaboration). While school psychology practitioners serving charter schools are likely well aware of NASP's practice recommendations, they are unlikely to be asked to provide these services within a tiered framework or to be afforded an opportunity to broaden their services (e.g., interdisciplinary teaming, consultative problem solving, implementing and evaluating effective interventions, designing and delivering effective curricula, or engaging in wellness enhancement for students). Since they are almost never part of the school's leadership team, they have very limited opportunity to frame an alternative system for school psychology service delivery. As will be described in greater detail, the fiscal imperatives of cost containment provide no incentive for charter schools to request comprehensive service delivery from school psychologists. This characteristically limits the school psychologist to a test-and-place function driven by whatever is the prevailing definition of "educational disability" and determined primarily by a school's regulatory obligations.

BASIC CONSIDERATIONS

Charter schools are tuition free, independent, public schools based on a "charter" agreement between the school and the community. This approach affords the charter school expanded freedom in return for a commitment to meet specific accountability standards.

Charter schools are public nonprofit, nonsectarian schools that operate independently of any school district and are under contract with an authorizer or sponsoring entity. The sponsor is the agent that establishes the charter school. A charter school develops when individuals acting as the founding coalition or governing authority seek backing from an authorized sponsor. As authorizers of community schools, sponsors serve as the central quality control manager in the development of the public charter schools. Charters are independently designed and operated, with each charter serving as its own LEA. Charter schools function and are ultimately overseen by each state's regulatory body created solely for that purpose.

Charter schools require an authorizer or sponsor. Yet, such entities only rarely are equipped by skill, staff, or experience to provide the routine services that a school needs to be functional. Most charter schools hire the services of a charter management company to administer the school's daily functioning, supervise or provide staff, buy or lease a building, select a food service plan, and in all ways cope with regulatory data reporting. Such providers are for-profit educational service delivery businesses. They access and deliver necessary specialized services (including school psychologists) either directly or through a subcontract. When buying books, desks, lunch snacks, or school bus transportation, services typically are put out for bid by vendors. That is also the case when charter schools seek specialty professional providers such as school psychologists. Most charter management companies hire third-party agencies as intermediaries to circumvent the legacy costs of a retirement system, tenure obligations and continuing contracts, and the necessity for negotiating employee compensation and benefit plans. The result is that a charter management company invests its staffing skills and capital and for a fee provides the services that the sponsors request, but no more than is contractually requested.

As schools-of-choice, charter schools must be responsive to the needs of students and communities. Some families choose a charter school because of an innovative curriculum, others because of its focus on academic achievement and smaller classes, and still others because it offers a promising alternative to an underperforming traditional public school (Zeehandelaar & Winkler, 2013). Charter schools appeal most to families dissatisfied with their traditional neighborhood public school. Eight of the nation's largest urban communities have at least 20% of their public school students in charter schools (National Alliance for Public Charter Schools, 2012). Ethnic minority students make up 60% of all students in public charter schools (Allen & Consoletti, 2010; National Alliance for Public Charter Schools, 2011, 2012).

What Makes Charter Schools Different

Charter schools are free to be innovative; that is, they have increased flexibility to adapt by implementing decisions about curriculum and structuring the school day compared to traditional LEAs. Plainly put, they are simply more nimble and agile at processing organizational change than are their traditional counterparts.

Accountability

Accountability for charter schools is codified in state and federal law, as well as in each school's contract with its sponsor. Charters are initially granted for renewable 3–5 year terms. Charter schools must define a curriculum and performance goals in their contract, commit to employ highly qualified educators, and administer state proficiency/graduation tests. They are open to all students, regardless of income, race, or religion. However, critics contend that selection bias may exist informally (Zimmer & Guarino, 2013).

Charters operate within a multitiered accountability system; that is, they are responsible to parents, authorizers, their state regulators, and to lenders of capital. Academic performance standards are negotiated prior to opening and are explicitly detailed in the charter. Parents elect to send their children to charters, and school psychologists and other educators can elect to work in them. Charter school administrators and operators are held accountable for improving student achievement and schools can be forced to close for consistent poor performance. Charters are also held accountable for their fiscal health and operational management. Historically, charter schools have experienced a 15% closure rate (Center for Education Reform, 2011). Of the approximately 6,700 schools that have ever received a charter across the United States, more than 1,000 have closed (Consoleti, 2011). There are 500 additional schools that received a charter that have been consolidated back into the LEA because they were unable to open (Consoleti, 2011). Critics often argue that charters lack accountability safeguards, suggesting that a charter education is inferior to the strictly monitored and regulated traditional public school model. Yet, failing schools have had their charters revoked. However, when a school fails its charter, students may lose critical instructional opportunities during the year or two leading to actual closure. There are five primary reasons for charter closures: financial irregularities (42%), organizational mismanagement (24%), academic failure (18%), district obstacles (6%), and facility problems (5%). Most charter schools that close for financial or operational deficiencies do so within the first 5 years or within their first charter contract (Peltason & Raymond, 2013).

Because each charter is established with a unique mission statement, the state regulator's job of overseeing charter schools is complicated. Authorizers are the first point of responsibility for ensuring that schools meet their own promises and are in accord with state and federal law. Charter documents provide the contractual authority for the school's operation and detail the school's mission, philosophy, students to be served, program and curriculum, goals, assessment methods, and indicators of success. State funding is received through a similar mechanism as provided to all public schools, although charter schools generally receive a smaller per pupil funding base (Peltason & Raymond, 2013).

While there are clear commonalities across schools in traditional LEAs (whether located in urban, suburban, or rural settings), differences also exist. A similar broad variety of formats exist for charter schools that ranges from a single school serving just a few grade levels with no affiliation to any other charter school to multiple schools organized under a common brand as franchisees to a large chain operator.

Charter schools are not uniform in size, census, educational orientation, or the children they serve. Charter schools can vary from bricks and mortar physical buildings to e-charters where teaching is done online and exist entirely virtually. The charter school concept is all about an alternative organization for school systems. It focuses on providing families with greater choice and creating schools that can be more innovative and responsive to families because of their independence. Thus, charters are not distinguished by a particular method or curriculum, mission, pedagogy or philosophy of education, or organization and enrollment.

Although charter schools may not discriminate in their student selection process, many serve a niche in the community. For example, some charters target late adolescents who have dropped out from traditional schools. Some charters specifically seek particular student characteristics, such as those previously suspended or expelled from public schools, students who are members of a particular heritage group (e.g., for an Afrocentric curriculum charter school), students with a history of behavioral challenge or noncompliance, and students whose parents are interested in secular "morality-based instruction" for their children. Charters may not discriminate in enrollment (e.g., refusing students with disabilities). While organizational parameters are determined through statute or the requirements of the school's sponsor, schools generally aim to satisfy what is perceived as a pressing educational need of the community.

Charter schools can generally be more responsive to changing local needs than traditional LEAs. One result can be a rapid initial development period with a charter school moving from the conception to opening stages in as short as 18 months. Similarly, if enrollment becomes severely reduced, a school may close or be reorganized over a single summer vacation period. Without an ability to attract a student body charters are not viable, since enrollment drives their income. Thus, schools must satisfy their customer base, since without new enrollees

and a stable census their continuation is in jeopardy. Consequently, compared to traditional neighborhood schools, they often appear aggressive in the recruitment and retention of their student body.

School Organization

There are many different approaches to the organization and instructional emphases among charter schools. Universally, charter schools are individualized and innovative. This means that even though charters may be similarly named, their approach can be radically different. Charter schools can be organized in a variety of ways to serve students, including from 1–12 grades (although most span K–8); year round or extended days; "back-to-basics" or contemporary technology emphases; environmental mission or an arts focus; business or labor partnership; specialized teaching strategies or clear pride in a spare, no nonsense approach to education; priority for special needs students; or the use of a racial or cultural specific curricula. Regardless of the school's organization, the primary method of instruction is classroom based. Multiage, nongraded classrooms are standard. Other, less common educational approaches include home-based instruction, work- or community-based learning, and distance learning (i.e., virtual or online schools). Most incorporate community service learning projects into their curriculum reflecting their community focus. Since the typical enrollment in charter schools is relatively small (averaging about 250 students), there are broad opportunities to be creative and innovative in instructional methodology and in grouping and tracking the student body. There is no requirement that the management talent and leadership be professional educators.

Enrollment in Charter Schools

Although seemingly numerous, particularly in urban or high-need areas, charter schools account for only 4% of the total number of young learners across the country (National Center for Education Statistics, 2013b). Most charter schools have no specific requirements for admission beyond the state minimum of proof of age and immunizations. Those few schools that do have admission requirements typically use personal interviews, residency determination, and basic biographic and demographic information.

Selecting a Charter School

Parents and professional educators have explicit reasons for choosing charter schools over the traditional public school. Their reasons may include a promise of smaller schools and classes, higher academic and behavioral standards (e.g., a "no-excuses" approach), a particular educational philosophy, an anticipation of enhanced parental involvement, and the existence of instructors who share their values, morality, or perspective.

Charter schools encourage substantial parent and community involvement. The format for parental involvement varies widely. It can be as simple as agreeing to visit the classroom when summoned by a teacher, or as complex as an enforceable contract requiring parents to help their child with schoolwork for a specified time each week.

Students recruited to charter schools disproportionately include those who have a history of low performance in public school, have already dropped out, are from communities experiencing marked poverty, have established gifts or talents, or have special educational needs. Nonetheless, proportionately fewer students with disabilities attend charter schools than are identified within the LEA population (excepting, of course, for those schools specifically targeting children with disabilities). Often, students with these characteristics gravitate to charters, even though the school is not attempting to be a magnet for them and may even try to dissuade a potential enrollee due to the complications and implied cost of services (National Center for Education Statistics, 2013a).

Selecting a Charter School for Employment

School psychologists contemplating employment in the charter movement should investigate carefully for a good match between their interests and the school's characteristics and mission. School psychologists' reasons for selecting charter school employment may include an attraction to the particular educational philosophy of the charter school, a desire to work for business-minded school managers, or a desire to work alongside colleagues with similar viewpoints about the role of education in children's lives. Others select charter schools for employment specifically because of the limited demand for an array of services and the availability of turn-key, short-term, clearly articulated service provision, including opportunities for part-time employment unavailable from the local LEA (Stein, 2009).

Since most charter schools do not have a census sufficient to justify the hiring of a full-time school psychologist or have no affiliation with other local entities that together can be combined into full-time employment, there is an entirely different pattern for the employment of school psychologists within charter schools. Most charter schools do not have a human resources department to which one can apply. Much of the employment is done by subcontracted, intermediary agencies that determine staffing. Many hiring decisions are last minute (since a school's census drives the funds available to hire specialty personnel such as school psychologists and reflect last minute student enrollment). Tenure protection for professional staff is atypical, and salaries are only rarely determined by seniority and are unrelated to local LEA employment terms. Bargained agreements and union representation are generally nonexistent, and contracts include fewer benefits and prerequisites than received by colleagues working locally in traditional LEAs. Employment is usually year by year and dependent upon performance as well as the changing nature of the school census. Supervision of a school psychologist's day-to-day work is generally provided by the school's administrator.

It is often the case that school psychologists are hired as independent contractors (sometimes called "1099 contractors" after the tax reporting classification). This is particularly common in western states without a heritage of unionization. Such school psychologists work as self-employed providers for tax and regulatory purposes and, for example, provide their own equipment and set their own schedules. In such cases the self-employed contractor generally provides only those special education eligibility determination data that state regulations do not allow teachers to gather (e.g., cognitive testing). It is standard for independent contractor school psychologists to be engaged by the case rather than by the day.

It is highly unusual for a school psychologist to be hired full time as a direct hire of a charter school, for all the above reasons. The contractual terms for specialty professional staff whose employment is governed by a third party agency bears no relationship to the employment terms of other locally employed LEA professionals. Any shortage of school psychologists in the charter school's catchment area influences the market cost of school psychologists and therefore employment and compensation terms. Part-time or as needed services are commonplace and result from a relatively low school census, limited involvement in comprehensive services (including restricted ability to engage in interventions, parent contact, and teaming), and cost-containment strategies instituted by the school's management.

It is common for the school psychologist in a charter school to be viewed as, and to be employed for, service as a psychoeducational gatekeeper; that is, solely for identifying special-education eligible students and absent any meaningful responsibility for implementing or monitoring interventions. It is rare for charter school psychologists to provide services to children without an identified disability. Specialty services provided by school psychologists to students with special educational needs incur significantly higher personnel expense than the average cost across typical children. Thus, school psychologists serving children with disabilities have their time audited and limited and framed by a close concern for the costs they incur. Counseling and other intervention services, provided for students experiencing emotional difficulties, is generally a role for social workers or licensed counselors. Mental health services are similarly not within the purview of most school psychologists employed in charter schools (Price & Lear, 2008).

When independence is missing in the determination of professional responsibilities (e.g., because duties are prescribed by a nonpsychologist school manager) then a school psychologist's ethical duty to children and families can become compromised. Consequently, the client for the school psychologist functioning in the majority of charter schools is predominantly the charter management company, school manager, or the employing contractual agency rather than children with special educational needs and their families. Also, the proprietary nature of the contractual agency's relationship with the service that hired them will likely be an influence that focuses the agency's attention first to their own employer, rather than the children that their agency directly serves. Thus, there is a potential for a subtle conflict or even proprietary dual relationship, for unless the school manager or charter management company feels cause to be satisfied, then the agency's contract might be withdrawn or not renewed. In turn, for the limited contract school psychologist serving the charter school, there is an incentive to just do what is requested since that is all that will be compensated.

Overall, there is far less autonomy for the school psychologist employed in charter schools when determining how each day will be organized. There is reduced involvement in preevaluation decision making and less opportunity for collaboration and consultation with instructional staff compared with traditional district hires. Since charter school psychologists are employed as part-time solo practitioners they have limited access to collegial support and employer-provided professional development opportunities.

The credentials, experience, and general preparation of professional educators in charter schools are a concern (Education Commission of the States, 2003). Hiring practices have been widely questioned as not contributing to identifying, cultivating, and retaining high quality professional staff. For example, some charters hire classroom educators without formal training or credentials in the subject areas they teach. Identifying individuals with minimum qualifications rather than established expertise becomes the norm when cost-containment drives decision making. Since the role of the school psychologist in the charter school is limited to test-and-place functions, then there is little incentive (and potentially a financial disincentive) for a charter school to employ a veteran, highly skilled, or otherwise expensive school psychologist.

BEST PRACTICES IN CHARTER SCHOOL ORGANIZATION, MANAGEMENT, AND SERVICE DELIVERY

Best practices can exist as a reality (what happens in a school is in accord with a learned society's evidence-based model) or as an aspiration (what professionals would like to have happen). By any reasonable accounting, the typical practice of school psychology in charter schools does not reflect the NASP Practice Model (NASP, 2010), nor does it appear to be evolving. While individual practitioners in charter settings may aspire to deliver contemporary, problem-solving, tiered-level services, there is scant infrastructure or platform for the school psychologist serving a charter school to be influential in introducing a new approach. Service options are constrained by funding imperatives that limit access only to students for whom the school has an obligation to identify as eligible for special education services and for whom there is a funding stream financially to justify the employment of the school psychologist.

There is an abundance of research on charter accomplishments in the aggregate with minimal evidence providing clarification on the relative effectiveness of the numerous formats within charter education, despite sophisticated analyses (e.g., Betts & Tang, 2011). There have been few successful attempts at identifying which charter initiatives yield the greatest benefit and why some strategies are effective and others are not. There is a broad contention among LEA-hired professionals (e.g., American Federation of Teachers, n.d.), unsupported by empirical evidence at this point, that charter establishments sponsored by a traditional LEA function with better overall outcomes than those without local LEA affiliation. Basically, the novel and creative ways in which charter schools are financed (e.g., the practice of funding capital expenses from operating budgets) makes it close to impossible to answer the following question: Is charter education capable of providing equivalent or even advanced outcomes based on reduced per pupil expenditure?

Because the majority of charter schools are standalone units without the support of an infrastructure supported by a team of educators and administrators, charter schools rarely have extended educational options in subject areas such as music, art, sports, foreign languages, and advanced proficiency instruction. Most charter schools emphasize a core of basic subjects and do not attempt to provide a wide ranging, comprehensive curriculum.

This centrality on a relatively narrow basic curriculum has implications for the delivery of special education services and particularly for related services such as school psychology provision. A typical charter school serving one or two classes across each of five or six elementary grades will likely employ one or two special education instructors to provide peripatetic specialized instruction or progress monitoring (Rhim, 2008). The focus at charter schools is upon the mainstream population. It is usual for special education services to be relatively limited compared to the variety available in traditional LEA settings.

The fiscal reality is that special education services are expensive and that the potential expenditure of charter school budgets can informally be influential at the stage of student recruitment. Unlike religious foundation schools that do not have a statutory obligation to provide comprehensive special education services, charter schools, which are publicly funded, are therefore liable for the expense of providing specialty instruction for children with disabilities. Yet, the base funding system for charter schools and the economies of scale in managing a relatively small enrollment limits the employment of a school psychology staff to serve the variety of disabilities children can present difficulties. One consequence is that the majority of charter schools contract for services from for-profit entities that engage and then sell the services of school psychologists. This model is also common in traditional LEAs in rural settings or in districts with small populations where services are purchased from regional service center providers (both public and private, for-profit and nonprofit).

Charter schools typically bid out their specialized needs for school psychology services based entirely on enrollments and the actual characteristics of children

with disabilities actually in attendance. Schools determine the services to be purchased based on their statutory obligations and budgetary imperatives and influenced by cost variables rather than the quality or comprehensive nature of the special services children need.

Improving services for students with special needs is one of the most active areas of district/charter collaboration. The Bill and Melinda Gates Foundation currently funds 14 large city LEAs that commit to Charter-District Collaborative Compacts with $40 million in competitive funding (Bill and Melinda Gates Foundation, n.d.). There are lessons emerging from traditional districts that have partnered with the charter providers so as to ensure high quality educational services for children in special education programs (Center on Reinventing Public Education, 2012). However, there is a dearth of reliable information specific to the role of school psychologists, and none discernible from established professional journals in the field, including NASP publications, to serve as a guide to school psychologists seeking to follow best practices specific to charter schools.

Highlights from these instances of effective partnering with charter schools to better serve students with special needs include agreements to place students with severe special needs in high performing charter schools and the provision of a menu of shared services, including a fund reserve to support charter schools serving students with special needs. District leaders have identified key lessons from their experiences in collaborating with charter schools on special education services: (a) numbers should inform, not drive, decisions; (b) build trust through demonstrating transparency about funding streams and student enrollment; (c) actively inform families that special education services are available in all charter schools; (d) engage charter schools to play a role in helping LEA schools think creatively about how to staff and serve students with special needs; (e) start collaborations around issues where district and charter leaders already agree; and (f) avoid waiting until the perfect solution arises and begin implementing partnerships around special education service provision and adjust programs and formulas as needed (Center on Reinventing Public Education, 2012).

Implications From Studies of Successful Charters

Several studies have addressed the question of how effective charter schools are at improving student outcomes (e.g., National Assessment of Education Progress, 2005). Large-scale studies of different charter models indicate that charters' performance varies widely by operator, geography, and school philosophy. In a recent comprehensive meta-analysis of charter school effect studies, Betts and Tang (2011) found that students in poverty and English language learners at charter schools earn higher test scores compared with statistically matched students in local public schools. Charters have a small positive impact on scores in elementary school math and reading and in middle school math, but none on high school or middle school reading scores. As a group, charter schools in urban settings seem to do best and virtual schools the worst in terms of student performance. There is almost nothing known about the learning trajectory of students in special education receiving their education in charter schools (Medina, 2007) and nothing published regarding outcomes for children based on the potentially influential variable of the availability of high quality school psychology provision to charter schools.

Some charter schools have adopted no-excuses strategies and are raising student outcomes, but the marginal increases in student outcomes may come with significant cost (National Alliance for Public Charter Schools, 2011). Paradoxically, an emphasis on back-to-basics can be marginalizing for those parents who originally became involved with a charter school so as to enhance their child's school options by seeking a comprehensive alternative education for their children. The monetary costs may not justify the minimal increments. Current information on costs of the programs and services that yield these marginal benefits is incomplete, poorly documented, and widely varied. No study has documented the power of school psychology to make a change in charter education and so there are no empirically validated guides to best practices.

Nonetheless, charter supporters contend that school practices from high quality charters can be migrated to previously failing traditional public schools to increase student achievement. For example, practices deemed successful in New York City charter schools have been migrated to low performing schools in Houston, Texas, including increased instructional time, stronger academic leadership, more skilled teachers, data-driven instruction, intensive tutoring, and a culture of high expectations (Center on Reinventing Public Education, 2012). Detractors question whether these imported practices are truly innovative or even result from innovations attributable to charter schools since most

have well-established histories (e.g., smaller class sizes and school-reform measures like intensive tutoring on core instruction, teacher coaching, extended school day, and clear behavioral policies with a no excuses regimen). Detractors contend that most success attributed to charters is not because of innovation but merely reflect common sense educational best practices (Schaeffer, 2012).

Researchers disagree whether charter education is superior or inferior to the traditional model. For school psychologists interested in the efficacy of the charter movement, particularly for children with disabilities, there is no credible database currently available to address this question. Yet, as is also the case for traditional public education, there are some strong charter schools and some weak ones. The actual variety in quality across charter schools is at least equally as broad as the differences between the best and the worst traditional public schools.

Charters originated with the promise of educational innovation and the potential for students' elevated academic performance. Retrospective analysis of the charter movement's results over 20 years is inconclusive regarding whether charter education is better or worse than traditional education in terms of student outcomes (National Alliance for Public Charter Schools, 2011). Yet, charters promote parental choice and provide an alternative to the traditional model. With the availability of the charter model, parents become decision makers about their children's educational options rather than just "decision thinkers." That is the core of every school choice debate.

Children attending charter schools will likely benefit from access to school psychologists with skills in the delivery of comprehensive services. It is axiomatic that charters must begin to appreciate the broader functions their staff team, particularly school psychologists, can play in serving all children using contemporary best practice models.

Teacher Quality

The credentials, experience, and general preparation of professional educators in charter schools are a concern (Education Commission of the States, 2003). Identifying individuals with minimum qualifications rather than established expertise has become the norm when cost containment drives decision making. Although charter schools typically take pride in their independence from governmental regulation when selecting an instructional methodology, this flexibility has too often led to laxity in the selection of gold standard, evidence-based instructional regimens. Even charter advocates are beginning to lobby for the closure of underperforming charter schools (California Charter Schools Association, 2012).

Finances

Because they are typically much smaller than their traditional LEA school districts, charter schools often have far less ability to compensate their professionals according to prevailing market rates. Most charters do not offer employment inducements comparable to traditional school districts. Fiscal mismanagement by individuals with little or no business expertise has been a frequent cause of charter school closure (Consoletti, 2011).

SUMMARY

As tuition free schools of choice, charter schools champion entrepreneurship and may serve as incubators of innovation. While accountable for achieving performance standards, they are exempt from most restrictions affecting traditional schools. Like neighborhood public schools, they have open admissions and similar demographics, albeit with a smaller overall population and class size and nontraditional grade arrangements.

The dramatic increase in the number of charter schools creates legions of strident supporters and detractors. Advocates highlight the benefits of choice and healthy competition, challenging standards, specialized approaches, innovative instructional practices, grass-roots governance, and a focus on community and parent involvement. Critics cite concerns with selective enrollment, accountability, staff qualifications, and experience, and they voice concern that charter schools reduce the fund balance available for traditional public schools. Current employment practices do not encourage the hiring of school psychologists able to exercise professional independence in decision making or incorporate contemporary best practices reflective of the NASP Practice Model (NASP, 2010).

The relatively new charter school initiative and its implementation remain a work in progress. Like most movements in education, it will take time to gather the data for reflecting upon the most efficient, culturally sensitive, and professionally supportable means for incorporating charter schools into the entire U.S. educational system. A critical element yet unaddressed is school psychologists' responsibility to be engaged in data gathering and model building to shape the future of psychological service delivery for children attending charter schools. Since the initiation of the charter movement, school psychologists have been almost totally disengaged from investigating charter school outcomes and formulating model professional practices to serve children and charter schools.

REFERENCES

Allen, J., & Consoletti, A. (2010). *Annual survey of America's charter schools.* Washington, DC: Center for Educational Reform. Retrieved from http://www.edreform.com/wp-content/uploads/2011/09/CER_Charter_Survey_2010.pdf

American Federation of Teachers. (n.d.). *A revolving door.* Washington, DC: Author. Retrieved from http://www.chicagoacts.org/charter-news/142-a-revolving-door

Betts, J. R., & Tang, Y. E. (2011). *The effect of charter schools on student achievement: A meta-analysis of the literature.* Washington, DC: National Charter School Resource Center. Retrieved from http://www.charterschoolcenter.org/resource/effect-charter-schools-student-achievement-meta-analysis-literature

Bill and Melinda Gates Foundation. (n.d.). *Gates Foundation announces investments for cities supporting collaboration, bold reform, and high performance.* Seattle, WA: Author. Retrieved from http://www.gatesfoundation.org/Media-Center/Press-Releases/2011/12/Foundation-Announces-Investments-for-Cities-Supporting-Collaboration-Bold-Reform-and-High-Performance

Bushaw, W. J., & Lopez, S. J. (2012). Public education in the United States: A nation divided. *Phi Delta Kappan, 94,* 8–25.

California Charter Schools Association. (2012). *Portrait of the movement: How charters are transforming California education.* Los Angeles, CA: Author. Retrieved from http://www.calcharters.org/PortraitoftheMovementReport2012.pdf

Center for Educational Reform. (2008). *Annual survey of America's charter schools, 2008.* Washington, DC: Author. Retrieved from http://www.edreform.com/edreform-university/resource/annual-survey-of-americas-charter-schools-2008/

Center for Education Reform. (2011). *Charter schools closure rate tops 15 percent.* Washington, DC: Author. Retrieved from http://www.edreform.com/2011/12/charter-schools-closure-rate-tops-15-percent/

Center on Reinventing Public Education. (2012, May 30). Lessons from compact cities on serving special education students. [Webinar]. Washington, DC: Author. Retrieved from http://www.crpe.org/updates/lessons-compact-cities-serving-special-education-students

Consoletti, A. (2011). *The state of charter schools: What we know—and what we do not—about performance and accountability.* Washington, DC: The Center for Educational Reform. Retrieved from http://www.edreform.com/wp-content/uploads/2011/12/StateOfCharterSchools_CER_Dec2011-Web-1.pdf

Education Commission of the States. (2003). *Charter schools and the teacher quality provisions of No Child Left Behind.* Washington, DC: Author.

Medina, J. (2007, December 20). Charter schools outshine others as they receive their first report cards. *The New York Times.* Retrieved from http://www.nytimes.com/2007/12/20/nyregion/20charter. html?ref=education

National Alliance for Public Charter Schools. (2011). *Measuring charter performance: A review of public charter school achievement studies.* Washington, DC: Author. Retrieved from http://www. publiccharters.org/data/files/Publication_docs/NAPCS_ AchvmntStdy_D8.pdf_20110330T165151.pdf

National Alliance for Public Charter Schools. (2012). *A growing movement: America's largest charter school communities.* (7th ed.). Washington, DC: Author. Retrieved from http://www.edweek. org/media/napcsmarketshare-13charters.pdf

National Assessment of Education Progress. (2005). *America's charter schools: Results from the NAEP 2003 pilot study.* Washington, DC: U.S. Department of Education. Retrieved from http://nces.ed.gov/ pubsearch/pubsinfo.asp?pubid=2005456

National Association of School Psychologists. (2010). *Model for comprehensive and integrated school psychological services.* Bethesda, MD: Author. Retrieved from http://www.nasponline.org/standards/ 2010standards/2_PracticeModel.pdf

National Center for Education Statistics. (2013a). *Children and youth with disabilities.* Washington, DC: Author. Retrieved from http:// nces.ed.gov/programs/coe/indicator_cgg.asp

National Center for Education Statistics. (2013b). *Fast facts: Charter schools.* Washington, DC: Author. Retrieved from http://nces.ed. gov/fastfacts/display.asp?id=30

Peltason, E., & Raymond, M. E. (2013). *Charter school growth and replication.* Stanford, CA: Center for Research and Education Outcomes. Retrieved from http://credo.stanford.edu/research-reports.html

Phi Delta Kappan. (2013). *Highlights of the PDK/Gallup poll.* Retrieved from http://pdkintl.org/noindex/2013_PDKGallup_HL.pdf

Price, Q. A., & Lear, J. G. (2008). *School mental health services for the 21st century: Lessons from the District of Columbia school mental health program.* Washington, DC: George Washington University. Retrieved from http://dmh.dc.gov/sites/default/files/dc/sites/dmh/publication/ attachments/SMHS21CenturyMentalHealthProgram.pdf

Rhim, L. R. (2008). *Special education challenges and opportunities in the charter school sector.* (NCRSP Working Paper #2008-12). Seattle, WA: Center on Reinventing Public Education, University of Washington. Retrieved from http://www.crpe.org/sites/default/ files/wp_ncsrp12_speced_feb08.pdf

Schaeffer, A. B. (2012). *The charter school paradox: How public-sector-only choice can increase costs, reduce educational diversity, and undermine competition, and how those unintended consequences can be avoided.* Washington, DC: Cato Institute. Retrieved from http://www. cato.org/sites/cato.org/files/pubs/pdf/charter-school-paradox. pdf

Stein, M. (2009, April). *Who chooses and why? Charter school choice patterns among Indianapolis parents.* Paper presented at the annual conference of the American Education Research Association, San Diego, CA. Retrieved from http://www.vanderbilt.edu/schoolchoice/ documents/who_chooses.pdf

Zeehandelaar, D., & Winkler, A. M. (2013). *What parents want: Education preferences and trade-offs. A national survey of K–12 parents.* Washington, DC: The Thomas Fordham Institute.

Zimmer, R. W., & Guarino, C. M. (2013). Is there empirical evidence that charter schools "push out" low-performing students? *Educational Evaluation and Policy Analysis, 35,* 461–480.

Section 2
Preventive and Responsive Services

Best Practices in Developing Prevention Strategies for School Psychology Practice

10

William Strein
Megan Kuhn-McKearin
Meghan Finney
University of Maryland

OVERVIEW

For evidence that prevention has become a major role and activity for school psychologists, school psychologists need to look no farther than a comparison of the National Association of School Psychologists' (NASP) own policy documents over the first decade of the 21st century. In NASP's (2000) *Professional Conduct Manual: Guidelines for the Provision of School Psychological Services*, the first reference to some form of the word *prevent* occurs 10 pages into the document. By contrast, NASP's *Model for Comprehensive and Integrated School Psychological Services* (NASP, 2010) references *prevention* on its first page: "School psychologists provide services to schools and families that enhance the competence and well-being of children, including...*prevention of academic and behavior problems* [emphasis added]..." (p. 1), and includes Preventive and Responsive Services as one of its five categories of Direct and Indirect Services.

The professional literature in school psychology has seen a steady growth in prevention-focused articles, chapters, and books. Since the publication of *Best Practices V*, there have been 101 articles (about 9%) addressing prevention in the primary school psychology journal literature, contrasted with 87 (8%) and 52 (7%) such articles in the preceding two 5-year periods (according to an ERIC search for articles with *prevention* as a descriptor in seven school psychology journals for three 5-year periods from 1998 to 2012). Recent years have seen the publication of edited volumes devoted entirely to prevention authored by recognized scholars in school psychology (e.g., Doll, Pfohl, & Yoon, 2010). The purpose of this chapter is to provide a broad overview of prevention as a major role for school psychologists and to present best practices for choosing and implementing prevention programs in schools.

Before continuing a discussion of prevention, we must start with a definition and some terminology. Notwithstanding the common usage that prevention refers to stopping something from happening, defining prevention with regard to psychological practice and research has been both difficult and contentious. For the purposes of this chapter, we define prevention both as interventions (a) that decrease the incidence (number of new cases) or prevalence (number of current cases) of some clearly defined, undesirable outcome (e.g., below-standard academic achievement, inappropriate special education placement, bullying, or suicide), or (b) that strengthen resiliency.

Prior to the mid-1990s, nearly all writings on prevention used a three-part terminology: primary, secondary, and tertiary prevention. Some authors continue to use this scheme. Beginning in the mid-1990s the prevention literature began to use terminology promoted by an Institute of Medicine report that focuses on which segment of the population an intervention targets: universal, selective, or indicated. The Institute of Medicine terminology corresponds closely to the now well-known three-tiered model used throughout many NASP publications. Simply put, the Institute of Medicine terminology and the three-tiered model correspond as follows (Institute of Medicine first;

three-tiered model second): universal → universal interventions; selective → targeted interventions; and indicated → intensive interventions. Terminology from the three-tiered model will be used throughout this chapter.

Need for Prevention Programs

Policy makers in education and mental health increasingly embrace prevention programs based on at least four rationales: (a) the recent development of numerous evidence-based prevention programs, (b) promotion of the well-being of youth, (c) resource limitations stemming from a complete reliance on treatment-oriented models, and (d) cost effectiveness. First, and perhaps most important, the number of evidence-based prevention programs has grown exponentially over the past 25 years. In its 1988 seminal publication on such programs, the American Psychological Association identified only 10 programs for children and youth that were evidence based (Price, Cowan, Lorian, & Ramos-McKay, 1988). Now hundreds of prevention programs are identified as evidence based (Cooney, Kratochwill, & Small, 2010), including programs that address academic and mental health goals. For example, Dombek and Connor (2012), in a study using randomly assigned matched schools, found that providing individualized reading instruction based on assessment results reduced the first-grade retention rate by nearly 50%. Likewise, prevention programs focused on social–emotional and behavioral outcomes have produced very positive results in terms of strengthening competencies and reducing problematic behavior (Durlak, Weissberg, Dymnicki, Taylor, & Schellinger, 2011).

Second, the potential to enhance the well-being of school-aged children by preventing academic, social, and behavioral problems has an inherent appeal to school psychologists. If large numbers of children can receive high-quality early educational experiences and mental health support, then the need for remedial interventions should decline. The idea of reducing the incidence and prevalence of academic and behavioral problems is at the heart of current thinking about school psychology practice, whether through the response to intervention (RTI) or the broader public health models. A preventive approach presumes that by providing appropriate levels of universal and targeted group interventions, the number of individuals needing Tier 3 intensive individualized interventions will be reduced.

Third, 4 decades ago, George Albee (1968), inarguably the key early figure in prevention psychology,

theorized that there will never be adequate numbers of direct-service mental health providers to treat all individuals in need of services. Albee concluded that prevention services provide the only feasible way to reach all individuals in need. In most areas of the United States the school psychologist-to-student ratio exceeds, or far exceeds, the NASP-recommended standard of 1:1,000 (Curtis, Castillo, & Gelley, 2012). Attempting to treat all students in need of school psychological services on an individual basis imposes an impossible task on school psychologists. Integrating prevention activities into their practice can help school psychologists to meet service demands. Finally, prevention programs can be cost effective. For example, studies indicate that programs that reduce outcomes such as school dropout rates or youth substance abuse may return financial benefits many times the cost of implementing the prevention program (Cooney et al., 2010).

Both leaders and practitioners in school psychology recognize the need for prevention as a major role for school psychologists and have done so particularly over the last decade. The 2002 Multisite Conference on the Future of School Psychology (Cummings et al., 2004) identified as one of its four underlying principles the recognition of a need for a greater emphasis on prevention and intervention. Of the 2002 conference's resulting 15 prioritized goals for a national agenda, three specifically target prevention issues. Ten years later the 2012 School Psychology Futures Conference continued this strong focus on prevention. Six of the seven 2012 conference's keynote or featured speakers (H. Adelman, B. Doll, J. E. Lochman, L. Taylor, R. Horner, and R. Weissberg) are known primarily for their work in prevention areas. As practitioners, school psychologists appear to be increasing their involvement in prevention activities. The most recent survey of NASP members indicates that school-based practitioners, on average, may be spending as much as one third of their time working to improve outcomes for all students and for those identified as being at risk (Castillo, Curtis, & Gelley, 2012), whereas earlier surveys showed much less such involvement.

Types of Prevention Programs

Prevention programs can be categorized according to scope or according to targeted domain. A program may focus on the individual person, be ecologically focused, or focus on multiple levels (Elias & Branden, 1988). In terms of targeted outcomes, historically school-based prevention programs have primarily targeted either academic or social–emotional domains. More recent prevention programs have adopted an integrative approach that simultaneously targets both domains.

Scope

Until recently, school psychologists likely were most familiar with person- (student-) focused programs, as they were historically the most commonly used type of prevention programs. Such programs typically use individual or group interventions focused on changing some aspect of the individual student. Person-focused programs target an array of intended outcomes; for example, increased academic skills (e.g., Individualizing Student Instruction; Connor, Morrison, Fishman, Schatschneider, & Underwood, 2007), changed social information processing (STORIES; Teglasi & Rothman, 2001), or altered discrete social behaviors (Skillstreaming; McGinnis, 2011). The unifying characteristic here is that individuals are targeted for change with little focus on changing anything on a broader level. Person-focused interventions apply to all tiers of a multitiered service delivery model but, when considered as a preventive intervention, are found at the universal and targeted interventions levels. For example, Second Step: Student Success Through Prevention (Committee for Children, 2008) is a person-focused prevention program used school-wide, whereas Skillstreaming is more typically delivered to small groups of students identified as being at risk (targeted intervention tier).

By contrast to person-focused programs, ecologically focused programs emphasize the need to have an impact on various layers of the student's environment to prevent or treat learning, social, emotional, and behavioral difficulties. Based broadly on an ecological framework, these programs assume that layers of the environment have differential effects on individual students. Though such programs were less well known until recently, many school psychologists now are familiar with ecologically focused programs. For example, Fast Track (Conduct Problems Prevention Research Group, 2011) is a well-researched prevention program to reduce conduct disorders that includes parent groups, parent–child sharing time, and home visitations as after-school and outside-of-school components, as well as an in-school focus on developing students' social and emotional competencies, and teacher classroom management.

Targeted Domains

There is a tendency in school psychology to equate prevention solely with programs that focus primarily on

social–emotional or mental health goals. This is inaccurate. Although it is true that much of the prevention literature has this focus, universal interventions to strengthen early academic skills and targeted interventions for those students at risk for school failure (e.g., Head Start) are clear examples of prevention programs focused on academic outcomes. Indeed, RTI can be characterized as a prevention-oriented system that most frequently targets academic outcomes. Academic prevention programs, such as instructional support teams, can be inexpensively implemented and used as instructional interventions aimed at preventing serious learning problems. An excellent example of a prevention program with an academic focus, Individualizing Student Instruction (Dombek & Connor, 2012), is described later in this chapter. School psychologists, with expertise in assessment and progress monitoring, are highly qualified to advocate for preventive instructional practices.

School-based social–emotional and mental health prevention programs focus most typically on the development of social competence by focusing on discrete skills (e.g., Skillstreaming; McGinnis, 2011); a social problem-solving model that enables students to make prosocial, functionally effective choices in interpersonal situations (e.g., I Can Problem Solve; Shure, 2001); or by altering social cognition (e.g., STORIES; Teglasi & Rothman, 2001). As mentioned above, some of these programs include work with families as well as with individual students (e.g., Conduct Problems Prevention Research Group, 2011).

BASIC CONSIDERATIONS

It is critical to consider the quality and evidence base for any prevention program before its implementation. School psychologists can now marshal substantial evidence in support of the effectiveness of prevention programs. The literature on the effectiveness of early intervention to promote academic success both universally and with targeted interventions is too vast to review here, even illustratively (see chapters on academic interventions in this edition of *Best Practices*).

Effectiveness research on prevention programs that target social, emotional, and behavioral outcomes is readily available. A recent meta-analysis of 213 universal (Tier 1) school-based social and emotional learning programs supports their effectiveness (Durlak et al., 2011). Universal social and emotional learning programs were found to have moderate positive effects (mean effect size [ES] = .57) on social and emotional learning skills and small, but meaningful, positive effects (mean ES = .23–.24) on positive social behavior, reduction of conduct problems, emotional distress, and attitudes. Importantly, these programs also demonstrated a small (mean ES = .27) positive effect on academic outcomes, although they were focused primarily on social and emotional learning goals. Programs led by classroom teachers were, on average, at least as good as those lead by nonclassroom personnel.

Evidence also supports the effectiveness of social and emotional learning programs for targeted (Tier 2) interventions. In a study of 80 such programs, Payton et al. (2008) found medium to large positive effects for social and emotional learning skills (mean ES = .77), other social–emotional outcomes (mean ES = .38–.50), and, again, academic outcomes (mean ES = .43). Other meta-analyses similarly have found positive results of intensive interventions for externalizing behavior problems both for individual interventions and group interventions, although individual interventions outperformed group interventions for the indicated population (Wilson & Lipsey, 2007).

Although thoroughly researching any program before adopting it is highly recommended, practicing school psychologists may not have time to conduct comprehensive literature searches in order to identify effective programs. So, it is helpful to know where to more easily obtain such information. Fortunately, there are several

sources, two of which are highlighted here. For academic interventions, school psychologists may find the Institute for Education Sciences' What Works Clearinghouse (http://ies.ed.gov/ncee/wwc) to be a valuable resource. The What Works Clearinghouse reviews evidence on intervention programs in education, with a heavy focus on literacy and math programs, and presents charts that evaluate the amount of evidence regarding a program's effectiveness and a measure of the degree of effectiveness indicated by the available evidence. For social–emotional programs, the Collaborative for Academic, Social, and Emotional Learning (CASEL; casel.org) reviews numerous prevention programs with regard to preset criteria and provides information on selected social and emotional learning programs for preschool and elementary school use. Table 10.1 summarizes the CASEL, What Works Clearinghouse, and two other Web-based sources of information on school-based prevention programs and their effectiveness that provide helpful guidance to school psychologists and school administrators. Numerous other Web-based compendia are available on specific prevention topics (e.g., teen pregnancy prevention, http://www.hhs.gov/ash/oah/oah-initiatives/teen_pregnancy/db/programs.html), that can be found easily by searching the Internet. However, caution is required. Each compendium uses its own guidelines for review and ratings of programs. Consumers need to

Table 10.1. Selected Sources of Information on Efficacy of Prevention Programs

Source	Age/Grade Levels	Prevention Program Information Provided
Collaborative for Academic and Social Learning Guide 2013 (http://casel.org/guide)	Pre-K–5	Reviews 24 social and emotional learning programs selected to meet preset criteria. Information on each program includes descriptions and ratings of program design and implementation support and of the evidence of the program's effectiveness.
Substance Abuse and Mental Health Services Administration National Registry of Evidence-Based Programs and Practices (http://www.nrepp.samhsa.gov)	Early childhood to young adult	Includes reviews of more than 120 school-based prevention programs, sortable by race/ethnicity, gender, age, setting (urban, suburban, rural, tribal), outcome type, and program focus. Entries for each program include program description, ratings of the quality of the research evidence and readiness for dissemination, and information on costs.
Office of Juvenile Justice and Delinquency Programs Model Programs Guide (http://www.ojjdp.gov/mpg)	Early childhood to young adult	Includes reviews and ratings of more than 160 school-based prevention programs, sortable by race, gender, age, setting (urban, suburban, rural, tribal), problem behavior, and program type. Entries for each program include program description, evaluation methodology and outcomes for one or more studies, references to the literature on the program, and an effectiveness rating of *promising, effective,* or *exemplary*.
What Works Clearinghouse (http://www.whatworks.ed.gov)	Pre-K–12	Reviews effectiveness of school-based intervention programs, including prevention programs, in both the academic and social/emotional (student behavior) domains. Includes specific category for dropout prevention.

review carefully each system's selection and evaluation criteria when considering the evidence provided by any of these sources. A good strategy for such review would be to consult several compendia and then consider the evidence as presented by more than one site.

Irrespective of what compendium of evidence-based programs is used, consideration of the compendium's criteria for inclusion and evaluation of evidence is critical. A program in one compendium might not even make the cut for another, or simply was not reviewed. Compendia also evaluate programs on differing outcomes or program characteristics. The Society for Prevention Research (http://www.preventionresearch.org) has developed a comprehensive set of standards for evaluating prevention programs' evidence of efficacy, effectiveness, and readiness for broad dissemination (Flay et al., 2005). School psychologists would do well to consult these standards before making a final decision on adopting a given program. Notwithstanding the importance of supportive evidence provided by experimental research, it is also critical to recognize that the implementation of prevention programs is highly contextual. Rigorous local program evaluation is essential for success.

Research on prevention indicates that there are several features of prevention programs that are likely to lead to successful outcomes (CASEL, 2012; Greenberg et al., 2003; Nation et al., 2003). These features are highlighted in Table 10.2.

Knowledge and Competencies

Following NASP's Practice Model (NASP, 2010) requires that school psychologists have basic competencies in prevention programming. Although NASP added this explicit expectation only in 2010, well-prepared and experienced school psychologists need not think of the implementation of prevention programs as requiring something substantially outside of their already-acquired competencies.

Many skills necessary for implementing prevention programs are competencies that have been at the core of school psychology practice for many years. Particularly relevant are competencies related to data-based decision making and accountability, consultation and collaboration, school and systems organization, policy development and climate, and program evaluation, all of which should seem familiar to most school psychologists. Depending on the target of a prevention program, interventions and instructional support to develop academic skills, and interventions and mental health services to develop social and life skills likely will inform the program's substance.

Most school psychologists considering involvement in prevention will be stronger in some of these competencies than in others. A careful approach to prevention work does not require expert-level competence in all of these areas. However, school psychologists whose current competencies focus nearly exclusively on psychoeducational assessment and/or direct services with students will need to acquire broader competencies before launching into prevention efforts. Workshops provided by NASP or other organizations can be used to strengthen such competencies. Partnering or consulting with colleagues who may have strengths in various areas is an excellent way to meet all of the skills that may be required without having to master all of the competencies oneself.

Table 10.2. Critical Features of Successful Prevention Programs

- *Program type/outcome match:* Programs may be differentially effective for particular outcomes (e.g., ecologically focused interventions may work particularly well for reducing substance abuse and delinquency).
- *Sufficient length:* Programs need to be long enough to accomplish what needs to be accomplished. Many programs are simply too short. Programs may also need booster sessions at later points after completion. Multiyear programs are especially desirable.
- *Appropriately timed:* Programs should be initiated early enough to have an impact on the development of the problem.
- *Socioculturally relevant:* Programs should be sensitive to the needs and cultural norms of the participants.
- *Comprehensive:* Programs using multiple interventions across multiple settings (includes both a person focus and an environmental or organizational change focus) are likely to be most successful.
- *Incorporate a variety of methods:* Programs should include sequential skills training with active student learning.
- *Structured manuals/curricula:* Programs should support consistency in delivery.
- *High quality implementation:* Programs should require staff to be well trained. This likely will require both initial and follow-up training for staff who join the program after its initial implementation.
- *Evidence of effectiveness:* Programs should provide clear research-based evidence of effectiveness that allow consumers to make deliberate choices regarding program adoption.
- *Outcome evaluation included:* Programs should have methods for formal evaluation of processes and outcomes.

School Variables

It would be naïve to believe that all schools are equally amenable to prevention programs or to prevention as a major role for the school psychologist. Several school-level variables contribute to implementation. First, the school's mission will affect the acceptability of prevention efforts. Universal prevention programs targeting social–emotional areas will be most successful in schools that include broad mental health goals as a stated mission (Elias & Branden, 1988). Universal or targeted preventive interventions targeting academic mastery are likely to be acceptable in nearly all schools.

Second, communication among staff will affect the fidelity of program implementation. Successful prevention programs are multifaceted and require that each component be implemented consistently and effectively. It is necessary, then, that administrators, teachers, support staff, and, when necessary, parents communicate about which program components are easily implemented and which are less feasible.

Third, higher parent involvement in the school's initiatives can improve prevention program success. Strong support for a program at home and at school can improve students' knowledge of the issue and attitude toward the program, and provides accountability for student behavior and involvement.

Fourth, competing initiatives within the school should be considered and, where present, can be dealt with by combining initiatives. For example, if a school desires to improve school climate and reduce bullying, the prevention program can combine the common goals and practices inherent in these initiatives, such as teaching school-wide expectations and establishing consistent consequences.

Fifth, a school's available resources are a key consideration and are detailed later in the chapter.

BEST PRACTICES IN DEVELOPING PREVENTION STRATEGIES

As an overall starting point, school psychologists should consider prevention strategies and programs using the tiered interventions model. This model provides guidance for evaluating potential problems and selecting suitable interventions.

Planning and Selecting Prevention Strategies and Programs

Prevention programs are most effective when tailored to the school's unique environment, resources, and needs.

Prior to selecting a program, school psychologists should conduct a needs assessment—a systematic assembly and evaluation of school-specific concerns and potential causes of these concerns—to determine what, if any, problem to target.

Needs assessments can range from informal (e.g., recognizing a need for a bully prevention program following numerous incidents of in-school bullying) to formal (e.g., a structured survey for students addressing major areas of concern in a school). While many types of needs assessments can be conducted in a school setting, surveys, by interview or questionnaire, are most commonly used. Highly structured questions, paper- or Web-based questionnaires, are most efficient when surveying large numbers of individuals. By contrast, interviews can provide rich qualitative information from a relatively small number of respondents. School psychologists may also assess needs by pulling information directly from the materials students are using. Although many school staff members may participate in creating a needs assessment, school psychologists, trained in research and evaluation methods, are highly qualified to conduct and evaluate such assessments.

Beyond providing insight into what school-specific problem should be addressed, results from a well-developed needs assessment help school psychologists and other school staff members determine at which level of implementation a prevention program will have the greatest impact. For example, if the results of a needs assessment indicate a school-wide issue with bullying, the prevention program should target the entire school. On the other hand, if the results indicate a problem only within a specific grade, the program should target only that grade. Determining the target level of an intervention can be challenging, but understanding school resources, and garnering the buy-in of administrators, can make this determination easier.

School psychologists should not rely solely on results of a needs assessment to select a prevention program. It is equally critical to consider whether the proposed prevention activities are appropriate for and suit the school environment. The suitability of a proposed prevention program is influenced by available resources, staff competencies, and how well the proposed activities mesh with the educational philosophy and general climate of the school and community. Designing school-based prevention programs that are highly congruent with the school's mission or culture can increase the acceptance, sustainability, and fidelity of the program (Biggs, Vernberg, Twemlow, Fonagy, & Dill, 2008). Some ways to do this might include (a) designing a program that is a regular component of the ongoing educational process, (b) integrating the activities into the school routine (e.g., a character education program that is a part of the language arts curriculum), and (c) focusing initial prevention efforts on targeted early interventions for at-risk students, rather than beginning with universal interventions because early interventions have greater acceptance. In addition, prevention work will often be more visible and acceptable if tied to tangible school outcomes (e.g., absenteeism, tardiness, or improving social relationships).

Once the school psychologist has completed the analysis of needs and fit, these results must be communicated to critical stakeholders in the adoption and implementation of the program. Effective implementation of prevention programs often requires the buy-in of multiple stakeholders. Well-developed communication skills and materials that support the need for and the evidence base of a prevention program are important components of a successful meeting with key decision makers. If a school-level prevention program is needed, the school administrators should understand the large impact that the program may have on the school environment and that school psychologists are prepared to be at the forefront of establishing and evaluating such programs. If administrators recognize the potential and provide support for such prevention programs, they can promote the idea to other school personnel and students' families (Biggs et al., 2008). If programs at the classroom level are needed, then the school psychologist can help teachers understand the importance of, and evidence base for, such programs. In these situations, the school psychologist can also provide meaningful information about how the program can be relevant for the teacher's classroom or department.

Implementation

Innovation requires leadership. Some school psychologists may already work in schools where prevention programs are institutionalized and an accepted part of the school's role. For others, a transition to target prevention will require considerable leadership. Johnson, Hays, Center, and Daley (2004) presented "champion roles and leadership actions" (p. 143) as one factor that is needed to initiate and sustain prevention programs. Research consistently emphasizes the importance of influential, proactive leaders in effective implementation and sustainability of interventions: "Formal and informal leaders within adopting systems, as well as champions who proactively promote an

innovation from inside or outside of a system, are critical to creating an environment that supports and facilitates sustaining innovations" (Johnson et al., 2004, p. 143).

Leadership Issues

When establishing new prevention programs, a core group of decision makers can provide a strong leadership structure. However, involving key stakeholders and offering leadership roles to future implementers of the program may increase program support and sustainability. Moreover, involving key leaders can help overcome barriers or resistance to new programs. School psychologists initiating prevention programs should seek champions for the program and support both from administrators and school staff (Johnson et al., 2004). Support from the building principal is critical. The principal can promote school-wide adherence to, and enthusiasm for, prevention programs. Indeed, without such support much success is unlikely. Further, both principal and district-level supports can increase the availability and acceptability of training for teachers and school staff which, in turn, promote effective program implementation.

Maintaining Implementation Integrity

Programs work only when actually implemented and are most effective when fully implemented as planned. This common sense statement belies a critical problem with prevention and other school-based intervention programs. Many programs are either only partially implemented or are implemented poorly. For example, Biggs et al. (2008) examined teacher reports of adherence to a violence prevention program and found varied levels of implementation ranging from teachers reporting daily use to others reporting no use of the program. Inadequate implementation leads to two problems. First, if *all* elements of a prevention program are necessary to produce an effect, poor implementation is a waste of time and resources because students will benefit little from the program. Second, if an *inadequately* implemented program does not result in the desired effects, policy makers may erroneously assume that the program or similar programs do not work and, therefore, should not be attempted in the future. Essentially, there is no way to accurately evaluate a partially implemented program.

Accordingly, prevention programs should include a mechanism for monitoring implementation integrity and providing support to staff where implementation is weak. Monitoring implementation integrity can be done through assessment; that is, the nature of the assessment is specific to the program. One common approach is to develop a checklist of required program components and then either have the implementer check off completion of each component and submit documentation to program leaders or have a program leader observe the program in action and check off appropriate completion of required program components. For example, a classroom-based, teacher-led social competency program might include as required components explanation of a skill, a wall-mounted poster reminding students of the skill, modeling by the teacher, and role-plays with feedback involving at least one third of the class. An observer could watch the teacher's session on this topic and complete a checklist regarding to what degree each of the required components actually occurred. For further examples see Castillo, Chapter 1. Although Castillo's discussion focuses specifically on multitiered support systems, the procedures are applicable broadly to school-based intervention programs.

Inservice training and ongoing consultation are ways the school psychologist can support school staff members in efforts to implement prevention programs (Fixsen, Naoom, Blase, Friedman, & Wallace, 2005). Inservice training through presentations provides staff with information about the program and allows members to practice necessary skills and problem solve through potential barriers to implementation. Ongoing consultation between the school psychologist and staff members facilitates the teaching of program components, assistance in planning for the staff member's role in the program, and problem solving through barriers to implementation in a dyad rather than the group environment of inservice training. Additional strategies that promote implementation fidelity include clear communication; explicit procedure and protocols; alignment with school culture, needs, and resources; and leadership and community support.

Program Evaluation

School-based prevention programs that explicitly include program evaluation procedures are more effective than those that have no such component (CASEL, 2012). Evaluation of prevention programs should include both formative and summative information. Formative evaluation refers to the collection of information while the program is being implemented and may include such information as implementation integrity, stakeholders' feedback on program operations, or assessment of intermediate goals. For example, in a

social competency development program the assessment of students' knowledge of problem-solving steps might provide corrective feedback for modifying the remaining sessions in the program. Summative evaluation refers to assessing the overall outcomes of the program. So, for the same example, summative evaluation might include an analysis of the number of disciplinary referrals for fighting before and after the program was implemented or data on the demonstrated social competency skills of students who participated in the program versus those who did not. Reporting evaluation results to school staff and parents in easily comprehensible, yet accurate, fashion is a critical piece of program evaluation. Additionally, both formative and summative evaluations need to be ongoing as the program continues to be implemented.

Institutionalization

Even when they produce desirable outcomes, school-based prevention programs are too often seen as time-limited projects. While projects fade, programs that are integrated into the fabric of the school endure. Several factors are key in institutionalizing successful programs. First, school psychologists should choose programs that address identified needs and goals that are integral to the school's defined mission. For example, decreasing academic failure will always be consistent with the school's mission, but a program to decrease adolescents' depression may endure only while there is enthusiasm from a particular staff member. Second, notwithstanding earlier comments about the importance of leadership, broader ownership and active involvement by multiple stakeholders (administration, teachers, parents) is more likely to result in institutionalization. In fact, leaders should try to sell the program to such stakeholders—particularly administration—early in the process, and, if unable to do so sufficiently, reconsider whether to pursue the program. Finally, programs must be sustainable. Those that require additional financial or labor resources beyond those normally available are likely to last only as long as external funding exists. Scope is an issue, so it is important to do what can be done with the available resources or resources that are likely to be obtained.

Examples of Effective Prevention Programs

Student retention is an intervention for students experiencing significant academic problems, but recent research suggests it is an ineffective intervention for improving academic achievement (Griffith, Lloyd, Lane, & Tankersley, 2010).

Individualizing Student Instruction

Research suggests providing individualized instruction may be more effective than class-wide approaches at improving skills and, ultimately, preventing retention (Dombek & Connor, 2012). Dombek and Connor (2012) explored this possibility using Individualizing Student Instruction (Connor et al., 2007). Individualizing Student Instruction combines teacher training on software used to link assessment results with recommendations for the amount and type of instruction needed for each child with ongoing professional development. It aims to assist teachers in differentiating reading instruction and implementing evidence-based reading practices. Studies show Individualizing Student Instruction to be effective for increasing students' word recognition and passage comprehension (Connor et al., 2007). In their study, Dombek and Connor (2012) matched and randomly assigned schools to implement Individualizing Student Instruction in first-grade reading classes or to continue with business as usual. Results showed that, after a year, students in Individualizing Student Instruction classrooms were less likely to be retained than their counterparts in control classrooms. The authors suggest that when teachers possess the resources to make informed instructional decisions via effective assessments and targeted instructional recommendations, student retention decreases, making it an effective prevention program.

Olweus Bullying Prevention Program

The Olweus Bullying Prevention Program (see Olweus and Limber, 2010, for detailed description) is a universal intervention for conduct problems. Bullying in schools is a problem that has gained increasing attention from school personnel and researchers over the past several decades. While many programs exist to deal with bullying, the Olweus Bullying Prevention Program shows particular promise to decrease student's involvement in bullying. The program began in Norwegian schools in the 1980s and has since been implemented and monitored in schools in South Carolina, Pennsylvania, Washington, and California.

The Olweus Bullying Prevention Program uses a multicomponent model working at four levels of implementation: school (e.g., establish a coordinating committee, conduct staff trainings), classroom (e.g., post and enforce rules against bullying, hold class-level meetings for parents), individual (e.g., meet with students involved in bullying, develop individual intervention plans for students), and community (e.g., involve community members on the coordinating committee, develop school–community partnerships to support the program). At each level of implementation, the program aims to reduce existing bullying, prevent future bullying, and improve peer relations at school.

As reviewed by Limber (2011), implementation of the Olweus Bullying Prevention Program in Norwegian schools has significantly decreased self-reported bullying victimization and bullying of others and has also increased student perception of positive school climate. When adapted for U.S. schools the core components of the program remained the same, but minor changes were made to implementation to suit the structure of U.S. schools. According to Limber (2011), implementation of the program in the United States has led to the following changes: significant decreases in self-reported bullying victimization and bullying of others, decreases in evaluator-observed bullying incidents, increases in student perception that teachers and other students actively intervened in bullying incidents, and increases in teacher perception that antibullying rules are clearly communicated and teacher self-confidence that they could effectively intervene in cases of bullying.

Diversity Issues

Given that diversity issues permeate all stages of prevention planning and implementation, school psychologists must consider ethnic and cultural diversity when selecting a program. A school psychologist should review literature on the program's effectiveness for the school population. In their study of school-based behavioral prevention programs for low-income urban youth, Farahmand, Grant, Polo, and Duffy (2011) found far fewer effective programs than were identified when examining programs for the whole population. Moreover, programs for low-income urban youth at a universal level were more effective than those implemented at a targeted level, a result not found when examining the effectiveness of these programs for the general population. As this study demonstrates, there is variability in program effectiveness for different populations.

Diversity issues are also important when implementing prevention programs. Aside from obvious difficulties encountered when implementing programs in settings with high populations of ethnic minorities (e.g., language barriers), school psychologists should educate themselves on the ways in which particular groups perceive the role of the school. Some groups may be reticent to accept prevention programs targeting mental health issues if they feel that schools are not the appropriate venue for such programs. Others may not see parents or families as having a major role in prevention initiatives. For these individuals, care should be taken to present the need for prevention in a thoughtful and meaningful way. School psychologists must work hard to create an environment where community members feel their voices are being heard and their needs are being addressed to the extent possible. To do this effectively, school psychologists must be cognizant of the diversity within their schools and knowledgeable about the best ways to reach all members of the community. Further, school psychologists must recognize the role of school culture, teacher attitudes, and their own cultural identity and biases when choosing, implementing, and evaluating prevention programs (Biggs et al., 2008).

Issues of Developmental Differences

During the planning phase of prevention programs, the age of the target group must be considered. The topic of the program must be developmentally appropriate if it is to be effective. For example, antibullying programs may be desirable to implement during early kindergarten and elementary school years since, for many children, this will be the first time they are spending much of their day in large groups of same-age peers, increasing the chances of bullying. Substance-abuse prevention programs, however, would be most appropriate in middle school since this is the time many students are confronted with substance use opportunities. The level of prevention program implementation can also contribute to disparate outcomes depending on age group. In their meta-analysis of school-based violence prevention programs, Wilson and Lipsey (2007) found universal programs to be more effective at reducing aggressive behavior in younger children than in older children while targeted and intensive programs more positively affected older children. As children age, their desire to be autonomous becomes stronger, potentially contributing to a greater effectiveness of prevention programs focused on the individual rather than the group during later childhood years and adolescence.

Overcoming Obstacles

Potential obstacles exist to implementing prevention programs. First, there may be resistance to prevention programs irrespective of who is implementing such programs. One of the most common negative views of prevention is a perceived lack of research support, a position that is no longer tenable. A second obstacle is administrators' often incorrect perception that special education resources, including school psychologists' time, cannot be used in prevention activities. However, since its inception, the 2004 Individuals with Disabilities Education Improvement Act (IDEA) has allowed for at least some prevention activities to be supported with IDEA funds, typically through early intervention efforts.

High student/psychologist service ratios may be a third obstacle to prevention work. School psychologists who serve several schools or who have high caseloads likely will have little time available for prevention program development and implementation. NASP recommends a ratio of 500–700 students for each school psychologist engaged in prevention, but this ratio is often significantly higher, although it has been improving incrementally over the past 20 years (Curtis et al., 2012).

A fourth obstacle is related to the perceived role of the school psychologist. Traditionally, school psychologists work primarily in special education assessment, thus administrators and staff may struggle to view them in a different, prevention-focused role and school psychologists may struggle to feel comfortable and confident expanding their role to be broader than just assessment.

Although obstacles to prevention program selection and implementation exist, there are ways to overcome them. School psychologists looking to reduce their testing role and move in more of a preventive direction may consider consultation as a starting point. Teacher consultation, most typically case centered, has emerged as the second-most common activity for school psychologists. Because training in consultation and collaboration is required for all NASP-approved school psychology training programs, many school psychologists have competencies in this area. Advocates of the consultation role stress the idea that consultation, although typically performed after a problem has been noted, inherently contains an element of prevention because helping the teacher to work more effectively with one student will likely also increased the teacher's effectiveness with future students. Furthermore, case-centered or teacher-centered consultation may evolve into systems-level consultation leading to the development of universal preventive efforts.

In overcoming obstacles related to time constraints, high student-to-school psychologist ratios, and uncertainty transitioning their roles to be more prevention-focused, school psychologists may consider forming working partnerships with the school counselor or social worker. Through partnerships, school psychologists can work collaboratively with other professionals on prevention activities that are more distal from the school psychologist's status quo role. School psychologists bring unique skills to the table through their training in assessing need and planning for intervention. Thus, while school-wide preventive programs around mental health, where present, have typically been the province of school counselors, school psychologists can collaborate to enhance the planning, implementation, and evaluation of these programs.

SUMMARY

Prevention is now a well-established role for school psychologists, as indicated by its emphasis in the NASP Practice Model and by the substantial growth of prevention-related works in the recent school psychology literature. As practitioners, school psychologists appear to be increasing their involvement in prevention activities.

Prevention is an intervention, and should follow the same careful steps that one would take when intervening with an existing problem. Considering the evidence base for any prevention program before its implementation is a critical first step. There is now ample evidence on the efficacy and effectiveness of prevention programs that target both the academic and the social, emotional, and behavioral domains at the universal and targeted levels of intervention. Including a robust program evaluation component is a critical piece of any prevention effort.

School characteristics are also important to consider when developing prevention activities. For example, how the school views its mission will affect the acceptability of prevention efforts, and communication among staff will affect the fidelity of implementation. Conducting a needs assessment and an environmental scan of available resources during the early planning phases can help determine what programs, if any, may work in any particular school. Critically, school psychologists must be aware of ethnic and cultural diversity when planning for and implementing a prevention program.

School psychology's long-standing broad core competencies provide well-prepared and experienced school psychologists with a solid basis for engaging in prevention. Innovation requires leadership. For school psychologists working in schools where prevention programs are a novelty, a transition to a prevention focus will require considerable leadership. Even with good leadership this transition may be a challenge, but increasingly school psychologists are making prevention an important part of their work.

AUTHOR NOTE

Special thanks to Dr. Jessica Koehler, coauthor of the previous edition of this chapter, for her many contributions to the current work.

REFERENCES

Albee, G. W. (1968). Conceptual models and manpower requirements in psychology. *American Psychologist, 23*, 317–320. doi:10.1037/h0026125

Biggs, B. K., Vernberg, E. M., Twemlow, S. W., Fonagy, P., & Dill, E. J. (2008). Teacher adherence and its relation to teacher attitudes and student outcomes in an elementary school-based violence prevention program. *School Psychology Review, 37*, 533–549.

Castillo, J. M., Curtis, M. J., & Gelley, C. (2012). School psychology 2010: Demographics, employment, and the context for professional practices: Part 2. *Communiqué, 40*(8), 4–6.

Collaborative for Academic, Social, and Emotional Learning. (2012). *2013 CASEL guide: Effective social and emotional learning programs—preschool and elementary school edition*. Chicago, IL: Author. Retrieved from http://casel.org/wp-content/uploads/casel_guide_summary.pdf

Committee for Children. (2008). *Second Step: Student success through prevention*. Seattle, WA: Author.

Conduct Problems Prevention Research Group. (2011). The effects of the Fast Track preventive intervention on the development of conduct disorder across childhood. *Child Development, 82*, 331–345. doi:10.1111/j.1467-8624.2010.01558.x

Connor, C. M., Morrison, F. J., Fishman, B. J., Schatschneider, C., & Underwood, P. (2007). The early years: Algorithm-guided individualized reading instruction. *Science, 315*, 464–465. doi:10.1126/science.1134513

Cooney, S. M., Kratochwill, T. R., & Small, S. A. (2010). Youth policy and politics in the United States: Toward an increased focus on prevention. In B. Doll, W. Pfohl, & J. Yoon (Eds.), *Handbook of youth prevention science* (pp. 445–460). New York, NY: Routledge.

Cummings, J. A., Harrison, P. L., Dawson, M. M., Short, R. J., Gorin, S., & Palomares, R. (2004). The 2002 conference on the future of school psychology: Implications for consultation, intervention, and prevention services. *Journal of Educational and Psychological Consultation, 15*, 239–256. doi:10.1207/s1532768xjepc153&4_3

Curtis, M. J., Castillo, J. M., & Gelley, C. (2012). School psychology 2010: Demographics, employment, and the context for professional practices—Part 1. *Communiqué, 40*(7), 1, 28–30.

Doll, B., Pfohl, W., & Yoon, J. (Eds.). (2010). *Handbook of youth prevention science*. New York, NY: Routledge.

Dombek, J., & Connor, C. (2012). Preventing retention: First grade classroom instruction and student characteristics. *Psychology in the Schools, 49*, 568–588. doi:10.1002/pits.21618

Durlak, J. A., Weissberg, R. P., Dymnicki, A. B., Taylor, R. D., & Schellinger, K. B. (2011). The impact of enhancing students' social and emotional learning: A meta-analysis of school-based universal interventions. *Child Development, 82*, 405–432. doi:10.1111/j.1467-8624.2010.01564.x

Elias, M. J., & Branden, L. R. (1988). Primary prevention of behavioral and emotional problems in school-aged populations. *School Psychology Review, 17*, 581–592.

Farahmand, F. K., Grant, K. E., Polo, A. J., & Duffy, S. N. (2011). School-based mental health and behavioral programs for low income, urban youth: A systematic and meta-analytic review. *Clinical Psychology: Science and Practice, 18*, 372–390. doi:10.1111/j.1468-2850.2011.01265

Fixsen, D. L., Naoom, S. F., Blase, K. A., Friedman, R. M., & Wallace, F. (2005). *Implementation research: A synthesis of the literature* (FMHI Publication #231). Tampa, FL: University of South Florida, Louis de la Parte Florida Mental Health Institute.

Flay, B. R., Biglan, A., Boruch, R. F., Castro, F. G., Gottfredson, D. C., Kellam, S., & Ji, P. (2005). Standards of evidence: Criteria for efficacy, effectiveness and dissemination. *Prevention Science, 6*, 151–176. doi:10.1007/s11121-005-5553-y

Greenberg, M. T., Weissberg, R. P., O'Brien, M. U., Zins, J. E., Fredericks, L., Resnik, H., & Elias, M. J. (2003). Enhancing school-based prevention and youth development through coordinated social, emotional, and academic learning. *American Psychologist, 58*, 466–474. doi:10.1037/0003-066X.58.6-7.466

Griffith, C. A., Lloyd, J. W., Lane, K. L., & Tankersley, M. (2010). Grade retention of students during grades K–8 predicts reading achievement and progress during secondary schooling. *Reading and Writing Quarterly, 26*, 51–66. doi:10.1080/10573560903396967

Johnson, K., Hays, C., Center, H., & Daley, C. (2004). Building capacity and sustainable prevention innovations: A sustainability planning model. *Evaluation and Program Planning, 27*, 135–149. doi:10.1016/j.evalprogplan.2004.01.002

Limber, S. P. (2011). Development, evaluation, and future directions of the Olweus Bullying Prevention Program. *Journal of School Violence, 10*, 71–87. doi:10.1080/15388220.2010.519375

McGinnis, E. (2011). *Skillstreaming the elementary school child: A guide for teaching prosocial skills* (3rd ed.). Champaign, IL: Research Press.

Nation, M., Crusto, C., Wandersman, A., Kumpfer, K. L., Seybolt, D., Morrisey-Kane, E., & Davino, K. (2003). What works in prevention: Principles of effective programs. *American Psychologist, 58*, 449–456. doi:10.1037/0003-066X.58.6-7.449

National Association of School Psychologists. (2000). *Professional conduct manual: Guidelines for the provision of school psychological services.* Bethesda, MD: Author.

National Association of School Psychologists. (2010). *Model for comprehensive and integrated school psychological services.* Bethesda, MD: Author. Retrieved from http://www.nasponline.org/standards/2010standards/2_PracticeModel.pdf

Olweus, D., & Limber, S. P. (2010). The Olweus Bullying Prevention Program: Implementation and evaluation over two decades. In S. R. Jimerson, S. M. Swearer, & D. L. Espelage (Eds.), *The handbook of school bullying: An international perspective* (pp. 377–402). New York, NY: Routledge.

Payton, J., Weissberg, R. P., Durlak, J. A., Dymnicki, A. B., Taylor, R. D., Schellinger, K. B., & Pachan, M. (2008). *The positive impact of social and emotional learning for kindergarten to eighth-grade students: Findings from three scientific reviews* (Technical Report). Chicago, IL: Collaborative for Academic, Social, and Emotional Learning. Retrieved from http://www.lpfch.org/sel/PackardES-REV.pdf

Price, R. H., Cowan, E. L., Lorian, R. P., & Ramos-McKay, J. (1988). *14 ounces of prevention: A casebook for practitioners.* Washington, DC: American Psychological Association.

Shure, M. B. (2001). *I can problem solve: An interpersonal cognitive problem solving program: Kindergarten and primary grades* (2nd ed.). Champaign, IL: Research Press.

Teglasi, H., & Rothman, L. (2001). STORIES: A classroom-based program to reduce aggressive behavior. *Journal of School Psychology, 39*, 71–94. doi:10.1016/S0022-4405(00)00060-1

Wilson, S. J., & Lipsey, M. W. (2007). School-based interventions for aggressive and disruptive behavior: Update of a meta-analysis. *American Journal of Preventive Medicine, 33*, S130–S143.

Best Practices in Population-Based School Mental Health Services

11

Beth Doll
University of Nebraska–Lincoln
Jack A. Cummings
Indiana University
Brooke A. Chapla
University of Nebraska–Lincoln

OVERVIEW

School shootings, suicides, and school dropout rates, along with the desire for higher academic test scores, have awakened policy makers, school administrators, teachers, and parents to the importance of attending to students' mental health needs. These needs are substantial. Epidemiological research has shown that 20% of school-age youth have a diagnosable psychiatric disorder (Centers for Disease Control and Prevention, 2013), and only a fourth of these students are receiving therapeutic services outside of the school (Hoagwood & Johnson, 2003). Given this significant gap between the need for and availability of mental health services, schools are the de facto mental health provider for most school-age children and adolescents. Concurrently, developmental research since the 1970s has demonstrated that mental health and psychological wellness are not ancillary to school success but are integral to it (Masten et al., 2005). In fact, schools cannot be successful unless their students are also developmentally, socially, and emotionally competent.

School psychologists must recognize their tacit responsibility for the mental health of their students. Adelman and Taylor (2010) argue strongly that school improvement efforts will not succeed until the reforms incorporate the efforts of school psychologists and other school mental health providers. This chapter will describe how population-based models can be used to align school psychological services with the mental health needs of children (Hoagwood & Johnson, 2003) and how doing so can strengthen students' school success. Emphasis will be placed on showing how population-based services are similar to and different from traditional school psychological services that focused on referred students. Emphasis will also be placed on what needs to happen to transition from traditional to comprehensive population-based school psychological services.

Population-based mental health services are those that have been carefully planned to meet the collective mental health needs of all students enrolled in a school. The services begin with monitoring students' mental health and then using the data from the monitoring to plan an array of services and interventions that promote psychological wellness. Students' wellness, in turn, is essential for optimal academic achievement. The array of population-based services represents a multitiered continuum of care. Universal screening and evidence-based interventions for all students serve as the foundation for all other mental health services in the school. Services promoting environments that nurture students at high risk correspond to the selected or targeted level of intervention. Finally, the intensive or indicated level of intervention is represented by remedial services that help students develop social, emotional, and behavioral competencies.

Traditional school psychological services had a clear goal: remediating social, emotional, or behavioral disturbances of referred students. With a population-based infrastructure, three additional goals are addressed: promoting the psychological well-being of all students, providing protective support to students at high risk for developmental failures, and promoting caretaking environments that allow students to overcome developmental risks and challenges (Doll & Cummings, 2008). Together, these four goals subsume both direct and indirect services described in the National Association of School Psychologists (NASP) *Model for Comprehensive and Integrated School Psychological Services* (NASP, 2010). Population-based services designed to promote mental health are at the central core of the NASP Practice Model. At the systems level, the domain of Preventive and Responsive Services requires that school psychologists work with others to enhance students' "learning, mental health, safety, and physical well-being" (NASP, 2010, p. 6). Likewise, at the student services level, the domain of Interventions and Mental Health Services to Develop Social and Life Skills requires that school psychologists work with others "to implement and evaluate services that support socialization, learning, and mental health" (NASP, 2010, p. 5). Additional references to mental health promotion are integral to the NASP Practice Model's domains of Data-Based Decision Making and Accountability and Consultation and Collaboration. These domains are also essential to the successful implementation of population-based mental health services.

BASIC CONSIDERATIONS

Within a population-based service model, systematic and objective needs assessments are conducted to create a portrait of the collective mental health of all students enrolled in a school or district (Doll & Cummings, 2008). The identified mental health needs are compared against a similarly comprehensive assessment of the mental health resources available in the school and community. Schools' mental health resources include the many social supports that are available through the teachers, administrators, and other school staff who interact with students in addition to the school mental health professionals. Next, a plan is constructed that prioritizes the needs of the school's students and allocates mental health resources to services that are frequently needed and those that will have high impact on the students' psychological wellness. Options for services may be expanded through collaborative

partnerships that integrate diverse mental health services into comprehensive systems of care and dismantle programmatic silos, which are narrowly construed programs that address a single risk factor or disturbance without regard for students' other risks or needs. Ongoing and rigorous evaluation of the impact of mental health services documents the plan's effectiveness and informs decisions about plan refinements. At the core of this cycle of assessment, planning, intervention, and evaluation are the principles that (a) students' mental health services must be intentional and empirically rigorous; (b) data should document the collective mental health needs of students in the district; (c) research should guide the match between interventions and those needs; (d) and evaluation should document the impact of the program's mental health services on students' psychological wellness and success.

Ultimately, all goals of population-based mental health services converge toward a single purpose: to foster the social, emotional, behavioral, and academic competence that students need to be successful in school and in life. The population-wide perspective allows school psychologists to exploit current and emerging research describing community-wide supports that strengthen students' developmental competence and psychological well-being. Schools are uniquely suited to implement population-based mental health services because their universal access to all children allows schools to detect students' early signs of social and emotional distress more readily than other mental health providers, and schools can incorporate appropriate mental health interventions into students' everyday routines.

BEST PRACTICES IN POPULATION-BASED SCHOOL MENTAL HEALTH SERVICES

This section will summarize the best practices available to school psychologists in population-based assessment, resource identification, planning, intervention, and evaluation. Figure 11.1 shows how these phases are revisited in an ongoing cycle of program renewal and refinement.

Population-Based Needs Assessment

A best practice is that school psychologists gather comprehensive, accurate data to describe the collective mental health of all students enrolled in their school or district. These population-based assessments address three questions: (a) What is known about the mental

Figure 11.1. Example of a School's Matrix Diagraming the Scope of Population-Based Mental Health Services and the Personnel Available to Support the Services

MAJOR AREAS OF FUNCTION	GENERIC COMPETENCIES	SPECIALIZED COMPETENCIES
DIRECT INTERVENTIONS	• Consulting with teachers regarding behavioral adjustment • Providing an evidence-based drug-prevention program within classrooms • Screening all students for suicide risk	• Developing and delivering a bereavement group for a student whose parent has died • Implementing a parenting intervention with parents of students with ADHD • Implementing a suicide prevention program for students at high risk
INTERVENTIONS TO ENHANCE SYSTEMS WITHIN SCHOOLS	• Consulting with building leadership and paraprofessionals to refine playground/recess practices • Consulting with building leadership to refine school policies for behavioral discipline	• Implementing a school-wide bullying prevention program • Establishing a crisis intervention team to respond to acts of violence or disturbing events
INTERVENTIONS TO ENHANCE SCHOOL–COMMUNITY LINKAGES AND PARTNERSHIPS	• Developing and staffing a parent resource center in the school	• Implementing a community–school service coordination team • Establishing a families and schools together intervention in the building
SUPERVISION/ADMINISTRATION	• Fostering a peer supervision network for school mental health professionals • Serving on the building mental health planning team	• Managing a supervision network for professionals • Conducting a systematic program evaluation of school mental health services

health of students who attend this school or schools in this district? (b) What are the needs of the population as a whole? (c) What are the needs of students identified as being at risk or in the early stage of developing problems? These may be unfamiliar questions for school psychologists who are accustomed to traditional one-child-at-a-time assessment procedures. Traditional child studies fully describe each student's academic, social, and emotional strengths and needs, and they point to the interventions that are needed for that student to be successful. Prior to 1980, school psychologists trusted that teachers and parents were referring the neediest students for assessment and that, collectively, the comprehensive child studies provided a complete and accurate assessment of schools' mental health needs. This confidence was shattered when subsequent epidemiological studies identified large numbers of unidentified children with significant mental health needs (Hoagwood & Johnson, 2003).

Population-based assessments identify students who would have slipped through the cracks in traditional referral-based services by proactively screening the full student population of a school with objective, empirically defensible measures of psychological wellness or disturbance (Doll, Haack, & Bieber, 2013). They identify students earlier than would otherwise be the case, and guide the planned development of school mental health services to match the collective students' needs.

Population-based assessments should only occur within an integrated student support plan (Dowdy, Furlong, Eklund, Saeki, & Richey, 2010). Even a highly sophisticated and well-implemented screening procedure has limited value without a follow-up plan to deliver services to students who demonstrate needs. Moreover, well-designed population-based screening requires concerted effort by a team and cannot be undertaken by a single individual. Thus, teachers, administrators, and noncertified staff in a school play essential roles in any population-based student support plan.

Population-based screening assessments should be selected with special attention to identification of the mental health needs that are not readily recognized within schools. Boys and some girls with externalizing symptoms are often identified by teachers in the traditional referral systems, while students of both genders who have internalizing symptoms are more often overlooked (Hoagwood & Johnson, 2003).

Population-based assessments must be highly accurate in describing the mental health of a school's students (Levitt, Saka, Romanelli, & Hoagwood, 2007). Accuracy is composed of the assessment's sensitivity and its specificity. Sensitivity refers to the percentage of students who are correctly identified as having a significant mental health need. In contrast, specificity describes the percentage of students correctly identified as not having a mental health need. A measure with high sensitivity (minimizing the number of false-negative identifications) will not overlook students with legitimate needs for school psychological services. Two other terms that school psychologists should be familiar with are *positive predictive value* (the proportion of true positives over the total of true positives added to the false negatives) and *negative predictive value* (the number of true negatives over the total of true negatives and false positives).

Finally, population-based assessments must be practical for use by teams of educators screening the full enrollment of a school or district (Doll et al., 2013). These assessments must be brief to administer so that the assessment of large numbers of students is neither time intensive nor prohibitively expensive. For example, it would be unreasonable to ask teachers to complete a 100-item symptoms checklist for every student in a class. The assessments must also be efficient to code and analyze. Hand scoring a brief, 20-item checklist from every child in a 500-student elementary school would be an onerous task. Many population-based assessments use multistage procedures in which the entire child population of a community is first screened to identify any evidence of a disorder. More time-intensive measures are then administered to students selected in the first stage and yield more comprehensive descriptions of their needs and strengths. At a minimum, the assessment results in a list of students with a demonstrated need for services and descriptive information about the identified group. The best assessments can be administered repeatedly without practice effects and are sensitive to intervention effects, so that the assessment results can verify reductions in the prevalence or severity of disturbances or increases in the prevalence or degree of psychological wellness once an intervention has been provided.

Four assessment strategies are used in population-based services to screen the full enrollment of a school or district. Measures may (a) identify students at high risk for disturbances based on their demographic or social risk, (b) describe students' access to very strong protective factors, (c) identify students with prominent symptoms of a disorder even though not all diagnostic criteria are met, or (d) identify students having a mental disorder or qualifying for special educational services for behavior disorders. Each of these strategies is described below, together with an example of a population-based measure that uses that strategy. Additional discussion of alternative population-based measures can be found in Doll et al. (2013).

Identifying Students With Chronic Life Stressors

Population-based assessment can be predicated on the developmental risk research, which has identified chronic stressors that place students at risk for limited academic and social success (Werner, 2013). Identification of children living with multiple stressors can aid in constructing effective prevention and intervention systems that target the specific needs of a school's enrollment. The most prominent of these stressors include poverty, low parent education, family conflict, ineffective parenting, child maltreatment, poor physical health of the child or parents, and parental mental illness or incapacity. Prevalence rates for some of these stressors can be identified through a systematic analysis of the cumulative file data available in school files (e.g., students' eligibility for free and reduced lunch or for Title I programs). Descriptions of other factors exist within other agencies in the community. For example, the police department can typically describe the incidence of violent and nonviolent crimes within the school's catchment area. A city planning department can describe the average home value in the community and the rate of rental versus owner-occupied properties.

The local employment office can describe the unemployment rate. Developmental risk research convincingly establishes that these community and family characteristics are primary determinants of developmental success or failure and that they are important indexes of the social need that exists within the community.

A very practical example of screening for chronic stressors can be found in Fairfax County, Virginia, where school psychologists, school social workers, and school counselors collaborated with community agencies and county government to gather information about the school enrollment's mental health needs (King & Jun, 2012). They distributed two surveys: Risk and Protective Factors (selected items from the Youth Risk Behavior Survey available from the Centers for Disease Control and Prevention, http://www.cdc.gov/healthyyouth/yrbs/index.htm) and Healthy Behaviors (selected items from the Communities That Care Survey available at the Substance Abuse and Mental Health Services Administration website [SAMHSA], http://store.samhsa.gov/product/Communities-That-Care-Youth-Survey/CTC020). Together, the surveys ask questions about students' mental health issues such as depression; suicide; body image; use of alcohol, tobacco, and other drugs; delinquent behaviors; bullying; sexual health; nutrition; and physical activity. The surveys were administered annually to 8th-, 10th-, and 12th-grade students, and staff members were then able to assess the impact of interventions. Then if a risky behavior was shown to be elevated in a specific high school, the school mental health team tailored interventions and prevention efforts for that school. More information about the program and a toolkit can be found on the Fairfax County School Psychology Services' website (http://www.fairfaxcounty.gov/ncs/prevention/toolkit.htm). The toolkit provides links to obtain support, a step-by-step guide for implementation, and contact information for the prevention staff. Also available on the site are prevention handouts and resources on substance abuse, bullying/cyberbullying, depression, suicide, and teen dating abuse.

Another risk survey report that represents a collaboration of the community and school resources is the Dane County (Wisconsin) Youth Assessment Overview Report (Dane County Youth Commission, 2012; reports are available at http://www.danecountyhumanservices.org/family/youth/dane_county_youth_commission.aspx). In the most recent report, 19.4% of Dane County middle and high school youth (7th to 12th grade) indicated *yes* when they were asked, "During the past 12 months, did you ever feel so sad or hopeless almost every day for at least 2 weeks in a row that you stopped doing some usual activities?" Girls reported depressive symptoms at a higher rate than boys, with a total of 25.6% of the girls reporting symptoms of depression. Of the high school students, anxiety symptoms were reported by 10.5% of the high school girls and 5.4% of the high school boys. Symptoms of an eating disorder were reported by 2.0% of the high school girls and 1.3% of the boys.

Whereas the Fairfax and Dane County surveys were anonymous, Eklund (2013) describes a screening procedure that was not. In an elementary school in the Fort Carson (Colorado) School District, specific students were identified as at risk using universal screening; and then school-wide social–emotional curricula were implemented. A large percentage of the district's students were dependents of active military parents, and, since students' parents were in various stages of deployment, this created significant stressors on the families. For example, when one parent was deployed to an active conflict, the other parent became a single parent, and there was also a shared fear that the deployed parent might not return or could be seriously wounded. Even when the deployed parents returned home, they were not the same as when they left. Working with teachers to identify and select social–emotional curricula, the program team decided that K–2 teachers would implement Second Step (Frey, Hirschstein, & Guzzo, 2000), while third- and fourth-grade teachers implemented Promoting Alternative Thinking Strategies (Greenberg, Kusche, & Mihalic, 1998), with the fifth-grade teachers opting for Stories of Us. Eklund used the Student Risk Screening Scale (Drummond, 1994) as well as the ClassMaps Survey (Doll et al., 2013). A total of 62 students were identified by the screening as having significant mental health needs. Thirty-nine of the students had been previously identified, while 23 students not currently identified were connected with services.

Describing Students' Protective Factors

Many of the same developmental studies that described demographic risk factors also identified protective factors that predict future life success in vulnerable students and could become the mechanisms underlying preventive interventions. Examples of such protective factors include close peer friendships, high self-efficacy, high level of engagement in productive activities, access to warm relationships and guidance from adults, or access to responsive schools. Consequently, a second form of population-based assessment identifies assets available to a school's students.

A promising example of asset assessment is the Resiliency Scales for Children and Adolescents (Prince-Embury, 2007). This is a 64-item self-report survey that describes the personal resources of students, including their senses of mastery and interpersonal relatedness, and also describes their emotional reactivity. The survey is based on very strong theoretical conceptualization and is nicely grounded in developmental research on adolescent resilience. Validity studies described in the Resiliency Scales for Children and Adolescents manual show that it discriminates well between students with and without a variety of psychiatric disorders. Moreover, comparison of the two strengths scales (sense of mastery and sense of relatedness) and the one liability scale (emotional reactivity) can yield a vulnerability index that represents students' personal capacity for coping with adversity.

By administering the Resiliency Scales for Children and Adolescents across enrolled students, schools could assess the collective personal resources of students. Prince-Embury (2010) explains how these results could guide interventions to strengthen students' resilience. Some students' ratings could trigger referral to cognitive–behavioral groups designed to strengthen their sense of mastery. Other interventions might help certain students identify their personal strengths. Still other students might be systematically directed toward activities and groups that could provide them with a social network of support. Reassessment with the Resiliency Scales for Children and Adolescents could establish the degree to which the school's services were contributing to gains in student resilience.

Identifying Early Symptoms of Later Disorders

Population-based assessments may also be based on evidence of early symptoms of dysfunction that do not satisfy the diagnostic criteria for mental disorders but nevertheless represent developmental problems that could impair students' life success (Albers, Glover, & Kratochwill, 2007). Early identification and intervention make it possible for schools to address adjustment problems when they are first evidenced and, in some cases, to mitigate long-term negative outcomes. While many risk-based assessments use surveys or rating scales to identify emerging symptoms, it is also possible to use existing school data as measures of functional risk. For example, information about office discipline referrals can be used to assess a school's safety and behavioral climate (Irvin et al., 2006).

As one example of an early identification assessment, the Check & Connect program compiles attendance and discipline data to identify middle school students who are in danger of disengaging from school (Christenson & Reschly, 2010). Disengaged students are paired with a mentor who then monitors the student's active participation in school, intervenes at critical points to keep the connection to school alive, and builds a meaningful partnership between home and school. The Check & Connect manual (Christenson, Stout, & Pohl, 2012) further explains the identification of students at risk for leaving school, indicators of student disengagement, desirable selection criteria for mentors, the role of the mentor, and detailed steps for implementing the program with fidelity. An innovative feature of the website (http://checkandconnect.umn.edu) is the availability of assistance to individuals writing funding proposals for a Check & Connect program within their school district.

Identifying Diagnosable Disorders

Results of epidemiological prevalence studies can be used to predict the most likely disorders that school psychologists will identify through population-based screening (Doll et al., 2013). The most prevalent psychosocial disorders in elementary-age students are anxiety disorders, attention deficit disorders, and, to a lesser extent, conduct and oppositional defiant disorders. By the secondary grades, the incidence of attention deficit hyperactivity disorder (ADHD) is somewhat lower, but the incidence of conduct disorders is at least twice that of elementary students, and mood disorders are three to four times as prevalent.

One prominent example of an assessment that identifies students with diagnosable disorders is the Systematic Screening for Behavior Disorders (Walker & Severson, 1992). This was used to screen the entire enrollment of a New Orleans school to identify students with behavior disorders who qualified for special educational services (Walker et al., 2010). Originally designed for use with elementary populations, recent research indicates the Systematic Screening for Behavior Disorders is also a promising tool for middle and high school populations (Lane, Kalberg, Parks, & Carter, 2008; Richardson, Caldarella, Young, Young, & Young, 2009). First, teachers attend a brief presentation alerting them to the distinctive internalizing and externalizing behaviors of students. Then each teacher identifies three students from his or her class who demonstrate externalizing behaviors and three who demonstrate internalizing behaviors. The teacher completes brief checklists to describe the nature and frequency of critical behaviors that characterize each of the six students. Those students with elevated ratings are systematically observed in both the classroom and the playground and are referred to the school's child study team for behavior planning if the students engage in excessive amounts of negative behavior, are unusually isolated, or are disengaged from classroom learning activities. Research conducted by the authors (Walker & Severson, 1992; Walker et al., 2010) shows that between 85% and 90% of a school's students can be correctly identified as having or not having internalizing or externalizing problems using the Systematic Screening for Behavior Disorders.

In prior decades, the administration, analysis, and interpretation of population-based measures such as those described above would be a prohibitively time consuming task. However, technology can substantially reduce the time and cost required for school staff to collect, organize, and analyze population-based data (Burns, 2013). Future advances in technology will only make population-based assessments even simpler. Measures administered using tablets or smartphones could save data directly to secure electronic spreadsheets and provide assistive technology for students with disabilities. As examples, the Dane County survey mentioned earlier was administered electronically, and the online ClassMaps survey reads questions aloud to students. Using current technology and cloud-based software, it can be a simple task to synchronize electronic data even when it is culled from multiple informants or uses different platforms. Integrated ratings across teachers, peers, and students can become powerful predictors of student mental health needs and school success. Population-based assessment is now a practical option of schools because of the potential of technologically enhanced assessment when collecting and examining large sets of data.

Even with technological enhancements, and regardless of the measures that are used, it is clear that a shift to population-based assessments cannot be made around the edges of traditional assessment. The strategies require considerable staff time up front in order to plan, collect, and analyze the school-wide data. At a minimum, this will require that schools redirect some of the resources currently allocated to referral-based service delivery. Moreover, population-based assessments do not replace traditional problem-based assessments of individual students; that is, population-based assessments rarely provide sufficient definitive information for a full behavior plan for any single student. Instead, population-based assessments provide different and important information about the overall mental health status of a school.

Identification of Mental Health Resources

A best practice is that school psychologists make effective use of existing resources of a school or district when describing services available to meet students' mental health needs. Questions about the school's mental health resources that parallel questions about students' needs. These are (a) What is being done already to support students' psychosocial development? (b) Who does it? (c) What else needs to be done? Underlying these questions is the very practical insight that, in most schools, transitions to population-based services will not be predicated on a substantial increase in the availability of mental health resources. Instead, most public schools face the prospect of continued tight budgets and unwavering pressure to cut expenses, particularly when these expenses are noninstructional. Community mental health centers face similar pressures, and private insurance carriers are inconsistent in their reimbursements for students' mental health services. Consequently, the shift from a traditional model to population-based school psychological services will often be made in the face of flat or even diminishing pediatric mental health resources.

Still, careful and deliberate planning might make it possible to use existing resources more efficiently and effectively (Adelman & Taylor, 2010). National policy makers have suggested that scarce resources could be leveraged if school psychologists, school counselors, school social workers, and community mental health professionals could coordinate their efforts rather than working independently to solve some of the same problems with the same subpopulations of students. Others point out that this coordination is sorely lacking between current school and community practice. Many note that teachers and other educators play a crucial role in fostering students' social growth and well-being, and so schools can draw upon many adults (not just school mental health professionals) when offering social–emotional learning programs for students. Schools are the sites for diverse social and mental health programs, including programs to prevent substance abuse and other risky youth behaviors, to promote school completion, to strengthen youth resilience, and to enhance parenting (Osher, Dwyer, & Jackson, 2004). Still, these programs have typically developed within programmatic silos, meaning that each works in isolation of the others

(Adelman & Taylor, 2010). They fail to take advantage of collaborative and coordinated ways of using each program to meet other programs' respective objectives. This is not to suggest that each program has an unimportant mandate or focus. However, a connection to other programs is too frequently missing from the mission of each program. At times, school and community programs partition services and compete for turf. Reshaping these programmatic silos into coordinated systems of care will require heretofore unknown flexibility and dedicated focus.

Resource mapping is a strategy for marshaling resources to address the needs of students who emerge from the assessment phase (Adelman & Taylor, 2010; Center for Mental Health in Schools at UCLA, 2008). Its purpose is to carefully analyze and plan the roles and functions of school counselors, psychologists, social workers, and other educators as a part of promoting collaboration and reducing fragmentation of services. As a systematic assessment of resources, resource mapping is, in itself, a major intervention and critical first step toward improving the effectiveness of the system's ability to anticipate and respond to students' psychological needs. The desired outcome is to free resources from their respective silos and leverage their impact.

The first step of resource mapping is describing the school's support staff: how staff members spend their time and when and where they provide services. In a typical school district, the staff could include school psychologists, counselors, attendance officers, social workers, dropout coordinators, school safety and violence prevention staff, resource teachers, crisis team members, school improvement team members, and staff from outside agencies that have programs that are school-linked or use school facilities. A map of services can be created by recording the nature of services provided by each individual or professional group, populations of students served, and when the staff is present in the school. Then, this description should be extended to include other educators and school staff who contribute in important ways to students' psychological wellness.

Once the map of school-based support staff resources is completed, the next critical step involves reframing roles to respond to the various needs identified during the initial assessment phase. For example, if four different mental health professionals are providing behavioral consultation in a school, and multiple professionals are often providing this service for the same students, realigning these services could free up resources for other needs. If, in this same school, a large

number of students were engaged in presuicidal behaviors, some of the freed-up professional time might be allocated to suicide prevention services. Adelman and Taylor (2010) describe this as weaving together the staff. An important component of this reframing process may be modifying existing policies to allow services to be combined in new ways and to allow professionals to interact in new ways.

The capacity of the school-based support staff can also be expanded by tapping community-based resources, including public and private agencies, personnel, and programs, for inclusion in the map. Community mental health professionals and school-based support staff are not the only resources for promoting students' healthy development. Teachers, parents, and mentors also provide critical support through their daily interactions with students. In some districts, the business community has shown much interest in promoting high-quality schools and may be a potential resource. In other districts, a local university represents yet another rich source of resources. Philanthropic groups may also be considered. As was the case for school-employed resources, the resource map should include the name of the program or professional, the nature of the service, and when the service is delivered.

Population-Based Planning

A best practice is that school psychologists' plan for population-based services is intentional, matching services and interventions to the highest priority mental health needs of the school's students. Reconciling students' needs with the available resources leads inevitably to a third set of questions: Which services should be provided to which students? When? By whom? For how long? With what result? By juxtaposing existing mental health resources with the needs of students in the school, it is possible to create a mental health service plan for the school. Mental health needs that are demonstrated by large numbers of enrolled students (e.g., anxiety symptoms) may indicate that school-wide services would be appropriate. Alternatively, very significant needs may justify the provision of high-intensity mental health services, even if these would be needed only by very few students. Matching resources against needs is a critical phase of population-based services.

The Center for Mental Health in Schools at UCLA (2001) provides a resource mapping matrix to conceptualize the match between students' needs and staff competencies and to describe the various facets of personnel preparation that will be necessary to implement the desired program. Their matrix has three dimensions: types of interventions, specificity of competencies, and levels of professional development.

Figure 11.1 is an example of one school's resource map using the first two dimensions. Interventions are classified as direct, including interventions that are individual, group, or classroom focused; those enhancing systems within school; those building or strengthening community–school partnerships; or interventions that are supervisory or administrative. Competencies are categorized as generic (held by many school staff or most school mental health professionals) or specialized (held by some or a few school mental health professionals).

Subsequent to a comprehensive mental health needs assessment in the school, the mental health team determined that there was a striking need to address the students' behavioral discipline, with a special emphasis on classroom behaviors of students with ADHD and on peer conflict occurring both within the classroom and on the playground. In addition, the team identified a high prevalence of presuicidal behaviors and frequent experimentation with substance use. The team decided that mental health services would be most appropriate if provided in partnership with the school's parents and with community mental health providers who were already engaged in family services. An array of interventions was identified by the team as important to provide in this school and community. At this point, the Center for Mental Health in Schools suggests that the team carefully consider the interventions relative to the professional development of the available personnel. For example, if the resource map described staff with mastery-level skill in the generic and specific competencies associated with suicide prevention, the team could move forward with a plan to target these services to the appropriate students. However, if available staff only had skills at the induction or preservice level, it would be necessary to locate other staff with more advanced skills. In the best of all possible worlds, there would be a one-to-one match between students' needs and staff skills. However, it is more likely that gaps in competence will be found. Although resource identification and professional development are represented as a second phase of the population-based service model, both must be continuous efforts that take place throughout the implementation of any program of mental health services.

In some cases, mental health service planning will document the need for new kinds of services that have

the potential to support multiple students simultaneously rather than one student at a time. One such program is Crone, Horner, and Hawken's (2010) school-wide behavioral support system that could be used with students whose behavioral compliance is a continuing problem. In other cases, school staff may decide that there are ecological factors that facilitate problems of a particular sort in a building. For example, a middle school used data to determine that large numbers of students were being expelled for behavioral conflicts that occurred at recess and that the playground's barren emptiness contributed to the disruptions. The school reduced expulsions significantly by adding more games to the noontime recess. In still other instances, mental health service planning will incorporate services that have not traditionally been thought of as mental health services. In particular, the emphasis on family and community factors as causal agents for students' mental raise disorders important questions about who is responsible for students' mental health and how healthy socioemotional development is promoted. Causal factors such as poverty, parental health, or community violence lay outside the traditional mental health and school authority in most communities, but their powerful links to psychological wellness suggest that services of police departments, social welfare agencies, community health departments, families, religious groups, schools, and neighborhoods are as essential to child mental health as the services of the school mental health professionals. Thus, a comprehensive plan for school mental health services will incorporate scores of adult caretakers who were not traditionally considered to be mental health providers.

Population-Based Intervention

A best practice is that school psychologists use population-based interventions that are evidence based and strategically selected to address the students' needs as identified in the plan. Selecting actual interventions for schools to implement raises another critical question: Which interventions are most likely to foster the changes the school psychologist is seeking in the students? Within the population-based model of school psychology, decisions about which interventions to provide and which students receive services are intentional decisions that are based upon the school-wide plan for services. Some, but not all, interventions will be delivered school-wide depending upon the needs of the school's students. The screening data can be especially helpful in making these decisions. Many, but not all, interventions will be preventive, because early intervention has the potential for greater impact at less cost. Some interventions will be therapeutic treatments for specific students with social or emotional disturbances that disrupt their learning or development. The NASP Practice Model (NASP, 2010) advocates for a continuum of school mental health services, arguing that school psychologists' focus should not remain at the individual level despite their history of collecting individual assessments of student learning.

The continuum of school mental health services needed for population-based services is likely to look very much like the three-tiered model of service described by Osher et al. (2004). The continuum must address the universal mental health needs of students with system-wide or building-wide services to promote psychological wellness and to prevent disturbance. For example, all students could benefit from instruction in social problem-solving strategies or from a school-wide bullying prevention plan. Planning for universal services can draw upon the very rich research in developmental competence that has begun to define factors that predict school learners' social, academic, and behavioral success (Masten et al., 2005). Notably, not all of these factors are services provided by mental health professionals. Instead, all of a school's teachers, administrators, or other staff members are potential sources of mental health support for students.

The second-tier services are targeted mental health services that are provided to identified students who are at high functional risk (i.e., early evidence of adjustment disturbances) or demographic risk (i.e., evidence of poverty, family violence, or other characteristics that predict poor outcomes). These services are more concentrated and more intense than universal services, address needs that are not broadly held by all students in a school, and have the purpose of strengthening competence as well as ameliorating risk. Examples of targeted services include programs to involve parents more fully in their students' schooling (e.g., Check & Connect; Christenson et al., 2012) or services to teach coping skills to highly aggressive students (e.g., Coping Power Program; Lochman, Wells, & Lenhart, 2008). In the typical school, 15–20% of the school enrollment will benefit from targeted mental health services. However, particular schools may have striking differences in the prevalence as well as the nature of targeted services that are needed. Both demographic and functional risk are not evenly distributed across all school communities but instead tend to concentrate into niches of very high risk, particularly in distressed urban schools or very isolated

rural communities (Hoagwood & Johnson, 2003). One function of population-based mental health service planning is to identify the nature and extent of a school's need for targeted services.

In every school, a few students will require more intensive services. This third tier of services is necessary for students whose dysfunction is pronounced and who are not able to benefit from schooling without substantial accommodations. In typical schools, these students represent between 1% and 5% of the enrollment. However, once again, the nature and extent of need can differ markedly from one school to the next. Adelman and Taylor (2010) argue for a fourth tier in the intervention continuum, that of infrastructure development and planning. Their point is well taken. Important systemic changes need to occur before students and adolescents will have access to mental health interventions in proportion to their demonstrated mental health needs. Practices that build the infrastructures to provide students with mental health services (including practices that promote population-based services in schools) are critically important mental health interventions.

The three-tiered model described by Osher et al. (2004) is distinctive in that it describes an array of services, whereas that described by Walker et al. (2010) describes groups of students. This difference is important. A three-tiered *service* model is useful for ensuring that a comprehensive program of mental health services is available for students enrolled in the school. It is simultaneously flexible, in that once services are available, the mental health team could allocate these services (or not allocate services) to individual students based on each student's need. Service allocation decisions can be made based on functional criteria (e.g., the frequency with which a child is sent to the office for disciplinary reasons) instead of diagnostic criteria (whether or not a child meets the diagnostic criteria for conduct disorder or the special education criteria for behavior disorders). Moreover, the same child might receive services at either or both Tiers 2 and 3, in addition to the universal services that are delivered to all students in a school.

Valuable resources are already available that describe the array of mental health services that might be implemented across the three tiers. Osher et al. (2004) provide a catalog of effective interventions, together with a program matrix that describes the nature of each intervention, its purpose and developmental level, and whether it is implemented within classrooms, schools, families, or communities. An accompanying CD provides additional references for the programs in an accessible PDF format.

Because population-based services incorporate universal services and interventions that interrupt developmental risk trajectories, these services have necessarily been interwoven with prevention services. Moreover, some of the strongest conceptual frameworks for population-wide interventions are included within the prevention literature. In particular, Nation et al. (2003) conducted a systematic analysis of the most effective prevention programs and, from this analysis, distilled a cogent description of key program characteristics. First, effective programs are comprehensive in that they incorporate multiple interventions and are implemented across school, home, community, and peer settings. Second, the most effective programs used varied and interactive teaching methods that actively engage participants in developing specific skills. Third, dosage of the best programs was matched to the severity of the problem. More severe problems require interventions that are more intense and of longer duration. Too often interventions are based on experience and what appears logical. However, Nation et al.'s (2003) fourth characteristic is that programs are most effective when the programs are theory driven, taking into account the etiology of the problem and drawing from an empirical evidence base. "Intervention theories focus on the best methods for changing the etiological risks" (Nation et al., 2003, p. 453). Finally, all effective programs promote strong, positive relationships between parents and students, teachers and students, and students and peers.

Skilled selection and implementation of preventive interventions are critical to the effectiveness of the intervention (Nation et al., 2003). Interventions may miss the mark if the interventions are delivered too early or too late. Traditional special education referral is a good example of waiting to intervene until failure is evident, when earlier and systematic steps might have avoided the failure altogether. Alternatively, an early elementary school curriculum on dating or substance use might be developmentally inappropriate for most students, and the effects might have washed out by the time students encounter those dilemmas. As a third example of the power of timing, HIV/AIDS programs have been shown to be effective prior to adolescents becoming sexually active but ineffective for those who are already sexually active. Skilled intervention planning will also select interventions that are consistent with local sociocultural norms as well as cultural beliefs and attitudes, and will embed evaluation into the intervention planning from the start. Finally, a well-trained staff is essential to effective interventions. Skilled interventionists will deliver a program with greater fidelity.

The emphasis on evidence-based interventions (Kratochwill & Stoiber, 2002) has drawn needed attention to the critical role that research plays in identifying the most powerful interventions to use with population-based services. Several very effective websites list interventions that meet rigorous standards for empirical evidence of effectiveness:

- SAMHSA's National Registry of Evidence-Based Programs and Practices: http://www.nrepp.samhsa.gov/
- What Works Clearinghouse of the Institute for Education Sciences: http://ies.ed.gov/ncee/wwc/
- Promising Practices Network: http://www.promisingpractices.net
- U.S. Department of Education's Office of Safe and Healthy Schools: http://www2.ed.gov/about/offices/list/oese/oshs/index.html
- Collaborative for Academic, Social, and Emotional Learning: http://casel.org
- Center for the Study and Prevention of Violence: http://www.colorado.edu/cspv (the site lists model or blueprint programs selected from more than 600 violence prevention programs at http://www.blueprintsprograms.com/)

Practitioners can easily consult these sites to identify promising intervention programs that match the mental health needs identified in a school.

Still, the criteria for methodological rigor differ substantially from one website to the next, and professional debates still rage over (a) whether or not cumulative small-n research can be adequate evidence of an intervention's effectiveness, (b) how critical it is that evidence of effectiveness be collected for populations in the United States, (c) whether promising interventions have been adequately evaluated for non-White populations, (d) whether interventions that proved promising in laboratory research settings will be equally effective in actual settings, and (e) whether results emerging from any single study have been sufficiently replicated in additional, independent studies. Ultimately, decisions about whether an intervention is sufficiently evidence based for use will rest with a school's mental health planning team. Although teams can evaluate the published evidence of an intervention, the definitive answer is really determined by the evidence and outcome data generated at that particular school.

Population-Based Evaluation

A best practice is that school psychologists conduct ongoing, data-based evaluations to demonstrate the impact that population-based services are having for students' psychological wellness. It is critically important that the school step back at regular intervals and examine the ultimate question: Have the services been effective in strengthening the social, emotional, behavioral, and academic competence of our students? Evaluation of a school's mental health service program is a complex undertaking and requires that team members clearly specify, in advance, the indicators of program success and how the program will be monitored over time. Within a population-based model, the essential evaluation question is whether students in the district are more successful, are less successful, or demonstrate no change in success once the school's comprehensive program of school mental health services is implemented. This question parallels questions asked about improvements or declines in individual students but places emphasis, once again, on the collective wellness of all students enrolled in the school.

This goal represents a special challenge: Even though it is possible to aggregate individual evaluation information across multiple students, time constraints make it impossible to conduct comprehensive individual evaluations of the full enrollment of a school. Consequently, school psychologists must identify and target key indicators of student wellness from the beginning, weaving evaluation into the implementation of the program of services. The most useful evaluation will be formative or ongoing and will inform continuous improvement in the mental health services program even while it is being implemented. The most effective evaluation is systematic, with methodologically rigorous designs and not antidotal or limited to a single case study.

Key considerations for evaluating population-based school mental health services can be adapted from Nastasi's and Hitchcock's (2008) recommendations for evaluating comprehensive and culturally specific programs. In many cases, data collection procedures will mimic those used in the original school mental health needs assessment, since these procedures lend themselves to broad assessment of the collective mental health of a school enrollment. Within the Nastasi and Hitchcock (2008) framework, a well-designed evaluation will describe the key features and impacts of all facets of the program, from the perspectives of multiple participants (providers, recipients, and other cultural brokers). Decisions will be made, in advance, about the kinds of

data that should be collected, how it should be managed, and steps that should be taken to ensure the validity and reliability of the data. In particular, data should be collected that describe the fidelity with which the intervention was conducted and the outcomes. The mental health team members should work to anticipate, in advance, unique challenges posed by evaluation and data collection in their particular school and community and the special opportunities for evaluation that might be present given other activities of the school and community. Key considerations for evaluating population-based school mental health services are included in Table 11.1.

Additional resources to support the evaluation of a population-based program of mental health services can be drawn from two approaches that illustrate the complex nature of program evaluation: Context, Input, Process, and Product (Stufflebeam & Shinkfield, 2007) and Comprehensive Mixed-Methods Participatory Evaluation (Nastasi & Hitchcock, 2008).

The Context, Input, Process, and Product model provides a useful framework to conceptualize evaluation. Within the model, context evaluations refer to the needs, assets, and opportunities that set the stage for a school's mental health goals and priorities. Input evaluations are assessments of alternative approaches or competing action plans along with their corresponding staffing plans and budgets. Process evaluations target how the program of services was implemented. Finally, product evaluations examine the intended and unintended consequences of the comprehensive services.

The Comprehensive Mixed-Methods Participatory Evaluation model is a mixed model approach. It takes advantage of the strengths of quantitative and qualitative. Nastasi and Hitchcock (2008) also characterize the approach as multisource, meaning that multiple stakeholders contribute to the evaluation. A strength of the Comprehensive Mixed-Methods Participatory Evaluation model is the importance that is placed on the cultural context of program implementation. Nastasi and Hitchcock (2008) note that successful program implementation requires an understanding of the shared beliefs, values, nuances of language, and behavioral norms. They define program success to include stakeholders' acceptance of the program, intervention integrity, outcomes, the degree to which the program is sustainable, and whether the program becomes part of the fabric of the institution.

SUMMARY

A population-based perspective on school mental health services provides alternative insights into how school

Table 11.1. Key Considerations for Evaluating Population-Based School Mental Health Services

Focus (key questions): Why?
- Was the program successful or effective?
- What is the impact of the program?
- Were program goals met?
- What were unintended positive and negative (iatrogenic) consequences (for individuals, groups, organizations)?
- Were there any unintended negative (iatrogenic) effects?
- What factors influenced program effectiveness?
- Was the program acceptable?
- Was the program implemented with integrity?
- Does the program have ecological–social validity? Was culture specificity achieved?
- To what extent did program acceptability, integrity, and ecological–social validity (culture specificity) influence program effectiveness or success?
- How do the multiple and potentially diverse perspectives of partners (planners, interventionists, and researchers; administrative, implementation, and evaluation staff; recipients, their caregivers, and community members) influence program success?
- How are evaluation data best used for data-based decision making and monitoring to ensure program success?

Participants: Who?
- Program planner or planners (researcher, interventionist, consultant)
- Professionals with expertise in mixed-method program evaluation
- Program implementation staff
- Cultural brokers (who can facilitate access and interpret culture)
- Representatives of stakeholder groups

Tasks or activities: What?
- Select or develop evaluation instruments or strategies
- Identify and secure existing data
- Data collection
- Data management
- Data analysis
- Data interpretation
- Data dissemination
- Participatory data-based decision making
- Staff development in evaluation methods, including accountability and monitoring

Strategies or methods: How?
- Data collection methods appropriate to specific program, using multimethod (combination of qualitative and quantitative methods), multisource (from various stakeholders) approach
- Recursive data collection, analysis, interpretation, and dissemination
- Systematic feedback process to facilitate program adaptation and staff development
- Participatory data-based decision making
- Facilitation of participatory process

Requisite skills (potential focus for recruitment and training)
- Program evaluation skills relevant to engaging in a participatory process, examination process and outcome variables, use of mixed methods (qualitative and quantitative), and seamless intervention–evaluation process
- Instrument development
- Data collection, management, and analysis
- Data interpretation and dissemination to varied stakeholder groups
- Participatory data-based decision-making skills
- Participatory problem-solving skills (communication, negotiation, consensus building)
- Group facilitation skills (e.g., engaging participants in idea generation, ensuring equitable participation, guiding group toward consensus)
- Professional and paraprofessional staff development and consultation skills

Challenges
- Identify or develop culture-specific instruments tied to program goals
- Ensure acceptability of evaluation by stakeholders
- Secure professional staff with expertise in evaluation
- Create seamless assessment–intervention process
- Access existing data within the system or organization
- Address ethical and legal issues related to data collection activities

Continued

Table 11.1. Continued

- Secure commitment to ongoing evaluation process
- Secure necessary resources
- Create a sustainable process and structure; build capacity within the system for sustainable program evaluation

Opportunities

- Ensure ecological validity and cultural specificity of mental health programs
- Develop sustainable and institutionalized evaluation systems
- Educate stakeholders about value of evaluation
- Build organizational–community capacity for program evaluation
- Engage in systematic evaluation of program acceptability, social validity, integrity, effectiveness, sustainability, and institutionalization
- Contribute to the understanding of how to implement successful programs (how it works; what contributes to its success) for the participating system and larger professional community
- Contribute to the knowledge base about intervention effectiveness and deployment of evidence-based programs in real-life settings
- Foster appreciation for the value and necessity of research, evaluation, and data-based decision making

Note. From *School-Based Mental Health Services: Creating Comprehensive and Culturally Specific Programs,* by B. K. Nastasi, R. B. Moore, & K. M. Varjas, 2004, Washington, DC: American Psychological Association. Copyright 2004 by the American Psychological Association. Reprinted with permission.

psychologists can best spend their time in schools, the purposes of their work, and the resources that are available to promote students' mental health. The shift in perspective can be dizzying at first and may cause school psychologists to lose sight of an important fact: School psychologists are already well prepared to function within population-based models. The responsibilities and skills are familiar, and the model's focus on data-based decision making takes good advantage of school psychologists' strong preparation in measurement, applied research, intervention, and evaluation. Indeed, population-based approaches to school psychological services weave together assessment and intervention procedures that are already available in the professional research literature. A principal value of the population-based perspective is in the very intentional and systematic planning that carefully matches services to student needs and in the careful attention that is paid to the mental health needs of all students enrolled in a school or community. Ultimately, the shift in perspective can maximize the impact of scarce school psychological resources.

AUTHOR NOTE

Disclosure. Beth Doll and Jack Cummings have a financial interest in books they authored or coauthored referenced in this chapter.

REFERENCES

Adelman, H., & Taylor, L. (2010, February). *Moving prevention from the fringes into the fabric of school improvement* Paper presented at the annual meeting of the National Association of School Psychologists, Anaheim, CA.

Albers, C. A., Glover, T. A., & Kratochwill, T. R. (2007). Where are we and where do we go now? Universal screening for enhanced educational and mental health outcomes. *Journal of School Psychology, 45,* 257–263.

Burns, M. K. (2013). *Using technology to enhance RTI implementation.* Washington, DC: National Center for Learning Disabilities. Retrieved from http://www.rtinetwork.org/getstarted/implement/using-technology-to-enhance-rti-implementation

Center for Mental Health in Schools at UCLA. (2001). *Framing new directions for school counselors, psychologists and social workers.* Los Angeles, CA: Author. Retrieved from http://smhp.psych.ucla.edu/pdfdocs/Report/framingnewdir.pdf

Centers for Disease Control and Prevention. (2013). *Mental health surveillance among children: United States, 2005–2011.* Washington, DC: Author.

Christenson, S. L., & Reschly, A. L. (2010). Check & Connect: Enhancing school completion through student engagement. In B. Doll, W. Pfohl, & J. Yoon (Eds.), *Handbook of youth prevention science* (pp. 327–348). New York, NY: Routledge.

Christenson, S. L., Stout, K. E., & Pohl, A. J. (2012). *Implementing Check & Connect with fidelity: What is Check & Connect? How is Check & Connect implemented?.* Minneapolis, MN: University of Minnesota, Institute on Community Integration.

Crone, D. A., Horner, R. H., & Hawken, L. S. (2010). *Responding to problem behavior in schools: The behavior education program* (2nd ed.). New York, NY: Guilford Press.

Dane County Youth Commission. (2012). *Dane County youth assessment overview report.* Madison, WI: Author. Retrieved from http://pdf.countyofdane.com/humanservices/youth/assessment_surveys/2012/youth_2012_overview.pdf

Doll, B., & Cummings, J. A. (2008). Why population-based services are essential for school mental health, and how to make them happen in your school. In B. Doll & J. A. Cummings (Eds.), *Transforming school mental health services: Population-based approaches to promoting the competency and wellness of children* (pp. 1–22; A joint publication with the National Association of School Psychologists). Thousand Oaks, CA: Corwin Press.

Doll, B., Haack, M. K., & Bieber, K. (2013). Population-based strategies for identifying school-wide problems. In R. Brown-Chidsey & K. Andren (Eds.), *Problem-based assessment for educational intervention* (pp. 77–100). New York, NY: Guilford Press.

Dowdy, E., Furlong, M., Eklund, K., Saeki, E., & Richey, K. (2010). Screening for mental health and wellness: Current school-based practices and emerging possibilities. In B. Doll, W. Pfohl, & J. Yoon (Eds.), *Handbook of youth prevention science* (pp. 70–95). New York, NY: Routledge.

Drummond, T. (1994). *The Student Risk Screening Scale (SRSS)*. Grants Pass, OR: Josephine County Mental Health Program.

Eklund, K. (2013, February). *Social emotional supports for military children and families* Paper presented at the annual meeting of the National Association of School Psychologists, Seattle, WA.

Frey, K. S., Hirschstein, M. K., & Guzzo, B. A. (2000). Second Step: Preventing aggression by promoting social competence. *Journal of Emotional and Behavioral Disorders, 8*, 102–112.

Greenberg, M. T., Kusche, C., & Mihalic, S. F. (1998). *Blueprints for violence prevention: Promoting alternative thinking strategies*. Boulder, CO: University of Colorado, Institute of Behavioral Science, Center for the Study and Prevention of Violence.

Hoagwood, K., & Johnson, J. (2003). School psychology: A public health framework: I. From evidence-based practices to evidence-based policies. *Journal of School Psychology, 41*, 3–21. doi:10.1016/S0022-4405(02)00141-3

Irvin, L. K., Horner, R. H., Ingram, K., Todd, A. W., Sugai, G., Sampson, N. K., & Boland, J. B. (2006). Using office discipline referral data for decision making about student behavior in elementary and middle schools. *Journal of Positive Behavior Interventions, 8*, 10–23. doi:10.1177/10983007060080010301

King, R., & Jun, M. K. (2012). *2011 Fairfax County youth survey risk and protective factors of 8th, 10th, and 12th grade students*. Fairfax, VA: Fairfax County and Fairfax County Schools. Retrieved from http://www.fairfaxcounty.gov/demogrph/pdf/2011_youth_survey_report.pdf

Kratochwill, T. R., & Stoiber, K. C. (2002). Evidence-based interventions in school psychology: The state of the art and future directions [Special issue]. *School Psychology Quarterly, 17*, 341–389.

Lane, K. L., Kalberg, J. R., Parks, R. J., & Carter, E. W. (2008). Student Risk Screening Scale: Initial evidence for score reliability and validity at the high school level. *Journal of Emotional and Behavioral Disorders, 16*, 178–190. doi:10.1177/1063426608314218

Levitt, J. M., Saka, N., Romanelli, L. H., & Hoagwood, K. (2007). Early identification of mental health problems in schools: The status of instrumentation. *Journal of School Psychology, 45*, 163–191. doi:10.1016/j.jsp.2006.11.005

Lochman, J. E., Wells, K. C., & Lenhart, L. A. (2008). *Coping power*. New York, NY: Oxford University Press.

Masten, A. S., Roisman, G. I., Long, J. D., Burt, K. B., Obradovic, J., Riley, J. R., … Tellegen, A. (2005). Developmental cascades: Linking academic achievement and externalizing and internalizing symptoms over 20 years. *Developmental Psychology, 41*, 733–746. doi:10.1037/0012-1649.41.5.733

Nastasi, B. K., & Hitchcock, J. (2008). Evaluating quality and effectiveness of population-based services. In B. Doll & J. A. Cummings (Eds.), *Transforming school mental health services: Population-based approaches to promoting the competency and wellness of children* (pp. 245–276; A joint publication with the National Association of School Psychologists). Thousand Oaks, CA: Corwin Press.

Nastasi, B. K., Moore, R. B., & Varjas, K. M. (2004). *School-based mental health services: Creating comprehensive and culturally specific programs*. Washington, DC: American Psychological Association.

Nation, M., Crusto, C., Wandersman, A., Kumpfer, K. L., Seybolt, D., Morrissey-Kane, E., & Davino, K. (2003). What works in prevention: Principles of effective prevention programs. *American Psychologist, 58*, 449–456. doi:10.1037/0003-066X.58.6-7.449

National Association of School Psychologists. (2010). *Model for comprehensive and integrated school psychological services*. Bethesda, MD: Author. Retrieved from http://www.nasponline.org/standards/2010standards/2_PracticeModel.pdf

Osher, D., Dwyer, K., & Jackson, S. (2004). *Safe, supportive, and successful schools: Step by step*. Longmont, CO: Sopris West.

Prince-Embury, S. (2007). *Resiliency Scales for Children and Adolescents*. San Antonio, TX: Harcourt Assessments. doi:10.1177/0829573507305520

Prince-Embury, S. (2010). Assessment for integrated screening and prevention using the Resiliency Scales for Children and Adolescents. In B. Doll, W. Pfohl, & J. Yoon (Eds.), *Handbook of youth prevention science*. New York, NY: Routledge.

Richardson, M. J., Caldarella, P., Young, B. J., Young, E. L., & Young, K. R. (2009). Further validation of the Systematic Screening for Behavior Disorders in middle and junior high school. *Psychology in the Schools, 46*, 605–615. doi:10.1002/pits.20401

Stufflebeam, D. L., & Shinkfield, A. J. (2007). *Evaluation theory, models, and applications*. San Francisco, CA: Jossey-Bass.

Walker, H. M., & Severson, H. H. (1992). *Systematic Screening for Behavior Disorders (SSBD): User's guide and administration manual*. Longmont, CO: Sopris West.

Walker, H. M., Severson, H. H., Naquin, F., D'Atrio, C., Feil, E. G., Hawken, L., & Sabey, C. (2010). Implementing universal screening systems within an RTI-PBS context. In B. Doll, W. Pfohl, & J. Yoon (Eds.), *Handbook of youth prevention science* (pp. 96–120). New York, NY: Routledge.

Werner, E. E. (2013). What can we learn about resilience from large-scale longitudinal studies? In S. Goldstein & R. B. Brooks (Eds.), *Handbook of resilience in children* (pp. 87–103). New York, NY: Springer.

Best Practices in Developing a Positive Behavior Support System at the School Level

12

Brian C. McKevitt
University of Nebraska at Omaha
Angelisa Braaksma Fynaardt
Great Prairie (IA) Area Education Agency

OVERVIEW

Educators and policy makers continue to recognize the pitfalls of commonly used discipline systems. School discipline tactics that include punishments for behavioral infractions, such as reprimands, suspensions, seclusionary time-out, and expulsions may stop a problem temporarily, but are rarely effective in producing long-lasting behavior changes and do not teach students skills to engage in desired behaviors (Bear, 2008). Lately, schools have been under increased pressure to adopt policies that incorporate evidence-based positive strategies for dealing with problem behaviors, including the use of positive reinforcement and effective social skill instruction. Recent U.S. Department of Education policy recommendations have encouraged the use of positive strategies to address problem behaviors (e.g., U.S. Department of Education, 2012), and the 2004 Individuals with Disabilities Education Act specifically mentions positive behavioral interventions and supports as recommended strategies. In addition, President Obama himself advocated for making schools safer using evidence-based strategies to prevent violence and improve school climate in his response to the Newtown, CT, school shooting (http://www.whitehouse.gov/now-is-the-time). A high degree of effective behavioral skill instruction and positive acknowledgment of students' appropriate behaviors not only promotes desired behaviors, but can also foster positive relationships between staff and students, which in turn could influence the overall climate of a

school and student outcomes (Caldarella, Shatzer, Gray, Young, & Young, 2011).

Over the last decade, school-wide positive behavior interventions and support (SWPBIS) strategies have been promoted as alternatives to traditional discipline for children and youth. SWPBIS is a broad set of research-validated strategies designed to create school environments that promote and support appropriate behavior of all students. These environments are brought about through the identification of common behavioral expectations that are valued by the school community and can apply to all students in all school settings and situations. Common expectations are directly and explicitly taught to all students to create an atmosphere in which students know what is expected of them at all times. Furthermore, in a SWPBIS framework, students are systematically and frequently acknowledged for their appropriate behavior. Undesired behavior, when it occurs, is responded to swiftly and consistently. A school environment is therefore created that (a) teaches students skills to behave appropriately, (b) positively acknowledges students engaging in those behaviors, and (c) provides consistency and stability in interactions among students and staff members (Sugai & Horner, 2006).

Ongoing data collection is a hallmark of SWPBIS. Data are collected to determine the need for SWPBIS, to analyze the fidelity of implementation and its effectiveness, and to make decisions about changes that should be made as SWPBIS is being implemented. Implementation of SWPBIS strategies with fidelity at a whole-school level has been shown to significantly reduce office discipline referrals (Bradshaw, Mitchell, & Leaf, 2010; Horner et al., 2009). Effectiveness of SWPBIS has been demonstrated across all grade levels, preschool (e.g., Benedict, Horner, & Squires, 2007) through high school (e.g., Bohanon, Flannery, Malloy, & Fenning, 2009), and has also been successful at reducing problem behaviors in other settings, such as playgrounds (Franzen & Kamps, 2008), summer recreation programs (McKevitt, Dempsey, Ternus, & Shriver, 2012), and alternative schools (Simonson, Britton, & Young, 2010).

The purpose of this chapter is to review the core features of SWPBIS as they are applied to a school building level. The chapter is applicable for those school psychologists who are looking for an overview of basic implementation requirements of SWPBIS. There is considerable information about systemic requirements for successful implementation of SWPBIS on national, state, and district levels offered by Sugai and Horner (2006) and on the website of the U.S. Department of Education's Office of Special Education Programs (OSEP) Technical Assistance Center on Positive Behavioral Interventions and Supports (http://www.pbis.org).

The primary focus of this chapter is on SWPBIS as it relates to school-wide implementation (i.e., universal primary prevention of problem behaviors in all school locations). As such, the chapter most appropriately addresses the Preventive and Responsive Services domain found in the National Association of School Psychologists (NASP) *Model for Comprehensive and Integrated School Psychological Services* (NASP, 2010). This domain focuses on school psychologists having the knowledge of principles and research related to resilience and risk factors in learning and mental health, services in schools and communities to support multitiered prevention strategies to promote students' well-being, and evidence-based strategies for effective crisis response. SWPBIS links closely with this domain given its multitiered, prevention framework.

It is important to recognize a SWPBIS system also addresses the behavioral needs of small groups of students (e.g., at-risk students in need of targeted secondary prevention) and individual students (i.e., those who are unresponsive to school-wide efforts and secondary level prevention efforts and are in need of intensive tertiary prevention). In fact, SWPBIS has gained momentum as response to intervention (RTI) has increased in its popularity and acceptance as a service delivery model. SWPBIS is highly related to RTI. The primary features of RTI (e.g., core instruction, universal screening, multitiered systems of support, and data-based

decision making and problem solving) are also core features of SWPBIS. For example, SWPBIS promotes the adoption and instruction of behavioral expectations school wide (i.e., core instruction) and the use of office discipline referral data (i.e., screening data) to identify students in need of more intense intervention (i.e., data-based decision making, multitiered supports).

In this chapter, basic considerations for systemic elements to have in place in a school desiring to implement preventive SWPBIS are discussed, followed by a review of best practices for successful implementation. Finally, brief examples of SWPBIS implementation are provided to solidify the basic tenets of the framework.

BASIC CONSIDERATIONS

To implement SWPBIS, there are several considerations that must be addressed. Some consideration (e.g., forming a team, gaining staff support, organizing training) must be done prior to implementation. Others (e.g., securing funding, engaging families, enhancing sustainability) are ongoing. These considerations are described below.

Team-Based Implementation

A school-based leadership team is in charge of developing and monitoring the implementation of SWPBIS. Teaming for SWPBIS is the process of "working as a cohesive, integrated, and representative collection of individuals who lead systems change and implementation process" (Technical Assistance Center on Positive Behavior Interventions and Supports [PBIS], 2010, p. 67). Sugai, Horner, Lewis-Palmer, and Todd (2005) recommend that the implementation of SWPBIS in schools be organized and monitored by a team of four to eight consisting of at least one administrator and other school staff committed to working on changing the behavioral and social climate of the school building. Staff from general education, special education, and special services such as school psychology or guidance counseling should be included on the leadership team. In addition, the team may want to consider having at least one family member on the team or creating a family advisory group to ensure that viewpoints and concerns of family members are taken into account. At a middle or high school level, it also can be beneficial to have a student advisory group or student member of the leadership team to provide student input on the development and implementation of SWPBIS (Young, Caldarella, Richardson, & Young, 2012).

The common belief underlying the use of teams in organizations is that group decision making and collaboration produce better outcomes than individual decision making. However, research suggests that the most effective teams are composed of personnel who have expertise in the team's topic (Iverson, 2002). Care should be taken to select members for the team who not only have interest in working toward a positive behavioral climate in school but also have skills in behavior, resource management, prevention, communication, and program development so they may be effective collaborators.

School psychologists are well suited to be team members given their training and expertise in each of these areas. They are often the behavioral experts in schools and have had specific training on consultation and collaboration. School psychologists can and should promote their unique training as members of SWPBIS teams.

Because there are so many teams in schools, it may be difficult to find the time to create a new team devoted to SWPBIS. Sugai et al. (2005) recommend a strategy of analyzing the roles, goals, and measurable outcomes of each school team, combining those that have similar goals and outcomes and eliminating those that cannot identify goals and measurable outcomes. In addition, schools often have many initiatives going on at one time. A similar approach should be taken to analyze initiatives; that is, to identify purposes and measurable outcomes of each initiative and combine similar ones or eliminate ones that do not have well-defined outcomes for students. For example, a school may have a school-wide bully prevention program but decide it wants to implement a SWPBIS framework as well. The respective teams that organize those approaches should analyze the purpose of each program and consider combining them, because bully prevention activities can often fall under the realm of SWPBIS.

To function effectively, team members should take on certain roles. There should be a team facilitator whose role it is to guide the conversation and ensure the group remains focused. There also should be a timekeeper and recorder to keep the group on track and organized. Someone should be responsible for creating an agenda and making sure all team members know the purpose of the meeting for that day. Teams should meet regularly (e.g., once every 2 weeks at a prescribed time) to ensure adequate planning time. Persons with skill in facilitating group communication and group participation also should be identified to ensure that the ideas of all team members are expressed and considered. Having these roles and activities will lead to more efficient team processing and decision making (Iverson, 2002).

The SWPBIS team has the main function of providing leadership for the school's SWPBIS efforts. The team works to assess school needs, develop and operationalize expectations, train staff to implement the strategies, and evaluate the effectiveness of efforts by reviewing student data regularly. Additional functions of the team are to address sustainability issues (e.g., replacing a team member when one leaves, training new staff), report to community stakeholders (e.g., parents, board of education), and obtain or allocate resources for SWPBIS work. The team should be formed at least a year prior to implementation to ensure adequate time for training and preparation and should create and maintain an action plan to guide its ongoing efforts (Sugai et al., 2005).

Staff Support and Buy-In

There must be sufficient acceptance among staff of the procedures and a willingness to implement the procedures with integrity because SWPBIS involves all personnel in a school. Sugai et al. (2005) recommend having a minimum of 80% of staff willing to implement SWPBIS procedures. This percentage can be obtained by a ballot, show of hands, or consensus. However, an anonymous ballot typically is the best way to obtain the most accurate count of staff in favor of SWPBIS. Schools that have fewer than 80% of staff committed may experience difficulties with implementation, sustainability, and effectiveness.

Obtaining 80% buy-in can sometimes be a daunting task. Scott (2002) recommends several strategies for responding to common arguments against using SWPBIS. Some school staff may believe their responsibility is only to teach academics. However, many researchers have demonstrated the strong correlation between academic performance and social skills. Therefore, they often must be taught simultaneously for some students to produce positive academic outcomes. With expertise in both behavior and academics, school psychologists can point out the relationship between these domains as they have buy-in conversations with school staff.

Time is another issue that confronts educators. In the long run, SWPBIS can save time because it prevents problems from occurring in the first place. Scott and Barrett (2004) found that administrators can save the equivalent of almost 16 days in a school year by not having to deal with office referrals and suspension issues.

Another common argument comes from teachers who may feel that what they are doing is already sufficient, that they are already meeting the behavioral needs of all students effectively. If this is the case, then the school's office discipline data should demonstrate this assertion and a more structured school-wide program may not be necessary. Having discipline data shared at staff meetings when discussing SWPBIS may be a powerful motivator for accepting that practices need to change, especially when those data demonstrate a pattern of problematic student behaviors. In addition, surveys such as the Effective Behavior Support Survey (Sugai, Horner, & Todd, 2000; available at http://www.pbis.org) can be useful to determine staff perception of components of SWPBIS already in place and priorities for making changes.

Finally, some school staff members do not believe that positive reinforcement and acknowledgement of desired behavior are appropriate for students. Some may believe these are even harmful activities. A detailed rationale against this belief is beyond the scope of this chapter. However, several researchers have demonstrated that rewards do not pose any negative effects on student motivation or performance. Akin-Little, Eckert, Lovett, and Little (2004) noted that no studies utilizing single-subject design research have found the use of reinforcement contingences to be harmful for students' motivation. Furthermore, believing that students will engage in certain behaviors simply because they should is unlikely to result in behavior change. School staff members who have arguments against the use of reinforcement strategies may benefit from reading more information about SWPBIS, visiting websites related to SWPBIS, talking to others who have used SWPBIS, or looking at outcome data from SWPBIS schools to help build their commitment.

School psychologists can be a go-to resource for gaining information about the issue of using rewards to reinforce desired behavior. Their training is replete with evidence-based interventions that capitalize on the merits of positive reinforcement for increasing desired behavior among students. Leadership teams may find it beneficial to model and practice buy-in conversations so they are prepared to address these common concerns.

Another necessity for buy-in among staff is to have a school administrator who actively supports SWPBIS efforts. Common practice suggests that at least one administrator should be part of the school leadership team, attend all meetings, and be a role model for staff in the school by modeling and using SWPBIS strategies. It is important to have the support of the building administrator who is able to dedicate resources (e.g., money, time) to the implementation of SWPBIS.

Finally, Sugai et al. (2005) suggest that a commitment to changing the behavioral climate of the school should be one of the top three goals of the school. The goal should be written into a school improvement plan so it is monitored frequently. Having a goal provides a level of accountability for implementation and effectiveness monitoring that otherwise would not be present. School psychologists are fluent at writing specific, objective, and measurable goals that can be used to track the effectiveness of SWPBIS efforts.

School and District Policy

It is important that school discipline policy is aligned to the tenets of SWPBIS. School policy regarding behavior should describe the proactive approach of the SWPBIS system in addition to the typical consequences found in a school or district discipline policy. For example, many school districts have policies around behavioral infractions (e.g., automatic suspensions for certain zero-tolerance behaviors) that will need to be included in the school discipline policy. It is recommended that schools develop a SWPBIS handbook that incorporates the school's overall approach to managing behavior at the primary, secondary, and tertiary levels of prevention. The handbook should clearly describe the steps for implementing SWPBIS at all three levels of the system.

With their knowledge of three-tier models of service delivery and effective behavioral practices, school psychologists can and should contribute to the development of these policy statements.

In addition, it is essential that the policy is supported by the local school district. The school district should have a district-wide leadership team in place to support efforts in multiple school buildings. With this leadership team should come district-level policy statements that support and promote SWPBIS throughout the district. Sugai and Horner (2006) provide further information about systemic leadership for promoting positive social, emotional, and behavioral outcomes for students. Because school psychologists often serve more than one school building in a district, they often are in a unique position to contribute to and comment on district-level policies that cut across multiple SWPBIS sites.

Team Training and Staff Development

Team training and staff development are major considerations when implementing SWPBIS in school buildings. All school staff, including certified and noncertified staff, as well as school volunteers who may come in contact with students, should be aware of SWPBIS and trained in at least the basics of implementation. For example, when a student walks down a hallway and demonstrates desired expectations for hallway behavior, a custodian who witnesses the behavior can acknowledge the student. Only if that custodian is knowledgeable about SWPBIS will he or she use the acknowledgement system that is part of the school's SWPBIS framework.

Training should first occur with the leadership team interested in implementing SWPBIS in the school. Sources for accessing training information include working through district- or state-level leadership teams or reading material about SWPBIS. The OSEP Center on Positive Behavioral Interventions and Supports (http://www.pbis.org) has information related to steps and procedures for SWPBIS implementation. It also contains information for each state's SWPBIS contact person. Leadership teams are highly encouraged to contact this person when thinking about implementing SWPBIS practices in their schools to ensure alignment with state efforts. Sullivan, Long, and Kucera (2011) found that most school psychologists (75% of those surveyed) have had some type of training in SWPBIS, so school psychologists are an obvious choice to help coordinate training for leadership teams.

When accessing trainings through district- or state-level leadership teams, school building teams will likely attend a sequence of trainings designed to introduce the logic behind SWPBIS, teach the core components of implementation, and enhance sustainability of the school's efforts by providing a number of checklists and tools for measuring implementation integrity and effectiveness. Teams also may be asked to identify a coach, a person internal or external to the building who has advanced training in behavioral theory (such as a school psychologist) and who can attend team meetings at least once per month (Sugai et al., 2005). The coach's role is to provide support and guidance to the team members as they work to implement and monitor SWPBIS efforts.

Team training typically occurs over a 3-year period (Sugai et al., 2005). The first year of training, often consisting of 4 days of training spread across the school year, addresses implementation of the universal prevention component of SWPBIS. The second and third years address implementation at the secondary and tertiary prevention levels, which are built on the foundation of the whole-school prevention system.

The school leadership team is then responsible for training the rest of the school staff in SWPBIS practices.

The training may occur during staff meetings, after school, or during special teacher work days when students are not there. School psychologists should play an active role in staff training given their understanding of learning processes and effective instruction. Techniques familiar to school psychologists who conduct professional development workshops or implement interventions (e.g., stating objectives, providing practice opportunities, providing feedback) are useful for staff-wide SWPBIS training. The leadership team also will need to plan follow-up trainings, or booster sessions, for staff after initial implementation of SWPBIS.

Finding adequate time to work with staff is often difficult for leadership teams. Teams may need to find creative ways to engage staff without overburdening them. For example, one leadership team member may take over for a classroom teacher while the teacher attends a brief training session to learn about a component of SWPBIS implementation.

Funding

SWPBIS work does not have to require significant monetary resources. Funding may be required for release time for professional development activities, materials (e.g., copying costs, posters, banners), reinforcement items (e.g., tokens, bookmarks with school expectations, T-shirts), and a data collection system. Schools should have a budget line item for funding SWPBIS work. While this may be difficult for many schools, having a specific budgeted allocation for SWPBIS demonstrates a strong commitment to this work and can enhance sustainability over time. Schools may obtain district, state, or federal grant money to start SWPBIS. However, it is unlikely that grant money will sustain the long-term implementation of this work.

Schools also should consider creative ways to obtain items for use in SWPBIS that ordinarily would require funding. For example, partnering with a local business such as a printing shop may help defray some of the copy and printing costs for posters and other materials. Asking students to donate gently used toys to a school store would enable the store to be stocked with rewards without cost. These are just two examples of creative thinking that can be displayed by SWPBIS leadership teams.

Engaging Families and Community Members

Stakeholders are very important contributors to successful implementation of SWPBIS at the school level (Technical Assistance Center on PBIS, 2010).

Stakeholders include parents, families, business leaders, community members, and school board members. These groups can be valuable resources to leadership teams by providing diverse perspectives, offering assistance (sometimes in the form of funding or donations), and ensuring that all voices are heard when discussing valued outcomes for students. In addition, teams should consider making annual reports to district-level leadership to promote activities and to ensure continued support from key stakeholders.

There are numerous ways to engage families and community members in SWPBIS efforts, ranging from providing information (e.g., newsletters, newspaper articles, parent meetings) to encouraging active participation in school activities related to SWPBIS (e.g., organizing assemblies, developing posters, donating resources). School leadership teams may want to develop surveys for families and community members to use as a source of input for their work and to solicit feedback. As families and community agencies learn about and understand what SWPBIS is, they may themselves adopt the framework in their own settings, thus creating a beneficial link between home, school, and community, a link that has been proven to produce better outcomes for children (Esler, Godber, & Christenson, 2008).

Sustainability

From the outset of SWPBIS implementation, leadership teams need to think about sustainability of efforts. Systemic changes brought about by SWPBIS should be expected to last at least 10 years (Sugai et al., 2005). Regularly evaluating the impact of the prevention system and using data to inform decision making about the effectiveness of implementation are crucial elements to the continuous regeneration of SWPBIS. In addition, having the universal prevention system is necessary, but not sufficient, for long-term impact of the school-wide program. As part of the system-wide three-tier framework, the universal prevention component of SWPBIS will not reach the 15–20% of the student population who need more intensive intervention efforts. Implementation of the secondary-level targeted group interventions and tertiary-level intensive individual interventions is necessary for long-term success of SWPBIS and school psychologists can play a critical role with implementation of these additional components.

Other techniques for enhancing sustainability over time include providing incentives for staff members who use the SWPBIS approach appropriately and consistently, sharing student data with staff regularly, and offering ongoing professional development and training related to SWPBIS. New staff members coming into a school implementing SWPBIS should be immediately oriented to the techniques so they know what is expected of them and their students. Having a SWPBIS handbook, such as the one described earlier, may help with sustainability as documentation of the school's work. The handbook can be given to all staff, including new staff and substitute teachers, to ensure consistency of implementation and understanding of the processes involved.

BEST PRACTICES IN SCHOOL-LEVEL POSITIVE BEHAVIOR SUPPORT

At the universal prevention level of SWPBIS, procedures to address school-wide issues and a system to support student success must be developed. The universal system is designed for all students in a school building. The universal system of SWPBIS must address five critical features: (a) establishing and defining clear and consistent school-wide expectations, (b) teaching the school-wide expectations to students, (c) acknowledging students for demonstrating the expected behaviors, (d) developing a clear and consistent consequence system to respond to behavioral violations, and (e) using data to evaluate the impact of school-wide efforts (Sugai et al. 2005). Table 12.1 summarizes these core features, and elementary and high school implementation examples are provided at the end of the chapter to further demonstrate these fundamental aspects of SWPBIS.

Table 12.1. Summary of Key Features of SWPBIS Implementation

Feature	Brief Description of Actions Needed
Expectations defined	Define three to five short, positively stated school-wide expectations.
Expectations taught	Provide direct and explicit instruction in each school location.
Acknowledgement system	Develop an easy and effective way for staff to reinforce expected behaviors.
Consequence system	Develop clear and consistent response to behavioral errors.
Data system	Use data to monitor the effectiveness of the system and to identify needs within the school-wide system.

Establishing and Defining Expectations

The first critical feature of a SWPBIS system is to establish clear and consistent school-wide expectations. The SWPBIS team and/or the school personnel should identify three to five behavioral expectations that are specific to the needs and culture within the school building. With their insight into the school's culture and climate, and often insight into the context of the overall school district as well, school psychologists can be very helpful in developing and defining relevant behavioral expectations. The expectations should be positively stated (e.g., be responsible, be safe) and void of a long list of negative rules (e.g., don't run, don't hit, don't kick). Expectations should be brief and memorable for students and staff and be developmentally appropriate for the age of the students. Expectations become more memorable for students if they are linked to an acronym or a logo (e.g., STAR students: safe, teachable, accept responsibility, respectful). However, a team should not spend an excessive amount of time trying to match the behavioral expectations to an acronym. The behavioral expectations are intended to be used in all locations within the school, should be posted throughout the school, and are intended to be used by all staff members (Sugai et al., 2005).

Teaching Expectations to Students

The second critical feature is to teach the behavioral expectations to students. The broadly stated behavioral expectations should be further defined as specific, observable behaviors for each location within the school. For example, "be responsible" in the cafeteria may be defined as putting garbage in the trashcan and trays in the sink. The same expectation in the classroom may be defined as bringing appropriate materials to class and turning in homework assignments. School staff may use a teaching matrix to assist with defining specific behavioral examples of the expectations (Sugai et al., 2005). For each location/expectation combination on the matrix, school personnel should identify the best example of the expectation in the location and an example that addresses the most problematic behavior in that location. The matrix may then be used to guide instruction.

Behavioral expectations must be taught to students. Effective teaching strategies include identifying the big ideas in a content area, making strategies conspicuous for learners, using scaffolding to support learning, strategically integrating essential information, linking instruction to students' background knowledge, and providing repeated opportunities to practice and master concepts (Coyne,

Kame'enui, & Carnine, 2010). The instruction should be direct and explicit, following a similar format of direct instruction for academics. As part of the leadership team, school psychologists should be active in teaching the expectations to students, and can also serve as consultants to other staff needing assistance with instruction.

Instruction should first identify the expectation or concept being taught (i.e., the big ideas). For example, "Today we are going to learn about being respectful in the hallway." Instruction should include modeling of the expected behaviors and modeling of nonexamples of the expected behaviors. Nonexamples of the expected behaviors are included so that students learn to discriminate between acceptable and unacceptable behaviors. Using self-talk while modeling examples and nonexamples makes the thinking strategy overt for students. It is good practice to have only adults demonstrate the nonexample behaviors during the instruction so students do not inadvertently practice undesired behaviors. Students should be given an opportunity to practice the expected behaviors repeatedly when being instructed. Corrective feedback and acknowledgement of demonstrating the expected behaviors during practice opportunities will allow students to build their accuracy and fluency in demonstrating the behavioral expectations. The method of delivering instruction should be matched to the students' developmental level. For example, it would be appropriate to use puppets to enhance instruction for preschool or primary grade levels and music or video production to enhance instruction at the high school level. The language used in the instruction also should be matched to the developmental level of the students.

It is important for the team to carefully consider the schedule of instruction. Each school should have a plan to provide initial instruction on the school-wide expectations for all students at the start of the school year. Schools often rotate students through instructional stations in each school location for this initial instruction. A well thought-out rotation schedule across multiple school days helps to ensure the efficiency of the instruction. Additional instruction or booster sessions should be provided throughout the school year, either in large groups or small groups, based upon needs identified from the data being collected to evaluate effectiveness of the SWPBIS system.

Acknowledging Students for Demonstrating Desired Behavior

Once students have been taught the behavioral expectations, they need to be acknowledged for demonstrating the expected behaviors. The universal primary prevention level of SWPBIS should include a positive reinforcement system to catch students behaving appropriately in order to maintain the desired behaviors. The team should determine the type and frequency of rewards that will be provided to students. The reinforcement system may include a variety of rewards. Some schools use tangible rewards (e.g., tickets that may be redeemed for prizes), access to privileges or preferred activities (e.g., time to use the computer), or social recognition (e.g., name announced at assembly and picture in the hallway). The team also should consider whether rewards will be delivered to individual students, groups of students, classrooms, grade levels, or all students. The developmental level of the students should be taken into consideration as the team creates the acknowledgement system. It is often beneficial to include students in the process of determining the rewards, particularly at the secondary grade levels. Regardless of the rewards chosen, the system must be easy and efficient for all staff members to use.

The school psychologist can provide insight to the team about best practices in using rewards as reinforcers appropriately. Initially, rewards should be delivered at a high frequency as students learn about SWPBIS in their school. The delivery of tangible rewards should be contingent upon desired behavior and accompanied by social praise to enhance the social desirability of the reward. Over time, the use of the tangible rewards may be decreased, but school staff should not limit the amount of verbal praise given to students engaging in desired behaviors. Using rewards responsibly not only increases desired behavior but also facilitates generalization of those behaviors in the long run (Akin-Little et al., 2004). For maintenance of desired behaviors and sustainability of SWPBIS efforts, the use of the acknowledgement system must continue.

SWPBIS is designed as a system to support the academic and behavioral success of all students. However, one key issue in developing the system is to change adult attitudes and adult behavior. It is important for the team to also consider developing a system to acknowledge staff for implementing the SWPBIS system.

Developing a Consequence System

Another component of a SWPBIS system is having clear and consistent responses by school staff to behavioral violations. While the majority of students will respond to the behavioral instruction and acknowledgements pro-vided to them, some students will still demonstrate varying degrees of behavior concerns. Therefore, a system must be put into place that provides students with corrective consequences when they demonstrate behavioral errors. The consequence or discipline system should clearly identify consistent staff responses for behavioral infractions and when staff members need to document behavioral issues. School teams often create a leveled consequence system that groups behaviors with similar severity levels or similar impact on the classroom. The team may then identify consequence options for each group of behaviors, ensuring that the intensity of the consequence options match the intensity and severity of the behaviors. Consequences may range from fairly minor, such as verbal reprimand or redirection, to more intense consequences, such as suspension and expulsion.

Consultation with the school psychologist can be especially helpful for school staff when dealing with students' ongoing behavioral infractions. The school psychologist can assist with implementing strategies that will likely work to improve behavior over time. For example, the consequence for behavioral infractions also should include a teaching component. The teaching component may range from reminding the student of the behavioral expectation to actually reteaching and practicing the expected behavior in the actual location in the school. Regardless of the type of consequences, the system should be easy for staff to use and all staff members should consistently use the system.

Along with identifying staff response to behavioral infractions, the team will need to identify when and how staff members will document inappropriate behaviors. Information collected about the behavioral incident should include the date and time of the incident, the student's name and grade, the classroom teacher's name, the referring person's name, the location of the incident, and consequence given. Some schools also choose to identify the potential function of the student's behavior on the referral form. These data should be entered into a database and should be used by the team to guide decision making about program effectiveness.

Using Data

Data about the implementation of the universal SWPBIS system and its effects on student outcomes should be collected. The School-Wide Evaluation Tool (SET; Sugai et al., 2001; available at http://www.pbis.org) is an instrument that measures the integrity of implementation of the universal level of SWPBIS in seven areas: behavioral expectations defined, behavioral expectations taught, behavioral expectations rewarded, systematic response to rule violations, information gathered to monitor student behavior, local management support for school-wide procedures, and district-level support for school-wide procedures. An independent observer completes the SET for a school. The observer completes a document review, observations within the school, and interviews with the administrator, staff, and students.

The SET yields a summary score for each of the seven areas and an overall mean score. The goal is to obtain at least 80% on the mean score and 80% on the subscale score of "expectations taught." Schools that are able to reach and maintain this level of implementation tend to experience the benefits of SWPBIS that have been reported in the effectiveness research (Horner et al., 2004). School personnel should use SET results to monitor the level of implementation of the universal prevention system over time. In addition, areas of improvement can be identified from the SET results. These areas of improvement should be addressed in the team's action plan. The SET has demonstrated good internal consistency, test-retest reliability, and construct validity (Horner et al., 2004).

The Team Implementation Checklist (TIC; Sugai, Horner, & Lewis-Palmer, 2001; available at http://www.pbis.org) is another tool that can be used to evaluate the implementation of the universal system. The team completes the TIC at least once per quarter. The TIC lists several steps to implementing the universal SWPBIS system. The team rates itself on each action step. Each step is rated as either achieved, in progress, or not started. The result is the percent of steps achieved. The goal is to have at least 80% of the steps achieved to indicate that SWPBIS is in place and functioning (Sugai et al., 2005). School personnel should include steps in the action plan to address items on the TIC that are marked as in progress or not started.

A comprehensive evaluation plan will also include evaluating the impact of SWPBIS on student behavior. Behavior incident or office referral data are efficient, effective, and naturally occurring ways to monitor the impact of the universal SWPBIS system on student performance. Office referral data should be entered into a data system on a regular basis. Analysis of the data should be readily available for decision making and should be available in graphic format to allow for the visual analysis of the data. An example of an efficient data system for housing office referral data is the School-Wide Information System (available at http://www.

Figure 12.1. Example of Office Discipline Referral Data Output

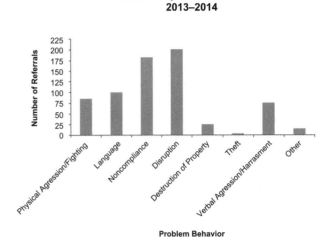

pbisapps.org). Figure 12.1 provides a sample of the type of data display obtained from a system such as this one. Data from the School-Wide Information System may be downloaded for use into a district's own student information system for further use.

School personnel should regularly review the office referral data at team meetings to determine if changes need to be made to the SWPBIS system. Office referral data can be analyzed regularly to look for trends or patterns of behavior. For example, school personnel can examine the types of problem behaviors being demonstrated, the locations of the problem behaviors, or problematic times throughout the school day. Regularly reviewing the data allows the team to use behavior referral data as a formative analysis tool. For example, if the data indicate an increase in the number of office discipline referrals in the hallway, then the team would want to address the issue. The team should collect additional data to determine why the problem is occurring and then implement an action plan to address issues in the hallway. The ongoing data collection can be used to evaluate the impact of the plan in the hallway.

Office referral data also should be reviewed at the end of the year as a summative evaluation tool. End of the year office referral data can be used to determine the overall impact of the SWPBIS system for the current year and can be compared to previous years. For example, the total number of office referrals or the rate of referrals per day per month could be compared across multiple years to determine if SWPBIS is affecting the overall demonstration of problem behaviors in the school building.

A school leadership team may want to consider using additional school-wide data to determine the impact of SWPBIS on student outcomes. The team may want to consider examining the impact of SWPBIS on attendance rates, suspension and expulsion data, and the number of students who drop out of school. Some schools use behavior screeners to identify students who need behavioral interventions, particularly those students who do not get frequent office discipline referrals but still are in need of assistance. Evaluating school-wide behavior using behavior screeners several times per year can be another useful strategy to assess the impact of SWPBIS over time.

The team also can examine the impact of the SWPBIS system on academic achievement, as research continues to demonstrate that schools that implement SWPBIS see correlations with higher academic achievement on statewide or district-wide assessment (e.g., Horner et al., 2009). It is believed that the reduction of behavior problems from SWPBIS allows for increased academic engaged time for students and more time for teachers to provide quality instruction without constantly managing problem behaviors, thus having a positive impact on students' academic achievement (Algozzine, Wang, & Violette, 2011). Given their expertise with data collection and analysis, school psychologists are in an excellent position to lead team discussions about collecting and using multiple sources of data to make decisions about the effectiveness of SWPBIS.

Establishing Targeted Group Interventions

Office referral data may be used to evaluate the overall impact of the SWPBIS system. The data also may be used to identify those students who need more support beyond the universal instruction provided to all students. A SWPBIS system also includes secondary and tertiary levels of support for students. A system of secondary or targeted support should be available for groups of students who need additional support. Typically, students with three to five office referrals in a given school year, but who are not displaying significantly disruptive or dangerous behaviors, need more instruction and support beyond the universal level of instruction. These students may need small group reteaching of and practice on the behavioral expectations in various locations in the school. These students also may be in need of small-group instruction in concepts such as anger management, social skills, problem-solving skills, and friendship-making skills in order to improve performance and master needed skills for school success.

School psychologists could coordinate or conduct social skills or problem-solving instruction groups or serve as coordinators of other group intervention or monitoring efforts. Numerous social skills programs exist that have strong empirical support for their effectiveness, and school psychologists are in an excellent position to evaluate such programs and make informed choices about those programs that could work in their schools (McKevitt, 2012).

Establishing Intensive Individual Interventions

A small number of students will require intense individualized instruction beyond the universal and/or secondary levels of a SWPBIS system. Typically these are the students with six or more office referrals in a given school year and/or the students who demonstrate significantly dangerous or disruptive problem behaviors. The SWPBIS system should include a way to proactively identify these students, determine their individual needs, and implement instructional interventions. Functional behavioral assessment should be used to identify the function of the student's problem behavior and the student's specific instructional needs. The information gathered should be used to develop a behavior intervention plan that identifies (a) the changes that will be made to the setting and antecedent events to prevent problem behaviors, (b) the new behavioral skills to be taught and how those skills will be reinforced, and (c) the behavior reduction strategies that will be implemented to reduce the frequency of the problem behavior. These behavior intervention plan elements are crucial to support the student and help him or her be successful in school (Crone & Horner, 2003). An individual monitoring plan should be developed for each student in need of individual support. The monitoring plan should evaluate the impact of the behavior support plan on the student's behavior and the treatment integrity of implementing the instructional plan. Clearly, the functional behavioral assessment process and behavior intervention plan development are areas of expertise for school psychologists.

Implementation Examples

To demonstrate the features of SWPBIS, two implementation examples are offered, one elementary school and one high school. While these examples are based on real schools, the school names have been changed.

Anderson Elementary School

Anderson Elementary School is located on the edge of a large city. It has approximately 350 students in grades K–6, with a teaching staff of 20. Because of escalating behavior problems and high student mobility (Anderson is located near a military base), the principal sought out training in SWPBIS. To demonstrate need and encourage staff buy-in, the staff completed the Effective Behavior Support Survey, and found that more than half of the staff believed school-wide behavior was in need of improvement.

During their training year, the SWPBIS leadership team, consisting of the principal, school psychologist, guidance counselor, and three classroom teachers, identified the following behavioral expectations: be safe, be kind, be responsible, and be respectful. They called their expectations the Fantastic Four. The team also

developed the teaching matrix they used to plan instruction of the Fantastic Four (see Figure 12.2). To acknowledge desired behaviors, the team planned to give out Fantastic Grams, slips of paper that students put in a box for a weekly prize drawing. Students earning Fantastic Grams also received public recognition at monthly celebration assemblies. To collect data on their progress, the team redesigned their office referral form (Figure 12.3) to align with their SWPBIS work and trained staff on proper procedures for referring students to the office. During the year prior to the SWPBIS implementation, the team recorded a total of 549 office discipline referrals and the school psychologist shared these data with staff along with updates about the team's progress.

At the beginning of the following school year, the staff taught the Fantastic Four in all school locations according to a schedule the leadership team developed.

Figure 12.2. Anderson Elementary School's Expectations Teaching Matrix

Fantastic Four	Be Safe	Be Kind	Be Respectful	Be Responsible
Classroom	• Hands/feet to yourself • Push chairs in • Sit in chairs safely	• Use nice words with each other • Raise your hand to speak	• Listen to the teacher • Follow instructions • Treat property with care	• Come to school prepared • Take care of classroom materials
Hallway	• Walk on the right side • Hands/feet to yourself • One step at a time	• Use nice words with each other • Greet friends quietly	• Give each other space • Hands/feet to yourself • Treat property with care	• Pick up litter • Move with a purpose
Lunchroom	• Yield to those with trays • Walk • Report spills to an adult	• Use nice words with each other • Use good table manners	• Use an inside voice • Eat only your lunch	• Keep area clean • Put trays and silveware in their place • Throw trash away
Playground	• Follow equipment rules • Take inside what you took outside	• Use nice words with each other	• Line up when called • Follow directions • Treat equipment with care	• Play in designated area • Organized games on the blacktop only
Bathroom	• Hands/feet to yourself • Wash hands • Report problems to an adult	• Maintain privacy	• Wait outside if stalls are full • One child per stall	• Clean up after yourself • Flush the toilet after use • Take care of needs quickly

Figure 12.3. Anderson Elementary School's Office Referral Form

Anderson Elementary School

Student Name_____

Date_____

Classroom Teacher _____

Grade_____

Referring Staff Member_____

Time_____

Location of Incident _____

Others Involved_____

☐ Be Safe ☐ Be Kind ☐ Be Responsible ☐Be Respectful

Description of the Situation_____

_____

Violation:
☐ Abusive language to students
☐ Abusive language to staff
☐ Destruction of property
☐ Disruption
☐ Noncompliance
☐ Physical aggression
☐ Possession of inappropriate items
☐ Theft

Probable Motivation:
☐ Obtain peer attention
☐ Obtain adult attention
☐ Obtain items/activities
☐ Avoid peer(s)
☐ Avoid adult
☐ Avoid task
☐ Unsure
☐ Other:_____

Staff Actions Taken:
☐ Teaching interaction/reteach skill
☐ Warning/verbal reprimand
☐ Loss of privileges
☐ Other: _____

☐ Break/time-out
☐ Parent contact
☐ Alternative behavior plan

Administrator Comments _____

_____

_____

Administrator's Signature/Date

The SET data revealed the school was implementing SWPBIS with fidelity, with an overall score of 97% of points earned (compared to 64% prior to implementation). After a year of implementation of the Fantastic Four, there was a considerable drop in office discipline referrals. By the end of the year, the total number of referrals was decreased to 276, a reduction of 50%. The staff perceived a noticeable positive change in the overall climate of the school and the students were excited to earn their Fantastic Grams. The high level of fidelity of implementation continued into the next school year, as did the decline in office referrals.

River Valley High School

River Valley High School is an urban high school of approximately 990 students in grades 9–12 and a teaching staff of 65. A district administrator learned about SWPBIS at an administrator meeting and thought it would be good for the high school, which was experiencing a large number of discipline problems, particularly related to tardiness. In fact, in a year, the school recorded more than 4,000 office referrals for tardiness alone. The district administrator spoke with the school principal who organized a team to learn about and develop SWPBIS. The team consisted of an assistant principal, school psychologist, guidance counselor, special education teacher, and three classroom teachers. The team accessed training through the local educational cooperative.

The team referred to its SWPBIS work as River Valley Pride and developed four behavioral expectations: be safe, be responsible, be respectful, and be there. The last expectation was specifically designed to address the tardiness issue. While the team did not find it difficult to develop expectations and a teaching matrix, it did find it challenging to identify a reward system that was appropriate for high schoolers. After much discussion, the team came up with the idea of putting stamps in students' planners for engaging in the expectations. Once students received 10 stamps, they could purchase candy from the school store or they could be entered into a monthly drawing for a gift card (e.g., $50 to a local gas station).

The other area of difficulty with SWPBIS planning the team experienced was in developing consistency with its consequence system. The team members found it challenging to gain agreement and consistency among 65 staff about what types of behaviors should be administrator managed versus staff managed. Again, after much discussion, the team came to an agreement and developed a set of consequence procedures that everyone could live with (see Figure 12.4). The school psychologist led a redesign in the office referral form to ensure it included adequate information for decision making about the SWPBIS efforts.

Because of the large staff size, staff buy-in was a challenge for the leadership team. The team was careful to keep staff informed of its efforts throughout their planning year, and had several days over the school year during which the school psychologist and one or two other team members met with small groups of teachers

Figure 12.4. River Valley High School's Consequence System

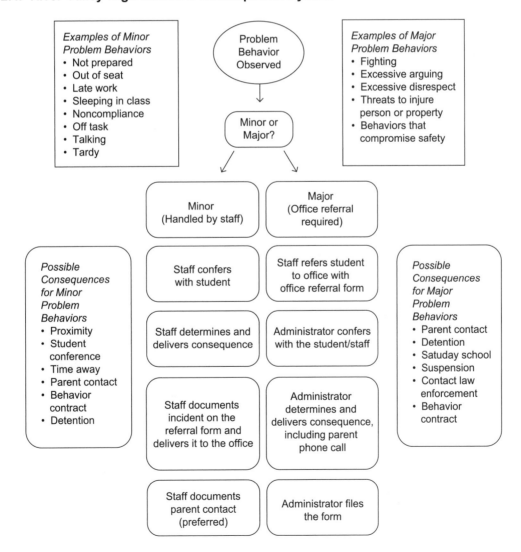

to explain SWPBIS and gain support. Although not all teachers expressed complete support, most liked the idea of consistency in language used with students as well as consistency in discipline procedures. By the end of the planning year, enough staff members demonstrated support for the team to feel confident they could proceed with implementation.

River Valley's SET data indicated fidelity of implementation, with an overall score of 95% of points earned after implementation, compared to a score of 59% prior to implementation. After one academic quarter of teaching and implementing River Valley Pride, the staff observed an overall decrease of problem behavior, but most impressively, the number of tardies was reduced by 75% over a comparable time the previous school year.

SUMMARY

SWPBIS is an effective framework for creating school environments that promote appropriate behavior for all students. Within that framework, preventive methods are incorporated that address the behavior of all students, including targeted groups of students and students needing intensive individualized support. The result is a school-wide system in which a culture of appropriate behavior is expected and demonstrated by students and acknowledged frequently by adults. Problem behavior is largely prevented and, when it occurs, is responded to swiftly and consistently. Data are collected and used to evaluate the effectiveness of the system and to make decisions about how to best address student behavior. Implementation of these components, combined with the foundational elements discussed earlier, will allow schools to promote and support the behavioral success of all students, which in turn can have a profound impact on the climate, culture, and achievement of the school community. School psychologists, with their knowledge and skills in assessment and intervention, behavioral principles, and data analysis, can play a large role in all components of a SWPBIS system.

REFERENCES

Akin-Little, K. A., Eckert, T. L., Lovett, B. J., & Little, S. G. (2004). Extrinsic reinforcement in the classroom: Bribery or best practice. *School Psychology Review, 33*, 344–362.

Algozzine, B., Wang, C., & Violette, A. S. (2011). Reexamining the relationship between academic achievement and social behavior. *Journal of Positive Behavior Interventions, 13*, 3–16. doi:10.1177/1098300709359084

Bear, G. G. (2008). Best practices in classroom discipline. In A. Thomas & J. Grimes (Eds.), *Best practices in school psychology V* (pp. 1403–1420). Bethesda, MD: National Association of School Psychologists.

Benedict, E. A., Horner, R. H., & Squires, J. K. (2007). Assessment and implementation of positive behavior support in preschools. *Topics in Early Childhood Special Education, 27*, 174–192. doi:10.1177/02711214070270030801

Bohanon, H., Flannery, K., Malloy, J., & Fenning, P. (2009). Utilizing positive behavior supports in high school settings to improve school completion rates for students with high incidence conditions. *Exceptionality, 17*, 30–44.

Bradshaw, C., Mitchell, M., & Leaf, P. (2010). Examining the effects of school-wide positive behavioral interventions and supports on student outcomes. *Journal of Positive Behavior Interventions, 12*, 133–148. doi:10.1177/1098300709334798

Caldarella, P., Shatzer, R. H., Gray, K. M., Young, K. R., & Young, E. L. (2011). The effects of school-wide positive behavior support on middle school climate and student outcomes. *RMLE Online: Research in Middle Level Education, 35*(4), 1–14.

Coyne, M. D., Kame'enui, E. J., & Carnine, D. W. (2010). *Effective teaching strategies that accommodate diverse learners* (4th ed.). Boston, MA: Pearson.

Crone, D. A., & Horner, R. H. (2003). *Building positive behavior support systems in schools: Functional behavioral assessment.* New York, NY: Guilford Press.

Esler, A. N., Godber, Y., & Christenson, S. L. (2008). Best practices in supporting home–school collaboration. In A. Thomas & J. Grimes (Eds.), *Best practices in school psychology V* (pp. 917–936). Bethesda, MD: National Association of School Psychologists.

Franzen, K., & Kamps, D. (2008). The utilization and effects of positive behavior support strategies on an urban school playground. *Journal of Positive Behavior Interventions, 10*, 150–161. doi:10.1177/1098300708316260

Horner, R. H., Sugai, G., Smolkowski, K., Eber, L., Nakasato, J., Todd, A. W., & Esperanza, J. (2009). A randomized, wait-list controlled effectiveness trial assessing school-wide positive behavior support in elementary schools. *Journal of Positive Behavior Interventions, 11*, 133–144. doi:10.1177/1098300709332067

Horner, R. H., Todd, A. W., Lewis-Palmer, T., Irvin, L. K., Sugai, G., & Boland, J. B. (2004). The School-Wide Evaluation Tool (SET): A research instrument for assessing school-wide positive behavior support. *Journal of Positive Behavioral Interventions, 6*, 3–12. doi:10.1177/10983007040060010201

Iverson, A. M. (2002). Best practices in problem-solving team structure and process. In A. Thomas & J. Grimes (Eds.), *Best practices in school psychology IV* (pp. 657–669). Bethesda, MD: National Association of School Psychologists.

McKevitt, B. C. (2012). School psychologists' knowledge and use of evidence-based social-emotional learning interventions. *Contemporary School Psychology, 16*, 33–45, Retrieved from http://www.casponline.org/pdfs/pdfs/school_psychologists'.pdf

McKevitt, B. C., Dempsey, J. N., Ternus, J., & Shriver, M. D. (2012). Dealing with behavior problems: The use of positive behavior support strategies in summer programs. *Afterschool Matters, 15*, 16–25.

National Association of School Psychologists. (2010). *Model of comprehensive and integrated school psychological services*. Bethesda, MD: Author. Retrieved from http://www.nasponline.org/standards/2010standards/2_PracticeModel.pdf

Scott, T. M. (2002). Removing roadblocks to effective behavior intervention in inclusive settings: Responding to typical objections by school personnel. *Beyond Behavior, 12*(1), 21–26.

Scott, T. M., & Barrett, S. B. (2004). Using staff and student time engaged in disciplinary procedures to evaluate the impact of school-wide PBS. *Journal of Positive Behavior Interventions, 6*, 21–27. doi:10.1177/10983007040060010401

Simonson, B., Britton, L., & Young, D. (2010). School-wide positive behavior support in an alternative school setting: A case study. *Journal of Positive Behavior Interventions, 12*, 180–191. doi:10.1177/1098300708330495

Sugai, G., & Horner, R. H. (2006). A promising approach for expanding and sustaining school-wide positive behavior support. *School Psychology Review, 35*, 245–259.

Sugai, G., Horner, R. H., & Lewis-Palmer, T. (2001). *Team Implementation Checklist*. Eugene, OR: University of Oregon, Educational and Community Supports.

Sugai, G., Horner, R. H., Lewis-Palmer, T., & Todd, A. (2005). *School-wide positive behavior support training manual*. Eugene, OR:

University of Oregon, Educational and Community Supports. Retrieved from http://www.pbis.org

Sugai, G., Horner, R. H., & Todd, A. (2000). *Effective Behavior Support Survey*. Eugene, OR: University of Oregon, Educational and Community Supports.

Sugai, G., Lewis-Palmer, T., Todd, A., & Horner, R. H. (2001). *School-Wide Evaluation Tool*. Eugene, OR: University of Oregon, Educational and Community Supports.

Sullivan, A. L., Long, L., & Kucera, M. (2011). A survey of school psychologists' preparation, participation, and perceptions related to positive behavior interventions and supports. *Psychology in the Schools, 48*, 971–985. doi:10.1002/pits.20605

Technical Assistance Center on Positive Behavioral Interventions and Supports. (2010). *Implementation blueprint and self-assessment: Positive behavioral interventions and supports*. Washington, DC: Author. Retrieved from http://www.pbis.org/common/pbisresources/publications/SWPBS_ImplementationBlueprint_vSep_23_2010.pdf

U.S. Department of Education. (2012). *Restraint and seclusion: Resource document*. Washington, DC: Author. Retrieved from http://www.ed.gov/policy/restraintseclusion

Young, E. L., Caldarella, P., Richardson, M. J., & Young, K. R. (2012). *Positive behavior support in secondary schools: A practical guide*. New York, NY: Guilford Press.

Best Practices in the Use of Learning Supports Leadership Teams to Enhance Learning Supports

13

Howard S. Adelman
Linda Taylor
University of California, Los Angeles

OVERVIEW

Case-oriented work has long dominated school psychology. While we are all concerned when a specific student manifests a learning, behavior, or emotional problem, a one-child-at-a-time focus has obvious limitations in schools where many are not doing well. As a result of a case-by-case orientation, many school psychologists and their student-support colleagues are not yet in tune with the concept of support staff leadership teams that focus on developing unified and comprehensive systems to address barriers to learning and teaching. In fact, some say to us: "What's that got to do with my job?" Others say: "What's that got to do with helping kids?"

Pursuit of best practices for carrying out leadership functions that are oriented to redeploying resources for system development is essential for ending the marginalization that continues to seriously impede the contribution of student support staff and that leads to reductions in force. Leadership teams focused on system development and enhancing how resources for addressing barriers to learning and teaching are used represent a major change in school operational infrastructure. This change enables the engagement of support staff in the type of analyses essential if school improvement planning and decision making are to create a unified and comprehensive system of student and learning supports at a school.

It is widely conceded that supports to address barriers to learning and teaching tend to be fragmented and narrowly focused and reach only a small proportion of those in need. Moreover, sparse budgets lead school psychologists, counselors, social workers, nurses, and other support staff into counterproductive competition with each other and with community professionals working with schools. Clearly, changes are needed. Support staff leadership teams can play a major role in altering this unacceptable status quo.

As school psychologists know, what happens for students depends first and foremost on who makes decisions about resources and who plans the details for school improvements. But the reality is that prevailing infrastructure mechanisms marginalize the influence of those most directly concerned about addressing learning, behavior, and emotional problems. So, pursuit of best practices makes it essential to rethink school and district leadership and operational infrastructure to correct this deficiency. We have addressed this and related systemic change matters in detail elsewhere (Adelman & Taylor, 2006a, 2008a, 2010; Center for Mental Health in Schools, 2005a, 2011a, 2012a). The focus here is on new leadership teams and workgroups designed to be a permanent part of a school and district infrastructure for unifying and developing a unified and comprehensive system of student and learning supports. Such mechanisms are essential to school improvement, and they provide a vehicle for school psychologists and other student support staff to expand their role and functions to encompass system development for school improvement. This is the key to moving from being seen as concerned only with providing services to a few of the struggling students to playing an essential leadership role in ensuring all students have an equal opportunity to succeed at school.

Pioneering work across the country conceives support staff leadership mechanisms from the school outward (Center for Mental Health in Schools, 2012a, 2012b, 2012c, 2012d). That is, first the focus is on school-level mechanisms. Then, based on analyses of what is needed to facilitate and enhance school-level efforts, mechanisms are conceived that enable clusters or families of schools to work together. The objectives in doing so are to increase efficiency and effectiveness and achieve the financial benefits that can be garnered from combining resources in pursuit of shared and overlapping functions. From this perspective, system-wide mechanisms are designed or redesigned to support the work at each school and among clusters of schools (e.g., those in feeder patterns).

The type of leadership mechanisms delineated in this chapter, at a school, for multiple school sites, and system-wide, enable school psychologists to play a critical role in school improvement efforts to unify and develop a comprehensive system of student and learning supports. Such mechanisms provide ways to (a) arrive at decisions about resource allocation; (b) maximize systematic and integrated planning, implementation, maintenance, and evaluation of student and learning supports; (c) outreach to create formal working relationships with community resources to bring some to a school and establish special linkages with others; and (d) upgrade and modernize the approach to providing student and learning supports in ways that reflect the best intervention thinking and use of technology. At each system level, these tasks require that all support staff adopt some new roles and functions and that parents, students, and other representatives from the community enhance their involvement. They also call for redeployment of existing resources as well as identifying new ones.

All schools have some activity focused on specific concerns, such as learning problems, substance abuse, violence, teen pregnancy, school dropouts, and delinquency. When viewed as a whole, an extensive range of activities oriented to students' needs and problems are found in many school districts. Some programs are provided throughout a school district, and others are carried out at or linked to targeted schools. The interventions may be designed to benefit all students in a school, those in specified grades, and/or those identified as having special needs. The activities may be implemented in regular or special education classrooms and may be geared to an entire class, groups, or individuals or they may be designed as pull-out programs for designated students. They encompass efforts to improve classroom and school-wide climate and a range of curricular and clinically oriented activities.

While schools can use a wide range of people to help students, most school-owned and operated services are offered as part of pupil personnel services. In large districts, school psychologists, counselors, social workers, and other specialists may be organized into separate units. Such units straddle regular, special, and compensatory education. Analyses of the situation find that the result is programs and services that are planned, implemented, and evaluated in a fragmented and piecemeal manner.

Service staff at schools tend to function in relative isolation of each other and other stakeholders, with a great deal of the work oriented to discrete problems and with an overreliance on specialized services for individuals and small groups. In some places, a student identified as at risk for grade retention, dropout, and substance abuse may be assigned to three counseling programs operating independently of each other.

Even in settings with relatively few services, such fragmentation not only is costly, it breeds counterproductive competition and works against developing cohesiveness and maximizing results. The problems inherent in all this have long been of concern to support staff and their professional organizations, as well as policy makers at state and federal levels (e.g., Fagan & Wise, 2000; Marx & Wooley, 1998).

With the intent of dealing with the above concerns, trailblazing schools across the country are pioneering the use of a leadership mechanism that focuses specifically on how resources are used and enhanced in order to improve how they provide student support activity (Center for Mental Health in Schools, 2012b). This mechanism differs in its functions from the case-oriented teams most schools have for reviewing individual student/family problems (e.g., a student support team, an Individualized Educational Program [IEP] team). The functions of such case-oriented teams include referral, triage, and care monitoring or management. In contrast, a student- or learning-supports leadership team at a school focuses on system development by enhancing use of all available resources associated with addressing barriers to student learning and promoting healthy development.

Two metaphors help differentiate the two types of mechanisms and the importance of both. A case orientation fits the starfish metaphor: The day after a great storm had washed up all sorts of sea life far up onto the beach, a youngster set out to throw back as many of the still-living starfish as he could. After watching him toss one after the other into the ocean, an old man approached him and said, "It's no use your doing that, there are too many. You're not going to make any difference." The boy looked at him in surprise, then bent over, picked up another starfish, threw it in, and then replied, "It made a difference to that one!" This metaphor, of course, reflects all the important efforts to assist specific students.

The leadership and resource-oriented focus is captured by a different metaphor: One weekend a group of school staff went fishing together down at the river. Not long after they got there, a child came floating down the rapids calling for help. One of the group on the shore quickly dove in and pulled the child out. Minutes later another child, then another, and then many more children were coming down the river. Soon everyone was diving in and dragging children to the shore and then jumping back in to save as many children as they could. In the midst of all this frenzy, one of the group was seen walking away. Her colleagues were irate. How could she leave when there were so many children to save? After long hours, to everyone's relief, the flow of children stopped, and the group could finally catch their breath. At that moment, their colleague came back. They turned on her and angrily shouted, "How could you walk off when we needed everyone here to save the children?" She replied, "It occurred to me that someone ought to go upstream and find out why so many kids were falling into the river. What I found is that the old bridge had several planks missing, and when children tried to jump over the gap, they couldn't make it and fell through into the river. So I got some folks to help fix the bridge." Fixing and building better bridges is a good way to think about prevention, and it helps underscore the importance of taking time for system development that improves and enhances use of limited resources.

Clearly, as the widespread policy and practice emphasis on Tier 1, Tier 2, and Tier 3 service levels suggests, schools need to pursue system development and resource-oriented functions in addressing learning, behavior, and emotional problems, as well as individual cases (Center for Mental Health in Schools, 2011b). Since case-oriented teams are widely implemented, it seems essential to increase understanding of the importance of ensuring there also is the type of system

development focus that leads to an increased emphasis on prevention and responding as early after problem onset as feasible. Such an emphasis is critical to reducing the number of students who end up needing to be responded to as cases. It also can help school psychologists as they strive to play a greater role in school improvement planning and decision making.

We initially demonstrated the feasibility of resource-oriented leadership teams in the Los Angeles Unified School District (Lim & Adelman, 1997; Rosenblum, DiCecco, Taylor, & Adelman, 1995). Currently, such a team is being introduced in many schools across the country (Center for Mental Health in Schools, 2012a; Education Development Center, 2011). Initially, the mechanism was designated by names such as Resource Coordinating Team and Resource Management Team. For purposes of this discussion, we will use the current preference to identify the mechanism as a Learning Supports Leadership Team.

Creation of leadership mechanisms focusing on learning supports at schools, for families of schools, and at the district level provides an often missing facet of the operational infrastructure (Center for Mental Health in Schools, 2005b). Where this facet is missing, certain functions may be given short shrift. Examples include analyses of how existing resources are deployed and clarification of how the various human and financial resources from public and private sectors can be woven together. When too little attention is paid to such functions, it hampers efforts to (a) weave together existing school and community resources; (b) enable programs and services to function in an increasingly cohesive and cost-efficient way; and (c) develop, implement, and evaluate over time a unified and comprehensive system of learning supports.

Available evidence suggests that, by transforming current approaches for addressing barriers to student learning and teaching, mechanisms for system development are vital in reducing marginalization and fragmentation of student and learning supports (Adelman & Taylor 2006a; Education Development Center, 2011; U.S. Department of Education, 1996). Moreover, when such mechanisms are created in the form of teams, they also can be vehicles for building working relationships and can help solve turf and operational problems. In all, a Learning Supports Leadership Team provides a structure for pursuing the type of functions specified in the National Association of School Psychologists (NASP) 2010 *Model for Comprehensive and Integrated School Psychological Services* (NASP, 2010).

BASIC CONSIDERATIONS

System development and improving and enhancing use of limited resources involve carrying out a variety of functions in a proactive way. These include providing leadership, capacity building, oversight for mapping and analyzing current resource use, establishing priorities for program development, making recommendations for resource deployment or redeployment and enhancement to improve programs and systems, and participating in decision making.

When the focus is on system development mechanisms for student and learning supports, the following intents are provided for:

- *All students:* Use resources to address the diverse needs of the many as well as the few and do so in ways that level the playing field and enable every student to have an equal opportunity to succeed at school.
- *Build a school-site infrastructure:* Establish and sustain organizational and operational mechanisms that are linked into an effective and efficient infrastructure at the school site.
- *Build infrastructure for a family of schools:* Connect schools in a complex or feeder pattern to maximize use of available resources and achieve economies of scale.
- *Connect with the district central office infrastructure:* Ensure that site-based and school cluster efforts are effectively linked to and nurtured by the central office.
- *Connect schools across districts:* In small rural school districts and where schools are organized into separate high school and elementary districts, this is both appropriate and necessary.
- *Build school–community collaborative:* Connect school and community infrastructures and braiding school–community resources.
- *Evolve a comprehensive, multifaceted, and cohesive system of learning supports:* Rethink and deploy resources in ways that evolve student support services into a unified and comprehensive learning supports component that is treated as a primary and essential facet of school improvement.

Team Composition

It is conceivable that one person can perform many of the basic functions described above. However, given the nature and scope of the work, it is preferable to have several stakeholders put their heads together and function as a formal Learning Supports Leadership Team.

Some schools find the idea of establishing another team unappealing. In such cases, an existing team (e.g., student or teacher assistance teams, school crisis teams, healthy school teams, or school improvement teams) can perform the system development functions. In adding these functions to another team's work, however, great care must be taken to structure the agenda so sufficient time is devoted to the leadership tasks. For small schools a large team often is not feasible, but a two-person team can still do much of the work. The point is to get started and build over time the type of team that fits the setting. The key is not to lose sight of the system development functions the team needs to pursue and what needs to be accomplished.

The team meets as necessary. Frequency of meetings depends on how ambitious the group's agenda is and time availability. Initially, this may mean once a week. Later, when meetings are scheduled for every 2–3 weeks, continuity and momentum are maintained through interim tasks performed by individuals or workgroups. Because some participants may be at a school on a part-time basis, one of the problems that must be addressed is that of rescheduling personnel so that there is an overlapping time for meeting together. Of course, the reality is that not all team members will be able to attend every meeting, but a good approximation can be made at each meeting, with steps taken to keep others informed as to what was done. Well-organized and well-trained teams can accomplish a great deal through informal communication and short meetings.

Where a new team is established, it might begin with only a few people. Then, as feasible, it can expand into an inclusive group of informed, able, and willing stakeholders. Although a Learning Supports Leadership Team might be created solely around psychosocial programs, the intent is to focus on resources related to all major learning supports programs and services. Thus, the team tries to bring together representatives from each of these programs and services. Because various teams at a school require the expertise of the same personnel, some people will necessarily be on more than one team. The following are the types of stakeholders who are candidates for such a team:

- Administrator responsible for student and learning supports (e.g., assistant principal)
- School psychologist
- Counselor
- School nurse

- School social worker
- Attendance and dropout counselors
- Safe and drug-free school staff
- Behavioral specialist
- Special education staff
- After-school program staff
- Bilingual and Title I program coordinators
- Health educators
- Representatives of community agencies involved regularly with the school (e.g., community entities involved with physical and mental health, welfare and protective services, juvenile justice)
- Student and family representation (when appropriate and feasible)
- Others who have a particular interest and ability to help with the functions, including regular classroom teachers, noncertificated staff (e.g., front office, food service, custodian, bus driver, school resource officer)

In establishing the team, school psychologists can play a key role in convening initial participants and facilitating the establishment of the mechanism.

For the team to function well, there must be a core of members who have or will acquire the ability to carry out identified functions and make the mechanism work (others are auxiliary members and workgroup participants). They must be committed to the team's mission. Building team commitment and competence is an ongoing task. The team must have a dedicated leader/ facilitator who is able to keep the group task-focused and productive. It also needs someone who records decisions and reminds members of planned activity and products. Whenever feasible, advanced technology (management systems, electronic bulletin boards and e-mail, clearinghouses) are used to facilitate communication, networking, program planning and implementation, linking activity, and a variety of budgeting, scheduling, and other management concerns.

A Learning Supports Leadership Team forms small workgroups as needed to address specific concerns (e.g., mapping resources, planning for capacity building, addressing problems related to case-oriented systems), develop new programs (e.g., welcoming and social support strategies for newcomers to the school), implement special initiatives (e.g., positive behavior support), and so forth. Such groups usually are facilitated by a member of the leadership team who recruits a small group of other stakeholders from the school and community who are willing and able to help. The group facilitator provides regular updates to the leadership team about workgroup progress and brings

back feedback from the team. Ad hoc workgroups take on tasks that can be done over a relatively short time period, and the group disbands once the work is accomplished. Standing workgroups focus on defined program areas and pursue current priorities for enhancing intervention in a given arena (e.g., helping design cohesive approaches to provide supports for various student transitions, enhancing home and school connections). Case-oriented teams such as student assistance or study teams and IEP teams, in effect, are standing workgroups and provide invaluable system data for the Learning Supports Leadership Team's deliberations.

Not an Isolated Mechanism but Part of an Integrated Infrastructure

System development mechanisms at all levels cannot be isolated entities. The intent is for each to connect to each other and be part of an integrated infrastructure. We focus here on the school level. Extrapolations can be made from there.

A Learning Supports Leadership Team must be a formal unit of a school's infrastructure. It must be fully connected with the other infrastructure mechanisms at the school (e.g., those associated with instruction and management/governance). Figure 13.1 illustrates relationships of such a team to other major infrastructure units.

Having at least one representative from the Learning Supports Leadership Team on the school's governing and planning bodies (e.g., the principal's decision-making team, school improvement planning team) ensures the type of infrastructure connections that are essential if student and learning supports are to be maintained, improved, and increasingly integrated with classroom instruction. In most cases, having the administrator who is responsible for student and learning supports on the team provides the necessary link with the school's administrative decision making related to allocation of budget, space, staff development time, and other resources. Moreover, as discussed below, where clusters or families of schools are working together, representatives from each of the schools meet together periodically (Adelman & Taylor, 2002; Taylor, Nelson, & Adelman, 1999).

A well-designed Learning Supports Leadership Team complements the work of a site's governance body by focusing on providing on-site overview, leadership, and advocacy for all activity specifically used to address barriers to learning and teaching. However, for this to

Figure 13.1. Learning Supports Leadership Team as Part of an Integrated Infrastructure at a School Site

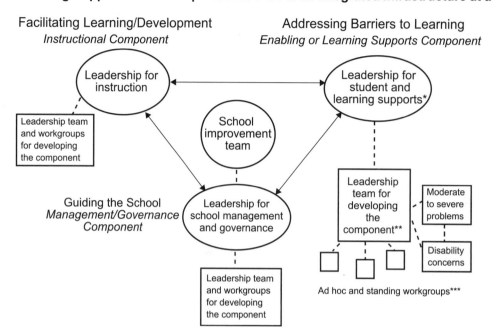

Note. For more on this, see the *Reworking Infrastructure* (Section B) of the Center's Toolkit for Rebuilding Student Supports Into a Comprehensive System for Addressing Barriers to Learning and Teaching: http://smhp.psych.ucla.edu/toolkitb3.htm
*Learning supports or enabling component leadership consists of an administrator and other advocates/champions with responsibility and accountability for ensuring the vision or the component is not lost. The administrator meets with and provides regular input to the Learning Supports Leadership Team. **A Learning Supports Leadership Team ensures component cohesion, integrated implementation, and ongoing development. It meets weekly to guide and monitor daily implementation and development of all programs, services, initiatives, and systems at a school that are concerned with providing learning supports and specialized assistance. ***Ad hoc and standing workgroups initially are the various teams that already exist related to various initiatives and programs (e.g., a crisis team) and for processing cases (e.g., a student assistance team, an IEP team). Where redundancy exists, workgroups can be combined. Others are formed as needed by the Learning Supports Leadership Team to address specific concerns. These groups are essential for accomplishing the many tasks associated with such a team's functions.

be the case, the team must be properly constituted, trained, and supported.

Establishing and building team capacity, of course, are not simple tasks. As a result, it is essential to think in terms of a phase-in process (Center for Mental Health in Schools, 2005a). Because establishing such a team involves significant organizational change, staff assigned to accomplish the tasks must have the skills of a systemic change agent. We designate this type of change agent as an *organization facilitator* and it is the type of role many school psychologists could learn to play (Adelman & Taylor 2006a; Lim & Adelman, 1997; Rosenblum et al., 1995).

Anyone chosen to create organizational change must be assured the full administrative support and be specially trained as a change agent. The training must include developing expertise to help school sites, families of schools, and districts implement and institutionalize substantively new approaches.

In brief, organization facilitators are catalysts and managers of change. As such, they strive to ensure that changes are true to the design for improvement and adapted to fit the local culture. Such a facilitator also must be an effective problem solver, responding quickly as problems arise and designing proactive strategies to counter anticipated barriers to change, such as negative reactions and dynamics, common factors interfering with working relationships, and system deficiencies. All this must be accomplished in ways that increase readiness and commitment to change while enhancing empowerment and a sense of community.

Organization facilitators also can help organize basic interdisciplinary and cross training to create the trust, knowledge, skills, and the attitudes essential for the kind of working relationships required if the resource-oriented mechanism is to operate successfully. Because the work of resource-oriented teams involves promoting systemic changes at a school, an organization facilitator helps team members understand how to be effective agents of change as they work with a site's stakeholders to restructure programs and infrastructure mechanisms. This includes matters such as planning, implementing, and formatively evaluating stakeholder development (coaching, with an emphasis on creating readiness both in terms of motivation and skills; team building; providing technical assistance) and ongoing capacity building and support.

We have focused here on an organization facilitator as a change agent for one school. Such an individual, however, might rotate among a group of schools. In large school districts, a cadre of such professionals might be used to facilitate change across an entire district.

BEST PRACTICES IN THE USE OF LEARNING SUPPORTS LEADERSHIP TEAMS TO ENHANCE LEARNING SUPPORTS

In keeping with the fundamental organizational principle emphasizing that structure (e.g., an operational infrastructure mechanism) follows function, we discuss best practices for a Learning Supports Leadership Team in terms of its major functions.

Functions

When we describe a Learning Support Leadership Team, some school staff quickly respond that they already have one (Center for Mental Health in Schools, 2011c). When we explore this with them, we usually find what they have is a case-oriented team (e.g., a student study team, student success team, student assistance team). To further clarify the difference between teams, we contrast the functions of each. In doing so, the intent is to highlight the differences in agenda and the need for

mechanisms to carry out both sets of functions listed in Table 13.1.

As noted already, the resource-oriented functions are pursued not just to enhance coordination, but to make progress toward the overall aim of developing a comprehensive, multifaceted, and cohesive system of learning supports (i.e., a learning supports component). In pursuing its functions, the team provides what often is a missing link for developing, implementing, managing, and enhancing programs and systems in ways that integrate, strengthen, or stimulate new and improved interventions (Higgins, Weiner, & Young, 2012).

For example, such a mechanism can be used to (a) map and analyze activities and resources to improve their use in preventing and ameliorating problems; (b) build effective systems for referral, case management, and quality assurance; (c) enhance procedures for management of programs and information and for communication among school staff and with the home; and (d) explore ways to redeploy and enhance resources, such as clarifying which activities are nonproductive, suggesting better uses for resources, and establishing priorities for developing new interventions, as well as reaching out to connect with additional resources in the school district and community.

About Mapping and Analyzing Resources

Schools have a variety of programs and services to address barriers to learning and teaching, and these consume a significant amount of resources. The interventions range from Title I programs, through extra help for low performing students, to accommodations for special education students. From what school administrators usually tell us, when the various sources of support are totaled at schools with substantial

Table 13.1. Different Functions of Case-Oriented and System Development Leadership Teams

Case-Oriented Team Functions	System Development Leadership Team Functions
Triage	Aggregating data across students and from teachers to analyze school needs
Referral	Mapping resources in school and community
Case monitoring/management	Analyzing resources
Case progress review	Identifying the most pressing program development needs at the school
Case reassessment	Coordinating and integrating school resources and connecting with community resources
	Establishing priorities for strengthening programs and developing new ones
	Planning and facilitating ways to strengthen and develop new programs and systems
	Recommending how resources should be deployed and redeployed
	Identifying where additional resources exist and developing strategies for accessing them
	Social marketing

amounts of federal and special project funding, learning supports account for about 25% of the resources. However, because school leaders are mainly focused on enhancing instruction in direct ways, essential efforts to provide a well-designed learning supports system continue to be marginalized, and resources are deployed in a fragmented and often wasteful and ineffective manner. One result of marginalizing supports for students is that school improvement efforts continue to pay little attention to the need for and potential impact of rethinking how these resources can be used to enable student learning by doing more to address barriers cited in the literature as risk factors (Adelman & Taylor 2006b; Center for Mental Health in Schools, 2004; Taylor & Adelman, 2004).

Whatever the actual percentage of resources used for student and learning supports, the fact is that in too many locales these resources are expended in ad hoc, piecemeal ways (Marx & Wooley, 1998). A Learning Supports Leadership Team can reverse this trend. The key to doing so involves mapping, analyzing, and managing resources with a clear emphasis on what needs to be done to help all students have an equitable opportunity to succeed at school (see Appendix A).

To determine high frequency needs of a school, the team uses aggregated data about student learning and behavior. For example, a team at an elementary school may find that 30% of the third graders have problems reading or a high school team might find that 40% of the students are not graduating. Awareness of such needs raises the question of what resources already are being expended to address the problems (Academy for Educational Development, 2002; Dewar, 1997; Kretzmann & McKnight, 1993).

Following initial mapping, the focus turns to analyzing how resources are currently used and considering how they might be redeployed to improve efforts to address barriers to learning and teaching. The goal is to develop specific recommendations for improving the work at each school through enhancing use of the school's existing resources, as well as enhancing resources through collaboration among the family of schools and with neighborhood entities (McKnight & Kretzmann, 1990). The tasks are to clarify what parts are in place, what is still missing, and how to braid and enhance resources to improve matters.

What Parts Are in Place

Discussion focuses on how effective and efficient current efforts are. Special attention is given to identifying redundant efforts, inefficient use of resources, and ineffective activities. With respect to what is seen as ineffective, analyses differentiate between activities that might be effective if they were better supported and more effectively implemented and those that are not worth continuing because they have not made a significant impact or because they are not well conceived. This facilitates generating recommendations about what should be discontinued so that resources can be redeployed to enhance current efforts and fill gaps.

What Is Still Missing

Every school has a wish list of needed programs and services. The analyses put these into perspective of the vision for a comprehensive, multifaceted, and integrated approach to addressing barriers to learning and promoting healthy development. By doing this, the analyses provide an appreciation of major gaps. Thus, rather than making ad hoc choices from a long list of wishes, recommendations can be based on systematic analyses of what current efforts require enhancement and what gaps need to be filled.

How to Braid and Enhance Resources to Improve Matters

Analyses focus first on how resources are being used at a school: Which resources are being used with the greatest impact and which are not? Is there redundancy? Ineffective activity? Programs where costs far outweigh benefits? Inefficiencies due to lack of coordination? Are there promising programs that are undersupported? Are there serious gaps in addressing high priority needs that have been identified by the school's governance body?

Based on the analyses, immediate priorities are set and recommendations are formulated with respect to how best to deploy and redeploy resources to have the greatest impact.

Essentially, the work involves conducting a gap analysis. That is, existing resources are laid out in the context of the adopted vision for a comprehensive, multifaceted, and integrated approach to addressing barriers to learning and promoting healthy development. This provides a basis for a discussion of matters such as (a) what is working and whether certain activities should no longer be pursued (because they are not effective or not as high a priority as other activities that are needed); (b) what are current priorities with respect to important areas of need and what resources might be redeployed and braided to meet the priorities, including enhancing existing promising practices and filling gaps; and (c) what are strategies and time lines for improving the system of learning supports.

Having accomplished a school-level analysis, the focus turns to how a family of schools (neighboring schools, especially those in a feeder pattern) might braid resources to address common concerns. At this juncture, the family of schools explores how community resources might be woven into the effort (Dedrick, Mitchell, & Roberts, 1994; Kingsley, Coulton, Barndt, Sawicki, & Tatian, 1997). Schools in the same geographic (catchment) area have a number of shared concerns, and feeder schools often are interacting with students from the same family. Furthermore, some programs and personnel are (or can be) shared by several neighboring schools, thus minimizing redundancy and reducing costs. Appendix B highlights the ways school-based Learning Supports Leadership Teams connect families of schools (e.g., feeder patterns) by establishing Learning Supports Leadership Councils.

Moving to the next level, recommendations are made for how to better use the resources district and community agencies offer at central locations or to a few select schools. And, finally, the work turns to whatever extramural grants are available to schools, districts, and community entities to help turn the vision of a comprehensive, multifaceted, and cohesive system of learning supports into reality.

Tools to Aid in Mapping and Analyzing Resources

Mapping and analyzing resources is a major systemic intervention. There are many tools that can aid the process.

One set of tools specifically designed to enhance school improvement planning for addressing barriers to learning and teaching is the self-study surveys developed by the Center for Mental Health in Schools at UCLA. These surveys focus on what currently is being done, whether it is being done well, and what else is desired. The set includes an overview Survey of System Status, which covers the leadership and coordination systems needed in developing an effective learning support component and surveys for each of the following six arenas for enhancing learning supports: (a) classroom-based strategies to enable learning, engagement, and reengagement of those with mild-moderate learning, behavior, and emotional problems; (b) support for transitions; (c) prescribed student and family assistance; (d) crisis assistance and prevention; (e) home involvement and engagement; (f) outreach to develop greater community involvement and support, including recruitment of volunteers. The

set also includes a special survey focusing on school–community partnerships.

Such self-study surveys can be used by any mechanism concerned with mapping and analyzing resources. For example, members of a Learning Supports Leadership Team initially might work separately in responding to survey items, but the major benefit comes from the shared understanding that arises during group discussions. The discussion and subsequent analyses also can provide a form of quality review.

As another tool in effectively mapping and analyzing resources and their deployment it is helpful to have a broad framework of the scope and content of learning supports. An example of such a framework is illustrated in Figure 13.2. This matrix integrates a conceptualization of primary areas of focus for intervention and traditional levels (e.g., promotion and prevention, early intervention, and treatment; Tier 1, Tier 2, and Tier 3 service levels) but conceives of them as integrated systems of intervention (Center for Mental Health in Schools, 2011b).

Role of a Learning Supports Leadership Team in Helping Establish a Unified and Comprehensive Learning Supports Component

Again, we stress that the ultimate aim of pursuing a Learning Supports Leadership Team is not only to end the fragmentation of student and learning supports but also to end the marginalization of the whole enterprise (Adelman & Taylor, 1997a, 2006a, 2012). Toward these ends, Learning Supports Leadership Teams can play a key role by rethinking and deploying resource use in ways that transform student support services into a unified and comprehensive enabling or learning supports component that is treated as a primary and essential facet of school improvement. Appendix C highlights the phases of such system development.

Major school improvement, of course, requires creating readiness, building consensus, and influencing action by key stakeholders for such a major systemic change (Adelman & Taylor, 1997b, 2008b; Center for Mental Health in Schools, 2005a). The information arising from mapping and analyses of resources provides an important database that can be communicated to key stakeholders to help them understand the benefits of change (Kretzmann & McKnight, 1996; Mizrahi & Morris, 1993). Also important to making effective change is the inclusion of the evidence base for moving

Figure 13.2. A Unifying Umbrella Framework to Guide Rethinking of Learning Supports

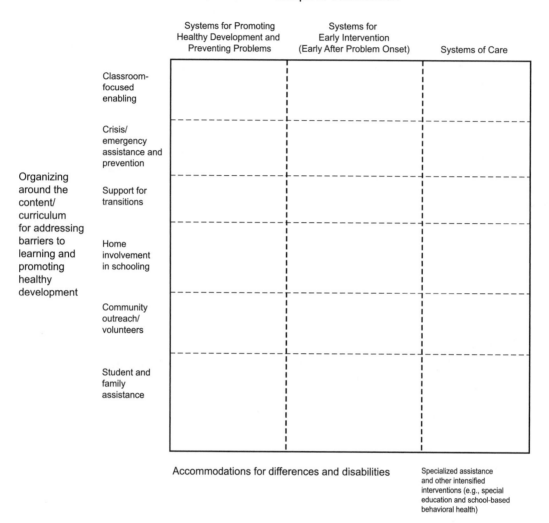

Scope of Intervention

Note. Specific school-wide and classroom-based activities related to positive behavior support, prereferral interventions, and the eight components of the Center for Prevention and Disease Control's Coordinated School Health Program are embedded into the six content areas.

in new directions (Center for Mental Health in Schools, 2004).

Data to Guide the Work and Evaluate Progress

All resource-oriented teams need data to enhance the quality of their efforts and to monitor their outcomes in ways that promote appropriate accountability. While new teams often do not have the resources for extensive data gathering, sound planning and implementation require that formative evaluation data be amassed and analyzed. In the process, data can be collected that provide a base for a subsequent evaluation of impact. All decisions about which data are needed should reflect clarity about how the data will be used.

The data for formative evaluation and team impact may already have been gathered from existing documents and records (base rate needs assessments, resource directories; budget information; census data; school, police; hospital; and other organization's reports).Where additional data are needed, they may be gathered using procedures such as checklists, surveys, semistructured interviews, focus group discussions, and observations. Of course, all data indicating that the team is having a positive impact should be widely shared as soon as it is available.

SUMMARY

System development leadership mechanisms are a key facet of school improvement efforts to transform and restructure daily operations for student and learning support. In some schools as much as 25% of the budget may be going to problem prevention and correction. Every school is expending resources to enable learning, and few have a mechanism to develop a unified and comprehensive system and ensure increasingly effective use of existing resources. Such a mechanism contributes to cost efficacy of learning supports activity by ensuring all such activity is planned, implemented, and evaluated in a coordinated and increasingly integrated manner. Creating system development leadership mechanisms also is essential for braiding together school and community resources and encouraging intervention activity to function in an increasingly cohesive way.

One of the primary and essential tasks a Learning Supports Leadership Team undertakes is that of taking stock of school and community programs and services that are in place to support students, families, and staff. A comprehensive gap assessment is generated as resources are mapped and compared with data on the unmet needs of and desired outcomes for students, their families, and school staff. Analyses of what is available, effective, and needed provide a sound basis for formulating priorities and developing strategies to link with additional resources at other schools, district sites, and in the community and enhance resource use. Such analyses also can guide efforts to improve cost effectiveness.

In a similar fashion, a Learning Supports Leadership Council for a complex or family of schools (e.g., a high school and its feeder schools) and one at the district level provides mechanisms for analyses on a larger scale. This can lead to strategies for cross-school, community-wide, and district-wide cooperation and integration to enhance intervention effectiveness and garner economies of scale.

Learning supports leadership mechanisms can reduce fragmentation and enhance cost efficacy. This mechanism can also guide school stakeholders in evolving the school's vision, priorities, and practices for learning supports and working to enhance resources in an integrative way. That is, with appropriate leadership from school psychologists and other student support staff, such a mechanism can play a key role in ending the marginalization of student and learning supports by transforming fragmented activity into a system of learning supports. In doing so, the focus needs to be on all school resources, including compensatory and special education, support services, adult education, recreation and enrichment programs, and facility use, as well as all community resources (including public and private agencies, families, businesses; services, programs, facilities; institutions of higher education; professionals in training; and volunteers including professionals making pro bono contributions).

The long-range aim is to weave all resources together into the fabric of every school and evolve a unified and comprehensive component that effectively addresses barriers to development, learning, and teaching. As leaders and policy makers recognize the essential nature of such a component, it will be easier to braid resources to address barriers. In turn, this will enhance efforts to foster healthy development. When resources are combined properly, the end product can be cohesive and potent school-community partnerships. These partnerships are essential to fulfilling society's aims of closing the achievement gap and ensuring all students have an equal opportunity to succeed at school and beyond.

AUTHOR NOTE

Disclosure. Howard S. Adelman and Linda Taylor have a financial interest in books they authored or coauthored referenced in this chapter.

REFERENCES

Academy of Educational Development. (2002). *Community youth mapping guide, tool kit, and informational video.* Washington, DC: Author.

Adelman, H. S., & Taylor, L. (1997a). Addressing barriers to learning: Beyond school-linked services and full service schools. *American Journal of Orthopsychiatry, 67,* 408–421. doi:10.1037/h0080243

Adelman, H. S., & Taylor, L. (1997b). Toward a scale-up model for replicating new approaches to schooling. *Journal of Educational and Psychological Consultation, 8,* 197–230. doi:10.1177/1049731507310195

Adelman, H. S., & Taylor, L. (2002, Autumn). So you want higher achievement scores? It's time to rethink learning supports. *The State Education Standard,* 52–56.

Adelman, H. S., & Taylor, L. (2006a). *The school leaders guide to student learning supports: New directions for addressing barriers to learning.* Thousand Oaks, CA: Corwin Press.

Adelman, H. S., & Taylor, L. (2006b). *The implementation guide to student learning supports: New directions for addressing barriers to learning.* Thousand Oaks, CA: Corwin Press.

Adelman, H. S., & Taylor, L. (2008a). *Rebuilding for learning: Addressing barriers to learning and teaching and re-engaging students.* New York, NY: Scholastic.

Adelman, H. S., & Taylor, L. (2008b). School improvement: A systemic view of what's missing and what to do about it. In B. Despres (Ed.), *Systems thinkers in action: A field guide for effective change leadership in education.* (pp. 55–76). Blue Ridge Summit, PA: Rowman & Littlefield.

Adelman, H. S., & Taylor, L. (2010). *Mental health in schools: Engaging learners, preventing problems, and improving schools.* Thousand Oaks, CA: Corwin Press.

Adelman, H. S., & Taylor, L. (2011). Turning around, transforming, and continuously improving schools: Policy proposals are still based on a two rather than a three component blueprint. *International Journal of School Disaffection, 8*(1), 22–34.

Adelman, H. S., & Taylor, L. (2012). Mental health in schools: Moving in new directions. *Contemporary School Psychology, 16,* 9–18.

Center for Mental Health in Schools. (2004). *Addressing barriers to student learning and promoting healthy development: A usable research base.* Los Angeles, CA: Author. Retrieved from http://smhp.psych.ucla.edu/pdfdocs/briefs/BarriersBrief.pdf

Center for Mental Health in Schools. (2005a). *Systemic change and school improvement: Designing, implementing, and sustaining prototypes and going to scale.* Los Angeles, CA: Author. Retrieved from http://smhp.psych.ucla.edu/pdfdocs/systemic/systemicreport.pdf

Center for Mental Health in Schools. (2005b). *School improvement planning: What's missing?* Los Angeles, CA: Author. Retrieved from http://smhp.psych.ucla.edu/whatsmissing.htm

Center for Mental Health in Schools. (2011a). *Key leadership infrastructure mechanisms for enhancing student and learning supports.* Los Angeles, CA: Author. Retrieved from http://smhp.psych.ucla.edu/pdfdocs/Report/resource_oriented_teams.pdf

Center for Mental Health in Schools. (2011b). *Moving beyond the three tier intervention pyramid toward a comprehensive framework for student and learning supports.* Los Angeles, CA: Author. Retrieved from http://smhp.psych.ucla.edu/pdfdocs/briefs/threetier.pdf

Center for Mental Health in Schools. (2011c). *"Not another team!" School improvement infrastructure viewed through the lens of addressing barriers to learning and teaching.* Los Angeles, CA: Author. Retrieved from http://smhp.psych.ucla.edu/pdfdocs/team.pdf

Center for Mental Health in Schools. (2012a). *Where's it happening: Examples of new directions for student support and lessons learned.* Los Angeles, CA: Author. Retrieved from http://smhp.psych.ucla.edu/summit2002/nind7.htm

Center for Mental Health in Schools. (2012b). *Blueprints for education reform: Have you analyzed the architects' vision?* Los Angeles, CA: Author. Retrieved from http://smhp.psych.ucla.edu/pdfdocs/blueprint.pdf

Center for Mental Health in Schools. (2012c). *Establishing a comprehensive system of learning supports at a school: Seven steps for principals and their staff.* Los Angeles, CA: Author. Retrieved from http://smhp.psych.ucla.edu/pdfdocs/7steps.pdf

Center for Mental Health in Schools. (2012d). *Common core state standards and learning supports.* Los Angeles, CA: Author. Retrieved from http://smhp.psych.ucla.edu/pdfdocs/comcorpol.pdf

Dedrick, A., Mitchell, G., & Roberts, S. (1994). *Community capacity building and asset mapping: Model development.* Edmonton, AB, Canada: Community Development Caritas.

Dewar, T. (1997). *A guide to evaluating asset-based community development: Lessons, challenges, and opportunities.* Chicago, IL: ACTA Publications.

Education Development Center. (2011). *Rebuilding for learning: Addressing barriers to learning and teaching, and re-engaging students.* New York, NY: Scholastic. Retrieved from http://www.smhp.psych.ucla.edu/pdfdocs/casestudy.pdf

Fagan, T. K., & Wise, P. S. (2000). *School psychology: Past, present, and future.* (2nd ed.) Bethesda, MD: National Association of School Psychologists.

Higgins, M. C., Weiner, J., & Young, L. (2012). Implementation teams: A new lever for organizational change. *Journal of Organizational Behavior, 33,* 366–388. doi:10.1002/job.1773

Kingsley, G., Coulton, C., Barndt, M., Sawicki, D., & Tatian, P. (1997). *Mapping your community: Using geographic information to strengthen community initiatives.* Washington, DC: U.S. Department of Housing and Urban Development.

Kretzmann, J., & McKnight, J. (1993). *Building communities from the inside out: A path toward finding and mobilizing a community's assets.* Chicago, IL: ACTA Publications.

Kretzmann, J., & McKnight, J. (1996). *A guide to mapping and mobilizing the economic capacities of local residents.* Chicago, IL: ACTA Publications.

Lim, C., & Adelman, H. S. (1997). Establishing school-based collaborative teams to coordinate resources: A case study. *Social Work in Education, 19,* 266–277. doi:10.1093/cs/19.4.266

Marx, E., & Wolley, S. F. (Eds.). (1998). *Health is academic: A guide to coordinated school health programs.* New York, NY: Teachers College Press.

McKnight, J., & Kretzmann, J. (1990). *Mapping community capacity.* Evanston, IL: Institute for Policy Research, Northwestern University.

Mizrahi, T., & Morrison, J. D. (1993). *Community organization and social administration: Advances, trends, and emerging principles.* Binghamton, NY: Haworth Press.

National Association of School Psychologists. (2010). *Model for comprehensive and integrated school psychological services.* Bethesda, MD: Author. Retrieved from http://www.nasponline.org/standards/2010standards/2_PracticeModel.pdf

Rosenblum, L., DiCecco, M. B., Taylor, L., & Adelman, H. S. (1995). Upgrading school support programs through collaboration: Resource coordinating teams. *Social Work in Education, 17,* 117–124. doi:10.1093/cs/17.2.117

Taylor, L., & Adelman, H. S. (2004). Advancing mental health in schools: Guiding frameworks and strategic approaches. In K. Robinson (Ed.), *Advances in school-based mental health.* (pp. 2-1–2-23). Kingston, NJ: Civic Research Institute.

Taylor, L., Nelson, P., & Adelman, H. S. (1999). Scaling-up reforms across a school district. *Reading & Writing Quarterly, 15,* 303–326.

U.S. Department of Education. (1996). *Putting the pieces together: Comprehensive school-linked strategies for children and families.* Washington, DC: Author.

APPENDIX A. ABOUT RESOURCE MAPPING AND MANAGEMENT

- *Why mapping resources are so important:* To function well, every system has to fully understand and manage its resources. Mapping is a first step toward enhancing essential understanding and, done properly, it is a major intervention in the process of moving forward with enhancing systemic effectiveness.

- *Why mapping both school and community resources are so important:* Schools and communities share (a) goals and problems with respect to children, youth, and families; (b) the need to develop cost-effective systems, programs, and services to meet the goals and address the problems; (c) accountability pressures related to improving outcomes; and (d) the opportunity to improve effectiveness by coordinating and eventually integrating resources to develop a full continuum of systemic interventions.

- *What are resources:* Among other resources are programs, services, real estate, equipment, money, social capital, leadership, and infrastructure mechanisms.

- *What we mean by mapping and who does it:* A representative group of informed stakeholder is asked to undertake the process of identifying what currently is available to achieve goals and address problems and what else is needed to achieve goals and address problems.

- *What this process leads to:* (a) Analyzing to clarify gaps and recommend priorities for filling gaps related to programs and services and deploying, redeploying, and enhancing resources; (b) identifying needs for making infrastructure and systemic improvements and changes; (c) clarifying opportunities for achieving important functions by forming and enhancing collaborative arrangements; and (d) creating social marketing.

- *How to do resource mapping:* First, do it in stages (start simple and build over time). Clarify people/agencies who carry out relevant roles/functions. Next, clarify specific programs, activities, services (including information on how many students/families can be accommodated). Then, identify the dollars and other related resources (e.g., facilities, equipment) that are being expended from various sources. Finally, collate the various policies that are relevant to the endeavor. At each stage establish a computer file and in the later stages create spreadsheets.

- Use benchmarks to guide progress related to resource mapping.

APPENDIX B. DEVELOPING AND CONNECTING MECHANISMS AT SCHOOL SITES, AMONG FAMILIES OF SCHOOLS, AND DISTRICT-WIDE AND COMMUNITY-WIDE

A multisite team can provide a mechanism to help ensure cohesive and equitable deployment of resources and also can enhance the pooling of resources to reduce costs. Such a mechanism can be particularly useful for integrating the efforts of high schools and their feeder middle and elementary schools. This clearly is important in addressing barriers with those families who have youngsters attending more than one level of schooling in the same cluster. It is neither cost-effective nor good intervention for each school to contact a family separately in instances where several children from a family are in need of special attention. With respect to linking with community resources, multischool teams are especially attractive to community agencies that often do not have the time or personnel to make independent arrangements with every school.

In general, a group of schools can benefit from a multisite resource mechanism designed to provide leadership, facilitate communication and connection, and ensure quality improvement across sites. For example, a multisite body, or what we call a Learning Supports Leadership Council, might consist of a high school and its feeder middle and elementary schools. It brings together one to two representatives from each school's Learning Supports Leadership Team (see Figure 13.B1).

The council meets about once a month to help (a) coordinate and integrate programs serving multiple schools, (b) identify and meet common needs with respect to guidelines and staff development, and (c) create linkages and collaborations among schools and with community agencies. In this last regard, it can play a special role in community outreach both to create formal working relationships and to ensure that all participating schools have access to such resources.

More generally, the council provides a useful mechanism for leadership, communication, maintenance, quality improvement, and ongoing development of a comprehensive continuum of programs and services. Natural starting points for councils are the sharing of needs assessments, resource maps, analyses, and recommendations for reform and restructuring. Specific areas of initial focus would be on local, high priority concerns, such as addressing violence and

Figure 13.B1. Connecting Mechanisms for Learning Supports Across All Levels

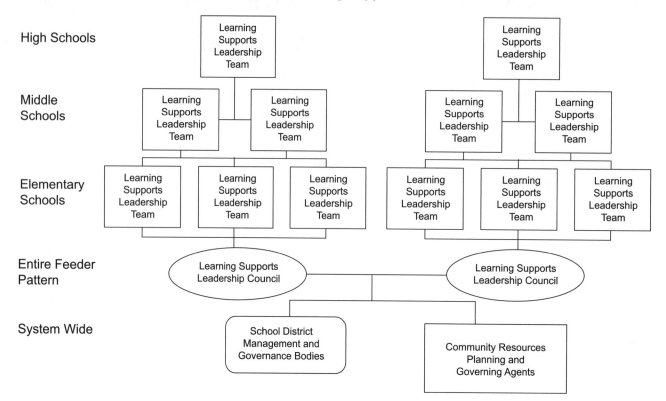

developing prevention programs and safe school and neighborhood plans.

Representatives from Learning Supports Leadership Councils would be invaluable members of planning groups (e.g., service planning area councils, local management boards). They bring information about specific schools, clusters of schools, and local neighborhoods and do so in ways that reflect the importance of school–community partnerships.

APPENDIX C. ESTABLISHING A COMPREHENSIVE LEARNING SUPPORTS SYSTEM

At all levels key stakeholders and their leadership must understand and commit to systemic changes for the proposed innovation. Commitment must be reflected in policy statements and creation of an infrastructure that ensures essential leadership, resources, motivation, and capability for developing an effective system of learning supports.

Developing such a system requires blending resources. Thus, the emphasis throughout is on collaboration—cooperation, coordination, and, where viable, integration—among school and community

stakeholders. Planning and accountability related to the following four phases of systemic change use data from evaluation of major antecedents, transactions, and outcomes.

First phase: Creating readiness and commitment

- Introduce basic ideas to relevant groups of stakeholders to build interest and consensus for the work and to garner feedback and support.
- Establish a policy framework and obtain leadership commitment. The leadership should make a commitment to adopt a comprehensive system for addressing barriers to learning and teaching as a primary and essential component of school improvement.
- Identify a leader (equivalent to the leader for the instructional component) to ensure policy commitments are carried out for establishing the new component.

Second phase: Start up and phase in—Building infrastructure and capacity

- Establish temporary mechanisms to facilitate initial implementation/systemic change (e.g., a steering group, an organization change facilitator) and develop the capacity of these mechanisms to guide and manage change and provide essential leadership during phase in.

- Formulate specific start-up and phase-in actions.
- Refine infrastructure so that the component is fully integrated with the instructional and management components. (a) Establish and train an administrative leader. (b) Ensure there is a resource-oriented mechanism (e.g., a Learning Supports Resource Team) and train those who staff it in how to perform major resource-oriented tasks (e.g., mapping, analysis, coordinating, planning, setting priorities for program development, enhancing intervention systems. (c) Help organize workgroups for each major arena of component activity and facilitate their initial mapping and analysis of resources and formulation of recommendations. (d) Develop ad hoc workgroups to enhance component visibility, communication, sharing, and problem solving.

- Establish a system for quality improvement and evaluation of impact and integrate it into school improvement planning, evaluation, and accountability.
- Attempt to fill program/service gaps and pursue economies of scale through outreach designed to establish formal collaborative linkages among families of schools (e.g., a feeder pattern) and among district-wide and community resources (e.g., through establishing a Learning Supports Resource Council).

Third phase: Sustaining, evolving, and enhancing outcomes

- Plan for maintenance and institutionalization.
- Develop strategies for maintaining momentum and progress.

Fourth phase: Replication to scale and generating creative renewal

14

Best Practices in School–Community Partnerships

John W. Eagle
Shannon E. Dowd-Eagle
Rhode Island College

OVERVIEW

It is nearly impossible in this current economic and educational climate to view effective schools as islands, independent and isolated environments in which students develop academically, socially, and behaviorally. As such, most districts and schools strive to develop meaningful relationships with members of the surrounding communities. Types of partnerships with community agencies, businesses, services, and programs are extremely varied and the ways to define school–community partnerships are equally diverse.

Part of the issue is attempting to define what the term *community* represents. In general, educators and researchers view the concept of community as something broader than the mere geographic proximity of organizations and available facilities. It incorporates all potential resources, including key stakeholders such as "youth, families, businesses, school sites, community-based organizations, civic groups, religious groups, health and human service agencies, parks, libraries, and other possibilities for recreation and enrichment" (Center for Mental Health in Schools, 2005, p. 9). Going beyond key stakeholders and resources, communities are also bound by a common set of values, cultures, and identity.

There are also several definitions of what a *partnership* between a school and community entails. One inclusive representation indicates that school–community partnerships "encompass various forms of temporary or permanent structured connections among school and community resources … [and] may be established to enhance programs by increasing availability and access and filling gaps" (Center for Mental Health in Schools, 2005, p. 9). School–community partnerships are most

beneficial when they are collaborative, empowering, proactive, and flexible.

Sheridan, Napolitano, and Swearer (2002) outlined several specific characteristics of school–community partnerships. They indicated that the interactions and relationships between the partners are collaborative, balanced, and cooperative/interdependent. There is a clear focus on maintaining a positive relationship with a commitment to cultural diversity and viewing differences in viewpoints as strengths, not hindrances. Finally, the actions between school and community groups are flexible, proactive, responsive, student focused, and emphasizing outcomes and goal attainment.

Background and Rationale for School–Community Partnerships

Schools are an inseparable part of a larger community, with members often sharing commonalities with regard to culture, history, and socioeconomic status. From an ecological perspective (Bronfenbrenner, 1979), the development and education of children is directly influenced by specific environmental contexts (i.e., family, school, peer, community, and societal), as well as indirectly via the reciprocal interactions and relationships between school, community, and family settings. Given the current educational climate, characterized by growing student needs and waning financial resources, the need for establishing strong school–community partnerships has never been greater.

These challenges affect youth from all walks of life and therefore are prevalent across urban, rural, and suburban communities. Although schools play an important role in meeting student academic, behavioral, social–emotional, and health needs, it is impractical to believe schools can meet all of these needs independently. The necessary resources are simply beyond the scope of what schools have available to them. Schools and communities must join forces and develop a comprehensive, integrated approach to the allocation of resources that supports the complex issues facing children, families, schools, and neighborhoods (Center for Mental Health in Schools, 2005). When these partnerships have been cultivated over time, benefits can include improved access to resources and services, a strengthening of social capital (Dryfoos, Quinn, & Barkin, 2005), and increased opportunities for learning to be reinforced across multiple settings.

The importance of developing school–community collaborations has been accentuated by recent federal education legislation and national practice standards from the National Association of School Psychologists (NASP). School–community partnership is a critical element in delivering effective services for the educational, social, and behavioral development of students, as well as the impactful roles schools play within communities.

Based upon federal legislation, such as the Individuals with Disabilities Education Improvement Act and the Elementary and Secondary Education Act (ESEA), schools have become increasingly accountable for providing appropriate services and creating positive educational outcomes. The outcome goals established by these acts of legislation cannot be achieved within a model that views schools as the sole provider of supports and services to students. The current constraints placed on schools by limited financial resources, personnel, and physical space necessitate that schools involve supports and resources of other systems (i.e., communities and families) to achieve these goals.

ESEA provides federal support to schools and districts for enhancing student academic and social development. Of the programs supported by ESEA, the ones most closely aligned to school–community partnerships fall within those supported under Title IV: 21st Century Schools. These programs include Safe and Drug-Free Schools and 21st Century Community Learning Centers. The current Blueprint for Reform reauthorization of ESEA sponsored by President Obama in 2010 identifies three programs related to school–community partnerships. The Successful, Safe, and Healthy Students program is designed to evaluate families' experiences and attitudes pertaining to school engagement, school safety, and school environment. The Promising Neighborhoods program provides comprehensive supports to students and families from

community organizations and resources. A priority of this program is to target high-poverty communities. The 21st Century Community Learning Centers program is continued through ESEA and supports the development of community learning centers that provide academic enrichment programs during hours that children are not in school.

The importance of fostering strong school–community linkages as part of school psychologists' professional practice is clearly endorsed in the NASP *Model for Comprehensive and Integrated School Psychological Services* (NASP, 2010) and outlines professional practices and organizational principles that guide the provision of psychological services by individual school psychologists and school systems to support (a) engaged learning and achievement, (b) high-quality instruction, (c) positive behavior, (d) diverse learners, and (e) safe school climates. Working independently, schools will not be able to achieve these desired outcomes. Collaboration with families, community members, and community agencies is an essential component to delivering comprehensive and integrated psychological services to children. This idea is expressed in the Preventive and Responsive Services domain of the NASP Practice Model (NASP, 2010), which indicates that school psychologists should have "knowledge of principles and research related to resilience and risk factors in learning and mental health, services in schools and communities to support multi-tiered prevention, and evidence-based strategies for effective crisis response" (p. 7).

The need to apply such knowledge arises when school psychologists face systemic challenges such as truancy, bullying, school violence, chronic mental health needs, or youth suicide. These complex issues can be mediated by preventive and responsive services delivered via a multitiered system that integrates school and community resources (NASP, 2010).

Types of School–Community Partnerships

The nature and purposes of school–community partnerships are important elements to consider. The degree to which schools and community partners collaborate falls along a continuum, not only in level of interaction with each other but also in physical location of service delivery, levels of communication (particularly related to confidential information), personnel delivering programs and services, and individuals supported via the collaboration (e.g., students, families).

School–community partnerships also exist between schools and a variety of different community agencies, organizations, or stakeholders. These community-based partners include, for example, businesses/corporations, universities and educational institutions, government and military organizations, healthcare organizations, faith-based organizations, volunteer and national service groups, senior citizens' organizations, and cultural and recreational institutions (Sanders, 2001). In practice, it is common that school–community partnerships include multiple types of community organizations.

Although there are several different forms of school–community partnerships, two general models have been developed: school-linked models and school-based models. Each model is distinct in the location that services are provided, either inside or outside the physical grounds of the school. Regardless of the model or form, partnerships between schools and community-based agencies are typically fluid and variable in format (Adger, 2001).

School-Linked Partnerships

A school-linked model is the most common form of partnership between schools and community agencies. This model represents a linkage of services between schools and community programs, organizations, and/or services. These often include human service organizations or family resource centers that are nearby but do not reside on a school campus (Sailor, 2002). School psychologist involvement with school-linked services include collaborative efforts between community mental health agencies (e.g., child guidance) and schools, health prevention and promotion programs (i.e., drug or pregnancy prevention collaborations), vocational training and business mentor programs in the community, and community-based after-school programs.

School-linked services have the benefit of not requiring a complete integration with the physical structure and resources of the school. However, services offered through school-linked programs may not be as physically or economically accessible for all students and families.

School-Based Partnerships

In contrast to school-linked services, school-based models incorporate services within the physical structure of the school, as the school itself becomes a full-service institution. This provision of comprehensive services offered within the school organization is often referred to as full-service or community schools.

Within a school-based model the school typically provides the physical space required for service delivery. However, the funding of programs is delegated among the service agencies involved. The intent of this model of school–community partnership is to provide the most efficient form of services "to all children within the context of a quality education" (Sailor, 2002, p. 15). A benefit of school-based models is that they provide a multitude of services to children and families that they may not otherwise be able to receive due to lack of transportation, difficulties navigating public health and social service agencies, time constraints, and in some situations health insurance concerns. However, potential barriers to school-based services include establishing consistent funding sources, physical space limitations, and the amount of time required to establish fully operational, comprehensive services on school grounds. Further, confidentiality issues related to the Health Insurance Portability and Accountability Act of 1996 also may produce a barrier related to information sharing among the child's "private" school-based provider and the school team.

Community schools are found at all levels of education (e.g., elementary, middle, secondary) and can consist of individual schools or district-wide initiatives, such as those in Cincinnati, Ohio; Providence, Rhode Island; and Dallas, Texas. Models of full-service schools have existed for many years. Examples of school-based services include the School Development Program at the Yale Child Study Center (Comer & Emmons, 2006) and the Children's Aid Society Community Schools partnership in New York City (Dryfoos et al., 2005).

Individuals Served by School–Community Partnerships

Regardless of whether school–community partnership programs are school based or school linked, these collaborations can support different populations within the community. A survey of more than 400 schools across the United States that were members of the National Network of Partnership Schools identified four major categories of services offered through school–community partnerships (Sanders, 2001): (a) student centered, (b) family centered, (c) school centered, and (d) community centered. Examples of student-centered partnerships included student tutoring, mentoring, and job shadowing. Family-centered collaborations consisted of family workshops, GED/adult education programs, and family counseling. School-centered services included the donation of equipment, beautification projects, staff development, and classroom assistance. Those partnerships with a community focus established outreach programs, artwork and science exhibits, and community revitalization.

Benefits of School–Community Partnerships

Effective school–community partnerships have provided substantial benefits to students, families, schools, and the local community (Coalition for Community Schools, 2003; Dryfoos et al., 2005). However, outcome studies are difficult to interpret since few school–community partnerships are either similar in structure or in outcome evaluation. Poorly defined models of partnerships, lack of clearly defined outcome goals, and inadequate research designs have made it difficult for researchers to empirically evaluate the effects of these partnerships.

Specific benefits for students include gains in academic achievement (i.e., higher grades, higher standardized test scores) (Coalition for Community Schools, 2009) and better access to mental health and health services (Colon, 2005). Families experience greater parental involvement with schools and improved family functioning (Blank, 2004). In a comprehensive review of school–community partnerships, Henderson and Mapp (2002) found that schools partnering with communities witnessed an increase in student attendance, decreased numbers of suspensions, increased teacher satisfaction, as well as reductions in the rates of substance abuse, teen pregnancy, and disruptive behavior. Additionally, schools engaging in community partnerships were found to have upgraded facilities, new resources, and new funding for new programs and family supports. Communities benefited through increased neighborhood safety and decreased community violence, and families within the community economically supported local businesses.

BASIC CONSIDERATIONS

School psychologists are in an ideal position to promote partnerships between school personnel and community organizations. They have a unique perspective that allows for knowledge of existing school resources, an awareness of the strengths and needs of students and their families, and an ability to identify potential community assets. Moreover, school psychologists' repertoire include training in program development, service coordination, collaboration, problem solving, and evaluation. Despite the multifaceted expertise of school psychologists, fostering effective relationships between school professionals and community leaders can be a complicated process that requires the consideration of several factors.

Awareness of Barriers

To be effective brokers of partnerships, it is critical that school psychologists become familiar with common barriers that may arise when developing school–community linkages. Entering the partnership with an awareness of potential pitfalls may help circumvent unnecessary challenges and facilitate successful partnering. Sanders (2001) identified seven common obstacles to school–community partnerships: participation, time, community partners, leadership, funding, communication, and focus.

Participation and Time Commitment

Time is a highly valued commodity that is often in short supply. Therefore, it is no surprise that insufficient time and difficulty securing participation from school staff and community members are two of the most frequently cited barriers to developing school–community partnerships. Being mindful of these challenges and respecting the time investment necessary for successful collaboration are critical. One way school psychologists may prevent overtaxing personnel is by reaching out to a wider range of volunteers to coordinate services. For example, soliciting volunteers from parent organizations such as the PTA/PTO may identify caregivers who are willing to share their expertise and provide input regarding the needs of other interested caregivers (Sheridan et al., 2002). In addition, providing compensation in the form of class coverage, transportation, and child-care services may go a long way in freeing up time for school staff or community members. Finally, organizing small committees to minimize the number of meetings requiring all parties can reduce time involvement while increasing efficiency.

Community Partners

The identification of community partners may be another challenge. In some resource-poor neighborhoods, there may be fewer available businesses, and therefore the competition to partner with those agencies is more prevalent. Expanding partnership options beyond local businesses is one potential solution. To achieve this goal, school psychologists may consider attending community events to identify fellow collaborators such as universities, healthcare organizations, government or military agencies, faith organizations, and senior citizen programs. Thinking broadly about connections within the community will maximize available resources and enhance partnership benefits.

Leadership

Skillful leadership plays a significant role in the development and preservation of school–community partnerships. The success of partnership activities depends heavily on the identification of an individual or group of individuals who can coordinate services and facilitate the relationship-building process (Sanders, 2001). Although school psychologists are ideal candidates to adopt a leadership role, administrative support for school–community partnerships is essential for success. By forming a trusting relationship with the principal, school psychologists will be in a position to launch important school supports and guide service delivery. Further, school psychologists can generate enthusiasm among the teaching staff by highlighting how partnership programs will allow for diverse learning opportunities for students. Partnerships characterized by consistent leadership and high levels of staff and administrative commitment are the most likely to meet with success (Sheridan et al., 2002).

Funding

An insufficient operating budget is another potential obstacle to developing school–community partnerships. Depending upon the individual needs of the school and community partner, funding is often necessary to provide materials, equipment, and professional development/training. A comprehensive management plan outlining specific activities and costs associated with those activities may increase the awareness of potential funding needs. In addition, the adoption of some creative problem-solving strategies may be necessary to address budgetary constraints, such as holding fundraisers, submitting grant applications, soliciting assistance from the PTA/PTO, and reallocating monies offered through Title I.

Communication

Effective bidirectional communication serves as the foundation for positive partnerships. Exchanges between partners can increase knowledge regarding each other's strengths and areas of expertise and serve to establish mutually beneficial objectives. Communication difficulties may arise due to linguistic differences or when there is intermittent or infrequent contact. To improve the interactions among school and community partners, school psychologists may employ reminder phone calls, newsletters, and interpreters.

Focus

The central purpose of school–community connections is the promotion of students' social, emotional, intellectual, and physical development. At each stage of program planning, an emphasis should be placed on maximizing the results for children. A lack of focus or temporary departure from preestablished goals is occasionally cited as a barrier to school–community partnerships (Sanders, 2001). Incorporating partnership objectives into school action plans can redirect attention to the outcomes for children. Moreover, Sheridan et al. (2002) outlined several questions that school personnel and community members may use to guide discussions and decision making:

> What do we want for the children in our school and their families? What do we know about their education and well-being now? What skills or resources do they need to successfully meet the goals we have for them? How will we know if we have made an impact? (p. 325)

Comprehensive Services

The integration of services can have a powerful effect on addressing risk factors facing students and families. To fully realize the benefits and extend the learning opportunities afforded to children, a comprehensive and multifaceted approach to service delivery is recommended. Comprehensive services have been conceptualized on a continuum ranging from (a) preventive services designed to enhance healthy development to (b) early intervention that addresses problems after initial onset to (c) intensive intervention supports for critical and chronic conditions (Taylor & Adelman, 2003).

This conceptualization of comprehensive school–community services is consistent with best practices within a multitiered model and offers numerous benefits. First, it adopts an ecological perspective that attends to the reciprocal interactions both within and between systems. To fully comprehend the complexity of factors influencing today's children and families, attention must be paid to all contexts within which the individual operates. Further, an ecological orientation allows for sensitivity to culture and ensures that vital intervention components reflect the values and belief systems of the targeted population and community. Second, offering a continuum of services increases the likelihood that the appropriate type and dose of intervention is administered. In keeping with the standard of intervening within the least restrictive environment, a range of services that provides support at various stages of risk ensures that treatment is appropriate for and responsive to the individual needs of children and families (Taylor & Adelman, 2003).

BEST PRACTICES IN SCHOOL–COMMUNITY PARTNERSHIPS

There are several aspects to consider when developing a best practices approach to school–community partnerships. These critical features include identifying specific objectives for school–community partnerships, developing relational and multicultural competencies required for effective partnerships within the community, establishing school–community partnerships within a problem-solving framework, understanding the process for evaluating the effectiveness of programs developed through this form of collaboration, and providing a continuum of school–community supports across a multitiered system of service delivery.

Objectives of School–Community Partnerships

School psychologists may look to partnerships with community agencies, organizations, programs, and stakeholders for a variety of reasons. Regardless of whether schools are located in wealthy or low-income districts, urban or rural districts, or high-achieving or low-achieving districts, school–community partnerships are valuable in providing supports for student development in the areas of (a) academic achievement, (b) behavioral and social development, (c) emotional and mental health development, (d) health promotion, and (e) transition planning and vocational training.

In practice, many school–community partnerships address multiple needs of students and families. For example, some drug prevention or substance abuse programs may incorporate elements of health or mental health support (e.g., counseling, remaining drug free, finding alternatives to drugs), academic support (e.g., tutoring, school completion), and vocational training (e.g., teaching functional job skills; Sheridan et al., 2002). Additionally, transition planning programs may include multiple services to address areas that magnify challenging transitions, such as learning disabilities, behavioral and emotional problems, and limited job skills.

Academic Achievement

Community organizations provide a wide range of opportunities to support the academic development of students (Epstein, 2011). After-school programs commonly provide additional guidance and time for completion of homework. Additionally, some programs may offer additional practice with adult guidance in specific academic areas that have been shown to enhance academic outcomes (Clark, 2002). Boys and Girls Clubs currently have several programs geared to academic success, such as Diplomas 2 Degrees (college readiness), BE GREAT: Graduate (at risk for dropping out), and Project Learn (academic enrichment and school engagement). Mentorship programs, supported by employees of local businesses, are also avenues for students to gain new perspectives of the necessary skill sets and motivation required for gainful employment. Further, academic programs may also target adults in parent-training workshops or adult education training programs, which can be facilitated by community-based organizations.

Behavioral and Social Development

School–community partnerships provide opportunities to support the social and emotional development of children and adolescents (Comer & Emmons, 2006). Partnerships between schools and after-school programs, such as Boys and Girls Clubs, YMCA/YWCA, and 21st Century Community Learning Centers provide seamless transitions from school to after-school care. Many of these organizations offer children and adolescents opportunities for further development in social skills, leadership skills, and character development. For example, YMCA/YWCA centers offer programs that target leadership, youth participation in government, and service learning. Big Brothers Big Sisters programs offer unique one-to-one mentorship for students. This mentorship can occur within the community, or in some cases at school through school-based mentoring available through agencies in certain locations, and have provided beneficial social and behavioral outcomes (Grossman & Tierney, 1998). A study of outcomes for Boys and Girls Clubs reported relatively positive results related to solving peer and school problems, being courteous to adults, and behaving ethically (St. Pierre, Mark, Kaltreider, & Campbell, 2001). Schools implementing a school-wide positive behavioral supports framework often partner with local community businesses. School psychologists can work with local restaurants, activity centers, museums/zoos, bike shops, and convenience stores to provide donations to schools in the form of incentives/acknowledgements given to students who follow behavioral expectations at school.

Emotional and Mental Health Development

Partnerships with community agencies are often essential in providing effective mental health services and counseling to students and families (Power, DuPaul, Shapiro, & Kazak, 2003). Although schools are a natural place to address mental health concerns, especially in urban and rural areas where families may have difficulty seeking out community services due to limited opportunities or a lack of resources, the reality is that schools are often unable to meet those needs independently. The individuals in schools who often work to meet these mental health needs (i.e., school psychologists, counselors, and school social workers) frequently have large caseloads divided between multiple schools. Therefore, to adequately meet these needs, the formation of school–community partnerships becomes critical. One example of such a partnership includes placing therapists from a local mental health agency within targeted schools to provide additional support in meeting the social and emotional needs of individual students. School psychologists' roles within the partnership may include enhancing parents' and teachers' awareness of available resources and/or identifying students and families who may benefit from services.

Health Promotion

School psychologists often encounter issues that have an impact on students related to health-related issues, such as allergies, obesity, sexual activity, substance abuse, and violence. The negative outcomes associated with many of these health-related concerns significantly influence the well-being of today's youth and highlight the need for establishing a community-based effort to support healthy development. Partnerships between local health clinics and schools can provide preventive efforts to promote healthy lifestyle choices (Colon, 2005). In such partnerships, interdisciplinary services can be provided in both the school setting (e.g., classroom instruction, small-group discussions) as well as the local clinic (e.g., group education, medical services). Many after-school programs (i.e., Boys and Girls Clubs, YMCA/YWCA) also offer opportunities for additional physical exercise outside of school. Local police and fire departments can also provide in-school educational training regarding safety, alcohol and drug abuse resistance, and violence prevention.

Transition Planning and Vocational Training

Effective school–community partnerships are important for transition planning and the coordination of services for major life changes, such as the transition to elementary school and the transition to adulthood (Center for Mental Health in Schools, 2005). Early childhood programs, such as Head Start, provide support for a child to enter the educational system ready to learn. School psychologists assist in transition-to-adulthood programs and coordinate services for youth who are in special education, foster care, and the juvenile justice system as these youth advance from youth service programs to more independent lifestyles or adult programs. A reciprocal relationship between community agencies supporting transitions and school systems assists in providing a smooth transition. Vocational training objectives target job skills and career needs of students by delivering on-the-job training or career planning services either within the school building or in the community. Local businesses, via coordination with school districts, can provide opportunities for students to engage in prevocational training and vocational experiences.

Relational Variables

Cultivating strong school–community relationships is a time-intensive process that cannot be forged overnight. The relationship must be nurtured, requiring time, patience, and a long-term commitment from all parties. A critical aspect for school psychologists in developing these successful partnerships is the adoption of an empowering communication style that promotes respect among key stakeholders. Swick (2003) outlined eight critical elements of communication that enhance relationship building and enrich interactions among partners:

- *Trust*: Necessary for the relationship to flourish. As school personnel and community members learn that they can depend upon one another, a trusting bond will be formed.
- *Role flexibility:* Refers to each partner's willingness to mutually support and nurture one another through joint decision-making activities.
- *Help exchange:* Centers on providing authentic assistance within the relationship. This assistance must extend past lip service and incorporate meaningful actions.
- *Responsive listening:* Based on the entirety of the interaction, emphasizes the importance of both verbal and nonverbal exchanges.
- *Individuation:* Defined as using the interactions with others (e.g., community agency representatives) as a means to develop one's own identity.
- *Group functioning skills:* Characterized by give-and-take communication. School and community leaders often enter the partnership with different perspectives and

objectives. Therefore, they must join forces to establish a mutually beneficial agenda, come together around common goals, and work toward a shared vision.

- *Nurturance:* Refers to treating one another with warmth and recognizing the unique expertise that each individual brings to the table. A nurturing communication style is devoid of judgment and negative stereotyping between school and community partners.

- *Problem solving:* Differing opinions and attitudes are to be expected when individuals with diverse viewpoints come together. Further, openly sharing those conflicting beliefs in a respectful manner can actually work to enrich the partnership. Therefore, it is essential that school personnel and community leaders discuss common approaches to the differing perspectives and challenges facing the partnership.

Multicultural Competencies

School psychologists benefit from a well-developed sensitive and responsive communication style that is particularly relevant when forming connections with students, families, and community members from culturally and linguistically diverse backgrounds. Culturally competent practice is not a one-size-fits-all approach (Guerrero & Leung, 2008), but rather it is a process that evolves over time as individuals and systems increase awareness, knowledge, and skill along a continuum of cultural competence. As part of this developmental process, school psychologists may use a conceptual framework to guide the values, attitudes, and behaviors needed to effectively deliver services cross-culturally. Within this framework, community engagement represents an important principle. Culturally competent practitioners must work jointly with natural and informal community supports to ensure that community members are equal partners in decision making and that local communities benefit from the partnership.

Wright Carroll (2008) outlined four practice elements, or multicultural flash points, that school psychologists can apply to support transformational change in schools. These flash points represent four general and interdependent skills: awareness, acknowledgment and knowledge, advocacy, and action. Awareness is a responsibility; that is, individuals must be cognizant of their own values and belief systems, the cultural identifiers of others, as well as systemic cultural bias. Similarly, awareness refers to an understanding that

decisions made today have implications for the future. Awareness promotes the acknowledgment and knowledge stage, whereby school psychologists engage in a cognitive process of coming to both realize and accept multiculturalism within the school climate. Advocacy is the process of using one's awareness, knowledge, and skill to actively develop a plan to promote change. Advocacy then leads to action, the act of behaving in a proactive manner to promote multiculturalism.

Implementing a Partnership-Based, Problem-Solving Approach

One of the key aspects of developing school–community partnerships is establishing an understanding of the potential key stakeholders within collaborating systems. There are several potential invested parties that can be identified within the school and community systems (Power et al., 2003). Key stakeholders in schools may include administrators, teachers, counselors, parents, and students. Constituents in the community may include primary care providers, mental health providers, faith-based leaders, youth development centers (e.g., 4-H, Boys and Girls Clubs), and staff in recreational centers. Additionally, prevention programs may also need to identify members of other institutions, such as hospitals, which might have physicians, nurses, physical and occupational therapists, speech–language therapists, social workers, patients, and families as key stakeholders.

The steps for following a partnership-based, problem-solving process have been outlined by Nelson, Amio, Prilleltensky, and Nickels (2000): (a) creating partnerships, (b) clarifying values and vision and deriving working principles, (c) identifying and merging the strengths of different partners and approaches, (d) defining the problem collaboratively, (e) developing the program collaboratively, and (f) researching and evaluating the program collaboratively. These steps are further described in Table 14.1 along with potential challenges to school psychologists.

Process for Evaluating School–Community Partnerships

An essential consideration in the development of school–community partnerships is to determine if the outcomes, objectives, and goals are being obtained. Marriott and Goyder (2009) provide a detailed process for monitoring and evaluating educational partnerships. Within their framework they identify six major stages: prepartnership, partnership building, partnership

Table 14.1. Steps in the Implementation of Partnerships for Program Implementation: Tasks, Processes, and Challenges

Roles of School Psychologists	Tasks and Processes	Challenges for School Psychology
Create partnerships	• Include community members and service providers from the community where the intervention is to take place • Create a welcoming and friendly climate for partners	• Abandon the role of expert and share power with partners • Reduce barriers to participation for partners • Learn to value and build relationships
Clarify values and vision and derive working principles	• Collaboratively clarify values and vision to guide the program • Derive working principles (ground rules) for how the group and program should work	• Engage in self-reflective analysis of personal values • Be open to being challenged by partners • Be aware of value incongruence and strive to reduce it
Identify and merge the strengths of different partners and approaches	• Identify and build on strengths of different partners • Merge deductive/nomothetic and inductive/experiential approaches to planning and implementation	• Work to overcome self-doubt and mistrust of community members • Value the experiential knowledge of community partners • Find common ground and respect differences to bridge the worlds of community members and professionals
Define the problem collaboratively	• Collaboratively define and analyze the problem in terms of risk and protective factors at multiple ecological levels • Focus on the strengths of the community	• Reconcile differing views and build consensus regarding a prevention program model
Develop the program collaboratively	• Collaboratively decide on what type of program to implement • Ensure that necessary hardware and software are available for program implementation	• Educate and train partners in research and evaluation • Be open to learning about new perspectives and ways of working from partners
Research and evaluate collaboratively	• Use both deductive (quantitative) and inductive (qualitative) approaches in program evaluation • Research and evaluate each of the steps	• Educate and train partners in research and evaluation • Learn to see community members as valuable partners in research and evaluation • Clarify roles of partners

Note. From "Best Practices in School–Community Partnerships," (pp. 321–336), by S. M. Sheridan, S. A. Napolitano, and S. M. Swearer, 2002, in A. Thomas and J. Grimes (Eds.), *Best Practices in School Psychology IV*, Bethesda, MD: National Association of School Psychologists. Copyright 2002 by the National Association of School Psychologists. Adapted with permission.

inception, partnership implementation, partnership assessment, and partnership transition.

Prepartnership

This is the earliest stage and occurs before any partnership has been initiated. At this stage a school psychologist may be considering developing a partnership with other key stakeholders, and would like to explore how monitoring and evaluation fit within the process. Although no formal partnership exists, the school psychologist, serving as a partnership facilitator, should establish a clear understanding of the value and importance that monitoring and evaluation processes have within the developing partnership. The distinction

between monitoring and evaluation also needs to be conveyed to stakeholders. *Monitoring* is an ongoing process that uses systematic data collection related to specific indicators to determine progress and achievement toward expected results. Monitoring provides essential inputs for evaluation and is considered to be part of the evaluation process. *Evaluation* is a systematic objective assessment of the attainment of specified outcomes. This includes timely assessments of efficiency, effectiveness, impact, and sustainability (Marriott & Goyder, 2009).

Building from the research in strategic planning, school psychologists can also assist in the development of a community and school needs assessment related to the partnership. An effective tool used in planning is a SWOT analysis. This includes listing the strengths, weaknesses, opportunities, and threats related to the goals and processes of the partnership. Each category indicates variables that are helpful or harmful to the objectives and originate internally or externally of the partnership. Strengths are viewed as helpful to obtaining outcomes and as internal to the partnership, weaknesses are harmful and internal, opportunities are helpful and external, and threats are considered to be harmful and external in origin. A SWOT analysis allows the partnership to explore possibilities, plan for potential challenges, and strategize the most appropriate course of action.

Partnership Building

During the building of the partnership, monitoring and evaluation principles are agreed upon by all key stakeholders. The school psychologist now focuses on helping the partners align monitoring and evaluation procedures with the anticipated outcomes. Each stakeholder should now have a clear understanding of his or her responsibilities regarding monitoring and evaluating the partnership, and the school psychologist assists in establishing buy-in. All participants then develop specified agreements related to monitoring and evaluation.

Partnership Inception

At this point the monitoring and evaluation system is created, and all parties agree to the outcomes that will be assessed. The school psychologist works with key members to ensure that the group develops outcomes that are SMART: specific; measureable; achievable and attainable; relevant and realistic; and time bound, timely, trackable, and targeted. Once these are established, baseline data are collected on the indicators. Examples of the baseline data collected by the school psychologist include interviews, review of official records, classroom observations, focus groups, questionnaires, self-assessment reports, and activity logs.

Partnership Implementation

When the inputs, activities, and outputs have been agreed upon, the actual practice of monitoring implementation and outcomes can begin. The health of the partnership, and the relationships within, are also assessed. To be effective, monitoring data need to have stakeholder ownership, be systematically managed, maintain consistency, and be credible (Marriott & Goyder, 2009). In this stage the role of the school psychologist is not only to participate in the development of monitoring procedures and management, but to also analyze the data collected.

Partnership Assessment

After engaging in the practice of monitoring, the partnership conducts formative and summative evaluation procedures. Formative assessments such as appraisals or midterm evaluations are used at specified intervals to determine how well the partnership is working and to assess outcomes up to that point. A summative evaluation reviews the progress of the collaboration related to end outcomes and is considered an end-of-term evaluation. School psychologists again collect and analyze evaluation data to establish if changes need to be made within the implementation of the partnership. There are three distinct forms of evaluation commonly used: internal evaluation (with a member of the partnership), joint evaluation (the partnership working together), and external evaluation (by someone outside the partnership). School psychologists may participate in internal and joint evaluations, and may assist in the selection of an external evaluator.

Partnership Transition

This final stage of monitoring and evaluation is related more to sustaining practices than to implementing practices. The partnership transitions from a temporary arrangement and becomes institutionalized and more permanent. Monitoring and evaluation procedures are reviewed and adapted to fit the ecology of the new institution.

Relation to a Multitiered Model

A multitiered model (e.g., universal, targeted, intensive) of service delivery provides a framework for the provision of school psychological services to all children. This multitiered model should not be viewed as existing within the structure of the school alone. It also extends to the delivery of services based upon collaborative school, community, and family partnerships. In fact, the practice domains of the NASP Practice Model (NASP, 2010) will not be effectively achieved if services exist solely within a school-centric framework. The supports available through community resources and agencies are essential for enhancing the academic and socioemotional development of all children.

The delivery of services to children through school–community partnerships parallels the multitiered model. The focus is not only on developing school–community partnerships for children with disabilities but on providing services through such collaborations for *all* students. Each level of support (e.g., universal, targeted, intensive) provides opportunities for schools to partner with community agencies or resources. And, each level of support offers opportunities for school psychologists to become involved in developing these collaborative services.

School–Community Partnerships Within a Multitiered System of Support

There are a variety of ways that schools and districts collaborate with community agencies, organizations, and businesses. Schools providing supports to students and families across a multitiered system of support often have a continuum of ways to partner with communities, based on the level of support needed. A nonexhaustive list of potential school–community collaborations across a multitiered system of support is listed in Table 14.2.

Universal Level of Support Partnerships
Examples of school–community linked services offered at the universal level of support include school-wide prevention and health promotion programs. One example is the 21st Century Community Learning Centers program. This program, funded by the U.S. Department of Education, is intended to develop community learning centers that provide additional support and learning opportunities to children and families (Anderson-Butcher, 2004). These community

supports are targeted for communities in which the students are underperforming in core academic subjects, such as reading and math. Community partners with 21st Century Community Learning Centers may include a variety of agencies, such as youth development organizations, faith-based organizations, settlement houses, businesses, and universities. The three major supports offered through 21st Century Community Learning Centers programs include academic tutoring and enrichment activities, youth development activities, and family literacy programs. Other services include violence and drug prevention, recreation, counseling, and character education programs. These supports are available to all children in the school during nonschool hours, such as afternoons and weekends.

An example of this type of community partnership is the Providence After School Alliance, a citywide, after-school partnership between the city of Providence, RI, Providence Public School System, and local communities (Kotloff & Korom-Djacovic, 2010). The Providence After School Alliance has developed citywide, after-school initiatives for both middle and high school students. These programs consist of expanded learning systems for youth arranged as campuses of after-school, in-school, and summer activities at schools and community locations throughout Providence. The program is available to all students on a first-come first-served basis and is free of charge to families. Since its creation, Providence After School Alliance estimates that the

Table 14.2. Examples of School–Community Partnerships Within a Multitiered System of Support Framework

System	School Resources	Community Resources
Universal/primary prevention	• General health education • Drug/alcohol education • Transition support • Parent involvement	• After-school programs • Safety programs (police and fire departments) • Local healthcare/dentists • Business donations for incentives, posters, announcements • Sports and recreation activities
Targeted/early intervention	• Pregnancy prevention • Violence prevention • Dropout prevention • Learning/behavior accommodations • Work programs	• Adult mentoring programs (Big Brothers Big Sisters) • Academic tutoring • Parent skills training (Second Step) • After-school classes (yoga, karate) • Career services
Intensive/care of chronic/ severe problems	• Special education for learning disabilities, emotional disturbance, and other health impairments	• Wraparound and family services • Summer behavioral camps • Individualized transitional services • Residential and day treatment programs

Note. From "Moving Prevention From the Fringes Into the Fabric of School Improvement," by H. S. Adelman and L. Taylor, (2000), *Journal of Educational and Psychological Consultation, 11,* pp. 7–36. Copyright 2000 by Taylor & Francis. Adapted with permission.

program has served 40% of middle school students in the city. On-site activities are linked to school coursework and include homework assistance, arts and music, and physical exercise options. Off-site activities also follow the three categories of programming: skills, arts, or sports. Examples of these include, but are not limited to, environmental activities (i.e., scientific skill development), local repertory theater, gymnastic studios, and aikido classes. Evaluative research has indicated that the after-school programs developed by the Providence After School Alliance are related to beneficial school engagement and social skills outcomes for students, particularly for those who participated in the program for more than 32 days per year (Kotloff & Korom-Djacovic, 2010).

At the universal level, school psychologists can identify and implement empirically supported academic, behavioral, and health promotion programs provided via partnerships with community agencies. Additionally, they can utilize their knowledge in grant writing to seek external funding to lead or assist districts and schools in applying for program support.

Targeted Level of Support Partnerships

Many targeted-level partnerships include school-linked services and referrals to community agencies for students considered at risk for academic, behavioral, or social–emotional difficulties. These can include either specific after-school classes or more extensive supports through group counseling programs for social skills or social–emotional development. Schools may also connect with community resources to provide additional supports for students through academic tutoring programs, adult mentorship opportunities, and specialized summer camps. One key to providing appropriate community supports for early intervention is the need to collect and maintain progress monitoring data to evaluate the effect of programs on student outcomes or to determine if more comprehensive supports are needed.

School psychologists can assist partnership programs at the targeted support level by identifying students appropriate for services, identifying evidence-based services, and helping to coordinate and implement services. At this level of support the school psychologist may play a major role in the referral process to an outside agency outside of the school or potentially coordinate supports available within the school.

Intensive Level of Support Partnerships

School–community partnership services offered at the intensive level provide systemic support for individual students whose needs require a greater degree of support. One such integrated program of support is wraparound services, which is a system of care that includes the collaboration of the family, school, and community agencies in establishing comprehensive and intensive treatment plans for the student and family (Eber, Sugai, Smith, & Scott, 2002). Wraparound services are a planning process in which key stakeholders, natural supports, and professionals operate in a team to enhance the availability and effectiveness of supports delivered to individuals and families (Eber et al., 2002). Members involved in implementing wraparound services often include case managers, school psychologists, social workers, teachers, school administrators, parents, community-based mental health professionals, and health professionals (i.e., nurse, physician). Wraparound services are often used at the most intensive level (i.e., individual) of support within school-wide positive behavioral support programs (Turnbull et al., 2002).

There are several ways that school psychologists can become involved in intensive support programs. Many school psychologists trained in a behavioral consultation model have extensive experience in delivering services through a problem-solving process. This training and experience can enable school psychologists to operate as leaders, ensuring that critical aspects of target behavior identification, functional behavioral assessment, intervention implementation, and intervention evaluation are followed. School psychologists can also provide individual therapeutic services to students. Further, school psychologists are well versed in operating within multidisciplinary teams and coordinating the integration of services across multiple systems.

SUMMARY

Communities are constantly changing, as are ways in which schools join together with community agencies, organizations, and key stakeholders. Educational legislation may determine how schools and communities operate together, whether it be providing evidence-based supports dependent upon student and family need, emphasizing early intervention and transition efforts, or focusing on college and business preparedness for the next generation of workers. However, there has been one constant. In order to provide the best educational and developmental opportunities for their student body, schools need the supports provided and available to them from their surrounding communities.

Collaborative partnerships between the multiple systems within which a student resides are essential in providing a congruent environment for a child's educational, social, and emotional development. Two major systems critical in a child's development are the school and the community. The more consistent the values, messages, expectations, and acknowledgments are between these two systems, the greater the possibility of enhancing and supporting child development. A parallel benefit of school–community partnerships is the ability to provide effective and comprehensive supports to the families of students.

There are two primary models for establishing school–community supports: school linked and school based. School-linked services provide families with referrals to community resources. However, school-based services offer comprehensive services (e.g., full service or community schools) to families that are based within the school's physical environment. School-linked services are the most common form of school–community partnerships.

Prevention and intervention programs developed through school–community partnerships typically focus on the areas of academic achievement, social and behavioral development, health promotion, transition planning, and vocational training. Overall, these collaborative efforts have demonstrated positive outcomes for students, families, schools, and communities. Benefits include higher academic achievement, greater family involvement, reduced rates of substance abuse and teen pregnancy, and decreased violence within the community.

REFERENCES

Adelman, H. S., & Taylor, L. (2000). Moving prevention from the fringes into the fabric of school improvement. *Journal of Educational and Psychological Consultation, 11*, 7–36.

Adger, C. T. (2001). School-community–based organization partnerships for language minority students' school success. *Journal of Education for Students Placed at Risk, 6*, 7–25.

Anderson-Butcher, D. (2004). Transforming schools into 21st Century Community Learning Centers. *Children & Schools, 26*, 248–252.

Blank, M. (2004). How community schools make a difference. *Schools as Learning Communities, 61*, 62–65.

Blank, M., Melaville, A., & Shah, B. (2003). *Making the difference: Research and practice in community schools*. Washington, DC: Coalition for Community Schools, Institute for Educational Leadership.

Bronfenbrenner, U. (1979). *The ecology of human development*. Cambridge, MA: Harvard University Press.

Center for Mental Health in Schools. (2005). *School-community partnerships: A guide*. (Rev.). Los Angeles, CA: Author. Retrieved from http://smhp.psych.ucla.edu/pdfdocs/guides/schoolcomm.pdf

Clark, R. (2002). Ten hypotheses about what predicts student achievement for African American students and all other students: What the research shows. In W. R. Allen, M. B. Spencer, & C. O'Conner (Eds.), *African American education: Race, community, inequality, and achievement: A tribute to Edgar G. Epps*. New York, NY: Elsevier Science.

Coalition for Community Schools. (2003). *Making the difference: Research and practice in community schools*. Washington, DC: Institute for Educational Leadership.

Coalition for Community Schools. (2009). *Community schools research brief 2009*. Washington, DC: Institute for Educational Leadership.

Colon, B. (2005). School-based services. In J. Dryfoos, J. Quinn, & C. Barkin (Eds.), *Community schools in action: Lessons from a decade of practice*. New York, NY: Oxford University Press.

Comer, J. P., & Emmons, C. L. (2006). The research program of the Yale Child Study Center School Development Program. *The Journal of Negro Education, 75*, 353–372.

Dryfoos, J. G., Quinn, J., & Barkin, C. (Eds.). (2005). *Community schools in action: Lessons learned from a decade of practice*. New York, NY: Oxford University Press.

Eber, L., Sugai, G., Smith, C. R., & Scott, T. M. (2002). Wraparound and positive behavioral interventions and supports in the schools. *Journal of Emotional and Behavioral Disorders, 10*, 171–180.

Epstein, J. (2011). *School, family, and community partnerships: Preparing educators and improving schools*. Boulder, CO: Westview Press.

Grossman, J. B., & Tierney, J. P. (1998). Does mentoring work? An impact of the Big Brothers Big Sisters program. *Evaluation Review, 22*, 403–426.

Guerrero, C., & Leung, B. (2008). Communicating effectively with culturally and linguistically diverse families. *Communiqué, 36*(8), 19.

Henderson, A. T., & Mapp, K. L. (2002). *A new wave of evidence: The impact of school, family, and community connections on student achievement*. Austin, TX: National Center of Family and Community Connections With Schools, Southwest Educational Development Laboratory.

Kotloff, L. J., & Korom-Djakovic, D. (2010). *AfterZones: Creating a citywide system to support and sustain high-quality after-school programs*. Philadelphia, PA: Public/Private Ventures.

Marriott, N., & Goyder, H. (2009). *Manual for monitoring and evaluating education partnerships*. Paris, France: International Institute for Educational Planning.

National Association of School Psychologists. (2010). *Model for comprehensive and integrated school psychological services*. Bethesda, MD: Author. Retrieved from http//www.nasponline.org/standards/2010standards/2_PracticeModel.pdf

Nelson, G., Amio, J. L., Prilleltensky, I., & Nickels, P. (2000). Partnerships for implementing school and community programs. *Journal of Educational and Psychological Consultation, 11*, 121–145.

Power, T. J., DuPaul, G. J., Shapiro, E. S., & Kazak, A. E. (2003). *Promoting children's health: Integrating school, family, and community*. New York, NY: Guilford Press.

Sailor, W. (2002). Devolution, school/community/family partnerships, and inclusive education. In W. Sailor (Ed.), *Whole-school success and inclusive education* (pp. 7–25). New York, NY: Teachers College Press.

Sanders, M. G. (2001). The role of "community" in comprehensive school, family, and community partnership programs. *The Elementary School Journal, 102*, 19–34.

Sheridan, S. M., Napolitano, S. A., & Swearer, S. M. (2002). Best practices in school–community partnerships. In A. Thomas & J. Grimes (Eds.), *Best practices in school psychology IV* (pp. 321–336). Bethesda, MD: National Association of School Psychologists.

St. Pierre, T. L., Mark, M. M., Kaltreider, D. L., & Campbell, B. (2001). Boys and Girls Clubs and school collaborations: A longitudinal study of a multicomponent substance abuse prevention program for high-risk elementary school children. *Journal of Community Psychology, 29*, 87–106.

Swick, K. J. (2003). Communication concepts for strengthening family-school-community partnerships. *Early Childhood Education Journal, 30*, 275–280.

Taylor, L., & Adelman, H. S. (2003). School-community relations: Policy and practice. In M. S. Fishbaugh, T. R. Berkeley, & G. Schroth (Eds.). *Ensuring safe school environments: Exploring issues, seeking solutions*. Mahwah, NJ: Erlbaum.

Turnbull, A., Edmonson, H., Griggs, P., Wickham, D., Sailor, W., Freeman, R., ... Warren, J. (2002). A blueprint for school-wide positive behavior support: Implementation of three components. *Exceptional Children, 68*, 377–402.

Wright Carroll, D. (2008). Toward multiculturalism competence: A practical model for implementation in the schools. In J. Jones (Ed.), *The psychology of multiculturalism in schools: A primer for practice, training, and research*. Bethesda, MD: National Association of School Psychologists.

15 Best Practices in School Crisis Intervention

Stephen E. Brock
California State University, Sacramento
Melissa A. Louvar Reeves
Winthrop University (SC)
Amanda B. Nickerson
University at Buffalo, State University of New York

OVERVIEW

School crisis intervention, as described in this chapter, is found within the National Association of School Psychologists (NASP) *Model for Comprehensive and Integrated School Psychological Services* (Preventive and Response Services domain; NASP, 2010a). This domain specifies that school psychologists "... have knowledge of principles and research related to ... evidence-based strategies for effective crisis response. School psychologists, in collaboration with others, demonstrate skills to ... implement effective crisis preparation, response, and recovery" (pp. 6–7).

This chapter addresses the school psychologist's response and recovery activities that collectively are considered crisis intervention. Its primary objective is to assist the reader to begin to acquire knowledge of the empirically supported best practices for helping school communities cope with crises. However, it is important to acknowledge that this chapter only provides the school psychologist with an introduction to this topic and that additional hands-on training and supervision should be obtained before attempting to provide crisis intervention.

As illustrated in Figure 15.1, school crisis intervention includes universal, selected, and indicated interventions and might also be considered primary, secondary, and tertiary prevention. Universal (or primary) crisis interventions are those services offered to all individuals exposed to a crisis. For those at low risk for psychological trauma, these may be the only interventions

required. Selected (or secondary) crisis interventions are those services offered to moderately to severely traumatized individuals who are having at least some difficulty coping independently with crisis circumstances. Following highly traumatic crises (e.g., acts of human violence with fatalities), this may include a substantial percentage of the student body. Indicated (or tertiary) crisis interventions, which often require collaboration with community-based mental health professionals, are those services provided to the most severely traumatized individuals. This is typically a minority of crisis survivors whose crisis reactions are so severe they require professional mental health treatment. However, if the crisis were highly traumatic it is possible (although rare) that a substantial percentage of a school's population may need this level of crisis intervention support (Brock et al., 2009).

As is further illustrated in Figure 15.1, school crisis interventions can be conceptualized as falling within a multitiered model of differentiated services, with the selection of specific interventions for individuals being based on temporal proximity to the crisis event (some are immediate interventions while others are offered days or weeks later), the magnitude of individual need for crisis intervention (not all individuals will require the same intervention), and the nature of the intervention provided (some interventions are more intense and directive than are others).

At Tier 1, and offered to all crisis-exposed individuals, the immediate/initial crisis interventions are designed to prevent or mitigate psychological trauma, to reaffirm

Figure 15.1. Levels of School Crisis Intervention From Least (Tier 1) to Most (Tier 3) Directive and Intense

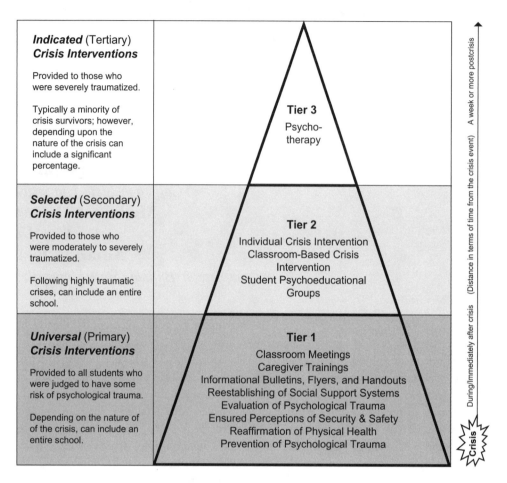

Note. From "Best Practices for School Psychologists as Members of Crisis Teams: The PREPaRE Model" (p. 1495), by S. E. Brock, A. B. Nickerson, M. A. Reeves, and S. R. Jimerson. In A. Thomas and J. Grimes (Eds.), *Best Practices in School Psychology V*, 2008, Bethesda, MD: National Association of School Psychologists. Copyright 2008 by the National Association of School Psychologists. Reprinted with permission.

physical health, and to ensure perceptions of safety and security. As these crisis interventions are completed, the next Tier 1 crisis intervention involves the evaluation of psychological trauma risk. It is from this psychological triage or risk screening that the need for all other crisis interventions are determined. For those identified as being at low risk for psychological trauma, additional Tier 1 crisis interventions may include reestablishing social support systems; disseminating informational bulletins, flyers, and handouts; providing psychological education to caregivers (e.g., parents and teachers) on how to help children cope with crises; and brief classroom meetings to promote understanding of crisis facts (Brock et al., 2009).

At Tier 2, and offered only to moderately to severely traumatized individuals (typically days to weeks after the crisis event), are interventions that provide more assertive or directive crisis intervention assistance. Specifically, this level of crisis intervention service includes student psychoeducational groups designed to provide direct instruction on addressing coping challenges; classroom-based crisis intervention designed to facilitate the processing of crisis experiences and reactions; and one-on-one individual crisis intervention, which strives to reestablish immediate coping (Brock et al., 2009).

Finally, at Tier 3, and offered only to the most severely traumatized (typically a week or more after the crisis event), are interventions that provide intensive and long-term mental health treatment. This psychotherapy addresses the most significant mental health challenges (e.g., posttraumatic stress disorder) that as a rule affect only a minority of crisis-exposed individuals (Brock et al., 2009).

Before moving on to a discussion of basic considerations and specific crisis intervention best practices it is important to acknowledge the importance of the collaboration called for in this domain of Preventive and Response Services from the NASP Practice Model (NASP, 2010a). While this chapter is focused on the work of school psychologists, much of this information presented is applicable to, and/or will require collaboration with, other school and community-based professionals. For example, psychological education activities require the support of the school principal and may include collaboration with curriculum coordinators. Similarly, while school psychologists should take a leadership role in the provision of mental health crisis interventions, with the appropriate training other school professionals (e.g., teachers) can and should be involved in the provision of these crisis intervention efforts. Further, collaboration among the various professional disciplines within the school setting is essential to the implementation of crisis interventions. Perhaps most importantly, the effective delivery of crisis intervention services requires that school psychologists be embedded within a multidisciplinary crisis response team of professionals, each of whom are focused on the crisis response procedures most closely aligned with their traditional job duties (e.g., school nurses would be focused on medical first-aid).

For a further discussion of the broader multidisciplinary school crisis team response, the reader is referred to Brock et al. (2009) and the standardized NASP workshop, *Crisis Prevention and Preparedness: Comprehensive School Safety Planning*. Additionally, professional development associated with the crisis interventions described in this chapter can be found in the NASP workshop, *Crisis Intervention and Recovery: The Roles of School-Based Mental Health Professionals*.

BASIC CONSIDERATIONS

Before the school psychologist can provide school crisis intervention, he or she will need to understand the defining features of a crisis event, the crisis state, and crisis intervention. The discussion that follows provides this essential background knowledge.

Crisis Event Characteristics

School psychologists must be able to recognize the characteristics of a crisis event. Brock et al. (2009) suggest that the types of events that may require a school crisis response are extremely negative (i.e., viewed as having caused physical or emotional pain), uncontrollable (i.e., generate feelings of helplessness, powerlessness, or entrapment), and unpredictable (i.e., occur suddenly, unexpectedly, and without warning). Members of the school community (i.e., students, staff, and parents) who experience or witness one of these events, or learn about a significant other being exposed to such an event, are potential psychological trauma victims and may require a school psychologist to provide one or more of the crisis interventions discussed in this chapter.

To best match the level of school crisis intervention response to the mental health needs of the school community, the school psychologist must also understand that some crisis events are more likely to generate psychological trauma than others. All other factors being equal, natural disasters and crises considered to be accidents are less traumatic than human-caused disasters and crises considered to have been intentional (e.g., assaultive violence). However, as illustrated in Figure 15.2, other factors interact with event type to determine an event's traumatic potential. These factors include the event's predictability, consequences, duration, and intensity. For example, a natural disaster or accident (events that typically do not generate significant traumatic stress), may become highly traumatic if they were not predicted (e.g., earthquake), had particularly devastating consequences (e.g., multiple fatalities), involved a relatively long duration of crisis-related coping challenges, and/or were associated with intense exposure to gruesome aspects of the crisis (Brock et al., 2009; Nooner et al., 2012).

The school psychologist's ability to estimate the number of students affected by a given crisis, and to subsequently determine the level of crisis intervention response needed, is critical as there are dangers associated with both overreacting and underreacting to a crisis. Overreacting may increase student threat perceptions, while underreacting may result in some needs being unmet. In addition to crisis-event variables, other factors will also be important in determining crisis-response level, such as the size of the school or school district and its available resources, the school's trauma history, and idiosyncratic threat perceptions (Brock et al., 2009).

Crisis State

The need for school crisis interventions will depend on the extent to which school community members enter into the crisis state. The importance of school

Figure 15.2. Crisis Event Variables Serve to Make Some Crisis Events More Traumatic Than Others

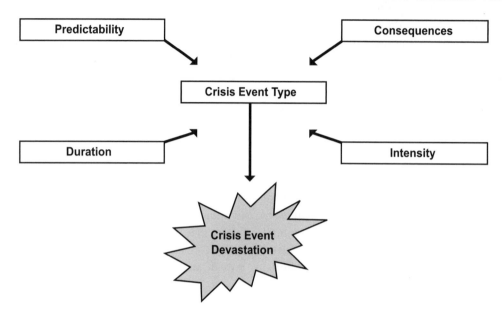

Note. From *School Crisis Prevention and Intervention: The PREPaRE Model* (p. 4), by S. E. Brock, A. B. Nickerson, M. A. Reeves, S. R. Jimerson, R. A. Lieberman, and T. A. Feinberg, 2009, Bethesda, MD: National Association of School Psychologists. Copyright 2009 by the National Association of School Psychologists. Reprinted with permission.

psychologists understanding what it means to be "in crisis" is underscored by the fact that whereas the occurrence of a crisis event should prompt consideration of the need to provide school crisis interventions, an event itself is insufficient to justify provision of such services. Rather, it is the personal consequences of the crisis event for the individual that generates the need to provide crisis intervention.

The crisis state can be described as the social, emotional, behavioral, and physical reactions associated with not being able to initially solve crisis-related problems (e.g., no longer feeling safe at school following a school shooting). The coping strategies developed to deal with crisis problems may be either adaptive (e.g., developing new coping skills) or maladaptive (e.g., avoiding school). It is also important for the school psychologist to recognize that the reactions associated with the crisis state are not necessarily signs of mental illness. Although reactions associated with the crisis state may look psychopathological, they are typically considered to be common reactions to unusual circumstances (Brock et al., 2009).

This is not to say that mental illness cannot evolve out of, or be exacerbated by, the crisis state. Although it typically resolves itself within several weeks (and recovery is the norm; National Institute of Mental Health, 2001), in some cases the crisis state may evolve into mental illness. If an individual develops such mental

health problems, there is a critical need for immediate and directive (Tier 2 and Tier 3) school crisis intervention. Thus, it is important for all school crisis team members to be aware of the psychopathologies that are a potential consequence of crisis exposure. Anxiety disorders, in general, and posttraumatic stress disorder, in particular, are the most common mental illnesses associated with exposure to a crisis event (Brock et al., 2009). Of particular interest to educators is the finding that posttraumatic stress disorder symptom severity has been linked to poor academic performance, declines in intellectual functioning, and increased dropout rates (Nooner et al., 2012).

Crisis Intervention

Finally, before school psychologists consider specific crisis-response and recovery strategies, they must understand the goals of crisis intervention and be knowledgeable about the range of intervention services that school crisis teams provide. The primary goal of school crisis intervention is to help restore the crisis-exposed student's basic problem-solving abilities and in doing so to return the student to his or her precrisis levels of functioning (Brock et al., 2009). Given this perspective, it is important for school psychologists to understand the role of coping in responding to a crisis.

Normal Coping

A useful framework for understanding normal coping has been offered by Moos and Billings (1984), who describe three domains of coping skills. The first coping domain, *appraisal focused*, involves rationally thinking through and preparing for crisis event consequences; possibly reframing the event; and, in some cases, mentally maintaining the event at a distance until an individual is ready to address it. It is important to acknowledge that this last appraisal-focused skill has intervention implications. It suggests that intervention must be sensitive to the possibility that not all school community members will be immediately ready to confront crisis facts. The second coping domain, *problem focused*, involves assertively striving to identify crisis facts and support systems, initiating efforts to address crisis-generated problems, and adjusting relationships and activities so that there are replacements for resources eliminated by the crisis. The third domain, *emotion focused*, involves the individual managing the emotions generated by the crisis, venting feelings in a way that brings some relief, and cognitively attempting to respond to crisis-generated problems.

The Range of School Crisis Interventions

The PREPaRE model of crisis intervention is consistent with guidance offered by the U.S. Department of Education (2010) and U.S. Department of Homeland Security (2008) and identifies the range of services that school psychologists need to be prepared to provide. From a comprehensive review of the literature (Brock et al., 2009), and incorporating elements from other community-focused protocols (e.g., Mitchell & Everly, 2001; National Organization for Victim Assistance, 1998), PREPaRE is the only model of school crisis intervention grounded in theory and research developed by, and specifically for, school psychologists. An especially helpful resource that provided important guidance to the model was the National Child Traumatic Stress Network and National Center for PTSD's *Psychological First Aid: Field Operations Guide* (Brymer et al., 2006).

The PREPaRE acronym stands for prevent and prepare, reaffirm, evaluate, provide interventions and respond, and examine. Specifically, the PREPaRE model emphasizes that school psychologists be involved in the following hierarchical and sequential set of activities. First, to the extent possible school psychologists strive to prevent crises from occurring in the first place and also prepare for or mitigate crises that cannot be prevented. Second, before beginning to focus on mental health, the initial response to crisis is helping to ensure physical health and perceptions of security and safety. Third, school psychologists evaluate the degree to which individuals have suffered psychological trauma. Fourth, from the evaluation of trauma, school psychologists facilitate the provision of increasingly more direct/intense crisis intervention services. Finally, the model calls for an examination of the effectiveness of crisis intervention efforts. The elements of PREPaRE are consistent with recent meta-analytic research suggesting that early interventions for trauma-exposed children should include risk screening and psychological education and offer multiple sessions to at-risk children (Kramer & Landolt, 2011).

BEST PRACTICES IN SCHOOL CRISIS INTERVENTION

Though crises have the potential to generate significant psychological injury, it is essential that school psychologists recognize that with the exception of the most extraordinary crisis circumstances and with the support of naturally occurring family, school, and community resources, the majority of individuals exposed to a crisis will recover (National Institute of Mental Health, 2001). Given this reality, most school crisis intervention services are indirect and often find school psychologists working behind the scenes, ensuring that students, staff, and parents are well positioned to realize their natural potential to overcome crisis. Of course, these naturally occurring resources do have their limits. Consequently, school psychologists need to be able to evaluate psychological trauma and respond accordingly. In other words, best practices for the school psychologist in crisis intervention involves working to foster natural recovery from psychological trauma while at the same time identifying severely distressed individuals and providing those individuals with appropriate crisis intervention.

Prevention and Preparedness

Initially and universally, school psychologists should engage in primary prevention. This involves working to prevent or mitigate circumstances that would require additional crisis interventions. This level of crisis intervention may find the school psychologist engaged in one or more of the following: (a) comprehensive school safety and crisis prevention activities; (b) preparing for those crises that cannot be prevented; (c) fostering student resiliency so that students are better protected from crises that are experienced; and (d) when faced with a crisis event, implementing emergency procedures in such a fashion that students are safe and exposure to frightening crisis scenes and images are minimized (Watson, Brymer, & Bonanno, 2011). Crisis preparedness must also include cultural sensitivity to the needs of children following crises.

Comprehensive School Safety and Crisis Prevention

School psychologists should help to ensure that both physical and psychological school safety are promoted (although they will likely have greater responsibility and expertise when it comes to the promotion of psychological safety). Among the strategies to be considered is Crime Prevention Through Environmental Design (Schneider, Walker, & Sprague, 2000). This approach details ways that schools can design the physical environment to increase (a) natural surveillance (b) natural access control, and (c) territoriality (or a sense of shared ownership of the school by students and staff, which in turn increases the likelihood of inappropriate behavior being challenged). Efforts to promote a sense of psychological safety at school may include the promotion of positive behavioral supports (e.g., http://www.pbis.org), social–emotional learning (e.g., http://www.casel.org), and school connectedness (e.g., http://www.cdc.gov/healthyyouth/adolescenthealth/pdf/connectedness.pdf).

Crisis Preparedness

Preparing for crises requires the school psychologist to help ensure that a comprehensive multidisciplinary crisis response team has been formed. The PREP<u>a</u>RE model recommends that the U.S. Department of Homeland Security's (2008) Incident Command System be used to structure team membership, with each team member having his or her own crisis preparedness tasks. By verifying that such a team is in place, the school psychologist will be better able to focus on the mental health crisis intervention activities that are the focus of this chapter. Specific preparedness activities that should take place include (a) obtaining all crisis response supplies and equipment (e.g., communication tools, first-aid supplies); (b) establishing search, rescue, and student accounting procedures; (c) establishing student assembly and release to parent procedures; (d) establishing crowd control and traffic management procedures; (e) developing the capacity to meet emergency medical needs; and, perhaps most relevant to the school psychologists; and (f) developing the capacity to provide crisis intervention to psychological trauma victims (and

reading this chapter is an example of such professional development). These roles should be detailed in a comprehensive school crisis plan that provides information for how to ensure an effective response to a wide variety of crises. Exercising and evaluating these plans through drills is essential to ensure necessary modifications can be made (Reeves, Kanan, & Plog, 2010).

Fostering Student Resilience

The primary prevention of psychological trauma also involves the school psychologist providing services that promote resiliency. For example, internal resiliency is promoted by helping students to (a) engage in active (versus avoidance) coping, (b) develop self-confidence, (c) regulate their emotions, and (d) develop internal loci of control. External resiliency can be promoted by facilitating (a) parent partnerships and parent engagement activities, (b) peer relationships, (c) access to positive adult role models, and (d) connections with prosocial institutions. To the extent that resilience is promoted, individuals will be less vulnerable to the adverse effects of crises (Brock et al., 2009; Cicero, Nooner, & Silva, 2011).

Implementing Emergency Procedures

Also referred to as *immediate prevention* (Brock et al., 2009), it is important for the school psychologist to understand that the effective implementation of emergency response procedures (e.g., lockdown, evacuation) can serve to prevent or mitigate psychological trauma by ensuring that students are kept safe and by minimizing student exposure to potentially traumatic scenes and images. This level of prevention should also include minimizing student exposure to potentially disturbing media images of the crisis event (Neria & Sullivan, 2011).

Reaffirming Physical Health and Perceptions of Safety

Immediately following a crisis event, the provision of practical help and physical support is also considered a universal intervention and always has precedence over the provision of psychological care. Crisis interventions that take place from this point forward are considered secondary prevention activities. Specifically, this next set of interventions requires school psychologists to engage in activities designed to meet basic physical health needs of students and helping to ensure that they believe they are safe (Watson et al., 2011).

Meeting Basic Physical Needs

This crisis intervention activity involves ensuring students are hydrated, fed, warm, and dry. To reduce feelings of helplessness it may be appropriate to encourage students to participate in getting supplies needed for comfort. For example, assuming it is safe to do so and students are able, selected students can be sent to the cafeteria or the office to get needed supplies rather than asking an adult to bring supplies to the classroom. In advance of a crisis, special consideration should be given to the physical needs of students with disabilities (Brock et al., 2009; Brymer et al., 2006).

Facilitating Perceptions of Safety

It is not enough for students to actually be physically cared for and safe immediately following a crisis. For recovery to begin, school psychologists must help students believe that they are no longer in danger. One approach for achieving this goal involves providing students with carefully selected crisis facts. Such knowledge can help them understand that the event, while very upsetting, has passed and is no longer a threat (Brymer et al., 2006). It is also critical to acknowledge that adult reactions are important influences on children's threat perceptions (Brock et al., 2009). This is particularly true among primary grade students. It has been reported that children within this age group may be led to view an event as personally threatening (even if it was not) if they observe adults behaving in a way that suggests the event was very dangerous (Shaw, 2003). Thus, it is critical that the school psychologist work with school staff members to ensure that their behaviors are not frightening. In particular, the school psychologist should strive to minimize student exposure to adult staff members who have lost emotional control. Once the crisis has ended, the situation has stabilized, and students' basic needs have been met, and students believe that crisis related dangers have passed, it will be appropriate for the school psychologist to begin planning for the provision of other school crisis interventions (Brock et al., 2009).

Evaluating Psychological Trauma

Prerequisite to the provision of crisis interventions is an understanding of the fact that different individuals will require different interventions (Watson et al., 2011). Thus, another universal intervention is the evaluation of psychological trauma risk, or psychological triage (Brock et al., 2009). The rationale for conducting such evaluation before offering additional crisis interventions is that (a) not all individuals will be equally affected by crisis exposure (with recovery being the norm; National Institute of Mental Health, 2001) and (b) the effectiveness of a given crisis intervention can be idiosyncratic. In other words, while some individuals will be highly traumatized, and will benefit from immediate and relatively intensive and highly directive crisis interventions, other individuals will be minimally traumatized and may find some of the more intense and directive crisis interventions counterproductive. For example, if crisis intervention were to take place in a group format, then there is a potential for students who are distressed to have a negative impact on otherwise unaffected students. Further, providing crisis intervention assistance to a student who does not need it may unintentionally send the message that the student is not capable of coping with the crisis independently.

As illustrated in Figure 15.3, psychological trauma is the result of an interaction between the crisis event and the individual's unique threat perceptions. Risk factors that influence threat perceptions are crisis exposure and personal vulnerabilities. Warning signs, which include both initial and durable crisis reactions (with the latter being more highly related to psychopathology), provide evidence that trauma risk has generated traumatic stress. Knowledge of these risk factors and warning signs allow school psychologists to make informed decisions about what crisis interventions are most appropriate for specific individuals.

Psychological Trauma Risk Factors

Risk factors include those variables that increase the probability of traumatic stress reactions. Their presence signals the need for school psychologists to increase vigilance for warning signs of psychological injury.

Physical exposure to the crisis event. The greatest risk for psychological trauma is found among those individuals who were physically proximal to the crisis event, who required medical attention, and who had particularly long and intense crisis exposures (Brock et al., 2009).

Vicarious exposure to the crisis event. After physical proximity, emotional proximity is the next most powerful predictor of traumatic stress that the school psychologist should evaluate. This includes those who had close emotional relationships with crisis victims. Those who are bereaved are an especially high-risk group (Brock et al., 2009). It is important to note that emotional closeness to a crisis may result from the viewing of media reports, as an association between such

Figure 15.3. Factors That Should Be Considered When Evaluating Psychological Trauma

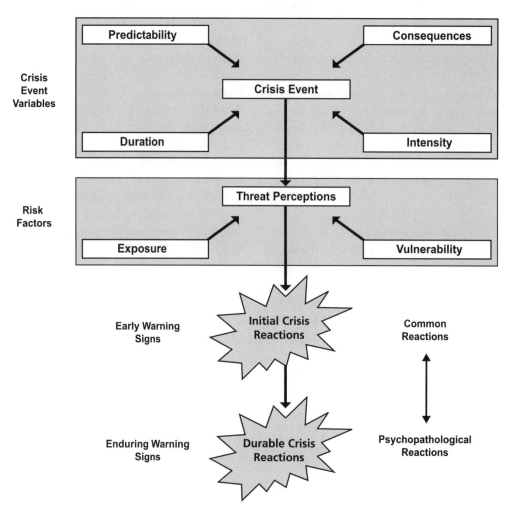

Note. From *School Crisis Prevention and Intervention: The PREPaRE Model* (p. 130), by S. E. Brock, A. B. Nickerson, M. A. Reeves, S. R. Jimerson, R. A. Lieberman, and T. A. Feinberg, 2009, Bethesda, MD: National Association of School Psychologists. Copyright 2009 by the National Association of School Psychologists. Reprinted with permission.

and symptoms of traumatic stress have been reported (Ben-Zur, Gil, & Shamshins, 2012).

Personal vulnerabilities. While physical and vicarious exposures are specific to the crisis situation, personal vulnerabilities are general risk factors that are applicable to all situations (not just the crisis event). This risk factor includes both internal and external vulnerabilities. Internal factors include having an avoidance coping style, a history of mental illness, prior traumatization, and developmental immaturity (although older teens have higher rates of posttraumatic stress disorder likely due to their increased trauma exposure). External factors are environmental variables and include having limited family, financial, social resources, and social connectedness (Brock et al., 2009; McDermott, Berry, & Cobham, 2012; Nooner et al., 2012).

Warning Signs of Psychological Trauma

The presence of risk factors should increase vigilance for the warning signs of traumatic stress. However, regardless of their presence or absence, warning signs are an indication that the individual is psychologically traumatized.

Severe crisis reactions. Some initial crisis reactions are to be expected among students exposed to a traumatic event and, at least initially, should not be pathologized. With the exception of the most severe crisis reactions, referrals for Tier 3 crisis intervention (psychotherapy) should not typically be considered for at least a week following the crisis event (Litz, Gray, Bryant, & Adler, 2002). However, there are exceptions to this rule, and Table 15.1 provides a list of the more severe crisis reactions that may necessitate immediate professional mental health treatment referrals.

Table 15.1. Crisis Reactions Indicating the Need for Immediate Mental Health Referrals

Peritraumatic dissociation
- Derealization (e.g., feeling as if in a dream world)
- Depersonalization (e.g., feeling as if your body is not really yours)
- Reduced awareness of surroundings (e.g., being in a daze)
- Emotional numbness (e.g., feeling emotionally detached/estranged; lack typical range of emotions; reduced interest in previously important/enjoyed activities; feeling as if there is no future career, marriage, children, or normal lifespan)
- Amnesia (i.e., failure to remember significant crisis event experiences)

Peritraumatic hyperarousal
- Panic attacks
- Disturbed memory and extreme difficulty concentrating
- Hypervigilance and exaggerated startle reactions
- Increased irritability (e.g., fighting or temper problems) and motor restlessness
- Difficulty falling and/or staying asleep (sometimes a result of the reexperiencing symptom of disturbing dreams)

Persistent reexperiencing of the crisis event
- Behaving and/or feeling as if the trauma were happening again (among children this may manifest as repetitive and automatic reenactment play[a])
- Extremely terrifying and reoccurring nightmares about the event (among children this may manifest as frightening dreams not specifically tied to the crisis)
- Reoccurring intrusive or distressing thoughts, images, or feelings associated with the event (among children this may manifest as repetitive play expressing crisis themes)
- Intense distress (both psychological and physiological) when presented with reminders (e.g., locations, sensations, symbols) of the trauma

Avoidance of crisis reminders
- Deliberate efforts to avoid thoughts, feelings, discussions, activities, places, or people that are associated with or bring back memories of the crisis event
- Agoraphobic-like social withdrawal
- Isolation from significant others

Depression
- Significant feelings of hopelessness and worthlessness
- Significant loss of interest in most activities
- Wakening early (sleeplessness; difficulty sleeping)
- Persistent fatigue
- Lack of motivation

Psychotic symptoms
- Delusions
- Hallucinations
- Bizarre thoughts or images
- Catatonia

Notes. From "Best Practices for School Psychologists as Members of Crisis Teams: The PREPaRE Model" (p. 1498), by S. E. Brock A. B. Nickerson, M. A. Reeves, and S. R. Jimerson. In A. Thomas and J. Grimes (Eds.) *Best Practices in School Psychology V*, 2008, Bethesda, MD: National Association of School Psychologists. Copyright 2008 by the National Association of School Psychologists. Adapted with permission.
[a] Among younger children, symptoms of reexperiencing the trauma may be primarily displayed through reenacting play and is considered pathological only when it appears to be repetitive and automatic.

Maladaptive coping behaviors. In addition to severe crisis reactions, the presence of maladaptive coping behaviors are also relevant to the school psychologist when determining who will need an immediate Tier 3 mental health crisis intervention referral. For example, some students may present with an acute risk of harm to self or others as a consequence of their crisis exposure. Others may attempt to cope with the trauma by extreme rumination about their role in the crisis event, excessive avoidance behaviors (e.g., refusing to leave the house), and/or the taking of excessive precautions (e.g., only sleeping with a light on or with a weapon nearby; Brock et al., 2009).

To summarize, Figure 15.4 offers a checklist that school psychologists can use to identify low, moderate, and high degrees of psychological trauma. While all

Figure 15.4. Psychological Trauma Risk Checklist for Determining Levels of Risk for Psychological Trauma

	Low Risk	Moderate Risk	High Risk
Physical Proximity	☐ Out of vicinity of crisis site	☐ Present on crisis site	☐ Crisis victim or eye witness
Emotional Proximity	☐ Did not know victim(s)	☐ Friend of victim(s) ☐ Acquaintance of victim(s)	☐ Relative of victim(s) ☐ Best friend of victim(s)
Internal Vulnerabilities	☐ Active coping style ☐ Mentally healthy ☐ Good self-regulation of emotion ☐ High developmental level ☐ No trauma history	☐ No clear coping style ☐ Uncertainty about pre-crisis mental health ☐ Some difficulties with self-regulation of emotion ☐ Appearance of immaturity at times ☐ Trauma history	☐ Avoidance coping style ☐ Preexisting mental illness ☐ Poor self-regulation of emotion ☐ Low developmental level ☐ Significant trauma history
External Vulnerabilities	☐ Living with intact nuclear family members ☐ Good parent/child relationship ☐ Good family functioning ☐ No parental traumatic stress ☐ Good social resources	☐ Living with some nuclear family members ☐ Parent/child relationship at times stressed ☐ Family functioning at times challenged ☐ Some parental traumatic stress ☐ Social resources/relations at times challenged	☐ Not living with any nuclear family members ☐ Poor parent/child relationship ☐ Poor family functioning ☐ Significant parental traumatic stress ☐ Poor or absent social resources
Immediate Reactions During the Crisis	☐ Remained calm during the crisis event	☐ Displayed mild to moderate distress during the crisis event	☐ Displayed acute distress (e.g., fright, panic, dissociation) during the crisis event
Current or Ongoing Reactions and Coping	☐ Only a few common crisis reactions displayed ☐ Coping is adaptive (i.e., it allows daily functioning at pre-crisis levels)	☐ Many common crisis reactions displayed ☐ Coping is tentative (e.g., the individual is unsure about how to cope with the crisis)	☐ Mental health referral indicators displayed (e.g., acute dissociation hyperarousal, depression, psychosis ☐ Coping is absent or maladaptive (e.g., suicidal or homicidal ideation, substance abuse)
Total:			

Note. From "Best Practices in School Crisis Intervention" (p. 785), by S. E. Brock and J. Davis. In A. Thomas and J. Grimes (Eds.), *Best Practices in School Psychology V*, 2008, Bethesda, MD: National Association of School Psychologists. Copyright 2008 by the National Association of School Psychologists. Reprinted with permission.

crisis interventions are potentially needed for the student at high risk (Tier 3), the student with a moderate risk may need only Tier 1 and Tier 2 interventions, while the individual with a low risk for psychological trauma may have his or her needs met by Tier 1 interventions.

Psychological Triage Protocol

The process of identifying individuals in need of specific crisis intervention services is dynamic. Thus, it is critical for school psychologists to develop and make use of a multistage psychological triage protocol and understand that triage is a process and not an event. A primary element of such a protocol is knowledge of the risk factors and warning signs described above. When combined with knowledge of crisis facts, school psychologists will be able to identify individuals at risk for psychological trauma. However, it is unlikely that even the most knowledgeable and well-informed school psychologist will be able to identify all crisis victims.

Thus, it is critical that an effective referral procedure be in place. Through such procedures parents, teachers, and other caregivers will be able to bring to the attention of the crisis intervention team individuals in need of Tier 2 and Tier 3 crisis interventions. For a sample psychological triage protocol and crisis intervention referral forms see Brock et al. (2009).

Provide Interventions and to Psychological Needs

From the evaluation of individual risk for psychological trauma, the school psychologist should provide crisis interventions that respond to psychological needs. The specific interventions to be considered, presented in order from least to most intense, directive and individualized are (a) reestablishment of naturally occurring social support systems; (b) providing psychological education that empowers students and their

Figure 15.5. The Relationship Between the Evaluation of Psychological Trauma and Specific Crisis Interventions

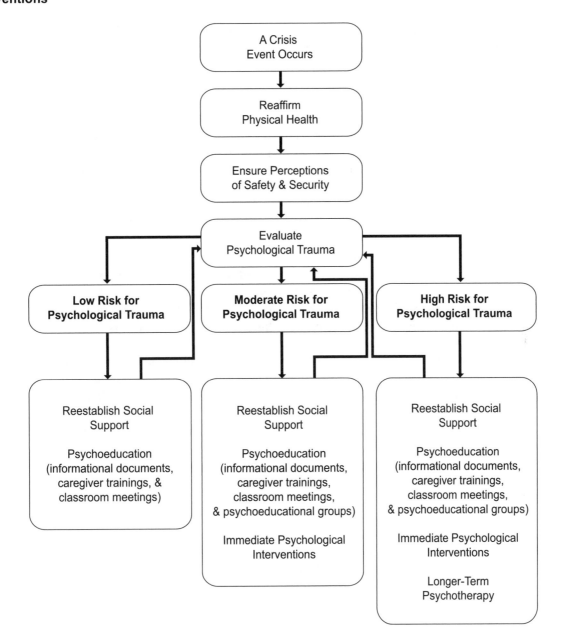

Note. From "Best Practices for School Psychologists as Members of Crisis Teams: The PREPaRE Model" (p. 1499), by S. E. Brock A. B. Nickerson, M. A. Reeves, and S. R. Jimerson. In A. Thomas and J. Grimes (Eds.), *Best Practices in School Psychology V*, 2008, Bethesda, MD: National Association of School Psychologists. Copyright 2008 by the National Association of School Psychologists. Reprinted with permission.

caregivers with knowledge that facilitates adaptive coping; (c) providing immediate psychological interventions; and (d) for the minority of students who may have been severely traumatized, providing and/or making referrals for longer term psychotherapeutic treatment. Figure 15.5 provides an illustration of relationships among the PREPaRE model elements and in particular how the evaluation of psychological trauma relates to the specific crisis interventions. As illustrated in Figure 15.5, these specific interventions should further inform the school psychologist's evaluation of psychological trauma.

Reestablishing Social Support Systems

Given expectations that most individuals will recover from their traumatic exposure (National Institute of Mental Health, 2001), reestablishing and empowering social support systems should be a primary school crisis intervention and in many cases is the only crisis intervention required. Being with and sharing crisis experiences with positive social supports facilitates recovery from trauma (Brock et al., 2009), and the level of such support is a strong predictor of traumatic stress (with more social support being associated with a lower likelihood of traumatic stress; Nooner et al., 2012).

Given these observations, all other school crisis interventions should complement the assets of naturally occurring social supports and be prepared to pick up where these supports end. Specific examples of this intervention include reuniting students with their parents, friends, and teachers and returning students to familiar environments and routines. Although social support systems are very powerful, they have limitations. For example, the duration and/or intensity of some crises may render natural support systems ineffective. In addition, individuals with preexisting mental health challenges are an especially high-risk group and often need more assistance than can be offered by naturally occurring social supports alone (Brock et al., 2009). Thus, school psychologists need to be prepared to offer or facilitate other school crisis interventions. In other words, school psychologists need to be prepared to not only empower and enable social support systems to facilitate natural recovery but also able to evaluate traumatic stress reactions and provide direct crisis intervention services when social supports are insufficient, ineffective, or unavailable.

Providing Psychological Education

Bridging the gap between Tier 1 and Tier 2 crisis interventions are a set of interventions collectively referred to as psychological education. At Tier 1 these include informational documents, caregiver trainings, and classroom meetings. At Tier 2 the crisis intervention is referred to as student psychoeducational groups. Through these crisis interventions school psychologists provide the factual information that helps caregivers and students understand, prepare for, and respond to a crisis event and resulting problems and reactions. Through such services, crisis survivors are provided guidance that will help them to take independent actions that mitigate traumatic stress (both in themselves and among others).

Psychological education strives to give crisis survivors control over the recovery process, can be used to promote social support, and facilitates approach-oriented coping, all of which are factors related to positive life change after victimization (Frazier, Tashiro,

Bennan, Steger, & Long, 2004). Further, these interventions reduce the stigma associated with mental health interventions, capitalize on personal strengths, and increase a sense of self-worth. Psychological education can also be beneficial in providing early connections to mental health resources.

Limitations of psychological education include the fact that the available research offers only preliminary support for this crisis intervention and that by itself it does not reduce crisis symptoms, especially the more severe traumatic stress reactions (Wessely et al., 2008). Thus, for the more significantly traumatized individuals, it is critical that this intervention be paired with other Tier 2 and/or Tier 3 crisis interventions, such as individual crisis intervention and psychotherapeutic treatment.

Informational bulletins, flyers, and handouts. The least intense or directive psychological education strategy is the dissemination of informational bulletins, flyers, or handouts. These materials can be made available through the school and/or the media (including social media). They facilitate an understanding of the crisis event, possible effects, and help to identify available supports. This crisis intervention strategy can parallel, complement, and/or supplement the information provided through other psychological education groups and trainings. It is recommended that elements of these documents (e.g., local referral and community support resource contact information) be developed in advance of a crisis.

Caregiver trainings. A second Tier 1 psychological education activity finds the school psychologist working with caregivers (e.g., parents and teachers) and helping the caregivers acquire the knowledge they need to help children exposed to a crisis event. Thus, providing caregivers with guidance about the effects of trauma exposure and how they can attend to and support their children is critical (Brock et al., 2009).

According to Brock et al. (2009), the goals of these trainings include ensuring that caregivers are (a) provided with the facts they need to help children understand the crisis event, (b) prepared for reactions that might be seen in their children or among themselves and informed that natural recovery is the norm, (c) provided strategies they can use to help children cope with crisis reactions and/or problems, (d) instructed on how to best respond to their children, and (e) able to identify psychopathological reactions and coping strategies and know how to make referrals for

Table 15.2. Sample Caregiver Training Session Outline

1. Introduction to the session.
2. Provide caregivers with the crisis facts that will allow them to help others gain cognitive mastery over the crisis event. When providing these facts it is important that caregivers be advised of the possibility of information transmission of posttraumatic stress disorder. Thus, it should be suggested that caregivers let student questions guide the information that is given. Caregivers should not give unasked-for detail. In particular, caregivers should avoid giving children information the children would not likely learn about on their own and that would unnecessarily frighten them.
3. Provide caregivers with information about the common crisis reactions likely to be seen among both children and the caregivers themselves.
4. Review strategies for helping children cope with crisis reactions. Specific strategies include:
   - Direct instruction regarding stress management and relaxation techniques
   - Bibliotherapy
   - Identifying existing supports (e.g., parents, teachers, school psychologists)
   - Identifying adaptive coping strategies and discuss how to redirect students away from maladaptive strategies (e.g., drinking)

Note. From "Best Practices in School Crisis Intervention" (p. 786), by S. E. Brock and J. Davis. In A. Thomas and J. Grimes (Eds.), *Best Practices in School Psychology V*, 2008, Bethesda, MD: National Association of School Psychologists. Copyright 2008 by the National Association of School Psychologists. Adapted with permission.

professional assistance. In addition, the direct contact with caregivers that this form of psychological education provides gives school crisis interveners an opportunity to identify those who may not be able to provide the social support that helps most children get through difficult circumstances. To help the school psychologist conduct a caregiver training, Table 15.2 provides an outline for this crisis intervention.

Classroom meetings. Also considered a Tier 1 intervention, this crisis intervention is comes from the experiences of Reeves et al. (2010) who have suggested that brief classroom meetings immediately following some crises are necessary to disseminate the crisis facts that can help to mitigate the trauma generated by crisis rumors. The now common use of social media among school-aged youth necessitates such meetings, as students are now able to immediately acquire information about a crisis (much of which is typically not vetted). Consequently, without this crisis intervention response, harmful and counterproductive rumors will proliferate (Flitsch, Magnesi, & Brock, 2012).

Classroom meetings, typically led by a classroom teacher who has been provided with a fact sheet developed by the school psychologist, have the following goals: (a) helping students to understand the crisis, (b) providing the teacher with the opportunity to identify what information (both rumor and fact) that students already have about the crisis event, (c) providing the teacher with the opportunity to assess how students in the classroom are initially coping with the crisis, and, as indicated, (d) allowing time for the school crisis team to organize additional crisis intervention supports. The classroom meeting has four steps: (a) a brief 5-minute introduction, (b) the reading of a crisis fact script that provides reassuring crisis event details, (c) an opportunity for students to ask questions, and (d) beginning to identify students who need additional crisis intervention assistance.

Student psychoeducational groups. This Tier 2 crisis intervention is similar to caregiver training; however, its focus is primarily on self-care (and secondarily on how to help others cope with the crisis event). According to Brock et al. (2009), these lessons have the following goals: (a) crisis facts are understood and rumors are dispelled, (b) common crisis reactions are identified and normalized, (c) psychopathological crisis reactions and maladaptive coping behaviors are identified and referral procedures specified, and (d) stress management strategies are identified and/or taught. In addition, the direct contact with students that this form of psychological education provides gives school psychologists an opportunity to identify those in need of more intensive Tier 2 psychological and Tier 3 psychotherapy interventions. To help the school psychologist conduct a psychoeducational group, Table 15.3 provides an outline for this crisis intervention.

Providing Psychological Interventions

For the more significantly traumatized students, simply providing instruction on how to manage crisis reactions and cope with crisis problems will not be sufficient. For these students, it is important that school psychologists provide more direct, intense, and individualized crisis interventions to help reestablish immediate coping.

Table 15.3. Student Psychoeducational Group Lesson Outline

1. Introduce students to the lesson.
2. Answer student questions about the crisis event.
   - It is important to be prepared to repeat crisis facts several times. Because these details can be so overwhelming, students often have difficulty understanding a given fact the first time it is presented.
   - The possibility of information transmission of traumatic stress must be kept in mind. In some cases even though a student was not personally exposed to a crisis or had seen others who were, having been told about an incident or event that constituted a direct threat to the life or well-being of someone else may be sufficiently traumatic to result in traumatic stress reactions.
   - It is recommended that student questions be the guide for determining what information is given. Do not give unasked-for details. In particular, avoid giving students information they would not have already known and that would unnecessarily frighten them.
3. Prepare students for the reactions that follow exposure to a crisis event.
   - Identify how crisis events affect people and prepare students for what to expect from themselves, their classmates, and their caregivers (e.g., teachers and parents).
   - Normalize most initial crisis reactions. It should be explicitly acknowledged that with time most reactions will become less intense and that recovery is the norm.
   - Acknowledge that if the reactions do not lessen with time (and/or are too intense to manage independently), then a referral for crisis intervention assistance will be needed.
   - Crisis interveners should identify those few severe crisis reactions that signal the need for immediate crisis intervention assistance (e.g., suicidal or homicidal ideation).
   - It is most important to explain how students can obtain crisis intervention assistance both for themselves and others.
   - With an understanding of how they are being effected and what some potential future concerns might be, students will be ready for instruction on how to cope with the event.

With an understanding of how they are being affected and what some potential future concerns might be, students will be ready for instruction on how to cope with the event.

4. Teach students how to cope with crisis reactions. Help students identify strategies that will help them (and those they care about) manage crisis reactions. Specific strategies to achieve this goal include:
   - Direct instruction regarding stress management and relaxation techniques
   - Identify existing supports (e.g., parents, friends, teachers, school psychologists, and counselors)
   - Identify adaptive coping strategies
5. Close the session by making sure that students have some idea of how they will manage the crisis reactions that they may experience. This can be done by having students write a list of activities they are engaging in to cope with the traumatic stressor. It will also be important to make sure that all students know how to obtain crisis intervention assistance. Assignment of homework that requires students to write their own self-care plan would be appropriate as the session ends. This would be an assignment, which like other schoolwork products, would be used by the instructor to gauge if a lesson has been understood. The completed assignment can also be used as an additional measure of psychological trauma. The content of individual student self-care plans may suggest which students need additional crisis intervention support.

Note. From "Best Practices in School Crisis Intervention" (p. 787), by S. E. Brock and J. Davis. In A. Thomas and J. Grimes (Eds.), *Best Practices in School Psychology V,* 2008, Bethesda, MD: National Association of School Psychologists. Copyright 2008 by the National Association of School Psychologists. Adapted with permission.

Specific examples of these interventions are classroom-based and individual crisis intervention. While both aim at helping students to reestablish immediate coping, group approaches also strive to help students feel less alone and more connected to their classmates (by virtue of their common experience) and to normalize crisis reactions (Brock et al., 2009). Even for the most severely traumatized students, these psychological interventions can be an important and necessary first step, for it is often through these interventions that students are placed in a position from which they can be provided Tier 3 interventions.

A limitation of psychological interventions includes the fact that these techniques are not psychotherapy, nor a substitute for such treatment. For the more severe psychological injuries, these crisis interventions are only the first step in the longer term treatment process. At the same time, however, for the less severely traumatized these interventions may prove sufficient.

Classroom-based crisis intervention. This Tier 2 crisis intervention is indicated when the number of crisis survivors outnumbers available crisis interveners. This type of crisis intervention is similar to the classroom-based student psychoeducational group described earlier. However, unlike these lessons, classroom-based crisis intervention finds the school psychologist helping students to actively explore and process individual crisis experiences and asks for sharing of individual crisis reactions. This specific crisis intervention is controversial and, as a result, particular care should be taken when it is deemed necessary. For example, because of requests that participants share their crisis experiences and reactions, it is recommended that classroom-based crisis intervention always be facilitated by a mental health professional. In addition, to ensure that necessary individual attention is given to students, classroom-based crisis interventions must be provided by a team (not an individual; Brock et al., 2009).

Brock et al. (2009) reviewed the literature regarding this crisis intervention and found no prior study that investigated its use with children. However, from research conducted with adults and adolescents, they suggested that classroom-based crisis intervention is contraindicated as a brief (less than 60 minutes), standalone, and individual intervention for acute physical trauma victims. On the other hand, they suggested that it is appropriate when used as a more involved (more than 60 minutes and/or combined with other interventions) group intervention for individuals who have experienced a crisis, but were not physically injured or otherwise acutely traumatized. Classroom-based crisis intervention is most appropriate for use with students who might be considered vicarious trauma victims.

An important reason for classroom-based crisis intervention's inclusion in the PREPaRE model is the reality that school-associated crises can simultaneously have an impact on a large number of students and make the provision of one-on-one crisis intervention extremely challenging. Thus, it is critical that the school psychologist have strategies designed to meet the needs of affected students in a group setting.

According to Brock et al. (2009), classroom-based crisis intervention groups should be homogeneous (in terms of crisis exposure and experience, crisis impact, and developmental level) and no larger than 30 students. Because these sessions can be quite lengthy (they can last more than 2 hours), this crisis intervention is not appropriate for younger primary grade students. Participation should be voluntary and attendance not mandatory. This is especially important given that, at least initially, denial of crisis magnitude and impact can serve an adaptive function. Requiring all students to

attend a group session may force some to confront the reality of the crisis before they are emotionally ready. In addition, it has been recommended that parental consent be obtained before students participate in classroom-based crisis intervention sessions (Everly, 2003).

It is essential that school psychologists recognize that a group setting is not appropriate for highly traumatized students (e.g., those who are very depressed, guilt ridden, intensely bereaved, psychotic, physically injured). These students must be given individual attention. In addition, if these individuals are placed in a classroom-based crisis intervention with other students who were not as seriously traumatized, there is the potential for contamination effects to occur, wherein individuals who are distraught may have a negative psychological impact on students who were not previously distressed (Everly, 2003).

While the classroom-based crisis intervention session should be facilitated by a mental health professional, the teacher of the participating students should be as active and involved as possible. However, it is important to recognize a teacher's limitations, and give the teacher the option of opting out of the session if the teacher feels his or her participation may be emotionally overwhelming. While it is appropriate for a teacher to shed a tear or two, it would be counterproductive if the teacher were to become hysterical in front of a classroom. Especially among young children, adult reactions are an important determinant of how traumatic the crisis event is judged to be. Thus, if significant adults, such as teachers, are viewed as being extremely distressed by the crisis event, young children may become more distressed (Dyb, Jensen, & Nygaard, 2011).

Elements of classroom-based crisis intervention are adapted from the group approaches originally put forward by Terr (1992) and Mitchell and Everly (2001). These elements are (a) an introduction to the session, (b) the provision of crisis facts and the dispelling of rumors, (c) the sharing of crisis stories, (d) the sharing of crisis reactions, (e) the empowerment of survivors, and (f) a closing. To help the school psychologist understand a classroom-based crisis intervention session, Table 15.4 provides an outline for this crisis intervention.

Following a classroom-based crisis intervention session, all caregivers and parents need to be informed about how they can help students cope. After the session has ended, at least one, but preferably all, of the facilitators should remain with the students. At the very least, a school psychologist should be available to students throughout the remainder of the school day

Table 15.4. Classroom-Based Crisis Intervention Elements

1. Introduction
   Duration: 10–15 minutes
   Activities/Goals:
   - Facilitators are identified.
   - Session purpose, sequence, and rules (including confidentiality) are explained.
   - Students are told that they are not allowed to leave the room without permission.
   - Students are told that attendance/active participation is voluntary.
2. Provision of crisis facts and the dispelling of rumors.
   Duration: up to 30 minutes
   Activities/Goals:
   - Provide crisis facts/dispel rumors: The novelty of the situation may make it difficult for students to understand facts. Thus, facilitators should be prepared to repeat them. Young children, in particular, may have difficulty understanding the event.
   - Let student questions determine the facts offered: Adults should not give unasked-for details that might unnecessarily frighten participants.
3. Sharing of crisis stories
   Duration: 30–60 minutes
   Activities/Goals:
   - Students share personal crisis stories.
   - Stories are validated.
   - Students are helped to feel more connected to each other by explicitly pointing out common experiences.
4. Sharing of crisis reactions
   Duration: 30 minutes
   Activities/Goals:
   - Students share personal crisis reactions.
   - Students are taught about common reactions.
   - Most initial stress reactions are identified as normal: Reactions are normalized by explicitly pointing out the commonalities of student reactions. Students are told what to do if they are unable to manage their reactions.
5. Empowerment of survivors
   Duration: up to 60 minutes
   Activities/Goals:
   - Help students regain some sense of control.
   - Help students identify coping strategies.
   - Teach basic stress management techniques.
6. Closing
   Duration: up to 30 minutes:
   Activities/Goals:
   - Development of memorials, preparation for attending or participating in funerals, the writing of get-well cards and letters to victims, and, if the class has experienced the death of a classmate or teacher, discussion of what to do with the deceased's desk and belongings.

to allow students additional opportunities to obtain support and answers to questions. This also gives facilitators additional opportunities to assess how individual students are coping.

Finally, as soon as possible after a classroom-based crisis intervention, facilitators should debrief the session. This debriefing typically occurs at the end of the school day and serves two purposes. First, it allows for discussion of student reactions and decisions regarding who will need additional crisis intervention. Second, facilitators must attend to their own reactions and coping. In particular, special attention needs to be directed toward the teacher who may have participated in the session. If needed, crisis intervention services should be made available to the teacher and other classroom-based crisis intervention team members.

Individual crisis intervention. This is the most intense and directive Tier 2 crisis intervention that the school psychologist provides and often serves as the gateway to Tier 3 interventions. It employs a basic problem-solving model and has as its primary purpose helping individuals who are in crisis reestablish immediate coping. Additional goals include (a) providing physical support and ensuring physical and psychological safety, (b) providing emotional support and beginning to contain distress, (c) identifying crisis-generated problems, (d) supporting adaptive coping and beginning the problem-solving process, and (e) assessing trauma risk and linking the student (or staff member) to helping resources (Brock et al., 2009).

Sometimes an immediate individual crisis intervention is all that is needed for the student (or staff member) to be able to solve crisis-related problems. However, it is important to point out that crisis resolution is not the goal of this intervention. Rather, it aims at making certain that the crisis survivor is moving in the right direction toward crisis resolution (which may include referral to a Tier 3 psychotherapy intervention).

General suggestions for providing individual crisis intervention, offered by Brymer et al. (2006), include helping children to verbalize their feelings, concerns, and questions and providing simple labels for common emotional reactions (e.g., "mad," "sad," "scared," "worried"). When providing individual crisis intervention it is also important for the crisis intervener's language to parallel the child's developmental level. For example, children 12 years and under typically have much less understanding of abstract concepts and metaphors compared to adults. Thus, it is critical to use direct and simple language. On the other hand, adolescents often appreciate having their feelings, concerns, and questions addressed in an adult-like rather than child-like manner.

Elements of an individual crisis intervention included in the PREPaRE model are adapted from the psychological first-aid techniques put forward by Brymer et al. (2006). These elements are (a) establish contact, (b) verify readiness to proceed, (c) identify and prioritize crisis-related problems, (d) address crisis problems, and (e) evaluate and conclude the intervention. As this is an individual intervention, the time frame for individual psychological first-aid can range from a few minutes to several hours. An outline for an individual crisis intervention is provided in Table 15.5.

Psychotherapeutic Interventions

While some combination of Tier 1 and Tier 2 crisis interventions will be sufficient for most students, it is important to recognize that for the most severely traumatized these interventions are only the first step in a longer term psychotherapeutic treatment process, a process that is considered tertiary prevention. It is essential for school psychologists to have knowledge of these Tier 3 crisis intervention treatments. In general, cognitive–behavioral approaches have been suggested to be most effective in the treatment of trauma-related psychopathology (Watson et al., 2011). Specific examples of empirically supported cognitive–behavioral

treatments include (a) Trauma-Focused Cognitive-Behavioral Therapy (Leenarts, Diehle, Doreleijers, Jansma, & Lindauer, 2012) and (b) School-Based Group Cognitive-Behavioral Therapy (Nadeem, Jaycox, Kataoka, Langley, & Stein, 2011; Silverman et al., 2008).

Given the long-term therapeutic nature of these interventions, parental consent is required before initiating any of these forms of treatment. In addition, while school psychologists have been identified as potential providers of trauma-focused cognitive–behavioral therapy (Rolfsnes & Idsoe, 2011), the psychotherapeutic skill required to successfully implement these intervention options may exceed that of many school psychologists. Supporting this observation, an examination of the NASP *Standards for Graduate Preparation of School Psychologists* (NASP, 2010b) reveals no specific expectation for the development of the cognitive–behavioral skills severely traumatized children and youth will require. Thus, while all school psychologists are expected to know about these treatments and make appropriate referrals, not all can be expected to provide these crisis interventions.

Examine

The effectiveness of crisis intervention employed following a school-associated crisis event needs to be examined. This should always be done by the school psychologist and other crisis team members after an incident and may include a focus group of those involved in the intervention to help gather feedback. Key questions to ask include: (a) Was the school's crisis intervention plan implemented as designed? (b) Were all appropriate crisis intervention roles and duties fulfilled? If not, why not? (c) Did the interventions address the physical and psychological needs of staff, students, and families? (d) Which interventions were most successful and why? (e) Did the crisis intervention address students with special needs? (f) What in the plan needs to be modified? (g) What other planning actions will facilitate future recovery efforts?

An all too often ignored element of concluding a crisis intervention is "caring for the caregiver." School personnel who respond to crisis situations will, as a result, also have been exposed to the event. For example, they will have experienced the emotional pain and trauma of those directly affected. Brock et al. (2009) report that it is the norm for school psychologists to report having experienced crisis reactions subsequent to their crisis intervention work, with physical reactions in general and fatigue or exhaustion being the most common. Thus, it is

Table 15.5. Elements of Individual Crisis Intervention

1. Establish psychological contact
    a. Introduction:
        i. Identify yourself
        ii. Inquire about and, as indicated, address basic needs
    b. Empathy:
        i. Identify crisis facts
        ii. Identify crisis-related feelings
    c. Respect:
        i. Pause to listen
        ii. Do not dominate the conversation
        iii. Do not try to smooth things over
    d. Warmth:
        i. Ensure verbal communication is congruent with nonverbal behaviors
        ii. Consider the use of and, as indicted, provide physical contact
2. Verify emotional readiness to begin problem identification and problem solving
    a. If not, stabilize the student
    b. If the student is ready, begin the problem-solving process
3. Identify and prioritize crisis-generated problems: Identify the most immediate concerns
    a. Inquire about what happened: Understand the crisis story
    b. Inquire about the problems generated by the crisis event
    c. Rank the order of crisis-generated problems
4. Address crisis-generated problems: Encourage the crisis survivor to be as responsible for coping with crisis-generated challenges as is possible
    a. Ask about coping attempts already made: Validate adaptive coping strategies already identified by the student
    b. Facilitate exploration of additional coping strategies: As indicated, encourage the student to identify his or her own adaptive coping strategies
    c. Propose other alternative coping strategies: As indicated, do not hesitate to explicitly direct the student toward adaptive coping strategies
        i. If lethality is low and the student is capable of action, then take a facilitative stance (i.e., the crisis survivor initiates and is responsible for coping actions)
        ii. If lethality is high or the student is not capable of acting, then take a directive stance (i.e., the crisis intervener initiates and is responsible for coping actions)
5. Evaluate and conclude the individual crisis intervention session: Ensure the student is moving toward adaptive crisis resolution
    a. Secure identifying information: Identify and ensure connection with primary natural social support systems (e.g., parents, teachers)
    b. Agree on a time for contacting again/follow up
    c. Assess if immediate coping has been restored
        i. Physical/emotional support has been obtained, and any lethality reduced
        ii. Crisis problems identified and adaptive coping initiated
        iii. From an assessed trauma risk level the student is linked to appropriate helping resources
            • If these goals have not been obtained, then recycle the individual crisis intervention process
            • If these goals have been obtained, the student should be complimented on his or her problem-solving skill, given the expectation that he or she will cope well with the trauma, and then the immediate psychological crisis intervention is concluded

Note. From *School Crisis Prevention and Intervention: The PREPaRE Model* (pp. 232–233), by S. E. Brock, A. B. Nickerson, M. A. Reeves, S. R. Jimerson, R. A. Lieberman, and T. A. Feinberg, 2009, Bethesda, MD: National Association of School Psychologists. Copyright 2009 by the National Association of School Psychologists. Adapted with permission.

critical that caring for the caregiver be an element of all school crisis intervention team protocols.

SUMMARY

While most crisis victims can be expected to recover independently and/or with the assistance of naturally occurring social support systems, some will require more direct crisis intervention. School psychologists are expected to be able to assess individual need for crisis intervention and match interventions to this need.

A hierarchical multitiered approach to school crisis intervention includes universal (Tier 1), selected (Tier 2), and indicated (Tier 3) interventions and spans primary, secondary, and tertiary levels of prevention. Universal primary prevention begins with efforts to prevent crises, to prepare for the fact that not all crises can be prevented, and keeping individuals safe and minimizing crisis exposure.

Immediately following a crisis, universal secondary interventions address physical safety and foster perceptions of safety. As immediate Tier 1 crisis interventions take place and conclude, the next step is to evaluate psychological trauma, and to then provide universal and selected secondary interventions. Still at Tier 1, these interventions begin with reestablishing social support. Recognizing that simply reconnecting individuals with friends and family is not always sufficient, the next level of crisis intervention involves providing psychological education on what happened and how to adaptively respond to the situation. At this point selected (Tier 2) interventions begin with the student psychoeducational group. Moving beyond instruction on how to cope with the crisis, and into activities that facilitate processing of experiences and reactions, are the psychological interventions (classroom-based and individual crisis interventions).

If an individual develops mental illness (e.g., post-traumatic stress disorder), the most directive and intense of the psychological interventions is psychotherapy. This indicated (Tier 3) intervention is a form of tertiary prevention, and cognitive–behavioral therapies were suggested to be the most effective treatments.

AUTHOR NOTE

The authors wish to acknowledge Julie Davis and Shane Jimerson, who contributed to the versions of this chapter that appeared in *Best Practices V* and to members of the NASP PREPaRE workgroup, who contributed to the model of crisis intervention described in this chapter. We also thank CSU, Sacramento, school psychology students Michelle Esparza, Audrey Larkin, Eric Vernon-Cole, and Olivia Weatherbee who assisted in writing this chapter.

Stephen E. Brock, Melissa A. Louvar Reeves, and Amanda B. Nickerson have a financial interest in books they authored or coauthored referenced in this chapter.

REFERENCES

Ben–Zur, H., Gil, S., & Shamshins, Y. (2012). The relationship between exposure to terror through the media, coping strategies and resources, and distress and secondary traumatization. *International Journal of Stress Management, 19*, 132–150. doi:10.1037/a0027864

Brock, S. E., & Davis, J. (2008). Best practices in school crisis intervention. In A. Thomas & J. Grimes (Eds.), *Best practices in school psychology V* (781–798). Bethesda, MD: National Association of School Psychologists.

Brock, S. E., Nickerson, A. B., Reeves, M. A., & Jimerson, S. R. (2008). Best practices for school psychologists as members of crisis teams: The PREPaRE model. In A. Thomas & J. Grimes (Eds.), *Best practices in school psychology V* (1487–1504). Bethesda, MD: National Association of School Psychologists.

Brock, S. E., Nickerson, A. B., Reeves, M. A., Jimerson, S. R., Feinberg, T., & Lieberman, R. (2009). *School crisis prevention and intervention: The PREPaRE model.* Bethesda, MD: National Association of School Psychologists.

Brymer, M. J., Jacobs, A., Layne, C., Pynoos, R. S., Ruzek, J., Steinberg, A., & Watson, P. (2006). *Psychological first-aid: Field operations guide* (2nd ed.). Los Angeles, CA: National Child Traumatic Stress Network and National Center for PTSD. Retrieved from http://www.nctsn.org/content/psychological-first-aid

Cicero, S. D., Nooner, K., & Silva, R. (2011). Vulnerability and resilience in childhood trauma and PTSD. In V. Ardino (Ed.), *Post-traumatic syndromes in childhood and adolescence: A handbook of research and practice* (pp. 43–60). New York, NY: Wiley-Blackwell.

Dyb, G., Jensen, T. K., & Nygaard, E. (2011). Children's and parent's posttraumatic stress reactions after the 2004 tsunami. *Clinical Child Psychology and Psychiatry, 16*, 621–634. doi:10.1177/1359104510391048

Everly, G. S. (2003). Early psychological intervention: A word of caution. *International Journal of Emergency Mental Health, 5*, 179–184. Retrieved from http://www.chevronpublishing.com/product.cfm?dispprodid=480

Flitsch, E., Magnesi, J., & Brock, S. E. (2012). Social media and crisis intervention. In S. E. Brock & S. R. Jimerson (Eds.), *Best practices in school crisis prevention and intervention* (2nd ed., pp. 287–304). Bethesda, MD: National Association of School Psychologists.

Frazier, P., Tashiro, T., Bennan, M., Steger, M., & Long, J. (2004). Correlates of levels and patterns of positive life change following sexual assault. *Journal of Consulting & Clinical Psychology, 72*, 19–30. doi:10.1037/0022-006X.72.1.19

Kramer, D. N., & Landolt, M. A. (2011). Characteristics and efficacy of early psychological interventions in children and adolescents after single trauma: A meta-analysis. *European Journal of Psychotraumatology, 2*, 1–24. doi:10.3402/ejpt.v2i0.7858

Leenarts, L. E., Diehle, J., Doreleijers, T. A. H., Jansma, E. P., & Lindauer, R. J. L. (2012). Evidenced-based treatments for children with trauma-related psychopathology as a result of childhood maltreatment: A systematic review. *European Journal of Child and Adolescent Psychiatry.* Advanced online publication. doi:10.1007/s00787-012-0367-5

Litz, B. T., Gray, M. J., Bryant, R. A., & Adler, A. (2002). Early intervention for trauma: Current status and future directions. *Clinical Psychology: Science and Practice, 9*, 112–134. doi:10.1093/clipsy.9.2.112

McDermott, B., Berry, H., & Cobham, V. (2012). Social connectedness: A potential aetiological factor in the development of child post-traumatic stress disorder. *Australian and New Zealand Journal of Psychiatry, 46*, 109–117. doi:10.1177/0004867411433950

Mitchell, J. T., & Everly, G. S. (2001). *Critical incident stress debriefing: An operations manual for CISD, defusing and other group crisis intervention services* (3rd ed.). Ellicott City, MD: Chevron.

Moos, R., & Billings, A. (1984). Conceptualizing and measuring coping resources and processes. In L. Goldberger & S. Breznitz (Eds.), *Handbook of stress: Theoretical and clinical aspects* (pp. 109–145). New York, NY: Macmillan.

Nadeem, E., Jaycox, L. H., Kataoka, S. H., Langley, A. K., & Stein, B. D. (2011). Going to scale: Experiences implementing a school-based trauma intervention. *School Psychology Review, 40,* 549–568. Retrieved from http://www.nasponline.org/publications/spr/index-list.aspx

National Association of School Psychologists. (NASP, 2010a). *Model for comprehensive and integrated school psychological services*. Bethesda, MD: Author. Retrieved from http://www.nasponline.org/standards/2010standards/2_PracticeModel.pdf

National Association of School Psychologists. (NASP, 2010b). *Standards for graduate preparation of school psychologists*. Bethesda, MD: Author. Retrieved from http://www.nasponline.org/standards/2010standards/1_Graduate_Preparation.pdf

National Institute of Mental Health. (2001). *Mental health and mass violence: Evidence-based early psychological intervention for victims/survivors of mass violence. A workshop to reach consensus on best practices*. Washington, DC: Author. Retrieved from http://www.nimh.nih.gov/health/publications/massviolence.pdf

National Organization for Victim Assistance. (1998). *Responding to communities in crisis*. Alexandria, VA: Author.

Neria, Y., & Sullivan, G. M. (2011). Understanding the mental health effects of indirect exposure to mass trauma through the media. *Journal of the American Medical Association, 306,* 1374–1375. doi:10.1001/jama.2011.1358

Nooner, K. B., Linares, O., Batinjane, J., Kramer, R. A., Silva, R., & Cloitre, M. (2012). Factors related to posttraumatic stress disorder in adolescence. *Trauma Violence Abuse, 13,* 153–166. doi:10.1177/1524838012447698

Reeves, M. A., Kanan, L. M., & Plog, A. E. (2010). *Comprehensive planning for safe learning environments: A school professional's guide to integrating physical and psychological safety: Prevention through recovery*. New York, NY: Routledge.

Rolfsnes, E. S., & Idsoe, T. (2011). School-based intervention programs for PTSD symptoms: A review and meta-analysis. *Journal of Traumatic Stress, 24,* 155–165. doi:10.1002/jts.20622

Schneider, T., Walker, H., & Sprague, J. (2000). *Safe school design: A handbook for educational leaders: Applying the principles of crime prevention through environmental design*. Eugene, OR: ERIC Clearinghouse on Educational Management. Retrieved from http://eric.ed.gov/?id=ED449541

Shaw, J. A. (2003). Children exposed to war/terrorism. *Clinical Child and Family Psychology Review, 6,* 237–246. doi:10.1023/B:CCFP.0000006291.10180.bd

Silverman, W. K., Ortiz, C. D., Viswesvaran, C., Burns, B. J., Kolko, D. J., Putnam, F. W., & Amaya-Jackson, L. (2008). Evidence-based psychosocial treatments for children and adolescents exposed to traumatic events. *Journal of Clinical Child Adolescent Psychology, 37,* 156–183. doi:10.1080/15374410701818293

Terr, L. C. (1992). Mini-marathon groups: Psychological "first aid" following disasters. *Bulletin of the Menninger Clinic, 56,* 76–86.

U.S. Department of Education. (2010). *School emergency management online course*. Washington, DC: Author. Retrieved from http://ebookbrowse.com/rems-course-emergencyplan-pdf-d82817160

U.S. Department of Homeland Security. (2008). *National incident management system*. Washington, DC: Author. Retrieved from http://www.fema.gov/national-incident-management-system

Watson, P. J., Brymer, M. J., & Bonanno, G. A. (2011). Post-disaster psychological intervention since 9/11. *American Psychologist, 66,* 482–494. doi:10.1037/a0024806

Wessely, S., Bryant, R. A., Greenberg, N., Earnshaw, M., Sharpley, J., & Hughes, J. H. (2008). Does psychoeducation help prevent post traumatic psychological distress? *Psychiatry, 71,* 287–302. doi:10.1521/psyc.2008.71.4.287

16 Best Practices in School Violence Prevention

Jim Larson
University of Wisconsin-Whitewater
Sarah Mark
Madison (WI) Metropolitan School District

OVERVIEW

"Am I doing everything that I can to ensure the safety of the children and adults in my school?" Who among us has not asked such a question after reading the latest heart-wrenching headline? There is arguably no greater responsibility that educators share than the physical and psychological well-being of the students under their care. In its many forms, school violence is dimensional in severity and manifests from mean-spirited teasing to targeted multiple homicide.

School violence prevention is the science and practice of managing what is knowable and mitigating the effects of what is not. The last half-century of prevention science has provided the blueprints for educators to create safer and more effective schools for all children. School psychologists now have access to a wealth of research-supported programs and procedures in areas such as social–emotional learning; bullying prevention; anger management; and crisis prevention, mitigation, and response. As data-based practitioners and child advocates, school psychologists can play critical roles in helping to bring that science forward and in doing so have a positive impact on the safety and well-being of the children and families they serve.

The purpose of this chapter is to assist school psychologists in that worthy effort. To that end, the information in this chapter will provide a brief overview of the status of violence in the schools, suggested areas of additional competencies to increase professional effectiveness, the structure and procedures for assessing and understanding the violence prevention needs of any particular school, and a discussion of violence prevention programs and procedures organized by the three prevention tiers.

Over the past decade, the subject of school violence prevention has evolved from a small niche for a few academics and interested school psychologists to a mainstream area of training and practice. A 2012 review of international online databases found that 771 peer-reviewed articles with the words *school violence* in the title have been published since the year 2000, up from only 21 in 1993 (Larson & Beckman, 2012). Assisting in this trend, a dedicated journal, the *Journal of School Violence*, began publication in 2001. In recent years, educators have come to recognize the link between safe environments and academic success and, along with that, the limitations inherent in relying primarily on the use of exclusionary discipline as a response to aggressive behavior. As a consequence, considerably more attention is now paid at the school level to positive behavioral supports, bully prevention, threat assessment and response, and anger management intervention. School psychologists, individually and collectively through the National Association of School Psychologists (NASP) initiatives and publications, have taken leadership roles in each of these areas.

There is no denying that the high profile school shootings that occurred in the late 1990s changed the face of public education in the United States. Doors that were once opened were now locked, and a new and chilling vocabulary emerged. Terms such as *threat assessment*, *risk factors*, *school shooter*, and *hit list* made their way into the school lexicon. Although the frequency of those tragic, multiple homicide events has abated, due in part to increased vigilance and organized prevention efforts by both students and school staff members, the tragedy in Newtown, CT, in December 2012, once again brought reminders of vulnerability and the recognition that school-associated homicide is still a fact of life both in the United States and internationally.

Between July 2009 and July 2010, there were 17 school-associated homicides of students ages 5–18 in American schools (Robers, Zhang, & Truman, 2012), a total that maintained a declining trend over the past 2 decades. In contrast to the rampage attacks that occurred in the late 1990s, more recent student homicides in and around school are much more likely to be the result of a conflict between two individuals that leads to the death of one of them. Whereas the likelihood of a targeted homicide occurring in any one particular school is exceedingly remote, the horrific prospect demands ongoing but reasoned vigilance. An essential feature of such vigilance is the provision of a safe and supportive learning environment for all students.

Consequently, it is not homicide directly, but rather the other more prevalent behaviors—chronic bullying, mean-spirited teasing, sexual harassment, relational aggression, and fighting—that school psychologists and other educators seek to prevent on a day-to-day basis. A fight between or among students in the school setting can be an extraordinarily disruptive and frightening event that can easily spiral out of control.

According to the National Center for Educational Statistics in its *Indicators of School Crime and Safety 2011* (Robers et al., 2012), in 2009, 31% of students in grades 9–12 reported that they had been in a physical fight in the past 12 months, and 11% reported that they had fought on school property. Although male students were more likely to have been in a fight, 23% of female students reported that they had been in a physical fight in the past year, and 7% of this fighting took place on school property, a slight decrease from previous reports (Robers et al., 2012). Students are not the only ones to face the problem of physical violence in school. During the 2007–2008 school year, 4% of teachers reported that they were physically attacked by a student (Robers et al., 2012).

This level of violence is not equally distributed among all students and all schools. Examining for racial differences, the *Indicators of School Crime and Safety 2011* (Robers et al., 2012) report found that 9% of Caucasian students and 8% of Asian students reported having been in a fight on school property compared to 17% of African American students, 14% of Hispanic students, and 21% of American Indian/Alaska Native students. The presence of gangs in the school environment shows

similar inequality of racial distribution, with 14% of Caucasian students reporting gang presence compared to 33% of Hispanic students, 31% of African American students, and 17% of Asian students.

The fact that many minority students tend to be concentrated in the largest urban school districts and poorest federal reservations helps to explain this disparity. Schools located in economically depressed neighborhoods where street crime, drugs, and gang activity thrive are at increased risk to experience problems with student behavior and school safety (Sprague, 2007). For example, during the 2011–2012 school year 882 students were arrested inside the New York City public schools (Lieberman, 2012). During the same period, 319 Chicago public school students were shot on city streets, 24 fatally (Sleven, 2012).

School psychologists are aware that students often bring unresolved neighborhood conflicts with them into the school building where they can erupt into violence. In describing life at a New York City high school, Mateu-Gelabert and Lune (2007) observed: "Students came to school with a set of expectations (learning in an academic environment without having to be concerned for their safety). Yet, many found, they needed first to deal with the street behavior they found in school" (p. 187).

No student should come to school routinely expecting to be bullied, sexually harassed, beaten up, or otherwise victimized, and yet many do. Understanding, addressing, and evaluating the many variables associated with preventing student violence presents challenges for school psychologists across communities and across individual schools. For some school psychologists, the dominant issue may be preventing verbal and relational bullying while others must struggle daily with how to prevent street violence from erupting in the school building. In either case, school psychologists recognize the importance that a safe, welcoming, and nurturing environment plays in the educational process and daily bring their training and expertise to the challenges presented.

In the Preventive and Responsive Services domain of the NASP *Model for Comprehensive and Integrated School Psychological Services* (NASP, 2010), school psychologists are urged to bring evidence-based prevention and intervention practices to address the academic, social– emotional, and behavioral needs of all students. Consistent with NASP recommendations, effective school violence prevention follows a multitiered, problem-solving model that brings both preventive services for all students as well as targeted, intensive supports for students with the greatest needs. Given the link between a safe school environment and positive student outcomes, it is critical that school psychologists, in collaboration with fellow educators, help all schools develop comprehensive, evidence-supported approaches to school violence prevention.

BASIC CONSIDERATIONS

What do school psychologists need to know and be able to do to address school violence? Not surprisingly, the answer to this question lies in the same competencies that school psychologists need to be successful in the other areas of professional practice. Preventing school violence is no longer an esoteric subspecialty of general practice. Rather, it is the outcome of effective modern day, prevention-oriented school psychology aimed at enhancing learning opportunities for all students. To understand the issues associated with school violence subsumes both an array of practice concerns with which most school psychologists have training and skill as well as less familiar, more focused areas. For many practitioners, functional assessment of anger-related student aggression, bullying prevention, needs assessment design, classroom/school-wide discipline procedures, and crisis management may be accustomed practice areas, whereas target hardening, threat assessment, primary and secondary prevention procedures, victim support, and school–community coalition building may be comparatively new ground. Four critical contextual areas of competency applied specifically to school violence prevention are summarized next.

Understand the Roots of Local Violence

In the school setting, violence manifests in numerous forms, often reflecting the socioeconomic condition of the surrounding neighborhood from where the students are drawn. If there are street gang problems, high criminality, heavy drug use, and/or racial strife outside of school, one can be comparatively certain that there will be spillover into the school buildings. In the same fashion, in low crime neighborhoods where perhaps extensive cyberbullying takes place outside of school and powerful social cliques regularly exert their negative influences, these schools must also prepare for the inevitable problems. Although the organizational and social structure of the school does influence the probability of some forms of violence (e.g., schools are fertile grounds for bullying but less so for fighting), it is often more useful to the practitioner to think of school

violence more broadly as violent behavior occurring on school property. Consequently, to achieve a deeper understanding and to prevent violence in the school setting, one must also strive to understand the social, cultural, psychological, and economic influences of the greater community context within which it occurs.

For instance, school psychologists should be alert to the ways in which violent street codes create social and psychological pressure on some students—including those otherwise doing well—to respond aggressively to perceived provocations from classmates or teachers. Big city or small, a change in recent immigration trends can foster growing racial divides, and these issues can raise tensions that students bring with them into the building. In many communities, the complicated access to oversubscribed community mental health service can have implications for service delivery priorities in the schools.

School psychologists are aware that the exterior influences on the level of violence in any given building are idiosyncratic to the community around it. It is important for school psychologists to acquire a firm understanding of the nature and extent of these influences by drawing upon community resources best positioned to be knowledgeable. For example, collaborative relationships with the mental health community, law enforcement, social services, or health providers can provide school personnel with alternative perspectives and open avenues to multitargeted prevention strategies.

Use Effective Data-Based Decision Making

Horrific occurrences in schools, such as those at Columbine, CO, in April 1999 and Newtown, CT, in December 2012, understandably frighten parents, students, educators, and the general public. At such times, media-fed rumors and misstatements of fact abound, and the potential for schools and communities to fall victim to recency bias and emotionally driven decision making is high. Should the school hire armed guards? Purchase metal detectors? Allow concealed carry in the school buildings? Aware of this, school psychologists can assist in bringing all violence prevention options under administrative consideration into the light of scientific inquiry, establishing what the published data say about *this* prevention measure under *these* circumstances. In such times, school boards and administrators are often under intense pressure to respond to community fears, and school psychologists are professionally and educationally well positioned to be of significant assistance.

Nurture a Strong Mental Health Focus

In the aftermath of every incident of homicidal violence in the school setting come the often justifiable hand wringing and finger pointing directed at the mental health delivery system. School psychologists are cognizant of the fact that a significant percentage of children's mental health needs are met in the school setting. Effective school violence prevention requires a vibrant and competent school-based mental health delivery system of skilled direct and indirect intervention and containing strong collaborative relationships with community mental health services. Efforts are directed at creating school connections and school bonding among all students, particularly those who show evidence of struggle in these regards. Such a system must avoid poorly informed calls for the use of student profiling as an alleged prevention method. Rather, school psychologists and other school professionals should provide ongoing, multisource mental health information to students, teachers, and the public and pursue efforts to ease child and adolescent access to treatment.

Prepare to Respond

In spite of the best efforts of schools to prevent all forms of violence, tragic occurrences are inevitable. No school, with full assurance, can prevent a highly motivated individual from inflicting deadly harm inside its walls. Although the statistical likelihood of a single or multiple homicide on school grounds is exceedingly remote, school psychologists must ensure that school personnel are prepared to respond, even in the unlikely eventuality. As Larson and Beckman (2012) observed:

> Homicide and other assaults with deadly weapons bring the danger of the outside world into the safety of the school building, and most often with forethought and purpose. The envelope of civility, rules, structure, and predictability becomes violated, and the coping mechanisms of individuals are put to the test. The traumatic effects on the larger population of the school will vary along multiple dimensions, including event exposure and predisposing psychological risk factors. (p. 224)

The full range of school violence prevention includes the need for school psychologists to become skilled in the many aspects of school crisis prevention and intervention as outlined in Brock (see Chapter 15). School personnel trained in NASP's PREPaRE model are well situated to assist in creating a structure to enhance prevention measures as well as manage the aftermath of a tragic incident of school violence.

BEST PRACTICES IN SCHOOL VIOLENCE PREVENTION

School violence prevention efforts are best conceptualized as the product of a problem-solving process applied to the now familiar multitiered model of service delivery. The application of problem solving to violence prevention involves a five-step process: Step 1, problem identification; Step 2, problem analysis; Step 3, problem response proposals; Step 4, response implementation; and Step 5, evaluation of prevention strategies. The foundations of this application have been described in depth elsewhere (e.g., Larson & Busse, 2012). While the process is typically recursive and may involve frequent loops back to previous steps for clarifying information, the directional flow is as follows: In Steps 1 and 2, an issue of school safety is identified, assessed, and reframed as a gap between existing conditions and desirable conditions of safety. In Step 3, assessment-informed changes or interventions are proposed to close the gap. In Step 4, they are implemented at one or more of the prevention tiers. In Step 5, the changes are evaluated in both a formative and summative fashion and recommendations for maintenance or additional changes are made.

Team Planning Structure

Planning and decision making for school violence prevention, like most other broadly based initiatives in the school, should be managed in a representative team format. The essential qualities of what may be called the School Safety Team are diverse representation among major stakeholders and enthusiasm for the task. School psychologists should take leadership roles in ensuring that the team is reflective of the cultural composition of the school and community. In addition to the school psychologist with skills in assessment and progress monitoring, core team membership should include individuals with one or more of the following competencies: (a) knowledge of the community, (b) teaching of social and emotional learning, (c) law enforcement, (d) counseling, (e) school discipline, and (f) concerns of parents (see Table 16.1). School psychologists who have overseen the implementation of NASP's incident command system model, PREPaRE, will have an identified group of professionals appropriate for membership on the School Safety Team.

Table 16.1. Sample School Safety Team Membership

Sample Core Prevention Coordinating Team
- Principal or designee (ex officio)
- School psychologist
- School social worker
- General education teacher representative
- Special education teacher representative
- Student (middle or high school)
- Parent representative (e.g., PTA leader, disability/ diversity advocacy group leader)
- Community representative (e.g., police liaison, clergy, local merchant)

Supplementary Coordinating Team Members
- School nurse (crisis planning)
- Curriculum specialist
- Behavior specialist
- Community agency representative
- University faculty

Assessment-Driven Decision Making

In a multitier, problem-solving model, the initial task for the violence prevention planning team involves defining the problem, and school psychologists can apply skills in data-based assessment to assist in the design and analysis of a comprehensive needs assessment. The results will generate important information from which to begin planning as well as provide a preintervention baseline to assist in ongoing program evaluation. National school violence prevalence studies have utility for forming broad national and regional public policy, but are not as helpful when it comes to helping a specific district or school to evaluate the most pressing needs on their school campuses. To plan effectively and implement a school violence prevention program, each school needs to conduct a needs assessment that is tailored to understanding the particular local concerns of all identified stakeholders.

The traditional mechanism used to gather this type of information is self-report surveys of staff, students, and parents. This assessment should provide data regarding the current level of prevention efforts from a multi-systemic viewpoint that looks at environmental modifications, school-wide programs, classroom initiatives, and targeted individual interventions. School psychologists may find it helpful to begin the needs assessment process with a series of listening sessions with teachers and other staff members during which participants are asked to raise their concerns regarding school safety. Open-ended questions are particularly useful, such as, "We are interested in making some changes so that our school is safer for everyone. Where do you think we

should start?" The information gleaned from these meetings can serve as a guide for school psychologists during the item development phase for the needs assessment survey. A useful guide for writing such surveys is available from the University of Kansas (http://ctb.ku.edu/en/tablecontents/sub_section_main_1042.aspx). A model needs assessment survey for school staff members was developed by the Melissa Institute for Violence Prevention and Treatment (http://www.teachsafeschools.org/checklist.html).

In addition, school safety climate data from student self-reports are useful for both prevention planning as well as formative and summative evaluations. *The California School Climate and Safety Survey–Short Form* (Furlong et al., 2005; http://www.michaelfurlong.info/CSCSS/cscss-forms) is a 52-item revision of an original 102-item form. This well-designed scale yields self-report information from students in three principal areas: school danger, school climate, and school victimization.

Information that is initially sought for needs assessment purposes can later provide feedback about the patterns, trends, and correlates of violence-related behaviors. For example, examining discipline data and assessing the campus settings where reported violence occurs can be useful to augment the validity of self-report data. Contextual information is important to gather because strategies to prevent or inhibit violent behavior on campus may include modification of setting variables such as the school's physical plant and supervision allocation. Web-based software is available to assist schools in the accumulation and analysis of these data. The School-Wide Information System (http://www.pbisapps.org/Pages/Default.aspx) is a Web-based office referral organization and monitoring system designed to help school personnel use office referral data in the development of student interventions.

Data from all sources need to be analyzed to develop hypotheses, with the ultimate goal of understanding why the problem is occurring. These results are then shared with faculty, students, and the community. An important task for the School Safety Team is to communicate the results in a manner so that all of the stakeholders understand the problem in the most useful and effective fashion. School psychologists can assume leadership in this area by (a) assisting all parties to understand issues associated with the validity and reliability of surveys and other forms of gathered data, (b) developing data-based conclusions from the information gathered, and (c) ensuring communication of the findings to students and other stakeholders in a developmentally and linguistically sensitive manner.

With the data gathered and analyzed, the time has come to consider prevention strategies. The target units of support are populations of students identified by relative risk status and the school, home, and community systems that can be effectively influenced to address those risks. In other words, the team will ask: "What do all of our students need?" (universal prevention programs); "What do some of our students need?" (selected prevention programs); and "What do a few of our students need?" (indicated prevention programs).

What follows are selected violence prevention programs and procedures appropriate for each prevention tier. Limitation of space prevents a more complete discussion of programs that could represent best practices in this area. Readers are referred to the National Registry of Evidence-Based Programs and Practices (http://www.nrepp.samhsa.gov) and the Hamilton Fish Institute (http://gwired.gwu.edu/hamfish) for additional resources.

Tier 1 Prevention Strategies

At the primary prevention level, universal prevention programs are concerned with providing all school building occupants with architectural/environmental modifications, information, strategies, and coping responses designed to prevent or mitigate the occurrence of violent, antisocial behaviors. Examples of school violence–oriented universal prevention efforts include architectural design features such as adequate lighting and open sightlines to discourage problem behavior and building access control policies that may include the presence of armed personnel. Well-conceived and enforced codes of school conduct and classroom-based socioemotional curricula are essential features of a universal prevention program.

Crime Prevention Through Environmental Design

Sprague (2007) posited four sources of school vulnerability that may be implicated in any incident of school violence: (a) design, use, and supervision of school space; (b) administrative practices; (c) characteristics of the surrounding neighborhood; and (d) characteristics of students enrolled. The most neglected of the four, he noted, is the design, use, and supervision of school space. When most schools in the United States were built, the issue of safety from assault did not figure into the architectural plans. Consequently, many school buildings can be easy targets for those who would do harm to the occupants.

The phrase *hardening the target* has entered the vernacular and refers to efforts aimed at making a structure such as a school building safer and less vulnerable to antisocial behavior. Locking exterior doors and increasing the adult presence on the playground are two common examples. In recent years, a more systematic approach to safety-oriented environmental and architectural design procedures can be found in an emerging knowledge base known as Crime Prevention Through Environmental Design (CPTED). CPTED refers to "the broad study and design of environments to encourage desirable behavior, heighten functionality, and decrease antisocial behavior" (Schneider, 2007, p. 4).

A CPTED analysis of a school building will examine (a) the natural surveillance provided by windows, and obstructions such as those afforded by corners and solid doors; (b) the natural access control and how to limit and control entry to the building; and (c) procedures for establishing and enhancing the message of who is in charge, known as territoriality (Schneider, 2007). Two useful surveys, the Basic School CPTED Survey and the Annotated School CPTED Survey are available in Schneider (2007).

School Resource Officers

Following the murders in Newtown, CT, in December 2012, the subject of providing armed adults (private security or local police) in all school buildings across the country was raised, and federal dollars were made available. A school resource officer is a certified law enforcement officer who is permanently assigned to a school or set of schools. School resource officers typically engage in three primary activities: law enforcement, law-related teaching, and mentoring (Myrstol, 2011). In a review of the literature, Myrstol (2011) found consistent support for school resource officers among administrators and teachers but a greater ambivalence among students. School psychologists should be alert to the finding that the presence of school resource officers has the potential to increase the criminalization of student behavior. Schools with school resource officers tend to show a greater number of arrests for disorderly conduct, particularly among students from lower socioeconomic backgrounds (Theriot, 2009). There is, however, emerging support for the role of school resource officers in reducing the incidence of more serious school violence, such as sexual assault, strong armed robbery, and aggravated battery (Jennings, Khey, Maskaly, & Donner, 2011).

Social–Emotional Education

Universal social–emotional curricula can lead to a decrease in student aggression and related behaviors, including disruption, conduct problems, and emotional distress (Durlak, Weissberg, Dymnicki, Taylor, & Schellinger, 2011). These curricula also can lead to an increase in social–emotional skills and positive social behaviors (Durlak et al., 2011). However, not all curricula are created equally. Researchers have identified four key factors that appear to differentiate more effective programs from less effective ones. More effective programs tend to have sequenced activities, use active forms of learning, focus on personal or social skills, and be explicit in targeting specific social–emotional skills (SAFE; Durlak et al., 2011).

Although social–emotional curricula have been shown to be effective in large and diverse samples of students, they seem to be more effective for some groups of students than for others. Students who might benefit more from these programs include younger students and students with higher initial levels of aggression (Conduct Problems Prevention Research Group, 2010). The literature is mixed about the possible effects of socioeconomic status. Some researchers have found that students with lower socioeconomic status benefit more from these programs while others have found that students with higher socioeconomic status benefit more (e.g., Conduct Problems Prevention Research Group, 2010). On the one hand, students with low socioeconomic status are at greater risk for aggressive behaviors and thus may have more potential for improvement with intervention. On the other hand, implementing social–emotional curricula in high poverty schools presents a unique set of challenges, including high mobility, higher levels of teacher stress, and greater difficulties with classroom management (Conduct Problems Prevention Research Group, 2010). More research is needed to understand how socioeconomic status affects the effectiveness of social–emotional curricula and what steps can be taken to best reach students across socioeconomic status levels.

Logistically, universal social–emotional learning programs are relatively low cost and easy to implement. Classroom teachers can successfully implement these programs and, indeed, may be in an ideal position to do so. On a practical note, teachers are already in their classrooms, reducing scheduling and staffing concerns. In addition, at least in the primary grades, teachers are with their students throughout the day, which allows them to help students generalize their new skills in naturally occurring opportunities. Perhaps it is not surprising then that students taught by their teachers, as opposed to other school or nonschool personnel, made gains in the most areas in a recent meta-analysis (Durlak et al., 2011).

Numerous social–emotional curricula are commercially available. Information on specific programs can be found in a variety of sources, including the *Collaborative for Academic, Social, and Emotional Learning 2013 Guide: Effective Social and Emotional Learning Programs* (http://casel.org/guide); the What Works Clearinghouse, maintained by the Institute of Educational Sciences of the U.S. Department of Education (http://www.ies.ed.gov/ncee/wwc); Blueprints for Violence Prevention Model and Promising Programs, maintained by the Center for the Study and Prevention of Violence at the University of Colorado (http://www.colorado.edu/cspv/blueprints); and the National Registry of Evidence-Based Programs and Practices, maintained by the Substance Abuse and Mental Health Services Administration (http://www.nrepp.samhsa.gov).

Tier 2 Prevention Strategies

As the number of potentially harmful risk factors increases and the mediating influence of available protective factors decreases, prevention and learning needs change. The second tier of prevention intensity targets those students who are at higher risk to become involved in serious school violence-related behaviors. These students receive selected prevention services. Students appropriate for such additional service may self-identify through the failure of universal efforts to help them inhibit their anger outbursts or predatory aggressive behavior or they may be proactively identified through systematic risk and protective factor screening procedures. This group may include the more obvious students who are chronic fighters or those who are engaging in bully-related behaviors but also younger students who have multiple identified risk factors who may as yet be drawing less attention. Selected prevention efforts involve coordinated programming that may include additional classroom or building-level positive behavioral supports, systematic skills training through pull-out groups, or community-based individual or family interventions. The goals of selected prevention efforts are to provide students with the knowledge and, importantly, the skills necessary to replace aggressive problem behaviors with more educationally and socially responsible behaviors in and out of the school. When these skills are taught effectively, with attention to maintenance and generalization, higher risk students are more able to participate in and benefit from the myriad school and community opportunities available to all students.

As noted earlier, students from certain ethnic groups are more likely to report involvement in violence at school. Compared with their Caucasian peers, African American and Latino students are also more likely to experience exclusionary discipline policies, including office referrals, out-of-school suspensions, and expulsions (Sullivan, Klingbeil, & Van Norman, 2013). Consequently, the potential for overrepresentation of students from diverse racial, cultural, and socioeconomic backgrounds in Tier 2 interventions must be considered. To offset this potential, it is important to clarify the skills and knowledge school psychologists, teachers, and other school staff members need to interact effectively with students from underserved populations.

Check-In/Check-Out

Check-in/check-out is an efficient, effective way to reach many of the students who require additional behavioral support beyond the universal level. These students are typically identified through the use of office referral data and teacher nominations. Students who participate in check-in/check-out meet briefly with a designated staff member each morning to receive their daily point sheet and discuss their behavioral goals. Students give their point sheet to each of their teachers during the day and receive feedback at the end of each class. At the end of the day, students review their point sheet with a staff member and take their point sheet home to be signed.

Check-in/check-out effectively reduces disruptive and other problematic behaviors of many, though not all, students who require support beyond the universal level (Filter, McKenna, Benedict, & Horner, 2007; McIntosh, Campbell, Carter, & Dickey, 2009). Teachers, students, and parents find it easy to implement, and school staff are able to successfully implement this intervention without outside support (Filter et al., 2007). Check-in/check-out appears to be an effective intervention for students who engage in problematic behaviors in order to receive attention, but might not be appropriate for students who wish to escape from academic activities (McIntosh et al., 2009). An in-depth functional behavior analysis is not necessary at the Tier 2 level and, indeed, would likely limit the number of students able to receive appropriate interventions. However, school psychologists or other staff should consider the function of a student's behavior before recommending that they participate in check-in/check-out.

First Step to Success

First Step to Success is collaborative intervention between the teacher and a student services professional designed for children from preschool to Grade 3 who are exhibiting significant levels of aggressive and/or oppositional behavior. The program uses visual feedback in the form of a bicolored card held up by the teacher and operant reinforcement in form of social praise and classroom reinforcers to modify specific problem behaviors. The student service professional (school psychologist or other, referred to as the consultant) models the intervention in the classroom for a series of 20–30 minute periods over 5 days, turning the intervention over to the teacher on the sixth day. The intervention lasts a minimum of 30 school days, and each day requires anywhere from 30 to 150 minutes of part-time teacher intervention time. There is also a parent education program that focuses on home–school cooperation. Sprague and Perkins (2009) evaluated previous research and found that all children improved on measures of problem behavior, academic engaged time, and teacher-rated behavioral adjustment.

First Step to Success is not a complex intervention, but it is comparatively labor intensive for a busy classroom teacher. Consequently, school psychologists need to be certain to secure a truly informed agreement with the teacher ahead of time so as to help ensure the highest possible intervention integrity.

Parent Management Training

School psychologists who choose to offer Tier 2 prevention services to younger students who are experiencing multisite aggressive behavior, in particular at home and in school, may find it essential to work directly with parents. Groundbreaking work by Patterson and others (e.g., Reid, Patterson, & Snyder, 2002) has provided insight into parenting practices that may unwittingly train and maintain aggressive behavior in children. Providing school-based treatment with students and ignoring possible counter training in the home may hinder or thwart the expected outcomes and lead to frustration for all involved.

Parent management training is a behaviorally focused intervention designed to train parents how to use social learning techniques, in particular operant conditioning, to alter child problem behavior (Kazdin, 2005). It is direct, well supported in the literature, and grounded in techniques with which most school psychologists are very familiar. Two of the most useful treatment manuals can be found in Kazdin (2005) and Kazdin and Rotella (2008). As most school psychologists know, the biggest challenge to school-based parent training is gaining consistent access to the parents with the greatest needs, and parents with the greatest needs often present the greatest challenges in this area. Successful implementation of this intervention may require contractual changes in the work day to allow for after school or evening hours, a budget for transportation and other incentives, and caregivers and facilities for child care.

Coping Power Program

The Coping Power Program is a small-group, cognitive–behavioral intervention for students in fourth through sixth grades. The program consists of 34 sessions with an additional 16 session parent component. The child component of Coping Power Program focuses on (a) goal setting, (b) anger regulation, (c) perspective taking, and (d) social problem solving. The parent component addresses (a) behavior management strategies, (b) family communication, (c) parental involvement in school matters, and (d) parental stress management (Lochman, Boxmeyer, & Powell, 2012). The Coping Power Program produced reductions in self-reported covert delinquent behavior and parent-reported substance abuse at the 1-year follow-up date and lower rates of teacher-reported aggressive behavior (Lochman & Wells, 2003).

Tier 3 Prevention Strategies

The third tier and smallest population requiring violence prevention services are students who will benefit from indicated prevention services. The needs of students at this level have typically proven unresponsive to prevention efforts at the universal or selected levels, and the school's and community's most focused and intensive services are indicated. At the Tier 3 level, prevention goals are typically a matter of maintaining current functioning strengths, with hopes for improvement in self-management skills. From a school violence prevention perspective, students appropriate for indicated prevention services may have repeatedly demonstrated or threatened behavioral aggression of such severity that they pose a danger to others in the school. When explosive anger and aggression are predictable components of a particular individual student's behavior, then school psychologists should take the lead in providing prevention strategies to ensure best the safety of all concerned.

Wraparound

Students whose behavioral self-regulation is so problematic that they pose a danger to themselves and others in the school and other settings are frequently the beneficiaries of a variety of services in and out of the school setting in what has come to be called a *wraparound*

organizational structure. In this context, multiple supports and services are wrapped around the student and, in many cases, the family in an effort to prevent problems from advancing to an even more serious level (see Eber, 2008; see also http://www.pbis.org/school/tertiary_level/wraparound.aspx for wraparound in the positive behavioral interventions and supports context). The wraparound teams are composed of differing memberships for each student and typically facilitated by the school psychologist or other student services professional. Among the primary objectives are to establish effective, problem-solving partnerships among the family, the school, and community resources with goals guided by the youth and family (Eber, 2008). Indicated-level school-based violence prevention strategies within the context of wraparound services might include interventions such as individual anger regulation counseling, aide accompaniment, adjusted school day, mentoring, alternative site placement, and academic support services.

Conflict Prevention and De-Escalation Strategies

Through consultation and inservice training, school psychologists can play an essential role in the task of reducing the potential for volatile student conflicts. Conflict prevention and de-escalation techniques have become an increasingly common topic of professional development for school staff, particularly as laws regarding restraint and seclusion have been enacted. Commercial crisis intervention training programs are available for training school personnel crisis antecedents, verbal de-escalation techniques, and restraint. The outcomes of these programs mostly have been studied in hospitals and mental health facilities and have typically focused on changes in restraint and seclusion use, rather than on changes in violent incidents (Livingston, Verdun-Jones, Brink, Lussier, & Nicholls, 2010). Useful information and techniques for school psychologists in efforts to develop crisis de-escalation inservices may be found in Colvin (2009). Additionally, training from the Crisis Prevention Institute (http://www.crisisprevention.com/Specialties/Nonviolent-Crisis-Intervention) has been well received by many school districts although systematic research on effectiveness is lacking.

Threat Assessment

Student threats of violence are prevalent in many schools. On average, 7–9% of teachers receive threats of injury from students over the course of a school year

(Robers et al., 2012). In 2002, a collaborative effort between the U.S. Secret Service and the Department of Education resulted in the publication of *Threat Assessment in Schools: A Guide to Managing Threatening Situations and to Creating Safe School Climates* (http://www.secretservice.gov/ntac/ssi_guide.pdf). This document held that school-based targeted violence could be largely prevented through a systematic process of investigation once a threat is brought to the attention of school personnel. The document provided a basic structure for implementing the process. Subsequently, *Guidelines for Responding to Student Threats of Violence* (Cornell & Sheras, 2006) was published and provided step-by-step organizational guidelines for the assessment and management of a credible threat of violence from a student or other party. These guidelines trace procedures from the initial assessment process through follow up and support for students who initiate threats of violence. Under the threat assessment model, school-based teams are created consisting of an administrator, the school resource officer, the school psychologist, a school counselor, and the school social worker. When a threat is brought to the attention of the team, it is categorized as either *transient* (easily resolved) or *substantive* (poses a serious danger to others). Substantive threats are further categorized as serious or very serious, depending in part on the potential severity of the threatened act. School psychologists play an essential role through their expertise in "psychological assessment and intervention that can be useful in responding to a student's aggressive behavior and addressing the social and emotional difficulties that frequently underlie threatening behavior" (Cornell & Sheras, 2006, p. 14).

Progress Monitoring and Evaluation of Prevention Activities

Most school psychologists are aware of programs in their districts that look good or are otherwise received positively by the stakeholders, but for which there is no evidence that demonstrable positive change is occurring. It is no less so in violence prevention than in other aspects of service delivery that decisions about maintaining, modifying, or discontinuing programs or procedures need to be linked to the continual analysis of acquired data. Occasionally, this can be a politically or socially difficult task, especially when entrenched or popular programs are called upon to show authentic outcomes, but answer they must. Few schools would continue a reading curriculum that failed to teach the

skill; the same must be true for any aspect of the school violence prevention effort. The time is too short, the resources too limited, and the stakes are too high.

In approaching this task, both formative and summative evaluations should be designed. Formative evaluations monitor ongoing progress toward program goals and inform critical changes to be made in implementation. Formative evaluations answer the question, "Is the prevention program on the right track?" The use of goal attainment scaling ratings adjusted for the expected progress can be a time-efficient and useful method for formative assessment. In addition, treatment integrity checks along with regular opportunities for staff discussion and problem solving will provide helpful and statistically defensible data regarding progress (see Turner-Stokes, 2010).

Goal attainment scaling is a criterion-referenced approach to behavioralizing problem definitions that also can be used to create testable hypotheses and document intervention effectiveness. Goal attainment scaling ratings can be used at either an individual or group level and involve operationally defining successive levels of program progress on a 5-point or 6-point scale (i.e., -2 to $+2$, wherein -2 indicates that a problem is much worse and $+2$ indicates a program goal is attained). For example, consider a student needs assessment survey item that states "I have avoided using the restrooms out of fear for my safety." Baseline data indicate that 20% of sixth- and seventh- grade students responded "true" to the item (20% becomes goal attainment scaling rating 0). The School Safety Team might agree that a decrease to a rate of 10% would indicate progress toward the program goal, and that would be entered as goal attainment scaling $= +1$. A decrease to less than 2% would indicate the program goal was attained, and entered as goal attainment scaling $= +2$. On the opposite side, no change or an increase up to 25% would indicate the prevention efforts were not having the desired effect (goal attainment scaling $= -1$), and an increase to above 30% might indicate that the efforts themselves may be iatrogenic and significantly worsening the problem, and a goal attainment scaling rating of -2 would be entered. There is no absolute formula for determining the criteria for each rating level, but reason, availability of intervention resources, and conservative judgment should prevail. Goal attainment scaling ratings can be used to gather outcome data on a number of different action hypotheses and subsequently combined to provide an overall progress index. Figure 16.1 provides an example of this procedure.

Multiculturalism and Child Development Issues

As noted, the potential for African American students and students of Hispanic heritage to be disproportionately identified for disciplinary consequences in part speaks to the need that all school psychologists involved in violence prevention activities have to maintain and grow their multicultural competencies. This is particularly true when the prevention work involves working with parents in programs such as in the aforementioned First Step to Success, Coping Power, or Parent Management Training. School psychologists need to be alert to any culturally imbedded parenting strategies, including those that may clash with their own experience or learning (e.g., Lansford, Deater-Deckard, Dodge, Bates, & Petit, 2004). In addition, school psychologists

need to have a firm understanding of child developmental pathways that may lead to aggressive behavior so as to better assist teachers and caregivers. Knowledge of the critical social and emotional competencies expected of early childhood learners can assist the school psychologist in the design of effective intervention strategies before problem behaviors become more difficult to change. A useful discussion of these developmental issues can be found in Bierman (2007).

SUMMARY

The emergence of school psychology as an influential force in national policy, research, program development, and service delivery in the area of school violence prevention has been one of the most significant and rapid changes in the profession over the past

Figure 16.1. Goal Attainment Scaling Example

Prevention Area: <u>Bullying Prevention</u>   Rater: <u>Principal</u>

Level of Expected Outcome	Goal 1 Reduction in Restroom Avoidance	Goal 2 Reduction in School Avoidance
Review date: May 23		
Goal attained (+2)	Reduction to 2% or less for same period in following year	Reduction to less than 3% for same period in following year
Expected improvement (+1)	Reduction to 10% or less for same period in following year	Reduction to 3% for same period in following year
Current status* (0)	20% of students reported they avoided restrooms for fear of bullies	5% of students reported staying home from school to avoid bullying
Less than expected outcome (−1)	No change or increase of less than 5% for same period in following year	No change or increase of 1% for same period in following year
Much less than expected (−2)	Increase of 5% or greater for same period in following year	Increase of greater than 1% for same period in following year

GAS Rating_____   GAS Rating_____

*Failure to achieve minimal criterion for positive movement is a 0 GAS rating

Note. GAS = goal attainment scaling.

number of years. Isolated, but high-profile violence in the schools in the late 1990s and at Sandy Hook Elementary School in Newtown, CT, in December 2012, caused educational staff in general and school psychology practitioners in particular to struggle with understanding the role of the school environment in the perpetration of violent behavior. Those horrific acts were the catalysts that sparked a renewed commitment to providing safe and nurturing learning environments for all students. While recognizing that targeted homicide in schools remains a reality, albeit a low probability one, school psychologists understand that school violence manifests itself in multiple forms—fighting, chronic bullying, mean-spirited teasing, sexual harassment, relational aggression—and that each has real and serious consequences for the lives of affected children and youth.

The current science and practice of school violence prevention involves understanding the multisystemic pathways that influence the development and maintenance of violent behavior and then applying effective prevention strategies across the broad spectrum of student needs. It involves recognition that highly publicized approaches that, for instance, rely on hypothesized profiles or on zero tolerance reactionary consequences are inadequate. Rather, best practices in school violence prevention involves recognition that collaboratively developed, empirically based, multicomponent, multilevel approaches rigorously applied and longitudinally maintained stand the best chances for success.

And finally, it involves a sobering understanding that in the end there is little a school can do to completely ensure that a committed individual will not be able to carry out his or her own plan of homicidal violence. Even in this reality, school psychologists must take an assertive leadership role to bring clear-eyed problem solving and the best available science to prevention decision making. In this manner will they be able to leave the building each day firm in the belief that they have done all that they can for the safety of the children in their care.

REFERENCES

Bierman, K. L. (2007). Anger and aggression: A developmental perspective. In T. A. Cavell & K. T. Malcom (Eds.), *Anger, aggression, and interventions for interpersonal violence* (pp. 215–238). Mahwah, NJ: Erlbaum.

Colvin, G. (2009). *Managing noncompliance and defiance in the classroom: A roadmap for teachers, specialists, and behavior support teams.* Thousand Oaks, CA: Corwin.

Conduct Problems Prevention Research Group. (2010). The effects of a multiyear universal social-emotional learning program: The role of student and school characteristics. *Journal of Consulting and Clinical Psychology, 78,* 156–168. doi:10.1037/a0018607

Cornell, D. G., & Sheras, P. L. (2006). *Guidelines for responding to student threats of violence.* Longmont, CO: Sopris West.

Durlak, J. A., Weissberg, R. P., Dymnicki, A. B., Taylor, R. D., & Schellinger, K. B. (2011). The impact of enhancing students' social and emotional learning: A meta-analysis of school-based universal interventions. *Child Development, 82,* 405–432. doi:10.1111/j.1467-8624.2010.01564.x

Eber, L. (2008). Wraparound: A key component of school-wide systems of positive behavior supports. In E. J. Bruns & J. S. Walker (Eds.), *The resource guide to wraparound.* Portland, OR: National Wraparound Initiative, Research and Training Center for Family Support and Children's Mental Health. Retrieved from http://www.nwi.pdx.edu/NWI-book/Chapters/Eber-5e.3-(school-wide-support-systems).pdf

Filter, K. J., McKenna, M. K., Benedict, E. A., & Horner, R. H. (2007). Check-in/check-out: A post-hoc evaluation of an efficient, secondary-level targeted intervention for reducing problem behaviors in schools. *Education and Treatment of Children, 30,* 69–84. doi:10.1353/etc.2007.0000

Furlong, M. J., Greif, J. L., Bates, M. P., Whipple, A. D., Jimenez, T. C., & Morrison, R. (2005). Development of the California School Climate and Safety Survey–Short form. *Psychology in the Schools, 42,* 137–149. doi:10.1002/pits.20053

Jennings, W. G., Khey, D. N., Maskaly, J., & Donner, C. M. (2011). Evaluating the relationship between law enforcement and school security measures and violent crime in schools. *Journal of Police Crisis Negotiations, 11,* 109–124. doi:10.1080/15332586.2011.581511

Kazdin, A. E. (2005). *Parent management training: Treatment for oppositional, aggressive, and antisocial children and adolescents.* New York, NY: Oxford University Press.

Kazdin, A. E., & Rotella, C. (2008). *The Kazdin method for parenting the defiant child.* New York, NY: Mariner Books.

Lansford, J. E., Deater-Deckard, K., Dodge, K., Bates, J. E., & Pettit, G. S. (2004). Ethnic differences in the link between physical discipline and later adolescent externalizing behavior. *Journal of Child and Adolescent Psychiatry, 45,* 801–812. Retrieved from http://www.nospank.net/landsford.pdf

Larson, J., & Beckman, S. (2012). Preventing student violence. In S. R. Brock & S. R. Jimerson (Eds.), *Best practices in school crisis prevention and intervention* (2nd ed., pp. 223–244). Bethesda, MD: National Association of School Psychologists.

Larson, J., & Busse, R. T. (2012). A problem-solving approach to school violence prevention. In S. R. Jimerson, A. B. Nickerson, M. J. Mayer, & M. J. Furlong (Eds.), *The handbook of school violence and school safety: International research and practice* (pp. 45–56). New York, NY: Routledge.

Lieberman, D. (2012, December 9). Schoolhouse to courthouse. *The New York Times.* Retrieved from http://www.nyt.com

Livingston, J. D., Verdun-Jones, S., Brink, J., Lussier, P., & Nicholls, T. (2010). A narrative review of the effectiveness of aggression management training programs for psychiatric hospital staff. *Journal of Forensic Nursing, 6,* 15–28. doi:10.1111/j.1939-3938.2009.01061.x

Lochman, J. E., Boxmeyer, C. L., & Powell, N. P. (2012). Cognitive-behavioral intervention for anger and aggression: The Coping Power Program. In S. Jimerson, A. B. Nickerson, M. J. Mayer, & M. J. Furlong (Eds.), *Handbook of school violence and school safety: International research and practice* (2nd ed., pp. 579–591). New York, NY: Routledge.

Lochman, J. E., & Wells, K. C. (2003). Effectiveness study of Coping Power and classroom intervention with aggressive children: Outcomes at a one-year follow-up. *Behavior Therapy, 34,* 493–515. doi:10.1016/S0005-7894(03)80032-1

Mateau-Gelbert, P., & Lune, H. (2007). Street codes in high school: School as an educational deterrent. *City & Community, 6,* 173–191. doi:10.1111/j.1540-6040.2007.00212.x

McIntosh, K., Campbell, A. L., Carter, D. R., & Dickey, C. R. (2009). Differential effects of a Tier 2 behavior intervention based on function of problem behavior. *Journal of Positive Behavior Interventions, 11,* 82–93. doi:10.1177/1098300708319127

Myrstol, B. A. (2011). Public perceptions of school resource officer (SRO) programs. *Western Criminology Review, 12,* 20–40.

Patterson, G. R., Reid, J. B., & Dishion, T. J. (1992). *Antisocial boys.* Eugene, OR: Castalia.

Reid, J. B., Patterson, G. R., & Snyder, J. (2002). *Antisocial behavior in children and adolescents: A developmental analysis and model for intervention.* Washington, DC: American Psychological Association.

Robers, S., Zhang, J., & Truman, J. (2012). *Indicators of school crime and safety: 2011* (NCES 2012-002/NCJ 236021). Washington, DC: National Center for Education Statistics, U.S. Department of Education.

Schneider, T. (2007). *Ensuring quality school facilities and security technologies: Effective strategies for creating safer schools and communities.* New York, NY: The Hamilton Fish Institute. Retrieved from http://gwired.gwu.edu/hamfish/merlin-cgi/p/downloadFile/d/20705/n/

Sleven, P. (2012, December 21). Chicago grapples with gun violence; death toll sores. *The Washington Post.* Retrieved from http://articles.washingtonpost.com/2012-12-21/national/36017398_1_gun-violence-homicide-rate-national-gun-debate

Sprague, J. (2007). *Creating school-wide prevention and intervention strategies: Effective strategies for creating safer schools and communities.* Washington, DC: The Hamilton Fish Institute, George Washington University. Retrieved from http://gwired.gwu.edu/hamfish/merlin-cgi/p/downloadFile/d/20707/n/off/

Sprague, J., & Perkins, K. (2009). Direct and collateral effects of the First Step to Success Program. *Journal of Positive Behavioral Interventions, 11,* 208–221. doi:10.1177/1098300780330935

Sullivan, A. L., Kilingbeil, D. A., & Van Norman, E. R. (2013). Beyond behavior: Multilevel analysis of the influence of socio-demographics and school characteristics on students' risk of suspension. *School Psychology Review, 42,* 99–114.

Theriot, M. T. (2009). School resource officers and criminalization of student behavior. *Journal of Criminal Justice, 37,* 280–287.

Turner-Stokes, L. (2010). Goal attainment scaling (GAS) in rehabilitation: A practical guide. *Clinical Rehabilitation, 2,* 191–205. doi:10.1177/0269215508101742

17 Best Practices in Bullying Prevention

Erika D. Felix
University of California–Santa Barbara
Jennifer Greif Green
Boston University (MA)
Jill D. Sharkey
University of California–Santa Barbara

OVERVIEW

In surveys of bullying, many students describe their concerns about the reactions of their peers and teachers to bullying: "A lot of the times, kids bully in small ways but after a year it all adds up and I think that no one really understands it." "It happens in the classroom. Sometimes, teachers don't notice. Other times, they ignore it." "Teachers never know when gossip is going around, and when they do find out, they most often say things like 'It will pass,' or they say 'Don't worry, no one believes it anyway' but people laugh at the person who the rumor is about, and no one even tries to help just the tiniest bit."

How schools, and the individuals within them, choose to address bullying has a substantial impact on students' feelings of safety and well-being. Approximately, 30–50% of U.S. students are involved as aggressors or as targets of bullying (Wang, Iannotti, & Nansel, 2009). The long-term effects of bullying on mental and physical health outcomes, for both bullies and victims, are well documented, and the potentially tragic consequences of bullying are frequently highlighted in the media.

School psychologists are increasingly involved in bullying prevention and intervention efforts, both at the request of their schools or districts and as required by some state legislatures. In response to these needs, there has been a surge of bullying prevention programs developed by university researchers and by private companies.

This chapter is designed to serve as a guide for school psychologists involved with bullying prevention and intervention activities. The National Association of School Psychologists (NASP) *Model for Comprehensive and Integrated School Psychological Services* (NASP, 2010) recognizes the importance of the domain of Preventive and Responsive Services in school psychologists' roles and delineates the comprehensive training school psychologists receive as problem solvers in the school context, which makes them ideally suited to address bullying in schools. First, school psychologists have knowledge in data-based decision making and accountability, which is important for accurately assessing and identifying school-wide and individual-level needs related to bullying prevention, selecting evidence-based interventions, and monitoring intervention success over time. Second, school psychologists are able to use consultation and collaboration skills to implement antibullying services as part of a team. Third, school psychologists are trained to implement interventions and mental health services to develop the social and life skills that can help bullies learn positive peer interaction and help victims avoid future bullying. Fourth, school psychologists' training in preventive and responsive services in multitiered prevention efforts is invaluable for planning to comprehensively address bullying, which cannot be successfully addressed at any one level exclusively. Fifth, school psychologists are trained in family–school collaboration so they can engage parents in the process.

Given the comprehensive training school psychologists receive to address student academic, social, and mental health problems in school, and the prevalence and negative consequences of bullying in schools, it is absolutely critical that school psychologists take a leadership role to address bullying in their schools. To help school psychologists accomplish this goal, this chapter provides information on the nature and consequences of bullying; the current state of bullying legislation as it is related to prevention efforts; and strategies that school psychologists can use to identify the most effective interventions for their schools and to be critical consumers of available programs. Several leading bullying prevention and intervention programs that school psychologists can implement as part of a comprehensive problem-solving team effort to address bullying in their schools are reviewed. Finally, a case study outlines the process of implementing bullying prevention and interventions at one school, with the role of the school psychologist highlighted.

Definitions of Bullying

There are many definitions of bullying. The most widely used definition was developed in the late 1970s by Dan Olweus, who pioneered research on bullying in Norway. This definition describes bullying as a subset of peer victimization that involves intentional aggression that is repeated over time and involves an imbalance of power between the person doing the bullying and the person being bullied (Olweus, 1996). Bullying can incorporate both physical and verbal aggression, as well as relational aggression (e.g., spreading rumors or gossip with the goal of harming a person's relationships), stealing and property damage, behaviors consistent with sexual harassment, and cyberbullying (i.e., using cyberspace as the vehicle through which to aggress against others). Throughout this chapter, when we use the term *bullying*, we are including any subtype a student can experience.

The specificity of the definition of bullying is designed to distinguish bullying behaviors from other forms of peer aggression, such as fighting between friends, or one-time events (Olweus, 1996). Bullying is considered to be a more pervasive and chronic form of victimization. It involves an ongoing aggressive relationship in which the child being bullied cannot defend himself or herself. Some equate bullying to abuse, because of the chronicity of victimization from which a target cannot escape. Although the three hallmarks of bullying (intentionality, repetition, power imbalance) may seem straightforward, in practice they can pose difficulties for schools aiming to identify and report acts of bullying. For example, does one severe incident of physical assault constitute bullying, even if it was not repeated? Decisions about which behaviors constitute bullying

can have consequences for school disciplinary responses and reporting regulations.

Cyberbullying is a recent phenomenon that poses a unique challenge to educators because it occurs largely outside of any potential visibility of adults, can happen instantaneously, opens the opportunities for multiple or repeated victimization within a short time period, and occurs in a context in which the victim may be relatively helpless to prevent or respond. In this regard, cyberbullying is more similar to verbal harassment (e.g., name calling or intimidation threats) and relational aggression (e.g., spreading demeaning rumors or causing ostracization from a group) than it is to physical forms of bullying (e.g., physical attacks or extortion of money). Currently, the most widely used definition of cyberbullying states it is the intentional and repeated harm of others through the use of computers, cell phones, and other electronic devices (Perren et al., 2012). As such, cyberbullying is considered to be a subset of verbal and relational aggression that involves the use of digital media to victimize others. This can include the use of social network sites, chat rooms, and e-mails to disseminate cruel or demeaning messages to individuals or to threaten or harass individuals using text, photos, videos, audio recordings, or multimedia forms.

Impact of Bullying

Bullying is widely prevalent among students and can have substantial long-term negative effects on psychological and physical health outcomes. Strong evidence links bullying and peer victimization with increased internalizing problems (e.g., depression, anxiety, withdrawal; Reijntjes, Kamphuis, Prinzie, & Telch, 2010) and later aggression (Sansone, Leung, & Wiederman, 2013). Bullies also show risk for mental health and aggressive behavior problems, and bully-victims—those who both bully others and are also targets of bullying themselves—show the greatest risk for mental health difficulties (Kumplainen et al., 1998).

Thus, school psychologists have good reason to be concerned about children involved in bullying (as both aggressors and victims). School psychologists have entered a period of increased recognition of the toll of bullying, as well as legislative and policy commitments to reducing bullying in schools. By championing bullying prevention and intervention efforts in their schools and school districts, school psychologists can play a central role in ensuring that policies and practices are based on solid evidence and thoughtful implementation.

BASIC CONSIDERTIONS

There are several basic considerations for school psychologists to attend to in selecting and adopting a bullying prevention program, including understanding the antibullying legislation in their state and common issues in successfully implementing a bullying prevention program.

Understanding Legal Mandates

In 1999 Georgia was the first U.S. state to enact bullying legislation, and most states have followed with their own legislation. These laws vary considerably in their definitions of bullying, purpose statements, scope of their laws, consequences for students, and expectations for schools (Stuart-Cassel, Bell, & Springer, 2011). However, the majority of state laws either mandate or encourage schools to implement bullying prevention programs or teacher training related to bullying (Stuart-Cassel et al., 2011). These laws have led schools and school districts to increasingly seek information about effective bullying prevention programs that will enable them to meet state mandates. Of the states with bullying laws, Stuart-Cassell et al. (2011) found that 45 states required school districts to adopt bullying policies, 36 explicitly prohibited cyberbullying, and 13 stated that schools have jurisdiction over behaviors occurring off of the school campus, if they contributed to a hostile environment at school.

As of 2013, there are no U.S. federal laws that specifically address bullying. However, there are federal laws requiring schools to respond to related victimization, including discriminatory harassment (harassment based on race, national origin, color, sex, age, disability, religion; see http://www.stopbullying.gov/laws/federal). These behaviors may overlap with bullying, requiring that schools address student conduct that may be considered discriminatory harassment.

The varying nature and scope of state bullying legislation has implications for the way school personnel conceptualize and respond to bullying, both at the school level and in individual cases. At times, these state mandates may be at odds with recommendations from research or the best practice standards of school psychologists. For example, schools may be required to enact specific no-tolerance disciplinary policies, whereas school psychologists may prefer flexibility in individualizing responses to bullying or remediating psychosocial challenges within a particular peer context. School psychologists are often integrally involved in ensuring that schools meet state mandates in regard to bullying legislation, and it is therefore important that they stay up to date with current laws and are aware of state-distributed model policies (this information can be found at http://www.stopbullying.gov/laws).

Adoption and Implementation of Programs

Recent research on the implementation of bullying prevention programs has found that educators vary in their preferences for methods of selecting antibullying programs. For example, Cunningham et al. (2009) found that teachers generally fell into three categories: those who are decision sensitive, those who are support sensitive, and those who are cost sensitive. Decision-sensitive teachers believe that individual schools, rather than districts or governments, should select prevention programs. This group is interested in the characteristics that define programs (e.g., simplicity, sustainability), believe in the effectiveness of prevention programs, and are the most supportive of prevention programs. Support-sensitive teachers are attuned to contextual factors that might influence the effective adoption and implementation of bullying prevention programs. This group prefers programs with a high level of staff and parent involvement, those that are supported by scientific research, and those that provide a comprehensive package of trainings, manuals, and supports. Cost-sensitive teachers prefer lower cost programs that minimize time demands for training and implementation. They anticipate fewer benefits of bullying prevention programs and are more likely than educators in the other groups to believe that bullying prevention is the responsibility of parents. These findings have important implications for selecting and designing bullying prevention programs, as they highlight the need for school psychologists to identify programs that will be most acceptable and feasible for implementation by the particular set of educators, staff, and families in their school.

Specificity of Programs

A final basic consideration to highlight is whether schools or districts should select programs specifically designed to address bullying or programs that are broader in scope. Although schools may work to accurately identify incidents of bullying and states may mandate that schools document and report bullying, many schools are much more interested in reducing peer aggression broadly and improving the social–emotional skills and well-being of their students in general rather than focusing on bullying alone. Similarly, many school-based prevention and intervention programs are also aimed at a broader base of behaviors than bullying alone. The decision of whether to select a prevention program that addresses a broader set of social–emotional goals (in addition to addressing bullying) or a program that focuses solely on bullying can be made by (a) considering the range of social–emotional programs being implemented in the school to determine how multiple goals can best be integrated and (b) conducting a comprehensive school-wide assessment of student social–emotional needs (including bullying) to determine the priorities of school intervention efforts. In some cases, schools will need to develop their own strategy for integrating multiple programs and goals, while in others they may be able to draw on existing resources. For example, a bullying prevention component has been developed to be implemented within the broader framework of positive behavior support (Ross & Horner, 2009). In this chapter, we will specifically focus on bullying prevention efforts, instead of broader violence prevention or social–emotional skills curricula.

BEST PRACTICES IN BULLYING PREVENTION

School psychologists can play a central role in selecting, implementing, and evaluating bullying prevention programs. Schools that consistently implement comprehensive strategies should be able to reduce bullying and victimization, while working to build a positive school climate that engages all students.

Where to Start

Collecting data on student experiences with bullying, victimization, and related behaviors is critical to planning for bullying prevention and intervention activities. The most widely used prevention program, the Olweus Bullying Prevention Program (described in more detail below; Olweus & Limber, 2010) begins by administering the Olweus Bullying Questionnaire to assess the current state of school bullying and guide school-level intervention planning. Information about, for example, where and when bullying is most likely to occur can play a central role in determining first steps for increasing teacher monitoring and planning for intervention.

There are many other measures with different strengths and limitations that school psychologists can use to identify the incidence of bullying and victimization. For example, the California Bullying Victimization Scale (Felix, Sharkey, Green, Furlong, & Tanigawa, 2011) is designed to be a school-wide anonymous bullying assessment that provides data on rates of student bullying and victimization. This scale does not use the term bullying, therefore eliminating concerns that students may have predefined notions of what the word bullying means that influence their survey responses. This strategy also addresses concerns that some surveys may be asking students to self-identify as bullying victims and that identifying as a victim of bullying may be an emotionally charged experience. Instead of using the word bullying and presenting a definition of bullying (as many bullying surveys do), the California Bullying Victimization Scale asks students whether they have experienced each of the key definitional components of bullying (i.e., aggression that is repeated, is intentional, and involves an imbalance of power between the aggressor and the target). Interestingly, this assessment strategy identifies a somewhat different group of students than other measures (Felix et al., 2011).

Regardless of the specific assessment tool selected, school psychologists should choose an assessment method with the following characteristics. First, assessments should be administered either school-wide or to a randomly selected group of students, rather than targeting students suspected to be involved in bullying, because bullying is often undetected by teachers and other adults. A school-wide or random assessment of students will provide school psychologists with a comprehensive picture of the nature of bullying and victimization. Second, assessments should include a wide range of victimization and aggressive behaviors (including physical, verbal, relational, sexual, and online aggression), so that school psychologists can identify the areas in which students are most in need of intervention. Third, school psychologists should select assessment tools that will provide key information that can guide interventions for students. This will likely include the location of bullying; the time of day at which it is most likely to happen; student help-seeking; and the reactions of school staff, teachers, parents, and uninvolved peers to bullying when it occurs. This type of information is critical to school safety planning. Fourth, schools also need to assess other related constructs (e.g., a range of forms of peer victimization, like conflict between friends or dating violence, and emotional well-being) in addition to bullying, in order both to understand the context of bullying and to inform the strategic selection of prevention and intervention programs. Fifth, we recommend that schools collect data from teachers and parents on their perceptions of bullying. Data collection from parents can be particularly useful for understanding experiences of younger students who may not be able to complete a self-report survey. Even in older grades, comparing data from student self-report with parent and teacher report can provide important information about potential gaps in perceptions of bullying. For example, if teachers report low rates of bullying, but students report high rates, these data can help to facilitate important conversations about how teachers understand student experiences.

General Strategies to Reduce Bullying

Ttofi and Farrington (2011) conducted an extensive review and meta-analysis of the effectiveness of antibullying programs in schools. Searching published and unpublished reports, 35 journals from 1983 through May 2009, and 18 electronic databases in various languages including English, the authors found 53 unique program evaluations, of which 44 allowed for the calculation of effect size. They concluded that school-based antibullying programs are generally effective in reducing bullying (average decrease 20–23%) and victimization (average decrease 17–20%). They found the following program elements were associated with a statistically significant decrease in bullying: parent

training/meetings, playground supervision, intensity for children, intensity for teachers, duration for children, classroom management, teacher training, classroom rules, a whole-school policy, school conferences, and having more than 10 components of bullying prevention. In light of these findings, we recommend the following general strategies. Note that these are components of a comprehensive effort and should not be simply implemented in isolation and then expected to be effective. As Ttofi and Farrington (2011) confirmed, intensity, duration, and comprehensiveness of antibullying programs are related to their success. (See Table 17.1 for a summary.)

A whole-school policy should be developed that discusses the goals of the school in reducing bullying behavior and the strategies school members should follow (Olweus, 1996). This should be a collaborative effort among school members for several reasons. In her efforts to implement the Olweus bullying prevention program, Limber (2004) found that (a) teacher commitment was paramount and that without it the program was not implemented with fidelity and, consequently, showed no effect; (b) when there was resistance from staff and parents, it was because some did not view bullying as a problem or considered it to be a rite of passage; and (c) the schools required extensive consultation to implement the program, so school psychologists should plan for this. As with many prevention efforts, care and planning must be taken to

Table 17.1. General Strategies for School Psychologists to Reduce Bullying and Victimization

- Form a group that includes teachers, parents, and students to coordinate the school's bullying prevention activities. With skills in consultation, collaboration, and data-based decision making, and expertise in direct and indirect services for children and families, a school psychologist is ideal to chair this group.
- Focus on the social environment of the school by creating a climate of respect and mutual support.
- Assess bullying at school with a survey designed to identify school-level needs.
- Using assessment results, work in collaboration with staff and parents to develop school-wide action plans.
- Select and implement a bullying prevention program that has evaluation data to support its effectiveness to address identified needs. Evidence-based programs have been shown to be effective and can protect against unintended negative consequences.
- Train staff in bullying prevention, because awareness and interest need to be supported with skills in how to respond and deal with bullying when it occurs.
- Establish and enforce school rules and policies associated with bullying by explicitly establishing positive behavior guidelines that prohibit bullying while defining positive behavioral expectations.
- Advocate for increased adult supervision in places where bullying is known to occur (e.g., playgrounds). Train staff to intervene consistently and appropriately in bullying situations, as this helps students feel safe. Failure to do so may inadvertently convey to students that bullying is tolerated.
- Consider a school-wide bully-victim screening to identify students who need more in-depth assessment and targeted or intensive intervention to address their bully-victim experiences and subsequent mental health consequences.
- Consult with teachers and other school staff around any challenges that prevent effective responses to bullying.
- Continue these efforts over time, as they need to be reinforced with each new cohort of students and to transcend any staff changes.

institutionalize the program, because staff turnover and leadership changes can result in the adoption of different programs each year. Limber (2004) stressed the importance of each school developing a committee to coordinate school-wide policies and activities. Using their expertise in data-based decision making, school psychologists can help the committee monitor bullying experiences of students and adjust practices to implement the optimal response based on individual schools' current needs and resources.

Part of a whole-school approach to bullying prevention should be attention to disciplinary methods (Ttofi & Farrington, 2011). Fair, firm, and consistently implemented consequences for bullying and victimization should be balanced with individualized intervention to address student concerns. Schools often implement zero tolerance policies that provide harsh consequences for breaking school rules, including bullying. However, zero tolerance policies may fail to correct behavior for students engaging in repeated rule violations and may even reinforce repetition of antisocial behavior. Thus, the use of the zero tolerance discipline approach for bullying is discouraged. The side effect of this philosophy of discipline is that it may affect staff and student willingness to report bullying because the punishment is so severe. Children who bully need prosocial role models, which they may not get if excluded from school (Limber, 2004). Instead of zero tolerance policies, students need opportunities to develop self-discipline, and schools must provide a positive climate for learning.

Playground supervision appears to be critical in the prevention of bullying (Ttofi & Farrington, 2011). This includes adult monitoring on the playground, lunch areas, hallways, and other open unstructured areas where students have increased opportunity to target each other. The hot spots identified by a school's bullying screening survey should receive increased monitoring, and a survey should reassess if hot spots change once increased monitoring is in place. Increasing monitoring alone will reduce rates of physical bullying, because this form of aggression is more likely to occur in the absence of adult observers. It is harder to monitor and intervene with the more subtle forms of aggression, such as spreading rumors or social exclusion as a way to hurt others. Playground supervisors interacting positively with youth and promoting prosocial play would likely prevent such social exclusion. In addition, strategies for monitoring and dealing with cyberbullying should be discussed, such as monitoring computer use on school campus and identifying discipline strategies for misuse.

Educational presentations and parent–teacher meetings appear to be important in the reduction of bullying (Ttofi & Farrington, 2011). Some antibullying programs include parent education. For example, the Bully Busters school-based program includes a manual for parents that helps them understand and respond to bullying. In addition to describing bullying and its impact on victims, the manual provides parents with techniques to help them communicate better within their families about the issue of bullying. Further research is necessary to determine specifically which aspects of parent training have the most impact on reducing the incidence of bullying.

Most prevention programs (e.g., Bully Busters and Steps to Respect) advocate dispelling myths about bullying among teachers and staff and training them how to effectively intervene when confronting a bullying situation. With their training in consultation, school psychologists are ideally positioned to lead this type of training and to offer booster trainings as needed. Steps to Respect offers video-based training that school psychologists can use. In addition to training specific to bullying, it is important to attend to the quality of classroom management, which may also help reduce bullying (Smith, Ananiadou, & Cowie, 2003). It is important that teachers model the skills they would like to see their students learn in terms of handling disagreements, treating others with respect, and using other prosocial behaviors. School psychologists can help impart classroom management skills that may not have been taught in educators' teacher preparation programs. In addition, classroom climate can be improved by directly addressing pupil-to-pupil relationships (Smith et al., 2003). Some programs (e.g., Steps to Respect) offer a social–cognitive curriculum that maps onto state standards that teachers can use.

Although most antibullying program components had the intended impact of reducing bullying behavior to some degree, there is some evidence that peer mediation and conflict resolution are ineffective interventions. Ttofi and Farrington (2011) found that the use of peers to tackle bullying, including peer mediation, increased rates of bullying. Similarly, Limber (2004) discouraged the use of peer mediation or conflict resolution curriculum to address bullying because, she argues, bullying is not a conflict or a matter of occasional interpersonal disagreements, but a form of chronic victimization. Limber (2004) suggests that peer mediation sends the wrong message to the bully if bullying is presented as a matter for conflict resolution (i.e., "You are both partly right and partly wrong").

Strategies to Reduce Cyberbullying

Many schools are specifically concerned about cyber-bullying, its impact on students, and strategies for effective intervention. Although cyberbullying appears to be less common than other forms of in-person bullying, there is some evidence that the effects of cyberbullying are particularly devastating for students because of the anonymous nature of aggression, the speed at which material can be spread to a large number of students, and 24/7 access to technology, which makes it more difficult for students to have a reprieve from bullying. As described by Perren et al. (2012), preventing cyberbullying typically involves two strategies. First, students involved in cyberbullying are often the same students who are involved in other forms of bullying. As such, addressing broader bullying behaviors will likely lead to a reduction in cyberbullying, and many bullying prevention efforts now incorporate cyberbullying in their general approach. Second, strategies to reduce cyberbullying often aim to reduce online risks more broadly. Increasing parental monitoring, teaching safe Internet use, and discussing Internet etiquette may effectively reduce cyberbullying in schools (Perren et al., 2012). Research on the effectiveness of strategies and interventions to reduce cyberbullying is still relatively new. Additional studies of these strategies are needed to determine how schools can successfully reduce cyber-bullying among students.

Review of Research-Supported Bullying Prevention Efforts

Although schools are clamoring for programs to address school bullying, and many commercial products make claims of efficacy, most programs currently used in U.S. schools have not undergone rigorous evaluation with a diverse student population. Programs to reduce student aggression in general may also reduce bullying to some degree. However, the chronic nature of school bullying, with its implicit power imbalance, may make it a more formidable problem to address. Therefore, general character education or violence prevention curricula may not adequately reduce bullying. Consistent with a multitiered problem-solving model, we describe prevention and intervention efforts for everyone at the whole-school level, for bullies and bully victims at the targeted level, and for chronic participants in bullying at the intensive level. The strategies for whole-school assessments can be starting points, but ultimately schools will also need to systematically collect data on students involved in bullying incidences to identify who may benefit from more targeted and intensive responsive services.

Whole-School Interventions

Table 17.2 summarizes the content, purpose, and evidence for the efficacy of six universal programs specifically focused on preventing bullying. These programs were selected because there was published evaluation data on them. These and other such programs are implemented throughout schools in order to increase bullying awareness, shape attitudes about bullying, and provide strategies for addressing bullying behavior. Components may include teacher training, classroom lessons, training videos, and social marketing. Schools can select a program based on what strategies are feasible and acceptable given their resources and needs.

Targeted Interventions

No universal prevention program can be 100% effective. Therefore, targeted programs to address the needs of chronic bullies and victims are crucial. For bullies, Limber (2004) warns against the use of group treatment as bullies may actually learn from and encourage each other. She also advocates the need for prosocial role models for bullies. Theory and research on aggression suggests that interventions to teach prosocial behavior to students who engage in bullying increase their feelings of empathy toward their victims, reduce peer group approval for aggression, improve problem solving for social situations, and reduce hostile attributions that can help reduce their aggressive behavior. Working with parents on developing consistent and fair discipline plans and increasing monitoring of their child's behavior should also reduce engagement in aggressive behavior. For victims, assertiveness training has been recommended and has shown modest empirical support (Smith et al., 2003). Other efforts focus on social skills training as a method to reduce the incidence of victimization by helping the student to be a less vulnerable target (see Table 17.2). Targeted interventions addressing the social dynamics in bullying, such as the Method of Shared Concern (Pikas, 2002), are showing some preliminary evaluation data supporting their effectiveness (Rigby & Griffiths, 2011).

Intensive Interventions

The available literature on interventions for chronic bullies and victims does not detail intensive interventions

Table 17.2. Evidence-Based Bullying Interventions

Program and Web Link	Grade Levels	Content/Purpose	Sessions/ Duration	State of Evidence
		Whole-School Interventions		
Bully Busters	K–5 or 6–8	A psychoeducational program targeting teachers in a group setting that focuses on increasing bullying awareness and prevention, personal power, identifying bullies and victims, recommendations and interventions for bullying behavior and helping victims, and relaxation and coping skills.	An ongoing workshop where teachers participate in a Bully Busters support team group	Evaluations showed significant changes in teachers' belief in skills and ability to influence students, sense of personal responsibility for students' learning/behavior, knowledge and use of bullying interventions, and reductions in disciplinary referrals (Newman-Carlson & Horne, 2004). Some efficacy was found with African American and Caucasian K–5 students (Orpinas, Horne, & Staniszewski, 2003). Studies have found overall decreases in bullying behavior and positive effects on teacher self-efficacy (Bell, Raczynski, & Horne, 2010).
Expect Respect http://www.expectrespectaustin.org/	5, 6–8, or 9–12	Addresses bullying, dating violence, and sexual harassment. Sessions focus on strengthening relationship and conflict resolution skills to improve school safety, school climate, student empowerment, and social support, and to prevent future violence.	Originally 12 weekly sessions; recently expanded to 24 weekly sessions	Bullying was not reduced among fifth graders, as students reported witnessing bullying more after the intervention. However, awareness of sexual harassment and intentions to intervene when observing bullying increased (Whitaker, Rosenbluth, Valle, & Sanchez, 2004). Both 6th–8th and 9th–12th graders increased their use of healthy conflict resolution behaviors, but victimization and perpetration were not reduced in this sample (Ball et al., 2012).
KiVa http://www.kivaprogram.net/	Primary and secondary school	Addresses bullying as a "group phenomenon" and emphasizes the role of witnesses of bullying. Includes universal interventions (e.g., teacher-implemented lesson plans, antibullying computer games, a virtual learning environment, a parent guide) and indicated interventions (discussions with students involved in bullying and selected classmates).	Ongoing	One of the newest bullying prevention programs shows promising results. Randomized controlled trials in Finland found that students in schools randomly assigned to the KiVa program were significantly less likely to report multiple forms of victimization at the end of the school year than students in control-group schools (Kärnä et al., 2011; Salmivalli, Kärnä, & Poskiparta, 2011). A pilot study is currently being planned in the United States by researchers at the University of Kansas.
Olweus Bullying Prevention Program http://www.violencepreventionworks.org/	K–9; 11–12 with program modifications	To reduce and prevent bullying in the schools and between students. The program is implemented at the student, parent, teacher, school, and community levels.	4–6 months to implement; ongoing boosters	Research shows mixed results. Some research has reported less victimization, bullying (Black & Jackson, 2007; Schroeder et al., 2012), and aggression (Limber, Nation, Tracy, Melton, & Flerx, 2004). However, research has also found increases in tolerance of bullying and decreases in bystander intervention (Limber et al., 2004).

Continued

Table 17.2. Continued

Program and Web Link	Grade Levels	Content/Purpose	Sessions/Duration	State of Evidence
Stories of Us: Promoting Positive Peer Relationships http://www.storiesofus.com/	Middle and high school	Brief, film-based program that includes a DVD and teacher's guide with lesson plans that are aligned with National Standards for English Language Arts, a supplementary make-your-own-film resource, and staff development and community education resources.	Five or eight lessons with optional classroom activities and homework	One study shows small effect sizes for attitudes toward bullying and perceptions of support for the intervention group compared to a control group. Implemented with fidelity and perceived as feasible and effective within the school context (Renshaw & Jimerson, 2012).
Steps to Respect (Committee for Children) http://www.cfchildren.org/steps-to-respect.aspx	3–5 or 4–6	Addresses bullying and friendship. Sessions focus on relationship skills, coping, assertiveness, empathy, positive social norms, socially responsive behavior, problem solving and emotion management.	11 student lessons, 2 literature units, teacher training video	Very well researched. Participating schools showed 33% reduction in physical bullying; 35% fewer teachers reporting fighting as a major problem (Brown, Low, Smith, & Haggerty, 2011); 72% decrease in malicious gossip (Low, Frey, & Brockman, 2010); and 70% reduction in destructive bystander behavior (Frey, Hirschstein, Edstrom, & Snell, 2009), for example.

		Targeted Interventions		
Method of Shared Concern http://www.readymade.com.au/method/	Not specified	Intervention for responding to identified cases of school bullying; an alternative to strict, punitive responses. Used for noncriminal cases that involve groups of students. Involves a series of meetings between trained practitioner and students involved. Aims to elicit concern about the bullied student, helps students develop a solution to the problem, and facilitates implementation of the solution.	A series of meetings, both individual and group	Evaluation evidence is emerging. A report of 17 case studies in Australia found that the majority of involved students reported an improvement in their situation, bullying students were positive about their involvement, and practitioners and school principals were positive about the program's effectiveness (Rigby & Griffiths, 2011).
Social Skills Group Intervention http://www.selmediainc.com/ssgrin/overview	Pre-K–10	A Tier 2 RTI antibullying intervention aimed toward bullies and victims. Aims to increase social–emotional skills among both groups, and to reduce incidences of bullying.	10 sessions	Research has found reductions in aggression, bullying, victimization (including relational; DeRosier, 2004), teasing by peers, depression, anxiety, and internalizing problems; and increases in social acceptance of others and self-esteem, self-concept, and self-efficacy (Harrell, Mercer, & DeRosier, 2009).

Note. RTI = response to intervention.

or treatments. Anecdotally, most often a student will present as having chronic problems with aggression (bullies) or clinical levels of depression, anxiety, or school avoidance (bully or victim). In this case, a thorough assessment by the school psychologist is indicated, and referral to the appropriate school mental health service or community-based treatment services is recommended. The school psychologist should take care to refer to community resources that are familiar with evidence-based treatments for the particular referral problem.

Developmental Differences

Studies consistently find that bullying increases from elementary to middle school and decreases again in later adolescence (e.g., Olweus, 1996). Types of bullying experienced change with age as well, with physical bullying among younger children giving way to relational bullying and sexual harassment among older adolescents. School psychologists can take into consideration the developmental needs of their students when selecting school-wide interventions, considering the role of parental involvement (e.g., explicit parental intervention may be more appropriate for younger students), determining the extent to which bullying behaviors are developmentally atypical (e.g., physical bullying is more atypical among older students), and designing individual intervention strategies.

School-wide bullying prevention programs typically shift with the age of their audience to address the most pressing developmental needs of students and to present strategies and materials in a format that is developmentally appropriate. Many commonly implemented programs consist of curricula designed for students at different grade levels (e.g., Olweus Bullying Prevention Program), or transition from a program geared toward younger students to a paired program aimed at older students. When addressing bullying with individual students, taking a developmental perspective can lead school psychologists to think about bullying within the context of an individual's social development and to determine whether skill building (such as empathy building and assertiveness training) may be beneficial. As noted earlier, students experiencing long-term chronic victimization are at greatest risk for a number of poor psychosocial outcomes. School psychologists can play an important role in monitoring (or collecting data to identify) involvement in bullying across many years of a child's development so that they can provide needed supports.

Multicultural Competencies Needed

Schools are a microcosm of society and can reflect societal attitudes about aggression, race relations, and diversity. Within the school context, youth learn from their peers, teachers, and other adults about acceptable behavior; how to handle conflict; ways to assert, manage, or limit power and control within relationships; and appropriate social behavior. A significant minority of youth are victimized by their peers due to race, ethnicity, or immigration status (for a review see Scherr & Larson, 2010). Research on trends in victimization and ethnicity show inconsistent patterns, as various studies have used different definitions of violence and victimization, measures, and samples. As bullying is a problem within every school, it is something that students and the adults in their lives learn to avoid, resolve, or endure. School psychologists can play an important role in making school a positive place for all.

Bullying Prevention Case Study

This case study combines experiences from various schools to provide practical direction as to how each aspect of bullying prevention should be considered and then implemented to meet the individual needs of a single school. School psychologists are encouraged to focus on the process of decisions rather than the ultimate interventions, as what is selected for implementation will depend on the needs of a particular school.

A junior high school of approximately 800 students is located in a suburban community and has a student population representative of the youth in the community, with about 50% Latino, 36% Caucasian, and 14% other or multiple racial background. About 40% are socioeconomically disadvantaged and 34% are English language learners. The campus was renovated less than 10 years ago and is well maintained. It has more than adequate instructional resources, including computer labs, a library, science labs, a theater, an activity room, and athletic fields and courts.

The school principal first identified the need to focus on bullying prevention by reviewing results of the California Healthy Kids Survey (http://chks.wested.org), a surveillance survey similar to the Youth Risk Behavior Surveillance Survey used nationwide, which indicated that a large percentage of students in the junior high school's county disagree that they feel safe in their school (19%), and many had experienced verbal harassment such as having been made fun of (35%) and having had sexual jokes made to them (39%), as well as physical violence such as having been in a fight (48%) and having been pushed or shoved (30%). The principal presented these results to the staff and the parents in separate meetings and found that there was agreement between stakeholders that bullying was a problem and should be addressed. Participants in the meeting shared anecdotes of verbal and physical aggression on campus, but the exact scope of the problem was unknown. Up to this point, the school treated incidents of peer victimization as disciplinary issues and interventions were limited to punishment of the aggressor by exclusion, such as suspension.

At the start of the school year, the school principal consulted with the school psychologist and formed a bullying prevention committee to understand and address the problem. The committee consisted of the principal, the school psychologist, the school counselor, and two interested teachers (physical education and social studies). The school psychologist encouraged the use of a school-wide screening to identify the most pressing needs, and the team agreed this was an important first step.

The team consulted with experts in bullying assessment and were offered the opportunity to administer the California Bullying Victimization Scale and have their data processed and analyzed without cost as part of an effort by the researchers to confirm the reliability and validity of the scale. The two teachers on the committee were selected to implement the scale to a large subsection of the entire school because they taught core courses required of all students. The survey was conducted anonymously and for the purposes of school safety planning, so passive instead of active parental consent procedures were used, and the results were not required to be included in the students' records. On the other hand, this meant the survey results could not be linked to individual students regardless whether incidences of bullying were reported, and thus action could not be taken to intervene.

Results of the survey indicated that 58% of males and 47% of females reported some kind of peer victimization in the past 30 days, and 16% of males and 23% of females reported victimization that was classified as bullying victimization (i.e., it was repeated and was done by someone more powerful than the victim). Victimization most often occurred in the lunch or eating areas (41%), followed by in the classrooms (28%), hallways (26%), and on the sports fields (25%). Victimization occurred less frequently in the bathrooms (17%), coming to/from school (8%), and on the bus (6%). Students reported that they most often talk to their friends about their victimization experiences (49%) followed by adults at home (27%), adults at school (10%), and no one (8%).

Reviewing these results, the bullying prevention committee determined that bullying and peer victimization was indeed a problem on their campus and affected a majority of students. The committee also identified certain areas of the school campus where incidents most often occur and determined that these areas could use better supervision. The committee presented these results to the entire school community along with some basic information about bullying and skits they developed with students to demonstrate what bystanders could do to intervene in victimization.

The bullying prevention committee made a wish list of prevention activities and prioritized them for implementation. This list included (a) updating policies on bullying and victimization, (b) adding structure and supervision for students during free periods, (c) teaching all school community members about bullying and about policies and practices to prevent and intervene with bullying, (d) identifying and implementing a universal bully prevention program, (e) developing and implementing a system for students to anonymously report bullying incidents, and (f) identifying the most effective responses for handling incidents of bullying.

The bullying prevention committee updated policies on bullying prevention before the end of the school year. In the committee's research, it determined that its previous approach focusing on zero tolerance for bullying is a popular but harmful approach to bullying prevention. Zero tolerance approaches promote punishment for specific infractions without taking into consideration the unique needs of a given situation. Students may be scared to report incidents for fear that peers will be treated harshly. The committee realized that the issue of bullying needed to be addressed openly through constant dialogue and that school community members needed to feel safe and empowered to report incidents and intervene when safe to do so.

The committee also realized that students who bully needed more support to stop hurtful behaviors and students who are victims may need help to overcome the psychosocial impacts of being bullied. Thus, the new policy focused on responsibilities of the school district to provide staff development and training on bullying and to encourage reporting of bullying incidents while maintaining confidentiality whenever possible. The policy made clear the punitive consequences of bullying but also noted the importance of empowering students to resolve bullying. The new policy was disseminated to teachers during professional development days prior to school the following school year and to parents and students through a handout in the annual student handbook that was required to be signed and returned. Classroom teachers reviewed the policy with students during the first week of school.

The bullying prevention committee also developed two key strategies to provide additional structure and supervision on school campus with a limited budget. First, the committee recruited parents to monitor hallways and the lunch areas during passing periods and breaks. To prepare the parent volunteers, they included them in staff training on how to recognize various forms of victimization, to intervene effectively, and to document incidents for administrator follow-up. Second, the committee recruited teachers to keep their classrooms open during lunch with planned activities such as playing board games or learning Morse code. Over time these classrooms became safe havens for students who had difficulty finding social connections in unstructured situations. Eventually, the school psychologist was able to incorporate this strategy with her work with students with autism spectrum disorders, developing lunch clubs for these students based on their particular interests and encouraging other students to join them.

For a universal bullying prevention program, the bullying prevention committee selected Promoting Positive Peer Relationships because of the enthusiastic endorsement of local bullying researchers who also offered to support implementation of the program free of charge in exchange for access to collect evaluation data. In addition, the program is brief and easy to implement so would not require extensive training or redevelopment of the curriculum in whatever class it was offered. The bullying prevention committee secured the participation of the health teachers, who were trained to implement the lessons and incorporate the lesson concepts into other aspects of their curriculum. The program was evaluated over 2 years, and results found small effect sizes for improving students' attitudes about bullying and their sense of social support in the school as well as strong social validity for ease of implementation and perceived benefit to students. The school continues to implement the Promoting Positive Peer Relationships program.

The school bullying committee identified a need to allow students to report bullying incidents anonymously because the committee did not have an efficient way to track bullying outside the standard office discipline referral process. The committee partnered with a local software company that developed an online system for school members to anonymously report bullying incidents and to prompt school administrators to investigate, respond to, and track each incident. Once a report is submitted, the system sends instant e-mail and text notifications to the administrator. The system also connects students and other participants to online resources to prevent and intervene with bullying. The system allows for aggregate data tracking at the school or across an entire district. The district has implemented the system for 2 years, helping provide feedback to the software company as they develop the software. There has not been a formal study of the impact of the software on incidents of bullying, nor has the software been used to help evaluate other bully prevention efforts, although these uses are possible. However, the administrators have expressed that using the software has helped them track and respond to incidents in a timely manner.

As the bullying prevention activities were being identified and implemented, the bullying prevention committee recognized a need to develop a more proactive and positive discipline strategy to respond effectively to bullying incidents when they occur and to prevent future occurrences of bullying and other discipline infractions. Initially the administration worked with the bullying prevention committee, and the school psychologist and school counselor in particular, to provide ad hoc intervention when needed. However, the committee recognized that a formal three-tiered approach to discipline would be more successful. Around this time, the school district notified the school that it decided to implement a restorative justice approach to discipline across the district, piloting it in one junior high school one year, expanding it to the other schools in subsequent years. Thus, the administrators of this school decided to maintain the current discipline approach to wait for the opportunity to engage in the district training and scale-up of restorative approaches, which will occur in the next school year.

The school continues to engage in the Promoting Positive Peer Relationships program and is beginning to implement the restorative justice approach. The school continues to use the software system to collect data about specific bullying incidences. The school also conducts school-wide annual assessments of bullying, to continue to track trends in bullying, where it is occurring, and whom students reach out to when they have been bullied. School administrators believe this annual assessment is crucial, because as a school serving seventh- and eighth-grade students, half of their student population changes every year. The administrators need current information for the student population they are serving that academic year.

These data have allowed the school to adjust and refine intervention efforts in response to the needs of specific groups of students. Bullying continues to occur at this school, but the rates of bullying have declined and school staff report much greater confidence in their ability to respond to bullying when it occurs.

SUMMARY

Studies estimate that 30–50% of U.S. students are involved as aggressors or targets of bullying (Wang, Iannotti, & Nansel, 2009), and the long-term negative effects of bullying on mental and physical health for both bullies and victims are well documented. Bullying is a subset of peer victimization that involves intentional aggression that is repeated over time and involves an imbalance of power between the person doing the bullying and the person being bullied (Olweus, 1996). School psychologists are often integrally involved in ensuring that schools meet state mandates in regard to bullying legislation, and it is therefore important that they stay up to date with current laws and are aware of state-distributed model policies (this information can be found at http://www.stopbullying.gov/laws). Collecting data on student experiences with bullying, victimization, and related behaviors is a critical starting point for planning bullying prevention and intervention activities. This can be done through a school-wide survey of students, staff, and parents. Then, it is important to select bullying prevention efforts that have evaluation data to support their success. Bullying prevention and intervention efforts that have some research and evaluation support are summarized in Table 17.1. Ttofi and Farrington (2011) found the following program elements were associated with a statistically significant decrease in bullying: parent training/ meetings, playground supervision, intensity for children, intensity for teachers, duration for children, classroom management, teacher training, classroom rules, a whole-school policy, school conferences, and having more than 10 components of bullying prevention. Bullying prevention efforts need to be continually monitored and evaluated by schools, as student populations and school staffing change with time. In sum, school psychologists play an essential role in making school a safe and positive place for all.

REFERENCES

Ball, B., Tharp, A. T., Noonan, R. K., Valle, L. A., Hamburger, M. E., & Rosenbluth, B. (2012). Expect Respect support groups: Preliminary evaluation of a dating violence prevention program for at-risk youth. *Violence Against Women, 18*, 746–762. doi:10.1177/1077801212455188

Bell, C. D., Raczynski, K. A., & Horne, A. M. (2010). Bully Busters abbreviated: Evaluation of a group-based bully intervention and prevention program. *Group Dynamics: Theory, Research, and Practice, 14*, 257–267. doi:10.1037/a0020596

Black, S. A., & Jackson, E. (2007). Using bullying incident density to evaluate the Olweus Bullying Prevention Programme. *School Psychology International, 28*, 623–638. doi:10.1177/0143034307085662

Brown, E. C., Low, S., Smith, B. H., & Haggerty, K. P. (2011). Outcomes from a school-randomized controlled trial of *Steps to Respect: A bullying prevention program. School Psychology Review, 40*, 423–443.

Cunningham, C. E., Vaillancourt, T., Rimas, H., Deal, K., Cunningham, L., Short, K., & Chen, Y. (2009). Modeling the bullying prevention program preferences of educators: A discrete choice conjoint experiment. *Journal of Abnormal Child Psychology, 37*, 929–943. doi:10.1007/s10802-009-9324-2

DeRosier, M. E. (2004). Building relationship and combating bullying: Effectiveness of a school-based social skills group intervention. *Journal of Clinical Child and Adolescent Psychology, 33*, 196–201. doi:10.1207/S15374424JCCP3301_18

Felix, E. D., Sharkey, J. D., Green, J. G., Furlong, M. J., & Tanigawa, D. (2011). Getting precise and pragmatic about the assessment of bullying: The development of the California Bullying Victimization Scale. *Aggressive Behavior, 37*, 234–247. doi:10.1002/ab.20389

Frey, K. S., Hirschstein, M. K., Edstrom, L., & Snell, J. (2009). Observed reductions in school bullying, nonbullying aggression, and destructive bystander behavior: A longitudinal evaluation. *Journal of Educational Psychology, 101*, 466–481. doi:10.1037/a0013839

Harrell, A. W., Mercer, S. H., & DeRosier, M. E. (2009). Improving the social–behavioral adjustment of adolescents: The effectiveness of a social skills group intervention. *Journal of Child and Family Studies, 18*, 378–387. doi:10.1007/s10826-008-9241-y

Kärnä, A., Voeten, M., Little, T. D., Poskiparta, E., Kaljonen, A., & Salmivalli, C. (2011). A large-scale evaluation of the KiVa antibullying program: Grades 4–6. *Child Development, 82*, 311–330. doi:10.1111/j.1467-8624.2010.01557.x

Kumpulainen, K., Henttonen, I., Almqvist, F., Kresanov, K., Linna, S. L., Moilanen, I., … Tamminen, T. (1998). Bullying and psychiatric symptoms among elementary school-age children. *Child Abuse & Neglect, 22*, 705–716. doi:10.1016/S0145-2134(98)00049-0

Limber, S. P. (2004). Implementation of the Olweus Bullying Prevention Program in American schools: Lessons learned from the field. In D. L. Espelage & S. M. Swearer (Eds.), *Bullying in American schools* (pp. 351–364). Mahwah, NJ: Erlbaum.

Limber, S. P., Nation, M., Tracy, A. J., Melton, G. B., & Flerx, V. (2004). Implementation of the Olweus Bullying Prevention Program in the southeastern United States. In P. K. Smith, D. Pepler, & K. Rigby (Eds.), *Bullying in schools: How successful can interventions be?* (pp. 55–79). New York, NY: Cambridge University Press. doi:10.1017/CBO9780511584466.005

Low, S., Frey, K. S., & Brockman, C. J. (2010). Gossip on the playground: Changes associated with universal intervention, retaliation beliefs, and supportive friends. *School Psychology Review*, *39*, 536–551.

National Association of School Psychologists. (2010). *Model for comprehensive and integrated school psychological services*. Bethesda, MD: Author. Retrieved from http://www.nasponline.org/standards/ 2010standards/2_PracticeModel.pdf

Newman-Carlson, D., & Horne, A. M. (2004). Bully Busters: A psychoeducational intervention for reducing bullying behavior in middle school students. *Journal of Counseling and Development*, *82*, 259–267. doi:10.1002/j.1556-6678.2004.tb00309.x

Olweus, D. (1996). Bullying at school: Knowledge base and an effective intervention plan. *Annals of the New York Academy of Sciences*, *794*, 265–276. doi:10.1111/j.1749-6632.1996.tb32527.x

Olweus, D., & Limber, S. P. (2010). Bullying in school: Evaluation and dissemination of the Olweus Bullying Prevention Program. *American Journal of Orthopsychiatry*, *80*, 124–134. doi:10.1111/j.1939-0025.2010.01015.x

Orpinas, P., Horne, A. M., & Staniszewski, D. (2003). School bullying: Changing the problem by changing the school. *School Psychology Review*, *32*, 431–444.

Perren, S., Corcoran, L., Cowie, H., Dehue, F., Garcia, D., Mc Guckin, C., ... Völlink, T. (2012). Tackling cyberbullying: Review of empirical evidence regarding successful response by students, parents, and schools. *International Journal of Conflict and Violence*, *6*, 283–293.

Pikas, A. (2002). New developments of the Shared Concern method. *School Psychology International*, *23*, 307–336. doi:10.1177/ 0143034302023003234

Reijntjes, A., Kamphuis, J. H., Prinzie, P., & Telch, M. J. (2010). Peer victimization and internalizing problems in children: A meta-analysis of longitudinal studies. *Child Abuse & Neglect*, *34*, 244–252. doi:10.1016/j.chiabu.2009.07.009

Renshaw, T. L., & Jimerson, S. R. (2012). Enhancing student attitudes via a brief, universal-level bullying prevention curriculum. *School Mental Health*, *4*, 115–128. doi:10.1007/s12310-011-9069-2

Rigby, K., & Griffiths, C. (2011). Addressing cases of bullying through the method of Shared Concern. *School Psychology International*, *32*, 345–357. doi:10.1177/0143034311402148

Ross, S. W., & Horner, R. H. (2009). Bullying prevention in positive behavior support. *Journal of Applied Behavior Analysis*, *42*, 747–759. doi:10.1901/jaba.2009.42-747

Salmivalli, C., Kärnä, A., & Poskiparta, E. (2011). Counteracting bullying in Finland: The KiVa program and its effects on different forms of being bullied. *International Journal of Behavioral Development*, *35*, 405–411. doi:10.1177/0165025411407457

Sansone, R. A., Leung, J. S., & Wiederman, M. W. (2013). Having been bullied in childhood: Relationship to aggressive behaviour in adulthood. *International Journal of Social Psychiatry*, *59*, 824–826. doi: 10.1177/0020764012456814

Scherr, T. G., & Larson, J. (2010). Bullying dynamics associated with race, ethnicity, and immigration status. In S. R. Jimerson, S. M. Swearer, & D. L. Espelage (Eds.), *The international handbook of school bullying* (pp. 223–234). New York, NY: Routledge.

Schroeder, B. A., Messina, A., Schroeder, D., Good, K., Barto, S., Saylor, J., ... Masiello, M. (2012). The implementation of a statewide bullying prevention program: Preliminary findings from the field and the importance of coalitions. *Health Promotion Practice*, *13*, 489–495. doi:10.1177/1524839910386887

Smith, P. K., Ananiadou, K., & Cowie, H. (2003). Interventions to reduce school bullying. *Canadian Journal of Psychiatry*, *48*, 591–599.

Stuart-Cassel, V., Bell, A., & Springer, J. F. (2011). *Analysis of state bullying laws and policies*. Washington, DC: Department of Education. Retrieved from http://www2.ed.gov/rschstat/eval/ bullying/state-bullying-laws/state-bullying-laws.pdf

Ttofi, M. M., & Farrington, D. P. (2011). Effectiveness of school-based programs to reduce bullying: A systematic and meta-analytic review. *Journal of Experimental Criminology*, *7*, 27–56. doi:10.1007/ s11292-010-9109-1

Wang, J., Iannotti, R. J., & Nansel, T. R. (2009). School bullying among adolescents in the United States: Physical, verbal, relational, cyber. *Journal of Adolescent Health*, *45*, 368–375. doi:10. 1016/j.jadohealth.2009.03.021

Whitaker, D. J., Rosenbluth, B., Valle, L. A., & Sanchez, E. (2004). Expect Respect: A school-based intervention to promote awareness and effective responses to bullying and sexual harassment. In D. L. Espelage & S. M. Swearer (Eds.), *Bullying in American schools* (pp. 327–350). Mahwah, NJ: Erlbaum.

18 Best Practices in Threat Assessment in Schools

Dewey Cornell
University of Virginia

OVERVIEW

Following the 1999 shooting at Columbine High School in Colorado, reports by the FBI (O'Toole, 2000) and U.S. Secret Service (Fein et al., 2002) recommended that schools establish threat assessment teams to prevent targeted acts of violence. Although an unfamiliar concept to most educators and psychologists at the outset of this century, threat assessment is a specialized form of risk assessment that is conducted when an individual threatens to commit a violent act or engages in threatening behavior. In the past decade, school shootings observed around the world have stimulated the adoption of threat assessment as a widely used international practice (Bondü, Cornell, & Scheithauer, 2011).

The concept of threat assessment has evolved to include the identification, assessment, and management of persons who have communicated threats of violence or engaged in some form of threatening behavior (Borum, Cornell, Modzeleski, & Jimerson, 2010). In school settings, the threat assessment team typically is concerned with understanding why a student made a threat or engaged in threatening behavior, and then identifying appropriate interventions that help address the underlying problem or concern that motivated the threat. For example, a student may be involved in bullying, upset over the end of a romantic relationship, or embroiled in some other conflict with peers. From this perspective, threat assessment can be viewed as a problem-solving approach to violence prevention. Threat assessment teams are concerned with helping students who may be frustrated, angry, distressed, and in need of assistance to prevent an act of violence. In many cases, the student's threat is a transient expression of frustration or defiance that does not pose a serious, substantive threat to safety. In other cases where the threat appears to be substantive and there is imminent danger, the threat assessment team takes appropriate protective actions, such as warning potential victims and contacting law enforcement.

Threat assessment is a flexible approach to violence prevention that requires the team to make reasoned judgments rather than follow a narrowly prescribed course of action that can lead to overreactions to ordinary student conflict and misbehavior. Threat assessment is especially useful as an alternative to zero tolerance discipline and reduces the use of school exclusion through suspensions, transfers, and expulsions.

Threat assessments are conducted in situations such as when an angry student threatens to beat up a classmate, a student is found with a knife or other weapon at school, or a student is reported by other students to have plans to kill someone. There must be sufficient grounds in the student's behavior to justify a threat assessment. Although there may be patterns of behavior that merit concern and prompt an informal assessment of how a student is doing, a threat assessment should be limited to cases in which a student has engaged in threatening communications or behavior. Threat assessments ordinarily are not conducted in situations such as if a student is disrespectful and angry in interactions with a teacher, a student wears a black trench coat and seems preoccupied with violent video games, or a student seems socially awkward and others describe the student as "creepy" or "strange."

School psychologists have a central role on threat assessment teams, which also may include school administrators, school resource officers, counselors, and social workers. As a team member, the school psychologist may contribute to the threat assessment process by interviewing the student identified as making a threat, as well as gathering information from parents, teachers, or witnesses to the threat. In many cases, the school psychologist will assist in clarifying the student's intentions and use counseling methods to address an underlying conflict or problem so that the threat is resolved. The school psychologist may also advise the team regarding student support needs or mental health concerns that merit further intervention. In the case of students receiving special education services, it will be appropriate to review the student's educational plan.

The school psychologist's role in threat assessment is consistent with the Preventive and Responsive Services domain of the National Association of School Psychologists (NASP) *Model for Comprehensive and Integrated School Psychological Services* (NASP, 2010) in multiple ways. The school psychologist provides student-level services in both evaluating a student's threatening behavior and identifying suitable interventions and mental health services to develop the student's social skills and coping capacity. At a systems level, the school psychologist consults and collaborates with the team members and other school staff members in helping to maintain a safe and supportive learning environment.

The purpose of this chapter is to give school psychologists an understanding of threat assessment as an approach to violence prevention that is well within their scope of practice and a valuable contribution they can make to maintaining a safe and supportive climate in their schools. Three objectives of the chapter are (a) to explain why threat assessment is a preferred alternative to other approaches that schools use to deal with potentially violent students, such as profiling and zero tolerance discipline; (b) to distinguish serious, substantive threats of violence from less serious, but more common transient threats; and (c) to alert school psychologists to the challenges and limitations of the threat assessment process.

BASIC CONSIDERATIONS

Threats of violence are common events in schools. A survey of 4,400 high school students found that approximately 14% reported being threatened by another student in the past 30 days (Nekvasil & Cornell, 2012). Despite the high frequency of threats experienced by high school students, few are reported to school authorities. Only 46% of public schools recorded a student threat of physical harm in the 2009–2010 academic year, with middle schools reporting the

highest rate of student threats, at more than 13 per 1,000 students (Neiman, 2011). The dilemma for school authorities is that, when a threat is reported, they must evaluate the seriousness of the threat and avoid two undesirable outcomes: overlooking a serious threat versus overreacting to a threat that is not serious.

School shootings are notorious events that raise great public concern and apprehension. School psychologists recognize that fear of a school shooting can bias judgments about the risk of violence (Cornell, 2006). Although numerous school shootings have occurred in the United States, the probability that any one of the nation's approximately 125,000 schools will experience a homicidal student attack is estimated as once every 6,000 years, and school homicides constitute less than 1% of the annual homicides of youth ages 5–18 (Borum et al., 2010). Nevertheless, the shootings at Sandy Hook Elementary School in Connecticut in 2012 prompted many state legislatures and communities to consider spending millions of dollars for armed guards, security cameras, and fortified entrances in our nation's elementary schools, even though youth are far more likely to be shot or killed outside of school than at school. School safety is an unquestionable priority, but effective safety practices and the allocation of limited resources must be based on a realistic understanding of the risk of violence.

Zero Tolerance Suspension Practices

School shootings have also propelled schools to adopt increasingly punitive and inflexible discipline practices (Cornell, 2006). The politically popular rubric of zero tolerance means that students are automatically suspended from school for even the slightest violations of school rules regarding weapons, drugs, or threats of violence (American Psychological Association Zero Tolerance Task Force [APA], 2008). There are frequent news reports of students being suspended for questionable reasons. For example, after the Sandy Hook Elementary School shooting in 2012, a 6-year-old boy was suspended from school for pointing his finger like a gun and saying "pow." One purpose of threat assessment is to provide an approach that permits school administrators to make reasonable judgments when it is evident that a student's behavior does not constitute a serious threat of violence.

Although school suspensions are widely used as a disciplinary strategy intended to maintain order and safety in schools, this practice has come under increasing scrutiny (Losen & Martinez, 2013). There is considerable evidence that school suspension does not achieve its stated objectives of reforming misbehaving students or deterring other students from breaking school rules (APA, 2008). A longitudinal study following 1 million Texas students from grades 6–12 found that suspensions did not have a positive impact on students, and instead raised the likelihood of school failure, dropout, and juvenile court involvement (Fabelo et al., 2011). Likewise, there is an absence of evidence that schools making high use of suspension are safer or more orderly environments. On the contrary, schools with high suspension rates have lower graduation rates than other schools, even after controlling for differences in school demographics (Losen & Martinez, 2013).

School Psychologists' Contribution to Threat Assessments

In their study of school shootings, the U.S. Secret Service observed that more than three quarters of the student perpetrators had communicated to someone, usually a friend or classmate, that they had an interest in making an attack at school (Vossekuil, Fein, Reddy, Borum, & Modzeleski, 2002). In more than two thirds of cases, the boys felt bullied or harassed by others and were motivated to take revenge. Similarly, the FBI study noted the frequent "leakage" of violent intentions in the communications of students before they carried out a school shooting (O'Toole, 2000). These observations supported the conclusion by law enforcement and education authorities that schools should focus on the identification and investigation of student threats as a violence prevention strategy (Vossekuil et al., 2002).

Threat assessments typically are conducted by multidisciplinary teams. School psychologists have a central role on threat assessment teams because of their expertise in assessing student behavior and socioemotional needs, formulating intervention plans, and emphasizing a data-based approach to decision making. A team is usually led by a school administrator such as the principal or an assistant principal who has responsibility for disciplinary matters. Other school staff members, such as school counselors and social workers, are often involved in carrying out interventions with students that address mental health and behavioral needs that are identified through the threat assessment. There should be a law enforcement officer on the team who is available in the most serious cases when there is a possible violation of law, need for a law enforcement investigation, or need for protective actions or security measures.

School psychologists may believe that they are not prepared to conduct threat assessments because their training did not teach them to predict violence. Indeed, there are many hazards and limitations to the prediction of violence (Borum, Bartel, & Forth, 2002; Heilbrun, Dvoskin, & Heilbrun, 2009). Nevertheless, there is strong interest in using profiles or checklists of warning signs to identify dangerous students. A federal government guide to school safety presented 16 warning signs that included items such as history of discipline problems, drug use and alcohol use, feelings of being picked on and persecuted, and excessive feelings of rejection (Dwyer, Osher, & Warger, 1998). Many school psychologists could identify students in their schools who meet these signs yet do not pose a threat for violence. The federal guide recognized the limitations of a warning signs approach and cautioned, "Unfortunately, there is a real danger that early warning signs will be misinterpreted" (Dwyer et al., 1998, p. 7). The guide urged school authorities to refrain from using the warning signs as a basis for punishing students or excluding them from school.

In their study of school shootings, the profiling experts with the FBI (O'Toole, 2000) concluded that schools should not rely on student profiling and noted, "Trying to draw up a catalogue or 'checklist' of warning signs to detect a potential school shooter can be shortsighted, even dangerous. Such lists, publicized by the media, can end up unfairly labeling many nonviolent students as potentially dangerous" (O'Toole, 2000, p. 2). The extraordinarily low base rate for severe violent behavior makes it unlikely that any psychological profile or assessment procedure could achieve respectable accuracy above chance levels (Heilbrun et al., 2009).

It is essential for school psychologists to help all school staff and administrators to remember that threat assessment is less concerned with the prediction of violence than the prevention of violence. The distinction between prediction and prevention has become increasingly important in the field of risk assessment in large part because of recognition that the risk of violence is not a static quality and is often amenable to intervention (Heilbrun et al., 2009). Moreover, many public health campaigns have demonstrated that prevention of many harmful outcomes (e.g., motor vehicle fatalities, smoking-related cancer, cardiovascular disease) can be achieved by addressing risk and protective factors in the population rather than attempting to make individual predictions. Prevention does not require prediction.

In an appropriately conducted threat assessment, the school psychologist should be concerned with prevention rather than prediction. This means the school psychologist will be on familiar ground in determining why a student engaged in a certain problem behavior (in this case, a threat). He or she will want to assess the student's mental state and sources of stress and support, appraise his or her coping strengths and weaknesses, and evaluate his or her need for mental health services. A referral for special education services may also be considered, if special education services may be relevant for the student and the student is not already receiving such services. If the student is receiving special education services, it would be appropriate to review the student's individual education plan, determine whether an appropriate functional behavioral assessment and behavior intervention plan are in place, and consider whether the plan might need adjustment. Rather than offer a questionable prediction that a student is "dangerous" or "not dangerous," the school psychologist should recommend interventions intended to reduce the risk of violence. Such interventions might range from mediating a peer conflict to seeking hospitalization for an emerging mental illness. These interventions are justified by the student's need for assistance and do not need to be based on a prediction of violence. Prevention of violence is achieved by serving the immediate needs of students in distress, without the need for prediction.

Research on Threat Assessment

Although many authorities recommend threat assessment as a violence prevention strategy in principle (Fein et al., 2002; O'Toole, 2000), there is little empirical research on threat assessment in practice. For example, the Colorado School Safety Resource Center (2013) has published a detailed description of the elements of threat assessment that draws upon recommendations from the Secret Service report (Fein et al., 2002). Another example is the Salem-Keizer school district in Oregon, one of many school systems that have developed their own threat assessment system (Van Dreal, 2011).

One of the first reports of a threat assessment model in schools was the Dallas Threat of Violence Risk Assessment (Van Dyke & Schroeder, 2006) developed in the Dallas, Texas, school system. The Dallas Threat of Violence Risk Assessment consists of 19 risk factors derived from a review of literature on risk factors for violence. Each item is rated as low (1), medium (2), or high (3), then summed into a total risk score in which

scores below 9 are considered low risk and scores above 14 are considered high risk. A structured system like this is appealing, but the authors cautioned that the scoring system and cutoff points were "arbitrarily chosen by the committee without empirical validation" (Van Dyke & Schroeder, 2006, p. 608).

The only threat assessment model that has been empirically examined in a series of studies is the Virginia Student Threat Assessment Guidelines (Cornell & Sheras, 2006). The Virginia model of threat assessment is an approach to violence prevention that distinguishes serious or "substantive" threats from the more frequent less serious threats termed "transient" threats. This model focuses attention on problems such as bullying, teasing, and other forms of student conflict that often underlie threats and emphasizes the need to address them before they escalate into violent behavior. School staff members are encouraged to adopt a flexible, problem-solving approach, as distinguished from a more punitive, zero tolerance approach to student misbehavior. Consistent with this goal, three studies found that Virginia workshop participants became less anxious about the possibility of a school homicide, more willing to use threat assessment methods to help students resolve conflicts, and less inclined to use a zero tolerance approach (Allen, Cornell, Lorek, & Sheras, 2008; Cornell, Allen, & Fan, 2012; Cornell, Gregory, & Fan, 2011).

Two year-long field tests demonstrated that school-based teams could conduct threat assessments in a safe and efficient manner, and that almost all students would be able to return to school without long-term suspension and no reports of threats being carried out (Cornell et al., 2004; Strong & Cornell, 2008). Subsequently, three controlled studies found strong support for the Virginia Guidelines. One study found that students at schools using the Virginia Guidelines reported less bullying, greater willingness to seek help for bullying and threats of violence, and more positive perceptions of school staff members than students in comparison schools (Cornell, Sheras, Gregory, & Fan, 2009). A second controlled study found large reductions in suspension rates and bullying infractions in a group of high schools after implementation of the Virginia Guidelines, while control group schools showed little change (Cornell et al., 2011). A third study was a randomized controlled trial. Over the course of a school year, students who made threats of violence in schools using the threat assessment model were much more likely to receive long-term suspension or an alternative school placement than students in the control schools (Cornell et al.,

2012). In addition, students in the threat assessment group schools were far more likely to receive school counseling services and parent conferences than students in the control group schools. Based on these studies, the Virginia Guidelines became recognized in 2013 as an evidence-based program by the National Registry of Evidence-Based Programs and Practices.

BEST PRACTICES IN THREAT ASSESSMENT

Both the FBI (O'Toole, 2000) and the Secret Service (Fein et al., 2002) reports recommended that schools adopt a threat assessment approach. Threat assessment is used by the Secret Service to investigate persons who might pose a threat to a government official, and it is used in the business field when there is concern about workplace violence (Borum, Fein, Vossekuil, & Berglund, 1999). In both settings, threats are often not serious and do not lead to criminal sanctions or loss of employment. The extension of this method to schools requires careful consideration of the developmental limitations of children and adolescents. Students frequently engage in threatening behavior that can range from being playful to being seriously angry. When angry, they may make statements that are expressions of feeling and not genuine intentions.

The practice of threat assessment has evolved to encompass more than just the assessment of whether someone poses a threat to others. When a threat is determined to be serious, threat assessment also includes threat management efforts to reduce the risk of violence. In urgent situations where violence appears to be imminent, the threat assessment team recommends immediate protective actions that typically involve law enforcement action. However, in most cases, the school psychologist can play a critical role in understanding why a student made a threat or engaged in threatening behavior, and then identifying appropriate interventions that help address the underlying problem or concern that motivated the threat. From this perspective, threat assessment can be viewed as a problem-solving approach to violence prevention. Threat assessment teams are concerned with helping individuals who are frustrated, angry, distressed, or in some way in need of assistance to prevent them from engaging in an act of violence. Threat assessment is a flexible approach to violence prevention that requires the team to make reasoned judgments rather than follow a narrowly prescribed course of action such as zero tolerance discipline. Threat assessment is ideally a process of threat resolution.

The threat resolution process is effective only when threats are reported to authorities, so it is essential that all school personnel understand the importance of reporting threatening statements, behaviors, or other observations that suggest the potential for violence. School personnel should be advised that they are not expected to make their own assessments of threats, but to provide information to the threat assessment team whenever they have a concern. Although a single observation may not seem significant, an accumulation of observations from multiple sources could indicate a significant concern to a threat assessment team.

Threat assessment teams, including school psychologists, are trained to encourage students, parents, and other members of the school community to report threats of violence so that the team can conduct an assessment and take appropriate action. In order to overcome the code of silence that affects many students, schools should educate students that there is a difference between snitching and seeking help (Syvertsen, Flanagan, & Stout, 2009). Students may be more willing to report threats when they see that school authorities are not taking a punitive, zero tolerance approach, but instead are concerned with solving problems and preventing conflicts from escalating into violence. Students are more likely to seek help in schools with a more positive and supportive climate (Eliot, Cornell, Gregory, & Fan, 2010). There should be multiple ways for students and other individuals to report behavior that concerns them: (a) Teachers, school psychologists, and other school staff should make known their interest and availability to hear concerns. (b) Information about safety matters and the importance of reporting threats should be included in school meetings and information routinely sent to parents at the outset of the school year. (c) There should be anonymous methods of making reports, such as a link on the school website. Some states and some large school systems have anonymous hotline reporting services (Payne & Elliott, 2011). (d) The school website should describe how and why concerns should be reported.

The term *threat* does not convey the broader function of the team and might discourage some individuals from reporting their concerns. Threat assessment teams do not have to be labeled or referred to as threat assessment teams. The functions of a threat assessment team could be carried out by teams identified by other labels, such as a conflict resolution team or student assistance team. Also, the threat assessment function could be incorporated into other team structures already in place in the school.

A key aspect of threat assessment is its emphasis on considering the context and seriousness of the student's behavior: What were the circumstances surrounding the student's actions and what did the student intend by these actions? If the investigation indicates that the threat is genuine, then the next step would be to take action to prevent it from being carried out.

One of the most important principles of threat assessment is that the team, including the school psychologist, should investigate whether the student *poses* a threat, not simply whether the student has made a threat (Fein et al., 2002). Many students will make threats that are not serious threats to the welfare of others. The investigation should look for behavioral evidence that indicates that the student is planning or preparing to carry out the threat. For example, has the student acquired weapons? Has the student developed a plan or practiced attack behaviors? Has the student recruited peers to assist in the attack?

Student Threat Assessment Guidelines

Basic principles of student threat assessment are found in the general literature on threat assessment (Fein et al., 2002; Heilbrun et al., 2009; O'Toole, 2000). These principles are more fully elaborated and used to establish a set of operational procedures in the Virginia Student Threat Assessment Guidelines (Cornell & Sheras, 2006). Guidelines give schools a flexible approach to student threats that can be adjusted to the seriousness of the student's behavior. There are many forms of aggressive behavior in the school-age population. Verbal aggression can range from playful teasing to arguments and abusive language, whereas physical aggression can range from playful jostling or horseplay to many levels of fighting, from pushing and shoving to serious attempts to hurt one another. Because student threats are a relatively common event, but rarely result in severe acts of violence, it is important that schools have a procedure to assess the seriousness of a threat rather than overreact with automatic suspension or expulsion. School authorities, including school psychologists, must always consider the context and meaning of the student's behavior. In many cases the threat is less serious than it may first appear. Research (reviewed above) indicates that schools using the Virginia Guidelines can make judgments about the seriousness of a threat that result in much lower rates of long-term suspension and fewer out-of-school placements than other schools.

A threat is defined broadly as any expression of intent to harm someone (Cornell & Sheras, 2006). A threat can be directly communicated to the target or indirectly communicated to third parties. Threats may be spoken or written, and increasingly they may be communicated through digital communication media such as websites or text messages. Threats can be specific ("I am going to kill you.") or vague ("I am going to hurt you."). Threats also can be veiled or implied ("You better watch your back." "You're going to be sorry."). Using abusive language or calling someone names is not considered a threat unless there is a statement expressing intent to harm someone.

Threats can also be expressed through behavior such as carrying a weapon, and here the presence of a threat requires more judgment. A student who brings a weapon to school is in violation of school prohibitions against weapons but may or may not intend to harm someone. Students may bring a weapon to school for protection, to impress others, or to make a sale. The definition of a weapon must also be carefully considered. Throughout the United States, students have been suspended, arrested, or expelled for bringing toy guns, water pistols, and even the tiny plastic accessories for military action figures that are shaped like guns (Cornell, 2006). Threat assessment allows school authorities to make commonsense judgments rather than rely on rigid rules.

Threat Assessment Team
It is recommended that each school have its own threat assessment team. A school-based team is recommended because local staff will know the students and be able to respond more quickly than an external team. In more complex cases, the team could draw upon consultation from outside the school. Memphis City Schools used a centralized threat assessment team to evaluate the most serious cases that were being considered for long-term suspension (Strong & Cornell, 2008). However, most student threats can be resolved without an extensive process, so that use of an outside team for all cases would be inefficient and could magnify the importance of a minor incident.

The team leader is typically an administrator who has responsibility for student discipline and safety. The assessment of a threat may involve one or more team members. Additional team members are engaged when it becomes apparent that the threat is more serious or requires more extensive investigation and intervention.

In more serious cases, a school psychologist conducts a mental health evaluation of the student. This evaluation has two main objectives: (a) to identify mental health problems that demand immediate attention, such as psychosis or suicidality, and (b) to determine why the student made the threat and make recommendations for dealing with problems or conflicts associated with the threat. Students typically make threats when they are frustrated and face a problem or situation that they cannot resolve. School psychologists, or other mental health professionals on the team, can help a troubled student resolve underlying conflicts or problems identified in the mental health assessment. It is best if the mental health professionals are staff members in the school because they will already know many of the students and staff members, and they will understand the culture of the school. In some school systems, however, the mental health services are provided by community-based professionals or staff from a central office serving all schools.

Each team should have a law enforcement representative, preferably a school resource officer who has been trained to work in schools (Clark, 2011). The school resource officer advises the team whether a student's behavior has violated the law, provides security, and can undertake criminal investigations in the most serious cases. It should be emphasized that most threat cases do not rise to the level of a criminal act and do not require criminal investigation. Many school authorities are concerned that law enforcement officers will be too quick to arrest a student for behaviors that ordinarily can be handled with school discipline (Kupchik, 2010). This concern should be addressed with law enforcement agencies so that there is a common understanding of roles and procedures.

Decision Tree

Threat assessment teams follow a seven-step decision tree (see Figure 18.1; Cornell & Sheras, 2006). One goal of the decision tree is to provide a flexible and efficient procedure that could be adjusted to the seriousness and complexity of the case. The first three steps of the assessment are a triage phase during which one or two team members determine whether the case can be quickly and easily resolved as a transient threat or will require more extensive evaluation and intervention as a substantive threat. In the most complex cases, there will be a comprehensive assessment of the student, interviews with witnesses, meetings with parents, and then the formulation of a safety plan that is administered over an extended period of time.

At Step 1 (see Figure 18.1), a member of the team begins by interviewing the student who made the threat,

as well as others who may have knowledge of it. The interviewer uses a standard set of questions that can be adapted to the specific situation. The interviewer must be concerned with the context as well as the content of the threat. In other words, what were the circumstances in which the student made a threat, what did the student mean, and what does the student intend in making the threat? The student's account is compared to what other witnesses report and how they experienced the threat.

At Step 2, the threat may be identified as transient, such as an expression of anger, frustration, or even inappropriate humor. The defining feature of a transient threat is that the student does not have a sustained intent to harm someone. In some cases, behavior that appears threatening to an observer might not be a genuine threat (e.g., when the student's statement was intended as a joke or a figure of speech). In such cases, the student and the school team member would seek ways to clarify the situation for all concerned parties.

At Step 3, transient threats are resolved when the student is able to offer an apology and explanation that makes amends for his or her behavior. In situations where there is an argument or conflict of some kind, the team may use available counseling resources. Many schools choose to use mediation or a conflict resolution process. The student may be reprimanded and disciplined in some other way if his or her behavior violated school rules. Most threats are resolved at this step, so the process is not too burdensome and the threat is not treated as a major problem if it is actually a minor incident.

A threat that cannot be easily resolved as a transient threat is regarded as a substantive threat, which means that there is a sustained intent to harm someone beyond the immediate incident. When it is not clear whether a threat is transient or substantive, the team considers the threat to be substantive. There are some presumptive, but not necessary or sufficient, indicators that a threat is substantive. Threats are more likely to be substantive when they are more specific in who will be attacked, when the attack will occur, and how it will be carried out. Likewise, threats are more likely to be substantive if the student has engaged in planning or preparation to carry out the threat, and if there is physical evidence of intent such as a weapon or written plan. In each case, the team must consider the totality of circumstances surrounding the threat and make reasoned judgments based on all the available information. The team should consider factors such as the student's age and capabilities, mental state, and history of aggression.

Figure 18.1. Decision Tree for Student Threat Assessment

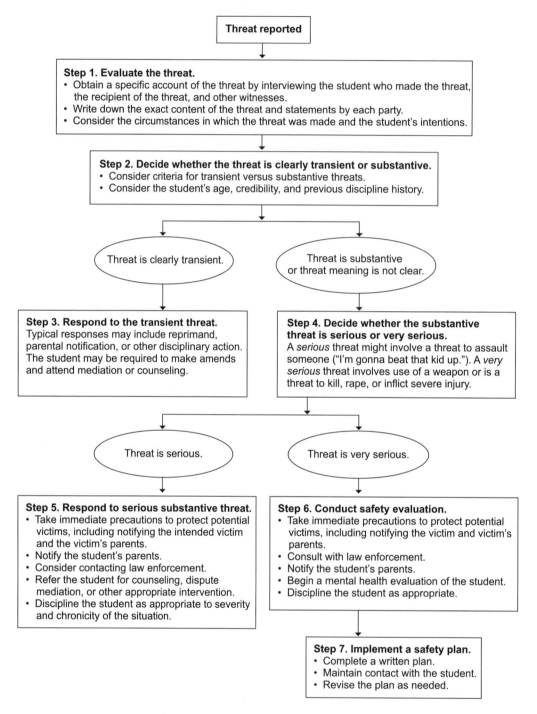

Threat reported

Step 1. Evaluate the threat.
• Obtain a specific account of the threat by interviewing the student who made the threat, the recipient of the threat, and other witnesses.
• Write down the exact content of the threat and statements by each party.
• Consider the circumstances in which the threat was made and the student's intentions.

Step 2. Decide whether the threat is clearly transient or substantive.
• Consider criteria for transient versus substantive threats.
• Consider the student's age, credibility, and previous discipline history.

Threat is clearly transient.

Threat is substantive or threat meaning is not clear.

Step 3. Respond to the transient threat.
Typical responses may include reprimand, parental notification, or other disciplinary action. The student may be required to make amends and attend mediation or counseling.

Step 4. Decide whether the substantive threat is serious or very serious.
A *serious* threat might involve a threat to assault someone ("I'm gonna beat that kid up."). A *very serious* threat involves use of a weapon or is a threat to kill, rape, or inflict severe injury.

Threat is serious.

Threat is very serious.

Step 5. Respond to serious substantive threat.
• Take immediate precautions to protect potential victims, including notifying the intended victim and the victim's parents.
• Notify the student's parents.
• Consider contacting law enforcement.
• Refer the student for counseling, dispute mediation, or other appropriate intervention.
• Discipline the student as appropriate to severity and chronicity of the situation.

Step 6. Conduct safety evaluation.
• Take immediate precautions to protect potential victims, including notifying the victim and victim's parents.
• Consult with law enforcement.
• Notify the student's parents.
• Begin a mental health evaluation of the student.
• Discipline the student as appropriate.

Step 7. Implement a safety plan.
• Complete a written plan.
• Maintain contact with the student.
• Revise the plan as needed.

Note. Copyright by Dewey Cornell. Used by permission.

At Step 4, a substantive threat is classified as serious or very serious, a distinction based on the intended severity of injury. A serious threat is a threat to assault, strike, or beat up someone. A very serious threat is a threat to kill, sexually assault, or severely injure someone. A threat involving the use of a weapon is generally considered a threat to severely injure someone, but teams must always use judgment. For example, if a student threatens to shoot someone with a water pistol, it would not make sense to treat such a threat as very serious.

At Step 5, the team responds to a serious substantive threat by taking protective actions to prevent the threat from being carried out. Immediate protective actions include cautioning the student about the consequences of carrying out the threat, providing supervision so that the threat is not carried out at school, and contacting the student's parents so that they can assume responsibility after school. A team member should also meet with the intended victim of the threat, both in an effort to resolve the underlying dispute and to warn the individual. If the intended victim is a student, that student's parents should be contacted as well. For serious substantive threats, threat assessment stops at this step.

In the case of very serious substantive threats, the team takes more extensive action at Step 6. Typically, the school psychologist will undertake a mental health evaluation of the student. The first goal of this evaluation is to assess the student's mental state and need for immediate mental health services. For example, does the student have delusional ideas that could motivate aggressive action? Is the student so depressed or suicidal that he or she might take desperate action without concern for the consequences? A second goal is to recommend strategies addressing the problem or conflict underlying the threat. For example, is the student a victim of bullying or involved in some other peer conflict? Although the use of long-term suspension is discouraged, a short-term suspension (typically a few days) is an appropriate safety precaution until the team can complete its evaluation. The school resource officer must determine whether law enforcement action should be taken.

At Step 7, the team integrates findings into a written safety plan. The plan may include a combination of mental health and counseling recommendations, findings from the law enforcement investigation, and disciplinary consequences. The safety plan is designed both to protect potential victims and to address the educational needs of the student who made the threat. These plans vary widely according to the circumstances of each case. A key feature of any plan is that it is oriented toward resolving the problem or conflict that stimulated the threatening behavior. Threats can be regarded as symptoms of a problem that a student is unable to resolve, such as bullying or intense conflicts with peers, or perhaps academic difficulties in school. In many cases the student is struggling with depression and suicidal feelings. Consequently, an effective plan will take a comprehensive, problem-solving approach.

Safety plans will include provisions for monitoring the student over a reasonable period of time and making sure that the plan is working. For example, a team member might be in regular contact with a student for several months to assess how things are going and whether efforts to address a problem with bullying have been successful. If the student has been referred for counseling or mental health services, then there should be provision to share information on the student's attendance and progress. For students who are receiving special education services, there may be changes in the student's Individualized Education Program (IEP). An IEP might include behavior support plans to help a student deal with anger or interpersonal conflict, or improve social skills.

Challenges School Psychologists Face in Doing Threat Assessments

Many school psychologists have provided feedback on the challenges they experience in participating on threat assessment teams. One of the most common concerns is a drift away from a team approach, often when there are changes in school administrators and the new administrators are unfamiliar with threat assessment. In these circumstances there may be a tendency to shift responsibility for conducting the threat assessment to the school psychologist. In some difficult cases, the school psychologist may be asked to make categorical predictions about a student's dangerousness or to certify that a student who has made a substantive threat is "safe to return to school." These expectations are unrealistic and inconsistent with the threat assessment approach, which recognizes that the risk of violence is not a static quality and is influenced by environmental factors. The school psychologist should recommend strategies for reducing risk rather than make a categorical determination of safety.

There is widespread agreement that a multidisciplinary team approach is essential to the threat assessment and management process. In substantive cases, the responsibility for conducting threat assessments should not rest with one person. A team is essential to considering multiple perspectives on a case and to examining assessment data as objectively as possible. Although the school psychologist may have the best understanding of the psychological factors involved in a student's behavior, disciplinary actions as well as decisions about the allocation of student support and IEP services require administrative support and engagement. In addition, the implementation of a safety plan often involves coordinated efforts by multiple staff members.

Another challenge arises when the school psychologist is asked to conduct a mental health assessment for a case that does not involve a very serious substantive threat.

For example, the case may involve a student who has been especially difficult for an administrator to discipline or perhaps the student has made angry remarks to a teacher and the teacher demands a comprehensive threat assessment as a kind of disciplinary consequence. Threat assessment guidelines are important because the school psychologist can use them to explain when a mental health evaluation is appropriate.

Information Sharing

School authorities are often unwilling to share information because of concerns about violating the Family Educational Rights and Privacy Act (FERPA). Confidentiality concerns were cited as one reason that critical information was not shared prior to the 2007 shooting at Virginia Tech (Virginia Tech Review Panel, 2007). However, soon after the Virginia Tech shooting, the U.S. Department of Education (2007) issued important clarifications about FERPA, affirming that an institution is permitted to release information from a student's educational records when it is determined that there is an articulable and significant threat to the health or safety of someone. At this point, the information can be disclosed to any person whose knowledge of the information is considered necessary to protect someone else's health or safety.

FERPA applies only to a student's educational records, and schools may have other sources of information about a student that are not restricted by FERPA (U.S. Department of Education, 2007). Most notably, FERPA does not apply to the personal observations or personal notes of a school psychologist (or any other school personnel) that are not derived from school records. In addition, schools can maintain records for law enforcement or security purposes, including threat assessment records, that are separate from and not part of a student's educational record.

Staff Training

The possibility of homicidal violence raises such concern that school authorities may believe that a threat assessment team requires extensive training and that only highly specialized experts can conduct threat assessments. On the contrary, the overwhelming majority of students who make threats of violence have ordinary problems that are familiar to experienced educators and mental health professionals (Cornell & Sheras, 2006). Some common peer problems include bullying, jealousy and rivalry between peers, romantic disputes, racial or ethnic bias, and gang-related conflict. Students may sometimes threaten school staff members

over disciplinary actions, academic requirements, and low grades. Although school-based teams should be able to deal effectively with most student threats, there may be exceptional cases that merit outside consultation with mental health professionals or law enforcement authorities. One example would be mental health consultation for cases that involve a student with unusual and severe psychological difficulties. Another example would be law enforcement consultation for a dispute between criminal gangs with a history of violence.

Overall, there are some special challenges to implementing a threat assessment model. Threat assessment is not a specific curriculum or prescriptive set of procedures but a set of guidelines to assist a team in its decision-making process. Moreover, threat assessment is not a routine activity, but an infrequent event that can occur unexpectedly at any time during the school year. As a result, it may take a year or more for some school team members to develop enough experience to trust the model and be comfortable using it.

Mental Health Evaluations of Threatening Students

As part of the threat assessment process, school psychologists should conduct a mental health evaluation of students who make very serious substantive threats. The term *mental health evaluation* is a generic term and school systems may prefer different terminology, but the purpose of the evaluation is always twofold: (a) identify mental health treatment needs, such as suicidal depression, psychosis, or intense anger; and (b) propose strategies for reducing the risk of violence by gathering information on the reasons for the student's threatening behavior.

The mental health evaluation ordinarily should be conducted as soon as possible after a student has been identified as making a very serious substantive threat. In an urgent or emergency situation, this evaluation might begin immediately without parental permission, just as one would begin an evaluation of a suicidal student. As soon as it is practical, however, the school psychologist would contact a parent for permission to continue the evaluation. Parents might be advised that a student making a very serious substantive threat will be suspended from school for disciplinary and safety reasons, and that completion of the evaluation is an important condition for the student to return to school. This information should already be a part of the school's discipline and safety policy, available to all students and parents.

Cornell and Sheras (2006) provide a detailed outline of topics for school psychologists to cover in a mental health evaluation of a student threatening violence. The student should be asked in detail about the reported threatening behavior. It is best to ask open-ended questions that are not judgmental or leading of the student. For example, it is better to ask "What happened today in the cafeteria?" rather than "Why did you threaten Robert in the cafeteria?" The school psychologist should find out as much as possible about the incident or behavior in question, but also explore the student's motives. Use questions like "I know you must have had some reasons to say that, but what led up to it?" It is also helpful to explore the student's understanding of the consequences of carrying out the threat, how others would be affected, and what would happen to the student. In cases where a specific individual (or group) is threatened, the interviewer should explore the relationship with the intended victims.

After gaining as much information as possible about the threat, the school psychologist should review the student's mental state and general mental health status, with special attention to symptoms of depression, including associated feelings of anxiety, irritability, and anger. The school psychologist should look for indications of delusions or hallucinations, too.

Another area of inquiry by school psychologists is the presence of risk factors that might be directly connected to the threat situation, such as the availability of weapons, especially access to firearms, and experiences of being bullied or teased by peers. It is also useful to review the student's history of aggressive behavior, delinquency, school discipline problems, and exposure to violence. Along with risk factors, the school psychologist should explore protective factors and coping capacity. Some of the most likely areas are family support, friendships and other forms of peer support, and personal strengths. It can be especially useful to assess whether the student feels pessimistic or hopeless about the future, or can conceive of a positive outcome. The threats of students who feel they have nothing to lose or nothing to look forward to in the future are concerning.

Another excellent resource is the Structured Assessment of Violence Risk in Youth (SAVRY; Borum et al., 2002). SAVRY can be used in conjunction with a threat assessment. SAVRY is an assessment tool, but not a formal test, designed to assist the mental health professional in assessing risk and protective factors. SAVRY purposely does not produce a risk score, because such scores are of questionable value and potentially misleading. A youth's risk for violence is much more situational and transitory than risk scores imply (Borum et al., 2002). Risk scores, as well as classifications of risk (e.g., high, medium, low) are static designations that ignore the variability in youth behavior and their responsiveness to their immediate environment. A youth who is low risk when supervised and feeling calm may be much more dangerous when angry, intoxicated, or surrounded by peers who encourage impulsive behavior. A student's level of risk rises when the student moves from a supervised classroom into the hallway between classes, and then rises again when he or she leaves school in the afternoon. Risk is not a fixed quality, but fluctuates over time.

Furthermore, there is little research on the risk of imminent violence in student populations. Many of the risk factors commonly identified in the literature are associated with general risk for violence that could be years in the future, rather than immediate risk to carry out a specific threat. Even youth who score high on risk assessment instruments do not engage in frequent acts of violence. As a result, school psychologists should be cautious about using instruments that reduce the risk of violence to a single score or categorical determination. No psychological test or instrument can replace the professional judgment that is essential to making decisions about interventions to prevent violence (Borum et al., 2002; Heilbrun et al., 2009).

Multicultural Issues

Ethnic minority students, especially African Americans, are suspended from school at much higher rates than Caucasian students (Losen & Martinez, 2013). This racial disparity in school discipline is of great concern because of the strong association between school suspensions and a series of negative outcomes for students, including further misbehavior, academic failure, dropping out, and juvenile court involvement (Fabelo et al., 2011; Gregory, Skiba, & Noguera, 2010). Although there is no single explanation that accounts for racial disparities in school discipline, the available evidence indicates that ethnic minority students are not suspended at higher rates because they engage in higher rates of serious misbehavior. On the contrary, they are suspended for relatively minor misbehavior such as being loud or disruptive in class (Losen & Martinez, 2013; Skiba, Michael, Nardo, & Peterson, 2002).

There also seems to be a link between the use of zero tolerance disciplinary practices and racial disparities in school suspensions (APA, 2008; Losen & Martinez, 2013). A school administrator using a zero tolerance approach would be less likely to assess or consider the reasons for a student's misbehavior, since the context and meaning of a student's behavior are minimized in applying the zero tolerance philosophy of punishment.

Teachers (and other school personnel) typically make continual assessments of student behavior and make judgments about whether behavior has crossed the line into a disciplinary infraction. The context and meaning of the behavior, the student's intentions, as well as the teacher's knowledge of the student and trust in the student, may influence these judgments. Similarly, the school administrator who receives the office referral and then determines whether a student is suspended from school may be influenced by these factors. Minority disparities could enter the process because teachers and administrators are less familiar with their minority students, less trusting or sympathetic in their view of them, or perhaps more concerned about their behavior. School psychologists can play an important role in reducing racial disparities in school discipline by considering the context and meaning of the student's behavior, recognizing that there are often cultural and socioeconomic differences in the style and manner of verbal expression that contribute to misunderstanding and conflict.

A statewide implementation study found that schools using the Virginia Student Threat Assessment Guidelines had fewer long-term and short-term suspensions than other schools, and that longer use of the Virginia Guidelines was associated with greater reductions in suspensions (Cornell & Lovegrove, 2013). There were similar reductions in suspension across schools with differing proportions of African American students. Threat assessment may be helpful in reducing suspension rates across racial groups because it guides school personnel to look carefully at the context for the student's behavior and to take a problem-solving approach rather than a punitive approach.

Evaluation of Outcomes

Prevention of violence is largely invisible when it is successful and brutally public when it fails. For this reason, it can be difficult to demonstrate the value of prevention efforts to school authorities and other observers. A school psychologist could be 99% successful at preventing student fights, yet one fight can create the impression that his or her services are not effective. Fortunately, there is a large body of scientific evidence

that school-based violence prevention efforts are effective and do improve student behavior (Wilson & Lipsey, 2007). As noted above, there is also evidence that threat assessment has a positive impact on school climate and reduces the use of school suspension (Cornell et al., 2012). It may be worthwhile to present such findings to school authorities.

More compelling than research articles may be firsthand evidence from the schools beginning to use threat assessment. Ideally, schools should have prior records of their disciplinary referrals and suspension rates so that trends can be examined over time and in comparison to state or regional norms. It would also be useful to evaluate the progress of students identified for threat assessment interventions. The field test of threat assessment in Memphis schools found a substantial reduction in the disciplinary referrals of students who received services following a threat assessment (Strong & Cornell, 2008). Schools should maintain records of threat assessments for three reasons. First, the record may be valuable if the student engages in threatening behavior several years later. Second, good record keeping can help maintain the quality of the evaluation process. The forms used in threat assessment records serve as a guide that helps ensure team fidelity to the model (Cornell & Sheras, 2006). Third, good records are important from a liability standpoint in order to demonstrate that school authorities took appropriate action in response to a threat of violence.

The threat assessment process focuses on understanding why a student made a threat. Usually the student is frustrated because the student has encountered a conflict or problem that he or she has not been able to resolve. One important benefit of a threat assessment approach is that the team can help the student to address the underlying problem and in this way prevent further frustration and potential difficulties. A student may have problems with anger, self-control, or social judgment that when addressed with counseling helps prevent future misbehavior. In other cases a threat assessment can have an impact on multiple students. For example, threats often occur in the context of bullying, and a threat assessment might lead to efforts to stop bullying among a group of students. Interventions initiated in response to a threat can have a widespread impact on other students and ultimately improve the overall school climate. There is some evidence for a broader impact of threat assessment because students report a more positive school climate and there is a decline in some disciplinary infractions (Cornell et al., 2009; Strong

& Cornell, 2008). School records also show a greater reduction in school suspensions than can be explained by the number of threat assessments conducted in a school (Cornell et al., 2011; Cornell & Lovegrove, 2013).

SUMMARY

Threat assessment is a problem-oriented approach to violence prevention that involves both evaluation and intervention to reduce the risk of violence. Threat assessment represents a form of risk assessment that places much more emphasis on risk management and prevention than on prediction of violence. There is a major focus on trying to understand the context and meaning of the student's threatening behavior, and then attempting to resolve the problem or conflict that often underlies a threat.

A series of field tests and controlled studies with the Virginia Student Threat Assessment Guidelines (Cornell & Sheras, 2006) demonstrated that school-based teams can be trained to conduct threat assessments that distinguish serious, substantive threats from less serious, transient threats. Using a seven-step decision tree, schools were able to respond to student conflicts, take necessary safety precautions, and administer appropriate disciplinary consequences that are calibrated to the seriousness of the situation. Threat assessment provides schools with a much-needed alternative to zero tolerance discipline and leads to substantial reductions in the use of long-term suspensions. Threat assessment also appears to have a beneficial impact on school climate, with associated reductions in bullying and greater willingness among students to seek help from school authorities (Cornell et al., 2009, 2011). In conclusion, threat assessment can be a valuable component of a comprehensive approach to school safety.

AUTHOR NOTE

Disclosure. Dewey Cornell has a financial interest in the Virginia Student Threat Assessment Guidelines and the manual described in this chapter.

REFERENCES

Allen, K., Cornell, D., Lorek, E., & Sheras, P. (2008). Response of school personnel to student threat assessment training. *School Effectiveness and School Improvement, 19*, 319–332. doi:10.1080/09243450802332184

American Psychological Association Zero Tolerance Task Force. (2008). Are zero tolerance policies effective in the schools? An evidentiary review and recommendations. *American Psychologist, 63*, 852–862. doi:10.1037/0003-066X.63.9.852

Bondü, R., Cornell, D., & Scheithauer, H. (2011). Student homicidal violence in schools: An international problem. *New Directions for Youth Development, 129*, 13–30.

Borum, R., Bartel, P., & Forth, A. (2002). *Manual for the Structured Assessment of Violence Risk in Youth (SAVRY)*. Lutz, FL: Psychological Assessment Resources.

Borum, R., Cornell, D., Modzeleski, W., & Jimerson, S. R. (2010). What can be done about school shootings? A review of the evidence. *Educational Researcher, 39*, 27–37. doi:10.3102/0013189X09357620

Borum, R., Fein, R., Vossekuil, B., & Berglund, J. (1999). Threat assessment: Defining an approach for evaluating risk of targeted violence. *Behavioral Sciences and the Law, 17*, 323–337.

Clark, S. (2011). The role of law enforcement in schools: The Virginia experience—A practitioner report. *New Directions for Youth Development, 129*, 89–102.

Colorado School Safety Resource Center. (2013). *Essentials of school threat assessment: Preventing targeted school violence.* Denver, CO: Author. Retrieved from http://www.colorado.gov/cs/Satellite/CDPS-SafeSchools/CBON/1251622848436

Cornell, D. G. (2006). *School violence: Fears versus facts.* Mahwah, NJ: Erlbaum.

Cornell, D., Allen, K., & Fan, X. (2012). A randomized controlled study of the Virginia Student Threat Assessment Guidelines in grades K–12. *School Psychology Review, 41*, 100–115.

Cornell, D., Gregory, A., & Fan, X. (2011). Reductions in long-term suspensions following adoption of the Virginia Student Threat Assessment Guidelines. *Bulletin of the National Association of Secondary School Principal, 95*, 175–194.

Cornell, D., & Lovegrove, P. (2013). *Student threat assessment as a method of reducing student suspensions.* Paper presented at the Closing the School Discipline Gap: Research to Practice conference, Washington, DC. Retrieved from http://civilrightsproject.ucla.edu/events/2013/copy_of_closing-the-school-discipline-gap-agenda

Cornell, D., & Sheras, P. (2006). *Guidelines for responding to student threats of violence.* Longmont, CO: Sopris West.

Cornell, D., Sheras, P., Gregory, A., & Fan, X. (2009). A retrospective study of school safety conditions in high schools using the Virginia Threat Assessment Guidelines versus alternative approaches. *School Psychology Quarterly, 24*, 119–129. doi:10.1037/a0016182

Cornell, D., Sheras, P., Kaplan, S., McConville, D., Posey, J., Levy-Elkon, A., … Cole, J. (2004). Guidelines for student threat assessment: Field-test findings. *School Psychology Review, 33*, 527–546.

Dwyer, K., Osher, D., & Warger, C. (1998). *Early warning, timely response: A guide to safe schools.* Washington, DC: U.S. Department of Education.

Eliot, M., Cornell, D., Gregory, A., & Fan, X. (2010). Supportive school climate and student willingness to seek help for bullying and threats of violence. *Journal of School Psychology, 48*, 533–553.

Fabelo, T., Thompson, M. D., Plotkin, M., Carmichael, D., Marchbanks, M. P., & Booth, E. A. (2011). *Breaking schools' rules:*

A statewide study of how school discipline relates to students' success and juvenile justice involvement. New York, NY: Council of State Governments Justice Center.

Fein, R. A., Vossekuil, B., Pollack, W. S., Borum, R., Modzeleski, W., & Reddy, M. (2002). *Threat assessment in schools: A guide to managing threatening situations and creating safe school climates.* Washington, DC: U.S. Department of Education and U.S. Secret Service, National Threat Assessment Center.

Gregory, A., Skiba, R. J., & Noguera, P. A. (2010). The achievement gap and the discipline gap: Two sides of the same coin. *Educational Researcher, 39*, 59–68.

Heilbrun, K., Dvoskin, J., & Heilbrun, A. (2009). Toward preventing future tragedies: Mass killings on college campuses, public health, and threat/risk assessment. *Psychological Injury and Law, 2*, 93–99.

Kupchik, A. (2010). *Homeroom security: School discipline in an age of fear.* New York, NY: New York University Press.

Losen, D., & Martinez, T. E. (2013). *Out of school & off track: The overuse of suspensions in American middle and high schools.* Los Angeles, CA: Center for Civil Rights Remedies at UCLA's Civil Rights Project. Retrieved from http://civilrightsproject.ucla.edu/resources/projects/center-for-civil-rights-remedies/school-to-prison-folder/federal-reports/out-of-school-and-off-track-the-overuse-of-suspensions-in-american-middle-and-high-schools/OutofSchool-OffTrack_UCLA_4-8.pdf

National Association of School Psychologists. (2010). *Model for comprehensive and integrated school psychological services.* Bethesda, MD: Author. Retrieved from http://www.nasponline.org/standards/2010standards/2_PracticeModel.pdf

Neiman, S. (2011). *Crime, violence, discipline, and safety in U.S. public schools: Findings from the school survey on crime and safety: 2009–10* (NCES 2011-320). Washington, DC: U.S. Department of Education.

Nekvasil, E., & Cornell, D. (2012). Student reports of peer threats of violence: Prevalence and outcomes. *Journal of School Violence, 11*, 357–375.

O'Toole, M. E. (2000). *The school shooter: A threat assessment perspective.* Quantico, VA: National Center for the Analysis of Violent Crime.

Payne, S. R. T., & Elliott, D. S. (2011). Safe2Tell: An anonymous 24/7 reporting system for preventing school violence. *New Directions for Youth Development, 129*, 103–111. doi:10.1002/yd.390

Skiba, R. J., Michael, R. S., Nardo, A. C., & Peterson, R. L. (2002). The color of discipline: Sources of racial and gender disproportionality in school punishment. *Urban Review, 34*, 317–342.

Strong, K., & Cornell, D. (2008). Student threat assessment in Memphis city schools: A descriptive report. *Behavioral Disorders, 34*, 42–54.

Syvertsen, A. K., Flanagan, C. A., & Stout, M. D. (2009). Code of silence: Students' perceptions of school climate and willingness to intervene in a peer's dangerous plan. *Journal of Educational Psychology, 101*, 219–232. doi:10.1037/a0013246

U.S. Department of Education. (2007). *Balancing student privacy and school safety: A guide to the Family Educational Rights and Privacy Act for elementary and secondary schools.* Washington, DC: Author. Retrieved from http://www2.ed.gov/policy/gen/guid/fpco/brochures/elsec.html

Van Dreal, J. (2011). *Assessing student threats: A handbook for implementing the Salem-Keizer system.* Lanham, MD: Rowman & Littlefield.

Van Dyke, R., & Schroeder, J. (2006). Implementation of the Dallas Threat of Violence Risk Assessment. In S. R. Jimerson & M. J. Furlong (Eds.), *The handbook of school violence and school safety* (pp. 603–616). Mahwah, NJ: Erlbaum.

Virginia Tech Review Panel. (2007). *Mass shootings at Virginia Tech, April 16, 2007.* Retrieved from http://www.vtreviewpanel.org/report/index.html

Vossekuil, B., Fein, R. A., Reddy, M., Borum, R., & Modzeleski, W. (2002). *The final report and findings of the Safe School Initiative: Implications for the prevention of school attacks in the United States.* Washington, DC: U.S. Department of Education and U.S. Secret Service. Retrieved from http://www.secretservice.gov/ntac/ssi_guide.pdf

Wilson, S. J., & Lipsey, M. W. (2007). School-based interventions for aggressive and disruptive behavior: Update of a meta-analysis. *American Journal of Preventive Medicine, 33*, 130–143. doi:10.1016/j.amepre.2007.04.01

Best Practices in Suicide Prevention and Intervention

Richard Lieberman
Los Angeles (CA) Unified School District
Scott Poland
Cheryl Kornfeld
Nova Southeastern University (FL)

OVERVIEW

In 2010, 38,364 Americans died by suicide, accounting for 1.6% of deaths in the United States (Centers for Disease Control and Prevention [CDC], 2011). In that same year, Americans 10–24 years old completed 4,867 (12.6%) of those deaths by suicide (CDC, 2011). The CDC (2012) Youth Risk Behavioral Surveillance Survey reported that while rates of students who have seriously contemplated suicide decreased between 1991 and 2009 from 29.0 to 13.8%, these rates have increased from 2009 to 2011 from 13.8 to 15.8%. Similar trends occurred among the same age group for making a suicide plan attempting suicide, having declined between 2001 and 2009 and then increasing between 2009 and 2011. Furthermore, 7.8% of high school students had attempted suicide in the previous 12 months. It is important to note that the number of reported suicides may be an underestimation of the actual number of deaths by suicide. Whereas the facts illustrate the dire need to focus on youth suicidal behavior, legislation pertaining to suicide prevention programs in schools serving K–12 has only been passed and enforced in few states (LaFleur & Poland, 2012). Thus, it is essential that schools become a skilled setting that enhances knowledge and methods for assessing for suicidal risk, seeking appropriate support/care, and intervening with at-risk youth.

School psychologists play a critical role as a consultant and trainer to other school personnel to ensure proper suicide prevention measures are taken. This translates to the school psychologist taking an active role in training the school staff on suicide screening, as well as in advocating for (and aiding in) the implementation of suicide prevention and intervention programs. The objective of this chapter is to provide the information, skills, model practices, and strategies that are critical to the services highlighted in the Preventive and Responsive Services domain of the National Association of School Psychologists (NASP) *Model for Comprehensive and Integrated School Psychological Services* (NASP, 2010).

Gender and Developmental Factors

Research illustrates that death by suicide is the third leading cause of death after accidents and homicides for males and females between the ages of 10 and 24 across all ethnicities (CDC, 2012). Whereas males accounted for 84% of completed suicide in this age range in 2010, their same-age female peers are more likely to seriously contemplate suicide (females: 19.3%, males: 12.5%), make a suicide plan (females: 15%, males: 10.8%), and attempt suicide (females: 9.8%, males: 5.3%; CDC, 2012). In other words, although females might contemplate, plan for, and attempt suicide at a rate two to three times higher than males, the rate that males tend to complete suicide is about five times higher than the rate of female completed suicide within the same age group. Males are less likely to seek support when in need and are more likely to use more lethal means than their same-age female peers.

Research continuously indicates that 100–200 suicide attempts are made for every young person who dies by suicide (CDC, 2012). Given these statistics, it is estimated that there are just about 1 million suicide attempts annually by young people. Given the aforementioned statistics, it is apparent that suicide prevention programs are necessary to reduce suicidal ideation, risk, and attempts among young people in addition to helping to increase knowledge and awareness about prevention.

Because this chapter examines suicide prevention and intervention in schools, it is also crucial to look at differential suicide rates across the differing ages of students attending school. It appears as though the risk in suicide increases with age (higher for 15 year olds than for those 10–14). While the rate of suicide among youth 10–14 years old has steadily declined over the past few years, the overall rate of suicide in this population is still higher than it has been in previous decades and continues to be of concern (Miller, 2011). Because the suicide rate among the population of 10–24 year olds is quite alarming, it is important to employ appropriate suicide prevention and intervention programs that target this age group.

Ethnicity and Cultural Factors

The prevalence of suicidal ideation and attempts also varies among individuals from different racial and ethnic backgrounds. American Indian and Alaska Natives have the highest rates of suicidal ideation, attempts, and planning among individuals between the ages of 15 and 19, followed by Hispanic, Caucasian, and African American individuals, respectively (CDC, 2012). In fact, while the prevalence of those seriously contemplating suicide among Hispanic individuals ages 15–19 was found to be at 16.7%, the prevalence rates for the same aged Caucasian and non-Hispanic Black populations were found to be 15.5% and 13.2%, respectively (CDC, 2012). However, the rates of completed suicide differ from the aforementioned statistics. The highest rate of completed suicide among youth is also within the American Indian and Alaska Natives; however, Caucasian youth, non-Hispanic Black youth, Asian/Pacific Islander youth, and Hispanic youth follow behind, respectively. The prevalence rates of American Indians and Alaskan Natives, the leading population of 10–24 year olds who are completing suicide, are doing so at rates of 31.27 per 100,000 among males and 10.16 per 100,000 among females. Additionally, it appears as though there has been an increase in suicide among the male population of African Americans over the past few decades that should be further addressed.

Sexual Orientation and Bullying

There has been a dramatic increase of media attention recently on the subject of the relationship between adolescents' sexual orientation and risk for suicidal behaviors (Hatzenbuehler, 2011). Though a question of mediating factors such as depression, hopelessness, and the social environment remains, gay, bisexual, and transgender (LGBT) children and adolescents are at a higher risk for suicidal ideation and attempts than their heterosexual peers (Hatzenbuehler, 2011). On average, Latino, immigrant, religious, and low-socioeconomic status families tend to have a lower acceptance of their child's sexual identity (Ryan, Russell, Huebner, Diaz, & Sanchez, 2010). Whereas 38.3% of LGBT children and adolescents with low family acceptance of their sexual orientation reported suicidal thoughts over the previous 6 months, only 18.5% of youth experiencing high family acceptance reported the same thoughts (Ryan et al., 2011). Reported lifetime suicide attempts reduced from 56.8 to 30.9% when a family engaged in high acceptance behaviors/attitudes versus those families demonstrating low acceptance. Furthermore, suicide risk declines (as psychological well-being increases) in LGBT children and adolescents who experience family connectedness, school safety, strong and positive associations to the LGBT community, and perceived caring from other adults (Eisenberg & Resnick, 2006).

Children and adolescents who are questioning their sexual orientation are also more likely to be bullied than their heterosexual counterparts, and bullied children and adolescents are more likely to contemplate and to attempt suicide (Hatzenbuehler, 2011). Social environment, such as the experience of verbal, physical, social, and cyberbullying, plays a considerable role in the association between LGBT children and adolescents and suicide. The likelihood that a child or adolescent with a minority sexual orientation has attempted suicide in the previous 12 months compared to his or her heterosexual peer is 21.5% to 4.2%, respectively. Further, a more supportive social environment significantly reduced the probability of a suicide attempt, especially those children and adolescents among the LGBT population, in comparison to a more negative environment (Hatzenbuehler, 2011).

BASIC CONSIDERATIONS

In order to adequately determine suicide risk, the school psychologist must carefully assess both risk and protective factors. Research that examines intrapersonal factors has found greater resilience among individuals with higher self-esteem (Sharaf, Thompson, & Walsh, 2009). In addition to this intrapersonal characteristic of resilience, interpersonal factors are also examined. When the availability of peer and family support is present, suicide risk decreases as self-esteem increases (Eisenberg & Resnick, 2006; Sharaf et al., 2009). Knowing that resilience can be defined as "the process of overcoming the negative effects of risk exposure, coping successfully with traumatic experiences, and avoiding the negative trajectories associated with risk" (Sharaf et al., 2009, pp. 160–161) increasing such protective factors (self-esteem and social support through peers and family) among youth in the United States may be a helpful tactic in suicide prevention programs.

Additionally, those students who feel as though they know adults who are trustworthy and capable of helping them with suicidal concerns maintain a positive attitude toward seeking help from school staff, are actively engaged in school and school activities, and are willing to potentially break promises of secrecy to talk with adults about suicidal ideation/behavior are major predictors of help-seeking behaviors for suicide (Eisenberg & Resnick, 2012; Pisani et al., 2012). As a result, designing suicide prevention strategies with the intent of strengthening self-esteem and social supports among students, as well as increasing their trust in school staff, may be effective in decreasing suicide risk among children and adolescents.

Risk Factors

There are numerous risk factors and trends for suicide among adolescents in the United States. These include but are not limited to gender; ethnicity; involvement in bullying; previous suicide attempts; a psychological disorder such as major depressive disorder or a substance abuse disorder; family history of suicide; family violence; sexual orientation minority/same-sex attraction; situational factors; and exposures to suicidal behavior of others, such as family members, peers, or the media (Miller, 2011). Furthermore, students who feel socially isolated, or a lack of connectedness to their peers or school, are also at risk for suicidal ideation and behaviors (Miller, 2011).

Psychopathological Disorders

A major risk factor for suicide among adolescents is the presence of a psychiatric disorder. There is an increased risk for suicide in adolescents with a mood disorder, most notably major depressive disorder (Miller, 2011).

While there is a high comorbidity rate with suicide in females with depression and alcohol/substance abuse, the highest comorbidity for males and suicide is with depression and conduct disorder. Further, since 3–5% of the adolescent population experiences a depressive disorder, it is important to be aware of this adverse and potentially fatal effect depression has. Hopelessness, or feeling as though life will never get better in the future, is a factor that significantly influences suicidal ideation and behaviors (Goldsmith, Pellmar, Kleinman, & Bunney, 2002).

The presence of impulsivity is another significant factor that influences suicidal ideation and attempts among children and adolescents according to research (Goldsmith et al., 2002). Higher scores in assessments measuring impulsivity, sensation-seeking attitudes, and aggressiveness are found to be significant risk factors for suicide, and male children and adolescents tend to rank higher on such scales. An impulsive adolescent may not exhibit signs of depression, hopelessness, or suicidal ideation prior to a suicidal attempt. Rather, the adolescent may just act on impulse in a crisis situation. Whether or not an adolescent is using and abusing substances as a means to numb himself or herself or escape from psychological distress, adolescents who use alcohol and/or drugs are at an increased risk for suicide than their non-substance-using peers (Miller, 2011). Further, adolescents with a depressed affect who use and abuse substances tend to be more impulsive, and are also at a greater risk for suicidal behaviors. Mental illness, which affects up to 20% of the teen population, is a significant risk factor for suicide among teenagers, with a strong emphasis on depressive disorders, the presence of impulsivity, and substance use disorders.

Familial and Biological Factors

Four of the major problem areas of childhood adversity factors that are associated with elevated risk for suicidal behavior are (a) childhood maltreatment or victimization, (b) problematic parenting or family environment, (c) socioeconomic hardships, and (d) childhood adversities such as difficult peer relationships, legal problems, loss of a parent or caregiver, and a history of mental disorder or suicide attempts in the child and/or family members (Hardt, Johnson, Courtney, & Sareen, 2006). It is unclear whether a family history of suicidal behaviors is linked to a genetic predisposition, to contagion, to gaining increased attention for such behaviors, or, more likely, to some combination.

Not only might there be a genetic factor increasing a risk of engaging in suicidal behaviors or a contagion effect, but there are also other aspects of family life that may contribute to an increased risk of suicide attempts among children and adolescents. As discussed previously, having family acceptance of their sexual identity was found to be a strong protective factor for an LGBT child or adolescent's mental and physical health. Parental acceptance of their child's sexual orientation, when he or she identifies as LGBT, also plays a significant role in their child's overall suicide risk by reducing overall suicidal ideation and risk three-fold (Ryan et al., 2010).

In 2003, the U.S. Food and Drug Administration (FDA) proposed a new warning pertaining to the association between the administration of antidepressants among children and adolescents with depression (ages 5–17) and increased risk of suicidal ideation/ behaviors. Further, the FDA (2004) then mandated that the manufacturers of 10 antidepressant drugs add such a warning to the label. While antidepressant medication has proven to be successful at helping to treat depression in children and adolescents, this black box label created an adverse effect on the prescription of these drugs. Because of these labels, there became hesitancy on the part of psychiatrists and physicians to prescribe antidepressant medication to children or adolescents suffering from major depression and suicidal ideation. While a principal goal of the proposal of the warning was for clinicians to more closely monitor children or adolescents on antidepressants, it actually created an overall doubt and a reduction in the prescription.

Bullying

Olweus (1993), creator of the Olweus Bullying Prevention Program, defines bullying as occurring when a person who has difficulty defending himself or herself, "is exposed repeatedly and over time, to negative actions on the part of one or more students" (p. 9). While 15–25% of students are being bullied, only one third of those students are reporting these incidents to the proper supports at school or home, such as teachers or caregivers. A child or adolescent's connectedness to his or her peers can play a significant role in his or her risk for suicide, and a higher feeling of victimization or isolation may lead to a higher risk for suicidal ideation and behaviors. Children or adolescents involved in bullying, as a victim or bully, were at a significantly higher risk for depression and suicide. According to Lieberman and Cowan (2011), "adolescents frequently cite interpersonal problems as a precipitant of suicidal behavior and, relevant to the issue of loss as a trigger, bullying causes a substantial loss of dignity and

humanity" (p. 13). Furthermore, the more frequently an adolescent was involved in bullying, the more likely that he or she was depressed, had feelings of hopelessness, had serious suicidal ideation, or had attempted suicide (Gould & Kramer, 2011).

Adolescents who are physically threatened or injured by peers report a higher frequency of suicidal thoughts and attempts than adolescents who were not victimized in such a manner, illustrating a significant connection between peer victimization and suicidal ideation/ attempts (Kaminski & Fang, 2009). This may contribute to the victimized student feeling a low sense of connectedness to his or her peers and school, further increasing his or her risk for suicide. Students experiencing bullying in conjunction with higher social isolation, depressed feelings, and/or suicidal ideation are at higher risk for subsequent suicidal ideation 4 years later than students who experience one of the factors exclusively (i.e., bullying without feelings of depression/ suicidality or feelings of depression/suicidality in the absence of bullying; Klomek et al., 2011).

As a dependence on technology is growing within the U.S. culture, there is a significant need to look at the impact that technology, particularly cyberbullying, has on suicide risk among children, adolescents, and young adults. Cyberbullying can be viewed as any act of bullying (i.e., mean or hurtful comments, spreading rumors, physical threats, pretending to be someone else, and mean or hurtful pictures) through a cell phone text, e-mail, or any social media outlet or online source (Hinduja & Patchin, 2012). About 20.8% of individuals ages 10–18 report having been victims of cyberbullying in their lifetimes and 19.4% report having cyberbullied others (Hinduja & Patchin, 2012). Low self-esteem, family issues, academic difficulties, school violence, delinquent behaviors, and suicidal ideation are all correlated with being a victim of cyberbullying (Hinduja & Patchin, 2012). As discussed previously, depressive symptoms and psychopathology have a grave impact on an individual's suicidal risk.

Self-Injury

While self-injurious behavior in itself may not necessarily be indicative of suicidal intention, an individual engaging in such behaviors is at greater risk for suicide because of it. Many children and adolescents typically engage in nonsuicidal self-injury, most commonly the cutting of the skin, as a means to release their emotional suffering and dissociate from psychological distress without the intention of dying (Lieberman & Poland, 2006). On the other hand, suicidal behavior is intended to end one's life under the belief that death is the only option. Self-harming is a chronic and repetitive risky behavior that many engage in at a high frequency.

Self-injury is, in fact, a risk factor for suicide and can lead to an individual being three times more prone to attempt or consider suicide at least once, if not multiple times in his or her life (Whitlock et al., 2012). If a child or adolescent who engages in nonsuicidal self-injury becomes suicidal, it is likely to be much easier for that individual to carry out the actions needed to cause lethal damage to himself or herself through possible desensitization (Whitlock et al., 2012). Furthermore, it is important to note that two factors that seem to lower suicidal risk among children and adolescents who have a history of engaging in nonsuicidal self-injury are (a) discussing their distress with their parents and (b) perceiving a meaning in life (Whitlock et al., 2012).

Situational Factors

Firearms were reported to be the leading cause of death by suicide among individuals between the ages of 10 and 24, followed by suffocation (CDC, 2011). The rates of the various methods for suicide among this population in the United States have changed over the past 2 decades. When broken down into specified ages and genders, the rates differ. For instance, whereas firearms are most often used for completed suicides among males ages 10–24 (49.7%), females within the same age range are more likely to commit suicide by suffocation. Suicide by firearms and poisoning has actually decreased significantly for females between the ages of 10 and 24 since 1990 (Berman et al., 2009). In 2004, hanging/suffocation became the leading cause of death by suicide for females (Berman et al., 2009). The rate of females utilizing suffocation as a means of suicide increased 233% between 1991 and 2009 and the rate of female usage of firearms has dramatically decreased since 1993 (Berman et al., 2009). While this may be the case for females between the ages of 10 and 24, male suicides among the same age group are still more often completed by firearm (Berman et al., 2009).

Whether or not a child or adolescent has an identifiable mental health disorder or other suicide risk factors, the presence of a firearm in a home, especially a loaded gun, is highly associated with an increased risk for youth suicide (American Foundation for Suicide Prevention, 2006). Further, 83% of gun-related deaths in homes containing firearms are the result of a suicide, and findings illustrate that someone other than the actual gun owner is often the individual completing

Table 19.1. Examples of Situational Crises

- Breakup with a significant other
- Trouble with authorities, such as school staff or the police
- Having a parent be deported
- Failing in school
- Bullying or victimization
- Death of a friend or loved one
- Anniversary of a death of a friend or loved one
- Unwanted pregnancy or abortion
- Embarrassment or humiliation in front of peers
- Parental divorce
- Relational, social, work, or financial loss
- Serious injury or illness that might change one's path in life
- Disappointment or rejection
- Family conflict or dysfunction
- High demands placed on the individual at school or at home
- Increased responsibilities of caregiving in the home
- Increased community violence in the surrounding area

Note. Based on information from Miller (2011), Kalafat and Lazarus (2002), and Miller and McConaughy (2005).

suicide in these cases (American Foundation for Suicide Prevention, 2006).

Another situational risk factor associated with child and adolescent suicidal behavior comes from social learning theory and is known as a contagion effect. Adolescents may learn that suicide is the only permanent solution to their problems by observing suicidal behaviors among celebrities, peers, or even family members.

Situational crises are also situational factors that can dramatically increase suicide risk, as these crises can be precipitating incidents for suicidal behaviors among children or adolescents. While these acute incidents are not the actual cause of a suicide attempt or completed suicide, they can lead to suicidal behaviors when in conjunction with other risk factors such as access to lethal means, substance use and abuse, depression, and/or past suicide attempts (Miller, 2011; Poland & Lieberman, 2002). Some specific examples of what constitutes a situational crisis are provided in Table 19.1.

BEST PRACTICES IN SUICIDE PREVENTION AND INTERVENTION

It is not only necessary for research to focus on a range of interventions for those at risk for suicide, but it is also important for school psychologists to understand the benefits of various prevention strategies. The numerous secondary intervention and postvention programs (i.e., those that play a significant role in aiding individuals who have been emotionally affected by a suicide) will, it is hoped, in turn, help thwart subsequent suicide attempts.

However, a principal focus on primary prevention is essential for school psychologists. The theme of Gene Cash's 2008–2009 NASP presidency was preventing youth suicide, affirming that suicidal behavior among youth is an urgent national public health concern that needs to be addressed. The conceptualization of youth suicide as a public health problem has allowed for the nation to adopt a public health model of its prevention.

> The public-health approach focuses on identifying patterns of suicide and suicidal behaviors in a group or population. It aims at changing the environment to protect people against diseases and changing the behaviors that put people at risk of getting them. (Yip, 2011, p. 118)

Although suicide is not a disease in the usual sense, it is a massive public health concern. Therefore, school psychologists must understand the importance of facilitating the development and adoption of suicide prevention programs through a public health lens in schools in order to reduce suicide risk and suicide rates among students.

Under Cash's NASP presidency, a call to action regarding youth suicide prevention, further advocates for a three-tiered public health model of prevention, intervention, and postvention that is explicated in his call to action (Lazarus, 2009). This multitiered model is based upon the severity and features of the suicidal risk, as well as the need for intervention. Each tier can each be thought of as (a) low risk: ideation; (b) moderate risk: current ideation and previous attempts or behaviors; and (c) high risk: current plan and intent with access to means (Lieberman, Poland, & Cassel, 2008).

There are two major goals of suicide prevention programs (CDC, 1994). The first goal is to look at individuals who are already at risk in order to make appropriate referrals and to provide effective treatment. The second goal is to reduce risk factors in general.

The American Foundation for Suicide Prevention maps out four evidence-based frameworks for ensuring success of suicide prevention strategies that incorporate these two goals. The first, gatekeeper training, involving educating individuals in the respective contexts (school staff and community members such as clergy, recre-

ational staff, clinical providers of healthcare to adolescents) to identify adolescents at risk for suicide. Approaches using this framework also teach the staff how to respond to suicidal individuals or other crises in their respective environments (American Foundation for Suicide Prevention, 2011).

The second recommended framework is general suicide psychoeducation, (i.e., teaching students about suicide, warning signs, and how to seek help for self or others). These strategies also often incorporate activities helping to boost the self-esteem of the adolescents involved. This framework can also be seen as one aspect of gatekeeper training, as the specified school staff members would be educated by a trained professional prior to educating the students on suicide.

The third recommended framework is the restriction of access to lethal means such as handguns and illicit substances to limit the accessibility of potential methods of self-harm. This is because ease of access to such measures increases the chance for a death by suicide to occur.

The fourth recommended framework is providing mental health treatment to individuals with depression and/or anxiety disorders, or those who are at-risk for such disorders. Screening programs are instruments or questionnaires that can be interpreted in order to identify high-risk individuals, as well as to provide further assessment and treatment. The Substance Abuse and Mental Health Services Administration, has provided *Preventing Suicide: A Toolkit for High Schools* (based on the Maine Youth Suicide Prevention Program; DiCara, O'Halloran, Williams, & Canty-Brooks, 2009) that recommends schools have screening programs in place as well as a plan to educate school staff, students, and parents on youth suicide/suicidal behaviors (Substance Abuse and Mental Health Services Administration, 2012). These are highly regarded methods for helping to uncover those adolescents who are possibly at risk for suicide, which will then lead to the utilization of appropriate protocols. Further, evidence-based suicide prevention programs are identified within the toolkit that can (and should) be implemented in schools in order to reduce student suicide. The two Tier 1 prevention approaches that most directly apply to schools are gatekeeper training and screening programs.

Gatekeeper Training and Screening Programs

Prevention programs have been proven to be successful Tier 1 strategies that properly train and educate school staff in suicide, as well as effectively screen for possible suicide risk, reduce suicidal ideation, decrease suicide attempts, and increase coping skills (Aseltine, James, Schilling, & Glanovsky, 2007; Brown & Goldstein Grummet, 2009). Signs of Suicide is a suicide prevention program for youth developed by the Substance Abuse and Mental Health Services Administration that utilizes a screening of adolescents to determine their risk for depression and suicidal tendencies.

The Signs of Suicide plan incorporates two frameworks: (a) increasing awareness through educating both students and school staff about recognizing the warning signs of depression and suicide and ways to intervene and (b) a screening that provides students with a short questionnaire to assess depression and suicide risk. This tool is used among eighth-grade and older students, and there is a distinct kit to use within each age group. While no formal training is necessary, the school psychologist is the appropriate staff member to serve as a key advocate and consultant for its implementation.

The Signs of Suicide kit includes teaching materials (a video and discussion guide) and a brief screening instrument for students (previously the Columbia Depression Scale and currently the Brief Screen for Adolescent Depression). The video, entitled *Friends for Life*, helps to teach students signs of suicidal ideation/ behaviors within themselves and others, to teach students that suicide is not the normal response to stressors, and to educate students about the specific actions to take in order to help someone in need. Additionally, the video focuses on current issues and risk factors among suicidal students, such as self-injurious behavior as it includes dramatizations of three adolescents who struggle with mental health issues. A peer-to-peer intervention strategy is suggested in the video in which students are taught to acknowledge a peer's suicidal ideation/behaviors, to care about the student in need through showing empathy and support, and to tell a responsible adult who will be able to help the depressed or suicidal student (Aseltine et al., 2007).

The video also encourages students to have open discussions about such issues with their parents in order to keep lines of communication open and honest, as well as to reduce the frequency and severity of such thoughts and feelings. Through these steps, this video increases awareness among students who may otherwise be ignorant of warning signs and actions to take. Children and adolescents are more apt to confide in peers than adults regarding depressive and suicidal thought. This video, along with the subsequent discussion, empowers its student audience and teaches

them how to intervene appropriately when a friend approaches them about such thoughts and emotions (Aseltine et al., 2007).

The other aspect of Signs of Suicide the Brief Screen for Adolescent Depression, is a self-screening tool that assesses depressive symptoms and suicidal ideation among eighth grade and older students. These students are asked to score the screenings themselves, and depending on the student's score on this screening, appropriate recommendations are made. A score of four or higher is considered to be an indicator of clinical depression, and students who receive such scores are encouraged to seek help immediately (Aseltine et al., 2007). Rather than limiting this referral solely to mental health professionals, the student may also be prompted to discuss personal issues and feelings with a trusted loved one or a trained school professional, such as a teacher or school psychologist.

Signs of Suicide has been found to be a straightforward and effective tool in reducing suicidal ideation and behavior among adolescents. The idea of a peer-to-peer intervention strategy is developmentally appropriate, as social interaction with peers and friends is the primary source of support among the majority of teenagers. Second, the implementation of this tool is relatively uncomplicated. It has been shown to be an effective method of preventing suicidal ideation and behaviors in adolescents. It is important to note that school staff members who carry out Signs of Suicide must be prepared properly in these areas through participating in the first of the previously mentioned methods of Tier 1 suicide prevention, gatekeeper training, and psychoeducation. By participating in effective training, faculty and staff will be able to assess properly for suicidal ideation and other mental health issues in adolescents.

Further, faculty and staff will be able to educate at-risk students and their peers suitably so that those students at risk are apt to seek out or to be referred to the appropriate mental health services. While teachers are trained to teach specific academic courses, the school psychologists (who are not necessarily in such close contact with numerous students on a daily basis) are experts in behavioral, emotional, and cognitive change. These school psychologists should utilize their knowledge in order to train the faculty and staff to be prepared to handle depressed or potentially suicidal students.

Identifying Suicidal Youth

It is imperative that schools put forth effort in identifying adolescents who are at risk for suicide. While many of such adolescents go unknown, the majority of them display warning signs and clues in some fashion that they are contemplating suicide. Because children and adolescents do not often refer themselves to treatment, a school psychologist's or other gatekeeper's effort to identify at-risk youth is vital. As previously discussed, gatekeeper training is an essential aspect of suicide prevention, and a strong effort should be made to ensure that these school staff members are properly trained and taught the various warning signs of suicide among youth. Warning signs can be understood as an acute risk factor such as a trait, attribute, or characteristic that has been found to be associated with suicidal ideation/ behavior. There are various warning signs of youth suicide (Poland & Lieberman, 2002; Rudd et al., 2006; Substance Abuse and Mental Health Services Administration, 2012):

- *Threats:* Can be either passive (e.g., "No one understands. What's the use?") or direct (e.g., "I wish I were dead"). Children and adolescents may utilize artistic outlets, such as creative writing or visual art pieces, to express thoughts of suicide. These threats may be made through cyber methods such as social media outlets or text messages. Whether direct or indirect communication, an individual who hears or reads such threats has the duty to take it seriously.
- *Plan/method/access:* The more specific the plan might be, the greater the probability for self-harming. Someone who has easier access to and is actively searching for access to means to hurt himself or herself with firearms, sharp objects, pills, drugs, and alcohol may be providing warning signs.
- *Final arrangements:* Someone who has a sense of purposelessness may begin to give away possessions and begin to write goodbye notes.
- *Sudden changes:* Dramatic changes in mood, behavior, friends, or personality should be looked at as a potential warning side of suicidal ideation/behaviors. While it is common for adolescents to go through mood changes, a dramatic shift that continues for days may be an indication of possible suicidal ideation. Withdrawal from friends, family, and society may also be a warning side of suicide.

There are various methods of Tier 2 and Tier 3 interventions that schools can utilize for suicidal youth, and it is important that each school plan in advance the steps to take with a potentially suicidal student. The Substance Abuse and Mental Health Services

Administration (2012) toolkit strongly advocates for the placement of protocols at each school in order to specify which staff will handle each of the tasks in the event of a suicide risk, suicide attempt, or completed suicide. Two crucial components that should be in place in every school, even if the school does not provide further suicide prevention strategies, are "protocols for helping students at possible risk of suicide" and "protocols for responding to a suicide death (and thus preventing additional suicides)" (Substance Abuse and Mental Health Services Administration, 2012, p. 17).

The school psychologist can take the lead role of developing a protocol to include necessary handouts and essential forms for documentation, risk assessment, notifying parents, providing referrals, and follow-up support. Some sample protocols for helping those students at risk that are provided within the toolkit include forms for parents and staff regarding at-risk adolescents; resources on properly assessing risk; information sheets for staff, students, and parents on various risk factors for youth suicide; suitable documentation examples; and methods for notifying parents of their child's suicide risk.

The school should have at least one appointed staff member who is properly trained at assessing a student's risk, such as the school psychologist. However, if the school did not designate someone, the school should contact a local mental health provider or National Suicide Prevention Lifeline (http://www. suicidepreventionlifeline.org) to identify a trained, local provider. Because school psychologists are trained in diagnostic assessment and interpretation of specific scales and instruments, the school psychologist may also be involved in risk assessment and may be best trained in using self-report questionnaires or screen scales referenced in Table 19.2. Through the utilization of such measures, school psychologists are more effective at screening for suicide potential, in addition to the presence of suicide risk factors, among students. These measures also aid in beginning to assess if a student's risk is at Tier 1, 2, or 3 for the school psychologist to act accordingly. Further, school psychologists may be trained in assessing student's suicide risk with many of the leading questions outlined in Table 19.3. The following general intervention for school-based crisis teams is recommended in order to assess for safety, identify the problem at hand, address the student's feelings and emotions, and ensure the student receives appropriate care (Lieberman et al., 2008; Miller, 2011; Substance Abuse and Mental Health Services Administration, 2012):

Table 19.2. Standardized Self-Report and Screening Scales for Assessment of Suicide

- The Columbia Suicide Severity Rating Scale (Posner et al., 2011)
- Beck Scale for Suicidal Ideation (Beck, 1991)
- The Suicidal Ideation Questionnaire (Reynolds, 1988; appropriate for students in grades 7–12)
- The Hopelessness Scale for Children (Kazdin, Rodgers, & Colbus, 1986)
- Signs of Suicide (http://www.mentalhealthscreening.org)
- Brief Suicide Risk Assessment Questionnaire (Miller & McConaughy, 2005)
- The Reynolds Adolescent Depression Scale-Second Edition (Osman, Gutierrez, Bagge, Fang, & Emmerich, 2010)
- MAPS: Measure for Adolescent Potential for Suicide (Eggert, Thompson, & Herting, 1994)

Note. Based on information from Lieberman et al. (2008), Miller and McConaughy (2005), and Substance Abuse and Mental Health Services Administration (2012).

Keep the student safe: A thorough assessment for safety and lethality is extremely important and so it is essential for a school to adequately supervise a student who is suspected to be at risk to himself or herself. As previously stated, a trained gatekeeper is a critical aspect of ensuring that the student is properly assessed for risk and brought into the school psychologist. In such a situation, it is important for the school staff to work together to best care for the student in need. No student at risk for suicide ought to be allowed to leave school unattended or to be left alone, even if just going to the restroom. This should begin with teachers and school staff not allowing at-risk students to even walk down the hall to the school psychologist unescorted by an adult.

Breaking confidentiality: When a student expresses suicidal risk, attention of the student's thoughts/behaviors should be immediately brought to the designated reporter (preferably a school psychologist) at the school. This reporter should be an individual who is properly trained to conduct risk assessments and make appropriate referrals. While some students at risk for suicide might ask to keep their suicidal ideation confidential, it is imperative that the designated reporter clearly make known that information regarding suicidal plan, ideation, or behavior must be disclosed to a third party, such as the student's parents. The student should be told that disclosing such information to the people who care most about him or her is extremely important. Keeping students informed of what actions are to be taken is a way to empower them and help them to feel as though their concerns will be both heard and understood.

Collaborate with administration or crisis team personnel: It is common for a school psychologist to need support from other staff. Difficult decisions made in such situations will be best made when discussed with and supported by other staff members, such as a nurse or psychologist, a school administrator, and other members of a school's crisis team.

Table 19.3. Areas to Address When Assessing a Student's Suicide Risk

- What are the current feelings of the student?
- What were the warning signs that initiated the referral?
- What is the student's current and past level of depression?
- What is the student's current and past level of hopelessness?
- Has the student currently, or in the past, thought about suicide (either directly or passively)?
- What is the method of any previous suicide attempt (any previous suicide attempts or prior self-injury may indicate higher risk)?
- Does the student have a current suicide plan or plan to harm himself or herself (the more specific the plan, if applicable, the higher the risk)?
- What method does the student plan to use and does the student have access to the means (higher risk when either or both of those are affirmed)?
- What are the student's perceptions on burdensomeness and belongingness?
- Is there history of alcohol or drug use?
- What are the student's current problems and stressors at home and at school?
- Has the student demonstrated any abrupt changes in behaviors?
- What is the student's current support system (higher isolation might indicate higher risk)?
- What is the student's current mental health status? Is there a history of mental illness?
- Is there a history of bullying, victimization, loss, or trauma (any affirmative response might indicate a higher risk)?
- What are the student's reasons to live (healthy answers to this question might indicate lower risk)?

Note. Based on information from Lieberman et al. (2008) and Miller (2011).

Suicide proof the environment and safety planning: When a student is suspected to be suicidal, it is a primary responsibility of the surrounding adults to remove access to lethal means. In addition to ridding the environment of access to weapons or anything that has potential to cause physical pain/death, it can be beneficial to prompt the suicidal student to commit to treatment. While no-suicide contracts are sometimes utilized, research illustrates that the utilization of written, signed safety contracts give mental health professionals and school psychologists a false sense of security and, further, a reduction of clinical caution with the student (Miller, 2011). In lieu of a contract, a safety plan can be made in collaboration with the school psychologist and student to ensure the student remains safe when he or she is feeling suicidal. This safety plan is to be used as a method of expressing direct, concrete, and nonsuicidal action. Stanley and Brown's Safety Planning Guide provides a six-step process for safety planning with suicidal students and can be utilized as a quick guide for school psychologists to refer to for such procedures (Stanley and Brown, 2008).

Utilize law enforcement and community supports when appropriate: It may be necessary to involve law enforcement in the process of taking care of the suicidal student depending on the severity of the suicidal risk, resistance/combativeness of the student, the student's attempt to flee the situation, and possible transportation needs. It is important for school psychologists to know the proper procedures in their state for involuntary hospitalization. When informing third parties, the gravity of the situation must be disclosed, making known that it involves a suicidal student.

Prepare a plan for reentry to the school: It is necessary for the facilitation of a student's reentry to school to be done in a careful, precise manner. A multidisciplinary approach is recommended that involves collaboration between the school psychologist, school personnel, the student, the student's parents or guardians, and professionals who have worked with the student in other fields, such as medical staff, hospital staff, and mental health professionals. While some might fight to hold the student from returning to school or find themselves anxious for a student's return, it has been found that a depressed person is much safer and better off in school than not. Additionally, school psychologists should check with their district's policies and guidelines.

Documentation

Documenting every step of this process is a crucial aspect for clinical, legal, and ethical reasons. When possible, the documentation should be done on the day of the assessment or incident and important information collected through interviews and assessments should be written down verbatim. These documents are an essential step of Tier 3 support when a referral of a suicidal student is made and a crisis team is utilized. There should be specified forms available within each school district in order to ensure proper records are kept of their responses, actions taken, recommendations, and referrals made to a suicidal student and/or the student's parents (Lieberman et al., 2008).

Suicide Intervention Model

Understanding how to properly conduct a risk assessment and knowing how to appropriately respond based on the student's level of risk are both significant factors in suicide prevention and intervention. Because early detection is extremely important, suicide risk assessment must be done carefully and accurately. Effective guidelines, as provided by Poland (1995) for the school psychologist to follow while assessing a student's suicide risk are (a) connect with student through providing empathy, support, and trust; (b) reflect feelings, remain nonjudgmental, and do not minimize the problems; (c) respect the student's developmental, cultural, and sexuality issues while collecting necessary information considering appropriate community referrals; (d) utilize an assessment worksheet; (e) be direct in questioning the student, staff member, and parents when collecting information; (f) never promise confidentiality; and (g) ensure that the school psychologist is maintaining the chain of supervision at all times.

Asking a student if he or she is thinking or has ever thought of suicide is vital, as it may lead to disclosure of risk that might otherwise have remained hidden. A multistage model can aid in early detection through the utilization of screenings and clinical interviews (Reynolds, 1991). While screenings should be brief, well validated, and reliable, the follow-up clinical interview with the student and the student's support system should be thorough in assessing ideation, plan, intent, risk factors, warning signs, and protective factors. Questions, indicators levels of risk, and general interventions are summarized in Table 19.4.

Notifying Parents

The failure of the school psychologist to notify parents or guardians when there is reason to suspect that the student is suicidal is quite a common source for lawsuits. The school psychologist has an obligation to report any

Table 19.4. Questions, Indicators, Levels of Risk, and General Interventions

Tier 1: Low risk (ideation)
- *Sample question to the student:* Have you ever thought about suicide or harming yourself?
- *Other possible indicators:* Current or recent thoughts; signs of depression; direct or indirect threats; sudden changes in personality, friends, or behaviors; evidence of self-harm in writing or artwork; dark Internet websites or social media posts
- *Actions:* Reassure and supervise the student; notify the parent; assist in connecting with school and community resources; suicide-proof environments; mobilize a support system; develop a safety plan that identifies caring adults, appropriate communication, coping skills, and resource numbers
- Document all actions.

Tier 2: Moderate risk (current ideation and previous behaviors)
- *Sample question to the student:* Have you ever tried to kill or harm yourself?
- *Other possible indicators:* Previous attempts; recent mental health hospitalizations; recent trauma (losses, victimization); recent medications for mood disorders; alcohol and substance addiction; running into traffic or jumping from high places; impulsivity; repetitive self-injury.
- *Actions:* See Tier 3.

Tier 3: High risk (current plan and access to method)
- *Sample question to the student:* Do you have a current plan to kill or harm yourself?
- *Other indicators:* Current plan with method/access; final arrangements; giving away prized possessions or written/e-mailed goodbye notes; refusal to agree to a safety plan.
- *Actions:* Supervise the student at all times (including restrooms); notify and release student only to (a) parent or guardian who commits to seek an immediate mental health assessment, (b) law enforcement, (c) psychiatric mobile responder; document all actions.
- *Prepare a reentry plan:* All students returning from mental health hospitalization should have a reentry meeting where parents, school, and community mental health personnel make appropriate follow-up plans.

student who is suspected to be at risk for suicide based on foreseeability. In other words, even if a student denies suicidal ideation/intent, it is the duty of the school to notify the parents if the information available infers that the student is likely suicidal and would, furthermore, be considered negligence for school personnel to refrain from doing so (Eisel v. Board of Education of Montgomery County, 1991).

The importance of informing the parents of a possible suicidal child is not just to prevent a potential lawsuit. It is critical for parents or guardians to be notified in order to best care for their child's safety (one caveat being if there are grounds to infer that the child would be abused or worsened by being in his or her home environment). Once the appropriate school staff member is with the student, preferably the school psychologist, it is vital to have that staff member get in touch with the parents or guardians. It is then essential to gain any further information from the parents or guardians that might contribute to the assessment of the student's risk if they are available and cooperative (Poland et al., 2008). The Substance Abuse and Mental Health Services Administration toolkit contains guidelines for notifying parents and for suicide prevention in high schools. It also provides a list of helpful steps for helping to engage parents and support them through this process (Table 19.5).

In addition to providing the information in Table 19.5, three essential aspects of involving the parents with their child who is possibly suicidal in order to ensure safety are stressed (DiCara et al., 2009). First, a school staff member, such as the school psychologist, should explicitly inform the parents or guardians that their child is at risk for suicide and explain the reasons as to why this is believed to be true. The school staff member(s) on this case should then explain the importance of removing access in the home to any lethal means.

It is crucial to educate the parents or guardians on how to properly rid access to lethal means and ways in which to keep the child safe at home for the time being. Appropriate referrals, with the level of care based on the severity of the case, should also be given to the child's parents or guardians at this time. In order for schools to provide the best practice for suicide prevention, policies for parental notification should be in place for students who are suspected to be suicidal, even if the student denies suicidal intent.

When it comes time to warn parents that their child might be suicidal, some issues may arise. First, if the team collaboratively decides that it is more of a risk to inform the student's parents based on potential neglect or abuse in the home, the school staff may skip to directly calling the state's child protective services

Table 19.5. Helpful Steps for a School Psychologist in Engaging and Supporting Parents of a Suicidal Student

- State what you have noticed in their child's behavior (not just results of your assessment) and ask how that fits with what they have seen in their child.
- Advise parents to remove lethal means from the home while the child is possibly suicidal. You can equate this to how you would advise taking car keys from their child who had been drinking.
- Provide empathy for this situation and comment on its scary nature.
- Acknowledge the emotional state of the parents.
- Acknowledge that it is essential for individuals to collaborate to help the child, as no one can do this alone.
- If the parent appears to be uncooperative or unwilling to take certain actions, find out the parent's beliefs about youth suicide risk/behavior and see if there are myths the parent believe are blocking the parent from taking proper action.
- Acknowledge and explore any cultural or religious concerns, or any other concerns, with accepting a referral to a mental health provider. Allow time to explain what it is the parent can expect.
- When possible, align yourself with the parent. It is important for the parent to understand where their child has gotten this idea without minimizing behaviors.

instead. Second, some parents are uncooperative and may refuse to come to the school to talk and/or personally pick up their children to bring them home safely.

We strongly advise against allowing students to walk or take the bus home alone, no matter what the parents suggest. If a parent or guardian refuses to ensure the safety of their child, refuses to seek out additional mental health services for their child, or does not take the suicide risk seriously, it is recommended that the school psychologist, or other school personnel, calls the state's respective child protective services.

Providing Referrals

School psychologists should keep a list of up-to-date community mental health resources to use as referrals for students who are possibly at risk for suicide in anticipation of suicidal crises. Once an action plan is in place for the student and his or her parent makes an appointment, it is recommended that the designated reporter or school psychologist contact the agency or mental health professional in order to ensure no relevant information be left out. Furthermore, various factors such as developmental, cultural, socioeconomic (potential need for provider who offers sliding scale rates), and sexuality issues should be considered when making such referrals (Lieberman, Poland, & Cowan, 2006).

Following Up and Providing Support

Whether or not the parents follow through with the school's referrals, it is important that there be follow-up services offered for the student and his or her family. A school should monitor the student's progress and make any modifications to the student's plan when necessary to meet the primary goal of ensuring the student's future safety. Additionally, the school's effort to provide continuous support and resources is necessary in order

to create a positive atmosphere for enhancing the student's success (Lieberman et al., 2008).

Postvention

The term *postvention* refers to events and activities that are planned for schools to put into action following a suicide as a means to assess the overall impact, identify at-risk students, prevent a contagion effect from occurring, and support survivors who are emotionally affected by the death to cope effectively. While schools are often unprepared to handle the aftermath of a suicide, what is implemented following a suicide is just as essential as the prevention efforts.

The American Foundation for Suicide Prevention and Suicide Prevention Resource Center (2011) created the *After a Suicide: A Toolkit for Schools*, which provides schools with appropriate postvention considerations and guidelines for addressing a suicide among the community. A strong collaboration between the school, parents, media, and community must exist in order to appropriately handle the situation at hand and minimize further suicide risk for others. Following a suicide, a collaborative effort is needed in order to provide the proper support to those survivors and to prevent contagion. Survivors of the suicide include friends, family, previously attempted survivors, classmates, and the school psychologist who might have worked with the student. Discussions and counseling for these survivors throughout the day following a suicide, as well as mental health referrals, are methods in which schools can support staff and students. In order to provide the best care to the school/community, this toolkit outlines very specific courses of action to take, and not to take, following a suicide. A summary of such guidelines can be found in Table 19.6.

Table 19.6. Suicide Postvention Guidelines

It is important to confirm suicide as cause of death with the coroner, medical examiner's office, and local law enforcement. The designated crisis team response leader should immediately meet with the team and assign duties.

Safety
- Keep standard school hours on the days following death.
- Discourage students from congregating in the hallway or bathroom and encourage the students to seek out appropriate counseling and help.
- Call on school resource officers to assist with keeping media off the grounds and assisting parents or others who might show up at the school.

Operations
- Contact the family, inform the family of the school's intervention efforts, offer support, and assist with funeral arrangements.
- Do not release information in a large assembly or over the intercom. Disseminate information to the faculty, students, and parents in small groups, up to the size of a small classroom. Be truthful, but avoid explicit details of the method and why the suicide happened. Instead, maintain focus on the general factors in suicide prevention and emphasize coping skills for survivors.
- Monitor activities throughout the school.
- Arrange for crisis counseling rooms for survivors and those affected by the death.
- Provide counseling and discussion opportunities for the faculty.
- Arrange for teachers and staff from local schools to assist if necessary.
- Identify and provide extra support to those who may be having a more difficult time.
- Provide tissues and water, and arrange for food to be available to staff and crisis workers on site.
- Track and respond to requests for memorialization by students and family members. It is important to balance between appropriate grieving and inappropriately glamourizing the death as a means to prevent contagion.

Community liaisons
- Provide primary contacts for working with the coroner or medical examiner, law enforcement to ensure safety, local government to facilitate a community-wide response to the suicide, mental health communities and grief organizations, and outside trauma/crisis responders to brief them as they arrive at the school.
- Contribute to a suicide prevention effort on behalf of the schools or community.

Funeral
- Encourage the family to hold funeral service off of school grounds and outside of school hours if possible.
- Contact the funeral director. Discuss the need to have crisis counselors at the service.
- Ensure that some school faculty is present at the funeral as a means to show support to affected students and survivors.
- Discuss with the family the importance of the funeral conductor/clergy placing emphasis on the connection between suicide and mental health issues (i.e., depression). It is important to refrain from romanticizing the death, contributing to contagion.
- Based on the family's wishes, assist in the distribution of information regarding the funeral to students, parents, and school staff.

Media relations
- Prepare a media statement including information on local support being provided, a list of possible suicide warning signs, as well as local and national mental health and suicide prevention resources.

Social media
- Consider bringing together a small group of friends of the deceased to work with school faculty and administration to monitor social networking sites and social media.
- Watch over the school's use of social media as an aspect of the crisis response.

Note. Based on information from American Foundation for Suicide Prevention and Suicide Prevention Resource Center (2011).

The postvention process can also be viewed as prevention method or a Tier 1 level of support, as it is an important step in limiting imitative behaviors following a suicide. It is important for the community to highlight the positive contributions and aspects of the deceased's life rather than glorifying the cause of death. A school should attempt to limit the amount and type of information used by the media when discussing the student's suicide.

This process should be one that is empathizing and psychoeducational in nature, discussing ways in which to identify and find help for potentially suicidal individuals and those suffering from mental illness. Resources such as the *After a Suicide* toolkit and American

Association of Suicidology (http://www.suicidology. org/home) provide letter templates and guidelines for the media and community in order to attempt to ensure that the suicide is handled properly to limit a contagion effect.

National Legislation and Initiatives

Because youth suicide is a national public health concern, an influx of initiatives and bills have been brought into recent action to address it. The 2004 Garrett Lee Smith Memorial Act was the first bill signed into law pertaining to youth suicide prevention, affirming that suicide is a national public health problem. The Act is an effort to provide funding to states, tribes, campuses, and behavioral mental health services for grants that support prevention and intervention efforts. A report from the U.S. Surgeon General describes an explicit strategy for taking action against suicide with a majority of the objectives pertaining to the implementation of suicide prevention protocols, in some fashion, within a school setting (U.S. Department of Health and Human Services Office of the Surgeon General & National Action Alliance for Suicide Prevention, 2012). This call to action places a strong emphasis on making suicide prevention a priority in the United States, and is a significant document for working toward the prevention of youth suicide.

SUMMARY

Suicide is now the third leading cause of death in the United States for 10–24 year olds. Many theories have been proposed to explain this increase: from the little black box on antidepressant medications to the explosion of social media, from economic strife to the trauma of military service, from the stigma surrounding having a mental illness to the stigma of asking for help. Undoubtedly, suicide remains a complex behavior, most often the result of numerous risk factors that come together in a perfect storm. While research has revealed little in the identification of predictors, it has provided rich data on the complex relationships of suicide to bullying and cyberbullying, self-injury, depression, substance abuse, trauma, and parental rejection of LGBT youth.

It is critical that all school psychologists be familiar with all aspects of suicide risk and suicide intervention in schools. They must continue to work with administrators to ensure safe campuses for all students and prepare their school personnel to recognize and intervene with students who present at all levels of risk for suicide. They must continue to work compassionately with parents on prevention and early intervention with children with mental health issues. They must continue to work collaboratively with their community mental health partners and law enforcement.

REFERENCES

American Foundation for Suicide Prevention. (2006). *About the cause: Suicide and depression facts*. New York, NY: Author.

American Foundation for Suicide Prevention and Suicide Prevention Resource Center. (2011). *After a Suicide: A Toolkit for Schools*. Newton, MA: Education Development Center. Retrieved from http://www.sprc.org/library/AfteraSuicideToolkitforSchools.pdf

Aseltine, R. H., James, A., Schilling, E. A., & Glanovsky, J. (2007). Evaluating the SOS suicide prevention program: A replication and extension. *BMC Public Health 2007, 7*(161). Retrieved from http://www.biomedcentral.com/1471-2458/7/161

Beck, A. (1991). *Beck Scale of Suicidal Ideation*. San Antonio, TX: Harcourt Assessment.

Berman, L., Eastgard, S., Gutierrez, P., Mazza, J., Poland, S., Roggenbaum, S., … Smith, J. (2009). *School suicide prevention accreditation resource guide* (2nd ed.). Washington, DC: American Association of Suicidology.

Brown, M. M., & Goldstein Grumet, J. (2009). School-based suicide prevention with African American youth in an urban setting. *Professional Psychology: Research and Practice, 40*, 111–117. doi:10.1037/a0012866

Centers for Disease Control and Prevention. (1994). Programs for the prevention of suicide among adolescents and young adults and suicide contagion and the reporting of suicide: Recommendations from a national workshop. *Morbidity and Mortality Weekly Report, 43*(6), 1–18.

Centers for Disease Control and Prevention. (2011). *Web-based injury statistics query and reporting system*. Atlanta, GA: National Centers for Injury Prevention and Control. Retrieved from http://cdc.gov/injury/wisqars/index.html

Centers for Disease Control and Prevention. (2012). Youth risk behaviour surveillance–United States, 2011. Surveillance summaries. *Morbidity and Mortality Weekly Report, 61*(4), 1–162. Retrieved from http://www.cdc.gov/mmwr/pdf/ss/ss6104.pdf

DiCara, C., O'Halloran, S., Williams, L., & Canty-Brooks, C. (2009). *Youth suicide prevention, intervention, and postvention guidelines*. Augusta, ME: Maine Youth Suicide Prevention Program. Retrieved from http://www.maine.gov/suicide/docs/Guidelines%2010-2009--w%20discl.pdf

Eggert, L. L., Thompson, E. A., & Herting, J. R. (1994). A Measure of Adolescent Potential for Suicide (MAPS): Development and preliminary findings. *Suicide and Life-Threatening Behavior, 24*, 359–381.

Eisel v. Board of Education of Montgomery County. 324 Md. 376, 597 A. 2d 447 (Md Ct. App. 1991).

Eisenberg, M. E., & Resnick, M. D. (2006). Suicidality among gay, lesbian, and bisexual youth: The role of protective factors. *Journal of Adolescent Health, 39*, 662–668.

Goldsmith, S. K., Pellmar, T. C., Kleinman, A. M., & Bunney, W. E. (2002). *Reducing suicide: A national imperative*. Washington, DC: National Academies Press.

Gould, M., & Kramer, R. A. (2011). Youth suicide prevention. *Suicide and Life-Threatening Behavior, 31*, 6–31. doi:10.1521/suli.31.1.5.6. 24219

Hardt, J., Johnson, J. G., Courtney, E. A., & Sareen, J. (2006). Childhood adversities associated with risk for suicidal behavior. *Psychology Times, 23*(7), 1–2.

Hatzenbuehler, M. L. (2011). The social environment and suicide attempts in lesbian, gay, and bisexual youth. *Pediatrics, 127*, 896–903. doi:10.1542/peds.2010-3020

Hinduja, S., & Patchin, J. W. (2012). *School climate 2.0: Preventing cyberbullying and sexting one classroom at a time*. Thousand Oaks, CA: SAGE.

Kalafat, J., & Lazarus, P. J. (2002). Suicide prevention in schools. In S. E. Brock, P. J. Lazarus, & S. R. Jimerson (Eds.), *Best practices in school crisis prevention and intervention* (pp. 211–223). Bethesda, MD: National Association of School Psychologists.

Kaminski, J. W., & Fang, X. (2009). Victimization by peers and adolescent suicide in three US samples. *The Journal of Pediatrics, 155*, 683–688. doi:10.1016/j.jpeds.2009.04.061

Kazdin, A. E., Rodgers, A., & Colbus, D. (1986). The hopelessness scale for children: Psychometric characteristics and concurrent validity. *Journal of Consulting and Clinical Psychology, 54*, 241–245.

Klomek, A. B., Kleinman, M., Altschuler, E., Marrocco, F., Amakawa, L., & Gould, M. S. (2011). High school bullying as a risk for later depression and suicidality. *Suicide and Life-Threatening Behavior, 41*, 501–516. doi:10.1111/j.1943-278X.2011. 00046.x

LaFleur, G., & Poland, S. A. (2012). Schools can be the difference in preventing suicide. *Education Week News, 32*(9), 24–25.

Lazarus, P. J. (2009). *Call to action to prevent youth suicide*. Bethesda, MD: National Association of School Psychologists. Retrieved from http://www.nasponline.org/advocacy/suicidecalltoaction.aspx

Lieberman, R., & Cowan, K. C. (2011). Bullying and youth suicide: Breaking the connection. *National Association of Secondary School Principals: Principal Leadership, 12*(2), 12–17.

Lieberman, R., & Poland, S. (2006). Self-mutilation. In G. G. Bear & K. M. Minke (Eds.), *Children's needs III*. Bethesda, MD: National Association of School Psychologists.

Lieberman, R., Poland, S., & Cassel, R. (2008). Best practices in suicide intervention. In A. Thomas & J. Grimes (Eds.), *Best practices in school psychology V* (pp. 1457–1473). Bethesda, MD: National Association of School Psychologists.

Lieberman, R., Poland, S., & Cowan, K. C. (2006). Suicide prevention and interventions: Best practices for principals. *National Association of Secondary School Principals: Principal Leadership, 7*(2), 11–15.

Miller, D. N. (2011). *Child and adolescent suicidal behavior: School-based prevention, assessment, and intervention*. New York, NY: Guilford Press.

Miller, D. N., & McConaughy, S. H. (2005). Assessing risk for suicide. In S. H. McConaughy (Ed.), *Clinical interviews for children and adolescents: Assessment to intervention* (pp. 184–199). New York, NY: Guilford Press.

National Association of School Psychologists. (2010). *Model for comprehensive and integrated school psychological services*. Bethesda,

MD: National Association of School Psychologists. Retrieved from http://www.nasponline.org/standards/2010standards/2_PracticeModel.pdf

Olweus, D. (1993). *Bullying at school: What we know and what we can do*. (1st ed.). Malden, MA: Blackwell.

Osman, A., Gutierrez, P. M., Bagge, C. L., Fang, Q., & Emmerich, A. (2010). Reynolds adolescent depression scale-second edition: a reliable and useful instrument. *Journal of Clinical Psychology, 66*, 1324–1345.

Pisani, A. R., Schmeelk-Cone, K., Gunzler, D., Petrova, M., Goldston, D. B., Tu, X., & Wyman, P. A. (2012). Associations between suicidal high school students' help-seeking and their attitudes and perceptions of social environment. *Journal of Youth and Adolescence, 41*, 1312–1324.

Poland, S. (1995). Best practices in suicide intervention. In A. Thomas & J. Grimes (Eds.), *Best practices in school psychology III* (pp. 155–166). Washington, DC: National Association of School Psychologists.

Poland, S., & Lieberman, R. (2002). Best practices in suicide intervention. In A. Thomas & J. Grimes (Eds.), *Best practices in school psychology IV* (pp. 1151–1167). Bethesda, MD: National Association of School Psychologists.

Posner, K., Brown, G. K., Stanley, B., Brent, D. A., Yershova, K. V., Oquendo, M. A., … Mann, J. J. (2011). The Columbia-Suicide Severity Rating Scale (C-SSRS): Initial validity and internal consistency findings from three multisite studies with adolescents and adults. *American Journal of Psychiatry, 168*, 1266–1277.

Reynolds, W. M. (1988). *The Suicidal Ideation Questionnaire: Professional manual*. Odessa, FL: Psychological Assessment Resources.

Reynolds, W. (1991). A school-based procedure for the identification of adolescents at risk for suicidal behaviors. *Family and Community Health, 14*, 64–75.

Rudd, M. D., Berman, A. L., Joiner, T. E., Nock, M. K., Silverman, M., Mandrusiak, M., … Witte, T. (2006). Warning signs for suicide: Theory, research, and clinical applications. *Suicide and Life-Threatening Behavior, 36*, 255–262.

Ryan, C., Russell, S. T., Huebner, D. M., Diaz, R., & Sanchez, J. (2010). Family acceptance in adolescence and the health of LGBT young adults. *Journal of Child and Adolescent Psychiatric Nursing, 23*, 205–213. Retrieved from http://familyproject.sfsu.edu/files/FAP_Family%20Acceptance_JCAPN.pdf

Sharaf, A. Y., Thompson, E. A., & Walsh, E. (2009). Protective effects of self-esteem and family support on suicide risk behaviors among at-risk adolescents. *Journal of Child and Adolescent Psychiatric Nursing, 22*, 160–168. doi:10.1111/j.1744-6171.2009.00194.x

Stanley, B., & Brown, G. K. (2008). *Safety planning: A brief intervention to mitigate suicide risk*. Washington, DC: U.S. Department of Veterans Affairs. Retrieved from http://www.sprc.org/library/Veteran_Safety_Plan.pdf

Substance Abuse and Mental Health Services Administration. (2012). *Preventing suicide: A toolkit for high schools*. (HHS Publication No. SMA-12-4669). Rockville, MD: Author. Retrieved from http://store.samhsa.gov/product/Preventing-Suicide-A-Toolkit-for-High-Schools/SMA12-4669

U.S. Department of Health and Human Services Office of the Surgeon General & National Action Alliance for Suicide

Prevention. (2012). *2012 National strategy for suicide prevention: Goals and objectives for action*. Washington, DC: Author.

U.S. Food and Drug Administration. (2004). *FDA launches a multi-pronged strategy to strengthen safeguards for children treated with antidepressant medications*. Washington, DC: Author. Retrieved from http://www.fda.gov/NewsEvents/Newsroom/PressAnnouncements/2004/ucm108363.htm

Whitlock, J., Muehlenkamp, J., Eckenrode, J., Purington, A., Baral Abrams, G., Berreira, P., & Kress, V. (2012). Nonsuicidal self-injury as a gateway to suicide in young adults. *Journal of Adolescent Health, 52*, 486–492. doi:10.1016/j.jadohealth.2012.09.010

Yip, P. S. (2011). Towards evidence-based suicide prevention programs. *Crisis: The Journal of Crisis Intervention and Suicide Prevention, 32*, 117–120. doi:10.1027/0227-5910/a000010

20 Best Practices in Crisis Intervention Following a Natural Disaster

Melissa Allen Heath
Brigham Young University (UT)

OVERVIEW

The World Health Organization (2013) reports the heavy toll of natural disasters. Around the world, natural disasters are responsible for approximately 90,000 deaths each year, with disasters directly affecting an additional 160 million survivors. Subsequent to immediate deaths, communicable diseases may threaten survivors' well-being. Rapidly escalating the death toll, inadequate and contaminated water and food cause diarrhea and malnutrition. This addendum to disaster tragically has an impact on young children, particularly those living in developing nations with limited medical care.

However, even with well-developed emergency services in place, recent hurricanes in the United States, such as Hurricane Katrina and Hurricane Rita in 2005 and Hurricane Sandy in 2012, demonstrate the immediate and ongoing needs of families and communities following such devastation and destruction. Regardless of a community's location, size, or financial stability, some type of natural disaster poses a potential threat to safety and well-being.

Natural disasters listed on the website for the Federal Emergency Management Agency (FEMA) include earthquakes, volcanoes, floods, landslides and debris flow, extreme heat, droughts, wildfires, severe weather, hurricanes, tornadoes, space weather (disrupting technology and communication), thunderstorms and lightning, and winter storms and extreme cold. Additionally, the World Health Organization (2013) offers the following definition for natural disaster:

[A natural disaster is] an act of nature of such magnitude as to create a catastrophic situation in which the day-to-day patterns of life are suddenly disrupted and people are plunged into helplessness and suffering, and, as a result, need food, *clothing, shelter, medical and nursing care and other necessities of life, and protection against unfavorable environmental factors and conditions. (para. 1)*

Because most natural disasters occur with minimal warning, both prevention and intervention are critical elements in mitigating chaos, property damage, injuries, and loss of life. In particular, this chapter summarizes major research findings related to natural disaster's impact on children's mental health and emotional well-being and provides implications for school-based crisis prevention and intervention.

In the event of a natural disaster, immediate and ongoing negative repercussions vary depending on the availability and effectiveness of immediate and sustained physical and social support. A school's preparation to address specific disasters buffers potentially negative outcomes. From a mental health perspective, prepared schools strengthen a community's stability and emotional recovery (Brock et al., 2009).

This chapter's information is related to the domain of preventive and responsive services, as conceptualized in the National Association of School Psychologists (NASP) *Model for Comprehensive and Integrated School Psychological Services*: "School psychologists have knowledge of principles and research related to … evidence-based strategies for effective crisis response" (NASP, 2010, p. 6). The NASP Practice Model offers specific examples of school psychologists' preventive and responsive services, including participation on school crisis teams by offering "direct services in the context of crisis prevention, preparation, response, and recovery" (NASP, 2010, p. 7). To better prepare school psychologists who offer these services, this chapter specifies evidence-based strategies for planning, preparing, and strengthening school-based responses to support children and youth vulnerable to and/or affected by natural disasters.

In particular, this chapter focuses on strategies for serving the whole school (Tier 1 interventions), small groups (Tier 2 interventions), and individuals (Tier 3 interventions). A multitiered service delivery model ensures that children's needs are carefully considered and adequately addressed. School psychologists must think in terms of severity and the degree of need for specific types of intervention, considering large group, small group, and/or individualized supervision, intervention, and ongoing support. Although school psychologists must be prepared and ready to assist on all levels of need, they must also prepare teachers and parents to assist students. This chapter emphasizes the importance of surveying the school's needs and preparing school psychologists to adequately address those needs.

BASIC CONSIDERATIONS

In regard to a given community and school, depending on location, some types of natural disasters are more likely to occur than others. For example destructive earthquakes commonly occur in Japan, Alaska, California, Oregon, and Washington, yet rarely occur in the upper Midwest portion of the United States. Moreover, earthquakes may trigger additional disasters, including tsunamis, avalanches, landslides, flashfloods, and fires.

Although not prone to earthquakes, states bordering the Gulf of Mexico and Atlantic Ocean are affected by hurricanes. Based on the National Hurricane Center's historical data (http://www.aoml.noaa.gov/hrd/tcfaq/J6.html), the deadliest recorded U.S. hurricane struck Galveston, Texas, in 1900, killing more than 8,000. In 2005, Hurricane Katrina affected more than 15 million people across seven states. The death toll was estimated at 1,836 (http://www.hurricanekatrinarelief.com/). More recently, the death toll from Hurricane Sandy in 2012 was estimated at more than 200, with 132 of those deaths occurring in the United States (Newman, 2012). Newman (2012) also reported that 8.51 million homes across 16 states and Washington, DC, were without electrical power following Hurricane Sandy.

Tornadoes commonly occur in portions of the United States, with an average of 1,000 tornadoes reported each year (National Climatic Data Center, 2012). The vast majority of tornadoes occur between the Rocky and Appalachian mountain ranges, commonly referred to as tornado alley. The highest number of tornadoes per square mile occurs in Florida and Kansas.

Research That Informs Best Practice

Based on an intensive review of disaster research, Bonanno, Brewin, Kaniasty, and La Greca (2010) summarized five major points:

- Few individuals affected by disasters suffer serious, long-term psychological harm (e.g., posttraumatic stress disorder, grief, depression, anxiety, suicidal ideation, and substance abuse). In the weeks and months following the disaster, chronic and severe psychological trauma is identified in less than 30% of exposed individuals. However, 1–2 years following the disaster this percentage drops to approximately 5% and is comparable across age. Even though children who are directly affected may display intense reactions during the first few months following a disaster, beyond the initial period of intense reaction, minimal to no differences are noted between exposed and unexposed children.

- Although a wide range of responses are noted immediately following a disaster, the vast majority of individuals are resilient and adapt, eventually returning to a normal trajectory of development.

- Although difficult to accurately predict outcomes following a disaster, it appears that outcomes are best predicted by a combination of factors, including cumulative trauma, preexisting risk factors, environmental factors, and resilience factors.

- Overall, it appears that disasters place some communities, families, and individuals at risk for social deterioration (weakening of community's social ties). Likewise, research demonstrates social support's powerful positive impact on postdisaster healing (for individuals and communities).

- The personal impact of far-removed disasters appears to be negligible, except in cases where an individual has a history of previous trauma or psychological illness. In other words, distant trauma may trigger intense responses in vulnerable individuals, but not typically in the general public.

Bonanno et al. (2010) also noted the negative aspects of debriefing (going in immediately after a traumatic situation and conducting mass crisis intervention counseling). These authors recommended offering psychological first-aid and psychoeducational materials during the first few weeks following a disaster. Bonanno et al. (2010) also encouraged a quick return to school, maintaining the strong social bonds that schools offer to children and families and offering opportunities to express feelings and discuss experiences.

Following a 1980 earthquake in central Italy, Galante and Foa (1986) investigated factors related to elementary school students' functioning. It appeared that a family member's death elevated the risk for emotional and behavioral problems in surviving children. Similar to Bonanno et al.'s (2010) findings, Galante and Foa emphasized the need to reestablish community stability by returning to daily routines and schooling as quickly as possible. Across the school year, treatment was offered in monthly 1-hour small group meetings (Tier 2 intervention). Activities included drawing and talking about the earthquake, ultimately building up to students acting out the earthquake.

McFarlane and Van Hoof (2009) conducted longitudinal research with children affected by Australian bushfires in 1983. Rather than the actual exposure to the disaster, presence of a child's posttraumatic symptoms was more related to the mother's intrusive memories and changes in parenting, particularly diminished parental supervision. A 20-year follow up demonstrated that the bushfires had minimal impact on the prevalence of survivors' psychiatric disorders and anxiety. This postdisaster research supported the following interventions: Offer resources and strengthen support for parenting (particularly for mothers), and help parents provide an emotionally stable home environment with sufficient parental supervision. The biggest finding in this longitudinal research was the warning for researchers to consider context and impact of cumulative trauma across a lifetime rather than focusing on one single traumatic event.

Following Florida's 1992 Hurricane Andrew, La Greca, Silverman, Vernberg, and Prinstein (1996) conducted longitudinal research with students in Grades 3–5. They noted minimal gender differences in children's responses to Hurricane Andrew. They also noted the decline in children's posttraumatic stress symptoms over time. Their findings supported maintaining strong social connections (parent–child, student–teacher, student–student) and providing long-term supportive services.

In 1992, Hurricane Iniki devastated Hawaii's Kauai Island. Two years after the hurricane, Chemtob, Nakashima, and Carlson (2002) screened students in Grades 2–6. Children with the highest levels of psychological trauma were randomly placed in one of three conditions: (a) small group treatment (Tier 2 intervention), (b) individual treatment (Tier 3 intervention), or (c) wait list (no intervention). Both group and individual treatments were equally effective in reducing trauma-related symptoms; however, students in group treatment were less likely to drop out of treatment. Although their research supports the use of both individual and group interventions, in school settings with limited mental health resources and limited funding, interventions provided in small group settings (Tier 2) offer effective therapeutic social support for students experiencing high levels of psychological trauma.

After Hurricane Georges devastated Puerto Rico, Felix et al. (2011) examined children's reactions at 18 months and then again at 30 months. Based on almost 2,000 parent–child dyad interviews, comparisons were made between children exposed and not exposed to the hurricane. Differences in internalizing disorders were evident at 18 months, but no differences were noted at 30 months. For children experiencing elevated levels of internalizing disorders (e.g., elevated anxiety and depression), this research indicated the potential need for supportive services across an extended period of time, up to 2 years following a disaster. An important finding from this research was that the majority of children's anxiety and depression naturally diminishes across time. Another finding was that poverty is associated with elevated risk for maladjustment, therefore extra monitoring, support, and resources should be available to this vulnerable group.

Fifteen to eighteen months after the 2004 Indian Ocean tsunami, Nastasi, Jayasena, Summerville, and Borja (2011) conducted research in southern Sri Lanka. Their research investigated a school-wide Tier 1 intervention project that was designed to support children's long-term psychosocial needs. Group lessons and activities were provided after school in classroom settings (school-wide, Tier 1 intervention). Local teachers and administrators were trained to teach lessons and lead group activities. Their research indicated the effectiveness of (a) long-term support of normative recovery for children's psychosocial needs, (b) the effectiveness of training teachers and administrators to offer group lessons and activities, and (c) the importance of providing culturally and contextually sensitive school-based services.

BEST PRACTICES IN CRISIS INTERVENTION FOLLOWING A NATURAL DISASTER

This section offers research-based intervention strategies to inform school psychologists in effectively supporting students' needs following a natural disaster. It is important to help schools return to a normal schedule as quickly as possible. Following natural disasters, rebuilding schools and getting children back in school are critical priorities in stabilizing communities (Greubel, Ackerman, & Winthrop, 2012). Additionally, research indicates the importance of social support in helping children recover following a traumatic event (La Greca & Silverman, 2009). Sources of social support include parent involvement (Cohen, Mannarino, & Deblinger, 2006, 2012), peer group support (Jaycox, Langley, & Dean, 2009), and supportive school and classroom environments (Nastasi et al., 2011).

Prepare in Advance

After identifying potential threats, school psychologists and crisis teams must prepare in advance to mitigate the impact of natural disasters. Although each natural disaster and each community's needs are unique, school psychologists can prepare their school's crisis plan to address potentially threatening situations.

One resource to assist schools in preparing and updating crisis plans is *Practical Information on Crisis Planning: A Guide for Schools and Communities* and is available on the Department of Education's website (http://rems.ed.gov/docs/PracticalInformationonCrisisPlanning.pdf). It provides guidelines for schools and communities to prepare for and manage crises. These guidelines are based on four phases of emergency management: prevention and mitigation, preparedness, response, and recovery. The introduction stresses the importance of advance planning and preparation, because in the midst of crisis response each person must be familiar with his or her role and responsibilities. It is critical for all participants to know each other, know the plan, and practice the drill.

Also relying on the same four phases of emergency management, Chapter 3 in the PREPaRE manual outlines the basic ingredients of creating and sustaining school crisis teams (Brock et al., 2009). The acronym PREPaRE stands for the following list of important strategies arranged in sequential order (Brock et al., 2009, p. ix): prevent and prepare for psychological trauma, reaffirm physical health and perceptions of security and safety, evaluate psychological trauma risk, provide interventions, respond to psychological needs, and examine the effectiveness of crisis prevention and intervention.

Prepare Disaster Services

In the prevention and mitigation phase, crisis teams must address potentially weak areas of response that might jeopardize the effectiveness of their school's disaster response efforts. After an extensive review of school crisis plans and an evaluation of required equipment, trained personnel, and means to carry out those plans, the U.S. Government Accountability Office (2007) identified common weaknesses that typically threaten the effectiveness of school-based crisis intervention. Their report recommended schools reassess their crisis plans, specifically attending to the following concerns: (a) attending to the safety needs of students with disabilities and special needs, particularly exiting and relocating students with limited mobility; (b) expanding emergency management drills to include community first responders and supportive community agencies; and (c) effectively communicating and coordinating crisis response efforts with parents and first responders during and following emergency situations. As part of a school crisis team, school psychologists must consider and address these concerns, making sure that crisis plans are responsive to these critical needs.

School personnel may require training in order to provide immediate assistance and assurance to both ambulatory and nonambulatory students. Some students will require both physical and emotional guidance due to handicapping conditions that may limit communication, understanding, and self-sufficiency. Furthermore, students with disabilities may lack adaptive coping skills to effectively address and manage their grief and loss, separation from caregivers, and changes in routine (Sormanti & Ballan, 2011). Additionally, an extended wait time for reuniting this vulnerable group of students with parents poses an added responsibility of keeping students comfortable and calm. Crisis teams must consider these challenges when preparing to face the necessity of immediate evacuation and relocation.

Natural disasters often threaten physical safety. Some students may require emergency medical attention. In advance of a natural disaster, school crisis teams must reach out and coordinate efforts with emergency medical professionals and local law enforcement. In planning for the potential needs of schools following a natural disaster, each community's unique strengths and vulnerabilities must be considered. As recommended by Annandale, Heath, Dean, Kemple, and Takino (2011), schools should begin planning by conducting a needs assessment. This involves considering who the crisis plan is intended to serve, taking into account the community's ethnic makeup; languages spoken in students' homes; religious preferences, values, and beliefs; and attitudes and perceptions regarding seeking help. A needs assessment should lead into problem solving, focusing on community resources that will strengthen resilience following a natural disaster. In identifying strategies to strengthen cultural sensitivity, planning must involve initiating and forming collaborative relationships with community agencies, local religious/faith leadership, and representatives from community groups (cultural brokers).

To assist in conducting a needs assessment, school psychologists may consider reviewing a planning and evaluation checklist included in U.S. Department of Health and Human Services (2003, pp. 57–58). This checklist identifies details to consider in advance of a disaster, including recruiting and training local individuals who are representative of the community's cultural and linguistic diversity. Other recommendations include advance planning to ensure that proposed disaster services are "accessible, appropriate, and equitable," considering the affected community (U.S. Department of Health and Human Services, 2003, p. 57).

The Minnesota Department of Health offers a resource, *Communicating Without English in an Emergency* (http://www.echominnesota.org/webinar-communicating-without-english). It breaks down emergency communication planning into seven action steps: (a) developing a commitment to planning; (b) locating families with limited English proficiency and identifying target languages; (c) encouraging and involving community participation; (d) selecting the preferred type of media for families and groups who speak the targeted languages; (e) summarizing, recording, and mapping information/data; (f) preparing messages and translating messages; and (g) testing the proposed communication plan. By following these steps, school crisis teams would be better prepared for the challenge of communicating with limited and non-English-speaking families.

These concerns regarding effective communication are especially relevant to school-based crisis planning. In advance of a natural disaster, schools must determine how they will communicate with all English speaking and non-English-speaking parents and how they will reunite children with their families. If schools are forced to relocate to another location, the identified setting and details about this decision must be communicated with parents and caregivers. Backup communication plans must be determined in advance of a disaster. These issues are complex in the planning stages, but unbelievably chaotic if plans are not clearly defined prior to the disaster.

Prepare Emergency Kits

Following Hurricane Katrina, more than 20,000 people sought refuge in the heavily damaged New Orleans Superdome. When emergency supplies were not delivered as anticipated, nor were individuals rescued as anticipated, conditions worsened. With no food, no water, no electrical power, and no working toilets, chaos ensued. Tragically, these individuals were not rescued until 6 days later. A major lesson was learned from this disaster: Each individual should take responsibility for his or her own welfare. It is impossible to ensure that FEMA or the Red Cross will be able to offer assistance to all individuals immediately after a natural disaster.

A very practical consideration is that school psychologists encourage teachers to prepare classroom emergency kits. Although these kits typically contain items listed in Table 20.1, each school and each teacher should identify additional items that best fit the students' and school's needs. As a whole, the school should consider storing water and packaged snacks that have a long shelf life. Spearheading these efforts may be delegated to parent–teacher organizations. Responsibility should also be clearly designated to specify who will prepare and maintain classroom emergency kits.

Additionally, school leadership, local religious/faith leaders, and community organizations can encourage and support families in preparing 3-day emergency kits for home use. Websites for the Red Cross (http://www.redcross.org/prepare/location/home-family/get-kit) and FEMA (http://www.ready.gov/sites/default/files/documents/files/checklist_1.pdf) recommend families make easily transportable 3-day emergency kits. These kits provide basic necessities to sustain families until relief agencies and emergency response teams arrive with additional supplies.

Table 20.1. Classroom Emergency Kit

- Laminated list of students and updated parent contact information
- Basic first-aid kit and emergency medication if needed for a specific student
- Flashlight with extra batteries
- Water bottles (one per student)
- Acceptable snacks that have a long shelf life; consider student allergies
- Whistle to alert others
- Paper/tablet and pencil/pen
- Favorite story book or activity
- Blanket/sheet
- Supplies for emergency toileting (bucket, plastic garbage sacks, toilet paper, moist wipes)
- Pack supplies in a rolling luggage and update the kit each year

Train for Emergency Preparedness

School psychologists must seek ongoing training opportunities for crisis prevention and intervention. NASP offers a well-researched training curriculum for crisis prevention and intervention in school settings based on the PREPaRE model (Brock et al., 2009). Details about obtaining this training are described on the NASP website (http://www.nasponline.org/prepare/).

Additionally, school psychologists should remain current in CPR certification through the Red Cross. This type of training is especially important in remote rural schools where access to emergency medical assistance is limited. In particular, physical injuries with excessive bleeding, shock, and blocked airways require immediate attention.

Although not singularly focused on school-based crisis intervention, three major national organizations—the Red Cross, FEMA, and the National Organization for Victim Assistance—offer training for disaster mental health and psychological first-aid. Each organization has specific sections of their training devoted to children and families. Details about training are provided on each organization's website.

- Red Cross: *Training for Red Cross Disaster Mental Health* is available through local and regional offices of the Red Cross. Information about signing up for training is available on the Red Cross website (http://www.redcross.org/take-a-class/disaster-training-registration).
- FEMA: The Emergency Management Institute (http://training.fema.gov/IS/crslist.asp) offers an independent study program. Courses are available online for U.S. residents and approved international students. The training is free and may count for continuing professional development hours. A limited number of slots for the online courses are available on a first-come, first-serve basis.
- National Organization for Victim Assistance: The training manual can be ordered on their website (http://www.trynova.org/wp-content/uploads/2012/07/OrderACRTManual.pdf) and the training ranges from 24 to 48 hours.

School psychologists must determine which types of training and resources are the best fit for their schools' specific needs. Additionally, taking into account that school psychologists may have a limited budget for training, free training materials and handouts for training are listed in Table 20.2.

Strengthen the Role of Teachers and School Staff

School psychologists are encouraged to strengthen the role of teachers and school staff in crisis intervention, helping teachers and staff provide emotional support in classroom settings (Tier 1 interventions). Students, in the event of a natural disaster, feel more comfortable with familiar adults, their teachers, and school staff (Wolmer, Hamiel, & Laor, 2011). Refer to Tables 20.3 and 20.4 for basic information geared to school psychologists helping teachers understand their role in crisis intervention following a natural disaster. Teachers are in a

---

Table 20.2. Free Internet Training Materials and Handouts for School-Based Crisis Intervention

- Quick training aids: http://smhp.psych.ucla.edu/qf/crisis_qt
  School-based crisis intervention; materials are offered for training or self-tutorial; site offers key points, fact sheets, and checklists to help school psychologists prepare presentations for teachers and school personnel

- NASP: http://www.nasponline.org/resources/crisis_safety/index.aspx
  School safety and crisis resources; list of resources; organized by topic; some handouts translated into other languages

- National Child Traumatic Stress Network: http://www.nctsn.org/trauma-types/natural-disasters
  Offers a variety of training materials related to natural disasters' impact on children, including psychological first-aid; free online training materials available at http://learn.nctsn.org

- FEMA: http://training.fema.gov/IS/crslist.asp
  Offers an online independent study program for U.S. residents; no cost and may count for continuing professional development hours

- Centers for Disease Control and Prevention: http://emergency.cdc.gov/mentalhealth/
  Provides handouts and distress helpline numbers; some handouts specific to schools, parents, and child-related needs; handouts include a variety of natural disaster topics; some handouts are translated into other languages

- U.S. Department of Education, Office of Safe and Drug-Free Schools: http://rems.ed.gov/docs/PracticalInformationonCrisisPlanning.pdf
  Helps schools prepare for potential disasters and trauma

Table 20.3. Tier 1 Intervention: Teachers' Roles in Supporting Students' Emotional Needs Following a Natural Disaster

Students' Emotional Needs	What to Say and Do
Insecurity	Provide directive leadership, remain calm, and reassure students: "We support one another." "I am here for you." "You are not alone." Return to a normal schedule as soon as possible. Stick to things that are predictable and familiar.
Isolation	Strengthen group cohesion in classrooms. Conduct classroom activities and discussions, providing options for student participation. Activities must be age appropriate. Consider drawing for younger students and journaling for older students. Encourage (but never force) students to talk or participate.
Anger and blame	Redirect negative emotions/energy into positive outlets: "We have control over our feelings." "We determine how this experience will have an impact on our lives."
Avoidance	Normalize the experience: "Many of us have difficulty thinking about this disaster. It is normal to escape the heavy sadness and fear, but we have to come back and work." "Each day, little by little, together we will work on getting better and feeling better."
Anxiety	Teach relaxation skills to the classroom. Even though some students may exhibit more anxiety than others, all benefit from this life skill. Build a relaxation activity into the daily schedule. Classroom participation helps build group cohesion. Minimally, teach students to take a deep breath, inhaling slowly and then exhaling slowly.
Helplessness	Help students move from being a victim to being a survivor. Assist students in planning service activities and projects to build community morale. Focus on what can be done rather than on what cannot be done. Start with the classroom; involve all students in beautifying the room (e.g., pictures, paintings, supportive quotes, plants, flowers, posters of favorite memories).
Pessimism and hopelessness	Read positive uplifting stories. Display positive statements about courageous individuals who rose above challenging situations. Offer students options of carefully selected (and approved) upbeat music to play as background music. Acknowledge that recovery takes time and patience. "Together we will move forward." Make posters titled "Possibilities." Ask students to list things they look forward to, including accomplishments, goals, and careers.

pivotal position to help carry out the general crisis plan for school-wide Tier 1 efforts, mostly addressing students' needs in the comfort of familiar classroom settings. More specifically, Tables 20.3 and 20.4 provide basic examples of what teachers may say and do when responding to students' emotional needs. It is important for school psychologists to carefully identify the most important information to guide teachers' participation in Tier 1 interventions. However, this information should not overwhelm school staff with myriad details and directives. School psychologists must guide teachers to focus on the most important aspects of emotional support. In advance of actually needing to use this information, school psychologists should discuss these strategies during staff meetings, taking a few minutes each month to help familiarize teachers and staff with basic Tier 1 interventions. It is important for school psychologists to practice role plays with teachers and staff to increase comfort in using recommended strategies, making the strategies familiar and ready to draw upon when needed.

Consider Children's Reactions

In addition to the uniqueness of each natural disaster, each setting is unique, and each individual is unique. However, some common reactions are anticipated and should be considered by school psychologists in preparation and response activities. Students will worry about the safety of their parents, siblings, friends, and pets more than they will worry about the safety of their home and personal belongings (New York University Child Study Center, 2006). They will want to reunite with their family as soon as possible. Students will need reassurance and strong leadership from their teachers and principal to help them feel safe and secure.

Fear and hysteria are magnified by visible physical injuries and blood, death of classmates or school adults, and uncertainty about who is in charge. Loud noises, particularly screaming, escalate the intensity of children's fear. It is important to soothe those who are highly volatile, even taking them to a separate room and providing one-on-one care with a trusted staff member.

Table 20.4. Teacher Roles in Supporting Adolescents Following a Natural Disaster

Observe students' emotional reactions: Be alert to a wide range of student reactions. Some students may be comfortable expressing emotions. Crying is a normal reaction. In contrast, some students may be especially quiet and appear dazed or aloof.

Know when to refer students: Students with inconsolable hysterical reactions may need to be referred to the school psychologist or counselor. Referrals may also be made for students who are withdrawn or appear especially affected by death. Talk with the school psychologist about concerns.

Listen to students: As students express their feelings, support their responses with sensitive comments:
- "Though we may express our sadness in different ways, we are all hurting inside."
- "I can see that you are really hurting."
- "It must be difficult to accept the death of someone you know and care about."
- "I am here for you. You are not alone."

Help students express their feelings: Support students in discussing their memories and expressing their feelings. Focus the discussion on the positive personal influence of the deceased person. Encourage students to write about their feelings.

Provide activities for students: Offer a variety of activities appropriate to the students' ages and situations. Action helps students move from the passive role (victim) to an active role (survivor).

Stick to facts: Avoid rumors and morbid details. Avoid blaming or speculating about who was responsible for or who could have prevented the death and injuries.

Accommodate classroom schedule to fit students' needs: Although school schedules provide a healthy structure and sense of normality, provide extra caring and emotional support for students. To decrease student stress and anxiety, consider extending deadlines and rescheduling tests.

Encourage students to take time for self-care: Self-care may include talking with friends and caring adults, making time for exercise and enjoyable activities, getting adequate rest, and eating healthy foods. These self-care strategies also apply to teachers.

Certain natural disasters and associated conditions also create intense fear. Examples include the incredible force of flood waters; shaking ground and loud noises associated with an earthquake; darkness (loss of electrical power); lightning, heavy rain, hail, and strong winds associated with hurricanes and tornadoes; and smoke and fire. While enduring uncomfortable conditions and awaiting parent–child reunification, teachers might encourage the class to sing familiar songs, color pictures, enjoy a snack, and play quiet games. Teachers might also read a favorite book to their students. As mentioned previously, school psychologists can assist teachers in preparing to fill this role.

Attend to Vulnerable Individuals

Bonanno et al. (2010) and Jaycox et al. (2010) emphasize the need to consider an individual's previous trauma in addition to focusing on the current trauma. This trauma history broadens the context for understanding an individual's response to current trauma and his or her resilience and ability to adjust following trauma. Jaycox et al. (2009) stress the importance of attending to the needs of children in foster care placements. These children are particularly vulnerable due to their extensive trauma history, typically involving sporadic and disrupted care, maltreatment and neglect, and limited family and social support.

Acknowledging these needs, a manual, *Support for Students Exposed to Trauma* (Jaycox et al., 2009), was designed for children in foster care who were affected by multiple and repeated trauma. The manual relies on trauma-focused cognitive–behavioral therapy. Based on recent research studies, Dorsey and Deblinger (2012) noted the particular effectiveness of trauma-focused cognitive–behavioral therapy with children in foster care. This type of therapy reportedly helped these vulnerable children make sense of trauma (change in thinking) and helped them build optimism and a sense of hope for the future (change in feelings). Ultimately, the changes in children's thoughts and feelings were also associated with improved behavior.

Consider Age Differences

During and immediately following a natural disaster, children's emotional reactions will vary depending on age, emotional maturity, level of understanding, gender, trauma history, personal beliefs about the disaster, and personal coping style. Younger children may become clingy and cry, ask a lot of questions, demand adult attention, and revert to immature behavior such as thumb sucking. Older students may understand the gravity of the situation and become fearful and worried. Some students may have been through previous natural disasters and struggle with triggers (i.e., smells and sounds may elicit flashbacks). Because teachers are the natural trusted leader, students of all ages will look to them for reassurance.

In the weeks following a natural disaster, students will struggle with emotional and physical symptoms of stress in response to the trauma they have experienced. Internalizing and somatic complaints include headaches, stomachaches, fear and worry about being separated from family members, clinginess, crying, difficulty concentrating, withdrawal, and generalized anxiety. Externalizing evidence of trauma response includes hyperactivity, impulsiveness, anger and aggression, and risk-taking behavior.

Additionally, children struggle when familiar schedules are disrupted. When the major pieces of a child's life are not in order, life becomes off balance. Ingredients that create stability include school attendance, scheduled meals, familiar food, consistent bedtime, sufficient time for relaxation and sleep, and leisure time for play and recreational activities with friends and family. When feelings of familiarity, safety, and stability are threatened, life is stressful and anxiety provoking. School psychologists must work with their schools to help reinstitute familiar routines, helping teachers and students settle back into their daily activities.

Monitor Children's Behaviors and Emotional Needs

Initially following a natural disaster, only the most extreme cases will be identified for immediate intervention. These cases may involve physical injuries that require immediate medical attention or extreme emotional reactions (e.g., screaming, inconsolable crying) that require immediate support. In the survival mode, the crisis team will help teachers and staff triage student needs, identifying the most critical needs for immediate attention. Most problems that arise over the following weeks will be red flagged by teachers and parents. School psychologists will follow up on these referrals.

Monitor and Assess Internalizing and Externalizing Behavior

Following a natural disaster, students may struggle with both externalizing behaviors (e.g., aggression, conduct problems, hyperactivity, impulsivity) and internalizing behaviors (e.g., depression, anxiety, social isolation). To help identify the severity of children's behavioral problems, school psychologists may rely upon behavior checklists, such as the Behavior Assessment System for Children-Second Edition and the Achenbach System of Empirically Based Assessment. If needed, other assessment instruments specific to depression (e.g., Children's Depression Inventory) and anxiety (e.g., Revised Children's Manifest Anxiety Scale) may be utilized. Information gathered from assessments and input from the referred student, parents, and teachers will assist school psychologists in identifying problematic behaviors and determining effective interventions to address student needs. For individual students who are especially traumatized and affected by the disaster, formal behavior intervention plans, individualized or small group counseling, and progress monitoring may be required. Specific behaviors may be carefully monitored and tracked for frequency and intensity.

Monitor Symptoms of Posttraumatic Stress Disorder

Some students may also struggle with symptoms related to posttraumatic stress. Posttraumatic stress disorder is a trauma and stress related disorder that may impact individuals of all ages. The disorder typically emerges following a traumatic event, such as a natural disaster. The traumatic event either directly or indirectly threatens the physical safety of self or others. Descriptors of the diagnostic criteria, as outlined in the *Diagnostic and Statistical Manual of Mental Disorders* (DSM-5; American Psychiatric Association, 2013, pp. 271–274) must be present for more than a month and must cause "clinically significant distress or impairment" in "important areas of functioning" (American Psychiatric Association, 2013, p. 272). In the year following a natural disaster, almost 30% of children may initially show symptoms related to posttraumatic stress disorder. However, this rate dissipates across time as children learn to adaptively cope with their intense feelings. Ultimately, approximately 8.7% of U.S. adults struggle with posttraumatic stress disorder (American Psychiatric Association, 2013, p. 276).

When observing young children's recovery (a month after disaster), school psychologists should watch for perseveration in children's play. Young children may repeatedly act out the traumatic incident and seemingly get stuck in playing out the trauma. Older youth may struggle with recurrent and intrusive floods of memories, as if they lack the ability to shift gears and move on to another topic. They may feel as if they are actually reliving the traumatic event. Frightening dreams may distress youth, causing intense fear and anxiety. Younger children may not recognize the content of their dream, but feel overwhelmed with fear.

Avoidance is also problematic. Adolescents may withdraw, avoiding social activities they previously enjoyed. They may lose their enthusiasm and appear drained by the trauma. They do not want to talk about it, think about it, or deal with it. They may feel emotionally, physically, and mentally numb. Children may avoid triggers that remind them of the trauma, including sounds, smells, places, people, and situations. In trying to avoid triggers that heighten anxiety, they become detached and isolated.

Students of all ages may struggle with hypervigilance and heightened arousal. They may overreact to minor distractions (easily startled). They may have trouble concentrating, feel edgy and irritable, and have difficulty sleeping or staying asleep. They may lash out in angry outbursts. Expressing their anger and frustration, adolescents my engage in risky, rebellious, and self-destructive behavior (e.g., drugs, alcohol, cutting, unprotected sexual activity). School psychologists should encourage teachers to watch for these types of behaviors and to refer students for individualized intervention as needed.

Additionally, two screening instruments specific to posttraumatic stress are commonly used. The University of California at Los Angeles Posttraumatic Stress Disorder Reaction Index helps identify posttraumatic stress symptoms in children and adolescents. This 48-item semistructured interview has been used both nationally and internationally. The instrument is intended for assessing youth ages 7–12 (child version) and ages 13 and older (adolescent version). This instrument takes approximately 20 minutes to administer, is available in three versions (parent, adolescent, and child), and is either completed as a self-report (paper and pencil) or during an interview (http://www.istss.org/UCLAPosttraumaticStressDisorderReactionIndex.htm).

The other instrument, the Child PTSD Symptom Scale (available in English and Spanish), measures the severity of posttraumatic stress disorder symptoms in children ages 8–18. This 24-item measure takes between 10 and 20 minutes to complete. This questionnaire may be completed by the student (paper and pencil) or may be read to the student and filled out by an adult interviewer. To gather another perspective of the child's symptoms, a companion parent report is also available.

Provide Interventions in School Settings

It is important to consider how, when, and where supportive services are offered. Immediate and intense debriefing, so popular in the 1980s, is not considered best practice for young children and adolescents exposed to trauma (Smith et al., 2013). Children need to be surrounded with familiar and trusted adults and friends. When intervention is deemed necessary, interventions must be evidence-based practices and must be delivered in an age-appropriate and culturally sensitive manner.

One year following Hurricane Katrina, Jaycox et al. (2010) offered two interventions: the Cognitive-Behavioral Intervention for Trauma in Schools, which included 10 group sessions and one to three individual sessions. These services were provided in the participating child's school, free of charge. The second intervention was Trauma-Focused Cognitive Behavioral Therapy, which was provided in a community clinic setting, free of charge.

Of those students whose parents signed permission for school-based treatment, 98% began the treatment. In sharp contrast, only 37% of those students whose parents signed permission for clinic-based intervention actually started treatment. Although parents may permit their children to participate in no-cost clinic-based counseling, services provided in school settings facilitate the likelihood of children's attendance and participation. Acknowledging this reality, Jaycox et al. (2010) noted the importance of schools offering services because this may be the only opportunity many children will have to counter trauma's negative impact. From a parent's or student's perspective, school-based mental health services may be perceived as carrying less stigma than services offered by therapists in community settings. Also, parents may not have the extra time to provide their child's transportation to outside services. Even with no cost involved, time constraints alone may deter parents from following through with community clinic-based services.

Provide Tier 1 Interventions

In preparation for unpredictable situations such as natural disasters, school psychologists should encourage teachers to practice relaxation skills with their students (as a classroom exercise). These skills, based on cognitive–behavioral therapy, can be referred to when needed. Cohen and colleagues (2006, pp. 75–86) describe using relaxation techniques with children who are struggling with symptoms associated with posttraumatic stress disorder and overwhelming emotions associated with trauma. Consulting with parents and teachers, school psychologists can encourage students to independently use relaxation skills, with minimal prompting.

Simple directions for relaxation often include the following elements:

- "Close your eyes."
- "Place all your worries and concerns aside."
- "Think of a positive and safe place. Imagine that you are there right now."
- "Think about something you enjoy, something that helps you feel happy and relaxed."
- "Very slowly, breathe in deeply, slowly count to five, then very slowly let your breath out, slowly count to five."

Encourage students to talk about the difference they feel after slowly inhaling and exhaling. Explain that this is one way they can control their tense feelings and anxiety. Younger children may want to draw a picture about an identified safe place and happy thoughts. In future counseling sessions, this picture could serve as a relaxation cue.

Additional strategies for relaxation include tensing certain muscles, then relaxing those muscles. Similar to the breathing exercise, counting slowly to five helps give structure to the relaxation exercise. An easy way to lead the student through muscle relaxation is to start with the toes and feet, moving to the calves, buttocks, stomach, hands, biceps, shoulders (raising and lowering), facial muscles and jaw, eyebrows, then total body (all muscles). Ask the children to tense their muscles as they inhale slowly (counting to five) and then relax their muscles as they exhale slowly (counting to five). Between muscle groups, encourage the student to notice the difference between tense muscles (burning tightness) and relaxed muscles (loose and a sense of relief). To encourage a peaceful feeling, those who lead relaxation exercises should talk quietly and slowly.

Provide Tier 2 and Tier 3 Interventions

For students struggling with posttraumatic stress symptoms beyond a month of the disaster/trauma, school psychologists may provide group or individual intervention based on cognitive–behavioral therapy strategies. Seek parent permission and student assent prior to students participating in school-based cognitive–behavioral groups (Jaycox, 2004). For more extreme cases, consider individual counseling based on the Trauma-Focused Cognitive Behavioral Therapy sessions outlined in Cohen et al. (2006). The same therapeutic strategies are further described in Cohen et al. (2012); however, the more recent book includes in-depth cultural modifications for use in international

settings and with special populations, including Latino, American Indian, and Alaska Native children. One chapter is designated specifically to modifications needed for children with developmental disabilities.

Cohen et al. (2012) and Jaycox (2004) provide intervention strategies based on cognitive–behavioral therapy, which have solid research demonstrating efficacy in countering children's posttraumatic stress disorder symptoms (Smith et al., 2013). Cohen et al.'s (2006, 2012) strategies are designed for a wider age range (preschool through high school) and consider cultural adaptations to sensitively account for varying opinions and beliefs linked to the individual's life experiences. Jaycox's (2004) outlined group sessions for ages 11–16 have proven effective in a variety of school settings following a range of traumatic events.

Assist Children in Developing a Trauma Narrative

A primary activity promoted in trauma-focused cognitive–behavioral therapy is helping children develop a story about their trauma, referred to as a trauma narrative (Cohen et al., 2006, 2012). Children are taught strategies that help them become aware of, observe, and manage their thoughts and feelings related to the trauma. With support, children then make changes in their thoughts and feelings so that their physical response and behaviors are more adaptive and align with healthy recovery across time. With support, children learn to manage their anxieties and fears related to traumatic events. They practice relaxation techniques and learn how to control their breathing and muscle tension. Table 20.5 summarizes the basic steps in developing a trauma narrative, as described by Cohen et al. (2006). Although the trauma narrative is typically conducted in a one-on-one setting (Tier 3 intervention), this intervention was also successfully conducted in small group settings (Tier 2 intervention; Galante & Foa, 1986).

Involve Parents or Caregivers in Children's Interventions

Involving parents or caregivers in the recovery process is critical because children look to them for guidance and support. Consistently, research findings support the important benefits of involving parents and guardians in children's treatment (Cohen et al., 2006, 2012). Likewise, in studying families affected by the 1983 Australian bushfires, McFarlane and Van Hoof (2009) noted that surviving children's posttrauma symptoms and problematic behaviors in school were more related to the

Table 20.5. Creating a Trauma Narrative: Recommended for Tier 2 and Tier 3 Intervention

Goal of Trauma Narrative

"…unpair thoughts, reminders, or discussions of the traumatic event from overwhelming negative emotions such as terror, horror, extreme helplessness, shame, or rage" (Cohen et al., 2006, p. 119).

Pre-Session

Introduce the trauma narrative's therapeutic basis (see Cohen et al., 2006, p. 121). Describe a scraped knee scenario. To avoid infection the injury must be washed clean, sprayed with an antibacterial spray, and a bandage applied. Ouch! That hurts! But cleaning the wound helps it to heal. Similarly, talking about the disaster may initially hurt, but in the long run it helps us heal. Read an age-appropriate story or news article that offers hope, an example of someone who experienced a similar trauma. Help them understand that they are not alone.

Writing the Narrative

Initial writing: Start with a general and nontraumatic introduction to the narrative, describing positive aspects of the child's life. The entire narrative takes several sessions. Gradually, help the child write a more detailed story about the traumatic event. Start with the facts about the disaster, later including the related emotional responses and fears.

Review the narrative: Once the first draft is completed, have the child read the narrative. As the details are described, include additional thoughts and feelings that may arise.

Identify the worst moment: Ask the child to describe the worst moment, worst memory, or worst part of the traumatic event. It may be helpful to draw a picture illustrating this moment. Talk about the feelings and physical sensations that are recounted, adding these to the narrative. If the child becomes overwhelmed with emotions during this part, use relaxation techniques. Take a slow deep breath and then slowly exhale. Explain that this is hard work and sometimes we need a short vacation, and change topics and move to another activity.

Conclusion: The narrative's ending may include lessons learned and what the child did to move from the victim role to the survivor role. End the narrative with optimism and hope for the future.

Options for Children With Multiple Traumas

Assist the child in creating a time line of life events. Include positive events and traumatic events. To avoid overwhelming the child, focus the trauma narrative on one selected trauma (which the child selects).

Cognitive Processing

While reviewing the narrative with the child, explore and correct inaccurate and unhelpful cognitions with progressive logical questioning. In addressing guilt, explore the differences between taking responsibility and regretting an action taken or not taken. Repair inaccurate cognitions; watch for words like "never," "always," "no one," "everyone," and "can't."

Note. The trauma narrative is based on information from Cohen et al. (2006).

mothers' functioning and changes in parenting than to the actual disaster itself. Empowering parents with effective strategies for meeting children's needs is mutually beneficial to parents and children, strengthening parent–child relationships (Cohen et al., 2006, 2012).

Suggestions for increasing parental involvement include consulting with parents about their child's progress at school and offering simple and direct recommendations for parents; that is, what to say to their children and how to encourage conversation about the disaster. School psychologists are encouraged to provide handouts that explain common reactions and what to expect.

Offer Interventions Sensitive to Unique Needs

Considering the challenges of identifying and treating posttraumatic stress disorder in children from diverse backgrounds, professionals must tailor traditional treatments to fit the specific needs of children, particularly taking into account issues such as poverty, health problems, and potential history of previous trauma (Dingfelder, 2008). Because of their life experiences, these children "may mask their fears and anxiety, presenting a facade of toughness," exhibiting minimal or no observable signs of posttraumatic stress disorder (Dingfelder, 2008, p. 34). Dingfelder (2008) also notes the importance of drawing on the community's resilience, such as spiritual or religious traditions, beliefs, and longstanding cultural connections.

Although research investigating disaster mental health services for children from diverse backgrounds is limited (Heath, Nickerson, Annandale, Kemple, & Dean, 2009), research indicates both Supporting Students Exposed to Trauma (Jaycox et al., 2009) and Cognitive-Behavioral Intervention for Trauma in Schools (Jaycox, 2004) have proven effective with children from a variety of cultural and socioeconomic backgrounds (Jaycox et al., 2010). This type of school-based group intervention appears to reduce posttraumatic stress symptoms by encouraging discussion of feelings about the traumatic event, building social support, reducing anxiety, teaching adaptive coping skills, and ultimately reducing maladaptive behavior.

SUMMARY

Regardless of a community's location, size, or financial stability, some type of natural disaster poses a potential threat to the safety and well-being of children. Because most natural disasters occur with minimal or no warning, both prevention and intervention are critical components in school crisis plans. This chapter summarized school psychologists' crisis prevention and intervention strategies to mitigate the impact of natural disasters and to strengthen social and emotional support for students. Prevention efforts must identify and address potentially vulnerable areas in crisis plans, including attending to the needs of students with disabilities, practicing the crisis plan, and coordinating efforts with emergency medical teams (U.S. Government Accountability Office, 2007).

Helping schools return to their normal schedule as soon as possible supports student recovery and stabilizes the community (Greubel et al., 2012). Additionally, research indicates the importance of social support in helping children recover following traumatic events (Brock et al., 2009). Sources of social support include parent involvement (Cohen et al., 2006), peer group support (Jaycox et al., 2009), and a nurturing school and classroom environment (Nastasi et al., 2011). Another aspect for school psychologists to consider is strengthening the role of teachers and school staff in crisis intervention and increasing emotional support for students in their familiar classroom setting (Wolmer et al., 2011). In regard to counseling strategies to address anxiety and posttraumatic stress in children and adolescents, the bulk of research supports cognitive–behavioral therapy. Therapy based on cognitive–behavioral strategies helps students understand the connection between thoughts, feelings, and behaviors (Cohen et al., 2012; Jaycox et al., 2009, 2010).

AUTHOR NOTE

The author appreciates the assistance of Julie Daye, Canyons School District, Utah, in summarizing the information that appears in Table 20.5.

REFERENCES

American Psychiatric Association. (2013). *Diagnostic and statistical manual of mental disorders* (5th ed.). Washington, DC: Author.

Annandale, N. O., Heath, M. A., Dean, B., Kemple, A., & Takino, Y. (2011). Cross-cultural sensitivity in state school crisis plans. *Journal of School Violence, 10,* 16–33.

Bonanno, G. A., Brewin, C. R., Kaniasty, K., & La Greca, A. M. (2010). Weighing the costs of disaster: Consequences, risks, and resilience in individuals, families, and communities. *Psychological Science in the Public Interest, 11,* 1–49. doi:10.1177/1529100610387086

Brock, S. E., Nickerson, A. B., Reeves, M. A., Jimerson, S. R., Lieberman, R. A., & Feinberg, T. A. (2009). *School crisis prevention and intervention: The PREPaRE model.* Bethesda, MD: National Association of School Psychologists.

Chemtob, C. M., Nakashima, J., & Carlson, J. G. (2002). Brief treatment for elementary school children with disaster-related posttraumatic stress disorder: A field study. *Journal of Clinical Psychology, 58,* 99–112.

Cohen, J. A., Mannarino, A. P., & Deblinger, E. (2006). *Treating trauma and traumatic grief in children and adolescents.* New York, NY: Guilford Press.

Cohen, J. A., Mannarino, A. P., & Deblinger, E. (Eds.). (2012). *Trauma-focused CBT for children and adolescents: Treatment Applications.* New York, NY: Guilford Press.

Dingfelder, S. F. (2008). Presidential initiatives: The smallest survivors. *Monitor on Psychology, 39*(9), 34, Retrieved from http://www.apa.org/monitor/2008/10/survivors.aspx

Dorsey, S., & Deblinger, E. (2012). Children in foster care. In J. A. Cohen, A. P. Mannarino, & E. Deblinger (Eds.), *Trauma-focused CBT for children and adolescents: Treatment applications* (pp. 49–72). New York, NY: Guilford Press.

Felix, E., Hernandez, L. A., Bravo, M., Ramirez, R., Cabiya, J., & Canino, G. (2011). Natural disaster and risk of psychiatric disorders in Puerto Rican children. *Journal of Abnormal Child Psychology, 39,* 589–600. doi:10.1007/s10802-010-9483-1

Galante, R., & Foa, D. (1986). An epidemiological study of psychic trauma and treatment effectiveness for children after a natural disaster. *Journal of the American Academy of Child Psychiatry, 25,* 357–363.

Greubel, L., Ackerman, X., & Winthrop, R. (2012). *Prioritizing education in the face of natural disasters.* Washington, DC: Brookings. Retrieved from http://www.brookings.edu/blogs/up-front/posts/2012/10/31-natural-disasters-winthrop

Heath, M. A., Nickerson, A. B., Annandale, N., Kemple, A., & Dean, B. (2009). Strengthening cultural sensitivity in children's disaster mental health services. *School Psychology International, 30,* 347–373.

Jaycox, L. (2004). *Cognitive-behavioral intervention for trauma in schools (CBITS).* Longmont, CO: Sopris West.

Jaycox, L. H., Cohen, J. A., Mannarino, A. P., Walker, D. W., Langley, A. K., Gegenheimer, K., ... Schonlau, M. (2010). Children's mental health care following Hurricane Katrina: A field trial of trauma-focused psychotherapies. *Journal of Traumatic Stress, 23,* 223–231. doi:10.1002/jts.20518

Jaycox, L. H., Langley, A. K., & Dean, K. L. (2009). *Support for students exposed to trauma: The SSET program: Group leader training manual, lessons plans, and lesson materials and worksheets* (Publication No. TR-675-NIMH). Santa Monica, CA: RAND. Retrieved from http://www.rand.org/pubs/technical_reports/2009/RAND_TR675.pdf

La Greca, A. M., & Silverman, W. K. (2009). Treatment and prevention of posttraumatic stress reactions in children and adolescents exposed to disasters and terrorism: What is the evidence? *Child Development Perspectives, 3,* 4–10. doi:10.1111/j.1750-8606.2008.00069.x

La Greca, A. M., Silverman, W. K., Vernberg, E. M., & Prinstein, M. J. (1996). Symptoms of posttraumatic stress in children after Hurricane Andrew: A prospective study. *Journal of Consulting and Clinical Psychology, 64,* 712–723.

McFarlane, A. C., & Van Hoof, M. (2009). Adult outcomes of childhood exposure to a disaster: A cohort study of the Ash Wednesday Bushfires of 1983. *British Journal of Psychiatry, 152,* 142–148.

Nastasi, B. K., Jayasena, A., Summerville, M., & Borja, A. (2011). Facilitating long-term recovery from natural disasters: Psychosocial programming for tsunami-affected schools of Sri Lanka. *School Psychology International, 32,* 512–532. doi:10.1177/0143034311402923

National Association of School Psychologists. (2010). *Model for comprehensive and integrated school psychological services.* Bethesda, MD: Author. Retrieved from http://www.nasponline.org/standards/2010standards/2_PracticeModel.pdf

National Climatic Data Center. (2012). *U.S. tornado climatology: Average annual number of tornadoes.* Asheville, NC: National Oceanic and Atmospheric Administration. Retrieved from http://www.ncdc.noaa.gov/oa/climate/severeweather/tornadoes.html

Newman, A. (2012, November 28). Comparing hurricanes: Sandy vs. Katrina. *The New York Times,* p. A-28. Retrieved from http://cityroom.blogs.nytimes.com/2012/11/27/hurricane-sandy-vs-hurricane-katrina

New York University Child Study Center. (2006). *Caring for kids after trauma, disaster, and death: A guide for parents and professionals* (2nd ed.). New York, NY: Author. Retrieved from http://www.aboutourkids.org/files/articles/crisis_guide02.pdf

Smith, P., Perrin, S., Dalgleish, T., Meiser-Stedman, R., Clark, D. M., & Yule, W. (2013). Treatment of posttraumatic stress disorder in children and adolescents. *Current Opinion in Psychiatry, 26,* 66–72. doi:10.1097/YCO.0b013e32835b2c01

Sormanti, M., & Ballan, M. S. (2011). Strengthening grief support for children with developmental disabilities. *School Psychology International, 32,* 179–193.

U.S. Department of Health and Human Services. (2003). *Developing cultural competence in disaster mental health programs: Guiding principles and recommendations* (DHHS Pub. No. SMA 3828). Rockville, MD: Center for Mental Health Services, Substance Abuse and Mental Health Services Administration.

U.S. Government Accountability Office. (2007). *Report to congressional requesters. Emergency management: Most school districts have developed emergency management plans, but would benefit from additional federal guidance* (GAO-07-609). Washington, DC: Author.

Wolmer, L., Hamiel, D., & Laor, N. (2011). Preventing children's posttraumatic stress after disaster with teacher-based intervention: A controlled study. *Journal of the American Academy of Child & Adolescent Psychiatry, 50,* 340–348. doi:10.1016/j.jaac.2011.01.002

World Health Organization. (2013). *Environmental health in emergencies: Natural events.* Geneva, Switzerland: Author. Retrieved from http://www.who.int/environmental_health_emergencies/natural_events/en/

21 Best Practices for Responding to Death in the School Community

Scott Poland
Catherine Samuel-Barrett
Angela Waguespack
Nova Southeastern University (FL)

OVERVIEW

When a school community is affected by the death of one of its members, the loss can represent a potential crisis that may affect many individuals in unique ways. The manner in which schools respond to a death can help minimize the negative impact on those affected and can set the stage for healing, recovery, and a return to relative normality. However, an effective response to a death in the school community requires advance planning through the development of procedures consistent with those of a comprehensive crisis intervention approach and that are sensitive to the needs of the school community. A school's level of preparedness to respond to and recover from a death is reflected in its ability to effectively (a) support those individuals grieving the loss of a teacher, colleague, or classmate; (b) return the school to its precrisis state; (c) identify those individuals who may be at risk for adverse social–emotional, behavioral, or academic reactions; and (d) refer to outside agencies those who may be at risk for maladaptive coping that cannot effectively be supported within the school.

It is estimated that most children will experience the death of a family member or friend before graduating from high school, almost 40% will experience the death of a peer (National Center for School Crisis and Bereavement, n.d.), and between 4% and 7% of children will experience the death of a parent before the age of 18 (Social Security Administration, 2000). Statistics such as these suggest that the experience of loss and death among children and adolescents is not uncommon and that school personnel are therefore likely to regularly encounter students who are experiencing levels of grief. Although not all students will exhibit outward signs of grief, and most children and adolescents will in fact display a normal adjustment to loss, as many as 15–20% of children can be expected to demonstrate significant difficulties after the loss of an important person in their lives (Worden, 1996). Failure to address the needs of these students can place them at greater risk for negative outcomes, including emotional and behavioral challenges and a decline in school performance. An awareness of the potential impact that a death may have on students is particularly important for school psychologists and others who work with children and adolescents so that they can appropriately respond to students' needs and help ensure a continued effective learning environment.

When a death affects the school community, schools can serve as optimal settings to provide services to students and faculty. Not only do schools provide members of the school community a familiar environment where supportive services can be readily provided, they can facilitate large numbers of students who may require support and also allow for ongoing monitoring of students who may require more intensive intervention. Moreover, classroom teachers, who are often on the front lines during a crisis, can be a tremendous source of support for their students and they can play a vital role in providing early and ongoing intervention when necessary. Unfortunately, many teachers and school personnel find themselves ill equipped to effectively respond to the needs of their students in the aftermath of a death.

303

Researchers have noted that school personnel, such as teachers, counselors, and administrators, often feel unprepared and inadequately trained to work with grieving students (Adamson & Peacock, 2007), highlighting the importance of improving training and education on grief and bereavement issues. At the very least, school personnel should be provided a basic knowledge of the grieving process of children and be offered ways in which to support those children. School psychologists can play an instrumental role in filling this knowledge and training gap by helping to raise awareness about issues related to crisis, loss, and bereavement, and by providing education, guidance, and support.

School psychologists play an integral role in preventive and responsive services, as outlined in the domain of Preventive and Responsive Services in the National Association of School Psychologists (NASP) *Model for Comprehensive and Integrated School Psychological Services* (NASP, 2010). NASP asserts that school psychologists should assist children with bereavement issues at school and that they should be knowledgeable about children's developmental differences in understanding death and specific helping behaviors to use in school.

Death in the school community involves the implementation of effective crisis preparation, response, and recovery, with a keen eye toward the recognition of risk and protective factors that may be precursors to future learning and social–emotional and behavioral difficulties. School psychologists must therefore demonstrate the ability to work collaboratively with school personnel, students, parents, and community providers to assist in the coordination of services to effectively respond to a death and to promote wellness and resilience in the aftermath.

The school psychologist should help minimize the development of potential difficulties or maladaptive reactions and promote students' readiness to learn. These goals are best achieved within a problem-solving and multitiered context, where general support and grief interventions are presented along a continuum of services ranging from universal school-wide prevention and intervention strategies to more individualized and intensive therapeutic interventions for those who fail to exhibit adequate adjustment to the death in spite of the provision of targeted supplemental supports.

This chapter addresses the broad role of schools, and of school psychologists in particular, in responding to death and delineates a framework for a proactive, comprehensive response to death-related loss. The primary objectives of this chapter are to impart a foundational understanding of the grieving process, particularly as it relates to children and adolescents, and

to provide a series of practical strategies that will assist in promoting successful outcomes for students as well as the larger school community. This chapter will aim to facilitate raising the competency and confidence levels of school psychologists in responding to a death so that they may assert themselves as knowledgeable consultants and as leaders who are integral members of the crisis response team.

BASIC CONSIDERATIONS

Schools must be prepared to respond to a range of potential crises and must have in place crisis intervention teams that can immediately mobilize and initiate a carefully developed crisis response plan. Consistent with guidelines by the U.S. Department of Education, an effective response to a death includes the concepts of *preparedness* or *readiness, response,* and *recovery* (U.S. Department of Education, 2007). It is helpful for school psychologists and crisis response teams to encourage schools to evaluate the school's ability to handle a crisis involving a death by assessing the degree to which the school has addressed the concepts of readiness, which is the school's current level of preparedness to respond to a crisis or emergency should such an event occur today; response, which is the activation of the crisis response team and utilization of the school's available skills and resources to act quickly and effectively in response to a death; and recovery, the restoration of stability within the school community through the promotion of positive coping strategies and interventions as needed.

Developmental Conceptions of Death

School psychologists must be knowledgeable about children's understandings of death. While most contemporary grief and loss paradigms reflect the importance of considering the uniqueness of the griever, understanding how children conceptualize death involves particular attention to developmental issues. Children's concepts of and reactions to death are significantly mediated by age and cognitive development level. Moreover, their understanding and perceptions of death, and their subsequent reactions to it, vary depending upon the degree to which they have acquired a mature concept of death. The development of a mature understanding of death evolves over time and involves the conceptualization of three key components: *irreversibility, nonfunctionality,* and *universality* (Hunter & Smith, 2008).

Irreversibility refers to the understanding that once a living thing dies it cannot become living again. Prior to achieving an understanding of this concept, younger children are more likely to view death as temporary and reversible, and they may believe that death can be spontaneously reversed through magical or wishful thinking. Nonfunctionality involves the understanding that all life functions of a living physical body end upon death. Children who have not acquired an understanding of this concept may believe that the person who has died may continue to perform certain functions after death, including external and readily observable functions such as breathing, speaking, or eating. Moreover, while children at this stage of development may understand that death is final and irreversible, they generally do not perceive death as being universal. As children's abstract thinking ability develops, however, they begin to form a more realistic, adult-like conception of death, and begin to understand the notion of universality, that all living things eventually die and that death is an inevitable aspect of life.

The specific age at which children achieve an adult understanding of the key components of death varies; however, the preponderance of the literature suggests that most children between the ages of 7 and 9 begin to develop a mature understanding of death. Regardless of the exact age that children acquire a mature death concept, it is paramount that school psychologists and other practitioners who work with children recognize the relationship between developmental level and manifestations of grief in children in order to effectively provide support.

Understanding the Grieving Process

A once commonly held view of the grieving process is that it occurs in separate and distinct stages that people generally work through in a linear progression to achieve resolution of their grief. However, in recent decades these views have been replaced with an understanding of grief as being more cyclical, where grief reactions may come and go in waves and the process of adjusting to the loss may continue across the life span to varying degrees in response to a variety of life circumstances. Worden (2008) outlined a framework for understanding the grieving process through his Tasks of Grief model. It is important to note that these tasks are not viewed as separate stages to be completed linearly, but rather can take place in any order and can be revisited many times. Worden's (2008) model is presented in Table 21.1 as one way of conceptualizing the complex nature of the grief process.

Central to working with individuals who have been affected by a death is an understanding of the key aspects of the grieving process and recognition of the complexity and individualized nature of grief. Although death is a common and universal experience, the way in which individuals respond to death is influenced by a myriad of factors, such as cultural and religious practices, age and developmental level, personality and emotional maturity, gender, experiences with death, available social support, relationship to the deceased, and concurrent stressful events. While a number of contemporary models of grief have been developed that provide a theoretical framework to help guide our understanding of how people respond to and recover from death-related loss (e.g., Doughty, 2009; Neimeyer, 2000; Servaty-Seib, 2004), an awareness of the complex nature of grief is paramount in effectively supporting individuals affected by a death.

While teachers and other school personnel who work directly with students can expect a range of affective reactions from children and adolescents in response to a death, those who are affected often present with a

Table 21.1. Worden's Tasks of Grief

- *Accepting the reality of the loss:* While some people may initially try to protect themselves by denying the facts of the loss, denying the irreversibility of the death, or minimizing the meaning of the loss, inevitably people must come to terms with the reality of the death and its finality.
- *Experiencing the pain of grief:* Although difficult, individuals must allow themselves to experience the pain associated with the loss rather than suppressing it. Understanding that grief is a normal process and that a wide range of thoughts, feelings, behaviors, and physical reactions are to be expected can help.
- *Adjusting to life without the deceased:* The process of adjusting to a loss may involve taking on new roles and adapting to a changed environment. Daily routines, holidays, and traditions once shared with the deceased will change and require adjustment.
- *Finding enduring connections with the deceased while moving forward with life:* This task is focused on revising rather than relinquishing the relationship with the deceased while embarking on a new life. Finding ways to remember the deceased allows for an ongoing connection while reorganizing one's life and adjusting to a new normal.

Note. Based on information from Worden (2008)

number of common immediate grief reactions, including shock, sadness, fear, guilt, crying, anger, anxiety, and denial. In addition, children express grief not only through their emotions but also through their behavior, physical reactions, and thoughts. Understanding the typical reactions of individuals who are affected by a death is not only an important step in identifying those who may require more intensive intervention, it also helps ensure that certain learning or behavior difficulties are not misinterpreted.

While each child or adolescent's grief response will be largely influenced by his or her chronological age and developmental level, there may be a great deal of overlap in expressions of grief between age groups. In addition, grief responses in younger children are especially influenced by the reactions of important adults in their lives, whose attitudes and behaviors play a significant role in how children perceive and interpret tragic events. For example, among children who have suffered the loss of a parent, the degree of risk for a child is most significantly predicted by the level of psychological and emotional adjustment of the surviving parent (Silverman & Worden, 1993). As previously noted, despite a great deal of variability in grief responses, children generally manifest a number of common physical, cognitive, and behavioral grief reactions as a part of the normal grieving process. Table 21.2 outlines common grief reactions that children may exhibit during the grief process.

While a variety of grief responses can be expected among children who have lost someone loved or important in their lives, children's grief can erupt in brief, intense episodes, with a sudden return to normal. Children may also appear to be performing well at school and adjusting to the loss, but may later experience difficulty when new changes or stressors arise. Children show marked variability in the onset of grief, with some grieving openly almost immediately while others may show no apparent sign of grief for months (Worden, 1996). Consequently, it is imperative that school psychologists actively participate in raising awareness among school personnel about the ongoing nature of the grief process.

BEST PRACTICES IN RESPONDING TO A DEATH

An effective school-based response to a death is one that is well planned and organized and that seeks to minimize adverse effects for those affected. Although not all deaths necessarily represent a crisis event within the school community, death is often sudden and unpredictable and can be overwhelming and sometimes traumatic for those affected by the loss. Consequently, a well-planned, proactive response to a death should be consistent with the key components of a comprehensive crisis prevention response plan, which includes establishing a multidisciplinary crisis response team, delineating

Table 21.2. Common Grief Reactions in Children and Adolescents

- Regressive behaviors in younger children, such as bedwetting or thumb sucking
- Increased fear and anxiety, which may manifest as clinginess or heightened fear of separation in younger children
- Changes in eating habits
- Sleep disturbance, such as nightmares or fear of the dark
- Somatic complaints, such as headache, stomachache, or muscle aches
- Inability to concentrate; difficulty listening and staying on task
- Restlessness
- Emotional shock
- Denial
- Sadness or despair
- Anger and acting out
- Reckless physical behavior, especially among adolescents
- Decrease in academic performance or school attendance
- Increased irritability, disruptive behavior, or aggressiveness
- Depression or guilt
- Longing for the deceased
- Resentment
- Isolation, withdrawal
- Concern about physical health
- Suppressed emotions

Note. Based on information from Fiorelli (2010).

team members' respective roles and responsibilities, providing staff training and parent education, collaboration with community agencies, and identification of the short- and long-term needs of school members in the aftermath of the death.

While remaining sensitive to the needs of the school community, school psychologists along with members of the crisis response team should be guided by a number of general goals when supporting schools through a tragic event such as a death. These goals include supporting those affected by the loss, restoring the psychological equilibrium of students and faculty as soon as possible by helping the school return to its normal routines, and identifying and referring individuals at risk for or exhibiting more severe responses who may require additional support that cannot be effectively provided at the school level.

Assessing the Degree and Range of Impact

When tragedy strikes a school, the school psychologist along with the crisis response team must assess the needs of the school community and determine the range and degree of impact of the death on school community members. The emotional impact of a death on the school community and the amount of subsequent support that may be required can be assessed by the school psychologist and school administrators by considering the following variables as outlined in Table 21.3.

Identifying At-Risk Students and Staff

To achieve the goal of supporting those affected by the loss of a classmate, teacher, colleague, or family member, and restoring the psychological equilibrium of students and faculty, an essential step is to identify potentially at-risk students and staff. School psychologists can play a key role in helping to identify individuals who may be in need of additional support. A useful trauma assessment model, Circles of Vulnerability (Lahad & Cohen, 2006), can be utilized by the school psychologist and school crisis response team as a screening tool to assist in identifying those individuals who may be at greatest risk of being emotionally affected by the death.

The concept of Circles of Vulnerability is based upon three dimensions that help determine an individual's level of vulnerability: (a) *physical proximity*, (b) *psychosocial proximity*, and (c) *population at risk*. Physical proximity is the physical distance an individual is from the death event, with those closest to the incident, such as an eyewitness, being more likely to be affected than those who experienced no direct exposure. Psychosocial proximity refers to the degree to which an individual identifies with or relates in some way to the deceased, such as cultural connections or team membership. Population at risk includes individuals who have been exposed to a traumatic event and who also have personal vulnerabilities, such as mental illness or

Table 21.3. Considerations in Assessing the Degree and Range of Impact of a Death Within a School Community

- *Status of the deceased within the school community and the length of time the deceased attended or worked at the school:* How well known and well liked the deceased student or staff member was can play a significant role in how the school is affected by the death. Often, the death of a popular student or staff member can elicit a strong initial grief response and may have an impact on a large segment of the school community. It is important, however, that schools demonstrate system-wide consistency in their responses to all deaths, regardless of the status of the deceased within the school.
- *The number of family members attending the school:* The range of impact on the school community may be greater when multiple members of the deceased's family, such as siblings and cousins, attend the same school.
- *The cause and manner of death:* Whether a death is sudden or anticipated will influence the grief response. Often, a death that occurs suddenly and unexpectedly, such as an accident, homicide, or suicide, may elicit a particularly intense emotional response. Violent deaths also increase the likelihood of a more severe grief response. In contrast, a death that is anticipated, such as one due to terminal illness, allows individuals the opportunity to prepare for the death and to experience anticipatory grief.
- *The location of the death:* A death that occurs on the school campus, traveling to and from school, or during a school-related activity may be particularly traumatic for students and staff, especially for those who witnessed the death.
- *Tragedies that have affected the school:* When schools have been affected by previous tragedy, the grieving process, healing, and recovery efforts may be complicated by the resurfacing of emotions from prior losses. The crisis response team should ascertain whether the school has been affected by any other recent tragedies, identify how the school handled those losses, and determine the effectiveness of past response and recovery efforts.

Note. Based on information from Poland and Poland (2004).

previous trauma exposure, that may contribute to the psychological and emotional impact of the death or traumatic event. Figure 21.1 illustrates the concept of circles of vulnerability.

Using this model as a guide, school psychologists and the crisis response team can begin to identify those who are potentially likely to be affected by the death and who may require additional support. Although each dimension of the model should be carefully considered, those individuals with the greatest degree of overlap across the three domains represent the highest risk for emotional impact and should be closely monitored in the aftermath of a death. The following groups may be particularly at risk for emotional distress and should be carefully monitored by school personnel:

- Family members of the deceased
- Close friends of the deceased
- Classmates of the deceased
- Students who participated in extracurricular activities with the deceased
- Students with a prior history of death-related losses
- Students who share a similar characteristic with the deceased
- Students with a difficult or strained relationship with the deceased
- Students at other schools where siblings of the deceased attend
- Students with history of mental health problems, particularly depression, anxiety disorder, and substance abuse
- Students currently receiving mental health or substance abuse treatment

Figure 21.1. Circles of Vulnerability

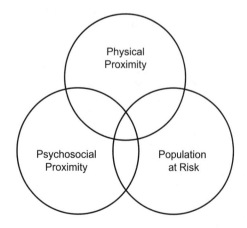

Note. Based on information from Lahad and Cohen (2006).

Identifying Potential Signs of Distress or Complicated Grief

Complicated grief, also referred to within the bereavement literature as traumatic grief or traumatic bereavement, is often associated with the development of trauma symptoms in response to a death (Cohen, Mannarino, Greenberg, Padlo, & Shipley, 2002) and is characteristic of a grief response that is prolonged, pervasive, and extreme. Moreover, the trauma symptoms that may accompany a complicated grief reaction often resemble symptoms of posttraumatic stress disorder. These intense responses, which may include intrusive and distressing thoughts or memories about the death itself or of the deceased, interfere with a child or adolescent's ability to proceed through the typical bereavement process and to function normally at home and school or with their peers.

Among those who may be at risk are individuals affected by a death that was sudden or traumatic, who witnessed the death under terrifying circumstances, who experienced the loss of multiple family members at one time, and individuals with a previous trauma history. In addition, children and adolescents who are already experiencing difficult life circumstances or who must endure additional death-related challenges, such as financial hardship, relocation, or family disruption, may be particularly vulnerable and at increased risk of experiencing complicated grief. The death of a parent or sibling also represents an especially difficult loss for children. Children who are not provided adequate support early in the grief process can develop significant emotional and behavioral problems that may lead to a number of psychiatric problems (Kirwin & Hamrin, 2005) and a host of school-related difficulties.

Symptoms associated with complicated grief may include intense focus on the loss and a preoccupation with how the deceased individual died; intense longing for the deceased and pervasive fantasies of his or her return; extreme withdrawal and detachment or isolation; difficulty accepting the reality of the death; persistent personality changes, such as a once passive, mild-mannered child who suddenly becomes a bully, or a well-groomed adolescent who completely abandons daily hygiene habits; extreme irritability or agitation; and excessive or inappropriate guilt (Corr, 2000). Individuals who exhibit any of these maladaptive behaviors may require more intensive support than those whose grief reactions appear to be more typical, and they should be immediately referred for professional assessment and potential treatment. These children may benefit from trauma-focused treatment in which they receive assistance and support in navigating the most distressing aspects of the death and learn specific strategies to regulate their thoughts, feelings, and behaviors (Cohen & Mannarino, 2011).

Taking Action: What Schools Can Do to Help

As illustrated in the scenario presented in Appendix A, responding to a death in the school community in a caring and effective manner requires not only a basic understanding of the general grief processes but also consideration of practical and critical crisis response procedures that will promote the school community's healing and timely return to relative equilibrium. A proactive response to a crisis greatly reduces the likelihood of negative outcomes for individuals and groups, and the school psychologist can take a lead role in helping schools plan in advance and cope with a death when it occurs by offering not only their support, but also, by integrating their roles and responsibilities into the broader school crisis response plan.

Notification Procedures

Verify the facts: In the wake of a death it is critically important to first verify the facts of the event. Prior to releasing any information regarding the circumstances of the death, appropriate law enforcement agencies and family of the deceased should be contacted by school administration to confirm that the student or staff member is deceased. With the wide use of texting and social media, it is particularly important to quickly disseminate the facts once the facts have been verified in order to dispel any rumors or prevent the spreading of inaccurate information, which can be a source of further trauma to the family of the deceased.

Establish a calling tree: It is important that both district and school personnel be notified of a death quickly and efficiently. A calling tree allows administrators to contact school staff and inform them of the event, the circumstances surrounding the event, and to provide information regarding the scheduling of a faculty meeting to review the school's response plan. A calling tree becomes particularly important when a death occurs during the weekend or in the evening after school hours so that school staff can be notified prior to returning to school. It is beneficial to regularly update the calling tree so that school staff can be notified of school-related emergencies in a timely manner.

Prepare an announcement to be distributed to the faculty: After school personnel have been notified of the death, it is

important to prepare a written statement and fact sheet to be distributed to faculty and staff so that students are provided with the same information. A fact sheet and/or statement containing the facts surrounding the death and other pertinent information will also allow front office staff, who are often on the front lines during a school crisis, to more effectively address and ease parental concerns.

Conduct a faculty meeting at the beginning or end of the school day: Depending upon when the death occurred, a faculty meeting should be held either at the beginning or end of the school day to provide teachers and staff with accurate information. Teachers should be provided with the prepared fact sheet and written announcement so that they can be consistent in the information they share about the death with their students. Teachers should also be notified of the location of any support rooms that have been established to provide additional care and support to students and staff. A follow-up faculty meeting should be scheduled to review the progress of the day, to identify and address any problems, as well as to identify students or staff who may be in need of additional support.

Notify students: Ideally, individual teachers should be responsible for announcing the death in their home-room classrooms so that students can grieve, express their feelings, and ask questions in small groups with a familiar and trusted adult. Alternatively, the principal or guidance counselor may visit each classroom to deliver the news, depending upon the nature and size of the school. News of the death should be given honestly and factually, using accurate and concrete terminology such as "killed" or "died." In most cases, announcing a death over the school intercom system should be avoided as it may cause panic and confusion among students. In addition, it is not advised to announce the death in a large group assembly because it offers little opportunity for teachers to provide personal support to students or to gauge students' individual reactions. Because of the importance of providing accurate information, teachers should use the prepared written statement to share the news with their students and should not deviate from the information.

If the individual's death is expected to have relatively little impact beyond the deceased's own class or classes, it may be beneficial to assign a counselor or other crisis team member to follow the deceased's class schedule for the day and to share details of the death only with those classes that will be affected. In addition, a teacher who has been particularly affected by the death or who is uncomfortable discussing the death with his or her students should be provided with a support person, such as a counselor, school psychologist, or crisis team member, to accompany the teacher to share the news of the death with students and to provide the teacher with additional support as needed.

Parental notification: Parents should be notified of a death in a timely manner so that they can respond to any potential needs or difficulties their child may experience. A letter should be sent home with students that explains what happened, what students have been told regarding the incident, typical emotional responses that parents can expect from their children, suggestions on how parents can best help their children, and possible resources. It is important to communicate to parents that their support of their grieving child will be most critical.

Roles of School Personnel

Principal's role: The principal should be immediately informed following the death of a student or faculty member. The principal will typically serve the role of verifying the facts of the death with appropriate law enforcement officials and providing an initial assessment of the impact that the death can be expected to have on the school community. Generally, the principal will be responsible for activation of the crisis response team and for initiating the protocol for notifying the student body of the death. In addition, the principal should designate a crisis team leader who will oversee and direct the crisis team's activities. The principal will also be responsible for regularly meeting with faculty to address any ongoing concerns and for meeting with the crisis response team within a few weeks following the death to determine the effectiveness of the response and to make appropriate modifications to the response plan.

In the event that the deceased student recently attended other schools or has siblings who attend other schools, the principal should immediately contact those schools to inform those schools of the death. While the principal will typically assume responsibility for calling the parents or family of the deceased to express the school's condolences, a visit with the family is also encouraged when appropriate. This serves as a critical and often appreciated outreach measure on behalf of the school and can be helpful in providing information regarding funeral arrangements, the role of any particular religious traditions or customs observed by the family, and what role, if any, students or faculty should play in the funeral process. Equally important, however, is the administration's role in setting the overall tone for the school's response. The principal

should impart a sense of unity and school cohesiveness during the response phase and should maintain visibility and availability to faculty, staff, and students.

School psychologist and counselor roles: The school psychologist and counselor can play a critical role during a school's response. During the initial few days school psychologists can be instrumental in identifying and gathering information about student and staff reactions to the death. It is important that they identify and make contact with students and staff who may have been well acquainted with the deceased and offer in-class assistance to those teachers who may need it or who request it. School psychologists and counselors should compile a list of all high-risk students including close friends, siblings, other relatives, neighbors of the deceased, students involved in the same extracurricular clubs or activities both at school and outside of school, students with a history of previous death-related losses or other significant life stressors, and high-risk students who were absent on the day of the death or when students were notified of the death. The school psychologist or counselor can meet with these high-risk students briefly so that subsequent decisions can be made regarding whether school-based interventions may be needed or whether referral to outside community mental health services may be required. See Appendix B.

Teacher's role: Concern about doing the right thing may sometimes cause teachers and school personnel to feel unsure of how to best support grieving students. However, failure to address students' needs can have detrimental short-term and potentially long-term consequences. With advance planning, teachers can play a critical role in helping their students cope with many of the difficulties often associated with the loss of someone they know. Whether a student is confronted with the loss of a beloved teacher, classmate, or close family member, teachers can provide a safe and nurturing environment for students to express their grief. Moreover, teachers are often in an ideal position to model constructive coping strategies and appropriate expression of emotions.

Most schools will not have enough counselors, school psychologists, or school social workers to simultaneously help large numbers of students cope with the death of a fellow student or teacher. Consequently, teachers must be empowered with knowledge about how to best support and work with grieving students within the classroom.

School psychologists can play a key role in sharing such information with teachers and in guiding them on how to facilitate referrals of students who exhibit complicated or traumatic grief. Table 21.4 provides general recommendations for teachers regarding how to support students following the death of a classmate, parent, or other significant person in a child's life.

Educating Students About Normal Grief Reactions

As discussed earlier in the chapter, those working with grieving students should have a basic knowledge of the grief process and an understanding of developmental issues that influence this process. However, students also benefit from receiving basic information regarding the grief process and normal reactions to death (Haine, Ayers, Sandler, & Wolchik, 2008). Providing students with basic, age-appropriate information regarding common responses to death helps normalize the

grieving process and can help reduce feelings of isolation, guilt, and anxiety.

School psychologists can instruct teachers on how to share with their students some of the most common grief reactions they may experience, including shock, fear, waves of strong feelings such as sadness or anger, and difficulty sleeping and concentrating. It should be noted that normalizing grief reactions are contraindicated for those who may be more acutely traumatized.

Emotional First-Aid

While teachers, administrators, and other school personnel may have varying roles and responsibilities depending upon the organizational structure of the school and the needs of the school community, one of the immediate priorities of school personnel and members of the crisis response team following the death

---

Table 21.4. Considerations for the Classroom Teacher in Supporting Grieving Students

- Provide students with accurate facts regarding the death, avoiding phrases or euphemisms such as "gone to sleep" or "gone to a better place."
- Allow students to ask questions, but offer brief, accurate answers without providing unnecessary details. Emphasis should be placed on students' reactions and feelings, not the details of the death or on the suspected perpetrators.
- Dispel any rumors.
- Encourage and allow opportunities for students to express feelings of grief and sadness while keeping in mind that not all students will necessarily have a need to talk about the loss or to express their feelings.
- Acknowledge the intensity of the loss. Share feelings of grief but avoid being overly emotional or dramatic about the details of the death.
- Help normalize students' feelings by reassuring them that their feelings are normal and to be expected (except with those exhibiting an acute response).
- Educate students regarding common grief reactions, including expecting to experience waves of strong emotions and a range of feelings.
- Provide coaching to students on how to effectively cope with strong feelings, such as talking with others or seeking help from a trusted adult.
- Model constructive coping strategies.
- Help relieve common feelings of guilt, particularly in younger children, by reassuring students that they are not responsible for the death. This is especially important for younger siblings of the deceased, who may feel guilty because of negative thoughts or feelings they may have had in the past toward their sibling.
- Encourage students to be supportive of one another and reassure them that adults are available to help.
- Allow students to reminisce and to share their memories about the deceased.
- Provide students who are reluctant to verbalize their feelings with alternative modes of communication (such as writing or drawing).
- Give students permission to cry if needed, as some students may perceive crying as an unacceptable public display of emotion.
- Do not immediately eliminate the deceased student's presence in the classroom (e.g., removing the student's desk).
- Be warm, open, and available to listen when needed.
- Listen in a noncritical and nonjudgmental manner.
- Temporarily adjust academic expectations to accommodate students who may need more time to grieve.
- Connect with students who have been affected by the death by regularly checking in with them and offering continued support.
- Minimize any additional anxiety by maintaining regular classroom and school routines whenever possible.
- Monitor students' behavior following the death, paying particular attention to the intensity and duration of their reactions.
- Refer any students exhibiting extreme emotions or behavior to the counselor or school psychologist.
- Recognize that anniversaries, holidays, and birthdays may be difficult and that students may require extra support and sensitivity during these times.

---

of a student or staff member is to assist in managing initial emotionality through the provision of emotional first-aid. Emotional first-aid is the initial support offered to those experiencing emotional distress prior to obtaining any specific therapeutic intervention. This emotional support should be offered quickly, soon after news of the death, in order to foster optimal adjustment.

The primary goals of emotional first-aid are to provide support and to give permission for the open expression of emotions in order to calm the individual and to ease immediate distress. Without pushing the grieving person or becoming invasive, it should involve reaching out physically and emotionally through the gentle use of simple and brief words such as those outlined in Table 21.5.

It is important to emphasize that the key aspect of emotional first-aid is simply the offering of genuine, empathic support, and giving the affected individual an opportunity to express a range of emotion. Those offering emotional first-aid should recognize that they are not expected to be an expert or to have all the answers, and they should not attempt to provide an explanation for the death. Additionally, the use of euphemisms such as "it will get better with time" or "they are in a better place" should be avoided as the euphemism can cause confusion, especially among younger children, who are more concrete in their thinking. Finally, those offering support should be aware that not all students will necessarily need to verbally express their emotions. These students should not be pressured to express their emotions and their initial lack of desire to verbalize their feelings should not be confused with complicated grief or lack of grieving.

Bereavement and Crisis Interventions

In the immediate aftermath of a death, it is important that students be informed about where and how they can receive support beyond that which is provided within the classroom. Depending upon the nature and impact of the death, schools may offer a designated support room that is designed as a drop-in site where students who have been referred by teachers or who self-identify as experiencing distress can receive a deeper level of support during the school day. It is important to note that immediately following a death, school psychologists and other mental health professionals who may facilitate support rooms should address immediate responses to the death and focus primarily on providing emotional first-aid. More structured bereavement interventions can be implemented in the following weeks and months.

The research base on bereavement interventions with children is somewhat limited with regard to empirical support for the degree of effectiveness of interventions in fostering positive adjustment after a death-related loss. Moreover, the current literature on bereavement interventions with children suggests that interventions may not necessarily be beneficial for all bereaved individuals, particularly for those who are experiencing normal grief (Currier, Holland, & Neimeyer, 2007). However, there is general consensus that targeted interventions may be beneficial for children identified as being at high risk for difficulties or who exhibit early signs of traumatic grief. Data such as these indicate the importance of utilizing screening measures, when possible, to select children who are showing signs of adjustment difficulties prior to implementing intensive grief or bereavement interventions.

Classroom-Based Crisis Interventions

In some cases the death may have occurred under traumatic circumstances, requiring support that specifically addresses symptoms of traumatic stress. When a death is traumatic and simultaneously affects a large number of students within the school (e.g., students who witness a death on school grounds), classroom-based crisis interventions, which are a form of immediate psychological first-aid offered within a group context and are designed to restore immediate coping skills in the aftermath of a traumatic event, may be beneficial.

Table 21.5. Strategies for Offering Emotional First-Aid

Reaching out physically
- Position yourself at the individual's side, at their level.
- Use the individual's name, using a soft voice.
- Provide a comforting physical presence through use of body language.

Reaching out emotionally
- Use brief comments: "This must be very painful for you." "You are not alone. We are here for you." "I'm sorry this happened, I'm here to listen." "I did not know the deceased but would like to know about [him or her]."
- Use brief suggestions: "It's okay to let your feelings out."
- Use brief questions: "How can I help?" "How are you feeling?"

The PREPaRE model suggests that classroom-based crisis interventions (see Brock et al., 2009) should be considered as an intervention option for reestablishing immediate coping of groups of students who have experienced a shared crisis event. Classroom-based crisis interventions are direct efforts by the crisis response team to highlight the commonality of students' reactions and to help students understand that their reactions are not necessarily abnormal. While classroom-based crisis interventions are not intended to address more severe traumatic responses requiring intensive psychotherapeutic intervention, these group interventions can help foster adaptive coping in nonacute responses to traumatic death and allow students to gain a better understanding of how they have been affected by the event, identify possible future concerns, and learn adaptive strategies to help them cope with the death.

While more intensive interventions are typically not a part of the school-based crisis response and commonly require collaboration with outside community-based mental health agencies, early intervention for students who have suffered the effects of death-related trauma can help students cope with the emotional aftermath of the trauma and prevent potential future psychological and academic difficulties. Cognitive Behavioral Interventions for Trauma in Schools (CBITS; National Child Traumatic Stress Network, 2008) is another school-based intervention developed for use addressing a wide range of trauma, including the witnessing of a death. CBITS is a structured skills-based group therapy approach focused on early intervention that can be provided by mental health professionals in school settings. CBITS has been designed to be implemented with an array of ethnically, culturally, and linguistically diverse populations.

Memorials and Other Rituals

A death within the school is often a tragic time when the entire school community comes together and grieves. Memorials and other rituals can help individuals honor and remember the deceased and can also help people begin to move through the grieving process and transition back to their daily routines. However, while memorials can be beneficial for some, for others they may serve as an ongoing reminder of the death and may trigger unwanted memories or fears. School psychologists should advise schools to give careful consideration before creating a permanent memorial or to avoid creating a permanent memorial structure or marker on school grounds. Instead, schools may provide opportunities for a series of memorial activities or allow for a temporary memorial site where the school community can place, for instance, notes, flowers, or letters.

Any memorial activities should be based on the needs and wishes of the school community and should include the input and involvement of administrators, teachers, parents, and students, especially those with personal ties to the deceased. Schools should also develop policies for memorials in advance, prior to being faced with a sudden death, and should consider planning and implementing a school-wide policy regarding memorials that is consistent and equitable regardless of the circumstances of the death.

In the case of suicide, it is particularly important to be cautious of inadvertently glorifying or romanticizing suicide through selected memorial activities. In a suicide toolkit for schools released by the American Foundation for Suicide Prevention and the Suicide Prevention Resource Center (2011), the principal recommendation for schools is to strive to treat all deaths the same.

Preparing for the Return of a Grieving Student
When a death has an impact on only one or a few students in a school, such as in the case of the death of a parent or close family member, teachers must prepare themselves and their students for the grieving student's return to school. In preparing for a grieving student's return, not only might the grieving student have concerns about returning to school, but classmates of the grieving child may also feel unsure about how to respond to the grieving student. Table 21.6 provides a summary of strategies that school psychologists can provide to teachers to help their students prepare for the return of a grieving classmate. School psychologists can advise teachers to also reflect on their own personal reaction to the death, their own level of comfort in discussing death and grief, and the closeness of their relationship to the deceased.

Parent Support and Education
It is not uncommon for people to feel unsure of what to do or say to comfort someone who is grieving. Whether a loved one within their family has died or whether their child has experienced the loss of a teacher or classmate, parents may need support in helping their child cope with the pain of grief. While each family's response to death will be shaped by its own cultural or religious beliefs and practices, providing parents with general guidelines regarding how to talk with their children about death and common grief reactions can be helpful in assisting parents as they navigate the grieving process

Table 21.6. Strategies for Preparing Students for the Return of a Grieving Classmate

- *Determine how the grieving student is coping with the loss:* It is important for the teacher to connect with the grieving student's family to find out how the student is coping with the loss. Obtaining this information prior to the student's return can help make the transition back to school more successful and can assist in gauging the level of preparation needed for classmates.

- *Discuss the topic of grief with students:* Teachers can discuss with the class the definition and nature of grief and the ways in which people may be affected by grief. Students should be encouraged to share their thoughts, feelings, and personal experiences on coping strategies that have been helpful to them in dealing with any past losses or challenges. Teachers can also provide guidance to students on how to express their sympathy and support.

- *Highlight potential difficulties the returning student may experience:* Teachers can share how difficult or uncomfortable it may be for the student to return to school, just as classmates may also feel unsure of how to respond to the grieving student. Some students may prefer to withdraw for a short period of time, some may want to be comforted and consoled, while others may want to be able to talk about their feelings. Consequently, teachers should gauge the returning students' needs and preferences upon return to the classroom.

- *Prepare students for possible behavior changes:* Students should be prepared to expect possible behavior changes in the grieving classmate upon the classmate's return to school, such as sadness, waves of emotions, social withdrawal, or anger. Teachers should explain that these behaviors are normal responses to grief and that these behaviors typically fade over time.

- *Be attentive to potential grief reactions of classmates:* Teachers should monitor the reactions other students may have to their classmate's loss. Friends and classmates may also feel sadness and strong emotions in response to the death. In addition, the death may cause feelings of grief and sadness to resurface in students who have suffered previous personal losses.

- *Provide opportunities to reach out to the grieving student:* Having students write cards or letters to the grieving student and his or her family can provide students with the opportunity to show their concern and help the grieving student feel supported and less isolated.

- *Teach students to respect the grieving process:* Help students understand that coping with grief may be a long process and a major challenge for their classmate.

with their children. It is important for school psychologists to emphasize to parents that their support during this time constitutes the most critical aspect of their child's adjustment and that simply acknowledging what has happened, listening empathically, expressing their concern, giving reassurance without minimizing the loss, being genuine about their own feelings, and offering their support can be instrumental in the healing process.

Schools may consider providing handouts to parents with basic information about the grieving process and local resources where additional help can be provided. The following suggestions outlined in Table 21.7 may be helpful when talking to children and adolescents about death.

Special Considerations

Support for students with special needs: Students with cognitive, emotional, or behavioral impairments may require additional support tailored to their unique needs in order to help them cope with and understand the feelings and changes associated with a death. Whether a student requires help understanding the finality of death, coping with confusion and distress as a result of the deceased's absence, or support in reducing increased problematic behaviors, establishing a safe and secure environment that promotes a timely return to normal routines and previous equilibrium is of primary importance (Jimerson & Huff, 2002). Using their knowledge, and consultation and collaboration skills, school psychologists can effectively support students with special needs by working closely alongside teachers of special education students, who will be the most familiar with the specific needs of each individual student.

Self-care: Caregivers cannot effectively care for others unless they also care for themselves. Coping with a death-related loss while also providing support to others can be physically, emotionally, and psychologically taxing, requiring people to identify their own needs and take the necessary steps toward meeting those needs in order to avoid becoming overwhelmed during periods of heightened stress. Strategies that may be effective in helping to reduce stress and to promote healing are outlined in Table 21.8.

Suicides: While any sudden death can be traumatic, suicides can have a particularly profound impact on the school community. The grief response following a suicide is inherently complex in nature and such deaths require schools to be aware of a number of issues. Owing to the traumatic nature of suicide, friends, family, acquaintances, and even those who were not

Table 21.7. Parent Strategies for Talking to Children and Adolescents About Death

- Provide reassurance to your child that he or she is safe and loved and that he or she will be taken care of.
- Be consistent with affection and support.
- Acknowledge and explain what has happened clearly and in a developmentally appropriate manner.
- During the initial conversation focus on what your child or adolescent thinks, feels, and understands about death. Understanding your child's own perception and feelings about the death can make it easier to meaningfully talk about it with your child.
- Avoid using euphemisms such as "he went to sleep and never woke up" or "she went away." Young children who hear "sleep" or "went away" used when a death has occurred may develop a fear of sleeping or of being separated even for short periods from their parents.
- Answer questions honestly in brief and simple terms, and more concretely with younger children.
- Do not force your child to talk if he or she temporarily feels like withdrawing, but assure your child that you will be there for them when they decide to talk.
- Allow your child to take the lead as to when, how long, and how much is discussed.
- Explain to your child that people may feel many different things, and that denial or disbelief, anger, sadness, or numbness are all normal feelings. Share with your child that it is also okay to feel sad and then to feel moments of happiness again.
- Model healthy coping strategies. It can be helpful for your child to know that although you are also saddened by the loss, you are willing to talk about how you feel.
- It is important to listen to your child's fears and normalize his or her reactions. If your child is an adolescent, be sure to acknowledge your child's fears before reassuring your child or your child may find it difficult to believe you.

acquainted with the deceased but who are otherwise vulnerable, may be at increased risk for a complicated grief response. In addition to feelings of intense shock and grief, survivors may feel a tremendous sense of guilt, regret, anger, and self-blame. It is especially important to provide supports to these individuals and to emphasize seeking help at school or through local service providers and crisis centers.

Cultural Considerations

Helping students and families cope in the aftermath of a death-related loss involves the provision of culturally sensitive care and support and the recognition that bereavement practices vary depending on the cultural background of the individual. Cultural traditions,

beliefs, and values play an integral role in a person's outward expression of grief and should be a key consideration in determining the type of support or interventions offered within both the school and community.

School psychologists and other mental health providers within the schools must possess an understanding of the specific cultural and religious perspectives on death of the students and families they serve. To gain better insight into these beliefs and practices, specific culture-related questions should be addressed: What, if any, cultural or religious rituals are practiced with regard to death, grief, coping, and honoring the dead? What are the cultural, spiritual, or religious norms as they relate to the expression of grief? What cultural, spiritual, or

Table 21.8. Strategies for Self-Care

- ***Take time for yourself:*** Incorporating quiet time into one's daily routine to rest or to perform a calming activity that helps reduce stress can be beneficial when coping with the impact of a death-related loss.
- ***Maintain a daily routine:*** Create and maintain a daily routine that incorporates current needs.
- ***Connect with others:*** Reaching out to trusted friends and family to share feelings related to the loss or simply to lean on for support with practical issues such as meal preparation can help reduce feelings of isolation and hopelessness.
- ***Take care of your body:*** Eating well, exercising regularly, getting adequate sleep, avoiding drugs or alcohol, and focusing on relaxed breathing techniques are simple yet effective strategies to help combat the physical toll of grief.
- ***Seek out support groups:*** Support groups can provide the opportunity to connect with others who are also grieving and can help reduce feelings of isolation.
- ***Draw on religious or spiritual beliefs:*** Solace and comfort can often be garnered by turning to one's spiritual beliefs and rituals during periods of heightened distress.
- ***Seek professional help if needed:*** Depending on the level of a person's existing support system and the degree of coping of the individual, seeking the help of a mental health professional can help address difficulties adjusting to a death and can assist in providing strategies for moving forward.

religious roles are typically ascribed to various family members? Are certain types of death, such as suicide, viewed differently than other types of death? Responding to questions such as these can provide valuable information about how people cope with death culturally and can facilitate the ability of school psychologists, teachers, and others who work with grieving students and families, to provide culturally appropriate support and interventions.

Setting the Stage for Resilience

In the aftermath of any tragic event it is important to begin the process of healing and recovery and to provide students with an environment that fosters the development of resilience. This is important because it can help students manage stress and feelings of fear or anxiety after trauma or a major loss. Resilience is described as the ability to thrive and to show positive adaptation despite significant adversity or challenging circumstances (Masten, 2001). Not surprisingly, children who are resilient are better able to adapt after experiencing highly stressful or traumatic events than less resilient children and also recover more quickly following exposure to stressful conditions.

Understanding this process of positive adaptation within the context of adversity and identifying specific sources of resilience in children can help parents, teachers, and other professionals who work with children promote and build resilience in children who have been affected by a death.

Schools can help foster resilience in students by promoting experiences that focus on building students' sense of competency, belonging, usefulness, and optimism. One of the most powerful and consistently observed protective factors that enhances resilience in children is the presence of a strong, supportive relationship with at least one caring adult (Luthar, 2005). Close bonds with people who provide stability, care, and attention are critical to the development of resilience. Consequently, in developing and implementing interventions designed to promote resilience, school psychologists should also incorporate measures aimed at improving child–parent interactions and fostering supportive relationships. School psychologists can assist schools in promoting resilience by facilitating the implementation of the following strategies outlined in Table 21.9.

When faced with circumstances beyond their control, it is important for students to hear from the adults that

Table 21.9. Strategies for Promoting Resilience

- *Help students identify supportive adults in their lives:* The importance of supportive personal relationships is essential to helping individuals cope with stressful life events and is a cornerstone of resilience. Teachers can help students identify sources of support, such as family members, peers, teachers, counselors, coaches, or clergy, and can encourage students to turn to their support network for comfort.
- *Help students make connections with peers:* Encourage students to be friends to others and teach skills of empathy. Connecting with others in this way strengthens social support and also helps build resilience.
- *Create positive classroom connections:* By developing classroom projects that promote teamwork and respect, students have the opportunity to develop a sense of belonging and contribution. Contribution directly fosters resilience as it helps students gain a sense of purpose and gives them the opportunity to strive toward a common goal.
- *Empower students by encouraging them to help others:* Students can feel empowered by helping others. Teachers and parents can engage students in discussions about ways they can help others and can actively promote such opportunities.
- *Help students increase a sense of competence by setting realistic goals:* Students acquire competence by mastering tasks and by facing challenges head on. By teaching students to work toward an achievable goal and by praising them for small steps made toward that goal, students begin to develop confidence in themselves and begin to learn that they can be successful in the face of challenges.
- *Encourage proper self-care:* Teaching students the importance of caring for oneself, including making time to eat properly and to get adequate rest and exercise, helps children stay balanced and better able to cope with stressful periods in their lives. Students should be encouraged to lead a balanced life that includes time for fun and relaxation.
- *Teach the importance of maintaining a daily routine:* Maintaining a daily routine can be comforting for children and provides a sense of structure in their lives, especially during times of crisis or challenging life circumstances.
- *Help nurture a positive self-view:* The manner in which children or adolescents view themselves influences how they react or respond to stressful life events. Teachers and parents can help children remember how they have successfully handled difficulties in the past and can assist them in understanding how coping with past challenges can help them manage future obstacles.
- *Encourage students to maintain an optimistic outlook:* It is important that students be encouraged to maintain a positive outlook on life and look forward to a positive future. Helping students learn to accept and anticipate changes in life can also promote better adjustment to future challenges.

although they may not always have control over events that occur in their lives, they do have control over how they respond to those events. School psychologists can play a critical role in promoting resilience by highlighting that students who develop a sense of inner control and who learn to take even small, positive actions to help themselves become more aware that they can have some control over outcomes in their lives, are less likely to be passive in the face of adverse circumstances, and are more likely to realize that they have the ability to bounce back after challenges.

Long-Term Follow Up

Ongoing monitoring of students and staff who have been affected by a death should be maintained to assess levels of coping and to assist with identification of individuals who may be in need of additional support or services. Continued communication among school staff and parents can also help facilitate monitoring of students' academic progress, social relationships, and overall adjustment. It is also important for schools to be aware that the resurfacing of grief reactions may occur during momentous occasions such as graduation, the anniversary of the death, or after another death within the school community. During these times schools may consider providing additional support to those who may be in need of continued services.

SUMMARY

Death-related loss within the school community is not an uncommon occurrence and schools must therefore be prepared to respond to the potentially profound and devastating impact that such an event can have on both individuals and the broader school community. The manner in which schools respond to the death of a teacher or classmate can help minimize the negative impact on those affected by the loss and can set the stage for healing and the building of resilience. However, an effective response to a death requires training, advance planning, and development of procedures consistent with those of a comprehensive crisis response plan.

School psychologists are skilled and trained to deliver a broad range of prevention and intervention strategies and to work collaboratively with other school-based clinicians, community agencies, students, and their families. Consequently, school psychologists should play a key role within a multidisciplinary crisis response team and can help lead efforts toward the effective response to a death in the school community and toward the promotion of healing and recovery.

REFERENCES

Adamson, A. D., & Peacock, G. G. (2007). Crisis response in the public schools: A survey of school psychologists' experiences and perceptions. *Psychology in the Schools, 44,* 749–694.

American Foundation for Suicide Prevention and Suicide Prevention Resource Center. (2011). *After a suicide: A toolkit for schools.* Newton, MA: Education Development Center. Retrieved from http://www.sprc.org/sites/sprc.org/files/library/AfteraSuicideToolkitforSchools.pdf

Brock, S. E., Nickerson, A. B., Reeves, M. A., Jimerson, S. R., Lieberman, R. A., & Feinberg, T. A. (2009). *School crisis prevention and intervention: The PREPaRE model.* Bethesda, MD: National Association of School Psychologists.

Cohen, J. A., & Mannarino, A. P. (2011). Supporting children with traumatic grief: What educators need to know. *School Psychology International, 32,* 117–131. doi:10.1177/0143034311400827

Cohen, J. A., Mannarino, A. P., Greenberg, T., Padlo, S., & Shipley, C. (2002). Childhood traumatic grief: Concepts and controversies. *Trauma, Violence, and Abuse, 3,* 307–327. doi:10.1177/1524838002237332

Corr, C. A. (2000). What do we know about grieving children and adolescents? In K. J. Doka (Ed.), *Children, adolescents, and loss: Living with grief.* Washington, DC: Hospice Foundation.

Currier, J. M., Holland, J. M., & Neimeyer, R. A. (2007). The effectiveness of bereavement interventions with children: A meta-analytic review of controlled outcome research. *Journal of Clinical Child & Adolescent Psychology, 36,* 253–259.

Doughty, E. A. (2009). Investigating adaptive grieving styles: A Delphi study. *Death Studies, 33,* 462–480. doi:10.1080/07481180902805715

Fiorelli, R. (2010). Grief and bereavement in children. In N. Kinzbrunner & J. Policzer (Eds.), *End-of-life-care: A practical guide.* (2nd ed., pp. 635–665). New York, NY: McGraw-Hill.

Haine, R. A., Ayers, T. S., Sandler, I. N., & Wolchik, S. A. (2008). Evidenced based practices for parentally bereaved children and their families. *Professional Psychology: Research and Practice, 39,* 113–121. doi:10.1037/0735-7028.39.2.113

Hunter, S. B., & Smith, D. E. (2008). Predictors of children's understandings of death: Age, cognitive ability, death experience, and maternal communicative competence. *Omega, 57,* 143–162. doi:10.2190/OM.57.2.b

Jimerson, S., & Huff, L. (2002). Responding to a sudden, unexpected death at school: Chance favors the prepared professional. In S. E. Brock, P. J. Lazarus, & S. R. Jimerson (Eds.), *Best practices in school crisis prevention and intervention.* (pp. 451–488). Bethesda, MD: National Association of School Psychologists.

Kirwin, K. M., & Hamrin, V. (2005). Decreasing the risk of complicated bereavement and future psychiatric disorders in children. *Journal of Child and Adolescent Psychiatric Nursing, 18,* 62–78. doi:10.1111/j.1744-6171.2005.00002.x

Lahad, M., & Cohen, A. (2006). *The community stress prevention center: 25 years of community stress prevention and intervention.* Kiryat Shmona, Israel: The Community Stress Prevention Center.

Luthar, S. S. (2005). Resilience at an early age and its impact on child psychosocial development. In *Encyclopedia on early childhood development.* Montreal, QC, Canada: Centre of Excellence for Early Childhood Development and the Strategic Knowledge Cluster on Early Childhood Development. Retrieved from http://www.child-encyclopedia.com/en-ca/child-resilience/perspectives.html

Masten, A. S. (2001). Ordinary magic: Resilience processes in development. *American Psychologist, 56,* 227–238. doi:10.1037/0003-066X.56.3.227

National Association of School Psychologists. (2010). *Model for comprehensive and integrated school psychological services.* Bethesda, MD: Author. Retrieved from http://www.nasponline.org/standards/2010standards/2_PracticeModel.pdf

National Center for School Crisis and Bereavement. (n.d.). Cincinnati children. In, *Guidelines for responding to the death of a student or school staff.* Cincinnati, OH: Author. Retrieved from http://www.stchristophershospital.com/pediatric-specialties-programs/specialties/690

National Child Traumatic Stress Network. (2008). *Cognitive behavioral intervention for trauma in schools: General information.* Los Angeles, CA: Author. Retrieved from http://www.nctsnet.org/nctsn_assets/pdfs/CBITSfactsheet.pdf

Neimeyer, R. A. (2000). Searching for the meaning of meaning: Grief therapy and the process of reconstruction. *Death Studies, 24,* 541–558. doi:10.1080/07481180050121480

Poland, S., & Poland, D. (2004). Dealing with death at school. *Principal Leadership, 4*(8), 8–12.

Servaty-Seib, H. L. (2004). Connections between counseling theories and current theories of grief and mourning. *Journal of Mental Health Counseling, 26,* 125–145.

Silverman, P., & Worden, J. W. (1993). Children's reactions to the death of a parent. In M. S. Stroebe, W. Stroebe, & R. O. Hansson (Eds.), *Handbook of bereavement theory, research and intervention.* New York, NY: Cambridge University Press.

Social Security Administration. (2000). *Intermediate assumptions of the 2000 trustees report.* Washington, DC: Author.

U.S. Department of Education. (2007). *Practical information on crisis planning: A guide for schools and communities.* Washington, DC: Office of Safe and Drug-Free Schools. Retrieved from http://rems.ed.gov/docs/PracticalInformationonCrisisPlanning.pdf

Worden, J. W. (1996). *Children and grief: When a parent dies.* New York, NY: Guilford Press.

Worden, J. W. (2008). *Grief counseling and grief therapy: A handbook for the mental health practitioner.* (4th ed.). New York, NY: Springer.

APPENDIX A. A STUDENT DIES IN AN ACCIDENT

The school psychologist received a call from the school principal on the eve of the 2-week Christmas holiday vacation. The principal stated that she was at the hospital and that a ninth-grade boy named Larry from the school had just been pronounced dead. Larry had borrowed a scooter in the neighborhood and been hit by an SUV. The accident was witnessed by four other students. The principal said that approximately 60 students were at the hospital and that they became very emotional when the death was announced. The hospital staff had requested that all students leave the hospital immediately as they were creating chaos. The principal asked for advice about what to do and what to say to the students.

The school principal is to be commended for being at the hospital to support the students and for asking for assistance from the school psychologist. The fact that the principal had all the contact information for the school psychologist indicated that prior planning had occurred and that the principal relies on the school psychologist in crisis situations.

There is no such thing as a perfect crisis response, but it is important to do something and not wait to respond. Tragic news travels quickly these days with almost every student possessing a cell phone and using text messaging and social networks. The school psychologist stressed the need to provide students an opportunity to express their emotions and that a range of emotions was to be expected. The school psychologist asked what plans the students had and the principal said that the grieving students were planning to gather in a local park. The school psychologist suggested that the school be opened that night and that students be encouraged to gather at the school instead of the local park. The school psychologist further stressed that a circle of care should be provided for the affected students and suggested that their parents be notified as quickly as possible and that students should be encouraged to call their parents and let them know about the tragedy. It was determined that many of the affected students were on sports teams and that the athletic parent booster organization would be a good way to get the word out to parents.

The school psychologist volunteered to meet the principal at the school and recommended that the crisis team for the school be alerted through the calling tree and encouraged the principal to alert as many staff members as possible. The teachers familiar to the grieving students would be helpful at the school that evening.

The school psychologist arrived at the school with a handout that had been prepared to give adults guidance for assisting children in the aftermath of tragedies. The first words the school psychologist heard when entering the school was, "Thank God you're here and let me get all the students for you." The school psychologist asked for a few minutes to gather thoughts and then, in partnership with the ninth-grade counselor, addressed the parents who were in attendance. The message to parents was to be there for their children, to reach out to them, to find the times when their child would talk to them, and to use reflective listening skills. The typical reactions that children have to tragedy were outlined, such as worries and fears about the future, sleeping problems, and academic and behavioral regression. Parents were encouraged to keep structure and routines in place for their children and to be patient and tolerant. Parents were encouraged to plan to attend the funeral with their children and to increase supervision over the holidays. Parents who had continuing concerns about their children were encouraged to call the school counseling office for assistance. A question-and-answer session followed, and a parent asked whether the fact that her child's grandmother had died last week would make this death especially difficult for her child. The answer was yes, and the school psychologist discussed that the individual crisis history for each student was important. The school psychologist said that those children who might have lost other friends or relatives to accidental deaths likely will be thinking about those previous tragedies now and may require even greater support.

Next, with all of the affected students gathered in a circle with the school psychologist and counselor seated, a session was held to encourage students to begin talking about the death. The school psychologist began by stating that she did not know their friend Larry but had helped students when other sad things had happened. All students were provided with the facts about the accident. In a focused effort to foster communication on the part of the students and not have them feel they were being talked at, the school psychologist asked the students to tell her about Larry. The students responded with many stories about Larry and his many positive characteristics. The school psychologist and counselor emphasized the need for students to share their thoughts and emotions with their parents and the fact that their parents were here because they cared so much about them.

The school psychologist said that in the session for parents it was emphasized that they talk less and listen more to their children. A few students wanted to determine who was at fault for the accident and were gently guided to focus more on the loss of their friend and classmate and on their own emotions, as the accident would be under investigation for some time.

One of the students asked if he could lead the group in a prayer and the school psychologist and counselor said yes. It was also emphasized that religion is a great source of support and comfort for many, but that everyone is encouraged to use whatever means that provides them with comfort.

Students were given permission for a range of emotions and religious beliefs, and were encouraged to let parents and school personnel know if their emotions were becoming overwhelming. Students were asked what sources of assistance had helped them when they had to deal with sad things in the past and were encouraged to utilize those sources of support now.

The school psychologist and counselor gave the hours that the school would be open the following day if any students wanted further assistance. The school psychologist and counselor stayed after the session to talk with students and parents who wanted individual attention.

Many additional steps were taken over the holidays as counselors and administrators called to check on how students were doing and also attended the funeral. Follow-up support for the victim's closest friends and for the two siblings of the victim, as they attended district schools, was a priority. A training session was held for all teachers on the teacher inservice day in January on how to best support students in the aftermath of death. Students also created a safety public service announcement in memory of the victim. School counselors were also especially alert to the needs of affected students and the family of the victim on significant anniversary dates such as Larry's birthday and on the anniversary of his death.

APPENDIX B. DEATH OF A STAFF MEMBER

The principal called the school psychologist at home at 9:00 p.m. to report that the school nurse was hit by a car and killed crossing the street in her neighborhood. The school psychologist responded with shock and sadness. Providing crisis intervention in the aftermath of the death of someone that the school psychologist knows is especially difficult. The nurse had been at the school for many years and was much beloved by staff. The principal and the school psychologist decided to implement the calling tree and e-mail notification procedures so that all staff would know the facts about the tragedy and informed them that a staff meeting would be held before school.

The school psychologist told the principal that the biggest impact would be on the staff, rather than the students, and stressed the importance of assisting the staff first. Plans were made for the school psychologist to be available to meet with small groups of staff throughout the day during their conference periods.

Previous responses to tragedies had taught the school psychologist that it is important to give everyone permission to experience and express a range of emotions and to provide opportunities to reminisce about the deceased. Staff and students would undoubtedly want to do something in memory of the deceased, and need to have input into the decision, but it might take several weeks to determine what would be best. Further, in

22 Best Practices in Using the DSM-5 and ICD-10 by School Psychologists

Susan M. Swearer
University of Nebraska–Lincoln
Kisha Radliff
Ohio State University
Paige Lembeck
University of Nebraska–Lincoln

OVERVIEW

Classifying mental health disorders has been a challenge that has spanned decades. Two similar, yet separate, systems have been developed for the classification of mental health disorders: the fifth edition of the *Diagnostic and Statistical Manual of Mental Disorders* (DSM-5; American Psychiatric Association [APA], 2013) and the 10th revision of the *International Classification of Diseases* (ICD-10; World Health Organization [WHO], 1992). Their most significant contribution is that they provide a common nomenclature that facilitates communication and treatment decisions, with similar goals for clinical use (First & Westen, 2007). These goals include making diagnoses and tracking their prevalence in order to facilitate improvements in clinical, research, and educational domains. Although the DSM-5 and the ICD-10 serve similar purposes, they are developed by separate organizations, APA and WHO, respectively.

This chapter will provide a brief review of both classification systems and make recommendations for school psychologists who may use the DSM and/or the ICD for educational classification, in communication with other mental health professionals, in research, or in private practice. Specifically, after reading this chapter, school psychologists will understand (a) the purpose of the DSM-5 and ICD-10, (b) similarities and differences between the DSM-5 and ICD-10, (c) the importance of the DSM-5 and ICD-10 in school psychology practice,

(d) how to integrate the DSM-5 and ICD-10 into data-based decision making, and (e) how the DSM-5 and ICD-10 can facilitate communication with other professionals (e.g., psychiatrists, pediatricians) to more effectively assess and treat youth with mental health needs.

The National Association of School Psychologists (NASP) emphasizes a comprehensive service delivery model that includes the provision of mental health services. In fact, the NASP *Model for Comprehensive and Integrated School Psychological Services* (NASP, 2010) includes domains that specifically address or refer to mental health. This chapter is related to the domain of Preventive and Responsive Services, which encompasses knowledge of factors that have an impact on mental health, services that promote prevention and intervention, and appropriate strategies for crisis intervention.

Knowledge of the DSM-5 and the ICD-10 is essential to effectively meet the mental health needs of youth in schools. In accordance with this viewpoint, the DSM-5 and ICD-10 include information beyond diagnostic criteria (e.g., prevalence, etiology, cultural features, and familial patterns) that can facilitate assessment, interpretation of results, and implementation of appropriate interventions. Given the use of the DSM and ICD systems in hospitals and practice settings, it is critical that school psychologists be familiar with the history and use of the DSM-5 and the ICD-10 to most comprehensively address the mental health needs of youth.

History and Development of the Classification Systems

This section presents the histories and descriptions of the DSM-5 and ICD-10 and compares them.

History of the DSM-5

The original classification system for mental health disorders emerged in the late 1800s (APA, 2000). From the release of the first edition of the *Diagnostic and Statistical Manual* by APA in 1952 to the fifth edition in 2013, the focus has been on developing objective criteria that lead to accurate diagnoses. Specifically, additional statistical consultation and gathering of empirical evidence were emphasized for the DSM-5 to ensure validity and reliablity (APA, 2012; Kraemer, Shrout, & Rubio-Stipec, 2007). Despite well-meaning intentions to develop criteria based on genetic, neuroscience, and behavioral science research (National Institute of Mental Health, 2008), the DSM-5 was confronted with criticism following its release in May 2013. Much of the criticism is political and due to changing the multiaxial system and several of the diagnostic categories. Despite the criticism, the DSM-5 is the result of an extensive history of revisions that has spanned approximately 200 years. (For a review of the DSM's history and development, please see the introductions of the two recent DSM manuals; APA, 2000, 2013.)

Description of the DSM-5

The DSM-5 has evolved into a well-organized classification system for mental disorders that influences assessment, diagnosis, and, pragmatically, insurance reimbursement. Most of the changes between the fourth edition (text revision) of the DSM (DSM-IV-TR) and the DSM-5 pertain to the DSM-5 manual's organization, the increased focus on developmental issues, and the addition of new disorders. The DSM-5 consists of three sections: (a) DSM-5 Basics, (b) Diagnostic Criteria and Codes, and (c) Emerging Measures and Models. It also has an Appendix that includes the changes between the two manuals; glossary of technical terms; glossary of cultural concepts of distress; and DSM-5, ICD-9-CM, and ICD-10-CM diagnoses and codes.

Specifically, the DSM-5 includes 21 diagnostic categories (to be more consistent with the forthcoming 11th revision of ICD [ICD-11], which will be issued in 2015) and a separate category encompassing other disorders that do not fit within these criteria (APA, 2013). For each disorder, information is provided about diagnostic features, associated features and disorders,

specific culture and gender features, prevalence, course, familial pattern, and differential diagnosis (APA, 2013). Departing from the ICD-10 and the DSM-IV-TR, the DSM-5 has shifted to a nonaxial sytem of diagnosis with separate notations for severity specifiers or psychosocial, contextual, and disability factors (APA, 2013). The DSM-5 also includes information about assessment measures and an alternative approach for personality disorders (i.e., a hybrid dimensional–categorical model). The alternative approach to identifying personality disorders "incorporates impairments in personality functioning as well as pathological personality traits" (APA, 2013, p. 731).

Of note for school psychologists, the DSM-5 more accurately depicts the developmental progression of mental health disorders (Narrow, First, Sirovatka, & Regier, 2007) and includes developmental differences in disorder presentation as well as lifespan considerations. The order in which each disorder is presented reflects the approximate timing of its developmental onset (APA, 2013). For example, separation anxiety, which is more common in childhood, appears earlier in the DSM-5, while dementia is described toward the end with other disorders that are more frequently diagnosed later in life. The organization of the DSM-5 was also affected by changes to chapter organization and grouping of specific disorders. Within the DSM-5's three sections, the disorders are structured based on their relatedness to one another. For example, new chapters include Neurodevelopmental Disorders, Substance Use and Addictive Disorders, and Obsessive–Compulsive and Related Disorders.

Additionally, a new metastructure is introduced to address the dilemma of overlapping criteria and high rates of comorbidity. For example, according to the DSM-IV-TR criteria, autism could not coexist comorbidly with attention deficit hyperactivity disorder (ADHD; Regier, Narrow, Kuhl, & Kupfer, 2009). The current system reflects the reality that prioritizing one diagnosis over others does not accurately represent most clients' presenting symptoms. Finally, research ultimately contributes to improvement in clinical utility (Reed, 2010). To demonstrate clinical utility means that sufficient meaningful information has been gathered to draw conclusions about a disorder's etiology, course, risk factors, and other information to inform effective practice. Evidence for poor clinical utility has been demonstrated through problems with the heterogeneity of criteria in that "not otherwise specified" (i.e., NOS) descriptors are made all too frequently (Regier, 2007; Regier et al., 2009). Therefore, it is not surprising that efforts have focused on strengthening the clinical utility of the DSM classification system in order to improve diagnostic decision making.

It is important to note the presence of several new disorders in the DSM-5. These include disruptive mood dysregulation disorder (to account for youth who are presenting with symptoms of bipolar disorder), excoriation (i.e., skin picking) disorder, and hoarding disorder. Disorders included in Section 3 include attenuated psychosis syndrome, Internet use gaming disorder, nonsuicidal self-injury, and suicidal behavioral disorder. Descriptions of changes to specific criteria can be found on the DSM-5 website (http://www.dsm5.org) and in the DSM-5 Appendix.

History of the ICD-10

The earliest versions of the ICD can be traced back to Jacques Bertillon's International List of Causes of Death (WHO, 2013). Over the years, this extensive document transformed into the *International Classification of Diseases*. A section devoted specifically to mental disorders was first included in the sixth revision of the ICD, which was released in 1948. It was not until the ninth revision of the ICD (ICD-9) in 1979 that a new classification manual was created that provided diagnostic criteria for each of the disorders. The release of the ICD-9 occurred soon before the release of the third edition of the DSM in 1980 and truly marked the beginning of the modern era of classification. (For an overview of the history of the ICD-10, see WHO, 1992, 2013.)

Description of the ICD-10

WHO is responsible for the creation and maintenance of the ICD. The ICD-10 consists of three volumes that serve different purposes. A clinical modification of the manual, the ICD-10-CM, was updated in the United States in 2013 to increase specificity of classification. However, it will not be implemented until 2014. The current manual that is predominantly concerned with mental disorders is the *Classification of Mental and Behavioral Disorders: Clinical Descriptions and Diagnostic Guidelines*, which was compiled primarily for clinical and educational use. The *Diagnostic Criteria for Research* manual, unsurprisingly, is intended to guide research endeavors. The first two manuals are intended to be used together. The third manual consists of a separate, short glossary to faciliate clercial tasks. With regard to its layout, blocks allow the disorders to be categorized. For instance, Block F30–F39 consists of mood disorders. Descriptions of clinical features and diagnostic guidelines follow these, which are similar to criteria outlined for each disorder in the DSM. Practioners are able to make diagnoses that are confident, provisional, or tentative based on the information they have available as well as on how well the patient's symptoms align with the diagnostic criteria provided. Unfortunately, problems with consistency have arisen because some countries, the United States included, have opted to make modifications that stray from the ICD's recommended original structure.

The principal function of the ICD is to "… permit the systematic recording, analysis, interpretation and comparison of mortality and morbidity data collected in different countries or areas and at different times" (WHO, 2004, p. 3). Although the ICD-10 is currently being used in more than 100 countries, it has yet to be implemented in the United States (Kupfer, First, & Regier, 2002). A few countries, the United States included, have favored the ICD-10-CM over the ICD-10 (Reed, 2010). This delay in adopting the most current version creates complications, particularly between the ICD-9-CM, the ICD-10-CM, and the forthcoming ICD-11. Several changes have been made from the ICD-9 to the ICD-10. An alphanumeric coding system has been incorporated to accommodate the increase in code options (Reed, 2010). In the forthcoming ICD-11 revision, the goal is to move toward an internationally universal system. This system will include additional descriptions of characteristics such as causal properties, genomic makeup, severity, and functional impact. Furthermore, care will be taken to coordinate revisions across countries, and the ICD may be revised biannually instead of on a 3-year cycle. However, the structure that is present in the ICD-10 will be maintained in the ICD-11.

Comparison of the DSM and ICD

Comparisons between the ICD-10 and the DSM-5 often focus on their conceptual and philosophical factors, discrepancies in how diagnostic criteria are defined, and organization. For instance, Kupfer and colleagues (2002) cite multiple deficiencies such as incompatibility between the two classification systems, the DSM's lack of cultural sensitivity, increased use of these systems in nonpsychiatric settings, and inconsistent empirical support for the included diagnoses. The classification systems are best described as evolving entities, in that proposed revisions that correspond to recent empirical research findings are almost constantly reviewed and incorporated. As these two classification systems continue to evolve, there is a movement toward more overlap in content, with the ultimate goal of integrating the two into one classification system. Given this goal for the future, it behooves school psychologists to be trained in both systems. Although the DSM-5 and ICD-10 have generally similar functions and overlapping priorities for classification, significant differences do exist. This is due in part to the fact that the DSM-5 was recently published while the ICD-10 has been available since the 1990s (ICD-11 will be available in 2015). Table 22.1 provides a brief presentation of similarities and differences between the DSM and ICD classification systems. (See First and Westen, 2007, for a more in-depth comparison of these two systems.)

BASIC CONSIDERATIONS

NASP states that school psychologists "provide direct educational and mental health services for children and youth" (NASP, 2010, p. 1) and addresses the delivery of mental health services in schools within the NASP Practice Model (NASP, 2010). Specifically, school psychologists engage in a broad range of practices (e.g., assessment, intervention, consultation, and counseling or other mental health interventions) to meet the mental health needs of youth at the individual, classroom, and school-wide levels. For example, school-wide interventions such as bullying prevention programming can be implemented to reduce bullying and improve overall school climate. Additionally, school psychologists play a key role in the process of determining educational classifications and identifying students for special education

services. This might include involvement in the evaluation of student response to interventions (e.g., through the response-to-intervention process) prior to assessment and conducting of multifactored assessments to determine eligibility for services under the 2004 Individuals with Disabilities Education Act (IDEA). School psychologists are also often involved in the development and implementation of social–emotional and behavioral interventions through the Individualized Education Program (IEP) process (e.g., individual counseling, social skills groups). Within this role, it is critical that school psychologists understand mental health issues, including criteria for diagnosis, relevant background information (e.g., etiology, associated features, cultural differences), and appropriate and empirically based interventions.

Given the scope and practice of school psychologists, the DSM and the ICD, while perhaps not primary diagnostic tools in school settings, are certainly valuable in helping school psychologists engage in best practices regarding assessing, identifying, classifying, and addressing mental health and related issues that have an impact on learning. Specifically, understanding the diagnostic criteria for child and adolescent mental health disorders helps guide data-based decision making in forming an appropriate assessment battery, assisting with determination of qualification for services under IDEA, and providing useful information for selecting appropriate and effective interventions. While criteria for educational classifications differ from those that determine

Table 22.1. Similarities and Differences Between the DSM-5 and ICD-10

DSM-5	ICD-10
• Developed by the American Psychiatric Association • Used by mental health practitioners	• Developed by the World Health Organization • Used by physicians and medical professionals, as well as mental health practitioners
• Primarily for use in the United States • A classification system specifically for mental health disorders	• International system of classification • Broader than the DSM; includes a wide range of morbidities and mortalities that are not limited to mental health diagnoses
• Mental illness is defined and explained in detail • Differences in criteria or duration or symptoms necessary for diagnosis • One manual	• Disorder is briefly and vaguely defined • Differences in criteria or duration or symptoms necessary for diagnosis • Multiple manuals (e.g., *Diagnostic Criteria for Research*, *Clinical Descriptions and Diagnostic Guidelines*)
• Disorders with typical child onset are dispersed throughout manual	• Specific section named, "Behavioural and Emotional Disorders With Onset Usually Occurring in Child and Adolescence"
• Takes into account impact of symptoms on social functioning • Supported by research and empirical studies • Not used for insurance reimbursement; codes bridged to ICD codes	• Does not emphasize social impairment • Supported by research and empirical studies • Codes used for insurance reimbursement

mental health diagnoses, there is some overlap and familiarity with diagnostic criteria that provides a broader understanding of child and adolescent mental health issues.

BEST PRACTICES IN THE USE OF THE DSM-5 AND ICD-10 BY SCHOOL PSYCHOLOGISTS

While most school psychologists working in school settings may not routinely provide DSM or ICD diagnostic codes for youth, having a thorough understanding of these classification systems is important for several reasons. School psychologists often work with youth who present with mental health symptoms that suggest the need for an outside evaluation. Thus, understanding the DSM and ICD will aid in effective referrals and will enhance effective communication with other professionals. Additionally, diagnostic criteria differ from educational classification requirements that must be met for a student to qualify for services under IDEA. It is important that school psychologists are familiar with the DSM and ICD criteria used to diagnose child and adolescent mental health issues that might also qualify under IDEA. Finally, school psychologists' knowledge of the DSM and ICD criteria guide appropriate decisions with regard to evidence-based assessment, school accommodations, and interventions for students who are diagnosed with mental health disorders.

Understanding the DSM and ICD: A Common Nomenclature

Understanding the DSM and ICD classification systems and the similarities and differences between diagnostic criteria and educational classification guidelines under IDEA is useful for making appropriate referrals and engaging in consultation with outside mental health professionals. In fact, the chair of the DSM-5 task force, David Kupfer, notes that the goal of the DSM is to provide a common language among clinicians and patients and that, despite shortcomings, the DSM-5 remains the best system available for providing coordinated patient care (Kupfer, 2013).

Mental health professionals outside of the school setting have expertise in the DSM and ICD. However, they are not often well versed in how diagnoses have an impact on learning and social and academic functioning in the school setting. This can lead to recommendations that are inappropriate or unrealistic. A common example of this occurrence is when a non–school mental health professional recommends or implies that a child qualifies for special education services as a result of his or her diagnosis. This recommendation is problematic for a variety of reasons, most notably because it may provide a family with potentially false information and create unnecessary tension between the family and the school if the child does not qualify, as indicated in the mental health report. When school psychologists are well versed in the DSM and ICD, they can interpret reports from outside mental health professionals and help families understand how this translates (or not) to educational services within the schools.

This situation can be examined through the case of Sally, whose parents bring an outside mental health evaluation report to a multidisciplinary team meeting and request that their daughter receive special education services. Sally has been diagnosed with Bipolar I Disorder, Severe, by a psychiatrist in the community. A school psychologist who is well versed in the DSM and ICD would be able to interpret and coordinate the information from the mental health evaluation with educational classification criteria. The school psychologist can help the family understand how this student might qualify for special education services through IDEA because he or she has knowledge about the symptoms of biplor disorder and an understanding of what the severity level means. In this case, the school psychologist can explain to Sally's teachers how to recognize specific signs associated with manic and/or major depressive episodes.

School psychologists are often confronted with the challenge of informing families that, despite their child being diagnosed with a mental health disorder, their child does not qualify for special education services. This dilemma stresses the importance of school psychologists engaging in proactive, preventative collaboration with outside mental health professionals to prevent these potential conflicts. School psychologists can play a role in familiarizing outside mental health professionals with the similarities and differences between IDEA and the DSM and ICD classification systems. For example, school psychologists often receive reports from the local community mental health centers and different private practice offices. Many times these reports conclude with a diagnosis and recommendations for educational services. Unfortunately, there is often not enough information included in the report about the educational impact of the diagnosis for the child, which can create a challenge with using the report to determine possible qualification. Additionally, the recommendations are not always feasible to implement in the school setting. Because school psychologists realize this is a recurring issue that negatively affects families, corrective action can be taken.

With their background in psychology and education, school psychologists have expertise in understanding mental health within the educational setting. Specifically, school psychologists can recognize the impact of various mental health issues on social and academic functioning. School psychologists are encouraged to consult with mental health professionals in their local communities to collaboratively identify what information should be included in reports to increase their utility for special education determination. In cases similar to Sally's, school psychologists may refer to input provided by community mental health professionals to create an explanatory packet of information that can be given to the community mental health centers and various private practice offices in the area. In addition to contact information for the school psychologist, this packet may include specific information about IDEA and the various educational classifications, and it may provide examples of where common child and adolescent mental health disorders might be classified under IDEA (e.g., ADHD might qualify under Other Health Impaired [OHI]). Further, school psychologists could provide suggestions as to how the impact of mental health functioning on educational performance can be discussed within the report. Last, school psychologists can provide examples of the types of data that can be gathered in the school (e.g., observations, teacher reports, progress monitoring data) to help determine the level of educational impact and make recommendations. Sally's example illustrates how school psychologists can use knowledge of the DSM and ICD to communicate with mental health professionals about the concordance and discordance between diagnostic considerations and educational classifications. Collaborating with outside mental health professionals is necessary so that information provided in their reports is able to be applied within the school setting.

Navigating the DSM, ICD, and IDEA

As indicated above, it can be challenging to navigate the differences between diagnoses (DSM and ICD) and educational classifications (IDEA). Despite this challenge, it is critical that school psychologists be familiar with the language of the DSM and ICD classification systems and how it relates to IDEA's educational classifications. An illustration of the differences in determination based upon each of these systems is presented in Table 22.2. Specifically, the table presents the IDEA criteria for OHI, the DSM-5 diagnostic criteria for ADHD, and the ICD-10 diagnostic criteria for hyperkinetic disorder.

A positive development reflected in the DSM-5 revision is the emphasis on defining the functional impact of the disability. Specifically, severity levels are indicated, which can be very helpful in communicating to school psychologists the extent to which the disorder has an impact on a student's educational or social functioning. Diagnoses now include diagnostic specifiers (e.g., hypoactivity or hyperactivity), subtypes (e.g., combined presentation, predominantly inattentive presentation), and severity (e.g., mild, moderate, severe) across many diagnoses. This allows for more in-depth information about individual presentation of a disorder. Additionally, these specifications will support school psychologists in making eligibility determinations, most notably with relation to diagnoses that have been collapsed or integrated into one disorder or for disorders that have broader criteria. For example, autism spectrum disorder now encompasses multiple other disorders, eliminating the diagnoses of Asperger's, Rett's disorder, and pervasive developmental disorder NOS. Therefore, school psychologists need to rely on specifiers and severity level when determining special education eligibility status (Grant & Nozyce, 2013).

Learning disabilities are an area of educational classification that often creates challenges when individuals receive an outside diagnosis of a learning disorder but do not meet eligibility criteria for IDEA. In these situations it is critical that school psychologists be able to effectively communicate to families why their child might not qualify and, more important, provide specific recommendations for the child given the symptoms they present with that warranted diagnosis (see Table 22.3 for a comparison of DSM-5, ICD-10, and IDEA criteria for learning disabilities). Recent studies suggest that approximately 5% of youth in schools have a learning disability classification (National Center for Learning Disabilities, 2009), which is based on the current definition under IDEA. The changes to diagnostic criteria for a Specific Learning Disorder in the DSM-5 are more aligned with the IDEA definition by considering student response to evidence-based intervention (Al-Yagon et al., 2013) and by emphasizing academic performance as a decisive factor (Scanlon, 2013) in determining a diagnosis of Specific Learning Disorder. Specifically, with regard to response to intervention, the DSM-5 Diagnostic Criterion A for Specific Learning Disorder states: "Difficulties learning and using academic skills, as indicated by the presence of at least one of the following symptoms that have persisted for at least 6 months, *despite the provision of interventions that target those difficulties*" (APA, 2013, p. 66, emphasis added). To illustrate the importance of school data, there is a note added at the end of the criterion that states, "The four diagnostic criteria are to be met based on a clinical synthesis of the individual's history (developmental, medical, family, educational), school reports, and psychoeducational assessment" (APA, 2013, p. 67). Colker, Shaywitz, Shaywitz, and Simon (2012) provide a detailed review of the changes to Specific Learning Disability criteria in the DSM-5, along with their legal and scientific implications.

The changes to the diagnostic criteria in the DSM-5 emphasize the importance of gathering data from the educational setting in making this diagnosis and attempting to merge IDEA guidelines and DSM criteria. Just as outside mental health professionals can provide school psychologists with crucial information about a student's functioning, school psychologists are in a position to offer outside mental health professionals information related to the impact of mental health issues on an individual's social and academic performance. Specifically, school psychologists could assist with gathering data to aid in appropriate diagnosis and specificity related to the impact on social and educational functioning. For example, school psychologists

Table 22.2. Comparing Diagnostic Criteria Across IDEA for Other Health Impairment, the DSM-5 for Attention Deficit Hyperactivity Disorder, and the ICD-10 for Hyperkinetic Disorder

IDEA: Other Health Impairment	DSM-5: Attention Deficit Hyperactivity Disorder	ICD-10: Hyperkinetic Disorder
(9) Other health impairment means having limited strength, vitality, or alertness, including a heightened alertness to environmental stimuli, that results in limited alertness with respect to the educational environment, that— (i) Is due to chronic or acute health problems such as asthma, attention deficit disorder or attention deficit hyperactivity disorder, diabetes, epilepsy, a heart condition, hemophilia, lead poisoning, leukemia, nephritis, rheumatic fever, sickle cell anemia, and Tourette syndrome; and (ii) Adversely affects a child's educational performance. (20 U.S.C. 1401(3); 1401(30), p. 13)	A. "A persistent pattern of inattention and/or hyperactivity-impulsivity that interferes with functioning or development, as characterized by (1) and/or (2) Inattention: Six (or more) symptoms have persisted for at least 6 months to a degree that is inconsistent with developmental level and that negatively impacts directly on social and academic/occupational activities: Note: Not due to oppositional behavior, hostility, defiance, or failure to understand instructions. For older adolescents and adults (ages 17 and older), at least five symptoms are required" (p. 59). a. Often fails to give close attention to details or makes careless mistakes. b. Often has difficulty sustaining attention in tasks or play activities. c. Often does not seem to listen when spoken to directly. d. Often does not follow through on instructions and fails to finish schoolwork, chores, or duties in the workplace. e. Often has difficulty organizing tasks and activities. f. Often avoids, dislikes, or is reluctant to engage in tasks that require sustained mental effort. g. Often loses things necessary for tasks or activities. h. Is often easily distracted by extraneous stimuli. i. Is often forgetful in daily activities.	G1. *Inattention.* At least six of the following symptoms of inattention have persisted for at least 6 months, to a degree that is maladaptive and inconsistent with the developmental level of the child: (1) often fails to give close attention to details, or makes careless errors in schoolwork, work, or other activities; (2) often fails to sustain attention in tasks or play activities; (3) often appears not to listen to what is being said to him or her; (4) often fails to follow through on instructions or to finish schoolwork, chores, or duties in the workplace (not because of oppositional behaviour or failure to understand instructions); (5) is often impaired in organizing taks and activities; (6) often avoids or strongly dislikes tasks, such as homework, that require sustained mental effort; (7) often loses things necessary for certain tasks or activities, such as school assignments, pencils, books, toys, or tools; (8) is often easily distracted by external stimuli; (9) is often forgetful in the course of daily activities.

Continued

Table 22.2. Continued

IDEA: Other Health Impairment	DSM-5: Attention Deficit Hyperactivity Disorder	ICD-10: Hyperkinetic Disorder

	2. "Hyperactivity and impulsivity: Six (or more) of the following symptoms have persisted for at least 6 months to a degree that is inconsistent with developmental level and that negatively impacts directly on social and academic/occupational activities:
	
	Note: The symptoms are not solely due to a manifestation of oppositional behavior, defiance, hostility, or a failure to understand tasks or instructions. For older adolescents and adults (age 17 and older), at least five symptoms are required" (p. 60)
	  a. Often fidgets with or taps hands or feet or squirms in seat.
	  b. Often leaves seat in situations when remaining seated is expected.
	  c. Often runs about or climbs in situations where inappropriate (may be restlessness in adults).
	  d. Often unable to play or engage in leisure activities quietly.
	  e. Often acts as if "on the go" or "driven by a motor."
	  f. Often talks excessively.
	  g. Often blurts out answer before a question has been completed.
	  h. Often has difficulty waiting his or her turn.
	  i. Often interrupts or intrudes on others.
	
	B. "Several inattention or hyperactive-impulsive symptoms were present prior to age 12 years.
	
	C. Several inattention or hyperactive-impulsive symptoms are present in two or more settings …
	
	D. There is clear evidence that the symptoms interfere with, or reduce the quality of, social, academic, or occupational functioning.
	
	E. The symptoms do not occur exclusively during the course of schizophrenia or another psychotic disorder and are not better explained by another mental disorder …" (p. 60).
		G2. *Hyperactivity.* At least three of the following symptoms of hyperactivity have persisted for at least 6 months, to a degree that is maladaptive and inconsistent with the developmental level of the child:
		  (1) often fidgets with hands or feet or squirms on seat;
		  (2) leaves seat in classroom or in other situations in which remaining seated is expected;
		  (3) often runs about or climbs excessively in situations in which it is inappropriate (in adolescents or adults, only feelings of restlessness may be present);
		  (4) is often unduly noisy in playing or has difficulty in engaging quietly in leisure activites;
		  (5) exhibits a persistent pattern of excessive motor activity that is not substantially modified by social context or demands.
		
		G3. *Impulsivity.* At least one of the following symptoms of impulsivity has persisted for at least 6 months, to a degree that is maladaptive and inconsistent with the developmental level of the child:
		  (1) often blurts out answers before questions have been completed;
		  (2) often fails to wait in lines or await turns in games or group situations;
		  (3) often interrupts or intrudes on others (e.g., butts into others' conversations or games);
		  (4) often talks excessively without appropriate response to social constraints.
		
		G4. Onset of the disorder is no later than the age of 7 years.
		
		G5. *Pervasiveness.* The criteria should be met for more than a single situation, e.g., the combination of inattention and hyperactivity should be present both at home and at school, or both school and another setting where children are observed, such as a clinic. (Evidence for cross-situationality will ordinarily require information from more than one source; parental reports about classroom behavior, for instance, are unlikely to be sufficient.)
		
		G6. The symptoms in G1–G3 cause clinically significant distress or impairment in social, academic, or occupational functioning.
		
		G7. The disorder does not meet the criteria for pervasive developmental disorders (F84.-), manic episode (F30.-), depressive episode (F32.-), or anxiety disorders (F41.-). (WHO, 1992, pp. 155–156)

Note. Some of the criteria described above (particularly lengthy descriptions of symptoms from the DSM-5 criteria) were summarized to conserve space. See APA (2012) and WHO (1992).

National Association of School Psychologists

Table 22.3. Comparing Diagnostic Criteria Across IDEA for Specific Learning Disability, the ICD-10 for Specific Developmental Disorder of Scholastic Skills, and the DSM-5 for Specific Learning Disorder

IDEA: Specific Learning Disability	DSM-5: Specific Learning Disorder	ICD-10: Specific Developmental Disorder of Scholastic Skills
"(A) IN GENERAL. – The term 'specific learning disability' means a disorder in 1 or more of the basic psychological processes involved in understanding or in using language, spoken or written, which disorder may manifest itself in the imperfect ability to listen, think, speak, read, write, spell, or do mathematical calculations. (B) DISORDERS INCLUDED – Such term includes such conditions as perceptual disabilities, brain injury, minimal brain dysfunction, dyslexia, and developmental aphasia. (C) DISORDERS NOT INCLUDED – Such term does not include a learning problem that is primarily the result of visual, hearing, or motor disabilities, of mental retardation, of emotional disturbance, or of environmental, cultural, or economic disadvantage" (20 U.S.C. §1401 [30], p. 2657–2658). Summary of criteria: • Elimination of the requirement for a "severe discrepancy" between intellectual ability (IQ) and achievement • Schools must use a "systematic process" to see if a child is responding to an evidence-based intervention (e.g., RTI) in the general classroom • Schools may also use alternative research-based procedures (20 U.S.C. §1401 [30], p. 2706).	A. "Difficulties learning and using academic skills, as indicated by the presence of at least one of the following symptoms that have persisted for at least 6 months, despite the provision of interventions that target those difficulties" (p. 66). • Inaccurate or slow and effortful word reading • Difficulty understanding the meaning of what is read • Difficulties with spelling • Difficulties with written expression • Difficulties mastering number sense, facts, or calculation • Difficulties with mathematical reasoning B. Skill is "substantially and quantifiably below those expected for ... age, and cause significant interference with academic or occupational performance, ... daily living, as confirmed by ... achievement measures and comprehensive clinical assessment. For individuals age 17 and older, a documented history of impairing learning difficulties may be substituted ..." (p. 67). C. Learning difficulties begin during school-age years, may not manifest until demands exceed limited capacities. D. Not better accounted for by intellectual disabilities, uncorrected visual or auditory acuity, other mental or neurological disorder, psychosocial adversity, lack of proficiency in the language of instruction, or inadequate educational instruction. "The four diagnostic criteria are to be met based on a clinical synthesis of the individual's history (developmental, medical, family, educational), school reports, and psychoeducational assessment" (p. 67). *Specifiers:* with impairment in reading, written expression, or mathematics *Severity:* mild, moderate, severe	Diagnostic guidelines: "... First, there must be a clinically significant degree of impairment in the specified scholastic skill ... judged on the basis of severity as defined in scholastic terms (i.e., a degree that may be expected to occur in less than 3% of schoolchildren); on developmental precursors (i.e., the scholastic difficulties were preceded by developmental delays or deviance—most often in speech or language—in the preschool years); on associated problems (such as inattention, overactivity, emotional disturbance, or conduct difficulties); on pattern (i.e., the presence of qualitative abnormalities that are not usually part of normal development); and on response (i.e., the scholastic difficulties do not rapidly and readily remit with increased help at home and/or at school). Second, the impairment must be specific in the sense that it is not solely explained by mental retardation or by lesser impairments in general intelligence ... this distinction can be made only on the basis of individually administered standardized tests of achievement and IQ that are appropriate for the relevant culture and educational system. Such tests should be used in connection with statistical tables that provide data on the average expected level of achievement for any given IQ level at any given chronological age ... the clinical guideline is simply that the child's level of attainment must be very substantially below that expected for a child of the same mental age. Third, the impairment must be developmental, in the sense that it must have been present during the early years of schooling and not acquired later in the educational process. The history of the child's school progress should provide evidence on this point. Fourth, there must be no external factors that could provide a sufficient reason for the scholastic difficulties ... children must have adequate learning opportunities. Accordingly, if it is clear that the poor scholastic achievement is directly due to very prolonged school absence without teaching at home or to grossly inadequate education, the disorders should not be coded here ... Fifth, the SDDSS must not be directly due to uncorrected visual or hearing impairments" (WHO, 1992, pp. 243–245).

Note. See APA (2012) and WHO (1992).

can engage in observations to learn more about how a student is functioniong in the classroom and determine what environmental factors, if any, relate to the observed behaviors.

How Diagnoses Fit Into Educational Classifications

School psychologists are in a position to play a leadership role in helping principals, teachers, other school staff, and families understand children who have various DSM or ICD diagnoses. In helping school administrators, teachers, and other school staff understand mental health issues, school psychologists could provide inservice training that targets the more common mental health issues seen in their district. Training could illustrate the diagnostic criteria and delineate similarities and differences between diagnoses and IDEA criteria for services, offer handouts with tips on what to look for and when to refer, and give information about general classroom management techniques that can be helpful in addressing a specific issue (i.e., ADHD). School psychologists might also provide guidance as to how to support youth who have diagnoses that have an impact on learning but do not qualify for special education. Another way that school psychologists could help to provide awareness about mental issues is by creating a friendly note from the school psychologist for teachers that includes general signs and symptoms of a specific mental health issue (e.g., obsessive–compulsive disorder), associated features that an individual might experience (e.g., low self-esteem, frustration), referral sources (e.g., school psychologist), and helpful accommodations that could easily be implemented in the classroom.

Another consideration is that the diagnostic label might not be consistent with the educational classification. For example, students may be verified for services under OHI or emotional disturbance, while their formal DSM-5 diagnosis may actually be ADHD or disruptive mood dysregulation disorder, respectively. School psychologists are better able to determine the appropriate educational classification when they understand the diagnostic criteria of the mental health issues that a child presents with. An example is the classification of emotional disturbance (also referred to as serious emotional disturbance or emotional and behavioral disturbance). Various mental health diagnoses (e.g., anxiety, depression) could allow a student to qualify for specialized services under the Emotional Disturbance classification if the mental health issue has an adverse impact on the child's educational performance.

Knowledge of the diagnostic criteria and the student's particular symptomatology could aid in determining identification as emotional disturbance and qualification for services under IDEA. School psychologists who use the DSM as a tool and are knowledgeable about diagnostic criteria can use this knowledge to guide more comprehensive assessment. Also, they are better positioned to interpret and integrate outside clinical reports into their comprehensive evaluation of students.

When Mental Health Diagnoses Do Not Result in Educational Classification

Many students receive outside evaluations or psychological treatment from providers in the community who rely on classification systems to describe diagnostic findings. Familiarity with the DSM and ICD is critical because educational classification and diagnostic criteria are not the same. A gap exists between mental health diagnosis and disability qualification through IDEA. Historically, the educational impact has not been a criterion that was strongly emphasized in the DSM in the same way that it is under IDEA regulations. Consequently, youth may be diagnosed by a community psychologist or mental health practitioner, but may not meet eligibility criteria for school intervention if their disability does not have a significant impact on their education. Especially at risk for not receiving services are youth diagnosed with internalizing disorders (i.e., depression and/or anxiety). These students often fly under the radar if they are well behaved and perform well academically. However, these students may be eligible to receive accommodations if their mood has a negative and significant impact on their functioning at school. In order to most effectively serve youth and their families, it is paramount that school psychologists understand the similarities and differences between DSM and ICD classification systems and IDEA.

As an example of mental health diagnoses that often do not meet educational classification, following is the case of Johnny. Johnny, an 8-year-old Caucasian male, is referred by his pediatrician to an outpatient clinic for an ADHD evaluation. Based on the results of a thorough evaluation, including parent, teacher, and self-rating forms, and careful consideration of DSM-5 diagnostic criteria, Johnny is diagnosed with ADHD, Combined Presentation, by a licensed psychologist. Johnny's symptoms are reportedly interfering with his social functioning (specifically, interactions with peers at school) and family relationships. During the feedback meeting, Johnny's psychologist recommended that

Johnny's parents pursue special education services for Johnny under the OHI verification. Johnny's parents convene a meeting with school personnel, who determine that Johnny does not qualify for special education services under IDEA since his grades are satisfactory (i.e., his educational performance is not deemed to be negatively affected). This decision leaves Johnny's parents feeling frustrated since they believe Johnny's inattentive and hyperactive/impulsive behaviors are not allowing him to reach his full academic or social potential at school.

At the suggestion of the psychologist, Johnny's parents request that Johnny be evaluated for a Section 504 Plan. Although school districts are not required to conduct an evaluation following solely the request of a parent, the administration and Johnny's teacher agree that Johnny's behavior appears to be interfering with his major life activities. A team meeting is held with Johnny's teacher, parents, and the school psychologist. Prior to this meeting, the school psychologist conducts a structured observation of Johnny's behavior in the classroom. At the meeting, the school psychologist interprets the outside evaluation report and DSM diagnosis, explains that the severity rating is "moderate" for Johnny's symptoms, and reviews the recommendations provided by Johnny's community psychologist. This information is reviewed in conjunction with other behavioral and academic evidence (i.e., results of a structured behavioral observation, Johnny's grades) that describes Johnny's functioning at school. It is decided that Johnny qualifies for services under the 504 Plan, and several accommodations are implemented (e.g., positive behavioral intervention strategies and extended time on tests). Throughout the school year, the school psychologist continues to consult with Johnny's teacher to monitor his grades and peer relationships, and to adjust interventions as needed.

This case example highlights the importance of the inclusion of dimensional indicators of severity in the DSM-5. The current DSM includes categorical classifications *with* a dimensional approach to psychopathology (First & Westen, 2007; Regier et al., 2009). Incorporating dimensional measures within the current DSM and ICD communicates information about impairment and impact on day-to-day functioning. Also, many youth experience subthreshold symptomatology, but do not meet formal criteria for a diagnosis when the minimum number of symptoms or functional impairment requirements are not met. This outcome would be similar to issues in educational classification in which individuals do not quite meet criteria to qualify for services, but clearly struggle academically. Therefore, dimensional components provide an indication of the severity of symptoms, possible targets for treatment, and an overall picture of functioning, which makes it easier to determine if treatment gains are being made (First & Westen, 2007; Kupfer et al., 2002).

Brian's case is an example. Brian is a 13-year-old African American male in the sixth grade who displays behavioral problems at home and, more recently, similar behaviors have been observed at school. The school psychologist notified Brian's family that the school wanted to proceed with a psychoeducational evaluation to evaluate the cause of the academic concerns. Brian's parents reported that they had recently met with Brian's pediatrician to discuss concerns at home and at school. They indicated to the school psychologist that the pediatrician had diagnosed Brian with ADHD and placed him on medication. What follows is a summary of the appointment.

Brian's parents had an appointment with the pediatrician three days earlier. At the appointment Brian's parents discussed his current behavioral problems that were occurring both at home and at school. The pediatrician asked the parents to complete a brief checklist. Specific behaviors they noted at home included: is constantly out of his seat (at the dinner table), has difficulty playing quietly, is often restless or fidgety (e.g., they cannot take him to restaurants because he will not sit still, he cannot sit through a movie), constantly interrupts others even when he is reminded not to interrupt, talks excessively, and has difficulty waiting in line (the parents noted a dislike for taking Brian to amusement parks because the lines are often long and Brian has difficulty waiting and becomes easily frustrated). They stated that his current teachers were reporting that Brian talks during independent work time, has difficulty staying in his seat, has become more fidgety than usual, seems easily distracted, and has started turning in incomplete homework and losing his classwork. The pediatrician also observed that Brian frequently interrupted, constantly moved about his office, seemed fidgety, and was very distractible.

The pediatrician was aware that there is a family history of ADHD (i.e., Brian's paternal aunt has a diagnosis of ADHD, Combined Presentation, and his paternal grandfather has symptoms of ADHD but has never been formally diagnosed). The pediatrician consulted with the family and determined a diagnosis of ADHD, Predominantly Hyperactive/Impulsive Presentation, as the cause for the presenting behaviors.

The pediatrician prescribed Adderall. The pediatrician told the family that he would check in with them at the end of the week to follow up and determine if changes needed to be made to the prescription. His parents started the medication on the following day.

In this case illustration, the school psychologist can use knowledge of the DSM/ICD criteria for ADHD to help build an assessment battery that will evaluate and monitor the symptoms of ADHD in addition to cognitive ability and academic performance. Further, the school psychologist will gather data from multiple sources (e.g., child, parents, and teacher). The school psychologist's expertise will help assess the educational impact of the symptoms that are occurring at home and in school. Additionally, the school psychologist could engage in progress monitoring to determine the effectiveness of the medication at reducing observed behaviors at school. The data gathered by the school psychologist would add to the pediatrician's information and lead to a more accurate assessment as to the underlying cause of Brian's behavior. Specifically, the school psychologist can engage in best practices by using multiple methods of assessment (e.g., cognitive, achievement, social–emotional and behavioral ratings, observations, and gathering background data). Comprehensive assessment in this case is particularly important due to the high comorbidity of ADHD and learning disabilities (DuPaul, Gormley, & Laracy, 2013).

The breadth of assessment procedures allows for multiple possibilities for outcomes. It could reveal a cognitive delay or academic difficulties that explain Brian's behavior more accurately than hyperactivity or implulsivity. A second possibility is that Brian's symptoms fit a diagnosis of oppositional defiant disorder instead of or in addition to ADHD. If grades, achievement test scores, and work samples indicate that Brian's academic performance is in fact affected by his symptoms, he would likely qualify for special education services, and an appropriate verification category would be determined. In general, the role of the school psychologist is to ensure that comprehensive, evidence-based approaches to assessment are used that align with diagnostic criteria, that effective interventions are implemented, and that interventions are monitored over time to ensure that Brian responds to them.

Using DSM/ICD Diagnoses to Inform Recommendations and Intervention Selection

Having a working knowledge of how these systems function and what the diagnostic codes mean allows school psychologists to use the information to improve interventions through consultation with other mental health and medical professionals. School psychologists are often involved in various levels of mental health promotion and intervention. Specifically, school psychologists practice across all three tiers of service delivery that fit within a problem-solving framework. For example, understanding of the DSM-5 and ICD-10 can facilitate the selection of assessments to screen for mental health issues school-wide (Tier 1) or to screen a targeted group of students (Tier 2) as a preventive measure. School psychologists could also use knowledge learned from these classification systems to develop a more effective assessment battery and treatment/ intervention plan for a student who is referred for evaluation due to mental health concerns (Tier 3). Data-based decision making is a key component of school psychological practice. Therefore, understanding the diagnostic criteria, etiology, and other features of mental health issues is of paramount importance to effectively engage in problem solving to address student mental health needs.

In addition to assessment and evaluation, DSM-5 and ICD diagnostic criteria can aid school psychologists in making appropriate recommendations for goals in the IEPs or 504 Plans. A diagnosis provides school psychologists with general information as to the symptom profile of the child, which can be used to support decisions about appropriate interventions. For instance, outside (i.e., community) psychological evaluations that result in a diagnosis often are summarized in a comprehensive report that provides recommendations. These reports can be shared by parents with school professionals, at which point the school psychologist can help implement the outlined recommendations and include such recommendations as accommodations in a student's 504 Plan, IEP, or less formal individual intervention plans.

Students may receive interventions outside of school that have an impact on school performance. With advancements in child psychiatry, many students diagnosed with behavior or mood disorders are prescribed medication to help manage their symptoms. If a student is receiving medication, then school psychologists can conduct behavioral assessments and, with permission from parents, share the results with the prescribing physician. For instance, the school psychologist may utilize a progress monitoring device to monitor the effectiveness of the medication as well as its side effects. This practice is especially important since many medications wear off by the time the school day ends, so parent reports may not provide accurate depictions of the child's reaction to the medication.

School Psychologists in Private Practice

Additionally, some school psychologists are also licensed by state boards of psychology or other state boards for licensure for practice outside of school settings. In order for a school psychologist to provide services outside of a school setting *and* receive third-party reimbursement, he or she must use the DSM-5 or ICD classification systems. The ICD-9-CM codes, not the DSM-IV-TR codes, are used for billing purposes by psychologists throughout the country, even though the DSM diagnoses may be referred to more frequently (Reed, 2010). Most companies have switched to the ICD-10 codes. Additionally, intellectual and cognitive testing can be reimbursed under ICD codes. Having this knowledge will open up additional potential practice opportunities for school psychologists outside of the school setting who have the appropriate credentials and training. Pragmatically, in order to receive third-party reimbursement, licensed practitioners must understand and use the DSM-5 and/or the ICD codes. Although many school psychologists may not use the DSM-5 and ICD classification systems in their work with students and their families in day-to-day practice in schools, the stated goal of the DSM, which is to facilitate communication and a common nomenclature surrounding diagnosis among professionals and their clients, still holds for school psychologists. School psychologists need to be at the forefront of school-based mental health services, and having an understanding and working knowledge of the DSM-5 and ICD classification systems is important, particularly in coordinating mental health treatment across professionals, including pediatricians, psychiatrists, and psychologists.

SUMMARY

The DSM-5 and the ICD-10 are distinct yet similar classification systems for identifying mental health disorders. The differences between the two classification systems range from subtle differences in diagnostic criteria to more obvious differences relating to their purposes for clinical and pragmatic use. Most hospital and insurance billing mechanisms use the ICD system, and most psychiatric practitioners and insurance providers use the DSM system. Despite these pragmatic differences, their noteworthy similarities lay the groundwork for the future goal of aligning the two systems.

ICD revisions are under way, and the goal is to align these revisions with the DSM-5. Current revisions focus on incorporating dimensional as well as categorical symptom profiles in both systems. It is evident that some of these changes will require a philosophical shift in approaching the diagnosis of mental disorders, which will ultimately advance the educational, research, and clinical utility of both the DSM and ICD classification systems.

The controversy between the two systems should be seen as part of systematic progress toward science informing diagnostic practice. School psychologists must be a part of this conversation in order to highlight the importance of understanding developmental processes in mental health functioning for youth. Thus, understanding the DSM and ICD classification systems is vital for school psychologists' involvement with and ability to communicate with other mental health professionals and their ability to be part of the functional utility of these classification systems for youth and their caregivers.

AUTHOR NOTE

The authors would like to thank Scott Napolitano for his helpful edits regarding the use of classification systems for third-party reimbursement.

REFERENCES

Al-Yagon, M., Cavendish, W., Cornoldi, C., Fawcett, A. J., Grünke, M., Hung, L., … Vio, C. (2013). The proposed changes for DSM-5 for SLD and ADHD: International perspectives: Australia, Germany, Greece, India, Israel, Italy, Spain, Taiwan, United Kingdom, and United States. *Journal of Learning Disabilities, 46,* 58–72. doi:10.1177/0022219412464353

American Psychiatric Association. (2000). *Diagnostic and statistical manual of mental disorders* (4th ed., text rev.). Arlington, VA: Author.

American Psychiatric Association. (2012, December 1). *American Psychiatric Association board of trustees approves DSM-5: Diagnostic manual passes major milestone before May 2013 publication* [Press release]. Retrieved from http://www.psychiatry.org

American Psychiatric Association. (2013). *Diagnostic and statistical manual of mental disorders* (5th ed.). Arlington, VA: Author.

Colker, R., Shaywitz, S., Shaywitz, B., & Simon, J. A. (2012). *Comments on proposed DSM-5 criteria for specific learning disorder from a legal and medical/scientific perspective.* Retrieved from http://dyslexia.yale.edu/CommentsDSM5ColkerShaywitzSimon.pdf

DuPaul, G. J., Gormley, M. J., & Laracy, S. D. (2013). Comorbidity of LD and ADHD: Implications of DSM-5 for assessment and treatment. *Journal of Learning Disabilities, 46,* 43–51. doi:10.1177/0022219412464351

First, M. B., & Westen, D. (2007). Classification for clinical practice: How to make ICD and DSM better able to serve clinicians.

International Review of Psychiatry, *19*, 473–481. doi:10.1080/09540260701563429

Grant, R., & Nozyce, M. (2013). Proposed changes to the American Psychiatric Association diagnostic criteria for autism spectrum disorder: Implications for young children and their families. *Maternal and Child Health Journal*, *17*, 586–592. doi:10.1007/s10995-013-1250-9

Kraemer, H. C., Shrout, P. E., & Rubio-Stipec, M. (2007). Developing the *Diagnostic and Statistical Manual 5*: What will "statistical" mean in DSM-5? *Social Psychiatry and Psychiatric Epidemiology*, *42*, 259–267. doi:10.1007/s00127-007-0163-6

Kupfer, J. (2013). David Kupfer, MD, responds to NIMH criticism of DSM-5 [Blog post]. Retrieved from http://www.nscmeblog.com/?p=1625

Kupfer, D. J., First, M. B., & Regier, D. A. (2002). *A research agenda for DSM-5*. Arlington, VA: American Psychiatric Association.

Narrow, W. E., First, M. B., Sirovatka, P. J., & Regier, D. A. (2007). *Age and gender considerations in psychiatric diagnosis: A research agenda for DSM-V*. Arlington, VA, American Psychiatric Association.

National Association of School Psychologists. (2010). *Model for comprehensive and integrated school psychological services*. Bethesda, MD: Author. Retrieved from http//:www.nasponline.org/standards/2010standards/2_PracticeModel.pdf

National Center for Learning Disabilities. (2009). *The state of learning disabilities*. New York, NY: Author. Retrieved from http://www.ncld.org/images/stories/OnCapitolHill/PolicyRelatedPublications/stateofld/StateofLD2009-final.pdf

National Institute of Mental Health. (2008). *The National Institute of Mental Health strategic plan*. Rockville, MD: Author. Retrieved from http://www.nimh.nih.gov/about/strategic-planning-reports/index.shtml#strategic-objective1

Reed, G. M. (2010). Toward ICD-11: Improving the clinical utility of WHO's international classification of mental disorders. *Professional Psychology: Research and Practice*, *41*, 457–464. doi:10.1037/a0021701

Regier, D. A. (2007). Dimensional approaches to psychiatric classification: Refining the research agenda for DSM-5: An introduction. *International Journal of Methods in Psychiatric Research*, *16*, S1–S5. doi:10.1002/mpr.209

Regier, D. A., Narrow, W. E., Kuhl, E. A., & Kupfer, D. J. (2009). Conceptual development of DSM-5. *American Journal of Psychiatry*, *166*, 645–650. doi:10.1176/appi.ajp.2009.09020279

Scanlon, D. (2013). Specific learning disability and its newest definition: Which is comprehensive and which is insufficient? *Journal of Learning Disabilities*, *46*, 26–33. doi:10.1177/0022219412464342

World Health Organization. (1992). *ICD-10: International statistical classification of diseases and related health problems*. Geneva, Switzerland: Author.

World Health Organization. (2004). *ICD-10: International statistical classification of diseases and related health problems* (2nd ed.). Geneva, Switzerland: Author.

World Health Organization. (2013). *History of the development of the ICD*. Geneva, Switzerland: Author. Retrieved from http://www.who.int/classifications/icd/en/HistoryOfICD.pdf

23 Best Practices in Pediatric School Psychology

Thomas J. Power
The Children's Hospital of Philadelphia, University of Pennsylvania School of Medicine
Kathy L. Bradley-Klug
University of South Florida

OVERVIEW

Success in school is critical to healthy development. Students who are engaged in school and who experience success academically and socially are likely to become competent, autonomous, and healthy adults. Being successful in school depends on many school factors, including student engagement in strong relationships with teachers, student engagement in developmentally appropriate and challenging curricular activities, and student involvement in mutually affirming peer relationships. In addition, family factors such as strong parent–child attachments and meaningful family involvement in student education are critical in promoting school success. Further, engaging in health-promoting behaviors, such as eating nutritious food, exercising on a regular basis, and getting an appropriate amount of sleep, are important for child development and school success. For children with chronic illnesses, it is important for them to be closely connected with health providers who can coordinate their care and minimize the likelihood that secondary or comorbid conditions will emerge.

Definition

Pediatric school psychology is a subset of child-serving psychology that is focused on promoting children's wellness and managing children's health conditions by coordinating systems of care (school, family, community, and health systems). Pediatric school psychology integrates aspects of school and pediatric psychology but is unique in that it focuses on health issues for the primary purpose of promoting success in school. Pediatric psychology focuses on health promotion and management, but it involves primarily the child, family, and health providers, and the emphasis on school is usually secondary. School psychology prioritizes successful school outcomes, but its focus is primarily on child, school, and family, and the emphasis on health factors historically has been secondary.

Emphasis on Coordination

A problem with service delivery to promote children's health is that care is typically fragmented. Services for the same child may be delivered in multiple systems, but there is little or no attempt to integrate care. For example, primary care practices and schools are major venues for the delivery of services for children with attention deficit hyperactivity disorder (Power, Blum, Guevara, Jones, & Leslie, 2013). However, primary care providers and school professionals typically offer services along a parallel course and there is little if any coordination of care across these systems. As a result, parents are often placed in the untenable position of having to coordinate care on their own, a responsibility for which some parents are not prepared.

The medical home model for primary care was designed in part to address this gap in service coordination for children with chronic health conditions. A medical home is a primary care practice that promotes coordination of services and continuity of care for all individuals, but especially those with chronic health conditions. Although this model generally has been successful in addressing the needs of children with common health conditions such as asthma, concerns have been raised about the adequacy of this approach for addressing behavioral health conditions (Toomey, Finkelstein, & Kuhlthau, 2008). Pediatric school psychology embraces the principles of medical home. It is an approach to promoting children's health that links multiple systems of care, in particular the family, school, and health system, to address a broad range of acute and chronic health conditions, including physical and behavioral health conditions. Further, pediatric school psychology is intrinsically interdisciplinary. It promotes partnerships across disciplines within systems of care (i.e., primary care, tertiary care health systems, schools, mental health centers) and across these systems. Additionally, the emphasis of pediatric school psychology on providing integrated services for children and adolescents in the community through interprofessional partnerships is highly compatible with key tenets of the 2010 Patient Protection and Affordable Care Act.

Emphasis on a Public Health Model

Consistent with the shift in school psychology to service delivery within the context of a public health framework, pediatric school psychology addresses children's health broadly along a continuum of care that includes multiple levels of prevention and intervention. As such, pediatric school psychology incorporates programming for all children. Health promotion and prevention efforts might include nutrition education, violence prevention, and social and emotional learning for all students. In addition, pediatric school psychology focuses on specialized, comprehensive care for children with identified chronic health conditions, such as traumatic brain injury, juvenile rheumatoid arthritis, and sickle cell disease.

Some school psychologists have chosen to become experts in pediatric school psychology. Several training programs have been developed to prepare school psychologists for the leadership skills needed to function in this role. However, the principles of pediatric school psychology can readily be applied by all school psychologists who are committed to promoting school success by addressing the development needs of the whole child.

The purpose of this chapter is to describe the hallmarks of pediatric school psychology and best practices for applying prevention and intervention strategies based on the principles of pediatric school psychology. This chapter focuses on the National Association of School Psychology (NASP) *Model of Comprehensive and Integrated School Psychological Services* (NASP, 2010) domain of Preventive and Responsive

Services. Best practices for promoting the health of all children, as well as those with chronic health conditions, are presented in the context of a multitiered, public health model.

BASIC CONSIDERATIONS

Pediatric school psychology is distinguished by its integration of multiple frameworks and perspectives. What follows are some of the principle hallmarks of pediatric school psychology.

Continuum of Services

Reflecting a strong emphasis on a public health model of care, pediatric school psychology affirms that services should be provided across a broad continuum, including multiple levels of prevention. A prevention framework can be applied to all students in a school, district, or community. Levels of prevention include universal (for all students), selective (for students with emerging risk), and targeted (for students with an identified problem). Also, a prevention framework has been adapted for children with chronic illnesses: Universal strategies are provided to all children with chronic illness regardless of whether the children demonstrate evidence of risk for psychological problems; targeted strategies are for children with evidence of emerging risk; and clinical/treatment strategies are for those with clear signs of functional psychological impairments (Kazak et al., 2007).

Positive Psychology

Historically, professionals in medicine and psychology have been oriented to identify diagnoses and develop strategies to solve problems. A deficit approach fails to acknowledge the wealth of research on protective factors that enable children to avoid risk and to be resilient in the face of risk. Also, a deficit approach does not acknowledge research showing that factors related to risk for emotional and behavioral disorders are relatively independent of protective factors (Suldo & Shaffer, 2008). As such, pediatric school psychology balances a problem solving orientation to intervention with a competence enhancing approach (Power, DuPaul, Shapiro, & Kazak, 2003).

Multisystemic Approach

Consistent with a developmental–ecological model, pediatric school psychology affirms the importance of using multisystemic models of intervention and prevention. The focus of such an approach is to promote child health and development by strengthening families, shaping the classroom and school climate, and building the capacity of health systems (e.g., strengthening primary care to serve as the child's medical home). In addition, a multisystemic approach emphasizes the importance of strengthening connections between systems, such as family–school, school–healthcare, and healthcare–family partnerships (Power & Bradley-Klug, 2013).

Partnership-Based Programming

A major emphasis of pediatric school psychology is to design interventions and develop programs using a partnership model, based on principles of the participatory intervention model (Nastasi, Bernstein Moore, & Varjas, 2004). Fundamental to a participatory model is the establishment of partnerships with key stakeholders (or intervention participants, such as youth, parents, teachers, and health professionals) and the involvement of these participants in all aspects of the program, including development, implementation, evaluation, and redesign. Evidence is emerging that interventions developed and implemented in partnership with key stakeholders may result in higher levels of implementation than programs using an expert model of training and consultation (Kelleher, Riley-Tillman, & Power, 2008).

Interprofessional Collaboration

Interventions for children with complex health conditions typically involve health professionals from multiple disciplines, who may be based in hospital and primary care settings, as well as school professionals from various disciplines. Effective management requires strong interprofessional partnerships within and across systems. In response to this need, the preparation of health professionals has increasingly emphasized competence in establishing and sustaining collaborative interprofessional relationships (Interprofessional Education Collaborative Expert Panel, 2011).

Evidence-Based Practices

Although efficacious prevention programs have been established for some problems, it is critically important to develop programs for other problems that are based on the most well-developed theory and empirical science available. In actual practice, research-based programs need to be adapted to respond to the specific circumstances of the population and setting, but it is critical for programs to incorporate the fundamental principles and components established through research.

Participant Engagement

The success of prevention programs depends on the extent to which participants are actively engaged and implement key program strategies. Potential barriers to engagement and implementation often include access issues (e.g., scheduling, transportation, child care) and beliefs (e.g., lack of trust in providers, stigma associated with illnesses and treatment). Health disparities related to socioeconomic factors and race/ethnicity also may contribute to barriers to care. For programs to be effective, it is essential to incorporate strategies to promote participant engagement and consistent implementation of interventions during the program and throughout follow up.

Progress Monitoring

A critical component of prevention and intervention is to monitor progress and make adjustments accordingly based on intended goals and outcomes. Progress monitoring requires the use of measures that are valid, sensitive to change, and feasible for repeated, frequent administration. Curriculum-based measurement techniques have a well-established track record for monitoring academic functioning, and daily behavior ratings are emerging as a valid and useful method of monitoring changes in behavioral and emotional functioning (Chafouleas, Volpe, Gresham, & Cook, 2010).

Programming for Sustainability

A problem with many interventions is that the effects diminish shortly after the targeted period of treatment has ended. For this reason, it is essential to work from the outset of intervention to promote sustainability. Strategies to promote sustainability might include providing training in organizational skills and time management to promote independent functioning, building peer networks and support groups for children and parents that can be maintained through their own efforts after the period of active intervention, and using innovative technology to provide coaching to children and parents (Jones, Forehand, McKee, Cuellar, & Kincaid, 2010).

BEST PRACTICES IN PEDIATRIC SCHOOL PSYCHOLOGY

Pediatric school psychology has a focus on promoting health for all children in school and addressing the special educational needs of students with chronic health conditions. Regardless of whether school psychologists have had formal training in pediatric school psychology, they have the expertise to apply the principles of pediatric school psychology to promote the health of all students and to address the needs of the subset of children with chronic health conditions.

Strategies for Prevention and Intervention

Application of a multitier, public health framework is highly appropriate in addressing the health needs of students, which can have an impact on achieving success in school. What follows is a description of strategies for developing prevention and intervention programs to promote health and reduce health risk that are applicable in the context of a multitier model for all students as well as those with identified chronic health conditions.

Promote Engagement and Build Partnerships

Engagement in prevention and intervention programs is essential for participants to benefit from evidence-based practices. The focus on engagement typically begins with efforts to connect with and educate the student. A key component of intervention is to promote health literacy, which refers to the ability to make informed health decisions in everyday life (Kickbusch, 2008). Development of health literacy promotes the active participation of youth in decisions related to their healthcare. Also, school psychologists can use motivational interviewing strategies to promote engagement in prevention and intervention programs (see Miller & Rollnick, 2002, for an in-depth description).

Successful intervention requires a strong commitment from the family. Barriers to family engagement may include time limitations and scheduling problems as well as lack of trust in school professionals. School psychologists can collaborate with teachers to identify strategies to promote greater family engagement by sending explicit invitations to families to become involved, being responsive to the time demands and schedules of parents, and affirming parents' efforts to be involved in their child's education at home and school. Alternative methods of communicating with caregivers using technology, such as Web portals for sharing progress reports (Jones et al., 2010), may help to reduce barriers to engagement. Further, enlisting community partners (i.e., adults living in similar neighborhoods who can serve as parent advocates and cultural brokers) can help to improve trust and overcome the stigma involved in service delivery.

School personnel, such as teachers, school nurses, and school counselors, have critical roles in developing and implementing prevention and intervention programs to promote health for all students and address the educational needs of children with special healthcare needs. Education of school staff is an important step in enabling the staff to address the health needs of students. Further, forming partnerships with school staff to develop prevention programs and intervention plans typically results in programs that are acceptable and feasible for staff to use.

Addressing the health needs of students also involves partnerships with community-based professionals, particularly pediatricians. Recent surveys of school psychologists and pediatricians found that both disciplines perceive the benefit of interdisciplinary collaboration, but partnership occurs infrequently in practice (Bradley-Klug et al., 2013; Bradley-Klug, Sundman, Nadeau, Cunningham, & Ogg, 2010). Feedback from school psychologists and pediatricians has indicated the need to educate health professionals about the role school psychologists can serve in promoting children's health in school. Face-to-face meetings with primary care providers, brochures outlining the roles of school psychologists, and presentations at grand rounds in community hospital settings may be useful in providing this education (Bradley-Klug et al., 2013).

Strengthen Systems

A key function of the school psychologist in promoting children's health is to strengthen the major systems in which children develop. Of course, the primary system in a child's life is the family. Supporting and guiding the family is important for prevention efforts to be successful, but it is essential in promoting the successful adaptation of children with chronic health conditions in the school. The collateral impact of a child's health condition can be overwhelming for caregivers and siblings. Many caregivers must take time off from their employment and risk losing their job to attend medical appointments and stay at home with their ill child. Lack of employment has obvious implications for the availability of health insurance to cover expenses associated with the treatment and ongoing management of a chronic health condition. Caregivers also experience significant levels of stress that can have an impact on other family members, particularly siblings, who may feel neglected or even guilty for being the healthy child. The school psychologist should be prepared to support families in stress by linking the family with support groups and community agencies, while also being aware that the stress of dealing with their child's illness can evoke highly adaptive responses that promote strong family relationships and successful coping by children.

Schools can be intimidating for children coping with a chronic illness and their families. The challenge of coping with school can be particularly stressful when a child's education is disrupted by a hospitalization or period of homebound instruction. A major role for the school psychologist is to ensure that school personnel have the knowledge and confidence needed to support the integration of children in school. Often the education of peers is also essential to promote successful coping in school. In addition, school psychologists can contribute to successful integration by working to establish a strong, trusting partnership between family and school (Power et al., 2003). In the context of this relationship, parents and school staff can collaborate to promote student competence and address problems as they emerge.

Successful coping with chronic illness requires that the child and family sustain key connections with health providers, including specialists and primary care providers. Over time, primary care providers serve a vital role in ensuring that these children have a medical home within which their health needs are being addressed and services are being coordinated. The school psychologist can help the family by monitoring the connection to key health providers, facilitating linkages when needed, assisting the family in overcoming barriers, and promoting child and parental self-efficacy in being able to successfully access health services when needed.

Strengthen Connections Across Systems

Collaboration across systems, particularly between the school and health system, is critical for effective prevention and intervention programming, but it can be highly challenging (Power et al., 2013). The Biopsychoeducational model (Grier & Bradley-Klug, 2011) was proposed as a comprehensive approach to assist school psychologists in coordinating the expertise of educators, health professionals, and families in promoting children's health and supporting a child with a chronic health condition. Based on an ecological framework emphasizing the problem-solving process, this model highlights the school psychologist's role as a liaison across systems to facilitate information sharing, data-based decision making, intervention development, and evaluation of response to intervention. (See Table 23.1 for a brief description of key components of this model.)

Nastasi and colleagues (2004) proposed the Participatory Intervention model as a framework to guide cross-system intervention planning, implementation, and evaluation. Emphasizing the importance of developing partnerships with students, parents, teachers, and primary care physicians, this model promotes the role of the school psychologist as one who engages participants in a dynamic, collaborative problem-solving process to identify the target concern, jointly develop interventions, and collectively evaluate outcomes. An example of how to promote competence and solve problems in the context of multisystemic partnerships is provided by Power and Bradley-Klug (2013).

Table 23.1. Key Components of the Biopsychoeducational Model

Component	Strategies
Systems-level understanding	The child with a chronic health condition must be considered within the context of relevant systems including the family, medical, and educational systems.
Communication and collaboration	The development of partnerships across these systems to facilitate interdisciplinary communication and collaboration is a key component of the Biopsychoeducational model.
School psychologist as liaison	Training in the areas of collaborative consultation, problem-solving, intervention development, and evaluation of response to intervention position the school psychologist to serve as a liaison between systems.
Collaborative problem solving and data-based decision making	In collaboration with members of the systems (e.g., child, parents, educators, medical personnel), steps of the problem-solving process (problem identification, problem analysis, intervention development, and progress monitoring) guide identification of concerns and development of evidence-based interventions.

Strengthen Resources and Solve Problems

Consistent with positive psychology, a major focus of pediatric school psychology is to identify student assets and system resources and to further strengthen them. In addition, there is an emphasis on collaborative problem solving. The strategies of applied behavior analysis and cognitive–behavioral therapy are especially useful in solving problems. Applied behavior analysis is highly familiar to most school psychologists and many resources have been developed to guide school psychologists in applying these strategies. In addition, cognitive–behavioral therapy may be used to address a number of cross-cutting issues that commonly arise among children with chronic health conditions, such as pain management, treatment adherence, school reintegration, and coping with stress and trauma (Power & Bradley-Klug, 2013). (See Table 23.2 for a brief description of intervention strategies for each of these common, cross-cutting issues.) It is strongly recommended that school psychologists receive advanced training in cognitive–behavioral therapy and application of these strategies individually and in groups. Incorporating the strategies described above to strengthen connections across systems is important in cognitive–behavioral therapy so that the family and all providers are aligned in advancing the goals of treatment, and consistent in supporting the implementation of therapy strategies.

Monitor Progress and Evaluate Outcomes

Consistent with a problem-solving approach, interventions must be monitored and evaluated to determine their overall outcomes. The plan for progress monitoring and program evaluation should be developed prior to implementation, and data collection throughout implementation should continually inform the overall evaluation. School psychologists have the knowledge and skills to consult with members of the intervention team to determine appropriate goals for behavior change and select formative and summative outcome measures to assess progress toward those goals. Goals for students with chronic health conditions might include attention to task as assessed through direct observation, completion of classroom assignments as measured through collection of permanent products, and improvement in school engagement as determined by attendance data.

Intervention evaluation also should include the assessment of treatment integrity and acceptability. Treatment integrity refers to the implementation of a strategy or intervention as planned. Measures of treatment integrity can be direct (e.g., observation and use of a checklist of intervention) or indirect (e.g., self-report of intervention implementation). Without data to indicate that the intervention was followed as intended, evaluation of outcomes may be compromised (Sanetti & Kratochwill, 2009). Intervention acceptability, referring to one's favorable perception of a particular intervention, also is a critical component of the evaluation process and has been linked to treatment adherence. Acceptability may be measured through informal interviews or published measures available in the empirical literature.

Developmental Considerations

School psychologists need to adapt prevention and intervention programs to be responsive to the developmental needs and challenges of the students they

Table 23.2. Efficacious or Potentially Efficacious Interventions for Treating Common Problems That Arise Among Children With Chronic Illnesses

Cross-Cutting Problems	Intervention	Reference
Improving adherence to medical regimen	• Behavioral interventions (problem solving; parent training) • Multicomponent approaches (behavioral interventions and education to youth and parents)	Kahana, Drotar, and Frazier (2008)
Promoting school reintegration	• Teacher education • Parent education • Comprehensive programs	Canter and Roberts (2012); Power et al. (2003)
Managing recurrent pain	• Anxiety reduction methods (relaxation; positive imagery; self-statements) • Biofeedback • Positive reinforcement methods	Dahlquist and Switkin Nagel (2009)
Coping with medical stress and illness	• Stepped model of prevention and intervention • Trauma-informed practice • Trauma-focused cognitive–behavioral therapy	Kazak et al. (2006)

serve. Family involvement is critical at every developmental level, but especially for preschool-age children. Effective programs for preschoolers actively involve parents in school-based activities and promote family–school collaboration on a highly frequent basis. Further, educators need to continually extend invitations for parents to be involved and offer guidance with regard to home-based family involvement activities. As students mature, and certainly by the middle school and high school years, the students themselves need to be actively involved in designing prevention programs and intervention strategies. Intervention strategies at this level typically include self-management and cognitive–behavioral strategies, such as self-evaluation, cognitive reframing, and problem-solving techniques.

Promoting Cultural Competence

Application of the Participatory Intervention model (Nastasi et al., 2004) virtually ensures that prevention programs and intervention strategies will be culturally competent. The key to this model is to include all of the relevant participants (e.g., parents, community leaders, key professionals) from the beginning and to actively collaborate with them throughout the process of program development, implementation, and evaluation. Through this ongoing partnership process, the program can be adapted as needed to promote the active engagement of all key participants and the delivery of services in a culturally effective manner.

Prevention Framework for All Children

As indicated, pediatric school psychology encompasses prevention and health promotion for all children as well as prevention for children with chronic health conditions. Prevention for all children can be conceptualized within a multitier framework, including strategies at the universal, selective, and targeted levels. Universal strategies are provided to all children. Selective strategies are offered to those who are vulnerable by virtue of the presence of risk factors (e.g., overweight, victim of teasing). Targeted strategies are provided to children who are demonstrating health problems or impairments (e.g., obesity, school avoidance). The following sections describe two examples of prevention programs for all students.

Example: Nutrition Education Program
A key strategy to promoting children's health and reducing the risk of cardiovascular disease, stroke, cancer, and obesity is to encourage and reward children for eating meals that are high in fruits and vegetables. A high percentage of children eat fewer than the recommended number of servings of fruits and vegetables (Guenther, Dodd, Reedy, & Krebs-Smith, 2006). Targeting children for health promotion efforts is important because food preferences develop early in life and eating behaviors are relatively stable over time.

Effective nutrition education programs involve multiple stakeholders in the planning process, including school administrators, educators, community leaders, and parents. These programs typically consist of multiple components. A good example is the Fruits and Vegetables Promotion program (Hoffman, Franko, Thompson, Power, & Stallings, 2010), a school-based program targeting young elementary-age students. The program consists of multiple components. First, in-class education is offered to teach the students about healthy eating habits and the importance of eating at least five servings of fruits and vegetables. Computer-assisted instruction can be useful in reducing the burden on teachers, standardizing the training, and promoting student engagement in game-like activities. Second, family involvement activities are important to ensure that children are receiving consistent messages about diet at home and school. Interactive children's books have been developed to guide parents through the family involvement process (Blom-Hoffman, Wilcox, Dunn, Leff, & Power, 2008). Third, collaboration with the food service staff is important to increase the fruit and vegetable content of school lunches. Fourth, including a behavior change component, which can be applied during lunchtime, is important to promote improvements in eating behavior in addition to knowledge change. Lunch supervisors are trained to observe students carefully and catch them being healthy by offering labeled praise and giving stickers or points when students are eating fruits and vegetables (Hoffman et al., 2010).

Although nutrition education programs typically are offered to all students, the programs can be directed to schools or school districts that have a relatively high percentage of children who are overweight. Also, with parent and youth permission, targeted programs can be developed for youth who are already displaying signs of risk by virtue of their obesity or cardiovascular status.

Example: Bully Prevention Program
Bullying in schools is prevalent. The consequences of aggression and violence are serious and may include injury, anxiety, and depression for the victim; a pattern

of antisocial behavior for the perpetrator; and academic underachievement for all involved.

Universal programs to prevent bullying are typically based in the classroom and include education to students, role playing, and opportunities for guided practice. A limitation of these programs is that they do not provide services in the contexts in which students often have their most significant peer conflicts; that is, the playground, lunchroom, hallways, and bus.

The PLAYS program was developed to promote adaptive social behavior and prevent aggression on school playgrounds (Leff, Costigan, & Power, 2004). The program was specifically designed for application in urban school settings. The program includes multiple steps. First, the school psychologist identifies key stakeholders, who may include the playground supervisors, principal, and perhaps physical education teacher. Second, the school psychologist collaborates with these participants to identify targets for prevention, which might include a reduction in rough play and an increase in cooperative play. Third, the school team develops the intervention plan, which might include (a) providing students with organized games to play with on the playground, (b) providing careful supervision of all areas of the playground, and (c) catching students being cooperative on the playground by offering praise and points for rewards. Fourth, a system of ongoing monitoring is applied to identify whether the intervention is being implemented in each area of the playground and whether students are exhibiting rough play and cooperative play in that area. Fifth, feedback is provided to the intervention team to determine whether adjustments in the intervention or implementation plan are needed.

The PLAYS program has been found to be effective when the interventions are provided. Specifically, cooperative play was shown to be three times more likely to occur on the playground when organized games were present as opposed to absent. Further, rough play was 50% less likely to occur when games were present (Leff et al., 2004).

Of course, a program like PLAYS is not sufficient for all students. Students who continue to demonstrate signs of risk (e.g., rough and uncooperative play) may benefit from selective prevention strategies that might include teacher instruction to the student before going out on the playground, heightened surveillance on the playground and the use of a daily report card by the playground supervisor, and evaluation of the daily report card by the teacher after recess with the provision of points and reinforcers based on playground behavior.

Students displaying evidence of bullying or victimization on the playground likely need more comprehensive programming, such as Friend-to-Friend (Leff et al., 2009), which provides experiential training in emotion regulation, conflict resolution, and friendship making in a small group context.

Prevention Framework for Children With Chronic Illnesses

The Pediatric Psychosocial Preventative Health model (Kazak et al., 2006) is recommended as a prevention framework for use by school psychologists for children with chronic health conditions. The model consists of three tiers, universal, targeted, clinical/treatment, with each tier addressing the increased healthcare needs of the child and family. Similar to other tiered models of prevention familiar to school psychologists, the Pediatric Psychosocial Preventative Health model is a dynamic model that allows for movement of children and families across levels as their needs change throughout the disease course (Kazak et al., 2007).

This model is applicable to all chronic health conditions, and addresses a broad range of cross-cutting issues including stress, pain management, social competence and self-advocacy, and adherence to treatments. The universal tier of this model focuses on children and families who may be functioning adequately, but may potentially be vulnerable due to health-related issues, such as a recent diagnosis of a chronic health condition in a child. Targeted prevention is aimed toward providing psychosocial services for children and families dealing with a chronic health condition who also have additional risk factors, such parental unemployment, lack of healthcare insurance, or limited access to pediatric care due to geographic location. The most intensive tier, clinical/treatment, is aligned with crisis prevention. Although relatively few students and families fall within this tier, the level of need and subsequent psychosocial support required is time consuming because these families are typically confronted with numerous risk factors. The following sections provide examples of the application of this model to Type I diabetes and childhood cancer.

Example: Students With Type 1 Diabetes

Type 1 diabetes is one of the most common chronic health conditions in school-age children (Bradley-Klug et al., 2013). Students with type 1 diabetes may experience difficulties in school related to variable academic performance, self-regulation of behaviors, and peer relationships owing to the symptoms of the disease, as well as the required blood glucose monitoring and treatment with insulin. A critical role at the universal level of the school psychologist for a student with type 1 diabetes is to ensure that school personnel, including all teachers and coaches who interact with the student, understand this specific type of diabetes. Important knowledge to share about this condition includes recognizing the signs and symptoms of high and low blood sugar, the necessity of monitoring blood glucose levels, the required treatment (e.g., glucose pump or injections), and how type 1 diabetes may have an impact on a student's progress and performance across settings. This information can be communicated by gathering all of the team members (e.g., classroom teachers, coaches, school nurse, parents, student) for an information sharing and planning session. Additional goals of this meeting might include determining the student's blood glucose check schedule, granting permission for the student to eat snacks in the classroom and take extra bathroom breaks, and deciding upon where the student will receive insulin injections during the school day if necessary. During this meeting team members also can be provided with important medical contact information.

At the targeted level, the role of the school psychologist would be to communicate and collaborate with the student's parents and medical team, particularly if the student's symptoms appear to be erratic and unmanageable in school. This may be indicative of poor diabetes management and possibly lack of adherence to treatment. The school psychologist can serve as a liaison by communicating across systems and developing partnerships with key individuals involved in healthcare management. School psychologists also can use their training in behavior management to develop interventions to promote treatment adherence. Strategies that have been found to promote treatment adherence include reminders and incentives, peer support, cognitive–behavioral interventions, motivational interviewing, and self-monitoring.

Adolescents with type 1 diabetes may have a particularly difficult time managing their chronic condition because of biological changes related to physical development as well as social pressures to engage in behaviors that may be particularly detrimental to their health. For example, adolescents with type 1 diabetes who engage in the consumption of alcoholic beverages may be particularly at risk due to inability to adequately self-manage their disease. Poor disease management may result in significant medical risk and functional impairment. The role of the school psychologist in this situation would be to immediately contact the family and medical professionals, and collaborate on the development of behavioral and medical interventions to address issues related to insulin management, treatment adherence, and training in coping skills to address peer pressure to engage in unhealthy behaviors. These individualized, intensive interventions would occur at the clinical/treatment level and clearly require collaboration across systems.

Example: Students With Cancer

According to the American Cancer Society (2012), the 5-year survival rate of childhood cancer is approximately 80%. Because of the high survival rate, childhood cancer is another common pediatric health condition found in schools. The role of the school psychologist will vary based upon whether a student is recently diagnosed, reentering school after treatment, or experiencing late effects of the disease and subsequent treatment.

For a student who is recently diagnosed, the school psychologist's role will focus on information gathering and sharing, with permission from the family, to appropriate school personnel. Part of this information sharing may include speaking with classmates to explain the student's medical condition, and discussing ways for peers to stay in touch with the student if the student is absent for an extended period as well as what to expect when the student returns to school. The school psychologist also should be mindful that any siblings of the student may be experiencing related stress and should work with siblings, teachers, and the parents to ensure that supports are in place in the school if needed.

It is critical that a reintegration plan be established for cancer survivors as they return to school as research has shown that adolescent cancer survivors, in particular, have difficulty reclaiming a sense of normality in school and indicate little support with the transition from patient to student (Duffey-Lind et al., 2006). Power and colleagues (2003) proposed a staged model of reintegration that calls for first educating and preparing the family, student, and school personnel on the process of reintegration. The role of the school psychologist in this stage may include apprising the family of the student's rights within the educational system, discussing with the student the plan for reentering the school and talking about any concerns or anxiety related to going back to school, and ensuring that school personnel are aware of the student's strengths and limitations. Using the steps of conjoint behavioral consultation (Sheridan & Kratochwill, 2008) in the second stage, the school psychologist might work with the family and educators to establish connections across these systems to best serve the needs of the student. As part of this process, the school psychologist should work with the family and school personnel to determine the most efficient ways to communicate as well as methods to promote rapport and trust. Finally, the last stage of the model should focus on maintaining and strengthening this connection, and extending the partnership to include community-based providers such as a primary care physician or pediatric oncologist to promote further collaboration.

It also is important as part of prevention planning to discuss with the student, parents, and teachers the possibility of late effects associated with cancer and treatment that may include physical, academic, and psychosocial concerns (Bradley-Klug & Sundman, 2010). The school psychologist could proactively develop a plan to progress monitor the student across grade levels to determine any changes in performance, communicate any changes to those who are working together in support of the student, and implement interventions as necessary.

Developing Leaders

Being effective in applying the principles of pediatric school psychology requires strong leadership skills. These skills include program development and evaluation, measurement development and grant writing.

Program Development and Evaluation

School psychologists not only provide services to children with identified needs but they develop programs for broad classes of children to promote health, prevent risk, and provide intervention. The process typically begins with a needs assessment to determine areas in need of program development and quality improvement. Once areas of programming have been identified, the participatory action research model offers a useful framework for involving relevant stakeholders in an iterative process of development, implementation, and evaluation. The school psychologist collaborates with professionals and community members to identify program goals, develop program components, design the evaluation plan, implement the program and evaluation methods, and make necessary adaptations of the program (see Power & Bradley-Klug, 2013, for a more elaborate description).

Measurement Development

Another role of the school psychologist is to identify measures for program evaluation. When existing measures are not adequate, it is useful to develop measures of critical variables. Measures are needed for screening, progress monitoring, outcome evaluation, assessment of intervention integrity and engagement, and assessment of acceptability. Measurement identification involves defining the purpose of assessment (i.e., screening, progress monitoring), determining the behaviors or functions to be assessed, and investigating existing measures to determine appropriateness and psychometric soundness for assessing the target behavior. Measurement development, when needed, consists of multiple steps including (a) understanding the theoretical and empirical research for the construct being assessed, (b) accounting for stakeholder perceptions of the construct, (c) generating a pool of potential items and a suitable response scale, (d) field testing items, (e) identifying the dimensions measured by the scale, and (f) evaluating reliability and validity (Power & Bradley-Klug, 2013).

Grant Writing

The development, implementation, and evaluation of prevention and intervention programs require resources that may not be readily available to the school psychologist. Thus, it is important to develop knowledge and skills in grant writing to access external funds, which can be obtained through grants or contracts. There are several types of grants available to support a variety of proposed projects, including service delivery, program development, training, career development, and research grants.

Grant writing can be highly challenging and typically involves professionals with expertise in multiple areas. Therefore, from the outset it is important to create a team with whom to collaborate in the development of the grant proposal. Also, familiarizing oneself with request for proposals and grants previously funded by the granting agency, communicating with the project officer, and getting feedback from peers and supervisors can be beneficial in increasing the odds of success.

SUMMARY

Pediatric school psychology integrates aspects of school and pediatric psychology and focuses on supporting children's success in school by promoting wellness and addressing health conditions that serve as barriers to learning. By its nature, pediatric school psychology is integrative and interdisciplinary. School psychologists can apply the principles of pediatric school psychology by continually working to establish connections between systems that serve children (family, school, and health system) and build interdisciplinary partnerships. Pediatric school psychology involves prevention for all students through health promotion activities such as nutrition education, promotion of physical fitness, and bully prevention. In addition, pediatric school psychology focuses on health promotion and risk prevention for students with identified chronic health conditions. Applying the principles of pediatric school psychology requires strong leadership skills, so investing in leadership development is essential. These skills may include program development and evaluation, measurement planning and development, and grant writing. Although most school psychologists likely have not received extensive training in health promotion and service delivery to children with chronic health conditions, their training in applying prevention and intervention strategies in the context of a multitier model will enable them to provide valuable and effective services to these children and their families. Finally, the principles of pediatric school psychology are highly consistent with the principles of integrated care and interprofessional partnerships emphasized by the Patient Protection and Affordable Care Act of 2010. For this reason, school psychologists with expertise in this area are well poised to respond to career opportunities that will emerge in response to unfolding healthcare reforms.

AUTHOR NOTE

Preparation of this chapter was supported by grants from the Department of Education, Office of Special Education Programs (H325D100019), and Health Resources and Services Administration, Maternal and Child Health Bureau (R40MC08964).

Disclosure. Thomas J. Power and Kathy L. Bradley-Klug have a financial interest in books they authored or coauthored referenced in this chapter.

REFERENCES

American Cancer Society. (2012). *Cancer facts and figures 2012*. Atlanta, GA: American Cancer Society.

Blom-Hoffman, J., Wilcox, K. R., Dunn, L., Leff, S. S., & Power, T. J. (2008). Family involvement in school-base health promotion: Bringing nutrition information home. *School Psychology Review, 37*, 567–577.

Bradley-Klug, K. L., Jeffries-DeLoatche, K. L., St. John Walsh, A., Bateman, L. P., Nadeau, J., Powers, D. J., & Cunningham, J. (2013). School psychologists' perceptions of primary care partnerships: Implications for building collaborative bridges. *Advances in School Mental Health Promotion, 6,* 51–67.

Bradley-Klug, K. L., & Sundman, A. (2010). Late effects of childhood cancer: Implications for school psychologists. *School Psychology Forum, 4*(3), 13–24.

Bradley-Klug, K. L., Sundman, A., Nadeau, J., Cunningham, J., & Ogg, J. (2010). Communication and collaboration with schools: Pediatricians' perspectives. *Journal of Applied School Psychology, 26,* 263–281. doi:10.1080/15377903.2010.518583

Canter, K. S., & Roberts, M. C. (2012). A systematic and quantitative review of interventions to facilitate school reentry for children with chronic health conditions. *Journal of Pediatric Psychology, 37,* 1065–1075. doi:10.1093/jpepsy/jss071

Chafouleas, S. M., Volpe, R. J., Gresham, F. M., & Cook, C. R. (2010). School-based behavioral assessment within problem-solving models: Current status and future directions. *School Psychology Review, 39,* 343–349.

Dahlquist, L. M., & Switkin Nagel, M. (2009). Chronic and recurrent pain. In M. C. Roberts & R. G. Steele (Eds.), *Handbook of pediatric psychology* (4th ed., pp. 153–170). New York, NY: Guilford Press.

Duffey-Lind, E. C., O'Holleran, E., Healey, M., Vettese, M., Diller, L., & Park, E. R. (2006). Transitioning to survivorship: A pilot study. *Journal of Pediatric Oncology Nursing, 23,* 335–343. doi:10.1177/1043454206293267

Grier, E. C., & Bradley-Klug, K. L. (2011). A Biopsychoeducational model of consultation for students with pediatric health disorders. *Journal of Education and Psychological Consultation, 21,* 728–742.

Guenther, P. M., Dodd, K. W., Reedy, J., & Krebs-Smith, S. M. (2006). Most Americans eat much less than recommended amounts of fruits and vegetables. *Journal of the American Dietetic Association, 106,* 1371–1379. doi:10.1016/j.jada.2006.06.002,

Hoffman, J. A., Franko, D. L., Thompson, D. R., Power, T. J., & Stallings, V. A. (2010). Longitudinal behavioral effects of a school-based fruit and vegetable promotion program. *Journal of Pediatric Psychology, 35,* 61–71. doi:10.1093/jpepsy/jsp041

Interprofessional Education Collaborative Expert Panel. (2011). *Core competencies for interprofessional collaborative practice: Report of an expert panel.* Washington, DC: Interprofessional Education Collaborative.

Jones, D. J., Forehand, R., McKee, L. G., Cuellar, J., & Kincaid, C. (2010). Behavioral parent training: Is there an "app" for that? *Behavior Therapy, 33,* 72–77.

Kahana, S., Drotar, D., & Frazier, T. (2008). Meta-analysis of psychological interventions to promote adherence to treatment in pediatric chronic health conditions. *Journal of Pediatric Psychology, 33,* 590–611. doi:10.1093/jpepsy/jsm128

Kazak, A., Kassam-Adams, N., Schneider, S., Zelikovsky, N., Alderfer, M., & Rourke, M. (2006). An integrative model of pediatric medical traumatic stress. *Journal of Pediatric Psychology, 31,* 343–355. doi:10.1093/jpepsy/jsj054

Kazak, A. E., Rourke, M. T., Alderfer, M. A., Pai, A., Reilly, A. F., & Meadows, A. T. (2007). Evidence-based assessment, intervention and psychosocial care in pediatric oncology: A blueprint for comprehensive services across treatment. *Journal of Pediatric Psychology, 32,* 1099–1110. doi:10.1093/jpepsy/jsm031

Kelleher, C., Riley-Tillman, T. C., & Power, T. J. (2008). An initial comparison of collaborative and expert-driven consultation on treatment integrity. *Journal of Educational and Psychological Consultation, 18*, 294–324. doi:Pii90593751410.1080/10474410802491040

Kickbusch, I. (2008). Health literacy: An essential skill for the twenty-first century. *Health Education, 108*, 101–104.

Leff, S. S., Costigan, T., & Power, T. J. (2004). Using participatory research to develop a playground-based prevention program. *Journal of School Psychology, 42*, 3–21. doi:10.1016/j.jsp.2003.08.005

Leff, S. S., Gullan, R. L., Paskewich, B. S., Abdul-Kabir, S., Jawad, A. F., Grossman, M., … Power, T. J. (2009). An initial evaluation of a culturally adapted social problem-solving and relational aggression prevention program for urban African-American relationally aggressive girls. *Journal of Prevention & Intervention in the Community, 37*, 260–274. doi:10.1080/10852350903196274

Miller, W. R., & Rollnick, S. (2002). *Motivational interviewing: Preparing people for change* (2nd ed.). New York, NY: Guilford Press.

Nastasi, B. K., Bernstein Moore, R., & Varjas, K. M. (2004). *School-based mental health services: Creating comprehensive and culturally specific programs*. Washington, DC: American Psychological Association.

National Association of School Psychologists. (2010). *Model for comprehensive and integrated school psychological services*. Bethesda, MD: Author. Retrieved from http://www.nasponline.org/standards/2010standards/2_PracticeModel.pdf

Power, T., Blum, N., Guevara, J. P., Jones, H. A., & Leslie, L. K. (2013). Coordinating mental health care across primary care and schools: ADHD as a case example. *Advances in School Mental Health Promotion, 6*, 68–80.

Power, T. J., & Bradley-Klug, K. (2013). *Pediatric school psychology: Conceptualization, applications, and strategies for leadership development*. New York, NY: Routledge.

Power, T. J., DuPaul, G. J., Shapiro, E. S., & Kazak, A. E. (2003). *Promoting children's health: Integrating school, family, and community*. New York, NY: Guilford Press.

Sanetti, L. M. H., & Kratochwill, T. R. (2009). Toward developing a science of treatment integrity: Introduction to the special series. *School Psychology Review, 38*, 445–459.

Sheridan, S. M., & Kratochwill, T. R. (2008). *Conjoint behavioral consultation: Promoting family-school connections and interventions* (2nd ed.). New York, NY: Springer.

Suldo, S. M., & Shaffer, E. J. (2008). Looking beyond psychopathology: The dual-factor model of mental health in youth. *School Psychology Review, 37*, 52–68.

Toomey, S. L., Finkelstein, J., & Kuhlthau, K. (2008). Does connection to primary care matter for children with attention-deficit/hyperactivity disorder? *Pediatrics, 122*, 368–374. doi:10.1542/peds.2007-2794

Best Practices in Medication Treatment for Children With Emotional and Behavioral Disorders: A Primer for School Psychologists

24

James B. Hale
University of Calgary
Margaret Semrud-Clikeman
University of Minnesota
Hanna A. Kubas
University of Calgary

OVERVIEW

School psychologists and educators are increasingly becoming aware that children in their classrooms are being treated with psychotropic medication for their emotional and behavior problems. Although the use of stimulant medication to treat children with attention deficit hyperactivity disorder (ADHD) has been common for several decades, children with social, mood, anxiety, and conduct problems are increasingly being treated with psychotropic medication. Although it is important to consider and implement other empirically based approaches in schools for children with emotional and/or behavioral disorders, such as cognitive–behavioral therapy and social skills interventions, medication treatment may also be needed for affected children. As a result, school psychologists need to understand how medication treatment can be used in conjunction with other empirically based approaches for helping children who struggle with psychosocial functioning in the classroom.

The causes of increased medication treatment are many, but the trend is clear: More children in schools are being treated with psychotropic medication for their emotional and behavioral problems than ever before. More than 9% of child visits to physicians are for psychotropic medication prescriptions, with the use of multiple psychotropic medications simultaneously to treat disorders (i.e., polypharmacy) increasing dramatically in recent years (Comer, Olfson, & Mojtabai, 2010). The science of using these powerful medications to treat child emotional and behavioral disorders has lagged behind the increased use of these medications, with off-label uses (i.e., uses not approved by the U.S. Food and Drug Administration [FDA] and other governing bodies) of psychotropic treatment commonplace among school-age children. Clearly, developmental, maturational, and diagnostic issues are significant concerns for practicing school psychologists, teachers, and parents when medication treatment is considered (Carlson, Demaray, & Hunter-Oehmke, 2006; Harper, 2012). As a result, school psychologists should be aware of the basic mechanisms, efficacy, and side effects of psychotropic medications, and engage in data-based decision making throughout the assessment and treatment process.

This chapter provides school psychologists with an overview of psychotropic medications used to treat emotional and behavioral disorders, and is intended to promote best practices in understanding and managing children who are prescribed these medications. Although school psychologists do not have prescription privileges, they are integral treatment team members who possess specialized knowledge and skills for accurately identifying disorders and coordinating service delivery between the home, school, and physician's office (DuPaul & Carlson, 2005). Unfortunately, regular communication between medical staff and schools regarding medication treatment is the exception, not the rule, so it is imperative that school psychologists play a critical role in developing communication channels and collaborating with teachers, parents, and medical personnel regarding use of psychotropics in children (Sulkowski, Jordan, & Nguyen, 2009). In addition, school psychologists are well prepared to augment medical treatment with effective behavioral and counseling interventions, and to determine the efficacy of both medication and other interventions (Kubiszyn, Mire, Dutt, Papathopoulos, & Burridge, 2012).

While understanding medication and what it is used for is important for practitioners, this chapter does more than just provide information about medication effects. It further increases practitioner knowledge related to school psychologists' competencies in the National Association of School Psychologists (NASP) *Model for Comprehensive and Integrated School Psychological Services* (NASP, 2010), particularly in the Preventive and Responsive Services domain. By providing current information about effective evidence-based strategies for children treated with psychotropic medication, this chapter will help school psychologists optimize interdisciplinary efforts that support the social and emotional well-being of children with emotional–behavioral disorders.

BASIC CONSIDERATIONS

As school mental health experts, school psychologists are important intermediaries between schools and medical staff and can provide critical information to inform physicians about disability identification and medication treatment response (DuPaul & Carlson, 2005). Unfortunately, many school psychologists do not have formal training in psychopharmacology (Gureasko-Moore, DuPaul, & Power, 2005) and may instead rely on their own independent research and informal workshops to learn about psychotropic medication (Carlson et al., 2006).

School Psychology and the Medical Model Approach for Treating Children

The use of psychotropic medication in children is related to symptom severity at initial presentation, the presence of co-occurring disorders, and the intensity of service necessary (Drilea et al., 2013), making school psychologists essential players in determining the presence of disabling conditions requiring medication treatment and other interventions.

In order to fully understand the unique role that school psychologists play in psychotropic medication treatment and management, it is important to recognize how the "medical model" influences physicians' understanding of psychological disorders and their resultant treatment practices. The medical model presumes that undesirable psychological and behavioral symptoms are caused by an underlying brain-based deficit. People ascribing to the medical model might conceptualize challenging emotional and behavioral problems as treatable brain chemical deficiencies. In the case of depression, one oft-used analogy is that antidepressant treatment for depression is similar to insulin treatment for diabetes. In this world view, emotional and behavioral disorders are best conceptualized as psychopathology, and this medical disorder requires a medical treatment, with psychopharmacology the answer to a child's psychosocial difficulties.

The assumption that child emotional and behavioral problems are medical problems that reside within the individual has led to the proliferation of psychotropic medication as an accepted treatment approach (Comer et al., 2010). Although the medical model approach has been maligned in school psychology for some time, it should not lead school psychologists to ignore neurobiological influences on emotions and behavior in children. In our opinion, dichotomous thinking about children's learning and socioemotional needs has no place in modern school psychology. There is now reliable evidence that most child disorders, such as ADHD, anxiety, mood, and conduct disorders, are associated with biochemical and functional brain abnormalities, which can be detected by neuropsychological, neuroimaging, and neurochemical measures (e.g., Reddy, Weissman, & Hale, 2013; Semrud-Clikeman & Fine, 2012). Specific brain patterns are associated with various disorders seen in schools, and these disorders can be evaluated with examination of historical, cognitive, neuropsychological, academic, and behavioral data (Koziol, Budding, & Hale, 2013).

Despite the allure of the medical model in conceptualizing and treating child emotional and behavioral disorders, it has serious limitations. The medical model may work well for medical disorders with affordable diagnostic tests that reliably differentiate typical from abnormal patterns (e.g., diabetes). In reality, however, most psychological and neuropsychological tests do not have sufficient specificity to differentiate between various childhood emotional and behavioral disorders (Hale, Reddy, Weissman, Lukie, & Schneider, 2013). Another serious limitation is that the medical model approach encourages reactive instead of proactive efforts to serve children with learning and behavior problems. The internal cause oversimplification may be appealing to the struggling parent or teacher, but the school psychologist must be cognizant that psychotropic medications do not always provide an easy solution for complex, multidetermined problems. Multimodal treatment approaches that combine medication with adjunct behavior therapy or cognitive–behavioral therapies are often most effective for children with emotional and behavioral disorders (e.g., DuPaul & Carlson, 2005).

Additionally, the medical model often negates the importance of a child's environment as a strong determinant of his or her behavior. For example, the medical model does not take into account the fact that various classroom stimuli and learned responses within family and social contexts lead to behavior problems that are difficult to manage. Using a problem-solving model, the school psychologist can augment a child's learning and behavioral response to intervention by conducting ecological and functional assessments, and by identifying classroom and other environmental variables that may be altered to produce meaningful behavior change (Watson, Steege, & Watson, 2011). School psychologists are uniquely effective in this role because they are trained to understand behavior as *functional* responses to environmental determinants rather than intrinsic to the individual.

A final drawback of the medical model is that the problems children experience are not static; that is, the brain's ability to change over time (i.e., plasticity) is remarkable and dramatic. Rather than being little adults, children have brains that are actively developing and changing in response to the environment (Harper, 2012). School psychologists must not only examine behaviors as being functionally determined by a particular external environmental context, they should also consider how they are a function of a particular *internal* environment, which is in essence the child's developing brain. What is clear from neuroimaging research is that cognitive, neuropsychological, and other brain strengths and weaknesses are common among children with disabilities, and that these patterns can be overcome, and in some cases even normalized, with successful intervention (e.g., Hale et al., 2013). However, the brain's remarkable ability to change in response to

the environment works in both directions. Correct interventions can change atypical brain patterns for the better, but if children are not given proper interventions, the likelihood of maladaptive behavior increases to the point that it becomes routinized in the brain, making it even more resistant to intervention (Koziol et al., 2013). The medical model suggests that only medication can change the brain for the better. In fact, less intrusive interventions and the resultant adaptive behavior patterns change the brain for the better, suggesting school psychologists and teachers can have a significant impact on brain function. In essence, research suggests that good teaching (and school psychological services) leads to good brain functioning.

Despite the limitations of the medical model and advantages of an environmental approach to understanding emotional and behavioral disorders in children, it is important to recognize that neither is sufficient alone to meet the needs of all children. There is a dearth of formal school psychology training in the biological bases of behavior (Reddy et al., 2013), particularly in the area of psychopharmacology (Carlson et al., 2006). As a result, school psychologists trained according to NASP standards may be more comfortable with using a problem-solving ecological approach to serving children with emotional and/or behavioral disorders, but to do so minimizes their potential impact in helping struggling children, especially those treated with psychotropic medication. Embracing the best of empirically based assessment and intervention approaches, including physiological, neuropsychological, cognitive, behavioral, and ecological, will maximize school psychologists' potential to serve all children with emotional and/or behavioral disorders. School psychologists should carefully consider all evidence-based interventions for emotional and/or behavioral difficulties and recommend interventions using a hierarchical procedure—with the least restrictive and intrusive interventions carried out first with integrity and fidelity—before psychotropic medication is considered. Further, school psychologists should attempt to be proactive and inquire about potential concerns regarding psychotropic medication use, including but not limited to potential side effects, abuse potential, possible drug interactions, and length of treatment.

Controversies Regarding Child Psychopharmacology

Despite the dramatic increase in psychotropic medication treatment for children, and evidence supporting biological correlates of child emotional and behavioral disorders, the practice of child psychopharmacology remains highly controversial. Given the limited empirical evidence for off-label treatment in children (Stoyanova-Beninska et al., 2011) and the challenges of conducting systematic psychotropic medication research in children, Harper (2012) suggests that a paradigm shift should occur from acceptance of psychopharmacological treatment in children toward increased scrutiny guided by empirical investigation to evaluate and validate the utility of psychotropic medication treatment. Without sufficient randomized controlled trials to document treatment efficacy and to evaluate untoward effects, it would be expected that psychotropic medication should be used less frequently in children, with alternative cognitive and behavioral interventions offered instead. Despite the dearth of research, trends suggest that psychotropic medication usage in children is gaining rather than losing momentum, so it is important for school psychologists to be well trained in the issues surrounding psychotropic medication use, and whenever possible advocate for less invasive interventions.

Regardless of these controversies regarding medication treatment in children, it is critical for school psychologists to take a leadership role in teaming with physicians. Identifying emotional and/or behavioral disorders and monitoring treatment response has become an important aspect of school psychological practice. Unfortunately, research suggests this is not common school psychology practice (Gureasko-Moore et al., 2005). When a school psychologist becomes aware of a child who needs psychotropic medication, the school psychologist may see the child as having "psychopathology" and may feel that he or she has limited input into differential diagnosis and treatment of the child. This assumption that medical and psycho-educational decisions are separate is, in our opinion, a mistake. This artificial segregation of professional turf works against the best interest of the child, because research suggests the school psychologist is in a better position than teachers or parents to serve as a liaison between the school and the medical doctor's office when it comes to the care of children treated with psychotropic medication.

Teachers are certainly a good source of information, but they seldom speak directly with physicians about a child's behavior on medication and instead communicate with parents (Koegel, Krasno, Taras, Koegel, & Frea, 2013), and few physicians seek sufficient input regarding a child's school behavior (Morgan & Taylor, 2007). Teachers have limited training and understanding of child emotional and/or behavioral disorders,

despite being the primary referral sources for such problems. Many teachers are also unaware or misinformed about the effects and potential problems associated with medication treatment in their students (Ryan & Katsiyannis, 2009). Although parents may serve as the primary informants for physicians making medical judgments, they too have very limited understanding of child disorders or medication effects, with the popular literature serving as their main source of information (Dosreis et al., 2003).

Of school-based personnel, school psychologists are likely to be most knowledgeable on psychopathology and medication treatment. School psychologists are the team members most likely to be involved in collecting, analyzing, and interpreting school-based data to help translate data and inform physician practice. School psychologist involvement is critical because physicians have limited resources, diagnostic tools, and time available for identifying and serving children with significant psychosocial needs. Therefore, they are often required to make quick judgments based on parent reports in making a diagnosis and choosing a treatment, a process that leads to poor diagnostic reliability and validity (Bickman, Wighton, Lambert, Karver, & Steding, 2012). In addition, child psychopharmacology practices are based on best guess approaches to medication choice and titration (i.e., dose choice). Although physicians and parents alike would prefer to choose the correct medication from the outset, the reality is medications are often chosen based on whether a good response has been achieved (Wall, Croarkin, Swintak, & Koplin, 2012). In addition, the clinical standard for judging medication response is parent report, which helps form the physician's global clinical impressions. In addition to subjective evaluation of behavioral medication response, physicians may not consider cognitive or neuropsychological effects of psychotropic medications, which could account for the limited long-term impact of psychotropic medication on academic achievement (Langberg & Becker, 2012).

BEST PRACTICES IN MEDICATION TREATMENT FOR CHILDREN WITH EMOTIONAL AND BEHAVIORAL DISORDERS

As noted earlier, there has been a dramatic increase in psychotropic medication treatment in children, with stimulant treatment for ADHD leading the way (Comer et al., 2010). Use of other psychotropic drugs has also proliferated. For example, increases in the use of atypical antipsychotic medications, which sometimes have serious side effects, has also been noted. Therapeutic and untoward side effects cannot be predicted for each individual. These are identified through clinical trials. Thus, each child is his or her own "*N* of 1" study for efficacy and safety. Complicating this issue further is the fact that teachers may be unaware of side effects, and children may lack the capacity to accurately appraise their own side effects or report concerns (Kubiszyn et al., 2012). In addition, psychotropic medications may have effects on neuro-development, which are seldom ascertained in children as most clinical trials have only been completed on adults (Harper, 2012). This could explain why treatment adherence tends to be poor for medication regimens (Quittner, Modi, Lemanek, Ievers-Landis, & Rapoff, 2008), which further undermines multidisciplinary intervention efforts for children with emotional and/or behavioral disorders. School psychologists can also provide essential family support services to educate, support, and advocate for family members who may struggle because of a child's emotional and/or behavioral disorders (Hoagwood et al., 2010).

Current Use of Child Psychotropic Medications

Owing to the increasing number of children taking prescription psychotropic medications, school psychologists need to be knowledgeable of the biological bases of behavior, and understand the risks and side effects associated with the various classes of medication used to treat different childhood emotional and behavioral disorders. Although an understanding of pediatric psychopharmacology is important for school psychologists, ethical and professional practice issues should be considered when assessing and treating children who have been prescribed psychotropic medications (Davis, Kruczek, & McIntosh, 2006). School psychologists should help facilitate communication and information sharing among team members, including physicians and parents, rather than provide advice regarding medication usage and dosage. Further, if school psychologists wish to monitor the cognitive, neuro-psychological, behavioral, emotional, and academic effects of psychotropic medications, they must be competent in providing such services (Roberts, Floress, & Ellis, 2009). School psychologists must also be competent in discussing psychotropic medication use with children and their families, whether they are completing evaluations, providing consultation, or conducting interventions, in order to fully understand

medication effects on academic performance, school behavior, or the overall child's well-being.

In the United States, the FDA provides prescribing information and probabilistic data for individual drugs on their website, http://www.FDA.gov. In addition to therapeutic effects, the probabilistic data indicate how likely certain side effects are compared to placebo. For example, for aripiprazole (Abilify), there are 77 pages of information, with a side effects incidence of 23% for sleepiness compared to 3% for the placebo, and 20% incidence for extrapyramidal (involuntary motor) signs compared to 3% for the placebo. For a child who is experiencing sleepiness or lethargy prior to medication use, these problems would likely increase. By using these psychotropic medication tables and collecting classroom data to evaluate treatment efficacy and side effects or determining which side effects may exacerbate extant symptoms, the school psychologist can assist the parent and physicians in making informed decisions regarding treatment continuation, modification, or discontinuation. It is important to note that the FDA only reports side effects that occur in 5% or more of the population. Generally only five common side effects are reported across all drugs in each drug category, providing a profile of commonly occurring side effects for that drug class.

Common Psychotropic Medications

The following section provides an overview of commonly used psychotropic medications in children to aid school psychologists in understanding and serving those treated. Table 24.1 provides the most common psychotropic medications used, the diagnoses that they are used for, and common side effects. There are also notes indicating where there is little empirical support or where there are black box warnings for specific medications used in children and adolescents. A black box warning is when the FDA provides warnings and advisories for serious but generally low-frequency events. Such black box warnings raise particular concerns regarding drug safety, suggesting it is critical for school psychologists to frequently monitor drug effects on children.

Stimulant Medications: Treatment of ADHD
Dopamine agonists (i.e., medications that increase dopamine), such as methylphenidate (e.g., Ritalin) and amphetamines (e.g., Dexedrine), are generally used for the treatment of ADHD. They have been well studied and have a long track record of efficacy. These medications are available in sustained release formulations. They have the strongest positive effect of any

Table 24.1. Common Psychotropic Medication Treatments and Side Effects for Different Child Emotional and Behavioral Disorders

Medication	Common Use	Manifestations	Side Effects
Stimulant medications:			
Methylphenidate (Ritalin, Concerta, Metadate, Daytrana)	ADHD	75% of children respond; increased attention	Initially insomnia, stomach aches, headaches
Dexmethylphenidate (Focalin)		Improved behavior	Rebound effect (worse behavior in late afternoon as it wears off); lowered seizure threshold; can exacerbate tics; slowed growth
Dextroamphetamine (Adderall, Dexedrine, Dextrostat, Vyanse, Procentra)	ADHD	Similar to methylphenidate	Similar to methylphenidate
Nonstimulant medications:			
Serotonin norepinephrine reuptake inhibitor (SNRI):			
Atomoxetine (Strattera)	ADHD	Efficacy not known for children under 6 years; better for children who have tics than stimulant medication; originally developed as antidepressant and was not helpful	Increased weight and appetite, sedation, irritability, heart palpitations, slowed growth, increased blood pressure and heart rate; black box warning present as to possible suicidal ideation in comorbid depression
Guanfacine (Tenex, Intuniv)	ADHD in rare cases	Improves severe impulsivity, unusual medication for ADHD	Safety for children under 12 has not been demonstrated; some reports of manic and aggressive behavior that stopped with discontinuation
Clonidine (Kapvay)			
Antipsychotic medications:			
Haloperidol (Haldol)	Psychosis; Tourette syndrome; ASD; PDD; ADHD with conduct disorder	Reduces aggression, psychotic symptoms; reduces tics; reduces fixations; increases social responsivity	Dystonia; extrapyramidal symptoms; dose reduction can decrease motor side effects
Chlorpromazine (Thorazine)	Psychosis; severe aggression, explosiveness in children with intellectual disabilities	Reduces hyperactivity; reduces aggression and overreactions; not effective for ASD	Similar to Haldol; lowers seizure threshold; cardiovascular problems; ophthalmological problems
Thiordazine (Mellaril)	Psychosis; extreme behavior problems	Improves schizophrenic symptoms	Similar to Haldol; cognitive dulling; sedation
Thiothixene (Navane)	Psychosis	Similar to Mellaril	Less sedating than Mellaril
Loxapine succinate, fluphenazine hydrochloride (Prolixin, Permitil)	Psychosis	Similar to Haldol	Similar to Haldol
Pimodine (Orap)	Psychosis	Clinical improvement	High doses may cause death and seizures
Clozapine (Clozaril)	Severe resistant psychosis	Clinical improvement	Life-threatening, hypertension, tachycardia, and EEG change; seizures

Continued

Table 24.1. Continued

Medication	Common Use	Manifestations	Side Effects
Atypical antipsychotic medications: Clozapine (Clozaril), Risperidone (Risperdal) Paliperidon (Invega), Quetiapine (Seroquel), Olanzapine (Zyprexa) Ziprasidone (Geodon), Aripiprazole (Abilify), Iloperidone (Fanapt) Lurasidon (Latuda) Asenapine (Saphris)	Schizophrenia; psychosis; manic state of bipolar disorder; off-label for OCD, disruptive behavior, eating disorders; risperidone and paliperidon possible use for ASD; quetiapine may be used for ADHD (off-label); ziprasidone off-label use for ADHD, depression; lurasidon and asenapine has no information as to use with children	Risperidone is the only medication approved for use with children with schizophrenia ages 13–17, approved for bipolar ages 10–17; aripiprazole approved for treatment of schizophrenia in children ages 13–17 and bipolar in children ages 6–17; also used off-label for children ages 10–12 for schizophrenia; also approved for children with ASD ages 6–17 for irritability, aggression, and self-injury	Weight gain; anxiety, sedation, insomnia, dsyphoria; risk of diabetes and hyperglycemia; many can cause extrapyramidal symptoms, extent unknown in children
Antianxiety medications: Alprazolam (Xanax), Lorazepam (Ativan), Diazepam (Valium), Clonazepam (Klonopin)	Anxiety	Reduces anxiety	Rarely used for children; if used, then for very brief periods of time
Antihistamines: Diphenhydramine (Benadryl), Hydroxyzine (Vistaril)	Anxiety	Reduces anxiety	Rarely used for children; sedation and sleepiness
Atypical antianxiety: Buspirone (BuSpar), Zolpidem (Ambien)	Anxiety	Reduces anxiety	Rarely used for children
Tricyclic antidepressant medications: Imipramine hydrochloride (Tofranil)	Depression; enuresis; ADHD; school phobia	Reduces separation anxiety; improves sleep disorders; improves depression	Potentially life-threatening cardiac complications; central nervous system complications (EEG changes, confusion delusions, psychosis)
Nortriptyline hydrochloride (Pamelor) Clomipramine hydrochloride (Anafranil)	Depression OCD; severe ADHD; enuresis; school phobia	Low rate of clinical improvement in children Reduces obsessions; reduces school phobia/anxiety; reduces aggression	Decreased appetite; sedation; tiredness EEG changes; seizure; withdrawal; cardiovascular effects
Selective serotonin reuptake inhibitors (SSRIs): Fluoxetine hydrochloride (Prozac)	Depression; OCD	Only SSRI approved by FDA for children	Nausea; weight loss; sleep disorders; anxiety
Serotonin norepinephrine reuptake inhibitors (SNRIs): Venlafaxine (Effexor, Pristiq), Duloxetine (Cymbalta)	Depression	Efficacy not proven for children	Unknown in children

Continued

Table 24.1. Continued

Medication	Common Use	Manifestations	Side Effects
Monoamine oxidase inhibitors (MAOIs):			
Phenelzine (Nardil) Tranylcypromine (Parnate)	Depression; bipolar disorder; panic disorder; PTSD	Efficacy not studied in children	Unknown in children
Other types of antidepressant medications:			
Buproprion hydrochloride (Wellbutrin)	Depression; ADHD	Adolescents 18 and older improve	Seizures; insomnia; tremors
Fluvoxamine (Luvox; SSRI)	Primary use is OCD; depression	Improves OCD symptoms in children and adolescents	Increased risk of suicidality and violence; nausea, anxiety, sedation, insomnia, headache, weight loss
Paroxetine (Paxil; SSRI)	Depression; anxiety	Not proven better for children than a placebo	Increased suicidality
Sertraline (Zoloft; SSRI)	OCD and social anxiety in children; depression; anxiety	Reduced OCD symptoms in children; cognitive–behavioral therapy and Zoloft found to be efficacious; improved attention and verbal fluency found	Increased suicidality; nausea, insomnia
Escitalopram (Lexapro; SSRI)	Depression; anxiety	Approved for children ages 12 and older	Increased suicidality; heart issues, sleepiness, insomnia, indigestion
Anticonvulsant and mood stabilizers:			
Lithium; Lithium carbonate (Eskalith)	Bipolar disorder; severe impulsive disorder	Improves mood swings, aggressive behavior	Thirst, weakness, restless movements
Valproic acid (Depakote, Depakene) Oxcarbazepine (Trileptal)	Seizure disorders; bipolar disorder	Improves aggressive behavior and mood swings; controls seizures	Adverse effects are dose related; weight gain, indigestion; liver and kidney damage in some cases
Carbamazepine (Tegretol)	Seizure disorder; ADHD (off-label); bipolar disorder (off-label); schizophrenia (off-label)	Used for partial seizures and tonic-clonic seizures; improves bipolar symptoms	Drowsiness, headaches
Lamotrigine (Lamictal)	Seizure disorders; bipolar disorder; depression (off-label)	Used for focal seizures, tonic-clonic seizures	Life-threatening skin rashes, anxiety, insomnia, memory and cognitive deficits

Note. ADHD = attention deficit hyperactivity disorder; ASD = autism spectrum disorder; OCD = obsessive–compulsive disorder; PDD = pervasive developmental disorder; PTSD = posttraumatic stress disorder.

stimulant medication on measures of attention, response inhibition, and social and classroom behavior, with smaller effect sizes found for academic improvement (DeVito et al., 2009). Despite these positive effects, the negative impact of stimulant medications is also important to consider. Consistent with animal models, studies have found that low doses of stimulant medications preferentially improve working memory, but higher doses hinder working memory performance (Schmeichel & Berridge, 2013). As a result, too high a dose can impair the working memory critical for reading comprehension, math word problem solving, and written expression, and may therefore limit long-term academic performance as a result (Kubas, Backenson, Wilcox, Piercy, & Hale, 2012). Adverse effects have been found with use of stimulants, as outlined in Table 24.1. Approximately 1% of children prescribed stimulant medication develop abnormal movements or tics, and careful administration is needed for children at risk for Tourette or other tic disorders. However, recent work suggests good stimulant tolerance in tic disorders, especially with comorbid ADHD. Height and appetite/weight suppression are generally dependent on dose and are also transient, with moderate growth suppression found after 24 months of use. However, drug holidays, perhaps over summer months, help counter this effect.

Nonstimulant Medications: Treatment of ADHD

For children who are resistant to stimulant treatment, selective norepinephrine reuptake inhibitors (SNRIs) have been found to be helpful. But, atomoxetine (Strattera) is the only nonstimulant drug therapy that has received approval by the FDA for the management of ADHD. Comparisons of atomoxetine (Strattera), which tends to have less serious side effects, and methylphenidate (e.g., Ritalin), which generally has more serious side effects, have found similar improvements in attention and activity level, but other results have been equivocal or have shown more favorable effects of methylphenidate (e.g., Ritalin). Therefore, methylphenidate (e.g., Ritalin) remains the first-line medication for ADHD treatment (Newcorn et al., 2008). While bupropion (Wellbutrin) has been found to reduce symptoms of ADHD with comorbid depressive symptoms, the side effects may contraindicate its use. Alpha-2 agonists, such as clonidine (Kapvay), provide reductions in activity level and decrease rebound effects following stimulant treatment. However, there have been rare reported instances of sudden death in children after taking clonidine (Kapvay) in conjunction with stimulants, but these rare cases may have been due to comorbid heart problems.

Antipsychotic Medications: Treatment of Schizophrenia, Tic Disorders, and Autism Spectrum Disorder

Antipsychotic medications have been classified as typical and atypical and are used to treat children and adolescents with schizophrenia, autism spectrum disorder (ASD), chronic motor tics, Tourette syndrome, severe aggression, and conduct disorders (Semrud-Clikeman & Ellison, 2009). Antipsychotic medications have many side effects, which children often find intolerable. This class of medications includes butyrophenones (Haldol), phenthiazines (Thorazine), and thioxanthenes (Navane). Atypical antipsychotic medications are prescribed for several uses beyond psychosis and schizophrenia in children. Atypical antipsychotics, including aripiprazole (Abilify), risperidone (Risperdal), quetiapine (Seroquel), and olanzapine (Zyprexa), were developed to treat other disorders, but there have been successful clinical trials for using them to treat psychotic behavior. They are sometimes prescribed for children who are aggressive, irritable, or disruptive, or who have been diagnosed with bipolar disorder, ADHD, or ASD, so it is not surprising that atypical antipsychotic prescriptions have increased 500% for children in the past decade (Olfson & Marcus, 2010). There is also an increased use of polypharmacy, which is the practice of combining antipsychotic medication with one or more other medications. Some of the combinations have been supported by clinical trials, while many other combinations are of unproven efficacy and may put the patient at increased risk of drug–drug interactions. Two atypical antipsychotics, aripiprazole (Abilify) and quetiapine (Seroquel), now carry black box warnings of increased suicidality in children.

Common side effects of antipsychotic medications include sleepiness, dizziness, extrapyramidal (motor) symptoms, increased appetite, and blurred vision. Sleepiness has been most closely associated with the use of aripiprazole (Abilify) with children with ASD and bipolar disorder, and with risperidone (Risperdal) for children with ASD, bipolar disorder, and schizophrenia. Of additional concern is that children who have ASD and bipolar disorder who are treated with aripiprazole (Abilify) have a high incidence of extrapyramidal side effects. Risperidone (Risperdal) carries a moderate risk for extrapyramidal side effects when used to treat ASD, bipolar disorder, and, to a lesser extent, schizophrenia.

Increased appetite appears to be associated with the use of olanzapine (Zyprexa) and risperidone (Risperdal) to treat ASD and bipolar disorder. Finally, blurred vision is a common side effect when aripiprazole (Abilify) or risperidone (Risperdal) are used to treat bipolar disorder. As these significant side effects are likely to interfere with school performance, they must be closely monitored by the school psychologist.

Mood (Depression and Bipolar Disorder) and Anxiety Disorder Treatment

Loss of peer relationships, poor or deteriorating academic performance, and loss of enjoyment in previously preferred activities (i.e., anhedonia) may be signs of major depression in children (Smiga & Elliott, 2011). Practitioners should be reminded that depression in children and youth may also be manifested as irritability and anger, rather than chronic sadness. As noted in Table 24.1, selective serotonin reuptake inhibitors (SSRIs) include fluoxetine (Prozac), sertraline (Zoloft), escitalopram (Lexapro), fluvoxamine (Luvox), and clomipramine (Anafranil). Of the SSRIs, only fluoxetine (Prozac) carries an FDA authorization for use with children. In a National Institute of Mental Health study on adolescent depression, significant reductions in depressive symptoms were found for fluoxetine (Prozac) but not for cognitive–behavioral therapy, with the combined cognitive–behavioral therapy and fluoxetine treatment offering the best effect (March, Silva, & Vitiello, 2006). It is important to note that information on antidepressant treatment efficacy and side effects for school-age children with depression and/or anxiety is extremely limited and inconsistent, so careful monitoring by the school psychologist is required.

In addition to the treatment of depression, antidepressant medications are also used for off-label uses such as for the treatment of obsessive compulsive disorder, other anxiety disorders, tic disorders, ASD, premenstrual dysphoric disorder, and ADHD (e.g., Chadehumbe, Greydanus, Feucht, & Patel, 2011). Serotonin-norepinephrine reuptake inhibitors such as venlafaxine (Effexor) are most commonly used to treat depression and bipolar disorder, and lithium (Eskalith) and anticonvulsants (e.g., Depakote, Tegrotol, Divalproex) are sometimes used to treat bipolar disorder (Thomas, Stansifer, & Findling, 2011). These medications have been poorly studied in children, and, therefore, may not prove efficacious or may result in significant side effects. However, some children diagnosed with ADHD may actually have pediatric bipolar with rapid cycling (Thomas et al., 2011), so increases in the use of these bipolar disorder medications may be

forthcoming. Of these medications, a randomized controlled trial found the anticonvulsant medication Divalproex superior to lithium (Eskalith) and placebo, which were not different from one another (Thomas et al., 2011).

More common side effects of antidepressants include sweating, sedation, upset stomach, decreased appetite, and nausea or vomiting. These physical difficulties may affect school performance and behavior and need to be carefully monitored. Tricyclic antidepressants are generally not used with children due to potential cardiological and anticholinergic side effects (i.e., dry mouth, blurred vision, memory deficits). In October 2004, the FDA required a black box warning on all antidepressant medications due to increased suicidality among children and adolescents. It may seem counterintuitive that antidepressant medicines could cause suicidal behavior. However, the theory behind this side effect is that reduction of depressive apathy and lethargy can lead to impulsive suicidal behavior. Therefore, children taking antidepressant medication must be monitored carefully for signs of suicidal ideation and/or behavior.

While SSRIs are frequently used to treat anxiety, a different class of medications, called anxiolytics, is more commonly used to control severe anxiety, sleep disorders, and aggression (Wilens, 2008). The most common medications used for these purposes are diazepam (Valium), chlordiazepoxide (Librium), and clonazepam (Klonopin). Buspirone (Buspar) has been found to work well with children in treating aggression (Wilens, 2008). Very few anxiolytic medications have been clinically demonstrated to improve anxiety in children. They tend to have severe side effects including cognitive blunting, impulsivity, and agitation, as well as addiction. Therefore, SSRIs and SNRIs are more likely to be used to treat anxiety in children.

Antiepileptic Medications

Antiepileptic (anticonvulsant) medications are essential for many children with seizure disorders, but are also sometimes prescribed to children with emotional and/or behavioral disorders. The side effects (cognitive slowing, sleepiness) of phenobarbital (Luminal) and phenytoin (Dilantin) have been known to have adverse effects on academic work. Phenobarbital also has significant negative effects on memory (Pliszka, 2003). Carbamazepine (Tegretol) has fewer side effects than the other two medications. Antiepileptic medications, particularly valproic acid (Depakote), carbamazepine (Tegretol), and oxcarbazepine (Trileptal), are also used to treat childhood psychiatric disturbances (Handen & Gilchrist,

2006). Additionally, valproic acid (Depakote) has been used to lessen the aggressive behavior of children with cognitive disabilities. It is suggested that valproic acid be used very sparingly, as this medication heightens the risk for hepatic failure and hemorrhagic pancreatitis, which are life-threatening conditions.

Antiepileptic medications are also used to reduce certain behavioral problems as noted above, but often side effects preclude their use. Studies for children with severe aggression have found carbamazepine (Tegretol) may be useful in children with significant aggression, but it also may increase mania, impulsive behaviors, and sedation, and also will likely impair cognition (Brown, 2005). For this reason the American Academy of Pediatrics recommends yearly psychological assessments to evaluate children's cognitive ability while they are treated with carbamazepine (Tegretol; Brown, 2005). While the FDA has approved the use of anticonvulsant agents only for seizure disorders and for manic phases of bipolar disorder, the clinical use of anticonvulsants for other behavior problems exceeds this recommendation (Brown, 2005). Multiple antiepileptic medications are sometimes utilized to treat severe emotional and behavior problems. Therefore, this polypharmacy treatment requires careful monitoring by the neurologist and school psychologist.

Monitoring of Medication Treatment

No one in the schools is better prepared to address monitoring of medication treatment and other interventions for emotional and/or behavioral disorders than school psychologists. Parents and teachers may have limited or inaccurate knowledge of medication and treatment (Carlson et al., 2006), and limited communication between physicians and schools is commonplace (Harper, 2012). As a result, school psychologists must spend considerable time educating parents about psychotropic medications, and carefully monitor academic and behavioral medication response. With skills in the identification of emotional and behavioral disorders, and in data collection for monitoring and evaluating treatment response (DuPaul & Carlson, 2005), school psychologists are an important bridge between the medical and educational worlds. In addition, school psychologists can monitor the cognitive and academic effects of psychotropic medication with direct (i.e., tests) or indirect (i.e., ratings) methods, both of which are critical additions in helping to determine treatment efficacy and monitor side effects. School psychologists are encouraged to monitor children's

psychopharmacological treatment by collecting, analyzing, interpreting, and communicating results with teachers and parents regarding cognitive and behavioral treatment response. This not only could facilitate data-based decision making regarding the efficacy of medication treatment, but it also could improve treatment adherence (Quittner et al., 2008). The results of this type of collaboration could be significant in improving the well-being of children with emotional and/or behavioral disorders.

An example of this type of treatment monitoring can be seen in an ongoing series of studies the authors have conducted on monitoring children's neuropsychological and behavioral response to stimulant medication. In a randomized, double-blind, placebo-controlled clinical trial of methylphenidate in ADHD, neuropsychological and behavioral medication response was examined, both at the individual and group level of analyses (e.g., Hale et al., 2011; Kubas et al., 2012). Measures of attention, working memory, executive function, classroom observation, as well as parent and teacher rating scales over a 4-week period were administered, and this information was given to physicians in brief reports so they could make more informed clinical judgment regarding treatment efficacy. The first week was used to collect baseline data, after which point the child was administered the following three conditions (each condition lasting 1 week) in random order: blinded placebo, low medication dose, or high medication dose. All individuals collecting data (i.e., psychometrician, parent, teacher, child) were blind as to the order of conditions. After all data were collected, parents and children were informed about the order of the trials, and a brief report was prepared for physicians, who subsequently met with parents to make clinical decisions about the medication treatment.

This research has revealed that children with ADHD and moderate or high baseline neuropsychological executive impairment were more likely to respond to stimulant medication than children who did not exhibit the same baseline executive impairment, suggesting that our protocol detects stimulant responders and nonresponders. Further, the sensitivity of our measures indicates that brief neuropsychological assessment measures and parent and teacher behavior ratings can be used by school psychologists to successfully monitor medication response. Our research also provided additional insight regarding medication response to guide physicians' medication practices. For example, for children with ADHD who responded well to stimulant medication, the best dose for their thinking or cognition proved to be lower than the best dose for their behavior, with working memory often compromised at higher doses of medication (Kubas et al., 2012). Since working memory has been shown to be an important predictor of academic achievement across various domains (e.g., reading comprehension, math word problems, written expression), this could explain why long-term academic treatment efficacy of stimulants has been limited (Langberg & Becker, 2012). Our studies illustrate how psychotropic medication dosing practices can be informed by neuropsychological, academic, and behavioral functioning. The school psychologist could conduct similar trials and present summary data to aid physicians in their clinical decision making regarding psychotropic medication dosing and treatment efficacy (Wall et al., 2012).

Figure 24.1 shows a typical response pattern for Lisa, a child diagnosed with ADHD. Although Lisa showed both cognitive and behavioral response to stimulant medication, the best dose for her cognitive functioning was actually lower than the best dose for her behavior (lower ranks equals better performance/behavior). If only behavioral criteria were used to identify ADHD and determine the best dose for Lisa, the high dose would be picked. However, when taking the higher dose, Lisa's cognition, particularly working memory, declined, and this could affect her academic achievement. This example illustrates the importance of cognitive and behavioral progress monitoring with regard to the effects of medication. If children with ADHD are treated only on the basis of their behavior, it is possible that cognition and long-term academic gains may be minimal. However, if a medication dosage was chosen that optimizes cognitive functioning and was supplemented with behavior therapy, these children may begin to demonstrate more consistent and lasting success in the classroom.

SUMMARY

School psychologists are likely to serve children who undergo medication treatment and other interventions for emotional and/or behavioral disorders. Their involvement is crucial because physicians need input from school personnel to accurately diagnose and treat children with emotional and/or behavioral disorders (Harper, 2012). In addition, parents and teachers may have limited or inaccurate knowledge regarding medication treatment (DuPaul & Carlson, 2005), which could explain why poor treatment adherence leads to questionable efficacy (Quittner et al., 2008). As a result, school psychologists not only need to collect data for physician and school-based decision making, but need to educate parents and school-based personnel as well. Thus, school psychologists are encouraged to seek out formal education in psychotropic medication treatment, so they can become more literate and provide much-needed educational and clinical services (Gureasko-Moore et al., 2005).

Figure 24.1. Lisa's Cognitive and Behavioral Response to Stimulant Medication

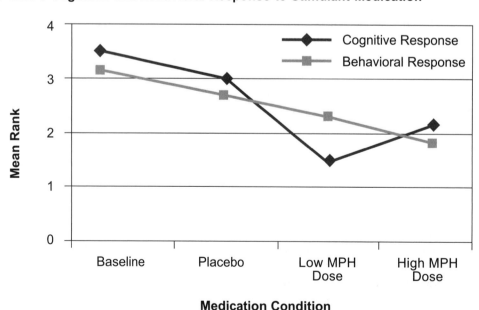

Note. MPH = methylphenidate (Ritalin).

School psychologists have well-developed skills in identifying emotional and behavioral disorders, as well as strong data collection skills that can be used to monitor and evaluate treatment response (DuPaul & Carlson, 2005). This allows school psychologists to act as collaborative problem solvers who can serve as a professional bridge between the medical and educational arenas. In addition, school psychologists can help monitor cognitive and academic effects of psychotropic medication using formal assessment, indirect informant reports, and observational procedures, which are critical in determining treatment efficacy and monitoring untoward medication effects (DuPaul & Carlson, 2005). This is especially critical given the limited research on the use of psychotropic medications in children (Stoyanova-Beninska et al., 2011) and the fact that some researchers are calling for a paradigm shift toward increased scrutiny guided by empirical investigation to evaluate and validate the utility of psychotropic medication treatment in children. School psychologists possess the skills necessary to carry out additional interventions, such as behavior management and cognitive–behavioral therapy, and to evaluate the effects of these interventions with or without additional psychotropic medication treatment (Gureasko-Moore et al., 2005). Through formal instruction in school psychology programs, supplemental training materials provided by NASP and other professional organizations, and continuing education workshops, school psychologists can be well prepared to bridge school, medical, and home settings to foster the well-being of children with emotional and/or behavioral disorders treated with psychotropic medication and other empirically based intervention programs.

AUTHOR NOTE

Disclosure. James B. Hale has a financial interest in books he authored or coauthored that are referenced in this chapter.

REFERENCES

Bickman, L., Wighton, L. G., Lambert, E. W., Karver, M. S., & Steding, L. (2012). Problems in using diagnosis in child and adolescent mental health services research. *Journal of Methods and Measurement in the Social Sciences, 3*, 1–26.

Brown, E. S. (2005). Bipolar disorder and substance abuse. *Psychiatric Clinics of North America, 28*, 415–425.

Carlson, J. S., Demaray, M. K., & Hunter-Oehmke, S. (2006). A survey of school psychologists' knowledge and training in child psychopharmacology. *Psychology in the Schools, 43*, 623–633.

Chadehumbe, M. A., Greydanus, D. E., Feucht, C., & Patel, D. R. (2011). Psychopharmacology of tic disorders in children and adolescents. *Pediatric Clinics of North America, 58*, 259–272.

Comer, J. S., Olfson, M., & Mojtabai, R. (2010). National trends in child and adolescent psychotropic polypharmacy in office-based practice, 1996–2007. *Journal of the American Academy of Child and Adolescent Psychiatry, 49*, 1001–1010.

Davis, A. S., Kruczek, T., & McIntosh, D. E. (2006). Understanding and treating psychopathology in schools: Introduction to the special issue. *Psychology in Schools, 43*, 413–417.

DeVito, E. E., Blackwell, A. D., Clark, L., Kent, L., Dezsery, A. M., Turner, D. C., … Sahakian, B. J. (2009). Methylphenidate improves response inhibition but not reflection-impulsivity in children with attention deficit hyperactivity disorder (ADHD). *Psychopharmacology, 202*, 531–539.

Dosreis, S., Zito, J. M., Safer, D. J., Soeken, K. L., Mitchell, J. W., Jr, & Ellwood, L. C. (2003). Parental perceptions and satisfaction with stimulant medication for attention deficit hyperactivity disorder. *Journal of Developmental & Behavioral Pediatrics, 24*, 155–162.

Drilea, S. K., Jowers, K., Lichtenstein, C., Hale, M., Blau, G., & Stromberg, S. (2013). Psychotropic medication use and clinical outcomes among children and adolescents receiving system of care services. *Journal of Child and Adolescent Psychopharmacology, 23*, 36–43.

DuPaul, G. J., & Carlson, J. S. (2005). Child psychopharmacology: How school psychologists can contribute to effective outcomes. *School Psychology Quarterly, 20*, 206–221.

Gureasko-Moore, D. P., DuPaul, G. J., & Power, T. J. (2005). Stimulant treatment for attention deficit hyperactivity disorder: Medication monitoring practices of school psychologists. *School Psychology Review, 34*, 232–245.

Hale, J. B., Reddy, L. A., Semrud-Clikeman, M., Hain, L. A., Whitaker, J., Morley, J., … Jones, N. (2011). Executive impairment determines ADHD medication response: Implications for academic achievement. *Journal of Learning Disabilities, 44*, 196–212.

Hale, J. B., Reddy, L. A., Weissman, A. S., Lukie, C., & Schneider, A. N. (2013). Attention deficit hyperactivity disorder. In L. A. Reddy, A. S. Weissman, & J. B. Hale (Eds.), *Neuropsychological assessment and intervention for youth: An evidence-based approach to emotional and behavioral disorders* (pp. 127–154). Washington, DC: American Psychological Association.

Handen, B. L., & Gilchrist, R. (2006). Practitioner review: Psychopharmacology in children and adolescents with mental retardation. *Journal of Child Psychology and Psychiatry, 47*, 871–882.

Harper, G. (2012). Psychopharmacology for children and adolescents: The paradigm shift. *Neuropsychiatrie de l'Enfance et de l'Adolescence, 60*(5), S8.

Hoagwood, K. E., Cavaleri, M. A., Olin, S. S., Burns, B. J., Slaton, E., Gruttadaro, D., & Hughes, R. (2010). Family support in children's mental health: A review and synthesis. *Clinical Child and Family Psychology Review, 13*, 1–45.

Koegel, L. K., Krasno, A. M., Taras, H., Koegel, R. L., & Frea, W. (2013). Is medication information for children with autism spectrum disorder monitored and coordinated across professionals? Findings from a teacher survey. *School Mental Health, 5*, 48–57.

Koziol, L. F., Budding, D. A., & Hale, J. B. (2013). Understanding neuropsychopathology in the 21st century: Current status, clinical application, and future directions. In L. A. Reddy, A. S. Weissman,

& J. B. Hale (Eds.), *Neuropsychological assessment and intervention for youth: An evidence-based approach to emotional and behavioral disorders* (pp. 327–346). Washington, DC: American Psychological Association.

Kubas, H. A., Backenson, E. M., Wilcox, G., Piercy, J. C., & Hale, J. B. (2012). The effects of methylphenidate on cognitive function in children with attention-deficit/hyperactivity disorder. *Postgraduate Medicine, 124*(5), 33–48.

Kubiszyn, T., Mire, S., Dutt, S., Papathopoulos, K., & Burridge, A. B. (2012). Significant differences in pediatric psychotropic side effects: Implications for school performance. *School Psychology Quarterly, 27*, 4–28.

Langberg, J. M., & Becker, S. P. (2012). Does long-term medication use improve the academic outcomes of youth with attention deficit hyperactivity disorder? *Clinical Child and Family Psychology Review, 15*, 215–233.

March, J., Silva, S., & Vitiello, B. (2006). The Treatment for Adolescents With Depression Study (TADS): Methods and message at 12 weeks. *Journal of the American Academy of Child and Adolescent Psychiatry, 45*, 1393–1403.

Morgan, S., & Taylor, E. (2007). Antipsychotic drugs in children with autism. *British Medical Journal, 334*, 1069–1070.

National Association of School Psychologists. (2010). *Model for comprehensive and integrated school psychological services*. Bethesda, MD: Author. Retrieved from http://www.nasponline.org/standards/2010standards/2_PracticeModel.pdf

Newcorn, J., Kratochvil, C., Allen, A., Casat, C., Ruff, D., Moore, R., & Michelson, D. (2008). Atomoxetine and osmotically released methylphenidate for the treatment of attention deficit hyperactivity disorder: Acute comparison and differential response. *American Journal of Psychiatry, 165*, 721–730.

Olfson, M., & Marcus, S. C. (2010). National trends in outpatient psychotherapy. *American Journal of Psychiatry, 167*, 1456–1463.

Pliszka, S. R. (2003). *Neuroscience of mental health clinicians*. New York, NY: Guilford Press.

Quittner, A. L., Modi, A. C., Lemanek, K. L., Ievers-Landis, C. E., & Rapoff, M. A. (2008). Evidence-based assessment of adherence to medical treatments in pediatric psychology. *Journal of Pediatric Psychology, 33*, 916–936.

Reddy, L. A., Weissman, A. S., & Hale, J. B. (Eds.). (2013). *Neuropsychological assessment and intervention for youth: An evidence-based approach to emotional and behavioral disorders*. Washington, DC: American Psychological Association.

Roberts, H. J., Floress, M. J., & Ellis, C. R. (2009). Training school psychologists in psychopharmacology consultation. *Psychology in the Schools, 46*, 827–835.

Ryan, J. B., & Katsiyannis, A. (2009). The importance of teacher involvement in medication therapy. *Teaching Exceptional Children Plus, 6*(2), 1–12.

Schmeichel, B. E., & Berridge, C. W. (2013). Neurocircuitry underlying the preferential sensitivity of prefrontal catecholamines to low-dose psychostimulants. *Neuropsychopharmacology, 38*, 1078–1084.

Semrud-Clikeman, M., & Ellison, P. A. T. (2009). *Child neuropsychology: Assessment and interventions for neurodevelopmental disorders* (2nd ed.). New York, NY: Springer.

Semrud-Clikeman, M., & Fine, J. G. (2012). Pediatric versus adult psychopathology: Differences in neurological and clinical presentations. In C. A. Noggle & R. A. Dean (Eds.), *The neuropsychology of psychopathology* (pp. 11–27). New York, NY: Springer.

Smiga, S. M., & Elliott, G. R. (2011). Psychopharmacology of depression in children and adolescents. *Pediatric Clinics of North America, 58*, 155–171.

Stoyanova-Beninska, V. V., Wohlfarth, T., Isaac, M., Kalverdijk, L. J., van den Berg, H., & Gispen-de Wied, C. (2011). The EU paediatric regulation: Effects on paediatric psychopharmacology in Europe. *European Neuropsychopharmacology, 21*, 565–570.

Sulkowski, M. L., Jordan, C., & Nguyen, M. L. (2009). Current practices and future directions in psychopharmacological training and collaboration in school psychology. *Canadian Journal of School Psychology, 24*, 237–244.

Thomas, T., Stansifer, L., & Findling, R. L. (2011). Psychopharmacology of pediatric bipolar disorders in children and adolescents. *Pediatric Clinics of North America, 58*, 173–187.

Wall, C. A., Croarkin, P. E., Swintak, C., & Koplin, B. A. (2012). Psychiatric pharmacogenomics in pediatric psychopharmacology. *Child and Adolescent Psychiatric Clinics of North America, 21*, 773–788.

Watson, T. S., Steege, M. W., & Watson, T. S. (2011). Functional assessment of behavior. In M. A. Bray & T. J. Kehle (Eds.), *The Oxford handbook of school psychology* (pp. 187–204). New York, NY: Oxford University Press.

Wilens, T. E. (2008). *Straight talk about psychiatric medications for kids* (3rd ed.). New York, NY: Guilford Press.

25

Best Practices in Assessing the Effects of Psychotropic Medication on Student Performance

John S. Carlson
Jeffrey D. Shahidullah
Michigan State University

OVERVIEW

The use of psychotropic medications (i.e., any medication that has an altering effect on behavior, mood, and/or emotions) to address the symptoms of mental health conditions in school-age children is clearly in the national spotlight. Spending for prescription medications (e.g., antipsychotics, psychostimulants) aimed at treating pediatric depression and attention disorders has increased significantly in recent years (Medco Health Solutions, 2011). Medications used to treat attention disorders (e.g., methylphenidate, atomoxetine) are among the most commonly prescribed psychotropic drugs, as nearly 3 million U.S. children ages 4–17 take them (Centers for Disease Control and Prevention, 2010; Merikangas, He, Rapoport, Vitiello, & Olfson, 2013).

Research findings clearly support the short-term efficacy of psychotropic medications in treating attention deficit hyperactivity disorder (ADHD), bipolar disorder, depression, generalized anxiety/social phobia, obsessive–compulsive disorder, Tourette syndrome, and symptoms of aggression/irritability in children with autism (Vitiello, 2012). Yet, the largely unknown long-term effects of these medications and the impact of chronic use in children and adolescents is a significant public health issue. A critical look at the use of these drugs within vulnerable child populations such as public child-serving agencies (e.g., foster care), low-income populations (i.e., Medicaid), and in children diagnosed with autism spectrum disorders has emerged recently within the literature (e.g., American Academy of Child and Adolescent Psychiatry, 2012). Moreover, the increasing practice of polypharmacy (i.e., use of more than one psychotropic medication) has raised a new set of concerns about the unintended side effects resulting from a combination of drugs acting on the rapidly developing child (Mojtabai & Olfson, 2010).

The importance of close monitoring and evaluation of medication effects (i.e., dose response) on students' functioning is clear. The need to isolate changes in target behaviors as a result of medication as well as monitoring for the emergence of unwanted or adverse side effects is well established (Vitiello, 2012). Psychotropic medications have the potential to have a negative impact on children's health and functioning in the home, school, and community (Kubiszyn, Mire, Dutt, Papathopoulos, & Burridge, 2012). Gathering data supporting the rewards versus risks of using psychotropic medications is essential to the treatment process.

With appropriate monitoring and safeguard procedures in place, the use of psychotropic medications can offer a safe and effective intervention for children who fail to respond to school-based services or for those who may need an adjunct to existing psychosocial treatments. Kubiszyn (1994) aptly recognized that the training and expertise that school psychologists possess in psychological assessment, evidence-based intervention, program evaluation, and consultation uniquely qualifies them to work with students who are prescribed medication as well as the students' families, the school staff, and the healthcare providers to ensure positive school outcomes. Further, he noted that appropriately trained school psychologists may be in the best position of any healthcare provider to serve as the knowledge brokers of psychotropic information by gathering the data needed to help others to initiate, evaluate, terminate, and integrate pharmacological, psychotherapeutic, and educational interventions into a comprehensive system of support.

The purpose of this chapter is to address how school psychologists may engage in best practices in evaluating the effects of psychotropic medication on school performance. Providing support to families and physicians in an effort to gather the data necessary to maximize the effectiveness of medication treatment in meeting parents' intended intervention goals is an important role to be undertaken by school psychologists. To assist in carrying out that role, a set of best practices by which the medication effects on student performance can be accurately and responsibly assessed are reviewed. This information is provided within the context of (a) current legal, ethical, and training standards pertinent to school-based medication evaluation; (b) the types of medications that are commonly prescribed to school-age children; and (c) a set of target behaviors and possible side effects that are commonly associated with each of these medications. Finally, a case example of a school-based evaluation of fluoxetine treatment of depressive symptoms in a high school student is presented in an effort to demonstrate how school psychologists can support data-based treatment decisions.

BASIC CONSIDERATIONS

At the systems level of service delivery, school psychologists have knowledge of the structure, organization, and theory of preventive and responsive services that facilitate the well-being of school-aged children. Within multilevel systems of support, such as school-wide positive behavioral interventions and supports (SWPBIS) and behavioral response-to-intervention (RTI) models, school psychologists are tasked with providing evidence-based interventions within a continuum of services. The progression through the levels of behavioral support within a school's student support services (e.g., SWPBIS/RTI) often necessitates school psychologists' involvement in the problem-solving process. Despite prevention support and responsive services targeting ecological variables and functional behavior assessment-indicated behavioral needs, a small percentage of students may still require a psychotropic medication in conjunction with school-based psychoeducational supports and family involvement for maximized gains and minimized dysfunction.

The National Association of School Psychologists (NASP) *Model for Comprehensive and Integrated School Psychological Services* (NASP, 2010a) lists the provision of Preventive and Responsive Services as a domain of practice that permeates all aspects of service delivery. Further, it recognizes the critical need for school psychologists to provide both direct and indirect services to those children requiring mental health intervention by working with parents, school personnel, and community resources to provide competent mental health support. These roles often require effective collaboration and consultation to take place with primary care providers (e.g., pediatricians, family physicians, child behavioral health consultants) to establish a continuity of care that bridges the gap between schools and medical settings.

Estimates indicate that roughly 25% of all students on school psychologists' caseloads are prescribed with one or more psychotropic medications (Carlson, Demaray, & Hunter-Oehmke, 2006). The importance of increasing professional training opportunities related to child psychopharmacology and the desire for additional training in this area are recognized by school psychology professionals as being essential for their work. It is important that school psychologists be readily available and well trained to engage in consultation, communication, and collaboration to evaluate the impact that these treatments have on school performance.

Without close monitoring and frequent feedback of treatment effects in the school setting, prescribing physicians often remain unaware if a medication is effective. Timely and needed adjustments are not typically made unless a child experiences unwanted side effects or adverse drug reactions. Parents also remain uncertain and anxious about whether their often tentative and reluctant decision to medicate their child was an appropriate one. Establishing the safest and most effective therapeutic dose is often an incremental titration process based on a child's response to the dosage prescribed. Close monitoring, particularly in the first few days/weeks, allows for a data-based approach to treatment decision making. HaileMariam, Bradley-Johnson, and Johnson (2002) found that pediatricians reported a preference for brief summaries of school-based data gathered from side-effect checklists, behavior rating scales, and systematic direct observation of classroom behavior. Parents too can benefit from easy-to-use and easy-to-understand graphs and tables summarizing the effects of medication on target behaviors in the school when compared to those same behaviors prior to initiation of medication and/or prior dosage.

There are a number of important steps for school psychologists to engage within their own schools and practices prior to providing leadership around monitoring the effects of psychotropic medication on student performance. These steps serve as important prerequisites to involvement in the medication evaluation process.

Step 1: Awareness of Legal, Ethical, and Training Issues

School psychologists need to be aware of local, state, and/or federal laws that may limit their consulting around issues of medication. Special education law clearly permits classroom personnel to speak with parents about a child's academic, behavioral, and functional performance at school and/or the potential benefit of an additional evaluation to determine the possible benefits that may be afforded through special education or related services. However, specific discussions with families about the need for medication treatment are not an appropriate role for school psychologists and should be left to the family's primary care physician.

There are a number of challenges in helping families to utilize services, such as combining medication and psychosocial approaches, that best address the complex etiology of a mental health condition. First, the principle of beneficence and nonmaleficence (i.e., do no harm) implies the need for progress monitoring. Second, school psychologists must engage in appropriate, professional relationships with students, parents, and other professionals. A clear explanation of the school psychologists' consultative role in school-based medication evaluation must be provided to all relevant stakeholders. Issues of confidentiality pertaining to the child's treatment and mental health condition must be clearly addressed in discussions with families. Determining who should know that the child is taking medications, what they should know, and how to engage them in collaborative efforts to examine school-based treatment response requires careful thinking, planning, and follow through by school staff. Third, school psychologists are obligated to use assessment tools that have adequate psychometric support (e.g., reliable assessment of treatment change) and evaluation procedures (e.g., continuous monitoring, data collection at baseline, during treatment, posttreatment) that are research based and appropriate for the condition being treated.

According to the guidelines of both the American Psychological Association (APA, 2010) and NASP (2010b), school psychologists have an ethical duty to practice within their limits of competence. To the extent that school psychologists have received formal training that is relevant to school-based medication evaluation (e.g., behavioral assessment, principles of psychopharmacology, progress monitoring, data-based decision making), then they are operating within appropriate ethical parameters. With respect to training guidelines regarding competencies pertaining to psychotropic medication evaluation, the recommendations put forth by APA (Smyer et al., 1993) are particularly relevant to the field of school psychology. APA recommends the following three levels of training in psychopharmacology for psychologists: Level 1: basic education in biological bases and principles of clinical psychopharmacology for all psychologists; Level 2: comprehensive training in professional and legal issues, assessment, treatment issues, and research in psychopharmacology for those who seek to engage in ongoing collaborative practice with physicians; and Level 3: intensive training and supervision in both didactic content areas and specific practicum requirements for those who seek to practice clinical psychopharmacology independently.

While NASP has yet to provide recommendations or competencies related to psychotropic medication or school-based medication evaluations, the NASP Practice Model (NASP, 2010a) does delineate specific competency domains for data-based decision making and accountability. Without proper training in these areas of competence and experience in carrying forward these responsibilities, school psychologists should seek to work collaboratively with others in the school who may possess these skills, such as the school nurse, social worker, or school counselor. When appropriate, postgraduate training should be sought to develop these competencies via conference attendance, coursework, and/or independent reading.

Step 2: Knowledge of Psychotropic Medication Treatments

Attention to evidence-based interventions within schools requires an interdisciplinary perspective and an awareness of the research base within other professions. Literature within the field of child clinical psychology, child and adolescent psychiatry, and pediatrics is highly relevant for school psychologists' practice. Accessing resources such as chapters or websites can help one stay informed about the latest findings pertaining to children's mental health treatments from across these disciplines. Staying current on pediatric medication efficacy studies and U.S. Food and Drug Administration (FDA) recalls and safety alerts, such as the black-box warnings for antidepressant use, school psychologists can play an active and informed role within treatment decision making.

Examples of the importance of this literature on the practice of psychological services for school-age children are found within ADHD treatment findings. It has been widely reported that methylphenidate treatment with intensive monitoring for the purpose of appropriate dosage titration is more effective in improving core symptoms of ADHD in the short term than are behavioral approaches, cognitive–behavioral therapy, parent training, educational interventions, or medication practices typically implemented by community-based physicians (MTA Cooperative Group, 2004). However, combining behavior therapy with medication results in long-term improved functioning across multiple settings, greater treatment acceptability as perceived by parents, and the possibility of a decrease in methylphenidate dosage (Pelham & Fabiano, 2008).

A review of the child psychopharmacology literature indicates that there are a number of classes of medication that are typically used with children. Table 25.1 provides an overview of each, including the types of potential benefits that may be targeted for intervention and possible side effects. Table 25.2 presents a listing of drugs that have been approved by the FDA for use in treating mental health disorders in children. Common practice within child psychiatry is to use medications that have been approved for adult populations, and thus many additional medicines that are commonly utilized with children are not present within this table. School psychologists should not be alarmed by this practice and instead should be motivated by the need and importance of gathering multiple sources of data to determine if such treatments are effective in child populations. Idiographic responses in school-aged children, given their unique and ever-developing biological systems, are more typically observed when compared to behavioral responses seen in adults and measuring individual change resulting from medication onset is paramount to the treatment process.

Step 3: Knowledge of Behavioral Assessment Techniques

Selecting measures that are sensitive to treatment change is essential to the evaluation process. Tools that gather information about children's thoughts, feelings, and actions across a number of different settings are ideal. An understanding of the importance of using multiple measures from multiple informants, across a multitude of classroom settings, is essential to school-based medication evaluation.

Collecting data that are specific to the intervention is also a hallmark of behavioral assessment. Thus, the knowledge of child psychopharmacology as mentioned in Step 2 is important to the selection of tools that clearly link to the target behaviors typically addressed by different classes of medication and the specific pre-scribed medication. Most likely this will include an assessment of academic performance, externalizing behaviors, internalizing behaviors, social skills, adaptive behaviors, and side effects. To measure these outcomes one or more of the following approaches should be considered and utilized: behavioral observations; direct measures of academic behavior such as those collected by curriculum-based measurement techniques; teachers' grade book to gather homework completion and accuracy rates; home–school notes including daily report cards; work samples; goal attainment scaling; treatment outcome ratings and specific teacher, parent, or child rating scales; side-effect rating scales; measures of treatment adherence; and measures of treatment acceptability.

Final selection of behavioral assessment tools to be used should be specific to the child, considerate of time and resource limitations, and agreeable to the student, parents, teachers, physicians, and other stakeholders within the medication monitoring process.

BEST PRACTICES IN EVALUATING MEDICATION IN SCHOOLS

There are a number of different models and guidelines that have been put forward within the literature pertaining to assessing the effects of psychotropic medication on student performance. Unfortunately, less attention has been given to what needs to happen prior to a child being prescribed a psychotropic medication. As a part of school psychologists' responsibility to carry out best practices in school-based medication evaluations, they must examine the following set of assumptions to ensure that only those children who are likely to benefit from medication treatment are receiving them. In some cases, providing data to suggest that medication treatment might not be the most appropriate would be a valuable contribution to the treatment decision-making team. Working closely with families and other school personnel to address these assumptions or to have these

Table 25.1. Psychotropic Drug Classes, Potential Target Behaviors, and Possible Side Effects

Class of Psychotropic Medication (Specific Example)	Potential Target Behaviors	Possible Side Effects
Anticonvulsants (carbamazepine)	• Seizures • Aggression • Irritability	• Memory difficulties • Inattention • Aggression
Antidepressants (imipramine, clomipramine)	• Enuresis • Depressive symptoms • Mood changes • Inattention	• Sedation • Dry mouth • Constipation • Weight gain
Selective serotonin reuptake inhibitors (fluoxetine, sertraline)	• Obsessive thoughts • Compulsive behaviors • Depressive symptoms	• Drowsiness • Stomach upset • Nervousness • Impulsivity
Atypical antidepressants (buproprion, venlafaxine, buspirone)	• Depressive symptoms • Anxiety symptoms • Panic attacks	• Dizziness • Headache • Insomnia • Drowsiness
Antihistamines (diphenhydramine)	• Anxiety • Sleep induction • Agitation	• Oversedation • Dizziness • Agitation
Antihypertensives (clonidine)	• Aggression • Hyperactivity • Impulsivity	• Dry mouth • Dizziness
Antimanics (lithium carbonate)	• Mood regulation • Aggression • Irritability	• Stomach upset • Headache • Sedation
Anxiolytics (alprazolam, diazepam)	• Anxiety symptoms • Seizures	• Sedation • Substance abuse • Memory difficulties
Atypical antipsychotics (risperidone, olanzapine, quetiapine)	• Schizophrenia symptoms • Mood regulation	• Hypotension • Motor impairments • Memory difficulties
Neuroleptics (chlorpromazine, haldol)	• Psychotic symptoms • Autism	• Sedation • Headache • Weight gain
Selective norepinephrine reuptake inhibitors (atomoxetine)	• Inattention • Hyperactivity • Impulsivity	• Headache • Fatigue • Stomach upset
Stimulants (methylphenidate, dextroamphetamine)	• Inattention • Hyperactivity • Impulsivity	• Diminished appetite • Weight loss • Sleep difficulties

Note. Based on information from U.S. Department of Health and Human Services (2012), Vitiello (2012), and Wilens (2008).

assumptions addressed by other mental health professionals before engaging in evaluation of the effects of psychotropic medication on school performance is important.

Assumption 1: A comprehensive diagnostic assessment has been completed by a highly qualified mental health professional. School-based treatment goals have been identified by the treating physician.

Assumption 2: Psychosocial and educational interventions have been previously developed to meet the child's needs at school and home, these interventions have been implemented with integrity, and data collected from these interventions have clearly demonstrated a lack of or a limited response and continued dysfunction exists. Yet, school psychologists also recognize and value parents' choice and decision about the sequence to

Table 25.2. U.S. Food and Drug Administration-Approved Mental Health Medications for Children and Adolescents

Trade Name	Generic Name	Approved Age
Stimulant medications for ADHD		
Adderall	Amphetamine	3 and older
Adderall XR	Amphetamine (extended release)	6 and older
Concerta	Methylphenidate (long acting)	6 and older
Daytrana	Methylphenidate patch	6 and older
Desoxyn	Methamphetamine	6 and older
Dexedrine	Dextroamphetamine	3 and older
Dextrostat	Dextroamphetamine	3 and older
Focalin	Dexmethylphenidate	6 and older
Focalin XR	Dexmethylphenidate (extended release)	6 and older
Metadate ER	Methylphenidate (extended release)	6 and older
Metadate CD	Methylphenidate (extended release)	6 and older
Methylin	Methylphenidate (oral solution and chewable tablets)	6 and older
Ritalin	Methylphenidate	6 and older
Ritalin SR	Methylphenidate (extended release)	6 and older
Ritalin LA	Methylphenidate (long-acting atomoxetine)	6 and older
Vyvanse	Lisdexamfetamine dimesylate	6 and older
Nonstimulants for ADHD		
Intuniv	Guanfacine	6 and older
Strattera	Atomoxetine	6 and older
Antidepressant and antianxiety medications		
Anafranil	Clomipramine	10 and older (for OCD)
Lexapro (SSRI)	Escitalopram	12–17 (for MDD)
Luvox (SSRI)	Fluvoxamine	8 and older (for OCD)
Prozac	Fluoxetine	8 and older
Sinequan	Doxepin	12 and older
Tofranil (tricyclic)	Imipramine	6 and older (for bedwetting)
Zoloft (SSRI)	Sertraline	6 and older (for OCD)
Antipsychotic medications		
Abilify	Aripiprazole	10 and older for bipolar disorder, manic or mixed episodes; 13–17 for schizophrenia and bipolar
Haldol	Haloperidol	3 and older
Mellaril	Thioridazine	2 and older
Orap	Pimozide	12 and older (Tourette's syndrome)
Risperdal	Risperidone	13 and older for schizophrenia; 10 and older for bipolar mania and mixed episodes; 5–16 for irritability associated with autism
Seroquel	Quetiapine	13 and older for schizophrenia; 10–17 for treatment of manic and mixed episodes of bipolar disorder
Thioridazine (generic only)	Thioridazine	2 and older
Zyprexia	Olanzapine	13–17 as second line of treatment for manic or mixed episodes of bipolar disorder and schizophrenia
Mood stabilizing medications		
Depakote	Divalproex sodium (valproic acid)	2 and older (for seizures)
Eskalith	Lithium carbonate	12 and older
Lithium citrate	Lithium Citrate	12 and older
Lithobid	Lithium carbonate	12 and older
Tegretol	Carbamazepine	any age (for seizures)
Trileptal	Oxcarbazepine	4 and older

Note. OCD = obsessive–compulsive disorder; MDD = major depressive disorder; SSRI = selective serotonin reuptake inhibitors. Based on information from U.S. Department of Health and Human Services (2012).

implement educational, psychological, ecological, and/or pharmacological approaches.

Assumption 3: The child's family has been presented with an overview of the risks and benefits associated with all of the evidence-based treatment approaches that are known to improve the child's current academic, social, emotional, and behavioral functioning. School psychologists understand parent perceptions of these treatment options and the potential cultural variations that may exist pertaining to medication treatment acceptability.

Assumption 4: Parents' decision to seek out medication treatment was based on their own beliefs, values, and interests. Parents have not reported being pressured by teachers or school staff to have their child put on medication. School psychologists should respect the decisions parents make for their child and support them in gathering the data necessary to support or refute their decision.

Assumption 5: Parental consent for involvement in the evaluation of medication effects on classroom learning and behavior has been obtained. Parents and guardians must have a clear understanding of what data will be gathered, who will be involved, and who will have access to the information collected.

Assumption 6: A consent for release of information has been obtained from parents so that open lines of communication are created across home, school, and community settings. The prescribing physician must be accessible and open to communications from the school in order for medication evaluation procedures to be effective.

Models for Evaluating Medication Effects

When the above assumptions have been met, school psychologists are then ready to engage in school-based medication evaluation. A number of formal school-based medication evaluation systems exist, including the School-Based Medication Evaluation Program (SBME; Gadow, 1993), the Methylphenidate Placebo Protocol (MPP; Hyman et al., 1998), and the Agile Consultative Model for Medication Evaluation (ACMME; Volpe, Heick, & Gureasko-Moore, 2005). Moreover, a number of similar research methods involving the use of placebo-controlled, crossover investigations of short- and long-acting stimulants in school settings are found in the literature (e.g., Pelham et al., 2013). The common theme across these programs/studies is to collect school-based data to find the minimum dosage that results in the maximum benefit on performance (i.e., lowest therapeutic dosage). Unfortunately, each of these approaches presents significant issues of feasibility and

usefulness for practicing school psychologists. Moreover, each has limited research supporting their utility within typical school settings and each has only demonstrated usefulness pertaining to treatment of ADHD symptoms. Yet, each provides important guidance to school psychologists for how to bring scientific principles into practice when engaging in school-based medication evaluation of student performance.

As stimulant medications are one of the most common types of medications taken by school-age children, and given that the majority of children's mental health disorders that come to the attention of service providers have to do with externalizing behavior problems, it is clear why most school-based evaluation programs focus on the use of these medications in the treatment of children who present with symptoms of inattention, hyperactivity, impulsivity, and other disruptive behaviors. Yet, it is also recognized that much work needs to be done to develop parallel medication treatment protocols or techniques for other prevalent childhood conditions, such as developmental delays associated with autism, social anxiety disorders, and pediatric depressive disorders. Currently, school-based evaluation models do not appear within the literature for these conditions. Much of this is due to difficulties in observing and measuring internal processes such as emotional distress, depressive or obsessive patterns of thinking, or feelings of anxiety. With those challenges in mind, there is much to be learned from the formal school-based medication evaluation models and practices found within the ADHD literature and a brief review of each is provided.

School-Based Medication Evaluation Program

The SBME model involves the use of behavioral ratings to provide a general measure of parent and teacher perceptions of behavior, and direct observations of students to provide a measure of context-specific behavior. Rating scales are completed within each phase, or dosage, of the evaluation. Most scales require respondents to rate characteristics on a scale from *not at all* to *very much*. Items reflecting core symptoms of ADHD might include excitability, impulsivity, inattentiveness, or disturbing other children. Associated or peripheral characteristics of ADHD might also be assessed. These would include behaviors related to aggression or social skills. Items reflecting side effects might include being overly quiet, having difficulty falling asleep, irritability, and appetite suppression. The advantages of these types of rating scales are that they are easy to use, easy to score, and usually cost effective.

The SBME model also uses direct observation codes conducted by trained observers to provide more precise descriptions of behavior across settings. While the observation codes produce specific descriptions of behavior, it is important to note that the use of the codes can be time consuming and expensive, since they require extensive training and are conducted by outside clinical observers. The use of these behavioral observation codes may also fail to detect changes in low-frequency behaviors that are not likely to occur during a particular observation session.

By combining rating scales and direct observations, the SBME model provides an opportunity for controlled, empirical data collection that includes multiple types and sources of data, with reports from parents, teachers, and trained observers, though it is important to note that limited attention is given to academic performance within SBME. In sum, feasibility issues and the intensive training required for SBME, especially the observational methods, present numerous challenges for use of this approach by practicing school psychologists.

Methylphenidate Placebo Protocol

The MPP model utilizes measures that can be implemented by school staff and parents with little additional training. It also attempts to measure changes in cognitive and academic performance unlike SBME. Rating scales assess the target effects of medication on core and peripheral symptoms associated with ADHD, as well as side effects. In place of the direct behavioral observation codes, this model uses the administration of functional tasks that measure cognitive skills (visual discrimination, digit span) and academic skills (listening comprehension, reading, math).

MPP uses both daily and weekly rating scales. Daily scales are completed by the student, parents, and teachers, and they include measures of attention, hyperactivity, social skills, and oppositional behaviors. Weekly parent and teacher rating scales of core ADHD symptoms and medication side effects are also gathered. Additionally, students are administered weekly assessments of functional tasks.

Behavioral ratings in this approach lack the rigor of the structured observations found within SBME. Also, many of the functional tasks may be subject to practice effects and the use of these tasks may not be an adequate measure of improvement in these areas. Yet differences in costs and resources needed to carry out MPP are likely to be viewed more favorably within school-based practices when compared to SBME.

Agile Consultative Model for Medication Evaluation

ACMME is a flexible model for school-based medication evaluation utilized in the context of a behavioral problem-solving framework. The flexibility of this approach is contingent upon the type of research design or dosage pattern prescribed by the physician (A [baseline], B [treatment], AB, or ABA design). Conceptually, this model has the potential for applicability beyond psychostimulants and treatment for ADHD. Target behaviors for intervention vary by case and can be individually developed in the context of problem identification, problem analysis, treatment implementation, and treatment evaluation interviews with parents. Unfortunately, this model has only been applied to ADHD treatment to date.

One substantial advantage of ACMME over other models is the inclusion of assessment pertaining to feasibility and acceptability, with specific attention to home–school–physician communication. A series of contact letters and rating scales are provided within ACMME to facilitate communication between the school psychologist and other stakeholders, including classroom teachers. Once resources and commitments have been obtained, interviews based on Bergan and Kratochwill's (1990) model of behavioral consultation are completed. Specifically, a hierarchy of target behaviors is identified, with specific attention given to differences between current levels of behavior and desired levels. Procedures for gathering data are agreed upon, including who will measure what and when, and then baseline data collection begins. Baseline data are reviewed and goals for treatment are established, so that the lowest dose required to obtain the desired behavioral effect may be realized. Opportunities to evaluate low, medium, or high doses in relation to baseline data exist, or different dosages of psychostimulant treatments may be administered within an alternating treatment design as determined in consultation with the prescribing physician. Data are then evaluated to determine the therapeutic dose that is prescribed. Finally, a follow-up data collection period occurs to ensure maintenance of the intended effects and to determine if medication is being administered and taken by the child as prescribed.

Summary

All three medication evaluation models have several characteristics in common. They all involve the use of varying medication dosages and the collection of baseline data. A single-subject design is utilized to account for varying symptom expression and response to medication. Parent and teacher rating scales, in addition to other measures, are completed at consistent intervals to provide ongoing measures of behavior. There is a focus on core behavioral symptoms of ADHD, such as hyperactivity and impulsivity, associated behaviors, and side effects of medication. Evaluation results are communicated clearly and efficiently to the prescribing physician for potential titration, continuation of current treatment, or discontinuation.

While all of these models demonstrate limitations when applied in a school setting, they provide a good starting place for thinking about designing school-based medication evaluation programs. Specifically, these models highlight the importance of multiple methods to measure behavior and use of rating scales as a means to monitor progress and collect data from both parents and teachers, and collaboration between home, school, and community providers is essential. Both teachers and parents should be involved because they can provide valuable information for examining the divergence or convergence of medication outcomes across settings. Moreover, treatment adherence and acceptability of

medication treatment are essential components to build into school-based evaluation procedures.

With these guidelines in mind, school psychologists can work with other key stakeholders, including physicians and school personnel (e.g., nurse, social worker, counselor), to create programs within existing school frameworks (e.g., SWPBIS, RTI) that evaluate student behavior in response to medication while balancing empirical data collection with practical concerns. Such procedures would be similar to other methods to evaluate students' response to intervention. A set of best practices to guide the development and involvement within these medication evaluation procedures is recommended in Table 25.3.

Important Considerations

Few school psychologists are afforded the time and resources necessary to engage in formal medication evaluation approaches like MPP, SBME, and ACMME. Thus, the predominant focus of school psychologists' efforts should be on issues of communication, collaboration, and consultation. Collaboration among parents,

Table 25.3. Best Practices in Evaluating the Effects of Medication on School Performance

- School psychologists work closely with parents, physicians, school personnel, and other stakeholders (i.e., progress-monitoring team) to design an individualized evaluation plan based on the child's target behaviors and the hypothesized impact of the psychotropic medication prescribed.

- A specific plan to operationalize the monitoring procedures is developed, along with a time line specifying a feedback loop to teachers, parents, and physicians.

- Data are gathered repeatedly across multiple settings and informants, including before medication onset. Parent, teacher, and student perspectives on symptom change are essential to the evaluation.

- Standardized measures of behavior (e.g., rating scales, curriculum-based measurement) are used concurrently with instruments demonstrating strong social validity and treatment sensitivity, such as a direct behavior rating scale. Treatment adherence and acceptability data are also gathered.

- Vigilance for changes in unintended beneficial effects for the child is maintained by progress-monitoring team members throughout the duration of the treatment evaluation.

- Assessment of any ecological changes within the classroom or home that may be the result of the child's medication treatment are gathered by parent and teacher reports.

- Side effects are assessed, based on medication type, and additional information from parents/teachers is gathered if they observe unintended effects. Side effect rating scales or side effect diaries should be completed by the student.

- Data are provided to parents in a user-friendly format through such means as graphs, tables, or brief summary reports. Visual representations can be developed easily using data management software such as ChartDog Graph Maker (http://www.interventioncentral.org/tools/chart_dog_graph_maker).

- Medication termination or maintenance guidelines and goals are operationalized at the point at which an optimal dosage (i.e., demonstrating maximum benefit and a minimum of side effects) has been obtained.

- Observations and data pertaining to concurrent educational and behavioral interventions are gathered. The adjunctive effects such approaches have in combination with medication treatment are identified.

- Follow-up skills training booster sessions are planned in anticipation of medication treatment termination in an effort to maintain treatment gains.

school personnel, and physicians is essential for effective medication treatment of childhood mental health disorders.

School psychologists are in an optimal position to facilitate the necessary communication among parents, school personnel, and the student's physician. As a facilitator of this process, the school psychologist has to overcome common barriers that may impede effective collaboration. Between parents and school personnel, there are barriers of limited knowledge, miscommunication, resistance, distance, and time. Parents sometimes have limited knowledge of the school's expectations and resources available to help evaluate their treatment decisions, which can lead to miscommunication between parents and the school system. Parents may experience resistance when interacting with schools. They may be uncertain about how much to reveal to schools about their home life when a problem arises, and they may be especially reluctant to disclose that their child has been prescribed medication. School personnel, including teachers and related service personnel, may also be presented with barriers, including a lack of time, limited knowledge of medication effects and side effects, or a lack of training in data collection methods. Finally, physical distance between home and school and time constraints can be barriers to effective communication and collaboration between families and school personnel.

There are similar barriers between parents and the treating physician. Parents often enter treatment situations for their children with limited knowledge of medication and treatment options. Parents may often prefer the use of behavioral treatment first, as a more conservative approach, but may agree to starting their child on a medication trial if that is what the physician recommends. Often, physicians are unaware of effective behavioral interventions and rely on those treatments for which they have been trained. Parents may have different expectations for their children than the physicians do, leading to miscommunication. Parents can experience resistance in interacting with the physician, because they are unsure about placing their child on medication or are unsure about seeking medical help at all. Finally, as in the interaction between parents and the school system, distance and time can impede collaborative efforts. School psychologists may be able to offer assistance to parents by collaboratively addressing these issues before the parent communicates with the child's physician.

Schools and physicians rarely interact. Typically, these lines of communication have not been established. Some exceptions include schools providing onsite health and mental health services or pediatric primary care settings that utilize an integrated approach to mental health treatment using child behavior health consultants to function as liaisons between the school and physician. Distance and time are also important barriers to overcome when attempting to collaborate between systems. Integrating information from parents, school personnel, and physicians, even when lines of communication are in place, is a difficult task.

As reported by DuPaul and Carlson (2005), there are several technologies and tools school psychologists can utilize to overcome the above barriers and effectively integrate information from all stakeholders. Specifically, Conjoint Behavioral Consultation (Sheridan, Kratochwill, & Bergan, 1996) procedures are recommended as potentially effective, and this recommendation parallels the problem-solving context for evaluation proposed within the ACMME protocol.

First Steps Toward Involvement

Through consultation with school psychologists, parents and teachers are ideal candidates to provide treatment progress-monitoring data through a number of published instruments. While there are many commercially produced rating scales available, a well-established example of an instrument that provides essential behavior progress monitoring data in response to medication treatment is the Behavior Assessment System for Children-Second Edition, Progress Monitor (BASC-2 PM; Kamphaus & Reynolds, 2009). The BASC-2 PM includes forms for teachers and parents and takes approximately 5 minutes to complete (15–20 items) and includes space for narrative comments. There is a preschool version (ages 2–5) and a school-age version (grades K–12). Also, there is a student self-assessment form for students in grades 3–12. The BASC-2 PM allows evaluators to organize input from multiple informants and to provide graphical illustration of results, and it gathers information about changes in identified target behaviors (externalizing/ADHD problems, internalizing problems, social withdrawal, adaptive skills) and treatment goals, emergent side effects, and changes in medication dosage. Its ease of use makes it amenable for frequent ratings during the treatment phase, using BASC-2 ASSIST scoring software that scores, analyzes, and graphs behavior ratings, observation data, and other school performance measures to provide progress reports of how behavior change correlates with treatment. Because the progress-monitoring forms are intended to track changes in behavior over time (daily, weekly, biweekly ratings), they provide useful data that can be shared with physicians for treatment planning and close monitoring of treatment changes, such as dosage titration and side-effect monitoring for potential contraindications. Specifically for use in school-based medication monitoring procedures, the teacher rates the student's behaviors during the active phase of the medication (i.e., typically 2–4 hours after ingestion for short-acting medicines) to assess for clinically significant changes in school performance (academic and/or behavior) at varying dosages.

Other psychometrically sound medication monitoring instruments are available, many of which can be used free of charge from the Massachusetts General Hospital School Psychiatry Program (http://www.massgeneral. org/schoolpsychiatry). A convenient tool for school psychologists to use may be the direct behavior rating scales found at Direct Behavior Ratings (http://www. directbehaviorratings.com). Also, the use of a daily report card (i.e., home–school note) provides a cost- and time-effective method of monitoring behavioral response to treatment in the classroom. When teachers are blind to a student's medication status, daily behavior ratings over the course of different treatment conditions (e.g., no treatment, placebo, low-dose treatment, high-dose treatment) provide an objective assessment of the treatments' effectiveness.

For the purposes of monitoring side effects, there are a number of excellent instruments (e.g., Stimulant Drug Side Effects Rating Scale; Barkley, 1998) that may more accurately target specific physiological effects not assessed in the progress-monitoring scales. In addition, there are comprehensive side effect rating scales available online for free from the Massachusetts General Hospital School Psychiatry Program (http://www2. massgeneral.org/schoolpsychiatry/pdfs/medications_ EvalSideEffects.pdf). In sum, the use of these assessment tools provides an exceptional way to help build a relationship between the school–home–medical provider and they may help set the stage for carrying out best practices in assessing the effects of psychotropic medication on student performance.

Case Example

A case example is presented below to illustrate what these practices might look like in order to gather the data necessary to adequately address these five important medication evaluation questions: Is medication effective compared to no medication? What dose results in the greatest improvement in functioning? Do the benefits of medication treatment outweigh the risks? Was medication treatment implemented as intended? Do parents and children find medication an acceptable method of treatment?

The school psychologist at Anderson High School volunteered to head up school-based efforts to work with the family of James, a 16-year-old tenth grader, who was struggling with school attendance, academic performance, poor peer relations, and depressive symptoms. His parents were especially concerned with his isolation and avoidance of social situations, including a tendency to spend countless hours playing video games.

According to his parents, James was recently diagnosed with major depressive disorder by a community-based clinical psychologist and referred to his family physician for medication consultation. James's parents were particularly concerned about recently well-publicized antidepressant side effects (i.e., black box warnings) and how his prescribed medication (i.e., fluoxetine) fell within that class of medications.

Articles on the Internet indicating that severe disinhibition, including homicidal and suicidal ideation, may occur within a small minority of children and adolescents taking fluoxetine were particularly worrisome to them. In addition, the idea that James could experience symptoms of depersonalization (i.e., watching yourself go through the day) or derealization (i.e., walking around in a dream) as a result of taking fluoxetine were also concerning.

In an effort to understand better the potential risks and benefits of this treatment approach, James's parents sought additional school-based data to support or refute their decision to move forward with medication treatment. They also requested help in locating accurate fluoxetine side-effect data, and they were referred to information that appears on the website of the FDA's Safety Information and Adverse Event Reporting Program, including a specific link on fluoxetine (http:// www.accessdata.fda.gov/drugsatfda_docs/label/2011/ 018936s091lbl.pdf).

Parental consent for data collection and a release of information was secured to allow for communication between home and school. James's parents would serve as the primary contact for school–physician communications. Based on discussions with James's parents and teachers, primary target behaviors included social withdrawal and depressed mood. A standardized, nationally normed rating scale with strong reliability and validity was selected for use in progress monitoring these two target behaviors. Secondary target behaviors included work completion and academic performance within his math class, a class in which he had been unexpectedly struggling as a result of his depressive symptoms. Weekly ratings from James, his mom, and his algebra teacher were obtained both prior to and following treatment onset. In addition, the Web-based grade book for algebra was monitored closely by the school psychologist with specific attention to baseline levels of work completion/performance and potential changes following medication treatment.

Specifically, rating scale data were collected twice within the 2 weeks leading up to James's scheduled appointment with his physician. Rating scale findings and performance in algebra clearly indicated the presence and stability of substantial difficulties in social withdrawal, depression, and impairment in school and home functioning. James and his parents decided to move forward with an 8-week trial of fluoxetine, the typical length of time necessary to see a maximum therapeutic response. Potential side effects of fluoxetine (disinhibition, lethargy, tiredness, stomach upset) were tracked in a daily side effect diary provided to James. James was instructed on which behaviors to look for by his primary care physician and the plan was to check in with the school psychologist at school if side effects emerged so that a determination could be made pertaining to the need to inform his primary care physician of possible serious side effects (e.g., vomiting, mania). It was established that the school psychologist would review the side effect diary weekly with James and his primary care physician would review it monthly during medication follow-up visits.

Within the first week of taking fluoxetine, James had written in his side effect diary that he had been feeling different from his usual self, in addition to symptoms of mild stomach upset. Upon review of the diary and follow-up questioning by the school psychologist, James appeared to be experiencing mild disinhibition symptoms, including blurting answers out in class and symptoms of impulsivity in his interactions with peers in the hallway. The school psychologist called James's parents and shared the information. Interestingly, James was also reporting feeling more comfortable and less shy around others compared to how he felt prior to taking fluoxetine. Unfortunately, his side effects (stomach upset, disinhibition) gradually increased and began to become problematic by the end of the second week of treatment. James's parents informed his primary care physician of this and a decision was made to reduce the dose of fluoxetine. Within a couple of days, stomach upset and disinhibition (e.g., silliness,

class disruptions) were no longer being reported by James or his teachers.

Prior to the first medication follow-up visit, the school psychologist provided James's parents a one-page "Medication Consultation Summary Report" to be shared with James's primary care physician, with the headings "Reason for Consultation," "Target Behavior Changes," "Emergent Side Effects in School," and "Conclusions." By the sixth week of treatment, and within the second medication consultation report, James's target behaviors showed initial signs of improvement according to behavioral rating data. James's parents, in conjunction with his primary care physician, decided to continue treatment until all treatment goals were met. Treatment adherence was strong and high levels of treatment acceptability were reported by James and his parents. The school psychologist's involvement gradually declined over the next 6 months as James's improvements (i.e., symptom reduction, improved performance in algebra) were maintained without the emergence of any additional side effects.

The school psychologist's reengagement with James occurred the following year after 18 months of successful fluoxetine treatment. Treatment goals had been met and James's parents decided to discontinue medication treatment. The school psychologist and school staff once again worked closely with the family to monitor the behavioral effects associated with a discontinuation of medication, and to offer psychosocial approaches (e.g., counseling, check ins, self-monitoring of academic performance) during the remaining school year.

SUMMARY

The push toward evidence-based practices within schools creates a context for school psychologists to develop the competencies necessary to examine treatments that might not ordinarily be a part of their graduate training. With the increasing rate of medication usage by school-age students, engaging in the evaluation of psychotropic medication treatment response is essential to promoting the academic, social, and emotional success of children struggling with mental health conditions. Best practices in evaluating medication effects on school performance, like most practices in the field of school psychology, are grounded in collaboration and communication with parents, physicians, and other treatment providers to create a comprehensive treatment plan that meets both the child's needs and the family's belief systems. Monitoring both the intended and unintended effects of these treatments is important as school psychologists help parents to be data-based decision makers in their quest to promote their children's development.

REFERENCES

American Academy of Child and Adolescent Psychiatry. (2012). *A guide for community child serving agencies on psychotropic medication for children and adolescents.* Washington, DC: Author. Retrieved from http://www. aacap.org/galleries/default-file/guide_for_community_child_ serving_agencies_on_psychotropic_medications_for_children_and_ adolescents_2012.pdf

American Psychological Association. (2010). *Ethical principles of psychologists and code of conduct.* Washington, DC: Author. Retrieved from http://www.apa.org/ethics/code/index.aspx

Barkley, R. (1998). *Stimulant Drug Side Effects Rating Scale.* New York, NY: Guilford Press.

Bergan, J. R., & Kratochwill, T. R. (1990). *Behavioral consultation and therapy.* New York, NY: Plenum Press.

Carlson, J. S., Demaray, M. K., & Hunter-Oehmke, S. (2006). A survey of school psychologists' knowledge and training in child psychopharmacology. *Psychology in the Schools, 43,* 623–633. doi:10. 1002/pits.20168

Centers for Disease Control and Prevention. (2010). Increasing prevalence of parent-reported attention-deficit/hyperactivity disorder among children: United States, 2003 and 2007. *Morbidity and Mortality Weekly Report, 59,* (pp. 1439–1443). Retrieved from http://www.cdc.gov/mmwr/pdf/wk/mm5944.pdf

DuPaul, G., & Carlson, J. S. (2005). Child psychopharmacology: How school psychologists can contribute to effective outcomes. *School Psychology Quarterly, 20,* 206–221.

Gadow, K. D. (1993). A school-based medication evaluation program. In J. L. Matson (Ed.), *Handbook of hyperactivity in children* (pp. 186–219). Boston, MA: Allyn & Bacon.

HaileMariam, A., Bradley-Johnson, S., & Johnson, C. M. (2002). Pediatricians' preferences for ADHD information from schools. *School Psychology Review, 31,* 94–105.

Hyman, I. A., Wojtowicz, A., Lee, K. D., Haffner, M. E., Fiorello, C. A., Storlazzi, J. J., & Rosenfield, J. (1998). School-based methylphenidate placebo protocols: Methodological and practical issues. *Journal of Learning Disabilities, 31,* 581–594. doi:10.1177/ 002221949803100609

Kamphaus, R. W., & Reynolds, C. R. (2009). *Behavior Assessment System for Children-Second Edition, Progress Monitor.* Bloomington, MN: Pearson.

Kubiszyn, T. (1994). Pediatric psychopharmacology and prescription privileges: Implications and opportunities for school psychology. *School Psychology Quarterly, 9,* 26–40.

Kubiszyn, T., Mire, S., Dutt, S., Papathopoulos, K., & Burridge, A. B. (2012). Significant differences in pediatric psychotropic side effects: Implications for school performance. *School Psychology Quarterly, 27,* 4–28.

Medco Health Solutions. (2011). *Drug trend report.* San Diego, CA: Mentus.

Merikangas, K. R., He, J., Rapoport, J., Vitiello, B., & Olfson, M. (2013). Medication use in U.S. youth with mental disorders. *Journal of the American Medical Association Pediatrics, 167,* 141–148. doi:10. 1001/jamapediatrics.2013.431

Mojtabai, R., & Olfson, M. (2010). National trends in psychotropic medication polypharmacy in office-based psychiatry. *Archives of General Psychiatry, 67,* 26–36. doi:10.1001/archgenpsychiatry.2009. 175

MTA Cooperative Group. (2004). The NIMH MTA follow-up: 24-month outcomes of treatment strategies for attention-deficit/hyperactivity disorder (ADHD). *Pediatrics, 113,* 754–761.

National Association of School Psychologists. (2010a). *Model for comprehensive and integrated school psychological services.* Bethesda, MD: Author. Retrieved from http://www.nasponline.org/standards/ 2010standards/2_PracticeModel.pdf

National Association of School Psychologists. (2010b). *Principles for professional ethics.* Bethesda, MD: Author. Retrieved from http://www.nasponline.org/standards/2010standards/1_ %20Ethical%20Principles.pdf

Pelham, W. E., & Fabiano, G. A. (2008). Evidence-based psychosocial treatments for attention-deficit/hyperactivity disorder. *Journal of Clinical Child and Adolescent Psychology, 37,* 184–214. doi:10.1080/ 15374410701818681

Pelham, W. E., Smith, B. H., Evans, S. W., Bulkstein, O., Gnagy, E. M., Greiner, A. R., & Sibley, M. H. (2013). The effectiveness of short- and long-acting stimulant medications for adolescents with ADHD in a naturalistic secondary school setting. *Journal of Attention Disorders.* doi:10.1177/1087054712473834

Sheridan, S. M., Kratochwill, T. R., & Bergan, J. R. (1996). *Conjoint behavioral consultation: A procedural manual.* New York, NY: Plenum Press.

Smyer, M. A., Balster, R. L., Egli, D., Johnson, D. L., Kilbey, M. M., Leith, N. J., & Puente, A. E. (1993). Summary of the report of the ad hoc task force on psychopharmacology of the American Psychological Association. *Professional Psychology: Research and Practice, 2,* 394–403.

U.S. Department of Health and Human Services. (2012). *Mental health medications.* Washington, DC: National Institute of Mental Health.

Vitiello, B. (2012). Principles in using psychotropic medication in children and adolescents. In Rey, J. M. (Ed.), *IACAPAP e-textbook of child and adolescent mental health.* Geneva, Switzerland: International Association for Child and Adolescent Psychiatry and Allied Professions. Retrieved from http://iacapap.org/wp-content/ uploads/A.7-PSYCHOPHARMACOLOGY-072012.pdf

Volpe, R. J., Heick, P. F., & Gureasko-Moore, D. (2005). An agile behavioral model for monitoring the effects of stimulant medication in school settings. *Psychology in the Schools, 42,* 509–523. doi:10. 1002/pits.20088

Wilens, T. E. (2008). *Straight talk about psychiatric medications for kids* (3rd ed.). New York, NY: Guilford Press.

26 Best Practices in Collaborating With Medical Personnel

Sarah E. Glaser
Steven R. Shaw
McGill University (QC)

OVERVIEW

Angela is a 13-year-old seventh-grade student. She has a history of severe, persistent, and poorly controlled asthma. Angela has been prescribed a variety of long-term and rescue medications, but she has developed symptoms such as headaches, nervousness, nausea, and sore throat. Seasonal allergies, colds, and stress often result in the return of symptoms and an overreliance on rescue inhalers. She has been hospitalized six times in the last year because of these medical problems. Angela's school performance has deteriorated to the point that she is receiving failing grades. School-based interventions have been ineffective because she is missing many days of school. When she attends school, there are severe limitations on her activity level and her ability to manage stress. School personnel have made the determination that Angela is eligible for a classification of Other Health Impaired in order to receive special education services. To develop the best possible educational program for Angela, medical, family, and school personnel (including the school psychologist) are required to share information and coordinate services. However, communication and collaboration among these multidisciplinary professionals is an activity with many barriers and challenges. Improving Angela's quality of life, including physical health and academic performance, requires a coordinated medical, psychosocial, and academic plan. To best serve Angela and students with similar medical needs, school psychologists must be knowledgeable about the best practices in collaborating with medical personnel.

Nearly every school psychologist has worked with students like Angela who have conditions such as asthma, attention deficit hyperactivity disorder, autism, or seizures that require continual collaboration with medical personnel. School psychologists are in a unique and important position to coordinate collaborative efforts and advocate for establishment of multidisciplinary services. Effective collaboration among educators and doctors is required to support the successful academic achievement and physical well-being of students with medical issues (McCabe & Shaw, 2010).

The purpose of this chapter is aligned with the domain of Preventive and Responsive Services in the National Association of School Psychologists (NASP) *Model for Comprehensive and Integrated School Psychological Services* (NASP, 2010) in that its purpose is to provide practical information to assist school psychologists in formulating treatment plans and collaborative professional relationships for students who require medical care or medication monitoring. These practices can ensure healthier academic, social–emotional, and physical outcomes among students. Barriers to collaboration with medical personnel, school policy relevance, and best practices will be discussed in detail.

Model of Collaboration

There are several relevant models of collaboration for doctors and school psychologists that provide relevant and productive frameworks of collaboration between educators and medical professionals (e.g., biopsychoeducational systems model; Grier & Bradley-Klug, 2011). Becoming familiar with these working models is a useful method of learning how to foster cooperation and effective consultation (Clemens, Welfare, & Williams,

375

2011; Glaser, Ouimet, & Shaw, 2010; McCabe & Shaw, 2010). Table 26.1 summarizes these models.

Figure 26.1 illustrates an overview of the unique collaborative role of each person involved in these models.

Barriers to Collaboration

There are many reasons why collaboration between medical and school personnel fail. Understanding and preparing for these barriers ensures that professionals are well versed in how to avoid and manage conflict. Table 26.2 summarizes examples of barriers to collaboration that can arise.

BASIC CONSIDERATIONS

Issues of school and physician collaboration are not a concern for most students, the majority of whom experience few, if any, serious health or mental health concerns during their school careers. When health and mental health concerns arise, students require significant amounts of staff time, home–school communication, and interaction with community providers. The types of collaboration between school psychologists, educators, and medical professionals are loosely organized into the multitier model of educational interventions.

Collaboration for Primary Prevention (Tier 1)

At the Tier 1 level, school-wide educational programming for the purposes of prevention of medical and mental health risks is a valuable form of collaboration. These programs combine the expertise of school psychologists and medical professionals with the access to a large population of school-age children in order to improve the overall well-being of communities. For example, medical personnel have partnered with school psychologists to develop programs in obesity prevention and reduction in transmission of cold and flu viruses. Recently, the issues of sports- and playground-related concussions have been a topic of concern. Medical professionals, neuropsychologists, and school psychologists have collaborated to improve playground design; improve coaching techniques for sports such as football, soccer, and cheerleading; instructed coaches, parents, and teachers to recognize signs of possible concussion; and educated teachers on short-term curricular adaptations for students with mild to moderate head injury.

Programs aimed at reducing the risk of serious mental health issues also offer the opportunity for school and medical personnel to collaborate. For instance, many school-based programs have been created that target prevention of anxiety disorders, depressive disorders, suicide and self-harm, drug and alcohol abuse, eating

Table 26.1 Summary of Collaborative Models

Model	Strategies
Collaborative team model	• Shared responsibility and decision making among all parties, including school psychologists, doctors, teachers, and school nurses • Encourages consistent and frequent interdisciplinary treatment of the child and allows for school psychologists and doctors to adopt different perspectives regarding their professional roles • Appropriate fit for students requiring long-term treatment collaboration between school psychologists and medical professionals • Organization and leadership among team members are established early in the process • School psychologists and educators can develop new and consensus-based strategies for identifying medical issues among students or learn to consider medical factors that may be contributing to educational difficulties
Systems models	• Take into consideration the planning of interventions at several different levels and involve active collaboration between medical professionals, educators, and family members • Involve the child's parents in the treatment process and encourage regular collaboration with all relevant individuals • Parents can provide educators and medical professionals with important information regarding the child's functioning in the home setting, which may differ from school behaviors; professionals can gain a deeper understanding of the child's difficulties and develop the most appropriate intervention plan • Collaboration among the student's school psychologist, teachers, family, and medical professional is most effective when it is ongoing throughout treatment and interactive between all members; the goal of this feedback loop is to improve the child's social, emotional, and academic functioning

Figure 26.1 An Integrated Model of Interprofessional Collaboration

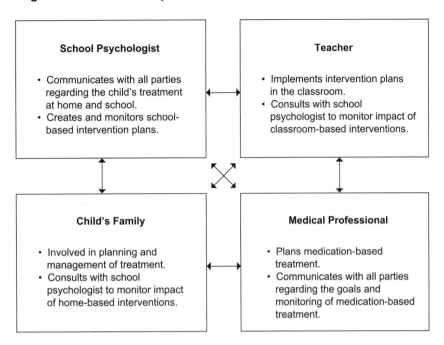

Note. From "Collaboration Between Educators and Medical Professionals: Models, Barriers, and Implications" (pp. 8–21), by S. E. Glaser, T. Ouimet, and S. R. Shaw, 2010. In P. McCabe and S. R. Shaw (Eds.), *Pediatric Disorders: Current Topics and Interventions for Educators,* Thousand Oaks, CA: SAGE. Copyright 2010 by SAGE. Adapted with permission.

disorders, and social–emotional problems stemming from peer bullying.

Collaboration for At-Risk Populations (Tier 2)

Tier 2 collaboration involves interventions for students who are at risk for physical or mental health issues. Many students encounter health issues that put them at risk for potential medical crises or significant problems such as frequent absences, unintended responses to medication, family disruption, fatigue, and pain. Physical and mental health conditions such as morbid obesity, mild concussions, seizure disorders, and eating disorders all put children at risk for these problems. For example, overweight children perform lower on math and reading test scores than nonoverweight children (Datar, Sturm, & Magnabosco, 2004). Given that medical consultation or treatment is often required for students with these conditions, frequent communication between school psychologists, educators, and medical professionals is necessary for collaborative programing. An introduction of changes in medication may result in unintended effects that may affect academic performance. Educational programs must be created that account for low energy, limitations of physical activity, pain, and frequent school absences. Because

school psychologists and educators spend so much time with children, they are in an ideal position to report changes in cognitive functioning (e.g., attention), mood, and physical health. Coordination among all parties can help to prevent medical and educational crises.

Schools are required by law to provide special services to students with disabilities. Educators and school psychologists are increasingly taking steps to protect students who are at risk for medical concerns. For instance, food and environmental allergies are a growing risk factor in schools. Most schools have made steps to minimize or eliminate commonly allergenic foods such as peanuts and strawberries. Hypoallergenic products ranging from crayons to paper to gym mats are also widely used. When students with potential for anaphylactic shock are present, educators are commonly trained in the injection of epinephrine. Modern heating, ventilation, and air-conditioning systems are also extremely effective in reducing symptoms of seasonal allergies for students affected. Similarly, for students with mental health concerns who are at risk for medical problems such as adverse side effects for medication or self-harm (which can affect academic performance), school psychologists may create specialized support groups or provide individual therapy.

Table 26.2 Barriers to Collaboration

Barrier	Issues	Example
Parallel diagnostic systems	Physicians typically use the ICD-10[a]. In contrast, school psychologists use the DSM-5[b], the guidelines set forth in the IDEA 2004, and local regulations.	A physician diagnoses ADHD based on ICD-10 criteria and requests educational assistance to treat the symptoms. However, the school psychologist finds that the same student is not eligible for an ADHD classification within the special education system per IDEA criteria. In addition, educational data and team decisions do not support special education services due to limited evidence that academic performance is impaired.
Decision-making process	• Physicians often make individual diagnoses whereas educators determine special education eligibility and other service needs via a team approach. • Physicians often do not use prereferral interventions or response-to-intervention models, or consider children's functioning in the context of the classroom. • The medical model assumes that the problem is predominantly within the child, whereas school psychologists also examine environmental factors. • School psychologists rarely consider family history, neurological findings, or lab results in making eligibility or program placement decisions.	A child with cancer has been avoiding school. The physician believes the avoidance is due to medical symptoms such as fatigue and nausea, whereas the school psychologist believes the avoidance is due to bullying by peers in the class.
Reimbursement	• Many physicians are under pressure to earn revenue to cover the massive overhead in any medical practice. As such, some feel pressured into engaging in activities that are likely to receive reimbursement from private insurance companies or government insurance. • Schools are under financial pressures due to shrinking budgets, personnel shortages, and growing school populations. Dedicating personnel to collaborative relationships with physicians can be difficult administratively.	A school psychologist plans an IEP meeting for a child with ADHD, but the school psychologist does not have adequate information from the physician about the child's medication regimen. The physician is not present at the meeting because the clinic does not allow for extra time spent in school consultation.
Ethical, legal, and privacy concerns	• Medical personnel may ask to be informed of confidential information obtained during a child's therapy sessions that is relevant to adherence to a medication regimen, but not as relevant to the actual physical illness. • Expectations about privacy may change over time, leading to the need for professionals to reconsider their approaches. • Each state has specific mandates for the scope of practice for medical professionals, psychologists, and certified educators, which vary widely. Some types of collaboration may be in conflict with the description of activities and limitations outlined in the licensing and certification guidelines.	An older adolescent with HIV and oppositional defiant disorder wishes to conceal his condition from school staff once he enters high school. The school must carefully consider the balance between privacy and "must-inform" policies regarding infectious diseases and risky behaviors.

Continued

Table 26.2. Continued

Barrier	Issues	Example
Time constraints and lack of resources	• School psychologists are the primary mental health care providers for many students, yet with a heavy assessment load and administrative work they are often not able to devote enough time to providing mental health interventions. • In the United States, the mean student to school psychologist ratio is 1,383:1 even though NASP recommends a ratio of 1,000:1[c]. • School psychologists cannot prescribe medication by law. Yet, many school psychologists are expected to monitor the medication effects of these students, often with little or no communication with the student's psychiatrist or physician. • Difficulty in managing these multiple roles and demands within limited time frames may lead to stress, burnout, poor work performance, and other issues.	A physician has requested that the school psychologist monitor medication treatment effects of a student with depression. The school psychologist is too overwhelmed with other duties to observe the student in class. The teacher is instead responsible for this task but has no training in this type of monitoring.
Blurring of professional boundaries	• Deviating from the codified scope of practice is an ethical and legal violation and can lead to disciplinary action. • Differences in professional training, tradition, and philosophies can create conflict between collaborators.	A school psychologist has requested to meet with the physician of a student with autism in order to discuss medication treatment, but the school psychologist has received no response. Because the school psychologist has taken extra training courses in psychopharmacology, the school psychologist feels prepared in providing the information to the student's parents. During a parent meeting, the school psychologist suggests different types of medications that can help with the student's symptoms, yet has unknowingly provided misinformation.
Lack of communication	• A physician might request that the school provide special education or therapeutic services for a patient. In this situation, educators may view the physician as disrespectful of school policies or ignorant of school law and regulation. • Physicians may also receive a copy of an IEP filled with educational jargon, rendering it difficult to interpret. Physicians might then view the educators as attempting to practice medicine without a license, providing information irrelevant to children's medical issues, or misinforming parents. • Frequent complaints from school psychologists and parents are that therapies conducted in one location may run contrary or interfere with therapies provided in another location, which can greatly affect treatment outcomes.	A physician receives an IEP report that is lengthy and contains specific jargon related to response to intervention. The physician is unable to interpret the terms and does not understand their relevance and disregards the report, even though it contains information that is relevant to the child's medical treatment.

Continued

Table 26.2. Continued

Barrier	Issues	Example
Lack of medical liaison	• A medical liaison is a point person who is able to translate jargon, oversee healthcare reimbursement, manage section 504 and OHI plans, oversee medication monitoring, instigate collaboration and negotiate barriers, develop prevention and intervention programs, and facilitate homebound instruction. Lack of a liaison can lead to diffusion of responsibility or lack of clear goals. • Given that there is rarely a formal case manager to coordinate educational and medical services and to ensure proper communication parents often fill the liaison role. However, parents differ in their skills in facilitating coordination of these services.	A mother of a child with Asperger's disorder has become the medical liaison because no professional point person is assigned. She does not tell school personnel that her child is receiving therapies through private- and hospital-based sources because of the fear of being excluded from school-based services. Unnecessary and contradictory overlaps in treatment subsequently result from this miscommunication.

Note. ICD-10 = International Clarification of Diseases; DSM-5 = *Diagnostic and Statistical Manual of Mental Disorders,* 5th edition; IDEA = Individuals with Disabilities Education Act; ADHD = attention deficit hyperactivity disorder; IEP = Individualized Education Program; OHI = Other Health Impaired.
[a]World Health Organization (2005). [b]American Psychiatric Association (2013). [c]See Curtis, Castillo, and Gelley (2010).

Collaboration for Significantly Involved Populations (Tier 3)

There are a small but significant number of children who have severe medical, psychiatric, or neurodevelopmental issues that impair school functioning. Table 26.3 summarizes examples of chronic and acute medical conditions and their required collaboration from school psychologists, educators, and doctors at the Tier 3 level.

School Policy Relevance

A basic understanding of school policy is useful when planning collaboration with other organizations. Table 26.4 summarizes the school policy relevance for collaboration between school psychologists and medical personnel.

BEST PRACTICES IN COLLABORATING WITH MEDICAL PERSONNEL

Why is effective collaboration important? Interdisciplinary collaboration is the essence of school psychology service delivery. Forging relationships between medical personnel and school psychologists is vital to the profession, as these relationships expand the role of school psychologists to provide increasingly comprehensive educational, psychological, and health services to all children (Nastasi, 2004).

Effective Collaboration

Lack of effective consultation between school psychologists and medical professionals can lead to poor decision making (Segool, Mathiason, Majewicz-Hefley, & Carlson, 2009). Barriers to effective collaboration can be overcome in a variety of ways that represent best practices in collaborating with medical personnel. These strategies can be cost-effective, improve service delivery, develop community relationships, increase academic performance and attendance, and provide a wider variety of service options.

Acknowledge the Benefits of Teamwork

How can professionals using two entirely different systemic approaches to diagnosis and service delivery work together? First, both professions understand that there are two equally legitimate and valid systems in place that can be complementary. Second, they must appreciate that in many cases neither physicians nor educators can provide effective services to children

Table 26.3 Medical Conditions and Need for Collaboration

Condition	Medical Collaboration Required	Examples
Chronic	• Preparing for transitions from a hospital stay or homebound schooling situation to school is important for students' physical, cognitive, and social–emotional recoveries. • Collaboration with parents and medical professionals to determine how well a child is adjusting to the demands of school after recovering from an illness or surgery is an important part of the intervention plan. • Psychotropic medications or medications for cancer can result in unwanted side effects such as impaired concentration, lack of appetite, weight gain or loss, sleep disturbances, agitation, personality changes, and sedation. Careful treatment monitoring by many different professionals, parents, and the affected child is required. • Mental health or neurodevelopmental conditions such as autism are often comorbid with medical conditions, requiring constant collaboration with physicians.	*Physical:* • HIV/AIDS • Sickle cell anemia • Seizure disorder • Asthma • Diabetes • Deafness/hearing impairments • Severe food allergies • Visual impairments • Orthopedic impairments • Genetic/developmental disability • Burns • Meningitis • Influenza • Concussion • Unexpected allergic reaction *Psychological:* • Attention deficit hyperactivity disorder • Encopresis or enuresis • Severe depression • Sleep disorders • Eating disorders • Conduct disorders • Anxiety disorders • Posttraumatic stress disorders • Psychotic disorders • Bipolar disorder • Autism spectrum disorders • Traumatic brain injury
Acute	• Acute illnesses and injuries are sudden and unexpected and typically require extensive hospitalization and rehabilitation and can result in a variety of school difficulties. Behavioral or medication monitoring must involve parents, teachers, and school psychologists. • Psychological and cognitive adjustment after accidents causing trauma may be challenging and require referral to external mental health services. • Medical professionals, school nurses, teachers, psychologists, and the family may all be involved in planning treatment for students. • If an outbreak of a contagious illness has caused the symptoms, then the school may need to implement a crisis intervention plan with the consultation of doctors.	

alone. Teamwork is a requirement and not simply a refinement or nicety. Teamwork is particularly important when addressing conditions that have an indirect impact on school performance. Strong collaborative efforts between the educational and medical communities result in improved community healthcare and more successful educational outcomes. Referring to the case example of Angela described in the Overview, it is clear that collaborative teamwork among her teachers, parents, school psychologist, and pediatrician is required

to manage her condition. It would be difficult and ineffective for one party alone to manage her condition and her resulting school problems.

Respect Professional Boundaries

All parties are legally and ethically required to respect the formal boundaries of the medical and educational professions as established by state certification and licensure laws. Physicians must refrain from dictating school educational placement decisions or educational

Table 26.4 Policy Issues and Collaborative Requirements

Policy	Overview	Example
Other Health Impaired	<ul><li>One of the designated special education categories under the Individuals with Disabilities Education Act of 2004</li><li>Defined as a medical issue that has an adverse effect on school performance</li><li>Aspects of determining eligibility for status include the documentation of the existence of a medical problem and the probability that this issue has significant impact on school performance</li><li>Must have evidence that the medical problem or the accompanying academic problems are chronic</li></ul>	Children diagnosed with attention deficit hyperactivity disorder, given that the disorder requires both medical and psychological monitoring in order to ensure effective treatment collaboration between school psychologists and physicians
Section 504 of the Rehabilitation Act of 1973	<ul><li>Civil rights law requiring that individuals who have or who are suspected of having handicapping conditions be granted equal access to employment, education, and all other aspects of community life</li><li>Developed to ensure equal access to educational opportunities</li><li>Collaboration with medical personnel is required to determine how a medical condition affects school performance</li></ul>	For students with medical issues, such as developing an appropriate system of mobility for a child with cerebral palsy or helping to improve the sound system for a child with a hearing aid

techniques, and school psychologists must abstain from suggesting medication decisions or making medical diagnoses. However, information can easily go across formal boundaries. For example, a teacher may state, "Since she started taking her medication for asthma, Samantha has started to fall asleep in class." Or a physician may state, "Since she started in the gifted class, Jennifer has had severe abdominal pain with no known medical origin." Although information sharing is important and needs to be encouraged, professional judgment and decision making about how to apply this information should be left solely in the hands of the appropriate professional.

Invite Active Participation

Although respect for formal boundaries is important, there must be an informal reaching across barriers. Physical presence goes a long way when establishing interdisciplinary relationships (Shaw & McCabe, 2008). In the case of Angela, if school psychologists and educators take time out of their busy schedules to meet with her physician to discuss medication effects, then they demonstrate a significant commitment to working as a collaborative team. When Angela's physician takes time to attend her Individualized Education Program (IEP) team meeting, the commitment to the collaboration is equally clear. Realistically, tight schedules and pressures to earn clinical revenue make personal appearances difficult for many doctors. Thus, it is

helpful to identify other means of participation. Inviting medical professionals to review reports or provide written input regarding a student's progress is one of the best ways to reach across barriers without the time demands of a personal appearance. Feedback from medical professionals can provide a much-needed different perspective on symptoms and treatment.

Teachers also play an important role in collaboration. For example, for students such as Angela, school psychologists can encourage teachers to be involved in medication monitoring. In Angela's case, medication side effects may be contributing to symptoms of anxiety and declining academic performance. Because teachers are knowledgeable in child development and spend a great deal of time with their students, they are often the first to identify signs of mental illness by changes in emotional, social, or behavioral functioning in the classroom (Segool et al., 2009). For instance, simple tracking charts with target behaviors and frequency checkmarks can be given to teachers in order to help with behavioral or academic treatment plans. School psychologists can give a short training workshop to educators to ensure that they are knowledgeable and comfortable using these systems.

Use Medical Liaisons

The use of a medical liaison apart from a child's parents can be a key factor in service delivery success (Glaser et al., 2010; Shaw, Glaser, & Ouimet, 2011). Because medical and educational systems have different vocabularies, using a medical–school liaison as a translator of information is often helpful throughout the consultation process to ensure smooth communication. Examples of professionals who are well prepared to act as liaisons are hospital-based teachers, school nurses, school social workers, and school psychologists. In Angela's case, a medical liaison is essential to create a comprehensive and integrated intervention plan. School psychologists and educators may not be fully aware of the symptoms of asthma, nor the side effects from her medications. Likewise, medical personnel involved in her case may be confused by terminology contained in her IEP or psychoeducational assessment.

Take Into Account Multiculturalism

School psychologists must always take into account multicultural factors among students and their families when engaging in consultation (Nuijens, 2004). The multicultural population in the United States is growing rapidly. For families in which English is not their first language, ensure that they are able to understand content presented in reports and during meetings. If necessary, find an interpreter or a translator. Recognize that different cultures view mental illness, education, and medication treatment differently. Students differ in their ability to complete academic tasks based on their multicultural or linguistic background. Labeling can lead to parents and students feeling blamed or helpless, and it is often more effective to focus on specific target behaviors.

Because the majority of school psychologists are not culturally or linguistically diverse, they need to pay special attention to their differing attitudes, practices, or privilege. They should recognize and acknowledge when clashes in culture contribute to strained or failed collaboration and work with families to rectify these situations. For instance, some cultures view behavior progress monitoring to be invasive and disrespectful. Some multicultural families have had negative experiences with systems or people of authority and may require reassurance and building of trust. Engage in consultation that respects differing perspectives and a feeling of safety, and be attentive and responsive to issues that arise. The specific culture of the school or community is also relevant. School psychologists should educate new immigrant families on the educational system and available resources and encourage teachers not to make culture the focal point when establishing perceptions of students. They should provide workshops for educators regarding multiculturalism and offer emotional support to teachers when teachers wish to discuss any related issues.

Engage in Treatment Integrity

Treatment integrity is a key component of effective school psychology delivery (Sanetti, Fallon, & Collier-Meek, 2011). There are several steps in designing or implementing an intervention for a child such as Angela. First, baseline data are to be collected via a functional behavior assessment, curriculum-based measurement, psychoeducational tests, or questionnaires administered to parents, teachers, and the student, among other tools. Interventions are then developed to address individual and systemic supports to improve the specific behavioral issues identified. Materials are then chosen and gathered, and implementers must be trained. All treatments are evaluated and then interventions are altered to maximize effectiveness. Assessment measures may include direct observation, parent report, test results, grades, or self-report questionnaires. School psychologists should keep in mind available resources and goodness of fit in measuring outcomes and establish early on the frequency of data collection and the criteria for an acceptable or unacceptable intervention. Following an intervention, they should consider factors that lead to success or failure, and solicit feedback from others regarding the feasibility of using the intervention in the future.

Communicate Effectively

The basics of effective communication are also extremely important among school psychologists. Following the strategies in Table 26.5 when collaborating with other professionals can be helpful.

Present Facts

There will also be times when school psychologists will be expected to present their findings through either a telephone conversation or face-to-face contact. In these situations, it may be most helpful for school personnel to adopt a medical model of case presentation (Power & Bradley-Klug, 2012) that organizes large quantities of information into the pertinent points, as summarized in Table 26.6.

Engage Parents and Respect Their Boundaries

School psychologists should ensure that parents have completed all appropriate release forms and that the parents understand the nature of the collaboration before it begins. School psychologists should confirm that parents comprehend the role of confidentiality

Table 26.5 Effective School Psychologist Communication Strategies When Collaborating With Medical Professionals

Strategy	Example
Be consistently available	Always return phone calls and e-mails in a timely manner and be easily available by phone, fax, e-mail, or other methods.
Provide relevant background and contact information	Present a brief fact sheet that outlines the school's general approach to collaborating with medical personnel and lists the names and contact information of appropriate staff. This sheet can easily be given to parents and sent directly to the medical provider's office.
Keep records	Keep consistent, secure, and detailed records of communication. Doing so not only keeps communication organized but also establishes a written record of all interactions and decisions. Back up all electronic information regularly.
Use technology	Use technology to organize record keeping, meetings, and sharing of information. Examples include Web-based tracking programs for intervention monitoring, group video conferencing, online calendars, and document sharing programs.
Use effective and jargon-free communication	Remind teachers and other staff to communicate without using jargon. When providing educational or psychological reports, provide one-page executive summaries to physicians that are easy to understand. Bullet points may be helpful in getting across key points. Electronic versions may be helpful as paper copies may be lost.
Schedule follow-up meetings	Schedule follow-up meetings with parents and doctors regularly in order to monitor progress and discuss any concerns. Establish a routine, such as meeting during the first Monday of every month or having a phone conference every 2 weeks.
Solicit feedback	Ask for feedback from parents and involved professionals throughout the collaboration process. What worked? What did not work and why? Use this information to improve collaboration protocols.

Table 26.6 Pertinent Facts to Present to Medical Professionals

Section	Content
Demographic information	Student's name, age, date of birth, school, grade, ethnic origin, sex, and reason for referral
Background information	All relevant historical findings (e.g., student's developmental and medical history, family history of mental health or medical disorders, academic progress over time, previous diagnoses, or placement in a special education curriculum)
Student's strengths and weaknesses	List relative weaknesses and strengths of the student as determined by assessment results and direct observations compared to other students in the class; share any diagnoses or classifications that were determined as a result of the assessment
Classroom requirements	Determine the behavioral, cognitive, social, and academic requirements of the classroom
Main recommendations	List the top three or four recommendations; the main goal is to communicate interventions that need to be addressed by the physician
Other recommendations	A quick statement regarding the other areas addressed in the recommendations contained in the full report might be helpful (e.g., "Several additional suggestions were made regarding IEP goals that might help this student improve her handwriting"); this additional information assures the physician that the more systemic issues are receiving attention

between professionals and have realistic expectations of collaboration. Most parents believe that an interdisciplinary relationship between professionals helps their child. However, some parents choose to keep medical and educational issues entirely separate. The parent's right to such a separation must be honored under the 1974 Family Educational Rights Privacy Act and the 1996 Health Insurance Portability and Accountability Act. In this case, the school might request that parents provide any critical information regarding treatment, medication, and symptoms to an appropriate staff member in order to facilitate the support of their child's scholastic needs.

Parents usually appreciate being informed regularly regarding their child's treatment formulation and progress, either by phone or e-mail or in formal meetings. School psychologists should establish a point person or medical liaison who will communicate with parents and answer any questions. Parents should be able to reach the appropriate professional, especially in an emergency situation involving medical issues. Parents should be invited to be a part of treatment planning and evaluation. Parent input is crucial because a child's behavior at home is often different from his or her behavior at school. Parents should be provided with educational materials as necessary, such as brief handouts regarding a new medical or mental health diagnosis, specific types of medication, or homebound instruction. Communicating the importance of open communication (e.g., sharing progress notes, developing a shared set of goals and therapeutic techniques, providing coordinated decision making) to parents sets a tone for professional collaboration and shared professional goals. For instance, in Angela's case her parents may be more familiar with the medical effects of asthma but less familiar with its psychological and educational effects. It is often up to the school psychologist to ensure that parents are well informed of these issues.

Engage the Student and Provide Support Based on Developmental Level

Developmental differences in children play a significant part in determining their involvement in their own treatment plan at school. For younger students or students with lower cognitive functioning, simply acquiring the experience in communicating preferences and claiming control can be productive. School psychologists should consider that some parents do not want their young children knowing about specific diagnoses, developmental concerns, medical history, or family history. Furthermore, many students will not be able to effectively process this type of information.

Often, older students are asked if they approve of their treatment plan. A better method is to have the student be a critical member of the team who helps develop programs right from the start. In cases such as Angela where students are more mature and have higher skill levels, they can be leaders in their own transition and collaboration team. Determining the nature of certain behaviors when the student is often the best source of this information is difficult. In Angela's case, determining the cause of her anxiety without her input is difficult. For instance, her anxiety may be related to a mediation side effect, social isolation or bullying because of her condition, fear of academic failure due to missed school, or fear of having an unexpected asthma attack. Such a simple investment of time with the student goes a long way toward ensuring the effectiveness of assessments and treatment plans. When students are enthusiastic participants in developing a treatment plan, then school psychologists and medical professionals have a far easier task.

Educating the student regarding the difficulties they are facing and providing support when needed is an important aspect of collaboration. Medical conditions can leave a child physically transformed, with severe medical side effects, and at risk for relapse. A new diagnosis of a medical or mental health disorder can be confusing, placing the student at risk for low self-esteem, learning problems, and social issues. The school psychologists should ensure that the student is aware of available school resources such as support groups, guidance counselors and school psychologists, and teachers. Even young students often understand when a certain set of behaviors or a physical trait sets them apart from their peers. Emotional support must be provided to children based on the child's developmental level. For instance, a young child with epilepsy may benefit from reading a story regarding the disease, whereas a teenager may benefit from individual or group counseling.

Reach Out to the Community

School psychologists can improve collaborative efforts with medical professionals by fostering strong community relationships. NASP (2008) highlights important steps that can be taken. Schools can work locally with parents, community clinics, and hospitals in order to clarify available needs and resources and develop shared goals for collaborative service delivery outcomes. An understanding of each community agency's role in these goals is helpful when addressing service limitations. School psychologists can also work with community agencies in order to create shared protocols that highlight issues related to confidentiality, professional ethics, and referrals. Furthermore, school psychologists and educators are advised to consult with lawyers and other knowledgeable professionals within the community whenever they are unsure about the legal, privacy, or ethical implications involved in a case.

Seek Additional Training

Conducting independent research in order to develop a basic understanding of concepts related to medical issues or psychotropic medications is a valuable activity. Keeping abreast of current literature on these issues and their evidence-based intervention approaches is crucial. Many professional organizations provide free academic journals that span a variety of topics. There may be workshops or conferences that focus on medical issues within the school setting. Contacting local hospitals and inquiring about relevant presentations by medical personnel may also yield excellent training opportunities. Likewise, medical personnel rarely receive training in the areas of school policy, learning disabilities, IEP planning, and other education-specific topics. Whenever possible, school psychologists can offer brief training workshops to local medical professionals.

Specific Applications of Collaboration

At the Tier 1, 2, or 3 levels there are specific applications of school psychologist–medical professional collaboration that rely on multidisciplinary partnerships in order to ensure successful educational and physical outcomes in students with special needs (Shaw & Brown, 2011). The best practices guidelines described previously should be used when engaging in specific collaborative applications.

School-Based Health Clinics

School-based health clinics continue to be a small but growing venue for collaboration between medical personnel and school psychologists. The scope of services among school-based health clinics varies widely. Some school-based health clinics are staffed with physicians, dentists, nurse practitioners, clinical psychologists, and social workers. This type of clinic is often referred to as a full-service school (Davis, Montford, & Read, 2005). Most school-based health clinics are staffed with nurse practitioners and with a supervising physician who may be occasionally onsite. Although school-based health clinics provide a useful service in improving access to healthcare, perhaps their most valuable function is as a multidisciplinary platform in which to develop widely reaching programs. For example, school psychologists can collaborate with medical personnel to develop programs that address chronic pain among adolescents, with the ultimate goal of reducing absenteeism. Although controversial in many communities, some school-based health clinics engage in sex education with the purpose of reducing sexually transmitted diseases. The variety of interdisciplinary programming possible through school-based health clinics is still being explored. However, all programming requires school collaboration with medical personnel.

Homebound Instruction

Homebound instruction is an educational accommodation that provides schooling outside of the school environment for children who have medical issues. For instance, children who are recovering from cancer may be homebound due to postsurgery care, compromised immune systems, or severe fatigue from chemotherapy.

Homebound instruction usually involves a certified teacher providing in-home instruction for up to an hour per day. Although the specific policies of homebound instruction vary across local educational agencies, nearly all involve consultation with physicians in order to determine eligibility. Medical information is required to estimate the duration of homebound instruction. In addition, accommodations are made during instructional activities in order to determine when the return to school is appropriate or when there is a potential threat to teachers and students due to contagion.

Managing Psychotropic Medications

An increasing number of schoolchildren are prescribed psychotropic medications (Thomas, Conrad, Casler, & Goodman, 2006). An important part of monitoring the efficacy and unintended side effects of medication is to monitor behaviors over the course of a child's day both in school and at home. Although there are many techniques and methods for educators to monitor behaviors that take place in schools, all methods require coordination with medical personnel and should involve systematic data collection. Few medical professionals have expertise in structured behavior observations, clinical interviewing, and behavioral assessment. Interpreting these data in light of dosage and unintended effects, while also controlling for confounding variables, are specialized skills that school psychologists are well trained to carry out with the input from medical professionals. School psychologists are also in the position to communicate behavioral observations, medical information, and treatment plans to others. For instance, teachers should be made aware of medical issues and medications that affect school performance so that they may differentiate curriculum and help monitor behavior.

Hospital-to-School Transition Teams

Some students spend a considerable number of days out of school due to psychiatric hospitalization and medical rehabilitation following injury or illness (Clemens et al., 2011). The transition from hospital to school can be overwhelming for children emotionally and academically. The responsibility is usually on the school to coordinate a successful reintegration. Effective communication among medical professionals, school psychologists, educators, and the family is critical to success. The use of a medical liaison may be required. A needs assessment to determine the needs of the student, school, and family can be helpful in ensuring that resources are allocated properly (Shaw & McCabe, 2008). Classmates may need to be educated regarding the student's illness to increase understanding and reduce social difficulties such as bullying. Furthermore, educators may need training regarding the child's difficulties in order to ensure that medical symptoms are not misinterpreted as low academic motivation or laziness.

Crisis Intervention Teams

Medical and school personnel will likely collaborate if there is a crisis in the school or community. Examples include natural disasters or violence or death within the school or community. These types of events are disturbing for students and may result in physical trauma, posttraumatic stress disorder, and other emotional problems. Members of the medical community may be brought into the school to help coping with the aftermath of a crisis, and doctors may be involved in the treatment of students who have been injured during such an event. Many school psychologists have the duty of ensuring that a strong crisis intervention model is in place. Effective training takes place on a regular basis with all school staff and involves drills and role-play with students. School psychologists also identify students who may be at risk for violence, use early intervention strategies to teach social skills and helping behaviors, and provide therapy for students with emotional disturbance.

School Prevention and Intervention Programs

In recent years, there has been a development of prevention and healthcare promotion programs being offered through schools (Power & Blom-Hoffman, 2004). Promoting school health through education and prevention programs is a growing area of collaboration between school psychologists and physicians. For instance, in addition to the school programs described in this chapter, early intervention initiatives have been designed to increase accident prevention, promote awareness of healthy nutrition, increase seatbelt use, encourage exercise, decrease substance abuse and cigarette smoking, curb violence, and reduce teen pregnancy. Medical personnel including physicians, nurses, dietitians, psychiatrists, physical therapists, and rehabilitation specialists have all made major contributions to the delivery of this information to schoolchildren. These programs are valued by the medical community in order to ensure healthy psychosocial outcomes in children.

SUMMARY

Despite differences in professional culture, vocabulary, training, systemic pressures, and other issues, medical personnel and educators have much in common when it comes to issues related to collaboration. This chapter provides an overview of the ways in which interdisciplinary collaboration and open communication are positive aspects of practice. To many professionals, collaboration is valued and the benefits appear to be self-evident. Despite the shared goal of providing the best service delivery to students with special needs, collaborative efforts can fail. Both medical and school professionals need to understand the systemic and other barriers to collaboration and develop approaches to overcome these obstacles. Medical and mental health issues of these children cannot be solved by one system or one profession.

AUTHOR NOTE

Disclosure. Steven R. Shaw has a financial interest in books he authored or coauthored that are referenced in this chapter.

REFERENCES

American Psychiatric Association. (2013). *Diagnostic and statistical manual of mental disorders* (5th ed.). Arlington, VA: Author.

Clemens, E. V., Welfare, L. E., & Williams, A. M. (2011). Elements of successful school reentry after psychiatric hospitalization. *Preventing School Failure, 55,* 202–213. doi:10.1080/1045988X.2010.532521

Curtis, M. J., Castillo, J. M., & Gelley, C. (2010). School psychology 2010: Demographics, employment, and the context for professional practices–Part 1. *Communiqué, 40*(7), 28–30.

Datar, A., Sturm, R., & Magnabosco, J. L. (2004). Childhood overweight and academic performance: National study of kindergarteners and first-graders. *Obesity Research, 12,* 58–68. doi: 10.1038/oby.2004.9

Davis, T. K., Montford, C. R., & Read, C. (2005). Interdisciplinary teamwork in a school-based health center. *Nursing Clinics of North America, 40,* 699–709.

Glaser, S. E., Ouimet, T., & Shaw, S. R. (2010). Collaboration between educators and medical professionals: Models, barriers, and implications. In P. McCabe & S. R. Shaw (Eds.), *Pediatric disorders: Current topics and interventions for educators* (pp. 8–21; A joint publication with the National Association of School Psychologists). Thousand Oaks, CA: Corwin.

Grier, B. C., & Bradley-Klug, K. L. (2011). Collaborative consultation to support children with pediatric health issues: A review of the biopsychosocial model. *Journal of Educational and Psychological Consultation, 21,* 88–105. doi:10.1080/10474412.2011.571522

McCabe, P., & Shaw, S. R. (2010). Trends in health care delivery: The increased burden on schools as health care providers. In P. McCabe & S. R. Shaw (Eds.), *Pediatric disorders: Current topics and interventions for educators* (p. 2–7; A joint publication with the National Association of School Psychologists). Thousand Oaks, CA: Corwin.

Nastasi, B. K. (2004). Meeting the challenges of the future: Integrating public health and public education for mental health promotion. *Journal of Educational and Psychological Consultation, 15,* 295–312. doi:10.1080/10474412.2004.9669519

National Association of School Psychologists. (2008). *The importance of school mental health services* [Position statement]. Bethesda, MD: Author. Retrieved from http://www.nasponline.org/about_nasp/positionpapers/iac.pdf

National Association of School Psychologists. (2010). *Model for comprehensive and integrated school psychological services.* Bethesda, MD: Author. Retrieved from http://www.nasponline.org/standards/2010standards/2_PracticeModel.pdf

Nuijens, K. L. (2004). *Culturally competent consultation in the schools: Information for school psychologists and school personnel.* Bethesda, MD: National Association of School Psychologists. Retrieved from http://www.nasponline.org/resources/culturalcompetence/cc_consultation.aspx

Power, T. J., & Blom-Hoffman, J. (2004). The school as a venue for managing and preventing health problems: Opportunities and challenges. In R. Brown (Ed.), *Handbook of pediatric psychology in school settings* (pp. 37–48). Mahwah, NJ: Erlbaum.

Power, T. J., & Bradley-Klug, K. (2012). *Pediatric school psychology: Conceptualization, applications, and strategies for leadership development.* New York, NY: Routledge.

Sanetti, L. M. H., Fallon, L. M., & Collier-Meek, M. A. (2011). Treatment integrity assessment and intervention by school-based personnel: Practical applications based on a preliminary study. *School Psychology Forum: Research in Practice, 5,* 87–102.

Segool, N. K., Mathiason, J. B., Majewicz-Hefley, A., & Carlson, J. S. (2009). Enhancing student mental health: Collaboration between medical professionals and school psychologists. *Communiqué, 37*(7), 1–4.

Shaw, S. R., & Brown, M. B. (2011). Keeping pace with changes in healthcare: Expanding educational and medical collaboration. *Journal of Educational and Psychological Consultation, 21,* 79–87. doi:10.1080/10474412.2011.571549

Shaw, S. R., Glaser, S., & Ouimet, T. (2011). Developing the medical liaison role in school settings. *Journal of Educational and Psychological Consultation, 21,* 106–117. doi:10.1080/10474412.2011.571479

Shaw, S. R., & McCabe, P. (2008). Hospital to school transition for children with chronic illness: Meeting the new challenges of an evolving health care system. *Psychology in the Schools, 45,* 74–87. doi:10.1002/pits.20280

Thomas, C. P., Conrad, P., Casler, R., & Goodman, E. (2006). Trends in the use of psychotropic medications among adolescents: 1994 to 2001. *Psychiatric Services, 57,* 63–69. doi:10.1176/appi.ps.57.1.63

World Health Organization. (2005). *International statistical classification of diseases and related health problems* (10th rev., 2nd ed.). Geneva, Switzerland: Author.

27 Best Practices in Meeting the Needs of Children With Chronic Illness

Cynthia A. Riccio
Jessica Beathard
William A. Rae
Texas A&M University

OVERVIEW

An increasing number of children experience medical issues that affect their functioning and are considered to constitute a chronic illness. Improving outcomes for children with chronic illness is one example of the need for school psychologists to have training in the National Association of School Psychologists (NASP) *Model for Comprehensive and Integrated School Psychological Services* (NASP, 2010) domain of Preventive and Responsive Services. Having the knowledge of principles and research related to resilience and risk factors for educational and mental health outcomes is important to identifying those services in schools and communities to best meet the needs of children with chronic illness. This chapter will discuss some of the issues to be considered in a multitiered system given the limited research on evidence-based practices with children with chronic illness.

How chronic illness is defined varies but, generally, a chronic illness is a medical condition that requires medical intervention on a continuing basis. It can be defined conservatively as a condition that is persistent and results in a substantial and major impairment in daily activities (National Center for Health Statistics, 2012). Common examples of chronic illness include asthma, leukemia, diabetes, epilepsy, cystic fibrosis, and sickle cell disease. Chronic illness also would include the medical complications associated with spina bifida, cerebral palsy, juvenile arthritis, HIV/AIDS, brain tumor and other forms of childhood cancer, and many congenital disorders. (For more information on specific chronic illnesses and school context, see Castillo, 2008.)

The number of children in schools with chronic illness is increasing, likely due to improved early identification, survival of high-risk infants, and other environmental factors (Brown, Daly, & Rickel, 2007). The overall prevalence of chronic illness ranges from 10 to 30% depending on the method used to collect data and how chronic illness is defined (Martinez & Ercikan, 2009) with estimates that 27% of children will experience a chronic condition that may or may not continue through their lifetime. Of these children, approximately 7% suffer from an illness severe enough to interfere with their normal school or life activities (National Center for Health Statistics, 2012). Based on the most recent report of the National Center for Health Statistics, for example, 14% of children under the age of 18 had a health problem that was being treated with medication within the previous 3 months of the survey. Of the chronic illnesses, the diagnosis of asthma, for example, is more frequent (14%) than a parent being told his or her child had a learning disability (7.6%) or attention deficit hyperactivity disorder (8.5%) as reported in the same survey. With asthma, those children who were non-Hispanic African American or living in poverty were most likely to continue to evidence the symptoms. Similarly, the prevalence of diabetes (any type) in children occurs in 1 in 500 school-age children and is the second most common chronic illness in childhood (Wodrich & Cunningham, 2008).

With the frequency of chronic illness among children, it is quite likely that a school psychologist will be in a position to work with, or collaborate with others about, a child with a chronic illness at some point in his or her professional career. The effects on school function vary from individual to individual (i.e., the severity, supports in place) and across time (i.e., when the effects of the illness or treatment are most acute). At a given time, a child with acute asthma may be more affected by the illness than a child with leukemia who is in remission. While there are clearly differences, oftentimes children with chronic illness face the same issues in school and in social situations, regardless of the illness. In many cases, the issues are more related to the acuteness of the disorder or disease or the treatment effects. Ultimately, chronic illness can affect children in all areas of functioning at school, home, and in the community. One study found that in their sample of 34 schools, a majority of children with chronic illness demonstrated lower academic motivation, more disruptive behaviors, and/or lower achievement (Forrest, Bevans, Riley, Crespo, & Louis, 2011).

School psychologists can serve as a critical resource in helping teachers and parents support children with chronic illness as they face both academic and social challenges. Some school psychologists choose to specialize in pediatric psychology to meet the needs of children with chronic illness. With or without the focus in pediatric psychology, the training in assessment, consultation, and both academic and mental health intervention can be useful in meeting the needs of these children and their families. School psychologists can foster and support school staff to promote and improve the psychological and educational outcomes for these children. The school psychologist may be part of the assessment team, be involved in intervention planning, serve as a liaison between the medical community and the school community, and assist teachers and parents through consultation and education.

This chapter provides information about responsive services and preventive activities related to academic and mental health for the child with a chronic illness. This chapter may be helpful when a child with a chronic illness is initially diagnosed and treatment is ongoing, when the child's medical history indicates the prior diagnosis of a chronic illness with no previously identified needs (e.g., identification of a child with sickle cell disease but no apparent need as yet for educational, psychological, or medical intervention), and when the child returns to school following a hospitalization or course of treatment, particularly if the illness is progressive or terminal.

BASIC CONSIDERATIONS

The impact of chronic illness may be the result of the disease itself or due to the various treatments that are used to address the disease, as well as issues related from any restrictions to activities. The impact of the illness itself will vary according to the illness, whether the disease process is acute or, in the case of cancer, in remission, as well as whether the condition is static or progressive. With some illnesses, the child will not be able to attend school at certain times due to fatigue or acute effects. In other cases, the child may attend but the child's level of engagement and learning may be affected. Children with a chronic illness that involves pain may be distracted from learning and unable to participate in physical activities (e.g., Compas et al., 2006). For example, children with sickle cell disease may suffer from frequent, and sometimes acute, pain episodes that affect sleep, activity level, and overall functioning; however, at other times, the child may be symptom free (Jacob et al., 2006). Although not pain related, students with insulin-dependent diabetes commonly have acute hypoglycemia or hyperglycemia. This means that the child's blood sugar levels are either too high or too low, either of which can affect the child's attention, learning, memory, and processing speed (Desrocher & Rovet, 2004). The fluctuations may result in inconsistency in the child's ability to function optimally in the classroom.

Regardless of the underlying disease process, effects of the disease or the treatment have the potential to affect the child's engagement in the learning process on a consistent basis and, ultimately, affect both academic and social growth. In another example, the child with asthma may have difficulty concentrating and be fatigued if oxygen levels are insufficient or may seem restless and inattentive as a side effect of medication. Children with asthma often have associated congestion that could affect their hearing some of the time despite passing a hearing test at another time. As with diabetes and sickle cell disease, the fluctuation in behavior and symptoms can be hard to understand for the classroom teacher or others who work with the child.

Not only the illness but the treatment used can have an impact on functioning, not only short term but long term. For example, common side effects of some treatments include drowsiness and fatigue, increased risk of infections, and cognitive effects. Similarly, individuals diagnosed with cancer may experience multiple side effects from their treatments (e.g., chemotherapy, radiation) including nausea, gastrointestinal problems, fatigue, hair loss, pain, anemia, and an increased risk of infection in the short term. In addition, some individuals with cancer develop impairments in their ability to learn and remember new academic information depending on the treatment protocol (Wade, Dang, Nelson, & Wasserberger, 2010). Medications used in the treatment of epilepsy (anticonvulsant medications) also commonly have effects on levels of alertness, distractibility, memory, and information processing (Wodrich & Cunningham, 2008). Similarly, treatments for cancer can lead to a decreased quality of life because of overwhelming side effects that include neuropsychological impairment, mood swings, irritability, and other psychological difficulties (Roddenberry & Renk, 2008). The school psychologist will need to consider effects of medical treatment in assessment and intervention planning as well as in consultation with teachers and school staff.

School Attendance

Chronic illness may result in increased absenteeism, decreased participation in activities at school, decreased participation in sports, and, related to these factors, fewer opportunities for the development of peer relations (Boonen & Petry, 2011). The average days absent varies significantly based on the disorder, the severity, and how the child and his or her family cope with the disease. For example, children with leukemia miss an average of 40 school days during the first stages of treatment, and attendance later will vary depending on the physical quality of life (Prevatt, Heffer, & Lowe, 2000). For children with type 1 diabetes, rate of absenteeism, as well as other factors, is predictive of academic skills and may be due not only to illness but also to clinic visits and the need to leave the classroom for glucose checks, injections, and snacks (for a review see Wodrich & Cunningham, 2008). Attendance issues across chronic illnesses will vary with the acuteness of the illness at a given time.

Attendance at school is important not only to ensure successful mastery of the curriculum but because frequent school absenteeism can cause disruptions in previously established friendships and make it difficult to establish new friendships. Children with chronic illnesses who are frequently absent from school are often viewed as being a less-preferred playmate or feel rejected (Reiter-Purtill, Waller, & Noll, 2009). In addition to the medical factors of the illness and treatment, the family's response to the child's illness was found to be a good predictive factor of school attendance and overall school impairment (Logan, Simons, & Carpino, 2011). Notably, some parents are highly vocal regarding their child's illness and advocate for modifications and accommodations; however, some parents may be reticent to share information about an illness due to cultural beliefs, fear, or a desire for their child to be treated as normally as possible. Similarly, while some parents may choose to restrict activities to protect their child, others encourage their children to participate fully. For example, some children with asthma engage in athletic and highly aerobic activities despite their illness.

Academic Performance

As noted, the disease process and treatment both can affect cognitive skills necessary for school success (Martinez & Ercikan, 2009). Children and adolescents with chronic illness are most likely to have academic deficits in school subjects that build on previous knowledge, possibly due to the high rates of absenteeism or memory deficits. Effects are not always evident immediately. In some cases such as leukemia, it may take up to 3 years after diagnosis and treatment to completely understand the effects of illness and treatment on a child's cognitive functioning even if the child continues to be in remission (i.e., is now "healthy"). The effects can include a decline in overall ability, as well as deficits in memory, organization, attention, processing speed, fine motor speed, and reading, spelling, and math skills (e.g., Castillo, 2008; Reiter-Purtell et al., 2009). This pattern of long-term effects is not only present with leukemia but with many chronic illnesses. As with academic skills in general, the extent of long-term effects could potentially be prevented, or at least reduced, with early recognition and appropriate service delivery (i.e., accommodations, modifications) prior to school failure.

Psychosocial and Behavioral Effects

Other potential contributing factors to lower academic achievement are the psychosocial and behavioral effects of chronic illness. Given the stressors and trauma often associated with medical management of the disease process, it is not surprising that children with chronic illness are at increased risk of emotional and behavioral problems (see Brown et al., 2007; Castillo, 2008). Some of these concerns may arise from restricted opportunities to develop social skills or maintain social relations over time. Parent concerns for the child and a tendency toward overprotection may further affect the child's functioning and level of involvement with peers and the school context. This may explain deficits in psychosocial and adaptive functioning in some children with chronic illness (e.g., Buelow et al., 2012; Sillanpää & Cross, 2009).

It is especially common to have an increased rate of internalizing problems such as depression, anxiety, and withdrawal in conjunction with chronic illness (e.g., Greydanus, Patel, & Pratt, 2010). Many children with chronic illnesses experience physical changes as a result of the disease or treatment and worry about their appearance (Saxe et al., 2005). This is especially important to consider with adolescents and the pressure to fit in and emphasis on social status. For children and adolescents with chronic illness, their anxiety may precipitate further withdrawal and depression, as well as subsequent peer rejection or neglect. Moreover, there is a direct link between poor peer relationships and later academic and behavioral problems such as externalizing problems (e.g., aggression, noncompliance, anger control), internalizing problems (e.g., anxious, fearful, depression, and solitary behaviors), and negative self-perceptions (Pinquart & Shen, 2011). There is also some research to suggest that for adolescents a chronic illness can lead to depression which can cause suicidal ideation or behavior (Greydanus et al., 2010).

There is some indication that the types of emotional or behavioral problems may be differentially associated with specific illnesses (Hysing, Elgen, Gillberg, & Lundervold, 2010). For example, it has been suggested that children with neurological disorders (e.g., epilepsy) may be more at risk for difficulties with emotional problems, inattention, conduct problems, and peer problems (Hysing et al., 2010; Rodenburg, Stams, Meijer, Aldenkamp, & Dekovic, 2005) as compared to those with other types of chronic illness (e.g., asthma) or healthy peers. Notably, in the Hysing et al. (2010) study, although children with asthma were found to have significantly higher rates of inattention than healthy peers, areas of home life, friendship, classroom learning, leisure, and family were comparable to their healthy peers. The outcome for children with epilepsy was not as positive relative to healthy peers. Less study has been done with regard to children with other chronic illnesses and the likelihood of mental health issues. School psychologists can play a critical role in identifying, circumventing, and treating mental health concerns for children and youth with chronic illness.

BEST PRACTICES IN MEETING THE NEEDS OF CHILDREN WITH CHRONIC ILLNESS

Jesse, a third grader, was struggling academically, and his teachers and parents expressed concern that he was falling farther and farther behind. Teachers also expressed concerns that he sometimes seemed unaware, confused, or very tired. Jesse's obtained scores on the benchmarking in September had been below expectancy and he participated in an intensive intervention. The teacher charged with implementing the program expressed concerns that Jesse was not able to focus sometimes and had been absent more than other students in the class. Both teachers expressed concerns about possible learning problems, attention deficit, hyperactivity, and/or home problems that could contribute to his fatigue and poor attendance. Progress monitoring did not indicate any improvement despite increased frequency and intensity of the intervention program.

The school psychologist completed a records review and contacted the parent. The school psychologist explained that as noted in a previous parent–teacher conference, Jesse was still struggling. The school psychologist obtained permission to do classroom observations and made an appointment to meet with the parent and the teachers to try to develop another or alternative plan to help Jesse. During the conference Jesse's mother shared with the teachers and school psychologist that Jesse has a seizure disorder but that he is on medication. This was not noted in Jesse's school records and the school nurse was not aware of the condition. Observations indicated that Jesse's attention and fatigue varied, as did his academic productivity. In particular, he seemed to have the most difficulty in the mornings and was most alert in the afternoons. Unfortunately, his academics were taught in blocks, mostly in the mornings. The school psychologist alerted the school nurse, and together with Jesse's mother they discussed the importance of having appropriate medical information available in the event that Jesse had a seizure during the school day. It was decided that the school nurse would contact Jesse's doctor and get the information needed for an individual health plan. The school psychologist also met with the teachers to see about shifting some of the academic load to later in the day when Jesse was more alert. Additional suggestions for varying the format of instruction to increase engagement and focus were provided to the teachers.

The school psychologist, together with the school nurse, provided the teachers and parents with information on seizure disorders and possible impacts on school functioning. Jesse's mother agreed to monitor his homework and any missed work more carefully as well. She also agreed to let the school nurse know if there were any changes in his medical situation. The teachers, parent, school nurse, and the psychologist agreed to see implement these changes in instruction, along with the intensive program, for a period of 6 weeks. At that time, they would all meet again to determine if a more formal academic plan (e.g., 504 Plan) or referral for comprehensive evaluation would be needed.

Importance of Training and Collaboration

Most training programs do not include a specific course on chronic illness, and most school psychologists do not know the effects of every chronic illness on the academic or psychological development of children. Further, as noted above, the disease process, treatments, and effects vary depending on the disease itself. Individual differences make it that much more difficult to be knowledgeable about each illness. School psychologists, however, have the skills and resources to garner the information needed for an individual child and his or her illness, identify key areas that warrant intervention, and monitor progress. The collaboration needed with children with chronic illness draws on school psychologists' knowledge of principles and research related to family systems, strengths, needs, and culture; evidence-based strategies to support family influences on children's learning and mental health; and strategies to develop collaboration between families and schools and extends it to include the medical community.

When a school psychologist or other school-based professional determines that a child has been diagnosed with a chronic illness, collaboration between the schools and the healthcare establishment is best practice. Ideally, the school psychologist should access information on that specific disease, as well as potential effects on achievement and mental health (see Table 27.1 for some starting points). In more complex cases, it may be appropriate, with parent permission, to discuss the child's case directly with the medical personnel involved (e.g., the physician, psychologist on staff at the medical facility, medical social worker) who can provide child-specific information. In this way, the school psychologist can play a key role in facilitating communication and involvement with parents and families to foster family–school collaboration.

Before any prevention or intervention strategies are implemented, a team approach is important. Because of

associated impairments in academic or social functioning, children with chronic illnesses are frequently eligible for special education services, often under the category of Other Health Impaired (Shaw & McCabe, 2008). For those students who are not served under special education, the appropriate student services team to meet that child's needs (e.g., response-to-intervention [RTI] team, 504 planning committee) would be appropriate, or a new student support services team identified. Alternatively, for some children with chronic illness, the issues in a given grade or at a given time may be so minimal that concerns and possible problems are only discussed less systematically as part of a parent–teacher conference with updates to the school nurse and school psychologist as needed. It is essential that the school psychologist, teacher, parent, and school nurse establish a process to address any ongoing and crisis situations that can occur with chronic illness and for the specific child. To address such situations, an individual health plan (e.g., what to do if the child has a seizure) may be in place, apart from or in addition to an Individualized Education Program (IEP) or 504 Plan.

The team (special education, RTI, 504, or other) needs to be multidisciplinary with key individuals who are involved in working with the child. Similar to the special education process, this support team should include teacher, parent or guardian, school administrator or designee, and school counselor, as well as the school nurse and school psychologist in order to best meet the needs and contexts in which the child functions. It is important that a child who already has a school-based team not have a separate team to address the health concerns. Not only would participation of the same individuals on multiple teams for the same child be unwieldy, it is important that the key individuals are not only involved in academic and mental health planning (i.e., IEP development, 504 Plan), but also with any individual health plan or discussion of how medical management may affect intervention planning. If possible, the team also would include someone on the child's medical team. It may or may not be possible for a representative of the medical team to be present, in which case someone on the school-based team will need to serve as the liaison. Just as the school-based team for the child will determine the person who serves as the liaison for the school, the medical team will determine who should be the appropriate contact person on the medical side.

The contact role and associated responsibilities of the members of the team will need to be determined and agreed to by the team members and may vary from

Table 27.1. Examples of More Common Chronic Illnesses and School Functioning

Chronic Illness	Symptoms	Frequent School Complications	Possible Supports Needed
Asthma (from Castillo, 2008)	• Shortness of breath, wheezing, gasping, chest tightness, and coughing • Possible dizziness or feeling faint	• Higher rates of absenteeism • Reduced play activity • Sleep disruption • Fatigue and inattention	• Reducing or eliminating the exposure to triggers (allergens, irritants, and chemicals) • Ensure easy access to necessary medications • Provide asthma education and awareness to students and staff • Provide safe physical activity opportunities • Provide education for the child and family
Diabetes (from Wodrich & Cunningham, 2008)	• Increased or decreased appetite with subsequent weight loss • Frequent urination and water intake • Lethargy	• Poor focus and concentration • Poor handwriting/fine motor skills • Inconsistent performance • Missing assignments • Long-term neurocognitive effects on learning and cognition • Difficulties in attention, learning, and memory tasks • Poor decision making • Higher rate of school absenteeism	• Establish individualized diabetes healthcare plan at school • Work in varied formats (interactive instruction, one to one, small groups) • Seating with fewer distractions • Minimize writing demands • Eliminate excessive drill/practice on work that student has mastered • Record how the student feels/behaves to better understand the effect of high and low blood sugar levels; rearrange schedule to accommodate such highs and lows • Allow the student to select the time of day when he or she feels best able to complete challenging tasks • Rearrange the schedule to accommodate fluctuations in functioning • Training for school personnel on management of diabetes at school
Epilepsy (from Buelow et al. 2012; Sillanpää & Cross, 2009; Wodrich & Cunningham, 2008)	• Seizures • Fatigue, possible confusion	• Problems with attention, vigilance, and motor control • Learning problems associated with otherwise normative ability • General cognitive delay • Motor and memory issues • Inattention/inability to focus • Poor peer relations • Decreased adaptive skills despite average cognitive ability • Behavioral side effects of medications such as drowsiness, lethargy, overactivity, confusion, and motor problems	• Determine if special education placement or 504 Plan is needed for academic problems • Individual health plan for response to seizure occurrence to ensure safety of student • Dispel disease-related myths • Psychosocial interventions that attempt to influence peer acceptance and understanding • Supports for social skills and activities in daily living regardless of cognitive ability as needed • Educate teachers and staff on what to look for and what to do (and what not to do) during seizure episodes • Monitor medication side effects

Continued

Table 27.1. Continued

Chronic Illness	Symptoms	Frequent School Complications	Possible Supports Needed
Cystic fibrosis (Drotar, 2006)	• Reduced pulmonary functioning • Increased sputum production and cough • Fever • Recurrent pulmonary infections • Weight loss • Reduced physical growth	• High rates of absenteeism due to doctors' appointments and hospital admissions • Due to high caloric needs, students may be unable to consume all necessary food during the school lunch time • Fatigue and inattention	• A specific IEP in order to anticipate possible medical needs that may rise • Specific plans for managing the completion of schoolwork in case of absenteeism due to illness • Coordinate with parents or caregivers to send work to the hospital when possible • Allow extra time to complete work or modify the amount of work • Homebound provisions or altered school schedules • Allow extra time to navigate the school halls and stairways • Encourage good hand hygiene in students and ask other parents to keep children home from school when they are ill • Allow students to bring extra snacks to school • Provide teachers with factual information about the illness
Cancer (Drotar, 2006)	• Fatigue • Hair loss • Diarrhea • Posttreatment and anticipatory nausea	• High rates of absenteeism due to doctors' appointments and hospital admissions • Problems with reintegrating to school after hospitalization • Emotional liability, poor emotion regulation • Lack of adherence to medical regimen when returning to school • Problems with socialization • Slowed academic processing speed • Psychological adjustment problems	• Implement school reentry procedures to reduce the negative impact of returning to school • Provide preventive education for teachers, staff, and students about the side effects of treatment (e.g., hair loss) that could complicate a positive reintegration • Allow student to wear head covering/cap • Social skills training • Counseling for child and family • Problem-solving skills training • Support and reinforcement of adherence to medical regimen
Sickle cell (Drotar, 2006)	• Extreme pain, frequent movement to try to alleviate the pain associated with crisis • Anemia and associated fatigue • Acute and chronic tissue injury • Frequent urination • Malnutrition • Cerebrovascular accidents (includes both overt and "silent" strokes)	• Frequent absences from school • Complaints of pain • Withdrawal from engagement in academic activities • Attentional deficits • Possible poststroke neurological impairment with associated cognitive or motor deficits	• Monitoring of academic progress with intervention, 504 Plan, and/or special education placement as needed • Specific plans for managing the completion of schoolwork and improve engagement in educational activities • Encourage hydration with allowance for frequent restroom use • Facilitate school reentry with appropriate and timely access to special education following stroke

team to team or school to school. Release of information forms that are two-way and cover communication with medical personnel are needed to be sure that there is appropriate communication. Communication between the home and school, as well as decisions about dissemination of information to relevant school staff, needs to be established up front. Given the medical nature of chronic illness, the school nurse is likely to be the best contact person for medically related problems and the school psychologist may be the best contact to addresses any psychosocial and academic problems. Further, it is helpful to establish a staffing pattern or schedule for routine progress monitoring that matches the current needs of the child. For example, the appropriate team might meet annually (i.e., for IEP meeting if in special education, review of the 504 Plan, and/or review of individual health plan depending on what is in place for a given child), which may be enough for conditions that are under control and have not changed substantially over the course of the year. In contrast, the plan for a child with multiple medical visits, frequent medication changes, or a medical crisis or change in condition will need to be reviewed more frequently. In particular, many children and youth with sickle cell disease may not experience overt problems, but then may experience crises that affect their functioning or, in more severe situations, the crisis may escalate to a cerebrovascular accident or stroke. In such instances, the changes in level of acuteness and severity would clearly warrant reconsideration of services needed. Similarly, the child who was hospitalized and treated for leukemia and returned to school with services in place may not need the same level of responses or the same type of responses over time.

Establishing how communication with team members is accomplished is important as well. For example, early on it would be important for face-to-face contact in order to establish appropriate rapport and connections with the medical team contact person. Over time, a telephone or electronic meeting, with confidentiality parameters disclosed and in place, may facilitate communication and may work well once that initial alliance is developed. With changes in condition or crisis, it may be helpful to have more face-to-face contact again.

During team collaboration, each member has an important role to play and each has essential information that will help the planning for the child. The parent knows how the child is at home and has the most immediate access to medical information. The school nurse can monitor medical conditions at school and

often may serve as the translator of medical information for parents and school personnel alike. The teacher will have the best knowledge of the child's day-to-day school functioning as well as a good sense of how medication or treatment may be affecting learning. The school psychologist is best trained in the area of psychosocial functioning and will be able to provide relevant information on the mental health status of the child. The school psychologist also will be able to provide ongoing assessment, conduct functional behavioral assessment, and monitor changes in the child's academic and socioemotional status. In the role of consultant, the school psychologist can assist the teacher in identifying appropriate accommodations, modifications, or interventions to address new issues as they arise.

Another key aspect of the team is providing relevant and at times critical information to others. For example, most teachers do not have in-depth knowledge of different types of chronic illness or the side effects of medication. They may question why a child who appears healthy most days needs accommodations or modifications, and they may not understand the fluctuations in function mentioned earlier. It is important to consider teacher perceptions of the illness, the teacher's expectations for the child, and whether the teacher understands the justification for any deviations from standard practice. One avenue to provide this information is through an inservice workshop about chronic illness (in general or a specific illness) and interventions. With individual teachers, the school psychologist can help school staff to understand the medical situation and how the child's illness or treatment may affect the child's ability to meet the demands of the curriculum, the classroom, and high-stakes testing.

For those illnesses that have recurring and remitting cycles, it may be important to highlight the variable level of functioning for the child and the need for expectations to be adjusted accordingly. The school psychologist also can act as a translator of educational terms to medical personnel. Providing good information to teachers, parents, and medical personnel, along with general guidelines for appropriate supports may be helpful. Table 27.1 provides some basic information on the most common chronic illnesses affecting children and a range of possible supports.

Together, the school psychologist and school nurse can provide useful information to all school personnel as needed, advocating for both preventive and responsive systems. In those situations where there is limited awareness of the illness or it is a new diagnosis, the school psychologist can provide information sheets to parents or staff about chronic illness in general, as well as specific illnesses from NASP (http://www.nasponline.org), the Centers for Disease Control (http://www.cdc.gov) and the Society of Pediatric Psychology (http://www.apadivisions.org/division-54). Finally, for teachers and staff who work with a child or children with terminal illness, inservice workshops on grief and appropriate supports following a child's death should be available.

Meeting the Needs of Children With Chronic Illness

It is important that the school psychologist make use of the best available research as well as utilizing clinical expertise and client characteristics, culture, and preferences (American Psychological Association, 2006). As part of the decision-making process by the school psychologist and team, the focus of treatment can be directed toward the student, classmates, parents, and/or school personnel (e.g., teachers, staff, administrators). The balance of treatment focus depends on the unique needs of the student, home–school communication, and the school climate. Regardless of the focus, the best interventions occur when all stakeholders (i.e., parents, teachers, child) are involved in the intervention and have a say in the decision-making process.

School psychologists can take both an advocacy and leadership role to identify and meet the academic and socioemotional needs of children with chronic illness. Because children with chronic illness are at increased risk of academic and mental health issues, it is important that assessment and intervention address both domains. Support is also needed for their parents, their teachers, and other school staff. School psychologists can be helpful in teacher consultation, facilitating parent involvement, and monitoring the child's social–emotional well-being in order to best understand and strengthen the systems in which the child functions (Power & Werba DeRosa, 2012). As part of the team, the school psychologist can assist in identifying medication effects, promoting and reinforcing child and parent adherence to medical treatment, and facilitating school integration/reintegration (DuPaul, Power, & Shapiro, 2009).

Assessment

When it becomes known that a child has a chronic illness, efforts should be made to gather information from the parents and medical professionals. In addition to the routine collection of developmental history, it may be important to discuss with parents how the child's illness has affected the child's functioning, family functioning, and even the wellness of siblings. From medical personnel it is important to clarify and document any restrictions on activities that need to be in place as well as any warning signs that might indicate the need for medical attention.

The level and content of further assessment needs to be determined on a child-by-child basis. For many children with chronic illnesses, benchmarking and universal screening of achievement through general education may be sufficient to ensure continued academic progress. Progress monitoring can occur as with any other child in general education. When children with chronic illness are struggling academically, more comprehensive assessment that covers the underlying skills involved in reading, writing, and mathematics, as well as broad cognitive abilities (e.g., memory, processing speed, language), is needed. Similarly, if the child is struggling socially or exhibiting behavioral problems, more individualized assessment may be appropriate to inform intervention.

In conducting formal cognitive and achievement testing, the school psychologist will need to consider what standardized measurements will work best given concerns for fatigue as well as the availability of alternate forms for reassessment. In contrast to a typical evaluation, given the frequency of concerns with attention and memory across disorders (Castillo, 2008), additional evaluation of these domains may be appropriate. In addition to formal testing, interviews with teachers and review of work products in the classroom can help to inform intervention planning. Teachers not only have a good sense of what is typical for that age group, they also have knowledge of the individual child's performance compared with peers and of the expected curriculum.

Similar to identification of academic deficits through the multitiered model, with universal screening of social–emotional and behavioral issues, students at risk for difficulties can be identified. For children with chronic illness, school psychologists can be involved in identifying appropriate evidence-based services at a group or individual level. In particular, there is potentially increased risk of depression that may result in suicide attempts in conjunction to chronic illness (Greydanus et al., 2010). Based on epidemiological data, Greydanus and colleagues found the relation of chronic illness, depression, and suicide attempts and completions to be of concern in adolescents and recommend that adolescents with chronic illness be screened for depression and other suicide risk factors on a regular basis. In this regard, the school psychologist may play a critical role in suicide risk assessment.

Once interventions are identified and implemented, the school psychologist can provide support for implementation and progress monitoring. In academic areas, whether progress will be monitored using teacher-developed, curriculum-based measures or the same measures as in RTI will need to be determined by the appropriate team. The school psychologist can be instrumental in helping the teacher to collect and evaluate the data over time for growth as part of the data-based decision-making. The information obtained from progress monitoring is critical in determining the level, type, and target of the services needed for the child's academic success and psychological well-being over time.

Because the health status of individuals with chronic illness often is not static, it is critical that review of progress be conducted at frequent intervals to meet any changing needs of the child. For children going through surgeries and multiple types of intervention (i.e., chemotherapy or radiation, significant changes in medications), more frequent assessment to provide real-time data on the child's functioning is needed. If at all possible, baseline data before treatment starts would be helpful. Immediate posttreatment measures and continued progress monitoring will be useful in data-based decision making regarding the level of services needed. Progress monitoring throughout the intervention process and in the weeks, months, and years that follow the medical protocol will be important. Similarly, for a child with a progressive or terminal illness, it will be important to monitor functional status on a frequent basis to ensure that the supports provided are appropriate to the child's changing needs.

Educational Intervention

Whether difficulties are a function of the illness, the treatment, or the ability to cope with the illness, children with chronic illness often struggle academically (Forrest et al., 2011). For those with academic deficits, one or more evidence-based practices may be identified to address the deficit. These will not differ significantly from the programs and principles identified. Additional evidence-based practices to address academic concerns are available through the What Works Clearinghouse (http://www.whatworks.ed.gov). In selecting interventions it is important to consider the length of time needed for the intervention and the need to account for

the likelihood of child absence if the intervention is sequenced and presented in group format.

To effectively address the educational needs of the child with chronic illness, it is also important to consider the role and needs of the teacher. Teacher consultation can help with issues of modifications/accommodations in the classroom as well as evidence-based interventions for specific academic deficits. Modifications to selected interventions may be necessary depending on the child's ability to sustain attention for the time period required, the extent of practice needed for information to be encoded, and the child's functional level (i.e., mastery of foundational skills). Through consultation and collaboration, the school psychologist also can provide the teacher with encouragement for continued interaction between the teacher and student during any extended periods of absences (Boonen & Petry, 2011). The school psychologist may be able to provide suggestions for increased engagement of the child as well. Another important factor is dealing with missed classwork and ensuring that teachers understand that the extent to which it is feasible for a child to complete both missed classwork and homework given fatigue. With knowledge and understanding, the teacher will be more effective with the student with a chronic illness.

School-wide practices also need to be considered and changes to policy advocated. To maximize instructional benefit, it is important to consider the child's class schedule in relation to identified side effects of any medications. For example, knowing that the child may become sleepy after taking a medication might be helpful in scheduling classes and activities that require more concentrated effort. If the sleepiness occurs during a more active class or during activities that do not require intense concentration, the effect on learning may be lessened. In the same way, the instructional schedule and medical visits can be coordinated so that the child is less likely to miss new material. When the teacher has a better understanding of the illness and medication effects, then the teacher can be better prepared to provide key work and instruction during those periods of optimal alertness.

Psychosocial Assessment and Intervention

School psychologists have the knowledge and skills to provide services that promote social–emotional functioning and mental health. The potential for psychological and social problems are the most challenging part of treating children with chronic illness in a school setting; however, consideration of a child's resilience, coping skills, and socialization should be an important part of student-level services. The school psychologist can be involved in the development and implementation of interventions designed to foster positive mental health and prevent maladjustment for children with chronic illness.

There are many programs that have been developed to address mental health issues for children with health conditions (see Drotar, 2006; Power & Werba DeRosa, 2012; Sansom-Daly, Peate, Wakefield, Bryant, & Cohn, 2012). Sansom-Daly et al. (2012) looked at 25 interventions with adolescents and young adults with chronic illness that were helpful in overall adjustment (see Table 27.2). Although there were limitations to the studies reviewed, they concluded that interventions that were longer than 3 months, had six or more sessions or contacts, and focused on skills such as communication as opposed to general coping seemed to have a greater impact. Tailoring the interventions to the individual along with gradually building skills was associated with better outcomes for students (Sansom-Daly et al., 2012).

As with academic programs, best practice is to use evidence-based programs to address emotional and behavioral concerns. With a variety of programs and approaches, the parameters for treatment can inform the decision-making process of the interventions that would be most appropriate for a given child with a

chronic illness. One consideration is any prior mental health interventions that the child has had in the past and the outcomes from that intervention. The goal or desired outcome of the intervention and the child's functioning level need to be considered in determining an appropriate program as well. For children with limited communication skills, a more behaviorally based program may be more appropriate than one that presupposes the ability to communicate effectively. Another consideration is whether the program is better administered in a group format or with the individual child. Individual intervention may be best for the child who is especially psychologically vulnerable or whose attendance is more sporadic and unpredictable. Group intervention may be best for the child who desires yet lacks peer interaction, who has more predictable attendance, and who has basic communication skills.

Power and Werba DeRosa (2012) proposed a multisystemic cognitive–behavioral intervention model that integrates ecological and cognitive–behavioral approaches, such that the interventions are most likely to be successful when developed in a collaborative partnership. Involvement of the stakeholders in choosing an intervention approach is critical. The evidence-based intervention may follow a structured script with sequenced tasks for a specific area (i.e., a manualized

Table 27.2. Summary of Effective Interventions for Adolescents and Young Adults With Chronic Illness

Target of the Program	Type of Intervention	Number of Studies	Findings
Facilitating psychological adjustment through peer support	Nondirective emotional and peer support	4	Three of four studies showed significant effects on at least one psychological measure.
Educational and counseling interventions	Education and/or psychoeducation models	8	Seven educational interventions showed small to very large improvement on at least one of the outcome measures; the intervention using one multisession counseling intervention yielded no significant results.
Practice of cognitive behavioral techniques (such as problem solving, cognitive restructuring, role-playing, and goal setting)	Adaptation and coping skills training interventions: coping skills for the student alone	7	Four of the seven skills-based interventions showed medium to very large significant effects.
Behavioral family systems therapy along with the multifamily discussion group format	Adaptation and coping skills training interventions: Multifamily/parent involvement in coping skills	6	Five of the six family-focused coping skills programs achieved medium to very large positive effects, but of the four studies that evaluated family variables (e.g., communication, conflict), only two showed significant effects.

Note. Compiled from 25 studies reviewed by Sansom-Daly et al. (2011).

program) but modified as needed to meet the needs and functioning level of the individual. For example, specific programs are intended for use with suggested ages but may be less appropriate if there are significant developmental issues. The pace and expectations also may need to be modified (e.g., breaking skills into smaller more manageable steps). Interventions may need to include some educational information (i.e., educating the child about his or her disorder) as well as direct teaching of skills (e.g., communication skills, coping skills). Unfortunately, there is not yet a body of conclusive outcome research on the effectiveness of many of these components, singly or in combination.

Many children and adolescents with chronic illness experience social rejection, possibly due to other children's concerns about the illness (Sentenac et al., 2012). The rejection may be most apparent following a period of hospitalization and convalescence. Restrictions from participation in some activities, the chronic nature of the illness, and other factors can have an impact on the development of social skills, further increasing the likelihood of rejection. With increased availability of social networking and e-mail, there are ways for children to continue to be in contact with peers while homebound or hospitalized and may result in less social isolation for the child with chronic illness (Straker, Pollock, & Maslen, 2009). It is not yet known, however, if social networking will facilitate the development of social skills and pragmatic communication. Certainly, in addition to an evidence-based social skills training program, consideration and identification of opportunities for the child to become involved in appropriate and structured peer activities, to the extent feasible, in addition to social networking, will be helpful.

For children with chronic illness and the likelihood that their illness will affect their ability for physical activity or socialization, consideration of quality of life, or a general sense of well-being, may be appropriate. Quality of life is being considered more and more as an outcome variable to represent overall well-being of children with chronic illness, not only in general terms but with regard to specific health issues. Quality of life has been studied in relation to many chronic illnesses including asthma, epilepsy, cancer, gastrointestinal disorders, and diabetes. Many factors, including coping strategies, relationship with parents, and parental quality of life have been found to be critical to child quality of life (e.g., Roddenberry & Renk, 2008). For those children with life-threatening illnesses, the school psychologist can be a support for the teachers in shifting from a focus on academic outcomes to consideration of

quality of life (e.g., the role of social interactions) while the child is able to participate, even minimally, in the school setting.

Systemic Intervention

School psychologists can assist in bringing about essential systemic intervention through their knowledge and understanding of how systems work. Specifically, the school psychologist can serve as an advocate for change to current school policies that might otherwise have a negative impact on the child with a chronic illness. Tardiness and attendance policies, for example, do not always serve children with chronic illness well. Often school policies related to attendance or tardiness that make sense for the typical child become barriers to school adjustment and psychosocial functioning. For example, a child with chronic illness might be tardy because of the illness itself or the side effects of treatment, but the same school policy (i.e., punishment) is applied. By being knowledgeable about these policies and the potential for conflicts due to a given chronic illness, the school psychologist can provide relevant information related to alterations in the discipline policy (e.g., as related to tardiness) and advocate for other modifications to policy as part of IEP, 504 Plan, or other individualized plan for the child with chronic illness.

In many states, the child must miss a specific number of days consecutively to qualify for homebound services or tutoring. This discourages the parents from having the child attend school whenever physically possible as the needed support of the homebound instruction is then lost. The flip side is that missing a given number of days may automatically result in a loss of credits or extensive make-up work. The mismatch between managed healthcare school policies on attendance and homebound instruction carry the potential to have a negative impact on the child with a chronic illness (Shaw & McCabe, 2008). In effect, considerable changes in the provision of medical care have occurred. In some instances (e.g., requiring some consecutive number of days prior to homebound instruction), school policies have not taken into account that chronic illnesses are more frequently treated with repetitive short stays rather than an extensive long-term hospitalization and convalescence.

Even for those who are eligible for homebound instruction, there is often no systematic plan for reentry to the school setting for the child. There may be limited consideration to beginning with half days and working up to full days, for example. As noted above, the teachers may not feel comfortable with the child returning from homebound and may need support. Given the potential for fatigue, the school nurse will need to be involved as well. The school psychologist can play a key role for those students who return to school following hospitalization and convalescence. Reintegration into the school, the curriculum, and social context can be particularly problematic after prolonged absence (see Boonen & Petry, 2011). Generally, components of reentry planning include programs for the child, support for the teachers and other school personnel, programming (i.e., education) for the child's peers, support for parents, and communication with medical personnel (Prevatt et al., 2000). Many evidence-based approaches to address child issues (e.g., coping skills, memory deficits, reading deficits) have been identified) and can be useful in meeting the needs of the child with chronic illness. There also are a number of intervention programs designed to facilitate school reentry and address the social–emotional issues of children with chronic illness. The school psychologist can have an active role in many aspects of service delivery. It is important to bear in mind that the social–emotional effects of having a chronic illness and appropriate interventions will differ as children enter adolescence and need to deal with increased social demands.

Many school districts and state education agencies have adopted a response to intervention approach using a multitier system. This framework is effective in terms of identification of at-risk students and provision of interventions within general education prior to referral for special education services. It is important to consider that this framework may not be in the best interest for the student whose chronic illness has resulted in relatively sudden and acute impairments (e.g., the student with sickle cell who has a stroke, the student with a brain tumor who has undergone surgery). For these students, and those with traumatic brain injury, it is critical that support services be in place as soon as possible in order to maximize rehabilitation. This is another instance when the school psychologist can help in the advocacy process by providing information to appropriate parties so that policy exceptions can be made.

Monitoring Student Outcomes

Assessment and intervention occur at multiple levels for the child with chronic illness as with any other child. For each child, the involvement of the school psychologist will be different and responsive to what is needed for that child. As noted earlier, there is a need for continuous monitoring and evaluation of student outcomes when interventions are implemented, including the provision of any accommodations or modifications. Progress monitoring for academic areas is easily accomplished through curriculum-based measurement and available benchmarking programs.

For social–emotional–behavioral concerns, school psychologists can best monitor and evaluate their own effectiveness when providing direct services (e.g., counseling) through the regular use of short self-report questionnaires to determine if the program being used is appropriate and effective. Various rating scales have shortened versions for parent and teacher perspectives as well as self-report by the child. These can be used to monitor treatment effectiveness on a monthly or school term basis. With some children with chronic illness, as noted, an added outcome component may be quality of life. It will be critical, however, to interpret the results of these measures in light of any changes in health status that occur.

Although not often considered in the context of student outcomes, the school psychologist also may want to obtain feedback from teachers and school staff with regard to the effects of any inservices or educational information on their respective comfort level and self-efficacy in teaching students with chronic illness. Similarly, it may be helpful to routinely check in with parents on how responsive they feel the plan and school are with regard to meeting the needs of their child. Getting input from primary stakeholders (parent, child, teacher) in terms of outcome over time is critical, given the potential change in children's needs, developmentally and medically, over time.

SUMMARY

The critical components of best practices for school psychologists working with children with chronic illness are based on ethical and professional standards and foster preventive and responsive services that focus on meeting the needs of individual children in a collaborative environment. Depending on the chronic illness, the disease course, and the resulting functional impairments, school psychologists are well placed to meet the academic and mental health needs of these children. The number of children with chronic illness is increasing, and more children with chronic illness are surviving into adulthood. Oftentimes, the disorder or illness is not obvious; that is, teachers or other school personnel may not understand why a child is absent so much or may need accommodations. In more acute situations, with a focus on medical and health issues, academic and mental health needs may not be identified early on. For this reason, implementation of multitiered assessment and progress monitoring to provide information on the child's educational progress is essential. Given research with regard to potential school problems associated with a chronic illness, prevention activities within a multitiered framework may be appropriate to reduce later, more long-term problems. Similarly, socialization and mental health issues need to be considered given the risk of internalizing and externalizing disorders as well as potential for peer neglect.

Some of the more critical components specific to meeting the needs of children with illness are (a) working in collaboration and serving as liaison between parents, schools, and the medical community; (b) being informed about and educating others about the illness; (c) providing support to teachers and school staff; (d) advocating for services and programs that meet the academic and mental health needs of students with chronic illness; (e) advocating for a change in policies that potentially negatively affect children with chronic illness; and (f) assisting in the transition for those children who reenter school following hospitalization and convalescence. School psychologists can play a critical role in establishing the collaborative team effort needed to help children with chronic illness obtain the services they need and be successful in school, home, and community. School psychologists can also take leadership and advocacy roles in the area of policy and system-wide change. The research base for programs specific to children with chronic illness is limited and summarized here. School psychologists have the skills and knowledge to add to this research base through program evaluation and case study.

REFERENCES

American Psychological Association. (2006). Evidence-based practice in psychology. *American Psychologist, 61,* 271–283.

Boonen, H., & Petry, K. (2011). How do children with a chronic or long-term illness perceive their school re-entry after a period of homebound instruction? *Child: Care, Health and Development, 38,* 490–496. doi:10.1111/j.1365-2214.2011.01279.x

Brown, R. T., Daly, B. P., & Rickell, A. U. (Eds.). (2007). *Chronic illness in children and adolescents.* Cambridge, MA: Hogrefe & Huber.

Buelow, J. M., Perkins, S. M., Johnson, C. S., Byars, A. W., Fastenau, P. S., Dunn, D. W., & Austin, J. K. (2012). Adaptive functioning in children with epilepsy and learning problems. *Journal of Child Neurology, 27,* 1241–1249. doi:10.1177/0883073811432750

Castillo, C. L. (Ed.). (2008). *Children with complex medical issues in schools.* New York, NY: Springer.

Compas, B. E., Boyer, M. C., Stanger, C., Colletti, R. B., Thomsen, A. H., Dufton, L. M., & Cole, D. A. (2006). Latent variable analysis of coping, anxiety/depression, and somatic symptoms in adolescents with chronic pain. *Journal of Consulting and Clinical Psychology, 74,* 1132–1142. doi:10.1037/0022-006X.74.6.1132

Desrocher, M., & Rovet, J. (2004). Neurocognitive correlates of type 1 diabetes mellitus in childhood. *Neuropsychology, 10,* 36–52. doi:10.1076/chin.10.1.36.26241

Drotar, D. (2006). *Psychological interventions in childhood chronic illness.* Washington, DC: American Psychological Association. doi:10.1037/11412-000

DuPaul, G. J., Power, T. J., & Shapiro, E. S. (2009). Schools and integration/reintegration into schools. In M. C. Roberts (Ed.), *Handbook of pediatric psychology* (4th ed., pp. 689–702). New York, NY: Guilford Press.

Forrest, C. B., Bevans, K. B., Riley, A. W., Crespo, R., & Louis, T. A. (2011). School outcomes of children with special health care needs. *Pediatrics, 128,* 303–312. doi:10.1037/11412-000

Greydanus, D., Patel, D., & Pratt, H. (2010). Suicide risk in adolescents with chronic illness: implications for primary care and special pediatric practice: a review. *Developmental Medicine & Child Neurology, 52,* 1083–1087. doi:10.1111/j.1469-8749.2010.03771.x

Hysing, M., Elgen, I., Gillberg, C., & Lundervold, A. J. (2010). Emotional and behavioural problems in subgroups of children with chronic illness: Results from a large-scale population study. *Child: Care, Health and Development, 35,* 527–533. doi:10.1111/j.1365-2214.2009-00967.x

Jacob, E., Miaskowski, C., Savedra, M., Beyer, J. E., Treadwll, M., & Styles, L. (2006). Changes in sleep, food intake, and activity levels during acute painful episodes in children with sickle cell disease. *Journal of Pediatric Nursing, 1,* 23–34. doi:10.1016/j.pedn.2005.06.002

Logan, D. E., Simons, L. E., & Carpino, E. A. (2011). Too sick for school? Parent influences on school functioning among children with chronic pain. *Pain, 153,* 437–443. doi:10.1016/j.pain.2011.11.004

Martinez, Y. J., & Ercikan, K. (2009). Chronic illnesses in Canadian children: What is the effect of illness on academic achievement, and anxiety, and emotional disorder? *Child: Care, Health and Development, 35,* 391–401. doi:10.1111/j.1365-2214.2008.0916.x

National Association of School Psychologists. (2010). *Model for comprehensive and integrated school psychological services.* Bethesda, MD: Author. Retrieved from http://www.nasponline.org/standards/2010standards/2_PracticeModel.pdf

National Center for Health Statistics. (2012). *Summary health statistics for U.S. children: National health interview survey, 2011.* Washington, DC: Author. Retrieved from http://www.cdc.gov/nchs/data/series/sr_10/sr10_254.pdf

Pinquart, M., & Shen, Y. (2011). Behavior problems in children and adolescents with chronic physical illness: A meta-analysis. *Journal of Pediatric Psychology, 36,* 1003–1016. doi:10.1093/jpepsy/jsr042

Power, T. J., & Werba DeRosa, B. (2012). Children with chronic health conditions: School-based cognitive-behavioral interventions. In T. J. Power & R. Werba DeRosa (Eds.), *Cognitive-behavioral interventions in educational settings: A handbook for practice* (2nd ed., pp. 531–555). New York, NY: Routledge.

Prevatt, F. F., Heffer, R. W., & Lowe, P. A. (2000). A review of school reintegration programs for children with cancer. *Journal of School Psychology, 45,* 217–236. doi:10.1016/s0022-4405(00)00046-7

Reiter-Purtill, J., Waller, J. M., & Noll, R. B. (2009). Empirical and theoretical perspectives on the peer relations of children with chronic conditions. In J. Reiter-Purtill, J. M. Waller, & R. B. Noll (Eds.), *Handbook of pediatric psychology* (pp. 672–688). New York, NY: Guilford Press.

Roddenberry, A., & Renk, K. (2008). Quality of life in pediatric cancer patients: The relationships among parents' characteristics, children's characteristics, and informant concordance. *Journal of Child and Family Studies, 17,* 402–426. doi:10.1007/s10826-007-9155-0

Rodenburg, R., Stams, G. J., Meijer, A. M., Aldenkamp, A. P., & Dekovic, M. (2005). Psychopathology in children with epilepsy: A meta-analysis. *Journal of Pediatric Psychology, 30,* 453–468. doi:10.1093/jepsy/jsi071

Sansom-Daly, U. M., Peate, M., Wakefield, C. E., Bryant, R. A., & Cohn, R. J. (2012). A systematic review of psychological interventions for adolescents and young adults living with chronic illness. *Health Psychology, 31,* 380–393.

Saxe, G., Stoddard, F., Chawla, N., Lopez, C. G., Hall, E., Sheridan, R., ...King, L. (2005). Risk factors for acute stress disorder in children with burns. *Journal of Trauma & Dissociation, 6*(2), 37–49. doi:10.1300/j229v06n02_05

Sentenac, M., Arnaud, C., Gavin, A., Molcho, M., Gabhainn, S. N., & Godeau, E. (2012). Peer victimization among school-aged children with chronic conditions. *Epidemiologic Reviews, 34,* 120–128. doi:10.1093/epirev/mxr024

Shaw, S. R., & McCabe, P. C. (2008). Hospital-to-school transition for children with chronic illness: Meeting the new challenges of an evolving health care system. *Psychology in the Schools, 45,* 74–87. doi:10.1002/pits.20280

Sillanpää, M., & Cross, J. H. (2009). The psychosocial impact of epilepsy in childhood. *Epilepsy and Behavior, 15,* S5–S10. doi:10.1016/j.yebeh.2009.03.007

Straker, L., Pollock, C., & Maslen, B. (2009). Principles for the wise use of computers by children. *Ergonomics, 52,* 1386–1401. doi:10.1080/00140130903067789

Wade, J. F., Dang, C. V., Nelson, L., & Wasserberger, J. (2010). Emergent complications of the newer anticonvulsants. *The Journal of Emergency Medicine, 38,* 231–237. doi:10.1016/j.jemermed.2008.03.032

Wodrich, D. L., & Cunningham, M. M. (2008). School-based tertiary and targeted interventions for students with chronic medical conditions: Examples from Type I diabetes mellitus and epilepsy. *Psychology in the Schools, 45,* 52–62. doi:10.1002/pits.20278

28 Best Practices in Working With Children With Traumatic Brain Injuries

Susan C. Davies
University of Dayton (OH)

OVERVIEW

Traumatic brain injuries (TBIs) can significantly affect student learning and behavior. School psychologists' knowledge about education, mental health, biology, and collaborative consultation put them in an excellent position to facilitate school-based response to known or suspected TBIs. The purpose of this chapter is to inform school psychologists about TBI etiology, incidence, and severity levels; possible outcomes following TBIs in school-age children; and best practices for students with TBI in terms of working with families, planning transitions, conducting assessments, and designing and monitoring interventions.

The content of this chapter is aligned with the National Association of School Psychologists (NASP) *Model for Comprehensive and Integrated School Psychological Services* (NASP, 2010), and, specifically, the Preventive and Responsive Services domain. School psychologists can be instrumental in educating the entire school population on brain injury prevention, recognition, and response. It is expected that this information will increase practitioner knowledge of TBI risk factors and variables that can affect recovery of academic skills, cognition, and social–emotional well-being. By engaging in the collaborative problem-solving process, practitioners can better coordinate evaluation of strengths and weaknesses and identify appropriate adjustments and accommodations during the recovery period and beyond. As described in the assessment and intervention sections of this chapter, school-based response to TBI is best framed within multitiered services, with the intensity of interventions increasing or decreasing based upon student need. For students with TBI, whose skills and abilities may be rapidly fluctuating, it is critical that school psychologists understand appropriate progress-monitoring techniques and issues that can affect resilience, risk, and recovery.

TBI is an acquired injury to the brain caused by an external physical force (e.g., a bump, blow, jolt to the head) or a penetrating head injury (Centers for Disease Control and Prevention [CDC], 2012). TBIs are generally labeled as mild (often used synonymously with the term concussion), moderate, or severe. The majority of individuals who sustain a mild TBI will return to normal activities without detectable problems (Bigler, 2012). Prognosis following TBI will vary and worsen with severity of injury, and survivors of severe TBIs are expected to have some degree of permanent impairment that would adversely affect behavior and, in children, learning at school.

In 1990, TBI was added as a disability category under the Individuals with Disabilities in Education Act (IDEA). This decision was in recognition that TBI occurs much more frequently than was previously thought and that educators needed specialized understanding of students with this type of disability. IDEA (2004) defines TBI as

> … an acquired injury to the brain caused by an external physical force, resulting in total or partial functional disability or psychosocial impairment, or both, that adversely affects a child's educational performance. The term applies to open or closed head injuries resulting in impairments in one or more areas, such as cognition; language; memory; attention; reasoning; abstract thinking; problem-solving; sensory, perceptual and motor abilities;

psychosocial behavior; physical functions; information processing; and speech. The term does not apply to brain injuries that are congenital or degenerative, or brain injuries induced by birth trauma. (34 Code of Federal Regulations 300.7(c)(12))

In order to be more effective in helping students with TBI, school psychologists need to understand the range of potential problems across injury severity level, developmental level, and setting (e.g., home, school, extracurricular venues, community). They may be called upon to assist in a variety of situations involving students with TBI, such as:

- Conducting evaluations of students suspected of sustaining a TBI
- Designing and monitoring interventions for students with TBI
- Explaining how TBI is different from other disability categories
- Helping students make the transition from hospital or rehabilitation back to school
- Consulting with medical professionals and other service providers
- Offering logistical and emotional support for parents and siblings
- Conducting brain injury prevention activities, such as Bike Helmet Awareness Week
- Providing inservice seminars on concussion awareness so faculty can learn concussion recognition and response

It is easy for school personnel to overlook the unique educational needs of students with TBI. Even if school psychologists have not received extensive training on TBI, they are still expected to be well versed in problem solving and working within a multitiered framework. This chapter will provide an overview of TBI and will illustrate how trainees and practitioners can build upon existing knowledge and skills to better serve students with TBI.

BASIC CONSIDERATIONS

The majority of TBIs are caused by falls (35.2%), followed by motor vehicle and traffic injuries (17.3%), struck by or against events (16.5%), and assaults (10%; Faul, Xu, Wald, & Coronado, 2010). Although a great deal of recent media attention has been on sports-related injuries, the majority of TBIs in children and adolescents occur off the playing field.

The incidents listed above can result in open head injuries, closed head injuries, or both. Open, or penetrating, head injuries occur when the skull becomes broken or an object, such as a skull fragment or bullet, penetrates the dura mater, the first of the brain's three protective layers inside the skull, or the deeper brain tissue. Closed, or nonpenetrating, head injuries can involve diffuse and/or focal injuries. Diffuse injuries are widespread injuries resulting from deformation of the brain within the skull. An example of this is a diffuse axonal injury. Rotational injuries occur when the brain rotates in the skull, which can result in shearing of axons, tearing of blood vessels, and/or compression of brain tissue. Focal injuries are compression injuries caused by collision forces that result in hematomas (bleeding) and contusions (bruising) on the surface or interior of the brain located at the site of impact or at isolated points in the brain (Andriessen, Jacobs, & Vos, 2010). Coup and contrecoup injuries are common with focal injuries. A coup injury is a compression injury at the site of impact, and a contrecoup injury is a compression injury at the site opposite the point of impact. Coup and contrecoup injuries are common during acceleration/deceleration injuries (e.g., a fall from a ladder, head-on automobile collision). The coup injury occurs at the site of impact when the brain compresses against the inside of the stopped skull. The contrecoup injury occurs when the brain bounces back, strikes the opposite side of the skull, and compresses the brain against the skull. Further injury occurs to the brain as it rubs back and forth against the ridges on the base of the skull.

Incidence

According to the CDC, incidences of TBI are higher among boys than girls: In preschool children, the ratio of boys to girls injured is 1.5 to 1, and in school-age children that difference increases to 2 to 1 (CDC, 2012). Males also tend to sustain more severe trauma, with the ratio for mortality being 4 to 1 (Anderson et al., 2001).

There are also age-related differences in the incidence and causes of TBI. The incidence of TBI has bimodal peaks in the pediatric population, with the first peak occurring in children younger than 5 years. The second peak in the pediatric population occurs in mid-to-late adolescence and is caused by motor vehicle accidents (Adelson, 1998; Gedeit, 2001).

Although in the educational setting TBI is often considered a low-incidence disability (because of the low numbers of students who qualify for special education services under this category), the overall occurrences of

TBI that are severe enough to result in permanent impairment occur with disproportionate frequency. In fact, TBI is a leading cause of death and disability in childhood and adolescence (CDC, 2012; Zaloshnja, Miller, Langlois, & Selassie, 2008). According to the CDC, approximately 1.7 million people sustain TBIs each year, and about 700,000 of those are children ages 0–19 (Faul et al., 2010). The majority of those who are injured are treated and released. On the other end of the continuum, more than 6,000 severely injured children die each year from complications related to their TBI (most of those are older adolescents). Approximately 29,000 children annually are left with persistent disability following TBI. Of those, about one third are estimated to have injuries so severe that those children require special education supports, which yields a cumulative total of 130,000 K–12 students (Glang et al., 2008). These data are congruent with Zaloshnja et al.'s (2008) estimation of 145,000 children ages 0–19 who have a disability from TBI. However, the federal special education census reported only 26,402 students were served under the TBI category of IDEA in 2007 (http://www.ideadata.org). Thus, only a small percentage of students with TBI who are estimated to need services are identified appropriately (Deidrick & Farmer, 2005; Glang et al., 2008; see Figure 28.1).

The reasons for underidentification may include one or more of the following:

- Students with TBI are being identified and served under a different special education category
- Scores on standardized instruments appear average because some skills remain intact
- Students may appear to have no difficulties if motor skills recover more quickly than cognitive abilities
- Belief in the myth that the students will bounce back
- Lack of educator awareness, knowledge, competence, and training on TBI
- Parents are not communicating with the school about the injury
- Misattribution of TBI-related difficulties to factors such as laziness, an oppositional nature, or emotional instability
- Difficulty obtaining a medical signature that there was a disability as a result of external force

Severity

TBI severity is often determined by a combination of measures, such as the Glasgow Coma Scale, length of loss of consciousness, and length of posttraumatic

Figure 28.1. Underidentification of Students With TBI

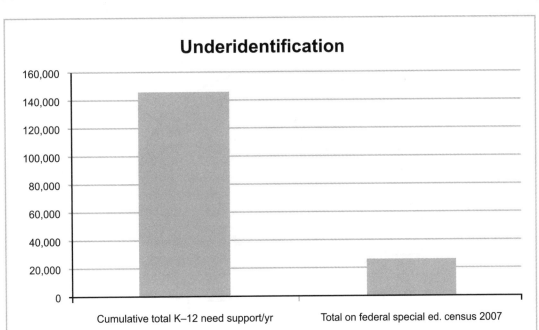

Note. From *TBI: Classroom Practices, Assessment and Eligibility*, by D. Ettel, 2012. Presentation at the TBI Summit at the annual Ohio Center for Autism and Low Incidence Disabilities conference in Columbus, OH. Reprinted with permission.

Table 28.1. Levels of TBI Severity

	Length of Loss of Consciousness	Glasgow Coma Score	Length of Posttraumatic Amnesia
Mild	None to approximately 30 minutes	13–15	< 1 hour
Moderate	30 minutes to hours (definitions range from 6–24 hours)	9–12	1–24
Severe	Typically > 24 hours (some say > 6 hours)	3–8	> 24 hours (some say > 1 week)

amnesia. The Glasgow Coma Scale rates patients' current level of functioning. It is scored between 3 and 15, 3 being the worst and 15 the best, and is composed of three parameters: eye response, verbal response, and motor response. The majority of TBIs (75–85%) are classified as mild. (See Table 28.1.) Another 8–10% are moderate, and 6–13% are severe (Peiniger et al., 2012). Because of advances in trauma medicine and surgical techniques, more children with serious brain injuries now survive. At the same time, length of stay in critical care facilities and rehabilitation has decreased (John, 2005). This results in students with more severe brain injuries returning to school and having subsequent educational needs.

Organization of the Brain

TBIs can result in injury to structural parts of the brain and/or to neurochemicals that communicate information throughout the brain. While a comprehensive neuroanatomy lesson is beyond the scope of this chapter, it is important that school psychologists have a basic understanding of brain structures and functions. (See Figure 28.2.)

The brain is divided into four lobes: the frontal lobe, the parietal lobe, the temporal lobe, and the occipital lobe. The frontal lobe, particularly the prefrontal cortex, has great vulnerability in a TBI. The prefrontal cortex is where executive functions are carried out; that is, a set of

Figure 28.2. Regions of the Brain

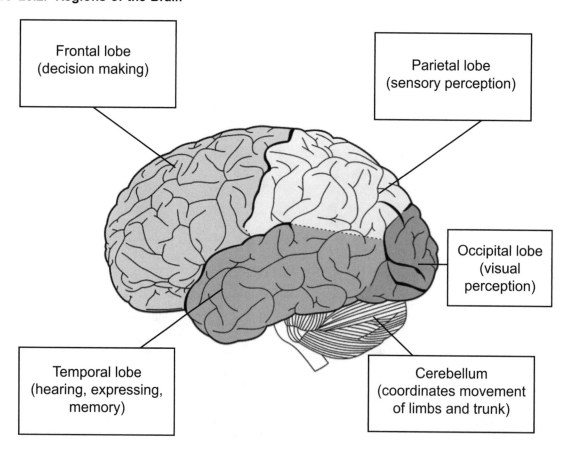

Frontal lobe (decision making)

Parietal lobe (sensory perception)

Occipital lobe (visual perception)

Temporal lobe (hearing, expressing, memory)

Cerebellum (coordinates movement of limbs and trunk)

processes that underlie flexible, goal-directed behavior. This includes skills such as planning and organization, inhibitory control, behavioral initiation, self-monitoring and self-correcting, working memory, flexibility in thinking, awareness of abilities and limitations, judgment and problem solving, and efficient search for information, such as retrieval of information from memory.

Also vulnerable in a TBI is the temporal lobe, particularly the medial and inferior temporal lobe structures (Tsang & Whitfield, 2012). This part of the brain is important for encoding new information into long-term storage, or memory. Damage to this part of the brain can cause anterograde amnesia (difficulty forming new memories and learning new information) or retrograde amnesia (loss of memory for events that occurred or skills that were acquired in the past).

The occipital lobe, which is primarily responsible for vision, can be injured in the contrecoup force when a person sustains a blow to the front of the head. Injury to this area might affect the processing of visual information or result in limited field of vision.

Damage to the parietal lobe may include, but is not limited to, such things as an inability to perceive when one is being touched or is touching something or someone. Students experiencing these symptoms might have trouble with such activities as typing on a computer keyboard or playing an instrument with their fingers.

Developmental Predictors of Outcomes

Developmental predictors of outcomes can include preinjury factors, the age of injury, and time since the injury.

Preinjury Factors

Children with preexisting conditions (e.g., mental health problems, substance abuse) are at higher risk of sustaining a TBI (Corrigan, 1995; Guskiewicz, Weaver, Padua, & Garrett, 2000; Saunders et al., 2009) and have poorer outcomes postinjury (Schwartz et al., 2003). Owing to inherent dangers, children exposed to physical violence, unsafe environments (e.g., dangerous neighborhoods), homes lacking supervision, or physical abuse may also be at increased risk for sustaining a TBI. Children who sustained severe TBIs and were in poorly functioning families have been shown to have slower recovery over time and lower overall functioning when compared to children from higher functioning families (Yeates et al., 1997). In terms of how the effects of preinjury factors can affect

postinjury outcomes, an example is a child with a preexisting condition such as attention deficit hyperactivity disorder (known to be associated with the frontal lobes) having even more problems sustaining attention following a TBI involving damage to the frontal lobe.

Age of Injury

One myth related to TBI is the idea that it is "better" to sustain an injury when one is very young because of the plasticity of the brain in the early years. However, although the young brain may allow short-term recovery by shifting functions to another area of the brain, later abilities might be compromised because normal developmental processes involving those areas that have been recruited may now be operating less efficiently. Thus, age of injury can predict certain kinds of recovery, but it does so in a complex manner.

Depending upon the severity and location of the injury, some children with TBI may never recover lost functions or acquire new functions, while others may but at a slower rate than is typical for their age and level of brain development. For these children, keeping up with same-age peers in school will likely be challenging. In addition, some children with TBIs show early recovery but then grow into symptoms as time passes. These children might seem fine for years but then have late-onset difficulties as the demands on the damaged brain structures increase. For example, a child who sustained a moderate TBI at age 2, with damage to areas of the brain involved in attention and concentration, might not experience difficulties until first grade, when demands for greater sustained attention to task is expected. In another example, a child who has sustained injury to the areas of the brain involved in executive function may be injured in early elementary school and show medical and neurological recovery, but then show signs of trouble in middle school, when increased demands for organization and planning of schoolwork increase. In these cases, delayed onset of symptoms may be attributed to other factors rather than to the injury that occurred several years before.

Time Since the Injury

The length of elapsed time between injury and assessment or intervention can affect outcomes (Jantz & Coulter, 2007). There is typically a rapid rate of recovery in the first 6 months after an injury, followed by a slower period of recovery throughout the first year, and finally a plateau (Ornstein et al., 2009). However, every child's recovery path is different, and reaching a plateau may not mean that recovery is complete. Long-term recovery at this point is generally more gradual, but can continue for months and years.

Outcomes Following TBI

Every brain injury is different and outcomes can vary greatly depending on type and severity of injury, as well as on quality of follow-up care and support. There may be significant gaps in memory and skills. There may be contradictory skills, with significant strengths in some areas but major difficulties in others.

Mild TBI

The child with mild TBI typically does not lose consciousness or loses consciousness very briefly and generally has normal neuroimaging (e.g., CT scans, MRIs; Bigler, 2010). However, these students may still demonstrate cognitive impairment on neuropsychological testing and/or ongoing metabolic abnormalities (Sady, Vaughan, & Gioia, 2011). Further, mild TBIs can have serious effects on learning, behavior, and memory (Buck, 2011). Subtle problems may go unrecognized, particularly if a child was not taken to the hospital for the blow to the head. The child may experience symptoms like headaches, difficulty concentrating, or mood swings.

Educators must be aware of appropriate adjustments that facilitate a safe recovery. Most symptoms of mild TBI resolve in a few weeks (Lau, Kontos, Collins, Mucha, & Lovell, 2011), but recovery rates are variable and some students have persistent postconcussive symptoms. Postconcussive symptoms are chronic cognitive and neurobehavioral difficulties that might include chronic headaches, fatigue, sleep difficulties, personality change in irritability and emotionality, sensitivity to light or noise, dizziness when standing quickly, short-term memory problems, difficulty in problem solving, and/or general academic difficulty (Moran et al., 2012). Best practices in facilitating short-term adjustments for students who have sustained a mild TBI/concussion and best practices in responding to students with more long-lasting problems appear later in this chapter.

Moderate to Severe TBIs

Moderate to severe TBIs can result in a number of problems that affect students, including cognitive deficits, emotional and behavioral problems (e.g., irritability, impulsivity, aggression), impaired social and adaptive functioning, declines in school performance, impaired alertness and orientation, fatigue, impaired language skills, executive functioning deficits (e.g.,

inattention, memory impairments, distractibility, difficulty following directions, poor organization), and corticosensory and motor skills deficits.

The location and severity of the injuries—and the quality of care after an injury—can determine how potential problems manifest in a student who sustained a TBI. Typically, physical problems resolve the fastest, leaving a child who may appear to have recovered when, in fact, a complicated constellation of invisible symptoms remain.

BEST PRACTICES FOR STUDENTS WITH TBI

Teachers who are experts in education often have little knowledge or training related to brain injuries. Conversely, many medical professionals who have expertise in brain injuries are not familiar with educational systems. Some schools try to address this problem through a one-time information session on TBI when an injured student returns to school. However, in order to be most effective, staff development practices should include training in evidence-based interventions, supervised practice with new skills, and continued mentoring, feedback, and consultation in the school setting (Glang, Todis, Sublette, Eagan-Brown, & Vaccaro, 2010). School psychologists are well positioned to provide these services, building a bridge between hospitals/rehabilitation facilities and schools and also collaborating with families.

Working With Families

School psychologists are familiar with the process of helping a family that is gradually realizing a child might have some type of disability. The situation for a family whose child sustained a TBI is often quite different: A tragic accident has in a moment changed the course of life. A family may be dealing with a mix of emotions, such as relief over the miraculous survival and recovery of a child after a life-threatening injury, grief over the loss of who that child once was or might have become, denial over issues of recovery and difficulties, and confusion over the sudden entry into the world of medical and educational jargon. A family may be dealing as well with the stress of injury or loss of other family members in an accident. Siblings at school may be frightened or resentful of a brother or sister who now acts differently or commands much of the parents' time and attention. Siblings may also have witnessed the injury and have new fears or problems sleeping. They may be embarrassed by their sibling's needs or behaviors in public. Older siblings may now be dealing with new responsibilities related to the care of others or household management.

School psychologists are in a unique position to not only help the child with a TBI, but also to provide support, resources, or counseling to any brothers or sisters in the school system. They know that many families are not prepared for the difficulties a child may face upon returning to school. The effective school psychologist provides care, support, and guidance for parents and siblings throughout the process of transition, assessment, and intervention.

One simple thing the school psychologist can do to help families cope is help parents set up a record-keeping system. Depending on an injury's severity and outcomes, the family may be meeting with various specialists and educators frequently and across a period of years. If the information is not stored in one place, then it can be very difficult to track down years later as additional problems emerge when a child grows into a disability, as described earlier. While the school will certainly keep its own careful records, a separate binder of information for the parents can provide a comprehensive record that is their exclusive property. It can track progress; note effective interventions; program results; and list important names, dates, and contact information for various professionals.

Another form of assistance by school psychologists is that of clarification. Children who were receiving intensive individualized speech, occupational, or physical therapy services in a rehabilitation program may also be eligible for them at school if they are related to educational needs. The school-based services, however, may differ in intensity or otherwise look different to the parents. The school psychologist can help explain the differences.

Transitions

A student with TBI faces numerous transitions: from hospital or rehabilitation back to school, within and between schools, and from school to postsecondary life. Any of these transitions can be difficult for any child, but they may be particularly challenging for one with a brain injury. Even the transitions of moving from one task to another or of returning to school after a vacation can lead to acting-out behaviors or academic struggles. School psychologists giving attention to these transitions in advance can help minimize such problems and facilitate adjustment to changes in environments, routines, and expectations.

Transition From Hospital or Rehabilitation to School

Many students with TBI are absent from school during rehabilitation or sustained their injuries during summer break. When such students return to school, teachers may not be aware of the injuries and subsequent educational needs, particularly if there is a lack of communication between hospital or rehabilitation facility and the school. The return to school is a critical time for putting appropriate services into place. A delay in services might lead to academic failure, social rejection, or exacerbation or mislabeling of difficulties. In fact, a staff's lack of knowledge about TBI and its related effects is a primary reason for a parent's dissatisfaction with his or her child's instructional services (McGrath, 2010).

School psychologists can ensure a smooth reintegration of students with TBI back into the school setting. They are well positioned to collaborate with medical professionals, parents, and the school team. For instance, rehabilitation team members may visit the school and, working with the school psychologist, provide inservice sessions to staff and classmates.

Because the transition process involves collaboration with agencies and other care providers, it is important to assign a case manager who can assist with scheduling meetings, communicating plans, and ensuring mutual respect for different perspectives. The case manager can help all members of the educational community understand how overwhelming it can be to enter the special education system when a previously so-called typical child suddenly has a disability.

Transitions Within and Between Schools

Transitions within and between schools require forethought and planning. Activities to help prepare the student might include visits to new settings, meetings with new teachers, and training for new teachers through inservice sessions or written information on brain injuries. A regular schedule of team meetings can provide a mechanism for easily making necessary changes to the program or plan of study.

Parents are critical for facilitating a successful transition, as they are the constant factor during school changes. They can ensure the school has updated copies of all records, communicate ongoing information from outside rehabilitation specialists or doctors, share particular transition concerns, and provide ongoing information about a child's adjustment to a new setting.

Transition From School to Postsecondary Life

The transition to college or independent living can be difficult for any young adult. The presence of a brain injury can certainly compound these difficulties. A student with TBI who successfully navigated high school with the help of parents and school staff may now be expected, for example, to independently get up on time, organize personal and class material, juggle multiple class syllabi, plan long-term projects, decipher social nuances of roommates, remember to change the oil in the car, and figure out how to pay for meals. School psychologists can ensure the development and implementation of a well-crafted, individualized transition plan, which is crucial for academic and social success.

IDEA requires transition services for students who are receiving special education services. This involves the development of a written plan as part of a student's Individualized Education Program (IEP) when the student is 16 (earlier in some states), which must be updated each year. The plan helps prepare the student for life after school and should consider the student's strengths, preferences, needs, and interests. A variety of postsecondary options are considered, including college, vocational training, employment, adult services, independent living, and participation within the community.

Two pieces of legislation influence the rights of individuals with TBI in the work place and special services offered at colleges and universities. Section 504 of the Rehabilitation Act of 1973 ensures that individuals with disabilities cannot be denied access to federally funded activities or programs solely based on disability. Thus, no college receiving federal funds can exclude a qualified applicant because of his or her disability. In Section 504, the Americans with Disabilities Act extends prohibition of discrimination on the basis of disability to all programs, activities, and services made available by state and local governments, regardless of whether those entities receive federal financial assistance. This law requires that accommodations are reasonable and timely. Reasonable accommodations are any modifications or adjustments to a work environment that make it possible for a qualified person with a disability to participate in and enjoy an opportunity. This deals with employment provisions and applies to colleges and universities.

The special education laws that provide funding to public schools do not apply to college. College staff may have limited experience in working with students with brain injuries. Thus, young adults with TBI need to take the initiative themselves to develop supports in college.

The presence of the disability does not, however, change the fact that the student must meet academic criteria for admission to the college. During the admissions process and after enrollment, it is important for students to research the resources, accommodations, and supports that are available. These might include a tutoring center, academic counselors who specialize in working with students with disabilities, support groups, writing assistance centers, or academic accommodations.

High school students injured close to graduation may be best served by not graduating right away, because graduating disqualifies them from additional special education services and because adult vocational rehabilitation services are not as readily available as special education services in public schools. Thus, a family with a high school student approaching graduation should receive careful guidance from the school psychologist to ensure that transition plans and programs optimally prepare the student for adulthood (Lash, Wolcott, & Pearson, 2005).

Assessment

School psychologists should regularly develop and test hypotheses about the potential cause of a student's struggles. Even if TBI is not originally a front line hypothesis, a previous head injury may be the underlying cause of academic and/or behavior problems. If a child has changes in academic performance or behavior following a blow to the head of any kind, regardless of how minor it may appear to be, an evaluation for a TBI may be warranted. Students with TBI can improve or decline significantly after an injury, so assessment must be frequent, flexible, and purposeful. Assessment and intervention for students with TBI is best addressed within a problem-solving framework. Multitiered practices such as response to intervention (RTI) and positive behavior interventions and supports allow for the early and ongoing assessment of skills, deficits, and educational needs. Selected assessments must be sensitive to uneven progress patterns (e.g., curriculum-based measures). School psychologists can then develop and implement appropriate interventions and accommodations, which can be altered as natural recovery takes place. Depending on the severity of the injury, a psychologist might consider approaching the RTI pyramid in reverse: providing the student with intensive supports and services upon return to school, and gradually reducing and withdrawing them as progress monitoring demonstrates improvement.

Observations and Interviews

During classroom-based observations, school psychologists can watch the teacher's management style and level of tolerance for inappropriate behavior, also determining the classroom structure and degree of classroom control. Students with TBI often do well with a calm, consistent approach. Teachers who present instructions in a clear, uncluttered manner—with few words and through visual examples—often do well with this group of students (Bowen, 2005).

When working with any student with academic or behavior problems, school psychologists must always inquire about a history of head injuries. A recent poll conducted on the NASP website revealed that only about half of respondents regularly asked parents about head injury, concussion, or mild TBI when collecting relevant background information about students. While the poll was nonscientific, it certainly points to a potential gap in everyday practice. Questions to parents might include: Has your child had a serious fall? Been in a car crash? Lost consciousness? Been dazed or confused after a sports accident? Parents know their children best and can give school psychologists preinjury comparisons of functioning. They can also describe their children's reactions and progress throughout treatment and recovery in a variety of settings and circumstances. This information is an essential part of a comprehensive evaluation. It is also important to get information on premorbid conditions, because TBIs can often exacerbate existing problems such as inattention, memory lapses, and impulsivity.

Checklists and Rating Scales

Behavioral checklists and rating scales can be useful for the school psychologist assessing the impact of a TBI. Instruments that are a regular part of training and practice (e.g., the Behavior Assessment Scale for Children-Second Edition, the Child Behavior Checklist) can provide useful data. Such rating scales can provide valuable information through both clinical subscales and item analysis. Because executive functioning deficits are common in students with TBI, a rating scale such as the Behavior Rating Inventory of Executive Function (Gioia, Isquith, Guy, & Kenworthy, 2000) might also be completed by parents, teachers, and students to give information on behavior regulation and metacognition.

Formal Assessment Measures

Because students with TBI often have uneven patterns of performance, a global standard score may not be fully representative of the child's ability. Many children with brain injuries have test scores that do not appear consistent with their daily functioning. This may happen for a variety of reasons. Children may perform well on some tests administered in a clinical setting but then not apply the ability in the context of daily life. Conversely, children may perform poorly on some tests but have sufficient compensatory strategies that allow them to perform better at home or school. Further, many intelligence tests focus on recalling old information. Children with a brain injury may be able to recall this old information but have great difficulty learning new information. They may also do better in a quiet testing room in a one-on-one setting but then have trouble paying attention, planning assignments, organizing materials, and ignoring distractions in the classroom.

Despite these limitations, norm-referenced assessments can provide school psychologists with a valuable tool in the evaluation process. For example, administering a traditional norm-referenced test of cognitive ability can allow the school psychologist to observe the child performing a variety of tasks in a relatively short period of time.

Curriculum-Based Measures

Curriculum-based measurement is a process of standardized testing that helps identify academic problems and allows progress monitoring in specific academic areas. Curriculum-based measurements are useful for students with TBI because they allow comparison between a student's preinjury and postinjury performance levels of academic functioning. For example, a student whose reading fluency was measured at 60 words read correctly per minute might read only 30 words correctly during the first week back at school. The student's progress back toward baseline can be monitored with weekly 1-minute reading probes. This is an inexpensive way to monitor academic progress quickly and frequently in a way that is less cognitively taxing than formal assessment measures and has been validated as a strong indicator of overall performance.

Functional Behavior Assessment

Functional behavior assessment is a way to gather information about situational variables that trigger or maintain a student's behavior. Through the use of observations, interviews, and manipulation of variables, the evaluator identifies the purpose (function) of the behavior and variables influencing the behavior. Functional behavior assessment helps identify slow and fast triggers, as well as consequences of behavior. Data are then used to develop an effective intervention plan. Impaired executive functions such as memory, attention, and concentration, as well as the student's stage of recovery from TBI, can all have an impact on the efficacy of interventions. Thus an intervention that includes only rewards or punishment for exhibiting appropriate behavior—without reteaching expected behaviors—may be unsuccessful. A functional behavior assessment might indicate a student with TBI is throwing his or her math book on the ground (behavior) because he or she can no longer solve the equations. Simply reinforcing the student to keep the book on the desk does not address the underlying issue of frustration.

Computer-Based Neurocognitive Tests

Computer-based neurocognitive tests allow school personnel to assess a student's condition at baseline and after a mild TBI/concussion. At present, these neurocognitive tests are typically conducted only with student athletes. They are administered during preseason to establish baseline levels of performance for athletes. If the athlete then sustains a mild TBI/concussion, the multicomponent test is readministered, and results are compared to baseline. This tool is used in conjunction with other measures to determine if the athlete needs further medical supervision and can be one part of a return-to-play decision. The expectation is that by objectively evaluating the concussed athlete's postinjury condition, there is a higher likelihood of tracking recovery for safe return to play (and therefore preventing the cumulative effects of multiple brain injuries).

Currently, the most widely used computerized neurocognitive test for student athletes is Immediate Post-Concussion Assessment and Cognitive Testing (Iverson, Lovell, & Collins, 2011). The test takes approximately 20 minutes and can be administered by an athletic trainer, school nurse, athletic director, team doctor, or psychologist who is trained in administration of the test. The test measures multiple aspects of cognitive functioning, including attention span, working memory, sustained and selective attention, response variability, nonverbal problem solving, and reaction time. It then produces a report of results that can be e-mailed or faxed for consultation. Data from repeated testing are stored, which can give the school psychologist access to historic data in a case of multiple concussions.

Intervention

School-based intervention plans for students with TBI are most effective when they are designed and monitored by a team of professionals. An effective intervention design will involve environmental support or modifications, the teaching of specific skills, and a reinforcement system to help motivate the child to use or practice the skills (Dawson & Guare, 2010). Clearly, there is a great deal of variability across individuals with TBI; therefore, there is little empirical validation for interventions specifically for TBI. Instead, school psychologists rely on evidence for effectiveness of types of categories of support.

Carryover and consistency between plans at home and school are beneficial so families and school teams can share and reinforce effective techniques. School psychologists can be instrumental in facilitating intervention collaboration among everyone who might be working with the child, including parents, teachers, medical professionals, clinical psychologists, nurses, school counselors, social workers, speech–language pathologists, occupational therapists, physical therapists, adaptive physical education teachers, coaches, athletic directors, and athletic trainers.

Adjustments for Mild TBI

Symptoms of mild TBIs have variable duration (minutes, days, weeks, months, or longer) and can include trouble thinking or remembering, physical symptoms, emotional or mood issues, and sleep-related problems such as fatigue or disturbed sleep. A child or adolescent who has sustained a concussion requires cognitive and physical rest to allow the brain time to heal (Halstead, Walter, & The Council on Sports Medicine and Fitness, 2010). This might include time off from school, no homework, computers, videogames, texting, cell phones, television, exercise, athletics, trips, social visits, or chores involving exertion. The student can begin to engage in light mental activity once symptoms subside.

The transition back to school and back to play after a concussion should be carefully considered by the family and school team. Students should engage only in cognitive activities that do not make symptoms worse. Thus, if computer work causes headaches, that activity should be decreased or stopped and the student should attempt more cognitive rest.

Return to School

Once physical symptoms subside, a reintegration to school may occur slowly. Once symptoms are close to preinjury baseline, the student can return to school, provided school personnel are willing to make appropriate adjustments to the educational environment.

Typical adjustments involve reducing cognitive and physical demands. These might include:

- Modified schedule: Shortened day or class periods, attendance of core classes only, rest periods during the day
- Modified assignments: Shortened assignments, extended time, postponed tests, excused tasks
- Avoidance of sensory overload: Avoidance of bright lights (sunglasses), avoidance of loud noises (quiet room, clinic)
- Excused activities requiring exertion: Gym, sports practice, carrying heavy loads
- Assistance: Reader, scribe, note taker, temporary tutor, assistive technology
- Minimized distractions: Quiet room for testing, preferential seating
- No penalties for incomplete work during recovery

Return to Play

In order to return to athletic practice and play, a child should first be cleared by a medical professional. The child should be symptom free both at rest and during physical or cognitive exertion. Neurological examination results should be normal and neuroimaging unremarkable. It is recommended that the child move through the following sequential steps to return to play (McCrory et al., 2009):

- No activity, meaning complete physical and cognitive rest
- Light aerobic activity only
- Sport-specific activities and training
- Noncontact drills
- Full-contact practice training only after medical clearance
- Game play

The athlete proceeds to the next level if asymptomatic at the current level for at least 24 hours. Generally each step takes 24 hours, so the complete rehabilitation protocol might take approximately 1 week. If symptoms occur in a phase, the athlete should drop back to the previous level and try to progress again after another 24 hours of rest. This protocol stems from an international consensus statement on concussion in sport (see McCrory et al., 2009, for more information on medical clearance).

Interventions for More Severe TBIs

There are two types of safeguards that are available to help students when returning to school following TBI.

Students who require ongoing accommodations in school may be eligible for a Section 504 plan (Rehabilitation Act of 1973, 29 U.S.C. 794). This plan documents accommodations that help the student access the curriculum. If the student's brain injury caused disability or impairments significant enough to have an adverse impact on educational performance to an extent requiring ongoing specialized instruction and services, he or she may be eligible for an IEP under IDEA. Few interventions that may appear on 504 plans or IEPs have been validated specifically for students with TBI. Instead, school teams often draw from academic and behavioral interventions that have been validated with populations of students exhibiting similar symptoms, such as trouble with attention, memory, or learning new concepts in specific academic areas. These may include strategies such as behavioral interventions, cognitive remediation, direct instruction, metacognitive strategies, family-centered approaches, or a combination of techniques. There is not a single phenotype with TBI, so the challenge school psychologists face is to match individual phenotypes to evidence-based interventions for the primary presenting problems.

When planning interventions, the team should prioritize concerns: Which areas most interfere with the ability to function? Which areas can be resolved quickly or compensated for easily? Which problem areas have been identified by the student, family, and school staff? How do we consider demands of new environments (bus, cafeteria, hall, gym) and the skills needed to be successful in those environments?

Table 28.2 lists strategies for different types of physical, emotional, executive functioning, and social/emotional/behavioral problems experienced by many students with TBI. An overarching goal of these accommodations and modifications might be to develop greater self-awareness. Strong interventions can help children with TBI recognize, understand, and learn to compensate for deficits.

Progress Monitoring

With any intervention, it is important to decide in advance how the team will determine whether or not the intervention was successful and whether it needs to be continued, changed, modified, or terminated. However, with TBIs this is particularly important because of the recovery trajectory. Intervention effectiveness can be determined first by evaluating whether the intervention was implemented as intended (treatment fidelity). If so, then the data can be evaluated through measurement of

Table 28.2. Accommodations and Modifications for Traumatic Brain Injury

Area	Type	Intervention
Physical	Orientation	• Provide a map/written schedule for tangible direction • Permit early class dismissal to avoid hall traffic • Provide consistent room arrangement and routines • Use a peer buddy to help with locating classes and following schedules • Provide cues to help with transitions ("In 3 minutes we will go to recess.")
	Fatigue	• Schedule a shortened school day • Provide breaks throughout the day • Have the student take a nap • Let the student listen to music • Remind the student to ask for help
	Motor (fine and gross)	• Help with written tasks • Reduce written work • Use dictation • Give extra time • Arrange for a peer to carry students books/backpack • Provide grips for writing utensils • Provide roller or gel pens for writing • Provide a peer note taker • Allow the student to use a computer for written assignments
	Sensory function	• Set calming strategies • Ensure proper lighting in the classroom • Provide a slant board/adjustable desktop to position books • Determine optimal font size for viewing text • Ensure optimal seating for listening • Minimize background noise • Provide written information to accompany verbal • Provide an outline of key points of lectures • Provide teacher-prepared notes • Allow additional time to complete tasks
Academic	New learning	• Provide longer viewing times and repeated viewing of new information • Present verbal information at a slower pace and with appropriate pauses • Provide a list of key words and concepts for lessons • Organize teaching concepts from concrete to abstract • Summarize information as it is being taught • Reinforce information with pictures or other images
	Language (expressive and receptive)	• Ask open-ended questions • Allow the student to dictate thoughts prior to writing • Teach the student appropriate expressions through role play • Practice sticking with a topic and sustaining conversation • Provide adequate time for the student to complete thoughts • Role-play real-life conversations • Encourage the student to use gestures, to move about when speaking, and/or to refer to visual aids to help pace and to increase comfort during speaking • Give initial sound cues • Use multiple-choice assessment when possible • Provide keywords for fill-in-the-blank tests • Provide headings, bullet points, or keywords for written work • Repeat instructions in a different order • Allow time to process verbal information and questions • Simplify and rephrase instructions

Continued

Table 28.2. Continued

Area	Type	Intervention
	Reading	• Use books on CDs • Adapt tests • Help with note taking • Give extra instruction • Use large print books • Use a slant board to modify the angle of books on the student's desk • Use a marker or cardstock with a window cutout to show only small sections of text at a time • Use a line marker to keep place while reading • Provide a written set of questions before reading • Review key vocabulary words prior to reading • Highlight keywords in colored marker • Give the student an outline to fill in while reading • Read written test items to the student • Provide summaries of complicated text
	Math	• Demonstrate concepts using concrete items • Create functional activities for practice of math concepts (e.g., purchasing items from a school store) • Use a calculator to aid multiple-step problems • Practice word problems with pictures or stories • Use marker or cardstock with a window cutout to display problems one at a time
	Processing speed	• Allow more time for a response • Control the amount of information that the student is to work with at one time • Set targets for quantity of work • Allow additional time to complete work and exams
Executive functions	Attention/concentration	• Shorten assignments • Minimize visual and auditory distractions (clear the desk, use a study carrel) • Use color coding or underlining to focus attention • Have the student recognize and communicate when presented with too much information at once • Ask teachers to repeat instructions slowly • Build in rest periods • Seat the student near the teacher • Provide verbal, visual, or physical redirection
	Behavior	• Avoid change in routine • Give choices • Be flexible • Adjust the schedule • Use time-out when necessary • Provide rest breaks • Arrange for positive interactions with peers • Focus on a student's strengths • Redirect the student away from source of frustration
	Memory/organization	• Provide an extra set of books (one for home, one for school) • Highlight important information • Provide an organization notebook with a written schedule, maps, homework, strategies • Provide graphic organizers and/or task checklists for academic information • Use a recorder or voice memo on a smartphone • Use repetition • Set up a buddy system

Continued

Table 28.2. Continued

Area	Type	Intervention
		• Reduce changes • Emphasize in advance any information that is to be remembered • Have the student focus on one task at a time • Use visual cues and/or provide written instructions • Teach the student to use external organizational aids (e.g., notes, memos, schedule sheets, an assignment planner) • Help the student complete a daily to-do list • Provide morning and end-of-day check-ins • Use flowcharts and mind-mapping techniques
	Problem solving, reasoning, and mental flexibility	• Teach explicit problem-solving steps • Use a checklist to identify choices and consequences • Model, rehearse, and role-play scenarios • Encourage the student to think about alternatives and consequences
	Self-awareness	• Use self-talk to ask whether a task is complete, what needs to be done, whether one was successful, etc. • Use a traffic light analogy and visual aid to help the student stop and ask: "Am I doing what I should be doing?"
	Initiation and planning	• Provide cues to begin a task • Provide the steps of a task • Praise any attempt to initiate the task • Provide assistance with getting started with schoolwork • Provide more frequent check-ins to ensure the student is completing work • Provide a written routine to assist/help the student begin work • Give a physical prompt to help the student get started
Social and emotional behavior	Social skills	• Organize a buddy system • Use real-life situations • Communicate and coordinate • Give reminders at transitions of what is next; use specific examples • Encourage the student to join a school-supported club or activity • Assign the student specific roles in group work • Role-play using a specific behavior
	Judgment	• Use and enforce clear rules and consequences for inappropriate verbal behavior and for drug/alcohol use • Involve students in structured activities that fill their time and introduce them to well-behaved peers • Teach the student how to appropriately express feelings in both language and behavior • Have the student check in with a teacher upon arrival at school • Use videos, daily situations, and the experiences of others to illustrate other points of view • Avoid topics that are likely to be highly emotional for the student
	Empathy	• Praise empathetic behavior (e.g., "It was nice of you to help your friend.") • Let the student know you care by listening intently • Teach the student to recognize when others behave kindly • Help the student tune into other peoples' emotions by making a game out of it • Play a game of guessing what other people are feeling • Give the student small jobs to do around the classroom • Show acts of kindness to set an example

effect size, percent of nonoverlapping data points, visual inspection of graphed data, trend line analysis, and/or goal attainment scaling (Hunley & McNamara, 2010).

The child's plan should be built around present levels of performance and then modified based on ongoing information acquired from a variety of assessments.

Special Considerations

Here will be discussed developmental differences, multicultural competencies, and evaluation of school psychology effectiveness.

Developmental Differences

School psychologists need to be mindful of developmental differences among children of different ages and how these can affect the outcomes after a brain injury. As discussed in the section on developmental predictors of outcomes, a child's age can affect manifestation of problems following a brain injury. A child's age might also affect factors such as responsiveness to interventions, self-awareness of disability, and level of involvement in transition planning. For example, while impaired self-awareness is often a side effect of TBI, it may also be a developmental issue because an elementary-age child would be expected to have less-developed frontal lobe (and subsequent executive functioning skills) than a high school student. Overall, the school psychologist must be prepared to address possible age-related issues, such as sexually inappropriate behaviors in the impulsive adolescent postinjury.

Multicultural Competencies

There is little research on how people from different cultures experience and understand traumatic brain injuries. In general, it seems there is a "universal experience of TBI that transcends individual cultures"; that is, across cultures, individuals with TBI and their families will likely value attentiveness, friendliness, and guidance from personnel (Simpson, Mohr, & Redman, 2000, p. 125). For families who speak a language other than English, school psychologists can facilitate communication with staff (i.e., by coordinating interpreters). This can help minimize the possibility of confusion and isolation.

Evaluation of School Psychologist Effectiveness

Many school psychologists are not adequately trained in brain injury recognition and response (Davies, 2013). Thus, it is important that school psychologists engage in self-evaluation of their knowledge and skills in serving this population.

SUMMARY

TBIs of all severity levels can adversely affect educational performance. They tend to be underidentified in schools, and educators may lack the knowledge of both signs and outcomes of TBIs. Many factors, including injury severity and location, age of injury, age at assessment, time since injury, and preinjury conditions may all affect student outcomes.

Close collaboration with families and medical professionals can have a positive impact on outcomes of students with TBIs of all levels of severity. The transition back to school must be carefully planned and monitored, and the assignment of a case manager, such as the school psychologist, can help with this process.

Students with mild TBIs/concussions typically recover from problems related to thinking/remembering, physical symptoms, and emotional/mood issues over time; however, it is critical that this recovery period occur in conjunction with appropriate adjustments to the school environment. The school psychologist can be instrumental in helping the school engage best practice surrounding responding to and preventing concussions among students, particularly student athletes. Students with more severe TBIs may have more long-lasting repercussions related to their TBIs that warrant ongoing accommodations or special education services. Interventions might target physical, academic, executive functions, and/or socioemotional–behavioral issues. Assessment and intervention of students with TBI should be frequent and flexible, including ongoing progress monitoring of the students' needs and response to academic and behavioral interventions.

REFERENCES

Adelson, P. D. (1998). Head injury in children. *Journal of Child Neurology, 13*, 2–15. doi:10.1177/088307389801300102

Anderson, V. A., Catroppa, C., Haritou, F., Morse, S., Pentland, L., & Rosenfeld, J. (2001). Predictors of acute child and family outcome following traumatic brain injury in children. *Pediatric Neurosurgery, 34*, 138–148. doi:10.1159/000056009

Andriessen, T. M., Jacobs, B., & Vos, P. E. (2010). Clinical characteristics and pathophysiological mechanisms of focal and diffuse traumatic brain injury. *Journal of Cellular and Molecular Medicine, 14*, 2381–2392. doi:10.1111/j.1582-4934.2010.01164.x

Bigler, E. (2012). Mild traumatic brain injury: The elusive timing of "recovery." *Neuroscience Letters, 509*, 1–4. doi:10.1016/j.neulet.2011.12.009

Bigler, E. D. (2010). Neuroimaging in mild traumatic brain injury. *Psychological Injury and Law, 3*, 36–49. doi:10.1007/s12207-010-9064-1

Bowen, J. M. (2005). Classroom interventions for students with traumatic brain injuries. *Preventing School Failure, 49*(4), 34–41. doi:10.3200/PSFL.49.4.34-41

Buck, P. W. (2011). Mild traumatic brain injury: A silent epidemic in our practices. *Health & Social Work, 36*, 299–302. doi:10.1093/hsw/36.4.299

Centers for Disease Control and Prevention. (2012). *Injury prevention and control: Traumatic brain injury*. Atlanta, GA: Author. Retrieved from http://www.cdc.gov/TraumaticBrainInjury/statistics.html

Corrigan, J. D. (1995). Substance abuse as a mediating factor in outcome from traumatic brain injury. *Archives of Physical Medicine and Rehabilitation, 76*, 302–309. doi:10.1016/S0003-9993(95)80654-7

Davies, S. C. (2013). School psychology programs: Graduate preparation in traumatic brain injury. *Trainers' Forum, 31*, 5–16.

Dawson, P., & Guare, R. G. (2010). *Executive skills in children and adolescents: A practical guide to assessment and intervention*. New York, NY: Guilford Press.

Deidrick, K. M., & Farmer, J. E. (2005). School reentry following traumatic brain injury. *Preventing School Failure, 49*(4), 23–33. doi:10.3200/PSFL.49.4.23-33

Ettel, D. (2012, November). *TBI: Classroom practices, assessment and eligibility*. Paper presented at the TBI Summit at the annual Ohio Center for Autism and Low Incidence Disabilities conference, Columbus, OH

Faul, M., Xu, L., Wald, M. M., & Coronado, V. G. (2010). *Traumatic brain injury in the United States: Emergency department visits, hospitalizations, and deaths*. Atlanta, GA: Centers for Disease Control and Prevention, National Center for Injury Prevention and Control.

Gedeit, R. (2001). Head injury. *Pediatrics in Review, 22*, 118–124. doi:10.1542/pir.22-4-118

Gioia, G. A., Isquith, P. K., Guy, S. C., & Kenworthy, L. (2000). *Behavior Rating Inventory of Executive Function*. Lutz, FL: PAR.

Glang, A., Todis, B., Sublette, P., Eagan-Brown, B., & Vaccaro, M. (2010). Professional development in TBI for educators: The importance of context. *Journal of Head Trauma Rehabilitation, 25*, 426–432. doi:10.1097/HTR.0b013e3181fb8f45

Glang, A., Todis, B., Thomas, C. W., Hood, D., Bedell, G., & Cockrell, J. (2008). Return to school following childhood TBI: Who gets services? *NeuroRehabilitation, 23*, 477–486.

Guskiewicz, K. M., Weaver, N. L., Padua, D. A., & Garrett, W. E. (2000). Epidemiology of concussion in collegiate and high school football players. *The American Journal of Sports Medicine, 28*, 643–650.

Halstead, M., Walter, K., & The Council on Sports Medicine and Fitness. (2010). Clinical report: Sport-related concussion in children and adolescents. *Pediatrics, 126*, 597–615. doi:10.1542/peds.2010-2005

Hunley, S., & McNamara, K. (2010). *Tier 3 of the RTI model*. Thousand Oaks, CA: Corwin.

Individuals with Disabilities Education Improvement Act of 2004. Pub. L. 108-446. 20 U. S. C. §§ 1400 et seq. (2004). Amendments to Individuals with Disabilities Education Act of 1990. Pub. L. 101-476. 20 U.S.C. §1401 et seq

Iverson, G. L., Lovell, M. R., & Collins, M. W. (2011). *Immediate post-concussion assessment and cognitive testing (ImPACT) normative data: Version 2.0 only*. Pittsburgh, PA: ImPACT Applications. Retrieved from http://www.impacttest.com

Jantz, P. B., & Coulter, G. A. (2007). Child and adolescent traumatic brain injury: Academic, behavioural, and social consequences in the classroom. *Support for Learning, 22*, 84–89. doi:10.1111/j.1467-9604.2007.00452.x

John, M. T. (2005). Hospitalizations for critically ill children with traumatic brain injuries: A longitudinal analysis. *Critical Care Medicine, 33*, 2074–2081. doi:10.1097/01.CCM.0000171839.65687.F5

Lash, M., Wolcott, G., & Pearson, S. (2005). *Signs and strategies for educating students with brain injuries: A practical guide for teachers and parents*. Wake Forest, NC: Lash.

Lau, B. C., Kontos, A. P., Collins, M. W., Mucha, A., & Lovell, M. R. (2011). Which on-field signs/symptoms predict protracted recovery from sports-related concussion among high school football players? *The American Journal of Sports Medicine, 39*, 2311–2318. doi:10.1177/0363546511410655

McCrory, P., Meeuwisse, W., Johnson, K., Dvorak, J., Aubry, M., Molloy, M., & Cantu, R. (2009). Consensus statement on concussion in sport. *British Journal of Sports Medicine, 43*, i76–i84. doi:10.1136/bjsm.2009.058248

McGrath, N. (2010). Supporting the student-athlete's return to the classroom after a sport-related concussion. *Journal of Athletic Training, 45*, 492–498. doi:10.4085/1062-6050-45.5.492

Moran, L. M., Taylor, H. G., Rusin, J., Bangert, B., Dietrich, A., Nuss, K. E., … Yeates, K. O. (2012). Quality of life in pediatric mild traumatic brain injury and its relationship to postconcussive symptoms. *Journal of Pediatric Psychology, 37*, 736–744. doi:10.1093/jpepsy/jsr087

National Association of School Psychologists. (2010). *Model for comprehensive and integrated school psychological services*. Bethesda, MD: Author. Retrieved from http://www.nasponline.org/standards/2010standards/2_PracticeModel.pdf

Ornstein, T. J., Levin, H. S., Chen, S., Hanten, G., Ewing-Cobbs, L., Dennis, M., … Schachar, R. (2009). Performance monitoring in children following traumatic brain injury. *Journal of Child Psychology and Psychiatry, 50*, 506–513. doi:10.1111/j.1469-7610.2008.01997.x

Peiniger, S., Nienaber, U., Lefering, R., Braun, M., Wafaisade, A., Borgman, M. A., & Maegele, M. (2012). Glasgow Coma Scale as a predictor for hemocoagulative disorders after blunt pediatric traumatic brain injury. *Pediatric Critical Care Medicine, 13*, 455–460. doi:10.1097/PCC.0b013e31823893c5

Sady, M. D., Vaughn, C. G., & Gioia, G. A. (2011). School and the concussed youth: Recommendations for concussion management and education. *Physical Medicine and Rehabilitation Clinics, 22*, 701–719. doi:10.1016/j.pmr.2011.08.008

Saunders, L. L., Selassie, A. W., Hill, E. G., Horner, M. D., Nicholas, J. S., Lackland, D. T., & Corrigan, J. D. (2009). Preexisting health conditions and repeat traumatic brain injury. *Archives of Physical Medicine and Rehabilitation, 90*, 1853–1859. doi:10.1016/j.apmr.2009.05.020

Schwartz, L., Taylor, H. G., Drotar, D., Yeates, K. O., Wade, S., & Stancin, T. (2003). Long-term behavior problems following pediatric traumatic brain injury: Prevalence, predictors, and correlates. *Journal of Pediatric Psychology, 28*, 251–263. doi:10.1093/jpepsy/jsg013

Simpson, G., Mohr, R., & Redman, A. (2000). Cultural variations in the understanding of traumatic brain injury and brain injury rehabilitation. *Brain Injury, 14*, 125–140. doi:10.1080/026990500120790

Tsang, K. K. T., & Whitfield, P. C. (2012). Traumatic brain injury: Review of current management strategies. *British Journal of Oral and Maxillofacial Surgery, 50*, 298–308. doi:10.1016/j.bjoms.2011.03.004

Yeates, K. O., Taylor, H. G., Drotar, D., Wade, S. L., Klein, S., Stancin, T., & Schatschneider, C. (1997). Preinjury family environment as a determinant of recovery from traumatic brain injuries in school-age children. *Journal of the International Neuropsychology Society, 3*, 617–630.

Zaloshnja, E., Miller, T., Langlois, J. A., & Selassie, A. W. (2008). Prevalence of long-term disability from traumatic brain injury in the civilian population of the United States, 2005. *Journal of Head Trauma Rehabilitation, 23*, 394–400. doi:10.1097/01.HTR. 0000341435.52004.ac

29 Best Practices in Responding to HIV in the School Setting

Tiffany Chenneville
University of South Florida St. Petersburg

OVERVIEW

Human immunodeficiency virus (HIV) is a worldwide epidemic with serious health and psychosocial consequences. Alarmingly, youth are among the fastest growing groups infected. School psychologists are in a unique position to respond to HIV given their expertise in the areas of child development, prevention, intervention, and problem solving and their training in the delivery of multitiered services. The purpose of this chapter is to describe best practices in responding to HIV in the school setting using a multitiered approach to problem solving. The information contained in this chapter is consistent with the National Association of School Psychologists (NASP) *Model for Comprehensive and Integrated School Psychological Services* (NASP, 2010a). Specifically, this chapter focuses on issues related to health and mental health, which is part of the model's Preventive and Responsive Services domain.

HIV Prevalence and Incidence

Since HIV emerged as a public health concern in the 1980s, the number of people living with HIV globally has risen to 33 million (UNAIDS, 2010). Prevalence reports estimate that approximately 1,148,200 people in the United States aged 13 and older have been diagnosed with HIV to date (Centers for Disease Control and Prevention [CDC], 2012a) and that 803,771 are living with an HIV diagnosis currently (CDC, 2010a). This does not include the number of people living with HIV who do not even know they are infected. Incidence reports estimate that approximately 50,000 new HIV cases are diagnosed each year (CDC, 2012a). Of these, recent data indicate that one in four

(26%) are youth between the ages of 13 and 24. In 2010, approximately 12,000 young people, or about 1,000 per month, were infected with HIV in the United States alone. These numbers do not include the number of AIDS cases, representing the end stage of HIV, diagnosed each year. Fortunately, with medical advances, including the use of highly active antiretroviral therapy, there has been a decrease in the number of AIDS-related deaths in the United States. This means more people are living with HIV longer.

Incidence data suggest the overall number of HIV infections has stabilized (CDC, 2010a). However, between 2008 and 2010, there was a significant increase in infections among youth, particularly among African American men who have sex with men. In fact, in 2010, the second highest number of new HIV cases occurred among 13- to 24-year-olds. Furthermore, a significant proportion of youth with HIV have been living with the disease their entire lives, with an estimated 22% having contracted the disease through mother-to-child transmission (CDC, 2011).

HIV Transmission

Transmitted by blood, semen, vaginal fluid, and, in some cases, breast milk, HIV infection often is categorized as perinatally acquired or behaviorally acquired. Perinatal infection, also referred to as mother-to-child transmission, results from childbirth—before, during, or after—or from breast-feeding. Behavioral infection results from sexual behavior or injection drug use. Understanding the distinction between perinatal and behavioral infection is important for school psychologists given, that the risk factors associated with each differ, which may affect the development and delivery of interventions. Most children with HIV who are under the age of 12 likely acquired HIV perinatally. Conversely, new diagnoses among adolescents most likely are the result of behavioral infection. Although less common given the screening practices of blood banks, transmission by blood transfusion also is possible.

The risk of HIV being transmitted at school is very low. It is not possible to transmit HIV through casual social contact such as hugging or holding hands. The behaviors most likely to result in HIV transmission—sexual behavior and injection drug use—are forbidden at school. And, while theoretically possible, the risk of HIV transmission by a human bite is extremely rare (CDC, 2010b). In fact, even in child-care settings, where biting is common, most bites do not break the skin (Canadian Paediatric Society, 2008), and there is no risk of HIV transmission from a human bite where the skin is not broken (CDC, 2010b). Further, while HIV has been detected in saliva, the quantities are very low. There are no known cases of HIV being transmitted by spitting (CDC, 2010b). Therefore, it is highly unlikely that HIV transmission would occur as a result of a bite at school. In addition, there are no known cases of HIV being transmitted during sports (CDC, 2010b). Use of universal precautions with any exposure to bodily fluids for any reason further reduces the very low risk of HIV transmission at school.

HIV Symptoms

HIV symptomatology varies widely. Given the potential psychoeducational consequences of these symptoms, school psychologists should be aware of the multitude of ways in which HIV affects the physical, cognitive, social, and emotional health of children and adolescents infected with HIV.

Medical Symptoms

HIV directly affects the immune system, which is responsible for helping the body fight disease. Immune functioning is determined by the number of blood cells, called CD4 + T cells, present at any given time. Higher numbers indicate greater immune functioning while lower numbers signal difficulty. A variety of factors may affect the presentation of symptoms associated with a suppressed immune system. For example, there are different types and strains of HIV that may affect treatment. Other factors that may affect immune functioning include length of time since HIV infection, medication adherence, medication resistance, and the

presence of comorbid diseases. In addition, behavioral health and lifestyle can affect immune functioning. A weakened immune system may result in fatigue, weight loss, diarrhea, or fever and, ultimately, place people with HIV at risk for opportunistic infections such as pneumonia or certain kinds of cancer. HIV can develop into AIDS, considered the last stage of HIV. In addition to the direct effects of HIV on physical functioning, there are mild to life-threatening side effects associated with the medications used to treat HIV.

Developmental Impact of HIV

The developmental challenges associated with HIV are well established in the literature (e.g., see Burns, Hernandez-Reif, & Jessee, 2008). In children born with HIV, the virus directly attacks a developing central nervous system that impairs brain growth, causing significant developmental delays. Young children with HIV are likely to experience cognitive, motor, and, in particular, language delays. In children and adolescents who acquire HIV later in life, the disease causes deterioration as opposed to delay. HIV-related neurological symptoms in adolescents include problems with memory, concentration, and motor skills as well as general mental slowing. Problems with multitasking also have been observed among individuals with HIV (Scott et al., 2011). In light of these difficulties, problems with academic achievement are likely (Burns et al., 2008).

Psychosocial Symptoms

Children and adolescents with HIV are at risk for a variety of psychological and social issues. Beyond addressing the psychoeducational needs of students with HIV, school psychologists are likely to be involved with the social–emotional needs of students who are infected with, or affected by, HIV. The stigma associated with HIV sets this disease apart from others. HIV-related stigma relates to the fact that HIV often is associated with homosexual behavior, promiscuity, and drug use, which are perceived negatively by many, and with fear of contamination. Stigma may result in fear of social ostracism, resulting in social isolation, and it is well known that internalizing behavior disorders such as anxiety and depression are common among people with HIV.

Across the age span, disclosure presents as a significant emotional issue facing youth with HIV. Many youth are afraid of disclosure because they fear rejection or the disruption of interpersonal relationships. In addition, many young children are encouraged by parents not to disclose for fear of inadvertent parental disclosure of HIV status and the social implications of openly living with HIV. This issue becomes particularly poignant for adolescents with HIV who are developing sexually. In fact, disclosure to dating partners was identified as the greatest concern among youth with HIV (Wiener & Battles, 2006). Despite a desire to share the "secret" and guilt about nondisclosure, fear of rejection is significant and may impede attempts to disclose (Michaud et al., 2009). Michaud et al. (2009) found that many choose not to disclose, especially to casual partners, in an effort to maintain their relationship. Also, some youth with HIV do not believe it is important to disclose their HIV status if they are using protection (Fernet et al., 2011). Siegel, Schrimshaw, and Lekas (2006) report that youth with HIV experience anxiety about transmitting the virus to others and a loss of sexual spontaneity and freedom surrounding their need to protect others. As Fernet et al. (2011) describe, youth with perinatally acquired HIV "have their first romantic and sexual experiences knowing that they are [HIV positive]" (p. 393), and the emotional burden and anxiety about rejection and loss can be great and may negatively affect intimate relationships among youth with HIV.

While there are many psychosocial issues that affect children and adolescents with HIV, regardless of mode of transmission, there are some important distinctions between children with perinatally acquired HIV and those with behaviorally acquired HIV, and school psychologists should be aware of these differences. Children born with HIV typically are living with a mother, and sometimes a father, who also is infected. Maternal guilt associated with HIV transmission to a child is common and can create a unique mother–child dynamic. Alternatively, a number of children with perinatally acquired HIV have been orphaned and, as a result, are placed in foster care or are raised by extended family.

In addition to the social–emotional issues associated with living with HIV, adolescents who acquire HIV behaviorally are likely to present with risky behaviors (e.g., sexual activity, substance use) that led to transmission in the first place. School psychologists should attend to these risk factors. Sexual activity without barrier protection—during intercourse or oral sex—is a significant risk factor for contracting a sexually transmitted infection, including HIV. Individuals with HIV may be coinfected with another sexually transmitted infection or reinfected with HIV, possibly with a different, more drug resistant strand of the virus, thus making secondary prevention important. Substance use is considered a risk factor for HIV. This includes both injection drug use, considered extremely risky, and noninjection drug use. Even alcohol use is associated with a decrease in inhibitions, which may lead to risky sexual behavior. School psychologists should be aware of the many factors correlated with risky sexual behavior and substance use. These factors include (a) limited access to comprehensive sexuality education; (b) the relationship between socioeconomic status and rates of drug use and sexual promiscuity; and (c) limited social skills, including assertiveness, which is needed to ask a partner to use protection or to overcome sex and substance use-related peer pressure.

Treatment

Despite challenges, the search for an HIV vaccine is under way, which could have dramatic implications for prevention. In the meantime, despite recent media attention about an infant being cured of HIV, there continues to be no known reliable cure. However, there have been significant advances in the treatment of HIV and, as indicated by the infant's case, research for a cure continues. The current standard of care is highly active antiretroviral therapy. The ultimate goal of treatment is to prolong survival. In addition, treatment goals include restoring normal growth and development, preventing opportunistic infections, and improving quality of life.

Drug therapy has been shown to be very effective, assuming medication adherence is good. Unfortunately, medication adherence often is problematic among youth with HIV. Some of the reasons for poor adherence include the poor taste of the medicine, the size of the pills (making swallowing difficult), and side effects, which may include nausea, dizziness, diarrhea, oral ulcers, hypersensitivity reactions, pancreatitis, and retinal damage (Ruest, 2011). These side effects may have an impact on school functioning. Fear of HIV disclosure further negatively affects medication adherence for many children with HIV. For some, taking medication is a painful reminder of their disease. These treatment issues are of particular importance for school psychologists working with children with HIV.

BASIC CONSIDERATIONS

School psychologists need to be familiar with HIV-related laws and professional standards in order to best serve children with HIV and their families. It is important for school psychologists to know, however, that many families opt not to share HIV status with schools because of the social stigma described above. As a result, most school personnel are unaware of students' HIV diagnosis and, therefore, many students infected with HIV live with the condition in secret without access to the academic, social–emotional, and behavioral supports available for youth with disclosed chronic health conditions.

Legal Issues

The rights of students with HIV are protected by federal and state laws. However, these laws may be interpreted differently by individual school districts, resulting in varied policies. In addition, conflicts sometimes arise between federal and state laws and NASP's ethical standards.

Federal Laws

School psychologists should be familiar with, at minimum, the following federal laws that offer protections to children with HIV in the school setting: (a) the 2004 Individuals with Disabilities Education Act

(IDEA), (b) Americans with Disabilities Act, (c) Rehabilitation Act of 1973, (d) Family Educational Rights and Privacy Act, and (e) Health Insurance and Portability and Accountability Act of 1996. A brief description of these laws, and how they apply to HIV in the school setting, is included in Table 29.1.

State Laws

Given that state laws vary widely with regard to policies affecting HIV education, testing, and treatment, school psychologists are encouraged to become familiar with their own state's laws. Clearly, individual state laws and policies will influence the ways in which school psychologists can intervene on issues related to HIV. For example, the types of Tier 1 interventions that can be developed will be affected by state policies regarding HIV education (e.g., does the state mandate abstinence education or are comprehensive sexuality education approaches permitted?). Interventions at Tiers 2 and 3 may be affected by HIV testing and treatment laws as well as prenatal screening laws.

Table 29.1. Description of Federal Laws as They Apply to HIV in the School Setting

Federal Law	Applicability to HIV in the School Setting
IDEA	• Children with HIV may qualify for special education programming under the classification of Other Health Impaired • Children with HIV may exhibit learning problems related to the neurological impact of the disease • Children with HIV may exhibit emotional or behavioral problems related to the psychosocial impact of HIV, which may affect learning • It is likely that many students with HIV receive special education services through IDEA • School psychologists are likely to encounter children with HIV receiving special education services under the classification of a learning disorder or an emotional or behavior disorder even if medical diagnosis has not been disclosed
ADA	• Protects children with HIV from being discriminated against in the school setting
Rehabilitation Act of 1973	• Section 504 expands on the requirements of the ADA for children with HIV in the school setting by allowing for modifications in the regular classroom • However, due to HIV-related stigma, many students with HIV cannot access these services as families are reluctant to disclose HIV status to schools unless, of course, there is another eligible diagnosis related to HIV
FERPA	• Also known as the Buckley Amendment, FERPA offers privacy protections to students with HIV by safeguarding the confidentiality of student records • Requires written consent before student records can be disclosed and, even then, disclosure can be made only to individuals with a legitimate need to know • Perceptions vary with regard to who has a need to know HIV status in the school setting and, in fact, this is a controversial issue
HIPAA	• Protects confidential health information and applies to public schools, colleges, and universities • Allows parents access to their children's medical information, which may be contained in school records • Affords parents of students with HIV the right to demand that erroneous information be corrected • The intentional or unintentional release of confidential health information, including HIV status, may result in serious consequences including heavy fines or time in prison

Note. IDEA = Individuals with Disabilities Education Act; ADA = Americans with Disabilities Act; FERPA = Family Educational Rights and Privacy Act; HIPAA = Health Insurance and Portability and Accountability Act.

Professional Standards

School psychologists should be aware of the ethical principles and standards that apply to HIV as outlined in the NASP (2010b) *Principles for Professional Ethics*. Of most relevance is Principle 1.2: Privacy and Confidentiality, which states that school psychologists should respect individuals' right to privacy (see Table 29.2 for a description of the applicable standards under this principle). Beyond their own professional behavior, school psychologists play a critical role in creating a culture of safety by stressing to school administrators and teachers the importance of maintaining the confidentiality of sensitive information. In addition to the ethical principles and standards described above, school psychologists should read and become familiar with the NASP position statement on *Supporting Students With HIV/AID* (NASP, 2012). The tenets of NASP's position statement are reflected in the best practice recommendations described in this chapter.

Table 29.2. Privacy and Confidentiality Standards

Standard	Emphasis
1.2.1	The importance of respecting the rights of individuals to determine for themselves when and how to disclose private information
1.2.2	The importance of minimizing privacy intrusions
1.2.3	The importance of discussing the limits of confidentiality at the onset of the professional relationship
1.2.4	The conditions under which confidentiality may be breached (e.g., threat of danger to self or others) and the importance of obtaining assent for the release of private information when possible
1.2.5	The importance of only discussing or releasing private information for professional purposes and on a need-to-know basis
1.2.6	The importance of respecting the students', parents', and colleagues' right to privacy with regard to sexual orientation, gender identity, or transgender status
1.2.7	The importance of respecting students', parents', and colleagues' right to privacy with regard to sensitive health information including the presence of communicable diseases

Note. From *Principles for Professional Ethics*, by National Association of School Psychologists, 2010, Bethesda, MD: Author. Copyright 2010 by the National Association of School Psychologists. Adapted with permission.

BEST PRACTICES IN RESPONDING TO HIV IN THE SCHOOL SETTING

Because youth spend a significant number of hours in school, schools are an optimal setting for promoting mental health and well-being among young people. Given the relationship between general health and wellness and mental health, schools also are considered by some to be the optimal setting for implementing HIV prevention and intervention efforts (Kann, Brener, McManus, & Wechsler, 2012). In order to most effectively prevent HIV transmission among students, school psychologists are urged to institute a continuum of preventive care whereby all students receive high-quality primary prevention efforts, students who are at risk for contracting HIV receive targeted prevention efforts, and students who are infected or affected by HIV receive intensive individualized interventions. Not only is this comprehensive approach to HIV prevention considered cost-effective, as it allocates prevention resources according to the level of student need, but it also ensures that all students receive high-quality preventions. This model fits nicely into the multitiered services paradigm currently emphasized in U.S. schools.

The best practice model described below applies most directly to school psychologists working in a school setting in the United States and may not apply to other settings in which school psychologists may work (e.g., hospitals, clinics, private practice). School psychologists working in countries outside the United States are referred to Walsh and Chenneville (2013) for a modified version of this model, intended for an international audience, that incorporates components of the World Health Organization's model of school change. Consistent with a multitiered services paradigm, the model described here includes a progression of services from Tier 1 to Tier 3 (see Figure 29.1). As described below, monitoring and evaluation of student outcomes are critical across all tiers.

Tier 1: Universal Interventions

Tier 1 represents the most proactive level of prevention. While the primary concern is educational outcomes for students, intervention at this level applies to all stakeholders. For example, there is concern not only for the physical and mental health of students, but also for the physical and mental health of teachers, recognizing the potential impact of teacher functioning on student success. At this level, we recognize that students may be affected by all members of the school community

Figure 29.1. Best Practices for Responding to HIV in the School Setting Using a Multitiered Services Model

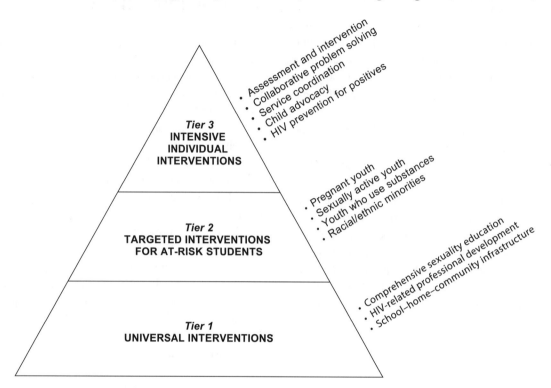

including teachers, administrators, staff, and parents. We also recognize the need for systems to be in place so that the school is in a position to respond to specific areas such as HIV. In addition, a school–home–community infrastructure is vital to the academic, behavioral, mental health, and physical health of all students. The interventions described at this level may require policy changes given the interplay between policy and practice. Policy-level research on both bottom-up (i.e., school-based policies and practices) and top-down (i.e., district-wide or statewide policy implementation) HIV-related practices represents an important component of Tier 1. School psychologists have a vital role to play in the development, delivery, and evaluation of Tier 1 services.

Comprehensive Sexuality Education for Students

The limited scope of education on sexuality and reproductive health in school systems is an issue for youth with HIV, not to mention a public health concern given that education about HIV and how to prevent it is often not occurring at home. This forces youth to learn about sexuality through their peers and the media. School psychologists should be aware that it is common for students to engage in sexual intercourse during their school-age years. In fact, it is estimated that upward of 50% of adolescents (ages 15–19) in developed countries engage in sexual intercourse (Abel & Fitzgerald, 2006). Additionally, the Youth Risk Behavior Surveillance System, a CDC surveillance system that monitors health behaviors that contribute to the leading cause of death and disability among youth and adults in the United States, found that 46% of high school students have engaged in sexual intercourse by the time they finish high school (CDC, 2009). Furthermore, 39% of students who were currently sexually active had not used a condom last time they had sexual intercourse. This suggests that a large proportion of students are engaging in risky sexual behaviors and putting themselves at risk for contracting HIV.

School psychologists also should be aware of the prevalence of sexually transmitted infections among adolescents. For example, data suggests one in five sexually active teens will acquire herpes (Alan Guttmacher Institute, 2006). Teens with sexually transmitted infections are at greater risk for HIV infection. Aside from sexually transmitted infections, teen pregnancy is correlated with unprotected sexual activity.

Despite incentives from the federal government for states to offer abstinence-only sexuality education programs (Title V), there is little evidence that such programs are effective (Hauser, 2008). Despite the fact that all states except California have used these federal dollars (Hauser, 2008), 68% of college students from two states receiving Title V funds reported in a retrospective study having received school-based comprehensive sexuality education (Walcott, Chenneville, & Tarquini, 2011). Consistent with NASP's position statement on support for students with HIV/AIDS (NASP, 2012), school psychologists should work within their schools to ensure that comprehensive sexuality education is being offered. School psychologists should be familiar with the benefits of abstinence as an important part of the curriculum, but they should be prepared to argue that "abstinence until marriage" is not realistic. School psychologists are in a prime position to provide facts surrounding the high rates of sexual activity among youth who are not married and may never marry. This is because of a rise in the number of people who choose not to marry and, for those who do, a rise in the age of first marriage or, for individuals who identify as homosexual, because gay marriage is still illegal in some states. School psychologists can argue that a comprehensive curriculum addresses these realities by providing youth with the information and skills necessary to prevent negative outcomes associated with unprotected sexual activity even as they enter adulthood. School psychologists can share NASP (2012) recommendations, which include the provision of developmentally appropriate comprehensive sexuality education at all grade levels as part of the school health curriculum. School psychologists also can share with administrators and others making curriculum decisions that school-based sexuality and reproductive health education at every age level is supported by the United Nations Educational, Scientific, and Cultural Organization (Goldman & Collier-Harris, 2012).

School psychologists also can become familiar with, and share with administrators and others involved with curriculum development, information programs specifically designed for HIV prevention, including those tailored for certain populations. For example, COMPAS is a school-based HIV prevention program that has been shown to be effective for reducing sexual risk among Spanish adolescents (Espada, Orgiles, Morales, Ballester, & Huedo-Medina, 2012). A program such as this might be useful in a school where the majority of students are Hispanic or Latino. Prevention programs tailored for specific populations also might be useful at Tier 2 as described later in this chapter.

HIV-Related Professional Development

School psychologists should work with health educators to educate school staff and administrators about the importance of HIV prevention education and intervention for creating a safe and healthy school culture. With proper ongoing training on health promotion topics, including HIV, a wide range of educators may be well suited to implement health promotion efforts; that is, not only school psychologists but also general and special education teachers, health and physical education teachers, guidance counselors, social workers, school nurses, and resource teachers. Because school personnel must not only be prepared to deliver health promotion curriculum, including comprehensive sexuality education, but also dispel myths surrounding HIV, a range of HIV topics are vital for educators.

School psychologists should encourage ongoing job-embedded professional development whereby training is focused on day-to-day practices as best practice for staff training. School psychologists may actively participate in this process, which can be useful for training school personnel to implement universal HIV prevention programs (Tier 1 interventions), targeted prevention programs for groups at high risk of contracting HIV (Tier 2 interventions), and individualized intervention plans for students living with HIV (Tier 3 interventions). Furthermore, school psychologists may join educators to form study teams with other colleagues to engage in ongoing learning about HIV as it relates to their experiences with specific high-risk groups. School psychologists can provide useful information about the importance of considering the developmental level of the students served (e.g., chronological age, cognitive functioning, social–emotional maturity) when designing professional development initiatives. Certainly, professional development initiatives may contain the same foundational information regardless of the developmental level of the students served in order to build educators' knowledge and understanding of health and mental health related to HIV. However, the specific health promotion efforts modeled will differ markedly depending on the age and developmental level of the students.

School–Home–Community Infrastructure

Comprehensive sexuality education and HIV-related professional development for staff will not be sustainable for meeting students' health and mental health needs in the absence of an infrastructure that aligns the goals of the school, the home, and the community. School psychologists may help to build this infrastructure by encouraging school personnel, parents and families, and the community to work collaboratively to prevent HIV and promote physical and mental resilience among those already infected or affected. In practice, this requires a high level of communication between schools and families that school psychologists can help to facilitate directly or indirectly through collaboration with health educators and school nurses. Families should be encouraged to reinforce concepts being taught within the health curriculum that may require educating families about HIV. For example, it might be helpful to invite families to attend HIV-related staff trainings. Alternatively, opportunities for parent training about HIV may be offered at the school, possibly sponsored by existing parent–teacher associations or cosponsored with community agencies. Community outreach is necessary to promote schools and community agencies work together to ensure best practices. School psychologists may be involved at a macro or micro level to implement these strategies and must be aware of resistance in the community to comprehensive sexuality education initiatives.

Tier 2: Targeted Group Interventions

Tier 2 focuses on highly efficient educational interventions for at-risk groups. School psychologists can help teachers and administrators to identify these groups by becoming familiar with the literature. Adolescents, injection drug users, racial and ethnic minorities, and those who do not know they are infected are known to be in greatest need of HIV prevention. In addition, students who are pregnant or who are known or thought to be sexually active might be targeted, as well as students who use substances other than injection drugs. Educational interventions at this level must be timely and developmentally appropriate and must take into consideration cultural differences. For example, school psychologists should be aware of the mistrust toward the government that is common among many in the African American community, which can have a negative impact on HIV prevention efforts.

At Tier 2, school psychologists should be careful to ensure that at-risk groups are defined based on behavior and not on labels. For example, tailoring interventions for men who have sex with men would be more appropriate than tailoring interventions for "gay" youth. This is more than a semantic distinction. Some people who identify as heterosexual engage in same-sex sexual behavior. This might be especially true during adolescence, which is a time marked by identity exploration, including sexual identity. Further, school psychologists do not want to foster the strong, negative association between HIV and the gay community due, in large part,

to the initial naming of the disease as Gay-Related Immune Disorder or the "gay plague." This had profound implications with regard not only to treatment of homosexuals, but also to perceptions of HIV in general. School psychologists should be aware of and sensitive to this history and should make efforts to avoid perpetuating the misperception that HIV is a gay disease. Further, because homosexuality may be particularly taboo in certain cultures, such as the African American community, African American youth who are gay, for instance, may fail to identify as homosexual. Youth such as these may be overlooked if groups are targeted based on sexual identity as opposed to high-risk behavior. School psychologists also should examine their own feelings and biases. It is not only important but ethically necessary for school psychologists who find themselves uncomfortable working with certain populations to seek training and supervision or, alternatively, to provide appropriate referrals for youth in certain high-risk groups.

HIV Testing

HIV testing is critical given that early detection and treatment have important prognostic implications. In addition to identification, HIV pretest and posttest counseling is known to be an effective prevention strategy. HIV counseling teaches people how HIV is transmitted and, in cases where HIV is diagnosed, how to prevent infecting others.

It is well established that many who are tested for HIV using traditional tests never return for their results. Therefore, rapid HIV testing is highly recommended. With rapid testing, results are available within minutes to hours, compared to several weeks for traditional tests. Positive results from rapid testing can be confirmed with more reliable tests such as the ELISA or Western blot. Because of the window period between infection and the development of HIV antibodies, false positives are possible. Retesting every 6 months for youth at high risk is, therefore, recommended.

School psychologists should be aware of HIV testing policies and procedures in the community within which they work so that they may make appropriate referrals for youth at risk for HIV either directly or through collaboration with the school nurse. Youth may have limited awareness of voluntary HIV testing and counseling. Further, school psychologists should be sensitive to the fact that youth may be resistant to HIV testing due to fear of knowing their HIV status, fear of HIV-related stigma and discrimination, or misconceptions about risk. For example, some may think only people showing symptoms of HIV need to be tested. School psychologists also can serve an important function after testing by providing support services such as counseling, collaboration with medical personnel, or consultation with staff (see section on Tier 3 interventions below).

Pregnant Youth

School psychologists can play a vital role, directly or indirectly through collaboration with the school nurse and administrators, in helping youth who are pregnant to access prenatal care. While prenatal care is important for all pregnant students, it becomes particularly important for youth with HIV. Proper prenatal and postnatal care is associated with a drastic reduction in perinatal HIV transmission rates. Therefore, HIV testing for women who are pregnant, including pregnant youth, is extremely important as a means of preventing mother-to-child transmission. In fact, testing and treating pregnant women is among the most effective and easy-to-implement HIV prevention strategies currently available. Ensuring that all pregnant women with HIV are tested and treated could eradicate perinatal HIV in the United States. School psychologists can work with local health departments and family planning agencies to help coordinate prenatal care for pregnant youth.

Youth Who Use Substances

Given high rates of substance use and abuse among people infected with HIV, school psychologists should be involved with school-based programs designed to identify and treat youth who use substances. Beyond injection drug use, which is directly correlated with HIV infection, the use of noninjection drugs also is problematic. Recreational drugs and alcohol are known to result in lack of inhibition, which may lead to risky behavior. It is well established that youth who use substances are more likely to engage in risky sexual behavior. Further, there is an indirect relationship between substance use and other risk factors associated with HIV (e.g., minority status, living in poverty, sex work).

School psychologists can collaborate with health educators to help to design, implement, and evaluate school-wide screening practices to identify youth at risk for substance use. Following identification, school psychologists may be involved in a needs assessment to determine the specific needs of youth. School psychologists also may be involved with the development, implementation, and evaluation of interventions tailored to the individual needs of the group. Interventions may include substance use education. Rather, more compre-

hensive approaches may include individual counseling, group counseling, peer mentoring, and behavioral skills training. Involving families is critical to the long-term success of these interventions. School psychologists will need to be familiar with community resources for youth who require more intensive treatment in which case collaboration is recommended to enhance, and avoid the duplication of, services.

Sexually Active Youth

Tier 2 interventions should focus on students who are sexually active. Guilamo-Ramos, Jaccard, Dittus, Gonzalez, and Bouris (2008) provide evidence of the utility of using a conceptual framework that relies on five major theories of human behavior to analyze sexual risk behavior among adolescents. Emphasizing behavioral intentions, including the factors that affect intentions and their impact on behavior, applying this framework to sexual behavior involves assessing the following: past sexual behavior, intentions to engage in sexual behavior, expectancies about the risks and benefits of engaging in sexual behavior, peer pressure to engage in sexual behavior, image implications of being sexually active, emotional and affective responses to being sexually active, and self-efficacy with regard to sexual behavior. This framework may be useful for school psychologists attempting to identify sexually active youth or those at risk for sexual activity.

Intensive comprehensive sexuality education, above and beyond what is offered at the Tier 1 level, should be provided to students found to be sexually active. Frank discussions should be held with youth at this level, and the content of education should be tailored to the individual needs of students identified at risk. The needs of these youth can be better understood by conducting a risk assessment including an assessment of facilitators and barriers to condom use. Depending on the climate within the community and within the school, it may be difficult for school psychologists to help address the needs of this population. In contexts where more explicit comprehensive sexuality education is not permissible within the school setting, students should be referred to community agencies such as Planned Parenthood. Therefore, it is important for school psychologists to be familiar with the resources available in their community.

Racial/Ethnic Minorities

School psychologists need to be aware of the risk factors related to HIV facing racial/ethnic minorities and provide appropriate interventions without perpetuating racial stigma and discrimination. Racial/ethnic minorities are at greater risk for becoming pregnant, with birth rates among 15- to 17-year-old non-Hispanic Blacks and Hispanics three and four times higher, respectively, than non-Hispanic Whites (Basch, 2011). Rates of HIV are higher among minorities than nonminorities despite the fact that minorities comprise a lower percentage of the population. Berkley-Patton, Goggin, Liston, Bradley-Ewing, and Neville (2009) describe a narrative-based HIV prevention intervention designed to increase use of HIV health and ancillary services (e.g., HIV testing, HIV treatment) among minorities. While outcome data on this strategy are needed, school psychologists may be able to modify or use aspects of this intervention to engage minority youth in school-based HIV prevention efforts or they may collaborate with health educators to ensure that evidence-based curricula are used.

Tier 3: Intensive, Individual Interventions

Tier 3 interventions are designed to prevent the development of additional problems that may result within groups already affected by the target problem. In this case, these groups may include the student infected or affected by HIV, family members, teachers, peers, and community agencies. Best practices require school psychologists to take on a wide variety of different roles (e.g., direct service provider, consultant, liaison) in order to provide comprehensive services to students and others affected by HIV. Unfortunately, as previously discussed, school psychologists often may be unaware of a student's HIV status, highlighting the importance of Tier 1 interventions designed to create safe and healthy school environments. This section focuses on the role of school psychologists who are aware of a student's HIV status. At Tier 3, the aim is to ameliorate problems associated with living with HIV, prevent HIV transmission to others, and prevent reinfection by delivering intensive individualized interventions.

School psychologists are encouraged to maintain consideration of the rights of children with HIV when developing and implementing Tier 3 interventions. Betancourt, Fawzi, Bruderlein, Desmond, and Kim (2010) describe a model called SAFE that incorporates minors' rights within a human security framework to promote the security, health, and development of children with HIV. Aspects of this model are demonstrated to varying degrees in the Tier 3 intervention described below.

Assessment

Because of the psychoeducational and psychosocial impact of HIV, school psychologists are most likely to encounter students with HIV for the purposes of determining eligibility for special education programming or for services through Section 504 of the Rehabilitation Act of 1973. This may require comprehensive assessment using traditional and nontraditional measures. School psychologists also are likely to be involved in the development of Individualized Education Programs (IEPs) and 504 Plans for students with HIV who are found eligible for these services. Best practices dictate the use of ecological assessment procedures to ensure positive outcomes for children.

Assessment practices will vary to some degree depending on the age of the student. Developmental evaluations may be necessary for infants and toddlers infected with HIV. It will be important, in these cases, to assess whether or not the child has met developmental milestones across the domains of cognition, language, adaptive behavior, gross and fine motor skills, and social–emotional functioning. As these children age, it might be advantageous to periodically reassess these domains to allow for an examination of changes in functioning over time. This may provide important information about disease progression. For older children and adolescents, the initial evaluation will provide a baseline upon which skills can be monitored over time. Again, this information may provide valuable information about disease progression. For example, while extreme fluctuations in IQ scores are not expected in the normal population, children with HIV may experience a decline in intellectual functioning because of HIV's effect on the central nervous system. In such cases, a change in services or placement in the school setting may be warranted. Thus, ongoing assessment using measures that allow for the direct comparison of skills over time is extremely important.

In addition to using nationally norm-referenced standardized tests of intelligence, academic achievement, adaptive behavior, and psychosocial functioning, other more ecologically valid measures of assessment are recommended. For example, assessment may include a thorough review of the student's school and medical records; student observations in a variety of settings; and interviews with students, parents, teachers, and, ideally, medical personnel. In addition, curriculum-based measurement and functional-based assessment methods are recommended. Hypotheses should be generated before, during, and after the evaluation process.

Interventions

Early intervention is critical for children diagnosed with HIV. Medical, developmental, and psychosocial interventions must be tailored to meet the individual needs of the family. Ideally, a physician who specializes in immunology will provide medical care. Medical intervention may include treatment using antiretroviral therapies. The goals of medical treatment for children with HIV are to prolong survival but also to promote or restore normal growth and development, to prevent opportunistic infections, and to improve overall quality of life. School psychologists working with students with HIV should become familiar with the common side effects of the drugs used to treat HIV (e.g., nausea, vomiting, diarrhea, and kidney stones). School psychologists are in a position to provide valuable information to physicians regarding the impact of side effects on academic and behavioral functioning. School psychologists also may play an important role in medication adherence either independently or in conjunction with the school nurse.

Beyond providing support that may benefit medical treatment for children with HIV, school psychologists may be called on to create and implement academic and behavioral interventions to address the direct effects of HIV on the body and the central nervous system. In addition to contributing to IEPs for students receiving services through IDEA, some students with HIV may require curricular modifications to succeed in school. School psychologists may intervene directly with the child or indirectly through consultation with the teachers and other school personnel.

Collaborative Problem Solving

School psychologists are encouraged to use a collaborative problem-solving process when working with students with HIV. School psychologists are well aware that collaboration can improve access to services, increase support for learning and for addressing barriers to learning, create opportunities for learning and development, and generate new approaches to strengthen connections between family, school, and community. When problem solving, it is critical that the problem-solving team is composed of people who know the student in many different settings in which the student functions (e.g., classroom, homeroom, lunchroom, extracurricular activities, home, community, clinic, hospital). It is critical for school personnel, parents, and in some instances community-based medical and mental health professionals to work together to identify the problem, establish shared goals related to HIV prevention and intervention, develop a feasible and acceptable intervention, and determine how and when progress will be evaluated.

Collaborative problem solving helps improve the quality of services provided and, ultimately, student outcomes.

School psychologists also may be called upon for crisis intervention and counseling for students infected with, or affected by, HIV. For example, school psychologists might be in a position to make a psychiatric referral for a child who is suicidal or to locate an emergency shelter for a family who has lost its home. When a child or family member dies from AIDS, school psychologists should assist with bereavement issues (NASP, 2012). In such cases, school psychologists may want to partner with a hospice if available in their community.

Individual counseling may be needed to address a variety of issues. Children and adolescents with HIV may need help dealing with their diagnosis. For example, individual counseling may provide an opportunity to process fears of abandonment, stress related to medical treatment, and the unique challenges associated with sexuality when living with HIV. For some, however, dealing directly with HIV and its consequences may be a secondary concern. Because of the high rates of internalizing behavior problems (e.g., anxiety, depression, social withdrawal, loneliness, anger, confusion, guilt, fear) among youth with HIV, individual counseling may be needed to address symptoms of anxiety and depression, which are among the common psychiatric manifestations experienced in this population. Family therapy also is often needed given the intergenerational nature of this disease. School psychologists may provide these services directly, depending on their role within the school setting, or may help coordinate services with other providers within or outside the school.

School psychologists might employ a wide variety of techniques, grounded in different theoretical backgrounds. Counseling should be developmentally appropriate, and it is important for psychologists to consider some of the common emotional reactions facing children and families affected by HIV. School psychologists are strongly encouraged to focus on the child and not the disease. Youth do not want to be identified by their disease. Further, as indicated above, often HIV status is secondary to more pressing concerns that need to be addressed. In this way, youth with HIV are no different than other youth school psychologists may encounter. It is important for school psychologists to be mindful of stereotyped opinions they may hold about this population and to avoid making assumptions based on disease status.

Service Coordination

The CDC (2012b) recognizes the importance of coordinating a school health framework based on the needs, resources, and standards of families and communities. Within this framework, healthy home and school environments can be fostered by helping families build leadership, decision-making, and, more generally, parenting skills that support healthy behavior among students. Coordination of communication between the school, the child's home environment, and medical/community agencies involved in the child's treatment is important in situations where HIV has been disclosed at school. Clearly, bidirectional dialogue between school personnel, parents, physicians, and community providers will allow for the best treatment outcomes for the child with regard to physical, intellectual, academic, and social–emotional functioning.

A liaison should be appointed within the school to serve as the primary contact person. This may be the school psychologist, the school social worker, or even the school nurse given the diagnosis and medical training nurses may have. The liaison's job is to ensure that school personnel are apprised of medical or other issues that may interfere with the child's performance at school. Similarly, the child and his or her family need to be aware of academic or psychosocial issues at school that may directly or indirectly affect the child's health. For example, outbreaks of communicable diseases such as chicken pox should be promptly and directly communicated to the family of a child infected with HIV given the implications of such diseases for individuals with a suppressed immune system. In addition, schools should notify parents of any signs of illness observed to allow for appropriate follow-up. Parenthetically, universal precautionary practices should be observed in the school setting.

Child Advocacy

Advocacy may be an important role for school psychologists dealing with a child infected with HIV and his or her family. One of the primary roles of the school psychologist in this regard is to ensure the child with HIV is treated as a person with a disease as opposed to a diseased person. In essence, this requires normalizing the school environment for the child as much as possible, which may require educating teachers and staff about HIV (see Tier 1 interventions above). Advocacy also may involve educating the child and his or her family about the child's educational rights under federal law. Transition planning and education of youth about postsecondary education options also are vital.

HIV Prevention for HIV-Positive Youth

It is well understood from a public health perspective that reducing the rates of HIV transmission depends, in large part, on changing the behaviors of those infected. As a result, HIV prevention programs increasingly are targeted toward people with HIV. Medical care and other community providers who treat people with HIV are encouraged to screen for high-risk behaviors and sexually transmitted infections, provide referrals for behavioral risk-reduction interventions such as substance abuse treatment programs, and facilitate partner notification, testing, and counseling.

School psychologists also should be screening for high-risk behaviors among youth with HIV and intervening accordingly where appropriate and allowed by school policy. In some ways, what is required is similar to the targeted group interventions outlined for Tier 2. However, there are some important distinctions. First, the target group is different. At Tier 2, the purpose of interventions is to identify students at risk for contracting HIV, whereas at Tier 3 the purpose of interventions is to identify students at risk for transmitting HIV. Second, because HIV has not yet been transmitted at Tier 2 in this paradigm, facilitation of partner notification is not necessary at that level, whereas it may be necessary at Tier 3.

School psychologists should become familiar with evidence-based packaged intervention programs for youth with HIV, which are available through the CDC. For example, as described in Walsh and Chenneville (2013), Choosing Life: Empowerment! Action! Results! (CLEAR) is one such program for youth with HIV ages 15 and older (see http://www.cdc.gov/hiv/topics/research/prs/resources/factsheets/CLEAR.htm). Collins et al. (2010) describe some of the successes and challenges in implementing packaged evidence-based interventions with this population. School psychologists are encouraged to familiarize themselves with some of these programs as well as difficulties that may be encountered when trying to implement these interventions.

Confidentiality

While important for all students, school psychologists should be mindful that confidentiality is extremely important for students with HIV given the stigma that continues to surround this disease. School psychologists may advocate for students with HIV by being aware of the practices surrounding the release of healthcare information at the schools in which they work. School psychologists may assist school administrators in setting up safeguards related to the way in which educational records are stored, transmitted, and accessed. Further, school psychologists may assist by helping to create a climate of safety where students with HIV and their families do not have to fear discriminatory social, behavioral, or attitudinal reactions.

Monitoring and Evaluating Student Outcomes Across Tiers

Monitoring and evaluating student outcomes is critical across all of the tiers described above. At Tier 1, school psychologists might be involved, either directly or through consultation and collaboration with school administrators and curricula specialists, with program evaluation for sexuality education programs delivered at the local or state level, HIV-related professional development, and initiatives designed to build home–school–community infrastructure. At Tier 2, school psychologists might be involved, again either directly or through consultation and collaboration with school administrators, curricula specialists, and others to evaluate interventions delivered at this level. For example, the effectiveness of interventions can be evaluated by tracking the number of students referred for HIV testing. At Tier 3, school psychologists are likely to be the most directly involved with monitoring and evaluating outcomes for the students. For example, school psychologists should monitor and evaluate the utility of academic and behavioral interventions designed for students with HIV just as they would for any of the students they serve.

SUMMARY

HIV represents a serious health crisis in the United States and globally, and youth are affected by this disease in vast numbers. HIV-related stigma is what sets this disease apart from other life-threatening and chronic illnesses. Even though educators may be unaware of their diagnosis, students with HIV are in school each day. School psychologists must be familiar with the medical, developmental, and psychosocial implications of HIV as well as applicable state and federal laws and professional standards, as they play a pivotal role in creating a safe and healthy school environment that supports HIV prevention and services for those affected by HIV. Best practices dictate a multitiered service delivery model. At Tier 1, comprehensive sexuality education and staff training about HIV are critical. At Tier 2, efforts should be made to identify

and intervene with students at risk for contracting HIV. And at Tier 3, interventions should be developed and implemented for students affected by HIV. School psychologists are in a unique position to positively affect this significant public health issue by developing interventions and monitoring and evaluating student outcomes at each level.

AUTHOR NOTE

The author would like to thank Audra Walsh, Elissa Lafond, and Amanda Sagarian for their assistance with aspects of this manuscript.

REFERENCES

Abel, G., & Fitzgerald, L. (2006). When you come to it you feel like a dork asking a guy to put a condom on: Is sex education addressing young people's understandings of risk? *Sex Education, 6*, 105–119.

Alan Guttmacher Institute. (2006). *Facts on sexually transmitted infections in the United States.* New York, NY: Author. Retrieved from http://www.guttmacher.org/

Basch, C. E. (2011). Teen pregnancy and the achievement gap among urban minority youth. *Journal of School Health, 81*, 614–618.

Berkley-Patton, J., Goggin, K., Liston, R., Bradley-Ewing, A., & Neville, S. (2009). Adapting effective narrative-based HIV-prevention interventions to increase minorities' engagement in HIV/AIDS services. *Health Communication, 24*, 199–209.

Betancourt, T. S., Fawzi, M. K., Bruderlein, C., Desmond, C., & Kim, J. Y. (2010). Children affected by HIV/AIDS: SAFE, a model for promoting their security, health, and development. *Psychology, Health, and Medicine, 15*, 243–265.

Burns, S., Hernandez-Reif, M., & Jessee, P. (2008). A review of pediatric HIV effects on neurocognitive development. *Issues in Comprehensive Pediatric Nursing, 31*, 107–121. doi:10.1080/01460860802272870

Canadian Paediatric Society. (2008). A bite in the playroom: Managing human bites in child care settings [Position statement]. *Paediatric Child Health, 13*, 515–519.

Centers for Disease Control and Prevention. (2009). *Youth risk behavior surveillance: United States.* Atlanta, GA: Author.

Centers for Disease Control and Prevention. (2010a). *HIV surveillance report: Diagnoses of HIV infection and AIDS in the United States and dependent areas, 2010.* Atlanta, GA: Author.

Centers for Disease Control and Prevention. (2010b). *Questions and answers: HIV transmission.* Atlanta, GA: Author. Retrieved from http://www.cdc.gov/hiv/resources/qa/transmission.htm

Centers for Disease Control and Prevention. (2011). *HIV among youth.* Atlanta, GA: Author. Retrieved from http://www.cdc.gov/hiv/youth/pdf/youth.pdf

Centers for Disease Control and Prevention. (2012a). *Monitoring selected national HIV prevention and care objectives by using HIV surveillance data—United States and 6 U.S. dependent areas—2010.* Atlanta, GA: Author. Retrieved from http://www.cdc.gov/hiv/surveillance/resources/reports/2010supp_vol17no3/index.htm

Centers for Disease Control and Prevention. (2012b). *Parent engagement: Strategies for involving parents in school health.* Atlanta, GA: Author. Retrieved from http://www.cdc.gov/healthyyouth/AdolescentHealth/pdf/parent_engagement_strategies.pdf

Collins, C. B., Hearn, K. D., Whittier, D. N., Freeman, A., Stallworth, J. D., & Phields, M. (2010). Implementing packaged HIV-prevention interventions for HIV-positive individuals: Considerations for clinic-based and community-based interventions. *Public Health Reports, 125*(Supplement 1), 58–63.

Espada, J. P., Orgiles, M., Morales, A., Ballester, R., & Huedo-Medina, T. B. (2012). Effectiveness of a school HIV/AIDS prevention program for Spanish adolescents. *AIDS Education and Prevention, 24,* 500–513.

Fernet, M., Wong, K., Richard, M., Otis, J., Lévy, J. J., Lapointe, N., ... Trottier, G. (2011). Romantic relationships and sexual activities of the first generation of youth living with HIV since birth. *AIDS Care, 23,* 393–400. doi:10.1080/09540121.2010.516332

Goldman, J. G., & Collier-Harris, C. A. (2012). School-based reproductive health and safety education for students aged 12–15 years in UNESCO's (2009) *International technical guidance. Cambridge Journal of Education, 42,* 445–461.

Guilamo-Ramos, V., Jaccard, J., Dittus, P., Gonzalez, B., & Bouris, A. (2008). A conceptual framework for the analysis of risk and problem behaviors: The case of adolescent sexual behavior. *Social Work Research, 32,* 29–45.

Hauser, D. (2008). *Five years of abstinence-only-until-marriage education: Assessing the impact.* Washington, DC: Advocates for Youth. Retrieved from http://www.advocatesforyouth.org

Kann, L., Brener, N., McManus, T., & Wechsler, H. (2012). HIV, other STD, and pregnancy prevention education in public secondary schools. *CDC Morbidity and Mortality Weekly Report.* Retrieved from http://www.cdc.gov/mmwr/

Michaud, P. A., Suris, J. C., Ralph Thomas, P., Kahlert, C., Rudin, C., & Cheseaux, J. J. (2009). To say or not to say: A qualitative study on the disclosure of their condition by human immunodeficiency virus-positive adolescents. *Journal of Adolescent Health, 44,* 356–362. doi:10.1016/j.jadohealth.2008.08.004

National Association of School Psychologists. (2010a). *Model for comprehensive and integrated school psychological services.* Bethesda, MD: Author. Retrieved from http://www.nasponline.org/standards/2010standards/2_PracticeModel.pdf

National Association of School Psychologists. (2010b). *Principles for professional ethics.* Bethesda, MD: Author. Retrieved from http://www.nasponline.org/standards/2010standards/1_%20Ethical%20Principles.pdf

National Association of School Psychologists. (2012). *Supporting students with HIV/AIDS* [Position statement]. Bethesda, MD: Author. Retrieved from http://www.nasponline.org/about_nasp/positionpapers/hivaids.pdf

Ruest, C. E. (2011). Common adverse effects of antiretroviral therapy for HIV disease. *American Family Physician, 83,* 1443–1451.

Scott, J., Woods, S., Vigil, O., Heaton, R. K., Schweinsburg, B. C., Ellis, R. J., ... Marcotte, T. D. (2011). A neuropsychological investigation of multitasking in HIV infection: Implications for everyday functioning. *Neuropsychology, 25,* 511–519. doi:10.1037/a0022491

Siegel, K. S., Schrimshaw, E. W., & Lekas, H. M. (2006). Diminished sexual activity, interest, and feelings of attractiveness among HIV infected women in two eras of the AIDS epidemic. *Archives of Sexual Behaviours, 35,* 437–449. doi:10.1007/s10508-006-9043-5

UNAIDS. (2010). *Global report: UNAIDS report on the global AIDS epidemic 2010.* Geneva, Switzerland: Author. Retrieved from http://www.unaids.org/en/

Walcott, C., Chenneville, T., & Tarquini, S. (2011). Relationship between recall of sex education and college students' sexual attitudes and behavior. *Psychology in the Schools, 48,* 828–842.

Walsh, A., & Chenneville, T. (2013). HIV in the school setting: Promoting mental health among youth through a school change model. *Advances in School Mental Health Promotion, 6,* 21–34. doi:10.1080/1754730X.2012. 760918

Wiener, L. S., & Battles, B. (2006). Untangling the web: A close look at diagnosis disclosure among HIV infected adolescents. *Journal of Adolescent Health, 38,* 307–309. doi:10.1016/j.jadohealth.2005.03.024

Section 3
Family–School Collaboration Services

30 Best Practices in Promoting Family Engagement in Education

Susan M. Sheridan
Brandy L. Clarke
University of Nebraska-Lincoln
Sandra L. Christenson
University of Minnesota

OVERVIEW

Pathways toward academic success, behavioral adaptation, and socioemotional health are predicated on both biological and environmental factors. Indeed, the environments within which children live and learn contribute significantly to their developmental trajectories, be they positive and productive or negative and unfulfilled. Among the developmental contexts that influence outcomes for children and adolescents, those related to the family and child-rearing environment are most critical. Therefore, school psychological practices that aim to enhance learning and development must, by design, focus on the environments in which children and adolescents live—including and importantly the home environment—and the adults who control them (Sheridan & Gutkin, 2000). The competence and confidence of significant adults who interact with and maintain responsibility for the welfare and well-being of children are necessary priorities. Services for children and adolescents will be maximally effective only if they include efforts to create conditions within which positive and healthy developmental experiences are evident. By extension, school-based services may be most effective when approaching practice in a manner that considers a student's learning and development as occurring within the context of his or her family.

Families are primary and essential facilitators of meaningful change, and they have significant impact on a child's growth and development over time. As a result, we contend that what is best for children is the opportunity to grow, develop, and learn in a positive, supportive family system. With that basic assumption in mind, we argue that school psychologists' front-line efforts at using best practices will always, by definition and default, involve a focus on engaging families in their child's overall development and learning. Furthermore, the domain of Family–School Collaboration Services in the National Association of School Psychologists (NASP) *Model for Comprehensive and Integrated School Psychological Services* (NASP, 2010) delineates that all school psychologists should have knowledge of evidence-based approaches for supporting family–school partnerships to support children's leaning and development. This approach to best practice requires school psychologists to have knowledge of family systems, strengths, needs, and culture, and to be guided by a set of values and beliefs that recognize parents and other caregivers as our primary clients who are responsible for promoting long-term growth in children.

Definitional Distinctions

Many terms have been used to capture how professionals—including school psychologists—think about and promote parents' roles in supporting their children's learning and behavior. Some of these include parent involvement or parent participation, where parents are given specific things to do to play a part. Others emphasize services to the family, such as family support or parent training programs. Still others stress working with the family—that is, parents and teachers working together—using phrases such as "home–school collaboration" or "parent–teacher partnership." These various approaches are characterized by unique goals, activities, and outcomes that differentiate involvement from engagement models.

Parent involvement refers to the participation of significant caregivers (including not only biological parents or legal guardians, but also grandparents, stepparents, foster parents, and others responsible for children's upbringing) in the educational process of children to promote their academic and social well-being (Fishel & Ramirez, 2005). When school efforts conform to an involvement philosophy, parents are encouraged to do specific and prescriptive things that tend to be supportive for any number or type of students. The focus is on attempts to "change parents" to fit educators' notions of what is important. Invitations to be involved are made in ways that are prescribed; that is, the message is often "be involved by doing things our way." Although such activities can be helpful in targeted ways, they often fail to sustain over time.

Parent engagement is conceptually and practically broader than parent involvement. It is defined as a relationship-based process by which parents connect with their child and other significant adults across many systems and contexts to support their child's development and help them learn and grow academically, behaviorally, and socioemotionally. Engagement concerns the connections and attachments between a parent and child, and between parents and other adults who share responsibility for children's well-being. The focus is on relationships formed with the intent of co-supporting children's healthy development and learning.

Parent Engagement

Parent engagement is a relational and dynamic construct composed of at least two dimensions that facilitate a child's healthy development: (a) relationships between a parent and child and (b) partnerships between parents and other care providers who share responsibility for their child's development. Parents are said to be engaged when they interact with their child with warmth and sensitivity and in ways that support their child's learning (Sheridan, Marvin, Knoche, & Edwards, 2008). First, parents' engagement with their children demonstrated through warmth, sensitivity, and responsiveness is associated with children's improved short-term cognitive, socioemotional, and language skills (Hirsh-Pasek & Burchinal, 2006), and long-term positive academic performance (Downer & Pianta, 2006). Children in highly connected parent–child relationships tend to display positive outcomes, such as strong

prosocial orientations, numerous and high quality friendships, and high levels of peer acceptance in kindergarten (Kerns, Klepac, & Cole, 1996). Alternatively, parenting interventions that are absent of highly responsive parent–child interactions have been found ineffective at achieving important behavioral outcomes (Mahoney, Boyce, Fewell, Spiker, & Wheeden., 1998).

A second dimension of parent engagement is characterized by partnerships between parents and other caregivers. An extensive amount of research corroborates the benefits of family–school partnerships in children's educational achievement, particularly for children who are at risk for or identified with disabilities (Lines, Miller, & Arthur-Stanley, 2011). The quality of family–school interactions has been shown to be positively related to student achievement and behavior to a greater extent than simply the number or amount of contacts families and teachers have with one another (Patrikakou & Weissberg, 1999). Furthermore, partnerships greatly enhance the amount, quality, and scope of services available to assist children in meeting their learning or behavioral goals (Clarke, Sheridan, & Woods, 2010). In potentially challenging situations, the establishment of positive, constructive relationships among family–school partners provides an opportunity for dialogue and problem solving, a window of opportunity not present when home and school systems operate in isolation from or counter to one another.

One manifestation of an engaged parent is evident in partnerships that form between parents and other caregivers who work together on behalf of a child's learning and development in a shared problem-solving and decision-making context. A family–school partnership is a child-focused approach wherein families and professionals cooperate, coordinate, and collaborate to enhance opportunities and success for children and adolescents across social, emotional, behavioral, and academic domains (Christenson & Sheridan, 2001). Partners are individuals who are united or associated with one another by virtue of a shared or common interest. The common goal or interest shared by parents and teachers surrounds the mutual desire to help a student succeed. As partners, parents and teachers are jointly responsible for achieving this goal. When problems are evident, parents and teachers as partners find ways to communicate effectively, provide ideas and input, and collaborate (give and take) until the issues are resolved. In these cases, it is not solely the teacher's job or the parent's role to ensure that a student is successful. Instead, teachers and parents share in the responsibility for identifying strengths in the student and in working together to address challenges and achieve academic, social, and emotional learning goals.

Partnerships with parents convey the message that not only are parents desirable in finding solutions to help students succeed, they are essential. Parents have information that is critical to understanding their children. As partners, teachers and parents can together set goals and explore concerns, develop specific strategies, follow through on plans at home and school, determine the progress made by students, and agree on ways to continuously improve or maintain improved performance.

BASIC CONSIDERATIONS

A useful framework when considering connections with families is characterized with five A's: approach, attitude, atmosphere, actions, and achievement. Importantly, each one represents a malleable factor that is completely within a school's control, thereby enhancing the opportunity to implement practices that are relevant and manageable within a particular system. The first three, approach, attitude, and atmosphere, emphasize conditions necessary for successfully engaging parents in actions that promote their child's learning and education. That is, the framework illustrates prerequisites (i.e., approach, attitudes, and atmosphere) that need to be in place before any actions can take hold. Actions will not be maximally beneficial or long lasting unless a meaningful approach, constructive attitudes, and a positive atmosphere are intact. When the first four are in place and reinforced, improvements in the fifth—achievement—is the result.

Approach

Approach represents the philosophy or orientation adopted by schools at a systems level. The approach used to promote parental engagement to interact with families establishes the tone, method, and manner by which relationships will unfold. To engage parents, a school-wide approach that fosters shared responsibilities, open dialogue, and promotion of family competencies is necessary (Christenson & Sheridan, 2001). When considering a systems approach to family–school engagement, the focus is on what schools do (to create and support engagement and partnership), not necessarily what is expected of parents or what parents do (to support school's goals, which is often the focus of an involvement approach).

The relationship schools develop with families takes center stage when considering whether parents will become engaged as partners. Schools and families are always in a relationship with one another; that is, the quality of the relationship is determined in large part by the approach used by schools. In other words, the approach can either attract, invite, reinforce, and reward families for their positive engagement, or it can diminish, discourage, and potentially sever positive connections between families and schools. Partnerships define relationships with families in ways that involve close cooperation between parties with clearly specified and joint roles, rights, and responsibilities (Christenson & Sheridan, 2001). The focus of the relationship is student centered, with the goal of improving learning experiences and developmental outcomes for children.

Attitude

The second aspect of the framework requires educators to consider the attitudes conveyed regarding family engagement and partnership. Attitudes are the underlying feeling, emotions, and positions held by family members and school personnel about each other, their relationships, and respective roles and responsibilities (Christenson & Sheridan, 2001). They include the underlying beliefs about children's and families' values, practices, and culture, and whether those are facilitators or deterrents toward growth and development. Attitudes include the messages communicated through actions and words that convey a school's approach to engage with parents. Although often subtle in form, attitudes act in significant ways to establish or abolish connections with parents.

An essential attitude that predicts whether families become engaged recognizes the inherent strengths in all families. Approaching families as partners emphasizes the attitude that parents are part of the solution (not problem), and thus leads to desires to partner with families rather than treat families (Dunst, 2000). In other words, a partnership approach requires the attitude that all families have strengths that can be tapped by soliciting information, listening actively, and sharing ideas cooperatively. This is in contrast to attitudes that consider family members as having deficits that need to be treated, trained, or altered. The latter approach (one where the focus is on changing parents because they are doing something that is "wrong" or insufficient) can quickly lead to the creation of condescending judgments and one-way prescriptive practices. Although parent education and skill building can be appropriate and valuable, the manner in which they are delivered can determine whether a partnership is possible (i.e., whether the parent will engage as a partner or a recipient of services).

Second, to achieve a true partnership that reinforces parental engagement assumes an attitude whereby there are shared goals and shared responsibility for success, rather than one that naturally assigns blame for challenges or problems. An attitude embracing the notion that the best opportunities for students will be possible when parents and teachers work together as partners is necessary. That is, each perceives himself or herself, and the other person, as a partner and equal in the relationship with unique strengths, perspectives, and resources to share. This does not assume that they bring identical expertise to the partnership. The unique roles each contribute in support of the student and the partnership is respected.

Finally, an attitude that perceives families as part of the solution, not the problem, is an essential aspect of engaging families. When families and schools are disconnected, an attitude that perceives parents as part of the problem (connoted by terms such as "hard to reach" or "uninvolved") may be typical. A proactive, constructive attitude recognizes that parents and educators desire many of the same outcomes, and engaging with one another as partners can result in shared success. There is no room to blame; that is, parents are part of the solution, not a deterrent, in students' abilities to achieve their goals.

Atmosphere

Atmosphere concerns both the physical and affective climate that exists in educational communities. It is an inherent aspect of the family–school relationship that predicts parents' feelings of comfort and acceptance, and ultimately their willingness to engage with educators. A school's atmosphere conveys a desire to be in a partnership with families, or sends a message (often implicit) discouraging engagement. In other words, the atmosphere can either set parents at ease, or can create discomfort and tension. It can serve as a prerequisite to engagement as it sets the stage for ensuring that parents can seize opportunities that are made available to connect and partner.

The physical climate is the outward manifestation of a school's orientation toward families, and communicates in an observable way the degree to which schools are inviting and family friendly. The physical atmosphere is often the focus of programs' efforts to involve parents. For example, bulletin boards, signs in various languages, pictures of different cultures, or family events often contribute to a school's physical atmosphere. These overt gestures at welcoming families are positive but may be short-lived unless they are integrated into an approach where clear and genuine attitudes that value families are conveyed.

The affective climate concerns the feelings parents experience upon engaging in interactions with school personnel, based largely on overtures made by educators. A school's affective climate is characterized by feelings of trust, respect, openness, and acceptance. The manner in which differences in backgrounds and cultures are supported within a school can contribute to the affective climate. Schools that recognize, appreciate, and respect various cultures and their contribution to a rich and rewarding learning opportunity promote a climate that is highly congruent for families and may enjoy greater levels of engagement.

Actions

Actions are the strategies or practices used to work effectively with parents to bring together all of the systems that support children. In the context of a supportive partnership-oriented approach, attitude, and atmosphere, actions that are adopted are likely to succeed in fostering positive and constructive connections. In general, actions that are responsive to the family and school, specific and appropriate to the goals and needs being presented, and reflective, planful, and solution-oriented are most conducive for encouraging family engagement and partnerships. They are defined by a partnership approach, constructive attitudes, and a positive atmosphere, and cannot be considered as an isolated set of activities. Thus, best practices for engaging families, presented next, must be understood within this broader context.

BEST PRACTICES IN PROMOTING FAMILY ENGAGEMENT

Rather than identifying a list of strategies or activities to suggest as a means for parents' involvement, the goal of engaging families is to create a seamless and integrated experience that brings families and schools together and promotes positive outcomes for students. Actions that are grounded in positive relationships between families and schools help establish seamless connections between home and school. Actions promote congruent values about education and consistent notions on the importance of student responsibility for learning.

The role of a school psychologist in promoting family engagement is akin to a systems consultant. Indeed, school psychologists are in an optimal position to serve as liaisons across systems (i.e., home and school), leading efforts to develop systemic action plans that will strengthen relationships with parents and achieve better outcomes for students. As a systems consultant, school psychologists can help schools and families co-create a plan for what the partnership will look like and how parents and teachers will support each other to achieve goals for a student. Practices at the school level, such as invitations extended to parents, communication patterns, assessment practices, intervention programs, and formal and informal opportunities provided to families are effective at encouraging parental engagement (Hoover-Dempsey & Sandler, 1997). Indeed, all practices in schools (e.g., prereferral assistance teams, assessment procedures, instructional and behavioral interventions, parent–teacher conferences) can be approached with a family–school focus (Christenson, 2004), and school psychologists have responsibilities to promote and guide an entire system in establishing and revamping practices within a school–family lens.

Useful tenets within systems consultation are to start early and target specific goals. Consulting practices that help school systems adopt a family engagement approach are most effective when parents are actively pursued early and actions are individualized. For example, some parents may only need information about the essential nature of their role and home support for learning strategies. Other families may need information and attention to a specific constraint, such as the need for increased reading resources in the home. Still other families may need ongoing support to maintain a connection with educators for their children's learning.

Systems consultants are often responsible for information sharing that creates effective climates for change and helping school leaders troubleshoot problems. School psychologists serving in this role are helping set the stage for partnerships when they explain the meaningful purpose of partnerships (i.e., partnering with families because of improved learning outcomes and school experiences for students), and provide examples of conditions within schools, homes, and the partnership that foster students' competence. When unique situations or challenges arise, school psychologists can model partnership-centered actions that allow for open dialogue, creative problem solving, and joint decision making.

Sjuts and Sheridan (2011) developed a family engagement interview that may be used by school psychologists as systems consultants to facilitate a self-reflection process pertaining to family engagement practices. This formative tool guides educators through self-reflection and planning regarding five core components of family engagement practices: (a) bidirectional communication, (b) foundational beliefs and attitudes, (c) respect and responsiveness, (d) cultural awareness and sensitivity, and (e) invitations for partnering. The measure helps educators identify areas of potential strength and need for improvement and guides planning for improving the quality of engagement practices, such as those outlined in this chapter.

Communication is perhaps the most outward and explicit practice that connects families and schools. Creating opportunities for families and schools to be engaged as partners starts with an evaluation of communication practices. School psychologists can examine invitations or overtures that reach out to parents and assess whether they, as school psychologists, convey a desire to achieve shared goals on matters that are of mutual priority (partnership) or suggest prescribed practices to be done in isolation (involvement). School psychologists can help school administrators and teachers emphasize the desire for constructive communication and create options for information sharing and two-way decision making, when appropriate. Beyond overtures made by schools, effective communication is foundational for sharing information between home and school, establishing goals, sharing expectations, helping parents and teachers understand each other's perspectives, and avoiding misunderstandings.

The practices described here are reflective of an overarching approach toward family engagement versus prescriptive step-by-step activities. The practices are categorized by those that are (a) foundational (i.e., school psychologists can perform as systems consultants) and (b) constructive (i.e., focused on promoting parent engagement and building positive relationships with individual families). Table 30.1 presents best practice guidelines and examples of strategies for school psychologists at both the foundational and constructive/individual levels.

Foundational Practices

Some basic relationship elements, including sincerity, trust, and respect, are foundational to the formation of positive home–school partnerships. Such elements are shaped through a series of communications and

Table 30.1. Foundational and Constructive Practices and Exemplar Strategies for Engaging Parents

Foundational Practices	Exemplars of Effective Strategies
Convey genuineness/sincerity	• Conduct an attitude assessment to establish a climate conducive to family engagement • Let parents know that they are necessary partners in their child's education • Invite parents to partner with educators in a meaningful role (e.g., decision-making and leadership roles) • Affirm parents' competencies
Build trust	• Demonstrate competence for meeting the child's learning needs and in interactions with families • Display positive personal regard or consideration for all families • Demonstrate consistency and transparency in words and actions that reflect a genuine desire to partner with parents • Consistently follow through with invitations and actions to engage parents
Convey respect	• Allow parents to choose how they would like to engage with their child and school • Ask parents to share information about themselves and their child, including learning goals they have for their child and strategies used to support learning • Actively listen to parents and demonstrate understanding of the message conveyed through their verbal and nonverbal cues • Validate parents' perspectives, even when different from those espoused by the school • Use information gathered from families in instructional planning • Demonstrate understanding and a desire to learn about family culture, upholding a strengths-based perspective to address cultural differences

Constructive Practices	Exemplars of Effective Strategies
Engage in effective, bidirectional communication	• Use parent-friendly language that avoids jargon, is easy to understand, and is in parents' native language • Provide families with various, bidirectional means to communicate with educators • Include positive messages in initial and ongoing contacts with families (e.g., good news phone calls or home–school notes) • Address issues or concerns with families calmly and honestly, avoiding blame and defensiveness.
Collaborate/partner	• Identify and explain roles, rights, and responsibilities of parents and educators in initial and ongoing interactions • Provide opportunities for joint decision making regarding the child's educational career (e.g., parent–teacher conferences, instructional/intervention planning, Individualized Education Program meetings) • Identify strengths within individuals (e.g., child, parent, and teacher) upon which to build skills/capacities • Identify strengths of systems (home, school, and community) and parent–teacher relationships upon which to foster partnerships • Offer supports and resources necessary for parents to engage in planning and partnership (e.g., offer flexible scheduling, provide information and data in advance of meetings, and explain planning/partnering processes) • Jointly develop and implement cross-setting plans to support the child's learning • Utilize structured, data-based processes to facilitate planning and partnering (e.g., conjoint behavioral consultation)

interactions that families experience with teachers and school staff over the course of a student's educational career. Conveying genuineness and sincerity, building trust, and demonstrating respect for families occurs through consistent, systematic positive parent–teacher interactions.

Convey Genuineness and Sincerity

Demonstrating sincerity and genuineness originates from internalized attitudes or beliefs that parent engagement is necessary to student success (Hoover-Dempsey et al., 2005). Sincerity is conveyed through a genuine message that all families have strengths and are competent and capable of helping their child achieve success with the right support. School psychologists can help establish policies and practices that ensure opportunities for families and educators to engage with one another. When family–school partnerships are valued by administrators, policies allowing flexible time and support for teachers and parents to interact with one another can go far in promoting these partnerships. Identifying and evaluating school policies supporting parent engagement (which may reflect the attitudes held by school leaders) are seminal for establishing practices that are genuine and sincere and therefore likely to be effective (Christenson & Sheridan, 2001).

School psychologists can help institute effective parent engagement practices by facilitating self-reflection and planning opportunities with school teams or administrators wherein current attitudes reflected in policies and practices are evaluated and modified if necessary. This will set the tone for an entire school body and elicit administrative support for teachers to practice in such a way that will strengthen their partnerships with families. The same self-reflection and planning is also important at a ground level to determine that the foundational attitudes are upheld across all school personnel as a prerequisite to any systematic action plans including constructive practices promoting family engagement. They might consider the use of an attitude assessment to ensure that family engagement practices are grounded in genuineness and sincerity. A number of useful surveys are available in Henderson, Mapp, Johnson, and Davies (2007).

Build Trust

Trust is often considered one of the most critical elements of home–school partnerships. Trust is a reflected through a stable sense of confidence that each partner will act in a manner that jointly supports the student and maintains the positive regard for the other and their contribution to the student's achievement. When parents have a high level of trust in their relationship with their child's educators, they have a more positive view of their role in their child's learning and are more likely to be engaged (Dunsmuir, Frederickson, & Lang, 2004).

Trust is a multifaceted and dynamic element of relationships. School psychologists can help build trust over time by creating a reliable and predictable environment through a series of positive interactions (Adams & Christenson, 2000). Unfortunately, parents tend to trust teachers and school personnel more than school personnel trust parents. Developing two-way

trust comes through a series of interactions between parents and educators (including school psychologists) where there is mutual respect and dependency, belief in each other's competencies, positive personal regard, accountability and dependability, and transparency between one's words and actions.

School psychologists play an important role in creating a trust-building environment for families. They can set a tone of commitment by communicating that family engagement is a priority. For example, school psychologists demonstrate a commitment to partnering with families by setting up opportunities for parents to participate with educators in making educational decisions at a time that respects their other obligations and allows parents to share their thoughts and input. Asking families about their goals for their child and developing home–school plans for achieving them also conveys a sense of commitment to partnering with families. Individualized treatment plans (e.g., Individualized Education Program) developed for students can incorporate parents' input in a meaningful way and establish a role for parents to remain involved in the implementation and evaluation of their child's progress, thus demonstrating that their participation is not just welcomed but necessary.

To build trust and partnerships with families, consistent positive interactions over time are important. Home–school communication is an important means by which trust is established. When communications with parents reflect a positive regard and consideration for their well-being, families develop a sense of trust that schools care about them and their children. Information shared through newsletters, personal communications, policies, and all other formats reflect a positive regard when delivered consistently and with a positive message. Positive regard is also reflected when educators seek parents' open and honest feedback and address questions and concerns responsively and promptly.

Some families may have developed a sense of distrust of schools owing to previous negative experiences from their own schooling or negative interactions with their children's previous educators. Developing a sense of trust in these situations requires time and commitment to establishing a new pattern of interactions. Initial efforts may not be received and reciprocated by all families as expected. Positive persistence and perspective taking are important for developing a renewed sense of trust in these situations.

School psychologists can model trust building behaviors in many ways. In a consulting role school psychologists can prioritize family involvement in decision-making meetings; encourage families to help identify and prioritize a student's educational needs; invite parents to share observations regarding their child's strengths, interests, and behavior at home and in other settings; and overtly validate the importance and value of parental perspectives. School psychologists can also help to establish a welcoming environment where parents are greeted pleasantly by name and in their native language (e.g., verbally or a bulletin board message), the building is clean and well maintained, and the parents are guided about where to go when they enter. School psychologists may be particularly effective at demonstrating persistence and commitment to parent engagement in instances when relationships are strained. This can be accomplished by modeling positive attitudes, sharing parents' and teachers' perspectives, establishing positive communication, ensuring follow through with parent requests, and providing opportunities to collaborate and problem solve with families to address difficulties when they arise.

The trust-building framework within Check & Connect (Christenson & Reschly, 2010), a targeted, structured mentoring program to engage students at risk of drop out, is characterized by the five A's. Mentors build relationships, emphasize problem solving, and are persistent with parents as they recognize that a trusting home–school relationship is a process that develops over time, especially for parents who feel alienated from the school system. Detailed trust-building actions used by mentors to establish relationships with parents are outlined within the program manual (Christenson, Stout, & Pohl, 2012) and provide an excellent additional resource for school psychologists looking to strengthen the family–school relationship or foster engagement with parents.

Convey Respect

Partnerships with parents are founded on a perceived sense of equality. Parents and teachers have unique expertise, skills, and experiences that they bring to the relationship and that they use to support students' success. School psychologists demonstrate and model respect for parents by valuing what parents bring to the partnership and creating meaningful opportunities for parents to share their input, resources, and ideas and make decisions on behalf of their child's education. Directly asking parents open-ended questions to share their thoughts and opinions, listening to their ideas, and affirming their role as decision makers in their child's education conveys a sense of respect (Gestwicki, 2000).

Interest and openness to understanding the child and family reinforces that families are valued.

Parents often enter into relationships with educators at a disadvantage. Within the educational system, teachers typically have the power to uphold their values and have clearly defined roles for making decisions on behalf of students, whereas parents often lack the resources, knowledge, and understanding for acting in such roles (Lareau & McNamara-Horvat, 1999). Thus, the responsibility falls on school psychologists, teachers, and administrators to establish a sense of equality by extending invitations to work together with parents to support their child's learning in ways that they find meaningful (Bryk & Schneider, 2002).

Parents may also need support to be able to engage in partnerships with schools. School psychologists can establish equality by providing parents with the necessary resources and information needed to engage with their child and partner with teachers (Hoover-Dempsey et al., 2005). For example, parents likely do not have access to curricula and assessment tools used to measure children's progress. They also do not receive training in how to use these tools to make data-based decisions or how to set developmentally appropriate goals across multiple domains of learning. Sharing these resources with families in a manner that they understand and desire to use helps prepare them to engage in a partnership with educators focused on student achievement. School psychologists can work to ensure that information shared with families is presented in a family-friendly manner and a format that is easily accessible to parents (e.g., brief pamphlet, online newsletter, mobile applications). Information that is shared with families is most useful when free from jargon and presented at a practical level that parents can understand and use in home settings (Blue-Banning, Summers, Frankland, Nelson, & Beegle, 2004).

Conversely, parents have a wealth of knowledge about their child and the home environment that is critical to their child's success, such as the child's interests, home routine, family culture, and traditions. Actively soliciting this information can be very informative for goal setting, individualized instructional planning, and problem-solving processes. Active attempts to convey a sense of respect and value in the role and expertise of families occur when school psychologists ask parents to share observations of their child's specific skills and elicit information about strategies that they have used to help foster those skills. Most importantly, affirming parent's efforts and utilizing information gathered from families in a meaningful way to support the child at school, such as using similar strategies to support the child in the classroom, conveys respect for parents (Byrk & Schneider, 2002; Minke, 2006).

Establish Connections Between Home and School

Continuity across home and school helps students transition among settings with ease. However, failure to note commonalities in goals may create disconnects or discontinuities for students. Parents are primarily concerned about the overall development of their child and often set goals and expectations for them to succeed in all domains, such as those associated with emotional security, friendships, and physical health. Schools typically emphasize students' learning and achievement as of primary importance. Continuity across home and school environments is achieved in part when school psychologists help parents and teachers recognize their shared desire to promote optimal outcomes, and work toward articulating common goals and expectations for children's learning and behavior (Henderson et al., 2007). For example, school psychologists can work with educators to promote positive outcomes for children across all domains (e.g., behavioral and mental health, cognitive development) and engage in practices that do so, such as antibullying, character building, physical fitness, and after-school enrichment programs. Similarly, they can encourage parents' roles in fostering children's academic skills along a continuum of supports (e.g., setting high expectations for learning, providing exposure to learning activities, interactively engaging in activities with their child). School psychologists have the opportunity to endorse evidence-based strategies that include a home and school approach in these and other systemic programs.

School psychologists can seize opportunities to promote connections by working to establish common messages to support a child's development (Henderson et al., 2007). Commonalities are more readily established when school psychologists and other educational personnel understand the families in their communities, know what they value, seek out their strengths, and recognize and appreciate their challenges in child rearing. Understanding families is only possible through bidirectional information sharing at all levels and communications focused directly on parents' goals and expectations for their child's educational experience. Practices that school psychologists can promote to create connections between home and school are presented in Table 30.2.

Constructive Practices

When foundational elements are in place, a positive, welcoming climate and a genuine and sincere desire to collaborate with families are established. Constructive practices then build upon these conditions to extend positive relationships with parents to cooperative and collaborative partnerships. Practices used to create such partnerships include effective bidirectional communication and collaborative planning.

Focused, Bidirectional Communication

Communication is the primary means by which relationships between families and schools are established. Traditional models of family involvement often utilize one-directional means of communicating whereby information is delivered from schools to families, but information from families is not typically elicited in a direct, consistent format. Establishing bidirectional means of communication that is focused and intentional demonstrates the belief that family input is valued and necessary for promoting student achievement. Directly soliciting parents' thoughts and concerns and providing them with a means for sharing resources with teachers helps parents to develop and establish an important role as an essential partner in their child's education.

The quality and quantity of communicative attempts are important to consider in establishing effective bidirectional communication (Clarke et al., 2010). This includes regular opportunities for parents and teachers to communicate specifically about the child's progress, including both successful experiences and concerns. Various modalities of written and/or verbal communication can be used to increase dialogue across home and school, such as e-mail, phone calls, text messages, newsletters, and two-way home–school notes. For example, weekly home–school notes can be sent home to inform parents of current events and upcoming assignments or projects, and then returned by parents with questions about the skills/materials and/or reports about how skills were practiced or observed in the home.

Positive comments are important, especially when children are facing challenges or when relationships have been strained (Blue-Banning et al., 2004). Avoiding jargon and messages that indicate judgment or blame also help to facilitate open lines of communication. Actively listening to what parents have to say fosters honest interactions that facilitate positive relationships. This is reflected when teachers not only hear what parents are saying, but communicate an understanding

Table 30.2. Best Practices for Creating Connections Between Home and School

Always consider parents/families as a resource and help them to recognize themselves as resources.

Provide the context for parents to feel empowered:
- Communicate to parents that they have power, dignity, and authority in rearing their children
- Empower parents in an intentional and ongoing way by demonstrating respect, belief, and expectations so that parents can gain greater access to and control over resources

Negotiate roles and responsibilities:
- Include parents in decision making for their child
- Explain to parents the importance of families to their child's learning, right away and often
- Expect parents to be involved
- Clarify how parents can help; provide options
- Encourage parents to be assertive
- Develop a parent–school agreement

Reduce barriers:
- Have contact with parents early in the school year
- Establish ongoing communication systems; include good news phone calls
- Use two-way communication formats that are both school to home and home to school
- Bridge the language gap; strive to have the best communication between school and home with all parents, including those who speak a language other than English

Create a spirit of cooperation:
- Explore what parents want school to accomplish
- Devise opportunities for engagement that parents see as practical and meaningful
- Reach out to parents with warmth and sensitivity
- Communicate to teachers and school administrators that sharing power with parents is not abdicating the school psychologist role; rather, it provides an opportunity to understand interests and goals of parents and learn how to achieve them

Take parents' perspectives:
- Identify why parents might not be involved:
  - Diverse background experiences of parents with schools
  - Economic and time constraints
  - Diverse linguistic and cultural norms
- Recognize that resistance is a form of communication:
  - Failure to achieve a connection between home and school highlights the lack of understanding about what is important to each party rather than the presence of resistance
  - Rather than defining parents as resistant, appreciate that they may simply hold different perspectives that need to be understood

Make the school welcoming and family friendly:
- Create a physical appearance that is inviting and open to all
- Consider whether the affective climate (unwritten and unspoken messages and attitudes about students and families) fosters warmth, sensitivity, and trust, or judgment and preconceived notions

Consider a range of other strategies:
- Use multiple efforts; no one way will work for all families
- Make events fun for families
- Plan for logistical barriers (e.g., work schedules, transportation, child care) and build in flexibility
- Invite parents to help determine the best way for them to be involved
- Meet parents on their turf
- Identify a parent in the school who can help spread positive messages
- Make sure roles for parents are meaningful to them

of the message that is being communicated and its relevance for the child's education.

Cultural and language differences can have an impact on communication efforts and the development of home–school partnerships. When such differences are viewed as strengths and opportunities for learning, rather than challenges to be overcome, families and teachers can enter into relationships with an open mind. To further promote open dialogue and prevent potential misunderstandings, communication should be in the family's native language as much as possible and respect for the family culture reflected in all interactions. Informal communication opportunities, such as drop off and pick up, may be especially important for reducing communication barriers with families who have reading difficulties or do not speak English.

School psychologists can not only model effective communication strategies, but may also provide training and support to school staff regarding their efforts to communicate with families. Proactively addressing communication challenges by anticipating language barriers and developing greater understandings of different cultural groups can help to prevent potential challenges in facilitating home–school partnerships. The Check & Connect implementation manual (Christenson et al., 2012) also provides some guidelines and examples for establishing effective communication, such as affirming parents' contributions to the child's success and encouraging parent input and dialogue, that school psychologists may find useful in shaping their communication practices with families.

Collaborative Planning / Partnering

Parents and teachers share a common purpose in helping children achieve their highest potential. As partners, there is a joint responsibility for supporting a child's learning and development. Collaborative planning provides a means by which parents and teachers together identify goals and develop cross-setting strategies for reaching these goals. As partners with unique perspectives about the child and his or her environments, parents and teachers make joint decisions about skills on which to focus and methods for working together to support them. They also share information and resources that will support one another and the child in pursuit of their objectives. For example, a parent and teacher may decide together that a child needs to increase reading fluency. The teacher may share information with the parent regarding the use of dialogic reading strategies when reading together at home and the parent may share information about the child's interests so that the teacher can capitalize on these during reading practice in the classroom. They might also discuss other naturally occurring opportunities for practice that occur across both settings, such as reading signs, billboards, and food labels, and develop similar strategies for prompting, supporting, and reinforcing the child to increase reading fluency.

Data-based decision making is a key feature of effective collaborative planning (Sheridan & Kratochwill, 2008). Objective measures of student progress are important in determining how to set goals and evaluating if strategies are effective in helping the student reach those goals. Teachers have expertise in collecting objective measures of student progress, whereas parents have extensive opportunities for directly observing their child's skill development across various contexts over time. Both forms of information are equally important to the planning process. Directly asking parents to share their observations and using these to inform decisions and develop instructional strategies for students reinforces respect for parents' expertise and helps develop a positive role construct for their participation in the educational process.

Conjoint behavioral consultation (Sheridan & Kratochwill, 2008) is one exemplar of an evidence-based collaborative planning model. Conjoint behavioral consultation is a problem-solving process facilitated by a school psychologist that brings together parents and teachers to jointly identify goals and develop cross-setting plans to address child-related concerns. It is defined as "a strength-based cross-system problem-solving and decision-making model wherein parents, teachers, and other caregivers or service providers work as partners and share responsibility for promoting positive and consistent outcomes related to a child's academic, behavioral, and social–emotional development" (Sheridan & Kratochwill, 2008, p. 25). The goals of conjoint behavioral consultation are threefold: (a) promoting positive academic, social–emotional, and behavioral outcomes for children through joint, cross-system planning; (b) promoting parent engagement through meaningful participation within a culturally sensitive context; and (c) establishing and enhancing home–school partnerships on behalf of children's development, both immediately and over time. The emphasis within this model is to develop and enhance home–school partnerships to effectively address the needs of the student.

Conjoint behavioral consultation is a four-stage process (i.e., needs identification, needs analysis and plan development, plan implementation, and plan evaluation) led by a school psychologist responsible for facilitating three semistructured interviews. Within the needs identification stage (or the Building on Strengths interview), school psychologists, parents, and teachers identify the strengths and needs of a student and jointly prioritize a target skill to address through the consultation process. Data collection procedures are established and used across settings to gather baseline information related to the target skill and environmental conditions that may have an impact on the child's progress. A partnership between the parent and teacher is forged by establishing equal roles and jointly making decisions. Commonalities across home and school are emphasized and differences in perspective are validated and addressed.

During the needs analysis stage (or the Planning for Success interview), baseline data are evaluated to determine a developmentally appropriate goal for the child and cross-setting plans are developed based on a functional assessment of environmental conditions hypothesized to influence the child's performance. Joint responsibility for plan development and implementation further fosters the partnership and builds a sense of accountability and trust in the parent–teacher relationship. Throughout the plan implementation stage, parents and teachers communicate regularly to identify and address potential issues with the plan and to share observations of the child's progress.

In the plan evaluation stage (or Checking and Reconnecting interview), parents and teachers evaluate the child's progress toward the goal, and the feasibility, acceptability, and effectiveness of the plan. Modifications are made as needed, and the team determines next steps in the process (e.g., making changes to the plan or terminating consultation). The importance of continued partnering and communication is emphasized and plans for maintaining the partnership are developed. Throughout the consultation process, the consultant focuses on building the capacities of the parent and teacher to promote skills for the child and to effectively partner with one another so that progress will be sustained beyond the consultation process.

All of the conjoint behavioral consultation interviews include both parents and teachers to facilitate conjoint planning. Each interview lasts approximately 45–60 minutes and the entire process requires approximately 6–8 weeks to complete. Although described in a stage-wise fashion, the data-based process is highly responsive to the presenting needs of the student, teacher, and family. As a result, the process is very fluid and the consultation team (i.e., consultant, parent, and teacher) may recycle through any stage of the process as warranted.

Conjoint behavioral consultation has been shown to be highly effective in addressing various concerns for students (Guli, 2005; Sheridan et al., 2012), including those with diverse backgrounds (Sheridan, Eagle, & Doll, 2006). The conjoint behavioral consultation manual (Sheridan & Kratochwill, 2008) includes a detailed description of the theoretical framework, procedures, and research behind the model, as well as an appendix of various reproducible implementation

tools. Implementation guidelines, materials, and resources are available on the Future of School Psychology Task Force on Family–School Partnerships' website (http://fsp.unl.edu/future_module3.html). With a background in consultation, behavioral principles, and data-based decision making, school psychologists are uniquely positioned to facilitate collaborative planning for parents and teachers.

Developmental Perspectives on Family Engagement

Best practices for engaging parents change over time based on the goals for the student and shifting roles and responsibilities for parents and educators. Although the manner in which parents engage with their child and their child's teachers may look different throughout the child's educational career, the importance of family engagement remains constant. Strong parent–child relationships characterized by warmth and responsiveness, supportive and clear expectations for the child's learning, and student-centered parent–teacher partnerships provide a strong foundation for student achievement at any age.

Early parent–child relationships and parent–teacher partnerships are especially important to the learning trajectory of a student. Parents are essentially their child's first teacher and early experiences set the stage for a child to view himself or herself as a learner and for parents to establish a positive role in their child's learning. Preschool is often the first interaction parents have with a formal educational system, and relationships formed therein set the stage for building trust and establishing a pattern of interactions and engagement that will likely carry forward as a parent and child move into elementary school. School psychologists working in early intervention programs are in an ideal position to capitalize on parents' innate interest in their child's early school experiences and create positive expectations for their active engagement and connection to school. School psychologists can also work with preschool teachers and early childhood interventionists to help them establish strong patterns of family engagement early on.

In the progression through elementary school and beyond, children will experience many transitions. Whereas teachers vary from year to year, school psychologists are often a constant person in a school and can create continuity to achieve successful transitions. As children age and develop more advanced skills, the emphasis on parental support for their child's learning shifts from direct instructional behaviors whereby parents establish and facilitate learning opportunities to more indirect support provided through high expectations for student performance and opportunities to demonstrate autonomy and independence. School psychologists' overtures and invitations for parent engagement will thus be increasingly determined by student need and desire (Hoover-Dempsey et al., 2005). Over time, students also assume increased roles and responsibility for their education and may participate in collaborative planning together with their parents and teachers. Although the need for frequent communication among parents and teachers may decrease over time as a result of increased student independence, regular interactions focused on building trust, conveying respect, and maintaining relationships remain important to promoting student achievement.

Multicultural Competencies

Respect for family background and values is inherent to the approach described herein. School psychological practices that are predicated on the belief that all families have strengths and are needed to support student achievement set the stage for engaging effectively with families of various cultures. Establishing a warm, inviting atmosphere and creating opportunities for educators to learn from families, with families, and about families so as to better engage with them and support educational success for all children are appropriate practices for school psychologists.

It is important for school psychologists to develop multicultural competencies including responsivity and a willingness to evaluate their practices. It is expected that diverse families will present a wide range of knowledge, skills, experiences, and values. School psychologists can adopt and model a strengths-based perspective that views parental differences as assets to the educational system. Perspective taking and openness to different cultures and ideas are important to developing an understanding of families. Conversely, it is also important for school psychologists to help families learn about and understand the culture of the school so that they can take full advantage of opportunities to engage (Christenson, Hurley, Sheridan, & Fenstermacher, 1997; Hoover-Dempsey et al., 2005).

Engaging in shared learning experiences allows parents and teachers to develop a better understanding of each other and further supports student achievement. Many of the practices described throughout this chapter create shared learning opportunities, such as asking parents to share their goals and expectations for their child and learning strategies employed at home. School psychologists can also ask families about cultural practices and family background as both relate to the child's educational experiences. Surveying families to determine what resources and information they need or want from the school may also help guide efforts to engage families. Specific information regarding school expectations, policies, curricula, instructional programming/strategies, and overall child development can be provided to families in various formats to help parents develop an understanding of school culture and consequently more fully engage in educational assessment and intervention (Christenson et al., 1997).

Evaluation of Practices/Outcomes

The purpose of family engagement is to support greater achievement on behalf of students. Thus, evaluation efforts should center on measuring benefits for students as the primary outcome. Increased learning support across home and school enhances opportunities for students to master skills effectively and efficiently. Comparing indicators of parent engagement with assessments of student achievement and performance, such as grades, achievement test scores, attendance records, and behavioral reports, can help to determine if efforts to engage parents are in fact benefiting students. Additional measures capturing noncognitive factors related to achievement, such as study skills, work habits, metacognitive strategies, and problem-solving skills (see Farrington et al., 2012) are also important to consider.

Indicators of parent engagement look at both engagement with the child and engagement with teachers. Evidence of engagement with the child falls along a continuum of activities and might include time parents spend in supporting of learning at home (e.g., reading together, checking homework, modeling and practicing skills) and methods they use to set and achieve goals. Evidence of partnerships parents have with teachers extend beyond traditional measures of attendance at school-based events and include positive communication and participation in decision making. Parent ratings of the home–school relationship and their role (i.e., role construct and self-efficacy beliefs) are important indicators as to whether engagement practices are indeed effective. Because parent engagement may vary from one family to the next in form and function, measurement will need to be sensitive to variations in practice. When parents are positively engaged, their behaviors are consistent and repeated over time developing a role construct and sense of self-efficacy as an effective educational partner regarding their child's learning.

When families and schools are engaged with one another, schools experience efficiency and effectiveness in instructional practices focused on student learning (Henderson et al., 2007). However, defining successful parent engagement with families may be idiosyncratic as it is an evolving process and not a one-time activity. Successful efforts to engage families establish administrative priorities reflected in goals set for the school, time and resources allocated to create opportunities for home–school partnerships, and progress monitoring and evaluation processes.

SUMMARY

As school psychologists, it is important to ask what we can do to aid in efforts to fully engage families. The role and extent of assistance necessary will be determined largely by the needs of the school system and the families of the children served. However, we assert that the school psychologist has a critical role in facilitating systematic reform efforts from traditional parent involvement practices to an approach that fully engages parents and develops lasting family–school partnerships.

A school's approach toward engagement and partnership determines in large part the attitudes and atmosphere experienced by families. Each of these is prerequisite to actions that either promote meaningful roles or discourage partnership practices. Together, the approach, attitudes, atmosphere, and actions set the stage for student achievement. Communication between school and home, and vice versa, is an operational means by which partnerships are realized. Family–school partnerships are a function of both foundational elements (such as trust and shared commitment to a student's success), and outward, constructive practices (such as home–school notes and joint problem solving). Engaging with families as partners requires an intentional approach predominated by a set of values held by professionals and not a prescribed set of isolated activities or practices. In the end, genuine and intentional efforts to link home and school in support of student learning define best practices in school psychological practice.

AUTHOR NOTE

Preparation of this chapter was supported in part by the Institute of Education Sciences, U.S. Department of Education, through Grant R324A100115 to the University of Nebraska-Lincoln. The opinions expressed are those of the authors and do not represent views of the Institute of Education Sciences or the U.S. Department of Education.

Disclosure. Susan M. Sheridan and Sandra L. Christenson have a financial interest in books they authored or coauthored referenced in this chapter.

REFERENCES

Adams, K. S., & Christenson, S. L. (2000). Trust and the family-school relationship examination of parent-teacher differences in elementary and secondary grades. *Journal of School Psychology, 38,* 477–497. doi:10.1016/s0022-4405(00)00048-0

Blue-Banning, M., Summers, J. A., Frankland, H. C., Nelson, L. L., & Beegle, G. (2004). Dimensions of family and professional partners: Constructive guidelines for collaboration. *Exceptional Children, 70,* 167–184.

Bryk, A. S., & Schneider, B. (2002). *Trust in schools: A core resource for improvement.* New York, NY: Russell Sage Foundation.

Christenson, S. L. (2004). The family–school partnership: An opportunity to promote the learning competence of all students. *School Psychology Review, 33,* 83–104.

Christenson, S. L., Hurley, C., Sheridan, S. M., & Fenstermacher, K. (1997). Parents' and school psychologists' perspectives on parent involvement activities. *School Psychology Review, 26,* 111–130.

Christenson, S. L., & Reschly, A. L. (2010). Check & Connect: Enhancing school completion through student engagement. In E. Doll & J. Charvat (Eds.), *Handbook of prevention science* (pp. 327–348). New York, NY: Routledge.

Christenson, S. L., & Sheridan, S. M. (2001). *Schools and families: Creating essential connections for learning.* New York, NY: Guilford Press.

Christenson, S. L., Stout, K., & Pohl, A. (2012). *Check & Connect: A comprehensive student engagement intervention: Implementing with fidelity.* Minneapolis, MN: University of Minnesota, Institute on Community Integration.

Clarke, B. L., Sheridan, S. M., & Woods, K. E. (2010). Elements of healthy family-school relationships. In S. Christenson & A. Reschly (Eds.), *Handbook of school-family partnerships* (pp. 61–79). New York, NY: Routledge.

Downer, J. T., & Pianta, R. C. (2006). Academic and cognitive functioning in first grade: Associations with earlier home and child care predictors and with concurrent home and classroom experiences. *School Psychology Review, 35,* 11–30.

Dunsmuir, S., Frederickson, N., & Lang, J. (2004). Building home-school trust. *Educational and Child Psychology, 21,* 110–128.

Dunst, C. J. (2000). Revisiting "rethinking early intervention." *Topics in Early Childhood Special Education, 20,* 95–104.

Farrington, C. A., Roderick, M., Allensworth, E., Nagaoka, J., Keyes, T. S., Johnson, D. W., & Beechum, N. O. (2012). *Teaching adolescents to become learners. The role of noncognitive factors in shaping school performance: A critical literature review.* Chicago, IL: University of Chicago Consortium on Chicago School Research.

Fishel, M., & Ramirez, L. (2005). Evidence-based parent involvement interventions with school-aged children. *School Psychology Quarterly, 20,* 371–402.

Gestwicki, C. (2000). *Home, school, and community relations: A guide to working with families* (4th ed.). Albany, NY: Delmar.

Guli, L. A. (2005). Evidence-based parent consultation with school-related outcomes. *School Psychology Quarterly, 20,* 455–472.

Henderson, A. T., Mapp, K. L., Johnson, V. R., & Davies, D. (2007). *Beyond the bake sale: The essential guide to family-school partnerships.* New York, NY: The New Press.

Hirsh-Pasek, K., & Burchinal, M. (2006). Putting language learning in context: How change at home and in school affects language growth across time. *Merrill Palmer Quarterly, 52,* 449–485.

Hoover-Dempsey, K. V., & Sandler, H. M. (1997). Why do parents become involved in their children's education? *Review of Educational Research, 67,* 3–42.

Hoover-Dempsey, K. V., Walker, J. M. T., Sandler, H. M., Whetsel, D., Green, C. L., Wilkins, A. S., & Closson, K. E. (2005). Why do parents become involved? Research findings and implications. *Elementary School Journal, 106,* 105–130.

Kerns, K. A., Klepac, L., & Cole, A. (1996). Peer relationships and preadolescents' perception of security in the child-mother relationship. *Developmental Psychology, 32,* 457–466.

Lareau, A., & McNamara-Horvat, E. (1999). Moments of social inclusion and exclusion: Race, class, and cultural capital in family-school relationships. *Sociology of Education, 72,* 37–53.

Lines, C., Miller, G. E., & Arthur-Stanley, A. (2011). *The power of family-school partnering (FSP): A practical guide for school mental health professionals and educators.* New York, NY: Routledge.

Mahoney, G., Boyce, G., Fewell, R. R., Spiker, D., & Wheeden, C. A. (1998). The relationship of parent-child interaction to the effectiveness of early intervention services for at-risk children and children with disabilities. *Topics in Early Childhood Special Education, 18,* 5–17.

Minke, K. M. (2006). Parent–teacher relationship. In G. G. Bear & K. M. Minke (Eds.), *Children's needs III: Development, prevention, and intervention* (pp. 73–85). Bethesda, MD: National Association of School Psychologists.

National Association of School Psychologists. (2010). *Model for comprehensive and integrated school psychological services.* Bethesda, MD: Author. Retrieved from http://www.nasponline.org/standards/2010standards/2_PracticeModel.pdf

Patrikakou, E. N., & Weissberg, R. P. (1999). The seven P's of school-family partnerships. *Education Week, 18*(21), 34–36.

Sheridan, S. M., Bovaird, J. A., Glover, T. A., Garbacz, S. A., Witte, A., & Kwon, K. (2012). A randomized trial examining the effects of conjoint behavioral consultation and the mediating role of the parent–teacher relationship. *School Psychology Review, 41,* 23–46.

Sheridan, S. M., Eagle, J. W., & Doll, B. (2006). An examination of the efficacy of conjoint behavioral consultation with diverse clients. *School Psychology Quarterly, 21,* 396–417.

Sheridan, S. M., & Gutkin, T. B. (2000). The ecology of school psychology: Examining and changing our paradigm for the 21st century. *School Psychology Review, 29,* 485–502.

Sheridan, S. M., & Kratochwill, T. R. (2008). *Conjoint behavioral consultation: Promoting family-school connections and interventions.* New York, NY: Springer.

Sheridan, S. M., Marvin, C. A., Knoche, L. L., & Edwards, C. P. (2008). Getting ready: Promoting school readiness through a relationship-based partnership model. *Early Childhood Services, 2,* 149–172.

Sjuts, T. M., & Sheridan, S. M. (2011). *Self-assessment of Parent Engagement Practices (SPEP).* Lincoln, NE: University of Nebraska-Lincoln, Center for Research on Children, Youth, Families, and Schools.

31

Best Practices in Systems-Level Organization and Support for Effective Family–School Partnerships

Laura Lee McIntyre
S. Andrew Garbacz
University of Oregon

OVERVIEW

Meaningful partnerships between families and educators are more than family nights and "Welcome Parents!" banners. Family–school partnerships represent a philosophy about work among families and educators that is focused on enhancing student performance (Christenson & Sheridan, 2001). A partner, by definition, is someone who has a joint share in something. Thus, when school psychologists work on behalf of students, families and educators develop a shared understanding of students' performance such that goals are cocreated, decisions are made in a joint fashion (Reschly & Christenson, 2012), and consistency across environments is emphasized (Crosnoe, Leventhal, Wirth, Pierce, & Pianta, 2010). The importance of family–school partnerships has been indicated by the National Association of School Psychologists (NASP). Specifically, family–school partnerships are linked to the NASP *Model for Comprehensive and Integrated School Psychological Services* (NASP, 2010) through the Family–School Collaboration domain.

Substantial empirical support exists to support family–school partnering. When families are engaged in their children's education, academic performance is enhanced (Jeynes, 2005), school and home behavior improves (Sheridan, Bovaird, Glover, Garbacz, & Witte, 2012), and behavior problems can be prevented (Domina, 2005). In addition, the parent–teacher relationship improves when parents and teachers partner (Sheridan et al., 2012). School psychologists can play a key role in promoting positive family–school partnerships.

Owing to the positive outcomes associated with family engagement and explicit NASP recommendations for family–school collaboration, it may be tempting for school psychologists to implement a stand-alone family–school partnership program to create positive outcomes. On the contrary, it is the case that family–school partnering can be aligned with common school-wide frameworks, such as school-wide positive behavior support (Fosco et al., in press) and problem-solving models (Sheridan & Kratochwill, 2008). Thus, we recommend that school psychologists embed family–school partnership programs into these school-wide frameworks, as systems-level supports are more likely to be sustainable and can cut across settings, such as home and school.

A systems perspective considers the school to be the level of analysis rather than an individual student, classroom, teacher, or parent. This shift allows for school-wide implementation of practices that are designed to meet common goals. In order for school-wide practices to be adopted, there must be formal support for implementation at the state, regional, and/ or school district level (Sugai & Horner, 2002). This top-down support may take many forms, including the administrative adoption of policies designed to encourage the implementation of practices, the establishment of district coordination teams, allocation of resources, and the prioritization of initiatives. Furthermore, these policies and practices are adopted by the superintendent, school board, and building administrators, providing additional administrative support. Although

455

administrator support is essential for implementing a school-wide set of practices, staff buy-in at the local level is crucial. Sugai and Horner (2002) argue for a top-down approach to implementation, yet stress the importance of staff buy-in and input regarding intervention practices and school culture values. In this chapter we argue that school psychologists can use a similar systems framework to support family–school partnering.

The purpose of this chapter is to provide school psychologists with foundational knowledge to implement practices that support family–school partnership activities within a systems framework. Specific learning objectives for school psychologists include (a) understand the key elements for fostering family–school partnerships, (b) apply a systems-level framework to an ecological approach to school-based family intervention, (c) understand how to adopt systems-level organization and support to the implementation of best practices in family–school partnering, and (d) apply knowledge of systems-level organization and support to best practices in family–school partnerships through a school psychology practice case example.

Family–school partnering within a systems-level organization will be reviewed in the sections that follow to highlight pragmatic and meaningful ways that school psychologists can engage families and educators in partnership to support students.

BASIC CONSIDERATIONS

There are key conceptual and contextual issues to consider when creating and maintaining systems-level organization and supports for family–school partnerships. Christenson and Sheridan (2001) provided an organizing framework for school psychologists and other school personnel to use when partnering with families. The conceptual framework Christenson and Sheridan articulated holds particular meaning for systems-level organization and support, as the themes they discuss reflect school-wide practices to enhance systems-level activities. Christenson and Sheridan's framework will be briefly reviewed and linked to relevant family–school partnership literature to indicate systems-level approaches for family–school partnering.

Key Elements for Family–School Partnerships

Christenson and Sheridan (2001) articulated four elements important for family–school work: approach, attitudes, atmosphere, and actions. Through an evaluation of each component, school psychologists can develop organizational strategies to enhance their work with families to best meet student needs. Christenson and Sheridan (2001) indicate that a partnering approach moves beyond identifying the influence of individuals and contexts in a child's life "to organizing these influences in a way that accounts for the reciprocal interaction among multiple influences" (p. 31). The approach school psychologists take with families sets the stage for how future work will be framed. When approaching work with families, school psychologists should consider their beliefs about the family's role in their child's education and their school's process for welcoming and supporting partnerships (Lines, Miller, & Arthur-Stanley, 2011). Attitudes held by school personnel can influence interactions with families. For example, school psychologists may consider families partners when responsibilities for educating children are shared. A school's view of families as *partners* rather than participants should be communicated to families (e.g., through invitations; Walker, Ice, Hoover-Dempsey, & Sandler, 2011) such that the contributions of all are emphasized (Sheridan, Rispoli, & Holmes, in press). A school's atmosphere is the tone of the school that is communicated to families. The atmosphere should communicate that active and meaningful partnerships among families and educators are valued. Central to the atmosphere of the school is how communication among families and educators occurs. Communication in family–school partnerships should be multidirectional (Sheridan et al., in press) to provide parents and educators the opportunity to share information (Garbacz et al., 2008). School psychologists can lead the efforts in facilitating communication that is inviting to all parties and stakeholders who are involved in educating children.

The final element in Christenson and Sheridan's (2001) framework is actions, or the ways families and educators share responsibility. Family–school partnership activities occur across settings and contexts. In schools, families can engage in school governance, go on class trips, and serve on school-based problem-solving teams. In homes, parents can work with their children on homework, provide rewards for meeting school expectations, and implement house rules that are aligned with school rules and expectations. Schools and homes establish consistency (Crosnoe et al., 2010) in healthy family–school partnerships such that the unique contextual factors are respected while coordinated systems of support for students are built.

Ecological Approach to Family Intervention and Treatment

To demonstrate elements of family–school partnerships, the Ecological Approach to Family Intervention and Treatment (EcoFIT; Fosco et al., in press) will be discussed as a model for framing systems-level organizational supports for partnering activities in schools. The EcoFIT approach was originally designed to be implemented in schools using school-wide positive behavior supports. However, the EcoFIT framework may also be suitable for school psychologists searching for an organizational, school-wide approach to family–school partnerships. In either instance, school psychologists may find it useful to establish organizational structures for family–school partnerships that are consistent with common school practices (e.g., identifying and acknowledging student appropriate behavior). Intervention approaches within EcoFIT will be briefly introduced and discussed within each tier of common systems frameworks (i.e., universal, selected, indicated) to demonstrate one approach to systems-level organizational supports for family–school partnerships. An expanded discussion of EcoFIT is available in other locations (e.g., Fosco et al., in press; Fosco, Dishion, & Stormshak, 2012).

At the universal level, EcoFIT uses three primary interventions: a family resource room, parent outreach activities (e.g., a parenting night on effective homework strategies), and school-wide detection and referral systems (e.g., a parent school-readiness screener; Fosco et al., in press). These activities address the school's approach to work with families by establishing proactive procedures, creating conditions to support multidirectional communication, and designing a parent-friendly and welcoming atmosphere. At the selected level, a family–school version of the Check-in/Check-out system (Crone, Hawken, & Horner, 2010) is used. This adapted framework allows parents and educators opportunities to discuss behavior concerns and address them together before concerns reach the indicated level.

The primary indicated intervention in EcoFIT is the family checkup (Fosco et al., 2012). The family checkup is a family-centered approach whereby a consultant guides a family through ecological assessments and assessment-derived interventions. The family checkup establishes conditions to support partnerships from the outset. Specifically, the decision to proceed with a family checkup is made as part of a collaborative set of interactions with families. A school psychologist,

in conjunction with the family and other educators, may initiate a family checkup. In a family checkup, interventions are linked to unique environmental strengths and needs reported by parents and teachers. Further, parents' and teachers' motivation to change is assessed and used to determine appropriate interventions and support strategies (Fosco et al., in press). School psychologists may serve as parent consultants and create partnership-centered atmospheres through (a) using a strengths-based orientation, (b) indicating that families are the experts about what will work for them and with their family, and (c) providing support and expertise about empirically supported strategies parents can use that meet their unique needs. These partnership-centered approaches are consistent with other indicated family–school partnership problem-solving models (e.g., Conjoint Behavioral Consultation; Sheridan & Kratochwill, 2008). Although the family checkup serves as the indicated intervention in the EcoFIT model, this intervention is situated within a tiered system of family–school partnership activities and interventions that provides a framework for providing all students, educators, and families with supports that promote family–school partnerships.

BEST PRACTICES IN SYSTEMS SUPPORT FOR FAMILY–SCHOOL PARTNERSHIPS

Figure 31.1 depicts our model of system-wide organization and support for effective family–school partnerships in promoting positive student and family outcomes. This figure is intended to be an organizing heuristic that highlights the relationship between implementing evidence-based strategies using a systems approach and key student and family outcomes.

As shown, system-wide organization and support provides a framework for implementing evidence-based strategies in schools. The focus of this chapter is on system-wide organization and support as it relates to best practices in family–school partnerships. It is beyond the scope of this chapter to review evidence-based instructional strategies and evidence-based behavioral strategies. Nevertheless, we see the implementation of all these evidence-based strategies (i.e., instructional, behavioral, and family–school partnering) as benefiting from system-wide organization and support. Thus, we are inclusive of evidence-based instructional, behavioral, and family–school partnering strategies within this model.

As shown in Figure 31.1, our model highlights the key role that system-wide organization and support plays in promoting positive outcomes. We include *both* student

Figure 31.1. Systems-Level Organization and Support for Effective Family–School Partnerships

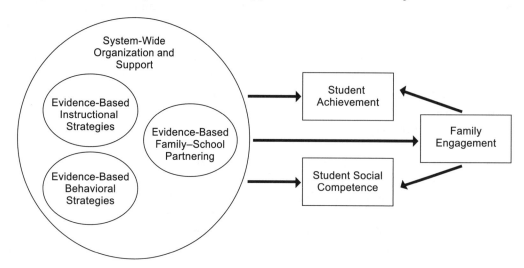

and family outcomes in our model given the literature linking evidence-based instructional and behavioral supports and family–school partnering activities to positive student and family outcomes. Indeed, when families and educators partner together, family engagement (e.g., parent–teacher communication and relationships) is enhanced (Sheridan et al., 2012). Adopting a systems approach in the implementation of evidence-based strategies at school may lead to gains in student achievement and social competence. When evidence-based family–school partnering activities are implemented, family engagement may be enhanced. We argue that family engagement can be considered a key outcome, as well as a variable that may influence student achievement and social competence. The arrows that point from family engagement back to student achievement and social competence highlight this relationship (see Figure 31.1).

Given the narrow scope of this chapter, the remainder of this section will focus on best practices in systems-level organization and support for promoting effective family–school partnerships. We note that this is only one part of the conceptual model depicted in Figure 31.1. We conclude with a discussion of multicultural competence, recommendations for partnering with families from diverse backgrounds, and evaluation of outcomes.

System-Wide Organization and Support

In order for stakeholders to adopt practices, policies, and procedures that promote the implementation of family–school partnering activities to improve outcomes for students and families, stakeholders must agree on common shared values. That is, they must agree that promoting family–school partnering is worthy of investing district resources.

Shared Value of Family–School Partnering

Evidence suggests that promoting family–school partnerships yields valuable outcomes for student achievement and social behavior (Jeynes, 2005) and is associated with lower rates of high school dropout (Barnard, 2004). This evidence creates a compelling argument for the need to invest in formal, system-wide supports to adopt and implement family–school partnering activities. School psychologists can promote the value of family–school partnering activities by engaging in conversations with families, school personnel, and district leaders about the benefits of family–school partnering. In so doing, school psychologists may serve as powerful advocates for investing in family–school partnerships.

Resource Allocation

In order for system-wide efforts to be effective in promoting the uptake of family–school partnering activities, adequate resources must be allocated to support family–school partnering activities (Christenson & Sheridan, 2001). Educational or district consultants may be needed to provide information to building administrators about partnering with families. We see school psychologists as uniquely positioned to function in this capacity. Additional resources should be requested for staff training, coaching, and technical assistance in partnering with families. Further, a district investment should be made to develop or implement an adequate data collection and monitoring system to track student outcomes and family engagement.

District- and Building-Level Policies and Procedures

Policies and procedures within districts and school buildings should be linked to relevant state and federal regulations and policies, and professional organization standards and position statements (e.g., *School–Family Partnering to Enhance Learning: Essential Elements and Responsibilities*; NASP, 2012). There are several considerations in determining how policies may be operationalized for universal procedures. First, it is important that key (e.g., an administrator) and representative staff (e.g., one teacher from each grade level) are involved in decision making. In addition, family needs and views of procedures should be sought (Raffaele & Knoff, 1999). For example, school psychologists may lead a school building or district town hall meeting or distribute surveys to parents to elicit suggestions and feedback (Raffaele & Knoff, 1999). After consensus is achieved for a set of explicit policies, school psychologists should communicate to the larger school community (e.g., teachers, support staff, parents, community stakeholders). Inclusive communication of this material should aim to reach all families directly (i.e., rather than rely on other parents to communicate it; Hill, 2010). In addition, school psychologists should use multidirectional communication methods that foster a free exchange of information (Sheridan et al., in press) such that all members of the school community have opportunities to ask questions and have their questions answered. These communication methods can encourage a shared understanding of goals and initiatives (Grimes & Tilly, 1996).

Establishing a Local Leadership Team

After policies have been agreed upon and disseminated, there are several considerations for local implementation. The first step is to establish a local team. The team should be representative of the school building, and include teachers and parents or caregivers from all grades, an administrator, and community stakeholders. A school psychologist could organize and lead the local leadership team or could serve as a team member. Organization of a local leadership team is similar to the creation of a school-wide positive behavior support team (Horner et al., 2009), but is expanded to include more family and community representation. The team's primary aim should be to promote a vision for shared responsibility and ownership of school community procedures among all community members.

Primary tasks of the school-wide team include common procedures, but will be operationalized for multitiered family–school partnership activities, specifically at the universal level. At this stage of implementation, readiness and consensus have been attained, and school psychologists would have communicated basic family–school initiatives to families. Specific team tasks at this juncture focus on identifying expectations, establishing a mechanism for collecting data on important outcomes, and engaging in data-based decision making.

Family–school partnering expectations should be operationalized across grade levels, as different partnering activities are relevant for certain grades (Christenson & Sheridan, 2001). For example, different home–school communication activities may exist across early childhood and kindergarten settings (Rimm-Kaufman & Pianta, 1999). Specifically, a partnering expectation in pre-K may include a daily home–school note or brief after school conferences whereas a home–school communication expectation in kindergarten may include biweekly contacts. Thus, general expectations may be the same across some grades (e.g., home–school communication), but will be operationalized differently. Rationales for the different approaches to partnering across grade levels should be communicated by school psychologists to families.

Communicating these rationales can serve at least two purposes. First, for families with children of different ages, it may help them discriminate partnering activities between their children. In addition, it can help parents understand their children's developmental processes. Owing to the multidimensional nature of partnering activities, expectations for partnering exist across settings (e.g., home, school), and include structural (e.g., reinforcing expectations) and relational (e.g., identifying the equal roles of families and educators) features.

District Coordination

System-wide supports should be formally managed at the district level (e.g., Sugai & Horner, 2002). In practice, this means that school districts coordinate and implement supports, both in terms of identifying and coordinating implementation of evidence-based instruction and behavioral supports and family–school partnering activities. Practices are adopted by the superintendent and school boards and implemented at the school building level with administrator support. In terms of family–school partnering activities, administrators establish expectations for partnering activities (Christenson & Sheridan, 2001) and communicate these expectations to stakeholders. In so doing, clear and coherent messages about partnering approaches are communicated to staff and families. Early on these messages should focus on establishing principles rather than procedures so that appropriate rationales are provided (Grimes & Tilly, 1996). Later, family–school partnering teams can establish policies and procedures based on input from all parties. Family–school partnering coordinators can hold office hours or drop-in times for families to allow a mechanism for families to provide input about school policies (Christenson & Sheridan, 2001). When establishing family–school partnering activities, it is important that at the outset administrators identify the roles of family and educators. We view school psychologists to be uniquely positioned to serve as family–school partnering coordinators given their background and training in education and psychology.

Staff Buy-In

It is important for school staff to have buy-in and input regarding family–school partnering activities. Although system-wide organization and support at the district level is crucial for implementing wide-scale policies and practices, educators and families should come together and be included in the process of creating their school culture for family–school partnering. Staff buy-in and district-level coordination stem from the positive behavior support literature (e.g., Horner et al., 2009). At a basic level, school psychologists can create opportunities for staff and family stakeholders to develop a common shared vision for supporting education intervention practices. Communication among stakeholders can help solidify what this vision will be. To garner staff buy-in and input, school psychologists can structure conversations to illicit feedback regarding what it means for parents and educators to be partners. True partners share responsibility for creating an inviting climate and school culture of family–school collaboration (Christenson & Sheridan, 2001). In establishing stakeholder buy-in, a shared vision for supporting educational outcomes for children within the community can be created.

Establishing Capacity

Establishing capacity is important for ensuring that educational practices remain relevant and are implemented with procedural fidelity (McIntosh, Horner, & Sugai, 2009). McIntosh et al. (2009) offer several

practical suggestions for establishing capacity for school-wide positive behavior supports. We suggest that establishing capacity for family–school partnering activities use a similar framework of system-wide organization and support. Specifically, McIntosh et al. (2009) suggest that the practices within a multitier framework have good contextual fit. That is, practices should address important problems in schools and be aligned with the values of the school building and larger system. Family–school partnering activities should be regularly evaluated to ensure that they continue to have a meaningful impact on family–school relations and student outcomes and that they reflect the needs and culture of the school and community context. Ongoing evaluation allows for continued review of the effectiveness of practices as well as the continued review of ease and efficiency of practice implementation. Ongoing evaluation of procedural fidelity can also inform staff training needs, as well as help teams interpret outcomes associated with practices.

McIntosh et al. (2009) suggest that districts provide adequate resources for staffing and leadership. In order to establish capacity for the implementation of family–school partnering activities, we suggest that districts invest money, faculty/staff time release, and training for educators to oversee the implementation of family–school partnering activities at the district and local levels. Further, we suggest that administrators make family–school partnering a priority and make this priority visible at the district and state levels. District support ensures that competing initiatives are minimized and that practices are sustainable and valued across systems (McIntosh et al., 2009).

Multicultural Competence

Systemic supports for family–school partnerships require that school personnel meet the needs of all families. Common educational practices in the United States may not provide sufficient opportunities for all families to engage in their children's education. For example, families who do not speak English fluently may not be able to benefit from a parent training session conducted in English. Thus, families who have unique or diverse background characteristics require that school psychologists and other school personnel give them special consideration and create structural supports to meet their needs.

All families want to support their children, but due to familial, background, or cultural characteristics they may not communicate this desire in a manner typically understood by school personnel. Specifically, families and school personnel may differ in how they understand a parent's role in his or her child's education (e.g., parental role construction; Walker, Wilkins, Dallaire, Sandler, & Hoover-Dempsey, 2005). For example, parents who engage in indirect home-based educational support for their child (e.g., creating a space at home where educational activities can occur) are engaging in valuable practices that may not be communicated to school personnel (Walker et al., 2011).

Significant barriers exist (e.g., lack of knowledge/participation in the education system) for developing and maintaining family–school partnerships, especially when families lack familiarity with common education procedures used in public schools in the United States. However, evidence suggests that families who recently immigrated to the United States can implement complex and systematic behavior intervention plans in a manner aligned with common educational practices (Swanger-Gagné, Garbacz, & Sheridan, 2009). In addition, families of diverse backgrounds may differ in terms of the type of support they want or need (Huntsinger & Jose, 2009). Recent reviews of the family–school partnership literature have sought to uncover evidence-based family–school practices to support families with diverse characteristics. Such reviews have indicated that although recommendations have emerged, the field is not yet able to specify cultural models of family engagement (Okagaki & Bingham, 2010). Nevertheless, some researchers (e.g., Walker et al., 2011) have been able to provide data-based recommendations for working with families of diverse backgrounds.

Recommendations for Partnering With Families From Diverse Backgrounds

Three recommendations for fostering family–school partnerships with families from diverse cultural backgrounds are communicate clearly and effectively (Sheridan et al., in press), use proactive rather than reactive strategies (e.g., Fosco et al., in press), and create a culturally inclusive school community (Hill, 2010).

Communication

School psychologists and other school personnel should use jargon-free language and use multidirectional communication methods (Sheridan et al., in press). Multidirectional communication strategies allow families and educators to share information in similar ways using language that does not rely on a specific set of

experiences (e.g., an advanced degree in education). Further, Hill (2010) indicates the importance of giving information to parents "freely, wholly, and willingly" (p. 120). This approach allows families of all backgrounds and roles in a school to access and understand key information. School psychologists can model this type of communication to school personnel and champion a school's efforts in facilitating positive family–school relationships with families from all backgrounds.

Use of Proactive Strategies

We recommend that school psychologists use proactive strategies when engaging with families from diverse backgrounds. The use of proactive rather than reactive strategies has at least three goals. First, building relationships with families prior to the development of specific concerns allows educators to set parameters and expectations for partnering and communicate partnering roles. Second, support plans that are collaboratively developed when target concerns arise may be more effective when expectations of shared responsibility for educational procedures are set. Third, the use of proactive strategies allows school psychologists and other educators the opportunity to address family concerns about their role in their child's education or specific concerns they may have for their child. Fosco and colleagues (in press) identify the utility of a parent readiness screener to gather initial information about parent-reported behavior concerns for children and their desire for assistance. School psychologists can use a similar screener to engage families in conversations about their concerns and desire for assistance. In addition, school psychologists can make explicit invitations to parents and teachers to discuss their shared goals for students. Such invitations, when made early on, can enhance family–educator relationships to increase parent involvement at school for parents of diverse cultural backgrounds (Walker et al., 2011).

Creation of Culturally Inclusive School Communities

School psychologists should work within their buildings and districts to create a culturally inclusive school community (Hill, 2010). Creating a culturally inclusive community is a complex task that involves validating cultural characteristics, integrating diverse cultural perspectives into academic material, and communicating to students that their individuality is valued (Hill, 2010). School psychologists can lead school personnel to engage in ongoing, honest assessments of their beliefs and the school community atmosphere to determine in what ways they may be explicitly or implicitly using approaches that favor families and students of certain backgrounds (Hill, 2010). The school-wide Caring School Community program (Battistich, Schaps, Watson, Solomon, & Lewis, 2000) aims to create a caring community that includes families and school personnel. Among other strategies, this approach seeks to engage each student in understanding certain family background characteristics, and connects families and educators in school-wide activities. Parents of certain backgrounds may also find it useful to connect with other parents in the school community. School psychologists can provide structured opportunities for these interactions to occur.

Evaluation of Outcomes

To evaluate the impact of systems support for family–school partnerships on key student outcomes, a mechanism for collecting data on important outcomes should be created. If schools are implementing school-wide positive behavior supports, the School-Wide Information System (May et al., 2000) can be used.

Data Collection

Specific outcomes that may be considered include school attendance, student achievement, student social competence, office discipline referrals, and family engagement. Family engagement should be collaboratively defined during team meetings with a building's family–school partnership team. Definitions of behavior outcomes and school practices should be based on family and educator priorities (Sheridan et al., in press). Many procedural details must be set before data can be used. For example, office referral forms need to be modified and aligned with the data entry system; individuals responsible for compiling, filing, and entering data should be identified; and procedures for summarizing and reporting data should be solidified. The data collection tasks can be coordinated by the family–school partnership team or can be coordinated by another ongoing team, depending on resources and priorities.

Data-Based Decisions

Once a data system is set, procedures for engaging in data-based decision making should be identified. Review of data include a discussion of the outcomes of interest, but should also note strengths of the school community. Family–school partnership programs that promote a strengths-based orientation can produce prosocial and adaptive outcomes (Sheridan et al., 2012). Hence, it may

be useful for the school system to focus first on building skills and competencies and second on reducing problem behavior. Based on the school team's outcomes of interest, data-based goals should be created so that future reviews of data can focus on evaluating progress toward goals. Goals should be observable and measurable, and represent a shared understanding (among school community members) of strengths and needs (Sheridan et al., in press). The school team should include representative parents and caregivers from all grade levels as well as community stakeholders. However, procedures for sharing data and progress toward goals with the larger school community must be set.

Discussion With Stakeholders

Discussions with the larger school community about activities such as progress toward shared goals, meaningfulness of outcomes, and engagement with the systems supports should be structured in an ongoing fashion. Many of the strategies that were used initially to create readiness and build consensus should be revisited at frequent intervals (as determined by the school team). School psychologists and other personnel may decide on a variety of ways to elicit feedback from the larger school community at this stage (e.g., town hall meetings). Similar to during implementation of universal supports, the focus should be on using proactive strategies that use multidirectional communication mechanisms.

Case Example

To illustrate how elements of systems-level organization and support for family school partnerships could be operationalized, we provide a fictional case example. Mary is a school psychologist with many years of experience working with children, families, and school personnel in a variety of capacities. During the summer, Mary was told she would be transferring to Sunnyside Elementary School. Sunnyside is a K–5 school in a suburban area of the United States. During her first meeting with the principal, Mary discovered that Sunnyside has been implementing the universal system of school-wide positive behavior supports to criterion for the previous 2 years. In addition, some selected and indicated strategies are used. The principal informed Mary that she recently attended a workshop about family–school partnerships and would like to do more to reach families in the school community. The principal gave Mary the task of forming organizational supports for family–school partnerships at Sunnyside.

We will describe conceptual approaches, as well as systems-level organizational supports for family–school partnerships at the universal, selected, and indicated tiers that we recommend Mary consider as she proceeds with the task.

Conceptual and Planning Considerations

Key initial considerations Mary will want to address include evaluating existing resources (e.g., systems-level organizational supports for students, parent–teacher associations) and identifying important stakeholders (e.g., administrators, district personnel, school personnel on school-wide teams, family members). Early discussions with important stakeholders should evaluate current relationships between families and school staff, possible strategies to encourage family–school partnerships, attitudes among school staff and families about partnering, and ways to align family–school partnership strategies with an existing school-wide positive behavior support framework.

After preliminary discussions have occurred, Mary should form a family–school team that includes representative individuals from the school community (e.g., administrators, teachers, parents). Together, the family–school team should develop shared goals and priorities for family–school partnerships within their school community that are aligned with the framework proposed by Christenson and Sheridan (2001). To guide the development of goals, the team should consider distributing a survey and/or engaging in focus groups with members of the school community to gather information about, for example, specific strengths and needs, school personnel and parent approaches to family–school interactions, and attitudes about partnering held by school personnel and parents. The Sunnyside family–school team identified specific needs regarding its general approach with all families in the school community, and minimal family–school connections within the school-wide positive behavior support framework.

Universal Strategies

The family–school team decided to initially target two primary universal organizational family–school strategies: (a) the school's approach with families and (b) the school's atmosphere. To target the school's approach with families, the family–school team used the family resource room concept proposed by EcoFIT (Fosco et al., 2012) and applied it to the whole school. Specifically, the team felt their school should function as a supportive environment for all members of the school community.

The family–school team partnered with other parents to create a welcoming atmosphere that is inclusive of family and educator cultural diversity. Multidirectional communication mechanisms were established (e.g., a parent school-readiness screener), effective parenting resources were made available (Fosco et al., in press), and teachers and administrators invited parents to visit the school and classrooms at any time and provide feedback about their visits. Finally, to build consistency with the school-wide positive behavior support framework, the family–school team began holding biweekly meetings with the school-wide positive behavior support team to identify ways to align family–school procedures with the school's universal school-wide positive behavior support strategies.

Selected and Indicated Strategies

As Sunnyside recently developed selected and indicated strategies within the school-wide positive behavior support framework, the school-wide positive behavior support team and the family–school team were able to easily identify family-centered strategies to use. Sunnyside adopted Check-in/Check-out (Crone et al., 2010), and together the two school teams determined that families would be contacted when Check-in/Check-out was considered for a student so discussions about the appropriateness of this strategy could be discussed with the family. If the family and school staff together determined Check-in/Check-out would be appropriate, they would develop the specific Check-in/Check-out procedures collaboratively (e.g., determine whether home-based incentives could be linked to performance at school).

At the indicated level, Sunnyside used behavioral consultation (Kratochwill & Bergan, 1990) to identify target concerns and develop functionally appropriate intervention plans. The family–school team proposed that the school-wide positive behavior support team should also adopt the family checkup for families that reported a need for additional support and the parent school-readiness screener to establish family-centered home–school connections. These more intensive interventions have been shown to enhance student outcomes across settings (e.g., Fosco et al., 2012).

Evaluation of Outcomes

Given that the school-wide positive behavior support team at Sunnyside adopted the school-wide information system (May et al., 2000) to aid in data collection, assist with monitoring key outcomes, and assist with data-based decision making, the family–school team proposed that the School-Wide Information System be used to monitor outcomes associated with the system-level family–school partnering activities. Specifically, the family–school team proposed that, in addition to collecting data on student attendance, office discipline referrals, and student achievement, that data on family engagement also be monitored. The team recommended that utilization of the Sunnyside family resource room be monitored and that family engagement in their child's selected and indicated strategies be recorded. The team recommended that these data be reviewed on an ongoing basis and be used to inform decisions about whether the family–school partnership strategies were associated with positive student and family outcomes.

Conclusion

The systems-level organizational supports Sunnyside initiated were linked to the strengths and needs of the school community. Thus, when considering organizational supports for family–school partnerships it is important school psychologists tailor the school's strategies with contextual factors and information gleaned from assessments. Finally, special consideration should be giving to cultural diversity within the school community to guide assessment approaches and organizational strategies. A plan for data collection, monitoring, and decision making must also be embedded into the organizational and systems support for family–school partnerships.

SUMMARY

Family–school partnerships represent a philosophy about how educators and family members work together to support student outcomes. Central to the implementation of family–school partnering activities is the identification of key stakeholders and the articulation of shared goals for working together. Evidence-based family–school partnering activities that reflect the culture, goals, and vision of families and educators can be implemented within a systems perspective if best practices in system-wide organization and supports are used. District resources must be allocated to support this initiative. Further, district- and building-level policies should be developed based on district priorities and input from key family and educational stakeholders. Local leadership teams should be developed with coordination occurring at the district level. Part and parcel of systems-level organization and support is ongoing evaluation of key outcomes, with data informing decisions about practices and school and district

policy. Finally, in order to be effective at partnering with families and other educators, school psychologists should strive to use culturally responsive practices that respect individual differences.

AUTHOR NOTE

Preparation of this chapter was supported in part by grant R01HD059838 from the National Institute of Child Health and Human Development awarded to the first author.

REFERENCES

Barnard, W. M. (2004). Parent involvement in elementary school and educational attainment. *Children and Youth Services Review, 26*, 39–62.

Battistich, V., Schaps, E., Watson, M., Solomon, D., & Lewis, C. (2000). Effects of the child development project on students' drug use and other problems. *The Journal of Primary Prevention, 21*, 75–99. doi:10.1023/A:1007057414994

Christenson, S. L., & Sheridan, S. M. (2001). *Schools and families: Creating essential connections for learning.* New York, NY: Guilford Press.

Crone, D., Hawken, L., & Horner, R. (2010). *Responding to problem behavior in schools* (2nd ed.). New York, NY: Guilford Press.

Crosnoe, R., Leventhal, T., Wirth, R. J., Pierce, K. M., & Pianta, R. C. (2010). Family socioeconomic status and consistent environmental stimulation in early childhood. *Child Development, 81*, 972–987. doi:10.111/j.1467-8624.2010.01446.x

Domina, T. (2005). Leveling the home advantage: Assessing the effectiveness of parental involvement in elementary school. *Sociology of Education, 78*, 233–249. doi:10.1177/003804070507800303

Fosco, G. M., Dishion, T. J., & Stormshak, E. A. (2012). A public health approach to family-centered prevention of alcohol and drug addiction: A middle school strategy. In H. J. Shaffer (Ed.), *APA addiction syndrome handbook: Volume 2: Recovery, prevention, and other issues.* Washington, DC: American Psychological Association.

Fosco, G. M., Seeley, J. R., Dishion, T. J., Smolkowski, K., Stormshak, E. A., Downey-McCarthy, R., ... Strycker, L. A. (in press). Lessons learned from scaling up the ecological approach to family interventions and treatment (EcoFIT) program in middle schools. In M. Weist, N. Lever, C. Bradshaw, & J. Owens (Eds.), *Handbook of school mental health* (2nd ed.). New York, NY: Springer.

Garbacz, S. A., Woods, K. E., Swanger-Gagné, M. S., Taylor, A. M., Black, K. A., & Sheridan, S. M. (2008). The effectiveness of a partnership-centered approach in conjoint behavioral consultation. *School Psychology Quarterly, 23*, 313–326. doi:10.1037/1045-3830.23.3.313

Grimes, J., & Tilly, W. D., III. (1996). Policy and process: Means to lasting educational change. *School Psychology Review, 25*, 465–476.

Hill, N. E. (2010). Culturally-based worldviews, family processes, and family–school interactions. In S. L. Christenson & A. L. Reschly (Eds.), *Handbook of school-family partnerships* (pp. 101–127). New York, NY: Routledge.

Horner, R. H., Sugai, G., Smolkowski, K., Eber, L., Nakasato, J., Todd, A. W., & Esperanza, J. (2009). A randomized, wait-list controlled effectiveness trial assessing school-wide positive behavior support in elementary schools. *Journal of Positive Behavior Interventions*, *11*, 133–144. doi:10.1177/1098300709332067

Huntsinger, C. S., & Jose, P. E. (2009). Parental involvement in children's schooling: Different meanings in different cultures. *Early Childhood Research Quarterly*, *24*, 398–410. doi:10.10116/j.ecresq.2009.07.006

Jeynes, W. H. (2005). A meta-analysis of the relation of parental involvement to urban elementary school student academic achievement. *Urban Education*, *40*, 237–269. doi:10.1177/0042085905274540

Kratochwill, T. R., & Bergan, J. R. (1990). *Behavioral consultation in applied settings: An individual guide.* New York, NY: Plenum Press.

Lines, C., Miller, G. E., & Arthur-Stanley, A. (2011). *The power of family–school partnering (FSP).* New York, NY: Routledge.

May, S., Ard, W., Todd, A., Horner, R., Glasgow, A., Sugai, G., & Sprague, J. (2000). *School-Wide Information System (SWIS).* Eugene, OR: University of Oregon, Educational and Community Supports.

McIntosh, K., Horner, R. H., & Sugai, G. (2009). Sustainability of systems-level evidence-based practices in schools: Current knowledge and future directions. In W. Sailor, G. Dunlap, G. Sugai, & R. Horner (Eds.), *Handbook of positive behavior support* (pp. 327–352). New York, NY: Springer.

National Association of School Psychologists. (2010). *Model for comprehensive and integrated school psychological services.* Bethesda, MD: Author. Retrieved from http://www.nasponline.org/standards/2010standards/2_PracticeModel.pdf

National Association of School Psychologists. (2012). *School–family partnering to enhance learning: Essential elements and responsibilities* [Position Statement]. Bethesda, MD: Author. Retrieved from http://www.nasponline.org/about_nasp/positionpapers/Home-SchoolCollaboration.pdf

Okagaki, L., & Bingham, G. E. (2010). Diversity in families. In S. L. Christenson & A. L. Reschly (Eds.), *Handbook of school-family partnerships* (pp. 80–100). New York, NY: Routledge.

Raffaele, L. M., & Knoff, H. M. (1999). Improving home-school collaboration with disadvantages families: Organizational principles, perspectives, and approaches. *School Psychology Review*, *28*, 448–466.

Reschly, A. L., & Christenson, S. L. (2012). Moving from "context matters" to engaged partnerships with families. *Journal of Educational and Psychological Consultation*, *22*, 62–78. doi:10.1080/10474412.2011.649650

Rimm-Kaufman, S. E., & Pianta, R. C. (1999). Patterns of family–school contact in preschool and kindergarten. *School Psychology Review*, *28*, 426–438.

Sheridan, S. M., Bovaird, J. A., Glover, T. A., Garbacz, S. A., & Witte, A. (2012). A randomized trial examining the effects of conjoint behavioral consultation and the mediating role of the parent-teacher relationship. *School Psychology Review*, *41*, 23–46.

Sheridan, S. M., & Kratochwill, T. R. (2008). *Conjoint behavioral consultation: Promoting family–school connections and intervention* (2nd ed.). New York, NY: Springer.

Sheridan, S. M., Rispoli, K. M., & Holmes, S. R. (in press). Treatment integrity in conjoint behavioral consultation: Conceptualizing active ingredients and potential pathways of influence. In L. Sanetti & T. Kratochwill (Eds.), *Treatment integrity: Conceptual, methodological, and applied considerations for practitioners.* Washington, DC: American Psychological Association.

Sugai, G., & Horner, R. H. (2002). The evolution of discipline practices: School-wide positive behavior supports. *Child and Family Behavior Therapy*, *24*, 23–50.

Swanger-Gagné, M. S., Garbacz, S. A., & Sheridan, S. M. (2009). Intervention implementation integrity within conjoint behavioral consultation: Strategies for working with families. *School Mental Health*, *1*, 131–142. doi:10.1007/s12310-009-9012-y

Walker, J. M. T., Ice, C. L., Hoover-Dempsey, K. V., & Sandler, H. M. (2011). Latino parents' motivations for involvement in their children's schooling. *The Elementary School Journal*, *111*, 409–429. doi:10.1086/657653

Walker, J. M. T., Wilkins, A. S., Dallaire, J. R., Sandler, H. M., & Hoover-Dempsey, K. V. (2005). Parental involvement: Model revision through scale development. *The Elementary School Journal*, *106*, 85–104. doi:10.1086/499193

32 Best Practices in Reducing Barriers to Parent Involvement

Patricia H. Manz
Julie C. Manzo
Lehigh University (PA)

OVERVIEW

Parents' involvement in their children's education is fundamental to their children's achievement and healthy development. Recognizing the pivotal influence of families on children's success, responsibilities for school psychologists are twofold: to engage parents in their children's education and to facilitate productive collaboration among parents and school personnel. Doing so requires school psychologists to be fully aware of the various ways in which parents are involved in their children's education and to apply this awareness in their practices for promoting family–school collaboration. This chapter is intended to facilitate school psychologists' engagement of families by reviewing fundamental theories of parents' involvement and the barriers that families may experience, with the emphasis on illustrating exemplar practices that align with the National Association of School Psychologists (NASP) *Model for Comprehensive and Integrated School Psychological Services* (NASP, 2010).

The NASP Practice Model (NASP, 2010) directly identifies Family–School Collaboration as a target domain for the systems-level services school psychologists provide. Students thrive in school climates that promote productive and positive family–school collaboration (Ollendick, 2005). Collaborative climates can be characterized as welcoming parents in the school and partnering with them in decision making and educational programming, as well as providing an infrastructure (e.g., space, resources) that enables them to work with school personnel (Mapp, Johnson, Strickland, & Meza, 2008). Expressions of mutual regard and trust among parents and school personnel are the hallmark of a collaborative school climate (Mapp et al., 2008).

Formulating and sustaining family collaboration at the systems level is necessary for school psychologists to provide effective services to individual students. Collaborative school climates are more likely to maximize parental involvement in student-level services (Christenson & Sheridan, 2001). Parent involvement at the student level is necessary for school psychologists to achieve their responsibility for providing data-based interventions to promote academic achievement and social competence for individual students. Recognizing the reciprocal interrelationship of parent involvement at student and systems levels, the NASP (2010) Practice Model includes family collaboration at both levels as key elements of school psychologists' roles and responsibilities.

BASIC CONSIDERATIONS

Parents, regarded as the adults who assume primary responsibility for children's healthy development, encourage and directly support their children's education through a variety of ways at home, in the community, and at school. Emanating from the seminal research conducted by Joyce Epstein (1995), educational involvement broadly spans behaviors such as parents fostering a nurturing home environment, directly teaching fundamental academic skills, providing resources for children, and serving as active contributors in schools through volunteering in classrooms or on decision-making committees. Fundamentally, parent involvement is seen as occurring at home, at school, and in the interpersonal relationships with school personnel (Manz, Fantuzzo, & Power, 2004).

Research conducted by Hoover-Dempsey and colleagues (Walker, Wilkins, Dallaire, Sandler, &

Hoover-Dempsey, 2005) illuminates the influences that shape the manner and frequency with which parents are involved in their children's education. Motivation for educational involvement is necessary. Motivation emanates from parents' sense that they are capable of being effectively involved in the manner they feel is most important for their child. Educational involvement is optimal when parents can fulfill roles that are associated with their values and perceived effectiveness. At the same time, the nature and frequency of parental involvement is shaped by external factors. Most simply, invitations to be involved guide and encourage parents' actions. Invitations can come from teachers as well as other school personnel. Children's expressed desire for their parents' involvement is also an invitation. The realities of parents' life circumstances largely shape their educational involvement. Their availability, the presence of other demands for their attention, as well as their perceptions of the skills and knowledge they can contribute to their children's education are determinants in how and where they are involved. In the end, parents' choices for involvement entail a balance of their motivation, perceived invitations, and life context.

Parents can experience an array of circumstances that constrain their involvement in their children's education. Kazdin's (2000) conceptualization of common barriers to treatment is helpful for understanding families' challenges in sustaining involvement in their children's education. Accordingly, parents' involvement in their children's education can be restricted by their life circumstances or by aspects of the involvement opportunity. Life circumstances entail a broad category including personal concerns, interpersonal difficulties within the family, or logistical obstacles. Additional potential barriers are related to the opportunities for involvement. The parents' perceptions that the involvement opportunity is associated with unattainable demands for their time or resources could deter their participation. Perceptions of the relevance of the involvement opportunity to the parents' values and expectations for the child may also determine their engagement. Last, trust among school personnel and parents can influence the nature and frequency of involvement. Although barriers may be described as distinctively associated with life circumstances, the level of demands, or trust of school professionals, in reality these barriers are intertwined. For example, a family experiencing the social hardships associated with living in poverty is less likely to have the emotional or financial resources for supporting their child's education. In this instance, the simplest request for involvement may feel too demanding for the parents. Table 32.1 provides an overview of the potential barriers, with illustrations of how they may be expressed at system and student levels.

The sheer number of barriers experienced by families is most often linked to their involvement in their children's education. Unsurprisingly, as families face a greater number of barriers, their involvement in their children's education diminishes (Mendez & Westerberg, 2012). At the same time, the barriers that parents

Table 32.1. Parental Involvement Barriers and Examples of Impact at System and Student Levels

Potential Barrier	Example of Systems-Level Impact	Example of Student-Level Impact
Life circumstances	Spanish-speaking parents in the community are unable to read communications or attend parent events in the school as all are presented in English.	Psychological distress in the family restricts adult support and monitoring of student's homework completion.
Demands of involvement opportunity	A large portion of the parents are unable to serve as classroom volunteers given that all opportunities require being present in the classroom during school hours.	The home component of a self-monitoring intervention requires the parent to block periods of time for observing the child and involves materials that are not readily available.
Relevance of involvement opportunity	The high school is presenting a parent information series on college planning, and not including other postsecondary experiences (e.g., vocational training).	The behavioral intervention requires the parent to praise and reward child behaviors that the parent feels should be routine.
Relationship with school personnel	The school principal rarely attends parent events or meetings and does not provide venues for routinely communicating school information to families.	During a multidisciplinary meeting, the teacher begins to write notes or leaves the table when the parent speaks.

Note. Based on information from Kazdin (2000).

experience may affect some expressions of educational involvement, but not others. A common pattern among low-income families is that their school-based involvement is more vulnerable to barriers than their involvement at home (Fantuzzo, Tighe, & Childs, 2000; Manz et al., 2004). Auerbach (2007) found that working-class parents were consistently supportive of their children's successful education, yet their expressed involvement in school settings varied. With regard to school contexts, some parents were not involved (e.g., moral supporter), others were inconsistent in the extent to which they expressed involvement (e.g., ambivalent companions), and others were more consistently involved (e.g., struggling advocates). Lower levels of school-based involvement among low-income parents has been attributed to several factors, including the unavailability of care for siblings, conflicting work schedules, or prior negative experiences with school personnel (Lamb-Parker et al., 2001).

On the other hand, increased involvement at home, relative to school, may be a reflection of parental values, not solely barriers. According to Zarate (2007), Latino parents perceive their involvement according to two complementary forms. Recognizing the value of formal education, the sample of Latino parents voiced involvement practices that directly supported their children's learning and achievement. Parents provided support and resources at home and were involved in school as directed by the teachers. In this vein, Latino parents viewed themselves as collaborating with the teachers in instructing the children. However, these Latino parents also constructed a role of involvement based on their perceived responsibilities for preparing their children for later life. Referred to as *life participation*, these parents assumed responsibility for monitoring children's social and moral development. Teaching their children life lessons and monitoring their social behavior are aspects of life participation. The Latino parents saw this form of

involvement as a unique responsibility for the family, yet necessary for the children's success at school.

Despite the range of potential barriers, more often families sustain, rather than diminish, involvement when personal challenges arise. Among a sample of low-income parents of preschool children, Lamb-Parker et al. (2001) reported that usually less than half of the parents who identified the presence of significant stressors in their life associated these stressors with reduced involvement in their children's learning. For example, 47% of the sample reported feeling overly sad, yet only 16% indicated that it interfered with their participation in their child's education. Similarly, a lack of electricity or heat at home was a stressor for 34% of the sample, yet only one parent claimed that it kept that parent from being involved with the child's schooling. Evidence of parental involvement despite the presence of personal stressors has been repeatedly demonstrated in other studies focused on low-income parents (Mendez, Carpenter, LaForett, & Cohen, 2009).

Unlike stressors related to life circumstances, parents are likely to restrict their involvement when they perceive services as irrelevant or demanding and when they do not share favorable relationships with the providers (Kazdin, 2000). This can be good news for school psychologists, as it is within their professional scope to enhance involvement opportunities and steer away from these barriers. School psychologists are challenged to formulate meaningful and attainable involvement opportunities in their assessment and intervention responsibilities that are congruent with the values, resources, and preferences of the parents they serve. At a systems level, school psychologists can lead and facilitate the formulation of a school climate that is welcoming, conveys appreciation of families' values by providing relevant involvement opportunities, and fosters positive relationships among parents and school personnel. Table 32.2 provides guiding principles for

Table 32.2. Guiding Principles for Understanding Potential Barriers to Parental Involvement

- Common to families of various cultures and socioeconomic status is an innate desire to support their children's learning and success at school.
- Parents engage in multiple forms of involvement spanning home, school, and community contexts.
- Parental involvement is an array of responsibilities, including meeting children's basic needs, providing resources, teaching fundamental academic skills, nurturing their moral and social development, volunteering at school, and communicating with teachers.
- Parents are faced with personal stressors that can impede their involvement, yet often parents are resilient in maintaining involvement.
- The barriers that are more likely to restrict involvement pertain to the demands and relevance of the opportunity as well as the parents' relationship with school personnel.

understanding parental involvement and the impact of potential barriers.

BEST PRACTICES IN REDUCING BARRIERS TO PARENT INVOLVEMENT

As illustrated in the NASP Practice Model (NASP, 2010), school psychologists infuse collaborations with families into assessment and intervention services directed toward individual students as well as those directed school-wide. The decision-making foundation for assessment and intervention is driven by data and conducted in a collaborative framework. Research regarding effective assessment and intervention practices that involve parents is growing. In this portion of the chapter, exemplary practices with related considerations for involving and collaborating with parents in the delivery of data-based and collaborative assessment and intervention services are presented, first for the systems level and then for the individual student level. This ordering is deliberate, emphasizing that a collaborative school climate is a catalyst for fostering parent involvement and collaboration on individual student levels.

Although exemplary best practices are offered for school psychologists to apply to student- and systems-level assessment and intervention, there is a critical need for school psychologists to be successful. School psychologists themselves need systems-level support to be able to function competently in their roles related to parent involvement and collaboration. Thus, critical needs for school psychologists' success in facilitating parent involvement are additionally identified in this chapter.

Systems Level

Barriers to parental involvement become most restrictive when schools operate without sufficient awareness of the community's perspectives and resources for educational involvement. When this occurs, schools may inadvertently offer opportunities for involvement that are not consistent with the goals of the larger community and those that may be too demanding. If school personnel are unfamiliar with the community's cultures and interpersonal styles, they may not approach families in a manner that elicits trusting relationships.

Assessment

An effective school is one in which professionals collaboratively engage families in devising a shared vision and associated goals. With this accomplishment,

the school can operate from a welcoming environment that provides opportunities that match families' values and resources and fosters the formation of trusting relationships. School-wide assessment of parents' perspectives and actions with regard to their educational involvement can guide the development of a school climate that is mutually acceptable and beneficial for families and schools. These assessments can demonstrate the ways and amount in which families are naturally involved with their children, direct reasonable goal setting for desired levels of involvement, and provide data for monitoring progress toward mutual goals. Moreover, school-wide assessments can illuminate the unique facilitators and barriers to parents' involvement for the community, thereby directing intervention programming to be responsive to families' needs and resources. School psychologists' unique expertise in child development, ecological systems theory, organizational leadership, and consultation procedures equips them to be natural leaders in conducting school-wide assessments with the objective to establish visions and goals relevant to family–school collaboration.

Our evolving understanding of family involvement is leading the development of assessment tools that will enable school psychologists to lead data-based efforts to promote and sustain educational involvement for families served by their schools. Several notable measures that possess basic psychometric quality have been developed for children representing diverse cultural backgrounds and ages. The Family Involvement Questionnaire is a series of rating scales that assesses home- and school-based involvement as well as home–school communication for preschool-age children (Family Involvement Questionnaire-Early Childhood; Fantuzzo et al., 2000) and elementary-age children (Family Involvement Questionnaire-Elementary; Manz et al., 2004). The Family Involvement Questionnaire has been shown to apply to families who are African American as well as Latino.

The content of the Family Involvement Questionnaire was derived in partnership with families of children from preschool through fifth grade to ensure its content was reflective of natural parental behaviors. Both the early childhood and elementary versions of the Family Involvement Questionnaire yield information for three forms of educational involvement: home based, school based, and home–school communication. Home-based involvement includes parents' engagement of children in academic activities, such as book reading or counting, as well as parents' provision of resources and home routines that are conducive for learning. School-based involvement

470

refers to parents' participation in school events and volunteer opportunities. Home–school communication includes a variety of exchanges between parents, educators, and school personnel for sharing information and discussing student progress. Measures such as the Family Involvement Questionnaire could be administered to families school-wide in an effort to obtain a broad perspective of the actual trends of parents' educational involvement and to direct intervention to achieve desired levels and forms of parental involvement. For instance, a school-wide assessment may show that home–school contact is the most frequent form of educational involvement, while the participation of parents in school activities is low. Further investigation could show that the common practice of the school is to contact parents when difficulties or concerns about their children arise. As parents' contact with school is most often problem-focused, the overall level of involvement in the school or collaboration with school professionals is dwindling. With this information, the school psychologist can guide the schools' administration in maintaining the high frequency of outreach to parents, yet ensuring that communication is balanced to present children's strengths and concerns. Additionally, ongoing assessment can reveal if the change in home–school contact did indeed increase parents' willingness to be involved in school-based activities. Other applications of school-wide assessments may show which groups of families are less involved, providing directions for targeted outreach by the school. Routine and repeated use of parent involvement measures could demonstrate the effectiveness of the schools' efforts and inform improvements.

Intervention

The first step toward system-wide interventions for promoting parent involvement and collaboration is to formulate a culture of trust among school professionals and the community of families served by the school. Adams and Christenson (2000) provide a rich account of the process of formulating trusting relationships among school personnel and families. Trust progresses from parents' and teachers' experience of the predictability of certain events, to an association of predictability to one another, to a general sense of trustworthiness. For example, a parent's first experience of trusting his or her child's teacher may come from the teacher's consistency in sending home weekly progress notes. Consistently engaging with the teacher around the progress notes, the parent may expand his or her trust of the activity to trusting the teacher more generally (e.g., trusting the teacher's grading, the teacher's impressions of the

student). These consistent experiences with the teacher can generalize into a more global sense of trusting the school and education processes. Thus the parent's trust is no longer solely linked to specific activities and persons.

Multiple opportunities for contact and communication between family members and school personnel are necessary to enable trust to form. Yet the quality of contact is more important than quantity (Adams & Christenson, 2000). When the focus or experience of contact is only negative, trust will not emerge. Many times, the contact and communication between families and schools arises when there are problems, which results in isolated and disconnected meetings. This common occurrence does not promote, but rather it can inhibit, the formation of trust. Shifting the pathway of interactions between families and schools from one that is problem-led to a routine for sharing about children's achievements as well as their needs is the way toward establishing family–school collaborations that are characterized by trust.

Barriers to partnerships between family members and school personnel often emanate from differences in perspectives, perceived situational demands, or cultural views. If these differences are to be transcended, the differences must be acknowledged and directly addressed. A challenging yet critical point of entry into a trusting relationship is to "partner with resistance" (Fantuzzo & Mohr, 2000). For example, a parent may feel that actively interacting with and teaching children in the classroom is taking on the teacher's role and reflects disrespect of the teacher's credentials and status. Therefore, the parent does not volunteer to assist with instructional activities in the classroom. In turn, the teacher may perceive the parent as disengaged in the child's education. In this example, a discussion between the teacher and parents at the start of the year that intentionally elicits their perspectives regarding their contributions and roles in the child's education would enlighten each another, make expectations for each other explicit, and likely minimize the occurrence of misperceptions that can undermine the formation of trust.

Effective communication between school professionals and parents is frequently prohibited by the professionals' use of language or jargon. Teachers and other school personnel share familiar labels as well as comfort levels in describing student concerns or disabilities (e.g., emotionally and behaviorally disordered, high risk). To the child's family, however, these labels and descriptions may not have meaning and, even worse, can be hurtful. Consequently, parents can respond in ways that seem inappropriate to the school personnel (e.g., parents may withdraw or outwardly reject them). In this example, recognizing the impact of professional jargon, as well as empathizing with the sadness and fears the parent may have regarding the child's situation, may enable school personnel to respond to the inappropriate parental response with patience, understanding, and a willingness to adjust their language. Thus, viewing the parent's response as a coping mechanism rather than as hostile or as uncaring about the child's education sets forth an avenue for collaboration.

School professionals' approach to communicating and relating to families can be enhanced by viewing barriers from a perspective of resilience, not deficit. Resilience is defined as competence in one's personal context (Fantuzzo & Mohr, 2000). For some families, effective actions in their personal context may not be effective actions in the school context. In these circumstances the actions of the families and parents are likely to be perceived negatively by each party. For example, many families in a low-income community may need to drop their children at school prior to school hours in order to arrive at work on time. Given the safety concerns, the school administrators may be critical of these actions. Yet, in working with the families and understanding their need to balance work responsibilities and child care, the school and community may be able to provide supervision in the early hours to assist families with care of their children.

Integrating natural helpers from the community, referred to as community paraeducators, is a promising approach for minimizing barriers that prohibit the formation of trusting relationships and productive communication among school professionals and families. Community paraeducators can serve a variety of roles, such as assisting teachers with instruction in the classroom or with individual students, or providing supervision for children during less structured activities such as lunch or recess. Most importantly, community paraeducators offer the dual benefits of fostering parent involvement and family–school collaboration.

The most meaningful contribution of community paraeducators is in guiding administrators and educators in acquiring an understanding of the barriers to parental involvement that are experienced in their school community (Monzó & Ruedo, 2003). Community paraeducators can minimize families' experiences of educational programming as less meaningful by guiding educators in infusing the cultural practices, values, and histories into the curricula. Community paraeducators can enlighten school personnel as to the life circumstances faced by many families and the community at large. Consequently, school professionals can incorporate actions or programs that enable families to be involved with their children's education, despite barriers associated their personal or community contexts. Moreover, community paraeducators can serve as the bridge for uniting family members and teachers. As community paraeducators share positive and productive relationships with educators and families, they can function to connect and foster direct relationships between educators and family members.

Manz, Power, Ginsburg-Block, and Dowrick (2010) provide a detailed and thorough process for directing school personnel and community members to collaboratively formulate roles and responsibilities for community paraeducators. The starting point is to develop clear definitions of the community paraeducators' roles and responsibilities, specifying how their contributions are interconnected with the school's mission. To be successful in fulfilling their roles and responsibilities, community paraeducators will require preservice training and ongoing supervision. Although the competencies specific to their responsibilities are focal points for training and supervision, equally important is attention to their working relationships with their professional colleagues. Community paraeducators' training and supervision activities can be conducted in partnership with their professional colleagues, which would foster communication between them and allow them the opportunities to integrate and complement their responsibilities. At the same time, professional school staff members will need training and guidance to serve as partners to the community paraeducators. Teachers, who are the most likely to work closely with community paraeducators, would benefit from training regarding the rationale for including community paraeducators in their classrooms as well as the specific strategies for effectively integrating them into instruction and management efforts. Finally, instilling a routine for data-based decision making and accountability that is collaboratively conducted by professional school staff and community paraeducators is a crucial mechanism for directing and ensuring the benefits of embedding community paraeducators in the school to the students' achievement as well as to the collaboration with families.

The Reading Partners program (Power, Dowrick, Ginsburg-Block, & Manz, 2004) is an example of a tutoring program that enlisted, supported, and integrated community paraeducators to provide instructional supports for first-grade students who were having difficulty in acquiring literacy skills. The Reading

Partners program was implemented by school psychologists, and it serves as an example of what their specific roles and responsibilities in a collaborative educational program may be. School psychologists provided training to community paraeducators in evidence-based instructional strategies in addition to curriculum-based assessment and progress monitoring. School psychologists also fostered routine meetings with the community paraeducators and teachers to review children's progress and to adjust instruction. Intervention integrity data demonstrated that the community paraeducators acquired the instructional competencies and implemented the program as planned. Outcome data showed increases in students' reading skills and teachers' acceptability of the program.

Individual Student Level

Multi-informant assessment that includes parents, educators, and related professionals is regarded as best practice in evaluating children's academic, emotional, and social functioning. As school psychologists are aware, parental input is a mandated component of evaluations related to special education eligibility determination. Parents' contributions to multi-informant assessment can include their report of concerns, description of their child at home and in the community, and provision of developmental and health histories. Further facilitating multi-informant assessment, parents can provide ratings of their children's social and behavioral adjustment on measures designed to complement parallel information that is obtained by the children's teachers. Complementary parent and teacher versions of behavioral rating scales are beneficial for facilitating problem identification and decision making.

Assessment

Despite the anticipated benefits of complementary parent and teacher measures, a frequent, yet insufficiently addressed barrier to conducting multi-informant assessment is the meaningful integration of parental input into a product that guides children's education. A common challenge to conducting fully synthesized and meaningful multi-informant assessments is that parent and teacher reports are often discrepant (Kerr, Lukenheimer, & Olson, 2007). This discrepancy between parents' and teachers' assessments is often attributed to the different contexts in which they interact with the child (e.g., home and school). Accordingly, the interpretation is that children actually behave or perform differently at home and school, given variation in demands, structure, and resources. This interpretation

can mislead school professionals to perceiving parental input as minimally relevant for planning children's education at school. Consequently, the assessment results or subsequent educational planning may appear less relevant or meaningful for the parent. Take for example a situation where a parent's report on a behavior rating scale portrays the child as withdrawn, which is not aligned with the school professionals' concerns. If the subsequent interventions do not include supports for the parent's concerns about the child's behaviors, the parent may feel unsupported and detached from a collective effort to address the child's needs. Consequently, the parent may limit involvement in collaborating with and reinforcing school professionals' efforts.

Until recently, little guidance in how to fully integrate findings across parents and teachers, especially when contradictory information is provided, has been available for school psychologists. Recent expansion of the causes for the discrepancy provides additional directions for school psychologists to manage the different perspectives and produce fully integrated multi-informant assessments. In addition to differences in the home and school settings, cognitive factors that influence parents' and teachers' reports of children's behaviors can lead to discrepant assessment information (De Los Reyes & Kazdin, 2005).

Parents' or teachers' understanding of the reasons for and potential consequences of assessing children can bias their recall and report when providing information. For example, wanting access to support services for students can bias their reports. Additionally, parents' and teachers' recall of children's behavior is affected by the source of information, like the immediacy of certain events. If either was in recent conflict with a child regarding the completion of a task, then he or she may be more likely to generalize that immediate experience to a global rating of the child as noncompliant, even if this is not characteristic of the child in all circumstances. Assumptions about the child, based on gender, socioeconomic status, or cultural background, are other examples of sources of information that could influence parents' and teachers' account of the child's behavior.

As seen in Table 32.3, several best practices for conducting multi-informant assessments emanate from this broadened conceptualization of the discrepancy between parent and teacher information (De Los Reyes & Kazdin, 2005). A multi-informant assessment should include methods and instruments that balance examination of children's internal states and contextual influences. This balance can entail behavioral ratings

Table 32.3. Best Practices for Synthesizing Parents' Report in Multi-Informant Assessment

- Interview parents and teachers to understand their expectations for the assessment and desired outcomes.
- Include assessments of the child's behavior as observed or perceived in home and school.
- Consider including parents during the child assessment.
- Balance assessment information that emphasizes context with that which emphasizes children's internal states.
- Report distinct perspectives rather than forcing a single conclusion.

Note. Based on information from De Los Reyes and Kazdin (2005) and Marcy, Thorndike-Christ, and Lin (2010).

and observations across informants (e.g., parents, teachers) and settings (e.g., home, school) as well as include direct assessments of children's skills and child self-report (Kerr et al., 2007). The conceptualization presented by De Los Reyes and Kazdin (2005) also highlights practices for understanding parents' and teachers' perspectives, possible biases, and sources of information related to their report of children's school performance and behaviors. Interviews with informants provide opportunities for the school psychologists to explore these cognitive factors and consider parents' and teachers' perspectives as they integrate assessment information. School psychologists can ask parents and teachers about their perspectives of the reason for and benefits of the assessment and their history with the child and long-term observations and impressions of the child's behavior. In addition they can ask parents and teachers to describe the home and school contexts.

Although the recommendations so far are geared to interpreting assessments across informants, alterations in the testing conditions may serve to minimize the parent–teacher discrepancy. When parents and teachers share an understanding of the skills or behaviors being assessed, greater agreement between their reports can be obtained. The authentic assessment approach, proposed by Marcy, Thorndike-Christ, and Lin (2010), elicits parent involvement in assessment and the opportunity for parents to be informed about the skills or behaviors targeted by the assessment. In contrast to conventional assessment, which entails trained professionals administering norm-based measures to children on an individualized basis, authentic assessment allows for parents to be present during the assessment and broadens the use of measures to include natural behaviors, interactions, and materials. In this study, parents rated the authentic assessment as more acceptable and relevant for intervention planning than conventional assessment. A potential best practice for school psychologists may be to engage parents more actively in the assessment planning and testing procedures so that they join teachers and other professionals as equal partners in intervention planning.

On a final note, the richness of a multi-informant assessment can identify a menu of options for addressing children's concerns (De Los Reyes & Kazdin, 2005). Therefore, school psychologists should not overly burden themselves to reduce the assessment to a single explanation or treatment approach for the child. Rather, the different perspectives may illuminate several potential pathways for addressing the concerns regarding the child at home as well as at school.

Intervention

As highlighted in this chapter, barriers to parental involvement in their children's education are largely associated with parents' perceptions that opportunities for their involvement are irrelevant to their personal goals for their child or overly demanding of their resources. Evidence for best practices for engaging parents in interventions to improve children's academic performance and school adjustment has grown. School psychologists have a range of intervention approaches and strategies that can enable them to establish interventions that engage family members and school professionals, most often teachers. In 2005, the American Psychological Association (APA) Division 16 Task Force on Evidence-Based Interventions thoroughly reviewed interventions involving family and school collaboration, which illuminated several effective features (Ollendick, 2005). Table 32.4 presents an overview of best practices for involving parents in student interventions. Allowing family members to co-construct the intervention with school personnel was more likely to result in student improvements than the alternative approach of delegating intervention responsibilities to families. Effective family–school interventions were also based in behavioral theory, using behavioral or cognitive–behavioral interventions. Last, in terms of specific strategies, intervention strategies that sought to foster two-way communication between home and school were noted as highly effective.

Daily report cards are widely used to foster communication across home and school. Daily reports enable teachers and family members to monitor and

Table 32.4. Best Practices for Involving Parents in Student Interventions

- Construct the intervention in collaboration with parents.
- Include means for reciprocal communication between parents and teachers.
- Use interventions with behavioral or cognitive–behavioral orientations, which are most effective.
- As appropriate, use empirically supported interventions that provide involvement opportunities for parents.
- Verify the effectiveness of interventions involving parents for the cultural and socioeconomic characteristics of students to whom they are applied.

communicate about children's behavior and academic progress, as observed at home and in school. Daily reports can be used in isolation or combined with other intervention strategies, such as providing reinforcement. Many resources are available to assist school psychologists in devising daily reports materials and procedures.

Advances in consultation procedures have provided a systematic framework for school psychologists to establish interventions, such as daily report cards, through collaboration with teachers and family members. Most notable, conjoint behavioral consultation (Sheridan & Kratochwill, 2008) is a problem-solving consultation framework for school psychologists to use in forming and directing family–school partnerships toward improving student outcomes. Conjoint behavioral consultation is a systematic process for identifying mutual goals and improving student outcomes through a data-driven intervention approach. The goals of conjoint behavioral consultation are threefold: to assist the individual student, to build a working alliance between the teacher and family members, and to enrich the competencies of the family members and teacher in addressing student concerns.

The advancement of conjoint behavioral consultation has influenced the development of intervention programs for specific populations and academic concerns, providing many evidence-based options for school psychologists. For instance, Power et al. (2012) have developed the Family School Success program as a means for guiding families of children with attention deficit hyperactivity disorder in managing their children's academic and behavioral needs at home and in collaboration with the school. Geared to early childhood education programs, the Getting Ready intervention (Sheridan, Knoche, Edwards, Bovaird, & Kupzyk, 2010) aims to bring parents and teachers together in identifying mutual goals and intervention approaches to enhance children's readiness for entry into kindergarten.

The APA task force's review of interventions involving family–school collaboration illuminated limitations in availability of evidence-based options for school psychologists. A glaring omission was the lack of empirical attention to understanding what intervention

works for whom (Ollendick, 2005). Low-income families who are ethnic or linguistic minorities have frequently been neglected in intervention development and evaluations. As an example, Dialogic Reading is a popular intervention that instructs parents and teachers in using a guided and interactive style of book reading. This intervention program has been shown to be highly effective in building children's vocabulary in a relatively brief period and with a reasonable amount of parent training (e.g., video instruction; Huebner & Meltzoff, 2005). Yet, Dialogic Reading for families who experienced socioeconomic risks and those who were an ethnic minority has been scarce. The small collection of studies with these families has demonstrated Dialogic Reading to be minimally effective (Manz et al., 2010).

Given that the most threatening barriers to parent involvement relate to the nature of the intervention itself, limitations in evidence-based interventions that include roles for parent involvement constrains school psychologists' efforts to engage parents and foster their collaboration with school personnel in devising student-level interventions. This is especially true when school psychologists are working with families from underrepresented groups. In these circumstances, school psychologists can utilize a collaborative, problem-solving framework that have elements shown to be effective (e.g., bidirectional communication, behaviorally based), like conjoint behavioral consultation, to devise interventions for individual students.

Critical Need: Advocating for Supports

Up until this point, the barriers to parental involvement have been presented from the perspectives of the families' experiences or the nature of the involvement opportunity at school. However, school psychologists face a unique set of barriers specific to their roles and functions. These barriers emanate from the restriction of supports and resources often encountered by school psychologists.

Professionals' sense of efficacy and their perceptions that the school climate is supportive are two main forces that shape their approach to engaging and collaborating with parents. Manz, Mautone, and Martin (2009) examined factors associated with school psychologists' perceptions of professional efficacy and school climate, specific to family–school collaboration. School psychologists reported higher levels of professional efficacy and positive perceptions of school climates when they received specialized training relevant to family–school collaboration, were in schools that were located in suburban areas, were employed by institutions other than school systems (even though their practice was in a school setting), were assigned to a single school, and had sufficient time (e.g., about 10 hours per week) available to collaborate with families.

The findings from Manz et al. (2009) are sobering, given that the typical training and employment parameters for school psychologists do not align with the factors that enhance their capacity to foster family–school collaborations. Consider, for example, the demands on school psychologists' time and their availability to foster family–school collaborations. Among the 544 school psychologists who completed the survey by Manz and colleagues, more than half reported having fewer than 5 hours per week available for working with families. Sadly, this finding is consistent with previous investigations, indicating that the field's progress in expanding school psychologists' role in parent involvement and collaboration has been insufficient.

Thus, while a primary responsibility of school psychologists is the application of best practices to enlist and collaborate with families, there is an imbalance of demands and supports. In this regard, the most pressing practice to put into place may be advocating for reconceptualization and prioritizing of school psychologists' roles and responsibilities and ensuring that they receive appropriate and sufficient resources from school districts (Lazarus, 2012). With the transformation of the prevention and school-based foci of federal healthcare initiatives, now is an optimal time to examine new directions for school psychology. The Affordable Care Act has provided more than $200 million for the development of school-based health clinics over the next few years. Yet, the need for school-based mental health providers who are highly skilled in integrating family, school, and healthcare systems to promote children's health development is reported as a primary barrier in establishing these clinics (Langley, Nadeem, Kataoka, Stein, & Jaycox, 2010). School psychologists are among the most equipped professionals to serve in this capacity, provided that their roles and responsibilities can adjust to this changing climate for promoting children's health and education.

SUMMARY

Involving parents in children's education and fostering their collaboration with school personnel is a central component of the student- and systems-level responsibilities for school psychologists, as illustrated in the NASP Practice Model (NASP, 2010). In fulfilling this crucial responsibility, school psychologists must overcome the barriers that prohibit parent involvement. Although potential barriers arise from the parents' personal circumstances, barriers also emanate from the nature of the involvement opportunity. In fact, barriers related to the nature of the involvement opportunity are more constraining than those posed by parents' life circumstances. On one hand, this reality is encouraging, as school psychologists are more likely to have an impact on the nature of the involvement opportunity than the family context. Yet, this presses school psychologists to offer involvement opportunities that are perceived as relevant and are within the parents' capacity. Further, forming trusting and positive relationships among families and school personnel is an imperative responsibility for school psychologists.

Although this chapter highlights exemplary best practices for student- and systems-level assessment and intervention services, several broad guiding principles are common across these services. School psychologists are called to be thorough and sensitive to complex contextual influences at the student or systems level. Contextually based assessment methods, such as interviewing and observing, and collection of social and behavioral measures across home and school are important. Parents should be engaged as partners in assessment and intervention, enlightening school psychologists about their perspectives and circumstances, and directing the development of meaningful intervention. This is applicable to student- and systems-level services. School psychologists can lead their professional colleagues in establishing a school environment that welcomes parents, reflects the strengths of their culture and community, and employs natural helpers. On a final note, the field of school psychology must advocate for and protect school psychologists' availability and resources for achieving high standards of parent involvement.

REFERENCES

Adams, K. S., & Christenson, S. L. (2000). Trust and the family–school relationship: Examination of parent-teacher differences in elementary and secondary grades. *Journal of School Psychology, 38,* 477–497.

Auerbach, S. (2007). From moral supporters to struggling advocates: Reconceptualizing parents' roles in education through the experience of working families of color. *Urban Education, 42*, 250–283.

Christenson, S. L., & Sheridan, S. M. (2001). *Schools and families: Creating essential connections for learning.* New York, NY: Guilford Press.

De Los Reyes, A., & Kazdin, A. E. (2005). Informant discrepancies in the assessment of childhood psychopathology: A critical review, theoretical framework, and recommendations for further study. *Psychological Bulletin, 131*, 483–509. doi:10.1037/0033-2909.131.4.483

Epstein, J. L. (1995). School/family/community partnerships: Caring for the children we share. *Phi Delta Kappan, 76*, 701–712.

Fantuzzo, J. W., & Mohr, W. (2000). Pursuit of wellness in Head Start: Making beneficial connections for children and families. In D. Cicchetti, J. Rapapport, I. Sandler, & R. Weissberg (Eds.), *The promotion of wellness in children and adolescents* (pp. 341–370). Washington, DC: CWLA Press.

Fantuzzo, J. W., Tighe, E., & Childs, S. (2000). Family involvement questionnaire: A multivariate assessment of family participation in early childhood education. *Journal of Educational Psychology, 92*, 367–376.

Huebner, C. E., & Meltzoff, A. N. (2005). Intervention to change parent-child reading style: A comparison of instructional methods. *Applied Developmental Psychology, 26*, 296–313.

Kazdin, A. E. (2000). Perceived barriers to treatment participation and treatment acceptability among antisocial children and their families. *Journal of Child and Family Studies, 9*, 157–174.

Kerr, D. C. R., Lunkenheimer, E. S., & Olson, S. L. (2007). Assessment of child problem behaviors by multiple informants: A longitudinal study from preschool to school entry. *Journal of Child Psychology and Psychiatry, 48*, 967–975.

Lamb-Parker, F., Piotrowski, C. S., Baker, A. J., Kessler-Sklar, S., Clark, B., & Peay, L. (2001). Understanding barriers to parental involvement in Head Start: A research-community partnership. *Early Childhood Research Quarterly, 16*, 35–51.

Langley, A. K., Nadeem, E., Kataoka, S. H., Stein, B. D., & Jaycox, L. H. (2010). Evidence-based mental health programs in schools: Barriers and facilitators of successful implementation. *School Mental Health, 2*, 105–113.

Lazarus, P. J. (2012). President's message. *Communiqué, 40*(8), Retrieved from http://www.nasponline.org/publications/cq/40/8/presidents-message.aspx

Manz, P. H., Fantuzzo, J. W., & Power, T. J. (2004). Multidimensional assessment of family involvement among urban, elementary students. *Journal of School Psychology, 42*, 461–475.

Manz, P. H., Mautone, J. A., & Martin, S. D. (2009). School psychologists' collaborations with families: An exploratory study of the interrelationships of professional efficacy and school climate, and demographic and training variables. *Journal of Applied School Psychology, 25*, 1–24.

Manz, P. H., Power, T. J., Ginsburg-Block, M., & Dowrick, P. W. (2010). Community paraeducators: A partnership-directed approach for preparing and sustaining the involvement of community members in inner-city schools. *The School Community Journal, 20*, 55–80, Retrieved from http://files.eric.ed.gov/fulltext/EJ891832.pdf

Mapp, K. L., Johnson, V. R., Strickland, C. S., & Meza, C. (2008). High school family centers: Transformative spaces linking schools and families in support of student learning. *Marriage & Family Review, 43*, 338–368.

Marcy, M., Thorndike-Christ, T., & Lin, Y. (2010). Parental reports of perceived assessment utility: A comparison of authentic and conventional approaches. *Infants & Young Children, 23*, 286–302.

Mendez, J. L., Carpenter, J. L., LaForett, D. R., & Cohen, J. S. (2009). Parental engagement and barriers to participation in a community-based preventive intervention. *American Journal of Community Psychology, 44*, 1–14.

Mendez, J. L., & Westerberg, D. (2012). Implementation of a culturally adapted treatment to reduce barriers for Latino parents. *Cultural Diversity and Ethnic Minority Psychology, 18*, 363–372.

Monzó, L. D., & Rueda, R. (2003). Shaping education through diverse funds of knowledge: A look at one Latina paraeducator's lived experiences, beliefs, and teaching practice. *Anthropology & Education Quarterly, 34*, 72–95.

National Association of School Psychologists. (2010). *Model for comprehensive and integrated school psychological services.* Bethesda, MD: Author. Retrieved from http://www.nasponline.org/standards/2010standards/2_PracticeModel.pdf

Ollendick, T. H. (2005). Evidence-based parent and family interventions in school psychology: A commentary. *School Psychology Quarterly, 20*, 512–517.

Power, T. J., Dowrick, P. W., Ginsburg-Block, M., & Manz, P. H. (2004). Partnership-based, community-assisted early intervention for literacy: An application of the partnership intervention model. *Journal of Behavioral Education, 13*, 93–115.

Power, T. J., Mautone, J. A., Soffer, S. L., Clarke, A. T., Marshall, S. A., Sharman, J., & Jawad, A. F. (2012). A family-school intervention for children with ADHD: Results of a randomized clinical trial. *Journal of Consulting and Clinical Psychology, 80*, 611–623.

Sheridan, S. M., Knoche, L. L., Edwards, C. P., Bovaird, J. A., & Kupzyk, K. A. (2010). Parent engagement and school readiness: Effects of the Getting Ready intervention on preschool children's social-emotional competencies. *Early Education & Development, 21*, 125–156.

Sheridan, S. M., & Kratochwill, T. R. (2008). *Conjoint behavioral consultation: Promoting family-school connections and interventions* (2nd ed.). New York, NY: Springer.

Walker, J. M. T., Wilkins, A. S., Dallaire, J. R., Sandler, H. M., & Hoover-Dempsey, K. V. (2005). Parental involvement: Model revision through scale development. *Elementary School Journal, 106*, 85–104.

Zarate, M. E. (2007). *Understanding Latino parental involvement in education: Perceptions, expectations, and recommendations.* Los Angeles, CA: The Toms Rivera Policy Institute.

33 Best Practices in Partnering With Parents in School-Based Services

Dawn D. Miller
Shawnee Mission (KS) School District
Nancy P. Kraft
Indian Head (WI) Community Action Agency

OVERVIEW

According to Mapp (2009), "Families play critical roles in student success. They support their children's learning, guide them through a complex school system, advocate for more and improved learning opportunities, and collaborate with educators and community organizations to achieve more effective educational opportunities" (p. 6). Collaborating with parents in meaningful and authentic ways can create a partnership that benefits an entire school community. Prerequisites to establishing quality partnerships are accepting parents as partners, making sure that all families feel welcome and invited by school staff, and finding ways to effectively communicate with them in support of children's learning.

The promotion of school psychologists to be leaders and advocates for family–school partnerships is viewed as an essential and expected practice. The National Association of School Psychologists (NASP) *Model for Comprehensive and Integrated School Psychological Services* (NASP, 2010) includes a domain specific to family–school collaboration, Family–School Collaboration Services. The expectation is that school psychologists will develop and utilize their understanding of family systems, strengths, and culture to promote the engagement of families in the educational process. For the purposes of this chapter, the process will be inclusive of practices across a multitiered system of support. Partnering with parents in this context will involve how school psychologists communicate with and engage parents early and intentionally.

Given this focus, this chapter will provide insight into what school psychologists need to know concerning family communication and involvement, both at the prevention and intervention level for children and also at the systems level, to bring about changes that will allow quality partnerships to be achieved. This chapter starts by examining the value of family involvement and sharing specific strategies to facilitate ongoing and effective communication to have a positive impact on and address students' academic, emotional, physical, and social needs. These issues are examined within the context of the current authorization of the Elementary and Secondary Education Act (ESEA), which shaped the 2004 reauthorization of the Individuals with Disabilities Education Act (IDEA), and within the context of a tiered system of support. The intent is to utilize the knowledge base regarding parent involvement and link this knowledge base to the legislative requirements in order for school psychologists to be effective leaders and advocates for stronger family–school partnerships.

What the Research Says About Parent Involvement

Parental and family involvement in schools matters, and the research is clear: When parents are involved, children do better in school (Hattie, 2009). Research on parent involvement and student achievement since the 1990s has borne this out. Henderson and Mapp's (2002) synthesis of the research on parent involvement, which included 51 studies conducted between 1993 and 2001, found that students with involved parents were more likely to earn higher grades and test scores, enroll in higher level programs, be promoted, attend school regularly, have better social skills and adapt well to school, and graduate and go on to postsecondary education. A more recent meta-analysis on the school–family connection, reviewing 58 studies conducted between 2003 and 2008, also found the key ingredient to quality public schools to be meaningful family involvement (Ferguson, 2008).

Understanding the nature of this involvement, however, is critical. Research has consistently shown that programs and interventions that engage families in supporting their children's learning at home are linked to higher student achievement over other forms, such as volunteering and attending school events, which have minimal impact (Henderson, Mapp, Johnson, & Davies, 2007). Schools have traditionally identified parent involvement as overt expressions of involvement, such as checking homework, establishing household rules, and participating in school-sponsored activities. But another recent meta-analysis, examining both the subtle and overt expressions of family participation, revealed that parental expectations—defined as the degree to which a student's parents believe that their child has great promise for achieving at high level—along with quality of parent–child communication and parental style, are more highly related to student achievement than various more overt expressions of this involvement (Jeynes, 2010).

A consistent finding from all the parent involvement research is that all families, regardless of their cultural backgrounds, education, and income levels, can have a positive impact on children's achievement and success in school (Phillipson & Phillipson, 2007). Parent involvement does matter in children's achievement, and schools can influence parent involvement processes, holding the keys to meaningful parent and family engagement (Epstein et al., 2009). The extent to which schools encourage and facilitate participation is a greater predictor of involvement than family characteristics. The National Center for Education Statistics' Parent and Family Involvement in Education Survey found that race and socioeconomic status affected how parents were involved (Herrold & O'Donnell, 2008). K–8 parents of Caucasian students were more likely than parents of African American or Hispanic students to attend a school event, volunteer or serve on a school committee, and participate in school fundraising. But, when it came to homework, survey data revealed that parents of Caucasian students trailed other groups in involvement, with 82% of parents of Caucasian students indicating that an adult checked their child's homework while 94% of African American and 91% of Hispanic students' homework was checked by a parent.

Consequently, educators should not hold preconceived notions about parent involvement.

Involvement will be higher when schools welcome parents and make it easy for them to be involved (Hanover Research, 2013). Parents report that feeling welcome and being treated with respect by school staff is the number one key to their connection with a school (Quiocho & Daoud, 2006). When school staff construct caring and trustful relationships with parents, treating parents as partners in their children's education, parents will be far more likely to become involved and stay involved. Fostering a sense of feeling welcomed into the school community is the first of six standards of the National Parent Teacher Association's (PTA) National Standards for Family–School Partnerships (PTA, 2009). These standards shift the focus from what schools should do to involve parents to what parents, schools, and communities can do together to support student success.

Another key to meaningful involvement is personal communication, as the foundation for effective partnerships is built on close collaboration and interaction (Allen, 2009). Communicating effectively is the second PTA national standard promoting quality family–school partnerships. According to Allen (2009), "schools can establish meaningful home–school dialogue when they expand communication to include more than routine practice and, whenever possible, tailor their communication to individual families" (p. 1). To create meaningful home–school communication Allen suggests that educators (a) invite dialogue (open a conversation about an important topic related to the curriculum, and invite specific family involvement), (b) monitor the tone and body language of face-to-face interactions, and (c) empathize (show families that school psychologists understand and respect demands on the families' time, finances, and family dynamics). Allen (2009) also stresses the importance of helping parents to get beyond past negative experiences with the school, which can hinder current effective communication between the school and home.

Effective communication is the second type of parent involvement identified by Epstein (2001), who categorized parent–school involvement programs into six broad types (see Table 33.1). Epstein (2001) suggests the following ideas about effective school-home communication:

- Make sure that memos and notices are written so that all parents can read and understand them.
- Make communication from school to home simple and readable, free of jargon, and in the language spoken by the family.

Table 33.1. Epstein's (2001) Framework of Six Types of Involvement

Type	Implementation Strategies
Parenting	Help all families establish home environments to support children as students
Communicating	Design effective forms of school-to-home and home-to-school communications about school programs and children's progress
Volunteering	Recruit and organize parent help and support
Learning at home	Provide information and ideas to families about how to help students at home with homework and other curriculum-related activities, decisions, and planning
Decision making	Include parents in school decisions, developing parent leaders and representatives
Collaborating with the community	Identify and integrate resources and services from the community to strengthen school programs, family practices, and student learning and development

- For example, use communications in print form; by e-mail and/or by phone; through TV, radio, and newspaper; and at extracurricular activities.
- Sponsor program or community events that allow educators and parents to interact socially in addition to standard parent–teacher conferences or school or program meetings.
- Implement feedback opportunities for parents and family members such as surveys on current program issues or special parent guest columns in the school newsletter.

Given these types of parent involvement, the report produced for the National Center for Family and Community Connections With Schools, *The School-Family Connection: Looking at the Larger Picture*, emphasizes the importance of focusing on creative and contextually relevant solutions that promote the efficacy of families to support their children's education (Ferguson, 2008).

As a first step to establishing meaningful family–school partnerships, educators and parents should examine their own beliefs, attitudes, and fears about each other that are barriers to coming together to support children's education. Henderson et al. (2007) have identified four core beliefs that serve as the foundation for the work of engaging families: (a) all parents have dreams for their children and want the best for them, (b) all parents have the capacity to support their children's learning, (c) parents and school staff should be equal partners, and (d) the responsibility for building partnerships between school and home rests primarily with school staff, especially school leaders. A starting point to establishing effective partnerships is an open and honest discussion about these core beliefs and an examination of educators' actions in relation to these beliefs. A useful tool to facilitate a discussion about

assumptions that hinder partnerships is found in Appendix A (Ellis & Hughes, 2002).

Parent Involvement in Federal Education Legislation

Parent involvement has always been a mainstay in ESEA. But it was not until the last reauthorization in 2001, the No Child Left Behind (NCLB) Act, when parent involvement was officially defined for the first time. In Title IX of NCLB, under General Provisions, parent involvement is defined as "the participation of parents in regular, two way, and meaningful communication involving student academic learning and other school activities," including the idea that parents play a key role in helping children learn and act as full partners in their child's education. The last reauthorization of ESEA also significantly shaped the 2004 reauthorization of IDEA.

For those districts that receive Title I funds, Section 1118 of NCLB has identified specific parent involvement activities at both the district and building level. While all schools receiving Title I funds are required to set aside a portion for parent involvement activities, school districts receiving more than $500,000 yearly in Title I funds must reserve at least 1% of these funds for activities to involve parents. Even possibly more important than sponsored activities, Section 1118 of Title I specifies that schools are required to develop, with parents, a parent involvement plan and to make the plan available to the parents of participating children. The plan must include the input of parents in shaping school-level policies, shared responsibility for bolstering student performance, and building more capacity for parent involvement. The plan should involve helping parents better grasp state and local standards, provide opportunities for involving all parents, provide materials and training to help parents promote learning at home, and, in general, build capacity for their involvement in their children's learning success. Another requirement is development of a parent–school compact that describes the school's responsibilities for providing high-quality curriculum and instruction, the parents' responsibilities for supporting children's learning, and the continuing home–school communication needed to achieve high standards. But long-term impact has been questionable, as compacts in the past have primarily focused on behavioral issues rather than being tied more closely to schools' improvement plans.

While NCLB has not yet been reauthorized, *A Blueprint for Reform: The Reauthorization of the Elementary and Secondary Education Act* was released in March 2010 and focuses on raising standards, encouraging innovation, and rewarding success (Duncan & Martin, 2010). Although the specific details outlining any changes for parent involvement will be included in the final legislation, the *Blueprint for Reform* acknowledges the importance of communities and families in supporting their children's education, stating that "a parent is a child's first teacher." This work in progress calls for the support of families, communities, and schools working in partnership to deliver services and supports that address the full range of student needs. In the meantime, however, the U.S. Department of Education has been issuing waivers to states concerning the Adequate Yearly Progress metrics that threatened to label the vast majority of schools as failing. A condition of receiving these waivers is that states must agree to a set of principles: (a) college and career-ready standards, (b) teacher evaluation systems that are linked to student achievement, and (c) new systems of accountability for raising achievement. Another condition is that states seeking flexibility under the federal legislation must work to turn around their lowest-performing 5% and 10% of their Title I schools as "priority" and "focus" schools. While one of the turnaround principles is increased family and community engagement, there has been little evidence to date that improvement plans have adopted meaningful strategies to establish authentic family–school partnerships (McAlister, 2012). The hope is that in the next reauthorization of ESEA, parent involvement will be buoyed up and be a centerpiece to enable meaningful and lasting school reform.

Reflections on the legislative maneuvers in ESEA over the past several decades demonstrate the clear desire for school and family partnerships to be genuine, relevant, and meaningful. While changes in IDEA over the same time span does not demonstrate as many changes to parent involvement, the intent of the law should be viewed as equally supportive of how families are to be involved in all aspects covered by IDEA. School psychologists play an instrumental role in promoting family and community involvement in the school improvement process and building on the family–teacher partnerships when the process involves individual students.

BASIC CONSIDERATIONS

Despite the benefits and the advantages of family–school collaboration and the requirements under federal legislation, both ESEA and IDEA, schools have been slow in implementing a coherent and systematic approach for parent engagement. A prerequisite to schools implementing parent involvement strategies is training in culturally responsive practices. Skills and practices like welcoming partnerships with families, building on family strengths, and positive communications should be folded into existing district systems of training (Rodriguez, Lopez del Bosque, & Villarreal, 2008). For example, district training sessions around reading instruction and strategies could include a section on how the information could be shared with families. This embedded focus has the advantage of demonstrating the expectation of family engagement as standard operating procedure within the school system as opposed to a spotlight on family engagement, which is often viewed as optional. Furthermore, ensuring that teachers make the information accessible to parents of their students is essential. This would mean having information in preferred formats for parents (e.g., printed, video, modeling in person) and accessible in their preferred language (Hanover Research, 2013).

Partnerships are built on close collaboration and interaction that is fostered through establishing and maintaining close communication. Thus, a first consideration in building partnerships and establishing close communication is to create a sense of community. Creating a sense of community will not emerge automatically within a school but needs to be "intentionally built by making every member feel welcomed and honored, and by ensuring that all are connected to the purpose of the school: students' learning" (Henderson et al., 2007).

An effective way to start building this sense of community, and increasing student achievement especially in low-performing schools, is through home visits.

One such model is the Parent/Teacher Home Visit project of Sacramento, California, that has been replicated in schools in 13 states. This model is founded on the core belief that "parents and teachers are equally important co-educators given that the parent is the expert on the individual child while the teacher is the expert on the curriculum that must be mastered for success" (http://pthvp.org). The goal of home visits, which can occur with children at all grade levels, is to build trust and to deepen relationships among all school staff, parents, and students. The visits are neither punitive nor focused on students' or parents' deficiencies, but rather provide an opportunity for school staff to meet with parents on their own turf and to learn about the expectations and dreams parents have for their children.

School staff visits to students' homes can take many forms. Staff can travel in pairs to their visits or they may visit one-on-one with the parent. Translators can accompany staff, if needed. In some instances, meetings have been set up in apartment complex clubhouses in preference of a family. School staff members who have participated in home visits, which last between 30 and 90 minutes, believe that the visits have mutually increased the teacher–parent relationship. Teachers and other school staff feel more comfortable picking up the phone, and families are more apt to call and talk to staff. When school staff get to know the students and their families, the parents become powerful advocates in their children's education as well as allies with school staff, working together to promote student learning.

Another effective strategy facilitating family–school partnerships is turning the family–school compact into a powerful tool to promote communication with families and authentic parent–school cooperation. Connecticut's State Department of Education has made great inroads into transforming a requirement under the federal education legislation, the Title I School–Parent Compact, into a useful document for meaningful communication with, and involvement of, families. Development of parent–school compacts has been a requirement of ESEA since the 1990s, but at the same time has been one of the weakest areas of Title I compliance (Stevenson & Laster, 2008). For the most part, compacts traditionally promoted general language in the law about parents' responsibility to support children's learning, and the language was vague and included monitoring school attendance, completion of homework, and television viewing. As this was a requirement under Title I, schools and parents complied, but the document for the most part was meaningless.

Instead, "Connecticut's Department of Education decided that if school–family compacts have to be created, schools should use the process to spark authentic conversations and list to parents' ideas about learning" (Henderson, Carson, Avallone, & Whipple, 2011). Compacts were grounded in student achievement data with the centerpiece of the compact focused on the school's improvement plan. Instead of generalities, compacts listed specific actions that parents, students, and teachers could take to improve student performance. They became a powerful tool for fostering effective communication between schools and families and for building lasting partnerships. Following a 10-step process, compacts are developed for each grade level, and parent meetings are held where teachers and parents together discuss specific strategies to achieve the school improvement and grade-level goals. If parents require assistance in implementing strategies, workshops are held to provide them the necessary training to support their children's learning.

BEST PRACTICES IN PARTNERING WITH PARENTS IN SCHOOL-BASED SERVICES

One of the most transformative heuristics that emerged in the field of education during the last decade is the framework for a multitiered system of supports (MTSS; McIntosh & Goodman, in press). While the roots associated with this framework have been traced and discussed in numerous articles and books, the transformative aspects have been the timely opportunity to meld what educators, researchers, and legislators have been promoting with evidence-based practices and data-based decision making for all students. Some of the most prominent and active researchers and leaders promoting this framework would include the work associated with positive behavioral interventions and supports (Sugai & Horner, 2009), which address social and emotional development, and response to intervention (RTI; Batsche et al., 2005), which is typically associated with addressing academic development. MTSS promotes an inclusive view of how academic and social learning is addressed along a continuum within the educational system. While differences exist in how states or districts depict a tiered system, the general features include universal, or primary, supports (Tier 1); supplemental, or secondary supports (Tier 2); and intense, or tertiary, supports (Tier 3).

Universal Level (Tier 1): Core Curriculum

Commonly accepted features of Tier 1 for academic and social learning include (a) focus on all students, (b) use of evidence-based and scientifically validated curricula and instruction, and (c) universal screening of all students to promote school and grade-level improvement planning with the problem-solving process and to identify students who may need additional support in a timely and more preventive manner. School psychologists can play an important role in their advocacy and demonstration of practices to support their buildings as they build or strengthen family engagement and involvement around these three key areas.

Focus on All Students

One of the first opportunities for school psychologists to engage in and promote best practices is to reinforce that a partnership with families starts with explicitly viewing each child as a part of the general educational community in the school. The central partnership is between the child's general education teacher and the family. The general education teacher is the child's primary teacher regardless of services the student may be receiving through Title I, English language support, and special education. Interactions between the school psychologist and general education teachers or parents need to promote this primary partnership. With school psychologists having more immediate access to resource personnel, it takes very intentional actions and words to foster this ownership. For example, when gathering data for a meeting, e-mails should be first addressed to the child's general education teacher. Additional support personnel (e.g., reading specialist, resource teacher) can be included, but the message should be clear that the classroom teacher is the primary teacher.

Evidence-Based Practices

It is from the school and the child's general education teacher that parents become informed of school and grade-level expectations. Researchers recommend that parents understand both what is expected and how they can support their child's education (Darling-Hammond, 2010). From a social learning standpoint, parents need to be informed of the school-wide expectations and what these expectations look like in each of the educational environments (e.g., classroom, hallway, lunchroom, playground), when the expectations are taught, and how a student's demonstration of the expectations will be acknowledged (e.g., specific praise and tangible tickets). This provides parents both the language and

understanding to enable them to support and reinforce their child's development of social competencies taught at school (Darling-Hammond, 2010). Social competencies taught school-wide revolve around expectations such as being safe, responsible, and respectful. In some instances, schools will use an evidence-based curriculum (e.g., Second Step) in order to teach more specific strategies that assist students in meeting these expectations (e.g., empathy and specific problem-solving skills). Whether it is school-wide expectations or social skill strategies, parents' being informed allows them to engage as partners by sharing what they know about their child and talking about how the information can transfer to the home setting (Ferguson, 2008).

The recent adoption of the Common Core State Standards by the vast majority of states provides perfect timing to revisit the discussion on developing meaningful family partnerships related to academic learning. With the Common Core providing a very clear and coherent picture of what students are expected to learn across K–12 and the emphasis for teachers to provide appropriate scaffolds for children so they are able to meet the standards, parents not only will understand the focus of instruction, but importantly will know what they can do to help them. The National PTA has created a guide for parents as they navigate Common Core, in the context of the National Standards for Parent–Family Partners referenced earlier (http://www.pta.org). As part of a building's Tier 1 efforts, principals and teachers will be able to elaborate on how the district's curricula, materials, and core instruction are aligned to meet Common Core and provide concrete examples of how skill development toward the standards can be reinforced by parents.

The expertise school psychologists have around child development provides an important opportunity for the discussion with general educators regarding differentiation of core instruction, materials, activities, and content. This discussion is critical given the expectation that teachers will provide appropriate scaffolding for individual students to meet grade-level expectations. School psychologists can provide strategies teachers can use during family conferences that will honor and promote teachers' learning from parents about a student's strengths and needs that leads to ideas for home–school connections (Ferguson, 2008). As an example, when schools or teachers are introducing the expectations around social learning using a building matrix that describes operationally defined behaviors by educational setting, a home matrix may be shared, with an example of how parents can use the matrix and acknowledgment system at home. Parents would generate their own specific examples related to the common broad expectations. For instance, if one of the expectations at school included being safe, safety at home may include wearing a helmet when riding a bike and only allowing an adult to answer the door.

Universal Screening

The last central component common to Tier 1 within an MTSS framework is the notion of universal screening. As stated previously, the purpose of universal screening is twofold: (a) to provide a school and grade-level profile to teams so they can engage in problem solving for school improvement and (b) to identify students who may need additional support in meeting grade-level expectations or those whose support would appropriately advance them when grade-level expectations are already demonstrated. While the latter has not commonly been addressed in the MTSS literature, we believe strongly that healthy schools consider the notion of a tiered system in meeting the needs of each child in the building, which includes children with advanced skills.

While progress has been made since 2000 regarding how buildings use data to make decisions and the professional development provided to teachers regarding assessment literacy, the comfort of teachers in using and interpreting data remains an area for improvement. Given that this chapter has been promoting the partnership between the child's primary teacher, their general education teacher, and the parent, school psychologists can play an important role in helping teachers translate universal screening results into understandable and family-friendly terms. Teachers and parents need to understand: (a) when the data suggest that the student may need additional support; (b) how to break down the data, if appropriate, to summarize areas of strength and possible focus areas; and (c) how to explain the difference between percentile scores, local versus national norms, and criterion-referenced scores. The talking points that will be shared related to progress monitoring data in the next section can serve as a template and be created around universal screening data.

When building- or grade-level teams are engaging in data dialogues and realize that a formal problem-solving process would be beneficial in determining how to craft a strong improvement plan (e.g., fourth-grade plan to address issues around vocabulary development, plan to address phonics when the majority of students are not at an acceptable level of accuracy, plan to support responsible behavior in the classroom), school psychologists can be logical and strong facilitators. The role of the facilitator is to make the process easy. School psychologists are often skilled at leading the problem-solving process, achieving consensus, and navigating discussions toward a mutually agreeable solution. Not only do they bring these facilitation skills to the table, but they also allow all directly involved parties to participate fully. While facilitating the planning process that will be done in classrooms, the school psychologist can facilitate the idea generation regarding how parents can be involved as partners. It is recommended to have school psychologists take the grade-level plans and ideas to a group of parents to engage in further discussion and exploration about how parents can partner with the school.

Supplemental and Intensive Instruction or Intervention (Tiers 2 and 3)

When universal screening data indicate that a student may need additional supports to achieve important academic or social competencies, the notion of MTSS is to have accessible and flexible supports available that will target the area of need, use evidence- or function-based interventions, and monitor progress frequently in order to know whether to keep or change something about the school psychologist's approach to the concern. While some states, districts, and buildings have made distinct decision rules regarding what is often referred to as Tier 2 and Tier 3, this chapter addresses them together and illustrates that the supports should be thought of more from the angle of a continuum, rather than as distinct steps in a process. As the intensity of the problem increases, so too will school psychologists likely increase (a) analysis of data, (b) time or frequency of the intervention, (c) personnel or agencies involved, and (d) customization of the intervention (McIntosh & Goodman, in press). Communicating and involving parents in the MTSS process highlighted for best practices revolve around the parents' role in understanding differentiated instruction and targeted intervention, how data are used to determine supports and make decisions, and how the problem-solving process is facilitated.

Family Understanding of Differentiation and Intervention

When designing a system of support around targeted intervention, building-level teams start to feel the difference in an MTSS system. The process of building infrastructure around an intervention system starts to make visible the before and after because it addresses what is done, how it is being done, and who does it. Because parents of current school-age students would not have had this type of system in place when they were in school, school psychologists need to make sure they are clear in their communication so parents do not associate school psychology practices with what parents remember as the way things were done. For example, some parents may have personally received Title I support as a student and associate that with being with other classmates needing help and with receiving support all year long. School psychologists need to ensure that parents understand that a cornerstone of MTSS is to try and act as preventively as possible, develop targeted intervention groups, and make group membership fluid and flexible (Burns & Gibbons, 2012).

When school psychologists share the notion of targeted intervention groups, parents need to understand (a) the specific focus of the intervention (e.g., fluency, phonics, resolving disagreements in a nonphysical manner), (b) how the intervention selected is designed to address this area, and (c) that the intervention is a supplement to the child's core instruction and not a replacement for the core instruction time. It is important to emphasize how and why this particular focus area fits into the bigger picture. For example, parents need to understand that the supplemental intervention may be targeting the area of phonemic awareness and that phonemic awareness is important in literacy development because being able to hear and manipulate sounds in words is a precursor to learning the graphemes associated with the sounds-phonics. Understanding the importance of the area targeted for support at the initial level of responding cannot be emphasized enough. If school psychologists find that a student is not responding to interventions, then they should want the urgency as a team to be increasing, and having already established a common understanding of the specific problem allows teams to focus on how to respond differently rather than playing catch-up with parents in the parents' initial understanding.

Building on the family-first partnership with the general education teacher, the discussion should also include how the teacher may be planning to differentiate during core instruction in light of the area being supported by intervention. With this information, parents will understand work the student brings home, be able to ask questions and engage in conversations with their child, and extend the intervention to the home setting, if appropriate. For example, the general behavior matrix that may have been created based on

the school's expectations may be modified if the child is receiving support based on recognizing and using a strategy to calm down when the child is frustrated or angry. For instance, the matrix that may have been created at home related to safety, referenced earlier, may need to include a modification of discussing the parents' calming strategy. This provides a nightly review of the strategy and discussion as to if and when the strategy was used that day. The parents would have the specific steps taught with the strategy (i.e., "stop and use your signal, name your feeling, and calm down") so they were reinforcing what was being taught at school.

Data-Based Decision Making

When teams are learning to use data to guide decisions regarding needing additional support, school psychologists are perfectly positioned to be sharing their expertise on an area of strength (e.g., assessment) and being a member who is a bit removed from daily discussion by virtue of their role. This once-removed role aids teams in breaking decision-making habits that exist in many buildings. Not only can school psychologists assist in the interpretation of data, but they also can advocate that teams remain neutral to some of the knowledge they have about a student that may, or may not, be supported by the data at hand. For example, when forming intervention groups using the data, a tendency has been for teams to not include students with disabilities or students who are English language learners. It is important that building-level teams include each student in the sort and articulate what the data indicate are each students strengths and needs, in order to make thoughtful decisions about appropriate intervention matches. The process is to be viewed as a dynamic process responsive to students' needs, and formally reviewing this effort several times a year is best practice.

In addition to data interpretation and advocacy for students when interpreting data, school psychologists can assist by supporting school dialogues with families regarding data. Teachers are often first to share that assessment, and data were not driving forces in their career choice. School psychologists in one school district made a set of talking points that could be used when sharing progress monitoring data (see Appendix B). It was intended to provide family-friendly language that makes the data accessible and understandable. The importance of having a common understanding of the student's strengths, needs, and response to intervention sets up opportunities for both celebrations and engagement in problem solving.

Individual Student Problem-Solving Process

While the problem-solving process is not intended to be reserved for individual students, we have elected to focus attention on best practices related to individual student problem solving because it is so vital to have strong family engagement when it comes to individual student planning. When parents have been involved early and created meaningful partnerships with their child's teachers, the critical areas to attend to related to family engagement is to (a) create the supports necessary to allow the parents' voice to be heard and understood with regard to their child, (b) make the process accessible so that the parents understand how their knowledge fits and adds value to the process, and have an overall outcome of shared ownership of the resulting plan.

A sobering reality as to the progress that remains to be made was shared by parents at a leadership forum hosted by the National Center for Learning Disabilities' RTI Action Network (http://www.rtinetwork.org/professional/forums-and-webinars/rti-leadership-forum). With parent panelists on every strand, a common and reoccurring desire was that they would not only be informed of the process but also be meaningfully included as a team member in problem solving. One panelist referred to teams being willing to "leave your egos at the door" in order for genuine partnerships to be formed.

Partnerships are strengthened when parents are fully included in the sharing of information and decision making within the problem-solving process. Parents would be involved in sharing and consensus around (a) identification of strengths and needs, (b) problem analysis, (c) intervention generation and selection, (d) goal setting and progress monitoring, and (e) plan evaluation. Engaging parents in the problem-solving process as a routine helps teams proceed in a systematic manner toward a mutually agreeable plan. This routine would be used as soon as data indicated that core and intervention supports did not appear sufficient to address the concern and would likely take place between the teacher and the parents. It would not have a heavy feeling of structure, but would start with strengths and needs, review of what has been working and not working, analyze what may be contributing most to the current trend in progress, generate ideas for improvement, and result in an agreeable plan for school and home. If progress remained unsatisfactory at the next progress review, the team may be expanded to include others whose expertise may be helpful in creating a stronger response plan. The importance of the routine is that parents will come to understand the process and know how their information about their child is helpful, and as more team members are added, the parents will be newcomers to the process. When parents are viewed as essential team members with the general education teacher, stronger relationships and ownership are fostered. The RTI Action Network provides a case study example of how this process unfolds over time (Miller, 2011).

SUMMARY

A central purpose of MTSS is to improve student outcomes by creating a strong educational system that is inclusive of all students, uses evidence-based practices, engages in data-based decision making, and uses the problem-solving process as a way to understand and build responsive plans. The standards provided by the National PTA and the central tenet discussed in this chapter illustrate how the work of school psychologists can be an important part of creating genuine and productive parent partnerships to improve student outcomes. Through their work with advocacy, facilitation, data interpretation and use, and engagement in the problem-solving process, school psychologists are positioned to make the standards visible in buildings. By engaging parents through partnerships at all levels of support within a tiered system, the standards related to creating welcoming schools and communicating and collaborating to support student success can be achieved more genuinely.

REFERENCES

Allen, J. (2009). Effective home–school communication. *FINE (Family Involvement Network of Educators) Newsletter, 1*(1). Retrieved from http://www.hwdsb.on.ca/e-best/files/2011/03/Home-School-Communication-BLAM.pdf

Batsche, G. M., Elliott, J., Graden, J., Grimes, J., Kovaleski, J. F., Prasse, D., ... Tilly, W. D., III. (2005). *Response to intervention: Policy considerations and implementation.* Alexandria, VA: National Association of State Directors of Special Education.

Burns, M. K., & Gibbons, K. (2012). *Implementing response-to-intervention in elementary and secondary schools: Procedures to assure scientifically-based practices.* New York, NY: Routledge.

Darling-Hammond, L. (2010). *Performance counts: Assessment systems that support high-quality learning.* Washington, DC: Council of Chief State School Officers. Retrieved from http://www.ccsso.org/Documents/2010/Performance_Counts_Assessment_Systems_2010.pdf

Duncan, A., & Martin, C. (2010). *A blueprint for reform: The reauthorization of the Elementary and Secondary Education Act.* Washington, DC: U.S. Department of Education, Office of Planning, Evaluation, and Policy Development.

Ellis, D., & Hughes, K. (2002). *Partnerships by design: Cultivating effective and meaningful school–family–community partnerships.* Portland, OR: Northwest Regional Educational Laboratory.

Epstein, J. L. (2001). *School, family, and community partnerships: Preparing educators and improving schools.* Boulder, CO: Westview Press.

Epstein, J. L., Sanders, M. G., Sheldon, S. B., Simon, B. S., Clark Salinas, K., Rodriguez Janson, N., … Williams, K. J. (2009). *School, family, and community partnerships: Your handbook for action* (3rd ed.). Thousand Oaks, CA: Corwin Press.

Ferguson, C. (2008). *The school–family connection: Looking at the larger picture.* Austin, TX: Southwest Educational Development Laboratory. Retrieved from http://www.sedl.org/connections/resources/sfclitrev.pdf

Hanover Research. (2013). *Parent participation in Title I schools.* Washington DC: Author.

Hattie, J. (2009). *Visible learning: A synthesis of over 800 meta-analyses related to achievement.* New York, NY: Routledge.

Henderson, A. T., Carson, J., Avallone, P., & Whipple, M. (2011). Making the most of school–family compacts. *Educational Leadership, 68*(8), 48–53.

Henderson, A. T., & Mapp, K. L. (2002). *A new wave of evidence: The impact of school, parent, and community connections on student achievement.* Austin, TX: Southwest Educational Development Laboratory.

Henderson, A. T., Mapp, K. L., Johnson, V. R., & Davies, D. (2007). *Beyond the bake sale: The essential guide to family–school partnerships.* New York, NY: The New Press.

Herrold, K., & O'Donnell, K. (2008). *Parent and family involvement in education, 2006–2007 school year, From the National Household Education Surveys program of 2007* (NCES 2008-050). Washington, D C: National Center for Education Statistics, U.S. Department of Education.

Jeynes, W. (2010). The salience of the subtle aspects of parental involvement and encouraging that involvement: Implications for school-based programs. *Teachers College Record, 112,* 747–774.

Mapp, K. (2009). The evidence is clear. In *State laws on family engagement in education: Reference guide* (p. 6). Washington, DC: Parent Teacher Association.

McAlister, S. (2012). *USDOE waiver policy should enforce meaningful compliance to parent engagement principle.* Providence, RI: Annenberg Institute for School Reform. Retrieved from http://annenberginstitute.org/print/495

McIntosh, K., & Goodman, S. (in press). *Multitiered systems of support: Integrating academic RTI and school-wide PBIS.* New York, NY: Guilford Press.

Miller, D. (2011). *Progress monitoring data review.* Washington, DC: RTI Action Network. Retrieved from http://www.rtinetwork.org/rti-blog/entry/1/174

National Association of School Psychologists. (2010). *Model for comprehensive and integrated school psychological services.* Bethesda, MD: Author. Retrieved from www.nasponline.org/standards/2010standards/2_PracticeModel.pdf

Parent Teacher Association. (2009). *PTA National Standards for Family–School Partnerships: An implementation guide.* Washington, DC: Author. Retrieved from http://www.pta.org/files/National_Standards_Implementation_Guide_2009.pdf

Phillipson, S., & Phillipson, S. N. (2007). Academic expectations, belief of ability, and involvement by parents as predictors of child achievement: A cross-cultural comparison. *Educational Psychology, 27,* 329–348.

Quiocho, A. M. L., & Daoud, A. M. (2006). Dispelling myths about Latino parent participation in schools. *The Educational Forum, 70,* 255–267.

Rodriguez, R. G., Lopez del Bosque, R., & Villarreal, A. (2008). *Creating culturally responsive parent engagement.* San Antonio, TX: Intercultural Development Research Association. Retrieved from http://www.idra.org/IDRA_Newsletter/November_-_December_2008_Enlightened_Public_Policy/Creating_Culturally_Responsive_Parent_Engagement/

Stevenson, Z., Jr., & Laster, C. (2008). *2003–2006 monitoring cycle report.* Washington, DC: U.S. Department of Education. Retrieved from http://www.ed.gov/admins/lead/account/monitoring/monitoringcyclerpt1008.pdf

Sugai, G., & Horner, R. H. (2009). Defining and describing school-wide positive behavior support. In W. Sailor, G. Dunlap, G. Sugai, & R. Horner (Eds.), *Handbook of positive behavior support* (pp. 307–326). New York, NY: Springer.

APPENDIX A. EXAMINING ASSUMPTIONS THAT HINDER FAMILY–SCHOOL PARTNERSHIPS

Instructions: Read each statement in the left column and check whether you feel this is or is not an assumption that hinders partnerships at your school. When done, discuss the assumptions the group considers most troublesome. Together, identify positive statements and strategies that will dispel preconceived notions, change attitudes, and help facilitate partnerships.

Assumptions That Hinder Family–School Partnerships		
Assumptions	School-based assumption	What may be the reality
1. Parents who don't attend school events don't care about their children's success in school.	☐ Yes ☐ No	
2. Parents who are illiterate or do not speak English can't help their children.	☐ Yes ☐ No	
3. Parents from different ethnic and racial groups don't understand the role they play in their children's education.	☐ Yes ☐ No	
4. It is up to parents to find out what is going on at school.	☐ Yes ☐ No	
5. Getting families involved takes a lot of time and energy, with the results not often corresponding to the effort.	☐ Yes ☐ No	
6. Children who are troublemakers often come from families that do not value education.	☐ Yes ☐ No	
7. It is all right for school staff to contact families only when a child is in trouble.	☐ Yes ☐ No	
8. The problem of hard-to-reach families and at-risk students is the fault of the families themselves.	☐ Yes ☐ No	
9. Teachers are expected to play the role of parents too much in their jobs.	☐ Yes ☐ No	

Note. From *Partnerships By Design: Cultivating Effective and Meaningful School–Family–Community Partnerships*, by D. Ellis and K. Hughes, 2002, Portland, OR: Northwest Regional Educational Laboratory. Copyright 2002 by Northwest Regional Educational Laboratory. Adapted with permission.

APPENDIX B. DATA TALKING POINTS FOR PARENT TEACHER CONFERENCES

Communicating With Parents – Topic: Progress Monitoring

The following talking points are intended to assist us as we help families understand progress monitoring and partner with them around their child's education. Please use these talking points as suggestions for explaining progress monitoring. *These talking points are not intended as a script.*

Overall Message

- Your child is valued at our school and in our district.
- Your child has strengths to build upon.
- As a team, we have the responsibility to help your child learn and achieve to high standards.
- You are an important part of the team.

What Is Progress Monitoring and Why Do It?

- Keeping track of _____'s progress will help us know if we are on track with our supports.

- We do several things to help us learn about _____'s reading skills. We have formal assessments, or tests, that give us a picture of his (or her) skills. As the teacher, I keep track of how students are learning on a daily basis during reading, and you and I both make observations that help us know about _____.
- It's common for parents to want to know how their child is progressing and how he (or she) compares to other children in the same grade. One way we look at progress is by assessing every week or every other week on a quick test called DIBELS. You can think of this as using a thermometer to check _____'s temperature. The test doesn't tell us everything we need or want to know, but it gives us an indication of overall health.
- Just like using a thermometer, we want to watch the temperature change over time to know if things are getting better or if we need to think about doing something different.
- We are committed to helping _____ become a strong and confident reader. Monitoring his (or her) progress helps us keep track of how well we are doing and when we need to put our heads together and change something.

34

Best Practices in Family–School Collaboration for Multitiered Service Delivery

Gloria Miller
Cathy Lines
Megan Fleming
University of Denver (CO)

OVERVIEW

School is a place where families and educators come together to share responsibility for raising, guiding, and teaching children in our society. Yet as Sara Lawrence-Lightfoot (2003) suggests, there is no more complex geography than the borderlands between home and school. The critical role of these overlapping spheres of influence has been cited as one of the most influential factors in student school success (Epstein, 1995). There is a great need for effective partnerships between families and schools, not only because students spend the majority of time out of school, but also because families have a dramatic influence on the degree to which children are engaged and perform in school.

The intentional practice of family–school collaboration embodies a relational equality between families and school professionals who work together to mutually support a child's development. Indeed, successful partnerships between families and schools involve a shared responsibility for a student's school success (Lines, Miller, & Arthur-Stanley, 2011). *Family* represents all primary caregivers in a child's life who perform essential parental functions. *School* refers to all teaching and nonteaching members of a school staff. Family–School Collaboration Services is one of the identified domains of practice in the National Association of School Psychologists (NASP) *Model for Comprehensive and Integrated School Psychological Services* (NASP, 2010a). Several other professional domains in school psychology (i.e., Consultation and Collaboration, Data-Based

Decision-Making, Academic Services, and Mental Health Services) also highlight the role school psychologists play promoting partnerships with families.

Numerous NASP position papers have focused on the family, school, and community collaboration role of school psychologists. *School–Family Partnering to Enhance Learning: Essential Elements and Responsibilities* (NASP, 2012) includes a concise review of these responsibilities. School psychologists (a) address concerns across the different contexts within which a child exist; (b) participate in school-based teams to plan and implement home–school efforts to improve educational outcomes for students; (c) implement systematic, evidence-based models of school–family intervention; (d) serve as liaisons to support two-way communication and coordination between school and home; (e) build partnerships between families and educators throughout screening, early intervention, and special education processes; (f) provide professional development opportunities for families and educators on the positive effects of partnering; and (g) support sustainable family–school partnerships through ongoing monitoring and accountability.

The newly revised NASP *Principles for Professional Ethics* (NASP, 2010b) also includes numerous standards associated with the ethical delivery of psychological services that highlight the role school psychologists have in building strong family–school partnerships. Standard II.3.10 most clearly summarizes this intent:

School psychologists encourage and promote parental participation in designing interventions for their children. When appropriate, this includes linking interventions between the school and the home, tailoring parental involvement to the skills of the family, and helping parents gain the skills needed to help their children succeed.

The purpose of this chapter is to review evidence-based family–school collaboration practices that can be implemented effectively by school psychologists within a multitiered system of supports. Relevant school-wide and upper tier examples are presented to improve family engagement and participation that can enhance students' academic and social–emotional outcomes. In addition, partnering strategies with families across grade levels and from culturally and linguistically diverse backgrounds are considered as are suggestions to overcome common implementation challenges.

BASIC CONSIDERATIONS

Considerable empirical evidence has accumulated demonstrating that families have a substantial influence on students' academic achievement and engaged learning from preschool to high school, with the greatest long-term benefits observed for ethnically diverse, low-income children and families (Christenson & Reschly, 2010). Family–school collaboration has been linked to improved school engagement, increased student motivation, long-term educational aspirations, and enhanced social–emotional learning as well as higher performance in math, science, reading, and English and a greater likelihood of school completion and college attendance (Nokali, Bachman, & Votruba-Drzal, 2010; Weihua & Williams, 2010).

Shift to Family–School Partnering

The reauthorization of general education (i.e., No Child Left Behind) and special education laws (i.e., Individuals with Disabilities Education Improvement Act) clearly point to the need to view parents/guardians as partners in all educational decision making. An important paradigm shift has occurred in regards to educator beliefs about families. There has been a distinctive move away from traditional unidirectional concepts of parent involvement to an emphasis on bidirectional coordination between homes and schools. The major characteristics of this shift and the many associated changes in school psychologists' roles and responsibilities are summarized in Table 34.1.

Multitiered Family–School Collaboration

A multitiered system of family–school collaboration incorporates universal as well as targeted or intensive practices to support students with and without disabilities. This service delivery model recognizes that one size does not fit all and allows for greater differentiation and allocation of resources (Edwards, 2011). The goal of a multitiered system of family–school collaboration is to create a continuum of coordinated partnership practices to support student success. This model is best reflected through an analogy. During the summer months, most people sleep with a minimum layer of warmth or support represented by a sheet. But with the advent of cooler weather, some people need to add a blanket for an additional layer of warmth and some, who have a greater sensitivity to cold, may require even more intensive layers through the addition of a comforter. Thus, most people benefit from a universal layer of family–school partnering support. However, supplementary layers may be needed for a smaller percentage of students, families, and staff owing to individual needs and reactions to changes in situations or conditions.

A well-developed family–school collaboration continuum includes an array of universal partnership practices infused throughout the school as well as selected supports offered strategically to families and students with identified personal or circumstantial needs. We have chosen to combine targeted and intensive family–school partnering efforts conceptually as upper tier supports. This not only removes the tendency to place or label students or families within one or another tier of service, it also more clearly demonstrates the idea that boundaries between tiers must remain permeable and fluid. Universal tier supports must filter throughout the school and upper tier supports must be intentionally available as needed.

One example of family–school collaboration within a multitiered service delivery model is the development of a system of supports for students and families during critical school transitions (i.e., preschool to elementary school to junior/middle school to high school). Universal practices might include school-wide and classroom information meetings as well as the development of materials and resources to meet the needs of most transitioning students and families. Additional group sessions could be planned for a smaller number of students and families who request or require further help to navigate these important changes. Even fewer students and families would be offered individually tailored interventions that could involve collaboration

Table 34.1. Shift From Parent Involvement to Multitiered Family–School Partnering

Traditional Parent Involvement[a]	Family–School Partnering
School is the typical site of involvement, usually with participants engaging in structured volunteering, such as fundraisers and organized events.	Home, school, and community settings are all partnering sites, with a focus on an array of opportunities to increase student learning and school success.
Education is viewed primarily as the school's responsibility with families often playing a limited or unclear role in supporting student school success.	Education is explicitly viewed as a shared responsibility between home and school with families playing a critical role in supporting student school success.
School–parent meetings and conferences tend to be formally initiated by the school, with a primary focus on information, program eligibility, and school-administered plans.	Family–school meetings can be initiated by the school or family members with a primary focus on joint planning; much discussion can occur outside of formal meetings; interventions and progress monitoring are mutually developed.
Homework is often given with the expectation of independent completion and with consequences for failure to comply.	Homework is given after families understand expectations and if a student fails to comply, solutions are jointly developed between the school and family.
Homework is directed and viewed primarily from the teacher's perspective.	Homework is viewed as a family–school communication touch point and is considered from the teacher, student, and family perspective.
Communication is often shared one-way from the school to the home, mostly through formal written formats.	Communication is shared two-way from school to home, then home to school through various means.
A few parents tend to participate at school-based events and on school committees.	Every family is given opportunities to participate and to gain information, with options to do so from home or work.
Sample School Psychologist Shift in Roles and Responsibilities	
System-wide social–emotional and behavioral standards, expectations, rewards, and curriculum are primarily presented at school to staff and students.	System-wide social–emotional and behavioral standards, expectations, rewards, and curriculum are shared with and understood by families; there is coordinated skill practice, recognition, and reinforcement at home and school.
Small intervention groups for academics and behavior require only signed parent permission.	Small intervention groups for academics and behavior require signed permission and personal outreach to every family, with two-way communication, regular progress updates, and opportunities for home skill practice.
Behavioral and other intervention plans are often developed by school staff and sent home for approval.	Behavioral and other intervention plans are developed collaboratively with staff, families, and students and include home–school–community coordination.

Note. From *Essential RTI Information Slides With Notes* by the Colorado Department of Education, 2012, Denver, CO: Author. Adapted with permission, Public Domain.
[a] In this table, "parent" refers primarily to parents and "family" refers to all caregivers and the student.

with community agencies and professionals. The latter two upper tier examples require more professional time and coordination across contexts. The need for upper tier efforts, however, is reduced and the effectiveness is enhanced when family-centered values, standards, and practices are ingrained in a school-wide core mission.

Data-Based Problem Solving and Family–School Collaboration

A major component of multitiered family–school collaboration is data-based problem solving focused on

student success. Families universally have a desire to help their children be successful in school and life. In fact, this dream is the essential glue of family–school partnerships (Lines et al., 2011). When this essential ingredient becomes a focus of data-based decision-making teams, there is greater intervention continuity across home and school settings and students across the developmental spectrum prosper. The most effective problem-solving teams collaborate with families to review formative and summative data, jointly establish targets and goals for student progress, and design and evaluate all interventions. Collaboration with families in this manner deepens each partner's understanding of expected educational outcomes and establishes joint responsibility for students' success.

While family–school collaboration has been an essential cornerstone of quality special education services, it also is now a mandated component of all general education response to intervention approaches (Turnbull, Turnbull, Erwin, Soodak, & Shogren, 2011). School psychologists, as essential members of data-based decision-making teams, must insist and reinforce the incorporation of families during all problem-solving sessions. Partnerships with families also can be evaluated over time in a variety of ways. Assessments could include quantitative disaggregation of the number of families who volunteer, participate in conferences, or attend school events. Additionally, family–school partnering data might be collected through parent perception and teacher satisfaction surveys, interviews with staff and families, analysis of school and home visits, and the simple collection of anonymous guest surveys to assess family member impressions of feeling welcomed and satisfied after visiting the school.

Implementing Multitiered Family–School Partnering

Despite clear legal and ethical obligations and the indisputable empirical evidence regarding the need for and long-term benefits of family engagement in student school success, researchers have continued to find limited and uncoordinated random acts of family–school collaboration (Weiss, Lopez, & Rosenberg, 2010). To avoid the common practice of selecting a hodgepodge of home–school activities not fully integrated into everyday routines, family–school collaboration must be systematically woven into the fabric of a school (Christenson, 2004). Multitiered checklists of family–school partnership practices can help in this regard (i.e., see http://www.cde.state.co.us/RtI/family).

From an implementation science perspective, the most successful schools carefully assemble a system of partnership practices with clear execution criteria in mind to support family–school collaboration (Fixsen, Naoom, Blase, Friedman, & Wallace, 2005). A framework for implementation includes developmental guidelines to increase the likelihood that school and district reforms can be sustained with confidence and fidelity. Each implementation stage overlaps with and supports later stages through a specific progression of emerging and developing practices as well as ideas to further operationalize and optimize efforts over time. Highly

successful reforms are those accompanied by clear structural, organizational, and leadership implementation criteria. Continual improvements are fostered through training, coaching, and other professional development, and sustainability is fostered by integrating new practices into established routines. A well-defined implementation framework is easily translated into an evaluation rubric to promote a cycle of ongoing assessment and data-based decision making. A national implementation science center has been established to ensure that evidence-based practices are successfully embedded into school-based organizational change efforts (see http://www.scalingup.org). School psychologists can advocate for the creation of clear criteria to promote family–school collaboration policy and practice. One such implementation rubric is currently in use in Colorado to foster the development of multitiered family–school support plans designed to improve student academic and behavioral success (see Table 34.2).

BEST PRACTICES IN FAMILY–SCHOOL COLLABORATION FOR MULTITIERED SERVICE DELIVERY

Evidence-based ideas for universal as well as upper tier family–school collaboration practices are reviewed and organized under four essential features. Owing to space limitations, only a few examples are highlighted here. Many other ideas relevant to a multitiered system of family–school partnership support can be found in highly regarded national resources (Center on School, Family, and Community Partnerships: http://www.csos.jhu.edu/p2000/center.htm; Harvard Family Research Project: http://www.hfrp.org; National Coalition for Parents in Education, http://www.ncpie.org; National Parent Teacher Association: http://www.pta.org).

Build Relationships

A strong relationship is at the heart of any partnership. Relationships are fostered when there is mutual respect, trust, sensitivity to, and appreciation of the role each partner plays in a student's life success. Family members must be recognized for their unique insights about their child's needs and talents and their enduring interest their child's future. Educators must be recognized for their knowledge of development, learning, and curriculum and their enduring interest in teaching and motivating students. Indeed, the quality of parents' relationships with educators as a child progresses

Table 34.2. Multitiered Family–School Partnering Implementation Rubric

Anchors and Questions	Emerging: Establishing Consensus	Developing: Building Infrastructure	Operationalizing: Gaining Consistency	Optimizing: Innovating and Sustaining
Structures:				
How is family, school, and community partnering established?	Staff, families, and community members review current partnering practices in policies, procedures, committee composition, forms, role descriptions, and communication. Strengths, challenges are identified.	Staff, families, and community members gather and disaggregate relevant family participation information and develop/revise current partnering structures and practices. All partnering roles and responsibilities are explicitly articulated.	Staff, families, and community members implement agreed-upon partnering plan consistently. The staff engages in a shared definition, understanding of rationale, and common expectations.	The entire school community has an embedded commitment to partnering. Systemic, school-wide partnering is infused within all organizational infrastructures.
How is ongoing support for and commitment to partnering ensured?	School leadership examines current roles of staff to identify ways to include staff liaison position.	School leadership identifies a staff person to support family, school, and community partnering.	Collaborative liaison and community support are offered as needed to staff and family members, with feedback as to effectiveness.	Collaborative liaison ensures ongoing support for all staff, students, families, and community members throughout the tiers.
How will staff and families know the partnerships are effective?	School leadership examines current data and data-collection methods to identify how useful they are for evaluating partnering practices.	Staff, families, and community members jointly examine and develop ways to measure the success of their partnering, using data (e.g., family/staff/student attendance, ratings, surveys, or visit and event feedback questionnaires).	Staff, families, and community members collect data on the success of their partnering. The collected data are examined regularly and adjustments to the school partnering plan are made accordingly.	School leadership collects, uses, and shares ongoing feedback and data from staff, community members, and families as an embedded practice for continuous improvement.
Processes and procedures:				
How is partnering used to benefit each student during universal, targeted, and intensive support?	Staff, families, and community members discuss and understand how collaborating together benefits every learner and family.	Staff, families, and community members create a tiered partnering framework. Guidelines for partnering with families and community members throughout the tiered framework are outlined.	Families are actively involved in the problem-solving process as equal partners throughout the tiers. Partnering with families increases as student needs increase.	All staff follow tiered partnering process. Families and staff pervasively and mutually share learner data and work together to solve problems with community members.
What is the partnering process if a student might have a disability?	Staff, families, and community members understand the law for identification of students with disabilities.	Staff, families, and community members have a mutual understanding of the law as it relates to problem solving and the tiers.	Staff and families consistently follow the guidelines for when a disability is suspected and collaborate when making decisions related to identification of disabilities.	Data are collected on clarity of and adherence to disability procedures. Adjustments are made accordingly as part of a continuous improvement cycle.

Continued

Table 34.2. Continued

Anchors and Questions	Emerging: Establishing Consensus	Developing: Building Infrastructure	Operationalizing: Gaining Consistency	Optimizing: Innovating and Sustaining
Professional development:				
How do staff, families, and communities build their partnering skills and knowledge?	Staff, families, and community members examine and understand the research behind partnering practices and their beliefs about school and home partnering.	Staff, families, and community members identify and receive professional development related to partnering practices, including ways to implement when differences in language, culture, or learning.	Staff, families, and community members implement the skills they are learning and receive ongoing professional development.	School-wide systems are well established. There is regular examination of professional development, using needs-based assessments and data to identify areas for further development.

Note. From *RTI Fidelity of Implementation Rubrics* by the Colorado Department of Education, 2010, Denver, CO: Author. Adapted with permission. Public Domain.

through school versus the frequency of contact has been a consistent predictor of academic and social development (Christenson, 2004). When strong relationships exist between parents and educators, both parties express positive intentions toward each other and feel confident that each will do whatever it takes to address a child's needs (Sheridan, Taylor, & Woods, 2008).

Universal Relationship Practices

School psychologists clearly play an important role in school-wide practices to encourage strong family–educator relationships. Such relations are fostered when educators hold positive perceptions about family capabilities and competence. Educators who capitalize on family strengths and existing resources are more likely to encourage passionate parent advocates (Lawrence-Lightfoot, 2003). Relationships between families and school staff are best developed through non-rushed, face-to-face conversations that instill respect for what each partner brings to the table and mutual confidence in each other's educational roles and child management preferences. Recognizing that time is a precious commodity, it is important to promote relationships during already established relational touch points between families and educators. Consider school registration, back to school nights, drop-off and pick-up times, and other routine classroom or special school events as prime occasions to foster relationships. Find ways to refocus and design such meetings so that they are not viewed solely as opportunities to provide information to families, but rather as opportunities to share personal interests, build trust, and gain an appreciation of home and school traditions and activities.

One of the most important and often overlooked chances to nurture relationships between families and schools is during parent–teacher conferences. Lawrence-Lightfoot (2003) interviewed effective parent and teacher collaborators from urban, suburban, and rural elementary to high schools for advice on how to enhance this relational touch point. Many ideas were forwarded to foster home–school relations during this critical meeting: (a) ensure that conferences are scheduled with enough time for questions and feedback; (b) invite families and then teachers to share their story and dreams for a child; (c) ask families to describe their child's strengths, needs, and preferences before teachers integrate their impressions; (d) give families an outline of what to expect; (e) go over key vocabulary and data to be discussed beforehand; (f) provide demonstrations of ongoing lessons and class procedures; and (g) ask students to lead the conference.

Upper Tier Relationship Practices

Upper tier relationship practices are essential to collaborate effectively when a child is not succeeding in school or with families whose child has a disability. School psychologists, as critical members of decision-making teams, often can help reduce the natural emotions and anxieties aroused when educators and parents come together to discuss a child's development or performance. Even well-seasoned teachers and parents who know how to advocate, communicate, and solve problems can become tentative and indecisive during such encounters. Strategies to develop trustful relationships take more time, especially during initial response-to-intervention or special education determination meetings or when family members or educators on the team have experienced less desirable partnering in the past. One upper tier practice proven helpful is to invite families and teachers to share personal photo albums, storybooks, or portfolios of information about the child (Turnbull et al., 2011). The extra time taken to develop a joint, strengths-based focus of the child from the perspective of both the home and the school before proceeding to a problem-analysis phase is especially critical if the confidence of either party has been eroded by previous negative exchanges.

School psychologists also play a vital role in reducing misperceptions and handling conflict between families or school staff members during and following meetings. One idea to quickly establish a cooperative rather than combative team atmosphere is to normalize the fact that there often are misunderstandings between families and schools even though both parties are working toward the same goal. Each person can then be asked to review one positive outcome expectation that would be in the best interest of the student. Another upper tier relationship building practice is to offer to hold meetings off campus at a convenient community location or in the family's home. Researchers are currently identifying how home visitation programs support family school engagement, what constitutes an effective program, and what age or type of student issue benefits most from this support (Meyer & Mann, 2006).

Create Welcoming Environments

Physically and psychologically inviting settings create a welcoming environment, foster perceptions of safety and friendliness, and convey that all families and family members are important to the school's mission. Welcoming environments increase family presence and participation at school. Family members who are treated as honored guests or valuable customers are more likely to feel engaged and positive about the school and confident about how to help their children succeed. Such impressions have a significant impact on parents' subsequent decisions to be involved at the school and in their child's education, especially for nonresident fathers (McWayne, Campos, & Owsianik, 2008).

Universal Welcoming Practices

School psychologists clearly play an important role in developing school environments that honor and encourage the involvement of all families. To ensure that a school is physically inviting, ask parents to carefully consider features such as lighting, safety, and comfort at entryways and places where people are greeted or congregate. From the moment someone walks into a school, it should be clear that families are critical to children's success. Well-trained, front-office staff appreciate the important role they play in fostering hospitable and welcoming school environments. Other welcoming strategies include the prominent display of a family-oriented mission statement, pictures of families and greetings in all native languages spoken at the school, and a school map with pictures to identify staff names, roles, locations, and contact information. To assess how welcome family members feel at the school, simple family guest satisfaction surveys could be developed and anonymously collected after visits through the addition of an entryway drop box. Handbooks, policies, and other written materials sent home at the beginning and throughout the year are important features of welcoming environments that should be checked for family-friendly language and comprehensibility. Families of different linguistic abilities could be asked to review and provide feedback on essential documents before and after distribution.

Another universal welcoming practice is to establish a designated space where families can gather and regularly meet. If not at the school, then neighborhood businesses, libraries, or community centers might donate a meeting place so that families can share educational information, locate community resources and services, watch educational or training videos, and borrow texts and other books. Besides increasing family participation at school, such spaces foster family support networks and increase parents' confidence about how to help their children succeed. Many community agencies and businesses will provide funding and other assistance to promote family–school–community partnerships that can be used to develop these assets or to offer childcare or travel stipends so families can attend school functions (Albright, Weissberg, & Dusenbury, 2011).

Upper Tier Welcoming Practices

School psychologists are instrumental in planning, implementing, and evaluating upper tier efforts to welcome families who regularly find it difficult to attend school functions, events, or conferences. Upper tier welcoming strategies are in order when teachers report limited family engagement after trying many universal strategies or when disaggregated records of parent attendance at school events indicate that one group of families is less engaged than others (Edwards, 2009). Potential new strategies should be developed to overcome common participation barriers (i.e., work, travel, childcare responsibilities). Some alternatives might include rotating meetings on and off campus, repeating meetings on different days and times, setting up a travel buddy system for families with transportation issues, asking high school students to assist with childcare, enlisting trained parent volunteers to call or meet with families individually, or requesting that students personally invite reluctant family members to attend school events and meetings.

Another upper tier welcoming strategy is to place more emphasis on the role families play in learning at home. While school participation is a worthy goal, families that are not as present at the school must be recognized for the many invisible ways they partner in their child's education (Gonzalez, Moll, & Amanti, 2005). Publicized lists of activities to enhance family involvement should not only include activities requiring a presence at the school but also those that foster learning at home and in the community. In fact, subtle aspects of parental engagement at home (e.g., monitoring free time) can have a larger impact on student achievement than overt involvement activities that necessitate being at a school (Jeynes, 2010). To further acknowledge the many things parents can do to support their child's learning, school psychologists could stress the importance of setting high educational expectations, instilling positive educational aspirations; reading with their children; conversing about current local, national, or world events; monitoring afterschool activities and homework; and praising persistence and effort. Seminars and parenting classes also could be offered on these topics and on how to promote consistent cross-setting discipline and positive behavior management.

Two-Way Communication

Two-way communication is the bidirectional sharing of meaningful information between homes and schools that serves as a conduit for family–school collaboration (Hiatt-Michael, 2010). Such communication must foster the free exchange of ideas and encourage open discussion, questions, and suggestions related to a student's schooling. Student performance increases when staff and families engage in regular, informative, and positive two-way communication that can originate either from the home or the school (Jeynes, 2010).

Universal Communication Practices

School psychologists play an important role in promoting school-wide family-to-school and school-to-family communication. As key members of many school-based teams, school psychologists are critical models of partnering language (e.g., using we, our, us; saying "What is best for our student?" "How will we know it is working?"). School psychologists also must champion the need for regular and constructive communication between the home and school. Positive home–school contact can improve family–school collaboration by demonstrating to students that everyone is working together to ensure success and celebrate accomplishments. A clear home–school communication policy should emphasize the importance of following up on all family inquiries within 48 hours and should encourage staff members to increase positive contact with all families. One idea is to regularly send home so-called good news notes to highlight student progress. These notes could be sent by normal mail as returnable postcards with a designated section for teacher comments as well as family feedback or as e-mail. Faculty could be reminded to send or could actually fill out such notes at regular staff meetings. To assess and acknowledge efforts made over the year to promote family–school collaboration, such activities could be documented on annual performance evaluations (Lines et al., 2011).

Offering a variety of ways to get in touch (i.e., written, face to face, telephone, video, e-mail) can also encourage two-way communication. At the beginning of the year, families and teachers could be asked to indicate a preferred time and method of contact. To further stress the importance of this issue, an invitation to communicate can be sent even before students officially return to school. Teachers/administrators and family members/students could be asked to share their hopes and dreams for the upcoming school year through introduction letters, phone calls, or personal visits. To further promote two-way communication after school hours, websites could be developed to provide 24-hour access to general information about upcoming projects and events that include a means to leave questions. In addition, secure and confidential links could be added to allow staff and families to access and leave personalized messages about individual students.

Homework has been described as the lynchpin of home–school communication (Patall, Cooper, & Robinson, 2008). School psychologists can help develop clear homework policies and guidelines with input from families. To enhance two-way communication, families could be asked to rate the acceptability and feasibility of their child's assigned work. Interactive assignments could be designed to further increase family awareness of what is being taught. In teach-to-learn assignments, students are asked to demonstrate something they just learned in class to a family member who then briefly summarizes what was taught and provides a rating of the "teacher's" success. Another interactive homework assignment is when a "class visitor" (e.g., a stuffed or real animal) is sent home with an accompanying journal so family members can record what the "visitor" did over the weekend. Interactive middle and high school homework assignments, called Teachers Involve Parents in Schoolwork (TIPS), invite students and family members to consider how to tackle real-world issues. Students who engage in such assignments earn higher grades and report increased self-efficacy and positive impressions of school and family members report an increased understanding of and ability to be involved in their child's schooling (Van Voorhis, 2011). Examples of TIPS assignments across content areas can be found at http://www.csos.jhu.edu/p2000/tips/index.htm.

Upper Tier Communication Practices

School psychologists often participate in collaborative meetings between families and educators when students need additional academic or social–emotional–behavioral support. Upper tier communication practices include active listening, empathic responding, and participant check-ins to assess ongoing impressions. To further appreciate issues across settings, parents and school staff could take and share brief video clips of a child at home and at school. Effective teaming also involves meditation and conflict management strategies to resolve misunderstandings and disagreements between team members. Mutually acceptable solutions are more likely to be developed when families and educators are encouraged to pay attention to each other's perspectives before intervention suggestions are offered (Lines et al., 2011).

Effective two-way communication is particularly important when students consistently struggle to complete or to turn in assignments. To avoid resistance and disengagement and to foster joint discussions about homework expectations, family members could be asked

to provide feedback about the appropriateness of assignments. The National Parent Teacher Association suggests that total nightly homework be limited to 10 minutes per grade level (i.e., 30 minutes for a third grader and 80 minutes for an eighth grader). Parents must be encouraged to alert teachers when children are not able to complete assignments within reasonable time limits since this may indicate other difficulties with schoolwork. Teachers must be encouraged to develop differentiated assignments to meet individual child and family needs and to provide examples of completed assignments, explicit scoring rubrics, and answers to frequently asked homework questions. To address practical constraints within a home, students could be allowed to select homework alternatives based on what works best in the context of their family (Van Voorhis, 2011). School psychologists could help coordinate after-school tutors to assist with homework and could offer workshops to teachers and parents on how to foster students' study and organizational strategies and provide appropriate levels of homework assistance and encouragement. These sessions could be videoed and posted online for later viewing.

Educate Partners

Educated partners feel informed and confident about their role in promoting a child's learning. They also are willing to share insights about what can be done at home and at school to enhance a student's learning and to openly discuss challenges and solutions to pressing issues. Educated families and staff believe that working together will indeed make a difference for students (Edwards, 2011). A family's eagerness to stay involved with their child's education is strongly linked to direct invitations to partner and to an understanding of key terms and systems used to communicate about and monitor their child's progress. This knowledge not only leads to role clarity, it also increases parental feelings of self-efficacy regarding what they can do to support their child's education (Hoover-Dempsey, Whitaker, & Ice, 2010). Families and school staff are more inspired to work together when they feel competent, supported, and invited to give input and perceive that their ideas will be fully recognized and considered.

Universal Educative Practices

School psychologists play an important role in helping families and educators mutually nurture a student's learning. Family members and school staff should be encouraged to learn about each other's respective values and customs through shared conversations and story-telling. Joint training opportunities between family members and staff are an effective means to promote educated partners who feel motivated and capable to share responsibility for student success. Workshops could be offered on topics of interest to both parties. Additionally, schools can design joint learning opportunities that are entertaining and educative for the whole family. School-wide family nights have been successfully developed where teachers demonstrate fun math, science, and literacy activities and family members share their vocational skills or hobbies. Separate educative sessions could be offered to families on child development topics and to teachers on effective family–school collaboration. Feedback on all educative efforts could be collected through routine surveys and then evaluated for ideas on how to modify and plan subsequent sessions.

To ensure that families and staff share important knowledge about student learning and how performance is monitored and assessed, families must understand the purpose of adopted school-wide academic and social–emotional curriculum and appreciate progress monitoring, grading, and testing data used in schools. Specific invitations can be sent to encourage direct observation, training, and participation in such learning activities or parent liaisons could be taught to share this information with families. When essential knowledge about standards, curriculum, and assessment is mutually understood, more meaningful conversations can be held to address issues and formulate practical suggestions for change (Albright et al., 2011).

Upper Tier Educative Practices

Educative practices at the upper tiers involve targeted strategies to address specific issues, groups, or individuals. School psychologists play a critical role in helping families understand their legal rights and ensuring that families are engaged as equal partners during any student decision-making meetings. When a child is struggling, parents often feel disenfranchised and alienated from the school and blame themselves for or expect to be blamed about their child's problems. Such worries and fears can make family members who attend team meetings appear guarded. School psychologists can anticipate and help allay such negative impressions by taking time to get together with families prior to any meeting to gain their perspectives and trust. Family members who will attend the meeting need to know what to review beforehand and must understand the essential information that will be shared. Visual or

graphic organizers, photographs, and action guides completed by teachers and families have been helpful (Turnbull et al., 2011). Family members are more likely to fully participate in educational decision making when they are treated as experts about their child and when their preferences are solicited. School psychologists are in the best position to encourage such teaming practices. Family–school collaboration leads to more successful outcomes when planned interventions fit into daily school and family routines and capitalize on complimentary home and school learning experiences.

Critical Implementation Issues

In this section, issues are considered for implementing a multitiered system of family–school collaboration across different age levels and with culturally and linguistically diverse families. Ideas for addressing common challenges to such practices are also presented.

Collaboration for Children at Different Age Levels

Family–school collaboration strategically differs for children from preschool to college. Partnerships with families are critically important when a child first enters into preschool. Successful early-childhood family–school collaboration can minimize home–school discontinuity, strengthen home–school relationships, and set a precedent for parental involvement at subsequent grade levels. School psychologists can help guide early childhood professionals to foster greater parental engagement through positive collaborative exchanges (Sheridan, Knoche, Kupzyk, Edwards, & Marvin, 2011). Interactions between preschool educators and families should promote a shared dialogue about child development and help family members appreciate their role in promoting language and early literacy and numeracy skills.

At school entry, family–school collaboration strategies are designed to help prepare families and children for school as well as ensure schools are prepared to be welcoming to families and children. During the transition into elementary school, when children face new requirements and higher academic expectations, parents who already know how to partner are more able to assist their child by providing an array of home educational experiences to enhance self-confidence and self-efficacy (Powell, Hee Son, File, & Froiland, 2012). Family–school collaboration at this time should focus on how to build a shared understanding of expectations, how to keep each other informed about a child's progress, and how to ensure there is regular communication about homework and behavior in and out of school.

As students transition to middle and high school there are unique partnership needs. Not only must students and families adapt to larger class sizes, new classmates, and more challenging and complex subject matter, there also are now a variety of teachers, many of whom may not reach out to families. As youth transition to middle and then high school, many may think the need for family–school collaboration declines, but this is not true (DeCastro & Catsambis, 2009). School psychologists must continue to highlight the importance and build support for partnerships between families and school professionals. Adolescents' school success is enhanced when parents and teachers express high academic and behavioral expectations and engage in positive collaboration. Higher levels of academic and social adjustment and greater academic efficacy, aspirations, and expectations for the future are found when there is consistent, positive two-way communication between families and teachers (Hiatt-Michael, 2010). Indeed, more not less contact between parents and school professionals in middle and high school has been found to enhance academic performance during these transitions, and such contact is especially important for English language learners and students from low-income families (Crosnoe, 2009).

Family–school collaboration often looks different in middle and high school. During this time, families play a critical yet less demonstrable monitoring and mentoring role by encouraging school completion and helping students consider postgraduation choices. School psychologists must continue to educate parents about their importance, even though they may feel insecure with their knowledge of upper level curricula and postsecondary options. Family–school collaboration during this transition regularly involves the provision of higher education and vocational information to both students and families. School psychologists typically are involved in a significant amount of outreach with local employers and postsecondary education programs within the community to plan trips to businesses, college campuses, and vocational schools. Secondary teachers also need guidance and encouragement in how to partner with families during this time. This topic is rarely covered in preservice training and many secondary teachers do not feel they have time to devote to individual student and family needs (Caspe, Lopez, Chu, & Weiss, 2011).

Collaboration With Culturally and Linguistically Diverse Families

School psychologists are in the ideal position to foster culturally sensitive and responsive family–school collaboration practices. Families from diverse cultural and linguistic backgrounds whose English is often limited are frequently overlooked, stigmatized, or viewed as disinterested or incapable of participating in their child's education, which is clearly not the case. Effective multicultural strategies have been developed to enhance relationships, create welcoming environments, and facilitate two-way communication and education with families. In general, school psychologists must ensure that greater efforts are taken to reach out to newcomer families who may feel overwhelmed, socially disenfranchised, isolated, or unqualified to participate in their child's schooling owing to a lack of confidence about communicating in English with their child's teachers (Vazquez-Nuttall, Li, & Kaplan, 2006).

Successful home–school relationships with ethnic minority families and families living in poverty across both rural and urban settings have been fostered through additional orientation sessions, meetings at community agencies where they receive other services, or home visitation programs (Edwards, 2009). Having a gathering place at the school where families can meet others and informally learn about schooling expectations also has led to stronger home–school relations. Welcoming practices that appeal to families from all cultural backgrounds include mentorships with similar speaking families; translated materials and information videos; invitations to share cultural stories, beliefs, and values and teach native crafts or skills; and a recognition of the many ways families already support their child's learning. When parents view schools as accepting of their cultural heritage and feel informed about school activities, they are more likely to demonstrate higher educational aspirations and greater involvement in their child's education across elementary, middle, and high school (Jeynes, 2012; Nzinga-Johnson, Baker, & Aupperlee, 2009).

Communication practices that can enhance family–school collaboration with culturally and linguistically diverse families include efforts to ensure that trusted translators, advocates, and cultural brokers from the community are invited to all meetings. This is especially important when children or families need more intensive services because of identified disabilities (Olivos, Gallagher, & Aguilar, 2010) or have been exposed to trauma or frequent displacements (i.e., immigrant, homeless, migrant, military, or refugee families; Yohani, 2013). Parent-to-parent visits or phone trees where families from the community call a small number of other families to share or solicit ideas also can enhance two-way communication. School psychologists must ensure that families who are newcomers to the United States understand nonobvious characteristics, distinctive customs, and technical terms associated with their new educational system. Productive two-way conversations should help illuminate and appreciate cultural similarities and differences in accepted behavior that may clash across settings. For example, ideas about personal space, resources, and communal property in the home are often viewed differently at school, where most possessions are individually assigned and not freely shared (e.g., food, books, utensils).

When a family has recently entered into the United States, it is important to ask about education experiences in order to understand what families might expect of educators and to clarify expectations about family involvement (Vazquez-Nuttall et al., 2006). In many cultures, teachers are entrusted as an authority on a child's academic development and family members do not feel they have the knowledge, skills or preparation to participate at school. This can be interpreted by some as nonengagement, when in reality it is simply a reflection of the family's view that their major partnering role is to dispense life advice and instill moral values and cultural traditions. Family–school collaboration is most successful when both parties are educated about each other's history and cultural values and when there is an effort to tap into and build upon cultural funds of knowledge (Gonzalez, Moll, & Amanti, 2005).

Overcoming Challenges to Family–School Collaboration

Structural and psychological factors can create individual and school-wide challenges that can interfere with educators' and families' ability to collaborate (Christenson, 2004). Structural challenges include time (i.e., work load demands, scheduling conflicts, mandated priorities, set hours) and logistics (i.e., transportation, language differences, funding for translators or cultural brokers, limited staff resources). Psychological challenges are more attitudinal in nature and include lower self-efficacy, confidence, expectations, fear of conflict, role ambiguity, limited buy-in, a lack of knowledge, and insufficient professional development. Recognizing that family–school partnering has positive effects on student achievement and that negative family–school exchanges can have a long-lasting impact on subsequent parental

involvement and ultimately students' school success, such challenges must be dealt with directly (Albright et al., 2011).

Many structural and psychological hurdles can be addressed through strong leadership; a clear family–school partnering vision; and effective organizational structures to support, reinforce, and educate staff and families. It is no longer prudent to allow family–school collaboration to occur without careful and systematic preparation of educators (Caspe et al., 2011). Professional development opportunities must be offered to teach effective strategies to enhance family–school partnerships and educators must be held accountable for their partnership efforts. Scheduling conflicts can be overcome by varying the time school events occur and by offering staff the flexibility to arrange meetings off campus and during nonschool hours. To address transportation issues, a travel buddy system could be developed where families share rides to key events. Alternative meeting formats could be arranged through conference calling, video sharing, and Skype sessions and off-site meeting facilities at neighborhood businesses, community centers, or libraries also could be considered. Schools with the most success in promoting strong family–school collaboration have developed a comprehensive, multitiered system of partnering supports based on foundational beliefs and expectations, an array of school-wide universal as well as upper level practices and services, and a systematic means to assess and evaluate overtime the impact of such efforts on student outcomes (Lines et al., 2011).

SUMMARY

A multitiered model represents a significant paradigm shift in how schools and families can mutually partner to support student school success. Family–school collaboration is now considered a critical aspect of any district or school reform effort applicable to general as well as special education students. There is a burgeoning, multidiscipline literature on evidence-based family–school collaboration processes that can promote student school achievement and lifelong success. Ensuring that family–school partnerships are developed within a multitiered system of supports allows for strategic resource allocation that will lead to greater sustainability overtime.

School psychologists are in the best position to impart attitudes, knowledge, and partnership skills to classroom teachers, administrators, and families and to develop strategies to confront challenges associated with involving families in their children's education. It also is clear that collaboration with families is a critical service delivery function of school psychologists since it is now considered one of 10 domains of professional competence. In the future, it is our hope that school psychologists further their role as leaders in the dissemination, application, and evaluation of effective practices to improve family, school, and community collaboration.

AUTHOR NOTE

Disclosure. Cathy Lines and Gloria Miller have a financial interest in books they authored or coauthored referenced in this chapter.

REFERENCES

Albright, M. I., Weissberg, R. P., & Dusenbury, L. A. (2011). *School-family partnership strategies to enhance children' social, emotional, and academic growth.* Newton, MA: National Center for Mental Health Promotion and Youth Violence Prevention, Education Development Center.

Caspe, M., Lopez, M., Chu, A., & Weiss, B. (2011, May). Teaching the teachers: Preparing educators to engage families for student achievement. *National PTA Issue Brief,* 1–16. Retrieved from http://www.hfrp.org/publications-resources/browse-our-publications/teaching-the-teachers-preparing-educators-to-engage-families-for-student-achievement

Christenson, S. L. (2004). The family–school partnership: An opportunity to promote the learning competence of all students. *School Psychology Review, 33,* 83–104.

Christenson, S. L., & Reschly, A. L. (2010). *Handbook of family-school partnerships.* New York, NY: Routledge.

Colorado Department of Education. (2010). *RTI fidelity of implementation rubrics.* Denver, CO: Author. Retrieved from http://www.cde.state.co.us/RtI

Colorado Department of Education. (2012). *Essential RTI information slides with notes.* Denver, CO: Author. Retrieved from http://www.cde.state.co.us/RtI/FamilyCommunityToolkit.htm

Crosnoe, R. (2009). Family-school connections and the transitions of low-income youth and English language learners from middle school into high school. *Developmental Psychology, 45,* 1061–1076. doi:10.1037/a0016131

DeCastro, B., & Catsambis, S. (2009). Parents still matter: Parental links to the behaviors and future outlook of high school seniors. In N. Hill & R. Chao (Eds.), *Families, schools, and the adolescents: Connecting research, policy, and practice* (pp. 91–109). New York, NY: Teachers College Press.

Edwards, P. A. (2009). *Tapping the potential of parents: A strategic guide to boosting student achievement through family involvement.* New York, NY: Scholastic.

Edwards, P. A. (2011). Differentiating family supports. In S. Redding, M. Murphy, & Sheley, P. (Eds.), *Handbook on family and community engagement* (pp. 113–115). Lincoln, IL: Academic Development Institute/Center on Innovation and Improvement.

Epstein, J. L. (1995). School/family/community partnerships: Caring for the children we share. *Phi Delta Kappan, 76,* 701–712.

Fixsen, D. L., Naoom, S. F., Blase, K. A., Friedman, R. M., & Wallace, F. (2005). *Implementation research: A synthesis of the literature* (FMHI Publication #231). Tampa, FL: University of South Florida, Louis de la Parte Florida Mental Health Institute.

Gonzalez, N., Moll, L. C., & Amanti, C. (2005). *Funds of knowledge. Theorizing practices in households, communities, and classrooms.* Mahwah, NJ: Erlbaum.

Hiatt-Michael, D. B. (2010). Communication practices that bridge home with school. In D. B. Hiatt-Michael (Ed.), *Promising practices to support family involvement in schools* (pp. 25–55). Charlotte, NC: Information Age.

Hoover-Dempsey, K. V., Whitaker, M. C., & Ice, C. L. (2010). Motivation and commitment to family-school partnerships. In S. L. Christenson & A. L. Reschly (Eds.), *Handbook of school-family partnerships* (pp. 30–60). New York, NY: Routledge.

Jeynes, W. H. (2010). The salience of the subtle aspects of parental involvement and encouraging that involvement: Implications for school-based programs. *Teachers College Record, 112,* 747–774.

Jeynes, W. H. (2012). A meta-analysis of the efficacy of different types of parental involvement programs for urban students. *Urban Education, 47,* 706–742. doi:10.1177/0042085912445643

Lawrence-Lightfoot, S. (2003). *The essential conversation: What parents and teachers can learn from each other.* New York, NY: Ballantine Books.

Lines, C., Miller, G. E., & Arthur-Stanley, A. (2011). *The power of family-school partnering (FSP): A practical guide for school mental health professionals and educators.* New York, NY: Routledge.

McWayne, C., Campos, R., & Owsianik, J. (2008). A multi-dimensional, multilevel examination of mother and father involvement among culturally diverse Head Start families. *Journal of School Psychology, 46,* 551–573. doi:10.1016/j.jsp.2008.06.001

Meyer, J. A., & Mann, M. B. (2006). Teachers' perceptions of the benefits of home visits for early elementary children. *Early Childhood Education Journal, 34,* 93–97. doi:10.1007/s10643-006-0113-z

National Association of School Psychologists. (2010a). *Model for comprehensive and integrated school psychological services.* Bethesda, MD: Author. Retrieved from http://www.nasponline.org/standards/2010standards/2_PracticeModel.pdf

National Association of School Psychologists. (2010b). *Principles for professional ethics.* Bethesda, MD: Author. Retrieved from http://www.nasponline.org/standards/2010standards/1_%20Ethical%20Principles.pdf

National Association of School Psychologists. (2012). *School–family partnering to enhance learning: Essential elements and responsibilities.* [Position Statement]. Bethesda, MD: Author. Retrieved from http://www.nasponline.org/about_nasp/positionpapers/Home-SchoolCollaboration.pdf

Nokali, N., Bachman, H., & Votruba-Drzal, E. (2010). Parent involvement and children's academic and social development in elementary school. *Child Development, 81,* 988–1005. doi:10.1111/j.1467-8624.2010.01447.x

Nzinga-Johnson, S., Baker, J. A., & Aupperlee, J. (2009). Teacher–parent relationships and school involvement among racially and educationally diverse parents of kindergarteners. *The Elementary School Journal, 110,* 81–91. doi:10.1086/598844

Olivos, E. M., Gallagher, R. J., & Aguilar, J. (2010). Fostering collaborations with culturally and linguistically diverse families of children with moderate to severe disabilities. *Journal of Educational and Psychoeducational Consultation*, *20*, 28–40. doi:10.1080/10474410903535372

Patall, E., Cooper, H., & Robinson, J. (2008). Parent involvement in homework: A research synthesis. *Review of Educational Research*, *78*, 1039–110. doi:10.3102/0034654308325185

Powell, D., Hee Son, S., File, N., & Froiland, M. (2012). Changes in parent involvement across the transition from public school prekindergarten to first grade and children's academic outcomes. *The Elementary School Journal*, *113*, 276–300. doi:10.1086/667726

Sheridan, S., Knoche, L., Kupzyk, K., Edwards, C., & Marvin, C. (2011). A randomized trial examining the effects of parent engagement on early language and literacy: The getting ready intervention. *Journal of School Psychology*, *49*, 361–383. doi:10.1016/j.jsp.2011.03.001

Sheridan, S., Taylor, A., & Woods, K. (2008). Best practices for working with families: Instilling a family-centered approach. In A. Thomas & J. Grimes (Eds.), *Best practices in school psychology V* (pp. 995–1008). Bethesda, MD: National Association of School Psychologists.

Turnbull, A., Turnbull, R., Erwin, E., Soodak, L., & Shogren, K. (2011). *Families, professionals, and exceptionality: Positive outcomes through partnerships and trust*. Upper Saddle River, NJ: Pearson.

Van Voorhis, F. L. (2011). Engaging families in student homework: Action steps for educators. In H. Kreider & H. Westmoreland (Eds.), *Family engagement in out-of-school time*. Charlotte, NC: Information Age.

Vazquez-Nuttall, E., Li, C., & Kaplan, J. (2006). Home-school partnerships with culturally diverse families: Challenges and solutions for school personnel. *Journal of Applied Psychology*, *22*, 81–102. doi:10.1300/J370v22n02_05

Weihua, F., & Williams, C. (2010). The effects of parental involvement on students' academic self-efficacy, engagement and intrinsic motivation. *Educational Psychology*, *30*, 53–74. doi:10.1080/01443410903353302

Weiss, H. B., Lopez, E. M., & Rosenberg, H. (2010). *Beyond random acts: Family, school, and community engagement as an integral part of education reform*. Cambridge, MA: Harvard Family Research Project.

Yohani, S. (2013). Educational cultural brokers and the school adaptation of refugee children and families: Challenges and opportunities. *International Journal of Migration and Immigration*, *14*, 61–79. doi:10.1007/s12134-011-229-x

35 Best Practices in Facilitating Family–School Meetings

Kathleen M. Minke
Krista L. Jensen
University of Delaware

If you had to identify, in one word, the reason why the human race has not achieved, and never will achieve, its full potential, that word would be "meetings."

—Dave Barry

OVERVIEW

School psychologists understand and embrace the need for collaboration, especially between families and schools, in order to support optimal outcomes for students. Such collaboration is highlighted within the National Association of School Psychologists (NASP) *Model for Comprehensive and Integrated School Psychological Services* (NASP, 2010) domain of Family–School Collaboration and is mandated through federal laws that require parent involvement in educational decisions across special education (the 2004 Individuals with Disabilities Education Act), compensatory education (Title I), and general education (Elementary and Secondary Education Act). Complying with these and other regulations produces the need for meetings. Producing positive results from these meetings, however, requires skilled facilitation.

Parents and educators meet for a variety of purposes that cut across the tiers of service delivery including school-wide planning and routine conferences (Tier 1); problem-solving meetings (Tier 2); and intensive, individualized intervention planning, including Individualized Education Program (IEP) meetings, person-centered planning, and wraparound services (Tier 3). Participants bring their own histories, cultures, and emotional investment to these meetings, but these differences may easily be unrecognized or discounted, leading to misunderstandings, miscommunications, and

poorer outcomes. Reflect for a moment on the family–school meetings you attended in the past month. Did parents and educators increase or decrease their trust in each other? Did anyone leave feeling angry, blamed, frustrated, and discouraged? Or did all participants leave feeling respected and that their views were heard and understood? Did they leave feeling energized, believing that other participants are dedicated to student success, that appropriate actions were planned, and that others will fulfill their commitments?

Family–school meetings, when conducted well, can produce these kinds of positive outcomes and be vehicles for building trusting relationships that support student success. However, most school psychologists have participated in meetings that did not go well and, in some cases, actually created more problems than they solved. Why does this happen?

The relationship between families and schools is an unusual one. These relationships tend to be emotionally charged, with the child's success at school seen not simply as an important goal for the child but also as a barometer of one's worth as a parent or teacher. Unlike most emotional relationships, this one is not entered into voluntarily, given that students are assigned to particular teachers without regard to the likelihood of a successful relationship match. In addition, it is a relationship that has a powerful influence on children, even when the partners interact infrequently. A relationship always exists between families and schools, whether or not it is recognized and acknowledged (Pianta & Walsh, 1996).

Families and educators may have widely disparate views on how this relationship should be structured, especially when there are cultural differences. Consider families that do not come to school for meetings. A frequent explanation is that these families do not care about their children's education. However, beyond even pragmatic barriers, such as getting time off work, transportation, or child-care difficulties, there are many other possible reasons parents may not attend. For example, among some Korean families, presence at the school can lead to rumors in the community that parents are trying to bribe teachers to secure more favorable treatment for their children (Lee, 2005). Some families delegate the responsibility for educating their children to teachers and see it as inappropriate and disrespectful to the teacher to come to the school (Lareau, 2011). Still other families, as a result of negative experiences, simply withdraw or take a position of "alienated advocacy" in efforts to support their children (Shapiro, Monzó, Rueda, Gomez, & Blacher, 2004, p. 44).

When families do attend meetings, differences in experiences and expectations, as well as the structure of the meetings, can create difficulties. In a typical problem-solving or IEP meeting, professionals out-number family members. The professionals also fre-quently have established relationships with each other, while parents may have few personal connections with the other attendees. Although there is usually a shared goal of supporting student success, there are also unshared (and often unstated) goals. Parents are concerned primarily with the success of their own child, while school personnel must be concerned with the success of all children. School personnel also may focus on resource constraints and worry that parents may demand more than they can deliver. The meeting processes may be complicated and poorly understood by parents, and parents often report feeling railroaded when their emotional reactions are not acknowledged or supported and when insufficient time is allocated (see Martin, 2005).

Myrsiades (2000) asked a group of employees at a large company to generate a list of ways to best sabotage a meeting. Their ideas included: fail to involve those who will be affected by decisions; do not provide an agenda; let people come and go, take phone calls, check e-mail, or otherwise interrupt the meeting; let the meeting drag on beyond its announced time; focus on personalities rather than issues; choose a bad meeting space that is of the wrong size, uncomfortable, or poorly arranged; and fail to provide for implementation and follow up on decisions made. Although these examples were developed in a business context, family–school meetings frequently are characterized by these elements. For example, in a qualitative study of parents' experiences in IEP meetings, Fish (2006) reported that

parents felt blamed and disrespected and cited lack of follow through on agreements reached as a major problem. Similarly, Lo (2008) observed a set of IEP meetings with Chinese families. In each meeting at least one professional arrived 10–35 minutes late and at least one left 30–90 minutes before the meeting was con-cluded. Parents reported feeling unprepared, confused, and criticized.

Clearly, no professional enters a meeting with parents with the intention of creating these kinds of negative outcomes. School psychologists are well positioned to promote more positive experiences, given their prepara-tion in consultative and collaborative services that support productive family–school collaboration. School psychologists typically have well-developed listening and communication skills that are essential to direct service delivery and deep understanding of the ways in which students', families', and educators' diverse backgrounds can influence the collaborative process. For many school psychologists, however, these skills are most often applied at the individual level (e.g., individual or small group counseling, behavioral consultation with one teacher). Facilitating complex meetings with relatively large numbers of individuals with competing needs may remain daunting, especially if development or preser-vation of the participants' relationships is one of the goals.

The focus in this chapter is to detail the ways in which efforts in these areas can be enhanced by the ability of school psychologists to lead productive family–school meetings through skilled facilitation. This chapter is intended to increase school psychologists' knowledge of facilitation from an ecosystemic perspective, encourage use of effective communication skills, and outline the ways in which effective facilitation can be applied at all levels of intervention in a multitiered, problem-solving approach.

BASIC CONSIDERATIONS

Facilitated meetings are highly structured processes in which the leader "guides the participants through a series of predefined steps to arrive at a result that is created, understood, and accepted by all participants" (Wilkinson, 2012, p. 5). Facilitation is based on the assumption that people will be more committed to plans, solutions, or interventions that they themselves developed. The facilitator carefully prepares for the meeting, ensures that participants are properly pre-pared, directs the meeting through its agenda, with particular attention to interpersonal and decision making processes, and closes the meeting being certain that next steps are clearly articulated and agreed upon. (Throughout the chapter the facilitator is assumed to be a school psychologist. However, the more generic term is used in some cases to recognize that many different professionals may serve in this role.)

According to Wilkinson (2012), the facilitator needs to be a motivator, guide, questioner, bridge builder, clairvoyant, peacemaker, taskmaster, and praiser. Although in many settings the facilitator is a neutral outside third party, school psychologists more typically will function as "citizen facilitators" (Garmston & von Frank, 2012, p. 6) who must, in addition, be accomplished in bringing their own voices into the discussion without dominating while guiding the group toward completion of its tasks. Clearly, a complex role.

In order to conduct productive, relationship-enhancing family–school meetings, school psychologists should begin by carefully considering their theoretical framework, communication skills, and multicultural competence.

Taking an Ecosystemic Strength-Based Approach

From an ecosystemic perspective, each individual is seen as functioning within a set of overlapping, interrelated systems (Bronfenbrenner, 1979). Behavior can only be understood by considering the context in which it occurs. Home and school represent two major contexts within which the child must function. When there are differing beliefs, expectations, rules for interaction, and so forth between these contexts, greater challenges for the child and for adult interactions can be anticipated. Family–school meetings represent an opportunity to link these two important developmental contexts in ways that are beneficial to students.

School psychologists in the facilitator role must work from a positive framework in which they actively elicit strengths of all participants and utilize these strengths in the problem-solving process. There are a number of excellent resources that outline the attitudinal underpinnings of collaborative approaches to family engagement (e.g., Christenson & Sheridan, 2001) and family-centered practices. In our work we have summarized the collaborative approach with the acronym CORE. That is, following any encounter between families and educators, the goal is for participants to leave feeling more connected, optimistic, respected, and empowered than they did at the start of the encounter.

Table 35.1 details a number of beliefs that support a strength-based, solution-oriented approach to families, students, and educators. When educators approach families with these kinds of positive, constructive attitudes, the opportunity for developing shared goals and problem solving effectively is enhanced (Christenson & Sheridan, 2001). These beliefs are consistent with those outlined by Bens (2006) that are more specific to the facilitation process, including the notion that better decisions emerge from groups than from individuals working alone and that the role of the facilitator is to elicit the best possible performance from each participant.

Table 35.1. Beliefs Associated With a Collaborative Approach

Element	Associated Beliefs
Connection	• I believe that trust develops when participants feel valued, listened to, and understood. • I feel confident in my ability to help families develop trust in our relationship.
Optimism	• When facing difficult situations, I believe that each person is doing the best he or she can and that every family has strengths and resources. • I believe that no one person is to blame for a problem. Blaming someone for a problem interferes with solving that problem. Effort should be directed at generating solutions, not figuring out why a problem exists. • I believe that problems are system problems; successes are system successes. Everyone has a role in both the problem and the solutions.
Respect	• In my interactions with families, I believe that each person (including me) is both an expert and a learner. • I believe that children should be active participants in the decisions that affect them.
Empowerment	• I believe that power, responsibility, decision making, and action should be shared when planning interventions. • I believe that families should be the main decision makers. • I believe that advice giving is disempowering and should be avoided.

Note. Adapted from "Preventing School Problems and Promoting School Success Through Family–School–Community Collaboration," by K. M. Minke. In *Preventing School Problems—Promoting School Success: Strategies and Programs That Work* (pp. 337–420) by K. M. Minke & G. G. Bear (Eds.), 2000, Bethesda, MD: National Association of School Psychologists. Copyright by the National Association of School Psychologists. Adapted with permission.

Using Effective Communication Skills

Communication, like all behavior, is not the property of a single individual. Rather, it is a transactional process where meaning is negotiated among the participants. It is also continuous and not always verbal. People can speak volumes without uttering a word through their nonverbal behavior. Impressions made from verbal and nonverbal communication are very hard to undo and so it is critically important that facilitators are highly intentional in the messages they send (see Fujishin, 2009, for further discussion).

The counseling microskills (Ivey, Ivey, & Zalaquett, 2010) familiar to most school psychologists are useful to review in preparation for facilitating meetings. School psychologists might also consider how to help other professionals utilize effective communication strategies, perhaps through professional development sessions, as these skills are often missing from teacher preparation programs (Graue & Brown, 2003). Minke (2006) outlined skills particularly relevant for teachers (see Table 35.2). It may also be helpful to review communication strategies to avoid, such as lecturing or moralizing, excessive self-disclosure, and approving/disapproving of the statements of others (Seligman, 2000).

In meeting facilitation, it is especially important to attend to the bidirectional nature of communication. That is, it is not sufficient for educators to communicate information clearly to families. Rather, educators must also work to understand what families are saying and communicate that understanding back to them. Active listening and empathic responding are essential to this process. Skilled facilitators use paraphrasing, summarizing, validating, redirecting, and probing so that all participants' views are available for problem solving. The purpose of a particular meeting will influence the selection of communication skills. Garmston and von Frank (2012) make a useful distinction between *dialogue*, which has the purpose of deepening understanding of participants' views and assumptions, and *discussion*, which has the purpose of making decisions. In many family–school encounters, a period of dialogue before attempting to make decisions would decrease the likelihood of misunderstandings and conflict.

Attending to the Influence of Culture

When families and educators come together, cultural differences should be expected and assumed. Family–school meetings typically are initiated by school personnel and are grounded within the school's culture.

Therefore, even in situations where parents have statutory decision-making authority (e.g., IEP meetings), the power dynamics of the meeting may be heavily tilted toward school personnel who have greater experience with the process. It is not uncommon for cultural differences to lead to a deficit view; that is, what looks like dysfunctional behavior to school personnel (e.g., interrupting, high emotionality) might be expressions of specific cultural communication patterns (Wilkinson, 2012). Therefore, care must be taken to specifically elicit family strengths (Zhang & Bennett, 2003) and to use good communication skills to understand rather than judge behaviors.

There is some evidence that it is easier for school psychologists to acquire technical consultation skills than relationship-building skills, particularly in multicultural situations (Newell, 2012). Facilitators and other educators must understand their own cultural background as well as how poverty, racism, and discrimination affect their work with others (Locke, 2003). Differences in areas such as parental expectations for their children, views on instruction and learning, and understanding of their roles and appropriate relationships with teachers vary markedly among families (Okagaki & Bingham, 2010). Through careful questioning and observation, educators can understand such differences more fully and tailor interactions to accommodate a wider variety of family preferences.

When interpreters are used, more time will be needed for preparation (e.g., to be sure that interpreters are familiar with technical terms, that other participants know to stop after a few sentences for interpretation) and for the meeting itself (Lo, 2008). It likely will be beneficial to spend additional time in relationship building through introductions and clarifying the process and to be especially careful to avoid idioms, slang, and jargon (Wilkinson, 2012). The use of interpreters who also have professional knowledge may be effective in encouraging bidirectional understanding of the influences of culture on problem solving and help bridge the differences between families and educators.

BEST PRACTICES IN FACILITATING FAMILY–SCHOOL MEETINGS

"Effective meetings are those in which the right people are present, the meeting's purposes are clear, important information is shared, new ideas are discussed, problems are solved, and accountability to tasks and outcomes is monitored" (Jorgensen, Schuch, & Nisbet, 2006, p. 110). The facilitator's goal is to create a collaborative process

Table 35.2. Basic Communication Skills

Skill	Description	Examples
Attending to nonverbal communication	• Increase your awareness of body language, tone, etc. • Notice nonverbal communication of all the participants, including your own	• "I noticed you were wringing your hands. I'm wondering if you are uncomfortable with what I just said." • "I'm worried that I might be talking too fast and I feel like I may have interrupted you. What more did you want to say?"
Listening to understand and reflect	• Be quiet and listen • Avoid giving your personal experience or opinion • Offer an empathic response	• "It sounds like you're pretty upset over what happened on the playground with Bill." • "You seem really worried about David. Tell me more about what you are seeing with his reading."
Modeling the collaborative role	• Resist the role of expert; ask for others' input before giving your ideas • Avoid labeling, jargon, laundry lists, etc. • Use effective questioning to elicit ideas from others	• "Were there any other ideas you had for helping Jane with her schoolwork?" • "Sometimes I find it hard to get him interested in class projects. What have you found at home that really sparks his interest?"
Searching for strengths and positive qualities	• When listening, identify strengths of the speaker • When talking, emphasize the positive, highlight the parent's contributions	• "He knows 24 of the 26 letters of the alphabet by heart. You have spent a lot of time helping him learn them." • "I can see that you have worked very hard to help Johnny be so respectful."
Reframing	• Reconstruct a negative statement to have a positive meaning	• "Johnny is very energetic" instead of "Johnny is very hyperactive." • "Jane really likes to be in charge" rather than "Jane is very controlling."
Delivering negative information	• Limit the amount of negative information delivered at any one time • Be calm and communicate openness to other views • Be brief, ask for a reaction after a few sentences	• "Jane seems to have a hard time getting started with her work, especially if it is math. Have you noticed that yourself?" • "Johnny has some trouble getting along with his classmates in the lunchroom and he sometimes gets into fights with other boys. What are your thoughts about that?"
Receiving negative information	• Actively listen and try to understand the main concern and speaker's goal • Reflect both content and emotion • Do not defend yourself	• "I can see you are really upset about Johnny's math grades, and you think he has been unfairly treated." • "It sounds like you are angry about what happened on the playground. Tell me more about what happened."
Blocking blame	• Validate others' viewpoints • Refocus the discussion • Summarize	• "I can see where constant questioning would distract you from your other responsibilities." • "Here's what I think everyone has agreed on so far. Where can we go from here?"

Note. Adapted from "Parent–Teacher Relationships," by K. M. Minke. In *Children's Needs III: Development, Prevention, and Intervention* (pp. 73–85), by G. G. Bear & K. M. Minke (Eds.), 2006, Bethesda, MD: National Association of School Psychologists. Copyright 2006 by the National Association of School Psychologists. Adapted with permission.

that is open and responsive to specific needs. The intent is to help the group accomplish its goals, whether the goals involve developing a school improvement initiative, revising an IEP, or conducting a functional behavior analysis. Although specifics will vary according to the particular tasks faced by the group, some elements are common to all facilitated meetings.

Preparation

Some of the most important meeting processes occur well before the meeting begins. Careful planning allows for greater clarity in goals and the roles participants are expected to play. The first steps involve personal preparation. Eller (2004) recommends taking stock of strengths in areas such as observation skills, interpersonal skills, ability to depersonalize anger, and staying calm under pressure. Wilkinson (2012) outlines "5 Ps of preparation" (p. 38) that anticipate important meeting processes including: (a) the purpose of the meeting, (b) the product or outcomes, (c) the participants, (d) probable issues or difficulties, and (e) the process or the strategies needed to accomplish the purpose.

Of particular significance is deciding who will participate in the meeting. Ideally, this process should itself be collaborative. For example, if the meeting involves school governance, then administrators should contact as many stakeholder groups as possible in seeking nominees for participation. If the meeting concerns the progress of a particular student, then parents should be encouraged to invite all individuals who they feel play an important role in the student's life. This invitation may result in a greater number of individuals important to the family attending and allow school professionals to gain better understanding of the student's support system (Minke & Anderson, 2003). Parents' preferences for which professionals participate should be respected. If certain individuals are mandated to participate, then it may be beneficial to have a conversation with parents to explain the role each person plays in the meeting and why they need to be there.

As noted above, the facilitator should also reflect on the role that cultural differences might play in the meeting and make plans to address issues directly. Most school psychologists will also need to carefully consider their prior relationships with the participants in the meeting. While their insider status allows greater understanding of the school culture and participants' histories with one another, such knowledge may actually inhibit problem solving (Eller, 2004). School psychologists must be careful not to act on untested assumptions about the participants and the process and may need to address directly whether the participants accept an insider in the facilitation role.

Preparation of other participants also is important. Facilitators should never assume that participants have shared understandings of the purpose of the meeting and the topics to be covered. Make personal contact in advance with key participants that describe the importance of their attendance and contribution (Adams, Means, & Spivey, 2007). Parents, especially, are more likely to attend if they clearly understand the benefit of their participation to their own children. Facilitators should develop and distribute the agenda in advance as part of the invitation process. A good agenda always focuses on the expected outcomes of the meeting

(Garmston & von Frank, 2012). Considering outcomes in advance will help you be sure you have both the right participants and tools needed to accomplish those outcomes. In many cases, participants can be asked to complete a short set of questions in advance that are directly related to the purpose of the meeting. Such requests convey the expectation that everyone will be an active participant in the meeting and that their views are important (Minke & Anderson, 2003).

Finally, it is important to prepare an environment appropriate to the meeting size and purpose. This can be particularly difficult to accomplish given space limitations in many schools. However, qualities of the environment can greatly influence the outcome of a meeting (Isenhart & Spangle, 2000). Consider the extent to which the meeting space contains sufficient numbers of adult-sized chairs, enough room to move around if needed, and a comfortable temperature. It is also important to think about the messages sent by the time and location chosen for the meeting (Isenhart & Spangle, 2000). A student with behavior problems may participate less in a functional behavioral assessment meeting held in the principal's office than in the library. Families may more readily participate in school governance meetings that are held in the evening rather than during school hours. The provision of refreshments or the use of soothing music as people enter the meeting may increase participants' comfort levels (Eller, 2004).

Starting the Meeting

The first few minutes of any meeting set the tone for what follows. These early minutes should be used to engage individuals and describe what is to come. In school settings it is particularly important to make introductions so that everyone knows who the other participants are, what each person's role is relative to the meeting's purpose, and how each person prefers to be addressed.

Consider the message about power and prestige that is sent if professionals address each other by their titles and surnames, while addressing parents as "mom" and "dad." Follow parents' lead if they prefer greater informality and use of first names. However, the manner of address should be the same for all participants.

The initial part of the meeting should involve structuring comments by the facilitator that clearly outline the purpose of the meeting, excite participants about the process by emphasizing anticipated results and how they will benefit, empower participants by describing their roles in the meeting, and involve participants quickly by asking an open-ended question that relates to the meeting goals (Wilkinson, 2012). Depending on the purpose, degree of formality, and level of emotionality of the participants, ground rules may be briefly stated or may need to be developed by the group and listed in writing (Wilkinson, 2012). Explicit ground rules are most likely to be needed in situations when a high level of conflict is anticipated. These rules might include keeping an open mind, criticizing ideas but not people, listening actively and respectfully, avoiding interruptions by turning off electronics, and staying the entire meeting (Martin, 2005). As structuring statements are delivered, the facilitator should make eye contact with all participants and note their reactions (Eller, 2004) so that early signs of participant discomfort or conflict can be noted and addressed. In some school meetings, it will also be important to consider issues of confidentiality and informed consent. Parents must be aware of who will have access to information discussed at the meeting and how the decisions made will be used.

Opening inclusion activities will vary depending on the purpose of the meeting. For meetings focused on school governance or other broader topics, Garmston and von Frank (2012) offer several opening activities that encourage commitment to the meeting, including the "group groan" (p. 152). Here, members list on a flip chart the best and worst things they think can happen in the meeting. The group agrees to groan loudly if any of the worst things occur. This can lighten the mood of a meeting and help the group if it gets stuck. If the focus is on an individual student, consider asking participants to state their best hopes for the meeting or for the student. This is a variation on the solution-oriented "miracle question" that can highlight strengths and promote optimism for problem solving (Ratner, George, & Iveson, 2012, p. 94).

Guiding the Process

Throughout the meeting, the facilitator must stay alert to both content and process. Often an early task is to give all participants a chance to express their views on the central concern of the meeting. In the case of a problem-solving meeting, start with the individual who asked for the meeting or with the parents and student who are the focus of the meeting. During this part of the meeting, empathic responding, validating individual perspectives, judicious questioning, and encouragement are likely to be needed. Intervene quickly if the discussion becomes focused on who is to blame for the

problem and refocus the discussion by probing for specific examples, solutions that have already been attempted, or student strengths that might be unrecognized. It can also be helpful to offer a summary of areas of agreement as a means to interrupt blaming. In some cases, it may be necessary to stop the process and instruct the participants specifically: "Everyone seems pretty frustrated with this problem. It's tempting to spend a lot of time blaming each other for how we've gotten to this point, but even if we could figure out who to blame, we would be no closer to a solution. Even though it is hard, it is important for us to spend the next part of our time thinking about ways in which each of us can contribute to improving the situation."

As the meeting progresses, the facilitator should make sure that everyone stays involved in the discussion. It is sometimes necessary to explicitly elicit comments from quiet participants and to limit the contributions of participants who may be too vocal. Throughout, the facilitator actively monitors process, clarifying information, and helping participants stick to the agenda and moving to new agenda items as appropriate (see Table 35.3 for strategies).

Managing Conflict

Facilitators also need to be prepared to manage emotionality and conflict in a constructive manner. Educators tend to see conflict as negative and to avoid it when possible, often leading to larger conflicts later on (Swap, 1993). It is important to distinguish between affective conflict, which focuses on people and personalities, and cognitive conflict, which focuses on ideas. Affective conflict is typically destructive and must be blocked. However, cognitive conflict is actually helpful as it brings divergent ideas to the problem-solving process (Garmston & von Frank, 2012).

The effective facilitator remains calm and focused when there is conflict (see Lee, Pulvino, & Perrone, 1998). Try a few deep, slow breaths, quick tensing/relaxing of major muscle groups, and silent positive self-talk statements (e.g., "I can handle this."). Be careful not to indicate verbally or nonverbally that you are suppressing the conflict, rushing to fix it, or lecturing the participants (Martin, 2005). Take a moment to think about what was happening just before the conflict became apparent so that you can plan an appropriate intervention.

The facilitator should be alert to miscommunications or perceptions that some participants are not behaving in a trustworthy manner. The use of empathic responding and other communication strategies will give the individuals involved a sense of being heard and

Table 35.3. Facilitation Techniques for Guiding the Process

Balancing
Ask those who have not spoken to weigh in; ask those who are speaking frequently to hold comments until all have spoken.

Stacking
Ask who wants to speak; assign the order in which people will speak.

Using the clock
Set a specific time limit for discussion of a given topic.

Calling for themes
Ask group members to identify shared perspectives they heard during a discussion.

Linking
If individuals make a comment that appears off topic, ask them to explain how their comment relates to the topic at hand.

Listening for common ground
Summarize both the similarities and differences in the views expressed; end with a check out of accuracy.

Bridging
Summarize and then state the next step.

Note. Based on information from Jorgenson (2006), Kaner et al. (2007), and Rees (1998).

respected, allowing emotionality to be reduced. Once this occurs, the facilitator can assess the readiness of the individuals to move on: "This issue has been a sore point in our school for a long time, so it may be hard for all of us to imagine things getting better. Our meeting today is one step in that direction but it will take time. I'm hoping we can continue to work together toward a solution using the energy and wisdom of the group. Is this plan O.K. with you?"

If communication strategies are unsuccessful, consider using an individual caucus, especially in the case of affective conflict. The group may take a break while the facilitator speaks privately and separately to the individuals involved in the conflict. The focus of the conversation should be on reminding the individuals of the goals and ground rules of the meeting and seeking their cooperation in completing the meeting. The outcome may be to try again, with the individual returning to the group, or to try again later, with the meeting continuing without this individual. If the individual having difficulty is a mandated participant, then the meeting may need to be rescheduled. If this happens, then the facilitator should address the difficulties with all participants before the next meeting, seeking ideas on how to get the agenda accomplished. Another strategy to use when there is an unexpected outburst of emotionality is to ask the group's permission to pause the agenda, ask all participants to state what they are thinking and feeling about what just happened, and then ask all participants to state what they believe needs to happen next so that the meeting can proceed. A break may be needed so that the facilitator can

consider whether the meeting can go forward under the new circumstances or if an alternative is needed (Wilkinson, 2012).

Making Contributions Collaboratively

One question that sometimes arises when school psychologists facilitate is how to include their insider expertise without dominating the meeting. A meeting may be conducted collaboratively throughout, but when it comes time to brainstorm ideas, participants look to the school psychologist as the expert who will define the solutions. In most cases, particularly as the intensity of the interventions contemplated increases, the school psychologist will have valuable suggestions to add to the process.

However, the likelihood of particular solutions being implemented is increased when all participants have a role in developing them. Therefore, it may be helpful to delay offering ideas until the group's ideas have been fully elicited. Drawing from solution-oriented approaches to counseling (Murphy & Duncan, 2010) the facilitator can explore past solution attempts (e.g., "What has already been tried to solve this problem? Did any of these solutions work even a little?") and unexpressed ideas (e.g., "Are there other ideas that maybe someone has recommended to you that you haven't tried yet?") to get as many solutions on the table as possible.

If the brainstorming process has not yielded ideas that the facilitator sees as important to consider, additional suggestions can be offered in a tentative way, with recognition that other participants may not find a particular intervention feasible or helpful. Whenever possible, options should be presented to the group (e.g., "When faced with similar problems to this one, some families have found it helpful to do _____, while other families have found it helpful to do _____. What do you think might work in your family?").

Making Decisions

Attention should also be given to the method by which decisions will be made within the meeting (see Fujishin, 2009, for more detail). It is wise to avoid use of administrative fiat, in which the leader simply makes the decision. Although this method is time efficient, it tends to lead to resentment. Voting/majority rule also has an element of efficiency, but it results in a perception of having winners and losers. Minority voices may not be adequately utilized.

Compromise involves some participants giving up preferred elements of a solution in order to get support from the group for other parts. It has the advantage of all participants getting something that they want, but it may also result in the discussion being shut down too soon and in less creative solutions. Arbitration involves having a neutral third party make a decision. This method can break an impasse but often leads to increased polarization of the sides and decreased capacity for consensus moving forward.

In most cases, decision making by consensus is preferred. In a consensus decision, all participants view the solution as acceptable and workable at least for a short period of time. To build consensus, the facilitator must be sure that all participants get a chance to express themselves, including those who disagree with a proposed idea or solution. Negotiation between differing viewpoints is encouraged through further brainstorming and questions such as, "Is there any way to combine the strengths of these two ideas?"

As solutions gain traction in the discussion, the facilitator must check in with all participants to see if they can live with the solution for a clearly defined trial period. In this way, individuals' commitment to follow through is likely to be increased. Kaner et al. (2007) suggest using a "gradients of agreement" scale (p. 212) that allows participants to rate on a Likert scale the degree of enthusiasm they have for a particular solution or decision. Kaner et al. (2007) note that the higher the stakes, the greater the degree of enthusiasm needed. Similarly, Wilkinson (2012) describes a quick "five finger consensus" technique (p. 213–214) in which participants are asked to show on their fingers the degree of support they have for a decision. This technique allows the group to reach consensus on a solution that has strong, but not unanimous, support.

Closing and Planning Follow Up

Ending the meeting effectively will enhance participants' feelings of accomplishment and provide clear guidance on the next steps. The facilitator should (a) summarize progress made in the meeting; (b) clarify the agreements and decisions made, pointing out specifically what each individual has agreed to do; (c) offer encouragement to all participants on following through with their agreements; (d) help the group determine the next steps; and (e) arrange to provide a summary of the meeting to all participants (Isenhart & Spangle, 2000).

Typically, there should be detailed discussion of evaluation. That is, participants should decide together how they will know that the plans made in the meeting were successful, how long they should wait before evaluating the outcomes, and what data they will need to determine success. Appropriate follow up may involve another meeting of all participants, a subgroup of participants, or some other method (e.g., phone conversations between parents and teachers).

Evaluation should also include assessment of the meeting process itself. Written satisfaction surveys can be helpful, but may result in the "happy diner response" in which everyone says it was fine to avoid making others uncomfortable while privately deciding never to participate again (Martin, 2005, p. xvi). It can be helpful to ask open-ended questions, preferably in an interview format, that allow participants to describe the extent to which they felt heard and respected in the meeting and make suggestions for improvement in future meetings. School psychologists can provide leadership in ensuring that data are gathered routinely following meetings and in locating venues in which these data can be utilized for planning improvements (e.g., school improvement team, positive behavior support team, instructional consultation team, or whole faculty).

Applications of Facilitation Skills

Meetings conducted as recommended here provide opportunities to build more constructive relationships between families and schools. In this section, we outline examples of family–school meetings that illustrate the principles described. We have tried to emphasize meetings that are not covered elsewhere in this edition of *Best Practices*. To the extent possible, evidence-based practices are highlighted. However, randomized control trials are rare, and practices can best be described as promising. In addition, the use of good facilitation skills often must be inferred in the studies cited, as these skills are infrequently the direct focus of investigations.

Tier 1

School-wide positive behavior support: The use of systematic, tiered approaches to developing and maintaining positive behavior in schools has grown dramatically over the past decade. School-wide positive behavior support is a promising approach to improving school behavior (Chitiyo, May, & Chityo, 2012) that emphasizes building-level teams, team decision making, effective communication, staff buy-in, and attention to sustainability (Sugai & Horner, 2009). Teams are encouraged to include parents as members; however, there is surprisingly little focus on the need for good facilitation skills in developing plans, monitoring implementation, and evaluating outcomes (Minke & Anderson, 2005). Skilled facilitation may be particularly needed at middle and high school levels where the teams are larger and more diverse, and schools may struggle to effectively engage students and families (Flannery, Sugai, & Anderson, 2009). There is some evidence of the importance of team leadership (and, by implication, good facilitation skills) in the implementation of this approach. For example, in a study of two New Zealand schools, cross-cultural understanding and empowerment of students, parents, and teachers were seen as critical for successful implementation (Savage, Lewis, & Colless, 2011). Students and parents were included in leadership teams, and their ideas were integral to improving school-wide practices. Although the facilitation skills of the team leaders were not described specifically, it seems likely that these successful teams had good communication and problem-solving strategies as part of their process.

Routine conferences: One of the most commonly occurring family–school meetings is the parent–teacher conference. Traditional conferences, in which parents come to listen to the teacher's report of their child's progress, can be stressful for both parents and teachers (Minke & Anderson, 2003), and the literature is full of survival tips for both teachers (e.g., Potter, 2008) and parents (e.g., Villaire, 2001).

In response, a number of alternative conference styles based on collaborative principles have appeared. Collaborative conferences involving students may increase parental attendance, improve parent–teacher relationships, and enhance students' ownership of their own learning (Tuinstra & Hiatt-Michael, 2004).

Although school psychologists do not typically participate in routine parent–teacher conferences, they can have an important role as consultants, providing inservice and individual training to teachers who are interested in improving this type of meeting.

Minke and Anderson (2003) developed an inservice training for elementary school teachers interested in implementing family–school conferences. Teachers completed 6 hours of training in communication and facilitation skills and learned a structured conference process that involved preparation and an active role for all participants, including the student. Conferences were structured to promote interactive conversation and a round-robin approach was used in which each topic, introduced first by the student, was fully discussed by everyone before a new topic was considered. Qualitative and quantitative analyses indicated that students (K–4) were active participants, and that student participation was one of the most highly valued aspects of the conference. Teachers and parents reported better, more positive communication, and increased learning about each other and the student. Although teachers found the facilitation skills challenging to learn and use, they planned to continue using the process. This style is a promising means for school psychologists to promote change at the school-wide level by helping teachers improve their communication and relationships with families.

Tier 2: Conjoint Behavioral Consultation

When students do not respond to universal supports, problem-solving meetings may be used to plan and implement more intensive supports. Often these meetings will bring families and school personnel together. Conjoint behavioral consultation, for example, involves a structured problem-solving process in which parents, teachers, and other caregivers work as partners to promote "positive and consistent outcomes related to a child's academic, behavioral, and social–emotional development" (Sheridan & Kratochwill, 2008, p. 25). The process is intended to strengthen relationships and improve parent engagement through collaboration. It is differentiated from other problem-solving meetings in that it involves families and focuses on difficulties the child is experiencing across settings. School psychologists frequently serve as consultants (facilitators) and are charged with managing a complex process of defining shared goals, planning and implementing changes across settings, and evaluating outcomes.

Effective facilitation skills are needed at each stage so that all participants feel heard, understood, and valued.

Sheridan and Kratochwill (2008) highlight many of the same communication, process, and conflict management skills detailed above as essential. Particular attention is given to helping participants understand others' perspectives and maintaining a positive, strength-based approach. Conflict is managed by focusing on mutual goals, reframing statements, providing structure, and responding to nonverbal communication. Building partnerships is important and can be promoted when facilitators model positive communication, highlight shared experiences among participants, and provide for meaningful participation by all.

Following consultation, parents report improved perceptions of communication and relationships with teachers (Sheridan et al., 2012). Similarly, teachers indicate "greater increases in relationships with parents" than teachers in the control group (Sheridan et al., 2012, p. 35). Importantly, the parent–teacher relationship had a mediating effecting on student outcomes, highlighting the significance of utilizing good facilitation skills that promote relationship development.

Tier 3

IEP: IEP meetings traditionally include parents, general education and special education teachers, related service providers, and other individuals as needed. Starting at age 14, students are also required to participate, which should promote students' self-determination skills and assist in transition planning. Unfortunately, these meetings have not always been characterized by the elements of successful facilitated meetings. Multiple difficulties for families have been documented including poor communication, use of jargon, and pressure to conform to preset decisions (e.g., Childre & Chambers, 2005). The lack of progress in this area is regrettable in that it has been known for more than 25 years that relatively minor changes in the IEP process can yield increases in parents' participation and improved relationships. For example, Brinckerhoff and Vincent (1986) asked parents to prepare by completing brief written assessments of their children's developmental levels. A school liaison met with parents briefly to describe the IEP process and prepare them for presenting their own assessment data. Increases were documented in joint decision making and additional attention to home-based programming compared to control group meetings, without increasing the amount of time spent in the meetings.

Student-led IEP approaches have been shown to be effective at increasing active student participation. Danneker and Bottge (2009) conducted a study with elementary students and provided them with six 20-minute sessions that included instruction on the purpose, format of IEPs, and all of the stages of conducting an IEP meeting. In the last session a script was also devised for the student to use. Meetings became more collaborative and student centered, and students displayed improvements in leadership and self-determination skills. Martin et al. (2006) utilized a video-modeling method for teaching high school students how to lead IEP meetings through the Self-Directed IEP instructional program. Students watched a video that modeled the 11 steps of the Self-Directed IEP process and received instruction from teachers on each step. Content of the lessons included introducing themselves and other team members, stating the purpose of the meeting, reviewing current goals and progress, expressing skills and limitations, and expressing options and new goals. Students took greater leadership roles, talked more, and had more positive perceptions of their IEP meetings. The Self-Advocacy Strategy (Van Reusen & Bos, 1994) includes teacher preparation in specific questioning and facilitation strategies designed to support students' success in the meetings. This approach is considered to have a moderate level of evidence (National Secondary Transition Technical Assistance Center, n.d.) showing that trained students provide more goals than untrained students and generally participate at a higher level. In addition, greater attention to students' learning strengths and a more positive tone in the meetings are observed.

School psychologists could consider collaborating with teachers who are training students in these skills. Teachers may benefit from training in how to support student leadership during the meetings. In addition, providing teachers inservice education on effective communication skills and perhaps adaptations of the guerrilla strategies described above might be useful in this regard. Studies to date have not addressed these issues. Still, available evidence supports use of these processes in schools where greater student participation in IEP meetings is a goal.

Person-centered planning: Person-centered planning is a method designed to promote self-determination and mobilization of support systems for individuals with disabilities and is often used for transition planning. Person-centered planning meetings bring together everyone who is important in the individual's life (e.g., family, teachers, community members, friends). Through a structured problem-solving process, the team develops a vision (dream) for the individual's life and plans how to achieve that dream. The facilitator is key to this process and must be creative and flexible, empower team members, and bring knowledge of community supports to the process (e.g., Butkus, Rotholz, Lacy, Abery, & Elkin, 2002). The facilitator must focus on self-determination of the individual while gaining participation of all team members. Strong facilitator skills led to adults with intellectual disabilities feeling listened to, having a greater understanding of and involvement in planning meetings, and developing increased self-determination. Their families and other supporters developed greater understanding of the aspirations of the adults and ways to help them achieve those aspirations (Espiner & Hartnett, 2012). Conversely, poorly trained facilitators are cited as one of the highest ranked organizational barriers for implementing plans (Robertson et al., 2007).

Wraparound: For students with severe difficulties, particularly emotional and behavioral concerns, wraparound services that involve families, educators, and community providers have been effective. Wraparound is a collaborative, strength-based, individualized approach to achieving positive outcomes through community services and natural supports (Eber & Keenan, 2004). It requires the development and maintenance of cooperative relationships between schools and community providers.

Facilitation skills are important for wraparound approaches to be successful. Particular emphasis is placed on initial conversations with families, blending perspectives of the team members, and clarifying the differences between needs and services (Eber, 2003, as cited in Eber & Keenan, 2004). Within the initial conversations, it is important to listen to and learn about all team members, including their histories, fears, preferences, and dreams.

Lyons and Rawal (2005) reviewed available evidence on the efficacy of wraparound programs. They cited studies documenting reductions in residential and inpatient treatment, out-of-state placements, and incarceration for participating youth. Wraparound services resulted in better adjustment, school attendance, and employment than traditional services. More recently, Painter (2012) found that youth and caregivers who received wraparound services reported significant improvements in youth "emotional and behavioral strengths and mental health symptoms" (p. 421) after a 6-month period. These improvements continued at 24-month follow up. Similarly, Mears, Yaffe, and Harris (2009) found that individuals receiving wraparound services demonstrated a decreased level of impairment and an improvement in functioning compared to those receiving traditional child welfare services. These data suggest that wraparound services represent a promising approach to service delivery for students with severe behavior problems.

SUMMARY

Families and educators must work together effectively to promote the healthy development of children. School psychologists are well positioned to assist in this endeavor through skilled meeting facilitation. These skills are developed within the context of an ecosystemic theoretical orientation that includes a strength-based, culturally sensitive approach to all families and well-developed listening and communication skills. Effective facilitators engage in careful premeeting planning and assist others, especially family members and students, in preparing as well. Meetings are characterized by clear goals, careful elicitation of all participants' views and ideas, resourceful conflict management, and consensus decision making. Decisions and commitments for follow up are made explicit.

These skills are tapped in a variety of meeting structures across tiers of service delivery. At the school-wide level, school psychologists can provide teachers training in communication and problem solving that allows for more productive and successful routine family–school conferences. Problem-solving meetings, such as conjoint behavioral consultation, can be structured to involve greater preparation and participation of students and their parents. Finally, at the most intensive level of service delivery, person-centered planning, IEP, and wraparound planning can bring informal and formal supports from both school and community together to address concerns in the least restrictive environment. Proficient meeting facilitation greatly increases the likelihood that families and educators will come away from their encounters with improved relationships, greater optimism, and more effective plans for student success.

AUTHOR NOTE

Disclosure. Kathleen M. Minke has a financial interest in books she authored or coauthored referenced in this chapter.

REFERENCES

Adams, T., Means, J., & Spivey, M. S. (2007). *The project meeting facilitator: Facilitation skills to make the most of project meetings.* Hoboken, NJ: Wiley.

Bens, I. (2006). *Facilitating to lead: Leadership strategies for a networked world.* San Francisco, CA: Jossey-Bass.

Brinckerhoff, J. L., & Vincent, L. J. (1986). Increasing parental decision making at the individualized educational program meeting. *Journal of the Division for Early Childhood, 11*, 46–58. doi:10.1177/105381518601100105

Bronfenbrenner, U. (1979). *The ecology of human development.* Cambridge, MA: Harvard University Press.

Butkus, S., Rotholz, D. A., Lacy, K. K., Abery, B., & Elkin, S. (2002). Implementing person-centered planning on a statewide basis: Leadership, training, and satisfaction issues. In S. Holburn & P. M. Vietze (Eds.), *Person-centered planning: Research, practice, and future directions.* Baltimore, MD: Brookes.

Childre, A., & Chambers, C. R. (2005). Family perceptions of student-centered planning and IEP meetings. *Education and Training in Developmental Disabilities, 40*, 217–233.

Chitiyo, M., May, M. E., & Chitiyo, G. (2012). An assessment of the evidence-base for school-wide positive behavior support. *Education and Treatment of Children, 35*, 1–24. doi:10.1353/etc.2012.0000

Christenson, S. L., & Sheridan, S. M. (2001). *Schools and families: Creating essential connections for learning.* New York, NY: Guilford Press.

Danneker, J. E., & Bottge, B. A. (2009). Benefits of and barriers to elementary student-led individualized education programs. *Remedial and Special Education, 30*, 225–233. doi:10.1177/0741932508315650

Eber, L., & Keenan, S. (2004). Collaboration with other agencies: Wraparound and systems of care for children and youth with emotional and behavioral disorders. In R. B. Rutherford Jr., M. M. Quinn, & S. R. Mathur (Eds.), *Handbook of research in emotional and behavioral disorders* (pp. 502–518). New York, NY: Guilford Press.

Eller, J. (2004). *Effective group facilitation in education: How to energize meetings and manage difficult groups.* Thousand Oaks, CA: Corwin.

Espiner, D., & Hartnett, F. M. (2012). 'I felt I was in control of the meeting': Facilitating planning with adults with an intellectual disability. *British Journal of Learning Disabilities, 40*, 62–70. doi:10.1111/j.1468-3156.2011.00684.x

Fish, W. W. (2006). Perceptions of parents of students with autism towards the IEP meeting: A case study of one family support group chapter. *Education, 127*, 56–68.

Flannery, K. B., Sugai, G., & Anderson, C. M. (2009). School-wide behavior support in high school: Early lessons learned. *Journal of Positive Behavior Interventions, 11*, 177–185. doi:10.1177/1098300708316257

Fujishin, R. (2009). *Creating communication: Exploring and expanding your fundamental communication skills* (2nd ed.). Lanham, MD: Rowman & Littlefield.

Garmston, R. J., & von Frank, V. (2012). *Unlocking group potential to improve schools.* Thousand Oaks, CA: Corwin.

Graue, E., & Brown, C. P. (2003). Preservice teachers' notions of families and schooling. *Teaching and Teacher Education: An International Journal of Research and Studies, 19*, 719–735. doi:10.1016/j.tate.2003.06.002

Isenhart, M. W., & Spangle, M. (2000). *Collaborative approaches to resolving conflict.* Thousand Oaks, CA: SAGE.

Ivey, A. E., Ivey, M. B., & Zalaquett, C. P. (2010). *Intentional interviewing and counseling: Facilitating client development in a multicultural society* (7th ed.). Belmont, CA: Brooks/Cole.

Jorgensen, C. M., Schuh, M. C., & Nisbet, J. (2006). *The inclusion facilitator's guide.* Baltimore, MD: Brookes.

Kaner, S., Doyle, M., Lind, L., & Toldi, C. (2007). *Facilitator's guide to participatory decision-making* (2nd ed.). San Francisco, CA: Jossey-Bass.

Lareau, A. (2011). *Unequal childhoods: Class, race, and family life* (2nd ed.). Berkeley, CA: University of California Press.

Lee, J. L., Pulvino, C. J., & Perrone, P. A. (1998). *Restoring harmony: A guide for managing conflict in schools.* Upper Saddle River, NJ: Prentice Hall.

Lee, S. (2005). Selective parent participation: Structural and cultural factors that influence school participation among Korean parents. *Equity & Excellence in Education, 38*, 299–308. doi:10.1080/10665680500299734

Lo, L. (2008). Chinese families' level of participation and experiences in IEP meetings. *Preventing School Failure, 53*, 21–27. doi:10.3200/PSFL.53.1.21-27

Locke, D. C. (2003). Improving the multicultural competence of educators. In P. B. Pederson & J. C. Carey (Eds.), *Multicultural counseling in schools: A practical handbook* (2nd ed., pp. 171–189). Boston, MA: Allyn & Bacon.

Lyons, J. S., & Rawal, P. H. (2005). Evidence-based treatments for children and adolescents. In C. E. Stout & R. A. Hayes (Eds.), *The evidence-based practice: Methods, models, and tools for mental health professionals* (pp. 177–198). Hoboken, NJ: Wiley.

Martin, N. R. M. (2005). *A guide to collaboration for IEP teams.* Baltimore, MD: Brookes.

Martin, J. E., Van Dycke, J. L., Christensen, W. R., Greene, B. A., Gardner, J. E., & Lovett, D. L. (2006). Increasing student participation in IEP meetings: Establishing the self-directed IEP as an evidenced-based practice. *Exceptional Children, 72*, 299–316.

Mears, S. L., Yaffe, J., & Harris, N. J. (2009). Evaluation of wraparound services for severely emotionally disturbed youths. *Research on Social Work Practice, 19*, 678–685. doi:10.1177/1049731508329385

Minke, K. M. (2000). Preventing school problems and promoting school success through family–school–community collaboration. In K. M. Minke & G. G. Bear (Eds.), *Preventing school problems—Promoting school success: Strategies and programs that work* (pp. 337-420). Bethesda, MD: National Association of School Psychologists.

Minke, K. M. (2006). Parent–teacher relationships. In G. G. Bear & K. M. Minke (Eds.), *Children's needs III: Development, prevention, and intervention* (pp. 73–85). Bethesda, MD: National Association of School Psychologists.

Minke, K. M., & Anderson, K. J. (2003). Restructuring routine parent-teacher conferences: The family-school conference model. *Elementary School Journal, 104*, 49–69. doi:10.1086/499742

Minke, K. M., & Anderson, K. J. (2005). Family-school collaboration and positive behavior support. *Journal of Positive Behavior Interventions, 7*, 181–185. doi:10.1177/10983007050070030701

Murphy, J. J., & Duncan, B. L. (2010). *Brief intervention for school problems: Collaborating for practical solutions* (2nd ed.). New York, NY: Guilford Press.

Myrsiades, L. (2000). Meeting sabotage: Met and conquered. *Journal of Management Development, 19*, 870–885.

National Association of School Psychologists. (2010). *Model for comprehensive and integrated school psychological services.* Bethesda, MD:

Author. Retrieved from http://www.nasponline.org/standards/2010standards/2_PracticeModel.pdf

National Secondary Transition Technical Assistance Center. (n.d.). Using the self-advocacy strategy to teach student involvement in the IEP. Retrieved from http://www.nsttac.org/sites/default/files/assets/pdf/SAS(moderate).final.pdf

Newell, M. L. (2012). Transforming knowledge to skill: Evaluating the consultation competence of novice school-based consultants. *Consulting Psychology Journal: Practice and Research, 64,* 8–28. doi:10.1037/a0027741

Okagaki, L., & Bingham, G. E. (2010). Diversity in families: Parental socialization and children's development and learning. In S. L. Christenson & A. L. Reschly (Eds.), *Handbook of family-school partnerships* (pp. 80–100). New York, NY: Routledge.

Painter, K. (2012). Outcomes for youth with severe emotional disturbance: A repeated measure longitudinal study of a wraparound approach of service delivery in systems of care. *Child Youth Care Forum, 41,* 407–425. doi:10.1007/s10566-011-9167-1

Pianta, R., & Walsh, D. B. (1996). *High-risk children in schools: Constructing sustaining relationships.* New York, NY: Routledge.

Potter, L. (2008). Difficult conversations: Parent-teacher conferences. *Principal Leadership, 8*(8), 32–35.

Ratner, H., George, E., & Iveson, C. (2012). *Solution focused brief therapy: 100 key points and techniques.* New York, NY: Routledge.

Rees, F. (1998). *The facilitator excellence handbook: helping people work creatively and productively together.* San Francisco, CA: Jossey-Bass/Pfeiffer.

Robertson, J., Hatton, C., Emerson, E., Elliott, J., McIntosh, B., Swift, P., & Joyce, T. (2007). Reported barriers to the implementation of person-centered planning for people with intellectual disabilities in the UK. *Journal of Applied Research in Intellectual Disabilities, 20,* 297–307. doi:10.1111/j.1468-3148.2006.00333.x

Savage, C., Lewis, J., & Colless, N. (2011). Essentials for implementation: Six years of school-wide positive behaviour support in New Zealand. *New Zealand Journal of Psychology, 40,* 29–37.

Seligman, M. (2000). *Conducting effective conferences with parents of children with disabilities: A guide for teachers.* New York, NY: Guilford Press.

Shapiro, J., Monzó, L. D., Rueda, R., Gomez, J. A., & Blacher, J. (2004). Alienated advocacy: Perspectives of Latina mothers of young adults with developmental disabilities on service systems. *Mental Retardation: A Journal of Practices, Policy and Perspectives, 42,* 37–54. doi:10.1352/0047-6765(2004)42<37:AAPOLM>2.0.CO;2

Sheridan, S. M., Bovard, J. A., Glover, T. A., Garbacz, S. A., Witte, A., & Kwon, K. (2012). A randomized trial examining the effects of conjoint behavioral consultation and the mediating role of the parent–teacher relationship. *School Psychology Review, 41,* 23–46.

Sheridan, S. M., & Kratochwill, T. R. (2008). *Conjoint behavioral consultation: Promoting family-school connections and interventions* (2nd ed.). New York, NY: Springer.

Sugai, G., & Horner, R. H. (2009). Responsiveness-to-intervention and school-wide positive behavior supports: Integration of multi-tiered system approaches. *Exceptionality, 17,* 223–237. doi:10.1080/09362830903235375

Swap, S. M. (1993). *Developing home-school partnerships: From concepts to practice.* New York, NY: Teachers College Press.

Tuinstra, C., & Hiatt-Michael, D. (2004). Student-led parent conferences in middle schools. *School Community Journal, 14,* 59–80.

Van Reusen, A. K., & Bos, C. S. (1994). Facilitating student participation in Individualized Education Programs through motivation strategies instruction. *Exceptional Children, 60,* 466–475.

Villaire, T. (2001). Preparing for a productive parent-teacher conference. *Our Children, 27*(2), 4.

Wilkinson, M. (2012). *The secrets of facilitation: The SMART guide to getting results with groups* (2nd ed.). San Francisco, CA: Jossey-Bass.

Zhang, C., & Bennett, T. (2003). Facilitating the meaningful participation of culturally and linguistically diverse families in the IFSP and IEP process. *Focus on Autism and Other Developmental Disabilities, 18,* 51–59. doi:10.1177/108835760301800107

36 Best Practices in Linking Families and Schools to Educate Children With Attention Problems

Jennifer A. Mautone
The Children's Hospital of Philadelphia (PA)
Kristen Carson
Lehigh University (PA)
Thomas J. Power
The Children's Hospital of Philadelphia and Perelman School of Medicine at the University of Pennsylvania (PA)

OVERVIEW

Attention problems are among the most prevalent difficulties affecting school children. For example, between 5, and 10% of children are diagnosed with attention deficit hyperactivity disorder (ADHD; Polanczyk, Silva de Lima, Horta, Biderman, & Rohde, 2007), but a much higher percentage of children have problems paying attention. There is an undeniable link between attention problems and academic underachievement. Although it can be difficult to sort out causative patterns between attention and academic deficits, the preponderance of evidence points to a strong causative connection between attention problems and learning deficits. Further, it has been shown that targeted academic interventions may not be as effective with children who have attention problems as compared to their peers. Research indicates that children with attention and learning problems need specialized instruction that focuses on improving both academic engagement and academic skills (Wolraich & DuPaul, 2010).

Interventions to address attention problems have primarily targeted children who have moderate to severe attention difficulties and who qualify for a diagnosis of ADHD. However, interventions might also be necessary for children who do not meet diagnostic criteria for ADHD. Indeed, interventions, including pharmacological and behavioral strategies, to support children with attention problems can be integrated into a multitiered model of service delivery and applied along a continuum of need. Pharmacological interventions, in particular stimulants, have been demonstrated in hundreds of studies to reduce attention problems among children with ADHD (Barbaresi, Katusic, Colligan, Weaver, & Jacobsen, 2007). Behavioral applications, including contingency management and academic interventions, have also been demonstrated to be effective in improving attention and school performance (Wolraich & DuPaul, 2010).

Intervention strategies to address children's attention problems often fail to involve the family, even though there is a large body of research demonstrating the impact that families can have on promoting their children's school success (Christenson & Reschly, 2009). Promoting family involvement in education is an important approach to address children's attention difficulties and promote academic success, and this strategy has been strongly affirmed by the National Association of School Psychologists (NASP) *Model for Comprehensive and Integrated School Psychological Services* (NASP, 2010), especially in the domain of Family–School Collaboration.

Intervention planning historically has targeted symptom reduction and the attainment of short-term goals.

This approach is problematic given that reducing impairments, as opposed to reducing symptoms, is more important to promoting school success, and attention problems tend to be chronic in nature. As such, intervention plans developed for students with attention difficulties ought to address areas of impairment rather than focus only on symptom reduction, and plans should incorporate a long-term perspective to address skill building across developmental levels (Evans, Owens, Mautone, DuPaul, & Power, 2014).

The focus of this chapter is on interventions school psychologists can offer to families to encourage ongoing, long-term family involvement in promoting child academic engagement, skill building, and success in school from the early elementary years through secondary school. These interventions include strategies that parents can implement at home with their children as well as approaches involving partnerships between families and schools across school years to address long-term goals.

BASIC CONSIDERATIONS

Children with attention difficulties frequently evidence impairment across multiple domains. Specifically, these children often have difficulties in school, such as problems listening during instruction, problems completing independent work and working accurately, and study skills deficits, which may result in academic underachievement (Wolraich & DuPaul, 2010). Additionally, compared with their peers, children with attention problems, particularly those with ADHD, are more likely to be placed in special education classes and are at higher risk for retention and drop out (Barkley, 2006). Children with attention problems frequently are referred for multidisciplinary evaluations and other supplemental school-based services, and school psychologists often are involved in assessment and intervention for children with these difficulties. Treatments for children with attention problems may include pharmacological, behavioral, and/or academic interventions.

Pharmacological Treatment

Children with moderate or severe attention difficulties who are diagnosed with ADHD frequently are prescribed psychotropic medications, particularly stimulants, to help manage their symptoms. Children with ADHD who are prescribed stimulant medications generally demonstrate marked reductions in core symptoms and related problems, such as off-task behavior and classroom disruptiveness (Barkley, 2006). However, the stimulants typically have more modest effects on areas of functional impairment, including educational and social functioning, and long-term benefits from stimulant treatment are limited, which is due in part to nonadherence to treatment over time (Jensen et al., 2007).

As physicians work with families to identify the best medication and dose for a child, school psychologists may assist by collecting teacher rating scales and/or conducting direct observations of students' classroom behavior. It should be noted that the use of stimulants without behavioral and academic interventions is sufficient in treating some children whose impairments are mild to moderate and who do not display comorbid conditions, in particular oppositional defiant disorder, conduct disorder, and mood disorders. However, when impairments are in the moderate to severe range and/or comorbid conditions are present, intervention packages that include targeted behavioral and academic interventions usually are required.

Behavioral and Educational Interventions

Behavioral interventions for children with attention problems include a variety of home- and school-based strategies that can be implemented by parents, teachers, or the child (e.g., self-management). Given that the behavioral difficulties of children with attention problems may reflect both skills and performance deficits, it is important to utilize strategies that identify targets for behavior change, teach appropriate replacement behaviors, and encourage the continued performance of newly acquired replacement behaviors. Furthermore, strategies to support students with attention problems should be developed based on the hypothesized function of the target behavior and individualized to address varied family and teacher goals and preferences for intervention (Wolraich & DuPaul, 2010).

Children who have attention problems are at risk for poor academic outcomes, so it also is critical that treatment include academic interventions within the classroom environment. Research indicates that academic interventions that alter the classroom environment, result in frequent and consistent feedback, and that are structured to match students' individual academic needs are effective in improving academic performance. Further, organizational skills training, including components to improve materials management, time management, planning, and work completion, have been shown to be effective with children as young as third grade (Abikoff et al., 2012). In addition, academic interventions can have positive effects on classroom behavior, and school-based interventions appear to be equally effective across general and special education settings (Wolraich & DuPaul, 2010).

As is the case with medication treatments, however, the long-term effects of behavioral and academic interventions appear to be limited. Therefore, it is important that intervention packages include a plan for sustainability, which might include organizational skills training for parents and students, follow-up intervention at the beginning of each school year to promote strong teacher–student and family–school relationships, and implementation supports (see below) designed to encourage ongoing and consistent adherence to the treatment plan.

Family Involvement in Education

Many behavioral parent training programs focus solely on change in the home environment and do not capitalize on the impact that families can have on the child's educational performance (Corcoran & Dattalo, 2006). Also, although school-based behavioral and academic interventions are effective methods for improving the performance of children with attention difficulties, to maximize intervention effectiveness it is critical that families be included as partners in the intervention process. For children with attention

problems, who are at risk for educational difficulty, family involvement in education, including family–school collaboration, serves as a protective factor. During preschool and kindergarten, family–school collaboration prepares children to enter school and supports healthy child development, and there is substantial evidence that a higher level of family–school collaboration is associated with greater student competence (Christenson & Reschly, 2009).

Models of family involvement in education suggest that families may be involved in their children's education through (a) home-based educational activities, (b) school-based activities, and (c) family–school partnership (see Table 36.1 for examples of each type of family involvement; Fantuzzo, McWayne, Perry, & Childs, 2004). The most effective programs consider all aspects of family involvement through a team approach and include family members at every level. When considering family involvement practices, it is critical that school psychologists acknowledge the home as an environment for learning and family–school partnerships as a means for building children's strengths and resolving their educational difficulties (Christenson & Reschly, 2009).

Implementation Supports

Current service delivery models for children often do not account for a family's readiness, willingness, and

Table 36.1. Sample Family Involvement Activities for Families of Children With Attention Problems

Domain	Family Involvement Activity	Suggested Implementation Supports	Developmental Considerations
Home-based involvement	• Engaging in daily family reading time • Studying with the child (i.e., parent tutoring) • Limiting television and videogame time • Parent coaching of homework sessions	• Post a daily family schedule in a visible location • Use a timer to monitor duration of activities • Monitor points earned by the child using an electronic format (e.g., spreadsheet on the family computer, notes application on a smartphone)	• Create "natural learning opportunities" for younger children • Increased use of self-monitoring strategies for homework as child matures
School-based involvement	• Volunteering in the classroom • Participating in the parent–teacher organization	• Electronic calendar with notifications enabled	
Family–school partnership	• Using parent–teacher conferences as an opportunity for problem solving and plan development • Regular communication between families and teachers about student performance	• Electronic communication between home and school • School website to monitor child progress (when available)	• Include adolescents in goal development

ability to engage in treatment (Dishion & Stormshak, 2007). As a result, many families fail to initiate treatment or drop out prematurely, limiting treatment effectiveness, especially with chronic conditions, such as ADHD. Increased attendance at treatment sessions alone, though, may be insufficient to have an impact on child outcomes at posttreatment in part because attendance does not sufficiently address the key mediating variable of intervention adherence (Clarke et al., 2013). Research suggests that adherence to recommended intervention strategies contributes to improvements in child and family functioning above and beyond attendance at treatment sessions. However, adherence to intervention strategies, as measured by completion of between-session homework assignments, often is variable (e.g., Clarke et al., 2013). Also, adherence to treatment recommendations declines significantly over the course of follow-up periods, and treatment gains observed during active intervention tend to decline during follow up as well (e.g., Power et al., 2012).

Recent research offers some insight into factors that contribute to lower rates of adherence to intervention plans for children with attention problems. For example, when children have ADHD, it is relatively common that at least one parent struggles with similar attention and organizational skills difficulties. In cases where parents have high levels of ADHD symptoms, improvements in child and family outcomes attenuate during intervention follow up (Dawson, Marshall, Wymbs, Mautone, & Power, 2013). In fact, families showed significant improvement immediately following treatment, whether parents had elevated ADHD symptoms or not. However, families in which there was a parent with elevated ADHD symptoms were less likely to maintain treatment gains during the follow-up period.

Developmental and Ecological Considerations

School psychologists working with families to support children with attention problems must consider the continually evolving context within which these interventions are implemented. Specifically, the child develops and matures, and the environments (i.e., family, school, community) supporting child development also change over time (Evans et al., 2014). In addition, interactions between these environments (e.g., family–school relationships) evolve throughout the child's education. For example, research suggests that teacher investment in family–school intervention and teacher invitations for family involvement tend to decline with advancing grade level (Hoover-Dempsey, Ice, & Whitaker, 2009).

Therefore, it is important that interventions are monitored and adjusted according to developmental and environmental changes.

Additionally, although most of the research related to children with attention problems focuses on school-age children, individuals as young as preschool age and those who are adolescents often exhibit similar difficulties. For example, research has shown that children ages 4–6 years who meet diagnostic criteria for ADHD have functional impairments in multiple domains (e.g., academic, social, and behavioral) and across settings compared to same-aged peers without ADHD, and these children are typically more impaired than children diagnosed at older ages (DuPaul & Kern, 2011). Additionally, symptoms, particularly inattention and impulsivity, and related impairments often continue into adolescence and adulthood; that is, about 75% of children with ADHD continue to meet criteria into adolescence (Barkley, 2006).

BEST PRACTICES IN LINKING FAMILIES AND SCHOOLS TO EDUCATE CHILDREN WITH ATTENTION PROBLEMS

When developing intervention plans, it is critically important that the long-term goals of the family and student are considered. In virtually every instance, the family articulates a desire for the child to develop into a competent individual who is able to function independently, be successful in the work place, and relate effectively to others. Therefore, it is critical to incorporate skill-building programs into the intervention plan to increase the likelihood that the child will have the skills necessary to become an autonomous, competent, happy adult. Maintaining a strong connection between the home, school, and healthcare system is a critical component of an effective intervention package that programs for future success. In some cases, especially when attention problems are moderate to severe and the response to educational and behavioral interventions is not adequate, medication may also be needed to promote skill development and the attainment of long-term goals.

There are a range of methods families can use to support their children's education. The following sections describe approaches that can be used to promote family involvement in education in the home and in the context of family–school partnerships. School psychologists can share this information with families during individual meetings with parents/caregivers or during a more structured family support program that could be offered in school for groups of families. Case examples are included to illustrate school psychologists' roles in working with families to support children with attention problems.

Family Involvement in the Home

Families vary greatly with regard to their willingness to support their children's education through involvement in school-based activities, and these variations are often related to cultural factors. However, families across ethnic and cultural groups generally are very willing to support their children's education by becoming involved with them at home. Further, there is some evidence that family involvement at home may have greater effects on student attention and motivation than family involvement in school (Fantuzzo et al., 2004). There are several ways in which parents can support their children's education in the home. What follows is a brief description of suggested empirically supported strategies for family involvement in education for children with attention difficulties. These strategies have been evaluated in several studies, both as separate interventions and as a treatment package designed to support family involvement in education, including family–school partnerships, for elementary-age children with ADHD (e.g., Power et al., 2012). School psychologists can partner with parents to encourage use of these strategies at home.

Creating a Context That Promotes Learning

Parental support of children's educational activities at home has been shown to promote children's success in school (Christenson & Reschly, 2009). Parents can promote academic success by communicating the importance of education and structuring the home environment so that educationally relevant activities are emphasized. For example, stressing the value of independent reading by scheduling a family reading time each evening can communicate the importance of literacy. Families can also utilize everyday activities, such as counting money while shopping, measuring ingredients needed for baking, and reading signs that appear along the road in the neighborhood, to foster learning in the natural context. Children learn the importance of education when parents communicate high and reasonable expectations for success and carefully monitor their children's academic performance. Further, children learn the value of studying when parents emphasize and reinforce effort on educational activities and point out examples of how effort results in strong performance (Christenson & Reschly, 2009).

Fostering Strong Parent–Child Attachments

Parents foster their children's success in school when they form and sustain strong parent–child attachments. Young children who develop in the context of warm, caring, and responsive parent–child relationships learn to orient and sustain their attention, regulate their behavior, and modulate their emotions (Pianta, 1997). Strong parent–child attachments prepare children to form successful relationships with teachers and peers, engage in academic instruction, and regulate their behavior in the school context. This may be particularly important for children with attention and behavior problems, who often struggle with developing social relationships outside of the family and regulating behavior and attention in school.

Families can strengthen the parent–child relationship through evidence-based strategies, such as the Child's Game (see McMahon & Forehand, 2003, for details), positive attending, and verbal praise. The Child's Game provides an excellent opportunity for parents and children to spend special time together through child-led interactive play. This activity ensures that, for approximately 10–15 minutes per day, parents are providing children with an abundance of positive attention at once, which may be especially important for children with attention problems, who often receive a great deal of negative feedback from adults. During the Child's Game, the parent should praise the child for adaptive behaviors, reflect back on the child's comments, imitate the child's play, and describe what the child is doing. The parent should avoid placing demands on the child, such as giving commands or directions, asking questions, or directing the child's play. In general, parents should provide positive or neutral statements during Child's Game and refrain from negative or critical statements.

Supporting Homework Performance

Children with attention problems generally have significant homework difficulties (Power, Werba, Watkins, Angelucci, & Eiraldi, 2006). Typically they struggle with homework at every step in the process, including remembering assignments and the materials needed to complete work, getting down to work at the appointed time, working efficiently and accurately, and returning completed assignments to school. Poor homework performance may contribute not only to academic difficulties but also parent–child conflict and strained parent–teacher relationships (Power et al., 2012).

Homework interventions can be differentiated into those focused on antecedent conditions and those emphasizing consequences (see Table 36.2). Several intervention strategies involve changing the antecedents of homework performance, which often requires some collaboration with the teacher. School psychologists can serve a consultative role to support this collaboration when necessary. It is essential for students to know what assignments have been given to them for homework. Requiring students to record assignments in a homework notebook and requesting teachers to review the notebook for accuracy are useful intervention approaches. For schools that post homework assignments on a website or make assignments available on a call-in hotline, the use of a homework notebook may not be necessary. However, in these cases, the child should be taught to use the website or homework hotline as he or she develops increased independence and takes responsibility for assignments. Also, assigning a peer to serve as a homework helper may be helpful, especially when the classmate receives guidance and support from the teacher to serve in this role.

Children with attention problems often take an unusually long amount of time to complete their assignments, which can be frustrating for students and their families. Part of the problem may be that the work assigned is too difficult for the student. When the purpose of the assignment is to promote further learning and mastery of material presented in class, the student should be able to accurately complete at least 85% of the assigned items independently. Another reason that

homework may take so long is that too much work has been assigned. School psychologists supporting families of children with attention problems might need to encourage the teacher to work with the parent to identify the proper homework difficulty level and amount of homework that is assigned.

Establishing a homework routine in the home is an important component of an effective intervention plan. School psychologists can work with families to set up a consistent routine for homework. Homework should be performed in a place that is relatively free of distractions and nearby to a parent to facilitate supervision. The timing of homework should take into account several factors, including the parent's availability for supervision, the child's schedule of extracurricular activities, and the duration of effect of medication, when it is used (Power, Karustis, & Habboushe, 2001). The development of a homework kit to include materials generally needed to complete homework, such as paper, pencils, assignment books, notebooks, worksheets, and school books, will ensure that the child is organized and prepared to begin homework tasks.

With regard to strategies for managing the consequences of homework performance, an effective and useful approach is goal setting and contingency contracting. This strategy entails multiple steps (see Power et al., 2001, for a further description). First, before homework begins, the parent and child consider all of the work assigned and divide it into subunits. In

Table 36.2. Strategies for Addressing Common Homework Problems of Children With Attention Difficulties

Homework Problem	Strategy
Difficulty recording assignments	• Teacher monitors use of a homework assignment book • Teacher posts homework assignments on a website • Teacher creates an electronic calendar for the child and the parent to monitor due dates
Trouble getting down to work	• Parent and child establish a consistent routine (time and location) for homework • If medication is being used, then the parent attempts to schedule homework when the medication is still having an effect • Parent attempts to minimize distractions during homework
Taking too much time on homework	• Teacher shortens assignments and intersperses additional, easy problems • Teacher shortens assignments and permits a choice among two or more options • Parent expects child to work on homework only for the maximum amount of time designated by teacher • Parents use a timer to monitor length of homework sessions
Trouble working efficiently	• Parent and child use goal setting strategy • Child receives positive reinforcement for completing assignments and working accurately
Difficulty returning homework to school	• Teacher provides immediate feedback for homework completion • Teacher and parent collaboratively establish an organizational system for the child • Teacher contacts the parent if problems continue

general, each subunit consists of work assigned in a particular subject area, although relatively long assignments should be divided into two or three subunits, taking into consideration the child's age and ability to sustain attention. Second, the child chooses which unit to work on first, and the parent and child negotiate goals for work completion and accuracy. The parent guides the child in selecting goals that are realistic with an 80% likelihood of being achieved. Third, the parent establishes the time limit for completion of the subunit of work and makes sure the child understands the directions and is able to do the work independently. Fourth, the child begins working while the parent monitors performance at a nearby location. During this period, the parent should offer praise on a periodic basis contingent upon clear evidence of attention and effort. It is essential for the parent to refrain from inadvertently reinforcing maladaptive behaviors. When the time limit expires, the parent and child evaluate the work together. The child can earn points for achieving established goals for each subunit of work. At some point in the near future, the child will be given an opportunity to exchange points for valued reinforcers. Fifth, once work on the first subunit has been completed, the child cycles through the steps once again, beginning with the first step. If the child does not achieve the goals for a particular subunit, then the family is to keep moving forward and not go back over the assignment. The child has the option of reviewing this work on his or her own later on, if desired.

Providing Tutoring at Home

Attention problems can result in repeated failure to take advantage of instructional opportunities provided at school and home. The outcomes of these continuous missed opportunities are that academic skills deficits can become magnified as children advance through the grades. Addressing the needs of children with attention problems involves more than designing targeted interventions to improve attention. Generally these children also require specialized academic instruction to reduce skills deficits and prevent failure in the future (Schnoes, Reid, Wagner, & Marder, 2006). Although school professionals have the primary responsibility for implementing academic interventions, parents can also be effective in providing instruction to their children using a wide range of tutoring strategies. School psychologists can support parents in utilizing these strategies effectively in the home.

Parents naturally assume the role of tutors when their children are confused about school work and request help. Although parents are well intentioned, they may use strategies that are minimally helpful and can lead to increased frustration for their children. For example, parents often encourage their children to use flashcard strategies to memorize information, such as math facts, spelling words, and state capitals. The stack of flashcards often contains a high percentage (e.g., greater than 20%) of items with answers that are unknown to the children. Research has repeatedly demonstrated that children perform more competently when they have increased opportunity to respond, such as while completing tasks that have a ratio of 80:20 of known to unknown material. Such activities result in relatively high levels of success, leading to an increased sense of self-efficacy and heightened levels of motivation and engagement.

Several instructional strategies have been developed that ensure that children experience high levels of success. For example, the folding-in technique is a useful and effective strategy for presenting flashcards that ensures high rates of success (Shapiro, 2010). Repeated reading techniques also have been found to be effective and rewarding for the child (Daly, Chafouleas, & Skinner, 2005). Repeated reading involves having the child read through passages with increasingly lower levels of support from the tutor. Additionally, cover-copy-compare is an effective strategy that can increase students' accuracy and fluency across a broad range of academic skills. In cover-copy-compare, the student first looks at and studies a model, such as a math problem or spelling a word. The student then covers the model, writes it from memory, uncovers the model, and checks his or her response. Parents can assist their child in using cover-copy-compare by providing error correction or encouraging their child to engage in self-correction.

For parent tutoring to be effective with children who have attention problems, it may be necessary to introduce strategies to improve attention and motivation. The goal setting and contingency contracting strategies presented above (as homework strategies) may be useful. The tutoring sessions can be broken into two or three discrete, relatively brief subunits. The parent and child can establish goals for work completion and accuracy, and reinforcers (e.g., points to be exchanged for privileges) can be provided depending upon the child's ability to achieve targeted goals.

Parent tutoring may not be appropriate for all families. School psychologists can assist families in determining whether these strategies are likely to be useful components of intervention plans given the child's primary areas of need. Certainly, if a child is struggling with homework, it is important to resolve these difficulties before allotting additional time for tutoring. Also, if the parent and child are experiencing some conflict in their relationship, the child may view parent tutoring as an imposition, resulting in oppositional child behaviors and heightened parent–child conflict. Parent tutoring is a reasonable option when the parent–child relationship is generally positive, homework challenges are being managed effectively, and the child expresses willingness to receive tutoring from the parent. Offering the child an opportunity to earn additional reinforcers by participating in tutoring may help to make this activity a more appealing option.

Limiting Screen Time

There is evidence that limiting the amount of time children spend watching television and playing video-games is associated with improved academic performance. When children engage in excessive amounts of screen time, there may be detrimental effects for parent–child attachment, homework completion, and health outcomes, such as decreased physical activity and childhood obesity. The American Academy of Pediatrics (2001) recommends that parents limit their children's screen time to no more than 2 hours per day.

Implementation Supports

Given the challenges families often experience related to intervention adherence, it is critical that treatment plans include a focus on implementation during and after treatment. It is recommended that intervention plans for children with attention problems include implementation supports designed to (a) account for parent and teacher readiness and willingness for change, (b) promote parent and teacher engagement in intervention, and (c) support high quality implementation over time (see Table 36.1). Also, in the context of a multitiered model of service delivery, it is important to consider whether the intervention plan was delivered as intended prior to making a decision to advance to a higher level of care.

Beyond providing skill instruction to families, school psychologists can play a vital role in supporting parental engagement in intervention and by providing guidance related to implementation. For example, telephone calls from the school psychologist on a periodic basis might be particularly useful in encouraging participation of families that are typically difficult to engage in intervention. Also, parents can be encouraged to spend several days implementing a specific strategy and recording successes and challenges on a worksheet or in a journal, or they can document specific details of their intervention plans at home (e.g., list components of the child's homework routine and post it in a visible location). Parents can then share permanent products with the school psychologist, and they can work together to celebrate successes or problem solve specific barriers.

Technology can also be used in innovative ways to provide ongoing support to parents. School psychologists can use technology to increase parent engagement, improve implementation, and facilitate better parent organizational skills and time management (Jones, Forehand, McKee, Cuellar, & Kincaid, 2010). For example, school psychologists can use e-mail and text messages to send reminders to families to practice strategies, share helpful tips, or provide additional support. Technology can also be used to check in with parents between meetings, provide access to handouts or materials, deliver video skill demonstrations to parents, offer feedback, or connect families with one another. Parents also might use technology to support organization, time management, and priority planning. As a result, technology can be an extremely useful tool in facilitating family routines. For example, virtual calendars allow parents to keep track of family appointments, deadlines, and events. Applications related to organization and time management are freely available on most smartphone and tablet devices.

Developmental Considerations

The homework and tutoring strategies described above are most useful for elementary-age children. During early childhood, parents can create a context that promotes learning without formal homework assignments from school. Parents can provide homework in the form of educational activities that align with the child's appropriate developmental level. For example, toddlers and preschoolers would benefit from alphabet and number books, nursery rhymes, and picture books with matching text (Dearing & Tang, 2010). Parents should be encouraged to participate in early literacy and numeracy activities with their children and engage in parent–child talk in order to promote cognitive development, language skills, school readiness, and parent–child attachment.

When working with adolescents, the strategies should be adjusted to take into account the student's desire for increased independence from adults and increased involvement with peers. Also, teens are usually capable of greater self-management of their attention problems than younger children, so the incorporation of cognitive–behavioral strategies that promote self-regulation is usually indicated at this age level. See Table 36.1.

During the transition to middle school, difficulties with attention may be more salient and may result in increased parent–child conflict over issues related to homework completion and autonomy. Therefore, it is important that parents continue to facilitate strong parent–child relationships by providing positive attention and verbal recognition to their children. Difficulties with homework completion and organizational skills may also become more apparent as children become increasingly more autonomous and responsible for materials, assignments, and adequate test preparation. Parents may need to take on more of a coaching role during homework completion in order to assist their children in independently setting goals and self-monitoring their behavior. As a result, families of children preparing to enter secondary education would benefit from intervention strategies focused on organizational skills, such as the Homework, Organization, and Planning Skills intervention. This school-based intervention provides students with skills instruction and problem-solving related to organizing school materials, accurate and consistent recording of assignments, and planning for task completion (see Langberg, 2011, for a further description). Parents participate by learning specific strategies and continuing to reward students at home for demonstrating skills following the conclusion of the intervention.

Family–School Collaboration

Collaboration between family and school can be an effective method of addressing children's attention problems and resolving related academic and behavioral difficulties. Unfortunately, families and school professionals often do not relate with each other collaboratively, particularly if the child is engaging in problematic behavior in the classroom and developing challenging relationships with adults and peers at school. In these cases, family–school relationships often become conflicted, and as conflict increases, it becomes impossible for families and schools to work together effectively (Power et al., 2012).

Traditionally, schools take on the primary responsibility for educating children, and goals may not be mutually developed with family expectations and values in mind (Sheridan & Kratochwill, 2008). Conjoint behavioral consultation is a methodology school psychologists can employ to forge partnerships between family and school and promote collaborative problem solving and shared decision making between parents and teachers and consistency between the home and school environments. Within the context of conjoint behavioral consultation, many useful strategies can be developed, including daily report cards. What follows is a description of conjoint behavioral consultation and daily report cards as they apply to children with attention problems.

Conjoint Behavioral Consultation

Conjoint behavioral consultation, which is based upon principles of systems theory and behavioral psychology, is a method for building partnerships across systems to promote competence and resolve problems (Sheridan & Kratochwill, 2008). Research suggests that conjoint behavioral consultation is highly acceptable to parents and teachers and effective at increasing adaptive behavior and social skills of students with disruptive behavior and attention problems. Also, teachers report significantly improved relationships with parents, and these improvements in parent–teacher relationships resulted in greater improvements in child outcomes (Sheridan et al., 2012).

Conjoint behavioral consultation provides a useful framework for family–school intervention for children with attention problems. Many interventions can be planned, implemented, and evaluated, including homework interventions, tutoring, and treatments to improve peer relationships. School psychologists serve a key role in the process, bringing families and teachers together for shared data-based decision making.

The initial goal is to build a collaborative relationship between the family and school. For cases in which there is an adversarial relationship between these systems, it is recommended that the consultant (i.e., school psychologist) work with the family and school professionals separately at the outset to address their concerns and prepare them for collaboration. Unfortunately, this often might be the case for children with attention problems owing to significant parental and teacher stress related to supporting these children.

If separate parent and teacher consultation sessions are necessary at the outset, the school psychologist should convey an understanding of individual parent and teacher perspectives, help the parents or teacher understand that all individuals involved in supporting the child share similar concerns and frustrations, help the parents or teacher understand the perspective of the other party, and develop strategies that the parents or teacher can use to promote effective collaboration between systems.

Once the family and school professionals have established a collaborative relationship, they are ready to engage in the process of behavioral consultation, which consists of four stages: problem identification, problem analysis, intervention implementation, and intervention evaluation (see Sheridan & Kratochwill, 2008, for an in-depth description of each stage).

Case Example

The following case example illustrates the conjoint behavioral consultation process resulting in the development and implementation of a daily report card. Daily report cards have been demonstrated to be effective in improving children's attention and performance in school (Volpe & Fabiano, 2013). Further, this strategy supports consistent family–school communication, and parents and teachers generally view this approach as acceptable and feasible for children with attention problems.

Daily report cards involve having the teacher evaluate the student's performance during the course of the school day and record this information on a report that is sent home to the parents. The parents and child review the report and determine whether the child's performance reaches the criteria for earning positive reinforcement. For details regarding daily report card development, see Volpe and Fabiano (2013).

Jake is an 11-year-old fifth-grade student experiencing attention difficulties at school. At a recent parent–teacher conference, Jake's teacher reported concerns that Jake is often off task, frequently talks out of turn with classmates, draws on his worksheets, and plays with objects in his desk during instructional time. As a result, Jake has difficulties completing class assignments within expected time limits and requires frequent prompts to continue working. Jake's parents inquired about what could be done in the classroom to address these behaviors. Jake's teacher suggested a meeting including the school psychologist to discuss potential strategies.

At the initial conjoint behavioral consultation meeting, the school psychologist and teacher discussed Jake's behavior problems and the teacher's response to them. It became apparent that the teacher unwittingly was providing Jake a great deal of attention for inappropriate behavior. The consultation included a discussion about principles of positive reinforcement. As part of this conversation, the school psychologist suggested that Jake may benefit from a daily report card intervention, which would allow Jake to gain adult attention for appropriate behavior. Specifically, the school psychologist explained that Jake could earn points for appropriate behavior, including completing work within expected time limits and raising his hand and waiting his turn to speak. Jake could also have the opportunity to earn rewards at home

contingent on meeting his daily points goal at school. Also, the daily report card would allow for ongoing communication between Jake's parents and teacher regarding his behavior in the classroom, and Jake would receive continuous feedback and reinforcement for appropriate behavior in class.

Jake's parents and teacher agreed that the daily report card might be a good fit for Jake, so they collaboratively designed the intervention in consultation with the school psychologist. The team decided that Jake's behavioral goals should be related to on-task behavior and work completion. Teacher observation prior to intervention indicated that Jake generally required four or more reminders to stay on task during each class period, so Jake's parents, teacher, and the school psychologist determined that Jake's first goal should be to stay on task with two or fewer reminders. The team decided that Jake would earn zero points if he required four or more reminders, one point for three reminders, two points for two reminders, and three points if he remained on task with two or fewer reminders. The rationale for including a range of point options was to ensure that Jake continued to feel motivated, even if he failed to fully reach his behavioral goal (i.e., two or fewer reminders). In addition to indicating number of points earned on the daily report card, the teacher was encouraged to provide positive attention on a highly frequent basis (i.e., at least four times more positive reinforcement than correction) for evidence that Jake was paying attention.

The teacher also noted that Jake tended to complete 50% or fewer of his daily seatwork assignments within expected time limits, so Jake's second goal was to complete assigned work during the class period. He earned zero points if he completed 50% or less of the assigned work, one point for 50–75% of the assignments, two points for 75–90%, and three points for 90–100%.

It was also determined that Jake would benefit from frequent feedback about his performance, so the team decided that the daily report card would be completed and reviewed with Jake during each core instructional period. Additionally, given Jake's age and grade, the school psychologist recommended that Jake evaluate his own performance to build skills in behavioral self-management and prepare him for the transition to middle school. The team decided that Jake should complete his own copy of the daily report card, and he could earn bonus points if his self-ratings matched those provided by his teacher.

The school psychologist assisted Jake's parents in designing a home-based reinforcement system in which points earned at school could be traded in for rewards at home daily. The school psychologist and parents also worked together to design implementation supports to ensure that the parents would remember to review the note and provide rewards contingent on performance on a daily basis.

Implementation Supports

At times, it might be difficult for parents and teachers to maintain contact consistently, and children with attention problems might also struggle to remember to bring the daily report card home to parents. In these cases, technological supports can be particularly useful. For example, in some school districts, Web-based interfaces for family–school connections are readily available. Parents and teachers use these websites to communicate routinely about child academic and behavioral performance. When using a daily report card, parents and teachers might consider e-mailing the report back and forth. This is especially useful for children who have significant organizational difficulty and who often forget to bring the daily report card home. School psychologists serving as consultants in the conjoint behavioral consultation process could be involved in this e-mail communication, which could also include e-mail reminders to follow the intervention plan consistently. Also, school psychologists can provide positive reinforcement for adherence to the intervention and guidance to parents and teachers about how to change the daily report card when this intervention is not working well. In addition, school psychologists can monitor the quality of interactions between parents and teachers and intervene when needed to strengthen this connection.

To increase the efficiency of conjoint behavioral consultation implementation, particularly given the limited amount of time available in teachers' daily schedules, school psychologists might consider meeting with a teacher and small group of parents if there are multiple students with similar needs in a classroom (Sheridan et al., 2012). This small group format not only addresses challenges with teacher schedules but also helps to establish supportive peer networks for parents, which is helpful in encouraging parental self-efficacy and autonomy in implementing interventions.

Developmental Considerations

Although conjoint behavioral consultation and daily report card strategies are most commonly used in the elementary years, these strategies can easily be adapted for the preschool and secondary school years. It is important that the age and developmental level of the child or adolescent be considered throughout conjoint behavioral consultation. Given the amount of time young children spend with their parents, it is critically important that parents be included in the intervention plan for preschool children to ensure consistency across the home and preschool settings. To meet the needs of older students, parents, teachers, and consultants might consider including the student in the conjoint behavioral consultation process. For example, student perspectives should be considered when identifying targets for intervention, acceptability of interventions, and perceived intervention effectiveness. Also, as students get older and become increasingly independent, self-monitoring strategies might be included in the plan.

Also, daily report cards can be modified in several ways to make them more effective and developmentally appropriate. One strategy that has been used effectively for students with more challenging behavior is to introduce response cost into the intervention. For example, the student could be given five points for paying attention to instruction at the beginning of class. Each time the child is clearly off task during instruction, the teacher takes one of these points away. The child earns the number of points left over at the end of the class period.

For students in middle school, it is often advisable to include a self-evaluation component. At the outset of the intervention, students evaluate their own behavior independent of the teacher evaluation. Students can earn points based upon the extent to which their ratings correspond with those of the teacher. Gradually over time, the frequency of teacher evaluations can be reduced so that the student is primarily responsible for evaluating his or her performance.

Family–School Collaboration in a Multitier Model

Every student can benefit from family involvement in education. Teachers and school psychologists have a critical role in fostering greater family involvement. Table 36.3 presents examples of activities for school psychologists related to supporting family involvement in education for children who have attention difficulties. Strategies at the universal level, which might be most useful for children with mild attention problems, include requiring students to use a notebook for accurate communication of homework assignments, encouraging families to promote independent reading in the home, inviting parents to raise questions and share their concerns with teachers before problems emerge, providing

Table 36.3. Sample Activities for School Psychologists Working to Link Families and Schools to Support Children With Attention Problems

Goal	Activity for the School Psychologist
Develop and monitor interventions across home and school settings	• Consult with families and teachers using the conjoint behavioral consultation model • Collect and evaluate outcome data (e.g., rating scales, work samples) to share with the team • Support consistent implementation by reviewing permanent products (e.g., parent homework worksheets; teacher documentation of intervention use) and providing performance feedback to address barriers to implementation • Encourage ongoing communication using electronic technology
Support family involvement in home-based activities	• Conduct workshops to help parents learn and practice strategies for home-based educational activities (e.g., parent tutoring) • Problem solve with parents to address barriers to implementation • Encourage parents to adjust strategies according to their child's developmental level and family preferences
Develop a homework routine	• Consult with parents and teachers to identify methods for assigning work (e.g., homework agenda), location and materials needed to do homework, and methods for returning work to school
Decrease the amount of time spent on homework	• Collaborate with the family to teach and implement goal-setting techniques • Use electronic technology, such as timers and calendars, to support adherence to homework schedules
Increase appropriate classroom behavior	• Consult with the family and teacher to develop a daily home–school report • Encourage use of organizational strategies to enhance consistent implementation • Remind parents and teachers to adjust the intervention according to student developmental level (e.g., include self-monitoring for adolescents)

parents tips about how to use naturalistic home and community activities to promote learning, and providing progress reports to families on a frequent basis. School psychologists can also monitor intervention integrity at all levels of the multitier intervention model and provide feedback and coaching to parents and teachers regarding consistent implementation. Interventions must be in place consistently and with high levels of integrity before decisions about student progress can be made accurately.

Some students will demonstrate problems sustaining an adequate level of academic engagement during the course of the school year, which likely will contribute to academic and/or behavioral difficulties. These students likely will require more intensive, targeted intervention (i.e., Tier 2) involving the family and school. In these cases, school psychologists can serve a valuable function by encouraging a more frequent exchange of information between family and school and guiding both parties through a process of problem solving and asset building, which might result in the development of a daily report card and a plan to promote protective factors (e.g., strengthening teacher–student relationships, and promoting student involvement in extracurricular activities). Also, consultation with parents on strategies to address

homework challenges using goal setting and contingency management techniques might be useful at this level.

A relatively few students will manifest clear problems with academic engagement that will impair academic, and perhaps social, functioning. These students require individualized, intensive intervention, which can be managed by a school psychologist. At this level of need, conjoint behavioral consultation, including a functional behavioral assessment to support plan development, will likely be necessary. The family may need intensive support to address homework issues and family issues that may be contributing to educational difficulties, which may require referral to an expert outside the school. Also, for cases in which attention difficulties are severe enough to warrant a diagnosis of ADHD, medication may be indicated. In these cases, conjoint behavioral consultation might also include the prescribing physician to ensure that the plan is well coordinated across systems of care.

Several tools may be useful for school psychologists involved in monitoring children's progress and determining the appropriate level of support. For example, the Homework Problem Checklist (see Power et al., 2006) and the Homework Performance Questionnaire (Power, Dombrowski, Watkins, Mautone, & Eagle,

2007) are useful in monitoring homework progress. The Academic Performance Rating Scale (DuPaul, Rapport, & Perriello, 1991) is helpful in assessing academic productivity and success on an ongoing basis. Also, the Parent-Teacher Involvement Questionnaire may be useful in monitoring the quality of the family–school relationship (Marcelle, Tresco, Mautone, & Power, 2013). In addition, intervention adherence can be assessed by monitoring parent completion of assigned homework (Clarke et al., 2013) and parent and teacher adherence to completing components of the daily report card. These methods can be used to indicate when additional supports are needed and when students have progressed to a point that a lower level of support is indicated.

SUMMARY

Attention problems are strongly associated with academic skills deficits and underachievement. A wide range of academic and behavioral strategies have been developed and validated to improve attention in the classroom. Efforts to improve the attention of children often fail to capitalize on the contributions that families can make to promote school success. Families can foster academic engagement through their involvement with their children in the home setting and by collaborating effectively with school professionals. Almost all families, regardless of cultural background, value education greatly and are willing to support their children's education through home-based strategies. These activities include emphasizing to children the importance of education, limiting television and recreational video and computer games, supporting children with homework, and providing tutoring at home when needed. Building family–school partnerships and sustaining these relationships is also critical. Conjoint behavioral consultation is a framework that is highly useful to school psychologists in fostering successful partnerships, promoting the development of competencies, and resolving problems when they arise. Within the context of conjoint behavioral consultation, useful strategies such as school–home daily reports can be developed and implemented. Several factors may serve as barriers to the implementation and maintenance of family involvement strategies. For this reason, it is important to provide implementation supports to parents, as well as teachers, to promote change. These supports should be tailored to fit the preferences and goals of parents and teachers. Further, it is important that school psychologists understand barriers to implementation, which may

be culturally determined, and to collaborate with families to overcome these challenges.

AUTHOR NOTE

The preparation of this chapter was supported by Grant R01MH068290 funded by the National Institute of Mental Health and the Department of Education, R34MH080782 funded by the National Institute of Mental Health, and R40MC08964 funded by the Maternal and Child Health Bureau, which were awarded to the senior author (Thomas J. Power). Also, The Children's Hospital of Philadelphia has received support from Shire for family education programs for children with ADHD, which contributed to the development of this chapter.

Disclosure. Thomas J. Power has a financial interest in books he authored or coauthored referenced in this chapter.

REFERENCES

Abikoff, H., Gallagher, R., Wells, K. C., Murray, D. W., Huang, L., Lu, F., & Petkova, E. (2012). Remediating organizational functioning in children with ADHD: Immediate and long-term effects from a randomized controlled trial. *Journal of Consulting and Clinical Psychology, 81,* 1–16. doi:10.1037/a0029648

American Academy of Pediatrics. (2001). Children, adolescents, and television. *Pediatrics, 107,* 423–426.

Barbaresi, W. J., Katusic, S. K., Colligan, R. C., Weaver, A. L., & Jacobsen, S. J. (2007). Modifiers of long-term school outcomes for children with attention-deficit/hyperactivity disorder: Does treatment with stimulant medication make a difference? Results from a population-based study. *Journal of Developmental and Behavioral Pediatrics, 28,* 274–287.

Barkley, R. A. (2006). *Attention deficit hyperactivity disorder: A handbook for diagnosis and treatment* (3rd ed.). New York, NY: Guilford Press.

Christenson, S. L., & Reschly, A. L. (Eds.). (2009). *Handbook of school-family partnerships.* New York, NY: Routledge.

Clarke, A. T., Marshall, S. A., Mautone, J. A., Soffer, S. L., Jones, H. A., Costigan, T. E., ... Power, T. J. (2013). Parent attendance and adherence predict treatment response to a family-school intervention for children with ADHD. *Journal of Clinical Child & Adolescent Psychology* Advanced online publication

Corcoran, J., & Dattalo, P. (2006). Parent involvement in treatment for ADHD: A meta-analysis of the published studies. *Research on Social Work Practice, 16,* 561–570. doi:10.1177/1049731506289127

Daly, E. J., Chafouleas, S., & Skinner, C. H. (2005). *Interventions for reading problems: Designing and evaluating effective strategies.* New York, NY: Guilford Press.

Dawson, A. E., Marshall, S. A., Wymbs, B. T., Mautone, J. A., & Power, T. J. (2013, May). Parental ADHD predicts poor maintenance after a family-school intervention for children with ADHD. Paper presented at the annual meeting of the American Psychological Association, Honolulu, HI.

Dearing, E., & Tang, S. (2010). The home learning environment and achievement during childhood. In S. L. Christenson & A. L. Reschly (Eds.), *Handbook of school-family partnerships* (pp. 131–157). New York, NY: Routledge.

Dishion, T. J., & Stormshak, E. A. (2007). *Intervening in children's lives: An ecological, family-centered approach to mental health care.* Washington, DC: American Psychological Association.

DuPaul, G. J., & Kern, L. (2011). *Young children with ADHD: Early identification and intervention.* Washington, DC: American Psychological Association.

DuPaul, G. J., Rapport, M. D., & Perriello, L. M. (1991). Teacher ratings of academic skills: The development of the Academic Performance Rating Scale. *School Psychology Review, 20,* 284–300.

Evans, S. W., Owens, J. S., Mautone, J. A., DuPaul, G. J., & Power, T. J. (2014). Toward a comprehensive, life course model of care for youth with ADHD. In M. S. Weist, N. A. Lever, C. P. Bradshaw, & J. S. Owens (Eds.), *Handbook of school mental health: Research, training, practice, and policy* (2nd ed.; pp. 413–426). New York, NY: Springer.

Fantuzzo, J., McWayne, C., Perry, M. A., & Childs, S. (2004). Multiple dimensions of family involvement and their relations to behavioral and learning competencies for urban, low-income children. *School Psychology Review, 33,* 467–480.

Hoover-Dempsey, K. V., Ice, C. L., & Whitaker, M. C. (2009). "We're way past reading together": Why and how parental involvement in adolescence makes sense. In N. E. Hill & R. K. Chao (Eds.), *Families, schools, and the adolescent: Connecting research, policy, and practice.* New York, NY: Teachers College Press.

Jensen, P. S., Arnold, L. E., Swanson, J. M., Vitiello, B., Abikoff, H. B., Greenhill, L. L., … Hur, K. (2007). Three-year follow-up of the NIMH MTA study. *Journal of the American Academy of Child & Adolescent Psychiatry, 46,* 989–1002. doi:10.1097/CHI. 0b013e3180686d48

Jones, D. J., Forehand, R., McKee, L. G., Cuellar, J., & Kincaid, C. (2010). Behavior parent training: Is there an "app" for that? *Behavior Therapy, 33,* 72–77.

Langberg, J. M. (2011). *Homework, organization, and planning skills (HOPS) interventions.* Bethesda, MD: National Association of School Psychologists.

Marcelle, E. T., Tresco, K., Mautone, J. A., & Power, T. J. (2013, February). Assessing the quality of the parent–teacher relationship. Paper presented at the annual meeting of the National Association of School Psychologists, Seattle, WA

McMahon, R. J., & Forehand, R. L. (2003). *Helping the noncompliant child: Family-based treatment for oppositional behavior* (2nd ed.). New York, NY: Guilford Press.

National Association of School Psychologists. (2010). *Model for comprehensive and integrated school psychological services.* Bethesda, MD: Author. Retrieved from http://www.nasponline.org/standards/ 2010standards/2_PracticeModel.pdf

Pianta, R. C. (1997). Adult-child relationship processes and early schooling. *Early Education and Development, 8,* 11–26.

Polanczyk, G., Silva de Lima, M., Horta, B. L., Biderman, J., & Rohde, L. A. (2007). The worldwide prevalence of ADHD: A systematic review and meta-regression analysis. *American Journal of Psychiatry, 164,* 942–948.

Power, T. J., Dombrowski, S. C., Watkins, M. W., Mautone, J. A., & Eagle, J. W. (2007). Assessing children's homework performance: Development of multidimensional, multiinformant rating scales. *Journal of School Psychology, 45,* 333–348. doi:10.1016/j.jsp.2007.02. 002

Power, T. J., Karustis, J. L., & Habboushe, D. F. (2001). *Homework success for children with ADHD: A family-school intervention program.* New York, NY: Guilford Press.

Power, T. J., Mautone, J. A., Soffer, S. L., Clarke, A. T., Marshall, S. A., Sharman, J., … Jawad, A. F. (2012). Family-school intervention for children with ADHD: Results of randomized clinical trial. *Journal of Consulting and Clinical Psychology, 80,* 611–623. doi:10. 1037/a0028188

Power, T. J., Werba, B. E., Watkins, M. W., Angelucci, J. G., & Eiraldi, R. B. (2006). Patterns of parent-reported homework problems among ADHD-referred and non-referred children. *School Psychology Quarterly, 21,* 13–33.

Schnoes, C., Reid, R., Wagner, M., & Marder, C. (2006). ADHD among students receiving special education services: A national survey. *Exceptional Children, 72,* 483–496.

Shapiro, E. S. (2010). *Academic skills problems: Direct assessment and intervention* (4th ed.). New York, NY: Guilford Press.

Sheridan, S. M., Bovaird, J. A., Glover, T. A., Garbacz, S. A., Witte, A., & Kwon, K. (2012). A randomized trial examining the effects of conjoint behavioral consultation and the mediating role of the parent–teacher relationship. *School Psychology Review, 41,* 23–46.

Sheridan, S. M., & Kratochwill, T. R. (2008). *Conjoint behavioral consultation: Promoting family-school connections and interventions* (2nd ed.). New York, NY: Springer.

Volpe, R. J., & Fabiano, G. A. (2013). *Daily behavior report cards: An evidence-based system of assessment and intervention.* New York, NY: Guilford Press.

Wolraich, M. L., & DuPaul, G. (2010). *ADHD diagnosis and management: A practical guide for the clinic and classroom.* Baltimore, MD: Brookes.

Index

P

Best Practices in School Psychology: Data-Based and Collaborative Decision Making

INTRODUCTION AND FRAMEWORK

DATA-BASED DECISION MAKING AND ACCOUNTABILITY

CONSULTATION AND COLLABORATION

Best Practices in School Psychology: Student-Level Services

INTERVENTIONS AND INSTRUCTIONAL SUPPORT TO DEVELOP ACADEMIC SKILLS

Best Practices in School Psychology: Systems-Level Services

SCHOOL-WIDE PRACTICES TO PROMOTE LEARNING

4. Best Practices in Curriculum Alignment
   Bradley C. Niebling and Alexander Kurz
5. Best Practices in Facilitating Professional Development of School Personnel in Delivering Multitiered Services
   Melissa Nantais, Kimberly A. St. Martin, and Aaron C. Barnes
6. Best Practices in Decreasing Dropout and Increasing High School Completion
   Shane R. Jimerson, Amy L. Reschly, and Robyn S. Hess
7. Best Practices in Focused Monitoring of Special Education Results
   W. Alan Coulter
8. Best Practices in Supporting the Education of Students With Severe and Low Incidence Disabilities
   Franci Crepeau-Hobson
9. Best Practices for Working in and for Charter Schools
   Caven S. Mcloughlin

PREVENTIVE AND RESPONSIVE SERVICES

10. Best Practices in Developing Prevention Strategies for School Psychology Practice
    William Strein, Megan Kuhn-McKearin, and Meghan Finney
11. Best Practices in Population-Based School Mental Health Services
    Beth Doll, Jack A. Cummings, and Brooke A. Chapla
12. Best Practices in Developing a Positive Behavior Support System at the School Level
    Brian C. McKevitt and Angelisa Braaksma Fynaardt
13. Best Practices in the Use of Learning Supports Leadership Teams to Enhance Learning Supports
    Howard S. Adelman and Linda Taylor
14. Best Practices in School–Community Partnerships
    John W. Eagle and Shannon E. Dowd-Eagle
15. Best Practices in School Crisis Intervention
    Stephen E. Brock, Melissa A. Louvar Reeves, and Amanda B. Nickerson
16. Best Practices in School Violence Prevention
    Jim Larson and Sarah Mark
17. Best Practices in Bullying Prevention
    Erika D. Felix, Jennifer Greif Green, and Jill D. Sharkey
18. Best Practices in Threat Assessment in Schools
    Dewey Cornell
19. Best Practices in Suicide Prevention and Intervention
    Richard Lieberman, Scott Poland, and Cheryl Kornfeld
20. Best Practices in Crisis Intervention Following a Natural Disaster
    Melissa Allen Heath
21. Best Practices for Responding to Death in the School Community
    Scott Poland, Catherine Samuel-Barrett, and Angela Waguespack
22. Best Practices in Using the DSM-5 and ICD-10 by School Psychologists
    Susan M. Swearer, Kisha Radliff, and Paige Lembeck
23. Best Practices in Pediatric School Psychology
    Thomas J. Power and Kathy L. Bradley-Klug
24. Best Practices in Medication Treatment for Children With Emotional and Behavioral Disorders: A Primer for School Psychologists
    James B. Hale, Margaret Semrud-Clikeman, and Hanna A. Kubas
25. Best Practices in Assessing the Effects of Psychotropic Medication on Student Performance
    John S. Carlson and Jeffrey D. Shahidullah
26. Best Practices in Collaborating With Medical Personnel
    Sarah E. Glaser and Steven R. Shaw

Best Practices in School Psychology: Foundations

DIVERSITY IN DEVELOPMENT AND LEARNING

9. Best Practices in Conducting Assessments via School Interpreters
   Emilia C. Lopez
10. Best Practices in Working With Children From Economically Disadvantaged Backgrounds
    Christina Mulé, Alissa Briggs, and Samuel Song
11. Best Practices in Providing School Psychological Services in Rural Settings
    Margaret Beebe-Frankenberger and Anisa N. Goforth
12. Best Practices in Working With Homeless Students in Schools
    Brenda Kabler, Elana Weinstein, and Ruth T. Joffe
13. Best Practices in Working With Children Living in Foster Care
    Tracey G. Scherr
14. Best Practices in Service to Children in Military Families
    Mark C. Pisano
15. Best Practices in Supporting Students Who Are Lesbian, Gay, Bisexual, Transgender, and Questioning
    Emily S. Fisher
16. Best Practices in Working With LGBT Parents and Their Families
    Julie C. Herbstrith
17. Best Practices in School Psychologists' Services for Juvenile Offenders
    Janay B. Sander and Alexandra L. Fisher
18. Best Practices in Planning Effective Instruction for Children Who Are Deaf or Hard of Hearing
    Jennifer Lukomski
19. Best Practices in School-Based Services for Students With Visual Impairments
    Sharon Bradley-Johnson and Andrew Cook

RESEARCH AND PROGRAM EVALUATION

20. Best Practices in Conducting School-Based Action Research
    Samuel Song, Jeffrey Anderson, and Annie Kuvinka
21. Best Practices Identifying, Evaluating, and Communicating Research Evidence
    Randy G. Floyd and Philip A. Norfolk
22. A Psychometric Primer for School Psychologists
    Cecil R. Reynolds and Ronald B. Livingston
23. Best Practices in Developing Academic Local Norms
    Lisa Habedank Stewart
24. Best Practices in Designing and Conducting Needs Assessment
    Richard J. Nagle and Sandra Glover Gagnon
25. Best Practices in Program Evaluation in a Model of Response to Intervention/Multitiered System of Supports
    Jose M. Castillo
26. Best Practices in the Analysis of Progress Monitoring Data and Decision Making
    Michael D. Hixson, Theodore J. Christ, and Teryn Bruni
27. Best Practices in Evaluating Psychoeducational Services Based on Student Outcome Data
    Kim Gibbons and Sarah Brown
28. Best Practices in Evaluating the Effectiveness of Interventions Using Single-Case Methods
    Rachel Brown, Mark W. Steege, and Rebekah Bickford

LEGAL, ETHICAL, AND PROFESSIONAL PRACTICE

29. Trends in the History of School Psychology in the United States
    Thomas K. Fagan
30. History and Current Status of International School Psychology
    Thomas Oakland and Shane Jimerson